CRIMINAL LAW

AUSTRALIA

The Law Book Company Ltd.
Sydney : Melbourne : Brisbane

CANADA AND U.S.A.

The Carswell Company Ltd.
Agincourt, Ontario

INDIA

N. M. Tripathi Private Ltd.
Bombay

ISRAEL

Steimatzky's Agency Ltd.
Jerusalem : Tel Aviv : Haifa

MALAYSIA : SINGAPORE : BRUNEI

Malayan Law Journal (Pte.) Ltd.
Singapore

NEW ZEALAND

Sweet & Maxwell (N.Z.) Ltd.
Wellington

PAKISTAN

Pakistan Law Journal
Karachi

HARRIS'S
CRIMINAL LAW

TWENTY-SECOND EDITION

BY

IAN McLEAN
Metropolitan Stipendiary Magistrate

AND

PETER MORRISH
of the Honourable Society of Gray's Inn,
Barrister, Deputy Clerk of the
Central Criminal Court

LONDON
SWEET & MAXWELL
1973

First Edition	1877
Second Edition	1881
Third Edition	1884
Fourth Edition	1886
Fifth Edition	1889
Sixth Edition	1892
Seventh Edition	1896
Eighth Edition	1899
Ninth Edition	1901
Tenth Edition	1904
Eleventh Edition	1908
Twelfth Edition	1912
Thirteenth Edition	1919
Fourteenth Edition	1926
Fifteenth Edition	1933
Sixteenth Edition	1937
Seventeenth Edition	1943
Eighteenth Edition	1950
Nineteenth Edition	1954
Twentieth Edition	1960
Second Impression	*1962*
Twenty-first Edition	1968
Twenty-second Edition	1973

SBN Hardback 421 16120 5
Paperback 421 16130 2

A/345

PRINTED IN GREAT BRITAIN

BY

THE EASTERN PRESS LTD.

OF LONDON AND READING

PREFACE

HARRIS'S *Criminal Law* has long been an established classic, giving to the student a broader prospect of the field of criminal law and a more practical approach than is possible in the average textbook. Nearly five years have elapsed since the last edition, and so fast has been the development of this branch of the law in these five years that this edition has had to be completely revised and rewritten. It is natural that social attitudes should change and that government policy should change with them; this is not peculiar to any particular period, but this state of affairs, combined with the gradual trend towards codification and simplification has resulted in a veritable torrent of new legislation. Again, the policy of keeping the law under review through the Criminal Law Revision Committee, and the welcome trend towards abandoning outworn and archaic provisions, all combine to render much of the previous edition obsolete. A new development is the increasing number of criminal appeals to reach the House of Lords, the consequent opinions shedding valuable light on many half forgotten by-ways of criminal liability.

In the forefront of the move towards codification stand the Theft Act 1968 and the Criminal Damage Act 1971, with their sweeping simplification of the law relating to offences against property. These enactments alone have required the complete rewriting of Chapters 35–42, with much consequential revision. The Road Traffic Act 1972 and the Firearms Act 1968 have consolidated and reviewed the law relating to these subjects (Chaps. 21 and 22).

The law relating to public safety, to consumer protection and the environment, is a fertile field for growth and change. In Chapter 17, particularly, wholesale revision has been required to allow for the changes wrought by the recent decisions on obscenity, and legislation such as the Fire Precautions Act 1971, the Trade Descriptions Acts 1968 and 1972, the Unsolicited Goods and

v

Services Act 1971, the Deposit of Poisonous Waste Act 1972 and a host of other enactments of a similar kind. The Gaming Act 1968 in Chapter 23, the Theatres Act 1968, the Industrial Relations Act 1972 are other important examples of new legislation which has required extensive revision of the text.

In the field of general principles one might expect little or modest change, yet there have been important decisions throwing new light upon the principles governing the exclusion of *mens rea* in criminal offences (*Sweet* v. *Parsley*, and *Warner* v. *Metropolitan Police Commissioner*). The cases of *Tesco Supermarkets* v. *Nattrass* and *R.* v. *Andrews-Weatherfoil* have called for careful reconsideration of the liability of corporations (Chap. 7). The case of *R.* v. *Hudson* in relation to duress (Chap. 6) is important, and in the area of homicide the sections on self-defence and provocation in Chapter 30 have had to be completely revised in the light of recent decisions.

We have sought to shed some of the more archaic material from this edition. It is not easy. Such is the vigour of the common law and some of the old statutes that crimes such as forcible entry and detainer (Chap. 16) have relevance even today in relation to the plethora of " sit-ins " and " squattings " which have become so fashionable in academic circles, and the Conspiracy and Protection of Property Act 1875 (Chaps. 16 and 27) is as relevant to the selfish industrial anarchy of today as it was when it was enacted. We have sought to change the emphasis on treason (Chap. 9) to accord more with the position since the last war and the situation in Rhodesia and Ireland today; piracy, also, has received a new lease of life, but we have tried to change the venue from the China Seas to London Airport, consonant with the provisions of the Tokyo Convention Act 1967 and the Hijacking Act 1971 (Chap. 10). We have relegated blasphemy and disturbing public worship to a lesser level and have ruthlessly pruned the law of criminal libel (Chap. 16). One must walk with care in this field—the 1970s have seen cases of false imprisonment and of kidnapping (Chap. 32). In seeking to relate to present-day conditions we have given greater consideration to the problems of obscenity (Chap. 17), the misuse of dangerous drugs (Chap. 20) and the intricate complexities of the former Road Safety Act 1967 (Chap. 22).

Of all the sweeping changes in the last five years none is more important than the reorganisation of the administration of the superior courts, and in consequence the last third of this edition (Part V) has had to be completely rewritten in the light of the Courts Act 1971. This Act, which came into force on January 1, 1972, was the product of the " Beeching " Commission on Assizes and Quarter Sessions, and it may be said to have given to the superior criminal courts the most drastic restructuring since the reign of King Henry II. It provides for the centralised control of the superior criminal courts under the auspices of the civil service. All trials on indictment now take place in the Crown Court (Chaps. 50–53) which sits concurrently at different places throughout England and Wales. It will be seen immediately that most of the law relating to venue and indictments (Chap. 50) becomes obsolete and has had to be revised. In addition to the Act itself, the Indictment Rules 1971 and the Indictment (Procedure) Rules 1971 have now been published, and much of the practice relating to committal for trial has been altered (Chap. 48). New Magistrates' Courts Rules appeared in 1968, and in 1970 the functions of the justices' clerk were given a more formal basis in the Justices' Clerks Rules (Chap. 48).

Sweeping changes in procedure were made by the Children and Young Persons Act 1969, and many ancillary matters were provided for in the Administration of Justice Act 1970 and the Attachment of Earnings Act 1971. These enactments required further revision of the text.

We have sought to restructure Part V on a more logical basis, by dealing first with magistrates' courts and then with the Crown Court, following this with matters of punishment and then dealing with appeals. Appeals have never received adequate treatment in previous editions, and we have sought to remedy this in Chapters 57 and 58, incorporating the provisions of the Criminal Appeal Act 1968, and the Courts Act 1971. We have added a section dealing in greater detail with the control of inferior courts by prerogative orders (Chap. 57).

The task of editing a work of this compendious nature is increased by the modern tendency to enact legislation in an enabling form, leaving it to the executive to bring it into force. Reliance on this practice has consigned to a form of " legal limbo " much major new legislation. It is on the statute book but is not yet in force. Some examples of this practice are the Medicines Act 1968 and the Misuse of Drugs Act 1971 in Chapter 20, and the Merchant Shipping Act 1970 and the Immigration Act 1971 in Chapters 25 and 9. It would be ridiculous not to include these statutes in the text, or only those sections which are in force, or to deal merely with the old law. To deal with both would simply lead to confusion once the new legislation becomes effective. We have written the particular statutes into the text in their proper sequence, showing by annotations in the footnotes where they are not yet in force. We have sometimes been forced to refer to the old law, we hope without undue emphasis, especially where decided cases may have some bearing on the interpretation of the new material. The Immigration Act 1971 will in fact come into force on January 1, 1973.

The Criminal Justice Act 1972 increases immensely the sentencing options available to the courts (Chaps. 54–56), including such important topics as community service orders, criminal bankruptcy orders, the deprivation of property connected with the commission of crime and much more besides, and it alters comprehensively the law relating to compensation (Chap. 56) and suspended sentences (Chap. 54). In addition, it makes many major alterations in other fields of the criminal law. We have also included the Costs in Criminal Cases Bill 1972. Although this is not yet an Act, without its provisions there would be a built-in obsolescence in this work.

We have done considerable research into the users of Harris. It is clear that they are law students, court officials and police officers. We hope that the students and others will find in this edition an authoritative and valuable introduction to the criminal law. For the police officer we have completely revised the approach to the investigation and prosecution of criminal offences (Chaps. 44–46), adding a comprehensive outline of police powers in Chapter 44. The exercise of these powers is constantly challenged and it is vital to have an understanding of their legal basis. The staff of the courts is increasingly drawn from persons without legal knowledge or experience, and we have tried to provide a *vade mecum* in this field, completely revising the sections on both the magistrates' courts and the Crown Court and approaching the topic from a more practical angle than hitherto. We have tried throughout to maintain a fair balance between that practical approach and academic legal theory, and to retain Harris's essentially compendious nature without losing its encyclopedic quality.

We are particularly grateful to the editorial staff of Sweet & Maxwell for their great patience and care in bringing out this new edition. The law is as it stood on July 1, 1972, with the addition of the Criminal Justice Act 1972 and the Costs in Criminal Cases Bill 1972.

I. McL.
P. J. M.

December 7, 1972.

ABBREVIATIONS

Kenny	*Kenny's Outlines of Criminal Law* (19th ed.)
Cross & Jones	*An Introduction to Criminal Law* (6th ed.)
Street	Street, *The Law of Torts* (5th ed.)
Salmond	*Salmond on Torts* (15th ed.)
Phipson	*Phipson on Evidence* (11th ed.)
Glanville Williams	Glanville Williams, *Criminal Law, The General Part* (2nd ed.)
Smith & Hogan	Smith and Hogan, *Criminal Law* (2nd ed.)
Russell	*Russell on Crime* (12th ed.)
Arch.	Archbold, *Criminal Pleading, Evidence and Practice* (37th ed.)
Paley	*Paley on Summary Convictions and the Magistrates' Courts Act,* 1952 (10th ed.)
Halsbury	Halsbury's *Laws of England* (3rd ed.)
Stone	*Stone's Justices' Manual,* 1972.
Patterson	*Patterson's Licensing* (80th ed.)
Smith	*Theft Act* (2nd ed.)

CONTENTS

PART ONE

CRIME

PART TWO

OFFENCES OF A PUBLIC NATURE

PART THREE

OFFENCES AGAINST THE PERSON

PART FOUR

OFFENCES AGAINST PROPERTY

PART FIVE

PROCEDURE UPON PROSECUTION OF INDICTABLE
AND SUMMARY OFFENCES

TABLE OF CASES

xxiii

TABLE OF STATUTES

xliii

PART I

CRIME

CHAPTER 1

INTRODUCTION

SECTION 1. THE NATURE OF CRIMINAL OFFENCES

Definition. The criminal law of England is that branch of *public law* which relates to offences that may be the subject of *criminal proceedings* instituted for the *punishment* of the offender.[1] Any act or omission which may be the subject of such proceedings is a criminal offence.[2]

Criminal and Civil wrongs compared. The distinguishing feature of a criminal offence is that it entails a liability to *punishment* by the state and not payment of damages to the injured party: " the domain of criminal jurisprudence can only be ascertained by examining what acts at any particular period are declared by the state to be crimes, and the only common nature they will be found to possess is that they are prohibited by the state and that those who commit them are *punished*." [3] The word " punishment " in the modern law does not, as will be seen, necessarily denote retribution as in the past. The object of punishment is the protection of the public which may be achieved in one of three ways, *i.e.* by deterring, isolating or reforming offenders or potential offenders.

When a *civil injury* has been committed the state affords to the injured person various remedies for the purpose of compensating him or restoring him to the position in which, but for

---

[1] *Burdett* v. *Abbot* (1811) 14 East at p. 162; *Mann* v. *Owen* (1829) 9 B. & C. at p. 602; *Att.-Gen.* v. *Radloff* (1854) 10 Ex. at p. 105; *Huntington* v. *Attrill* [1893] A.C. 150.

[2] The terms " crime " and " offence " (see *Horsfield* v. *Brown* [1932] 1 K.B. at p. 367) or " criminal offence " are sometimes used synonymously of all acts and omissions entailing liability to punishment. Sometimes, on the other hand, the word " crime " is restricted to indictable offences, and the terms " offence " or " criminal offence " are applied to offences punishable on summary conviction: see *Lee* v. *Dangar, Grant & Co.* [1892] 2 Q.B. at pp. 347, 348. Nevertheless the terms " crime," " criminal offence " and " offence " are used in this book as terms of general description and not in any special or limited interpretation.

[3] *Proprietary Articles Trade Association* v. *Att.-Gen. for Canada* [1931] A.C. at p. 324.

3

the injury, he would have been. Here the matter is one of *private law*, and the state intervenes only at the instance of the injured party who may at any time, even after the institution of proceedings, abandon or compromise his claim. In some civil actions exemplary damages may be awarded in order to mark the court's strong disapproval of the defendant's conduct.[4] Such damages are in excess of the actual loss suffered and are, therefore, more in the nature of punishment than compensation. But the real object of such proceedings is, nevertheless, to compensate the injured party, although the defendant may be incidentally punished for his wrongdoing.

A civil injury, as will be seen later, may also constitute a criminal offence. An assault, for example, is a civil injury for which the injured person may obtain compensation and is also a criminal offence. But, whenever a *criminal offence* is committed, then, irrespective of whether it also involves a civil injury, the offender becomes liable to *punishment by the state*, not for the purpose of affording compensation or restitution to anyone who may have been injured but as a penalty for the offence and in order to deter the commission of similar offences and, in some cases, for the reform of the offender. Here the matter is one of *public law*; the proceedings against the offender may be instituted by the Crown without the consent of any person who has been injured, the Crown alone can remit the punishment, and the mere fact that compensation has been made to a person injured by the offence does not exempt the offender from punishment.[5]

Just as civil courts have limited powers of punishment by awarding exemplary damages, so criminal courts have limited powers of awarding compensation. Thus a criminal court may, upon conviction of any offence, make an order requiring the offender to pay compensation in respect of any personal injury, loss of, or damage to, property caused by the offence or any offence which the offender has taken into consideration.[6] Here

---

[4] Examples of such actions are breach of contract and torts where the defendant has been actuated by malice: In *Broome* v. *Cassell & Co. Ltd.* compensatory damages of £15,000 and exemplary or " punitive " damages of £25,000 were awarded in a libel action, and upheld in the House of Lords [1972] 2 W.L.R. 645.

[5] *Smith* v. *Dear* (1903) 88 L.T. 664.

[6] Except where the damage is due to an accident arising out of the presence of a motor-vehicle on a road.

the compensation is merely incidental to the real object of the proceedings, which is the punishment of the offender.[7]

As a general rule there is nothing in the character of an act or omission which determines whether it is a criminal offence or merely a civil wrong but, in most cases, it is not difficult to decide into which category it falls. In cases of difficulty it is necessary to examine the nature both of the punishment provided for the wrong and of the proceedings that can follow the commission of the wrong and then, having regard to the various characteristics which are normally associated with a criminal offence, decide whether it is one or not.[8]

It must be borne in mind that many acts which were formerly criminal offences are no longer punishable as such, and, conversely, many acts which formerly were not punishable have become criminal offences. Again, since by-laws, " which are enforceable as part of the law of the land," [9] vary very much in different districts, an act which is not punishable in one place may, in another district, amount to a criminal offence.

In particular, nothing in the moral character of an act or omission can distinguish it from a civil wrong or make it a criminal offence. There are, for example, many breaches of statutory regulations and by-laws which, because they are punishable in criminal proceedings, must be classed as criminal offences although they do not involve the slightest moral blame, as, for example, " not carrying a light on a bicycle or . . . keeping a pig in a wrong place," [10] or the neglect in breach of a by-law to cause a child to attend school during the whole of the ordinary school hours.[11] And, conversely, acts which may be regarded as immoral are not necessarily criminal offences [12] as, for example, adultery. Even incest was not a criminal offence before the Punishment of Incest Act 1908.

---

[7] See p. 820 *post*. In a magistrates' court the amount is limited to £400 in respect of any one offence: Criminal Justice Act 1972, s. 1 (5).

[8] *Cattell* v. *Ireson* (1851) E.B. & E. 91 ; Glanville Williams, " The Definition of Crime " [1955] C.L.P. 107. Since the Administration of Justice Act 1960, ss. 1 and 13 (amended by the Courts Act 1971, Scheds 8 and 11) it has been of less practical importance to know whether, in a difficult case, a wrong is punishable criminally or merely civilly.

[9] *Mellor* v. *Denham* (1880) 5 Q.B.D. at p. 469.

[10] *Wiffen* v. *Bailey* [1915] 1 K.B. at p. 614.

[11] *Mellor* v. *Denham* (1880) 5 Q.B.D. 467 (although this is now an offence under the Education Act 1944, s. 39, as amended).

[12] See *R.* v. *Price* (1884) 12 Q.B.D. at p. 255.

Section 2. The Growth of the English Criminal Law

A thousand years before the Norman Conquest the law of the Germanic tribes, in common with many unsophisticated systems of law, recognised the distinction between offences of a public character and offences against the person or property of individuals. For the former class, such as treachery and desertion, the punishment of death was inflicted: for the latter class a fine was imposed, of which part was paid to the King or some other tribal authority and part to the injured person, or, in case of murder, to his relatives.

This fundamental distinction characterised the law that existed in England at the time of the Norman Conquest. Most injuries to the person or property were expiable by payment of compensation (*bôt*) to the injured person and a fine (*wite*) to the King or some other public authority. Some, however, were inexpiable (*bôtless*) and were punishable by loss of life or limb or by outlawry. There were also certain offences against the person, the peace and the prerogatives of the King that placed the property, the life and limbs of the offender at his mercy. All serious offences gradually fell into this category and were included among Pleas of the Crown.[13]

There was, however, no law, either civil or criminal, which was common to the whole kingdom. The greater part of the law was of Anglo-Saxon origin and was founded upon the customs of the petty kingdoms of the Heptarchy. These kingdoms had, however, passed under the domination of either Wessex, Mercia or the Danes so that there were three main bodies of law, the Wessex law, the Mercian law and the Danish law which, though similar in their general characteristics, differed in detail and were modified by a variety of local customs. All ordinary jurisdiction was vested in local courts, of which the most important were the courts of the shire and hundred, and was exercised in accordance with local custom. But the King and Witenagemot exercised jurisdiction over persons of high rank and in cases in which justice had been denied by the local courts.

After the Norman Conquest the ecclesiastical courts were separated from the lay courts and henceforth claimed cognisance of all offences of a spiritual character, including those against

---

[13] Until the coming into operation of the Indictments Act 1915, every indictment concluded with the allegation that the offence was committed " Against the peace of our lord the King, his crown and dignity."

sexual morality, over many of which, however, the lay courts subsequently reasserted jurisdiction.

Apart from this change the law was, in all ordinary matters, still administered in the local courts, now consisting principally of the county courts (the former courts of the shire), the Hundred Courts, the Manorial Courts and the Borough Courts.

The Witenagemot was, however, replaced by the Curia Regis, which was both King's Council and King's Court, and, in the latter capacity, exercised jurisdiction over all matters affecting the King's interests.

By the end of the reign of Henry III the court became separated from the Council and divided into the three courts of King's Bench, Common Pleas and Exchequer, in the first of which was vested the supreme control of all criminal justice. But before this time there began a series of changes as a result of which the old local courts sank into insignificance and their criminal jurisdiction was either taken away or fell into disuse. The first and perhaps the most important of these changes was the permanent institution of **itinerant justices**.

Soon after the Conquest the Norman kings adopted the practice of sending out commissioners to transact Royal business of various kinds and, in particular, to inquire into the performance by the local authorities of their duties and to enforce the collection of the Crown revenue from fines, forfeitures, feudal dues and other sources.

The procedure employed by these commissioners was that of the inquest (*inquisitio*), *i.e.* an inquiry made by summoning recognitors or jurors to declare upon oath their knowledge of the matters which were the subject of investigation.

At first these commissions were used only for some special purpose, the most famous instance being for the compilation of the Domesday Book, but under Henry I the practice was begun of sending commissioners from the Curia Regis to make circuits through the country for various fiscal and judicial purposes. Under Henry II this practice became systematic and the kingdom was divided into circuits into which itinerant justices were sent regularly, sometimes to hold a general eyre for the purpose of inquiring into all " Pleas of the Crown," that is to say, all Crown business, whether administrative, fiscal or judicial, sometimes, on the other hand, with a more limited authority.

Of these limited commissions the most important was the Commission of Assize. This was of itself merely a commission to take the possessory assizes, which were civil proceedings for the recovery of the possession of land. To it, however, there was annexed by the Statute of Westminster II the power to try certain actions that had been commenced in the courts of Common Pleas and King's Bench,[14] and also, by later statutes, the commissions of Oyer and Terminer and of Gaol Delivery, under which the criminal jurisdiction of the judges of assize was exercised until the passing of the Courts Act 1971.

With the growth of the power of the justices of assize and the transfer to other authorities of the financial and administrative business of the country the general eyres fell into disuse and were given up at the end of the fourteenth century.

In 1166 a further step was taken which ultimately had the effect of transferring to the itinerant justices the trial of all serious offences and thus creating a criminal law common to the whole kingdom. By the **Assize of Clarendon** of that year the itinerant justices were directed to use the procedure of the inquest for the discovery and punishment of all persons guilty of murder, robbery and larceny or the harbouring of criminals, and it was ordained that presentment of such offenders should be made in the county court by twelve men from each hundred and four from each township. By the **Assize of Northampton** of 1176 this procedure was extended to forgery and arson. Thus was begun the list of those Pleas of the Crown which became known as felonies [15] and thus also originated the system of prosecution by the presentment or indictment of a grand jury. All felonies involved forfeiture of the felon's goods to the King, to whom also his lands were forfeited for a year and a day, after which they escheated to his lord, except in cases of treason, when they were forfeited to the King for ever. All except petty larceny and mayhem became ultimately punishable by death. The term " felony " came to include all offences which were punishable as such by statute, or which, whatever the punishment, were made felonies by statute. This might occur where the statute so provided in express terms, or where the definition of

---

[14] This was the origin of the *nisi prius* jurisdiction, so termed because in such actions the jurors were summoned to Westminster only *unless before* the date named in the writ the justices should come into their county.

[15] At a later date forgery became a misdemeanour.

the offence described it as being feloniously committed.[16] Forfeiture for treason and felony were abolished by the Forfeiture
Act 1870, and the punishment of death now applies to very few
offences.[17-18]

By the reign of Edward I all serious criminal offences, including
not only felonies but also many lesser offences which were subsequently known as misdemeanours, were ordinarily dealt with by
the itinerant justices. Misdemeanours were indictable offences
other than treason or felonies. As a broad generalisation, which is
subject to numerous exceptions, it is true to say that misdemeanours
were less serious than felonies. The principal differences between
those two classes were:

   (i) the distinction between principals and accessories was only
      recognised in felonies;

  (ii) to compound a felony was a criminal offence, but there
      was no similar offence in relation to a misdemeanour;

 (iii) powers of arrest without warrant were wider in the case
      of a felony than in that of a misdemeanour;

 (iv) a trial for felony could not take place in the absence of
      the accused who was required to be present in court
      throughout the trial.[19] This rule did not apply in the case
      of trials for a misdemeanour, although in practice it was
      usually followed [20];

  (v) a person convicted of felony might be ordered to pay
      compensation not exceeding £400 for any loss of property
      caused by his felony;

 (vi) conviction of felony involved disqualification from holding
      certain offices;

(vii) civil proceedings could not, as a rule, commence before the
      prosecution of the felon.

The power of the county courts and hundred courts to try
Pleas of the Crown had been taken away by Magna Carta and
the criminal jurisdiction of the former had entirely ceased, but that
of the latter was still exercised in the court which was held by the
sheriff twice a year in his tourn (tour) of the hundreds and at which
presentment was made of criminal offences, those of a minor
character being dealt with at once, but the more serious crimes

[16] *R.* v. *Johnson* (1815) 3 M. & S. 539.   [17-18] See p. 759, *post.*
[19] *R.* v. *St. George* (1840) 9 C. & P. 483.
[20] *R.* v. *Lovett* (1839) 9 C. & P. 462.

being reserved for the King's justices; the manorial and borough courts also continued to exercise jurisdiction over petty offences.

During the reign of Edward III the surviving powers of the old local courts were still further weakened by the creation in every county of **justices of the peace** to whom authority was given to hear and determine felonies and trespasses against the peace and who were required, for this purpose, to hold general sessions at least four times a year.

The procedure in these quarter sessions was by indictment in the same manner as before the judges of assize and, except as to treason, their jurisdiction was unlimited, but they were directed to send all difficult cases to assizes, and in the eighteenth century it became the practice to send all capital offences to assizes.

In the course of the fourteenth and fifteenth centuries a similar power of holding quarter sessions was acquired by many boroughs under their charters, by which the mayor and leading officials were usually made justices of the peace. After the creation of these courts of quarter sessions the term " Pleas of the Crown " was extended to all offences within their cognisance and practically included all criminal offences except such minor misdeeds as still continued to be dealt with in the old local courts until they fell into disuse. The sheriff's tourn was abolished in 1887 but had in fact been obsolete for at least two centuries before that date: the manorial and borough courts were never abolished but ceased to exercise jurisdiction, the latter usually merging into the borough sessions.

In the course of the sixteenth century a new class of criminal offence began to come into existence, consisting of petty offences created by penal statutes which provided that they should be heard and determined by the justices of the peace out of quarter sessions in a summary manner and without the intervention of a jury. Henceforth, accordingly, there were two classes of criminal offences, those which were triable on indictment and those which could be dealt with summarily under statutory powers.

SECTION 3. THE DIVISIONS OF CRIMINAL OFFENCES

(a) Indictable and Summary Offences

Subject to one exception [21] all criminal offences are either tried on indictment, that is, by a jury at the Crown Court, or summarily,

[21] Post, p. 176.

that is, in a magistrates' court. A criminal offence may be indictable either at common law or by statute, but no matter is cognisable by a magistrates' court unless expressly or impliedly made so by statute.

Some offences are only triable on indictment. Other indictable offences can be tried summarily. For example, theft, an indictable offence, can be tried summarily. Likewise some summary offences can be tried only summarily whereas others can be tried on indictment. And there is another class of offences which are both indictable and summary. These differences will be explained fully later.[22]

(b) *Treason, Felonies and Misdemeanours*

Criminal offences were formerly, as we have seen, divided into treason, felonies and misdemeanours. Treason still remains in a category of its own, the essence of the offence being a breach of that allegiance due to the Crown from every person under its protection. **Section 1** of the **Criminal Law Act 1967,** however, abolished all distinctions between felony and misdemeanour, and provided that from January 1, 1968, the law and practice in relation to felonies should be the law and practice relating to misdemeanours. The expression " felony " is no longer used.[23] The expression " misdemeanour " although still in use in certain isolated instances [24] is to all intents and purposes obsolete and is replaced by the expression " indictable offence " which is found in modern statutes.

(c) *Arrestable Offences*

Section 2 of the Criminal Law Act 1967 created a new category of offence known as " an arrestable offence." An arrestable offence is an offence for which the sentence is fixed by law or for which a person (not previously convicted) may under or by virtue of

---

[22] *Post*, p. 646.

[23] By the Criminal Law Act 1967, s. 12 (5), any enactment creating an offence by directing it to be a " felony " shall be read as directing it to be an " offence," and any enactment relating to " felonious " stealing shall be read as referring to mere " stealing." See the Second Schedule to the Act for adaptations of existing statutes.

[24] *e.g.* Indictments Act 1915, s. 4.

any enactment be sentenced to imprisonment for a term of five years, and includes attempts to commit any such offence.[25]

(d) *Common Law and Statutory Offences*

An offence may be *indictable* either at common law or by statute.

Common law criminal offences consist of such actions and omissions as, by common custom, have from early times been considered as of a criminal character. The definitions of criminal offences of this kind are to be found in a long series of judicial decisions commencing from the time of the itinerant justices, to whose declarations of the common custom is due the creation of the common law.[26] Those which remain at the present time are very few in number and their punishments and consequences are in most cases now governed by statute.

A statutory offence, on the other hand, is one that has been created and defined by some particular statute or statutes, or by regulations or orders made under statutory authority, as, for example, the numerous regulations and orders that were made under the Emergency Powers (Defence) Act 1939.

Where a statute declares any act or omission to be treason, felony, misprision of treason, or misdemeanour, an indictment lies in respect thereof. And, even though a statute does not use express terms describing the nature of the offence, if it prohibits a matter of public grievance or commands a matter of public convenience, all acts or omissions contrary to the prohibition or command of the statute are misdemeanours at common law and punishable by indictment unless the statute has prescribed a particular remedy in such terms as to exclude, either expressly or by implication, the remedy by indictment.[27] Where, in such a statute, there is a substantive prohibition or command, an indictment will lie for disobedience to the statute although another particular remedy is provided by a subsequent section, but if the prohibition or command and the particular remedy are in the same section the remedy by indictment is excluded.[28]

[25] Arrestable offences include *e.g.* obtaining by deception and causing death by dangerous driving, which were not previously felonies.

[26] There were, however, certain offences of a common law character, such as perjury, which for a long time were dealt with only by the ecclesiastical courts. *Ante,* p. 6.

[27] *R.* v. *Hall* [1891] 1 Q.B. at p. 753 ; Arch. paras. 2–8.

[28] *R.* v. *Hall* (*ubi supra*) ; and see *R.* v. *Buchanan* (1846) 8 Q.B. 883 ; Arch. para. 8.

Where, however, in the case of an act or omission which is already indictable at common law, a statute prescribes a new mode of proceeding or punishment, without altering the quality of the offence, the new mode is alternative, and the offender may still be indicted at common law.[29] But if the statute alters the quality of an offence, *e.g.* by varying the punishment, the new mode of proceeding and punishment is the only one that can be adopted. Similarly, if a later statute alters the quality of an offence created by an earlier statute or alters the procedure or the punishment prescribed by that earlier statute, proceedings can no longer be taken under the earlier statute.[30]

(e) *Criminal Offences which are or are not Civil Wrongs*

A criminal offence may or may not also amount to a civil wrong against some particular person. Thus, on the one hand, the criminal offence of smuggling and many coinage offences do not necessarily involve any civil wrong to any individual person. On the other hand, an assault or a libel are both criminal offences and violations of the private rights of individuals. But the wrong and the remedy are different. " When a person sues in an action for libel or assault, he does not sue on behalf of the public, or because the public are injured by the libel or assault, or because there was a danger of producing a breach of the peace, which is the ground on which an indictment is founded; but he sues for the injury done to him by the libel or assault." [31] So far also as concerns the civil remedy the right to exact compensation rests with the person injured, who cannot, however, by any bargain " defeat proceedings instituted by the Crown in the interests of the public. . . . He may compromise his own civil rights, but he cannot compromise the public interests." [32]

Civil proceedings in respect of criminal offences. Where an act constitutes both a civil wrong and a criminal offence, there is no longer any reason [33] why the civil proceedings should not be commenced before, or indeed concurrently with, the criminal proceedings.

[29] *R.* v. *Richard Carlile* (1819) 3 B. & Ald. 161 ; Arch. para. 8.
[30] Arch. para. 9.
[31] *Att.-Gen.* v. *Bradlaugh* (1885) 14 Q.B.D. at p. 691.
[32] *R.* v. *Coney* (1882) 8 Q.B.D. at p. 553.
[33] Since the passing of the Criminal Law Act 1967.

In the case of an assault the fact that criminal proceedings have been taken may, under **sections 44** and **45** of the **Offences against the Person Act 1861,** be a bar to subsequent *civil* proceedings. Those sections provide (i) that if justices, upon the hearing, upon the merits, of any *summary proceedings* for assault or battery *on complaint preferred by or on behalf of the person aggrieved* under sections 42 and 43 of the Act, deem the offence not proved, or justified, or so trifling as not to merit a punishment, and dismiss the complaint, they shall forthwith make out and deliver to the person against whom the complaint was made a certificate stating the fact of such dismissal; (ii) that if a person against whom such a complaint has been preferred obtains such certificate, or, having been convicted, pays the fine imposed or suffers the imprisonment awarded, he shall be released from all further or other proceedings, *civil or criminal*, for the same cause.[34]

[34] Arch. paras. 442–443.

CHAPTER 2

GENERAL PRINCIPLES OF CRIMINAL RESPONSIBILITY

SECTION 1. INTRODUCTION

FROM early times, in common with many less sophisticated systems of law, the common law of England paid scant regard to matters of intention. Crimes were of strict or absolute liability, and were punishable, usually in terms of compensation, for the effect caused rather than for the intention with which they were committed. The practical difficulties of operating such a system justly are obvious. In the fourteenth century, by which time many crimes were punishable with death, a need arose for some way of differentiating between those of evil intention and others less blameworthy. It was as a result of the social and religious pressures of the time that one of the cardinal principles of English criminal law developed. It is expressed in this way: *actus non facit reum, nisi mens sit rea,* that is to say, " that a person cannot be convicted and punished in a proceeding of a criminal nature unless it can be shown that he had a guilty mind." [1] The criminal law is not usually concerned with whether the accused knew that what he was doing was wrong—indeed, ignorance of the criminal law is no defence.[2] However, we take from this maxim the two phrases " *actus reus* " and " *mens rea* " and use them, so to speak, as pegs upon which to hang the basic principles of the criminal law.

The *actus reus* is sometimes said to be that physical element of a crime which is prohibited by law, but it may be said to comprehend all the ingredients of a crime other than the required mental state of the accused, which is called *mens rea*.[3] If there was no *actus reus* or if the accused had no *mens rea* at the time that he caused the *actus reus* [4] then the accused must be acquitted,

---

[1] *Chisholm* v. *Doulton* (1889) 22 Q.B.D. at p. 739.

[2] *Post*, p. 52.

[3] The requirement of " voluntariness " has also been included in this book as part of the *mens rea*. Some writers define *actus reus* and *mens rea* differently: see *e.g.* Kenny, p. 17 *et seq.*

[4] The requirement that the *actus reus* and *mens rea* must exist at the same time is subject to exceptions: see *post*, pp. 34, 453 and *Fagan* v. *Metropolitan Police Commissioner* [1969] 1 Q.B. 439.

unless *mens rea* has been expressly or impliedly excluded by the definition of the crime.

SECTION 2. ACTUS REUS

It is an offence to assault a police officer in the execution of his duty.[5] The *actus reus* of this offence is: (i) an assault (ii) upon a police officer (iii) in the execution of his duty. So if A strikes B, who is dressed up as a police officer but is not in fact one, A has not committed this offence (although he may have committed another) because one of the ingredients of the crime—that the victim be a police officer—is missing.

It is bigamy[6] for any person, being married, to marry any other person during the lifetime of the former husband or wife. The *actus reus* of this offence is: (i) the accused must "marry" some other person (ii) while married. So if A, married to B, decides bigamously to marry C but, unbeknown to A, B dies on the day before the ceremony, then A does not commit bigamy.

It is an offence for a man to have sexual intercourse with a girl under the age of 16.[7] If the girl with whom the accused had intercourse was in fact 18, then the offence will not have been committed, notwithstanding that the accused may have thought that she was under 16.

Even the time of the day may constitute part of the *actus reus*. Thus the offence of taking fish by night[8] can only be committed where the accused did the act of poaching between one hour after sunset and one hour before sunrise.

To commit most offences the accused must have either:

    (i) done an act,[9] in the sense of executing some bodily movement, or

    (ii) omitted to do an act.

The problem of omissions is given separate treatment below.

Although hardly to be considered as a separate category, the statute creating some offences defines the *actus reus* not as the

---

[5] *Post*, p. 71.
[6] *Post*, p. 260.
[7] *Post*, p. 467.
[8] Para. 2 (2) of Sched. 1 of the Theft Act 1968.
[9] Sometimes the act must be of a specified kind (*e.g.* in bigamy, going through a ceremony of marriage). But this is not true of all crimes. For example, homicide may be committed by shooting, stabbing, assaulting, etc.

commission of an act, or the omission to do an act, but rather as "a state of being." Thus an offence may be committed by the accused *being in* a particular place, or *being in possession* of something or *being in charge* of something.

In a number of offences it must be shown not only that the accused did an act, or omitted to do an act, but also that certain consequences resulted from that act or omission.[10] For example, if A and B each decide to kill a different person by shooting but, whereas A kills one, B misses the other, then only A can be guilty of murder. So likewise if A and B decide to set fire to different buildings, but, whereas A's efforts to set light to the building are successful, B's are not, then only A can be guilty of the offence of arson under the Criminal Damage Act 1971. When consequences are an ingredient of a crime, it must be shown that the accused's act or omission *caused* those consequences. The problem of causation is given separate treatment below.

Finally, all offences include a number of various other ingredients, which must be present. For example, some offences may only be committed (i) by a particular class of person, *e.g.* a reputed thief under the Vagrancy Act 1824; or (ii) against a person of a particular age, *e.g.* indecency with a child; or (iii) against a particular class of public servant, *e.g.* an assault on a constable; or (iv) in respect of property of a particular type, *e.g.* theft of a motor-vehicle under section 12 of the Theft Act 1968; or (v) without the consent of the victim, as in rape; or (vi) in a particular place, *e.g.* the removal of articles from places open to the public, under section 11 of the Theft Act 1968; or where (vii) there is a particular relationship between the accused and the victim, *e.g.* incest; or (viii) at a particular time, *e.g.* at night, under the Night Poaching Act 1828; or (ix) even the negative ingredient of absence of lawful authority or reasonable excuse.

Section 3. Omissions

The common law, as opposed to statute, does not usually make it an offence to omit to do something.[10a] Thus, if A sees a child

---

[10] In some offences the consequence must flow from certain specified conduct, *e.g.* causing death by dangerous driving (*post*, p. 296); in other offences the consequence may flow from any conduct, *e.g.* murder.

[10a] Misprision of felony (abolished by the Criminal Law Act 1967) is an example.

drowning in a shallow pool, then, in the absence of any relationship between A and the child, he is not guilty of any offence if he allows the child to die.

In some circumstances, however, the common law imposes a duty to act. Except in regard to the law of murder and manslaughter, these common law duties are no longer of importance because they have been superseded and, to a considerable extent, supplemented by statute. Thus it is now a statutory offence to fail to provide the necessary care for children [11] or to fail to assist a constable to suppress a breach of the peace [12]—both of which duties existed at common law. Among the new duties created by statute there is, for example, the duty to stop after an accident or to report the accident to the police.[13] Some of these statutory offences will be dealt with later in the book in the appropriate places.

Usually it will be clear whether a particular offence can be committed by, or only by, omission. In some cases, however, it may be difficult to decide this point. In *Green* v. *Cross*,[14] for example, it was held that a person who *omitted* to take a dog out of a trap could be convicted of " causing a dog to be cruelly ill-treated," contrary to the Cruelty to Animals Act 1849.[15]

However, once it has been shown that a particular offence can be committed by omission, this is not the end of the question. It must then be shown that the accused was, *in the circumstances*, under a duty to act. So having decided, for example, that it was possible to " cause a dog to be ill-treated " by omission, it had to be decided whether the accused was under a duty to release the dog from the trap which the accused had himself lawfully set to capture rabbits. Often those circumstances in which the accused has a duty to act are set out in the offence, but in this case they were not. Notwithstanding this, the accused was held to have been rightly convicted. We can perhaps, therefore, suggest that if a person carelessly or accidentally causes certain prohibited consequences, he is under a duty to prevent (so far as he is able to do

[11] *Post*, p. 481. Children and Young Persons Act 1933, s. 1 (2) (*a*).
[12] *Post*, p. 173.
[13] *Post*, p. 315.
[14] (1910) 74 J.P. 357.
[15] See now Protection of Animals Act 1911, s. 1, as extended by the Protection of Animals (Amendment) Act 1954, which specifically mentions omissions, *post*, p. 417.

so) those consequences from continuing. So, possibly, a person could be convicted of causing unnecessary suffering to animals (contrary to section 1 of the Protection of Animals Act 1911)[16] if, after knocking an animal down on the road and wounding it, he failed to stop and do something to relieve the suffering (assuming that it was possible for him to do so).

Murder and manslaughter. Until recently if a person in the course of unlawful conduct caused the death of another, he was automatically guilty of manslaughter, notwithstanding that he did not foresee death or even any harm occurring to the deceased. This applied equally to criminal omissions as well as to criminal acts. Thus in *R.* v. *Senior*[17] it was held that if a parent failed to comply with his statutory duty to provide medical care for his child and his omission caused or accelerated the death of the child, it was necessarily manslaughter. We shall see later[18] that the better view is that death in the course of an unlawful act is not now necessarily manslaughter. It is therefore not safe to assume that *R.* v. *Senior* will be followed on that point.[19]

Quite apart from this rule, it is clear that if a person's omission causes the death of another and *there is a duty cast upon him to prevent harm to that person*, then it will be either murder, if he foresaw that death or grievous bodily harm would be likely to follow from the omission, or manslaughter, if he foresaw some harm or was " criminally negligent."[20]

The precise circumstances in which the common law imposes a duty to prevent harm are not clear, but it would appear that in the cases enumerated below there is such a duty. However, notwithstanding that there may, in a particular case, be a duty, there is, apparently, a general principle that if a person to whom a duty to prevent harm is owed by the accused is able to take care of himself, or remove himself from the dominion of the accused, but does not do so, the accused is not criminally liable.[21] Subject

A/345

[16] *Post*, p. 417.
[17] [1899] 1 Q.B. 283.
[18] *Post*, p. 443.
[19] But see *R.* v. *Watson and Watson* (1959) 43 Cr.App.R. 111.
[20] See *R.* v. *Gibbins and Proctor* (1918) 13 Cr.App.R. 134; *R.* v. *Bonnyman* (1942) 28 Cr.App.R. 131. See further, *post*, p. 444.
[21] *R.* v. *Charlotte Smith* (1865) 10 Cox at p. 94; *R.* v. *Bonnyman* (1942) 28 Cr.App.R. at pp. 136–137.

to this proviso, the cases in which a duty is owed appear to be as follows:

(1) Parents are under a duty to prevent harm to their children by taking care of them and providing them with food, clothing, medical care and accommodation. So in one case it was held to be murder where a father deliberately refrained from providing his daughter of seven with the necessaries of life knowing, and indeed desiring, that she would suffer grievous bodily harm.[22] It is not clear whether a failure to provide medical care because of religious beliefs will sustain a conviction for either murder or manslaughter today.[23] During the period when any unlawful omission resulting in death was automatically manslaughter,[24] the problem did not arise because religious beliefs are not a defence under the statutory provisions requiring parents to provide medical care for their children. But, even assuming that this rule has now gone, if a parent allows his child to die in the belief that God will cure the child better than man, he will still be guilty of manslaughter if his omission is found to be " criminally negligent." [25] If, on the other hand, the parent foresees that without medical aid his child will die but believes that it is God's will that no such medical aid be provided, it may well be murder or, at least, manslaughter.

(2) Every person is under a duty to prevent harm to a person by taking care of him and providing the necessaries of life for him, if he has undertaken, whether by contract or not, to look after him and that person is helpless or infirm. So persons, such as nurses and foster-parents, who undertake to look after children are under this duty.[26] The courts are apparently ready to imply an undertaking from the fact that the parties live together in the same house. Thus it has been held that a husband who failed to look after his infirm wife,[27] a woman who failed to look after the seven-year-old child of a man with whom she shared a house,[28] a woman who failed to look after an elderly aunt with whom she was

---

[22] R. v. *Gibbins and Proctor* (1918) 13 Cr.App.R. 134. See also Children and Young Persons Act 1933, s. 1 (2) (*a*), *post*, p. 481.

[23] See R. v. *Downes* (1875) 1 Q.B.D. 25.

[24] *Ante*, p. 19.

[25] *Post*, p. 444.

[26] See also the old cases in which employers were convicted of manslaughter for not taking proper care of their servants and apprentices: Russell, pp. 406–408.

[27] R. v. *Bonnyman* (1942) 28 Cr.App.R. 131.

[28] R. v. *Gibbins and Proctor* (1918) 13 Cr.App.R. 134.

living [29] and parents who failed to look after a twenty-five-year-old daughter [30] could be convicted of either murder or manslaughter, as the case may be. In these cases, even though a person may be under no obligation to take a person into his household, having done so, the courts are prepared to imply the undertaking to look after him if he should become helpless or infirm.

(3) A person is under a duty to do something if he has undertaken to do it and his failure to do it may be dangerous. So it was held to be manslaughter when the " criminal negligence " [31] of a railway-crossing gate-keeper in failing to close the gate caused the death of a person crossing the line.[32] So also employees whose failure to observe safety procedures (particularly in coal mines) caused the death of fellow-employees have been convicted of manslaughter.[33]

Section 4. Causation

Introduction

Where the *actus reus* of an offence includes certain consequences of conduct (whether act or omission), it must be shown that the accused *caused* those consequences. So in homicide where the prohibited consequence is death, it must be shown that the accused caused the death.

A person can be said to *cause* something to happen only if that thing would not have occurred at the time and in the manner in which it did occur if he had not done what he did. So if A puts poison in B's drink, intending thereby to kill him, but before B drinks it, or a fatal amount of it, B dies of a heart attack, A cannot be guilty of murder.[34]

Apart from this rather obvious case, even if a person's conduct can be said, in this sense, to have caused a thing to happen, he may not be held to have caused it for the purpose of the criminal law. From now on, unless it is either expressly stated or otherwise clear that the expression " cause " is being used in the wide sense of

---

[29] *R.* v. *Instan* [1893] 1 Q.B. 450.
[30] *R.* v. *Chattaway* (1922) 17 Cr.App.R. 7.
[31] *Post,* p. 444.
[32] *R.* v. *Pittwood* (1902) 19 T.L.R. 37 ; but *cf. R.* v. *Smith* (1869) 11 Cox 210.
[33] See, *e.g. R.* v. *Lowe* (1850) 3 C. & K. 123 ; *R.* v. *Hughes* (1857) Dears. & B. 248. See further Russell, pp. 410 *et seq.*
[34] See *R.* v. *White* [1910] 2 K.B. 124 although he might be convicted of the attempt. See also Russell, pp. 54–55.

being a " factor," it will be used in this latter sense, *i.e.* " cause " means " cause " for the purposes of the criminal law.

Problems of causation do not often arise in criminal law. One reason for this is that, as we shall see in the next Section, most crimes require *mens rea*. This means that the accused must normally have foreseen that the consequences prohibited by the crime would be likely to result from his conduct.[35] If the accused did not have this necessary foresight he will be acquitted because of lack of *mens rea*. On the other hand if he did foresee that these prohibited consequences would be likely to result from his conduct and he caused (in the wide sense) those consequences, he will normally have *caused* those consequences for the purposes of the criminal law. However, as the following examples show, a problem of causation may still arise even in these circumstances.

(1) A assaults B, intending to kill him, and B jumps out of a window to escape from A and kills himself. This kind of problem will be dealt with immediately below.

(2) A, intending to kill B, shoots B but only wounds him very slightly. A clearly has the requisite *mens rea* for murder, that is, he foresees and desires B's death. Now let us assume that on being taken to the hospital in an ambulance, a piece of masonry from a building falls on the ambulance and " kills " B; or, alternatively, that B has a rare blood disease which prevents his blood from coagulating so that the slight wound leads to his death, which it would not have done if he had not been suffering from this disease; or, alternatively, that B refuses to have the wound treated and dies of blood poisoning, which would not have occurred if B had had the wound treated. In all these cases, a problem of causation arises, *i.e.* did A cause B's death for the purposes of the criminal law so that he can be convicted of murder? This kind of problem will be examined below under the heading of " Subsisting and supervening causes."

The Prohibited Consequences Occur in a Way other than the Accused Expected

Assuming that the accused has the necessary *mens rea* for a crime and assuming that his conduct caused (in the wide sense) the prohibited consequences of that crime, the fact that the accused

---

[35] In the case of homicide, however, it is *not* necessary that the accused should have foreseen death: *post*, p. 433.

did not foresee the precise way in which those circumstances occurred does not affect his criminal liability. This principle is illustrated by a number of cases.

If B, under apprehension of immediate violence from A and in an attempt to escape, does an act,[36] *e.g.* jumps out of a window or into a river, which causes his death, A is regarded as having caused B's death, for the purpose of the criminal law, even though he may not have foreseen this possibility. The test is, not whether the accused foresaw the effect of his actions, but whether the action of the victim was the natural result of what the accused said and did, in the sense that it could reasonably have been foreseen. The test is an objective one. If, of course, the victim does something silly or unexpected that no reasonable man could be expected to foresee, the chain of causation will be broken.[37] It follows, therefore, that if A has the *mens rea* for murder and B dies this way, A is guilty of murder.

This same principle has been held to apply where, in similar circumstances, B accidentally fell out of a window to which he had gone to call assistance.[38]

In another case [39] B, who was riding a horse, was assaulted by A. To avoid a further attack B spurred the horse, which then in fright threw B, who died. It was held that A had caused B's death.

In another case [40] the accused, intending to kill a child, gave the child's nurse some laudanum, telling the nurse that it was a medicine and that she should give it to the child. The nurse decided that the child did not require medicine and left the laudanum on a mantelpiece. Subsequently the nurse's daughter, aged five years, removed the laudanum and administered it to the child and the child died. It was held that the accused had been rightly convicted of murder.

Subsisting and Supervening Causes

It can be seen from the examples that have been given above that a court, when dealing with this kind of problem of causation, has

---

36 There is some slight authority that B's action must have been such as a reasonable man might take: see *R.* v. *Pitts* (1842) C. & M. 284.
37 *R.* v. *Roberts* (1971) 56 Cr.App.R. 95 and see *R.* v. *Pitts* (1842) C. & M. 284; *R.* v. *Halliday* (1889) 61 L.T. 707; *R.* v. *Beech* (1912) 7 Cr.App.R. 197.
38 *R.* v. *Curley* (1909) 2 Cr.App.R. 109.
39 *R.* v. *Hickman* (1831) 5 C. & P. 151.
40 *R.* v. *Michael* (1840) 9 C. & P. 356.

to decide whether the existence of *another* factor broke the chain of causation, so that the accused's conduct was not a cause for the purposes of the criminal law. In other words, even though A may have foreseen death as being the likely result of his conduct and even though his conduct may have been a cause (in the wide sense) of the death, still he is not regarded in the criminal law as having caused the death because some other factor has broken the chain of causation. Of course, B's death is the result of many other causes (in the wide sense) besides A's conduct but only substantial causes can break the chain of causation.

Assuming that an accused person did foresee the likelihood of the prohibited consequences of his conduct, this possibility of something breaking the chain of causation is, in practice, only rarely likely to lead to difficulties. Among the crimes which require that certain consequences must have followed the accused's conduct, it is unusual for a distinction to be made between serious and less serious consequences. For example, the offence of arson under the Criminal Damage Act 1971 is complete when the accused sets fire to the building. The amount of damage is irrelevant otherwise than as to punishment. It would not therefore matter that a third party had come along after A had started the fire and caused it to burn harder. Most of the offences involving damage to property draw no distinction between destruction, serious damage and less serious damage.[41]

However, in offences against the person a distinction is made between death and injuries less than death.[42] Thus if A intends to kill a person but only wounds him, A is not guilty of murder, there having been no death. It follows that if A wounds a person intending to kill him and that person later dies because of the wound and another cause (*e.g.* incompetent medical aid) the problem arises. Although it is possible for problems of causation to arise otherwise than in the law of homicide, it is invariably only in homicide that the problem does arise in practice.

In homicide the problem is further complicated by the fact that, as we shall see later,[43] it is not *necessary* in either murder or manslaughter for the accused to have foreseen death, the prohibited

---

[41] See p. 530, *post.*
[42] A distinction is also made between actual bodily harm and grievous bodily harm, and it would be possible to envisage a problem of causation arising under s. 18 of the Offences against the Person Act 1861.
[43] *Post*, pp. 433, 442.

consequence, as being the likely result of his conduct. To be guilty of murder it is sufficient that the accused foresaw only grievous bodily harm. Manslaughter can be committed even though the accused had no foresight of the consequences at all.

It is difficult to gather from the authorities any clear solution to the problem of causation. Furthermore, in a work of this size it is not possible to give the problem adequate consideration. Only the more common problems will be examined and they will be examined from the standpoint of the law of homicide. However, the general principles could be applied to other crimes. It must also be remembered that the present discussion is based on the premise that the accused had the necessary *mens rea* for homicide. Manslaughter by criminal negligence will be dealt with separately below.

One preliminary point ought to be made. If two or more people acting in concert have the required *mens rea* for homicide, it does not matter who acted first or that the act of only one of them in fact killed the deceased. So if A and B assault C intending to kill him, A will still be guilty of murder even though his blow *on its own* would not have killed C.[44]

As we have already seen, the court in dealing with a problem of causation is concerned principally with trying to decide whether some other factor is of sufficient importance to prevent the accused's conduct from being a cause of the death. Other factors may either be subsisting at the time of the accused's conduct, *e.g.* the victim was suffering from a rare blood disease which prevented even a trivial wound from healing, or supervene after the accused's conduct and before the death.

Causes subsisting at the time of the accused's conduct do not, apparently, break the chain of causation. If A shoots at B intending to kill him, and inflicts a slight wound which does not heal because of a rare blood disease and B dies, A is guilty of murder.[45] It is also clear that it would be murder if A's conduct merely accelerated B's death which was bound to occur in a short time anyway.[46] But this is not a true problem of causation, unless A's conduct would not have killed B *then*, but for B's condition.

[44] See *R.* v. *Garforth* [1954] Crim.L.R. 936; and see *Ghosh* v. *King-Emperor* (1924) 41 T.L.R. 27.
[45] See *R.* v. *Woods* (1921) 85 J.P. 272; Russell, pp. 416–417; *cf. R.* v. *Johnson* (1827) 1 Lew. 164.
[46] See *R.* v. *Dyson* [1908] 2 K.B. 454.

Unlike subsisting causes, causes which supervene after the accused's conduct will sometimes break the chain of causation. If a victim dies of loss of blood it can make no difference that medical aid would have saved the victim's life. Nor would it make any difference that it was the victim who refused to submit to medical aid.[47]

The effect of improper medical treatment upon the chain of causation will be dealt with separately below. Apart from this, a cause subsequent to the accused's conduct will only break the chain of causation if it is not *likely* to occur in the circumstances *and*

    (i) is not foreseen by the accused, or

    (ii) does not merely combine with the antecedent cause so that both are contributory causes.

Not likely to occur. If a subsequent cause is likely to occur in the circumstances it cannot break the chain of causation. If, for example, A shoots B intending to kill him, and B subsequently dies of hunger, or of exposure,[48] or of a disease brought on by infection in the wound, or of a disease brought on by the wound itself,[49] A is guilty of murder. But if, for example, B is killed by a piece of falling masonry, or by lightning or by a flood, in the place where A had left him, A would not be guilty of murder. If A wounded B and while B was lying wounded, C came along and cut off B's head, A would not be guilty of murder unless A and C were acting in concert.[50]

What is "likely" in the circumstances is probably objective, *i.e.* the accused himself need not have foreseen the subsequent cause. It must be so where the accused abandoned his victim thinking he was dead, and it would seem to make no difference that A abandoned B realising that he was still wounded.

Not foreseen by the accused. If the accused abandoned his victim helpless after wounding him knowing that he was only wounded and foreseeing that some particular event or circumstance would cause his death, that event or circumstance would not break the chain of causation.

[47] *R.* v. *Holland* (1841) 2 Mo. & R. 351.
[48] *Thabo Meli* v. *R.* [1954] 1 W.L.R. 228; discussed *post*, p. 440.
[49] *Brintons Ltd.* v. *Turvey* [1905] A.C. at p. 233.
[50] Above, p. 25.

Contributory cause. If the intervening cause would not have killed the victim but for the weakened condition in which he was as a result of the accused's conduct, the accused is still guilty.

So if A, intending to kill B, wounded him and, acting quite separately,[51] C also wounded B, then A will be guilty of murder if it was the combined effect of the acts of A and C that killed B.

Death in the course of improper medical treatment. Improper medical treatment is probably treated differently from other supervening causes of death. The Courts-Martial Appeal Court in *R.* v. *Smith*[52] said:

> " It seems to the court that if at the time of death the original wound is still an operating cause and a substantial cause, then the death can properly be said to be the result of the wound, albeit that some other cause of death is also operating. Only if it can be said that the original wounding is merely the setting in which another cause operates can it be said that the death did not result from the wound. Putting it another way, only if the second cause is so overwhelming as to make the original wound merely part of the history can it be said that the death does not flow from the wound." [53]

In that case the accused had stabbed a fellow-soldier. While being carried to the medical centre he was dropped twice and, at the centre, the medical officer, who at the time was very busy, ordered certain treatment which was " thoroughly bad and might well have affected his chances of recovery." [54] The victim died. The accused's appeal against a conviction for murder was dismissed.

It may be that the less serious the injury, the easier it will be to find that the chain of causation is broken by treatment which is utterly wrong; whereas the more serious the injury, the harder it will be to come to that conclusion.

Manslaughter by criminal negligence. As we shall see later,[55] it is possible to commit manslaughter even though the accused

---

[51] See above, p. 25.
[52] [1959] 2 Q.B. 35. *Cf. R.* v. *Jordan* (1956) 40 Cr.App.R. 152, which the court in *R.* v. *Smith* said (at p. 43) was " a very particular case depending upon its exact facts." And *cf. R.* v. *Davis* (1883) 15 Cox 174.
[53] At pp. 42–43.
[54] *Ibid.* at p. 42.
[55] *Post*, p. 444.

did not himself foresee any harm to the deceased, provided that the accused was " criminally negligent." Where it is shown that the accused was criminally negligent, the negligence of the deceased [56] or of the third parties [57] does not prevent it from being manslaughter.

Section 5. Mens Rea

Introduction

The importance of the doctrine of *mens rea* cannot be over-emphasised.

> " The full definition of every crime contains expressly or by implication a proposition as to a state of mind. Therefore, if the mental element of any conduct alleged to be a crime is proved to have been absent in any given case, the crime so defined is not committed; or again, if a crime is fully defined, nothing amounts to that crime which does not satisfy that definition."

This succinct statement of the law by Stephen J.[58] although apparently overlooked for many years received the express approval of the House of Lords as late as 1969.[59] Many crimes are defined almost entirely in terms of the *actus reus* and, but for the doctrine of *mens rea*, anyone who caused the *actus reus* would be guilty of the offence. For example, it is an offence for any person being married to marry any other person during the lifetime of the husband or wife.[60] The *actus reus* of this offence is complete if A marries B while still married to C. But A will be acquitted because of lack of *mens rea* if A thought that C was dead.[61] Again it is an offence to be in unlawful possession of prepared opium.[62] If A is found with opium on him and has no lawful reason for having the opium on him, then he has committed the *actus reus* of the offence. But A should be acquitted for lack of *mens rea* if he did not know that he had any opium

---

[56] *R.* v. *Swindall and Osborn* (1846) 2 C. & K. 230.
[57] *R.* v. *Benge* (1865) 4 F. & F. 504.
[58] In *R.* v. *Tolson* (1889) 23 Q.B.D. 168 at p. 187.
[59] In *Sweet* v. *Parsley* [1970] A.C. 132.
[60] *Post,* p. 260.
[61] *Post,* p. 261.
[62] *Post,* p. 266.

on him (*e.g.* it had been planted on him) or did not know that the substance that he had on him was a drug at all.[63]

The doctrine of *mens rea* originated in the idea that a man should not be held criminally [64] responsible and so liable to punishment unless he is morally blameworthy. The doctrine as it is applied today may be summarised in this way: a man will not, as a general rule, be held to be criminally responsible unless: (i) he was acting voluntarily; (ii) knew what he was doing, and (iii) in those offences where particular consequences form part of the *actus reus* he foresaw the likelihood of those consequences. So a man cannot, in the obvious case, be guilty of murder if, at the time he does the act which kills his victim, he is sleepwalking, for he does not know what he is doing. Nor can a person who strangles another in the throes of an epileptic fit be convicted of murder, for his acts cannot be said to be voluntary.

The application of the doctrine of *mens rea* does not *always* achieve what is really the basic purpose of the criminal law—the protection of persons and property. This protection is best achieved by (i) deterring potential violators, (ii) reforming actual violators and (iii) protecting society from potential violators, for example, by keeping them in a place from which they cannot escape. By imprisoning a person who did have *mens rea* when he killed someone, all three (deterrence, reform and protection) may be achieved. But, instead of simply *acquitting* such a person because he had no *mens rea*, it may be that he should be detained for reform or that society should be protected from him.

For example, A kills B while driving negligently. He did not realise that he was driving in a manner that might result in B's death. He would therefore have no *mens rea* for murder. Yet society may have to be protected from him. So his driving licence ought, perhaps, to be taken away from him. Secondly, further punishment ought, perhaps, to be provided if it is thought that people can be made to avoid killing others by driving more carefully if negligent drivers are punished.

Again, the insane person may well have no *mens rea*, being quite unaware of what he was doing. But if he is dangerous, he ought to be removed from society.

---

[63] And see *post*, pp. 36–38.
[64] He may be held civilly responsible, because the civil law is concerned primarily with compensation.

To overcome the deficiencies of the doctrine of *mens rea*, the legislature and, to a certain extent, the courts, have now created crimes of negligence of which the motor-vehicle crimes are a clear example. Secondly, the courts have developed a doctrine of insanity,[65] the relevant part of which may be summarised thus: if a person has no *mens rea* because he was suffering from a disease of the mind, then he ought to be acquitted, *but*, being a danger to society, he ought to be kept confined until cured.

To sum up, excluded from criminal responsibility because of the doctrine of *mens rea* are: (i) persons who have no *mens rea* and who are neither negligent nor insane; (ii) persons who have no *mens rea* but who are negligent, and (iii) persons who have no *mens rea* because they are insane. It will be seen below [66] that even persons in category (i) may be liable for certain offences. If society feels that it can reform persons in category (ii) or that society should be protected from them, then crimes should be created to catch them. As regards the persons in category (iii), if they are a danger to persons or property, they ought to be confined until cured.

One final introductory comment ought to be made. It must not be forgotten that, even if the accused has the necessary *mens rea*, the *actus reus* of the offence charged must still be proved. A person who attempts to kill another may be as morally guilty as a person who succeeds in killing another. However, only the latter is guilty of murder and will accordingly be punished more severely.

What is Mens Rea?

After that brief introduction, the doctrine of *mens rea* may now be discussed more fully. As we saw earlier [67] when examining *actus reus*:

To commit most offences the accused must have either:

(i) done an act, in the sense of executing some bodily movement, or
(ii) omitted to do an act.

To commit some offences it is sufficient to show that the accused was in some " state of being," *e.g was in possession* of something, or *was* in some specified place.

[65] *Post*, p. 90.
[66] p. 40, *post*.   [67] *Ante*, p. 16.

In a number of offences it must be shown not only that the accused did an act, or omitted to do an act, but also that certain consequences resulted from that act or omission.

Finally, all offences include a number of various other ingredients, which must be present.

The doctrine of *mens rea* can be said to superimpose itself upon the *actus reus* by laying down the particular mental state, *vis-à-vis* each element of the *actus reus*, that the accused must have had at the time of the alleged commission of the offence. The doctrine may now be more fully stated as follows:

(1) Where the *actus reus* requires some conduct (whether act or omission) on the part of the accused, then it must be proved that:

    (i) the conduct was voluntary,

    (ii) in the case of acts, the accused knew that he was doing that act,

    (iii) in the case of omissions, the accused did not believe that he was doing what he was under a duty to do.

(2) Where certain consequences form part of the *actus reus*, it must be proved that the accused foresaw those consequences as likely to result from his conduct.

(3) Where having " possession " of something forms part of the *actus reus* it must be proved that the accused was voluntarily in possession and that either he knew or must have known that he was in possession, or he was indifferent as to whether he was in possession or not.[68]

(4) As regards all the other ingredients of the *actus reus*, there is no general principle that the accused must know that they are present.

Before discussing these rules in detail, it should be mentioned that the definition of a particular offence may expressly or by implication exclude *mens rea* in respect of a particular ingredient of the *actus reus* or even of all the ingredients. This aspect of certain statutory offences will be examined later [69] but two examples may suffice to illustrate the principle, both of them taken from road traffic legislation. It is an offence to use a

---

[68] *Lockyer* v. *Gibb* [1967] 2 Q.B. 243 and see *Warner* v. *Metropolitan Police Commissioner* [1969] 2 A.C. 256; and see *R.* v. *Buswell* [1972] 1 W.L.R. 64.
[69] See p. 40, *post*.

motor vehicle without there being in force in relation to the user
of the vehicle a valid policy of insurance to cover third parties.
This offence is committed whether or not the accused realised
that he was uninsured, if in fact there was no valid insurance.
The same applies to an offence under the Road Traffic Act 1972 [70]
of driving or attempting to drive a motor vehicle on a road
having consumed alcohol in such a quantity that the proportion
in his blood as ascertained from a laboratory test etc. exceeds
the prescribed limit. The accused may be convicted of this
offence whether or not he knew that he had taken that quantity
of alcohol.

(1) Conduct. Where the *actus reus* requires the accused to have
done an act (in the sense of executing a bodily movement), then
as a general rule it must be proved that the act was *voluntary* [71]
and the accused must have known that he was doing that act.[72]
So if X takes A's hand which has a knife in it and forces A to
stab B or if A stabs B while he, A, is asleep or having an epileptic
fit (*i.e.* acting as an automaton), A has no *mens rea*.[73] So, as was
said by Pearson J. in *Hill* v. *Baxter*,[74] a person in the driving seat
of a car while the car is in motion cannot be said to be " driving "
that car (and so cannot be driving dangerously [75]): if

" (1) [He] . . . is having an epileptic fit, so that he is unconscious and there are merely spasmodic movements of his
arms and legs. (2) By the onset of some disease he has been
reduced to a state of coma and is completely unconscious.
(3) He is stunned by a blow on the head from a stone which
passing traffic has thrown up from the roadway. (4) He is
attacked by a swarm of bees so that he is for the time being
disabled and prevented from exercising any directional control

---

[70] See p. 304, *post*.
[71] Voluntariness is sometimes classified as part of the *actus reus*: see Smith
and Hogan, p. 31. See also *Bratty* v. *Att.-Gen. for Northern Ireland* [1963]
A.C. at p. 407.
[72] A person may know what he is doing and yet his conduct may not be
voluntary: X seizes A's hand which has a knife in it and forces A to stab
B. A may know that he is stabbing B but is not guilty of any offence
because his conduct was not voluntary.
[73] For a full discussion of automatism, see *Bratty* v. *Att.-Gen. for Northern
Ireland* [1963] A.C. 386. Provided that a person was acting voluntarily at
the time, loss of memory afterwards does not affect his responsibility (see
ibid. at p. 409). If a person has no *mens rea* because he has a disease of
the mind, then he will be acquitted but found insane; *post*, p. 90.
[74] [1958] 1 Q.B. at p. 286.   [75] For this offence, see *post*, p. 297.

over the vehicle, and any movements of his arms and legs are
solely caused by the action of the bees."

Similarly, it has been said that a person is not " driving " if, owing
to a mechanical defect of which he did not have any knowledge,
the steering fails completely.[76]

So also, as was said in *R.* v. *Charlson* [77] :

" A man in the throes of an epileptic fit does not know what
he is doing. Thus if a friend bends over to assist the epileptic
and in the midst of his fit the latter grips that friend by the
throat, not knowing what he is doing, and in so doing throttles
him and causes his death, no offence has been committed
against the criminal law. . . ." [78]

It is not every involuntary act which can be said to negative
mens rea. Two examples spring to mind. Where an involuntary
act arises from self-induced drunkenness, it is well settled law [79]
that if the accused is so drunk that he does not know what he is
doing, he has a defence to a charge which requires to constitute
mens rea a specific or ulterior intent [80] but not to an offence where
no such specific intent is required. This somewhat artificial distinction between offences requiring a specific or ulterior intent and
those where no such intent is required leads to the curious result
that drunkenness or intoxication by reason of drugs taken may
operate as a defence to a charge of wounding *with intent to cause
grievous bodily harm* (contrary to section 18 of the Offences
Against the Person Act 1861), but not to a charge of unlawful
wounding (contrary to se ion 20 of the same Act).

There may well be another important proviso to the principle that a person acting involuntarily has no *mens rea*. A
person who, at the time of the alleged commission of the offence,
was acting involuntarily may well still be criminally responsible
if, knowing that he was suffering under some condition (*e.g*
epilepsy) which was likely to cause him to act involuntarily, he

---

[76] *R.* v. *Spurge* [1961] 2 Q.B. at p. 211.
[77] [1955] 1 W.L.R. at p. 320.
[78] An epileptic would also not satisfy (2) (foresight of consequences).
[79] See *R.* v. *Lipman* [1970] 1 Q.B. 152. This case has been severely criticised
as has the artificial distinction referred to, ([1969] Crim.L.R. 547; [1970]
Crim.L.R. 132) and there is a convincing argument that the principle ignores
the provisions of the Criminal Justice Act 1967, s. 8 (see p. 52, *post*).
[80] See pp. 39–40, *post*.

allowed himself to be in a position in which he knew that he was likely to commit the *actus reus* of an offence. So if A knows he is subject to epileptic fits and still drives, he will not be able to plead involuntariness to a charge of dangerous driving if he should suffer an epileptic fit while driving.[81] He could, of course, still plead involuntariness if he was hit by a stone and knocked unconscious. So again a driver who falls asleep is not driving in the sense indicated above, but will not be able to plead automatism if he knew he was getting sleepy.[82] This proviso would seem to be of general application and not only apply to driving cases.

Some authority for this proviso is to be found in *Att.-Gen. for Northern Ireland* v. *Gallagher*.[83] In that case it was said that a person charged with murder cannot plead that he did not know what he was doing because he was so drunk if he formed an intention to kill before getting drunk and became drunk in order to kill.[84] In that case the accused intended to kill while drunk. The principle would seem to apply if he foresaw that he was likely to kill and did not care whether he killed or not (*i.e.* was reckless). The principle would also seem to apply to crimes other than murder and also to automatism induced otherwise than by drunkenness.[84a] What, in other words, a court is doing in this kind of case is joining an earlier *mens rea* to a later *actus reus*,[84b] *i.e.* making an exception to the rule that the accused must have the necessary *mens rea at the time* that he caused the *actus reus*. It was said in *R.* v. *Lipman*[85] that for the purposes of criminal responsibility, there is no reason to distinguish between the effects of drugs taken voluntarily and drunkenness which is voluntarily induced.

The requirement of voluntariness applies as much to omissions as to acts. Thus a person cannot be convicted of refusing to aid a police officer in the preservation of the peace if he was physically unable so to aid him.[86]

---

[81] See *Hill* v. *Baxter* [1958] 1 Q.B. at pp. 286–287 and *R.* v. *Sibbles* [1959] Crim.L.R. 660. For a different explanation of these cases, see [1959] Crim. L.R. 661.

[82] *Ibid.*   [83] [1963] A.C. 349.

[84] " So also when he is a psychopath, he cannot by drinking rely on his self-induced defect of reason as a defence of insanity " (*ibid.* at p. 382).

[84a] See, *e.g. Bolton* v. *Crawley* [1972] Crim.L.R. 222.

[84b] In *Fagan* v. *Metropolitan Police Commissioner* [1969] 1 Q.B. 439, the Divisional Court held that the *mens rea* of assault could be superimposed upon an existing continuous *actus reus*.

[85] [1970] 1 Q.B. 152.

[86] *Post*, p. 173.

However, although a person must know what he is doing, it is not necessary to show that he knows what he is *not* doing. This follows from the maxim, which is discussed more fully later,[87] that ignorance of the criminal law is no defence. So, if it is an offence not to do X, A will be guilty if he did not do X (even if he did not know that he had to do X) unless his omission was involuntary or he mistakenly believed that he was doing X.[88]

(2) Foresight of consequences. The doctrine of *mens rea* imports intention, knowledge, or recklessness. Where certain consequences form part of the *actus reus*, the accused must have foreseen those consequences as likely to result from his conduct. If he had the necessary foresight, then it will not affect his criminal responsibility that he either (i) desired the consequences, or (ii) was indifferent as to whether they occurred or not, or (iii) did not want them.[89]

As a matter of terminology, a person is said to *intend* consequences if he had this foresight and desired the consequences.[90] A man is said to be *reckless* if he foresaw that the consequences were likely to result and was indifferent as to whether they occurred or not or did not desire them.[91]

In *R.* v. *Cunningham* [92] the accused had torn away a gas-meter in the cellar of an empty house, intending to steal the contents. Gas leaked from the fractured pipe and partly asphyxiated a Mrs. Wade, an occupant of the next-door house. The accused was charged with unlawfully and maliciously causing a person to take a noxious gas (the term " maliciously " merely expressly imports *mens rea*).[93] It was held that he could only be convicted of this offence if, assuming that he did not intend the injury to Mrs. Wade, he foresaw that the removal of the gas-meter might cause injury to someone [94] but nevertheless removed it.[95]

In *R.* v. *Pembliton* [96] the accused had thrown a stone at persons with whom he was fighting. The stone broke the window of a

[87] *Post*, p. 52.
[88] As to mistake, see further, *post*, p. 47.
[89] See, *e.g. R.* v. *Roberts* (1971) 56 Cr.App.R. 95.
[90] The presumption of intent is dealt with later (*post*, p. 51).
[91] See Glanville Williams, p. 30 *et seq.*
[92] [1957] 2 Q.B. 396.
[93] *Post*, p. 42.
[94] Not necessarily Mrs. Wade : see *post*, p. 48.
[95] At p. 401.
[96] (1874) L.R. 2 C.C.R. 119.

public-house and he was charged with unlawfully and maliciously committing damage to property.[97] It was held that he could be convicted only if he " knew that the natural consequence of his act would be to break the glass," [98] whether he desired to break the glass or not.

Finally, a person charged with a crime must have foreseen the prohibited consequences of *that* crime (or that class of crime). A person, therefore, is not guilty of murder if he foresees that he is likely to shoot an animal but in fact shoots another person.[99]

(3) " State of being." Where some " state of being," *e.g.* being in a certain place, or being found in a certain place, or being in charge of, or in possession of something, forms part of the *actus reus* of an offence, it must be proved that the accused was voluntarily in that state and either that he must have known that he was in that state, or that he was indifferent as to whether he was in that state or not.

The decision in *R.* v. *Larsonneur* [1] is often said to conflict with the first half of the proposition, *i.e.* the accused must have been voluntarily in that state. In that case the Court of Criminal Appeal confirmed the conviction of an alien for being in England when leave to land in the United Kingdom had been refused, although she had been brought into England forcibly by the police. The decision can only be understood if it is appreciated that it depends upon the exact wording of a particular statute.

R. v. *Cugullere* [2] is authority for the second half of the proposition. In that case it was held that a person could not be convicted of possessing an offensive weapon in a public place [3] unless he knew that he had the offensive weapon with him.[4] He would presumably be convicted if he was indifferent as to whether he was in possession or not.

---

[97] Now criminal damage to property, see p. 530, *post*.
[98] At p. 122.
[99] See further, *post*, p. 48.
[1] (1933) 97 J.P. 206.
[2] [1961] 1 W.L.R. 858. See also *R.* v. *Sleep* (1861) L. & C. 44.
[3] *Post*, p. 294.
[4] Contrary to the present submission there are a number of cases in which it was held that persons completely incapacitated through drink could still be *in charge* of a vehicle (see, *e.g. Duck* v. *Peacock* [1949] 1 All E.R. 318; *Haines* v. *Roberts* [1953] 1 W.L.R. 309). These cases are no longer of much practical importance because of a change in the wording of the offence (*post*, p. 297).

Difficulties frequently arise in those " possession cases " where the *actus reus* consists of acquiring or being in possession of some prohibited article or substance, such as a forged banknote, an offensive weapon or dangerous drugs. When possession of such an article or substance is penalised by statute, what is the nature and extent of the knowledge or awareness which must be proved against the person in actual or constructive possession of the prohibited article or substance in order for the particular section of the Act to apply?

The concept of " possession " itself has caused, both in its interpretation and in the principles lying behind it, innumerable difficulties. " English law has never worked out a completely logical exhaustive definition of possession." [5] Distinctions and inconsistencies have arisen under various statutes, and the only thing that is clear is that the definition of the term, and " *mens rea* " to be attributed to it has to be derived in each instance from the particular statute creating the offence.

It may be stated as a general principle that in all " possession cases " it must be proved that the accused was voluntarily in possession of the prohibited article or substance or, possibly, that he was indifferent as to whether he was in possession or not. In *Lockyer* v. *Gibb* [6] Lord Parker C.J. said:

> " In my judgment it is quite clear that a person cannot be said to be in possession of some article which he or she does not realise is, for example, in her handbag, in her room, or in some other place over which she has control. That I should have thought was elementary; if something were slipped into your basket and you had not the vaguest notion it was there at all, you could not possibly be said to be in possession of it."

This first step causes little difficulty. The real problem arises when the possessor knows that he has something in his possession, that is, he is in voluntary possession of some article or substance, but is mistaken as to its nature or quality. In *Warner* v. *Metropolitan Police Commissioner* [7] the appellant was found in pos-

---

[5] Per Lord Jowitt in *United States of America and Republic of France* v. *Dollfus Mieg et Cie S.A.* [1952] A.C. 582 at p. 605.
[6] [1967] 2 Q.B. 243, at p. 248, a case under the Dangerous Drugs Act 1964.
[7] [1969] 2 A.C. 256, a case under the Drugs (Prevention of Misuse) Act 1964; and see also *R.* v. *Buswell* [1972] 1 W.L.R. 64.

session of two packages. He alleged in his defence that he thought both contained scent. When the packages were opened, one was found to contain scent and the other was found to contain prohibited drugs. The principle to be drawn from the opinions seems to be this: that while mere "ignorant possession" as postulated by Lord Parker C.J. in *Lockyer* v. *Gibb* will not satisfy the requirements of *mens rea* in a "possession offence" yet *mens rea* may be satisfied by knowledge of the existence of the article or substance in the control of the possessor even without knowledge of its specific qualities. Thus, if the possessor knows that he is in possession of an unlawful or prohibited substance he may be convicted of possessing the actual substance, say, dangerous drugs, even though he did not know that the substance was *e.g.* heroin or cannabis.[8]

A further difficulty arises in regard to packaged goods, that is, where the possessor has been handed a parcel, or a suitcase or some kind of container. It was suggested in *Warner's* case that while possession of a package was a strong inference of possession of its contents, the necessary *mens rea* of possession would not be satisfied if, for instance, where the accused was the owner of the package, it was shown that he was genuinely mistaken as to its actual contents and of their illicit nature, and received them innocently, provided that he had had no reasonable opportunity since receiving the package to acquaint himself with the contents. In the case of a servant, or a bailee, the inference of *mens rea* might be rebutted by raising a real doubt as to the fact that he had no right to open the package and no reason to suspect that the contents were illicit.

(4) All the other ingredients of the actus reus. There is no general rule that an accused must have known that all the other ingredients of the *actus reus* are present. This may seem illogical but expediency as much as historical accident is probably responsible. The necessity for *mens rea* as to these ingredients will depend in each case upon the nature of the offence and in relation to statutory offences may depend upon the exact wording of the statute and even the subject-matter of the enactment.[9] It is settled

---

[8] This general principle is now enshrined insofar as dangerous drugs are concerned, in the Misuse of Drugs Act 1971, s. 28 (3) (*a*) (not in force on July 1, 1972).

[9] See below p. 42.

law that where an accused is charged with assault upon a police officer in the execution of his duty, it is clear from the definition of the offence that it need not be proved that he *knew* either that the victim was a police officer or that he was acting in the execution of his duty.[10]

Among the ingredients of the *actus reus* of any crime involving personal violence is the requirement that the accused was not acting in self-defence. So if A thinks that B is making such an attack on him as would, whether A knew this or not, justify A killing B. A is not guilty of murder.[11]

Specific or Ulterior Intent

A number of crimes require not only *mens rea* as to the *actus reus* but also a further ulterior, or specific, intent.[12] For example, in burglary it must be shown that the accused entered a building as a trespasser and that he intended to steal or commit certain specified offences.[13] In theft it must be shown that the accused intended permanently to deprive the owner.[14] A number of the aggravated assaults also require a particular intent, *e.g.* wounding with intent to do grievous bodily harm,[15] assault with intent to rob.[16]

" Doing ' X ' with intent to ' Y ' " means that the accused must have done " X " *desiring* " Y " or *desiring* thereby to facilitate the accomplishment of " Y." In other words, he assaulted the woman desiring thereby to facilitate raping her. It is, apparently, not sufficient that, in doing " X," he was indifferent as to whether it would facilitate the accomplishment of " Y." If A hits B, indifferent as to whether B dies or not, he cannot be convicted of wounding with intent to murder. But if B dies, he can be convicted of murder, because for murder it is only necessary to

---

10 See p. 171, *post.*

11 See *R.* v. *Rose* (1884) 15 Cox 540. Some straining of the meaning of the word " know " is necessary. If A kills B when there is no question of self-defence, A would not have been consciously aware that he was not acting in self-defence—but he is still, of course, guilty of murder. It is difficult, however, to think of a word which would be better than the word " know."

12 See Smith and Hogan, 2nd ed., p. 42, for the reasons why the expression " ulterior intent " is to be preferred.

13 *Post*, p. 508.

14 *Post*, p. 502.

15 *Post*, p. 458.

16 *Post*, p. 507.

show that he foresaw that death was likely to occur and it does not matter that A did not desire it.[17]

It appears that even if A realises that " Y " is substantially certain to occur if he does " X," he will not be guilty of " doing ' X ' with intent to ' Y ' " if he did not desire " Y ". So in *R.* v. *Steane* [18] the accused was charged with doing an act likely to assist the enemy with intent to assist the enemy. The accused had broadcast for Germany during the war but only under threats that he and his family would be beaten up if he did not do so. It was held that on this evidence the jury were entitled to find that he did not intend to assist the enemy.[19] But there is some doubt as to whether this decision is right. It seems clear that Steane would have been guilty if, realising that broadcasting would have assisted the enemy, he broadcast with no desire to assist the enemy but in order to make money for himself.[20] If this is so, *Steane's* case cannot be regarded as laying down a general principle.

Finally, a person intends to do " Y " if his intent is conditional, *i.e.* he intends to do " Y " if certain circumstances arise. So for example, a person is guilty of burglary if he enters a building as a trespasser, intending to steal one particular thing *if it is there*, or to rape a woman if she is there.

SECTION 6. EXCLUSION OF MENS REA

At common law, as we have seen, *mens rea* was an essential element of every crime [21] and there would seem to be no case in which Parliament in giving statutory form to an old common law crime has dispensed with the need for *mens rea*.[22] Nevertheless there is a long line of authorities which hold that Parliament has intended in one particular field or another to penalise persons, whether or not it can be said that they had *mens rea* for the

---

[17] See *R.* v. *Bourdon* (1847) 2 C. & K. 366: *post*, p. 433; *contra, Covington* v. *Wright* [1963] 2 Q.B. 469; which, it is submitted, is of doubtful authority; *cf. Fraily* v. *Charlton* [1920] 1 K.B. 147; *R.* v. *Berner* (1953) 37 Cr.App. R. 113.

[18] [1947] K.B. 997.

[19] See also *R.* v. *Ahlers* [1915] 1 K.B. 616.

[20] See *Chandler* v. *Director of Public Prosecutions* [1964] A.C. at p. 805, where Lord Devlin said that a person does something *with a purpose* if he knows that his act will probably achieve that purpose, whether he wants it to be achieved or not.

[21] *Warner* v. *Metropolitan Police Commissioner* (1968) 52 Cr.App.R. 373.

[22] *Ibid.* p. 376.

particular offence.[23] Offences of this kind are known as offences of strict or absolute liability, and in such cases it has been held that the belief, intention or state of mind of the accused person is immaterial and irrelevant, if he has in fact done the *actus reus* which constitutes the offence.

Most of these offences of strict liability arise under regulatory legislation, controlling such matters as the sale of food and drink, the use of false weights and measures, and the use of misleading or false trade descriptions. Similarly, many of the offences in the statutes regulating road traffic have been held to come within this category. For example, it has been held that a person commits the offence of driving whilst uninsured [24] even though he believes that he is insured,[25] and that a driver commits the offence of using a motor vehicle with a defective braking system [26] even though he has no knowledge of the defect.[27]

It will only be in exceptional circumstances that a serious offence of a truly criminal nature will be held to have been committed in the absence of *mens rea.* Such a situation was discussed by the House of Lords in 1968 in a case involving possession under the Drugs (Prevention of Misuse) Act 1964,[28] in *Warner* v. *Metropolitan Police Commissioner.*[29] In this case and the subsequent cases of *Sweet* v. *Parsley* [30] and *Tesco Supermarkets Ltd.* v. *Nattrass* [31] the principles were examined in some detail.

The reason for the creation of offences of strict liability is an obvious one. Where *mens rea* is a constituent of an offence, the burden of proving it is upon the prosecution; and while the proof of the *actus reus* is generally effected by merely calling witnesses to the facts, the burden of proving *mens rea* is often a difficult and onerous one.[32] Nevertheless the courts are naturally reluctant to recognise such offences, as Lord Goddard put it in an oft-quoted passage:

[23] The cases are reviewed *in extenso* in *Warner* v. *Metropolitan Police Commissioner (supra)* and in *Sweet* v. *Parsley* (1969) 53 Cr.App.R. 221; also in *Lim Chin Aik* v. *R.* [1963] A.C. 160.
[24] Road Traffic Act 1972, s. 143, *post*, p. 314.
[25] *Quelch* v. *Collett* [1948] 1 K.B. 478.
[26] Road Traffic Act 1972, s. 40 and the Construction and Use Regulations 1969, as amended.
[27] *James & Son Ltd.* v. *Smee; Green* v. *Burnett* [1955] 1 Q.B. 78.
[28] Repealed by the Misuse of Drugs Act 1971. Not in force July 1, 1972.
[29] (1968) 52 Cr.App.R. 373. [30] (1969) 53 Cr.App.R. 221.
[31] [1971] 2 All E.R. 127 where the particular difficulties arising in relation to the liability of employers for the acts of their servants are examined.
[32] *Tesco Ltd.* v. *Nattrass* [1972] A.C. 153 at p. 169.

" It is of the utmost importance for the protection of the liberty of the subject that a Court should always bear in mind that, unless a statute, either clearly or by necessary implication, rules out *mens rea* as a constituent part of a crime, the Court should not find a man Guilty of an offence against the criminal law unless he has a guilty mind." [33]

Having stated this general principle, however, it should be realised at once that the courts are prepared, given the necessary circumstances, to hold that Parliament has intended to rule out *mens rea* as an element of an offence.[34] The *locus classicus* on the subject is to be found in the judgment of Wright J. in *Sherras* v. *De Rutzen* [35] and his statement of the law has been expressly approved both by the Privy Council [36] and by the House of Lords [37] in the last decade.

" There is a presumption that *mens rea* . . . is an essential ingredient in every offence; but that presumption is liable to be displaced either by the words of the statute creating the offence or by the subject-matter with which it deals, and both must be considered."

Clearly one must first look at the actual words of the section of the Act which creates the offence in order to extract the intention of Parliament. The words of the section may show immediately an intention to create an absolute offence, or they may show that *mens rea* is required in some form or other in regard either to the offence as a whole, or to some particular part of the *actus reus*. This they may do explicitly by the use of such qualifying adverbs [38] as " maliciously," " fraudulently," " negligently," " knowingly " or " recklessly." [39] The mere fact that such words do not appear does not necessarily exclude *mens rea*, however.[40]

---

[33] In *Brend* v. *Wood* (1946) 62 T.L.R. 462, approved in *Lim Chin Aik* (*supra*) and in *Warner's* case (*supra*).
[34] *R.* v. *Bishop* (1880) 5 Q.B.D. 259 ; *R.* v. *Pierre* [1963] Crim.L.R. 513, *post*, p. 294 ; *Yeandel* v. *Fisher* [1966] 1 Q.B. 440 ; *Lockyer* v. *Gibb* [1967] 2 Q.B. 243, *post*, p. 269 ; *Warner* v. *Metropolitan Police Commissioner* [1969] 2 A.C. 256 ; but *cf. Sweet* v. *Parsley* [1970] A.C. 132.
[35] [1895] 1 Q.B. 918.
[36] In *Lim Chin Aik* (*supra*).
[37] In *Warner's Case* (*supra*).
[38] Per Lord Diplock in *Sweet* v. *Parsley* (*supra*).
[39] As to " wilfully " see below.
[40] In *Roper* v. *Taylor's Central Garages* [1951] 2 T.L.R. 284 at p. 288 Lord Devlin said " all that the word ' knowingly ' does is to say expressly what is normally implied."

There is a great deal of confusion in this branch of the law and the cases are conflicting.[41] An example is the use of the word " wilfully." It has been held [42] that a person does not " wilfully " obstruct a highway by opening his car door if he does not foresee that his action will cause an obstruction; yet it has been held [43] that a person " wilfully " kills a house pigeon when he shoots a bird which he honestly believes is a wild pigeon.

Apart from the use of qualifying adverbs, the words used by the Act may themselves connote some particular mental elements. It has been held for instance that the word " permit " connotes knowledge of the prohibited act permitted [44]; that the word " contravenes " implies knowledge of the prohibition which is said to have been contravened [45]; " possess " means knowingly possess [46] and " carries " means carries " to his knowledge " [47] in the context of certain particular statutory offences. Of course the mere fact that such a word is held to bear that meaning in the context of one statutory enactment does not mean that it will be held to bear that meaning in the context of another wholly different enactment.

Where no clear indication of the intention of Parliament is given by the words of the statute,[48] the courts will then, but only then, go on to examine all relevant circumstances in order to decide whether Parliament intended to create an offence of strict liability. Wright J. in *Sherras* v. *De Rutzen* [49] said that the presumption of *mens rea* could be displaced by the " subject-matter " of the enactment. He had in mind three separate classes of exception to the general rule.

(1) acts which are not criminal in any real sense [50] but are acts which in the public interest are prohibited under a penalty;

---

[41] See *Lim Chin Aik, Warner* and *Sweet* v. *Parsley, supra.*
[42] *Eaton* v. *Cobb* [1950] 1 All E.R. 1016.
[43] *Cotterill* v. *Penn* [1936] 1 K.B. 53; see also *Wells* v. *Hardy* [1964] 2 Q.B. 447.   [44] See p. 272, *post.*
[45] *Sambasivam* v. *Public Prosecutor, Federation of Malaya* [1950] A.C. 458.
[46] *Warner's* case.
[47] *R.* v. *Cugullere* [1961] 1 W.L.R. 858.
[48] In *Att.-Gen.* v. *Lockwood* (1842) 9 M. & W. 378 at p. 398 it was said that where no clear indication is given either way, there is a presumption that Parliament did not intend to make criminals of persons who were not blameworthy, and the courts might be forced, where the section is silent as to *mens rea*, to read appropriate words into the section to give effect to the will of Parliament.   [49] [1895] 1 Q.B. 918 at p. 921.
[50] It was said in *Warner's* case that only exceptionally would the subject-matter of the Act operate to exclude the need for *mens rea* in a serious case of a truly criminal offence.

(2) some, and perhaps all, public nuisances;
(3) cases in which, although the proceeding is criminal in form, they are really only a summary mode of enforcing a civil right.

The statutes regulating the sale of food and drink have been held to come within that category, and those applying to licensing, although even here there is confusion in applying the principle. Thus it has been held that a licensee commits an offence under the licensing legislation of serving alcoholic liquor to a drunken man even though he was unaware of his customer's condition [51]; while under the same legislation it has been held that a licensee does not commit the offence of serving drinks to a police officer on duty if he reasonably supposed that the officer was off duty.[52]

An interesting example of the way in which the courts approach this question of " subject-matter " is to be found in the opinion of Lord Pearce in *Warner's* case. Here the question was whether there was a need for *mens rea* in relation to the possession of dangerous drugs under the Drugs (Prevention of Misuse) Act 1964.[53] In the course of his opinion Lord Pearce said this :

" Parliament was clearly intending to prevent or curtail the drug traffic. Having defined a series of persons who may lawfully possess the drugs, it makes possession by all others unlawful, thus putting the drugs out of the reach of unauthorised persons. It was not merely forbidding them to possess drugs for unlawful or guilty objects. It was forbidding them to possess the drugs at all. Thus it would block up all unauthorised channels through which drugs might flow and would thereby establish a strict control of their dissemination. It was forbidding unauthorised possession even for worthy motives. . . . There is an assumption that the Act was intending to penalise those with no guilty intention . . . it cannot, I think, have been intended that it should be a defence for an unauthorised person to show that he may have possessed the drugs for a laudable object or with no guilty intentions. For the unauthorised person is simply not allowed to have them for any object whatever."

---

[51] *Cundy* v. *Le Cocq* (1884) 13 Q.B.D. 207.
[52] *Sherras* v. *De Rutzen* (*supra*).
[53] Repealed by the Misuse of Drugs Act 1971. (Not in force on July 1, 1972.)

The Privy Council, in *Lim Chin Aik* v. *R.*,[54] added to the principles laid down in *Sherras* v. *De Rutzen* this further one:

" It is not enough . . . merely to label the statute as one dealing with a grave social evil and from that to infer that strict liability was intended. It is pertinent also to inquire whether putting the defendant under strict liability will assist in the enforcement of the regulations. That means there must be something he can do, directly or indirectly, by supervision or inspection, by improvement of his business methods or by exhorting those whom he may be expected to influence or control, which will promote the observance of the regulations. . . . Where it can be shown that the imposition of strict liability would result in the prosecution and conviction of a class of persons whose conduct could not in any way affect the observance of the law, their Lordships consider that, even where the statute is dealing with a grave social evil, strict liability is not likely to be intended."

Much of the confusion that has arisen with these less serious offences is due to the fact that courts have traditionally thought in terms of " *mens rea* " or " no *mens rea*." But the purpose of many of these crimes is to catch the negligent person—*e.g.* the negligent seller of food. To catch him the courts have tended to adopt a formula which catches the non-negligent person—*e.g.* the person who took all reasonable care to see that his milk was unadulterated. Little public benefit but much individual harm can be achieved by convicting such a person. The non-negligent person will get as much publicity in local newspapers as the negligent person and the explanations that he will offer in mitigation may not be noted by the readers. The fine may be small or nothing but the resulting publicity may be very damaging. In order to mitigate the injustice which may be involved in offences of strict liability, whereby a careful and conscientious person who is in no way morally to blame is subjected to punishment,[55] Parliament frequently provides that it shall be a defence to a prosecution for such an offence for the person upon whom the statutory duty is imposed to prove that he exercised all due diligence to avoid a

[54] [1963] A.C. 160.
[55] *Per* Lord Diplock in *Tesco Supermarkets Ltd.* v. *Nattrass* [1972] A.C. 153.

breach of the duty concerned.[56] Even this is perhaps no ideal
solution. It would often be easier to infer that Parliament had
intended that negligence should be the necessary mental element,
than to infer that the creation of an absolute offence was intended;
nevertheless English law has not developed in this way.[57] The
English courts might have worked their way towards a liability for
negligence as the Australian courts have done.

Murder and Manslaughter

Ironically, murder and manslaughter have always provided and
still do provide an exception to the general principle of *mens rea*.
The *mens rea* of these two crimes will be examined in Chapter 30.

SECTION 7. CRIMES OF NEGLIGENCE

Sometimes, however, instead of replacing *mens rea* by strict responsibility the courts and, to a greater extent, the legislature have
replaced *mens rea* with liability for negligence, *i.e.* the accused will
be liable if the reasonable man in the circumstances would not have
conducted himself as the accused has done.

At common law a person can commit manslaughter by an act
or omission which is " criminally negligent " or, in other words,
grossly negligent. Apart from manslaughter, the development of
negligence as a basis of responsibility has primarily been the work
of the legislature. For example, in the Sexual Offences Act 1956,
the legislature have in some crimes replaced common law *mens rea*
as to one of the ingredients of the crime with liability for negligence.
So if a man under twenty-four years of age has intercourse with
a girl under sixteen contrary to section 6 of that Act,[58] he will be
guilty unless he believes her to be over the age of sixteen and has
reasonable cause for the belief. So he will commit the offence if
he knew that she was under sixteen, or if he had no idea what age
she was, or if a reasonable man would have thought her to be

---

[56] Examples are to be found in the Food and Drugs Act 1955, the Weights and
Measures Act 1963 and the Trade Descriptions Act 1968 (*post* p. 395).

[57] See the Australian cases quoted in *Sweet* v. *Parsley* (*supra*) based upon the
judgment of Cave J., in *R.* v. *Tolson* (1889) 23 Q.B.D. 168. See also the
article by Professor Howard at (1960) 76 L.Q.R. 547; also *Burns* v. *Bidder*
[1967] 2 Q.B. 227, *post*, p. 317.

[58] *Post*, p. 467.

under sixteen. However, if neither the accused believed nor a reasonable man would have believed that the girl was under sixteen, he is not guilty.[59]

A clear example of liability for negligence are the offences of dangerous driving and of driving without due care and attention.[60] The driver must be driving in the sense that he is voluntarily controlling his movements,[61] but apart from that, the standard by which the accused's driving is judged is that of a reasonable driver.[62]

Ideally, negligence should be the basis of responsibility for many of these minor offences. For example, it would have been far better if those road traffic offences which have been interpreted as imposing strict liability [63] had been interpreted as imposing liability only for negligence. The tendency, however, has been to impose liability for negligence only where the legislature clearly intended this.[64]

SECTION 8. MISTAKE

Mistake Negativing Mens Rea

If the accused is acting under a mistake of fact which prevents him from having *mens rea* as to a particular part of the *actus reus* of a crime, then, as we have seen, he should be acquitted of that crime, provided, of course, that *mens rea* as to that part of the *actus reus* of the crime is necessary. So where a particular consequence forms part of the *actus reus* (*e.g.* death in murder) the accused will not be guilty if he foresaw another consequence than that which occurred.[65] If A stabbed a person honestly believing that that person was a theatrical dummy, he is not guilty of murder because he did not foresee that his conduct would result in a person's death.[66] So also, for example, a person should not be convicted of being in unlawful possession of a particular drug if he thought that he was in possession of soda.[67] Similarly, a person

---

[59] *Cf.* Sexual Offences Act, s. 7 (2), *post*, p. 423, which was interpreted as retaining the subjective test in *R.* v. *Hudson* [1966] 1 Q.B. 448.

[60] *Post*, p. 297.   [61] *Ante*, p. 32.

[62] *McCrome* v. *Riding* [1938] 1 All E.R. 157: *post*, p. 300; *R.* v. *Gosney* [1971] 2 Q.B. 674.

[63] *Ante*, p. 41.

[64] But *cf. Leicester* v. *Pearson* [1952] 2 Q.B. 668, and see *post*, p. 317.

[65] Exceptionally in murder, it is sufficient if the accused foresaw grievous bodily harm (*post*, p. 433).

[66] See *Att.-Gen. for Northern Ireland* v. *Gallagher* [1963] A.C. 349 at p. 381.

[67] *Post*, p. 268.

is not guilty of murder if he honestly thought that the deceased was making a violent attack on him.[68] Nor is he guilty of bigamy if he honestly thought that his first wife had died.[69]

Where it is not necessary to prove *mens rea* as to a particular part of the *actus reus*, then the accused's mistake will not prevent him from being convicted. If *mens rea* has been replaced by strict responsibility then the accused will be convicted.[70] If *mens rea* has been replaced by negligence, as in section 6 of the Sexual Offences Act,[71] then the accused will be convicted unless a reasonable man could have entertained the same belief as the accused.

It is often said that only a reasonable mistake of fact will negative *mens rea*.[72] The better view is that the reasonableness of the mistake is a consideration which the jury should take into account when determining whether the accused *honestly* held the belief.[73] The more unreasonable the belief, the more unlikely it is that it is honestly held, but it does not follow that the accused *could* not have held that belief. To hold otherwise is to impose liability for negligence, which, as far as serious crimes are concerned, is contrary to principle.

Transferred Malice

In the examples given above, the accused's mistake negatived *mens rea*. Some mistakes do not have this effect and do not prevent the accused from being convicted. If A intends to kill B but mistakenly kills C, he is still guilty of murder. He foresaw that his conduct would be likely to result in one person's death, and it does not affect his liability that some other person was killed by him. In *R. v. Latimer*[74] A had aimed a blow at B and severely injured C. A's conviction for unlawful and malicious wounding of C was affirmed.

This principle does not, however, apply if A mistakenly causes the *actus reus* of one crime but has the *mens rea* for another. Thus in *R. v. Pembliton*,[75] the accused could not be convicted of unlawfully and maliciously causing damage to a window under the

[68] *Post*, p. 439.
[69] *Post*, p. 261.
[70] *Ante*, p. 45.
[71] *Ante*, p. 46.
[72] See, *e.g. R. v. Rose* (1884) 15 Cox 540 at p. 541, *post*, p. 388; *R. v. Tolson* (1889) 23 Q.B.D. 168 at pp, 181, 183; *R. v. King* [1964] 1 Q.B. 285 at p. 292.
[73] *Wilson* v. *Inyang* [1951] 2 K.B. 799.
[74] (1886) 17 Q.B.D. 359.
[75] (1874) L.R. 2 C.C.R. 119.

Malicious Damage Act 1861,[76] because he did not have the necessary *mens rea* for this offence. Nor could he be convicted of an unlawful wounding, for which he had the necessary *mens rea*, because there had been no wounding

Mistake of Civil Law

Sometimes the *actus reus* of a crime includes an ingredient the existence or non-existence of which depends upon some rule of civil law.[77] For example, bigamy can only be committed if the accused is already married to someone else.[78] To find out whether or not he is married one must look to the civil law regarding the creation and termination of marriages. Similarly a person does not commit theft if he is entitled to take the goods. If X seizes A's purse in the street and immediately A seizes it back again, A, obviously, cannot be guilty of theft.[79]

It follows that if the accused honestly believed that the civil law regards him as unmarried [80] or as entitled to take the goods alleged to be stolen, then he is not guilty of bigamy or respectively theft. In both cases the accused would not have the necessary *mens rea*. It is not clear, however, that there is a general principle that mistakes of the civil law will, as a general rule and in the appropriate circumstances, negative *mens rea*.

The definition of the offence may, of course, expressly or impliedly exclude such a defence. In *Wells* v. *Hardy* [81] the accused was charged with unlawfully and wilfully taking fish from the River Thames. It was held by the Divisional Court that it was no defence that the accused honestly believed that he had a right to fish, although whether or not the fishing was *in fact* unlawful was a matter of civil law.[82]

Section 9. Proof

More will be said about proof later in the book,[83] but a short summary is necessary here. Throughout a criminal trial the burden

---

[76] Mostly repealed by the Criminal Damage Act 1971.
[77] See *post*, p. 52, as to ignorance of the criminal law.
[78] See *post*, p. 260.   [79] *Post*, p. 500.
[80] He is said to have a " claim of right," *post*, p. 500. As to a claim of right in a charge involving criminal damage see *post*, p. 532.
[81] [1964] 2 Q.B. 447. To the same effect, see *Hudson* v. *MacRae* (1863) 4 B. & S. 585.
[82] The court held that only if the accused did not intend to fish would he be not acting " wilfully."   [83] *Post*, p. 592.

of proof remains upon the prosecution to prove their case beyond a reasonable doubt,[84] except in the *very few* cases in which the burden is cast upon the accused either because of some rule of law [85] or because the definition of the crime so enacts.[86] So although self-defence, automatism, duress and even mistake are spoken of as defences, this is misleading. If the accused acted in legitimate self-defence, he will not have committed the crime. Since the prosecution must prove the commission of the offence beyond a reasonable doubt, it follows that they must prove beyond a reasonable doubt that the accused was not acting in self-defence.

This often gives rise to difficulties. They are best explained by Lord Goddard C.J. in *R.* v. *Lobell* [87]:

"It must, however, be understood that maintaining the rule that the onus always remains on the prosecution does not mean that the Crown must give evidence-in-chief to rebut a suggestion of self-defence before the issue is raised, or indeed need give any evidence on the subject at all. If an issue relating to self-defence is to be left to the jury there must be some evidence from which a jury would be entitled to find that issue in favour of the accused, and ordinarily no doubt such evidence would be given by the defence. But there is a difference between leading evidence which would enable a jury to find an issue in favour of a defendant and in putting the onus upon him. The truth is that the jury must come to a verdict on the whole of the evidence that has been laid before them. If on a consideration of all the evidence the jury are left in doubt whether the killing or wounding may not have been in self-defence the proper verdict would be not guilty. A convenient way of directing the jury is to tell them that the burden of establishing guilt is on the prosecution, but that they must also consider the evidence for the defence which may have one of three results: it may convince them of the innocence of the accused, or it may cause them to doubt,

84 *Woolmington* v. *Director of Public Prosecutions* [1935] A.C. 462. In *Tesco Supermarkets Ltd.* v. *Nattrass* [1972] A.C. 153 at p. 169 Lord Reid suggested that this rule might one day have to be reconsidered.
85 *e.g.* the defence of insanity; *post*, p. 90. For other examples, see *post*, pp. 592–594.
86 Where the burden is cast upon the accused, he need only discharge it on the balance of probabilities; *post*, p. 595.
87 [1957] 1 Q.B. at p. 551. For another explanation, see *Bratty* v. *Att.-Gen. for Northern Ireland* [1963] A.C. at pp. 413–414.

in which case the defendant is entitled to an acquittal, or it may and sometimes does strengthen the case for the prosecution. It is perhaps a fine distinction to say that before a jury can find a particular issue in favour of an accused person he must give some evidence on which it can be found but nonetheless the onus remains on the prosecution. . . ."

SECTION 10. INFERENCES OF MENS REA

Because it is difficult to investigate the state of a man's mind and because, wherever *mens rea* is necessary, it must be proved that the accused had a particular state of mind (such as knowledge or foresight) it follows that courts must be able to draw inferences from a person's conduct. If A shoots B from a yard away and kills him, it is reasonable to infer that A foresaw that his conduct would be likely to result in B's death. So if the prosecution prove the shooting in these circumstances, *mens rea* may be inferred and, if there is no evidence, given by the accused or otherwise, to rebut this inference, then the accused *could* be convicted. In other words, the facts plus the inference are *sufficient* to convict the accused. But if there is some evidence to suggest that the inference should not be drawn *e.g.* A thought the gun to be unloaded and this evidence is sufficient to raise a doubt as to guilt in the minds of the jury, then the accused should, in principle,[88] be acquitted. The burden of proof does not, however, shift to the accused, although, *as a matter of common sense*, the accused may be obliged to lead some evidence.[89] Exactly the same reasoning would apply to a person found in possession of opium. Assuming that a person must know[90] that he is in unlawful possession of opium (*i.e. mens rea* must be shown), an inference would arise from the fact that it was found on him that he did so know, but this inference could be rebutted.

One important inference is sometimes called the " presumption of intent," although it would be better called a presumption of foresight. Unfortunately, there has been a judicial tendency to say that this presumption *must* be drawn. This is wrong, as Lord Denning has said:

[88] But see further below.
[89] See *R.* v. *Lobell* [1957] 1 Q.B. at p. 551 (above).
[90] But see now, *ante*, p. 36.

"When people say that a man must be taken to intend the natural consequences of his acts, they fall into error: there is no 'must' about it; it is only 'may.' The presumption of intention is not a proposition of law but a proposition of ordinary good sense. It means this: that as a man is usually able to foresee what are the natural consequences of his acts, so it is, as a rule, reasonable to infer that he did foresee them and intend them. But, while that is an inference which may be drawn, it is not one which must be drawn. If on all the facts of the case it is not the correct inference, then it should not be drawn." [91]

However, the error was recently adopted by the House of Lords in *Director of Public Prosecutions* v. *Smith*.[92] As a result of the decision in that case and following a report of the Law Commissioners,[93] **section 8** of the **Criminal Justice Act 1967** was enacted. This section expressly provides that a court or jury, in determining whether a person has committed an offence—

(a) shall not be bound in law to infer that he intended or foresaw a result of his actions by reason only of its being a natural and probable consequence of those actions; but

(b) shall decide whether he did intend or foresee that result by reference to all the evidence, drawing such inferences from the evidence as appear proper in the circumstances.

SECTION 11. IGNORANCE OF THE CRIMINAL LAW

In Section 8, we saw that a mistake of civil law may prevent a person from having the necessary *mens rea*. Ignorance or mistake of the criminal law is treated quite differently in that neither will, as a general rule,[94] provide a defence. Even if a person could not possibly have known the law, he is still guilty. So in one case a person was convicted of an offence which he committed on the high seas although the statute creating the offence was passed while

---

[91] *Hosegood* v. *Hosegood* (1950) 66 T.L.R. (Pt. 1) at p. 738.
[92] [1961] A.C. 290. *Post*, p. 433, fn. 32.
[93] Imputed Intent, H.M.S.O. 1967.
[94] An exception is made in favour of people suffering from a disease of the mind and infants of a certain age (*post*, pp. 90, 104). See also *Lim Chin Aik* v. *R.* [1963] A.C. 160.

he was on the high seas and he could not possibly have known about it.[95]

The difference between a mistake of law and a mistake of fact is illustrated by the following example. A policeman has the right to arrest a person who has committed an arrestable offence.[96] If A, a policeman, arrests a person mistakenly thinking that he has committed crime " X," an arrestable offence, he should not be liable for false imprisonment, because his mistake of fact would negative *mens rea*.[97] But if he had arrested a person for committing crime " Y," which he wrongly thinks is an arrestable offence, then he might be liable for false imprisonment, his mistake being one of law unless he was otherwise given a power to arrest for crime " Y." [98]

The solution to these two examples does, of course, involve the proposition that the right to arrest is part of the criminal law.[99] Similarly the right to use force to eject trespassers must be treated as part of the criminal law. So a person who intentionally kills a trespasser, thinking wrongly that he has the right to kill trespassers, will be guilty of murder.

SECTION 12. VICARIOUS RESPONSIBILITY

Vicarious responsibility means responsibility for the conduct of another, such as that which arises under the civil law between principal and agent.[1] At common law, subject to two possible exceptions (*e.g.* criminal libel and common law nuisance [2]) there was no vicarious responsibility. In a large number of statutory offences creating strict or absolute liability, however, the courts have been prepared to recognise vicarious responsibility. In *Tesco Supermarkets Ltd.* v. *Natrass* [3] Lord Diplock said:

" To constitute a criminal offence, a physical act done by any person must generally be done by him in some reprehensible

[95] *R.* v. *Bailey* (1800) R. & R. 1.
[96] *Post*, p. 555. [97] *Ante*, p. 47.
[98] But see *R.* v. *Dadson* (1850) 2 Den. 35, discussed in Smith and Hogan, 2nd Ed. p. 29.
[99] It is also part of the civil law, the person wrongly arrested having an action for damages.
[1] A clear distinction must be made between vicarious responsibility and ordinary responsibility under the principles examined in this chapter and the next (relating to accomplices).
[2] *Post*, pp. 206 and 216.
[3] [1971] 2 All E.R. 127 at p. 155.

state of mind.[4] Save in cases of strict liability where a
criminal statute, exceptionally, makes the doing of an act a
crime irrespective of the state of mind in which it is done,[5]
criminal law regards a person as responsible for his own crimes
only. It does not recognise the liability of a principal for
the criminal acts of his agent; because it does not ascribe
to him his agent's state of mind."

So for example a master does not commit the offence of handling
stolen goods merely because his servant is in possession of them,
knowing them to have been stolen,[6] for the *mens rea* required
by the Theft Act cannot be attributed to the master. Any number
of similar examples might be given.

In the field of statutory offences giving rise to strict or absolute
liability,[7] however, vicarious responsibility is readily recognised.
Coppen v. *Moore* [8] is a good illustration of the position. A owned
a number of shops. In one of the shops an employee, contrary
to express instructions, sold some American ham as " Scotch
ham." A was convicted of selling goods to which a false trade
description had been applied.[9] It was held that A " sold " the
ham in question although the actual transaction was carried out
by his servant. The policy behind such a decision is clear. In
the field of regulatory legislation [10] such as that governing the
sale of food and drinks, false trade descriptions, weights and
measures, and road traffic, the courts do not feel that employers
should be able to avoid criminal responsibility for offences of
strict liability because they employ persons to do the actual selling.
This seems a proper attitude, provided that responsibility is limited,
wherever possible, to the careless or negligent employer, which
is in fact the trend adopted in the modern statutes.[11]

The courts are reluctant to interpret statutes as creating
vicarious responsibility, and must be able to find such a principle

---

[4] *i.e. mens rea* is required.
[5] See pp. 40–46, *ante.*
[6] *R.* v. *Pearson* (1908) 1 Cr.App.R. 77.
[7] See pp. 40–46, *ante.*
[8] [1898] 2 Q.B. 306. See also *Goodfellow* v. *Johnson* [1965] 1 All E.R. 941.
[9] See now the Trade Descriptions Act 1968 *post*, p. 395.
[10] See pp. 40–46, *ante.*
[11] See *e.g.* Food and Drugs Act 1955, s. 113 (1); Weights and Measures Act
1963, ss. 16, 26, 27, 28; Trade Description Act 1968, s. 28, but see *Commissioners of Police* v. *Cartman* [1896] 1 Q.B. 655; *Grade* v. *D.P.P.* [1942] 2
All E.R. 118.

in the words of the statute itself. A master can be said to "sell" something which is actually sold by his servant, but he can hardly be said to "drive" a vehicle driven by his employee. Thus it would be unlikely that an employer could be held vicariously responsible for the act of his servant in driving a vehicle in excess of the speed limit, or of driving when he had taken too much to drink. The courts have held that the word "use" indicates an intention to create vicarious responsibility. An employer "uses" a motor vehicle with defective brakes if his servant is driving on his master's business.[12] This is an offence of absolute liability and is committed by either the servant or the master, even though neither of them knew of the defect. Other words which have been held to create vicarious responsibility include "in possession"[13] "presents" *e.g.* a play[14] and "fails."

It is exceptional to find vicarious responsibility being imposed if *mens rea* is necessary, but it is so in the case of licensing offences.[15]

Where a person who holds a public licence delegates to his servant the management of the business in respect of which the licence is granted, the licensee may be vicariously liable for the conduct of his delegate.[16] In these cases the licensee is deemed to have done what the delegate did and, where necessary, with the same state of mind as the delegate. So, for example, if a person left in charge of a public-house during the publican's absence from the house supplies liquor either to a constable on duty knowing that the constable is on duty[17] or to a drunken person,[18] the publican is vicariously responsible.[19] Similarly a licensee may be vicariously responsible if, in his absence, a delegate

---

[12] *James & Son Ltd.* v. *Smee*; *Green* v. *Burnett* [1955] 1 Q.B. 78. A problem arises if the employee uses the motor vehicle for his private and unauthorised use: see *Strutt* v. *Clift* [1911] 1 K.B. 1; *Phelon & Moore Ltd.* v. *Keel* [1914] 3 K.B. 165; *Griffiths* v. *Studebakers Ltd.* [1924] 1 K.B. 102.

[13] *Melias* v. *Preston* [1957] 2 Q.B. 380.

[14] *Grade* v. *D.P.P.* [1942] 2 All E.R. 118.

[15] See, *e.g. Mullins* v. *Collins* (1874) L.R. 9 Q.B. 292 and *Allen* v. *Whitehead* [1930] 1 K.B. 211—both licensing cases. See also *Mousell Brothers Ltd.* v. *London and North Western Ry.* [1917] 2 K.B. 836; *G. Newton Ltd.* v. *Smith* [1962] 2 Q.B. at p. 284. The authority of these cases has recently been doubted, see *Vane* v. *Yiannopoullos* [1965] A.C. 486, *per* Lords Morris and Donovan; but *cf. Ross* v. *Moss* [1965] 2 Q.B. 396.

[16] See Smith and Hogan, 2nd Ed. pp. 98, 99.

[17] *Post*, p. 363.

[18] *Post*, p. 362.

[19] *Mullins* v. *Collins* (1874) L.R. 9 Q.B. 292; *Commissioners of Police* v. *Cartman* [1896] 1 Q.B. 655.

" permits " or " knowingly permits " unlawful activities such as unlawful gaming to continue on the premises.[20] But where the licensee is himself in charge he will not be vicariously responsible [21] for the conduct of a servant in another room.[22] The policy behind these decisions is clear. Licences are only granted to persons of good personal character and the purpose of so restricting the grant would be defeated if the licensee could, by delegating the management, free himself from responsibility.[23]

---

[20] *Allen* v. *Whitehead* [1930] 1 K.B. 211.
[21] If the licensee knows about the unlawful activities he will usually be guilty either of a substantive offence (*e.g.* offences of " permitting " or " suffering ") or as an accomplice.
[22] *Somerset* v. *Hart* (1884) 12 Q.B.D. 360; *Vane* v. *Yiannopoullos* [1965] A.C. 486.
[23] *Massey* v. *Morris* [1894] 2 Q.B. at p. 414. The master is not liable if an employee has no authority to make any sales: *Adams* v. *Camfoni* [1929] 1 K.B. 95.

CHAPTER 3

ATTEMPTS, INCITEMENT AND CONSPIRACY

SECTION 1. ATTEMPTS

AN attempt to commit any offence,[1] other than a summary offence,[2] is itself an offence. Section 7 (2) of the Criminal Law Act 1967 provides that a person convicted on indictment of an attempt to commit an offence for which a maximum term of imprisonment or a maximum fine is provided by any enactment shall not be sentenced to imprisonment for a term longer, nor to a fine larger, than that to which he would be sentenced for the completed offence.[3]

Section 19 (9) of the Magistrates' Courts Act 1952 provides that where a person is convicted of attempting to commit an indictable offence by a magistrates' court before which he has elected summary trial[4] and the offence is both an indictable and a summary conviction offence, the maximum penalty that he may be given is that to which he would have been liable if he had been proceeded against summarily.[5] Where a person is convicted of attempting to commit an indictable offence by a magistrates' court before which the accused has elected summary trial[6] and he is remanded for sentence to the Crown Court, section 7 (2) of the Criminal Law Act will apply.[7]

---

[1] But see *R.* v. *Moran* (1952) 36 Cr.App.R. 10. It is said (Russell, p. 172) that in the case of treason no distinction is drawn between attempt and the full offence because an attempt to commit treason would amount to an overt act of treason. *Sed quaere* whether this is true of all the different kinds of treason. See Stephen's *Digest of the Criminal Law*, 1877, art. 50. It is submitted that there is no offence of attempted manslaughter in practice, whatever the theoretical possibilities may be. *Cf.* Smith & Hogan, *op. cit.*, 2nd ed., p. 178. See also *R.* v. *Bruzas* [1972] Crim.L.R. 367 and the commentary thereon.

[2] However, both conspiracy and incitement to commit summary offences are themselves indictable offences; *post*, pp. 62, 63. Statute may, of course, provide that an attempt to commit a summary offence is itself an offence.

[3] This gives statutory force to the decision in *R.* v. *Pearce* [1953] 1 Q.B. 30.

[4] By virtue of s. 19, *post*, p. 647.

[5] Under s. 18, *post*, p. 650.

[6] By virtue of s. 19 of the Magistrates' Courts Act 1952; if he is sentenced by a magistrates' court, the maximum sentence is six months.

[7] Criminal Justice Act 1948, s. 29 (3) (*a*).

Where a person is being tried on indictment for any offence,[8] the jury may find him guilty of an attempt to commit that offence.[9] A magistrates' court trying an indictable offence summarily may not find the accused guilty of attempt if the completed offence is charged,[10] since a magistrates' court, subject to certain exceptions, may only try one information at a time.

Where a person is charged on indictment with attempting to commit an offence or with any assault or other act preliminary to an offence, but not with the completed offence, then (subject to the discretion of the court to discharge the jury with a view to the preferment of an indictment for the completed offence) he may be convicted of the offence charged, notwithstanding that he is shown to be guilty of the complete offence.[11] The same principle (*i.e.* a person may be convicted of attempt even though he succeeded) presumably applies to summary trials of indictable offences.[12]

Mens rea of attempt. Where a crime prohibits certain consequences, such as death or injury to the person, or certain conduct, such as administering noxious gas or setting fire to something, then, in order to be convicted of attempt, it appears that the accused must have foreseen that the consequences were likely to occur and desired that they should or intended to conduct himself in the prohibited manner.[13] For example, the crime of arson under the Criminal Damage Act 1971 [14] requires a setting fire and some burning. To be guilty of the attempt, therefore, the accused must have intended to set fire to the house, foreseen that burning was a likely consequence and desired that consequence. If there had been

---

[8] With the possible exception of treason, to which s. 6 (3) of the Criminal Law Act 1967 does not apply.

[9] *Ibid.* s. 6 (2) (3) (4).

[10] *Pender* v. *Smith* [1959] 2 Q.B. 84 at p. 88. And see *Lawrence* v. *Same* [1968] 2 Q.B. 93.

[11] Criminal Law Act 1967, s. 6 (4). *Sed quaere* whether a person may be convicted of attempt when he is charged with, and is found to have committed, the completed offence: *R.* v. *Harden* [1963] 1 Q.B. 8.

[12] But see *Rogers* v. *Arnott* [1960] 2 Q.B. 244, doubted in *R.* v. *Males* [1962] 2 Q.B. 500 and discussed in Smith and Hogan, 2nd ed., p. 163.

[13] See *R.* v. *Whybrow* (1951) 35 Cr.App.R. 141. See also *R.* v. *Cook* (1963) 48 Cr.App.R. 98. But the law is certainly not very clear and there seems no reason in principle why recklessness should not be sufficient. If A shoots at B foreseeing that he may kill him, but not desiring it, why should he not be guilty of attempted murder?

[14] *Post*, p. 530.

someone in the house, the accused could only be convicted of attempted murder if he foresaw that *death* was a likely consequence of the burning and desired it.[15] Mere intention to cause grievous bodily harm, although sufficient for murder,[16] is not sufficient for attempted murder.

There is some authority to the effect that even though the definition of a crime does not require *mens rea* as to one or more of the ingredients of the crime (*e.g.* it is a crime of strict liability),[17] an attempt to commit that crime requires *mens rea*.[18] If this is so, it would be in line with the decisions on aiding and abetting [19] and conspiring to commit [20] such crimes.

Actus reus of attempt

" An attempt to commit a crime is an act done with intent to commit that crime, and forming part of a series of acts which would constitute its actual commission if it were not interrupted." [21]

The difficulty arises not in stating the principle but in its application. In *R.* v. *Miskell*,[22] the Courts-Martial Appeal Court said:

" Not all acts which are steps towards the commission of a crime can be regarded as attempts. Some may be too far removed from the commission of the crime to be regarded as attempts to commit the crime; but just where the distinction is to be drawn between preliminary acts of preparation and acts which are nearly enough related to the crime to amount to attempts to commit it is often a difficult and nice question. . . .

" The principle to be applied by the court in deciding the question was stated by Parke B in *R.* v. *Eagleton*.[23] That statement of the principle was approved and followed in *R.*

---

[15] See *R.* v. *Whybrow* (1951) 35 Cr.App.R. 141.
[16] *Post*, p. 433.
[17] *Ante*, p. 41.
[18] See *Gardner* v. *Akeroyd* [1952] 2 Q.B. 743.
[19] *Post*, p. 73.
[20] *Post*, p. 63.
[21] Stephen's *Digest*, 5th ed., art. 50, approved by Lord Parker in *Davey* v. *Lee* [1968] 1 Q.B. 366 at p. 370.
[22] [1954] 1 W.L.R. 438 at p. 440; and see *R.* v. *Gammon* (1959) 43 Cr.App.R. 155.
[23] (1855) Dears. 515.

v. *Robinson*[24] and *R*. v. *Woods*[25] in the following words:
' The mere intention to commit a misdemeanour is not criminal. Some act is required, and we do not think that all acts
towards committing a misdemeanour are indictable. Acts
remotely leading towards the commission of the offence are
not to be considered as attempts to commit it, but acts
immediately connected with it are.' "

The application of this admittedly nebulous principle may be
seen in the following cases. In *R*. v. *Robinson*[26] a jeweller, with
the object of fraudulently obtaining insurance moneys, hid his
stock of jewellery, tied himself up and represented to the police
that a burglary had taken place at his shop. The police having
found the jewellery, he was arrested and charged with having
attempted to obtain money from the insurers by false pretences
(now, " by deception " under the Theft Act 1968). It was held
that what he had done was merely " preparation for the commission of a crime, not a step in the commission of it." [27] However, the court also said that a claim for the money from the
underwriters or a communication to them of the pretended burglary
would have been sufficient to make him guilty of attempt.

The Divisional Court held in *Comer* v. *Bloomfield*[28] that the
justices were entitled to reach the conclusion that a mere preliminary inquiry as to insurance cover for a stolen vehicle made
with fraudulent intention will not constitute an act, sufficiently
proximate to the obtaining of compensation to amount to an
attempt to obtain money by deception. The facts were that the
defendant seriously damaged his van due to his own fault. He
knew his insurance policy did not cover damage caused by his
own fault, but was uncertain as to what it did cover. He left the
van in some woods, told the police it had been stolen and told
the insurance company the same thing. He then asked his insurance company whether he could claim under his policy for theft.
The insurance policy in fact, did not cover him for theft. On a submission of no case the justices dismissed the charge of attempting
to obtain money by deception on the ground that there was merely

[24] [1915] 2 K.B. 342.
[25] (1930) 22 Cr.App.R. 41 at p. 44.
[26] [1915] 2 K.B. 342.
[27] At p. 349.
[28] [1971] R.T.R. 49, D.C. ; [1971] Crim.L.R. 230, D.C.

an inquiry which was insufficiently proximate to the obtaining of money by deception to constitute an attempt.

In *Hope* v. *Brown*[29] the accused, a butcher, was charged with attempting to sell meat above a maximum permitted price. The accused had prepared meat for delivery to customers and placed on each package a ticket specifying a price that it was lawful to charge. However, it was admitted that before delivery these tickets would be removed and another set of tickets specifying a higher unlawful charge would be substituted. The preparation of the fake tickets and placing them in a drawer was alleged to constitute an attempt. The court held that these acts were too remote from the intended sale to constitute an attempt. To constitute an attempt, it was said, the false tickets would have to have been affixed to the meat.

In *R.* v. *Button*,[30] on the other hand, the court held that the accused was properly convicted of attempt. In that case, the accused, who was a good runner, entered for two handicap races at an athletic meeting in the name of another person who was a less good runner, whereby he was given a long start to which he was not entitled. He won both races, but there was no evidence that he had applied for the prizes. *R.* v. *Button* was distinguished in *R.* v. *Robinson*[31] on the grounds that the accused in the *Button* case had made a false pretence " directly to the race authorities with the intent to make them part with the prize."

In *R.* v. *Cook*[32] the accused was found in another person's car and there was evidence that he was fiddling with the ignition lock on the dashboard. It was held that there was sufficient evidence on which the accused could be convicted of attempting to take and drive away a vehicle without the owner's consent.

In each case the nature of the act which is immediately connected with the commission of the offence will be a matter of fact. In a recent case, the Divisional Court approved a passage from Archbold which described such an act as an act " the doing of which cannot reasonably be regarded as having any other purpose than the commission of the specific crime." [33]

---

[29] [1954] 1 W.L.R. 250.
[30] [1900] 2 Q.B. 597.
[31] [1915] 2 K.B. 342 at p. 348.
[32] (1963) 48 Cr.App.R. 98.
[33] *Davey* v. *Lee* [1968] 1 Q.B. 366 at p. 371. See also *Jones* v. *Brooks* (1968) 52 Cr.App.R. 614.

Impossibility of objective. The mere fact that the accused was attempting to do something that was, in the circumstances, physically impossible does not prevent a conviction for attempt. Thus a person who puts his hand into a pocket with intent to steal can be convicted of attempt although the pocket is empty [34] and it has recently been held by the Court of Appeal (Criminal Division) in *R. v. Crispin* [35] that a person who assisted in the removal of stolen goods without handling them was guilty of an offence. So equally was one who attempted to do so, as where the defendant arrived at a garage to remove stolen skirts and the police had already removed them. Having gone to the place where the stolen property was believed to be with transport and with the purpose of moving it, it was sufficient to convict him of attempting to handle stolen skirts by assisting in their removal or disposal, and it mattered not whether the property was in fact there or had been recovered by the police.

Law and fact. Where an attempt to commit an offence is charged, it is for the judge to rule whether there is evidence capable of constituting an attempt, and for the jury to say whether they accept the evidence as amounting to an attempt.[36]

SECTION 2. INCITEMENT

Soliciting or inciting (or attempting to solicit or incite [37]) a person to commit any offence including a summary offence,[38] or to conspire to commit any offence,[39] is itself an **indictable** offence [*fine and Imp.*] [39a] at common law. Section 19 (8) of the Magistrates'

---

[34] *R. v. Ring* (1892) 17 Cox 491. *cf. R. v. Easom* [1971] 2 Q.B. 315 distinguishing *R. v. Ring* (*supra*); in which it was held that a defendant charged with stealing a handbag and its contents was entitled to be acquitted where it appeared that he might have taken it to see whether it contained anything worth stealing and then, being disappointed, left it near its owner with its contents intact because his " conditional appropriation " was neither theft nor attempted theft. *Quaere* whether he might have been convicted on a differently worded indictment. It should be observed that the extension of the law of receiving by s. 22, Theft Act 1968, was intended to catch persons involved in the " conduit pipe."

[35] (1971) 55 Cr.App.R. 310.

[36] *R. v. Cook* (1963) 48 Cr.App.R. 98.

[37] *R. v. Ransford* (1874) 13 Cox 9.

[38] *R. v. Curr* [1968] 2 Q.B. 944. As to the distinction between summary and indictable offences, see Chap. 48, *post*.

[39] *R. v. De Kromme* (1892) 17 Cox 492.

[39a] As to fines at common law, see p. 201, *post*, fn. 52.

Courts Act 1952, provides that where a person is convicted of inciting to commit a summary offence by a magistrates' court before which he has elected summary trial, the maximum penalty is that which could be given on conviction for that offence. In the case of certain offences, *e.g.* murder,[40] special provision is made for incitement to commit those offences.

The offence is proved in the same manner as the offence of giving assistance, encouragement, etc., to a principal offender before the commission of an offence, *i.e.* as an accomplice.[41] But whereas an accomplice to an offence cannot be convicted unless that offence is actually committed or attempted, this does not apply to a person charged with incitement. The incitement itself constitutes the offence.[42]

It has been held sufficient that the incitement was published in a newspaper and not addressed to any particular person.[43]

SECTION 3. CONSPIRACY

Conspiracy is an **indictable** offence at common law [*fine and Imp*].[44] It has been held that a higher sentence should not be passed for conspiracy than could be passed for the substantive offence except in very exceptional cases.[45] Conspiracy to murder is punishable by ten years' imprisonment.[46]

Actus reus. Conspiracy consists in the agreement between two or more persons to achieve an unlawful object—the word " unlawful " being used here in a special sense. This concept of conspiracy is based upon the legal fiction that the offence lies not in the overt acts themselves but in the agreement to commit them.[47] The *actus reus* lies in the agreement itself. Mere knowledge of a plan is not sufficient; nor the mere intention to achieve the unlawful object.[48]

---

[40] *Post*, p. 446.
[41] Arch. para, 4095. For the law regarding accomplices, see *post*, p. 73.
[42] *R.* v. *Assistant Recorder of Kingston-upon-Hull, ex p. Morgan* (1969) 53 Cr.App.R. 96, at p. 98.
[43] *R.* v. *Most* (1881) 7 Q.B.D. 244.
[44] See fn. 59 to p. 201, *post*.
[45] *Verrier* v. *D.P.P.* [1967] A.C. 195 H.L.
[46] *Post*, p. 446.
[47] *D.P.P.* v. *Bhagwan* [1970] 3 All E.R. 97 *per* Lord Diplock at p. 104.
[48] *Mulcahy* v. *R.* (1868) L.R. 3 H.L. 306 at p. 317.

For there to be a conspiracy more than one person must agree. Husband and wife are not more than one person for this purpose [49]; nor are a director of a limited company and the company itself, where the sole responsible person in the company is that director.[50]

A conspiracy may be complete even if no further act is done in pursuance of the agreement, and provided that the stage of negotiation has been passed [51] even though the parties have not yet settled the means to be employed.[52] Again, an agreement which would otherwise amount to a conspiracy is not necessarily prevented from being one by the fact that it contains some reservation, express or implied, although this will depend upon the nature and extent of the reservation. In R. v. Mills [53] it was suggested that if the reservation were merely that the crime should not be attempted if a policeman were on the scene, then the conspiracy would still be complete; but if the matters left outstanding or reserved were of a substantial nature, the arrangements might be said to be negotiations only.

There need be no direct communication between the members in order to constitute conspiracy [54]; nor need it be proved that any particular accused concocted the scheme or was present at its origins.[55] " The conspirators may join in the conspiracy at various times; any one of them may not know all the other parties; . . . and any one may not know the full extent of the scheme to which he attaches himself." [56] It is sufficient if it is proved that each conspirator knows that there is in existence or coming into existence a scheme which goes beyond the illegal acts which he agrees to do,[57] and attaches himself to the scheme. Quite a slight participation in the scheme will suffice.[58] There is no need that the conspirator should be an accomplice in the crime.[59]

Mens rea. Conspiracy to commit an unlawful act, even an offence of strict liability, requires *mens rea*. The Crown must prove

[49] *Mawji* v. *R.* (1957) 41 Cr.App.R. 69 P.C..
[50] *R.* v. *McDonnell* [1966] 1 Q.B. 233 but *cf. R.* v. *I.C.R. Haulage* [1944] 1 K.B. 551.
[51] *R.* v. *Walker* [1962] Crim.L.R. 458.
[52] *R.* v. *King and King* [1967] 2 Q.B. 338.   [53] [1963] 1 Q.B. 522.
[54] *R.* v. *Meyrick* (1929) 21 Cr.App.R. 94.
[55] *R.* v. *Murphy* (1837) 8 C. & P. 297 at 311.
[56] *R.* v. *Griffiths and Ors.* (1965) 49 Cr.App.R. 279.
[57] *Ibid.*
[58] Glanville Williams, p. 668.   [59] See p. 73.

not only an agreement amounting to a conspiracy between the conspirators to carry out an unlawful purpose, but also an intention in the mind of the individual conspirator to carry out that unlawful purpose.[60] In *Churchill* v. *Walton* [61] Viscount Dilhorne, delivering the opinion of the House of Lords, said:

> " The question is, ' What did they agree to do? ' If what they agreed to do was, on the facts known to them, an unlawful act, they are guilty of conspiracy and cannot excuse themselves by saying that, owing to their ignorance of the law, they did not realise that such an act was a crime. If, on the facts known to them, what they agreed to do was lawful, they are not rendered artificially guilty by the existence of other facts, not known to them, giving a different and criminal quality to the act agreed upon."

Proof of conspiracy. Only rarely will direct evidence of the agreement be available. In the words of the House of Lords, therefore [62]: " Proof of a conspiracy in most cases depends on inferences to be drawn from the conduct of the parties."

The existence of the conspiracy itself " may be shown by the detached acts of the several conspirators." [63] Moreover, on a trial for conspiracy, there is an exception made to the hearsay rule.[64] On the trial of A for an offence other than conspiracy, what B said or wrote to C about A would normally be inadmissible to prove, *as against A*, the truthfulness of the statement. So if A, a public officer, is charged with taking bribes from B and C, a letter from B to C stating that A was asking for his monthly cheque and that he wished the matter to be kept confidential would be inadmissible on the trial of A to prove the truthfulness of its contents, *i.e.* that A was taking bribes. The rationale for this is that A cannot cross-examine B and this evidence is, therefore, potentially very dangerous. But if A is charged with a conspiracy with B and C to take bribes, then once " the prosecution have laid a sufficient foundation by evidence to go to the jury, of several persons having conspired together," [65] the letter would be admissible against A to

---

[60] *R.* v. *Thompson* (1965) 50 Cr.App.R. 1.
[61] [1967] 2 A.C. 224 at p. 237.
[62] *Ibid.*, at p. 232.
[63] *R.* v. *Blake* (1844) 6 Q.B. 126 at p. 139.
[64] *Post*, p. 605.
[65] *Cf. Phipson on Evidence*, 11th ed., para. 266.

prove the truthfulness of its contents.[66] However, this exception applies only to acts or statements of any of the conspirators *in furtherance of the common design*.[67] So if B and C then confessed to the police that A had received bribes from them, that confession would be inadmissible to prove that A had conspired with B and C because the confession would not be in furtherance of the common design.[68]

The unlawful object. An agreement to commit any indictable or summary offence [69] is a conspiracy. It is far from clear what other kinds of unlawful objects are sufficient. There are two main categories of unlawful object. Into the first category fits the type of object which affects the public at large, or the state [70] or the administration of justice. Conspiracies of this kind may be compendiously referred to as conspiracies to effect a public mischief. That such a conspiracy is an offence has only recently been affirmed by the House of Lords in *Shaw* v. *Director of Public Prosecutions*.[71] Into the second category fits the type of object which injuriously affects an individual or group of individuals. The first category will now be dealt with.

The very nature of this kind of conspiracy makes it difficult, if not impossible, to offer any definition of what kind of conduct constitutes a public mischief. The following have been held to be indictable conspiracies of this kind:

   (i) A conspiracy to obtain a passport from the Foreign Office by means of false representations as to the identity of the person by whom it is to be used.[72]

  (ii) A conspiracy to enable a person to obtain admission to the Inner Temple as a student by means of forged documents.[73]

---

[66] See *R.* v. *Whitaker* (1914) 10 Cr.App.R. 245.
[67] *R.* v. *Blake* (1844) 6 Q.B. 126.
[68] See *R.* v. *Pepper* (1921) 16 Cr.App.R. 12.
[69] *R.* v. *Blamires Transport Ltd.* [1964] 1 Q.B. 278. But see *R.* v. *Barnett* [1951] 2 K.B. 425. Any time limitation on the right to commence proceedings for the substantive offence does not apply to conspiracy: *R.* v. *Simmonds* [1967] 1 Q.B. 685. See also *R.* v. *Hunter & Ors.* [1972] Crim.L.R. 369 (conspiracy to prevent the burial of a corpse).
[70] But see *D.P.P.* v. *Bhagwan* (1970) 54 Cr.App.R. 460. H.L.
[71] [1962] A.C. 220; and see *R.* v. *Knuller, etc.* [1972] 2 Q.B. 179.
[72] *R.* v. *Brailsford* [1905] 2 K.B. 730.
[73] *R.* v. *Bassey* (1931) 22 Cr.App.R. 160.

   (iii) **An agreement by an accused person to indemnify his bail so that he would have no interest that the accused was forthcoming to take his trial.**[74]

   (iv) **A conspiracy to publish matter calculated to interfere with a fair trial.**[75]

   (v) **A conspiracy to defeat a Defence Regulation by diverting goods intended for export to the home market.**[76]

   (vi) **A conspiracy by police officers to obstruct the course of public justice by taking bribes for the purpose of preventing or hindering prosecutions.**[77]

   (vii) **A conspiracy to obstruct public justice by making false statements to the police.**[78]

  (viii) **A conspiracy to corrupt public morals by the publication of a directory of prostitutes,[79] or by publishing advertisements in a magazine with a wide circulation encouraging homosexual practices.**[80]

It is interesting to note that in all these cases the accused were agreeing to commit criminal offences and that all the cases *could*, therefore, have been decided on narrower grounds.[81]

In a case where there is no question of public standards of morality, no question of fact or degree or opinion, but a simple straightforward case in which the act complained of is an act

---

[74] *R.* v. *Porter* [1910] 1 K.B. 369; approved in *R.* v. *Foy and others* (1972) 116 S.J. 506.

[75] *R.* v. *Tibbits and Windust* [1902] 1 K.B. 77.

[76] *R.* v. *Newland* (1953) 37 Cr.App.R. 154, where the authorities are reviewed. But it was said in *D.P.P.* v. *Bhagwan* (1970) 54 Cr.App.R. 460 that the use of dishonest devices such as those employed in *Newland's* case is an essential ingredient of a criminal conspiracy against the state, or to defeat the intention of a statute.

[77] *R.* v. *Hammersley* (1958) 42 Cr.App.R. 207.

[78] *R.* v. *Field and Others* [1965] 1 Q.B. 402.

[79] *Shaw* v. *Director of Public Prosecutions* [1962] A.C. 220.

[80] *R.* v. *Knuller, etc.* [1972] 2 Q.B. 179, C.A.; affirmed on appeal *sub nom.* *Knuller (Publishing, Printing and Promotions) Ltd.* v. *Director of Public Prosecutions* [1972] 3 W.L.R. 143, H.L. A conviction based upon the same facts for " outraging public decency " was however quashed. Lord Diplock was of opinion that no such offence as conspiracy to corrupt public morals had existed prior to the decision in *Shaw's* case and urged that that case should not be allowed to stand; a majority of the House decided, however, that it would be improper to overrule it.

[81] Nos. (i) and (v) constituted obtaining by false pretences under the Larceny Act 1916 (repealed by the Theft Act 1968). No. (ii) constituted forgery. Nos. (iii) and (iv) constituted contempt of court. No. (vi) constituted the offence of bribery. No. (vii) constituted obstruction of a police officer. No. (viii) constituted an offence against the Obscene Publications Act 1959. See also *R.* v. *Simmonds* [1967] 1 Q.B. 685.

previously held illegal as a matter of law, it is for the judge to direct the jury as a matter of law that, if they are satisfied as to the facts, that they must conclude that the case is one of conspiracy to effect a public mischief. He is not, in such a case, bound to leave the question " public mischief or no?" to the jury.[81a]

The scope of the second category is far from clear. It appears that any agreement to defraud an individual or a group of individuals will be conspiracy. Thus it has been held to be an indictable conspiracy—

(i) For A and B, the latter being a partner with C, to enter into an agreement for the purpose of depriving C of his share of partnership property.[82]

(ii) For A and B to conspire to obtain goods or credit without intending to pay for them.[83]

In the case of example (i), this would be a crime now, although not at that time.[84] In the case of example (ii), the conduct of the accused probably constituted an offence.[85]

In *R*. v. *Clucas*[86] the accused was charged, *inter alia*, with conspiracy to defraud certain bookmakers. The accused and another represented that they were placing bets on behalf of a large number of workmen, whereas they were in fact doing it on their own behalf. It appears by inference from the judgment and more clearly from a later case involving the same man[87] that by making these representations the bookmakers concerned gave the conspirators credit. Then " when they won they collected their bets and when they lost they moved on to the next place."[88] The court held that although the accused was not guilty of obtaining the winnings by false pretences, he was guilty of conspiracy to defraud. However, it is interesting to note that the accused was in fact also guilty of an offence against section 17 of the Gaming Act 1845,[89] of which he was convicted in a later trial.[90]

[81a] *R*. v. *Foy and others* [1972] 116 S.J. 506; *cf. Joshua* v. *The Queen* [1955] A.C. 121, P.C.   [82] *R*. v. *Warburton* (1870) 1 C.C.R. 274.
[83] *R*. v. *Orman* (1880) 14 Cox 381.
[84] The offence was completed before the passing of 31 & 32 Vict. c. 116, by which a partner could be convicted of stealing partnership property (see now s. 5 (1) of the Theft Act 1968).
[85] The offence of obtaining a pecuniary advantage by deception, see p. 514, *post.*
[86] [1949] 2 K.B. 226.   [87] [1959] 1 W.L.R. 244.
[88] *Ibid.* at p. 245.   [89] *Post*, p. 351.
[90] *R*. v. *Clucas and O'Rourke* [1959] 1 W.L.R. 244, following *R*. v. *Leon* [1945] K.B. 136.

In *R. v. Fountain* [91] it was alleged that the accused had conspired together and with other persons unknown to defraud such persons as should be induced to accept bets made by or on behalf of themselves on certain football matches by agreeing to ensure that certain teams lost the matches. The accused were charged with conspiracy to defraud. The trial judge ruled, on a motion by defence counsel that there was no case to answer, that there was such an offence as conspiracy to defraud. Once again, however, it should be pointed out that the accused were agreeing to commit what was anyway a criminal offence, *i.e.* an offence contrary to section 17 of the Gaming Act 1845.

Where the acts which form the subject of the conspiracy are not criminal, nor prohibited by legislation, nor tortious at common law, an agreement to do them is not an offence because the court considers that they will defeat, frustrate or evade the purpose or intention of an Act of Parliament. In *Director of Public Prosecutions* v. *Bhagwan* [92] the appellant was convicted of conspiracy to evade the controls on immigration imposed by the Commonwealth Immigrants Act 1962. He agreed with the master of the ship and others to be landed at a deserted beach and thereby avoid examination by an immigration officer. The House of Lords said that there was nothing in the Act to limit the time or place where such a person's entry to the United Kingdom must be made and there was no duty on the immigrant to seek out an immigration officer on his arrival.

Acquittal or immunity of the conspirators. One person may be convicted alone of conspiracy with persons who are unknown or not in custody, or dead, or whose trial has been postponed.[93] But if two persons are *jointly* indicted for conspiring together both must be convicted or both acquitted [94]; so, also, if three persons are jointly indicted for conspiring together and two are acquitted, the third cannot be convicted even on his own confession.[95] It is not yet clear whether this applies to separate trials. It is difficult to justify the rule because, if there is enough evidence to prove beyond a reasonable doubt that A conspired with B, A should not

[91] [1966] 1 W.L.R. 212.
[92] (1970) 54 Cr.App.R. 460. *Cf. R. v. Knuller, etc.* [1971] 3 W.L.R. 633.
[93] See *R. v. Plummer* [1902] 2 K.B. 339 at p. 344.
[94] *R. v. Manning* (1883) 12 Q.B.D. 241.
[95] *R. v. Plummer* [1902] 2 K.B. 339.

be acquitted merely because there is not enough evidence to prove as against B that he conspired with A.

It would necessarily seem to follow from this rule that if A is indicted alone on a charge of conspiracy with B, A should be acquitted if B would have had to have been acquitted had he, in fact, been charged with conspiracy. For example, it could be proved on A's trial that B was insane at the time of the agreement, or that B was a policeman who had no intention of carrying out the agreement but was seeking evidence against A,[96] or that B had diplomatic immunity. Or, again, assume that A agrees to have intercourse with B, a girl under sixteen.[97] It seems clear that B could not be convicted of conspiracy[98]; can A, therefore, not be convicted of conspiracy either?

There is some authority to the effect that A may be convicted in these circumstances.[99] Although this is apparently inconsistent with the rule that if all the conspirators are tried together they must either all be convicted or all acquitted, it would seem to be right in principle. In the case of one individual, the criminal law quite properly requires more than a decision to commit a crime in order to convict him of attempt.

The rolled-up charge. The practice of charging conspiracy where the substantive offence has been committed has been heavily criticised by the courts on a number of occasions. In *R.* v. *Griffiths*[1] the Court of Criminal Appeal said:

> " The practice of adding what may be called a rolled-up conspiracy charge to a number of counts of substantive offences has become common. We express the very strong hope that this practice will now cease and that the courts will never again have to struggle with this type of case, where it becomes almost impossible to explain to a jury that evidence inadmissible against the accused on the substantive count may be admissible against him on the conspiracy count once he is shown to be a conspirator.
>
> " We do not believe that most juries can ever really understand the subtleties of the situation. In our judgment, except

[96] See *e.g. R.* v. *Birtles* (1969) 53 Cr.App.R. 469, C.A.
[97] *Post*, p. 467.
[98] *Post*, p. 82.
[99] See *R.* v. *Duguid* (1906) 70 J.P. 294.
[1] [1966] 1 Q.B. 589 at p. 594.

in simple cases, a conspiracy count (if one is needed at all) should be tried separately to substantive counts."

Recently the House of Lords stated that only in the very exceptional case should an indictment include a count for conspiracy to commit an offence and a count for the offence itself.[2]

SECTION 4. PROCURING WITH INTENT

A number of offences prohibit possession of certain things either absolutely or conditionally, *e.g.* offences concerning offensive weapons, dangerous drugs, forged documents and implements of forgery. A number of other offences prohibit possession of certain things if the possession is accompanied by a particular intent. Other offences prohibit the procuring of certain things if the procuring is accompanied with a certain intent, *e.g.* procuring poisons, etc., with intent to procure a miscarriage thereby.[3]

Where a person is in possession of or procures something with which he intends to commit an offence, it is probable that he is not thereby and without any further action on his part guilty of an attempt to commit that offence.[4] Such possession or procuration would only amount to an act of preparation.

Although such conduct may not constitute an attempt, there is some authority to the effect that *procuring* anything with intent to commit an offence is itself a common law offence. In *R*. v. *Gurmit Singh*[5] the accused was alleged to have procured a rubber stamp bearing the words "Magistrate First Class Jullundur." With this he intended to prepare an affidavit for the income tax authorities proposing to show that he had dependants in India. Such affidavit would, if accepted, entitle him to a remission of income tax. The accused, who was arrested immediately after he had collected the rubber stamp from the shop, was charged, *inter alia*, on one count with attempted forgery and on another with procuring a stamp with intent to commit forgery. The learned trial judge ruled that there was no evidence of attempted forgery, but that there was such an offence as procuring with intent and that there was sufficient

---

[2] *Verrier* v. *Director of Public Prosecutions* [1967] 2 A.C. 195 at pp. 223–224. These criticisms have made no difference, the practice continues.

[3] Offences against the Person Act 1861, s. 59 (*post*, p. 451).

[4] See [1965] Crim.L.R. 720.

[5] [1966] 2 Q.B. 53; [1965] Crim.L.R. 718.

evidence of that offence having been committed. The accused was duly convicted on this count.

Notwithstanding that there is some authority to support the existence of such an offence,[6] it is open to doubt whether there is, or should be, such an offence. Certainly the decision " suggests a possible general extension of criminal liability beyond what has generally been supposed for many years to be its proper limits." [7]

---

[6] R. v. *Fuller and Robinson* (1816) R. & R. 308; *Dugdale* v. *The Queen* (1853) Dears. 64.
[7] [1965] Crim.L.R. 720.

CHAPTER 4

DEGREES OF RESPONSIBILITY

SECTION 1. ACCOMPLICES

UNTIL the Criminal Law Act 1967, the law relating to accomplices depended upon whether the principal was guilty of a felony or of a misdemeanour. The difference was primarily one of terminology. An aider, abettor, counsellor or procurer to an offence which was a misdemeanour would have been called either a principal in the second degree or an accessory before the fact if the offence had been a felony. There was one difference in substance. There was no equivalent in the law relating to misdemeanours to an accessory after the fact.

With the abolition of the distinction between felony and misdemeanour, the governing legislation is section 8 of the Accessories and Abettors Act 1861, which provides that every person who shall aid, abet, counsel or procure the commission of any misdemeanour is liable to be tried, indicted and punished as a principal. As far as summary conviction offences are concerned the governing legislation is section 35 of the Magistrates' Courts Act 1952, which provides that a person who aids, abets, counsels or procures the commission by another person of a summary offence shall be guilty of the like offence. The important point to note is that the aider, abettor, counsellor or procurer is guilty of the same offence as the principal and is liable to the same penalties. In this chapter such persons will be called " accomplices."

The accessory after the fact to a felony has now disappeared and a new offence has been created to deal with those who give assistance to persons who have committed arrestable offences.[1]

Principals

Before discussing accomplices, a brief reference should be made to principals in the first degree, called hereafter simply principals. A principal is a person who actually perpetrates or takes part in the perpetration of the offence. A person who employs an *innocent*

---

[1] This offence will be dealt with in s. 2 of this chapter.

agent is liable as a principal although he is not actually present at the completion of the transaction, nor does anything with his own hands.

Thus in *R.* v. *Michael* [2] the accused was indicted for the murder of her infant child. The child was in the charge of a woman to whom the accused had given a bottle of laudanum, telling her it was a medicine and asking her to give the child a teaspoonful every night. The woman placed the bottle on a mantlepiece and in her absence one of her own children gave the accused's child about half the contents of the bottle, causing its death. It was held that the accused was rightly convicted, that is as a principal of murder. [3]

Actus Reus and Mens Rea of Accomplices

Actus reus. In order to be an accomplice, that is an aider and abettor, the accused must do an act; although where he has the power to control the principal and is actually present when the offence was committed, mere acquiescence may amount to assistance or encouragement. [4] Assistance by omission is illustrated by the following case. Where a person is the owner of the car in which he is travelling as a passenger and he does not prevent the driver from driving dangerously, the owner may be convicted as an accomplice because he has the right to control the driver's actions. [5] The same principle would presumably apply if an owner of a car took no steps to prevent a drunken person from driving his car even though he was not a passenger. So also a publican's failure to stop customers from drinking outside permitted hours may make him an accomplice to that drinking. [6]

Where A watches B assault C, A's failure to prevent the assault would not *in itself* make him an accomplice [7] or, where A learns that B will assault C, A's failure to inform the police would not, in itself, make him an accomplice although in the latter example it might be different if A was himself a policeman.

[2] (1840) 9 C. & P. 356.
[3] Further problems that can arise with the use of an innocent agent are discussed *post*, p. 81.
[4] *Per* Slade J. in *National Coal Board* v. *Gamble* [1959] 1 Q.B. 11 at p. 25, approved in *Tuck* v. *Robson* [1970] 1 W.L.R. 741.
[5] *Du Cros* v. *Lambourne* [1907] 1 K.B. 40.
[6] *Tuck* v. *Robson* [1970] 1 W.L.R. 741.
[7] See *R.* v. *Atkinson* (1869) 11 Cox 330; *R.* v. *Coney* (1882) 8 Q.B.D. 534.

The act or omission must constitute assistance or encouragement.[8] It is no criminal offence to stand by, a mere passive spectator of a crime, even of a murder. Mere presence at the commission of an offence is not enough. It must be proved at the very least that the accused by some means or other *encouraged* the participants.[9] Mere *intention* to encourage is not in itself enough, there must also be *encouragement* in fact.[10]

In *R.* v. *Coney*[11] the accused were spectators at a prize fight. The Court for Crown Cases Reserved held that although mere presence unexplained is evidence of encouragement (and therefore of guilt) it is not conclusive proof of encouragement. Hawkins J. said[12]:

"In my opinion, to constitute an aider and abettor some active steps must be taken by word, or action, with the intent to instigate the principal, or principals. . . . Non-interference to prevent a crime is not itself a crime. But the fact that a person was voluntarily and purposely present witnessing the commission of a crime, and offered no opposition to it, though he might reasonably be expected to prevent and had the power so to do, or at least to express his dissent, might under some circumstances offer cogent evidence upon which a jury would be justified in finding that he wilfully encouraged and so aided and abetted. But it would be purely a question for the jury whether he did so or not."

Under this principle, a passenger of a car being driven dangerously may be guilty of dangerous driving as an accomplice. But it would be more difficult to find the evidence of encouragement in this case than in the *Coney* case, because in the *Coney* case the incentive to the fighters was the presence of the accused. The presence of the passenger would not necessarily be an encouragement to the driver but it might be.[13]

Mens rea. In order to be an accomplice, a person must have *mens rea*. In addition to encouragement in fact, there must be an

[8] *Per* Devlin J. in *National Coal Board* v. *Gamble* [1959] 1 Q.B. 11 and see *Tuck* v. *Robson* [1970] 1 W.L.R. 741.
[9] *R.* v. *Allan* [1965] 1 Q.B. 130 at p. 138.
[10] *R.* v. *Clarkson* [1971] 1 W.L.R. 1402.
[11] (1882) 8 Q.B.D. 534. See also *Wilcox* v. *Jeffrey* [1951] 1 All E.R. 464; *R.* v. *Allan* [1965] 1 Q.B. 130. *Cf. Smith* v. *Baker* [1972] Crim.L.R. 25.
[12] (1882) 8 Q.B.D. 534 at pp. 557–558.
[13] See *R.* v. *Baldessare* (1930) 22 Cr.App.R. 70.

intention to encourage. A person does not become an accomplice by assisting another person to commit an offence unless he is voluntarily and knowingly giving that assistance and knows that the offence is being or is likely to be committed. This is so even though the offence itself is one of strict liability.[14] Provided that the accused knows that the offence is being or is likely to be committed, it does not matter whether he desires the offence to be committed or is indifferent as to whether the offence is committed. Nor should it make any difference (although there is authority to the contrary [15]) that he does not want the offence to be committed. In *National Coal Board* v. *Gamble* [16] Devlin J. said:

> " If one man deliberately sells to another a gun to be used for murdering a third, he may be indifferent about whether the third man lives or dies and interested only in the cash profit to be made out of the sale, but he can still be an aider and abettor. To hold otherwise would be to negative the rule that *mens rea* is a matter of intent only and does not depend upon desire or motive."

The person alleged to be an accomplice must know the essential *facts* which must be proved to show that an offence has been committed.[17] It is not necessary that he should know that those facts constitute an offence, but he must know at least what the person abetted is doing.[18] It must be proved that he knew that the type of crime which was in fact committed was intended, but it is not necessary to prove that he knew that a particular offence on a particular date and at a particular premises was intended.[19] So a person was convicted as an accomplice where he provided oxy-acetylene cutting equipment with the knowledge that it was going to be used for breaking and entering premises although he did not

---

[14] See *National Coal Board* v. *Gamble* [1959] 1 Q.B. 11; *John Henshall (Quarries) Ltd*. v. *Harvey* [1965] 2 Q.B. 233; *R*. v. *Churchill* [1967] 2 A.C. 224 at p. 235.

[15] *R*. v. *Fretwell* (1862) L. & C. 161. This is the same kind of problem as raised in *R*. v. *Steane* [1947] K.B. 997, discussed *ante*, p. 40.

[16] [1959] 1 Q.B. 11 at p. 23.

[17] *Johnson* v. *Youden* [1950] 1 K.B. 544; *Pope* v. *Minton* [1954] Crim.L.R. 711; *Davies Turner & Co*. v. *Brodie* [1954] 1 W.L.R. 1364.

[18] *Thomas* v. *Lindop* [1950] 1 All E.R. 966; *Ferguson* v. *Weaving* [1951] 1 K.B. 814; *R*. v. *Patel* [1970] Crim.L.R. 274.

[19] *R*. v. *Bainbridge* (1959) 43 Cr.App.R. 194; *R*. v. *Payne* [1965] Crim.L.R. 543; *R*. v. *Bettles* [1966] Crim.L.R. 503.

know that it was going to be used, as it in fact was, against the Stoke Newington Branch of the Midland Bank.[20]

A problem arises where a person knows that one type of offence is likely to be committed and then, during the commission by the principal of that offence, some further offence is committed. For example, if a person assists a robber (*e.g.* by being a look-out) and the principal kills someone in circumstances which make him guilty of murder, is the look-out then guilty of murder? The applicable principle of law may be stated thus:

". . . where two persons embarked on a joint enterprise, each was liable for the acts done in pursuance of that joint enterprise including liability for unusual consequences if they arose from the agreed joint enterprise, but that, if one of the adventurers went beyond what had been tacitly agreed as part of the common enterprise, his co-adventurer was not liable for the consequences of the unauthorised act, and it was for the jury in every case to decide whether what was done was part of the joint enterprise or went beyond it and was an act unauthorised by that joint enterprise." [21]

This principle was applied in *R.* v. *Lovesey*; *Peterson.*[22] In that case, the appellants with a number of other men attacked and robbed a jeweller, who later died from his injuries. There was no direct evidence of the individual roles of the various persons concerned. Since neither of the appellants' parts could be identified the Court of Appeal held that neither could be convicted of an offence which went beyond the common design to which he was a party.

In *R.* v. *Smith* [23] the appellant and three others had been causing a disturbance in a public-house. The appellant went outside to pick up bricks with a view to wrecking the premises. While he was outside, one of his associates inside took out a knife and fought with and killed the barman. Smith knew that the principal had the knife on him. Dismissing his appeal against a conviction for manslaughter, the Court of Criminal Appeal held that the use of the knife could not be said to be outside the scope of the

[20] *R.* v. *Bainbridge* (1959) 43 Cr.App.R. 194.
[21] Headnote to *R.* v. *Anderson and Morris* [1966] 2 Q.B. 110.
[22] [1970] 1 Q.B. 352.
[23] [1963] 1 W.L.R. 1200; applied in *R.* v. *Betty* (1964) 48 Cr.App.R. 6.

concerted action. The court said further [24] that the use of a loaded revolver unknown to Smith might possibly have been outside the scope of the concerted action.

Where it is alleged that an accused person's continuing and non-accidental presence during the commission of an offence constitutes aiding and abetting it is not enough that the presence of the accused has in fact given encouragement. It must be proved that the accused intended to give encouragement; that he *wilfully* encouraged. This was the position in *R.* v. *Clarkson* [25] where the defendants who had been drinking heard indications that a woman was being raped in a room and they entered it and remained while the offences were committed. There was no evidence of direct physical participation or verbal encouragement.

Mens rea of accomplices and manslaughter. It will be seen later [26] that a person is guilty of manslaughter if death results from the commission by him of an unlawful and dangerous act even though he did not foresee that death was likely to occur. Thus an accomplice to an *unlawful* abortion will be guilty as an accomplice to manslaughter if death results, although he did not foresee that death was likely to occur.[27]

Joint possession and accomplices. It is possible to have more than one person in possession of something, such as an offensive weapon. If A is holding a knife, B may be in joint possession with A if he knew about the knife and had some control over the knife.[28] But even if B is not a joint possessor, he may be an accomplice to A's possession. In *R.* v. *McCarthy* [29] the Court of Criminal Appeal said:

> ". . . it is possible to envisage circumstances in which A may have the sole possession and control over an explosive while B, without having any share in such possession or control, is present actively encouraging A or helping him in some way to maintain his possession or control.

24 [1963] 1 W.L.R. 1200 at p. 1207.
25 [1971] 1 W.L.R. 1402, Ct.M.A.C.
26 *Post*, p. 441.
27 *R.* v. *Creamer* [1966] 1 Q.B. 72; *R.* v. *Buck* (1960) 44 Cr.App.R. 213; As to counselling and procuring death by dangerous driving, see *R.* v. *Millar* (*Contractors*) *Ltd. and Anor*. (1970) 54 Cr.App.R. 158, at pp. 163–165.
28 See *R.* v. *Irala Prevost* [1965] Crim.L.R. 606.
29 [1964] 1 W.L.R. 196 at p. 200.

" In the view of this court a man may properly be convicted of aiding and abetting this offence [unlawful possession of explosives] if it is found: (a) that he knew that the principal offender had explosives in his possession or under his control; (b) that he knew facts giving rise to a reasonable suspicion that the principal offender did not have such explosives in his possession or under his control for a lawful object; (c) that he was present actively encouraging or in some way helping the principal offender in the commission of this offence."

Persons Present at the Commission of the Offence

A person who is *present* at the commission of an offence but who, without committing the offence, assists or encourages its commission is guilty of the like offence as the principal. It is not necessary that the alleged aider and abettor should be actually present as an eye-witness of the event, provided that he is somewhere in the vicinity ready to give help if needed, or acting as a watch, or as driver of the " getaway " car.[30]

Persons Giving Assistance Before the Commission of the Offence

A person who is not present at the commission of the offence but who, *before its commission*, encourages, advises, assists or arranges the commission of the offence is guilty of the like offence as the principal.

It has been shown above that the supplier of equipment to a principal may be convicted as an accomplice, provided that he was aware of the type of crime that the equipment would be used for.[31] A company and a director of the company, with knowledge that a vehicle was in a dangerous condition, sent a servant with like knowledge to drive a vehicle from Scotland to England. In consequence of the dangerous condition a fatal accident occurred. The Court of Appeal held,[32] *inter alia*, that even where dangerous driving arose from some defect in the vehicle, rather than from the manner of driving, a person could be convicted of procuring

---

[30] See, *e.g.* R. v. *Betts and Ridley* (1930) 22 Cr.App.R. 148 and p. 75, *ante.*
[31] A person is not an accomplice if he merely hands over equipment which the principal has a right to demand, *e.g.* because he owns it: see *National Coal Board* v. *Gamble* [1959] 1 Q.B. 11 at p. 20 and the authorities there cited.
[32] R. v. *Millar (Contractors) Ltd. and Another* [1970] 2 Q.B. 54; (1970) 54 Cr.App.R. 158.

the offence. There might be participation in an offence by a person who was not present, and for that purpose it sufficed that the employers had set the crime in motion by instructing the servant to drive, knowing that the vehicle was in a dangerous condition.

Accomplices to Principals Who Have Themselves Been Either Acquitted or Not Convicted

On the trial of A as an accomplice to the commission of a crime by B, it may happen that the court which is trying A is satisfied beyond a reasonable doubt that A was an accomplice and that B committed the crime but that B has not yet been convicted of the crime. May the jury still convict A? Although there was some doubt in the case of a felony,[33] it seems clear now that the answer is that the jury may convict A in these circumstances. It was said in *R.* v. *Humphreys and Turner* [34]:

> " It may seem anomalous, at any rate to laymen, that even if a principal offender is acquitted, a conviction of aiding and abetting him may still be valid, but the logic of the situation is wrapped up in the rules of evidence. In a case where two people are charged a jury is always directed to consider each case separately. This is because the evidence as against one accused or another may be quite different in validity (*i.e.* admissibility) or strength. A statement by accused A is normally inadmissible as evidence against accused B; but may well be conclusive. It would be anomalous if a person who admitted to a substantial part in the perpetration of a misdemeanour as aider and abettor could not be convicted on his own admission merely because the person alleged to have been aided and abetted was not or could not be convicted."

Accomplices to Principals Who Are Guilty of Crimes of a Greater Degree

Where the court is satisfied that the principal is guilty of a crime, it may properly convict an accomplice of a lesser degree of that crime. So it is possible for a person to be convicted of murder and his accomplice of manslaughter.

---

[33] See *R.* v. *Anthony* [1965] 2 Q.B. 189.
[34] [1965] 3 All E.R. 689 at p. 692.

Innocent Agents

In the situations envisaged in the examples given above, the court could convict A, provided that they were satisfied beyond a reasonable doubt that B committed the crime in question or a greater crime. A much more difficult problem arises if B cannot or could not be convicted of the crime because in law B did not commit the offence. For example, it will be seen later that a boy under fourteen cannot be convicted of rape. Let us assume that A, a woman, is present encouraging a thirteen-year-old boy, B, to have intercourse with a woman without her consent. B is not guilty of rape but can A be convicted of rape? Technical considerations apart, A should obviously be convicted of rape. One solution to the problem is to say that A is guilty of the rape of the woman by an innocent agent, in the same way that a person can murder another through an innocent agent.[35] The indictment would then read that " A [a woman] . . . had sexual intercourse with . . . , without her consent." Although this seems strange, the same form could be used if the boy, B, was over fourteen and himself guilty of rape. It was usual to indict accomplices to misdemeanours as principals [36] and the same rules of practice now apply to those offences which were, before the passing of the Criminal Justice Act 1967, felonies. It is no stranger to indict A as a principal if she uses an innocent agent, than if she was an accomplice to B.

In one case this result was reached,[37] but in another,[38] the court refused to convict a person in these circumstances. In this case the driver of a bus was acquitted of careless driving after a bus that he was reversing had knocked down two pedestrians, on the grounds that it was the conductor's duty to signal that the road was clear. The conductor's appeal against a conviction for aiding and abetting was allowed, the court holding that a person cannot aid another in doing something which that other has not done. Why could not the conductor be convicted of himself driving without due care via an innocent agent? The court did not deal with the point. If the driver had been guilty of careless driving and the conductor had been an accomplice, the conductor could have been charged as a principal, *i.e.* that he (the conductor) did drive

---

[35] *Ante*, p. 74.
[36] See Arch. para. 4172.
[37] *R.* v. *Bourne* (1952) 36 Cr.App.R. 125.
[38] *Thornton* v. *Mitchell* [1940] 1 All E.R. 339. See also *Morris* v. *Tolman* [1923] 1 K.B. 166; *Liddon* v. *Stringer* [1967] Crim.L.R. 371.

without due care.[39] The difficulty is really a verbal one. If A can murder via an innocent agent, there is no good reason why he (or she) should not be able to " rape " or " drive " via an innocent agent. This would not mean that all conductors have to have driving licences because the person who has to have the licence is the person at the wheel. A conductor who encouraged a six-year-old child to steer the conductor's bus down a hill could, it is submitted, be convicted of driving without a licence, via an innocent agent, whether he had a licence or not. It is the combined activity of the two which constitutes the crime.

This suggested solution to the problem may only be used where A has done more than assist in the commission of the offence. A must have employed or used B to commit the offence. If there is an absence of such employment or use, another solution must be found. It has been suggested that A may be convicted as an accomplice to B, if B produces the *actus reus* of the crime albeit without the necessary *mens rea*.[40] For example, A assists B to go through a form of marriage, A knowing that B's first wife is still alive and knowing that B thinks she is dead. Although B is not guilty of bigamy, it is suggested that A is still guilty as an accomplice.

It is not clear whether A may be convicted if he has assisted B and B is not guilty because, for example, he has diplomatic immunity or comes within a class of persons who have a special exemption from liability for the particular offence. So, in the example given above of the woman assisting the boy to " rape," if the woman's assistance is insufficient to make her the principal, it is not clear whether she could be convicted as an accomplice.

Victims as Parties

In *R.* v. *Tyrrell* [41] the Court for Crown Cases Reserved held that it is not a criminal offence for a girl between the ages of thirteen and sixteen to aid and abet a male person in committing, or inciting him to commit, the offence of having unlawful sexual intercourse with her contrary to, what is now, section 6 of the Sexual Offences Act 1956.[42] The court was of the opinion that it was not intended that the women or girls for whose protection the Act was passed

---

[39] Above, note 30.
[40] Smith and Hogan, p. 80 *et seq.*
[41] [1894] 1 Q.B. 710.
[42] *Post*, p. 467.

should be punishable under it for offences committed upon themselves.

It is not clear how far this principle extends. This immunity does not extend to women upon whom abortions are performed,[43] presumably for the reason that the laws against abortion are not designed to protect women. But it might well extend to tenants paying premiums which are illegal under the landlord and tenant legislation,[44] or to a member of the public dealing with unqualified " solicitors." [45]

Withdrawal by an Accomplice

It has been held that to free a person from liability for a crime which he has assisted, encouraged, etc., he must expressly countermand or revoke the assistance previously given before the commission of the crime.[46] Where this revocation is not possible, it would presumably be enough to tell the police. In any event the person may be guilty of conspiracy or incitement.

SECTION 2. ASSISTING OFFENDERS

Section 4 of the **Criminal Law Act 1967,**[47] provides that, where a person has committed an arrestable offence,[48] any other person who, knowing or believing him to be guilty of the offence or of some other arrestable offence, does without lawful authority or reasonable excuse any act with intent to impede his apprehension or prosecution shall be guilty of an offence. It must be established therefore that a person has committed an arrestable offence; that the accused knew or believed that that person had committed it, even if he did not know his identity; that the accused did an act with intent to impede the apprehension or prosecution of that person; and that that act was done without lawful authority or reasonable excuse.[49] It is not an offence to assist persons guilty of offences other than arrestable offences.

The punishment for the offence depends upon the gravity of the other person's offence. The appropriate sentence is determined as follows:

[43] *R.* v. *Sockett*, 1 Cr.App.R. 101.
[44] See *Grace Rymer Investments Ltd.* v. *Waite* [1958] Ch. 831 and *post*, p. 411.
[45] *Post*, p. 375.
[46] *R.* v. *Croft* [1944] 1 K.B. 295.
[47] Extended by the Theft Act 1968, s. 12 (3).　　　　[48] *Post*, p. 558.
[49] *R.* v. *Brindley and Long* (1971) 55 Cr.App.R. 258.

" (a) if that offence is one for which the sentence is fixed by law, he shall be liable to imprisonment for not more than ten years;

(b) if it is one for which a person (not previously convicted) may be sentenced to imprisonment for a term of fourteen years, he shall be liable to imprisonment for not more than seven years;

(c) if it is not one included above but is one for which a person (not previously convicted) may be sentenced to imprisonment for a term of ten years, he shall be liable to imprisonment for not more than five years;

(d) in any other case, he shall be liable to imprisonment for not more than three years." [50]

According to the Criminal Law Revision Committee which drafted the Bill, the exception for " lawful authority " is intended to cover an executive decision against prosecution.[51] The exception for " reasonable excuse," the Report states, will avoid extending the offence to acts such as destroying the evidence of an offence (for example, a worthless cheque) in pursuance of an agreement to refrain from prosecuting in consideration of the making good of the loss caused by that offence, which agreement is now lawful by virtue of section 5 (1) of the Act,[52] discussed later.[53] The Report states that the Committee decided not to make provision granting immunity to the family of a criminal or a person in a professional relationship with the criminal but instead to recommend that the consent of the Director of Public Prosecutions be required before proceedings may be instituted. This requirement of consent is achieved in section 4 (4) of the Act.

This offence requires, as did the offence of being an accessory after the fact, that the accused do something active. It is not sufficient that he merely fails to report the offender to the police or arrest the offender. The offence covers " such conduct as driving a criminal away after a crime, providing a car for the purpose, hiding him from the police or destroying fingerprints or other traces of the crime." [54] It should be noted, however, that the section

---

[50] s. 4 (3).
[51] 7th Report, Felonies and Misdemeanours, Cmnd. 2659, para. 28.
[52] Ibid.
[53] Post, p. 175.
[54] Cmnd. 2659, para. 28.

does not require that the act actually assisted the offender—it is the intent that is important.[55]

In order to commit the offence the accused must do the acts with intent to impede his apprehension or prosecution. In other words it must be proved that the accused desired this impediment or, *semble*, foresaw this impediment as substantially certain to occur.[56] It does not matter that the assistant did not know the *nature* of the person's offence.[56a] Difficulties arise with a person who handles stolen goods received from a thief who could be, but has not yet been, apprehended. It might be supposed that he would almost always now be guilty of an offence against section 4 and, before this Act, have been an accessory after the fact to the theft or receiving. In the words of one writer:

> " One of the greatest problems facing any thief, or guilty receiver, is that of disposing of the goods. Until he does so, he is vulnerable. The mere finding of them in his possession directs upon him the searchlight of police suspicion, and even if the police dig up no other evidence against him, that possession alone is evidence upon which a jury may convict him. Probably the greatest service anyone can render him in the way of avoiding justice is to take the goods off his hands. One would suppose that if an accessory after the fact is one who receives, relieves, comforts or assists a felon, then one who occasions a sigh of relief in the felon by relieving him of the incriminating goods must clearly be such an accessory." [57]

However, there has been some judicial reluctance to convict in this kind of case. In *R.* v. *Andrews and Craig* [58] the accused were found in possession of four " jumpers," part of a consignment of stolen jumpers in the possession of M, on whose behalf they were looking for buyers. The accused were convicted of receiving the four jumpers and of being accessories after the fact to the receiving of the remainder of the property. Their appeals against

---

[55] At common law the accessory had to both assist and intend to assist: Arch. para. 4155.

[56] *Ante*, p. 31.

[56a] Nevertheless it is necessary to specify in the indictment the particular offence committed in order that the court's jurisdiction to entertain it and the maximum punishment to which the accused is liable is known at the outset: *R.* v. *Morgan* [1972] 1 Q.B. 436.

[57] D. W. Elliott, " The *Mens Rea* of Accessories after the Fact " [1963] Crim.L.R. 159.

[58] [1962] 1 W.L.R. 1474. See also *R.* v. *Brown* [1965] Crim.L.R. 108.

convictions as accessories were allowed on the grounds of a misdirection to the jury. The Court of Criminal Appeal said [59]: " the
mere fact that the accused is making money for himself out of the
transaction does not necessarily mean that he is not at the same
time assisting and intending to assist the felon to escape by disposing of the goods." But if what was done was done without regard
to what happened to the felon, and what he did was merely for the
purpose of making money for himself, this would not constitute
him an accessory after the fact. With respect to the court, this
seems right. But, it is submitted, the court should also have pointed
out that if the accused did assist the offender to impede apprehension or prosecution, there is a presumption that he intended this
result. This presumption is, of course, rebuttable [60] but, in practice,
it would be difficult to rebut.[61]

Another problem arises if a person, knowing that X has committed an arrestable offence, harbours him *merely* by providing
or continuing to provide X with accommodation at ordinary rates
or in the ordinary way. The view of the Criminal Law Revision
Committee was that the person would not be guilty of an offence
against section 4.[62] But it would be difficult to rebut the presumption of intent when harbouring with knowledge is proved. If no one
harboured the offender he would be found much more quickly.

On the trial of a person on indictment for an arrestable offence,
the jury, if satisfied that that offence was committed may, on
acquitting the accused of the offence charged, find him guilty of
assisting etc. the offender.[62a]

SECTION 3. TREASON

The Criminal Law Act 1967 retains the separate category of
treason.[63] Any person who is present at the commission of the
offence assisting the traitor, or who knowingly gives assistance
before the commission of treason, or who, knowing that a treason

[59] [1962] 1 W.L.R. 1474 at p. 1477, explaining a passage in Lord Denning's
judgment in *Sykes* v. *Director of Public Prosecutions* [1962] A.C. 528.
[60] *Ante*, p. 51.
[61] See further Elliott, *op. cit.*
[62] 7th Report, Felonies and Misdemeanours, Cmnd. 2659, para. 30.
[62a] It is wrong that this issue should be raised by the judge for the first time
after the evidence is closed: *R.* v. *Cross* (1971) 55 Cr.App.R. 540. When
the jury return their verdict they should be asked whether they find the
accused guilty of the substantive count or by virtue of s. 4 (2). *Ibid.*
[63] s. 12 (6).

has been committed, assists the traitor in order to hinder his apprehension or trial is guilty of treason as a principal and punishable in the same way.[64] Since treason is an arrestable offence, a person giving assistance after the treason has been committed could alternatively be convicted of an offence against section 4 of the Criminal Law Act 1967.

[64] Arch. para. 4141.

CHAPTER 5

INSANITY, INTOXICATION

SECTION 1. INSANITY

Civil detention. In certain circumstances persons suffering from mental disorder may be compulsorily detained for observation or treatment on the recommendation of two medical practitioners or, in an emergency, of only one.[1] Authority for the compulsory detention of a person for treatment must be renewed at the end of one year and thereafter every two years.[2] These provisions can apply irrespective of whether the person detained has committed a criminal offence.

Unfit to plead and to stand trial on indictment.[3] A person thought to have committed an offence may be so mentally disordered or otherwise incapable of understanding criminal proceedings that he ought not to stand trial. The question whether a person is fit to plead is usually decided by a jury at the time of the trial. In exceptional cases, however, an alternative procedure is followed. This will be examined first.

Where a person has been remanded in custody to await a preliminary inquiry or to await trial at the Crown Court, the Home Secretary may direct that that person be removed to a hospital, if he is satisfied by reports from at least two medical practitioners that the person in question is suffering from mental illness or severe abnormality of a nature or degree which warrants his detention in a hospital for treatment. If he has not already been remanded for trial, the magistrates' court may still commit him for trial in the normal way, except that it may do so without him being brought to court.[4] When the case is considered at the Crown Court, that court may either direct that he should be tried,[5] or instead, if it appears impracticable or inappropriate to

---

[1] Mental Health Act 1959, ss. 25, 26, 29.
[2] *Ibid.* s. 43.
[3] As to summary proceedings, see *post*, p. 93.
[4] If he is not committed for trial, the Home Secretary's direction lapses, but the person is still liable to be detained under the same circumstances and on the same conditions as a civil detainee (above): *ibid.* s. 77 (4).
[5] In which case his fitness to plead may well be put in issue.

88

bring him before the court and if certain conditions are satisfied, make a " hospital order " (with or without an order restricting discharge) without convicting him. Hospital orders are dealt with later.[6] The Home Secretary's direction then ceases to have effect.[7]

The normal procedure is for a jury to decide at the time of trial whether an accused person is unfit to plead. A person is unfit to plead if, by reason of mental disorder or for some other reason (*e.g.* he is a deaf mute), he is incapable of understanding and following the proceedings and of communicating with or being communicated to by others.[8] A person suffering from amnesia has been held not unfit to plead.[9] The issue may be raised by either the judge, the prosecution or the defence.[10] If the defence raises the issue and the matter is disputed, then the onus is upon the defence to prove on a balance of probabilities that the accused is unfit.[11] The question of fitness to plead is normally raised at arraignment [12] and decided there and then by a jury specially sworn for the purpose. If the jury find the accused fit to plead, then another jury must be empanelled for the trial.[13] However, the court has a discretion to postpone consideration of the issue of fitness until any time up to the opening of the case for the defence.[14] This is done when it is possible that the accused would be found " not guilty " anyway. When the question of fitness to plead falls to be determined otherwise than on arraignment, then it is not necessary for a separate jury to try the issue.[15]

---

[6] *Post*, p. 796.
[7] Mental Health Act 1959, ss. 72–77, as amended by Criminal Procedure (Insanity) Act 1964, s. 4 (7), the Criminal Appeal Act 1968 and the Children and Young Persons Act 1969, Sched. 6; Courts Act 1971, Sched. 8, Pt. II, para. 38.
[8] *R.* v. *Pritchard* (1836) 7 C. & P. 303; *R.* v. *Governor of Stafford Prison, ex p. Emery* [1909] 2 K.B. 81; Arch. paras. 463–466.
[9] *R.* v. *Podola* [1960] 1 Q.B. 325.
[10] See Criminal Procedure (Insanity) Act 1964, s. 4 (1), as amended by the Criminal Justice Act 1967, s. 98 (6) and Sched. 4. This subsection applies to any disability, such that, apart from the Act, would constitute a bar to the accused being tried: *R.* v. *Burles* [1970] 2 Q.B. 101. See also *R.* v. *McCarthy* [1967] 1 Q.B. 68, interpreting this subsection.
[11] *R.* v. *Burles*, *supra*.
[12] But may be postponed until any time up to the opening of the defence: Act of 1964, s. 4 (2). See *e.g. R.* v. *Webb* [1969] 2 Q.B. 278 and *R.* v. *Burles* [1970] 2 Q.B. 191.
[13] Criminal Procedure (Insanity) Act 1964, s. 4 (4) (*a*).
[14] *Ibid.* s. 4 (2). See *R.* v. *Webb* (*supra*); *R.* v. *Burles* (*supra*) for the factors to be considered by the judge in deciding whether it is expedient and in the interests of the accused to postpone the trial of this issue.
[15] *Ibid.* s. 4 (4) (*b*); Courts Act 1971, s. 35 (5) (*b*).

Where a person is found unfit to plead, he is detained in a hospital until ordered by the Home Secretary to be discharged.[16] An appeal lies to the Court of Appeal against a finding that the accused was unfit to plead. Where the appeal is allowed, the court may direct that he should be tried.[17]

Found by a jury to be not guilty by reason of insanity.[18] A person who is not found unfit to plead may still be acquitted [19] by the jury on the grounds that he was *insane* at the time of the commission of the offence. The expression " insane " has here a particular legal meaning and it must not be thought that the word is being used in any medical sense. The purpose of classifying an accused as " insane " in the legal sense is twofold:

(1) If a person has no *mens rea* because he is suffering from a disease of the mind, it is right that he should be acquitted but it is wrong that he should be allowed to go at large. A person who has killed another may honestly have believed that the other was making a violent attack on him. If his belief is not induced by any disease of the mind, then he ought, probably, to be allowed to go free. On the other hand, if his belief was induced by a disease of the mind, the public ought to be protected from him until he is cured or unlikely to do it again. The classification into " sane " and " insane " has, therefore, this first purpose of making sure that persons suffering from a disease of the mind are treated differently from persons not so suffering.

(2) A person may have *mens rea* and yet, due to a disease of the mind, be utterly unaware that he is doing wrong. Again society must be protected from him, although it is thought wrong to punish such a person; rather he should be detained in a hospital. As a matter of practice, this is no longer of such great importance.

---

[16] Criminal Procedure (Insanity) Act 1964, s. 5 and Sched. 1, substituted by the Criminal Appeal Act 1968, s. 52 (1) and Sched. 5. The expression " Her Majesty's pleasure " is no longer used. S. 5 (4) provides that he may later be committed for trial again, if the Home Secretary is satisfied that he can properly be tried.

[17] Criminal Appeal Act 1968, s. 15 (1). If the issue of fitness to plead was determined later than on arraignment, the court may, alternatively, direct an acquittal: *ibid.* However, in that case, the court may also order that the accused be detained in a hospital for observation for at least a limited period: *ibid.* s. 14 (2).

[18] As to summary proceedings, see *post*, p. 93.

[19] Until 1964, the verdict was guilty but insane: Criminal Procedure (Insanity) Act 1964, s. 1.

As we shall see,[20] courts have wide powers to order a convicted person to be detained in hospital for mental treatment, and the Home Secretary may remove a prisoner from prison to a mental hospital.

Test of insanity. This is to be found in the answers of the judges given to the House of Lords in *M'Naghten's* case.[21] Their answer to the question " In what terms ought the question to be left to the jury as to the prisoner's state of mind at the time when the act was committed? " was as follows: " Every man is to be presumed sane until the contrary is proved . . . to establish a defence on the ground of insanity it must be clearly proved that at the time of the committing of the act the party accused was labouring under such a defect of reason from disease of the mind as not to know the nature or quality of the act he was doing, or if he did know it, that he did not know he was doing wrong."

It must be proved, first, that the accused was suffering from a disease of the mind. What constitutes a disease of the mind is not entirely clear. In *R.* v. *Kemp* [22] Devlin J. held that the accused was suffering from a disease of the mind when he attacked a person during a temporary loss of consciousness caused by a congestion of the blood in the brain itself caused by arteriosclerosis.[23] In *R.* v. *Clarke* [23a] it was said that depression causing absent-mindedness and confusion, although a minor mental illness fell short of being a disease of the mind causing a defect of reason such as that envisaged in *M'Naghten's* case. Lord Denning has said that epilepsy or cerebral tumours, as well as the major mental diseases, are diseases of the mind, but that concussion and sleep-walking are not.[24]

Secondly, it must be proved that the accused did not know the

---

[20] *Post*, p. 769.

[21] (1843) 10 Cl. & F. 200 and 4 St.Tr. 847, where it is spelt " M'Naghton." See Arch. paras. 32–36 where the actual questions and answers are set out. The M'Naghten Rules relate to accused persons who, by reason of a disease of the mind are deprived of the power of reasoning. They do not apply to persons who retain their power of reasoning but who, in moments of confusion or absent-mindedness fail to use their powers to the full: *R.* v. *Clarke* [1972] 1 All E.R. 219, C.A.

[22] [1957] 1 Q.B. 399.

[23] Approved in *Bratty* v. *Att.-Gen. for Northern Ireland* [1963] A.C. at pp. 410–412, *per* Lord Denning, disapproving *R.* v. *Charlson* [1955] 1 W.L.R. 317.

[23a] [1972] 1 All E.R. 219, C.A.

[24] *Bratty* v. *Att.-Gen. for Northern Ireland* (*supra*) at pp. 412, 414.

nature or quality of the act he was doing. The effect of this appears
to be that where a crime requires *mens rea*, then, if, owing to a
disease of the mind, the accused did not have the necessary *mens
rea* at the time that he is alleged to have committed the offence,
he should be acquitted but found insane.[25] So if, owing to a disease
of the mind, a person is acting quite involuntarily (as in *Kemp*),
or does not know what he is doing or thinks that he is sawing a log
when he is, in fact, sawing a person's head off,[26] then he will be
found not guilty by reason of insanity. If, on the other hand, he
only thinks that he is killing a girl when he is in fact killing a boy,
he will be convicted because his mistake does not prevent him from
having *mens rea*.[27] In one exceptional case, a person can, in these
circumstances, still be convicted. If, prior to the alleged commission of the offence, the accused had the necessary *mens rea* for that
offence, knowing it to be wrong, and subsequently he voluntarily
put himself in such a state or position that he was likely to, and
did in fact, produce the *actus reus* of that offence, then he can be
convicted.[28] In the words of Lord Denning[29]:

> " So also when he is a psychopath, he cannot by drinking
> rely on his self-induced defect of reason as a defence of
> insanity. The wickedness of his mind before he got drunk is
> enough to condemn him, coupled with the act which he in-
> tended to do and did do. A psychopath who goes out
> intending to kill, knowing it is wrong, and does kill, cannot
> escape the consequences by making himself drunk before
> doing it."[29a]

Thirdly, if the accused knew the nature or quality of the act,
then it must be proved that he did not know he was doing wrong.
Wrong for the purposes of this rule has been held to mean contrary

---

[25] This part of the M'Naghten Rules " appears to be only a particular statement
of the doctrine of *mens rea* ": Lord Devlin, " Criminal Responsibility and
Punishment " [1954] Crim.L.R. at p. 679.

[26] Glanville Williams, p. 479.

[27] See the fourth answer given by the judges in *M'Naghten's* case, Arch. para.
35.

[28] *Att.-Gen. for Northern Ireland* v. *Gallagher* [1963] A.C. 349; *ante*, p. 36.

[29] At p. 382.

[29a] See *Bolton* v. *Crawley* [1972] Crim.L.R. 222 where the accused took drugs
with the intention of rendering himself irresponsible and when under the
influence of those drugs assaulted a shop manageress, causing her actual
bodily harm.

to law.[30] So if the accused knew that what he was doing was against the law, it will not matter that he thought that what he was doing was morally right.

If a person knows the nature or quality of the act and knows he was doing wrong, then the fact that he was acting under an impulse, however strong, will not afford him a defence under the rules.[31] To mitigate the harshness of this, a defence of diminished responsibility, available only to persons charged with murder, has now been created.[32] The fact that a person was acting under such an impulse may, of course, incline the judge to make a hospital order in lieu of imprisonment.[33]

Where the defence raise the issue of insanity, it is for the defence to prove on the balance of probabilities that the accused was insane.[34] The prosecution may contend that the accused is insane if the defence contends that he was suffering from diminished responsibility.[35] and also if the defence contends that the accused was acting involuntarily or otherwise did not have the necessary *mens rea*.[36]

Where the jury find the accused not guilty by reason of insanity, he is detained in a hospital until ordered by the Home Secretary to be discharged.[37] There is now a right of appeal against a verdict to this effect.[38]

Insanity and summary proceedings. In contrast to the provisions applicable to trials on indictment, the provisions dealing with mentally disordered persons being tried summarily are quite

---

[30] *R.* v. *Windle* [1952] 2 Q.B. 826.

[31] See *Att.-Gen. for South Australia* v. *Brown* [1960] A.C. 432, where the authorities are reviewed. If the impulse is completely irresistible and the result of a disease of the mind, then the accused will not know the nature or quality of the act.

[32] *Post*, p. 434.

[33] *Post*, p. 796.

[34] This rule does, however, give rise to a problem. If the prosecution must prove beyond a reasonable doubt that the accused had the necessary *mens rea*, it is difficult to see how the defence can also prove that by reason of a disease of the mind the accused did not know the nature or quality of the act: Smith and Hogan, p. 122 *et seq.*

[35] Criminal Procedure (Insanity) Act 1964, s. 6.

[36] See *Bratty* v. *Att.-Gen. for Northern Ireland* [1963] A.C. at p. 411; Criminal Law Revision Committee, 3rd Report, Cmnd. 2149, para. 41.

[37] Criminal Procedure (Insanity) Act 1964, s. 5 and Sched. 1, substituted by the Criminal Appeal Act 1968, s. 52 and Sched. 5.

[38] Criminal Procedure (Insanity) Act 1964, ss. 2, 3. The court may confirm the jury's verdict, or direct a simple acquittal or substitute a verdict of guilty.

different.[39] **Section 60 (2)** of the **Mental Health Act 1959,**[40] provides that where a person is charged before a magistrates' court with any act or omission as an offence punishable by imprisonment, and the court is satisfied on the evidence of two medical practitioners that the accused is suffering from mental illness or severe subnormality and is also satisfied that the accused did the act or made the omission charged, then the court may make a hospital order without convicting him. Hospital orders are dealt with later.[41-42]

SECTION 2. INTOXICATION THROUGH DRINK OR DRUGS

The general principle of English law is that, subject to certain very limited exceptions, self-induced drunkenness is no defence to a criminal charge.[43] The Court of Appeal (Criminal Division) has expressed the view [44] that for the purpose of criminal liability there is no reason to distinguish between the effects of drugs voluntarily taken and drunkenness voluntarily induced.

Perhaps the most lucid exposition of the subject of drunkenness in relation to criminal liability is that by Lord Denning in *Att.-Gen. for Northern Ireland* v. *Gallagher.*[45] Lord Denning reviewed the circumstances in which drink (and one must now include drugs) might affect a man's mind, and the manner in which the criminal law dealt with each situation.

First, Lord Denning said, drink may impair a man's powers of perception so that he may not be able to foresee or measure the consequences of his actions as he would if he were sober. The law does not permit him to set up this self-induced want of perception as a defence. Even if he did not himself appreciate that what he

---

[39] The issue of fitness to plead can in theory be raised on summary proceedings (see *R.* v. *Pratt, ex p. Rigau* [1954] Crim.L.R. 551) but there is no statutory provision equivalent to the Criminal Procedure (Insanity) Act 1964. That Act, also, does not apply to persons being tried summarily who are found insane within the M'Naghten Rules. Such a person is entitled simply to be acquitted, unless the magistrate exercises his power under s. 60 (2) of the Mental Health Act 1959.

[40] See also Magistrates' Courts Act 1952, s. 26, as amended, which gives the court power to remand him, either in or out of custody, for medical examination.

[41-42] *Post,* p. 796.

[43] *Att.-Gen. for Northern Ireland* v. *Gallagher* (1961) 45 Cr.App.R. 316.

[44] *R.* v. *Lipman* [1970] 1 Q.B. 152.

[45] *Att.-Gen. for Northern Ireland* v. *Gallagher* (1961) 45 Cr.App.R. 316 at p. 342.

was doing was dangerous, if a reasonable man in his place who was not befuddled with drink would have appreciated it, he is guilty of the offence charged.[46]

Secondly, drink may impair a man's power to judge between right and wrong, so that he may do a thing when drunk which he would not dream of doing while sober. He does not realise he is doing wrong. Again, he may not set up his self-induced want of moral sense as a defence. It is not a defence for a drunken man to say he did not know he was doing wrong.[47]

Thirdly, drink may impair a man's power of self-control so that he may more readily give way to provocation than if he were sober. Again, he is not allowed to set up his self-induced want of control as a defence. The acts of provocation are to be assessed not according to their effect on him personally, but according to the effect they would have on a reasonable man in his place.[48]

To these three propositions, Lord Denning added two exceptions:

(a) If a man is charged with an offence in which a specific or ulterior intent is essential (as in murder though not manslaughter), evidence of drunkenness which renders him incapable of forming that specific or ulterior intent is an answer to the charge.[48a] This degree of drunkenness is reached when a man is rendered so stupid by drink that he does not know what he is doing, as where a drunken man thought his friend lying in his bed was a theatrical dummy placed there, and stabbed him to death.

(b) If a man by drinking (or taking drugs) brings on a distinct disease of the mind, so that he is temporarily insane within the M'Naghten Rules, that is, he does not know what he is doing or that it is wrong, then he has a defence on the grounds of insanity.[49]

[46] See also *R.* v. *Meade* [1909] 1 K.B. 895 as explained in *D.P.P.* v. *Beard* [1920] A.C. 479, 502–504.

[47] That is wrong in the moral sense. *Ibid.* at p. 506.

[48] *R.* v. *McCarthy* [1954] 2 Q.B. 105; *Bedder* v. *D.P.P.* [1954] 1 W.L.R. 1119 and see Homicide Act 1957, s. 3.

[48a] In *Bolton* v. *Crawley* [1972] Crim.L.R. 222 the Divisional Court held that the offence of assault occasioning actual bodily harm contrary to the Offences against the Person Act 1861, s. 47, does not require a specific or ulterior intent, and therefore drugs voluntarily taken provide no answer.

[49] *R.* v. *Davis* (1881) 14 Cox C.C. 563 and *Beard's* case, *supra.* Here wrong must mean wrong in law.

It would seem that involuntary drunkenness whereby the accused is made drunk by the acts of another will be a defence to a criminal charge.[50]

To the general rule that drunkenness can negative any specific or ulterior intent, there is an exception. A person who, prior to the commission of the offence, had the necessary *mens rea* for that offence and who subsequently puts himself in such a position that he is likely to, and does in fact, produce the *actus reus* of that offence can still be convicted.[51] In the words of Lord Denning [52]:

> " If a man, whilst sane and sober, forms an intention to kill and makes preparation for it, knowing it is a wrong thing to do, and then gets himself drunk so as to give himself Dutch courage to do the killing, and whilst drunk carries out his intention, he cannot rely on this self-induced drunkenness as a defence to a charge of murder, nor even as reducing it to manslaughter. He cannot say that he got himself into such a stupid state that he was incapable of an intent to kill."

Finally, if, as a result of alcoholic excess, insanity within the meaning of the M'Naghten Rules supervenes, the accused must be treated in the same manner as any other insane person.[53]

[50] 1 Hale 32.
[51] *Att.-Gen. for Northern Ireland* v. *Gallagher* [1963] A.C. 349.
[52] *Ibid.* at p. 382, and see *Bolton* v. *Crawley* (*supra*).
[53] *Director of Public Prosecutions* v. *Beard* [1920] A.C. 479 at pp. 500–501.

CHAPTER 6

DURESS, COERCION, NECESSITY

SECTION 1. DURESS

WE have seen earlier [1] that *mens rea* may be lacking where the act of the accused person is involuntary. Thus where A seizes B's hand which has a knife in it, and so forces his hand that it kills C, B should be acquitted. A further problem in *mens rea* arises where A threatens B in such a manner that B feels compelled to commit a criminal offence in order to avoid A carrying out his threats, in which case he is said to be acting under duress.

It is clearly established that duress provides a defence to any criminal charge,[2] with the exception possibly of murder [3] and treason as a principal.[4] The authorities show that it has been held to be a good defence to charges of perjury,[5] criminal damage to property,[6] handling stolen goods [7] and theft.[8]

Not every form of cajolery or persuasion will amount to duress and clearly the more serious the offence committed the graver the pressure applied will have to be to excuse its commission. Present threats of death [9] or grievous bodily harm [10] may constitute duress. Threats of imprisonment may well do so.[11] It has been said that threats to property merely will not suffice.[12] The concept of duress is based upon the theory that the accused is acting in this manner because his will has been neutralised or overborne by the threats held out. Thus the threat must be a

---

[1] p. 32, *ante*.
[2] *R.* v. *Hudson* [1971] 2 Q.B. 202.
[3] *R.* v. *Taylor* (1838) 8 C. & P. 616.
[4] *R.* v. *Steane* [1947] K.B. 997 at p. 1005; *contra R.* v. *Stratton* (1779) 21 St.Tr. at p. 1223 and *R.* v. *Purdy* (1946) 10 J.Cr.L. 182. Duress may of course be restricted by statute. See the Unlawful Oaths Acts 1797, s. 2 and 1812, s. 2.
[5] *R.* v. *Hudson*, *supra*.
[6] *R.* v. *Crutchley* (1831) 5 C. & P. 133.
[7] *Att.-Gen.* v. *Whelan* [1934] Ir.R. 518.
[8] *R.* v. *Gill* [1963] 1 W.L.R. 841.
[9] *R.* v. *McGrowther* (1746) Fost. 13; *R.* v. *Purdy*, *supra*.
[10] *Att.-Gen.* v. *Whelan*, *supra*, and see *R.* v. *Kray* (1969) 53 Cr.App.R. 569 *cf.* pp. 576–578.
[11] *Per* Lord Goddard C.J. in *R.* v. *Steane*, *supra* at p. 1005.
[12] *R.* v. *McGrowther*, *supra*.

97

" present " threat and must be effective at the time when the
crime is committed, and effective to " neutralise the will of the
accused at the time." [13] Whether a threat of future violence
will amount to duress will depend upon the particular circumstances. A threat of future violence may be so remote as to be
insufficient to overpower the will at the moment when the offence
was committed,[14] again the accused may have elected to commit
the crime in order to rid himself of the threat hanging over
him and not because he was driven to act by immediate and
unavoidable pressure.[15] Nevertheless where there is no opportunity
for delaying tactics and the person threatened must make up his
mind whether he is to commit the offence or not it has been said
that :

> " the existence at that moment of threats sufficient to destroy
> his will ought to provide him with a defence even though
> the threatened injury may not follow instantly, but after an
> interval." [16]

In *Subramaniam* v. *Public Prosecutor* [17] the appellant was held
to have a defence fit to go to the jury to a charge of unlawfully
possessing ammunition, on his plea that he had been compelled by terrorists to accept the ammunition and feared for his
safety if they returned. In *R*. v. *Hudson* [18] the appellants were
charged with perjury, on the basis of their failure to identify an
accused on trial. The basis of their defence was that one of
them had been approached by a man with a reputation for violence
who threatened her that if she " told on " the accused in court
she would be cut up. They said in evidence that they were
frightened and decided to tell lies to the court to avoid the consequences which might follow if they gave evidence against the
accused. Their resolve was strengthened when they saw the man
who had uttered the threats in the public gallery of the court during
the trial. It was held by the Court of Appeal (Criminal Division)
that the issue of duress had been wrongly withdrawn from the jury.
The Lord Chief Justice, Lord Parker, commented :

---

[13] *Per* Lord Parker C.J. in *R*. v. *Hudson, supra.*
[14] *Ibid.* at p. 206.
[15] *Ibid.*
[16] *Ibid.*
[17] [1956] 1 W.L.R. 965 P.C.
[18] *R*. v. *Hudson* [1971] 2 Q.B. 202.

" The threats . . . were likely to be no less compelling, because
their execution could not be effected in the court room, if
they could be carried out in the streets . . . the same night."

In each case it will be a matter of degree depending upon the
circumstances.

In *Hudson's* case it was suggested by the Crown that the
appellants ought to have taken steps to neutralise the threats by
seeking police protection, either when they came to court or
beforehand, and submitted that duress ought not to be a good
defence if the accused was in a position to appeal for police protection. Not unreasonably, this wholly unrealistic argument did
not appeal to the court. It was said however that it was always
open to the Crown to prove that the accused failed to avail himself
of an opportunity which was reasonably open to him to render
the threat ineffective, in which case the threat in question might not
be relied upon by the accused.

In every case, the burden of proving lack of duress, if the
matter is raised, lies upon the prosecution.[19]

SECTION 2. COERCION

In the case of a married woman, the common law presumed that
a felony or misdemeanour, other than homicide and treason, committed by her *in the presence of* her husband was committed under
his coercion. Unless the prosecution proved that the wife had
taken an independent part in the commission of the crime she
was entitled to be acquitted. Coercion was, therefore, regarded
as something much wider than duress.

Now by **section 47** of the **Criminal Justice Act 1925,** it is
provided that any *presumption of law* that an offence committed
by a wife in the presence of her husband is committed under his
coercion is abolished, but on a charge against a wife for any
offence other than treason or murder it shall be a good defence
to prove that the offence was committed in the presence of, and
under the coercion of, the husband. Although there is some doubt
about this,[20] the effect of this section would seem to be not to alter
the substantive law but merely to shift the burden of proof.[21] In

[19] *R.* v. *Gill* [1963] 1 W.L.R. 841 and see pp. 49, *ante,* and 595, *post.*
[20] Glanville Williams, *op. cit.,* pp. 764, 767.
[21] But see also, *ante,* p. 49.

practice the defence of coercion appears to be raised very rarely. At least one reason for this is that to-day it would, presumably, be much more difficult for a wife to show that she had not taken an independent part.

SECTION 3. NECESSITY

In certain circumstances a person who would otherwise be guilty of a criminal offence will be acquitted if, faced with the alternative of either committing that crime or allowing a greater evil to occur, he chooses to commit that crime. One particular form of necessity, that is, duress, was examined in Section 1, and the same policy considerations mentioned in that section apply here.

It is difficult to find any clear judicial statement to the effect that a person will, in these circumstances, be acquitted. But there are a number of cases in which the existence of necessity of this kind has been held to excuse—although the word " necessity " has not always been used. Justifiable use of force in self-defence, in defence of property, in making an arrest or in preventing flight from detention may be regarded as examples of necessity—the " greater evils " in these cases, sometimes but not always, being criminal offences by the other person. But apart from these cases, the judicial approach to the problem has been, understandably, piecemeal.

Sometimes a person may be forced to commit what would otherwise be a criminal offence to avoid committing a more serious offence. In this case he should, in principle, be acquitted of the lesser offence. For example, it is an offence to fail to provide proper medical care for a child and, if death follows from the omission, it can, sometimes, be manslaughter.[22] It is also a common law misdemeanour to take an infected person through a public place.[23] If a person could not provide proper medical care for his infected child at home, he might have to take the child through a public place to reach a doctor or hospital,[24] in which case he should be acquitted of the common law misdemeanour.[25] He might, otherwise and in the appropriate circumstances, be guilty of manslaughter, should the child die. Similarly,

[22] *Ante*, p. 20.
[23] *Post*, p. 220.
[24] It would, of course, be rare today for a person to *have* to take the child through a public place.
[25] See *R*. v. *Vantandillo* (1815) 4 M. & S. 73.

to avoid a child in the road, a driver of a car might have to take the car across a double white line, contrary to section 22 of the Road Traffic Act 1972. It would be quite wrong, in principle, to convict the driver of the motoring offence, since, if he had killed the child, he might, in the appropriate circumstances, have been convicted of manslaughter.

Sometimes the "greater evil" will not involve anyone in criminal liability but would still justify a person committing what would otherwise be a criminal offence to avoid it. It has often been said that a prisoner who escaped from a burning jail to save his life or a person who pulled down a house to prevent a fire from spreading would not be guilty of what would otherwise be criminal offences.[26]

In some cases, a statutory provision makes it clear that a necessity of a particular kind will result in an acquittal. For example, section 1 of the Infant Life (Preservation) Act 1929, provides that causing an unborn child to die is justified in order to preserve the life of the mother.[27] Again, section 79 of the Road Traffic Regulation Act 1967, provides that no statutory provision imposing a speed limit on motor-vehicles shall apply to any vehicle on an occasion when it is being used for fire brigade, ambulance or police purposes, if the observance of those provisions would be likely to hinder the use of the vehicle for the purpose for which it is being used on that occasion.[28]

In the light of the authorities and having regard to general principles, it is difficult to accept the decision in *R.* v. *Kitson.*[29] In that case the accused, who was intoxicated, was sleeping in a car the driver of which had just parked and alighted. The car had been improperly braked and started to roll down the hill. The accused managed to get himself into the driving seat and eventually steered the car into the verge. He was convicted of driving under the influence of drink,[30] and his conviction was upheld on appeal. Presumably an offence would also have been committed if the accused had not had a licence to drive or had been uninsured. It should, however, be pointed out that no reference was, apparently, made to necessity.

[26] As to which, see *post*, pp. 190, 530.
[27] *Post*, p. 451.
[28] But *cf. Whittall* v. *Kirby* [1947] 1 K.B. at p. 201. See also s. 36 (3) of the Road Traffic Act 1972.
[29] (1955) 39 Cr.App.R. 66. [30] *Post*, p. 301.

Usually it will be clear which of the two evils from which the accused had to choose was the greater. But in the famous case of *R. v. Dudley and Stephens* [31] the problem arose in an acute form. The two accused, another sailor, Brooks, and the deceased, a boy of eighteen, were shipwrecked and had to take to an open boat. Twenty days later the accused, being some 1,000 miles from land without any prospect of rescue and having been seven days without food and five without water, killed the deceased and ate him. No lots were drawn, but the deceased was much weaker than the others and the jury found that the others would probably have died if they had not killed the boy. Four days after the killing, they were rescued. On arrival in England they were charged with and convicted of murder.[32] The case was argued before a court of five judges. The court refused to accept that necessity excused the murder. Understandably, perhaps, the court felt that it was impossible to set a standard by which the comparative value of lives could be measured.[33] Less acceptably, the court felt that " such a principle once admitted might be made the legal cloak for unbridled passion and atrocious crime.[34] "

Although necessity is usually referred to as a defence, like duress, the burden of proof remains on the prosecution.[35]

---

[31] (1884) 14 Q.B.D. 273.
[32] The sentence of death was commuted to six months' imprisonment.
[33] (1884) 14 Q.B.D. 273 at p. 288.
[34] *Ibid.*
[35] *Ante,* p. 99.

CHAPTER 7

MISCELLANEOUS VARIATIONS IN LIABILITY

SECTION 1. SOVEREIGN, DIPLOMATIC AND OTHER IMMUNITIES

NEITHER the reigning sovereign of this country nor foreign sovereigns are amenable to the jurisdiction of the courts of this country.[1] Foreign sovereigns may, however, waive their immunity from criminal proceedings.[2]

Immunity is granted to diplomatic personnel representing foreign governments in the United Kingdom and, in certain circumstances, in transit through the United Kingdom. This immunity extends to their families. The nature and extent of this immunity and the right to waive [3] this immunity are now to be found in the **Diplomatic Privileges Act 1964,** as extended by the **Consular Relations Act 1968** and amended by the **Diplomatic and other Privileges Act 1971.** A list of the names of diplomatic personnel residing in England is kept by the Foreign Office; but the fact that a person's name is not on the list does not mean that a court cannot hold that he is entitled to immunity.[4]

It is fundamental to the claiming of immunity that the agent should have been accepted or received by this country. A foreign state's unilateral action in appointing a diplomatic agent does not confer diplomatic immunity on that agent until he has been accepted and received as *persona grata* in this country.[5]

A certificate granted by the Foreign Office that a person is entitled to immunity is conclusive of that fact in the courts.[6]

By a number of statutes immunity has been extended to members of international organisations and representatives of Commonwealth countries.[7]

---

[1] Russell, p. 96.
[2] See *Sultan of Johore* v. *Abubakar* [1952] A.C. 318.
[3] On the right of waiver see also *R.* v. *Madan* [1961] 2 Q.B. 1.
[4] *Hitchcock's Case* (1958) 7 I.C.L.Q. 562.
[5] *R.* v. *Governor of Pentonville Prison, ex p. Teja* [1971] 2 Q.B. 274 at p. 282. As to trade representatives, see also *Fenton Textile Assn. Ltd.* v. *Krassin* (1921) 38 T.L.R. 259.
[6] *Duff Development Corporation* v. *Kelantan* [1924] A.C. 797; *Engelke* v. *Musmann* [1928] A.C. 433; see also Diplomatic Privileges Act 1964, s. 4.
[7] See Diplomatic Immunities (Conference with Commonwealth Countries and Republic of Ireland) Act 1961, the Commonwealth Secretariat Act 1966, the

Finally, in certain circumstances, members of foreign visiting forces are not liable to be tried by a United Kingdom court.[8]

SECTION 2. ALIENS

Aliens cannot normally be tried for offences committed otherwise than within the United Kingdom, or on British ships within the Admiralty jurisdiction. Special provisions apply in relation to piracy *jure gentium* and the hijacking of aircraft.[8a]

SECTION 3. INFANTS

Procedure. Special provisions have been made for the trial and punishment of children under the age of seventeen. These will be dealt with later.[9]

Criminal responsibility. A child under the age of ten cannot be guilty of any offence.[10] So a child of five who takes another child's toy cannot be convicted of stealing. Since the passing of the Theft Act 1968, however, the child's parent can be convicted of theft if he decides to keep the toy and thereby dishonestly appropriates it.

As regards children who are under fourteen but more than ten, it must be proved not only that the child had the necessary *mens rea* but also that the child knew what he was doing was wrong.[11] Exceptionally, boys under fourteen may not be convicted of certain sexual offences.[12]

SECTION 4. CORPORATIONS

Procedure. Special provisions have been made for the trial, either summarily or on indictment, of corporations.[13] Corporations appear and plead through a representative.

International Organisations Act 1968, and the Diplomatic and other Privileges Act 1971.

[8] Visiting Forces Act 1952, s. 3, as amended.

[8a] See Chap. 10, *post*.   [9] *Post*, pp. 680, 799.

[10] Children and Young Persons Act 1933, s. 50, as amended by the Children and Young Persons Act 1963, s. 16 (1). Until 1963, the age was eight. The Children and Young Persons Act 1969, s. 4, provides for it being raised to fourteen, except in the case of homicide, but this section is not yet in force.

[11] *R.* v. *Gorrie* (1919) 83 J.P. 136; Arch. para. 29.

[12] *Post*, p. 466.

[13] *Post*, p. 757. Roughly speaking, a corporation is an organisation which has a legal personality quite apart from its members; *cf.* a partnership.

Criminal responsibility. We have seen how corporations may be held vicariously responsible [14] in exactly the same circumstances as a natural person,[15] but the liability of corporations is not limited exclusively to vicarious responsibility.

Corporations, being legal fictions, can only act and think through their officers and servants. For the purposes of imposing criminal responsibility upon corporations *other than vicarious responsibility*, only the conduct and accompanying mental state of senior officers, acting in the course of their employment, can be imputed to a corporation. If a senior officer, for example, makes a false statutory return on behalf of the corporation, knowing it to be false, the corporation can be convicted of the offence which is thereby committed.[16] So also, it has been held, a corporation may be convicted of a common law conspiracy to defraud [17]—the conduct and the guilty mind of the senior official involved being imputed to the corporation.

As Lord Reid put it in *Tesco Supermarkets Ltd.* v. *Nattrass* [18]:

" A living person has a mind which can have knowledge or intention or be negligent and he has hands to carry out his intentions. A corporation has none of these: it must act through living persons, though not always one or the same person. Then the person who acts is not speaking or acting for the company. He is acting as the company and his mind which directs his acts is the mind of the company. There is no question of the company being vicariously liable. He is not acting as a servant, representative, agent or delegate. He is an embodiment of the company or, one could say, he hears and speaks through the persona of the company, within his appropriate sphere, and his mind is the mind of the company. If it is a guilty mind then that guilt is the guilt of the company."

The following limitations upon the liability of corporations must be noted however. First, only the conduct and accompanying

---

[14] *Ante,* p. 53.

[15] *Mousell Bros.* v. *London and North Western Ry.* [1917] 2 K.B. 836; *Griffiths* v. *Studebakers Ltd.* [1924] 1 K.B. 102.

[16] *Director of Public Prosecutions* v. *Kent and Sussex Contractors Ltd.* [1944] K.B. 146; *Moore* v. *I. Bresler Ltd.* [1944] 2 All E.R. 515.

[17] *R.* v. *I.C.R. Haulage Co. Ltd.* [1944] K.B. 551.

[18] [1971] 2 W.L.R. 1166 at p. 1176.

mental state of persons in control of the corporation may be imputed to the corporation.

> " Knowledge of a servant cannot be imputed to the company unless he is a servant for whose actions the company are criminally responsible and . . . that only arises in the case of a company where one is considering the acts of responsible officers forming the brain. . . ." [19]

Again, " it is not every ' responsible agent ' or ' high executive ' or ' agent acting on behalf of the company ' who can by his actions make the company criminally responsible. It is necessary to establish whether the natural person or persons in question have the status and authority which in law makes their acts, in the matter under consideration, the acts of the company so that the natural person is to be treated as the company itself." [20] This is a matter of law [21] and it has been suggested [22] that in order to discover what natural persons are to be treated in law as being the company for this purpose, one must look for the persons who, by the memorandum and articles of association of the company, or as a result of action taken by the directors or by the company in general meeting, are entrusted with the exercise of the powers of the company. Secondly, these officers must be acting within the scope of their employment. Thirdly, " a company and its director cannot be convicted of conspiracy, when the only human being who broke the law or intended to do so was the director." [23] Fourthly, corporations cannot be convicted of the few crimes which cannot be punished by a fine, e.g. murder.[24] Finally, it is difficult to see how corporations could commit certain offences, e.g. sexual offences. But it is not impossible that a corporation could be convicted of crimes involving personal violence,[25] e.g. the directors order an unlawful trap to be built on corporation property to catch trespassers.[26]

---

[19] Per Lord Parker C.J. in Magna Plant v. Mitchell quoted in Tesco Ltd. v. Nattrass, supra at p. 1179.
[20] R. v. Andrews-Weatherfoil Ltd. [1972] 1 W.L.R. 118, C.A. per Eveleigh J.
[21] Ibid.
[22] Per Lord Diplock in Tesco Ltd. v. Nattrass, supra at pp. 1203–1204.
[23] R. v. McDonnell [1966] 1 Q.B. 233 at p. 245.
[24] Post, p. 429.
[25] R. v. I.C.R. Haulage Ltd. [1944] K.B. at p. 556, doubting R. v. Cory Bros. & Co. Ltd. [1927] 1 K.B. 810.
[26] For this offence, see post, p. 461.

Section 5. Husband and Wife

As to husband and wife the following points, to which further reference has been made or will be made later, may here be noticed briefly:

(i)   A married woman who commits an offence in the presence of her husband has a wider defence than the general defence of duress.[27]

(ii) A husband and wife, being regarded as one person, cannot by themselves be convicted of conspiracy.[28]

(iii) Spouses are liable for offences under the Theft Act 1968, by one spouse against the property of another, as if they were not married. Also, they are now enabled to prosecute each other for any offence (whether under the Theft Act 1968, or not) as if they were not married, subject in certain cases to the consent of the Director of Public Prosecutions.[29]

Section 6. Offences Committed outside the United Kingdom

Offences committed outside the United Kingdom by British subjects are not triable in England unless there is statutory provision to the contrary. There are now many exceptions to this general rule and the subject is dealt with later in this book.[30]

[27] *Ante*, p. 99.
[28] *Ante*, p. 64.
[29] Theft Act 1968, s. 30.
[30] *Post*, p. 690.

CHAPTER 8

COURTS OF CRIMINAL JURISDICTION

SECTION 1. MAGISTRATES' COURTS

IN criminal matters the functions of magistrates' courts are twofold, namely:

(i) as a **court of trial** to deal with certain classes of offences triable summarily,[1] and

(ii) as **examining justices** before whom a charge is made against a person for an indictable offence.

A magistrates' court is defined in section 124 (1) of the Magistrates' Courts Act 1952 as " any justice or justices of the peace acting under any enactment or by virtue of his or her commission under the common law."

The summary jurisdiction of magistrates rests entirely upon statute, no matter being cognisable by justices in a summary manner unless expressly or impliedly made so by Act of Parliament. This jurisdiction exists (i) over summary offences which are not indictable, and also (ii) over certain indictable offences.[2]

The Office of magistrate or justice of the peace. Before the Norman Conquest the police organisation was based upon the principle of the collective responsibility of each group of kinsmen or neighbours for the offences of its members and the duty of every man to join in the hue and cry in pursuit of offenders. This principle was maintained for some time after the Conquest, and was supplemented, in the reign of Richard I, by the appointment in every shire of knights to receive from all men an oath for the preservation of the peace, and, in the thirteenth century, by the occasional appointment of *custodes pacis*. These " conservators of the peace " were made permanent by 1 Edw. 3, st. 2, c. 16, which provided that thenceforth in every county certain persons should be assigned (*i.e.* by commission) to keep the peace.

---

[1] As to proceedings before examining justices and summary trial, see *post*, pp. 663 *et seq.*; pp. 654 *et seq.*

[2] See *post*, pp. 646 *et seq.*

By 18 Edw. 3, st. 2, c. 2, *judicial* powers were conferred upon these commissioners, this statute providing that "two or three of the best of reputation in the counties shall be assigned *keepers of the peace* by the King's commission; *and* at what time need shall be, the same, with others wise and learned in the law, shall be assigned by the King's commission *to hear and determine felonies and trespasses* done against the peace in the same counties." By 34 Edw. 3, c. 1, their powers were further regulated, and they acquired the title of "justices of the peace"; from this time also separate commissions were issued for each county. By subsequent statutes it was provided that they should hold general sessions at least four times a year.

In boroughs the mayors and other chief officers formerly held office under the terms of the grant or charter creating the borough, but since the Municipal Corporations Act 1835, justices of the peace for boroughs having a separate commission of the peace are assigned like justices for counties by commissions issued by the Crown.[3] By section 1 (2) of the Justices of the Peace Act 1968, the Lord Mayor and Aldermen of the City of London by virtue of the charter granted by King George II in 1741 continue to be justices of the peace for the City of London, but additional justices of the peace may be appointed under a commission of the peace which is issued for the City, as a county of itself.

Formerly, many people, such as Mayors and Chairmen of County Councils, were *ex officio* justices by virtue of their offices but by schedule I to the Justices of the Peace Act 1968, stipendiary magistrates and the Commissioner and Assistant Commissioners of Police for the Metropolis are the only *ex officio* justices remaining.

The criminal jurisdiction of justices became threefold, namely:

1. A jurisdiction exercised in quarter sessions [4];
2. A jurisdiction to deal summarily with certain offences and complaints [5];
3. A preliminary jurisdiction in respect of indictable offences.[6]

---

[3] See now s. 157 of the Municipal Corporations Act 1882, as amended (replacing s. 107 of the Act of 1835) and the Courts Act 1971, s. 3.

[4] Now the Crown Court.

[5] *Post*, pp. 646 *et seq.*

[6] *Post*, p. 663.

The growth of summary jurisdiction was due to the number of summary offences created by penal statutes. In the absence of any special statutory provision, such offences could be dealt with only by the common law method of trial. But in order to avoid the inconvenience of either postponing the trial of petty offenders until the next sessions or summoning a jury at more frequent intervals, it became the practice to provide by new statutes that petty offences should be heard and determined by justices out of quarter sessions in a summary manner, without the intervention of a jury.

By other statutes they were given power to hear and determine certain civil complaints.

Summary jurisdiction accordingly falls under two heads:

(1) Criminal, in which the proceedings begin by an information and may end with a conviction. This jurisdiction now exists over (i) offences originally indictable, with which a magistrates' court can deal without committal for trial [7]; (ii) summary offences.[8]

(2) Civil, in which the proceedings are begun by complaint and may conclude with an order. The principal jurisdiction of this kind is under the Affiliation Proceedings Act 1957, the Guardianship of Minors Act 1971, and Matrimonial Proceedings (Magistrates' Courts) Act 1960.[9]

For many years the same justices of the peace who exercised summary jurisdiction in magistrates' courts met also in quarter sessions to try indictable offences as a bench of justices sitting with a jury. Their functions in this regard declined with the years, and they were eventually confined to county quarter sessions only, and functioned (apart from duties in their appellate jurisdiction) as assessors on questions of sentence. The Administration of Justice (Miscellaneous Provisions) Act 1938, permitted the Lord Chancellor on the application of quarter sessions to appoint a legally qualified chairman and deputy chairman. The Criminal Justice Administration Act 1962, s. 5, provided that a chairman of quarter sessions for a county must be legally qualified. Persons filling the post of recorder, deputy recorder or assistant recorder had to be barristers.

[7] See *post*, p. 647.
[8] See *post*, p. 646.
[9] See also the Magistrates' Courts Act 1952.

Justices in the Crown Court

The Courts Act 1971 provides for the participation as judges of justices of the peace at the Crown Court on the hearing:

(a) of any appeal, and

(b) of proceedings on committal to the Court.[10]

The number of justices to constitute the court [11] and the qualifications of such justices are prescribed by the Crown Court Rules. In such a court any judge of the High Court, Circuit Judge or Recorder sitting with them presides, and has a casting vote in the event of the Bench being equally divided.[12] Also, a justice of the peace is not disqualified from acting as a judge of the Crown Court for the reason that the proceedings are not at a place within the area for which he was appointed as a justice, or because the proceedings are not related to that area in any other way.[13]

Appointment and qualification of justices of the peace. Except those who are justices *ex officio*, all justices sit by virtue of a commission issued under the Great Seal, in a form settled by an Order in Council of 1878, made under the Crown Office Act 1877. It is this commission and numerous statutes which determine the powers of justices.

A separate commission is issued for every (administrative) county, county borough and such non-county boroughs as satisfy certain conditions.[14] Separate provisions apply to Greater London.[15]

Most magistrates, therefore, hold office by having their names added to the Commission of the Peace for their particular county or borough. They are appointed by the Crown on the recommendation of the Lord Chancellor in accordance with the Justices of the Peace Acts 1949 and 1968. The Lord Chancellor acts after consultation with an advisory committee. Any person who is not disqualified [16] may be appointed a justice of the peace for any area

---

[10] Courts Act 1971, s. 5 (1).

[11] Subject to there being not less than two but not more than four.

[12] Courts Act 1971, s. 5 (8).

[13] *Ibid.* s. 5 (9).

[14] Justices of the Peace Act 1949, s. 10 and Sched. 3, as amended by the Courts Act 1971, Sched. 11.

[15] See Administration of Justice Act 1964, s. 2, as amended by the Courts Act 1971, Sched. 11.

[16] *Post*, p. 113.

if he resides in or within fifteen miles of that area.[17] This residence qualification does not apply to *ex officio* justices.

In the City of London, the Lord Mayor and Aldermen still retain their ancient rights to sit as justices.[18]

In the inner London area [19] salaried magistrates (called stipendiary magistrates), limited to forty in number,[20] are appointed by the Crown on the recommendation of the Lord Chancellor. To be qualified for appointment, a person must be a barrister or solicitor of not less than seven years' standing.[21] The commission is the same as that of *county* justices.

In boroughs having a separate commission of the peace or counties or parts of counties (exclusive of any borough having a separate commission of the peace) or " joint districts " comprising two or more areas for which separate appointments might be made, stipendiary magistrates may be appointed by the Crown on the recommendation of the Lord Chancellor, on a petition being presented to the Secretary of State by the council or councils of the area concerned.[22] The qualification is seven years' standing as a barrister or solicitor.[23] In addition there are a few special statutes regulating the appointment of stipendiary magistrates in certain areas. In practice, there are less than twenty areas outside London which have stipendiary magistrates. In areas which have stipendiary magistrates, lay justices continue to share the work with them, but stipendiary magistrates have greater powers and, whereas for the trial of an offence there must usually be at least two justices present, a stipendiary magistrate may sit alone.[24]

Local limits of the jurisdiction of justices. The authority of a justice of the peace is in general limited to the county, borough or district for which he is appointed and is not attached to the person so as to be exercisable elsewhere.[25] However, county justices

---

[17] Justices of the Peace Act 1949, s. 1 (1).
[18] Justices of the Peace Act 1968, s. 1 (2).
[19] This consists of the 12 inner London boroughs: Administration of Justice Act 1964, s. 2, and the London Government Act 1963, as amended by the Courts Act 1971, Sched. 11.
[20] Administration of Justice Act 1964, s. 10, as amended by the Courts Act 1971, Sched. 11.
[21] *Ibid.*
[22] Justices of the Peace Act 1949, s. 29.
[23] *Ibid.*
[24] As far as London is concerned, see Administration of Justice Act 1964, s. 9.
[25] For exceptions to this rule and the jurisdiction of justices generally, see *post*, pp. 641 *et seq.*

have certain concurrent jurisdiction, although in practice this is not exercised.[26] It is interesting to note that under the Courts Act 1971,[27] a justice of the peace is not disqualified from acting as a judge at the Crown Court for the reason that the proceedings are not at a place within the area for which he was appointed as a justice, or because the proceedings are not related to that area in any other way.

Disqualifications. At common law a justice is disqualified from acting in any matter with regard to which he has an interest, and the mere presence on the Bench of an interested justice has been held to invalidate the proceedings.[28] Any pecuniary interest, however small, is, in the absence of any statutory provision to the contrary, a bar to the justice acting [29]; but where it is not pecuniary, it must be such as to afford a real likelihood of a bias.[30] The right to object to a justice on the ground of his interest may be waived by the parties, in which case the proceedings are validated.[31]

The following statutory disqualifications also exist:

(i) A person convicted of treason forfeits any civil office under the Crown.[32]

(ii) A person reported by an election court as personally guilty of any corrupt practice at a parliamentary or municipal election is disqualified from being a justice for five years from the date of the report.[33]

(iii) A person adjudged a bankrupt cannot be appointed or act as a justice of the peace, even though he is an *ex officio* justice. This disqualification is removed if the

[26] Municipal Corporations Act 1882, s. 154 as amended by the Courts Act 1971, Sched. 11; and see *Lawson* v. *Reynolds* [1904] 1 Ch. 718.

[27] s. 5 (9).

[28] *R.* v. *Lancashire JJ.* (1906) 75 L.J.K.B. 198. See also *R.* v. *Suffolk JJ.* (1852) 18 Q.B. 416; *Frome United Breweries Co.* v. *Bath JJ.* [1926] A.C. 586. An *acquittal* cannot, however, be quashed on this ground: *R.* v. *Simpson* [1914] 1 K.B. 66.

[29] In the absence of any such statutory provision even the fact that as a ratepayer the justice is interested in the result of the proceedings is sufficient to disqualify him: *R.* v. *Gaisford* [1892] 1 Q.B. 381.

[30] *R.* v. *Rand* (1886) L.R. 1 Q.B. 230; *R.* v. *Sunderland JJ.* [1901] 2 K.B. 357; *R.* v. *Bath Compensation Authority* [1925] 1 K.B. 685.

[31] *Wakefield Local Board of Health* v. *West Riding, etc., Ry.* (1865) L.R. 1 Q.B. 84.

[32] Forfeiture Act 1870, s. 2; Criminal Justice Act 1948, Sched. 10; Criminal Law Act 1967, Sched. 3.

[33] Representation of the People Act 1949, ss. 140 (3), 141 (1), 163.

adjudication is annulled or the bankrupt obtains his discharge with a certificate that the bankruptcy was caused by misfortune without any misconduct on his part, or in any case at the end of five years from the date of his discharge.[34]

(iv) A sheriff cannot while he is sheriff act as a justice of the peace for the county of which he is sheriff.[35]

(v) The offices of clerk to the justices and of justice of the peace for the same county are incompatible.[36]

(vi) Also certain classes of persons are disqualified by statute from acting as justices in particular cases, *e.g.* a member of a local authority is usually disqualified from acting as a justice in a case involving the local authority.[37]

SECTION 2. THE CROWN COURT

Immediately before the passing of the Courts Act 1971, original criminal jurisdiction in relation to trials on indictment was vested in the Courts of Quarter Session and the Courts of Assize. Of the former, County Quarter Sessions were held by virtue of the commission of the peace and consisted of a number of justices presided over by a legally qualified chairman. Borough quarter sessions were held by a recorder, as a sole judge. In Cheshire, Durham, Greater London, Kent and Lancashire special provisions applied, and the courts were presided over by full-time chairmen and deputy chairmen. The criminal jurisdiction of quarter sessions was both original and appellate. In its original jurisdiction it tried all indictable offences, other than a number of the more serious, which were reserved for trial at the assizes. In its appellate jurisdiction, apart from hearing appeals under various enactments, a general right of appeal to quarter sessions by persons convicted in a magistrates' court, was conferred by the Magistrates' Courts Act 1952.

The courts of assize were the direct descendants of the itinerant justices set up by Henry II. In so far as criminal cases were

---

[34] Bankruptcy Acts 1883, s. 32; 1890, s. 9, as amended.
[35] Sheriffs Act 1887, s. 17, modified by the Administration of Justice Act 1964, s. 19 (4), 36 (4); and see Justices of the Peace Act 1949, Sched. 1.
[36] *R.* v. *Patteson* (1832) 4 B. & Ad. 9; and see *R.* v. *Douglas* [1898] 1 Q.B. 560.
[37] Justices of the Peace Act 1949, s. 3, as amended by the Administration of Justice Act 1964, Sched. 5.

concerned, the commissioners, who included judges of the High
Court and Queen's Counsel, appointed by letters patent, sat under
the commissions of oyer and terminer and general gaol delivery.
The former empowered them to hear and determine the indictable
offences committed within their jurisdiction, and the latter to try
any prisoner in gaol or released on bail. The Central Criminal
Court at the " Old Bailey " was the assize court for Greater
London, and further had power to try all offences committed
within the jurisdiction of the Admiralty.

The Criminal Justice Administration Act 1956, set up Crown
Courts in Liverpool and Manchester, which exercised jurisdiction
both as courts of Assize and courts of quarter session. The full-
time recorders of Manchester and Liverpool were commissioned
to sit as judges of assize with the judges of the High Court.

Both quarter sessions and assizes were abolished by the Courts
Act 1971.[38] In their place, the Act established a Crown Court in
England and Wales, to be a superior court of record. The Crown
Court, together with the Court of Appeal and the High Court form
the Supreme Court.[39] The jurisdiction and powers of the Crown
Court are exercised by a judge of the High Court, a Circuit judge
or a Recorder, or in certain cases by one of those judges sitting
with justices of the peace.[40] Circuit judges in order to serve in the
Crown Court and the county courts must be barristers of ten years'
standing, or a Recorder who has held that office for at least five
years,[41] appointed by the Queen on the recommendation of the
Lord Chancellor. The Recorders under the Act have little in
common with their predecessors apart from their name. They are
part-time judges of the Crown Court appointed by the Queen on
the recommendation of the Lord Chancellor from barristers and
solicitors of ten years' standing.[42]

The Crown Court is a single court which sits in a number of
different locations.[43] It has the power to sit at any place in England
and Wales as determined by directions given by the Lord

[38] ss. 1 and 3, as were the Crown Courts established under the Criminal Justice
Administration Act 1959, s. 3 : Courts Act 1971, Sched. 11, Pt. IV.
[39] s. 1 (1).
[40] ss. 4 and 5.
[41] s. 16.
[42] s. 21.
[43] A useful account of the administrative background of the Crown Court is
to be found in " The Crown Court " by D. Robinson at [1972] Crim.L.R.,
pp. 14–24.

Chancellor.[44] Those locations are divided into centres described as first-tier, second-tier and third-tier centres. First-tier centres deal with both civil and criminal cases and are served by High Court and Circuit judges; second-tier centres deal with criminal cases only but are served by judges of the High Court and Circuit judges. Third-tier centres deal with criminal cases but are served by Circuit judges only.[45] The class of case suitable for trial by any particular category of judge, that is High Court judge or Circuit judge, is determined by directions given by the Lord Chief Justice with the concurrence of the Lord Chancellor.[46] When the Crown Court sits in the City of London it is known as the Central Criminal Court.[47] The Lord Mayor and Aldermen of the City of London are entitled to sit as judges of the court with any judge of the Crown Court.[48]

All proceedings on indictment must now be brought before the Crown Court and jurisdiction is conferred on the Crown Court in proceedings on indictment, wherever committed, and including in particular proceedings on indictment for offences within the Admiralty jurisdiction.[49]

Schedule 1 to the Courts Act 1971, transfers to the Crown Court all the appellate jurisdiction (with minor exceptions) of the former courts of quarter session.

SECTION 3. THE QUEEN'S BENCH DIVISION OF THE HIGH COURT
OF JUSTICE

The Queen's Bench Division is the successor of the Court of Queen's Bench and had a common law jurisdiction to try all criminal offences against the law of England. Its jurisdiction was in general concurrent with that of assizes and quarter sessions but by particular statutes it had exclusive jurisdiction over certain offences. Its jurisdiction to try cases at first instance, that is by trial at bar before more than one judge, was seldom used, the last occasion being the trial of Sir Roger Casement in 1916. This jurisdiction was limited by section 11 of the Administration of

---

[44] Courts Act 1971, s. 4 (4).
[45] H.L. Written Ans., May 5, 1971, col. 448.
[46] Courts Act 1971, ss. 4 (5), 5 (4) and Sched. 10. See the Directions dated October 1971 reported at [1971] 3 All E.R. 829, and p. 708, post.
[47] s. 4 (7).
[48] Ibid.
[49] s. 6.

Justice (Miscellaneous) Provisions Act 1938, and the whole has been abolished by the Courts Act 1971.[50]

However, the Queen's Bench Division has a very important appellate jurisdiction, exercised by a Divisional Court in respect of the proceedings of magistrates' courts and the Crown Court.[51] This is the procedure for appeal by way of case stated.[52] Appeal lies from a Divisional Court in a criminal case to the House of Lords.[53]

In addition to its original and appellate jurisdiction, the Queen's Bench Division exercises all the powers of control over inferior courts and tribunals which is vested in the High Court and which is exercised by means of the writ of *habeas corpus* and the prerogative orders of *mandamus, certiorari* and *prohibition.*[54]

SECTION 4. THE COURT OF APPEAL (CRIMINAL DIVISION)

The Court of Criminal Appeal was established by the Criminal Appeal Act 1907, and gave a person convicted on indictment an appeal for the first time; a convicted person having had no right of appeal to the Court of Crown Cases Reserved, which it replaced. It was left to that court to review cases where a point of law was reserved to them by the trial judge. The jurisdiction of the Court of Criminal Appeal was transferred to the Criminal Division of the Court of Appeal by the Criminal Appeal Act 1966. The court has no original jurisdiction and can only deal with criminal cases coming before it by way of appeal, or in certain circumstances, by reference from the Home Secretary or the Attorney-General.[55] An appeal lies, with leave, and on a certificate of the court, to the House of Lords.[56]

SECTION 5. THE HOUSE OF LORDS

The judicial functions of Parliament in criminal matters are vested in the House of Lords, which operates as a final court of appeal.[57] Appeals lie to the House of Lords both from the Queen's Bench Division of the High Court and from the Criminal Division of the

---

[50] Sched. 11.
[51] s. 10.
[52] See p. 833, *post.*
[53] See p. 837, *post.*
[54] s. 10.
[55] The whole subject of appeals to this court is dealt with in Chapter 58, *post.*
[56] See p. 859, *post.*
[57] See pp. 837, 859, *post.*

Court of Appeal. They are regulated by the Appellate Jurisdiction Acts of 1876 and 1887 and the Administration of Justice Act 1960. Appeals from the Court of Appeal are governed by Part II of the Criminal Appeal Act 1968.

SECTION 6. COURTS OF PARTICULAR JURISDICTION

(i) The coroner's court. The court of the coroner is a common law court, but the duties and authority of a coroner are now regulated by the **Coroners Act 1887,** as amended by the **Coroners (Amendment) Act 1926** and the **Courts Act 1971.**[57a]

By **section 3** of the Act of **1887** he is required to hold an inquest whenever there is the dead body of a person lying within the area of his jurisdiction and there is reasonable cause to suspect that such person has died a violent or unnatural death or a sudden death the cause of which is unknown, or has died in prison, or in such place or under such circumstances as to require an inquest.

Proceedings at the inquest are governed by the **Coroners Rules 1953,** which provide that proceedings and evidence at the inquest shall be directed solely to ascertaining (i) who the deceased was; (ii) how, when and where he came by his death; (iii) the persons (if any) to be charged with murder, manslaughter or infanticide [58]; and (iv) the particulars to be registered concerning the death; and neither the coroner nor the jury are to express any opinion upon any other matter.[59]

Where a person is charged by a coroner's inquisition with murder, manslaughter or infanticide the coroner has, by **section 5** [60] of the Act of **1887,** power to issue a warrant for his arrest, and under **section 25** [61] of the Act of **1926** power to commit him for trial.

A coroner has also at common law jurisdiction to hold an inquest on treasure trove, and this jurisdiction is preserved by **section 36** of the Act of **1887,** which provides that " a coroner

---

[57a] The coroners courts have recently been under inquiry by the Brodrick Committee which reported in November 1971. See Cmnd. 4810 (Report of the Committee on Death Certification and Coroners).

[58] But if someone has already been charged before examining magistrates with one of these offences or with an offence against the Suicide Act 1961, or with causing death by dangerous driving, the coroner must adjourn the inquest until the conclusion of the criminal proceedings: Coroners (Amendment) Act 1926, s. 20; Suicide Act 1961, Sched. 1; Road Traffic Act 1972, s. 1 (2).

[59] r. 26.

[60] As amended by the Courts Act 1971, Sched. 8.

[61] As amended by the Courts Act 1971, Sched. 8.

shall continue as heretofore to inquire of treasure that is found, who were the finders, and who is suspected thereof."

(ii) Courts-martial. The Army Act 1955, the Air Force Act 1955, the Naval Discipline Act 1957, and the Armed Forces Act 1971 provide for the trial of soldiers, airmen and sailors by courts-martial for offences against military, air force or naval discipline and subject to certain restrictions, for ordinary criminal offences.[62]

The Acts do not exempt soldiers or airmen from punishment by the ordinary criminal courts. They expressly provide that nothing therein is to exempt any officer, soldier or airman from being proceeded against by the ordinary course of law when accused of any offence.[63] This is subject, however, to an exception in favour of sailors. The Naval Discipline Act provides that where a person is convicted of an offence by naval disciplinary proceedings, a civil court is barred from subsequently trying him for the same offence.[64] In the case of soldiers and airmen, if a person who has been sentenced for an offence by a court-martial is afterwards tried by a civil court for the same offence, that court in awarding punishment shall have regard to the military punishment he may have already undergone.[65] No person acquitted or convicted by a competent civil court is to be tried by court-martial for the same offence.[66]

(iii) Courts-Martial Appeal Court. This court was created by the Courts-Martial (Appeals) Act 1951, and is now governed by the Courts-Martial (Appeals) Act 1968 and consists in general, of the same judges who comprise the Court of Appeal (Criminal Divi-

---

[62] See, for example, *R.* v. *Page* [1954] 1 Q.B. 170, where a British soldier who murdered an Egyptian national in Egypt was held to have been rightly convicted by court-martial, murder being an offence " triable in England when committed abroad." See also *Cox* v. *Army Council* [1963] A.C. 48, where a British soldier serving in Germany was held to have been rightly convicted at a court-martial of the offence of driving without due care and attention, although, at the time, he had been driving in Germany—this offence being one " which, if committed in England, would be punishable by [English] law."

[63] Army Act 1955, s. 133; Air Force Act 1955, s. 133; Naval Discipline Act 1957, s. 129, as amended by the Armed Forces Act 1971, ss. 45, 55 and 57.

[64] Naval Discipline Act 1957, s. 129, as amended by the Armed Forces Act 1971, ss. 45, 55 and 57.

[65] Army Act 1955, s. 133; Air Force Act 1955, s. 133.

[66] Army Act 1955, s. 134; Air Force Act 1955, s. 134; Naval Discipline Act 1957, s. 129, as amended by the Armed Forces Act 1971, ss. 45, 55 and 57.

sion).[67] The court acts on the same principles as those applied by the Criminal Division of the Court of Appeal so far as they apply.[68] An appeal lies from the decision of a court-martial of any of the three services of the court against conviction only [68a] and not against sentence. An appeal lies from this court to the House of Lords in certain circumstances.[69]

---

[67] Courts-Martial (Appeals) Act 1968, ss. 2, 3. The court may be differently constituted in the case of appeals heard in Scotland or Northern Ireland : *ibid.* s. 1 (1).

[68] *R.* v. *Condon* (1952) 36 Cr.App.R. 130.

[68a] Courts-Martial (Appeals) Act 1968, s. 8.

[69] Courts-Martial (Appeals) Act 1968, ss. 39–48.

PART II

OFFENCES OF A PUBLIC NATURE

CHAPTER 9

OFFENCES AGAINST THE CROWN AND GOVERNMENT

SECTION 1. TREASON AND MISPRISION OF TREASON

THE unilateral declaration of independence, in 1965, by the leaders of the Crown Colony of Southern Rhodesia, has drawn attention to the difficulty of applying to modern conditions the existing law of treason, based as it is upon the Treason Acts 1351–1817. The modern law is vague and ill-defined.[1] At common law treason might be high treason or petit treason but the separate offence of petit treason disappeared in 1828.[2]

High treason. Disregarding its more colourful anachronisms[3] the offence of treason today, considered in the context of the two world wars, consists of:

  (i) levying war against the King[4] in his realm[5];

  (ii) being adherent to the King's enemies in his realm, giving them aid and comfort in the realm or elsewhere[6] and,

---

[1] See " Rhodesia Crisis—Criminal Liabilities " by B. A. Hepple, P. O'Higgins and C. C. Turpin [1966] Crim.L.R. 5 and " Rhodesia Crisis—Criminal Liabilities " by Prof. O. Hood Phillips [1966] Crim.L.R. 68.

[2] Offences against the Person Act 1828, s. 2, re-enacted by s. 8 of the Offences against the Person Act 1861.

[3] A man is still guilty of treason if he (a) compasses or imagines the death of the King's wife *and* manifests such compassing or imagining by some overt act (Treason Act 1351); or (b) violates the King's wife or his eldest daughter unmarried, or the wife of the King's eldest son and heir (*ibid.*); or (c) slays the Chancellor, Treasurer or the King's justices of the one Bench, or the other (*i.e.* the judges of the King's (Queen's) Bench Division), justices in eyre, or justices of assize, and all other justices assigned to hear and determine, being in their places, doing their offices (Treason Act 1351); or (d) attempts by any overt act to prevent the person next in succession under the Act of Settlement from succeeding to the Crown (Treason Act 1702, s. 3).

[4] The term " King " includes a Queen Regnant: Interpretation Act 1889, s. 30. The person to whom allegiance is due is the King or Queen *de facto*, that is to say, the King or Queen for the time being in actual possession of the Crown; no allegiance is therefore owed to a King *de jure*, who has merely a right to the Crown: Treason Act 1495, s. 1.

[5] *i.e.* England and Wales; the operation of the statute was, however, extended to Scotland by the Treason Act 1708, s. 1, and to Ireland by Poyning's Act 1494.

[6] *Ibid.* and see Arch. para. 3003.

possibly, in the context of the Rhodesian situation and the Irish troubles of the eighteenth and nineteenth centuries.

(iii) either within the realm or without, compassing, imagining, devising or intending the death, maiming or wounding, imprisonment or restraint of the person of the King or of his heirs and successors *and* expressing, uttering or declaring such compassings, etc., by publishing any printing or writing, or by any overt act or deed.[7]

Certain important points arise from this definition.

(1) Who can commit treason? Treason being a breach of allegiance owed to the Crown, it can be committed only by those persons who owe allegiance to the Crown.[8] The authorities state that all British subjects owe this allegiance and therefore can commit treason.[9] However, the category " British subjects " today includes, as well as citizens of the United Kingdom and Colonies, citizens of independent Commonwealth countries, some of which are republics.[10] These territories have their own legislation relating to treason. A court would probably now hold that the only British subjects who can be tried for treason in England *as British subjects* are citizens of the United Kingdom and Colonies. If a British subject, who is not however a citizen of the United Kingdom and Colonies, commits an act, outside England, which would have amounted to treason under English law, he could not now be convicted of treason in England, since he does not owe the necessary allegiance, although he could be proceeded against in accordance with the law of his own country.[11] This contention is supported by the Rhodesian situation between 1965 and 1972. Aliens, and those British subjects who are not citizens of the United Kingdom and Colonies, can only exceptionally commit treason. They can do so while owing the allegiance to the Crown which arises from the fact of protection by the Crown. An alien is said to enjoy that protection while he is in British territory.[12] This rule probably now only

---

[7] Treason Act 1351; Treason Act 1795, made perpetual by the Treason Act 1817.   [8] See *Joyce* v. *D.P.P.* [1946] A.C. at pp. 365, 374.
[9] *R.* v. *Casement* [1917] 1 K.B. at p. 130.
[10] See the British Nationality Act 1948, s. 1, as amended by subsequent statutes.
[11] See British Nationality Act 1948, s. 3.
[12] *De Jager* v. *Att.-Gen. of Natal* [1907] A.C. 326. In that case the accused, an alien resident within British territory, had assisted invaders while Her Majesty's forces had temporarily withdrawn. His conviction for high treason was affirmed by the Judicial Committee of the Privy Council.

applies if he is in the United Kingdom and Colonies. This allegiance continues if he has left British territory but his family and effects remain behind [13] or, it was decided in *Joyce* v. *D.P.P.*,[14] if he is in possession of a British [15] passport. In that case the accused, an alien, had obtained a British passport by misrepresenting himself as a British subject.

(2) Levying war against the Queen in her realm. To constitute a levying of war " there must be an insurrection, there must be force accompanying such insurrection, and the object of it must be of a general nature." [16] The number of persons engaged is not material, nor need they be armed with military weapons, nor is actual fighting necessary.[17] Levying of war may be either actual or constructive, for " not only those who directly rebel against the King and take up arms in order to dethrone him but . . . those who in a violent and forcible manner withstand his lawful authority, or endeavour to reform his government, are said to levy war against him." [18] There is therefore a constructive levying of war whenever any insurrection or disturbance takes place for the purpose of effecting innovations of a *public and general character* by an armed force or in order to redress any *public grievance*, as *e.g.* to obtain the repeal of a statute,[19] to alter the religion established by law, or to pull down *all* enclosures, or *all* prisons, or *all* dissenting chapels.[20]

But it is not treason, though it may be a *riot*, if the object of a disturbance be of a private nature, *e.g.* to throw down the enclosures of a particular manor or common, or to destroy a particular building, or to make a demonstration to secure the liberation or mitigation of the punishment of particular political prisoners.[21]

---

[13] See *Joyce* v. *D.P.P.* [1946] A.C. at pp. 366–369, 374–375.

[14] [1946] A.C. 347.

[15] Again the rule in *Joyce's* case would probably now only apply if the alien had obtained a United Kingdom and Colonies passport.

[16] *R.* v. *Frost* (1839) 9 C. & P. at p. 161.

[17] *R.* v. *Gallagher* (1883) 15 Cox 291, where the jury were directed that to destroy public buildings by explosive with the intent of compelling the Queen to change her counsels and to intimidate Parliament into doing what it otherwise would not have done would be a levying of war; see also Arch. para. 3023 and authorities there cited.

[18] 1 Hawk. c. 17, s. 23.

[19] *R.* v. *Gordon* (1781) 2 Dougl. 590.

[20] *R.* v. *Dammaree* (1710) 15 St.Tr. 522 at p. 605; *R.* v. *Purchase, ibid.* at p. 699.

[21] *R.* v. *Frost* (1839) 9 C. & P. 129.

An overt act of levying war, actual or constructive, must be proved in order to support the indictment, but a conspiracy to levy war directly against the Queen, as we shall see, may be charged as an overt act of compassing the Queen's death.[22]

(3) Being adherent to the Queen's enemies in the realm, giving them aid and comfort in the realm, or elsewhere. This is, in modern times perhaps the form of treason most frequently to reach the courts, and was the charge faced by Joyce and a number of other traitors after the Second World War. The words " giving them aid and comfort " in the realm are in apposition to and explain what is meant by the words " being adherent to." Therefore, " if a man be adherent to the King's enemies in his realm by giving to them aid or comfort in his realm, or if he be adherent to the King's enemies elsewhere, that is, by giving them aid or comfort elsewhere, he is equally adherent to the King's enemies, and if he is adherent to the King's enemies, then he commits the treason which the statute of Edward II defines." [23]

Thus in the case of *R*. v. *Casement* [24] a British subject went to Germany during the First World War and there actively endeavoured to persuade other British subjects, who were prisoners in Germany, to join the German forces; he also took part in an expedition from Germany with the object of landing arms in Ireland for the use of German forces. *Held*, by the Court of Criminal Appeal, that he was guilty of treason by adhering to the King's enemies elsewhere than in the realm and that he could be tried in this country.

An overt act which is evidence of aiding or comforting must be proved.[25] Examples of such overt acts are becoming naturalised in an enemy country in time of war [26]; raising forces for the Queen's enemies; sending them arms, money or intelligence; or joining them in acts of hostility.[27] It is not however sufficient to prove by some overt act that the accused in fact aided or comforted the enemy, unless it is also proved that the accused intended so to aid and comfort.[28]

---

[22] *Post*, p. 127.
[23] *R*. v. *Casement* [1917] 1 K.B. at p. 137.
[24] [1917] 1 K.B. 98.
[25] The mere conspiracy to adhere might, however, as we shall see (*post*, p. 127), be an overt act of compassing the Queen's death.
[26] *R*. v. *Lynch* [1903] 1 K.B. 444.
[27] Arch. paras. 3029–3031.   [28] *R*. v. *Ahlers* [1915] 1 K.B. 616.

The term " enemies " means only subjects of a foreign state at war with the Queen,[29] and therefore assistance given to British subjects in rebellion is not an adherence to the Queen's enemies.[30]

(4) Compassing, etc., the death, or any harm tending to the death, wounding, imprisonment or restraint of the Queen. It may be, when one considers the Rhodesian situation between 1965 and 1972, that this particular form of treason is not wholly anachronistic.[31] In this species of treason the offence is constituted by the compassing or imagining, which must however be manifested and proved by some overt act.[32] The actual killing of the Queen is therefore the overt act by which the compassing is established.[33] Everything wilfully done or attempted whereby the Queen's life may be endangered is an overt act of compassing her death,[34] as, for instance, consultations of conspirators on the means of killing the Queen.[35]

The Treason Act 1351, did not make treasonable, for example, the mere compassing to depose the Queen or to levy war or to adhere to the Queen's enemies. The courts remedied these deficiencies by holding that a conspiracy is itself an *overt act*, and therefore conspiracies, for example, to depose the Queen, to levy war against her or to adhere to her enemies are overt acts of compassing her death, and therefore high treason.[36] The crime of treason was further defined and extended to include these and other conspiracies by the Treason Act 1795. By the Treason Felony Act 1848, all the offences specified in the 1795 Act were made felonies, with

---

[29] Arch. para. 3035: It does not appear necessary that war should have been formerly proclaimed: *ibid.* During the Korean war, the Attorney-General stated in a written answer in the House of Commons that the presence of British journalists with North Korean forces constituted an act of treason. (1950) *House of Commons Debates*, Vol. 478, p. 203.

[30] *Ibid.*

[31] See the extended interpretations placed upon the section in *R.* v. *Sheares* (1798) and in particular in the case of *Earl of Essex* (1600) 1 St.Tr. 1334 at col. 1355 " in every Rebellion the law intendeth as a consequent the compassing the death and deposition of the King." Both these cases are referred to in the first of the articles mentioned in fn. 1 on p. 123.

[32] Although the Treason Act 1351, did not specify that the compassing or imagining must be manifested and proved by an overt act, this was held to be necessary by the courts (1 Hawk. c. 17, s. 29) and is now necessary by virtue of the Treason Act 1795.

[33] (1660) 5 St.Tr. at p. 982.

[34] Fost. 195.

[35] *R.* v. *Tonge* (1662) 6 St.Tr. 225 and see, further, Arch. para. 3016.

[36] *Mulcahy* v. *R.* (1868) L.R. 3 H.L. 306.

the exception of the section which is set out in (iii) above,[37] which remains treason. These offences are considered below.[38] However, the 1848 Act did nothing to affect the judicial interpretation of the 1351 Act, so that it is still technically possible to convict persons of treason, by compassing the Queen's death, if they conspire, for example, to depose the Queen or to levy war.

Punishment for treason. Formerly of a particularly barbarous character,[39] the sentence is now death by hanging, unaccompanied by any forfeiture of property.[40]

Misprision of treason. An account of what constitutes misprision can be found elsewhere.[41] This offence consists in the bare knowledge and concealment of treason without any assent thereto.[42] As has been already pointed out,[43] there is in treason no distinction between principals and accessories, and at common law the mere non-disclosure of treason was deemed to be an assent to it and consequently to amount to treason.[44] But by the Treason Act 1554,[45] it was provided that the mere " concealment or keeping secret of any high treason " shall be deemed only misprision of treason.

In order to be guilty of misprision of treason the accused must have had knowledge not merely of a treasonable design but of its nature and of the persons engaged in it and must have failed to make disclosure.[46]

The offence is a common law misdemeanour, punishable by *imprisonment for life.*[47]

---

[37] *Ante*, p. 124.
[38] *Post*, p. 129.
[39] Women were burnt. A male traitor was drawn on a hurdle to the place of execution and hanged, but while still alive was cut down and disembowelled; his head was then severed from his body which was quartered, and the head and quarters were at the King's disposal and were usually exposed in some conspicuous position.
[40] Forfeiture Act 1870, s. 1.
[41] Arch. para. 4152.
[42] Kel. (J.) 21 ; see also Arch. para. 4152.
[43] *Ante*, p. 86.
[44] 1 Hawk. c. 20, s. 2.
[45] This Act was repealed by the Criminal Law Act 1967, Sched. 3.
[46] Kel. 21, 22 ; 1 Hawk. c. 20, s. 6 ; 1 Hale P.C. 372, *i.e.* to the judge of assize (now presumably a judge of the Crown Court) or justice of the peace or some other responsible official: *ibid.*
[47] Arch. para. 4152. Forfeiture for this offence was abolished by Criminal Law Act 1967, s. 7 (5).

Special rules relating to prosecutions for treason and misprision of treason

(1) No one can be prosecuted for any treason or misprision of treason committed *within the realm* unless the bill of indictment is signed within three years after its commission, except when the treason consists in designing or attempting the assassination of the Queen.[48]

(2) Bail can be allowed in treason only by order of a Secretary of State, or by a judge of the High Court.[49]

(3) By **section 12 (6)** of the **Criminal Law Act 1967,** it is provided that in all cases of treason and of misprision of treason the procedure shall be the same as the procedure on trials for murder.

SECTION 2. TREASON FELONY ACT 1848

By the **Treason Felony Act 1848,** it is an offence [*Imp. life*] for any person,[50] either within the realm or without, to compass, imagine, devise or intend—

(i) to deprive or depose the Queen or her heirs and successors from the style, honour or queenly name of the imperial crown of this realm, or of any other of Her Majesty's dominions or countries; *or*

(ii) to levy war against the Queen, her heirs and successors, within this realm, in order, by force or constraint, to compel him or them to change his or their measures or counsels, or in order to put any force or constraint upon, or to intimidate or overawe both Houses or either House of Parliament; *or*

(iii) to move or stir any foreigner or stranger with force to invade this realm or any other of Her Majesty's dominions or countries under the obeisance of Her Majesty, her heirs or successors,

and to express, utter or declare such compassings, imaginations and inventions, devices and intentions, or any of them, by publishing any printing or writing, or by any overt act or deed.

---

[48] Treason Act 1695, ss. 5, 6.
[49] Magistrates' Courts Act 1952, s. 8.
[50] Presumably the term " person " means the same as in treason.

At first sight, the Treason Felony Act 1848 seems to do little but duplicate the Treason Acts in another form. It is more readily understandable when one realises that the purpose of its enactment was to allay doubts as to whether the Treason Act 1795 applied to Ireland, and to clarify doubts as to how far words alone could be treasonable.[51]

As has already been pointed out,[52] it has been held that the requirement of an overt act is satisfied if the accused (merely) *conspired* with others to commit the offence that he is charged with compassing.[53]

We have already seen what the words " levying war " mean.[54] An illustration of what amounts to " compassing to depose " is afforded by the case of *R*. v. *Gallagher*.[55] The jury were directed that if the accused intended to separate Ireland from the Crown of England by force, then they were compassing to depose. In that case the overt act, which manifested and proved that the accused had both compassed to depose and to levy war, was the preparation of high explosive for the purpose of blowing up public buildings.[56]

If on the trial the facts proved amount to a treason, the prisoner may, nevertheless, be convicted, but he cannot afterwards be prosecuted for treason on the same facts.[57]

SECTION 3. ATTEMPTS TO ALARM OR INJURE THE QUEEN

In consequence of various assaults and other acts of annoyance to which Queen Victoria was subjected at the beginning of her reign it was by **section 2** of the **Treason Act 1842,** made an offence [*Imp.* 7 *years*] for any person:

(i) Wilfully to discharge or attempt to discharge or point, aim or present at or near to the person of the Queen [58] any gun, pistol or any other arms, whether or not containing any explosive or destructive material, or to dis-

---

[51] See Crim.L.R. [1966], *op. cit.* at p. 7.
[52] *Ante*, p. 127.
[53] *Mulcahy* v. *R*. (1868) L.R. 3 H.L. 306.
[54] *Ante*, p. 125.
[55] (1883) 15 Cox 291.
[56] See further, *ante*, p. 127.
[57] Treason Felony Act 1848, s. 7.
[58] This section in terms referred only to the Queen, but it must be construed as referring to the Sovereign for the time being: Interpretation Act 1889, s. 30.

charge or cause to be discharged or attempt to discharge, etc., any explosive substance near to the person of the Queen, or

(ii) Wilfully to strike or strike at or attempt to strike, etc., the person of the Queen in any manner, or

(iii) Wilfully to throw or attempt to throw any matter or thing at or upon the person of the Queen, with the intent in any such cases to injure or alarm the Queen, or to break the public peace, or whereby the public peace may be endangered, or

(iv) Wilfully to produce or have near the person of the Queen any firearms or other arms, or any explosive, destructive, or dangerous matter or thing, with intent to use the same so as to injure or alarm the Queen.

SECTION 4. SEDITION

Any person who *with a seditious intention* either speaks, writes or acts is guilty at common law of an offence [*Fine* [58a] *and Imp.*]. If the seditious matter is in a permanent form, *i.e.* constitutes a libel,[59] and (*semble*) is published,[60] then the offence is called seditious libel.[61] Otherwise it is simply called sedition.

A seditious intention is an intention:

(i) to incite the Queen's subjects to attempt otherwise than by lawful means the alteration of any matter in Church or state by law established, to create public disturbance or to incite civil war, or

(ii) to bring into hatred or contempt or to incite disaffection against the person of the Queen, her heirs, or successors, or the Government and Constitution of the United Kingdom,[62] as by law established, or either House of Parliament, or the administration of justice,

---

[58a] See p. 201, *post*, n. 59.

[59] *Post*, p. 206 and see the Theatres Act 1968, s. 4.

[60] There is doubt as to whether there must be publication: see *R.* v. *Burdett* (1820) 4 B. & Ald. 95.

[61] When a person is convicted of seditious libel a search warrant may be issued authorising the search of his premises and the seizure of all copies of the libel: Criminal Libel Act 1819, ss. 1, 2.

[62] A document published in this country which is calculated to disturb the government of a *foreign* country is not a seditious libel, nor punishable as a libel at all: *R.* v. *Antonelli* (1905) 70 J.P. 4.

or to incite ill will between different classes of the Queen's subjects.[63]

Everyone may lawfully criticise or censure the conduct of the servants of the Crown or the acts of the Government, provided that he does so without malignity, and does not impute corrupt or malicious motives, and avoids defamation, obscenity or blasphemy.[64]

As in all cases where intention is a matter to be considered by the jury, section 8 of the Criminal Justice Act 1967 applies.[65]

Truth is no defence if a statement is seditious.[66] However it is a defence to show that the statement was made on a privileged occasion, as, for example, in the Houses of Parliament.[67]

No prosecution can be commenced against any proprietor, editor, publisher or any person responsible for the publication of a newspaper for any libel published therein without the order of a judge in chambers, notice of the application for which must be given to the accused.[68]

Seditious conspiracy. A conspiracy to commit sedition or to publish a seditious libel is an offence, as indeed is any conspiracy to commit a crime. However a number of particular seditious conspiracies are now also punishable by statute.[69]

SECTION 5. OFFENCES AGAINST THE OFFICIAL SECRETS ACTS

By **section 1 (1)** of the **Official Secrets Act 1911,** as amended by the **Official Secrets Act 1920,**[70] it is an offence [71] if any person for any purpose prejudicial to the safety or interests of the state:

    (i) approaches, inspects, passes over or is in the neighbourhood of, or enters, any prohibited place within the Act, or

---

[63] See the authorities cited in Arch. paras. 3147–3149; and see *R.* v. *Burns* (1886) 16 Cox 355.
[64] *Ibid.*
[65] *Ante,* p. 51.
[66] *R.* v. *Burdett* (1820) 4 B. & Ald. 314; *R.* v. *Duffy* (1846) 2 Cox 45.
[67] Arch. para. 3162.
[68] Law of Libel Amendment Act 1888, s. 8.
[69] *Post,* p. 138.
[70] s. 10 and Sched. 1. By s. 11 of the Act of 1920 the two Acts are to be construed together.
[71] For the punishment, see *post,* p. 138.

(ii) makes any sketch, plan, model or note calculated or intended to be useful to an enemy,[72] or

(iii) obtains, collects, records, publishes or communicates to any other person any secret official code word or pass word or any sketch, etc., or other information calculated or intended to be useful to an enemy.

Section 1 (2) states that on a prosecution under this section it is not necessary to show that the accused person was guilty of any particular act tending to show such prejudicial purpose, and he may be convicted if from the circumstances of the case or his conduct or known character [73] as proved it appears that his purpose was prejudicial; and that if any sketch, etc., or information relating to any prohibited place, or any official code word, etc., is made, obtained, collected, recorded, or published, or communicated by any person not acting under lawful authority, *it is deemed to have been made, etc., for a prejudicial purpose unless the contrary is proved.*

In *Chandler* v. *D.P.P.*[74] the House of Lords held that if a person enters an airfield which comes within the definition of a " prohibited place," [75] with the purpose (that is, the intention or desire [76]) of obstructing or interfering with the operational activities of that airfield, then he can be convicted of an offence against this section even though he had no intention of spying. The fact that his motive for wishing to interfere is to persuade the Government to change its policy on nuclear weapons was held to be immaterial. The House of Lords also held that a person accused under this section cannot bring evidence to prove that *his* interference was not prejudicial because the maintenance of the base *itself* was prejudicial to the safety and interests of the state. This follows, it was held, from the rule of law that the disposition and order of the armed forces are within the exclusive prerogative of the Crown, and cannot be challenged in the courts.

By **section 2** of the **Act of 1920,** in any proceedings against a person for an offence under section 1 of the Act of 1911, the fact

---

[72] The term " enemy " includes a potential enemy: *R.* v. *Parrott* (1913) 8 Cr. App.R. 186.

[73] This is an exception to the general rule that evidence of the accused's bad character is not admissible: see *post,* p. 603.

[74] [1964] A.C. 763.   [75] *Post,* p. 136.

[76] [1964] A.C. at p. 790, *per* Lord Reid; but see *per* Lord Devlin: *ibid.* at p. 805.

that he has been in communication with or has attempted to communicate with a foreign agent,[77] either within or without the United Kingdom, is evidence that he has, for a purpose prejudicial to the safety or interests of the state, obtained or attempted to obtain information calculated or intended to be useful to an enemy. And, unless he proves the contrary, a person is deemed to have been in communication with a foreign agent if he has within or without the United Kingdom visited the address of a foreign agent as defined by the section, or associated with a foreign agent, or the name or address of any foreign agent or any information regarding a foreign agent is found in his possession or has been supplied by him to any other person or to him by any other person.

By **section 2** of the **Act of 1911**,[78] it is an offence if any person having in his possession or control any secret official code word, etc., or sketch, etc., or other information which relates to or is used in a prohibited place or which is made or obtained in contravention of the Act or which was entrusted to him in confidence by any person holding office under Her Majesty[79] or obtained by him or to which he had access as a person holding office under Her Majesty or as a Government contractor or through employment under a Government contractor,

    (i) communicates such secret official code word, etc., or sketch, etc., to any person to whom he is not authorised or to whom it is not his duty to communicate it;

    (ii) uses the information in his possession for the benefit of any foreign Power or in any other manner prejudicial to the safety, etc., of the state;

    (iii) retains such sketch, etc., in his possession when he has no right, or when it is contrary to his duty, to retain it or fails to comply with all directions issued by lawful authority with regard to the return or disposal thereof;

---

[77] The expression " foreign agent " is defined by s. 2 (2) (*b*) of the Act of 1920.

[78] As amended by s. 9 of and Sched. 1 to the Official Secrets Act 1920. See the remarks of Caulfield J. in the *Sunday Telegraph* secrets case reported in *The Times* on February 3, 1971, which have led to the government setting up an inquiry into the operation of this section.

[79] A police officer is a person " holding office under Her Majesty " for the purposes of this section: *Lewis* v. *Cattle* [1938] 2 K.B. 454. Certain directions made by the Bank of England to bankers are deemed to be made by a person holding office under Her Majesty: Bank of England Act 1946, s. 4.

(iv) fails to take reasonable care of, or so conducts himself as to endanger the safety of, such code or pass word, etc., or information.

It is also an offence

(i) for any person having in his possession, etc., any sketch, plan, etc., or document or information relating to munitions of war to communicate it to any foreign Power, or in any other manner prejudicial to the safety, etc., of the state;

(ii) for any person to receive any secret official code word, etc., sketch, etc., knowing or having reasonable grounds to believe that it is communicated to him in contravention of the Act, *unless he proves* that the communication was contrary to his desire.

By **section 1** of the **Act of 1920,** it is made an offence for any person, for the purpose of gaining admission or assisting any other person to gain admission to any prohibited place, or for any other purpose prejudicial to the safety or interests of the state, to do certain acts specified in the section, as, for example, to make an unauthorised use of any uniform, to make any false statement in any declaration, application or document, to forge or alter any passport or official document, to personate any person holding office under the Crown, to use or have in possession without authority the die, seal or stamp of any government department or any imitation thereof.

By the same section it is also made an offence (i) for any person to retain for any purpose prejudicial to the safety, etc., of the state any official document, or to fail to comply with any official directions as to its return; (ii) to allow any other person to have possession of any official document issued for his use alone, or to communicate any secret official code word, etc., so issued, or without lawful authority or excuse to possess any official document, etc., issued for the use of some other person; (iii) without lawful authority, etc., to sell or possess any Government die, seal, or stamp, or imitation thereof. On any prosecution under this section involving proof of a purpose prejudicial to the safety, etc., of the state the provisions of section 1 (2) of the Act of 1911 apply.[80]

[80] See *ante*, p. 133.

By **section 3** of the **Act of 1920** any person who in the vicinity of [81] a prohibited place interferes with the police or members of Her Majesty's forces on guard is guilty of an offence.

The expression " prohibited place " is defined by **section 3** of the **Act of 1911,** as amended by **section 10** of and the **First Schedule** to the **Act of 1920.** It includes (i) any work of defence, arsenal, naval or air force establishment, factory, dockyard, camp, ship, or aircraft, telegraph, telephone, wireless or signal station, belonging to or occupied by or on behalf of Her Majesty, and any place belonging to, etc., Her Majesty and used for munitions of war, or sketches, plans, models, or documents relating thereto, or for getting any metals, oil or minerals for use in time of war; (ii) any place not belonging to Her Majesty where any munitions of war or sketches, etc., are being made, repaired, gotten or stored under contract with, or with any person on behalf of, Her Majesty or otherwise on behalf of Her Majesty; (iii) any place belonging to or used for the purposes of Her Majesty which is for the time being declared by order of a Secretary of State to be a prohibited place; (iv) any railway, road or other means of communication by land or water, or any other place used for gas, water, electricity or other public works, or any place where any munitions of war or sketches are being made, repaired or stored, otherwise than on behalf of Her Majesty, which is for the time being declared by order of the Secretary of State to be a prohibited place. **Section 6** of the **Atomic Energy Authority Act 1954,** enables a place used by the authority to be declared a prohibited place for the purposes of section 3 of the Act of 1911.

By **section 7** of the **Act of 1911** a person who knowingly harbours any person whom he knows or has reasonable grounds for supposing to be a person who is about to commit or who has committed an offence under that Act, or who, having harboured any such persons wilfully omits or [82] refuses to disclose to a superintendent of police any information in relation to such person, is guilty of an offence.

By **section 6** of the **Act of 1920,** as substituted by **section 1** of the **Official Secrets Act 1939,** a chief officer of police who is satisfied that there is reasonable ground for believing that an offence under

---

[81] The words " in the vicinity of " mean " in or in the vicinity of ": *Adler* v. *George* [1964] 2 Q.B. 7.

[82] The word " omits " was added by Sched. 1 to the Act of 1920.

section 1 of the Act of 1911 has been committed and for believing that a person is able to furnish information as to the offence or suspected offence may with the permission of the Secretary of State, or, in a case of great emergency, without such permission, authorise a superintendent of police or any police officer not below the rank of inspector to require that person to tender information and, if necessary, on tender of expenses, to attend at such reasonable time and place as may be specified. Failure to give information or attend is an offence.[83]

By **section 7** of the **Act of 1920** any person who attempts to commit or *incites* another person to commit, or *aids or abets*, and [84] does anything preparatory to the commission of any offence under either Act is liable to the same punishment as if he had committed the offence.

By **section 6** [85] of the **Act of 1911** a person found committing an offence under the Acts, or suspected of having committed, or attempted to commit, or being about to commit, such an offence, may be arrested.

By **section 8** of the **Act of 1911** no prosecution for any offence under that Act can be instituted without the consent of the Attorney-General. A suspected person may, however, be arrested and remanded without any preliminary consent.

By **section 9** of the **Act of 1911**, if a justice is satisfied by information on oath that there is reasonable ground for suspecting that an offence under the Acts has been or is about to be committed, he may grant a search warrant authorising the search of any premises named in the warrant and the seizure of any sketch, etc., which is evidence of an offence under the Act. In cases of emergency a superintendent of police may by a written order give a constable the same authority.

By **section 10** of the **Act of 1911** the Acts apply (i) to offences committed in any part of Her Majesty's dominions; (ii) to offences committed anywhere by British officers or subjects. An offence committed out of the United Kingdom may be tried in any competent British court where it was committed or in England.[86]

---

[83] This is an exception to the common law rule that a person cannot be *required* to accompany the police to answer questions, unless he is arrested: *post*, p. 554.
[84] The word "and" must be read as meaning "or": *R. v. Oakes* [1959] 2 Q.B. 350.   [85] As amended by Criminal Law Act 1967, Sched. 3.
[86] Criminal Justice Act 1948, Sched. 10, and Criminal Law Act 1967, Sched. 3. In England and Wales proceedings on indictment must be brought in the Crown Court.

By **section 5** of the **Act of 1920,** provisions are made for the registration and regulation of persons carrying on the business of receiving postal packets for delivery or forwarding to the persons for whom they are intended, and any failure to comply with these provisions is punishable on summary conviction by *imprisonment for* 1 *month and a fine of* £10.

Punishments. By **section 8** of the **Act of 1920** the maximum punishment for an offence against section 1 of the 1911 Act is 14 *years' imprisonment* and for other offences, on conviction on indictment 2 *years' imprisonment* and on summary conviction 3 *months' imprisonment and* £50 *fine.* Consecutive sentences in all totalling 42 years of imprisonment for a series of offences against section 1 (1) (*c*) of the Act of 1911 were in one case awarded and confirmed by the Court of Criminal Appeal.[87]

This section also provides that no offence which may be tried on indictment may be tried summarily except by consent of the Attorney-General.

Section 6. Unlawful Oaths

By the **Unlawful Oaths Acts of 1797** and **1812,** it is an offence for any person or persons, in any manner or form whatsoever, either (i) to take (except under compulsion), or (ii) to administer, or (iii) cause to be administered, or (iv) to be aiding or assisting at or present at and consenting to the administering or taking of, any oath or engagement purporting or intended to bind the person taking the same to do any of the following things:

(1) Mutiny, sedition. To engage in any mutinous or seditious purpose or to disturb the public peace, or to be of any association, society or confederacy formed for any such purposes [**Act of 1797;** *Imp.* 7 *years*].

(2) Treason, felony. To commit any treason, murder [**Act of 1812** [88]; *Imp. life*].

---

[87] *R.* v. *Blake* (1961) 45 Cr.App.R. 292; and see *R.* v. *Britten* [1969] 1 W.L.R. 151.

[88] As amended by the Punishment of Offences Act 1837, s. 1, and the Penal Servitude Act 1857, s. 2, and Criminal Law Act 1967, Sched. 3.

(3) Obedience to superiors. To obey the orders or commands of any committee or body of men not lawfully constituted, or of any leader or commander or other person not having authority by law for that purpose [**Act of 1797**; *Imp. 7 years*].

(4) Evidence. Not to inform or give evidence against any associate, confederate or other person [**Act of 1797**; *Imp. 7 years*].

(5) Unlawful combinations. Not to reveal any unlawful combinations or any illegal acts done or to be done [**Act of 1797**; *Imp. 7 years*]. This has been interpreted as not being confined either to combinations formed for mutinous or seditious purposes or to illegal acts of the same nature. It has been held to include, for example, an oath taken by a group of poachers that they would not inform against each other.[89]

(6) Unlawful oaths. Not to reveal or discover any illegal oath or engagement which may have been administered, or tendered to, or taken by, such person or persons, or to or by any other person or persons, or the import of such oath or engagement [**Act of 1797**; *Imp. 7 years*].

It is not an offence under either Act if the oath is taken under compulsion. But under neither of the Acts, however, is compulsion any justification or excuse to a person taking such an oath unless within, under the first Act, four days, and under the second Act, fourteen days, he discloses all the circumstances to a justice of the peace, or one of the Secretaries of State, or the Privy Council, or if he is in actual service in Her Majesty's forces, to his commanding officer.[90]

It is not necessary, under either Act, that the oath or engagement should be in any particular form if the parties understand it to have the force and obligation of an oath.[91]

SECTION 7. INCITING TO MUTINY AND DISAFFECTION

By **section 1** of the **Incitement to Mutiny Act 1797,** anyone who maliciously and advisedly [92] endeavours to seduce any person serv-

---

[89] *R.* v. *Brodribb* (1816) 6 C. & P. 571; *cf. R.* v. *Ball, ibid.* 563 and *R.* v. *Dixon, ibid.* 601.

[90] Unlawful Oaths Act 1797, s. 2; Unlawful Oaths Act 1812, s. 2.

[91] Act of 1797, s. 5; Act of 1812, s. 6. The oath need not be on a Testament: *R.* v. *Brodribb* (1816) 6 C. & P. 571.

[92] As to the meaning of " advisedly," see the old ecclesiastical case of *Heath* v. *Burder* (1862) 15 Moo.P.C.

ing in Her Majesty's forces from his duty and allegiance, or to incite any such person to commit any act of mutiny,[93] or to make any mutinous assembly, or to commit any traitorous or mutinous practice, is guilty of an offence [*Imp. life*].[94]

Where the incitement is in a publication addressed to British soldiers generally, it is not necessary to specify in the indictment any particular person who has been incited.[95]

By **section 1** of the **Incitement to Disaffection Act 1934,** any person is guilty of an offence under the Act who maliciously and advisedly endeavours to seduce any member of Her Majesty's forces from his duty or allegiance to Her Majesty.

By **section 2** any person is guilty of an offence under the Act who, with intent to commit or to aid, abet, counsel or procure the commission of an offence under section 1 of the Act, has in his possession or under his control any document of such a nature that the dissemination of copies thereof among the members of Her Majesty's forces would constitute such an offence.

By the same section it is provided that if a judge of the High Court is satisfied by information on oath that there is reasonable ground for suspecting that an offence under the Act has been committed within three months before the laying of the information and that evidence of its commission is to be found at any premises or place specified in the information, he may, on the application of an officer of police of a rank not lower than that of inspector, grant a *search warrant,* authorising the search of such premises or place and of any person found therein and the seizure of anything which the officer conducting the search has reasonable ground for suspecting to be evidence of the commission of such an offence.

By **section 3** any offence against the Act is an offence punishable on **indictment** [*Imp. 2 years and £200 fine*] and on **summary conviction** [*Imp. 4 months and £20 fine*].

No prosecution under the Act can take place without the consent of the Director of Public Prosecutions. Where a prosecution is being carried on by the Director of Public Prosecutions a

---

[93] Mutiny amounts to collective insubordination, collective defiance or disregard of authority, or refusal to obey authority: see *R.* v. *Grant* [1957] 1 W.L.R. 906, a case decided on the Army Act 1881.

[94] Punishment of Offences Act 1837, s. 1. The Act was extended to the Air Force by an Order made under the Air Force (Constitution) Act 1917 (S.R. & O. 1918, 548).

[95] *R.* v. *Bowman* (1912) 22 Cox 729.

court of summary jurisdiction may not deal with the case summarily without his consent.

By various statutes the offences of procuring or persuading a person belonging to Her Majesty's forces to desert or of knowingly assisting or concealing or assisting to conceal such a deserter are punishable on **summary conviction.**

By **section 53** of the **Police Act 1964,** any person who causes or attempts to cause, or does any act calculated to cause disaffection amongst the members of any police force, or induces, or attempts to induce, or does any act calculated to induce any member of a police force to withhold his services or to commit breaches of discipline, is guilty of an offence and is punishable on **indictment** [*Imp. 2 years and fine*] and on **summary conviction** [*Imp. 6 months and £100 fine*].

By **section 3** of the **Aliens Restrictions (Amendment) Act 1919,** any *alien* who attempts or does any act calculated or likely to cause sedition or disaffection amongst any of Her Majesty's forces or the forces of Her Majesty's allies or the civilian population is guilty of an offence punishable on **indictment** [*Imp. 10 years*] or on **summary conviction** [*Imp. 3 months*]. By the same section if any alien promotes or attempts to promote industrial unrest in any industry in which he has not been bona fide engaged for at least two years immediately preceding in the United Kingdom, he is liable on **summary conviction** to 3 *months' imprisonment.*

SECTION 8. ILLEGAL TRAINING AND DRILLING

By **section 1** of the **Unlawful Drilling Act 1819,** as amended by **section 16** of the **Firearms Act 1920,** all meetings and assemblies for the purpose of training or drilling to the use of arms, or of practising military exercises, without any lawful authority from Her Majesty or a Secretary of State, or any officer deputed by him for that purpose, are prohibited.

Any person present at such a meeting for the purpose of training others is guilty of an offence [*Imp. 7 years*]: a person present for the purpose of being trained is also guilty of an offence [*Fine and Imp. 2 years*].[96]

Any justice of the peace or constable or other person acting in their assistance may disperse any such unlawful meeting and

[96] Unlawful Drilling Act 1819, s. 1.

arrest and detain any person present.[97] Any prosecution under the Act must be commenced within six months after the commission of the offence.[98]

SECTION 9. ILLEGAL WEARING OF UNIFORMS—ILLEGAL MAINTENANCE OF ASSOCIATIONS OF MILITARY CHARACTER

In the year 1936 the members of a quasi-political organisation had acquired notoriety by wearing a costume the colour of which indicated their political creed and, thus clad, holding meetings for its propagation. Those meetings frequently resulted in serious disturbances and breaches of the peace, the prevention and suppression of which required large numbers of police. Consequently the **Public Order Act 1936,** was passed in which Parliament sought to legislate against certain methods of promoting political objects.

By **section 1** of the Act it is an offence punishable on **summary conviction** [*Imp. 3 months and £50 fine*] [99] for any person in any public place or at any public meeting to wear uniform signifying his association with any political organisation or with the promotion of any political object.[1] A constable may without a warrant arrest any person whom he reasonably suspects to be committing an offence against this section.[2]

The chief officer of police in the area [3] may, however, with the consent of a Secretary of State, by order permit, subject to such conditions as may be specified in the order, the wearing of such a uniform on any " ceremonial, anniversary or other special occasion " if he is satisfied that it is not likely to involve public disorder.

Where a person is charged before any court with an offence under this section no further proceedings in respect thereof may be taken against him without the consent of the Attorney-General except such as the court may think necessary to secure his due appearance: if, however, he is remanded in custody, he is entitled

---

[97] *Ibid.* s. 2.
[98] *Ibid.* s. 7.
[99] Public Order Act 1936, s. 7 (2) amended by the Public Order Act 1963, s. 1.
[1] The terms " public meeting " and " public place " are defined by s. 9 of the Act, as amended by the Criminal Justice Act 1972, s. 33 (not in force at July 1, 1972) and see p. 196, *post,* which does not, however, define either " uniform " or " political."
[2] s. 7 (3).
[3] See the Police Act 1964.

to be discharged in eight days on entering into a recognisance without sureties unless within that period the Attorney-General has consented to such further proceedings.

By **section 2** it is provided that, if the members or adherents of any association of persons, whether incorporated or not, are—

(i) organised or trained or equipped for the purpose of enabling them to be employed in usurping the functions of the police or of the armed forces of the Crown; or

(ii) organised and trained or organised and equipped either for the purpose of enabling them to be employed for the use or display of physical force in promoting any political object, or in such manner as to arouse reasonable apprehension that they are organised and either trained or equipped for the purpose [4];

then any person who takes part in the control or management of the association, or in so organising or training as aforesaid any members or adherents thereof, shall be guilty of an offence punishable on **indictment** [*Imp.* 2 *years and* £500 *fine*] or on **summary conviction** [*Imp.* 6 *months and* £50 *fine*].[5] The Crown must prove in order to establish an offence under the section, first, that there was an association of persons; secondly, that the members or adherents of the association were organised or trained, or organised and equipped; thirdly, that this was in such a manner as to arouse reasonable apprehension that they were organised and trained, or organised and equipped for the purpose of enabling them to be employed for the use or display of physical force in promoting a political object; then fourthly as to individuals charged, not that they were merely members or adherents of such an organisation, but that they were taking part in the control or management, or in the organising and equipping of the organisation. The prosecution need not show that they *intended* the use or display of physical force, but that apprehension arose as to their intentions. Reasonable apprehension is the test.[6] The fact that there is no evidence of actual attacks on opponents does not of course remove grounds for reasonable apprehension.[7] Provided, however, that in any pro-

---

[4] For the first conviction for an offence against this subsection, see *R.* v. *Jordan and Tyndall, The Times,* November 10, 1962.
[5] Public Order Act 1936, s. 7 (1).
[6] *Per* Thompson J. at the trial of *R.* v. *Evans & Ors.* (the Free Wales Army Trial) Swansea, April 16, July 1, 1969.
[7] *R.* v. *Jordan and Tyndall* [1963] Crim.L.R. 124.

ceedings against a person charged with the offence of taking part in the control or management of such an association it shall be a defence to that charge to prove that he neither consented to nor connived at the organisation, training or equipment of members or adherents of the association in contravention of the provisions of this section.

No prosecution may be instituted under this section without the consent of the Attorney-General.

In any criminal or civil proceedings under this section, proof of things done or of words written, spoken or published (whether or not in the presence of any party to the proceedings) by any person taking part in the control or management of an association or in organising, training or equipping members or adherents of an association shall be admissible as evidence of the purposes for which, or the manner in which, the members or adherents of the association (whether those persons or others) were organised or trained or equipped.

Nothing in the section, however, is to be construed as prohibiting the employment of a reasonable number of persons as stewards to assist in the preservation of order at any public meeting held on *private premises* or their being furnished with badges or other distinguishing signs. Provisions are made by this section for the issue of a search warrant where there is reasonable ground for suspecting that an offence under this section has been committed.[8]

Section 10. The Foreign Enlistment Act 1870

The object of the **Foreign Enlistment Act 1870,** is to regulate the conduct of Her Majesty's subjects during the existence of hostilities between foreign states with whom Her Majesty is at peace and to prevent the commission of acts which might be injurious to the public because of their tendency to provoke misunderstandings with foreign Powers.

By this statute two classes of acts are made offences [*Fine and Imp*. 2 *years*], namely, (1) illegal enlistment, and (2) illegal shipbuilding and expeditions.[9]

---

[8] The provisions are substantially the same as those contained in s. 2 of the Incitement to Disaffection Act 1934 (*ante*, p. 140) and see *Ghani* v. *Jones* [1970] 1 Q.B. 693, C.A. for the requisites which must be established to justify the taking of an article by police when no man has been arrested or charged.

[9] *Ibid.* s. 13.

Any person who aids, abets, counsels or procures the commission of any offence against the Act may be tried and punished as a principal.[10]

(1) *Illegal enlistment.* It is an offence against the Act for **any British subject,** without the Queen's licence, within or without the Queen's dominions, to accept, or agree to accept, or for **any person,** whether a British subject or not, to induce within Her Majesty's dominions any other person to accept or agree to accept, any commission or engagement in the military or naval service of a foreign state at war [11] with a friendly state [**section 4**]. It is also an offence for a British subject to leave the Queen's dominions with intent to accept such a commission or for any person to induce a British subject to leave with the like intent [**section 5**]. It is also an offence for a master or owner of a ship to take an illegally enlisted person on board [**section 7**].[12]

(2) *Illegal shipbuilding and illegal expeditions.* It is an offence against this Act to build or otherwise fit out, etc., any ship to be used in the service of a foreign state at war [13] with a friendly state [**sections 8, 9, 10**] or to prepare any naval or military expedition against the dominions of any friendly state [**section 11**].[14]

SECTION 11. OFFENCES RELATING TO PUBLIC STORES

The law relating to unlawful dealings with public stores was consolidated by the **Public Stores Act 1875.**

Certain marks described in the Act are appropriated for public stores, *i.e.* all stores under the care or control of a Secretary of State, or the Admiralty, or any public department or office, or any person in the service of Her Majesty: if anyone without lawful authority, *proof of which lies on the accused,* applies these marks to any other stores, he is guilty of an offence [*Imp. 2 years*] [**section 4**].

If anyone, with intent to conceal Her Majesty's property in such stores, obliterates any such mark, either wholly or in part, he is guilty of an offence [*Imp. 7 years*] [**section 5**].

---

[10] *Ibid.* s. 14.

[11] A Foreign Office certificate stating whether or not two foreign countries were " at war " would (*semble*) be conclusive: *Kawasaki Kisen Kabushiki Kaisha of Kobe* v. *Bantham S.S. Co.* [1939] 2 K.B. at p. 554; Oppenheim's *International Law*, Vol. I (8th ed.), p. 766.

[12] See further Arch. paras. 3081–3091.   [13] *Ante*, n. 11.

[14] See *e.g. R.* v. *Jameson* [1896] 2 Q.B. 425; also Arch. paras. 3081–3091.

Anyone who has possession of any of Her Majesty's stores reasonably suspected of being stolen or unlawfully obtained and does not give to the court a satisfactory explanation of his possession is guilty of an offence [£5 *fine or Imp. 2 months*] and is also punishable on summary conviction [*to the same extent*] [**section 7**].[15]

By **section 9** dealers and other persons who are in possession of Her Majesty's stores, and fail to satisfy that they came by them lawfully, are liable on a **summary conviction** to a penalty of £5.

By **sections 195** of the **Army Act 1955,** and of the **Air Force Act 1955,** and **section 98** of the **Naval Discipline Act 1957,** it is an offence punishable on **indictment** [*Imp. 2 years and £500 fine*] or on **summary conviction** [*Imp. 3 months and £100 fine*] for any person to purchase, take in pawn or otherwise receive or solicit any person to sell, pledge or otherwise hand over military, air force or naval stores *unless he proves* that he satisfies one of certain specified conditions set out in the sections.

Under all the three above-mentioned Acts a search warrant may be issued by a justice of the peace.[16] Under the Public Stores Act 1875, any person may arrest without a warrant a person found committing any offence under the Act. The other three Acts provide that a constable may arrest a person whom he has reasonable grounds for believing has committed an offence against these sections.[17]

SECTION 12. COUNTERFEIT MONEY

Banknotes. The forging and altering of banknotes is an offence under the **Forgery Act 1913,** and is dealt with in Chapter 43 (*post*).

Coins. The law on this subject has been consolidated by the **Coinage Offences Act 1936.**[18] The following are the principal offences under the Act:

---

[15] For the powers of arrest in relation to offences under the Act, and the powers of a justice to issue a search warrant, see s. 12 as substituted by the Theft Act 1968, Sched. 2, Part II.

[16] Public Stores Act 1875, s. 12, substituted by Theft Act 1968, Sched. 2, Part II; Army Act 1955, s. 195; Air Force Act 1955, s. 195; Naval Discipline Act 1957, s. 106 (2).

[17] Army Act 1955, s. 195 (3); Air Force Act 1955, s. 195 (3); Naval Discipline Act 1957, s. 106 (1).

[18] The whole range of coinage offences is now receiving the attention of the Law Commission.

Section 1. Counterfeiting. Falsely to make or counterfeit any coin resembling any current coin is an offence [*gold and silver* [19] *coin, Imp. life; copper,* [20] *Imp.* 7 *years*].[21] This offence, and also any offence against sections 5 and 6 (*infra*), is deemed to be complete although the coin made or counterfeited is not in a fit state to be uttered or the making or counterfeiting has not been finished or perfected. It is also an offence under section 5 (3) of the Act to have in one's possession counterfeit coins with intent to utter them. It has been held that to utter a counterfeit coin means to pass it or try to pass it as genuine.[22]

The counterfeiting can generally only be proved by circumstantial evidence; for example, by proof of finding coining tools in the prisoner's house, together with pieces of the money, some in a finished, some in an unfinished state, or such other circumstances as may fairly warrant the jury in presuming that the prisoner either counterfeited, or caused to be counterfeited, or was present aiding and abetting in counterfeiting the coin in question.[23]

Section 2. Gilding and silvering coin and metal; filing and altering coin. To gild, silver, wash, case over or colour:

    (i) any coin, whatsoever resembling any current gold or silver coin; or

    (ii) any current copper coin, with intent to make it resemble or pass for any current gold or silver coin; or

    (iii) any piece of silver, copper, coarse gold or silver, or metal, with intent that it shall be coined into false and counterfeit coin resembling any current gold or silver coin; or

To gild, wash, etc., any current silver coin with intent to make it resemble, etc., any current gold coin; or

---

[19] By s. 12 (1) of the Coinage Act 1971, the term " silver " includes cupro-nickel, the metal now used to make all current coins except two new pence pieces, new pennies and new halfpennies.

[20] By s. 17 of the 1936 Act " copper coins " are those made of any metal not used for gold or silver coins, *i.e.* two new pence pieces, new pennies and new halfpennies.

[21] By s. 17 of the 1936 Act, a coin is deemed to be current if it has been coined in any of Her Majesty's mints, or is lawfully current, by virtue of any proclamation or otherwise, in any part of Her Majesty's dominions, whether within the United Kingdom or otherwise, *or is lawfully current* in any foreign country.

[22] *R.* v. *Selby* [1972] A.C. 515 (H.L.).

[23] Arch. para. 3103.

To file or in any manner alter any current silver coin with intent to make it resemble, etc., any current gold coin, or any current copper coin with intent to make it resemble, etc., any current gold or silver coin, is an offence [*Imp. life*].

Section 3. Impairing gold and silver coin. Unlawful possession of filings, etc. To impair, diminish or lighten any current gold or silver coin with intent that it shall pass for current gold or silver coin is an offence [*Imp. 14 years*].

Unlawfully to have in possession any filings, chippings, dust, bullion or solution obtained by any such process, knowing that it has been so obtained, is an offence [*Imp. 7 years*].

Section 4. Defacing and uttering defaced coins. Defacing any current coin by stamping thereon any names or words, although the coin is not thereby diminished or lightened, is an offence punishable on **indictment** [*Imp. 1 year*] or on **summary conviction** [*Imp. 6 months and £400 fine*].[24]

Coin so defaced is not legal tender and, provided that the consent of the Attorney-General has been given to the institution of proceedings against the person tendering or uttering it, he may, on **summary conviction,** be fined £2.

Section 5. Uttering and possession with intent to utter. To tender, utter or put off[25] any false or counterfeit[26] coin resembling any current coin knowing it to be false or counterfeit is an offence punishable on **indictment** [*Imp. 1 year*] or on **summary conviction** [*Imp. 6 months and £400 fine*].[27]

To tender, utter or put off any false or counterfeit coin resembling any current gold or silver coin, knowing it to be false or counterfeit and either:

(a) at the time of the tendering, etc., to have in possession any other such false or counterfeit coin; or

24 Magistrates' Courts Act 1952, s. 19 and Sched. 1.
25 There is an uttering and putting off if a counterfeit coin is offered in payment, even if it is refused as bad by the person to whom it is offered: *R.* v. *Welch* (1851) 2 Den. 78. But see *R.* v. *Selby* [1972] A.C. 515 (H.L.) and p. 147, *ante*.
26 Certain coin is deemed to be counterfeit: s. 17 of the Act; see also *R.* v. *Hermann* (1879) 4 Q.B.D. 284.
27 Magistrates' Courts Act 1952, s. 19 and Sched. 1.

    (b) on the day of the tendering, etc., or within the next ten
        days to tender, etc., any other such false or counterfeit
        coin, knowing it to be false or counterfeit,

is an offence punishable on **indictment** [*Imp. 2 years*] or on
summary conviction [*Imp. 6 months and £400 fine*].[28]

To possess three or more false or counterfeit coins resembling
any current coin, knowing them to be false or counterfeit, and with
intent to utter them is an offence punishable on *indictment*
[*gold or silver coin—Imp. 5 years*; *copper coin—Imp. 1 year*] or on
summary conviction [*Imp. 6 months and £400 fine*].[29]

To commit any of the offences under this section, except
in so far as it applies to copper coin, after a previous conviction
for any such offence or of any offence under sections 1, 2, 3, 6, 7
(*a*), 9 or 10 of the 1936 Act is punishable with life imprisonment.[30]

Everyone who, *with intent to defraud*, tenders, utters or puts
off [31] as or for any current gold or silver coin;

    (a) any coin not being that current coin and being of less
        value than that current coin; or

    (b) any medal or piece of metal resembling that current coin
        and being of less value than the current coin

is guilty of an offence punishable on **indictment** [*Imp. 1 year*]
or on **summary conviction** [*Imp. 6 months and £400 fine*].[32]

**Section 6. Buying or selling, etc., counterfeit coin for a lower
value than its denomination.** Without lawful authority or excuse
(proof of which lies on the accused) to buy, sell, receive, pay or
put off or offer to buy, etc., any false or counterfeit coin resembling
any current coin at a lower rate of value than its denomination is
an offence [*gold or silver coin, Imp. life*; *copper coin, Imp. 7 years*].

Section 7. Importing and exporting counterfeit coin. For any
person without lawful authority or excuse (proof of which lies on
the accused) and knowing the same to be false or counterfeit

    (a) to import or receive into the United Kingdom from beyond
        the seas any false or counterfeit coin resembling any cur-

---

[28] Magistrates' Courts Act 1952, s. 19 and Sched. 1.
[29] *Ibid.*
[30] s. 5 (5).
[31] *Ante*, n. 25.
[32] Magistrates' Courts Act 1952, s. 19 and Sched. 1.

rent gold or silver coin [33] is an offence [*Imp*. 14 *years*]; and

(b) to export or put on board any ship or vessel for the purpose of export any false or counterfeit coin resembling any current coin,[34] is an offence punishable on **indictment** [*Imp*. 14 *years*] or on **summary conviction** [*Imp*. 6 *months and* £400 *fine*].[35]

Section 8. Making, etc., medals resembling gold or silver coin.
For any person without lawful authority or excuse (proof of which lies on the accused) to make, sell, offer for sale or have in his possession for sale any medal, cast, coin or other thing made wholly or partially of metal and (a) resembling in size, figure and colour any current gold or silver coin or (b) having thereon a device resembling a device upon any such current coin or (c) so formed that it can by gilding, silvering, washing or other like process be so dealt with as to resemble any such current coin is an offence punishable on **indictment** [*Imp*. 1 *year*] or on **summary conviction** [*Imp*. 6 *months and* £400 *fine*].[36]

Section 9. Making, mending or having possession of coining implements. For any person without lawful authority, etc. (proof of which lies upon him), knowingly to make or mend, buy or sell, or have in his possession any stamp, die, mould, etc., or various specified implements for the false making of any current *gold* or *silver* coin is an offence [*Imp*. *life*]. Similar conduct in relation to current *copper* coin is also an offence [*Imp*. 7 *years*].

Section 10. Conveying coining implements, coin, bullion or metal out of the Mint. This, if done without lawful authority, etc. (*proof of which lies on the accused*), is an offence [*Imp*. *life*].
Miscellaneous provisions of the Act
By **section 11** any person found committing an offence against the Act, except an offence against section 8, may be arrested without warrant by any person and a search warrant may be issued by a justice of the peace.

Any person who finds in any place or in the possession of any person, without lawful authority or excuse, any counterfeit coin,

---

[33] The wide definition of current coin as including coins lawfully current in any foreign country should be noted: *ante*, n. 21.   [34] *Ibid.*
[35] Magistrates' Courts Act 1952, s. 19 and Sched. 1.   [36] *Ibid.*

counterfeiting instrument or counterfeiting material must seize it and take it before a justice of the peace.

By **section 14,** when any coin is tendered as current gold or silver coin to a person who suspects it to be diminished otherwise than by reasonable wear or to be counterfeit, it may be cut, bent, broken or defaced by him, and, if it is found to be so diminished or to be counterfeit, any loss will fall on the person tendering it, but if it is of due weight and appears to be lawful coin, the person to whom it is tendered must receive it at its denominational value. Any dispute as to whether it is so diminished, etc., shall be heard in a summary manner by a justice of the peace.

By **section 10** of the **Coinage Act 1971** it is an offence punishable on **indictment** [*Imp. 2 years and a fine*] or on **summary conviction** [£400 *fine*] except under the authority of a licence granted by the Treasury, to melt down or break up any metal coin which is for the time being current in the United Kingdom or which, having been current there, has at any time after May 16, 1969, ceased to be so.

SECTION 13. CUSTOMS AND EXCISE

The existing law on this subject is contained chiefly in the **Customs and Excise Act 1952.** This Act deals with smuggling, the collection of excise duty and the granting of certain excise licences.

Smuggling is the importing or exporting of either (i) dutiable goods on which the duty has not been paid, or (ii) goods the importation or exportation of which is forbidden or restricted.

It is an offence for any person to import into the United Kingdom any goods (a) liable to duty, the duties for which have not been paid, or (b) contrary to any prohibition or restriction for the time being in force with respect to those goods,[37] with intent either to defraud Her Majesty or to evade such prohibition or restriction [**section 45**[38] as amended by **section 26** of the **Misuse of Drugs Act 1971**][39]; and such goods are liable to forfeiture [**section 44**].

---

[37] There are a large number of such prohibitions and restrictions; see, *e.g.* Halsbury, Vol. 33, p. 50 *et seq.* As to the importing of dangerous drugs and the penalties therefor, see Chap. 20, *post*.

[38] Although it is for the prosecution to prove the necessary intent, once it is proved that the accused is in possession of uncustomed goods, there may well be a conviction unless the accused can give some explanation from which the jury may infer that he did not know duty had not been paid: *R.* v. *Cohen* [1951] 1 K.B. 505; *Sayce* v. *Coupe* [1953] 1 Q.B. 1.

[39] Not in force as at July 1, 1972.

It is an offence for any person with fraudulent intent to ship for export goods of which entry [40] is required if such entry has not been duly made. Whether there is fraudulent intent or not the goods are liable to forfeiture [**section 47**]. A similar penalty is provided by **section 56** as amended by **section 26** of the **Misuse of Drugs Act 1971** [41] for the improper exportation of goods with intent to evade any prohibition or restriction.[42] "Goods" include money or bank notes; the smuggling or attempted smuggling of money or banknotes being made an offence by the Exchange Control Act 1947.[43]

The above offences are punishable on **indictment** [44] [*Imp. 2 years and either* £100 *fine or fine equivalent to three times the value of the goods, whichever is greater*] or upon **summary conviction** [*as upon indictment but maximum imprisonment of* 1 *year*].[45]

Any person who makes any signal to any other person in a ship or aircraft or across a boundary in connection with any smuggling of goods into or out of the United Kingdom is liable on **summary conviction** to a penalty of £100 and imprisonment for one year [**sections 71 and 283**].[46]

Any person who fires upon any vessel, aircraft or vehicle in the service of Her Majesty while that vessel, aircraft or vehicle is engaged in the prevention of smuggling is guilty of an offence [**section 72;** *Imp. 5 years*].

If any person engaged in the commission of any such offence is armed with offensive weapons, or is in any way disguised, or being so armed or disguised is found in the United Kingdom with any goods liable to forfeiture under the customs Acts, he is liable either on **indictment** [*Imp.* 3 *years*] or on **summary conviction** [*Imp.* 1 *year*] [**sections 73 and 283**].[46]

The term "offensive weapons" includes all such things as are not in common use for any other purpose than as weapons,[47] but not an article like an ordinary whip.[48]

---

[40] *i.e.* notification to the proper officer.
[41] Not in force as at July 1, 1972.   [42] Above, n. 37.
[43] Fifth Sched. 2, Pt. III, para. 1 (i) and see *R.* v. *Goswami* [1969] 1 Q.B. 453.
[44] Except where special penalties are imposed by s. 26 of the Misuse of Drugs Act 1971 in relation to Class C drugs. (Not in force as at July 1, 1972.)
[45] Customs and Excise Act 1952, s. 283, as amended by Misuse of Drugs Act 1971, s. 26. (Not in force as at July 1, 1972.)
[46] As amended by Misuse of Drugs Act 1971, s. 26. (Not in force as at July 1, 1972.)
[47] *R.* v. *Hutchinson* (1784) 1 Leach at p. 342n.
[48] *R.* v. *Fletcher* (1742) 1 Leach 23.

Excise duty is charged on the manufacture or production of the following items: intoxicating drink, hydrocarbon oils, tobacco, mechanical lighters and matches.[49] Numerous criminal offences relating to the collection of these duties are to be found in the Act of 1952 and other Acts.[50]

The following provisions of the Customs and Excise Act 1952 are of general application to both smuggling and the collection of excise duty.

(1) Knowingly or recklessly to make a false declaration, etc., is an offence [**section 301**] punishable on **indictment** [*Imp. 2 years, £500 fine, forfeiture*] or on **summary conviction** [49] [*as on indictment but maximum imprisonment 1 year*].

(2) To make any false statement *otherwise than knowingly or recklessly* [52] is an offence [**section 301**] punishable on **summary conviction** [53] [*£300 fine*].

(3) To counterfeit or falsify any document, seal, etc., is an offence [**section 302**] punishable on **indictment** [*Imp. 2 years, £500 fine*] or on **summary conviction** [54] [*Imp. 1 year, £500 fine*].

(4) It is an offence [**section 304** as amended by **section 26** of the **Misuse of Drugs Act 1971**] [55] (i) knowingly and with intent to defraud Her Majesty, in any way to handle, deal with, etc., goods which are either chargeable and upon which duty has not been paid or are subject to a prohibition or restriction which has not been satisfied or (ii) in relation to any goods, to be in any way knowingly concerned in any fraudulent evasion or attempted evasion of any duty chargeable thereon or any prohibition or restriction applicable thereto. This offence is punishable upon **indictment** [*Imp. 2 years,*[56] *£100 fine or fine equivalent to three times the value of the goods*] or on **summary conviction** [57] [*as upon indictment but maximum imprisonment 1 year*].

(5) Proceedings for any offence under these Acts must be commenced within three years after the date of the offence [**section 283**].

[49] See Halsbury, Vol. 33, pp. 183 *et seq.*, and the current Supplement.
[50] For a recent example, see the Hydro-Carbon Oil (Customs and Excise) Act 1971.
[51] s. 283 as amended.
[52] This is a clear, if rather incredible, example of an offence of strict liability.
[53] s. 283 as amended.
[54] *Ibid.*
[55] Not in force as at July 1, 1972.
[56] See fn. 43 on p. 152, *ante*. See *R.* v. *Ardalan* [1972] 1 W.L.R. 463.
[57] s. 283 as amended.

(6) Where anything has become liable to forfeiture under the Customs and Excise Acts, any ship (other than certain larger ships), aircraft, vehicle container, etc., in which the thing so liable was carried is liable to forfeiture [**sections 277–279**]. Knowledge on the part of the owner or operator is apparently immaterial.[58]

Excise licences are required under various Acts (i) for mechanically-propelled vehicles which are used or kept on public roads in Great Britain,[59] (ii) for the production and manufacture of those items on which excise duty is paid, and (iii) to run or carry on certain trades, businesses, etc., *e.g.* bookmaking,[60] selling intoxicating liquor (on or off licence)[61] or tobacco, owning clubs where intoxicating liquor is sold,[62] moneylending[63] and pawnbroking.[64] Licences (not all of which are strictly excise licences) are also required for, among other things, dogs,[65] radio and television receivers.[66] Failure to take out a licence where necessary is made a criminal offence by the appropriate Act.

SECTION 14.   OFFENCES AGAINST THE IMMIGRATION LAWS

The **Immigration Act 1971**[67] is intended to replace with a single code of permanent legislation the Aliens Restriction Act 1914, the Commonwealth Immigrants Acts 1962 and 1968, and the Immigration Appeals Act 1969. **Part I** of the Act regulates entry into, and stay in the United Kingdom, and **Part II** provides for a system of appeals in relation to the operation of the Act. A number of offences are created in **Part III.** Thus under **section 24** it is an offence punishable on **summary conviction** [*Imp. 6 months and £200 fine*] for a person who is not a patrial[68] to contravene the restrictions imposed by the Act on entry and embarkation, to overstay a limited leave to enter or remain, or to fail to observe

---

[58] See *Commissioners of Customs and Excise* v. *Jack Bradley (Accrington) Ltd.* [1959] 1 Q.B. 219; D. W. Elliott, "Forfeiture under the Customs Laws" [1958] Crim.L.R. 786.

[59] *Post*, p. 316.

[60] *Post*, p. 329.

[61] *Post*, p. 354.

[62] *Post*, p. 354.

[63] *Post*, p. 381.

[64] *Post*, p. 384.

[65] *Post*, p. 415.

[66] See generally on this topic Halsbury, Vol. 33, pp. 201 *et seq.*

[67] In force fully January 1, 1973.

[68] The expression "patrial" is used of persons having the right of abode in the United Kingdom under ss. 1 and 2 of the Act: see s. 2 (5).

conditions attached to such leave.[69] By **section 26** a number of miscellaneous offences (similarly punishable) are created in connection with the administration of immigration control.

By **section 25 (1)** it is an offence punishable on **summary conviction** [*Imp. 6 months and £400 fine*] or on **indictment** [*Imp. 7 years and fine*] [70] for any person to be knowingly concerned in making or carrying out arrangements for securing or facilitating the entry into the United Kingdom of anyone whom he knows or has reasonable cause for believing to be an illegal entrant.[71] A constable or immigration officer may arrest without warrant anyone who has, or whom he, with reasonable cause suspects to have, committed an offence under that subsection: **section 25 (3).** Section 25 (1) applies specifically [72] to things done outside as well as to things done inside the United Kingdom where they are done (a) by a citizen of the United Kingdom and Colonies; (b) by a British subject by virtue of section 2 of the British Nationality Act 1948; (c) by a British subject without citizenship by virtue of section 13 or 16 of the Act of 1948 and (d) by a British subject by virtue of the British Nationality Act 1965, and (e) by a British protected person. The extended time limit provided by section 28 (below) applies in relation to prosecutions for this offence.

It is an offence under **section 25 (2)** punishable on **summary conviction** [*Imp. 6 months and £200 fine*] for a person knowingly to harbour anyone whom he knows or has reasonable cause for believing to be either an illegal entrant or a person who has committed certain offences under section 24 (1). By **section 27** it is an offence punishable on **summary conviction** [*Imp. 6 months and £200 fine*] for persons connected with ships or aircraft or with ports, to act in certain circumstances in contravention of the Act.

In the case of offences under parts of section 24, under section 25 (1) and parts of section 26, it is provided by **section 28** that an information may be tried by a magistrates' court [in England and Wales] if it is laid within six months of the commission of the offence, or if it is laid within three years after the commission of

---

[69] Powers of arrest without warrant are relevant under s. 24 (3).

[70] Under s. 25 (6) and (7) the court is given powers of forfeiture in relation to ships, aircraft or vehicles.

[71] This is defined in the Act, s. 33 (1), as a " person unlawfully entering or seeking to enter in breach of a deportation order or of the immigration laws, and includes a person who has so entered."

[72] s. 25 (5).

the offence and not more than two months after the date certified
by a chief officer of police to be that date on which evidence
sufficient to justify the proceedings came to the notice of his police
force.

SECTION 15. OFFENCES AGAINST INCOME TAX ACTS, ETC.

The statutes regulating the collection of income and other similar
taxes, of purchase tax and stamp duties all create criminal offences
which are too detailed and specialised for inclusion in this book.

CHAPTER 10

PIRACY AT SEA AND IN THE AIR

PIRACY is an offence *jure gentium* or by statute. The former is part of the common law of England [1] and consists in the commission of any robbery within the jurisdiction of the Admiralty,[2] without the authority of any state, by means of the dispossession of the master of the ship and the seizure or destruction of the ship itself or of any of the goods carried in the ship, or in the attempt so to do.[3] If a ship on the high seas is unlawfully taken possession of by violence or by threat of violence, whether by persons from outside the ship or members of the crew, or passengers in the ship, and the ship is thereafter appropriated to the use of those who have seized it, that is piracy [4] *jure gentium*. **Section 4** and the **Schedule** to the **Tokyo Convention Act 1967** applies the following definition of piracy *jure gentium* to proceedings for such an offence before a court in the United Kingdom:

(1) Any illegal act of violence, detention or any act of depredation, committed for private ends by the crew or passengers of a private ship or a private aircraft, and directed: (a) on the high seas, against another ship or aircraft, or against persons or property on board such ship or aircraft; (b) against a ship, aircraft, persons or property in a place outside the jurisdiction of any State;

---

[1] And of Scotland. In *Cameron and Ors.* v. *H.M. Advocate*, 1971 S.L.T. 70, five members of the crew of a registered British ship were indicted in that, when at sea, they did " unlawfully deprive the skipper of his command, surround and menace him, order him to his cabin, threaten to injure him, rob him of his keys, take possession of the bonded stores of the vessel, put the skipper and other members of the crew ashore, wrench the microphone from the radio broadcasting equipment of the vessel, destroy the ship's log and the skipper's fishing book and navigated the vessel onto the high seas and ' did thus take masterful possession ' of the vessel and appropriate it to their own use."

[2] See p. 692, *post*.

[3] *Att.-Gen. for Hong Kong* v. *Kwok-a-Sing* (1873) L.R. 5 P.C. 179; *Re Piracy Jure Gentium* [1934] A.C. 586.

[4] *Cameron and Ors.* v. *H.M. Advocate* (*supra*) per Lord Cameron. The fact that the offence occurred in territorial waters does not apparently affect the situation, at least in Scotland, *ibid.*, per Lord Milligan in the High Court of Justiciary. *Cf.* the provisions of the Tokyo Convention Act 1967.

(2) Any act of voluntary participation in the operation of a ship or of an aircraft with knowledge of facts making it a pirate ship or aircraft;

(3) Any act of inciting or intentionally facilitating an act described in (1) or (2) above.

Acts of piracy committed by a warship, government ship or government aircraft, whose crew has mutinied and taken control are assimilated to acts committed by a private ship. A ship or aircraft is considered to be a pirate ship or aircraft if it is intended by the persons in dominant control to be used for one of the acts set out above. The same applies if the ship or aircraft has been used to commit any such act so long as it remains under the control of the persons guilty of that act.

Piracy *jure gentium* is justiciable in the courts of every nation,[4a] and any court having jurisdiction in respect of piracy committed on the high seas has jurisdiction in respect of piracy committed by or against an aircraft, wherever that piracy is committed.

By **section 7** of the **Piracy Act 1698** it is piracy for any natural born subject or denizen of Her Majesty to commit any such act, or act of robbery or act of hostility against any of Her Majesty's subjects on the sea under colour of any commission from any foreign prince or state. By **section 8** of the same Act it is piracy for any commander or master of a ship, or seaman, in any place within the Admiralty jurisdiction, " piratically and feloniously " to run away with his ship, or any boat, ammunition or goods, or yield them up to any pirate, or to bring any seducing messages from any pirate, enemy or rebel, or to conspire with or attempt to corrupt any commander, master, officer, or mariner to do any of the above acts or to turn pirate, or for any reason to lay violent hands on his commander whereby to hinder him from fighting in defence of his ship, or to confine his master or to make or endeavour to make a revolt in his ship.

By **section 1** of the **Piracy Act 1721,** it is an offence for any commander or master of a ship or any other person to trade with any pirate or to supply any pirate, felon or robber upon the seas with any ammunition, provisions or stores, or knowingly to fit out any ship for any such purpose, or for any person to conspire with any pirate, etc., on the seas, knowing him to be such, or any persons

---

4a See Arch. paras. 3051–3058.

belonging to any ship forcibly to board any merchant ship upon the
high seas, or in any port, and to throw overboard or destroy any
goods or merchandise belonging thereto.

Piracy under the **Piracy Acts 1698** and **1721** is an offence
punishable on **indictment** with **life imprisonment,** or if accompanied by any assault with intent to murder any person on or
belonging to the ships, or by wounding or endangering the life
of any such person, by **death.**[5]

By **section 1 (1)** of the **Hijacking Act 1971,** a person on board
an aircraft in flight,[6] who unlawfully, by the use of force or by
threats of any kind, seizes an aircraft or exercises control of it
commits the offence of hijacking [*Imp. Life*]; whatever his nationality, whatever the State in which the aircraft is registered and
whether the aircraft is in the United Kingdom or elsewhere. If the
aircraft is used in military,[7] customs or police service, or both,
the take-off place and the place of landing are in the territory[8] of
the State in which the aircraft is registered. In these particular
circumstances an offence is not committed within the meaning of
section 1 unless (i) the person seizing or exercising control of the
aircraft is a citizen of the United Kingdom and Colonies or a
British subject or protected person within certain specified categories,[9] or (ii) the act is committed in the United Kingdom; or (iii)
the aircraft is registered in the United Kingdom, or is used in the
military or customs service of the United Kingdom or in the service
of a police force in the United Kingdom.

By **section 1 (4)** of the Act, a person in the United Kingdom
who induces or assists the commission elsewhere of an act which
comes within the definition of hijacking (but for the exceptions in
section 1 (2)) also commits an offence [*Imp. Life*].

By **section 2** of the Act, where a person, of whatever nationality,
does on board an aircraft, wherever registered, and while outside
the United Kingdom, an act which if done within the United

---

[5] Piracy Act 1837, ss. 2, 3, as amended by the Criminal Justice Act 1948, s. 1
(1).
[6] This includes any period from the moment when all its external doors are
closed following embarkation until the moment when any such door is
opened for disembarkation, and in the case of a forced landing any period
until the competent authorities take over responsibility for the aircraft, and
for persons and property on board: s. 1 (5).
[7] Including naval and air force service: s. 1 (7).
[8] Including its territorial waters: s. 1 (6).
[9] See s. 3.

Kingdom would amount to murder, attempted murder, man-slaughter,[10] or assault, or an offence under sections 18, 20, 21, 22, 23, 28 or 29 of the Offences against the Person Act 1861, or section 2 of the Explosive Substances Act 1883, his act shall constitute that offence if it is done in connection with the offence of hijacking committed or attempted on board that aircraft.

[10] And culpable homicide in Scotland.

CHAPTER 11

GENOCIDE

BY **section 1** of the **Genocide Act 1969** it is an offence to commit genocide. Genocide means any of the following acts committed with intent to destroy, in whole or in part, a national, ethnical, racial or religious group, such as:

 (a) killing members of the group;

 (b) causing serious bodily or mental harm to members of the group;

 (c) deliberately inflicting on the group conditions of life calculated to bring about its physical destruction in whole or in part;

 (d) imposing measures intended to prevent births within the group;

 (e) forcibly transferring children of the group to another group.

The offence of genocide is punishable on **indictment** [*Imp. Life*] if the offence consists of the killing of any person; or in any other case [*Imp.* 14 *years*].

It is doubtful whether genocide committed abroad by a British subject would be an offence under the Act, because it is silent as to jurisdiction. **Section 2** of the **Act** makes provision as to extradition and evidence for foreign courts in regard to any offence of genocide and any attempt or conspiracy to commit such an offence and any direct and public incitement to commit such an offence.

Chapter 12

OFFENCES WITH RESPECT TO PUBLIC OFFICE

Section 1. Introduction

This chapter deals with offences which can be committed by public officers in their capacity as public officers, offences committed by any person against public officers and bribery and corruption.

Section 2. Bribery

The offence of bribery comprises acts of three classes, namely,

    (1) Bribery of public officers;

    (2) Bribery at elections;

    (3) Bribery of and by agents.

(a) *Bribery of Public Officers, Sale of Offices and Honours*

Bribery of public officers. It is a common law offence punishable by *fine and imprisonment*:

    (i) to bribe or offer a bribe to any public officer, judicial or ministerial, in order to influence him in the performance of his duty or the conduct of his office;

    (ii) for any such officer to accept such a bribe.[1]

Thus it is an offence to attempt to procure an appointment by offering a bribe to a Privy Councillor.[2] The offence is not, however, restricted to the bribery of the higher officers, such as judges or Ministers of the Crown, but includes the bribing of those in subordinate positions. So, for example, the colonel of a regiment is a public ministerial officer and it is a common law offence for him to receive, or for anyone to pay him, a bribe to show favour in respect of catering contracts for his regiment.[3] So also a constable is a public officer.[4]

---

[1] Arch. paras. 3483, 3992; and see *R.* v. *Whitaker* [1914] 3 K.B. 1283.

[2] *R.* v. *Vaughan* (1769) 4 Burr. 2494.

[3] *R.* v. *Whitaker* [1914] 3 K.B. 1283.

[4] *R.* v. *Lehwess*, 140 Cent.Crim.Ct.Sess.Pap. 731.

By **sections 1** and **2** of the **Public Bodies Corrupt Practices Act 1889,** it is also an offence [*Imp.* 2 *years* [5] *and fine,*[6] *forfeiture of any bribe received and of any public office held at time of conviction and certain disabilities from holding public office*]:

(i) for any person [7] corruptly [8] to solicit, receive or agree to receive, for himself or any other person, any gift, loan or advantage as an inducement to, or reward [9] for, or otherwise on account of any member, officer or servant of a public body [10] as defined by the Act doing or forbearing to do anything in respect of any matter or transaction in which that public body is concerned;

(ii) for any person corruptly to give, promise or offer any gift, etc., for any such purpose.[10a]

The mischief aimed at by this Act is to prevent public officers or public servants being put into a position where they are subject to temptation. The word " corruptly " . . . denotes that the person making the offer does so deliberately and with the intention that the person to whom it is addressed should enter into a corrupt bargain.[11] It is not necessary that the offeror should intend to see the transaction through, and the motive of the offeror is immaterial.[12]

No prosecution under this Act can be instituted without the consent of the Attorney-General or Solicitor-General [*ibid.*, **s. 4**].

---

[5] Or in cases within s. 1 of the Prevention of Corruption Act 1916, imprisonment for 7 years; see *post,* p. 169.

[6] In the case of an offence against s. 2 there is no limit on the amount of fine: Criminal Justice Act 1967, s. 92 (8).

[7] As to bribery by a limited company see *R.* v. *Andrews-Weatherfoil Ltd.* [1972] 1 W.L.R. 118.

[8] The meaning of the word " corruptly " is not defined in the Act. See " The Corruption of ' Corruptly ' " by F. D. Shyllon [1969] Crim.L.R. 250.

[9] " Reward " covers the receipt of payment for a past favour without any antecedent agreement: *R.* v. *Andrews-Weatherfoil Ltd.* [1972] 1 W.L.R. 118.

[10] By s. 7 of the Act the term " public body " means any council of a county or county of a city or town, any council of a municipal borough, also any board, commissioners, select vestry or other body which has power to act under and for the purposes of any Act relating to local government or the public health or to poor law, or otherwise to administer money raised by rates in pursuance of any public general Act.

[10a] See *Mayor, etc., of Salford* v. *Lever* [1891] 1 Q.B. 168.

[11] Parker C.J., in *R.* v. *Smith* [1960] 2 Q.B. 423 at p. 428. *Cf. R.* v. *Lindley* [1957] Crim.L.R. 321 and *R.* v. *Calland* [1967] Crim.L.R. 236.

[12] *R.* v. *Smith (supra).*

Sale, etc., of office and honours. By the **Sale of Offices Acts 1551** and **1809,**[13] it is an offence [*Fine and Imp. 2 years and forfeiture of or disqualification from the office in question*] for any person to sell or purchase, or bargain for the sale or purchase of, any office or employment in the gift of the Crown, or to receive or give, or agree to receive or give, any money, reward or profit for any appointment or nomination to or resignation from any such office or for the consent or support of any person to any such appointment or resignation.

By the **Honours (Prevention of Abuses) Act 1925,** it is an offence [*Fine of £500 and Imp. 2 years or, on summary conviction, Fine of £50 and Imp. 3 months, and in either case forfeiture to the Crown of any gift, etc., which is capable of forfeiture*] for any person to accept or give, or to agree to accept or give, or to attempt to obtain from, or to offer to, any other person any gift, money or valuable consideration as an inducement or reward for procuring or assisting or endeavouring to procure the grant of a dignity or title of honour to any person, or otherwise in connection with such a grant.

(b) *Bribery and Corrupt, etc., Practices at Elections*

Bribery and attempted bribery at parliamentary or municipal or parish council elections are common law offences,[14] but are now, with other illegal and corrupt practices, punishable by statute.

The law relating to **parliamentary, municipal and parish elections** is contained in the **Representation of the People Act 1949,**[15] which consolidated the law with regard to elections. Only a few of the numerous offences created by the Act can be mentioned here. In particular the offences concerning election expenses have been omitted.

The following offences are punishable either on **summary conviction** [*Fine of £100 and Imp. 3 months*] or on **indictment** [*Fine of £200 or Imp. 1 year*] [**section 146**] [16]:

---

13 As to these statutes, see *Hopkins* v. *Prescott* (1847) 4 C.B. 578; *R.* v. *Charretie* (1849) 13 Q.B. 447.
14 *R.* v. *Plympton* (1724) 2 Ld.Raym. 1377; *R.* v. *Pitt and Mead* (1762) 1 Wm. Bl. 380; *R.* v. *Lancaster and Worrall* (1890) 16 Cox C.C. 737 (bribery at the election of an assistant overseer of a parish, to which the same common law rules are applicable).
15 As amended by the Representation of the People Act 1969.
16 Alternatively a person may be *summarily convicted* of any of these offences by an election court (the court in which elections may be questioned) and be

(1) Treating. This includes (i) the corrupt giving, or paying the expenses of giving, meat, drink, entertainment, or provision to *any person*, before, during or after an election, in order corruptly to influence his vote or the vote of any other person or on account of such person or any other person having voted or refrained from voting; (ii) the corrupt acceptance by an *elector* of such treating [**section 100**].

(2) Bribery. This is exhaustively defined and includes (i) the giving, lending, agreeing to give or lend, offering, promising, or promising to procure, any money or valuable consideration, or office, place, or employment to or for any voter, or to or for any person, in order to influence any voter, or corruptly to do any such act on account of any voter having voted or refrained from voting; (ii) the making of any such gift, etc., to any person in order to induce him to procure or endeavour to procure the return of any person at an election or the vote of any voter; (iii) the advance or payment of any money to any person with intent that it shall be expended in bribery or the payment of any money to any person in discharge or repayment of any money expended in bribery [**section 99**].

(3) Undue influence. This consists of the use or infliction of, or threat to use or inflict, any force, violence, injury or loss on any person in order to influence his vote, or on account of his having voted or refrained from voting, or the employment of any duress or fraudulent device [17] to prevent the free exercise of the franchise by any voter [**section 101**].

Personation is an offence [*Imp. 2 years*].[18] This includes not only voting as some other person (whether that person is living, dead or fictitious), but also applying for a ballot paper in the name of another person [**section 47**].[19]

The following offences are punishable on **summary conviction** [£100 *fine*] [**sections 147, 153**]:

fined £200 or imprisoned six months: s. 146 (4). But by s. 149 (2) the accused must be given the option of being tried by a jury.

[17] Fraud is an essential ingredient of an offence under s. 101 (2) (*b*): *Roberts* v. *Hogg* [1971] S.L.T. 78 J.C. at p. 83.

[18] s. 146 (3).

[19] This offence is not committed by a person who, being properly appointed a proxy under s. 14 of the Act, votes *by post* as proxy.

(i) Voting in person or by post or by proxy with knowledge of a legal incapacity to vote or voting twice [**section 48**].[20]

(ii) Use of television or wireless stations abroad with intent to influence persons to give or refrain from giving their votes at a parliamentary or local government election, otherwise than in accordance with the provisions of the Act [**section 80**].[21]

(iii) Acting, or inciting others to act, in a disorderly manner at a lawful public meeting for the purpose of preventing the transaction of the business for which the meeting was called [**section 84**].

(iv) Making false statements of fact in relation to the personal character or conduct of any candidate for the purpose of affecting the return of the candidate at the election [**section 91**].

(v) Payments to electors, other than advertising agents, on account of the exhibition of election notices [**section 94**].

(vi) Printing, publishing, posting or distributing by an election agent or candidate election publications not bearing the name and address of the printer and publisher [**section 95**].

(vii) Inducing a candidate to withdraw from being a candidate in consideration of any payment, and a candidate so withdrawing [**section 92**].

(viii) Using prohibited premises [22] as a committee room [**section 93**].

(ix) Employing paid canvassers, and being so employed [**section 96**].

(x) Payments on account of bands of music, torches, flags or banners [**section 97**].

(xi) Providing money for any payment which is contrary to the provisions of the Act [**section 98**].

Miscellaneous offences under the Act include:

(i) Fraudulently defacing, fraudulently destroying nomination papers or ballot papers; supplying any ballot paper without due authority; putting into a ballot box any ballot paper other than that which he is authorised by law to put in;

---

[20] As amended by the Representation of the People Act 1969.
[21] As amended by the Representation of the People Act 1969, s. 9 (5).
[22] *e.g.* any premises used for sale of food or intoxicating liquor (*ibid.*).

fraudulently taking any ballot paper out of a polling
station; interfering with any ballot box or packet of ballot
papers, without due authority [*Imp. 2 years if the offender
is an official*: *Imp. 6 months in respect of offence at a
parliamentary election*: *fine of £20 and Imp. 6 months in
respect of offence at a local government election*] [**section
52**].[23]

(ii) Contravening the provisions of the Act with regard to
secrecy. Section 53 contains numerous provisions, which
are beyond the scope of this book, designed to maintain
the secrecy of voting and to ensure that no information is
sought or obtained with regard to the candidate for whom
any particular voter has voted—*summary offence* [*Imp. 6
months*] [**section 53**].

(iii) If any constable reasonably suspects any person of committing an offence under section 84 (1) of the Act (acting in
a disorderly manner at a public meeting [24]) he may, if
requested so to do by the chairman of the meeting, require
that person to disclose his name and address. Failing to
disclose his name and address or giving a false name and
address renders that person liable to a *fine of £2 on summary conviction*. Further on such failure or where the constable reasonably suspects that the name and address given
is false, the constable may arrest the person without warrant
[**section 84 (3)**].

(iv) Police officers illegally canvassing—*summary offence* [*Fine
of £100*] [**section 87**].

(c) Bribery of and by Agents

By **section 1 (1)** [25] of the **Prevention of Corruption Act 1906,** it is
made an offence [*Imp. 2 years and fine or, on* **summary conviction,**
Imp. 4 months and £200 fine]:

(i) for any agent *corruptly* [26] to accept or obtain, or agree to

[23] These offences are, with the exception of defacing or destroying nomination
papers at a local government election (punishable on summary conviction),
punishable either on indictment or summary conviction: *ibid.*
[24] Above.
[25] As amended by the Criminal Justice Act 1967, s. 92 (8), 106 (2) and Sched. 3.
[26] In *R.* v. *Calland* [1967] Crim.L.R. 236 Veale J. directed the jury that corruption under this section meant dishonestly trying to wheedle an agent away
from his loyalty to his employer; if they thought the defendant's conduct
was sharp practice but not dishonest the defendant should be acquitted.

accept, or attempt to obtain, from any person, for himself or for any other person, any gift or consideration as
an inducement or reward for doing or forbearing to do,
or for having done or forborne to do, any act in relation
to his principal's affairs [27] or business, or for showing or
forbearing to show favour [28] or disfavour to any person in
relation to his principal's affairs or business;

   (ii) for any person *corruptly* to give or agree to give or offer
any gift or consideration to an agent as an inducement or
reward for acting in any such manner;

   (iii) for any person *knowingly* to give to any agent, or for any
agent *knowingly* to use, with intent to deceive his principal,
any receipt or other document in respect of which the
principal is interested, and which contains any statement
which is false or erroneous or defective in any material
particular, and which, to his knowledge, is intended to
deceive the principal.

   In the case of *Sage* v. *Eicholz* [29] it was held that the
word "knowingly" in this clause is used deliberately
instead of the word "corruptly" in the other clauses, so
that, in order to establish the offence of knowingly giving
to an agent such a document, it is not necessary to prove
that the agent was corrupted or had a guilty knowledge of
its falsity.

To constitute an offence under this section it is not necessary
that the person who accepted the bribe did what he was bribed to
do.[30]

By **section 1 (2)** the term "agent" includes any person employed
by or acting for another, and also a person serving under the Crown
or under any corporation, municipal borough, county or district
council.

No prosecution for an offence under this Act can be instituted
without the consent of the Attorney-General or Solicitor-General
[*ibid.* **s. 2**].

---

[27] As to the ingredients of this section see *R.* v. *De Rable* (1948) 33 Cr.App.R.
5 and also *Morgan* v. *D.P.P.* [1970] 3 All E.R. 1053.
[28] It is sufficient that the bribe is given to the accused as an inducement to show
favour. It does not matter if he did in fact show favour: *R.* v. *Carr* [1957]
1 W.L.R. 165.
[29] [1919] 2 K.B. 171.
[30] *R.* v. *Carr* [1957] 1 W.L.R. 165.

By **section 1** of the **Prevention of Corruption Act 1916,** it is provided that, where an offence under the Prevention of Corruption Act 1906, or under the Public Bodies Corrupt Practices Act 1889,[31] has been committed in relation to a contract or proposal for a contract with Her Majesty, or any government department or any public body, or a sub-contract to execute such work, *imprisonment for seven years may be inflicted.*

By **section 2** of the same Act it is provided that, in any proceedings under the Act of 1906 or 1889, any money, gift or consideration given or received by a person in the employment of Her Majesty, etc., by or from a person or agent of a person holding or seeking to obtain a contract from Her Majesty, etc., shall be deemed to have been given or received corruptly unless the contrary is proved.

Section 3. Local Government

By **section 76** of the **Local Government Act 1933,** as amended, it is provided that when any contract, in which a member of a local authority has any pecuniary interest, is being discussed at a meeting, any such member must disclose his interest and refrain from speaking or voting on the matter.[32] Failure to comply with the section is punishable on **summary conviction** [£200 *fine*].[33]

The 1933 Act was quite general as to what was meant by "interest." This has since been modified as follows:

> (i) A member is not debarred from speaking or voting when the only interest which he has in the contract or other matter is a beneficial interest in shares of a company or other body, provided that the total nominal value of the shares does not exceed £500 or one-hundredth of the total nominal value of the issued share capital of the company, whichever is the less.[34] His duty to disclose the interest, however, still remains.[35]

[31] *Ante*, pp. 163 and 167 respectively.
[32] The Act does not say that a member must not speak or vote in his own interest. It says that if he has any pecuniary interest in any contract under consideration he must not speak or vote *at all*. Hence a member may be liable even though he speaks or votes to his own disadvantage: *Brown* v. *Director of Public Prosecutions* [1956] 2 Q.B. 369.
[33] Local Government (Pecuniary Interests) Act 1964, s. 1 (4).
[34] Local Government Act 1948, s. 131, as amended by the Local Government (Miscellaneous Provisions) Act 1953, s. 15.
[35] Local Government Act 1948, s. 131.

(ii) The definition of pecuniary interest does not include any
interest which is so small that it could not reasonably be
expected to influence the member in discussing, or voting
on, the matter.[36]

A prosecution under section 76 may not be brought except by
or on behalf of the Director of Public Prosecutions.[37]

In certain circumstances the Minister of Housing and Local
Government may allow a member to speak and vote notwithstanding that he has a pecuniary interest in the matter under
discussion.[38]

SECTION 4. OPPRESSION AND NEGLECT

The common law offence of extortion under colour of office or
franchise was abolished by the Theft Act 1968, s. 32 (1) (a).

Any form of **oppression or misconduct** by a public officer by
colour of his office is an offence.[39] Thus, a judicial officer is indictable for any illegal act committed by him from fraudulent, corrupt
or vindictive motives, or for manifest illegality and oppression, or
gross abuse of power, or partiality and wilful abuse of discretion;
but he is not criminally liable for oppression where he acts under
a mistake, uninfluenced by any corrupt or improper motive, and
believing that he is acting in a fair and legitimate exercise of his
office.[40] So also a ministerial officer is indictable for any act of
oppression or any illegal act committed in the execution of his
duty, from corrupt or other improper motives, but not where he
acts from ignorance or mistake.

Any **unjustifiable neglect or refusal** by a public officer to perform his duties is also a similar offence,[41] as, *e.g.* the neglect of a
magistrate to take such steps as are in his power and could be
expected from a man of ordinary prudence, firmness and activity,
in order to suppress a riot,[42] or the refusal of a sheriff to execute
a criminal.[43] Likewise, it is a similar offence for a person to

---

36 Local Government (Pecuniary Interests) Act 1964, s. 1.
37 Local Government Act 1933, s. 76 (7).
38 *Ibid.* s. 76 (8).
39 *R.* v. *Williams and Davis* (1762) 3 Burr. 1317; *R.* v. *Llewellyn-Jones* [1968]
1 Q.B. 429.
40 *R.* v. *Borron* (1820) 3 B. & Ald. 432; *R.* v. *Badger* (1843) 4 Q.B. 468.
41 Arch. para. 3491.
42 *R.* v. *Pinney* (1852) 5 C. & P. 254.
43 *R.* v. *Antrobus* (1835) 2 Ad. & El. 788

refuse to serve in any public office to which he has been duly appointed and from which he has no ground of exemption.[43a]

SECTION 5. ASSAULTING OR OBSTRUCTING A CONSTABLE

Assault

By **section 51 (1)** of the **Police Act 1964,** it is an offence punishable on **summary conviction** [*Imp.* 6 *months*[44] *and* £100 *fine*] or on **indictment** [*Imp.* 2 *years and fine*] for any person to assault a constable in the execution of his duty, or a person assisting a constable in the execution of his duty.

A number of points arise as to the meaning of this section.

(1) The term " assault " is defined later.[45]

(2) The term " constable " includes a prison officer.[46]

(3) Knowledge that the person assaulted is a police constable or knowledge that he is acting in the execution of his duty is not necessary; the offence is assaulting a constable *being* in the execution of his duty, not *knowing* him to be in the execution of his duty.[47]

(4) Whether or not an officer is in the execution of his duty is discussed later[48] but it may be said generally that he is so when

    (i) lawfully arresting or detaining a person,[48a] or

    (ii) preventing the commission of any crime or breach of the peace in public[49] or on private premises,[50] or

    (iii) lawfully effecting a search or seizure of goods.[51]

[43a] Arch. para. 3942.

[44] For a second or subsequent offence it is nine months: *ibid.*

[45] *Post*, p. 453.

[46] Prison Act 1952, s. 8.

[47] *R.* v. *Forbes and Webb* (1865) 10 Cox 362; *R.* v. *Maxwell and Clanchy* (1909) 2 Cr.App.R. 26; *McBride* v. *Turnock* [1964] Crim.L.R. 456. However, a genuine mistake based on reasonable grounds, that the constable was a thug and not a police officer would be material in judging the reasonableness of the resistance in relation to the defence of self defence: *Kenlin* v. *Gardiner* [1967] 2 Q.B. 510; and see *R.* v. *Mark and Mark* [1961] Crim.L.R. 173. Self defence is open to a defendant on a charge under s. 51, as it is in any case of assault (*Kenlin* v. *Gardiner* (*supra*)) unless the assault resisted is itself justifiable. See *R.* v. *Fennell* [1971] 1 Q.B. 428.

[48] *Post*, pp. 555 *et seq.*

[48a] As to the powers of arrest, see *post*, p. 555 *et seq.*

[49] *Duncan* v. *Jones* [1936] 1 K.B. 218, *post*, p. 197.

[50] *Thomas* v. *Sawkins* [1935] 2 K.B. 249. It was held in this case that the police have a right to enter into and remain on private premises if there are reasonable grounds for belief that a breach of the peace might occur.

[51] Russell, pp. 688–689. As to powers of search and detention, see *post*, p. 562.

If the police are exceeding their authority resistance is not an assault within this section.[52]

Obstruction or Resistance

By **section 51 (3)** of the **Police Act 1964,** it is an offence punishable on **summary conviction** [*Imp.* 1 *month, Fine* £20] for any person to resist or wilfully obstruct a constable in the execution of his duty, or a person assisting a constable in the execution of his duty. Obstruction of constables in the exercise of certain specified powers is also punishable summarily under other Acts.[53]

To " obstruct " is to do any act which makes it more difficult for the police to carry out their duty.[54] Thus it is an obstruction to consume alcohol after an accident with the deliberate intention of frustrating the breathalyser procedure under the Road Traffic Act 1972.[55]

It has been held that to attempt to hold a meeting prohibited by the police in the execution of their duty [56] is an obstruction. It has also been held that to warn a person who is committing a crime (in this case driving at a speed in excess of the limit) of the presence of the police, with the intention of preventing the police from getting evidence of the commission of the crime, is, likewise, an obstruction.[57] However, contrary to popular belief, refusal to answer questions put by the police or refusal to accompany a constable to a police station or other place (unless an arrest is being made) is not an obstruction of the police in the execution of their duty, unless the police have statutory powers to ask the particular question or order the person to accompany them.[58]

The obstruction must be " wilful " to come within the section. It must therefore be deliberate and intentional.[58a] Where the

---

[52] *Davis* v. *Lisle* [1936] 2 K.B. 434; *R.* v. *Waterfield* [1964] 1 Q.B. 164. For a discussion of when an officer is acting in the execution of his duty see p. 552, *post.*

[53] See, *e.g.* Licensing Act 1964, s. 186.

[54] *Hinchcliffe* v. *Sheldon* [1955] 1 W.L.R. 1207; *Rice* v. *Connolly* [1966] Q.B. 414 at p. 419; and see *Ingleton* v. *Dibble* [1972] 1 Q.B. 480 at p. 487.

[55] *Ingleton* v. *Dibble* (*supra*).

[56] *Duncan* v. *Jones* [1936] 1 K.B. 218, discussed *post,* p. 197.

[57] *Betts* v. *Stevens* [1910] 1 K.B. 1.

[58] *Rice* v. *Connolly* [1966] 2 Q.B. 414. For examples of these statutory powers, see p. 137 and see the " picketing " cases: *Piddington* v. *Bates* [1961] 1 W.L.R. 162 and *Tynan* v. *Balmer* [1967] 1 Q.B. 91.

[58a] *Rice* v. *Connolly* (*supra*).

obstruction consists of a refusal to do an act which the constable has asked the defendant to do, such as refusing to give information or assistance, such refusal cannot amount to a "wilful" obstruction under the Act unless the law imposes on the person concerned some obligation in the circumstances to act in the manner requested by the officer. When, however, the obstruction consists of some positive act, there is no such qualification.[58b]

Duty to Aid Constables

To **refuse to aid a constable** in the execution of his duty to preserve the peace is a common law offence, provided that it is proved that (i) a breach of the peace[59] was being committed in the presence of the constable, and (ii) there was a reasonable necessity for the constable to call upon the accused for his assistance, and (iii) that the accused was duly called on for his assistance, and without any physical impossibility or lawful excuse refused to give it: whether the aid of the accused would have proved sufficient or useful is immaterial.[60]

SECTION 6. ASSAULTING OR OBSTRUCTING OTHER PUBLIC OFFICERS

There are numerous other statutory offences concerning assaults on or obstruction to public officers in the execution of their duty, of which the following are the more important: assaulting or obstructing in the execution of their duty (i) bailiffs of inferior courts,[61] (ii) county court officers,[62] (iii) regular members of the army[63] and air force,[64] and (iv) customs and excise officers.[65] Also resisting a sheriff while lawfully executing a writ is an offence.[66]

[58b] *Rice* v. *Connolly* as explained in *Ingleton* v. *Dibble* (*supra*).
[59] *Post*, p. 194.
[60] *R.* v. *Brown* (1841) 1 C. & M. 314.
[61] Inferior Courts Act 1844, s. 7.
[62] County Courts Act 1959, s. 30.
[63] Army Act 1955, s. 193.
[64] Air Force Act 1955, s. 193.
[65] Customs and Excise Act 1952, s. 10.
[66] Sheriffs Act 1887, s. 8 (2).

CHAPTER 13

OFFENCES AGAINST THE ADMINISTRATION
OF JUSTICE

SECTION 1. EMBRACERY AND INTERFERENCE WITH WITNESSES

Embracery. Any attempt to corrupt or influence a jury by " money, promises, letters, threats or persuasions, except only by the strength of the evidence and the arguments of counsel in open court," constitutes the offence of embracery, which is a common law offence punishable by *fine and imprisonment*. It may be committed not only by a party to the cause or his agent but by one of the jurors. A juror who allows himself to be so corrupted or influenced is guilty of the same offence. It is also a common law offence to induce a juror not to appear.[1]

Interference with witnesses. It is a common law offence punishable by *fine and imprisonment* to attempt to pervert the due course of justice by threatening or persuading a witness [2] not to give evidence or to give evidence of a particular character. This offence is also punishable summarily as a contempt of court.[3]

By **section 2** of the **Witnesses (Public Inquiries) Protection Act 1892,** it is an offence punishable by a *fine of £100 or imprisonment for three months* to threaten, punish, injure or attempt to punish or injure any person for having given evidence upon any inquiry held under any Royal Commission, or by any committee of either House of Parliament, or pursuant to any statutory authority, or upon account of the evidence given by him upon any such inquiry, unless such evidence was given in bad faith. This offence is triable summarily or, upon the request of the prosecution or the accused, upon indictment.

---

[1] Arch. para. 3447; 1 Hawk. c. 85.

[2] Witness includes a potential witness: *R.* v. *Grimes* [1968] 3 All E.R. 179n.; and is not confined to a person actually called to give evidence: *ibid.* See also *Moore* v. *Clerk of Bristol Assizes* [1971] 1 W.L.R. 1669; as to contempt of court by threatening a witness.

[3] Arch. para. 3451; 1 Hawk. c. 21, s. 15; *R.* v. *Lawley* (*Lady*) (1731) 2 Stra. 904; *R.* v. *Greenberg* (1919) 26 Cox C.C. 466.

174

SECTION 2. CONCEALING OFFENCES

The offence of compounding a felony has now been abolished.[4] **Section 5 (1)** of the **Criminal Law Act 1967,** provides that where a person has committed an arrestable offence,[5] it is an indictable offence for any other person who, knowing or believing that the offence or some other arrestable offence has been committed, and that he has information which might be of material assistance in securing the prosecution or conviction of an offender for it, accepts or agrees to accept for not disclosing that information any consideration other than the making good of loss or injury caused by the offence, or the making of reasonable compensation for that loss or injury. The consent of the Director of Public Prosecutions is required before proceedings for this offence may be instituted.

It was no offence merely to take back stolen goods without agreeing to show any favour to the thief.[6] But by **section 23** of the **Theft Act 1968,** where any public advertisement of a reward for the return of any goods which have been stolen or lost uses any words to the effect that no questions will be asked, or that the person producing the goods will be safe from apprehension or inquiry, or that the money paid for the purchase of the goods or advanced by way of loan on them will be repaid, the person advertising the reward or any person who prints or publishes the advertisement commits an offence punishable on **summary conviction** [*Fine* £100].

Giving false information. At common law there was some doubt as to whether it was an offence for a person to make false reports to the police about the commission of an offence.[7] However, for two or more persons to agree to do this is a common law conspiracy.[8] **Section 5 (2)** of the **Criminal Law Act 1967,** now provides that it is an offence punishable on **summary conviction** [*Imp.* 6 *months and* £200 *fine*] for any person to cause any wasteful employment of the police by knowingly

---

[4] Criminal Law Act 1967, s. 5 (5). The offence of compounding treason still remains.

[5] *Post*, p. 555.

[6] 1 Hawk. c. 59, s. 7.

[7] *R.* v. *Manley* [1933] 1 K.B. 529; *R.* v. *Newland* [1954] 1 Q.B. 158; and *cf. R.* v. *Bailey* [1956] N.I. 15, a Northern Ireland case.

[8] *Ante*, p. 67.

making to any person a false report tending to show that an offence has been committed, or to give rise to apprehension for the safety of any persons or property, or tending to show that he has information material to any police inquiry. Proceedings for this offence may not be instituted without the consent of the Director of Public Prosecutions.[9]

SECTION 3. CONTEMPT OF COURT [10]

What is known as contempt of court may be either civil contempt, which is said to consist of disobedience to the order of a court made in civil proceedings, or criminal contempt which consists of any words or acts obstructing, or tending to obstruct, the administration of justice in any court, whether civil or criminal. In the recent case of *Morris* v. *The Crown Office* [11] Salmon L.J. said this:

" The archaic description of these proceedings as ' contempt of court ' is in my view unfortunate and misleading. It suggests that they are designed to buttress the dignity of the judges and protect them from insult. Nothing could be further from the truth. No such protection is needed. The sole purpose of proceeding for contempt is to give to our courts the power effectively to protect the rights of the public by ensuring that the administration of justice shall not be obstructed or prevented." [12]

Criminal contempt is punishable both at common law and, to a limited extent, by statute and appeal now lies, subject to certain provisos [13] from the punishment imposed.

Common Law. Criminal contempt is punishable at common law upon **indictment** [14] [*Fine and Imp.*] [15] but this procedure now seems to have fallen into disuse.[16] Far the more usual method of

---

[9] s. 5 (3).
[10] It was announced on May 27, 1971 that the government proposed to set up an inquiry into the law of contempt.
[11] [1970] 2 Q.B. 114.
[12] Referring to *Skipworth's* case (1873) L.R. 9 Q.B. 230 and *R.* v. *Davies* [1906] 1 K.B. 32.
[13] Administration of Justice Act 1960, s. 13.
[14] *Att.-Gen.* v. *Butterworth* [1963] 1 Q.B. 696; nor is the power to imprison restricted by the provisions of the Criminal Justice Acts 1948 and 1967, *Morris* v. *Crown Office* (*supra*).
[15] As to the punishment for common law misdemeanours see p. 201, n. 59.
[16] Halsbury, Vol. 8, p. 4 n. (*o*) and p. 5 n. (*a*).

dealing with criminal contempt is by summary process, "the possible recourse to indictment . . . is too dilatory and too inconvenient to afford any satisfactory remedy."[17] The jurisdiction in regard to summary process is, however, limited in the following ways:

(i) Magistrates may not punish summarily for contempt, although they may, by means of an oral complaint, bring the matter before a separate bench.[18] They may, of course, eject the wrongdoer, or where the conduct complained of consists of disrespectful or unmannerly expressions used in the face of the court or in the obstruction of their officers in the execution of their duty, they may bind the offender over under the Justices of the Peace Act 1361.[19] Where the misconduct amounts to an assault, it has been said[20] that the proper course is to issue a summons returnable *instanter*.

(ii) Any civil or criminal court of record has jurisdiction to punish contempt committed "in the face of the court"— a term defined later.

(iii) Any division of the Supreme Court[21] has the jurisdiction set out in (ii) but also has jurisdiction to punish any other[22] contempt committed against it or any inferior court. The Queen's Bench Division can punish contempt of a magistrates' court.[23]

Criminal contempt of court is of four main classes, namely:

(i) where some contempt is committed in the face of the court, as where a defendant in addressing the jury used

---

17 *Per* Wills J. in *R.* v. *Davies* (*supra*) referring to the unpublished judgment of Wilmot C.J. in *R.* v. *Almon* (1765) Wilm. 243.

18 *R.* v. *Lee* (1701) 12 Mod. 514.

19 Hawk. P.C.C. 61, s. 237 but see *R.* v. *Aubrey Fletcher, ex p. Thompson* [1969] 2 All E.R. 846.

20 By Lord Goddard C.J. in *R.* v. *Butt* (1957) 41 Cr.App.R. 82.

21 The Supreme Court consists of the Court of Appeal, the High Court and the Crown Court: Courts Act 1971, s. 1.

22 If the inferior court has jurisdiction to punish a contempt then the Supreme Court does not have jurisdiction to punish the same contempt. See *e.g. R.* v. *Judge* [1931] 2 K.B. 442.

23 See *e.g. R.* v. *Parke* [1903] 2 K.B. 432 applied in *R.* v. *Duffy, ex p. Nash* [1960] 2 Q.B. 188; *R.* v. *Daily Mail* [1921] 2 K.B. 733 and see *R.* v. *Evening Standard* [1954] 1 Q.B. 578. By virtue of the Courts Act 1971, ss. 4 (8) and 10 (5) the Crown Court is not an inferior court for this purpose, even in its appellate jurisdiction. *Cf.* the position as to the issue to it of the prerogative orders at p. 835, *post.*

language of a blasphemous character and also directly insulted the judge,[24] or where a witness[25] or a juror[26] fails to attend when served with a process, or where a witness remains in court after the witnesses have been ordered to leave the court,[27] or, after being sworn, refuses to answer,[28] or where jurors toss a coin to determine their verdict[29];

(ii) where there has been a publication of matter scandalising the court, as, e.g. scurrilous abuse of a judge with reference to remarks made by him in the course of a case[30];

(iii) where any act done or writing published is calculated to obstruct or interfere with the due course of justice or the lawful process of the courts, as, for example, the intimidation of or interference with jurors, parties or witnesses,[31] or the publication of comments relating to pending cases which are calculated to prejudice their fair trial and so interfere with the course of justice[32]; but by **section 11** of the **Administration of Justice Act 1960,** it is not an offence for a person *either* to publish such matter if, at the time of the publication (having taken all reasonable care), he did not know that a case was pending *or* to distribute

[24] R. v. *Davison* (1821) 4 B. & Ald. 329; see also R. v. *Pater* (1864) 5 B. & S. 299.
[25] See also *post*, pp. 668, 742.
[26] See now the Courts Act 1971, s. 38, p. 180 *post.*
[27] *Chandler* v. *Horne* (1842) 2 Mood. & R. 423.
[28] *Ex p. Fernandez* (1861) 10 C.B.(N.S.) 3.
[29] Halsbury, Vol. 23, p. 44.
[30] R. v. *Gray* [1900] 2 Q.B. 36. See also *McLeod* v. *St. Aubyn* [1899] A.C. 549, but see R. v. *Griffiths, ex p. Att.-Gen.* [1957] 2 Q.B. 192.
[31] *Ante*, p. 174; see also R. v. *Stowell* (1843) 5 Q.B. 44; *Re Johnson* (1887) 20 Q.B.D. at p. 74; *Att-Gen.* v. *Butterworth* [1963] 1 Q.B. 696; *Moore* v. *Clerk of Bristol Assizes* [1971] 1 W.L.R 1669; *Chapman* v. *Honig* [1963] 2 Q.B. 502.
[32] R. v. *Payne* [1896] 1 Q.B. 577; R. v. *Tibbits and Windust* [1902] 1 K.B. 77; R. v. *Duffy* [1960] 2 Q.B. 188. On the same principle it has been held that it is a contempt of court to publish in a newspaper a photograph of a person charged with a criminal offence when a question of identity may arise at the trial, and the publication of the photograph might prejudice a fair trial: R. v. *Daily Mirror* [1927] 1 K.B. 845. See also R. v. *Thomson Newspapers Ltd.* [1968] 1 W.L.R. 1. A criminal cause remains *sub judice* until the expiration of the time within which notice of appeal to the Court of Appeal may be given and, if such notice has been given, until the appeal has been heard and determined (R. v. *Davies* [1945] 1 K.B. 435), but if the matter would not influence the appellate judges, it is not a contempt: R. v. *Duffy, supra.*

such matter if, at the time of the distribution (having taken all reasonable care), he did not know that it contained such matter and had no reason to suppose that it was likely to do so. A motion for leave to issue a writ of attachment against a newspaper editor on the ground that matter published by him might prejudice a fair trial should be made only by the Law Officers [33];

(iv) where matter relating to proceedings in private is published [34]; but by **section 12** of the **Administration of Justice Act 1960,** the publication of such matter constitutes contempt only in five cases (these include, *inter alia,* wardship and adoption proceedings and those occasions when the court sits in private for reasons of national security) and can, in any other case, constitute contempt only if the court (having power to do so) expressly prohibits publication.

Statutes. By **section 157** of the **County Courts Act 1959,** it is provided that if any person

(i) wilfully insults the judge of a county court, or any juror or witness, or any officer of the court during his sitting or attendance in court, or in going to or returning from the court; or

(ii) wilfully interrupts the proceedings of a county court or otherwise misbehaves in court,

any officer of the court, with or without the assistance of any other person, may, by order of the judge, take the offender into custody and detain him until the rising of the court, and the judge may, if he thinks fit,

(i) by a warrant under his hand commit the offender for any period not exceeding one month to any prison to which he has power to commit, or

(ii) impose upon the offender a fine not exceeding £20 for every offence.[35]

[33] *R.* v. *Hargreaves* [1954] Crim.L.R. 54.
[34] See, *e.g. Alliance Perpetual Building Society* v. *Belrum Investments Ltd.* [1957] 1 W.L.R. 720.
[35] The power of the county court to punish for contempt is limited to this Act: *R.* v. *Lefroy* (1873) L.R. 8 Q.B. 134.

Any person summoned as a witness to a county court who fails to attend or refuses to be sworn or give evidence may, subject to certain provisos, be fined the sum of £10 by the court.[36]

By the **Courts Act 1971, section 38,** it is an offence [*Fine of £100*] if a juror duly summoned under the Act fails to attend (on the first or any subsequent day on which he is required to attend by the summons or by the appropriate officer) in compliance with the summons or if, after attending in pursuance of a summons is not available when called on to serve as a juror, or is unfit for service by reason of drink or drugs. By **section 38 (2)** such an offence is punishable either on summary conviction or as if it were criminal contempt committed in the face of the court. A person is not liable to be so punished if he can show reasonable cause for his failure to comply with the summons or for not being available when called on to serve.[37]

The provisions of **section 77** of the **Magistrates' Courts Act 1952** and of the **Criminal Procedure (Attendance of Witnesses) Act 1965,** which regulate the attendance of witnesses and set out punishments for non-attendance are dealt with in Chapters 47, 51 and 54.

Sketching, etc., in court. By **section 41** of the **Criminal Justice Act 1925,** it is made an offence punishable on **summary conviction** by a *fine of* £50 for any person

    (i) to take or attempt to take in any court any photograph, or, with a view to publication, to make or attempt to make in any court any portrait or sketch of any person being a judge of the court or a juror or a witness in or a party to any proceedings before the court, whether civil or criminal: or

    (ii) to publish any photograph, portrait or sketch taken or made in contravention of the foregoing provisions, or any reproduction thereof.[38]

[36] s. 84.
[37] s. 38 (4).
[38] A photograph, etc., is deemed to be taken, etc., in court if taken, etc., in the court room, or in the building or precincts of the building in which the court is held, or if taken, etc., of the person while entering or leaving the court room, etc. (*ibid.*).

Section 4. Restrictions on the Reporting of Cases

By the **Judicial Proceedings (Regulation of Reports) Act 1926,** extended by the **Domestic and Appellate Proceedings (Restriction of Publicity) Act 1968,** it is an offence punishable on **summary conviction** [*Imp.* 4 *months and fine* £500] for any proprietor, editor, master printer or publisher to print or publish or cause or procure to be published

   (i) in relation to any judicial proceedings, any indecent matter or indecent medical, surgical or physiological details the publication of which would be calculated to injure public morals;

   (ii) in relation to any judicial proceedings for dissolution of marriage, nullity of marriage, for judicial separation, restitution of conjugal rights or proceedings by a wife against her husband for maintenance,[39] any particulars except (a) the names, addresses and occupations of the parties and witnesses; (b) a concise statement of the charges, defences and countercharges in support of which evidence has been given; (c) submissions on any point of law arising in the proceedings and the decision of the court thereon; (d) the summing-up of the judge and the finding of the jury and the judgment of the court and observations of the judge in giving judgment;

   (iii) in relation to proceedings for the declaration of legitimacy and the like, any particulars other than particulars of the declaration sought by the petitioner.[40]

By **section 58** of the **Magistrates' Courts Act 1952,** it is an offence punishable on **summary conviction** [*Imp.* 4 *months and fine* £400] for any proprietor, etc., of a newspaper or periodical to print or publish, or cause to be printed or published, in it any particular of *domestic proceedings* [41] in a magistrates' court other than the items mentioned in (ii) (a)–(d) above.

By **section 39** of the **Children and Young Persons Act 1933,**[42]

---

[39] Added by the Domestic and Appellate Proceedings (Restriction of Publicity) Act 1968, s. 2 (3).

[40] *Ibid.*

[41] The term " domestic proceedings " is defined in s. 56 of the Act, as amended by the Guardianship of Minors Act 1971, Sched. 1, and includes, *inter alia,* guardianship, matrimonial and affiliation proceedings.

[42] As amended by the Children and Young Persons Act 1963, Sched. 5.

it is provided that in relation to any proceedings in any court, the court may direct that, except so far as it may by direction permit,

> (i) no newspaper report of the proceedings shall reveal the name, address, or school, or include any particulars calculated to lead to the identification of any child or young person concerned in the proceedings; and
>
> (ii) no picture shall be published in any newspaper as being or including a picture of any such child or young person.

Any person publishing any matter in contravention of any such direction is punishable on **summary conviction** [*Fine* £50].

By **section 49** [43] of the same Act [44] it is a similar offence for any newspaper report of **any** proceedings in a **juvenile court** [45] to publish any such matter or picture. If it is appropriate to do so for the purpose of avoiding injustice to a child or young person [46] the court or the Secretary of State may by order dispense with the requirements of this section to the extent specified in the order.

By **section 3** of the **Criminal Justice Act 1967,** restrictions have been placed on the reporting of committal proceedings. These restrictions are dealt with later.[47]

---

[43] As extended by the Children and Young Persons Act 1963, s. 57 to appeals from such proceedings.

[44] As amended by the Children and Young Persons Act 1969, s. 10.

[45] s. 10 (1) (*b*) of the 1969 Act extends the restrictions to proceedings relating to supervision orders in respect of persons who have attained 18 years, in magistrates' courts.

[46] *e.g.* where a child or young person has attended a court as a witness the restrictions might be lifted to scotch rumours that he was the accused person.

[47] *Post,* p. 665.

CHAPTER 14

PERJURY AND OFFENCES AKIN TO PERJURY [1]

SECTION 1.   OFFENCES AGAINST THE PERJURY ACT 1911

THE law relating to perjury, which was a common law misdemeanour, was consolidated by the **Perjury Act 1911,** by which
any person who, having been lawfully sworn as a *witness* or an
interpreter in a judicial proceeding, wilfully makes a statement
material in that proceeding, which he knows to be false or does
not believe to be true, commits the offence [*Fine and Imp.* 7 *years*]
of **perjury [section 1 (1)].** [2]

The term " judicial proceeding " includes a " proceeding before
any court, tribunal, or person having by law power to hear,
receive, and examine evidence on oath " [**section 1 (2)].** [3]

Where a statement made *for the purposes of* a judicial proceeding is not made before the tribunal itself, but is made on oath before
a person authorised by law to administer an oath to the person
who makes the statement, and to record or authenticate the statement, it is for the purposes of section 1 of the Act to be treated
as having been made in a judicial proceeding [**section 1 (3)].**

A statement made by a person lawfully sworn in England
for the purposes of a judicial proceeding (i) in another part of
Her Majesty's dominions; (ii) in any lawfully constituted British
tribunal outside Her Majesty's dominions; (iii) in a tribunal of
a foreign state, is for the purposes of section 1 to be treated as
a statement made in a judicial proceeding in England [**section 1 (4)].**

---

1 These offences are receiving the attention of the Law Commission.
2 Where the making of a false statement is an offence not only under this Act but
also by virtue of some other Act, the liability of the offender under this Act is
in addition to his liability under such other Act: *ibid.* s. 16 (1).   Where the
making of a false statement is by any other Act made punishable on summary
conviction, proceedings may be taken either under this Act or under such other
Act, unless by any such other Act passed before the commencement of this Act
the offence is punishable *only on summary conviction: ibid.* s. 16 (3).
3 By the Evidence Act 1851, s. 16: " Every court, judge, justice, officer, commissioner, arbitrator, or other person . . . having by law or by consent of parties
authority to hear, receive, and examine evidence, is . . . empowered to administer
an oath to all such witnesses as are legally called before them . . ." Two Special
Commissioners of Income Tax sitting to hear an appeal against an assessment
to surtax constitute such a tribunal: *R.* v. *Hood-Barrs* [1943] K.B. 455.

Conversely, if for the purposes of a judicial proceeding in England a person is lawfully sworn under the authority of an Act of Parliament (i) in any other part of Her Majesty's dominions; (ii) before a British tribunal or British officer in a foreign country, or within the jurisdiction of the Admiralty, it is to be treated as having been made in the judicial proceedings in England for the purposes of which it was made [**section 1 (5)**].

From the words of section 1 of the Act it will be seen that, in order to constitute perjury—

(1) the person making the statement must have been lawfully sworn;

(2) the statement must have been made wilfully;

(3) it must have been material in the judicial proceeding;

(4) he must have known it to be false *or* not believed it to be true.

(1) For the purposes of the Act, the forms and ceremonies used in administering an oath are immaterial if the court or person before whom the oath is taken has power to administer an oath for the purpose of verifying the statement in question, and if the oath has been administered in a form and with ceremonies which the person taking the oath has accepted without objection, or has declared to be binding on him [**section 15 (1)**].

In the case of persons who are allowed [4] by law to affirm or declare instead of swearing, the expression " oath " includes " affirmation " and " declaration," and the expression " swear " includes " affirm " and " declare " [**section 15 (2)**].

Nothing, however, in this Act applies to a statement made without oath by a child under the provisions of the Children and Young Persons Act 1933.[5]

(2) The statement must have been made, not by inadvertence or mistake, but wilfully or deliberately, and after the attention of the person making it has been sufficiently called to the subject.[6]

(3) The statement must have been material.   The question whether a statement was material is a question of law to be determined by the court of trial [**section 1 (6)**].

---

[4] This would, presumably, include a person who, under the Oaths Act 1961, may be *required* to make a solemn affirmation instead of being sworn.

[5] Provision is, however, made by this Act for the punishment of a child who wilfully gives false evidence.

[6] *R*. v. *Stolady* (1859) 1 F. & F. 518; *R*. v. *London* (1871) 24 L.T. 232.

All statements made for the purpose of affecting the decision of a tribunal are material, that is to say, not merely statements as to matters which are directly in issue, but also statements as to matters which affect the credit of a witness [7] or which tend to corroborate the evidence of a witness [8] or which, after conviction, are made by an accused person in order to obtain a mitigation of sentence.[9]

Thus in *R.* v. *Baker* [10] B was charged with selling beer without licence. Being sworn as a witness, he admitted that he had been previously convicted of the same offence, but swore that, on the previous occasion, his solicitor had pleaded guilty on his behalf without his knowledge or consent. In fact he had authorised his solicitor to plead guilty. He was indicted for perjury and convicted. *Held*, by the Court for Crown Cases Reserved, that, as his statements affected his credit as a witness, they were material and therefore he was guilty of perjury.

In *R.* v. *Tyson*,[11] upon the trial of S for robbery, T, in support of an alibi set up by S, swore that S was in a certain house at the time of the robbery, that he had lodged there for nearly two years preceding that time, and during that time he had never been absent for more than a night or two. In fact S had been in prison for one of those two years. *Held*, by the Court for Crown Cases Reserved, that the last two allegations were material as tending to render more probable the truth of the first and that T was accordingly guilty of perjury.

In *R.* v. *Wheeler* [12] W, having pleaded guilty to a charge under the Sale of Food and Drugs Act 1875, was sworn as a witness and wilfully made a false statement in the hopes of influencing the court to mitigate his sentence. He was indicted for perjury and convicted. *Held*, by the Court of Criminal Appeal, that the statement was material and that the conviction was right.

(4) The defendant must have known his statement to be false *or* not believed it to be true. Hence also a person can be convicted of perjury if he wilfully asserts a fact of which he is ignorant even

[7] *R.* v. *Baker* [1895] 1 Q.B. 797.
[8] *R.* v. *Tyson* (1867) L.R. 1 C.C.R. 107.
[9] *R.* v. *Wheeler* [1917] 1 K.B. 283.
[10] *Ubi supra.*
[11] (1867) L.R. 1 C.C.R. 107.
[12] [1917] 1 K.B. 283.

though his assertion is true.[13]   And, although a mere statement of opinion cannot amount to perjury, a person may be indicted for perjury if he swears that he thinks or believes certain facts to be true, but in fact knows that they are untrue or has no belief at all as to their truth.[14]

At common law the false statement must have been made before a court of competent jurisdiction, but under the Act it seems that perjury may be committed although the court has no jurisdiction in the matter.[15]

If any judge of a court of record or a petty sessional court, or any justice of the peace sitting in special sessions, is of opinion that any witness in a proceeding before him has been guilty of perjury, he may order him to be prosecuted for perjury if he thinks there is sufficient cause for such a prosecution, and he may commit him for trial [**section 9**].[16]

Section 89 of the **Criminal Justice Act 1967,** makes it an **indictable** offence [*Imp. 2 years and fine*] for any person in a written statement tendered in evidence in criminal proceedings by virtue of section 2 or 9 of the Act wilfully to make a statement material in those proceedings which he knows to be false or does not believe to be true.   Section 2 deals with written statements admitted in the preliminary enquiry (Chap. 48) and section 9 deals with written statements admitted in trials on indictment (Chap. 52).   This section is deemed part of the Perjury Act 1911.

False statements made otherwise than in a judicial proceeding. At common law and under the Act, perjury can be committed only in judicial proceedings.   But by **section 2** of the **Perjury Act 1911,** it is provided that if any person—

(i) being required or authorised by law to make any statement on oath for any purpose, and being lawfully sworn (otherwise than in a judicial proceeding) wilfully makes a statement which is material for that purpose and which he knows to be false or does not believe to be true; or

(ii) wilfully uses any false affidavit for the purposes of the Bills of Sale Acts

he shall be guilty of an offence [*Fine and Imp. 7 years*].

---

[13] 2 Hawk. c. 69, s. 6; *R.* v. *Mawbey* (1796) 6 T.R. 619 at p. 637.
[14] *R.* v. *Schlesinger* (1847) 10 Q.B. 670; *Roe* v. *Bradshaw* (1866) L.R. 1 Ex. 106.
[15] s. 1 (2), *ante*, p. 183; Arch. para. 3504.
[16] As amended by the Courts Act 1971, Sched. 11.

By other sections of the Act various *false statements and declarations* are also offences, *e.g.* :

(i) For any person knowingly and wilfully to make a false oath, or to make or sign a false declaration, notice or certificate, for the purpose of procuring a marriage or a certificate or licence for marriage, or to make or cause to be made, for the purpose of being inserted in any register of marriage, a false statement as to any particular required to be registered [*punishable as perjury, and also on summary conviction, by a fine of* £100] [**section 3**].

(ii) For any person wilfully to give to any registrar of births or deaths any untrue particulars or false information, or to make any false certificate or declaration under or for the purposes of any Act relating to the registration of births or deaths [*similarly punishable*] [**section 4**].[17]

(iii) For any person knowingly and wilfully to make—otherwise than on oath—a statement false in any material particular (*a*) in any statutory declaration, or (*b*) in any abstract, account, balance-sheet, certificate, declaration, report, return, etc., which by any Act of Parliament he is required to make, attest, or verify, or (*c*) in any oral declaration or answer which by any Act of Parliament he is required to make [*punishable on* **indictment** *by Imp.* 2 *years and fine and on* **summary conviction** *by Imp.* 6 *months and* £400 *fine*] [**section 5**].[18]

(iv) For any person by wilfully making or producing or causing to be made or produced either verbally or in writing any declaration, certificate or representation which he knows to be false or fraudulent (*a*) to procure or attempt to procure himself to be registered on any register kept under any Act of Parliament of persons qualified by law to practise any vocation or calling, or (*b*) to procure or attempt to procure a certificate of the registration of any

---

17 In offences within ss. 3 and 4 a penalty of £50 on summary conviction was imposed by s. 28 of the Criminal Justice Act 1925, which in this respect amended the Perjury Act 1911. The penalty was increased to £100 by the Criminal Justice Act 1967, Sched. 3. S. 28 of the 1925 Act also provides that summary proceedings for offences under ss. 3 and 4 of the Act of 1911 may be commenced at any time within 12 months after the commission of the offence.

18 Magistrates' Courts Act 1952, s. 19 and Sched. 1.

person on any such register [*Fine and Imp.* 12 *months*] [**section 6**].

Subornation of perjury. By **section 7** of the **Perjury Act 1911,** every person who aids, abets, counsels, procures or suborns another person to commit any offence against the Act is liable to be indicted, tried and punished as if he were a principal offender; every person who incites or attempts to procure or suborn another person to commit an offence against the Act is also guilty of an offence [*Fine and Imp. for* 2 *years*].[19]

Evidence. On a prosecution for perjury alleged to have been committed on the trial of an indictment for any offence or for procuring or suborning the commission of perjury in any such trial, the fact of the former trial shall be sufficiently proved by the production of a certificate containing the substance and effect (omitting the formal parts) of the indictment and trial purporting to be signed by the appropriate officer of the Crown Court or other person having the custody of the records of the court, or the deputy of such appropriate officer or person, without proof of the signature or official character of the appropriate officer or person appearing to have signed the certificate [**section 14**].[20]

Corroboration. No person can be convicted of any offence against the Act, or of any offence declared by any other Act to be perjury or subornation of perjury, or to be punishable as such, solely upon the evidence of one witness as to the falsity of any statement alleged to be false [**section 13**].

Accordingly, under this section, which is declaratory of the common law rule, the falsity of any statement must be proved either by two witnesses or by one witness who is substantially corroborated by proof of other material and relevant facts.[21]

It is not, however, necessary that there should be two independent witnesses to contradict the particular fact if there be two *pieces of evidence* in direct contradiction.[22]

Thus, where the defendant has sworn to a fact he may be convicted of perjury:

[19] Subornation of perjury is also an offence at common law: 1 Hawk. c. 69, s. 10.
[20] As substituted by the Courts Act 1971, Sched. 8.
[21] See *R.* v. *Yates* (1841) C. & M. 132; *R.* v. *Threlfall* (1914) 10 Cr.App.R. 112.
[22] *R.* v. *Hook* (1858) D. & B. 606.

(i) by the evidence of two witnesses directly contradicting him [23];

(ii) by the evidence of one witness directly contradicting him and a second witness corroborating the first [24];

(iii) by the evidence of one witness directly contradicting him and proof that he himself has on another occasion made a statement contradicting his evidence [25];

(iv) by evidence that he has on other occasions made statements contradicting his evidence and proof of facts tending to show that those statements were true [26];

(v) by the evidence of two witnesses that he has on two occasions made statements contradicting his evidence.[27]

But he cannot be convicted merely by proof that he has on another occasion made a contradictory statement.[28]

SECTION 2. OFFENCES AKIN TO PERJURY

(1) At common law it is an indictable offence **to fabricate evidence with intent to mislead a judicial tribunal.**[29]

(2) At common law it is an indictable offence **to defraud the Crown,** even though the particular fraud might not have been indictable if it had been a fraud by one subject upon another.[30] The only recent examples of prosecutions for this offence are apparently in connection with false statements relating to income tax made with intent to defraud the Revenue, when such statements are not otherwise an offence by statute.[31]

(3) By numerous statutes it is an offence **to make false statements with regard to particulars required by those statutes:** see, *e.g.* Mental Health Act 1959, Bankruptcy Act 1914, Registration of Business Names Act 1916, Customs and Excise Act 1952, Criminal Justice Act 1967.

---

[23] *R.* v. *Roberts* (1848) 2 C. & K. 607.
[24] *R.* v. *Gardiner* (1839) 8 C. & P. 737.
[25] *R.* v. *Mayhew* (1834) 6 C. & P. 315.
[26] *R.* v. *Hook* (1858) D. & B. 606.
[27] *Ibid., per* Byles J. at p. 616.
[28] *R.* v. *Wheatland* (1838) 8 C. & P. 238; *R.* v. *Hughes* (1844) 1 C. & K. 519.
[29] *R.* v. *Vreones* [1891] 1 Q.B. 360; Arch. para. 3544.
[30] *R.* v. *Hudson* [1956] 2 Q.B. 252; Arch. para. 3547.
[31] *Ibid.*

CHAPTER 15

ESCAPE, RESCUE AND OBSTRUCTING ARREST

SECTION 1. ESCAPE

IF a prisoner escapes from lawful custody or a criminal charge without using any force or violence, he commits the common law offence of **escape** [*Fine and Imp.*].[1] It is not clear whether this applies also to civil custody.[2]

At common law a person who is lawfully detained or imprisoned on a charge of treason or any other offence or in the course of civil process and who escapes using either personal violence or any force against property in order to effect his escape commits the common law offence of **breach of prison** [*Fine and Imp.*].[3] In either case if the prisoner merely gets over a wall or goes through an open door then, in the absence of personal violence, he is guilty only of the misdemeanour of escape.[4] But the breaking need not be intentional, so that a prisoner was held to be guilty of prison breach where he accidentally threw down from the top of a prison wall some loose bricks placed there in order to impede escape and give an alarm.[5]

Although on an indictment for breach of prison it is not strictly material whether the accused was innocent or guilty of the offence for which he was imprisoned, it is a good defence if he can prove that he was indicted for that offence and acquitted.[6]

Whether the offence be the offence of escape or the offence of breaking prison, the fact that the accused was not in prison is immaterial. It is only necessary that in some way his liberty was restrained.[7]

By **section 38** of the **Offences against the Person Act 1861,** a person who assaults any person with intent to resist or prevent the lawful detainer of himself for any offence commits an offence

---

[1] Arch. para. 3421; and see *R.* v. *Hinds* (1957) 41 Cr.App.R. 143.
[2] See Russell, p. 323.
[3] 2 Hawk. c. 18, ss. 12, 21.
[4] Arch. para. 3436.
[5] *R.* v. *Haswell* (1821) R. & R. 458.
[6] Arch. para. 3436.
[7] Arch. para. 3434.

[*Imp.* 2 *years*], and by **section 18** of the same Act it is an offence [*Imp. life*] unlawfully and maliciously to wound or to cause grievous bodily harm [8] to any person, or shoot or attempt to shoot at any person with the like intent.

SECTION 2. ALLOWING OR AIDING ESCAPE

To assist or allow a person to escape is an offence both at common law and by statute.

Common law. A custodian, whether officer or private person,[9] who *negligently* allows a prisoner lawfully in his custody upon a criminal charge to escape is guilty of the offence of **escape** [10] [*Fine and Imp.*].[11]

A custodian, whether officer or private person, who voluntarily permits such a prisoner to escape is guilty of the offence of **escape** which is:

(i) a **treason,** if the prisoner had been *convicted* of treason,

(ii) an **indictable** offence, if the prisoner had been *convicted* of such an offence or if the prisoner *had not as yet been convicted*.[12]

In both cases if the prisoner has been convicted, then the custodian is liable to be punished in the same degree as the prisoner.[13]

Any person, whether custodian or not, who assists another to escape from lawful custody on a criminal charge is guilty:

(i) if the prisoner was guilty of *treason*, then of treason as a principal,[14] or

(ii) in any other case, is guilty either as an accomplice to the escape or, in the appropriate circumstances, of an offence against section 4 of the Criminal Law Act 1967.[15]

Any person who *forcibly* liberates another from lawful custody on a criminal charge is also guilty of the offence of **rescue.**[16] If,

---

[8] *Post*, pp. 458, 459.

[9] It is the duty of a private person to deliver over to a proper officer anyone whom he has lawfully arrested, and, until he has done so, his liability is the same as that of an officer: 2 Hawk. c. 20.

[10] Arch. para. 3421.

[11] Arch. paras. 3421, 3427–3428.

[12] Arch. paras. 3421, 3429–3430.

[13] Arch. para. 3429.

[14] 2 Hawk. c. 21, s. 7; Russell, p. 332.

[15] *Ante*, p. 83.

[16] Arch. paras. 3444–3446.

however, the prisoner was in private custody, the rescuer is not liable criminally unless he knew that such custody was on a criminal charge.[17] The offence is a **treason** and punishable as a treason if the rescued person had himself been *convicted* of treason.[18] In any other case it is an **indictable** offence [*Fine and Imp.*].

Any person who aids a prisoner to escape from lawful custody on a civil process is guilty of a misdemeanour.[19]

Statute. By **section 39** of the **Prison Act 1952,**[20] it is an offence [*Imp. 5 years*] to aid any prisoner to *escape or attempt to escape* from any prison [21] or, with intent to facilitate the escape of any prisoner, to convey anything into any prison (other than the excepted prisons).[22] **Section 22 (2)** of the **Criminal Justice Act 1961,** makes it an offence to harbour escaped prisoners.

By **section 32 (3)** of the **Children and Young Persons Act 1969** it is an offence [*Imp. 6 months and £100 fine*] for a person knowingly to compel, persuade, incite or assist another to become, or continue to be, absent from a place of safety which is a community home, a remand home, special reception centre or training school; or a person who has been committed to the care of a local authority or a fit person, under the Act.

By **section 1** of the **Prisoners of War Escape Act 1812,** it is an offence [*Imp. life*] to aid a prisoner of war to escape.

By **section 129** of the **Mental Health Act 1959,** it is an offence to induce or knowingly to assist any person liable to be detained under that Act to absent himself without leave or to escape (as the case may be), or knowingly to harbour such a person who has absented himself without leave or escaped, or to give him assistance to prevent or hinder him being retaken [**summary conviction**—*Imp. 6 months and fine £100; conviction on* **indictment**—*fine and Imp. 2 years*].

---

[17] Arch. para. 3444.
[18] Arch. para. 3445.
[19] *R.* v. *Allan* (1841) C. & M. 295.
[20] As amended by the Criminal Justice Act 1961, Sched. 4.
[21] This Act does not apply to naval, military or air force prisons, which are governed by special statutes: see the Naval Discipline Act 1957, s. 82 (3) amended by the Armed Forces Act 1971, s. 52; the Army Act 1955, ss. 54, 56; the Air Force Act 1955, ss. 54, 56.
[22] For the offence of bringing liquor, etc., into prison, see Prison Act 1952, s. 40 and *R.* v. *Ashley* (1968) 52 Cr.App.R. 42.

Section 3. Obstructing or Resisting an Arrest

At common law a person who obstructs the arrest of a person who has committed treason becomes thereby a principal.[23] Obstructing the arrest of a person for an arrestable offence may constitute an offence against section 4 of the Criminal Law Act 1967.[24]

By **section 38** of the **Offences against the Person Act 1861,** an assault upon any person with intent to resist or prevent the lawful *apprehension* of himself or of any other person for any offence is an offence [*Imp. 2 years*]. By **section 18** of the same Act it is an offence [*Imp. life*] unlawfully and maliciously to wound or cause grievous bodily harm to any person, or shoot or attempt to shoot at any person with the like intent.

---

[23] Foster 341; and see Russell, p. 332.
[24] *Ante*, p. 83. See also assaulting, resisting or obstructing a constable contrary to Police Act 1964, s. 51, p. 171, *ante*.

CHAPTER 16

OFFENCES AGAINST THE PUBLIC PEACE

SECTION 1. BREACH OF THE PEACE

BREACH of the peace is not a separate offence in England [1] but
(i) it is a constituent part of a number of offences discussed in this
and other chapters, (ii) a person may be lawfully arrested if he is
committing or about to commit such a breach,[2] (iii) it is part of a
constable's duty to prevent such breaches,[3] (iv) refusal to aid a
constable in the execution of this duty is an offence [4] and (v)
magistrates have the power to bind over a person to keep the
peace.[5]

" Strangely enough, what constitutes a ' breach of the peace '
has not been authoritatively laid down." [6]   It apparently involves
some danger to the person.[7]

Disorderly conduct likely to lead to a breach of the peace is
prohibited by **section 5** of the **Public Order Act 1936** as substituted
by **section 7 of the Race Relations Act 1965,** [8]   The Act is intended
to preserve not only public order in the sense of many persons
being involved, but also public order in the sense of preserving
order in a public place.[9]

SECTION 2. PUBLIC MEETINGS AND PROCESSIONS

Public Meetings [10]

The holding of public meetings. Many statutes and by-laws
prevent or regulate the holding of public meetings in public parks

---

[1] It is an offence in Scotland.
[2] *Post*, p. 556.
[3] *Ante*, p. 173.
[4] *Ante*, p. 173.
[5] *Post*, p. 791.
[6] Kenny, p. 578.
[7] Hawk.P.C. c. 60, s. 6.   See also Kenny, p. 578, and Russell, p. 257.   For a
definition of the offence in Scotland, see [1959] Crim.L.R. 438.
[8] See, *post*, p. 212.   See also the Theatres Act 1968, s. 6.   Conduct of this nature
is frequently punishable under local statutes.
[9] *Ward* v. *Holman* [1964] 2 Q.B. 580, but does not apply to quarrelling neighbours: *Wilson* v. *Skeock* (1950) 113 J.P. 294 D.C.
[10] For a useful summary of the law on this topic, see D. G. T. Williams, " Police,
Public Meetings and Public Order " [1963] Crim.L.R. 149.

and in or around public buildings. Thus, for example, meetings cannot be held in Trafalgar Square without the permission of the Department of the Environment.[11]

The holding of public meetings on highways will often constitute a civil trespass to the owners of the highway, usually the adjoining landowners, in which case they could request the police to move the trespassers on. If the local authority own the highway, then perhaps the police could also move trespassers on, but this is not clear.[12]

More important, any obstruction of the highway may constitute the offence of public nuisance,[13] and by **section 121** of the **Highways Act 1959,** the wilful obstruction of free passage along a highway is punishable on **summary conviction** [£50 [14] *fine*].

Certain public meetings are prohibited specifically by statute. In particular all meetings for the purpose of illegal drilling are prohibited.[15] Also by **section 23** of the **Seditious Meetings Act 1817,** meetings of more than fifty persons within a mile of Westminster Hall during sittings of Parliament or of the superior courts [16] for the purpose or on the pretext of considering or preferring a petition, complaint, remonstrance or address to the Queen or either House of Parliament, for alteration of matters in Church or state, are unlawful assemblies.[17]

The conduct of public meetings. By **section 4** of the **Public Order Act 1936,** it is provided that any person who, while present at any public meeting or on the occasion of any public procession, has with him any offensive weapon, otherwise than in pursuance of lawful authority (as defined by the section), shall be guilty of an offence [18] punishable on **summary conviction** [*Imp.* 3 *months and* £50 *fine*].[19]

Insulting words and behaviour. By **section 5** of the **Public Order Act 1936** [20] any person who in any public place or at any

---

[11] Trafalgar Square Act 1844; S.I. 1970, No. 1681.
[12] See Street, *Freedom, the Individual and the Law,* p. 43.
[13] *Post,* pp. 216, 217.
[14] The fine was increased by the Criminal Justice Act 1967, Sched. 3.
[15] *Ante,* p. 141.
[16] See, now, s. 224 of the Supreme Court of Judicature (Consolidation) Act 1925.
[17] As to what constitutes an unlawful assembly, see, *post,* p. 200.
[18] See also Prevention of Crime Act 1953, s. 1, *post,* p. 292.
[19] s. 7.
[20] As substituted by the Race Relations Act 1965, s. 7.

public meeting uses threatening, abusive or insulting words or behaviour,[21] or distributes or displays any writing, sign or visible representation which is threatening, abusive or insulting, with intent to provoke a breach of the peace or whereby a breach of the peace is likely to be occasioned is made guilty of an offence [22] punishable on **indictment** [*Imp. 1 year and £500 fine*] or on **summary conviction** [*Imp. 3 months and £100 fine*].[23] The term " public place " is defined in section 9 (1) [24] to include, *inter alia*, any highway and other premises or place to which, at the material time, the public have, or are permitted to have, access, whether on payment or otherwise. If a person uses insulting language he will be liable under this section if, having regard to the particular audience he is addressing, a breach of the peace might occur. The fact that a reasonable man might not break the peace is immaterial.[25]

A constable may arrest without a warrant any person suspected by him to be committing an offence against either section 4 or 5.[26]

By **section 1** of the **Public Meetings Act 1908**,[27] it is an offence

---

[21] As to the meaning of these terms see the article by A. Dickey at [1971] Crim.L.R. 265 and the articles by D. G. T. Williams, " Threats, Abuse and Insults " at [1967] Crim.L.R. 385 and " Protest and Public Order " [1970] C.L.J. 96. The word " insulting " is to be given its ordinary meaning and the question of whether the speech or the behaviour has been insulting is a question of fact for the court: *Brutus* v. *Cozens* [1972] 3 W.L.R. 521 H.L. Vigorous, distasteful or unmannerly speech or behaviour is permitted provided it is not threatening, nor abusive, nor insulting: *ibid.*, *per* Lord Reid.

[22] In *R.* v. *John and Another* [1971] Crim.L.R. 283 a county court judge sitting at Inner London Quarter Sessions is said to have held: that the words " threatening, abusive or insulting words or behaviour " were adjectival in their nature, being descriptive of a course of conduct conducive to a breach of the peace and as such they created one offence, but . . . that the words " with intent to cause a breach of the peace or whereby a breach of the peace was likely to be occasioned " envisaged such different situations and such different intents that although certain situations existed where it could describe two ways of committing the same offence, two offences were created. As to the first proposition see also *Vernon* v. *Paddon*, *The Times*, February 12, 1972, D.C.

[23] However, it is more usual to prosecute, not under this Act, but under local Acts and by-laws for this kind of conduct. Behaviour of this nature is also punishable under the Metropolitan Police Act 1839, s. 54, and the Town Police Clauses Act 1847.

[24] As substituted by the Criminal Justice Act 1972, s. 33, thus presumably negativing the decision in *Cooper* v. *Shield* [1971] 2 Q.B. 334 that a railway platform is not a " public place." As to conduct by a person in a private place which is likely to result in a breach of the peace in a public place, see *Wilson* v. *Skeock* (1949) 113 J.P. 294, D.C.

[25] *Jordan* v. *Burgoyne* [1963] 2 Q.B. 744.

[26] s. 7.

[27] Amended by the Representation of the People Act 1949, s. 175 (1) and Sched. 9; and by the Public Order Act 1963, s. 1 (2).

punishable on **indictment** [*Imp*. 1 *year and* £500 *fine*] or on **summary conviction** [*Imp*. 3 *months and* £100 *fine*] [28] for any person at a lawful public meeting to act in a disorderly manner for the purpose of preventing the transaction of the business for which the meeting was called together. Inciting a person to commit an offence under this section is similarly punishable on **summary conviction.** [29]

By **section 84** of the **Representation of the People Act 1949,** it is an offence punishable on **summary conviction** [£100 *fine*] [30] for any person at a political meeting for a parliamentary or local government election [31] to act, or incite others to act, in a disorderly manner for the purposes of preventing the transaction of the business for which the meeting was called together.

If a constable reasonably suspects a person of committing an offence against either of the two preceding sections, he may, upon request of the chairman, ask the person to declare his name and address. If he refuses to do so or gives a false name he is punishable on **summary conviction** [£2 *fine*]. Furthermore if he refuses to do so or the constable reasonably suspects him of giving a false name and address, the constable may arrest him without warrant. [32]

Apart from these statutory provisions a public meeting may at common law constitute an unlawful assembly, rout or riot—all of which are discussed in the next section.

Also, at common law, the police may prevent a meeting from being held if they reasonably apprehend that it will cause a breach of the peace, although such breach of the peace may not occur at the meeting itself. So, in *Duncan* v. *Jones* [33] A had in May held a meeting near an unemployed training centre, with the result that a disturbance had taken place in the centre. In July she proposed to hold a similar meeting at the same place but was forbidden to do so by a police inspector. In defiance of this prohibition she attempted to hold the meeting and began to address those who were present. She was taken into custody and charged with and

---

[28] Public Order Act 1963, s. 1.
[29] s. 1 (2) of the Public Meetings Act 1908, as amended by the Public Order Act 1963, s. 1.
[30] s. 147.
[31] This is further defined in s. 84.
[32] s. 1 of Public Meetings Act 1908, as amended by s. 6 of the Public Order Act 1936; s. 84 of the Representation of the People Act 1949.
[33] [1936] 1 K.B. 218.

convicted of unlawfully and wilfully obstructing the police inspector when in the execution of his duty. It was not alleged that she, or any of the persons present, had committed, incited or provoked any breach of the peace. *Held*, *by* the Divisional Court, that she was rightly convicted. Since the police inspector reasonably apprehended a breach of the peace it was his duty to prevent anything by which, in his opinion, it would be caused. While he was taking steps to do this he was wilfully obstructed.[34]

Notwithstanding the case of *Beatty* v. *Gillbanks*,[35] which is discussed later,[36] the police could probably prevent a meeting likely to lead to a breach of the peace (at least if there was no other way of securing the peace) even though the speaker and the organisers themselves were not guilty either of unlawful assembly[37] or of any other offence. If in these circumstances the orders of the police were disobeyed, an offence against section 51 of the Police Act 1964 (obstructing a constable in the execution of his duty[38]), might be committed.

Public Processions

Little need be added here to what has been said above about public meetings. Although a procession would not normally constitute a trespass, it might constitute a public nuisance[39] or an obstruction.[40] Sections 4 and 5 of the Public Order Act 1936,[41] apply to processions, as would also the common law duty of the police to prevent a breach of the peace.[42] A procession might also constitute an unlawful assembly, rout or riot, all of which are discussed in the next section.

By **section 3** of the **Public Order Act 1936,** provisions are made for enabling a chief officer of police to impose conditions upon the conduct of public processions and also for enabling them, in certain circumstances, to be prohibited for a limited period.[43]

---

[34] See also *Wise* v. *Dunning* [1902] 1 K.B. 167.
[35] (1882) 9 Q.B.D. 308.
[36] *Post*, p. 200.
[37] *Post*, p. 200.
[38] *Ante*, p. 172.
[39] *Post*, p. 216.
[40] *Ante*, p. 195.
[41] *Ante*, p. 195.
[42] *Ante*, p. 194.
[43] For an example of the use of this power, see Williams, *op. cit.*, p. 152.

Any person who knowingly fails to comply with any such conditions or organises or assists in organising [44] any public procession held or intended to be held in contravention of such a prohibition is made guilty of an offence punishable on **summary conviction** [*Imp. 3 months and £50 fine*].[45]

Power of Binding Over

The power that a magistrates' court has to bind over a person to keep the peace or to be of good behaviour is discussed more fully later.[46] However, it is worth pointing out here that it can be used to good effect to prevent assemblies likely to lead to a breach of the peace. So in *Wise* v. *Dunning* [47] the appellant, a Protestant, had held meetings in Liverpool attended by large crowds and at which he made highly insulting gestures and remarks about Roman Catholics. As a result breaches of the peace had been committed by his supporters and opponents. Having threatened to hold further meetings he was bound over by a stipendiary magistrate to keep the peace and be of good behaviour and this order was confirmed by the Divisional Court.

SECTION 3. INTIMIDATION

By **section 7** of the **Conspiracy and Protection of Property Act 1875** every person [48] who, with a view to compelling any other person to abstain from doing, or to do any act [49] which such other person has a legal right to do or abstain from doing, wrongfully and without legal authority [50]:

(a) uses violence to, or intimidates, such other person, or his wife or children, or injures his property [51]; or

(b) persistently follows him about from place to place; or

---

[44] A person indicating, planning or pointing out the route by which others are to go is " organising " a procession: *Flockhart* v. *Robinson* [1950] 2 K.B. 498.

[45] s. 7.

[46] *Post*, p. 791.

[47] [1902] 1 K.B. 167.

[48] See *Lyons* v. *Wilkins* [1899] 1 Ch. 255.

[49] The particular act must be specified in the summons and conviction: *R.* v. *McKenzie* [1892] 2 Q.B. 519 at p. 521.

[50] As to the significance to be attached to the words " wrongfully and without legal authority " see the article by R. J. Coleman at [1970] Crim.L.R. 608.

[51] The particular property injured must be specified in the summons and conviction: *Smith* v. *Moody* [1903] 1 K.B. 56.

(c) hides his tools, clothes or other property, or deprives him of or hinders him in the use thereof; or

(d) watches and besets [52] his house, or other place where he resides, or works, or carries on his business, or happens to be, or the approach to such house or place; or

(e) follows him with two or more other persons in a disorderly manner through any street or road,

commits an offence punishable on **summary conviction** [*Imp.* 3 *months or* £20 *fine*].

This section, although normally arising in connection with industrial disputes is not in fact limited to such matters and is of general application.[53]

SECTION 4. UNLAWFUL ASSEMBLY—ROUT AND RIOT—AFFRAY

Unlawful assembly. An unlawful assembly at common law is an assembly of three or more persons (i) for purposes forbidden by law or (ii) with intent to carry out any common purpose, lawful or unlawful, in such a manner as to endanger the public peace or under such circumstances of alarm, either from the numbers or language or behaviour of the assembly as to give to persons of reasonable firmness and courage ground to apprehend a breach of the peace.[54] The moment when persons in a crowd, however peaceful their original intention, commence to act for some shared common purpose supporting each other and in such a way that reasonable citizens fear a breach of the peace, the assembly becomes unlawful. In particular that applies where those concerned attempt to trespass or to interrupt or disrupt an occasion where others are peaceably and lawfully enjoying themselves or show preparedness to use force to achieve the common purpose.[55]

A lawful assembly is not, however, rendered unlawful merely because those participating in it are aware that the unlawful acts of *other* persons, who are hostile to the assembly, will probably cause a breach of the peace. Thus in *Beatty* v. *Gillbanks* [56] it was

---

[52] Watching and besetting are not defined in the Act; *cf. R.* v. *Wall* (1901) 21 Cox C.C. 401 and *Charnock* v. *Court* [1899] 2 Ch. 35.

[53] As to the possible application of the Act to " sit ins " by students, see R. J. Coleman, *op. cit.* As to industrial disputes see p. 407, *post.*

[54] See *R.* v. *Vincent* (1839) 9 C. & P. 91; *R.* v. *Graham and Burns* (1888) 16 Cox 420.

[55] *R.* v. *Caird and Others* (1957) 54 Cr.App.R. 499.

[56] (1882) 9 Q.B.D. 308.

held that leaders of the Salvation Army who organised Sunday processions through the streets of a town were not guilty of unlawfully assembling merely because from previous experience they knew that riots would be caused by the physical opposition of a rival organisation, such riots not being the natural consequence of any acts of the defendants.[57] It would, however, be an unlawful assembly if a procession or meeting was organised with the intention of using language insulting and abusing persons holding different views, and therefore being *provocative* of a breach of the peace.[58]

All persons who take part in an unlawful assembly or give any help or encouragement in the prosecution of its purpose are guilty of an offence [*Fine and Imp.*].[59] Whether there has been any such encouragement is a question for the jury. Mere presence without encouragement is not sufficient.[60]

Rout. A rout is a disturbance of the peace by three or more persons who assemble with an intention to do something which if executed will amount to a riot, and who actually make a move towards the execution of their common purpose but do not complete it.[61] It constitutes a similar offence.

Riot. A riot is a tumultuous disturbance of the peace by three or more persons who assemble together of their own authority, with an intent mutually to assist one another against any who oppose them in the execution of an enterprise of a *private nature whether lawful or unlawful*, and afterwards actually execute the same in a violent and turbulent manner to the terror of the people.[62] Riot is a common law offence[63] punishable on **indictment** [*Fine and Imp.*].[64]

---

[57] The decision in *Beatty* v. *Gillbanks* has, however, been doubted or restrictively interpreted: see, *e.g. Wise* v. *Dunning* [1902] 1 K.B. 167 and *Duncan* v. *Jones* [1936] 1 K.B. 218. See also *ante*, p. 197.

[58] *Wise* v. *Dunning* [1902] 1 K.B. 167.

[59] At common law the punishment for a misdemeanour was at large. The term of imprisonment or the amount of the fine was at the discretion of the court provided that the punishment was not inordinate: see Arch. para. 659, also *R.* v. *Morris* [1951] 1 K.B. 394 where Lord Goddard C.J. traces the origin of the rule. And generally see *Verrier* v. *D.P.P.* [1967] 2 A.C. 195.

[60] *R.* v. *Atkinson* (1869) 11 Cox at p. 332; *R.* v. *Caird and Others* (1957) 54 Cr.App.R. 499. Any person who actually encourages or promotes an unlawful assembly or riot, whether by words, by signs or by actions or by participating in it, is guilty of an offence.

[61] Arch. paras 3572 and 3577.

[62] Arch. para. 3581.

[63] The Riot Act 1714 was repealed by the Criminal Law Act 1967, Sched. 3.

[64] See note 59, *ante*.

From the cases it is clear that there are five necessary elements of riot [65] (i) the number of persons concerned must be at least three; (ii) they must have a common purpose; (iii) the execution or inception of the common purpose must be proved; (iv) there must also be proved an intent on the part of the persons in question to help one another, by force if necessary, against any person who may oppose them in the execution of that common purpose; and (v) there must be proved force or violence, not merely used in and about the common purpose, but displayed in such a manner as to alarm at least one person of reasonable firmness and courage.[66]

Thus, during the public rejoicings which occurred on peace night, 1919, a crowd of 150 or 200 people assembled and lighted a bonfire. Some of them, armed with crowbars and pick-axes, obtained fuel by taking the woodwork and flooring of an empty house belonging to the plaintiff. Here the first three elements of a riot were clearly satisfied and it was found by Bailhache J. (iv) that there was no doubt that anyone who interfered with the crowd would have been subject to rough usage and (v) that there was force and violence which alarmed at least one neighbour who was a man of reasonable firmness and courage. *Held*, accordingly that there was a riot.[67]

The common purpose must, however, be of a private nature and not of such a public or general character as to make the offence amount to treason.[68]

The essence of the offence is that the assembling is accompanied with circumstances either of actual force and violence or of such an apparent tendency thereto as are calculated to inspire terror; if an assembly is not accompanied with such circumstances it is not a riot, however unlawful the intent of the persons assembled

---

[65] *Per* Pritchard J. in *Munday* v. *Metropolitan Police Receiver* [1949] 1 All E.R. 337, following *Field* v. *Receiver for the Metropolitan Police District* [1907] 2 K.B. 853 and *Ford* v. *Receiver for the Metropolitan Police District* [1921] 2 K.B. 344.

[66] In *R.* v. *Sharp & Johnson* [1957] 1 Q.B. 552 at p. 560 Lord Goddard C.J. said that the requirement of proving that at least one person, etc., was alarmed might have to be reconsidered. In *Dwyer* v. *Metropolitan Police Receiver* [1967] 2 Q.B. 970 at p. 978 Lyell J. said he would have been prepared to hold, in the absence of direct evidence, that the conduct of the rioters was such as would have alarmed such a person.

[67] *Ford* v. *Receiver for the Metropolitan Police District* [1921] 2 K.B. 344.

[68] 2 Hawk. c. 65, s. 6.

or the acts which they commit [69]; it may, however, be punishable as a conspiracy.[70]

The moment when persons in a crowd, however peaceful their original intention, commence to act for some shared common purpose supporting each other and in such a way that reasonable citizens fear a breach of the peace, the assembly becomes unlawful. In particular that applies when those concerned attempt to trespass, or to interrupt or disrupt an occasion where others are peacefully and lawfully enjoying themselves, or show preparedness to use force to achieve the common purpose. The assembly becomes riotous at latest when alarming force or violence begins to be used.[71]

Unlawful assembly, rout and riot form three stages. Thus, if parties assemble in a tumultuous manner and actually execute their purpose with violence it is a riot; if they meet for a purpose which, if executed, would make them rioters and make any move towards its execution, it is a rout; but if, having done nothing, they separate without carrying their purpose into effect, it is an unlawful assembly.[72] But, as already pointed out, an assembly is unlawful if its purpose is illegal, so that an assembly for treasonable or seditious purposes, although not riotous, is nevertheless an unlawful assembly.[73]

In *R. v. Sharp & Johnson* [74] Lord Goddard C.J. pointed out that " riot " is a term of art, and contrary to popular belief, a riot may involve no noise or disturbance of the neighbours, although there must be some force or violence. " For example " he said " if three men enter a shop and forcibly or by threats steal goods therein, technically they are guilty . . . also of riot." [75]

It is to be observed that the offence of riot is distinct from any other offences, such as assaults or criminal damage to property, that may be committed in the course thereof.

---

[69] 2 Hawk. c. 65, s. 5; Arch. para. 3585.

[70] *Ante*, p. 63.

[71] *Per* Sachs L.J. in *R. v. Caird and Others* (1957) 54 Cr.App.R. 499.

[72] 1 Hawk. c. 65, ss. 1, 8, 9; Arch. 3572; *R. v. Birt* (1831) 5 C. & P. 154.

[73] 2 Hawk. c. 65, s. 9; see however, Arch. para. 3571.

[74] [1957] 1 Q.B. 552.

[75] See also *London and Lancashire Fire Insurance Co.* v. *Bolands Ltd.* [1924] A.C. 836. But see the distinction between the two forms where compensation arises under Riot (Damages) Act 1886, and the article by A. Samuels at [1970] Crim.L.R. 336.

Affray. The common law offence of affray [*Fine and Imp.*] [76] consists of two or more persons fighting together to the terror of the Queen's subjects [77] " Where two or more people fight in the presence of persons who neither participate in nor encourage the fighting and thereby some of these persons are frightened or put in fear, the offence of affray is complete." [78]

Such offences will for the most part take place in places to which the public can go as of right or by leave and licence [79] but the offence need not be committed in a public place.[80] The essential factor is that there should be innocent bystanders who do not participate in the fighting. There must be evidence that at least persons *appeared* to be alarmed.[81] It is not an affray if one of two persons fighting in the street is merely defending himself against attack.[82]

In order for a spectator to be convicted of being a principal in an affray there must be proof that at the very least, by some means or other, he *encouraged* the participants. Mere physical presence is not sufficient.[83]

At common law and by the Assize of Northampton [84] persons who arm themselves with dangerous weapons so as to terrify the Queen's subjects are guilty of an offence in the nature of an affray. Whether they would be prosecuted under those provisions today or whether the prosecution would be brought under the Prevention of Crime Act 1953 is another question.

But " if persons, innocently assembled together, do afterwards upon a dispute happening to arise among them, form themselves into parties, with promises of mutual assistance, and then make an affray, they are guilty of a *riot*." [85]

Anyone may arrest persons guilty of an affray if it is actually continuing in his presence or he has reasonable ground to believe

---

[76] As to the punishment for common law misdemeanours see, *ante*, p. 201 at note 59.
[77] ". . . affray is derived of the French effraier which signifieth to terrifie, or bring feare," Lambard's *Eirenarcha* (1614) at pp. 125–125 and see generally *R.* v. *Button & Swain* [1966] A.C. 591.
[78] *Ibid., per* Marshall J. at p. 609.
[79] *Ibid.*
[80] *Ibid.*
[81] *R.* v. *Sharp & Johnson* [1957] 1 Q.B. 552.
[82] *Ibid.*
[83] *R.* v. *Allen* [1965] 1 Q.B. 130. *Cf. R.* v. *Clarkson* [1971] 1 W.L.R. 1402.
[84] 2 Edw. 3, c. 3.
[85] 1 Hawk. c. 65, s. 3.

that it will be renewed, or the arrest is upon fresh pursuit immediately after the affray.[86]

The mere use of quarrelsome and threatening language does not constitute an affray.

SECTION 5. FORCIBLE ENTRY AND DETAINER

By the **Forcible Entry Act 1381** [87] it is an offence punishable on **indictment** [*Fine and Imp.*] [88] for any person to make entry " with strong hand " or with " multitude of people " into land or premises of which another is in possession.

In a prosecution under this statute it is immaterial whether the person making the forcible entry had or had not a right to enter, so that an indictment will lie where a landlord forcibly ejects a tenant whose term has expired.[89] The statute does not, however, apply where the person ejected had the bare *custody* of the land or premises, *e.g.* as servant of the person making entry, nor, probably, where he was a mere trespasser who had previously ejected the person making entry.[90]

A similar offence punishable on **indictment** [91] [*Imp. and Fine*] [92] known as **forcible detainer** is created by the **Forcible Entry Acts 1391** [93] *and* **1429** [94] making it criminal for a person who has entered either forcibly or even peaceably to " hold with force ", thus detaining land or premises from the prosecutor, unless the latter is a mere trespasser who has ejected him.[95]

An indictment for a forcible entry cannot be supported by evidence of a mere trespass, but there must be some actual force, as by breaking doors or windows or doing personal violence to the

---

[86] *Price* v. *Seeley* (1843) 10 Cl. & F. 28; *R.* v. *Marsden* (1868) L.R. 1 C.C.R. 131; 1 Hawk. c. 68, ss. 13, 14, 16. A constable, though without a warrant, is bound to exercise these powers: 1 Hawk. c. 63, s. 13; *R.* v. *Brown* (1841) C. & M. at p. 318.

[87] 5 Ric. 2, Stat. 1, c. 7.

[88] See note 59 on p. 201, *ante.*

[89] At common law an indictment for forcible entry lay only when it was by a person who had no title, and the statute was passed to prevent persons from the use of " violent methods of doing themselves justice ": 1 Hawk. c. 64, ss. 1, 2.

[90] 1 Hawk. c. 64, s. 32; Arch. para. 3603; *Browne* v. *Dawson* (1840) 12 Ad. & El. 624; *Hemmings* v. *Stoke Poges Golf Club* [1920] 1 K.B. 720.

[91] *R.* v. *Mountford* [1972] Q.B. 28.

[92] See note 59 on p. 201, *ante.*

[93] 15 Ric. 2, c. 2.

[94] 8 Hen. 6, c. 9.

[95] *Hemmings* v. *Stoke Poges Golf Club* [1920] 1 K.B. 720.

prosecutor or his family or servants, or there must be at least some show of force which is calculated to intimidate the prosecutor and prevent resistance. But it was said in *Milner* v. *MacLean* [96] that

> " if persons either take or keep possession of either house or land, with such number of persons and show of force, as is calculated to deter the rightful owner from sending them away, and resuming his own possession, that is sufficient in point of law to constitute a forcible entry or a forcible detainer ".

The intention of the statute was to prevent breaches of the peace in the case of forcible entry, whether or not the person entering had the right to do so peaceably. It is immaterial whether or not there is an intention to occupy the premises. [96a] Accumulating an unusual number of people or unusual weapons or making other preparations of such a kind which indicate in themselves that any attempt to enter will be opposed by force may amount to the use of force in detaining premises even though the owner is deterred and never makes the attempt at all. [97]

Restitution. In either case the court in which the proceedings take place may by writ of restitution restore possession to the prosecutor unless the person indicted has been in quiet possession for three years before the date of the indictment. [98]

SECTION 6. CRIMINAL LIBEL [99]

Defamation consists in the publication, without justification or excuse, of that which is calculated to injure the reputation of another, by exposing him to hatred, contempt or ridicule, [1] or tending to lower the victim in the estimation of right thinking members of society, [2] as for instance, a charge of any criminal offence, or of any fraud, dishonesty, immorality or dishonest conduct.

---

[96] (1825) 2 C. & P. 17, *per* Abbott C.J., approved by the Court of Appeal in *R.* v. *Robinson* [1971] 1 Q.B. 156 at p. 162.

[96a] *R.* v. *Brittain* [1972] 1 Q.B. 357 (gate-crashers at a party).

[97] *Per* Widgery L.J. in *R.* v. *Robinson* (*supra*), where it was held that the erection of barricades might amount to the use of force within the Act.

[98] 8 Hen. 6, c. 9; 31 Eliz. 1, c. 11; 21 Jac. 1, c. 15.

[99] It was announced on May 27, 1971, that the government proposed to set up an inquiry into the law of defamation.

[1] *Parmiter* v. *Coupland* (1840) 6 M. & W. at p. 108.

[2] *Per* Lord Atkin in *Sim* v. *Stretch* [1936] 2 All E.R. 1237 at p. 1240.

If published in writing, printing, pictures, effigy or any other *permanent* form it is a **libel**[3]; if by mere words it is a **slander.**

Libel is both a civil wrong and a criminal offence[4]; slander is only a civil wrong. " A person libelled may pursue his remedies for damages, or prefer an indictment, or he may both sue for damages and indict. The whole topic of defamation belongs essentially to the law of tort, and reference should be made to books on that subject for a detailed consideration of it. Nevertheless, libel, may in certain circumstances amount to a criminal offence, because of its supposed tendency to arouse angry passions, provoke revenge, and thus endanger the public peace; but the libeller is not the less bound to make compensation for the pecuniary or other loss or injury which the libel might have occasioned to the person libelled. In this respect libel stands on the same footing as an assault." [5]

The publication of a criminal libel is a common law offence [*Fine and Imp.* 1 *year,*[6] *or, if the publication is with knowledge of its untruth,* 2 *years* [7]].

By **section 8** of the **Law of Libel Amendment Act 1888,** no criminal prosecution can be commenced against any proprietor, publisher, editor, or any person responsible for the publication of a *newspaper* [8] for any libel contained therein without the order of a judge in chambers, the application for which must be made on notice to the person accused, who must have an opportunity of being heard against it.

---

[3] See *Monson* v. *Tussaud's Ltd.* [1894] 1 Q.B. 671. S. 1 of the Defamation Act 1952, by which broadcasting is deemed to be a publication in a permanent form, has no application in the case of criminal libel: The common law rule applies therefore. This is thought to be that it is libel if the broadcast was made from a written script, whereas only slander if it was not: see O'Sullivan and Brown, *The Law of Defamation,* p. 7. The Theatres Act 1968, s. 4, provides that for the purposes of the law of defamation, including the law of criminal libel, publication of words in the course of a play shall be treated as publication in permanent form, subject to the exceptions in s. 7 of the Act.

[4] The Defamation Act 1952, which modifed the common law rules in certain respects, does not affect the law relating to *criminal* libel: see s. 17 (2).

[5] *R.* v. *Holbrook* (1878) 4 Q.B.D. at p. 46.

[6] Libel Act 1843, s. 5.

[7] *Ibid.,* s. 4. A person who is indicted under s. 4 may, if knowledge is not proved, be convicted under s. 5: *Boaler* v. *R.* (1888) 21 Q.B.D. 284.

[8] The term " newspaper " is defined by s. 1 of the Newspaper Libel and Registration Act 1881.

It has been held that one spouse cannot take criminal proceedings against the other for a defamatory libel,[9] but it is submitted that, in view of section 30 (2) of the Theft Act 1968, this is no longer the case.

As a general rule, all libels are both civil wrongs and also indictable offences. Since, however, the essence of the criminal offence is the danger to the public peace, criminal proceedings may possibly not lie,[10] and certainly ought not to be brought,[11] for a libel which, although actionable, was of such a character or published in such circumstances that it could not endanger the public peace, and in such a case a jury might be entitled to acquit the defendant, although he would have no defence in a civil action.[12] Conversely, and for the same reason, criminal proceedings are possible in some classes of cases in which no action could be brought, e.g.:

(1) Libels on deceased persons, intended to injure or provoke their families.[13]
(2) Libels tending to degrade and defame persons in situations of power and dignity in foreign countries, as likely to interrupt pacific relations with such countries.[14]
(3) Libels against a body or class of individuals tending to excite hatred against them.[15]
(4) Libels published only to the prosecutor.[16]
(5) Libels which are true (unless for the public benefit).

In an ordinary prosecution for libel **the prosecutor must prove:**

(1) The publication of the libel. The essence of the offence being its tendency to cause a breach of the peace, it is sufficient if the libel is published to the prosecutor; it is *not necessary,* as it is in civil proceedings for damages, *to prove publication to a third person.*[17] Nor is it necessary, in order to constitute a publication, that the libel should have in fact reached the prosecutor.[18]

---

[9] *R.* v. *Lord Mayor of London* (1886) 16 Q.B.D. 772.
[10] See *Wood* v. *Cox* (1888) 4 T.L.R. at p. 654.
[11] *R.* v. *Wicks* (1936) 25 Cr.App.R. 168.   [12] *Ibid.* at p. 172.
[13] 1 Hawk. c. 73, s. 1; Arch. para. 3631. But see *R.* v. *Labouchere* (1884) 12 Q.B.D. at p. 324, where it was said that there must be some very unusual publication to justify an indictment for aspersing the character of the dead.
[14] Arch. para. 3631; *R.* v. *Peltier* (1803) 28 St.Tr. 529.
[15] *R.* v. *Gathercole* (1838) 2 Lew.C.C. 237; *R.* v. *Williams* (1822) 5 B. & Ald. 595; see also *Le Fanu* v. *Malcolmson* (1848) 1 H.L.C. 637.
[16] See *infra* n. 17.   [17] *Clutterbuck* v. *Chaffers* (1816) 1 Stark. 471.
[18] *R.* v. *Adams* (1888) 22 Q.B.D. 66; *R.* v. *Burdett* (1820) 4 B. & Ald. 95.

(2) **That it refers to himself,** *i.e.*: "That the words published, whether by name, nickname, or description, are such as reasonably to lead persons acquainted with . . . [him] to believe that he is the person to whom the libel refers." [19]

(3) **The libellous character of the publication.** The matter which is charged to be libellous must be " calculated to provoke a breach of the peace " by casting upon the prosecutor an injurious imputation.[20] But, except perhaps in trivial cases, it is not necessary for the prosecution to adduce any evidence of circumstances by reason of which the imputation was in fact likely to provoke a breach of the peace.[21]

By **Fox's Libel Act 1792** it is provided that in all criminal proceedings for libel the jury may give a general verdict of guilty or not guilty upon the whole matter put in issue. Before this Act it was held that the question of libel or no libel was a question of law for the court, and that only the questions of fact were for the jury. But the Act does not prevent the judge from directing the jury to *acquit* if the case fails in law because the words are not capable of any defamatory meaning. Accordingly, " if the defendant can get either the court or the jury to be in his favour he succeeds. The prosecutor . . . cannot succeed unless he gets both the court and the jury to decide for him." [22]

Falsity. The falsity of the libel is immaterial except where the charge is of publication with knowledge of its untruth [23] or where justification is pleaded.[24]

The required mental element. It is not clear whether in criminal libel the accused's reference to the prosecutor must have been either intentional or reckless or whether, alternatively, the offence is one of strict liability.[25] Strictly, criminal libel, being a common law offence, should require either intention or recklessness,[26] but there

---

[19] *Jones* v. *Hulton* [1909] 2 K.B. at p. 477; affirmed [1910] A.C. 20; see also *Le Fanu* v. *Malcolmson* (1848) 1 H.L.C. 637.

[20] *R.* v. *Adams* (1888) 22 Q.B.D. 66; *Monson* v. *Tussaud's Ltd.* [1894] 1 Q.B. 671.

[21] *R.* v. *Wicks* (1936) 25 Cr.App.R. 168.

[22] *Capital and Counties Bank* v. *Henty* (1882) 7 App.Cas. 741 at p. 776.

[23] *Ante*, p. 207.

[24] *Post*, p. 210.

[25] As to the position in civil law, see *Street on Torts*, 5th ed. p. 298.

[26] *Ante*, p. 33. But it is worth noting that also contrary to general principles criminal libel can, at common law, be committed vicariously: see *post*, p. 210.

is some authority for saying that this is not necessary.[27]   In those cases where qualified privilege attaches to a publication, the prosecution may still succeed if it can be proved that the publication was in reality actuated by " *express* malice " or " malice in fact "; that is to say, that the occasion was used not for the purposes which render the publication lawful, but for the gratification of ill-will or some improper motive.[28]

Defence. The defendant may prove:

(1) That the publication was on a privileged occasion.[29]

(2) That the matter was a " fair comment " on a matter of public interest.[30]

(3) That the publication was accidental or without his authority or knowledge.

(4) That the libel is true, and that its publication was for the public benefit.

The first three defences may be proved under the plea of not guilty, but the defence of justification must be specially pleaded.

Accidental or unauthorised, etc., publication. The accused may escape liability if he is able to show that the publication was accidental,[31] or made without his authority or knowledge.

---

[27] *R.* v. *Munslow* [1895] 1 Q.B. 758.

[28] *Royal Aquarium* v. *Parkinson* [1892] 1 Q.B. 431; *Wright* v. *Woodgate* (1835) 2 C.M. & R. 573.

[29] Privilege may be absolute or qualified. In the first case the existence of *express malice* is immaterial; see *Royal Aquarium* v. *Parkinson* (*ubi supra*); in the second case the privilege is lost if the publication was actuated by any malice in fact. Absolute privilege attaches to *e.g.* statements made in the course of judicial proceedings, whereas qualified privilege attaches to *e.g.* confidential communications between solicitors and clients made while that relationship is in existence or in contemplation and for the purpose of getting or giving professional advice: *More* v. *Weaver* [1928] 2 K.B. 520. Some doubts have, however, been expressed in the House of Lords as to whether this privilege is absolute or qualified. See *Minter* v. *Priest* [1930] A.C. 558.

[30] The defence of " fair comment " is that the matter complained of is a fair and bona fide *criticism on a matter of public interest.* That is (i) that the matter commented upon was of public interest; (ii) that the publication is criticism, *i.e.* an expression of *opinion* on existing *facts* which are truly stated: *Davis* v. *Shepstone* (1886) 11 App.Cas. 187 at p. 190; (iii) that the criticism is " fair comment." This does not, of course, mean that the comment must be a *correct* criticism but that the mode of expression must be fair and the opinion honestly held: *Merivale* v. *Carson* (1887) 20 Q.B.D. 275 at p. 281. But " proof of malice may take a criticism prima facie fair outside the right of fair comment, just as it takes a communication prima facie privileged outside the privilege ": *Thomas* v. *Bradbury, Agnew & Co.* [1906] 2 K.B. 627 at p. 640.

[31] *R.* v. *Munslow* [1895] 1 Q.B. at p. 765.

A person, such as a newsvendor or bookseller, who is not the first or main publisher but takes a subordinate part in disseminating a libel is not responsible if he did not know that it contained a libel and his ignorance was not due to negligence.[32] Contrary to the ordinary rule by which a man is criminally responsible only for his own acts, the proprietor of a newspaper was criminally liable for the publication of libels by his servants.[33] But by **section 7** of the **Libel Act 1843,** whenever on the trial of an indictment or information for libel evidence has been given which establishes a presumptive case of publication against the defendant by the act of any other person by his authority, the defendant may prove that the publication was made without his authority, consent or knowledge, and did not arise from want of care on his part.

Justification.   By **section 6** of the **Libel Act 1843** it is a defence to criminal proceedings for defamatory libel that the libel is *true and that it was for the public benefit that it should be published.* This defence must be specially pleaded in writing, and cannot be set up in cases of blasphemous, seditious or obscene libel.

Evidence of the truth of a libel can be given only at the trial and not in proceedings before magistrates except:

(i) Under **section 4** of the **Newspaper Libel and Registration Act 1881,** which provides that, on the hearing of a charge against a publisher, proprietor or editor or person responsible for the publication of a newspaper for a libel published therein, a court of summary jurisdiction may receive evidence of any matters of defence, including evidence of its truth, and that its publication was for the public benefit, and if of opinion that a jury would probably acquit it may dismiss the charge.

And, under **section 5** of the Act, if on the hearing of such a charge a court of summary jurisdiction is of opinion that, although the person charged is shown to have been guilty, the libel was of a trivial character and may be adequately punished under the section, it may, with the

---

[32] *Emmens* v. *Pottle* (1885) 16 Q.B.D. 354; *Vizetelly* v. *Mudie's Library* [1900] 2 Q.B. 170.
[33] *R.* v. *Holbrook* (1878) 4 Q.B.D. at p. 47.

consent of the accused, deal summarily with the charge and inflict a fine not exceeding £50.[34]

(ii) Where the charge is under **section 4** of the **Libel Act 1843,** a magistrate may receive evidence of the truth with a view to committing the accused for trial under section 5.[35]

SECTION 7. INCITEMENT TO RACIAL HATRED

At common law incitement to racial hatred can constitute sedition [36] or criminal libel.[37] If the incitement takes place in public, then an offence against the Public Order Act 1936, may be committed if a breach of the peace is likely.[38]

Section 6 of the Race Relations Act 1965 [39] provides that a person shall be guilty of an offence [40] punishable either on **summary conviction** [*Imp.* 6 *months and* £200 *fine*] or on **indictment** [*Imp.* 2 *years and* £1,000 *fine*] if, with intent to stir up hatred against any section of the public [40a] in Great Britain distinguished by colour, race, or ethnic or national origins—

(a) he publishes or distributes written matter [41] which is threatening, abusive or insulting; or

(b) he uses in any public place or any public meeting [42] words which are threatening, abusive or insulting,

being matter or words likely to stir up hatred against that section on grounds of colour, race, or ethnic or national origins. No prosecution may be instituted except with the consent of the Attorney-General.[43]

[34] But in view of s. 8 of the Law of Libel Amendment Act 1888, *ante*, p. 207, these sections are of little practical importance : see Arch. para. 3625.

[35] *R.* v. *Carden* (1879) 5 Q.B.D. 1.

[36] *Ante*, p. 131.

[37] *Ante*, p. 206.

[38] *Ante*, p. 195.

[39] Discussed in " Racial Incitement and Public Order " [1966] Crim.L.R. 320 and the article by A. Dickey at [1968] Crim.L.R. 489 ; and S. M. Partington at [1967] Crim.L.R. 497. See also the Race Relations Act 1968.

[40] In all probability, s. 6 creates no civil rights whatever; even if it does, they reside in the Attorney-General only : *Thorne* v. *B.B.C.* [1967] 1 W.L.R. 1104.

[40a] Members of an association may be a section of the public : *R.* v. *Britton* [1967] 2 Q.B. 51, 55 ; *Race Relations Board* v. *Charter and Others* [1972] 1 Q.B. 545 at p. 555.

[41] The expression " written matter " includes any writing, sign or visible representation : s. 6 (2).

[42] These words have the same meaning as in the Public Order Act 1936, as substituted by the Criminal Justice Act 1972 (*ante*, p. 196): s. 6 (2).

[43] s. 6 (3). It was said in Parliament on a number of occasions that the offence would only be used in extreme cases (D. G. T. Williams, *op. cit.*, p. 325).

The expression "national" in national origins means national in the sense of race and not citizenship.[44] The expressions "publish" and "distribute" mean publish or distribute to the public at large or to any section of the public not consisting exclusively of members of an association of which the person publishing or distributing is a member.[45] It has been held that to leave a pamphlet at the house of a Member of Parliament in order to persuade him to change his policy on racial matters did not, in itself, constitute a distribution to the public at large or any section of the public.[46]

Section 5 of the **Theatres Act 1968** provides that a person shall be guilty of an offence punishable either on **summary conviction** [*Imp. 6 months and £200 fine*] or on **indictment** [*Imp. 2 years and £1,000 fine*] if, with intent to stir up hatred against any section of the public in Great Britain distinguished by colour, race, or ethnic or national origins, he presents or directs, whether for gain or not, a public performance of a play[47] involving the use of threatening, abusive or insulting words[48] and that performance, taken as a whole, is likely to stir up hatred against that section on grounds of colour, race, or ethnic or national origins.

Proceedings may not be instituted in England and Wales without the consent of the Attorney-General.

SECTION 8. BLASPHEMY

Blasphemy is a common law offence, punishable by *fine and imprisonment*.[48a] It consists in the irreverent denial or ridicule of the *Christian* religion, or contumelious reproaches of Jesus Christ, or scurrilous and profane scoffing at the Holy Scriptures or exposing any part thereof to hatred and ridicule.[49] If published in writing it constitutes a **blasphemous libel.** Attacks on other religions are not blasphemy[50]; nor is the mere denial of the Christian religion or the

---

44 *Ealing London Borough Council* v. *Race Relations Board* [1972] 2 W.L.R. 71.
45 s. 6 (2).
46 *R.* v. *Britton* [1967] 2 Q.B. 51.
47 s. 5 does not apply in relation to those performances exempted under s. 7 of the Act.
48 " Words " includes pictures, images, gestures and other methods of signifying meaning: s. 4 (3).
48a See p. 201, *ante*, n. 59.
49 See *R.* v. *Bradlaugh* (1883) 15 Cox 217; *R.* v. *Ramsay and Foote, ibid.,* 231; *Bowman* v. *Secular Society Ltd.* [1917] A.C. 406 (reviewing the authorities).
50 *R.* v. *Gathercole* (1838) 2 Lew. 237.

propagation of doctrines hostile to the Christian faith; the gist of the offence is the use of ribald language calculated to deprave public morality and to endanger the peace.[51] Accordingly, publications discussing with decency and gravity questions as to Christian doctrine or statements in the Hebrew Scriptures, and even questioning their truth, are not punishable as blasphemy; but publications which in an indecent and malicious spirit assail and asperse the truth of Christianity, or of the Scriptures, in language calculated and intended to shock the feelings and outrage the belief of mankind are punishable as blasphemous libels.[52]

If the decencies of controversy are observed, even the fundamentals of religion may be attacked without a person being guilty of blasphemy.[53] But the limits of decent controversy would be passed if the circumstances in which words were published were such that their publication was likely to lead to a breach of the peace.[54]

No prosecution can be commenced against any proprietor, etc., of a newspaper for any blasphemous libel contained therein, without the order of a judge in chambers.[55]

SECTION 9. OBSTRUCTING PUBLIC WORSHIP

To strike any person in a church or churchyard is a common law offence.[56] The offences of brawling and obstructing, etc., the celebration of divine service, etc., are also punishable by various statutes,[57] of which the following are the most important.

By **section 2** of the **Ecclesiastical Courts Jurisdiction Act 1860,** the offence of brawling, *i.e.* of riotous, violent or indecent behaviour in places of Worship of the Church of England, or certified under the Places of Worship Registration Act 1855, whether during the celebration of divine service or at any other time, or in any churchyard or burial ground, or disturbing any clergyman or minister authorised to minister therein, is punishable on **summary conviction** [*Fine £20* [58] *and Imp. 2 months*].

---

[51] *Bowman* v. *Secular Society* (*supra*).
[52] *R.* v. *Bradlaugh* (*ubi supra*).
[53] *R.* v. *Ramsay and Foote* (1883) 15 Cox at p. 238.
[54] *R.* v. *Gott*, 16 Cr.App.R. 87.
[55] Law of Libel Amendment Act 1888, s. 8.
[56] Arch. para. 3411.
[57] For these statutes see Arch. paras. 3412–3416.
[58] The fine was increased by the Criminal Justice Act 1967, Sched. 3.

If a person is in fact guilty of riotous, violent or indecent behaviour in church, it is no defence to a charge against him under the Act for him to allege that he was setting up a claim of right which he thought he had.[59] The offence may be committed by a clergyman who acts in such a manner in the churchyard of his own parish church.[60]

By **section 36** of the **Offences against the Person Act 1861,** it is an offence [*Imp. 2 years*] for anyone, by threats or force, to obstruct or prevent, or endeavour to obstruct or prevent, any clergyman or other minister in or from celebrating divine service or otherwise officiating in any church, chapel or other place of divine worship, or in or from the performance of his duty in the lawful burial of the dead in any churchyard or other place, or to strike or offer violence to any clergyman, etc., who is engaged in, or to the knowledge of the offender is about to perform, any such rites or going to or returning from the performance thereof.

By **section 7** of the **Burial Laws Amendment Act 1880,** any person who, in any churchyard in which parishioners have a right of burial, delivers any address not being part of or incidental to a religious service permitted by the Act or otherwise permitted by any lawful authority, or who in any such place wilfully endeavours to bring into contempt the Christian religion or the belief or worship of the members or minister of any church or denomination of Christians or any other person, or is guilty of any riotous, violent or indecent behaviour at any burial under the Act, or wilfully obstructs such a burial or a burial service, is guilty of an offence.

---

59 *Asher* v. *Calcraft* (1887) 18 Q.B.D. 607; *Kensit* v. *St. Paul's (Dean and Chapter)* [1905] 2 K.B. 249.
60 *Vallancy* v. *Fletcher* [1897] 1 Q.B. 265.

CHAPTER 17

OFFENCES AGAINST PUBLIC ORDER

SECTION 1. PUBLIC NUISANCES

THIS section and the following five sections are concerned with what are commonly called public nuisances. A number of activities which constitute a public nuisance at common law are now either alternatively or exclusively penalised by statute. Each of the following sections will examine a particular kind of nuisance and this section will merely give an introduction to public nuisances in general.

A nuisance may be either public or private. A **private** nuisance is the subject only of civil proceedings.[1] A **public** nuisance constitutes both a civil wrong[2] and at common law an offence [*Fine and Imp.*[3]]. A private nuisance is one which affects a particular individual (or individuals) in the enjoyment of his land. A public nuisance is one which affects the public or a considerable portion[4] of the public, but not necessarily in their enjoyment of their land. It follows that the same activity may (but will not necessarily) constitute a private and public nuisance at the same time.

No length of time can authorise a public nuisance,[5] though a prescriptive right may be acquired to do some act amounting to a private nuisance.[6]

A statute may authorise a nuisance, but the mere fact that a statute gives permission or power to do a certain act does not necessarily take away the liability for any nuisance created thereby. Thus the fact that a canal company is empowered by a special Act to make a canal and supply it with water from certain streams does not exempt it from the liability for nuisance caused by the

---

[1] See generally Salmond, p. 83 *et seq.*
[2] The right of an individual to sue in respect of a public nuisance is limited.
[3] See note 59 on p. 201.
[4] If a nuisance affects only a few individuals, it will not constitute a public nuisance: *R.* v. *Lloyd* (1803) 4 Esp. 200.
[5] *Dewell* v. *Sanders* (1619) Cro.Jac. 490.
[6] See *Sturges* v. *Bridgman* (1879) 11 Ch.D. 852, applied in *Davies* v. *Du Paver* [1953] 1 Q.B. 184.

polluted condition of the water so taken.[7] So also locomotives
cannot be used on highways unless they conform to certain regulations, but they nonetheless may be a public nuisance though there
has been conformity with such regulations.[8] To create immunity
from liability it must be shown that either the statute expressly
authorises or directs the nuisance or that the use of the powers given
by the statute, in the manner contemplated and sanctioned by the
statute, " necessarily involves the creation of what would otherwise
be a nuisance at common law." [9] Thus where a statute gave a
company authority to construct a railway by the side of a highway
and to use locomotives on the railway, it was *held* that, the
authority being absolute and unqualified the company could not
be indicted for a nuisance because the use of the railway, in the
manner contemplated by the Act, frightened horses upon the
highway.[10]

Section 2. Highway Obstruction

Common law. The obstruction [11] of any highway constitutes a
public nuisance,[12] and the obstruction itself can be removed if there
is no other reasonable method of passing by it.[13] A highway is any
way along which the public generally has a right to pass, whether
path, road, river,[14] or bridge.

A person may be responsible whether he himself obstructs the
highway or whether he attracts such crowds that they obstruct
the highway. A trader, therefore, who blocks the way with his
stall or with lorries [15] or by attracting crowds [16] may commit
nuisance.

---

[7] *R.* v. *Bradford Navigation Co.* (1865) 6 B. & S. 631.
[8] *Att.-Gen.* v. *Scott* [1904] 1 K.B. at p. 408.
[9] *London, Brighton and South Coast Ry.* v. *Truman* (1885) 11 App.Cas. at p. 50.
See also *Metropolitan Asylum District* v. *Hill* (1881) 6 App.Cas. 193; *Canadian
Pacific Ry.* v. *Parke* [1899] A.C. 535.
[10] *R.* v. *Pease* (1832) 4 B. & Ad. 30.
[11] *Non-repair* of a highway no longer constitutes a public nuisance: s. 59 (1) of
the Highways Act 1959. Ss. 59–61 as amended by the Courts Act 1971, Sched.
11, provide a special procedure for enforcing a liability to maintain highways.
[12] See *Trevitt* v. *Lee* [1955] 1 W.L.R. 113 at p. 117; *Dymond* v. *Pearce* [1972]
1 Q.B. 496. As to evidence in such proceedings see the Evidence Act 1877,
s. 1, as amended by the Highways Act 1959, Sched. 25.
[13] *Dimes* v. *Petley* (1850) 15 Q.B. 276; Russell, p. 1391.
[14] *Att.-Gen.* v. *Terry* (1874) L.R. 9 Ch. 423; *Orr Ewing* v. *Colquhoun* (1877)
2 App.Cas. 839.
[15] See *R.* v. *Russell* (1805) 6 East 427; *R.* v. *Jones* (1812) 3 Camp. 230.
[16] *R.* v. *Carlile* (1834) 6 C. & P. 636; *R.* v. *Moore* (1832) 3 B. & Ad. 184.

But no obstruction can constitute nuisance unless it " appreci-ably " prevents free passage.[17] Thus a stall *may* be erected in such a way [18] or a public meeting *may* be held in such a way that no nuisance is committed.[19]

Even if the obstruction is " appreciable " it will not necessarily constitute a nuisance if the inconvenience is not unreasonable in extent or prolonged for an unreasonable time.[20] This would apply, for example, to the use of a pavement coal-hole, the erection of scaffolding for repairs,[21] the formation of a queue,[22] parking for the purposes of loading and unloading,[23] or to processions.[24] *Prima facie*, however, sitting down in the highway is an unreasonable obstruction [25] as is leaving a car standing in a street; or a person standing on the pavement.

Finally, it has been held that to park in a designated parking area cannot constitute an obstruction.[26]

Statute. By **section 121** of the **Highways Act 1959**, it is an offence punishable on **summary conviction** [£50 [27] *fine*] for any person without lawful authority or excuse wilfully to obstruct free passage along a highway.[28] The accused must apparently intend to cause an obstruction [29] but the fact that he thought he had a right to do so is irrelevant.[30] The question depends on whether the occasioning of the obstruction was reasonable, *i.e.* did the person causing it have lawful excuse.[31] Under the Motor Vehicle (Con-struction and Use) Regulations 1969 [31a] the Queen's Bench Division held that leaving a car for a reasonable time, although an obstruc-

---

[17] *R.* v. *Bartholomew* [1908] 1 K.B. 554, and the authorities there cited.
[18] *Ibid.*
[19] *Burden* v. *Rigler* [1911] 1 K.B. 337.
[20] See *Nagy* v. *Weston* [1965] 1 W.L.R. 280, and the cases cited in the following three footnotes.
[21] *R.* v. *Jones* (1812) 3 Camp. 230.
[22] *Dwyer* v. *Mansfield* [1946] K.B. 437; *cf. Fabbri* v. *Morris* [1947] 1 All E.R. 315.
[23] *R.* v. *Jones* (1812) 3 Camp. 230; *R.* v. *Clark* [1964] 2 Q.B. at p. 321.
[24] *R.* v. *Clark* [1964] 2 Q.B. 315.
[25] *R.* v. *Moule* [1964] Crim.L.R. 303.
[26] *Anderson* v. *Hargreaves* [1962] 1 Q.B. 425.
[27] The fine was increased by the Criminal Justice Act 1967, Sched. 3.
[28] See also to similar effect Town Police Clauses Act 1847, s. 28 (of limited application).
[29] *Eaton* v. *Cobb* [1950] 1 All E.R. 1016.
[30] *Arrowsmith* v. *Jenkins* [1963] 2 Q.B. 561.
[31] *Scarfe* v. *Wood and Another* [1969] Crim.L.R. 265.
[31a] As amended.

tion was not an unnecessary obstruction within the meaning of the Regulations. It was for the justices to decide whether the duration of the parking was reasonable.[32] A constable may arrest without a warrant any person whom he sees committing an offence against this section.[33]

It is also an offence punishable on **summary conviction** [£20 *fine*] for any person to cause or permit any motor-vehicle or trailer of which he is in charge to cause any unnecessary[34] obstruction.[35]

As far as both these offences are concerned the term " obstruction " has the same meaning as in common law nuisance.[36]

Other sections of the **Highways Acts 1959 and 1971,** penalise a variety of other obstructions. In particular, by **section 127** of the 1959 Act, it is an offence punishable on **summary conviction** [£50[37] *fine*] without lawful authority or excuse: (i) for any person to deposit on certain specified highways any dung or rubbish, or to deposit, on any highway, anything whatsoever to the interruption of any user of the highway, and (ii) for any hawker or other itinerant trader or gipsy to pitch his booth or camp, etc., on any highway. By **section 129**[38] a duty is imposed upon highway authorities to remove from a highway any obstruction caused by snow, soil or arising from any other cause, either from time to time or after an order to that effect made by a magistrates' court upon a complaint made by any person.[39] Failure to comply with this section is punishable on **summary conviction** [£5 *fine*]. Other offences of obstruction in relation to builders' skips are created by the **Highways Act 1971;** it is an offence punishable on **summary conviction** [£100 *fine*] to deposit a skip on a highway without permission[40]; or not to comply with the conditions of permission granted[41]; or to fail to remove or to reposition a skip [£50] when required to do so.[42]

---

[32] *Evans* v. *Baker* [1972] Crim.L.R. 53. [33] Highways Act 1959, s. 121.
[34] The precise meaning of this word has not, apparently, been defined: see *Police* v. *O'Connor* [1957] Crim.L.R. 478.
[35] Motor Vehicles (Construction and Use) Regulations 1969 (S.I. 1969, No. 321), reg. 95. [36] See *R.* v. *Clark* [1964] 2 Q.B. at p. 320.
[37] See n. 27 above.
[38] As substituted by the Highways (Amendment) Act 1965.
[39] The court may require the authority to remove the obstruction within such period (not being less than 24 hours) from the making of the order as the court thinks reasonable, having regard to all the circumstances of the case.
[40] s. 31 (3).
[41] s. 31 (4). [42] s. 32 (8).

SECTION 3. ACTS ENDANGERING PUBLIC SAFETY

Common law. Acts endangering the safety of the public or any appreciable portion of the public are common law nuisances. For example:

   (i) Allowing a house near a highway to be ruinous [43] or an excavation near a highway to be unfenced.[44]

  (ii) Keeping a fierce and unruly bull in a field crossed by a public footway or keeping a ferocious dog in public unmuzzled.[45]

 (iii) Blasting stone in a quarry so as to throw stones on adjoining houses and highways.[46]

 (iv) Carrying on the manufacture of arsenic so as to poison cattle in adjoining fields by particles of arsenic falling from a vapour produced in the manufacture.[47]

  (v) Unlawfully bringing a person suffering from an infectious disease into a public thoroughfare to the danger of the public,[48] or removing him to a place where the public would be exposed to infection, or maintaining a hospital in such a way as to endanger health.[49]

 (vi) Supplying, exposing for sale, or possessing with intent to sell, food unfit for consumption.[50]

(vii) Keeping explosives or other inflammable articles in circumstances which cause public danger.[51]

Statute. **Part V** of the **Public Health Act 1936,** as amended by the **Public Health Act 1961,** has numerous provisions for preventing the spread of certain specified diseases. In particular it is an offence punishable on **summary conviction** [£10 *fine*] for any person, knowing that he or someone within his care is suffering from one of these diseases, to expose other persons to the risk of infection by his presence or the presence of the person within his

---

[43] *R.* v. *Watts* (1704) 1 Salk. 357.
[44] *Barnes* v. *Ward* (1850) 9 C.B. 392.
[45] Arch. para. 3831.
[46] *R.* v. *Mutters* (1864) L. & C. 491.
[47] *R.* v. *Garland* (1851) 5 Cox 165.
[48] *R.* v. *Vandtandillo* (1815) 4 M. & S. 73.
[49] *Metropolitan Asylum District* v. *Hill* (1881) 6 App.Cas. 193.
[50] *Shillito* v. *Thompson* (1875) 1 Q.B.D. 12; *R.* v. *Dixon* (1814) 3 M. & S. 11. Also summarily punishable under the Food and Drugs Act 1955 (*post,* p. 387).
[51] *R.* v. *Lister* (1856) D. & B. 209.

care in any public place, shop, etc.[52] Other provisions are designed to prevent (i) a person in this condition carrying on certain occupations and (ii) the spread of infection via, for example, laundries, libraries, public conveyances and accommodation.[53]

The manufacturing, keeping, selling and importing of gunpowder, nitro-glycerine, and other explosive substances, are regulated by the **Explosives Acts 1875** and **1923,** which contain a number of provisions enforceable by forfeitures, fines and imprisonment.[54] The Acts do not affect any common law liability for nuisance. The Explosives Act 1875 forbids the sale of gunpowder and explosives (including fireworks) to any child apparently under the age of 13[55] and also forbids the throwing or lighting of fireworks in any highway, street or public place[56] **[summary conviction—£20** *fine].*[57]

By the **Petroleum (Consolidation) Act 1928** the keeping of petroleum spirit is governed by numerous regulations, the breach of which is, as a rule, punishable on **summary conviction.** However, failure to give notice on entering a harbour that a ship is carrying petroleum spirit is punishable by **section 8 [Indictment:** *Fine of* £500; **summary conviction:** *Fine of* £100].[58]

By the **Atomic Energy and Radioactive Substances Acts of 1946–1960** the sale and use of radioactive substances and the accumulation and disposal of radioactive waste are regulated. In particular, failure to register premises on which radioactive substances are being used or kept and failure to register mobile radioactive apparatus is punishable on **indictment** [*Imp. 5 years and fine*] or on **summary conviction** [*Imp. 3 months and* £100 *fine*].[59] Under the **Nuclear Installations Act 1965**[60] it is an offence to fail to license or insure nuclear installations.

---

[52] s. 148. The fine was increased by the Criminal Justice Act 1967, Sched. 3.
[53] ss. 152–159.
[54] The Emergency Laws (Miscellaneous Provisions) Act 1953, s. 3, empowers the Secretary of State by order to extend the statutory control; failure to comply with the order is punishable on *summary conviction* by 3 months' *imprisonment* and *fine* of £50. The control of Explosives Order 1953 (S.I. No. 1598), provides that, subject to certain exceptions, a person shall not acquire gunpowder or safety-fuse unless licensed by the chief officer of police.
[55] ss. 3, 31, 39.
[56] s. 80.
[57] ss. 31, 80. The fine was increased by the Criminal Justice Act 1967, Sched. 3.
[58] The latter was raised from £50 by the Criminal Justice Act 1967, Sched. 3.
[59] Radioactive Substances Act 1960, ss. 1, 3, 13.
[60] As amended by the Nuclear Installations Act 1969 and the Atomic Energy Authority Act 1971.

Section 11 of the **Civil Aviation Act 1949** provides that where an aircraft is flown in such a manner as to be the cause of unnecessary danger to any person or property on land or water, the pilot or the person in charge of the aircraft, and also the owner thereof, unless he proves to the satisfaction of the court that the aircraft was so flown without his actual fault or privity, are punishable on **summary conviction** [£200 *fine and Imp. 6 months*].[61]

Dangerous driving on the highway is dealt with later.[62]

A number of Acts and by-laws have provisions designed to prevent the public from being injured in places of entertainment,[63] *e.g.* cinemas,[64] fairs,[65] platforms and balconies used on public occasions.[66]

Finally, **section 28** of the **Town Police Clauses Act 1847**[67] punishes on **summary conviction** [£20[68] *fine*], among other things a failure to fence or light cellar flaps and coal-holes in streets, the throwing or lighting of fireworks in streets and the lighting of bonfires in streets.

SECTION 4. ACTS INJURIOUS TO PUBLIC COMFORT, HEALTH AND ENJOYMENT

Common law. A public nuisance may be caused by any noise, vibration, stench or effluvia which creates serious public discomfort or injury to health.[69] This form of nuisance is usually prevented by civil action but it may also (or sometimes only) constitute a criminal offence.

" The time during which the business has been carried on or the reasonableness of the steps taken to avoid noise or smell [etc.] do not afford any criterion for deciding whether the trade is or is

---

[61] The expression " owner " in relation to an aircraft includes any person by whom the aircraft is hired at the time of the offence: s. 11 (2). The Act does not apply to aircraft belonging to or exclusively employed in the service of Her Majesty: *ibid.*, s. 61.

[62] *Post*, p. 297.

[63] The Fire Precautions Act 1971 strengthens and rationalises the law relating to fire precautions in places of public entertainment and resort, and in certain kinds of residential premises. Most of the Act came into force at March 20, 1972. See p. 410, *post*.

[64] Cinematograph Act 1952, s. 2, as amended by the Courts Act 1971, Sched. 11.

[65] Public Health Act 1961, s. 75.

[66] Public Health Acts (Amendment) Act 1890, s. 37.

[67] As amended, this Act is only of limited application.

[68] The fine was increased by the Criminal Justice Act 1967, Sched. 3.

[69] Russell, pp. 1404–1405.

not a public nuisance."[70] Nor, likewise, does it affect the issue
that the complainant came to the nuisance and not vice versa.[71]
However, a person who lives in a town or industrial area cannot
expect the peace, quiet and pure air of the countryside, although
an excess of smoke, smell or noise will constitute a nuisance:
" in each of such cases it becomes a question of degree." [72]

Statute. Various nuisances of the kind being dealt with in this
section are also punishable by numerous statutes and by-laws.
Many of these are taking on a new significance in view of the
growing awareness of the dangers from pollution to the environment. This growing awareness has increased the numbers of
statutes imposing criminal sanctions. Only a few can be mentioned.

Section 92 of the **Public Health Act 1936** [73] declares the following
(among others) to be " statutory nuisances ": any premises, animals,
accumulations, deposits, dust or effluvia, which either are, or are
kept in such a manner or place as to be, prejudicial to health or a
nuisance. The local authority may serve an " abatement notice "
on the person responsible for a statutory nuisance [74] and if this is
disregarded may complain to a justice of the peace, who may make
a " nuisance order " requiring the person to prevent the nuisance
and also fine him £20.[75] Alternatively, a complaint may be made
directly to a justice by any person aggrieved by the nuisance, and
the same procedure then applies as if the local authority had made
the complaint.[76] If, in either case, the nuisance order is disregarded,
then the person responsible may be fined £50 and a further £5
for each day on which the offence continues after conviction
therefor.[77]

Nuisances caused by certain kinds of smoke and by noise and
vibration have also been made " statutory nuisances " within the

---

[70] *Ibid.*, p. 1407, relying on *Att.-Gen.* v. *Cole and Sons* [1901] 1 Ch. 205.

[71] *Fleming* v. *Hislop* (1886) 11 App.Cas. at p. 697.

[72] *Colls* v. *Home and Colonial Stores* [1904] A.C. at p. 185; approved in *Polsue and Alfieri* v. *Rushmer* [1907] A.C. at p. 123.

[73] As amended.

[74] See s. 93.

[75] s. 94. The fine was increased by the Criminal Justice Act 1967, Sched. 3; and see the extended powers conferred on local authorities by the Public Health (Recurring Nuisances) Act 1969. As to the nature of this offence, and the procedure applicable to it see *Northern Ireland Trailers Ltd.* v. *Preston Corporation* [1972] 1 W.L.R. 203.

[76] s. 99.

[77] s. 95. The fine was increased by the Criminal Justice Act 1967, Sched. 3. See also the Public Health Act 1936, s. 83.

meaning of the Public Health Act 1936, by, respectively, the **Clean Air Acts 1956 and 1968,** and the **Noise Abatement Act 1960.** Both Acts, however, add further special provisions to the Public Health Act.

In particular **section 2** of the **Noise Abatement Act** makes restrictions on the use on highways of loudspeakers, etc. Loudspeakers are not to be operated on highways between 9 p.m. and 8 a.m. (subject to exceptions in favour of the police, etc.) and not to be operated at any time for the purpose of advertising any entertainment, trade or business [**summary conviction**—£10 *fine*]. An exception, however, is made in favour of loudspeakers operated between noon and 7 p.m. from vehicles selling a perishable commodity for human consumption (for example, ice cream), provided that they are operated so as not to give reasonable cause for annoyance. The loudspeaker must be used solely for informing members of the public (otherwise than by means of words) that the commodity is on sale from the vehicle.[78]

Section 1 (5) of the **Deposit of Poisonous Waste Act 1972** makes it an offence punishable on **summary conviction** [*Imp. 6 months and £400 fine*] or on **indictment** [*Imp. 5 years and fine*] for a person to deposit [78a] waste on land, or to cause or permit waste to be deposited, where the waste is of a kind which is poisonous, noxious or polluting, and its presence on the land is liable to give rise to an environmental hazard.[78b] A defence is provided to a charge of depositing if the defendant proves (i) that he acted under the instructions of his employers, or (ii) that he relied on information given by others (without any reason to suppose that such information was false or misleading) and (iii) in either case, that he neither knew nor had any reason for sup-

---

[78] s. 2 (3).

[78a] A person is treated as depositing waste if he deposits any substance (solid, semi-solid or liquid) in such circumstances, or for such a period that he may reasonably be supposed to have abandoned it where it is deposited or to have brought it to that place for the purpose of its being disposed of (by him or others) as waste: s. 1 (2).

[78b] The presence of waste is treated as giving rise to such a hazard if the waste has been deposited in such quantity (whether by itself or accumulating with other deposits of the same or different substances) as to subject persons or animals to material risk of death, injury or impairment of health, or as to threaten the pollution or contamination (whether on the surface or under the ground) of any water supply; and where waste is deposited in containers, this is not of itself to be taken to exclude any risk which might be expected to arise if the waste was not in containers: s. 1 (3). The degree of risk is assessed in accordance with s. 1 (4).

posing that the waste was of such a kind that it would be an offence to deposit it.[78c]

Under the **Rivers (Prevention of Pollution) Acts 1951 to 1961** it is an offence to cause or knowingly permit to enter a stream any poisonous, noxious or polluting matter; or matter which impedes the proper flow of water in a manner leading or likely to lead to a substantial aggravation of pollution [**summary conviction**—£100 *fine*: **Indictment**—£200 *fine*].[79] This offence is in the nature of a public nuisance and belongs to that class of offences which cannot strictly be described as *criminal* but are rather acts prohibited by statute under a penalty.[79a] The prosecution need not establish knowledge, intention or negligence on the part of the defendant in order to establish that he *caused* such a result.[79b]

The **Prevention of Oil Pollution Act 1971** punishes on **summary conviction** with fines of up to £50,000 offences of discharging certain specified oils into the sea, whether outside territorial waters,[80] in United Kingdom waters[81] or from pipe lines or as the result of exploration[82]; and renders necessary the use of specified equipment and records in ships to prevent oil pollution. The Act also punishes the obstruction of the authorities in dealing with oil from shipping casualties.[83]

Section 1 of the **Litter Act 1958**, as amended by the **Dangerous Litter Act 1971**,[84] makes it an offence punishable on summary conviction [£100 *fine*] to deposit and leave in any place in the open air to which the public are entitled or permitted to have access without payment anything whatsoever in such circumstances as to cause, contribute to, or tend to lead to, its defacement by litter. In sentencing a person convicted under the **Litter Acts 1958 to 1971** the court must have regard not only to the purpose of the Acts

---

[78c] Where the charge is causing or permitting, it is a defence if the defendant proves that he took all such steps as were reasonably open to him to ensure that no offence was committed: s. 1 (6).

[79] Increased penalties are provided for repeated or continued offences. A number of other minor offences arise under these Acts.

[79a] See the judgment of Wright J. in *Sherras* v. *De Rutzen* [1895] 1 Q.B. 918 considered at p. 43, *ante*.

[79b] *Alphacell Ltd.* v. *Woodward* [1972] 2 W.L.R. 1320.

[80] s. 1.

[81] s. 2.

[82] s. 3.

[83] s. 14.

[84] This Act also makes better provision for the abatement of dangerous litter and empowers local authorities to promote the abatement of litter by means of publicity.

in preventing the *defacement* by litter of places in the open air, but also the *nature* of the *litter* and any *resulting risk* (in the circumstances of the offence) of *injury* to *persons* or *animals* or of *damage* to *property*. In order to abate litter a Local Authority may take such steps as it thinks appropriate for bringing the attention of the public of their area to the effect of section 1 of the Acts. The deposit of rubbish, etc., is also punished by section 127 of the Highways Act 1959, which was noted in Section 2 (above [85]).

Section 28 of the **Town Police Clauses Act 1847,**[86] punishes on **summary conviction** [*Imp.* 144 *days or* £20 [87] *fine*] a number of nuisances committed in any *street*. These include, in particular, throwing any dirt, litter, offal or rubbish, or shaking any carpet (except doormats before 8 a.m.), or causing any offensive matter to run from any manufactory, butcher's shop, etc.

In conclusion, mention should also be made of the **Diseases of Animals Act 1950,**[88] and regulations made thereunder, which create a variety of offences designed to prevent the spread of disease among animals.

Section 5. Indecent Exposure

Common law. All open lewdness or whatever outrages decency or is offensive and disgusting [89] is an indictable offence at common law [*Fine and Imp.*].[90] So any public exposure of the naked person [90a] is an indictable nuisance, as, *e.g.* by bathing naked near a public footway or inhabited houses, although there is no exposure beyond what is necessarily incidental to bathing, and although such houses were of recent erection and had been built near a place where as long as living memory extended there had been a usage to bathe.[91] The exposure must be public; indecent exposure to only one person is not a common law offence.[92] But it need not be in a public place

---

[85] *Ante,* p. 219.
[86] This Act is only of limited application
[87] See above, n. 57a. The fine was increased by the Criminal Justice Act 1967, Sched. 3.
[88] As amended by subsequent legislation.
[89] It is not necessary for the prosecution to prove actual disgust or annoyance on the part of the observer: *R.* v. *Mayling* [1963] 2 Q.B. 717 where the older cases are considered.
[90] Russell, p. 1423. As to punishments at common law see note 59 at p. 201.
[90a] As to the statutory offence under the Vagrancy Act 1824, s. 4, and the meaning of " person " thereunder, see p. 241, *post.*
[91] *R.* v. *Crunden* (1809) 2 Camp. 89; *R.* v. *Reed* (1871) 12 Cox 1.
[92] *R.* v. *Webb* (1848) 2 C. & K. 933.

if it is in a place where the public go, whether by right or not, or which can be seen by a number of persons.[93]

Statute. Public exposure of the naked person is punishable **summarily.**[94]

SECTION 6. OBSCENITY

Anything which outrages public decency and is injurious to public morals (as opposed to the decency or morals of a particular individual [95]) is said to be an offence at common law,[96] subject perhaps to the proviso that it must be obscene.[96a] This would include, for example, words, pictures, books, films, exhibitions, plays, signs and effigies. The essence of the offence being the likely injury to public morals it follows that the thing in question must be published or otherwise displayed.[97]

The need to distinguish, for example, between the picture of a nude in a medical textbook and in a salacious magazine inevitably leads to difficulties. To overcome these difficulties, the courts have slowly developed a test for obscenity. In the case of books and most other articles this common law test has been, to a certain extent, superseded by the statutory definition in the Obscene Publications Act 1959 (below) and in relation to plays by the Theatres Act 1968. But the common law test is still of some importance because these Acts do not cover all forms of obscenity. The **Obscene Publications Act 1959** has been held not to alter the law on conspiracy to publish,[98] and the **Theatres Act 1968** prevents the prosecution of an offence at common law of conspiring to corrupt public morals, or of any act contrary to public morals or decency, in respect of an agreement to present or give the performance of a play, or to cause anything to be said or done in the course of such a performance.

---

[93] *R.* v. *Wellard* (1884) 14 Q.B.D. 63; *R.* v. *Thallman* (1863) L. & C. 326.
[94] *Post*, p. 241.
[95] *Shaw* v. *Director of Public Prosecutions* [1962] A.C. at p. 233 (H.L.).
[96] *R.* v. *Wellard* (1884) 14 Q.B.D. at p. 67.
[96a] In *Knuller (Publishing, Printing and Promotions) Ltd.* v. *Director of Public Prosecutions,* [1972] 3 W.L.R. 143, H.L., where the appellants were alleged to have conspired to outrage public decency by inserting lewd, disgusting and offensive advertisements in a magazine, Lord Reid was of opinion that the offence did not extend to a case where it was said that ordinary decent-minded people, who were not likely to be corrupted or depraved, would be outraged or utterly disgusted by what they read.
[97] Arch. para. 3837.
[98] *Post*, p. 232.

What exactly constitutes obscenity *at common law* is far from clear. It can be tentatively suggested that the following rules apply:

(1) The tendency of the matter charged as being obscene must be such as to deprave and corrupt.[99] The precise meaning of these words is not clear.[1] It has been held that obscenity is not confined to sexual matters and that a book about drug-taking can be obscene.[2]

(2) It is not clear whether the accused must have *intended* to deprave and corrupt.[3]

(3) The tendency of the matter must be such as to deprave and corrupt the class of persons who, having regard to the methods of distribution, publication or exhibition, are likely to come into contact with it.[4] For example, the mere fact that an adolescent, if he were to read a particular book, might be corrupted and depraved by it does not necessarily make it obscene at common law.[5] If, however, the book was aimed at or likely to be sold to children, it might well be.

(4) It has been suggested that nowadays, particularly in view of section 4 of the Obscene Publications Act 1959 (below), it is unlikely that serious scientific, medical, historical or religious matter would be regarded as obscene at common law.[6] But again this would depend upon the circumstances of publication, etc. Whereas a picture in an historical book in a library would probably not be regarded as obscene at common law, the same picture peddled in the streets might well be.[7]

(5) It has been said that the purpose of the author is a relevant consideration. Was he being " honest " and following an " honest thread of thought " or not?[8] Although it is difficult to define this suggested rule further, it is presumably designed to distinguish either " good " literature from " bad " or the " honest suggestion,"

---

99 *R.* v. *Hicklin* (1868) L.R. 3 Q.B. at p. 371.
1 But see p. 233, *post.*
2 *John Calder (Publications) Ltd.* v. *Powell* [1965] 1 Q.B. 509.
3 *Cf. Shaw* v. *Director of Public Prosecutions* [1962] A.C. at p. 233 (C.C.A.) and *R.* v. *de Montalk* (1932) 23 Cr.App.R. 182.
4 See Russell, p. 1425; *R.* v. *Hicklin* (1868) L.R. 3 Q.B. 360; *R.* v. *Thomson* (1900) 64 J.P. 456.
5 *R.* v. *Martin Secker and Warburg* [1954] 1 W.L.R. at pp. 1139–1140; *cf R.* v. *Hicklin* (1868) L.R. 3 Q.B. at p. 371.
6 See Russell, pp. 1426–1427, and *R.* v. *Thomson* (1900) 64 J.P. 456.
7 *R.* v. *Thomson* (1900) 64 J.P. 456.
8 *R.* v. *Martin Secker and Warburg* [1954] 1 W.L.R. at p. 1143.

for example, that premarital intercourse might not be wrong, from salacious writing encouraging promiscuity.[9]

Rough and ready as the common law test might be, it does at least *try* to distinguish the serious, honest and good from the pornographic, dishonest and bad. Unfortunately, in *Shaw* v. *Director of Public Prosecutions,* Viscount Simonds [10] put the whole matter into doubt again when he said [11]:

> " Let it be supposed that at some future, perhaps, early, date homosexual practices between adult consenting males are no longer a crime. Would it not be an offence if, *even without obscenity*, such practices were publicly advocated and encouraged by pamphlet and advertisement? " [12]

Viscount Simonds then went on to answer his question in the affirmative. The italicised words are, with respect, disturbing in that they effectively get round both the terms of the Obscene Publications Act 1959 and the common law test, as it is usually stated.

Having examined the general common law principles we now turn to an examination of different kinds of obscenity.

Obscene Plays

Any obscene play or other exhibition to which the public are admitted whether on payment or otherwise, may amount to a public nuisance.[13] Censorship of plays by the Lord Chamberlain was abolished by **section 1** of the **Theatres Act 1968,** and instances of contravention of the laws relating to obscenity are more likely. **Section 2 (4)** of the Act provides that no person shall be proceeded against in respect of the performance of a play [14] or anything said or done in the course of such a performance, (a) for an offence at common law where it is of the essence of the offence that the performance or what was said or done was obscene, indecent, offensive, disgusting or injurious to morality; or (b) for an offence under section 4 of the Vagrancy Act 1824 for wilfully exposing to public view an indecent exhibition; and no person shall be pro-

---

9 To the obvious riposte: " how can you decide?," one can only answer that, if censorship is accepted as necessary, such a decision must be made.
10 With whose judgment Lords Morris of Borth-y-Gest and Hodson agreed.
11 [1962] A.C. 220 at p. 268.
12 Italics added.
13 *R.* v. *Saunders* (1875) 1 Q.B.D. 15.
14 Defined, s. 18 (1).

ceeded against for an offence at common law of conspiring to corrupt public morals or to do any act contrary to public morals or decency, in relation to a play. However, **section 2 (2)** makes it an offence punishable on **summary conviction** [*Imp. 6 months and £400 fine*] or upon **indictment** [*Imp. 3 years and a fine*] to present or direct in public or private an obscene performance of a play (whether for gain or not). A prosecution on indictment shall not be commenced more than two years after the commission of the offence: **section 2 (3).**

The test of obscenity under **section 2 (1)** is that a performance of a play shall be deemed to be obscene if, taken as a whole, its effect is such as to tend to deprave and corrupt persons who are likely, having regard to all the relevant circumstances, to attend it. This test is similar to that contained in section 1 (1) of the Obscene Publications Act 1959.[15]

The defence of public good **(section 3)** [16] is open to a person charged under the Act as it is to a person charged under the Obscene Publications Act 1959,[17] and similar provisions as to the calling of expert witnesses apply [18]; but their opinions are confined to the artistic, literary or other merits of the performance of the play. Plays given on a domestic occasion in a private dwelling are excluded from the section [19] as are performances given solely or primarily for the purposes of rehearsal, or to enable a record or a film to be made, or for the purposes of making a broadcast or a transmission to subscribers to a diffusion service.[20]

Proceedings may not be commenced without the consent of the Attorney-General **(section 8).**

Where the performance of a play was based on a script, then in proceedings under section 2, an actual script on which that performance was based is admissible as evidence of what was performed and of the manner in which the performance was given, or any part of it, and if such a script is given in evidence, then except in so far as the contrary is shown by evidence, the performance is to be taken to have been given in accordance with

---

[15] See p. 233.
[16] On the grounds that the performance was justified in the interests of drama, opera, ballet or any other art, or of literature or learning.
[17] See p. 235, *post.*
[18] See p. 235.
[19] Theatres Act 1968, s. 7.
[20] *Ibid.*; and as to what is meant by solely or primarily for one of those purposes.

the script **(section 9).** A police officer of or above the rank of superintendent may, if he has reasonable grounds for suspecting an offence under section 2 to have been committed, or is likely to be committed, make an order in writing, and signed by him, authorising any police officer to require a person named in the order to produce an actual script on which a performance is based, and if it is produced to require such a person to afford the police officer the opportunity of having a copy made. Failure to comply with the requirements of such an order renders such person liable on **summary conviction** to a fine of £100.

Other Obscene Exhibitions

The display of indecent exhibitions in any street or window situate in any street is punishable summarily under the Vagrancy Act 1824, s. 4.

Obscene Films

The exhibition of obscene films can no doubt constitute a public nuisance at common law. However, as far as most film-shows are concerned this is of no importance in practice because local authorities, in the exercise of their power to license cinematograph exhibitions, impose conditions upon the showing of films both as to their suitability for children and adults.[21] However, private clubs (other than children's clubs) are exempted from the requirement of licensing [22] and an exhibition at such a club might constitute a public nuisance at common law.

The position at common law is not affected by the Obscene Publications Act 1959 (below), which does not apply to exhibitions of films, *other than* exhibitions in private houses to which the public are not admitted. In the case of such private exhibitions the accused would be prosecuted under the Act.[23]

The distribution, selling, letting, etc., of obscene films is now governed by the Obscene Publications Act 1959 [24]; and their importation by the Customs Consolidation Act 1876.[24a]

---

21 Cinematograph Act 1909, s. 2, as amended by the Cinematograph Act 1952, s. 3 and Sched. See further Street, *op. cit.*, p. 68 *et seq.*
22 Act of 1952, s. 5.
23 s. 2 (4).
24 *Ibid.* s. 1 (3).
24a s. 42; see p. 237, *post.*

Obscene Articles

At common law the publication of obscene matter in a permanent form (for example: books, pictures, effigies) constitutes the offence of **obscene libel**—a species of public nuisance. The test for obscenity for such matter is now to be found in the Obscene Publications Act 1959. This Act provides in section 2 (4) that

> " A person publishing an article shall not be proceeded against for an offence at common law consisting of the publication of any matter contained or embodied in the article where it is of the essence of the offence that the matter is obscene."

Although it might be thought that this subsection would effectively dispense with the need to use the common law test for such matters, the House of Lords held in *Shaw* v. *Director of Public Prosecutions* [25] that a *conspiracy* to publish an obscene libel did not come within section 2 (4) and that the common law test might still be applied.[26] In that case, as we have seen,[27] Viscount Simonds also went further and suggested that in an appropriate case it is possible to by-pass the accepted common law test for obscenity.[27a]

Now by **section 2 (1)** of the **Obscene Publications Act 1959,** as amended by **section 1 (1)** of the **Obscene Publications Act 1964,** it is an offence punishable on **summary conviction** [28] [*Imp. 6 months or* £100 *fine*] or on **indictment** [*Imp.* 3 *years and fine*] to publish an obscene article or to have an obscene article for publication for gain (whether for gain to oneself or to another).

Publication. By **section 1 (3)** of the Act, a person publishes an article who:

> " (a) distributes, circulates, sells, lets on hire, gives, or lends it, or who offers it for sale [29] or for letting on hire; or

---

[25] [1962] A.C. 220 at pp. 268, 269, 290, 291.

[26] See further [1961] Crim.L.R. at pp. 474–475.

[27] *Ante*, p. 229.

[27a] On June 3, 1964, the Solicitor-General gave an assurance in the House of Commons that a " conspiracy to corrupt public morals " would not be charged so as to circumvent the statutory offence under s. 4; see the observations of Lord Reid in *Knuller, etc.* v. *Director of Public Prosecutions* [1972] 3 W.L.R. 143.

[28] A prosecution must be brought within 12 months: Act of 1959, s. 2 (2). The limitation period in respect of proceedings on indictment is two years: *ibid.* s. 2 (3).

[29] An article in a shop-window is not offered for sale because, according to the law of contract, the placing of an article there constitutes only an invitation to treat: *Mella* v. *Monahan* [1961] Crim.L.R. 175; *Fisher* v. *Bell* [1961] 1 Q.B. 394.

(b) in the case of an article containing or embodying matter
to be looked at or a record, shows, plays or projects it."
It is provided, however, that paragraph (b) does not apply either
to anything done in the course of an exhibition of films (other than
exhibitions in private houses to which the public are not admitted)
or to anything done in the course of television or sound
broadcasting.[30]

Article. By **section 1 (2),** as amended by **section 2 (1)** of the
Obscene Publications Act 1964, the term " article " means:

(i) any article which can be read or looked at, or
(ii) any article from which it is intended to reproduce an
article which can be read, looked at [31] or listened to, or
(iii) any sound record, or
(iv) any film or other record of a picture or pictures.

Obscenity. By **section 1 (1)** it is provided:

" For the purposes of this Act [32] an article shall be deemed
to be obscene if its effect or (where the article comprises two or
more distinct items) the effect of any one of its items is, if
taken as a whole, such as to tend to deprave and corrupt
persons who are likely, having regard to all relevant circumstances, to read, see or hear the matter contained or embodied
in it."

This test is somewhat similar to that at common law although
more precisely defined.[33] The precise meaning of the words " deprave and corrupt " is not clear, but the words are probably used as
synonymous, and " corrupt " does not merely mean to lead astray
morally.[34] A book is not necessarily obscene merely because it
is in bad taste or is undesirable [35]; nor is obscenity confined to

[30] Obscenity in the course of television or sound broadcasting might constitute a
public nuisance at common law. See also ss. 3 and 4 of the Television Act
1964 and see Theatres Act 1968, s. 7.
[31] *e.g.* a photographic negative. *Cf. Straker* v. *Director of Public Prosecutions*
[1963] 1 Q.B. 926, D.C. and *Derrick* v. *Customs and Excise Commissioners*
[1972] 2 Q.B. 28, D.C.
[32] *Cf.* the position under the Post Office Act 1953, s. 11. See *R.* v. *Anderson*
[1972] 1 Q.B. 304.
[33] *Ante,* p. 228.
[34] *Per* Lord Reid in *Knuller etc.* v. *Director of Public Prosecutions* [1972] 3
W.L.R. 143.
[35] *R.* v. *Martin Secker and Warburg* [1954] 1 W.L.R. 1138.

sexual matters, and it has been held that a book about drug-taking can be obscene.[36]

The tendency of the article must be " such as to tend to deprave and corrupt persons who are likely, having regard to all the relevant circumstances, to read, see or hear the matter contained or embodied in it." [37] If the article in question was not such as to deprave or corrupt the person to whom it was published, then no offence against section 2 (1) will have been committed [38] " unless it could reasonably have been expected that the publication by . . . [that] person would follow from publication by the person charged " [39] and the other ingredients of the offence are satisfied. So in R. v. Clayton and Halsey [40] it was held that no offence against section 2 (1) had been committed when two police officers had bought some photographs from the accused, because they admitted in cross-examination that such photographs did not arouse any feelings in them whatsoever. The Court of Criminal Appeal, however, upheld the accused's conviction for conspiracy to publish obscene articles, contrary to section 2 (1), because there was no evidence that the sale of the photographs would be restricted to persons not susceptible to their influence.

Where a written article consists of a number of distinct items, the test must be applied to each individual item. If the test shows one item to be obscene that is enough to make the whole article obscene.[41]

Expert evidence, such as is permitted under section 4 of the Act in relation to the defence of " public good " is not admissible in relation to the matter of obscenity. This is a matter exclusively in the hands of the jury.[42]

Having an obscene article for publication for gain. This offence was added by the 1964 Act because of the decision in R. v.

36 John Calder (Publications) Ltd. v. Powell [1965] 1 Q.B. 509.
37 In reference to a book the test is whether its effect is to tend to deprave and corrupt a " significant proportion of those likely to read it ": R. v. Calder & Boyars Ltd. [1969] 1 Q.B. 151.   38 s. 2 (6).
39 Ibid.   40 [1963] 1 Q.B. 163.
41 R. v. Anderson [1972] 1 Q.B. 304.
42 R. v. Calder & Boyars Ltd. [1969] 1 Q.B. 151 ; R. v. Anderson [1972] 1 Q.B. 304, distinguishing D.P.P. v. A.B.C. Chewing Gum Ltd. [1968] 1 Q.B. 159. In R. v. Anderson (supra) the Court of Appeal said that when obscenity was alleged the " aversion argument " was a proper defence for the jury to consider, namely that the matter was " so disgusting and filthy that it

Clayton and Halsey. For the purpose of this offence, an article is deemed to be obscene if its effect would be such as to tend to deprave and corrupt either the persons to whom it may reasonably be inferred the accused contemplated publication or the persons to whom a further republication might reasonably be expected to be made.[43] The term " having " is widely defined.[44]

> " . . . a person shall be deemed to have an article for publication for gain if with a view to such publication he has the article in his ownership, possession or control."

Intent. It has been held that the 1959 Act does not require an intention to deprave or corrupt.[45]

No reasonable cause to believe article obscene. It is a good defence for the accused to prove that he had not examined the article *and* had no reasonable cause to suspect that either his publication of it or his having it (as the case may be) would constitute an offence against section 2.[46]

Public good. It is a good defence for the accused to prove " that publication of the article in question is justified as being for the public good on the ground that it is in the interests of science, literature, art or learning, or of other objects of general concern." [47] In considering this defence the jury must consider on the one hand the number of readers whom they believe would tend to be depraved and corrupted by the publication; the strength of the tendency to deprave or corrupt and the nature of the depravity or corruption; on the other hand they should assess the strength of the literary, sociological, or ethical merit which they consider the book to possess. Weighing up all these factors they are required to decide whether on balance the publication is proved to be justified as being for the public good.[48] Experts may give evidence as to

would not corrupt and deprave, but rather cause persons to revolt from activity of that kind." See also *Director of Public Prosecutions* v. *White* [1972] 3 All E.R. 12.

[43] See s. 1 (3) (*b*) of the 1964 Act.   [44] s. 1 (2) of the 1964 Act.

[45] *Shaw* v. *Director of Public Prosecutions* [1962] A.C. at p. 227 (C.C.A.); *R.* v. *Penguin Books Ltd.* [1961] Crim.L.R. 176.

[46] ss. 2 (5) of the 1959 Act and 1 (3) (*a*) of the 1964 Act.

[47] s. 4 (1) of the Act of 1959. As to this section, see *R.* v. *Penguin Books Ltd.* [1961] Crim.L.R. 176.

[48] *R.* v. *Calder & Boyars Ltd.* (*supra*).

whether in their opinion it is in such interests,[49] and to whether in their opinion the publication is for the public good.[50]

By **section 3** of the **Obscene Publications Act 1959,** provision is made for the forfeiture of obscene articles upon summary conviction. If there are reasonable grounds for suspecting that in any premises or on any stall or vehicle there are obscene articles which are, or are from time to time, kept for publication, then a search and seizure warrant may be issued by a justice of the peace.[51] Any offending articles are to be brought before a justice of the peace, who may order their forfeiture if he is satisfied that they are obscene and kept for publication for gain [52] and that the accused has not proved public good.[53]

Merely because a person has been convicted of publishing an obscene article or keeping such an article for publication for gain or such an article has been forfeited, it does not follow that an identical article will be adjudged obscene by another jury or, as the case may be, another magistrates' court. However, in practice, some uniformity is achieved, because the Director of Public Prosecutions must be informed by the chief officer of police of any case (in his police district) of indecent libel, exhibition or publication in which it appears to him that there is a prima facie case for prosecution.[54] And although the consent of the Director of Public Prosecutions to a prosecution is not required, in practice his advice is no doubt taken.[55]

By **section 11** of the **Post Office Act 1953** [56] it is an offence punishable on **indictment** [*Imp.* 12 *months*] or on **summary conviction** [£100 *fine*] for any person to send or attempt to send a postal packet which encloses any indecent or obscene book, picture, or

---

49 *Ibid*. s. 4 (2) and such evidence is restricted to this question: *R*. v. *Anderson* [1972] 1 Q.B. 304, distinguishing *D.P.P.* v. *A.B.C. Chewing Gum Ltd.* [1968] 1 Q.B. 159.

50 *John Calder (Publications) Ltd.* v. *Powell* [1965] 1 Q.B. 509; *R*. v. *Anderson* (*supra*).

51 *Ibid*. s. 3 (1). S. 3 (2) provides that if such material is seized, then documents relating to the trade or business found in the same place may also be seized. However, no search or seizure warrant may be issued except on an information laid by the Director of Public Prosecutions: Criminal Justice Act 1967, s. 25.

52 *Ibid*. s. 3 (3). S. 3 (3) and (4) lays down who must be summoned and who, apart from the person summoned, may appear to show cause why the articles should not be forfeited.

53 s. 4.

54 Prosecution of Offences Regulations 1946 (S.R. & O. No. 1467), reg. 6 (2) (*d*).

55 (1960) 23 M.L.R. at p. 290.

56 As amended by the Post Office Act 1961, the Criminal Justice Act 1967, Sched. 3, and the Post Office Act 1969, s. 76 and Sched. 4.

other article, or has on the packet or cover any indecent or offensive words or designs.

The 1959 Act does not apply here. The words "indecent or obscene" in section 11 "convey one idea, namely offending against the recognised standards of propriety, indecent being at the lower end of the scale and obscene being at the upper end." [57] Again, "obscene" here bears its ordinary dictionary meaning, including things which are shocking or lewd.[57a] The test to be applied is objective and the character of the addressee is immaterial,[57b] it is to be decided by the jury without assistance from persons who might have views on the matter, or might be able to speak as to the effect of the material on them.[57c]

A newspaper proprietor who inserts advertisements inviting people to send for obscene publications may, if he knows their character, be convicted of aiding and abetting this offence.

By **section 4** of the **Unsolicited Goods and Services Act 1971** it is an offence [58] punishable on **summary conviction** [£100 *fine for first offence*; £400 *for a subsequent offence*] for any person to send [59] or cause to be sent to another, any book, magazine or leaflet (or advertising material for any such publication) which he knows or ought reasonably to know is unsolicited [60] and which describes or illustrates human sexual techniques.

By **section 42** of the **Customs Consolidation Act 1876** [61] the importation into the United Kingdom of any indecent or obscene [62] prints, books, articles, etc., is prohibited, and any such print, etc., is liable to be forfeited, and any person who tries to evade the prohibition will commit an offence against section 45 of the Customs and Excise Act 1952.[63]

By **section 2** of the **Venereal Disease Act 1917** [64] the publication

---

[57] *R.* v. *Stanley* [1965] 2 Q.B. 327 at p. 333.
[57a] *R.* v. *Anderson* [1972] 1 Q.B. 304.
[57b] *R.* v. *Straker* [1965] Crim.L.R. 239 (C.C.A.).
[57c] *R.* v. *Stamford* [1972] 2 W.L.R. 1055.
[58] No prosecution to be instituted except by, or with the consent of, the Director of Public Prosecutions: s. 4 (3).
[59] " Send " includes deliver: s. 6 (1).
[60] *i.e.* sent without any prior request made by that person or on his behalf: s. 6 (1).
[61] As amended.   [62] *Ibid.*
[63] *Ante*, p. 151. Reels of film come within the section: *Derrick* v. *Customs and Excise Commissioners* [1972] 2 Q.B. 28, D.C. *Cf. Straker* v. *Director of Public Prosecutions* [1963] 1 Q.B. 926, D.C.
[64] s. 2 will be amended by s. 135 of and Sched. 5 to the Medicines Act 1968, when that Act comes into force.

by anyone [65] of advertisements offering to treat or recommending remedies for venereal disease is an offence punishable on **indictment** [*Imp.* 2 *years*] or on **summary conviction** [£100 *fine or Imp.* 6 *months*].

To affix to or inscribe on any building, gate, fence, tree, etc., so as to be visible to anyone on any street, highway, etc., or to affix to, etc., any public urinal or to deliver or attempt to deliver or exhibit to any person in any street, highway, etc., or throw down the area of any house or exhibit to public view in the window of any house, any indecent or obscene printed or written matter is punishable on **summary conviction** [£20 *fine or Imp.* 1 *month*].[66]

The exposure to view in any public place of obscene prints, etc., is also punishable under the Vagrancy Acts.[67]

By the **Children and Young Persons (Harmful Publications) Act 1955,** provision is made for preventing the publication of harmful matter to children. The Act applies to any book, magazine or other like work which is of a kind likely to fall into the hands of children or young persons and consists wholly or mainly of stories told in pictures (with or without the addition of written matter), being stories portraying (a) the commission of crimes, or (b) acts of violence or cruelty, or (c) incidents of a repulsive or horrible nature, in such a way that the work as a whole would tend to corrupt a child or young person into whose hands it might fall [**section 1**].

Any person who prints, publishes, sells or lets on hire such work, or has in his possession for the purpose of selling or letting for hire such work, is guilty of an offence punishable on **summary conviction** [*Imp.* 4 *months and* £100 *fine*]. It is a defence for the accused to prove that he had not examined the contents of the work and had no reasonable cause to suspect that it was one to which the Act applied [**section 2**].

A prosecution may not be commenced under the Act except by, or with the consent of, the Attorney-General [**section 2 (2)**].

---

[65] Except local authorities: s. 2, proviso.

[66] Indecent Advertisements Act 1889, s. 3, as amended by the Criminal Justice Act 1967, Sched. 3 and the Indecent Advertisements (Amendment) Act 1970. By s. 5 advertisements relating to complaints arising from sexual intercourse are deemed to be indecent if so affixed, etc., to any building, etc., or affixed to, etc., any public urinal or delivered or attempted to be delivered to any person in any street, etc.

[67] *Post,* p. 241.

Section 7. Disorderly Houses

Keeping a disorderly house is a common law offence [*Imp. and fine*].[68] There is no comprehensive judicial definition of what constitutes a disorderly house.[69] It has been held that a disorderly house need not constitute a public nuisance.[70] But there must be some evidence of persistent user.[71]

A house has been held to be disorderly if persons resort there for such illegal practices as cock-fighting or playing any unlawful sport [72] or indulging in unnatural practices.[73]

But illegality on the part of the persons resorting to the house is not necessary.[74] So, recently, prosecutions for keeping a disorderly house have been used to prevent certain strip-tease shows. In *R. v. Quinn* [75] it was held that where indecent performances or exhibitions are alleged as rendering the premises a disorderly house it must be proved that the premises are

> " conducted contrary to law and good order in that matters are performed or exhibited of such a character that their performance or exhibition in a place of common resort (a) amounts to an outrage of public decency or (b) tends to corrupt or deprave or (c) is otherwise calculated to injure the public interest so as to call for condemnation and punishment." [76]

At common law a common gaming-house could constitute a disorderly house, but this is no longer so, as a result of section 38 of the Betting, Gaming and Lotteries Act 1963. Brothels are dealt with separately in Section 10, below.

Section 8. Public Mischief

There is old authority to the effect that, *quite apart from the law of conspiracy*, which was dealt with above,[77] " all offences of a public nature, that is, such acts or attempts as tend to the prejudice

---

[68] As to common law punishments, see note 59 on p. 201.
[69] *R. v. Quinn* [1962] 2 Q.B. at p. 254.
[70] *Ibid.* at pp. 254–255.
[71] *R. v. Brady and Ram* [1964] 3 All E.R. 616.
[72] *R. v. Higginson* (1762) 2 Burr. 1232.
[73] *R. v. Berg* (1927) 20 Cr.App.R. 38.
[74] *R. v. Quinn* [1962] 2 Q.B. at p. 254.
[75] [1962] 2 Q.B. 245.
[76] *Ibid.* at p. 255. For a criticism of this, see [1961] Crim.L.R. at pp. 611–612.
[77] *Ante*, p. 63.

of the community," [78] constitute the indictable misdemeanour of public mischief at common law. However, the offence fell into desuetude until 1933, when the Court of Criminal Appeal held in *R. v. Manley* [79] that causing the police to waste their time in investigating false allegations is a public mischief.[80] Subsequently it was held in another case [81] that publishing scandalous matter about the Jews also constituted a public mischief.

The authorities have been criticised, both as contravening the principle " *nulla poena sine lege* " and as an unwarranted judicial encroachment upon the province of the legislature.[82] In *R. v. Newland*,[83] Lord Goddard C.J. said, *obiter*, that " In our considered opinion the safe course is no longer to follow [*Manley's* case]." [84]

SECTION 9. VAGRANCY

The law relating to this subject is contained principally in the **Vagrancy Act 1824.** Vagrants are of three classes, namely:

(1) **Idle and disorderly persons.** This class includes:

    (i) Hawkers and pedlars wandering abroad and trading without licence.[85]

    (ii) Prostitutes behaving in public places in a riotous and indecent manner.[86]

    (iii) Persons wandering abroad or placing themselves in any public place to beg, or causing or encouraging any children to do so.[87]

Such persons may be arrested by any person without a warrant if found committing one of these offences [88] and are punishable on **summary conviction** [*before one justice or in an occasional court*: *Imp.* 14 *days or* £1 *fine*; *before a petty sessional court*: *Imp.* 1 *month or* £5 *fine*].[89]

---

[78] *R. v. Higgins* (1801) 2 East 5.
[79] [1933] 1 K.B. 529.
[80] See also *R. v. Bailey* [1956] N.I. 15 to a similar effect. See now *ante*, p. 175.
[81] *R. v. Leese* (1936) 82 L.J. 310.
[82] See *e.g.* Stallybrass, " Public Mischief " (1933) 39 L.Q.R. 183.
[83] [1954] 1 Q.B. 158 at p. 168.
[84] But *cf. Sykes* v. *Director of Public Prosecutions* [1962] A.C. 528 at p. 562, where Lord Denning classified *Manley's* case as a common law offence of interfering with the course of justice; *R. v. Bailey* [1956] N.I. 15.
[85] Vagrancy Act 1824, s. 3.   [86] *Ibid.* See also *post*, p. 243.
[87] Vagrancy Act 1824, s. 3.   [88] *Ibid.* s. 6.
[89] Vagrancy Act 1824, s. 3; Magistrates' Courts Act 1952, ss. 27 (3), 98 (5) and Sched. 3.

(2) **Rogues and vagabonds.** This class includes:

    (i) Persons committing any of the foregoing offences a second time.[90]

    (ii) Persons wandering abroad, and lodging in any barn or outhouse, or unoccupied building, or in the open air, or under a tent, or in any cart or wagon, *other than a tent, cart or wagon in which or with which they travel,* and not giving a good account of themselves.[91]

    (iii) Persons wilfully exposing to view in any street, road, highway or public place (or in the window of any shop or other building situate in any street, etc.) any obscene picture, print or other indecent exhibition.[92]

    (iv) Any person wilfully, openly, lewdly and obscenely exposing his person with intent to insult any female.[93]

    (v) Any person wandering abroad and endeavouring by the exposure of wounds or deformities to obtain alms.[94]

    (vi) Any person collecting alms, or endeavouring to procure charitable contributions of any kind under any false or fraudulent pretence.[95]

    (vii) Every person pretending or professing to tell fortunes or using any subtle craft, means or device, by palmistry or otherwise, to deceive and impose upon any of Her Majesty's subjects.

    (viii) Any person armed with an offensive weapon, or having upon him any instrument, with intent to commit an arrestable offence.[96]

[90] Vagrancy Act 1824, s. 4.

[91] Vagrancy Act 1824, s. 4, amended as to the words in italics by the Vagrancy Act 1935, s. 1 (3), which also provides that a person so wandering about, etc., is not to be deemed a rogue and vagabond unless certain facts therein set out are proved.

[92] Vagrancy Act 1824, s. 4, Vagrancy Act 1838, s. 2, and Theatres Act 1968, s. 2. See also Town Police Clauses Act 1847, s. 28 (only of limited application).

[93] Vagrancy Act 1824, s. 4, as amended by the Criminal Justice Act 1925, s. 42. The offence can be committed in a private room as much as in public: *Ford* v. *Falcone* (1971) 115 S.J. 365. See also Town Police Clauses Act 1847, s. 28 (only of limited application). Under s. 28 there is no requirement that the accused should intend to insult a female. The word " person " in the section means penis and not any other part of the body, notwithstanding that there may be an intention to insult a female: *Evans* v. *Ewels* [1972] 1 W.L.R. 671, D.C. It is doubtful if this restriction applies in the case of indecent exposure at common law.

[94] Vagrancy Act 1824, s. 4.

[95] *Ibid.*

[96] *Ibid.*

(ix) Any person found [97] in any dwelling-house, warehouse, etc., or in any enclosed yard, garden, etc., for any unlawful purpose.[98] Unlawful means criminal.[99] It is not necessary that the accused intended to commit a crime in the place where, or at the time when, he was found.[1]

(x) Every person apprehended as an idle and disorderly person and violently resisting apprehension, if convicted of the offence for which he is apprehended.[2]

(xi) Any suspected person or reputed thief frequenting or loitering about any river, canal, dock, etc., or any quay, warehouse, etc., adjoining thereto, or any street or highway leading thereto, or any place of public resort,[3] or any street or highway or any place adjacent thereto, with intent to commit an arrestable offence.[4] A person is a suspected person if by reason of previous convictions [5] or by reason of his conduct on a *previous* occasion he has become the object of suspicion.[6] Any acts relied on to show that he was a suspected person must be separate from the acts which are relied on to show that he was loitering with intent to commit an arrestable offence. It is not necessary that the previous occasion should be on an earlier day or be separated from the present occasion by any great lapse of time, provided that his conduct on the two occasions constitute two separate transactions.[7]

---

[97] The accused must be found but not necessarily apprehended there: *R.* v. *Lumsden* [1951] 2 K.B. 513.

[98] Vagrancy Act 1824, s. 4.

[99] *Hayes* v. *Stevenson* (1860) 25 J.P. 39.

[1] *Re Joy* (1853) 22 L.T.J. 80.   [2] Vagrancy Act 1824, s. 4.

[3] A place *may* be a place of public resort notwithstanding that there is a charge for admission and that the occupier has a right to refuse admission: *Glynn* v. *Simmonds* [1952] 2 All E.R. 47.

[4] Vagrancy Act 1824, s. 4, as amended by the Penal Servitude Act 1891, s. 7. It is not necessary to show that the person suspected was guilty of any particular act or acts tending to show his intent if from the circumstances of the case and his known character it appears that his intent was to commit an arrestable offence: Prevention of Crimes Act 1871, s. 15.

[5] *R.* v. *Fairbairn* [1949] 2 K.B. 690.

[6] *Ledwith* v. *Roberts* [1937] 1 K.B. 232.

[7] *Hartley* v. *Ellnor* (1917) 26 Cox 10; *Pyburn* v. *Hudson* [1950] 1 All E.R. 1006. *Cosh* v. *Isherwood* (1970) 52 Cr.App.R. 53. *Cf. Fitzgerald* v. *Lyle* (1971) 114 S.J. 929 D.C. See further Wood, " Street Offences Act 1959 " [1960] Crim.L.R. at pp. 524–526. See also the commentary to *Fitzgerald* v. *Lyle* at [1972] Crim.L.R. 125.

Such persons may be arrested by any person without a warrant if found committing one of these offences [8] and are punishable on summary conviction [*before one justice or in an occasional court*: *Imp.* 14 *days or £1 fine*; *before a petty sessional court*: *Imp.* 3 *months or £25 fine*].[9]

(3) **Incorrigible rogues.** This class includes:

(i) Any person convicted for the second time as a rogue and vagabond.

(ii) Any person apprehended as a rogue and vagabond and violently resisting apprehension, if subsequently convicted of the offence for which he is apprehended.

(iii) Any person breaking or escaping out of any place of legal confinement before the expiration of the term for which he has been committed or ordered to be confined by virtue of the Vagrancy Act 1824.[10]

One justice may convict a person of being an incorrigible rogue. When so convicted by a justice or justices he may be committed on bail or in custody to the Crown Court.[11] The Crown Court may then, after examination into the circumstances of the case, order him to be imprisoned for a maximum of one year.[12]

SECTION 10. OFFENCES RELATING TO PROSTITUTION [13]

In this chapter we are only concerned with those offences relating to prostitution which can be said to be violative of public order. A number of other offences dealing with prostitution are dealt with in the chapter on sexual offences.[14] It should be noted that prostitution itself is not a criminal offence.

---

8 Vagrancy Act 1824, s. 6. However, where the crimes require a specific intent (*e.g.* intent to commit an offence) it is sufficient to show that the person effecting the arrest honestly and on reasonable grounds believed that the arrested person had the necessary intent: *Ledwith* v. *Roberts* [1937] 1 K.B. at p. 251.

9 Vagrancy Act 1824, s. 4; Magistrates' Courts Act 1952, ss. 27 (3), 98 (5) and Sched. 3. 10 Vagrancy Act 1824, s. 5.

11 *Ibid.*, as supplemented by the Criminal Justice Administration Act 1962, ss. 14 and 15; as amended by the Criminal Justice Act 1967, Sched. 6.

12 *Ibid.* s. 10; Criminal Justice Act 1948, Sched. 10. Note that an incorrigible rogue is not *indicted* at the Crown Court. In order to give that court jurisdiction he must have been convicted by a court of summary jurisdiction under s. 5: *R.* v. *Evans* [1915] 2 K.B. 762. See, for procedure at the Crown Court, *R.* v. *Holding and Long* (1934) 25 Cr.App.R. 28, and *R.* v. *Billington* (1942) 28 Cr.App.R. 180. The Crown Court must investigate the facts fully before passing sentence.

13 See the article by A. Dickey at [1969] Crim.L.R. 538. 14 *Post*, p. 465.

Before discussing the various offences, it is necessary to define the expressions " prostitute " and " brothel."

The expression " prostitute," or " common prostitute," has been defined as a woman who " offers her body commonly for lewdness for payment in return." [15]   The expression " commonly " involves the notion of (at least some) indiscriminancy.   " Lewdness " has been held not to be confined to sexual intercourse but to include other sexual acts [16] and, it has been suggested *obiter*,[17] may include even a lewd or obscene strip-tease.

Brothels are either premises which are used by persons of the opposite sex [18] for the purposes of illicit sexual intercourse (although the women may not be prostitutes [19]) or premises which are used by *two or more* women for the purposes of prostitution.[20]   If two prostitutes use the same room or flat, no difficulty arises.   Some difficulty arises if there are a number of rooms or flats in a building, each (or some of each) of which are exclusively occupied by one prostitute.   The *building* will then, it appears, constitute a premises itself, and so a brothel, if :

(i) for the purposes of their trade, there are a number of prostitutes occupying rooms, which " are sufficiently close to each other to constitute a nest of prostitutes, be that nest large or small," [21] or

(ii) the landlord takes an active part in managing the prostitutes.[22]

But if a building, for example, consists of only two flats and each is exclusively occupied by one prostitute and there is no management by the landlord, then it may well not be a brothel, because in that case it is the flat and not the building which constitutes the " premises." [23]

---

15 *R.* v. *De Munck* [1918] 1 K.B. at p. 637; approved in *R.* v. *Webb* [1964] 1 Q.B. 357. For the problems that can arise in trying to prove that a woman is a common prostitute, see Wood, " Street Offences Act 1959 " [1960] Crim.L.R. at pp. 523–527.
16 *e.g.* masturbation, whipping : *R.* v. *Webb* [1964] 1 Q.B. 357, and at p. 366.
17 *Ibid.* at p. 360, *per* Widgery J.
18 As to " male brothels," see p. 245, *post.*
19 *Winter* v. *Woolfe* [1931] 1 K.B. 549.
20 *Singleton* v. *Ellison* [1895] 1 Q.B. 607; *Gordon* v. *Standen* [1964] 1 Q.B. 294.
21 *Donovan* v. *Gavin* [1965] 2 Q.B. 648 at p. 650.
22 *R.* v. *Webb* (*supra*).
23 *Strath* v. *Foxon* [1956] 1 Q.B. 67.

Section 6 of the **Sexual Offences Act 1967** provides that, for the purposes of sections 33–35 of the Sexual Offences Act 1956 (below), premises shall be treated as a brothel if people resort to it for the purpose of lewd homosexual practices in circumstances in which resort thereto for lewd heterosexual practices would have led to its being treated as a brothel for the purposes of those sections.

By **section 1** of the **Street Offences Act 1959** it is an offence punishable on **summary conviction** for a common prostitute to loiter or solicit in a street or public place for the purpose of prostitution [£10 *fine*; 2nd *conviction, £25 fine*; 3rd *or subsequent conviction, £25 fine and Imp. 3 months*]. A constable may arrest without a warrant anyone he finds in a street or public place and suspects, with reasonable cause, to be committing an offence under this section.[24] " Street " is defined widely to include any bridge, road, footway, alley, etc., which is for the time being open to the public, the doorways and entrances abutting on a street (as thus defined) and any ground adjoining and open to a street.[25]

Attracting the attention of men by making noises while standing on a balcony or at a window, whether the window be open or closed, has been held to amount to soliciting.[26] However, the display by a prostitute of a card on a notice-board in a street offering her services does not amount to soliciting.[27] Soliciting by men is dealt with in the chapter on sexual offences.[28]

Section 2 of the Act provides that a woman who is cautioned by a constable to the effect that if she persists in her conduct she may be charged with an offence under section 1 may apply to a magistrates' court within fourteen days to have the caution set aside on the grounds that she was not committing an offence against this section. The Act does not otherwise regulate the system of cautions, nor does it make such a system compulsory. Practice, therefore, can vary from area to area.[29]

---

[24] *Ibid.* s. 1 (3).

[25] *Ibid.* s. 1 (4). For " public place," see, *post*, p. 334.

[26] *Smith* v. *Hughes* [1960] 1 W.L.R. 830.

[27] *Weisz* v. *Monahan* [1962] 1 W.L.R. 262; *Burge* v. *Director of Public Prosecutions* [1962] 1 W.L.R. 265.

[28] *Post*, p. 479. The punishment for this offence is considerably greater than the punishments provided in the Street Offences Act 1959, and reflects the alleged " immoral " nature of the crime.

[29] Wood, " Street Offences Act 1959 " [1960] Crim.L.R. 521.

Sections 33–36 of the **Sexual Offences Act 1956** enact a number of offences concerning brothels. All these offences are similarly punishable on **summary conviction** [*Imp*. 3 *months and* £100 *fine*; 2*nd or subsequent conviction*,[30] *Imp*. 6 *months and* £250 *fine*].[31]

Section 33 makes it an offence to keep a brothel, or to manage, or act or assist in the management of, a brothel.

Section 34 makes it an offence for a lessor or landlord of any premises or his agent [32] to let the whole or part of the premises with the knowledge that it is to be used, in whole or in part, as a brothel, or, where the whole or part of the premises is used as a brothel, to be wilfully a party to that use continuing.

Section 35 makes it an offence for the tenant or occupier, or person in charge, of any premises knowingly to permit the whole or part of the premises to be used as a brothel.

Section 36 makes it an offence for the tenant or occupier of any premises knowingly to permit the whole or part of the premises to be used for the purposes of habitual prostitution. However, it has been held that a woman who uses premises of which she is the sole occupier for her own habitual prostitution cannot be convicted under this section.[33]

Section 11. Drunkenness

Drunkenness is not of itself a criminal offence, but being drunk in certain circumstances can constitute an offence. In this chapter we are only concerned with those offences which can be said to violate public peace and order.

The following offences are punishable on **summary conviction:**

(1) Being found drunk in any highway or other public place, whether a building or not, or on any licensed premises [£5 *fine*].[34] A person found committing this offence may be apprehended.[35] The term " public place " includes any place to which the public have access, whether on payment or otherwise.[36] The term

---

[30] A previous conviction under any of these sections (or their predecessors) is sufficient: Sched. 2.
[31] Sched. 2.
[32] This would include a porter: *Durose* v. *Wilson* (1907) 71 J.P. 263.
[33] *Mattison* v. *Johnson* (1916) 80 J.P. 243.
[34] Licensing Act 1872, s. 12, as amended by the Penalties for Drunkenness Act 1962, s. 1. A single justice may try this offence: Criminal Justice Administration Act 1914, s. 38.
[35] Licensing Act 1902, s. 1.
[36] *Ibid*. s. 8.

"licensed premises" means any premises in respect of which a justices' licence or an occasional licence for the sale of intoxicating liquor is in force.[37]

(2) While drunk, guilty of riotous or disorderly behaviour in any highway or other public place [38] or, while drunk, being in possession of any loaded firearm [£10 *fine or Imp.* 1 *month*].[39] A person found committing either of these offences may be apprehended.[40] This offence and similar local offences will be replaced by **section 91** of the **Criminal Justice Act 1967** when it comes into force. This section provides that any person, who in any public place (defined in section 91 (4)) is guilty, while drunk, of disorderly behaviour, commits an offence punishable upon **summary conviction** [£50 *fine*]. An order bringing this section into force is not to be made unless the Secretary of State is satisfied that sufficient suitable accommodation is available for the care and treatment of persons convicted of being drunk and disorderly.

(3) Being drunk, violent, quarrelsome or disorderly in a late night refreshment house,[41] or in licensed premises, *and,* in either case, failing to leave when requested to do so [£5 *fine*].[42] In either case a constable is under a duty, upon being requested to do so, to help expel an offender.[43]

The **Criminal Justice Act 1972** [44] provides that a constable, in any case in which he has power to arrest a person found drunk

---

[37] See *Stevens* v. *Dickson* [1952] 2 All E.R. 246 and Licensing Act 1964, s. 200.
[38] See note 36, above.
[39] Licensing Act 1872, s. 12, as amended by the Penalties for Drunkenness Act 1962, s. 1. See also to similar effect Metropolitan Police Act 1839, s. 58, and Town Police Clauses Act 1847, s. 29 (both as amended by the 1962 Act). These two Acts are not of general application.
[40] Licensing Act 1872, s. 12.
[41] *Post*, p. 251.
[42] Respectively the Late Night Refreshment Houses Act 1969, s. 9 (4) and the Licensing Act 1964, s. 174. The term "licensed premises" is defined by s. 200 of the Act as any place for which a justices' licence is in force and any premises (other than licensed canteens) where intoxicating liquor is sold by retail or under licence. See also for other similar offences drunkenness in aircraft, Air Navigation Order 1966, art. 41; drunken, violent quarrelsome or disorderly behaviour in a betting office, Betting, Gaming and Lotteries Act 1963, s. 10; drunk in charge of a child, Licensing Act 1902, s. 2 (1), as amended by the Penalties for Drunkenness Act 1962, s. 1; in passenger steamers, Merchant Shipping Act 1906, s. 76; of postal officers, Post Office Act 1953, s. 59 (*b*); of railway servants under the Railway Regulation Acts 1840 and 1842.
[43] Respectively the Late Night Refreshment Houses Act 1969, s. 10 (2), and the Licensing Act 1964, s. 174.
[44] s. 34, not in force as at July 1, 1972.

in a public place [45] may, if he thinks fit, take him to a treatment
centre for alcoholics, such person being deemed to be in lawful
custody. Such a person will not be liable to be detained at such a
place, and the fact of his being taken there will not preclude him
from being charged with any offence.[46] No treatment centres have
yet been set up.

Section 12. Swearing

By **section 28** of the **Town Police Clauses Act 1847** (which applies
in all urban areas [47] and certain other areas), it is an offence punishable on **summary conviction** [£20 [48] *fine or Imp*. 14 *days*] to use in
any street any profane or obscene language or sing any profane or
obscene song or ballad to the annoyance of any person.[49] A constable may arrest without a warrant anyone found committing these
offences.[50]

Section 13. Licensing of Places of Entertainment

Theatres

Section 12 of the **Theatres Act 1968** provides that no premises [51]
shall be used for the public performance [52] of a play [53] except under

---

[45] Including any highway and other premises to which at the material time the
public have or are permitted to have access, whether on payment or otherwise:
Criminal Justice Act 1972, s. 26 (3). Powers in this regard are conferred by
Criminal Justice Act 1967, s. 91 (1), the Licensing Act 1872, s. 12, the Metropolitan Police Act 1839, s. 58, the City of London Police Act 1839, s. 37,
the Town Police Clauses Act 1847, s. 29, and certain local Acts.
[46] Criminal Justice Act 1972, s. 34 (2).
[47] Public Health Act 1875, s. 171. See also the Metropolitan Police Act 1839,
s. 54 (12).
[48] The fine was increased by the Criminal Justice Act 1967, Sched. 3.
[49] Clearly the definition of " obscene " in the Obscene Publications Act 1959,
s. 1 (1) does not apply here, and it is submitted that the approach adopted
by the courts to s. 11 of the Post Office Act 1953 (see p. 237, *ante*) would
be adopted, " obscene " bearing its ordinary dictionary meaning, and including
things which are shocking or lewd (see p. 237, *ante*). Whether the words of
the language or song are obscene is a matter for the justices. It suffices to
show that the words were *calculated* to annoy; *proof* of annoyance is not
required: *Myers* v. *Garrett* [1972] Crim.L.R. 232. It is not necessary to call
as a witness a person who has been annoyed: *Wooley* v. *Corbishley* (1860)
24 J.P. 773. It is sufficient if a constable is annoyed: *Brabham* v. *Wookey*
(1901) 18 T.L.R. 99.
[50] Town Police Clauses Act 1847, s. 28.
[51] " Premises " includes any place: s. 18 (1).
[52] " Public performance " includes any performance in a public place within the
meaning of the Public Order Act 1936 (see p. 196, *ante*) and any performance
which the public or any section thereof are permitted to attend whether on
payment or not.   [53] " Play " is defined in s. 18 (1).

and in accordance with the provisions of a licence [54] granted by the licensing authority.[55] There is no longer any requirement [56] that new stage plays be submitted for censorship.[57] By **section 13,** if a public performance of a play is given at premises in respect of which a licence under the Act is not in force, an offence punishable on **summary conviction** [*Imp. 3 months and £200 fine*] is committed by any person concerned in the organisation or management of that performance, and by any other person who, knowing or having reasonable cause to suspect that such a performance would be given at those premises without such a licence being in force, either allowed the premises to be used for the giving of that performance or let, or otherwise made available the premises to any person for that purpose.

The holder of a licence and any person who allows, lets or otherwise makes available the premises also commits an offence (similarly punishable) [58] if while a licence is in force, the terms, conditions, or restrictions [59] imposed by the licence are contravened or not complied with. There must be knowledge or reasonable cause for suspicion that the premises would be used otherwise than in accordance with the licence. It is a defence for a licenceholder to prove that the contravention took place without his consent or connivance and that he exercised all due diligence to prevent it: **section 13 (2).** A licenceholder convicted of such an offence may have his licence revoked by the licensing authority: **section 13 (5).**[60]

The **Sunday Theatre Act 1972,** exempts from penalty under the Sunday Observance Act 1781 performances of plays on a Sunday, and any person managing, conducting, assisting at, or otherwise taking part in or attending or advertising such a performance at premises licensed under the Theatres Act 1968 (or premises where plays are performed by authority of letters patent). **Section 2,** how-

---

[54] Except in the case of letters patent theatres and certain military entertainments: s. 17.

[55] The relevant local authority.

[56] As there was under the Theatres Act 1843, s. 12.

[57] See p. 229, *ante.*

[58] s. 14.

[59] The licensing authority may only impose terms, restrictions or conditions which they consider necessary in the interests of physical safety or health, or any condition regulating or prohibiting the giving of an exhibition, demonstration or performance of hypnotism within the meaning of the Hypnotism Act 1952, s. 1 (2).

[60] But not before the time for bringing an appeal has expired: s. 13 (5).

ever, lays down certain restrictions on the hours of such performances, contravention of which is punishable on **summary conviction**
[*Imp.* 3 *months and* £200 *fine*].

Cinemas

We have already seen that, subject to certain exceptions, cinematograph exhibitions must be licensed. It is an offence not to have
such a licence.[61] A constable, or any officer appointed by the
licensing authority, may enter any premises in which a cinematograph exhibition is being given to see whether an offence against
the Cinematograph Acts is being committed.[62] Obstructing the
entry of a constable or other officer is an offence.[63]

Places Selling Intoxicating Liquor

Public-houses and clubs and restaurants selling intoxicating liquor
are dealt with separately later.[64]

Late Night Refreshment Houses

By **section 2** of the **Late Night Refreshment Houses Act 1969**
premises which are kept open for public refreshment, resort and
entertainment (other than premises licensed for the sale of beer,
cider, wine or spirits), at any time between 10 p.m. and 5 a.m. must
be licensed by the appropriate local authority. Keeping such
premises without a licence is an offence [65] punishable on **summary
conviction** [*Imp.* 3 *months and* £200 *fine*].[66] **Section 7** permits
the licensing authority to impose a condition prohibiting
the keeping open of the premises at any time between 11 p.m. and
5 a.m. to avoid unreasonable disturbance of residents in the neighbourhood. Breach of such a condition is an offence [similarly
punishable].[67] A register is kept of the licences concerned. A
licensee who fails to notify the local authority within two weeks
of a change of address affecting the register commits an offence [68]
[£20 *fine*].

---

[61] Cinematograph Act 1909, s. 3, as amended by Cinematograph Act 1952, Sched.
[62] Cinematograph Act 1909, s. 4, as amended by Cinematograph Act 1952, Sched.
[63] Cinematograph Act 1909, s. 4.
[64] *Post*, Chap. 24.
[65] s. 2 (3).
[66] s. 11 (1).
[67] s. 11 (1).
[68] s. 6 (3).

By **section 8** the licensing authority may make it a condition of the grant or renewal of the licence that no charge at all (except a reasonable charge for cloakroom or toilet facilities) be made between 10 p.m. and 5 a.m. unless a tariff of charges is displayed on the premises. Where such a condition is imposed, touting for custom outside is unlawful. The licensing authority is also empowered to impose a condition that the tariff be so displayed that it may be read before entry. Breach of these conditions is an offence punishable on summary conviction [*Imp. 3 months and £200 fine*].

By **section 9 (1)** it is an offence [punishable as above] for a licensee knowingly to permit unlawful gaming [69] on the premises, or knowingly to permit prostitutes, thieves or drunken and disorderly persons to assemble at or continue upon the premises. A constable is empowered to visit a late night refreshment house, and refusal to admit him is an offence under **section 10 (1).**

Music and Dancing

In most areas any house or place kept for public dancing, music or other entertainment of the like kind must be licensed (and the licence be displayed) and failure to have a licence or observe the conditions of the licence is an offence. This will be by virtue of either a local Act [70] or Part IV of the Public Health Acts Amendment Act 1890, if that Part of the Act has been adopted or applied to a particular area.[71] Section 51 of that Act makes a failure to have a licence or comply with the conditions of a licence punishable on summary conviction [£200 *fine* [72]].

The statutory regulations do not, however, apply to premises in respect of which a justices' licence [73] is in force so as to require any licence for wireless or television broadcasts, or music and singing provided by the reproduction of recorded sound or by not more than two performers.[74] Nor do these statutory regulations normally apply to cinematograph exhibitions.[75]

---

[69] Within the meaning of s. 53 and Pt. I of Sched. 11 to the Gaming Act 1968.
[70] See, *e.g.* London Government Act 1963, Sched. 12; Home Counties (Music and Dancing) Licensing Act 1926.   See further Halsbury, Vol. 37, p. 41 *et seq.*
[71] See Halsbury, Vol. 37, p. 46.
[72] The fine was increased by the Criminal Justice Act 1967, Sched. 3.
[73] *Post*, p. 360.
[74] Licensing Act 1964, s. 182.
[75] Cinematograph Act 1952, s. 7.

It has been held that it is not necessary to have a licence when customers themselves play or sing round a piano.[76] Nor will clubs normally be required to have a licence because clubs are, usually, not "public." However, a club may require a licence if any member of the public can be admitted to the premises immediately upon filling in his application without any process of selection.[77]

For the numerous other cases in which it has been held that a licence is or is not necessary, reference should be made to more specialised works.[78]

Private Places of Entertainment

The **Private Places of Entertainment (Licensing) Act 1967** provides for the licensing of premises used for dancing, music or any other entertainment of the like kind which is not public and which is promoted for private gain. The Act must be adopted by a local authority before it comes into force for that area.

Boxing and Wrestling

Provision for licensing public boxing and wrestling has been made only in a number of local Acts.[79]

Billiards

Section 11 of the **Gaming Act 1845,** as amended by section 56 of the Betting, Gaming and Lotteries Act 1963, provides that places kept for public billiards (other than premises in respect of which a justices' on-licence is in force [80]) must be licensed [81] and that failure to have such a licence is punishable on **summary conviction** [£50 *fine*; *2nd or subsequent conviction, Imp. 2 months and* £100 *fine*] or upon **indictment** [£300 *fine*; *2nd or subsequent conviction, Imp. 6 months and* £500 *fine*]. Notice of the licence must be posted in some conspicuous place near the door and on the outside of the house, and failure to do so is punishable on **summary conviction** [£10 *fine*].

---

76 *Brearley* v. *Morely* [1899] 2 Q.B. 121.
77 See *Panama (Piccadilly) Ltd.* v. *Newberry* [1962] 1 W.L.R. 611.
78 Paterson, *Licensing Acts*, 80th ed., 1972.
79 See, *e.g.* London Government Act 1963, Sched. 12. See further Halsbury, Vol. 37, pp. 50–51.
80 With the exception that the holder only of a beer-house licence needs a billiards' licence to allow playing.
81 By the justices.

A holder of a billiards' licence who fails to comply with the conditions set out therein,[82] *e.g.* allows drunkenness or disorderly behaviour, etc., or who refuses to admit a constable is punishable on summary conviction [£10 *fine*; *2nd or subsequent conviction,* £20 *fine*].[83]

It is an offence for the holder of a billiards' licence or justices' on-licence to allow playing before 8 a.m. or after 1 a.m.[84] It is also an offence to allow any playing on Sundays, Christmas Day, Good Friday or any day appointed for a public fast or thanksgiving, but the holder of a justices' on-licence may allow playing on those days at times at which playing is allowed on other days.[85] These offences are punishable in the same manner as failure to have a licence.[86]

It is also an offence, punishable as a breach of the conditions of the licence, for the holder of a billiards' licence to keep open the premises at the times, or on the days, when playing is not allowed.[87]

SECTION 14. HYPNOTISM

Section 1 of the **Hypnotism Act 1952**[88] provides that conditions regulating or prohibiting the giving of an exhibition or demonstration of hypnotism[89] may be attached by the licensing authority to licences granted to a theatre, or[90] for public music, dancing and entertainment.[91]

Where, in respect of a place, such a licence is *not in force,* then **section 2** prohibits any such demonstration at that place in connection with an entertainment to which the public are admitted, whether on payment or otherwise, unless:

---

[82] See Gaming Act 1845, Sched. 3.

[83] Gaming Act 1845, ss. 12 and 14; Licensing Act 1872, s. 75; Licensing Act 1964, s. 117.

[84] Gaming Act 1845, s. 13.

[85] Gaming Act 1845, s. 13, as amended by the Licensing Act 1964, s. 182 (2).

[86] Gaming Act 1845, s. 13. In the case of the holder of a billiards' licence these offences are also punishable as breaches of the conditions of the licence: *ibid.* s. 12.

[87] Gaming Act 1845, s. 13, as amended by the Betting and Gaming Act 1960, s. 26 (2).

[88] As amended by the Theatres Act 1968, s. 19 and Sched. 2.

[89] Defined in s. 6.

[90] Theatres Act 1968, s. 1 (2).

[91] *Ante,* p. 251.

(i) in areas where licences are required for public music, etc.,
the authority having the power to grant those licences has
authorised the demonstration; or

(ii) in areas where such licences are not required,[92] the local
authority has authorised it.

Conditions may in either case be attached to this authorisation.[93]

Section 3 makes it an offence for any person to give a demonstration of hypnotism on a person who has not attained the age
of 18 [94] years at or in connection with an entertainment to which
the public are admitted, whether on payment or otherwise, unless he
had reasonable cause to believe that the person had attained that
age.

Offences against sections 2 and 3 are punishable on **summary
conviction** [£50 *fine*].[95]

Nothing in the Act prevents the demonstration of hypnotism
for scientific or medical purposes.[96]

SECTION 15. FRAUDULENT MEDIUMS AND FORTUNE-TELLING

By **section 4** of the **Vagrancy Act 1824** " every person pretending
or professing to tell fortunes, or using any subtle craft, means or
device, by palmistry or otherwise, to deceive and impose upon any
of [her] Majesty's subjects," is deemed a rogue and vagabond
and punishable accordingly.[97]

Section 2 of the **Fraudulent Mediums Act 1951** has repealed
so much of section 4 as extends (i) to persons purporting to act
as spiritualistic mediums or to exercise any powers of telepathy,
clairvoyance [98] or other similar powers, and (ii) to persons who,
in purporting so to act or to exercise such powers, use fraudulent
devices.

Section 1 (1) of the Act provides that such persons shall be
guilty of an offence, provided that in the case of persons in category

---

92 *Ante*, p. 251.
93 s. 2 (2).
94 Substituted by the Family Law Reform Act 1969, s. 1 (3) and Sched. 1.
95 ss. 2, 3.
96 s. 5.
97 *Ante*, p. 241. The prevalence of genuine " Gipsy Rose Lees " at fairs suggests
that prosecutions for this offence are rare.
98 Defined in the *Shorter Oxford English Dictionary* as " the faculty of mentally
perceiving objects at a distance or concealed from sight. . . ."

(i) they had an intent to deceive and that in the case of persons in either category it is proved that they acted for reward. The offence is punishable on **summary conviction** [*Imp.* 4 *months and* £50 *fine*] or on **indictment** [*Imp.* 2 *years and* £500 *fine*].[99]

Nothing in this section applies to anything done solely for the purpose of entertainment.[1]

SECTION 16. STREET AND HOUSE-TO-HOUSE COLLECTIONS

Section 5 of the **Police, Factories, etc. (Miscellaneous Provisions) Act 1916**[2] provides that a police authority[3] may make regulations with respect to the places where and the conditions under which persons may be permitted in any street,[4] or public place, within the police area, to collect money or sell articles for the benefit of charitable or other purposes. These regulations do not apply to the sale of articles in the ordinary course of trade for the purpose of earning a livelihood when no representation is made that any proceeds will be devoted to charity.[5] Failure to comply with the regulations is punishable on **summary conviction** [£2 *fine*; 2nd or subsequent conviction, £5 *fine*].[6]

Sections 1, 2 and 3 of the **House to House Collections Act 1939**[7] provide that it shall be an offence to promote a collection[8] made by means of visits from house[9] to house for a charitable purpose,[10] or to act as a collector for such a collection, unless the promoter is authorised to promote the collection either:

(i) by a licence granted by the police authority of the area; or

(ii) in the case of certain local charitable purposes, by a certificate granted by the chief officer of police for the area; or

---

[99] The consent of the Director of Public Prosecutions is required before proceedings can be brought: s. 1 (4).

[1] s. 1 (5).

[2] As amended by the Police Act 1964, ss. 21 (3), 25 (4).

[3] Defined in Sched. 8 to the Police Act 1964.

[4] Defined in s. 5 (4).

[5] s. 5 (1) (*b*).   [6] s. 5 (1).

[7] As amended by the Police Act 1964, s. 64 (3), Sched. 10, Part I.

[8] As to the meaning of " collection " see *Carasu Ltd.* v. *Smith* [1968] 2 Q.B. 383 where it was held to include an activity where a person was induced to purchase one article on the representation that part of the proceeds would go to a charitable purpose.

[9] The expression " house " is defined to include a place of business: s. 11.

[10] The expression " charitable purpose " is defined in s. 11.

(iii) in the case of collections over wide areas, by an exemption order made by the Secretary of State.

If the promoter is not so authorised, then he is guilty of an offence punishable on **summary conviction** [*Imp. 6 months and £100 fine*], and so also is the collector [*£5 fine; 2nd or subsequent conviction, Imp. 3 months and £25 fine*].[10a]

Section 4 empowers the Secretary of State to make regulations [11] regulating the manner in which collections may be carried out and the conduct of promoters and collectors, *e.g.* use of prescribed badges and certificates of authority, prohibiting persons below a prescribed age from collecting and requiring a return of proceeds and expenses, etc., to be made. Breach of these regulations is punishable on **summary conviction** [*£5 fine*].[12]

The unauthorised use of prescribed badges or certificates of authority or the use of badges or certificates so nearly resembling the prescribed ones so as to be calculated to deceive is punishable on **summary conviction** [*Imp. 6 months and £100 fine*].[13]

A person whom a constable believes to be a collector is required to give his name and address to the constable on demand.[14] Failure to do so is punishable on summary conviction.[15]

10a s. 8 (1) (2).
11 See House to House Collection Regulations 1947 (S.R. & O. 1947 No. 2662), as amended by S.I. 1963 No. 684.
12 s. 8 (3).
13 ss. 6, 8 (4).
14 s. 6.
15 s. 8 (5).

CHAPTER 18

REGISTRATION OF BIRTHS AND DEATHS—OFFENCES RELATING TO CORPSES

SECTION 1. REGISTRATION OF BIRTHS AND DEATHS

THE **Births and Deaths Registration Act 1953** provides for the compulsory registration of all births [1] and deaths with the registrar of the sub-district where that birth or death occurred. The Act specifies [2] the persons qualified to register a birth and provides that it must be registered within forty-two days.[3] It also specifies [4] the persons qualified to register a death and provides that a death must be registered within five days, unless an inquest is held.[5] Where a person dies who has been attended in his last illness by a medical practitioner, **section 22** provides that that practitioner must sign a death certificate and deliver it to the registrar.[6]

Among the offences created by the Act are (i) failure on the part of the parents [7] to register a birth, (ii) failure on the part of a person to register a death when it is his duty to do so, and (iii) failure to comply with section 22.[8] All offences are punishable on summary conviction [£10 and, in the case of an offence within (i), £20 *fine*].[9]

The making of false declarations, statements and certificates in connection with the registration of births and deaths is punishable by the Perjury Act 1911.[10]

SECTION 2. NOTIFICATION OF DEATHS TO CORONERS

It is a common law offence to dispose of a dead body in order to prevent a coroner's inquest being held upon it.[11]

---

[1] Notice of births must also be given to the local medical officer of health [£1 *fine*]: Public Health Act 1936, s. 203.
[2] The father of the illegitimate child is not *required* to register: s. 10. In the case of a still-birth, the birth need only be registered if it took place after the 28th week of pregnancy: ss. 2, 41.
[3] Provision is made in ss. 6 and 7 for late registration.   [4] s. 16.
[5] Provision is made in ss. 19–21 for late registration.   [6] s. 22.
[7] Failure on the part of any other person to register a birth, when it is his duty to do so, is not, apparently, an offence.
[8] s. 36.
[9] *Ibid.* The fine was increased by the Criminal Justice Act 1967, Sched. 3.
[10] s. 4.   [11] For footnote, see p. 258.

Statutes impose duties upon certain persons in certain circumstances to notify the coroner of a death. These persons include registrars, persons in charge of certain institutions, *e.g.* prisons, mental homes, and foster parents.[12] Some of these statutes make it an offence to fail to comply with these duties.[13]

SECTION 3. OFFENCES RELATING TO BURIALS AND CREMATIONS

To leave unburied the corpse of any person for whom the defendant was bound to provide and was able to provide decent burial is a common law offence.[14]

It is also a common law offence (i) to dispose of a corpse so as to prevent the holding of a coroner's inquest [15]; (ii) without lawful authority to remove a corpse from a grave in a burying ground, whatever the motive or object for its removal [16]; (iii) without lawful authority to dispose of a corpse for dissection.[17]

It has also been held to be a common law nuisance to expose the naked dead body of a child in or near, and within view of, a highway.[18]

By **section 7** of the **Burial Laws Amendment Act 1880** it is an indictable offence to act riotously, violently or indecently at a burial or wilfully obstruct a burial.[19]

The burning of dead bodies is now governed by the **Cremation Act 1902,** as amended by the **Cremation Act 1952.** Under this Act a number of Regulations have been made regarding the conditions under which cremation may take place. They are, in particular, designed to prevent cremation from taking place until the cause of death has been properly ascertained.[20]

---

[11] Arch. para. 3907. As to conspiracy to prevent the burial of a corpse see *R.* v. *Hunter and Others* [1972] Crim.L.R. 369. The Report of the Committee on Death Certification and Coroners (Cmnd. 4810) published on November 10, 1971 reviews the certificate of death as well as the future of the Coroner. Its conclusions are to be found summarised at [1972] Crim.L.R. 70 *et seq.*

[12] For a list of these statutes, see Halsbury, Vol. 8, p. 485 *et seq.*

[13] *Ibid.*

[14] Arch. para. 3906.

[15] Arch. para. 3907.

[16] *R.* v. *Sharpe* (1857) D. & B. 160; Arch. para. 3908.

[17] *R.* v. *Lynn* (1788) 1 Leach 497.

[18] *R.* v. *Clark* (1883) 15 Cox 171.

[19] See also Cemeteries Clauses Act 1847, s. 59, which makes it an offence to play games or sports in a cemetery or unlawfully disturb any persons assembled in a cemetery [£10 *fine*]. The fines were increased by the Criminal Justice Act 1967, Sched. 3.

[20] See Halsbury, Vol. 4, p. 120 *et seq.*, for these regulations.

By **section 8** of the Act, as amended by the Perjury Act 1911, and the Cremation Act 1952, the following are offences:

(i) for any person wilfully to make any false representation or to sign or utter any false certificate with a view to securing the burning of human remains [*Imp.* 2 *years*];

(ii) for any person, with intent to conceal the commission or impede the prosecution of any offence, to procure or attempt to procure the cremation of any body, or, with such intent, to make any application or give any certificate under the Act [*Imp.* 5 *years*].

The same section also provides that any person who contravenes any regulation made under the Act, or knowingly carries out or procures or takes part in the burning of any human remains, except in accordance with such regulations or the provisions of the Act, shall be liable on **summary conviction** [£50 *fine*].

Certain summary offences arise under the **Births and Deaths Registration Act 1874**.[21]

By **section 1** of the **Births and Deaths Registration Act 1926** it is an offence to dispose of a body before delivering to the person effecting the disposal a registrar's certificate [22] or coroner's order,[23] or a written declaration that the certificate or order has been issued [£20 *fine*].[24]

---

[21] See ss. 17–19.

[22] This is granted by the registrar upon registration of a death or a still-birth: Births and Deaths Registration Act 1953, ss. 11, 24.

[23] See S.I. 1954, No. 1596, rr. 82, 88 ; Coroners (Amendment) Act 1926, s. 14 (2).

[24] If the body is disposed of by cremation, failure to comply with this requirement will also be an offence against the Cremation Act 1902, s. 8 (1), as being a breach of the Cremation Regulations 1930, r. 6. The fine was increased by the Criminal Justice Act 1967, Sched. 3.

CHAPTER 19

BIGAMY AND OFFENCES AGAINST THE MARRIAGE LAWS

SECTION 1. BIGAMY

By **section 57** of the **Offences against the Person Act 1861** it is provided that " whosoever, being married, shall marry any other person during the life of the former husband or wife, whether the second marriage takes place in England or Ireland [1] or elsewhere, shall be guilty of an offence " [*Imp. 7 years*] except

(1) where a second marriage is contracted elsewhere than in England or [Northern] Ireland by anyone other than a British subject;

(2) where a second marriage is contracted by any person whose husband or wife has been continually absent for seven years and has not been known by such person to be living within that time.[2]

(3) where the second marriage is after a divorce or after the first marriage has been declared void by a court of competent jurisdiction.[3]

The second husband or wife may, if aware of the bigamous character of the marriage, be indicted as an accomplice to the bigamy.

To commit an offence against section 57 the accused must, at the time of the second marriage, *be married*. This means that his first marriage must be:

(i) valid [4] and not yet terminated by: (a) a valid [5] divorce decree,[6] or (b) the death of the other spouse; or

---

[1] This means exclusive of Eire (the Republic of Ireland): Irish Free State (Consequential Adaptation of Enactments) Order 1923.

[2] The prosecution must prove that the accused knew his wife to be alive at some time during the seven years: *R.* v. *Curgerwen* (1865) L.R. 1 C.C.R. 1; *R.* v. *Lund* (1921) 16 Cr.App.R. 31.

[3] It is not clear why this provision is included since in neither case would the accused then be " married."

[4] Whether or not a marriage is valid can be a difficult question of law, particularly where the marriage was celebrated abroad or the spouses were domiciled abroad at the time of the marriage: see Bromley, *Family Law*, 3rd ed., p. 30 *et seq.*

[5] A divorce obtained abroad may not be recognised as valid in England: Bromley, *op. cit.*, p. 88 *et seq.*

[6] The marriage subsists until the decree absolute has been granted. It is also possible for a valid marriage to be terminated by a foreign nullity decree: *Salvesen* v. *Austrian Property Administrator* [1927] A.C. 641.

(ii) valid and the proviso in (2) above does not apply (seven years' absence); or

(iii) voidable [7] and not yet terminated by a valid [8] nullity decree,[9] and,

in any case, must also be monogamous.[10] It follows that if the accused had contracted a void [11] marriage, a second marriage is not bigamous.[12]

It is no defence that the second marriage was itself void independently of its bigamous character. So, where A, being married, went through a ceremony of marriage with his niece, it was held that he could be convicted of bigamy.[13]

Mistake.[14] The accused will not be guilty of bigamy if he mistakenly thought, and that mistake was one of fact and was reasonable, that

(i) his first wife was dead [15]; or

(ii) his first marriage was void [16]; or

(iii) his first marriage had been dissolved or annulled.[17]

There is no clear English authority on what would be the effect of a (reasonable) mistake as to the (civil) law of marriage,[18] e.g. a mistaken belief that a foreign divorce would be recognised in England.[19] All the above authorities concerned mistakes of fact,

---

[7] A marriage may be either valid, voidable or void. Only death or a divorce terminates a valid marriage. Voidable marriages can be terminated either by death or a decree (absolute) of nullity. Void marriages, on the other hand, can be treated by *anyone* as never having existed without the necessity for any decree, although a nullity decree *can* be obtained to clear up any confusion that may exist or in order to ask for such ancillary orders as maintenance and custody: see further Bromley, *op. cit.*, p. 55 *et seq.*

[8] A nullity decree obtained abroad may not be recognised as valid in England: Bromley, *op. cit.*, p. 78.

[9] A voidable marriage subsists until the decree absolute has been given and a second marriage before that time is void and bigamous: see *Wiggins* v. *Wiggins and Ingram* [1958] 1 W.L.R. 1013.

[10] *R.* v. *Sarwan Singh* [1962] 3 All E.R. 612.

[11] Above, note 7.

[12] Arch. para. 3790. See also *R.* v. *King* [1964] 1 Q.B. 285.

[13] *R.* v. *Allen* (1872) L.R. 1 C.C.R. 367.   [14] *Ante*, p. 47.

[15] *R.* v. *Tolson* (1889) 23 Q.B.D. 168.

[16] *R.* v. *King* [1964] 1 Q.B. 285. See also the earlier authorities cited in that case.

[17] *R.* v. *Gould* [1968] 2 Q.B. 65, overruling *R.* v. *Wheat and Stocks* [1921] 2 K.B. 119.

[18] In *R.* v. *Lolley* (1812) R. & R. 237 and *Earl Russell's Case* [1901] A.C. 446 there was no argument on the question of mistake. See further, *ante*, p. 47.

[19] Presumably such a belief might well now be a valid defence: *R.* v. *Gould, supra.*

although there is no suggestion in the cases that there would be any difference if the mistakes had been mistakes of law.

SECTION 2.   OFFENCES AGAINST THE MARRIAGE ACTS 1949 TO 1970

Under **section 75** of the **Marriage Act 1949** any person who knowingly and wilfully solemnises marriage otherwise than as required by subsection (1) [20] of that section is guilty of an offence [*Imp.* 14 *years*], and any person who knowingly and wilfully solemnises a marriage otherwise than as required by subsection (2) [21] of that section is also guilty of an offence [*Imp.* 5 *years*].

Every prosecution under this section must be commenced within three years from the date of the offence.

The essence of these offences seems to be that the accused intended that persons present at the ceremony would believe that a valid monogamous [22] marriage was being performed by him.[23] If therefore " the person who is alleged to have solemnised the marriage honestly believes that he is only taking part in what is known by everyone present to be a charade, the foundation of the offence must go." [24]

The Marriage (Registrar-General's Licence) Act 1970 permits marriages on unregistered premises on the authority of the Registrar-General's licence where he is satisfied that one of the persons to be married is seriously ill and is not expected to recover, and cannot be moved to registered premises. It is an offence punishable on **summary conviction** [£100 *fine*] or on **indictment** [*Imp.* 3 *years* and £500 *fine*] (i) to solemnise such a marriage in a place other than that specified in the licence; (ii) to solemnise such a marriage [25] without the presence of a registrar; or (iii) after the expiration of one month from the date of entry in the marriage notice book; (iv) to give false information by way of evidence of legal capacity for the marriage; (v) or to give a false medical certificate in regard to the matter.

---

[20] *e.g.* solemnising a marriage according to the rites of the Church of England without banns of matrimony having been duly published or solemnising a marriage according to the said rites falsely pretending to be in Holy Orders.
[21] *e.g.* solemnising a marriage in a place in which marriages may not be celebrated.
[22] *R.* v. *Bham* [1966] 1 Q.B. 159.
[23] *R.* v. *Kemp* [1964] 2 Q.B. 341.
[24] *Ibid.* at p. 349.
[25] Except in the case of a Jewish or Quaker marriage: s. 16 (1) (*b*).

CHAPTER 20

DANGEROUS DRUGS AND POISONS

SECTION 1. DANGEROUS DRUGS

THE **Misuse of Drugs Act 1971** [1] repeals all that legislation solely
concerned with the control of dangerous drugs,[2] and seeks to
consolidate the law relating to dangerous and otherwise harmful
drugs. The Act seeks to achieve two broad purposes, namely the
control of dangerous drugs and the prevention of their abuse. It
specifies as " controlled drugs " [3] the substances set out in Parts I,
II, and III of the **Second Schedule** and divides them, according
to their harmfulness, into three classes, A, B, and C. It is not
surprising to find substances such as cocaine, heroin, LSD, mor-
phine and opium in class A. The amphetamines, codeines,
cannabis and cannabis resin are found in class B; while class C consists of a number of the less familiar substances. There is provision
in the Act for amending this schedule or removing any substance
from one class to another, as the necessity arises. A number of
offences of varying seriousness are created by the Act and these
are clearly set out in a table in the **Fourth Schedule** showing the
section creating the particular offence, the general nature of the
offence, the mode of prosecution and the punishment specified
according to the class of drug involved. These offences seek to
control the importation and exportation,[4] the possession,[5] the production and the supply [6] of controlled drugs; the use of premises
for certain activities relating to controlled drugs such as opium and
cannabis [7] and also the cultivation of the plant cannabis.[8] Further,

---

[1] Not in force on July 1, 1972, except for ss. 1 (Advisory Council); 32
(research); 35 (financial provisions); 37 (interpretation); 38 (special provisions
affecting Northern Ireland); and 40 (short title and commencement) and Sched.
I (the constitution of the Advisory Council) which were brought into operation
on February 1, 1972, by the *Misuse of Drugs Act* 1971 (*Commencement No.* 1)
Order 1971, *S.I. No.* 2120 (c. 57).
[2] The Drugs (Prevention of Misuse) Act 1964, the Dangerous Drugs Acts 1965
and 1967 and the regulations under those Acts.
[3] s. 2.
[4] s. 3.
[5] s. 5.
[6] s. 4.
[7] ss. 8 and 9.
[8] s. 6.

263

in attempting to prevent the abuse of drugs, the Act confers power upon the Secretary of State to make regulations [9] governing the safe custody of controlled drugs [10] and to give directions prohibiting a practitioner [11] or pharmacist [12] convicted of certain offences from possessing or supplying etc. controlled drugs [13] or prohibiting a practitioner who is prescribing, administering or supplying etc. such drugs in an irresponsible manner from so doing.[14]

The Act also gives the Secretary of State power [15] to obtain information regarding the prescription etc. of drugs from a doctor or the supply of drugs by a pharmacist and to prevent such a person furnishing him with false information.[16] Assisting in or inducing the commission outside the United Kingdom of an offence under a corresponding law [17] is also made an offence; as is obstructing the exercise of powers of search etc. or of concealing books and drugs etc.[18] An attempt to commit any offence under the Act, or to incite or to attempt to incite another to commit such an offence is also punishable.[19] This then is the general scheme of offences provided under the Act. It is only possible to deal with a few of the more important points in a work of this size.

Specific Offences

By **section 3** the importation or exportation of a controlled drug is prohibited (except under regulations made in accordance with **section 7** of the Act, or under or in accordance with the terms of a licence issued by the Secretary of State and in compliance with any conditions attached thereto). Improper importation and improper exportation are punishable under the **Customs and Excise Act 1952, sections 45 (1)** and **56 (2)** [20] respectively, on **indictment** [*Imp.* 14 *years and fine in respect of class A and B drugs* [21]; *Imp.* 5 *years and fine in respect of class C drugs* [22] *or on* **summary**

---

[9] s. 10.

[10] s. 11.

[11] " Practitioner " except in the expression " Veterinary practitioner " means a doctor, dentist, veterinary practitioner or veterinary surgeon.

[12] " Pharmacist " has the same meaning as in the Medicines Act 1968.

[13] s. 12.

[14] s. 13.

[15] s. 17.

[16] s. 18.

[18] s. 23 (4).

[20] See generally p. 151 *et seq., ante.*

[22] See, *ante,* p. 263.

[17] s. 20 (2).

[19] s. 19.

[21] See, *ante,* p. 263.

conviction *Imp. 12 months and a penalty of three times the value of the goods or £400 whichever is the greater, in respect of all classes of drug*].[23]

Section 4 (2) makes it an offence punishable in respect of class A and B drugs on **indictment** [*Imp. 14 years and fine*] or on **summary conviction** [*Imp. 12 months and £400 fine*] and in respect of class C drugs punishable on **indictment** [*Imp. 5 years and fine*] or on **summary conviction** [*Imp. 6 months and £200 fine*] for a person to produce or be concerned in the production of a controlled drug in contravention of **section 4 (1).**

Section 4 (1) makes it unlawful (subject to any regulation made under section 7 of the Act) for a person to produce [24] a controlled drug or to supply [25] or offer to supply such a drug to another.

Section 4 (3) makes it an offence [*punishable as under section 4 (2)*] for a person to supply or offer to supply a controlled drug, or to be concerned in the doing of either activity by another person, in contravention of section 4 (1).[26]

Section 5 (3) makes it an offence [*punishable as under section 4 (2)*] for a person to have possession [27] whether lawfully or not, of a controlled drug with intent to supply it to another in contravention of section 4 (1).[28]

Section 5 deals with possession. **Section 5 (1)** makes it unlawful (subject to regulations made under section 7) for a person to have a controlled drug in his possession.[29] **Section 5 (2)** makes it an offence punishable on **indictment** [*Imp. 7 years and fine in respect of class A drugs; Imp. 5 years and fine in respect of class B drugs; Imp. 2 years and fine in respect of class C drugs*]; or on **summary conviction** [*Imp. 6 months and £250 fine*] for a person to have a controlled drug in his possession in contravention of section 5 (1).[30] **Section 5 (4)** provides a defence for a person charged with an offence of possession under section 5 (2) if he proves—

---

[23] See generally, *ante*, p. 151.
[24] " Produce " where the reference is to producing a controlled drug, means producing it by manufacture, cultivation, or any other method, and " production " has a corresponding meaning: s. 37 (1).
[25] " Supplying " includes distributing: s. 37 (1).
[26] Subject to s. 28, *post*, p. 268.
[27] See, *post*, p. 267.
[28] Proof of lack of knowledge under s. 28 is a defence: see p. 269, *post*.
[29] See p. 267, *post*.
[30] Subject to s. 28, *post*. See the cases cited at p. 267, *post*.

(a) that knowing or suspecting it to be a controlled drug, he took possession of it for the purpose of preventing another from committing or continuing to commit an offence in connection with that drug and that as soon as possible after taking possession of it he took all such steps as were reasonably open to him to destroy the drug or to deliver it into the custody of a person lawfully entitled to the custody of it; or

(b) that knowing or suspecting it to be a controlled drug, he took possession of it for the purpose of delivering it into the custody of a person lawfully entitled to the custody of it, and that as soon as possible after taking possession of it he took all such steps as were reasonably open to him to deliver it into the custody of such a person.[31]

Section 6 (1) makes it unlawful (subject to any regulation made under section 7) for a person to cultivate any plant of the genus cannabis.[32]   A person who does so [33] commits an offence under **section 6 (2)** punishable on **indictment** [*Imp. 14 years and fine*] or on **summary conviction** [*Imp. 12 months and £400 fine*]. **Section 9** makes it an offence punishable on **indictment** [*Imp. 14 years and fine*] or on **summary conviction** [*Imp. 12 months and £400 fine*] for a person

(a) to smoke or otherwise use [34] prepared opium [35]; or

(b) to frequent a place used for the purpose of opium smoking; or to have in his possession [36]—

> (i) any pipes or other utensils made or adapted for use in or connected with the smoking of opium, being pipes or

---

[31] s. 5 (5) modifies the wording of s. 5 (4) so that the defence may apply to a charge of attempting to get or attempting to take possession of a controlled drug under s. 19 (1).   s. 5 (6) provides that nothing in ss. 5 (4) and 5 (5) shall prejudice any defence which is open to a person charged under s. 5.

[32] " Cannabis " (except in the expression " cannabis resin ") means the flowering or fruiting tops of any plant of the genus cannabis from which the resin has not been extracted, by whatever name they may be designated : " Cannabis resin " means the separated resin, whether crude or purified, obtained from any plant of the genus cannabis : s. 37 (1).

[33] Proof of lack of knowledge under s. 28 is a defence : see p. 269, *post.*

[34] No count should charge a user for more than one activity : *Ware* v. *Fox* [1967] 1 W.L.R. 379.

[35] Prepared opium means opium prepared for smoking and includes dross and any other residues remaining after opium has been smoked : s. 37 (1).

[36] See, *post*, p. 267.

utensils which have been used by him or with his knowledge and permission in that connection; or

(ii) any utensils which have been used by him or with his knowledge and permission in connection with the preparation of opium for smoking.[37]

Possession

Possession, which is the subject of the greatest number of proceedings under the previous legislation, is not specifically defined in the Act [38] but **section 37 (3)** provides that for the purposes of the Act the things which a person has in his possession shall be taken to include anything subject to his control which is in the custody of another. There are authorities under the former legislation which are clearly relevant to the new Act. Possession involves not only physical possession but an element of control. Control is clearly important in those cases where the accused is said to be in constructive possession of the substance concerned. Thus, where drugs are found concealed on an accused person's premises it must be proved, if he was absent when they arrived, either that on his return he had become aware of them and exercised some control over them or that the drugs or the package containing them had come, albeit in his absence, at his instigation or by arrangement with him.[39] It was held in *R.* v. *Buswell* [40] that where a person mislaid an article or thought erroneously that it had been destroyed or disposed of, if in fact it remained in his care and control he did not lose possession. The defendant, who was under treatment for drug addiction, was given amphetamine tablets on a prescription and he lost those tablets and obtained more on a second prescription to replace those he thought he had lost. Ten months later he rediscovered the tablets on the first prescription in the back of a drawer in his room. He consumed some and was found in possession of the remainder. His possession was held to be lawful.

Possession implies that there must be something to possess, that is to say, that it is of sufficient quantity to be seen in order that the accused may be said to have the necessary *mens rea* or

---

[37] Proof of lack of knowledge under s. 28 is a defence: see p. 269, *post*.
[38] As to possession generally, see pp. 36–38, *ante*.
[39] See, *e.g. R.* v. *Cavendish* [1961] 1 W.L.R. 1083, a decision on stolen goods.
[40] [1972] 1 W.L.R. 64. The charge was laid under s. 1 (1) of the Drugs (Prevention of Misuse) Act 1964.

knowledge that he has possession of it.[41]   Thus it was held in
R. v. Worsell [42] that possession of a tube, to all intents and purposes
empty, which was empty to the naked eye although it contained a
few droplets of a drug which were only discernible microscopically
and were impossible to measure or pour out, did not constitute
possession of a drug.[43] Where there is sufficient of the drug to be
measured so that it can be weighed in milligrammes it has been
held that this can amount to possession.[44] It is submitted that, in
view of section 28, to constitute possession under the Act, there
must be sufficient traces or residue of a controlled drug for the
accused to know that he has not only an illicit substance but a
substance which is a controlled drug. In Hambleton v. Callinan [45]
where traces of amphetamine powder could only be detected in
the urine of the accused by chemical analysis after its consumption
by them, the prosecution should have alleged possession prior to
arrest to have been successful. The presence of amphetamine
powder in the urine would be prima facie evidence of earlier
possession. Any reference in the Act to misusing a drug is a reference to misusing it by taking it; and a reference to the taking of it
is a reference to the taking of it by a human being by way of any
form of self-administration, whether or not involving assistance by
another.[46]

Mens Rea

Section 28 of the Act clarifies the requirements of *mens rea* in
relation to offences under sections 4 (2) and (3), 5 (2) and (3), 6 (2)
and 9 (1) and thereby clears up the uncertainty as to the degree
of knowledge which had to be proved in those offences involving
possession under the old law. The decisions in *Warner* v. *Metropolitan Police Commissioner* [47] and *Sweet* v. *Parsley*,[48] although

---

[41] A conviction was quashed in R. v. Marriott [1971] 1 W.L.R. 187 on the grounds
of misdirection, where on scientific examination minute traces of cannabis resin
had been found on a penknife in the possession of the accused, but the
prosecution had failed to prove that the accused had reason to believe that
the knife contained any foreign substance.

[42] [1970] 1 W.L.R. 111.

[43] For the purposes of reg. 9 of the Dangerous Drugs (No. 2) Regulations 1964
and the Dangerous Drugs Act 1965, s. 13.

[44] R. v. Graham [1970] 1 W.L.R. 113; see also R. v. Frederick [1970] 1 W.L.R.
107.

[45] (1968) 132 J.P. 461.

[46] s. 37 (2).

[47] [1969] 2 A.C. 256.   [48] [1970] A.C. 132.

demonstrating that a mental element was required in such offences,[49] which were said to be offences of strict liability,[50] failed to spell out the degree of knowledge required. Under the previous enactments the mental element required proof of two stages. First, it had to be proved that an accused knew that he had actual or constructive possession of the article which contained the drugs. Secondly, although it could not be proved that the accused knew the exact nature of what he had, it had to be proved that there were facts from which it could be inferred that he knew he had a substance of an illicit nature, though not necessarily what kind of illicit substance it was.[51]

By **section 28 (2)** [52] it is provided that in any proceedings for an offence to which the section applies [53] it shall be a defence for the accused to prove that he neither knew of nor suspected nor had reason to suspect the existence of some fact alleged by the prosecution which it is necessary for the prosecution to prove if he is to be convicted of the offence charged; and by **section 28 (3)** it is expressly provided that it is necessary, if the accused is to be convicted of the offence charged,[54] for the prosecution to prove that some substance or product involved in the alleged offence was the controlled drug which the prosecution alleges it to have been, and if it is proved that the substance or product in question was that controlled drug, the accused—

(a) shall not be acquitted of the offence charged by reason only of proving that he neither knew nor suspected nor had reason to suspect that the substance or product in question was the particular controlled drug alleged; but

(b) shall be acquitted thereof—

(i) if he proves that he neither believed nor suspected nor had reason to suspect that the substance or product in question was a controlled drug; or

(ii) if he proves that he believed the substance or product in question to be a controlled drug, or a controlled

---

[49] Unauthorised possession, contrary to reg. 9 of the Dangerous Drugs (No. 2) Regulations 1964 and s. 13 of the Dangerous Drugs Act 1965 or contrary to s. 1 (1) of the Drugs (Prevention of Misuse) Act 1964.
[50] *Lockyer* v. *Gibb* [1967] 2 Q.B. 243, D.C.
[51] See generally " Drugs and the Guilty Mind " by P. J. Morrish, 134 J.P. 201.
[52] Subject to s. 28 (3).
[53] See n. 54 *infra*.
[54] That is an offence under s. 4 (2) and (3), 5 (2) and (3), 6 (2) or 9 (1).

drug of a description, such that, if it had in fact been that controlled drug or a controlled drug of that description, he would not at the material time have been committing any offence to which the section applies.[55]

The importance of section 28 is this, that by importing a specific *mens rea* into these sections, an " innocent possessor " of a receptacle containing drugs, whether he be a carrier innocently carrying it, or a recipient innocently receiving it for safe custody, cannot be convicted of possessing the drug merely because he knew he had possession of the receptacle.

In *R*. v. *Fernandez* [55a] the defendant was a merchant seaman who was given a package to take to England. He was told it contained " smoking sticks " and he had an idea that this referred to marijuana cigarettes; he saw the contents, for the package broke open while he had it and he thought he might get into trouble with the customs authorities. The Court of Appeal dismissing his appeal, pointed out that although it was clear that he did not know the precise nature of the contents, his conduct indicated that he was prepared to take the package into his possession whatever its contents and therefore possession was proved for all purposes.

Section 21 provides that where an offence under the Act is committed by a body corporate, and it is proved to have been committed with the consent or connivance of, or is attributable to any neglect on the part of any director, manager, secretary, or other similar officer of the body corporate, or any person purporting to act in such a capacity, he, as well as the body corporate, shall be guilty of that offence.

Lawful Possession

The old concept of " without lawful excuse " which was a part of the former legislation is not re-enacted in the present statute. In sections 3, 4 (1), 5 (1) and 6 (1) it will have been seen that the offence is committed only " subject to regulations under section 7." **Section 7** empowers the Secretary of State to authorise activities in regard to controlled drugs which would otherwise be unlawful

---

55 Nothing in the section prejudices any other defence which it is open to an accused person to raise: s. 28 (3).
55a [1970] Crim.L.R. 277, C.A. As to aiding and abetting see *R*. v. *Patel* [1972] Crim.L.R. 274. (Both of these decisions are under the old law.)

under those sections.[56] Further the regulations may exempt from those sections [57] certain specified controlled drugs.[58] In particular the regulations may provide for certain things to be done under licence or authority issued by the Secretary of State and in compliance with any conditions attached thereto.[59] They must provide, by virtue of **section 7 (3),** that it is not unlawful under section 4 (1) for a doctor,[60] dentist,[61] veterinary practitioner or veterinary surgeon [62] acting in his capacity as such to prescribe, administer, manufacture, compound or supply a controlled drug, or for a pharmacist [63] or a person lawfully conducting a retail pharmacy business,[64] acting in either case in his capacity as such, to manufacture, compound or supply a controlled drug; and under section 5 (1) for a doctor, dentist, veterinary practitioner, veterinary surgeon, pharmacist or person lawfully conducting a retail pharmacy business to have a controlled drug in his possession for the purpose of acting in his capacity as such. Under **section 7 (4)** the Secretary of State may by order,[65] if he considers it in the public interest, direct that a controlled drug be removed from those drugs which may be prescribed by a doctor, dentist etc. or which may be manufactured etc. by a pharmacist etc. under subsection (3). Except, however, that such a drug can be kept for the purposes of research or other special purpose,[66] or under a licence or authority issued by the Secretary of State.[67]

Management of Premises

By **section 8** it is an offence punishable on **indictment** [*Imp.* 14 *years and fine*] in respect of class A and B drugs; [*Imp.* 5 *years and fine*] in respect of a class C drug and on **summary conviction**

---

[56] Except under s. 3.
[57] Other than s. 6 (1).
[58] s. 7 (1).
[59] s. 7 (2).
[60] Doctor means a fully registered person within the meaning of the Medical Acts 1956–1969.
[61] Meaning a person registered in the dentists' register under the Dentists Act 1957.
[62] The former means a person registered in the supplementary register kept under s. 8, and the latter a person registered in the register of veterinary surgeons kept under s. 2, of the Veterinary Surgeons Act 1966.
[63] Which has the same meaning as in the Medicines Act 1968.
[64] See s. 7 (5).
[65] See also s. 7 (5), (6) and (7).
[66] s. 7 (4) (*a*).
[67] s. 7 (4) (*b*).

[*Imp.* 12 *months and* £400 *fine*] in respect of class A and B drugs;
[*Imp.* 6 *months and* £200 *fine*] in respect of class C drugs for a
person being the occupier or being concerned in the management
of any premises, *knowingly* to permit [68] or to suffer the production
or attempted production of a controlled drug in contravention of
section 4 (1), the supply or attempted supply of a controlled drug
to another, or the offer to supply a controlled drug to another in
contravention of section 4 (1), the preparation of opium for smoking
and the smoking of cannabis, cannabis resin or prepared opium.
This section contains the word " knowingly " which imports into
the section *mens rea*, thereby clarifying the unsatisfactory situation
under the former legislation.[69]

Enforcement

Powers of search and arrest. By **section 23 (1)** [70] a constable or
other authorised person has the authority to enter the premises of
persons carrying on the business of a producer or supplier of
controlled drugs and to demand the production of, and to inspect,
any books or documents relating to dealings in any such drugs and
to inspect any stocks of any such drugs without a search warrant.
Under **section 23 (2)** a constable who has reasonable grounds to
suspect that any person is in possession of a controlled drug in
contravention of the Act or regulations made under it, may

(*a*) search that person, and detain him for the purpose of
searching him;

(*b*) search any vehicle or vessel [71] in which the constable suspects that the drug may be found and for that purpose may
require the person in control of the vehicle or vessel to
stop it;

(*c*) seize and detain, for the purpose of proceedings under the
Act, anything found in the course of the search which
appears to the constable to be evidence of an offence under
the Act.

---

[68] " Permit " connotes *at least* knowledge or reasonable grounds for suspicion:
Sweet v. *Parsley* [1970] A.C. 132 at p. 162, *per* Lord Diplock; but reasonable
grounds for suspicion should not be equated with suspicion or suspicion with
knowledge: *R.* v. *Souter* [1971] 1 W.L.R. 1187.

[69] See, *e.g.* the case of *Sweet* v. *Parsley* (1969) 133 J.P. 188; [1970] A.C. 132.

[70] Without prejudice to any other powers, etc.

[71] " Vessel " includes a hovercraft within the meaning of the Hovercraft Act 1968.

Section 23 (3) provides for the issue of a search warrant by a justice in certain cases. It is an offence [72] punishable on **summary conviction** [*Imp*. 6 *months and* £400 *fine*] or on **indictment** [*Imp*. 2 *years and fine*] for a person intentionally to obstruct a person in the exercise of his powers under section 23; or to conceal from a person acting in the exercise of his powers, any books, documents, stocks or drugs, or without reasonable excuse (proof of which lies on him) to fail to produce any such books or documents where their production is demanded by a person in the exercise of his powers.

By **section 24 (1)** [73] a constable may arrest without warrant any person who has committed, or whom the constable with reasonable cause suspects to have committed an offence under the Act if

(*a*) he believes, with reasonable cause, that that person will abscond unless he is arrested; or

(*b*) the name and address of that person are unknown to, and cannot be ascertained by, him; or

(*c*) he is not satisfied that a name and address furnished by that person as his name and address are true.

The Advisory Council on the Misuse of Drugs [74] has a general duty under the Act to keep under review the drug situation in the United Kingdom and to give advice [75] on measures which it thinks ought to be taken for preventing the misuse of drugs or for dealing with social problems connected with their misuse.

SECTION 2. POISONS AND OTHER DANGEROUS SUBSTANCES

The sale of poisons is regulated by the **Pharmacy and Poisons Act 1933,** as amended, and regulations made thereunder. Those poisons included in the " Poison List " may only be sold by authorised sellers of poisons. Subject to certain exceptions, to be an authorised seller a person must be a registered pharmacist carrying on a business which comprises the retail sale of drugs, which sale is under his personal control or that of some other registered pharmacist.[76] In the case of a company, the keeping, selling etc. of poisons must be under the control of a superintendent, who

[72] s. 23 (4).
[73] Without prejudice to any other powers, etc.
[74] Set up under s. 1 of the Act and constituted in accordance with Sched. I.
[75] See s. 1 (2).
[76] s. 8. To be repealed by the Medicines Act 1968, Sched. 6. (Not in force on July 1, 1972.)

shall be a registered pharmacist, and the retail sale of drugs must be under his personal control or under the personal control of another registered pharmacist.[77]

Part II of the **Therapeutic Substances Act 1956** [78] controls the sale, supply etc. of penicillin and certain other substances which may endanger health unless used with proper safeguards.

The use of poison to endanger life or injure is also specifically provided for in the Offences against the Person Act, 1861.[79]

Medicinal Products

The object of the **Medicines Acts 1968** [80] to **1971,** which came into force on October 25, 1968,[81] is the control of:

(1) The sale, supply or export of any medicinal product including the procuration of not only for such sale, supply or exportation but the manufacture or assembly of such a medicinal product for such a purpose;

(2) the import of any medicinal product without a product licence [82];

(3) the use of medicinal products in clinical trials and medicinal tests on animals; and

(4) the manufacture, sale, supply, importation or exportation of any articles or substances used wholly or partly for a medicinal purpose which are not medicinal products.[83]

Control is achieved generally by the issue of licences and certificates, ministerial orders and regulations and the creation of enforcement agencies.[84]

Medicinal product means any substance or article (not being an instrument, apparatus or appliance) which is manufactured, sold, supplied, imported or exported for use wholly or mainly in either or both of the following ways, that is to say:

[77] s. 9. To be repealed by the Medicines Act 1968, Sched. 6.
[78] To be repealed by the Medicines Act 1968, Sched. 6.
[79] *Post,* p. 460.
[80] As amended by the Medicines Act 1971.
[81] Except for ss. 63–65, 77, 85 (5), 86 (3), 90 (2), 93, 97 and 135 which are to come into operation on such day or days as the Ministers may by order appoint.
[82] ss. 8 and 9.
[83] s. 104.
[84] *e.g.* the Pharmaceutical Society, every County, County borough council in England and Wales, every London borough council and the common council of the City of London, the overseers of the Inner and Middle Temples, etc.

(a) use by being administered [85] to one or more human beings or animals for a medicinal purpose;

(b) use,[86] in circumstances to which this paragraph applies, as an ingredient in the preparation of a substance or article which is to be administered to one or more human beings or animals for a medicinal purpose.[87]

Medicinal purpose means the treating or preventing of disease; diagnosing disease or ascertaining the existence, degree or extent of a physiological condition; contraception; inducing anaesthesia and otherwise preventing or interfering with the normal operation of a physiological function, whether permanently or temporarily, and whether by way of terminating, reducing or postponing, or increasing or accelerating, the operation of that function or in any other way.[88] The 1968 Act is divided into eight parts. **Part I** sets up the Medicines Commission and defines its general functions, establishes various committees and defines which Ministers are responsible for the administration of the Act. **Part II** deals with licences and certificates relating to medicinal products. Certain sections in Part II create offences as follows:

Section 45 (1) to (6) inclusive makes it an offence for any person to contravene any of the provisions of **section 7** (general provisions as to dealing with medicinal products); **section 8** (provisions as to manufacture and wholesale dealing); **section 31** (clinical trials); **section 32** (medicinal tests on animals); **section 34** (restrictions as to animals on which medicinal tests have been carried out); **section 40** (general provisions relating to medicated animal feeding stuffs); and **section 45 (6)** (making statements known to be false when giving information to the licensing authority required under section 44). It is also an offence under **section 45 (1)** for any person to be in possession of any medicinal product or animal

---

[85] " Administer " means administer to a human being as an animal, whether orally, by injection or by introduction into the body in any other way, or by external application, whether by direct contact with the body or not. Administering a substance or article is a reference to administering it either in its existing state or after it has been dissolved or disposed in, or diluted or mixed with, some other substance used as a vehicle.

[86] Use in a pharmacy or in a hospital, or by a practitioner, or in the course of a business which consists of or includes the retail sale, or the supply in circumstances corresponding to retail sale, of herbal remedies.

[87] ss. 130 (1) and 130 (4) to (7) inclusive define what a " medicinal product " does not include.

[88] s. 130 (2).

feeding stuff for the purposes of selling, supplying or exporting it in contravention of any of those sections. By **section 45 (8)** any person who is guilty of any of those offences is liable on conviction on indictment [*Imp. 2 years and fine*]; or on **summary conviction** [£400 *fine*] (the normal penalty).

By **section 45 (7)** it is an offence on **summary conviction** [£50 *fine*] for any person without reasonable excuse to fail to comply with a requirement imposed on him by a notice under section 44 (2).

By **section 46** special defences are provided for in offences committed under section 45.

Part III makes further provisions relating to dealings with medicinal products and creates certain offences as follows:

Section 67 (4) makes it an offence on conviction on indictment or on summary conviction (normal penalty) for any person to contravene any of the provisions of section 52 (the sale or supply of medicinal products not on the general sales list); section 58 (provisions relating to medicinal products which may be sold by retail, or supplied in circumstances corresponding to retail sale etc. on prescription only); section 63 (adulteration of medicinal products) [89]; section 64 (sale of medicinal products to the prejudice of the purchaser) [90]; section 65 (failure to comply with standards specified in monographs in certain publications) [91]; and for any person to contravene any regulations made under section 60 or 61 and section 67 (6) (unauthorised provision of medicinal products sold, supplied or imported in contravention of an order made under section 62).

By **section 67 (5)** it is an offence on **summary conviction** [£100 *fine*] for any person to contravene section 53 (sale or supply of medicinal products on the general sales list); or section 54 (1) (sale of medicinal products from automatic machines); or an order made under section 54 (2) (restrictions as to the quantities of a medicinal product sold etc. in a container by automatic machines).

By **section 67 (6)** it is an offence on **summary conviction** [£400 *fine or such lesser sum as may be specified in the regulations*] for any person to contravene any regulations made under section 66 (further powers to regulate dealings with medicinal products).

[89] Not in force on July 1, 1972.
[90] *Ibid.*
[91] *Ibid.*

By **section 68** a person may be disqualified (in certain specified circumstances [92]) on conviction of offences under section 67 (6) from using premises used for carrying on a retail pharmacy business for such a purpose for a period not exceeding two years.

By **section 67 (4)** it is an offence on **summary conviction** [£400 *fine*] for a person disqualified under such an order to use those premises for the purposes of a retail pharmacy business carried on by him.

Part IV deals with pharmacies and under this Part of the Act certain offences are created as follows:

By **section 84 (1)** it is an offence on **summary conviction** [£50 *fine*] for any person to contravene section 77 (annual return of premises to the registrar).[93] Also by **section 84 (2)** it is an offence on **summary conviction** [£100 *fine*] for any person to contravene any regulations made under section 79 (2) (the imposition of further restrictions or other requirements with respect to the use of titles, descriptions and emblems).

Part V deals with containers, packages and the identification of medicinal products and the following offences are created under that Part. By **section 91 (1)** it is an offence [94] on conviction on indictment (normal penalty) or on summary conviction for any person to contravene the provisions of section 85 (5) [95] (labelling and marking of containers and packages so as to falsely describe the product or likely to mislead as to the nature or quality of such product or to its uses or effects); section 86 (3) [96] (the supply etc. of a leaflet falsely describing the product or likely to mislead as to the nature or quantity of such product or as to its uses or effects); or section 90 (2) [97] (false and misleading descriptions as to medicated animal feeding stuffs). Also, by section 91 (2) if any regulations made under Part V so provide, it is an offence on conviction on indictment [98] [*Imp. 2 years and fine*] and on **summary conviction**

---

[92] The court must not make such an order unless it thinks it is expedient so to do having regard: (*a*) to the gravity of the offence of which he has been convicted, or (*b*) the unsatisfactory nature of the premises, or (*c*) to any offences under s. 67 (6) of which he has previously been convicted.

[93] Not in force on July 1, 1972.

[94] Subject to (*a*) the defence that the contravention is due to the default of another person, s. 21, or (*b*) the defence of warranty, s. 122.

[95] Not in force on July 1, 1972.

[96] *Ibid.*

[97] *Ibid.*

[98] If the regulations so provide.

[£400 *fine or such lesser sum as may be specified in the regulations*] for any person to contravene the regulations or to contravene the provisions of section 85 (3) (sell or supply or possess any medicinal product for sale or supply so as to contravene any requirements [99] as to labelling and marking containers and packages imposed by the regulations); section 86 (2) (supply with any medicinal product or possess for the purpose of so supplying, a leaflet so as to contravene any requirements [1] imposed by regulations); section 87 (2) (sell or supply or possess any medicinal product for sale or supply so as to contravene any requirements as to containers imposed by the regulations) or any of those provisions as applied by section 90 (1).

Part VI deals with the promotion of sales of medicinal products.

Section 92 explains the scope of Part VI and defines the meaning of advertisement.

Section 93 [2] creates certain offences in relation to false or misleading advertisements and representations and makes them punishable on conviction on indictment or on summary conviction (normal penalty).

Section 94 creates a summary offence [3] [£100 *fine*] relating to advertisements requiring the consent of the holder of a product licence.

Section 95 creates further offences in relation to regulations regulating advertisements and representations and makes them punishable on conviction on indictment if the regulations so provide [*Imp.* 2 *years and fine*] and on **summary conviction** [£400 *fine or such lesser sum as may be specified in the regulations*].

Sections 96 and 97 both create summary offences [£50 *fine*] in relation to advertisements and representations directed to practitioners and the power for a licensing authority to require copies of advertisements, respectively.

Part VII deals with *British Pharmacopoeia* and other publications and **Part VIII** deals with miscellaneous and supplementary provisions.

More particularly **section 111 (1)** confers on any person duly authorised in writing by an enforcement Authority [4] at any reason-

[99] " Requirements " includes restrictions.
[1] *Ibid.*
[2] Not in force on July 1, 1972.
[3] Subject to the defence that the contravention is due to the default of another person: s. 121.   [4] *Ante,* p. 274.

able time the right to enter any premises on production, if required, of his credentials for the purposes of ascertaining whether there is or has been, on or in connection with those premises,[5] any contravention of any provisions, regulations or orders which by or under the provisions of sections 108 to 110 of this Act that Authority is required or empowered to enforce, or generally for the purposes of the performance by the Authority of their functions under the Act or under any such regulations or order.[6]

By **section 111 (5)** a justice of the peace may issue a search warrant on a sworn information in writing if he is satisfied that there are reasonable grounds for entry and that admission to the premises [7] has been refused, or that a refusal is apprehended (provided that in either case) notice of its intention to apply for a warrant has been given to the occupier, or that an application for admission, or the giving of such a notice, would defeat the object of the entry, or that the case is one of urgency, or that the premises are unoccupied or the occupier is temporarily absent.[8] By **section 112** power is given to inspect, take samples and to seize goods and documents.

Section 114 (2) makes it a summary offence [£50 *fine*] for any person,

(a) to wilfully obstruct a person acting in pursuance of the Act and duly authorised so to act by an enforcement Authority,

(b) to wilfully fail to comply with any requirements properly made to him by a person acting under section 112 (power to inspect, take samples and seize goods and documents) or

(c) to fail without reasonable cause to give to a person so asking any other assistance or information which that person might reasonably require of him for the purpose of the

---

[5] s. 111 (2) gives similar power to enter any ship, aircraft or hovercraft and to enter any vehicle other than a hover vehicle, any stall or place other than premises, or any home-going ship; s. 111 (3) gives a further right in similar circumstances to enter any premises occupied by an applicant for a licence or certificate under Pt. II for the purpose of verifying any statement contained in the application for the licence or certificate; s. 111 (4): admission to a private dwelling house cannot be demanded as of right unless 24 hours' notice of the intended entry has been given to the occupier.

[6] s. 111 (7): valid for one month.

[7] Includes any ship, aircraft, vehicle, stall or place.

[8] Where premises, etc., are unattended the enforcement officer must leave them as effectively secured against trespass as he found them: s. 114 (1).

performance of his functions under the Act. It is further provided by

Section 114 (3) it is an offence on conviction on indictment or on summary conviction [normal penalty] for any person who is giving any such information [9] as is mentioned in subsection (2) (*a*) above to make any statement which he knows to be false.

By **section 118** it is an offence on conviction on indictment or on summary conviction [normal penalty] for any person to disclose to any other person (save in the performance of his duty) any information with respect to any manufacturing process or trade secret obtained by him in premises which he has entered by virtue of section 111 or any information obtained by or furnished to him in pursuance of the Act. **Section 123** creates offences on conviction on indictment or on summary conviction [normal penalty] in relation to warranties and certificates of analysis. **Section 124** provides that where an offence which is committed by a body corporate is proved to have been committed with the consent and connivance of, or to be attributable to any neglect on the part of, any director,[10] manager, secretary or other similar officer of the body corporate, or any person who was purporting to act in any such capacity he, as well as the body corporate, is guilty of that offence. Where such a body corporate is carrying on a retail pharmacy business, a superintendent or a pharmacist acting under his directions (within the terms of section 71 of the Act) although not officers of such body corporate shall be deemed to be such.

Under **section 125** a magistrates' court [11] may try an information for an offence if it is laid within twelve months from the commission of the offence.

Section 126 deals with presumptions and **section 127** with service of documents. The meaning of various words used in the Act are defined under **section 132.**

---

[9] No person is required to answer any question or give any information if to do so might incriminate him (or if that person is married) the husband or wife of that person.

[10] In relation to a body corporate established by or under any enactment for the purpose of carrying on under national ownership any industry or part of an industry or undertaking, being a body corporate whose affairs are managed by its members, means a member of that body corporate.

[11] Notwithstanding anything in s. 104 of the Magistrates' Courts Act 1952.

CHAPTER 21

FIREARMS AND OTHER OFFENSIVE WEAPONS

SECTION 1. THE FIREARMS ACT 1968

THE **Firearms Act 1968** [1] consolidates the former legislation on this topic [2] and briefly, provides that

1. Certain kinds of firearms, such as machine guns for instance are prohibited without written Defence Council Authority;
2. All firearms other than shot guns or air guns require a firearms certificate;
3. Shot guns require a shot gun certificate;
4. Carrying firearms in public, using and carrying them while committing certain offences, and their possession by persons with bad criminal records are all punishable with heavy penalties; and
5. The use of all guns, including air guns, by young persons is closely regulated.

Schedule 6 of the Act sets out a table of offences and mode of trial and punishments for the various offences presented by the Act. [3]

Apart from the control of firearms, there are restrictions on the carrying of offensive weapons imposed by the Prevention of Crimes Act 1953; also there are restrictions on their sale by virtue of the Restriction of Offensive Weapons Act 1959; and provisions exist as to offences committed by armed robbers, armed burglars, poachers and smugglers, all of which are dealt with elsewhere in this book. [4]

Definitions

" Firearm " is defined in the Act [5] as meaning, except where otherwise provided, a lethal barrelled weapon of any description from

---

[1] As amended by the Courts Act 1971, Scheds. 9 and 11; the Criminal Damage Act 1971, and the Criminal Justice Act 1972, s. 28 and Sched. 6.
[2] The Firearms Acts 1937 and 1965 and the Air Guns and Shot Guns Act 1962, and Pt. V of the Criminal Justice Act 1967, all of which are repealed by s. 59 and Sched. 7.
[3] See Arch. paras. 2312–2314.
[4] See pp. 507, 510, 420, 151 respectively.   [5] s. 57 (1).

which any shot, bullet or other missile can be discharged, and includes any prohibited weapon, whether it is such a lethal weapon or not, any component part of any such lethal or prohibited weapon, and any accessory to such weapon designed or adapted to diminish the noise or flash caused by firing. A lethal weapon is a weapon which, whether used properly or misused, could cause death.[6]

A " prohibited weapon " is defined [7] as any firearm which is so designed or adapted that, if pressure is applied to the trigger, missiles continue to be discharged until pressure is removed from the trigger or the magazine is empty, or any weapon of whatever description designed or adapted for the discharge of any noxious liquid, gas or other thing. " Ammunition " is defined [8] as meaning except where otherwise provided, ammunition for any firearm within the meaning of the Act, and includes grenades, bombs and other like missiles, whether capable of use with such a firearm or not, and also prohibited ammunition. " Prohibited ammunition " is defined [9] as any ammunition containing or designed or adapted to contain any noxious liquid, gas or other thing. "Imitation firearm" is defined [10] as anything which has the appearance of being a firearm (other than a prohibited weapon of the second kind, *i.e.* a weapon designed to discharge any noxious gas etc.) whether or not it is capable of discharging any shot, bullet or other missile.[11] The definitions of " shot gun " and " air weapon " are described in the text, below.

Possession without Authority

Possession of Prohibited Firearms. Section 5 of the Act makes it an offence [**summary conviction:** *Imp. 6 months and £400 fine*; **indictment:** *Imp. 5 years and fine*] for any person, without the

---

6 *Moore* v. *Gooderam* [1960] 1 W.L.R. 1308, where it was held that a low-power Diana air gun was a firearm for the purposes of the 1937 Act. In *R.* v. *Freeman* [1970] 1 W.L.R. 788, the Court of Appeal held that a ·38 starting pistol, of solid construction with a revolving chamber, the firing chamber of which had constrictions in the front end, and the barrel of which was solid except for an exhaust port on top for the escape of gas was a firearm for the purposes of s. 1 (1). Although the features referred to were intended to prevent the discharge of missiles, they could be readily removed by drilling, in which event the pistol would be capable of firing ammunition with lethal force. (Part of the barrel had in fact been drilled.)

7 ss. 5 (1) and 5 (2).

8 s. 57 (2).   9 ss. 5 (1), 5 (2).

10 s. 57 (4) and see *R.* v. *Titus* [1971] Crim.L.R. 279.

11 It includes a real firearm which is incapable of firing: *R.* v. *Debreli* [1964] Crim.L.R. 53.

authority of the Defence Council to have in his possession, or to purchase, acquire,[12] manufacture, sell or transfer any prohibited weapon or prohibited ammunition.[13]

Possession without a certificate. **Section 1** makes it an offence punishable on **summary conviction** [*Imp. 6 months and £400 fine*] [14] or on **indictment** [*Imp. 3 years and a fine*] [15] for a person to have in his possession, or to purchase or acquire, any firearm or ammunition to which section 1 of the Act applies without holding a firearm certificate in force at the time, or otherwise than as authorised by such a certificate. The section applies to all firearms except a shot gun (*i.e.* a smooth bore gun with a barrel of not less than twenty-four inches in length not being an air gun) and an air weapon (*i.e.* an air rifle, air gun, or air pistol) not of a type declared by rules made by the Secretary of State under **section 53** to be specially dangerous.[16] The section applies to all ammunition except (a) cartridges containing five or more shot none of which exceeds ·36 inch in diameter; (b) ammunition for an air gun, air rifle or air pistol; and (c) blank cartridges not more than one inch in diameter measured immediately in front of the rim or cannelure of the base of the cartridge.

Section 2 makes it an offence [**summary conviction:** *Imp. 6 months and £400 fine*] [17] to possess, purchase or acquire, without exemption, a shot gun without holding a certificate of authorisation to possess shot guns, and it is an offence punishable in a similar manner to fail to comply with a condition subject to which a shot gun certificate is held. The manner in which firearms certificates are obtained and the conditions under which they are issued are to be found in Part II of the Act. Certificates are obtainable from the Chief Officer of Police for the area in which the applicant resides, and when granted are usually in force unless revoked for a period of three years.[18] The general principle is that a certificate should

12 " Acquire " means here, accept, as a gift or borrow, and " acquisition " shall be construed accordingly: s. 57 (4).

13 The authority must be in writing and may be subject to conditions: ss. 5 (3) and 5 (4).

14 Increased from £200 by the Criminal Justice Act 1972, s. 28 (5), not in force July 1, 1972.

15 Or where the offence is committed in an aggravated form within the meaning of s. 4 (4) then on indictment [*Imp. 5 years and a fine*].

16 Firearms (Dangerous Air Weapons) Rules 1969, S.I. 1969, No. 47.

17 Increased from £200 by the Criminal Justice Act 1972, s. 28 (5), not in force July 1, 1972.   18 s. 26.

be granted if the chief officer of police is satisfied that the applicant has a good reason for having or acquiring the firearm or ammunition without danger to the public safety or to the peace, but it should not be granted to a person prohibited from possessing a firearm [19] or a person of intemperate habits or unsound mind, or a person who for any other reason is unfitted to be trusted with a firearm.[20]   Conditions may be attached to the issue of the certificate [21] and it may subsequently be varied [22] or revoked.[23]   A person dissatisfied by the refusal or revocation of a certificate or the imposition of conditions has a right of appeal against the decision to the Crown Court.[24]

In relation to firearms certificates, offences are committed by persons who sell, transfer to any other person (other than a registered firearms dealer) in the United Kingdom any firearm or ammunition to which section 1 applies or a shot gun unless that person shows that he is authorised under the Act to purchase or acquire it, either by certificate or otherwise, **section 3 (2);** by persons who undertake to repair such firearms or shot guns for such other person, **section 3 (3).**   Both these offences are punishable: [**summary conviction:** *Imp.* 6 *months and* £400 [25] *fine*; **indictment:** *Imp.* 3 *years and fine*].[26]   It is an offence, carrying similar punishment, for a person, with a view to purchasing, acquiring, or procuring the repair, test or proof of such a firearm or shot gun, to produce a false certificate, or one in which a false entry has been made, to personate a person to whom a certificate has been granted, or to make any false statement, **section 3 (5).**   It is an offence [**summary conviction:** *Imp.* 6 *months and* £400 [25] *fine*] for a person to make any statement which he knows to be false for the purpose of procuring, whether for himself or another, the grant or renewal of a certificate under the Act, **section 26 (5).**

It is an offence punishable [**summary conviction:** *Imp.* 3 *months and* £50 [27] *fine*] for a pawnbroker to take in pawn any firearm or

---

[19] *i.e.* under s. 21 (amended by the Courts Act 1971, Sched. 9) after conviction of certain grave crimes.

[20] s. 27.   [21] s. 27 (2).

[22] s. 29.   [23] s. 30.

[24] s. 44, as amended by the Courts Act 1971, s. 53 and Sched. 9.

[25] Increased from £200 by the Criminal Justice Act 1972, s. 28 (5), not in force July 1, 1972.

[26] Substituted for £200 by the Criminal Justice Act 1972, s. 28 (4), not in force July 1, 1972.

[27] Increased from £20 by the Criminal Justice Act 1972, s. 28 (5), not in force July 1, 1972.

ammunition to which section 1 applies or a shot gun, **section 3 (6).**

Registration of Dealers

The Act provides [28] for a register of firearms dealers, and also for the compulsory registration of transactions in firearms.[29]   A person commits an offence: [**summary conviction:** *Imp. 6 months and £400* [30] *fine*; **indictment:** *Imp. 3 years and fine*] if he manufactures, sells, transfers, repairs, tests or proves any firearm or ammunition to which section 1 refers or exposes for sale, transfers or has in his possession for sale, transfer, repair, test or proof, such a firearm, or ammunition or shot gun, without being registered as a firearms dealer, **section 3 (1).**

A person commits an offence [**summary conviction:** *Imp. 6 months and £400* [31] *fine*] who, for the purpose of procuring the registration of himself or another as a firearms dealer; or procuring, whether for himself or another, the entry of any place of business in the register, makes a statement which he knows to be false, **section 39 (1).**   Also, a registered firearms dealer commits an offence, punishable similarly, who has a place of business which is not entered in the register: **section 39 (2),** or who fails to comply with any of the conditions of registration: **section 39 (3).**   It is an offence, similarly punishable for a person to fail to comply with the provisions regarding compulsory registration of firearms transactions (section 40 (5)).

Section 4 of the Act makes it an offence [**summary conviction:** *Imp. 6 months and £400* [32]; or on **indictment:** *Imp. 5 years and fine*] for a person to shorten the barrel of a shot gun to a length less than twenty-four inches.[33]   It is further an offence, punishable in the same manner for a person, other than a registered dealer to convert into a firearm anything which, though having the appearance of being a firearm, is so constructed as to be incapable of discharging any missile through its barrel.   Where a person

---

[28] ss. 34–39.   [29] ss. 40–42.
[30] Increased from £200 by the Criminal Justice Act 1972, s. 28 (5), not in force July 1, 1972.
[31] Increased from £200 by the Criminal Justice Act 1972, s. 28 (5), not in force July 1, 1972.
[32] Increased from £200 by the Criminal Justice Act 1972, s. 28 (5), not in force July 1, 1972.
[33] There is an exemption in favour of a registered dealer when replacing a defective part of a barrel: s. 4 (2).

commits an offence under section 1 of the Act by having such weapons as the above in his possession, or purchasing or acquiring them, without a firearms certificate, then he shall be treated as having committed that offence in an aggravated form.[34]

Certain persons are exempted from the foregoing provisions [35] of the Act.   Thus a person who has received a police permit under section 7 of the Act does not require a firearms certificate. Authorised dealers are exempted in certain circumstances [36] as are carriers, warehousemen, auctioneers and their servants.[37]   Animal slaughtering instruments are exempted when kept in a slaughter house or knacker's yard.[38]   There are exemptions in favour of sporting purposes, athletic meetings, rifle clubs and cadet corps, miniature ranges and shooting galleries.[39]   There are certain exemptions for persons taking part in theatrical performances, or rehearsals, or in films [40] and in relation to equipment for ships and aircraft [41]; and for persons resident in Great Britain for not more than thirty days in all in the preceding twelve months to possess, or purchase or acquire a shot gun without holding a shot gun certificate.[42]

Prevention of Crime and Preservation of Public Safety

The following offences of possessing a firearm with intent to injure; using a firearm to resist arrest and carrying a firearm with criminal intent are triable only on indictment. Thus, **section 16** [42a] makes it an offence [*Imp. Life* [43] *and fine*] for a person to have in his possession any firearm or ammunition [44] with intent, by means thereof to endanger life, or to enable another person by means thereof to do so, whether any injury has been caused or not.[44a]

Section 17 [45] makes it an offence [*Imp. Life and fine*] for a person to make or attempt to make any use whatsoever of a firearm [44] or imitation firearm [46] with intent to resist or prevent the lawful arrest or detention of himself or another.   A further offence [*Imp.* 14 *years* [47] *and fine*] is committed by any person who, at the time of

---

[34] See n. 15 on p. 283.   [35] ss. 1–5.   [36] s. 8.
[37] s. 9.   [38] s. 10.   [39] s. 11.
[40] s. 12.   [41] s. 13.   [42] s. 14.
[42a] As amended by the Criminal Damage Act 1971, s. 11 and Sched. Pt. I.
[43] Substituted for 14 years by the Criminal Justice Act 1972, s. 28 (2).
[44] Defined in ss. 57 (1) and (2) respectively.
[44a] See *R. v. Bentham* [1972] 3 W.L.R. 398.
[45] Amended by the Criminal Damage Act 1971, s. 11 (8) and the Sched.
[46] Defined in s. 57 (4).
[47] Substituted for 7 years by the Criminal Justice Act 1972, s. 28 (3).

committing or being arrested for certain offences has in his possession a firearm or imitation firearm, unless that person shows that
he had the firearm or imitation firearm in his possession for a
lawful object: **section 17 (2).** The offences to which this subsection
applies are set out in the First Schedule to the Act.[48]

Section 18 makes it an offence [**indictment:** *Imp.* 14 [49] *years and
fine*] for a person to have with him a firearm [50] or imitation firearm [51] with intent to commit an indictable offence or to resist
arrest or prevent the arrest of another, in either case while he has
the firearm with him. Proof that the accused had a firearm or
imitation firearm with him and intended to commit an offence, or to
resist or prevent arrest is evidence that he intended to have it with
him while doing so, **section 18 (2).**

The following offences are triable either summarily or on indictment. **Section 19** makes it an offence [**summary conviction:** *Imp.*
6 *months and* £400 [52] *fine*; and **indictment** [53]: *Imp.* 5 *years and fine*]
for any person who, without lawful authority or reasonable excuse
(the proof whereof lies on him) [54] he has with him in a public
place [55] a loaded shot gun [56] or loaded air weapon [57] or any other
firearm [50] (whether loaded or not), together with ammunition
suitable for use in that firearm.

Section 20 makes it an offence for a person (punishable as in
section 19) while he has a firearm with him, to enter or be in any
building or part of a building as a trespasser and without reasonable
excuse (the proof whereof lies on him).[54] The same section makes
it an offence [**summary conviction:** *Imp.* 3 *months and* £200 [58] *fine*]
for a person to trespass armed on land or land covered with water,
subsections 2 and (3) of section 20.

Reasonable excuse: a person is exempted from the provisions
of section 17 if he shows that he had possession of the weapon
with a "lawful object." Under section 19 above a person is

---

[48] As amended by the Theft Act 1968, s. 33 (3) and Sched. 3.
[49] Substituted for 10 years by the Criminal Justice Act 1972, s. 28 (3), not in
force July 1, 1972.
[50] Defined in s. 57 (1).   [51] Defined in s. 57 (4).
[52] Increased from £200 by the Criminal Justice Act 1972, s. 28 (5), not in force
July 1, 1972.
[53] Except where the firearm is an air weapon.
[54] As to the standard of proof see p. 594, *post.*   [55] Defined in s. 57 (4).
[56] Defined in s. 57 (1).   [57] Defined in s. 57 (6) (*b*).
[58] Increased from £100 by the Criminal Justice Act 1972, s. 28 (5), not in force
July 1, 1972.

exempted from the penal provisions if he shows that he had
" lawful authority or reasonable excuse."   Reasonable excuse is
also an exemption under section 20.   A person, presumably, has
lawful authority when he is authorised by statute or delegated
legislation to carry firearms.[59]   Servants of the Crown and the
police, carrying firearms in their capacity, respectively, as servants
or police are, anyway, exempt from the provisions of the Act.[60]
The expression " reasonable excuse " is much wider.   It would,
presumably, exempt a person going hunting or carrying a firearm
to be repaired or from a shop where he has just bought it.   It has
been held to exempt the temporary possession of a person using a
gun at a miniature shooting gallery [61] and it might exempt the
possession of a firearm for self-defence in special circumstances,
e.g. armed couriers of money.[62]   It would also exempt the person
handing in an unauthorised gun to a police station.[63]   However,
a decision under the Prevention of Crime Act 1953 suggests that,
even though a person has a reasonable excuse, he will lose it if
he uses the firearm in an unlawful manner.

Mens rea.   It has been held that section 23 (and, presumably,
therefore, other sections) of the 1937 Act (now repealed and replaced
by sections 17 and 18 of the 1968 Act), creates offences not requiring full *mens rea*.   Although the accused must know that he is
carrying the thing which is a firearm,[64] it has been held that he need
not know of the facts which make it a firearm within the meaning of
the Act.[65]   " Suppose (to take a perhaps unlikely case) that D
believes the thing he is carrying is a hair-drier.   In fact, it is a gas
pistol.   On being arrested, he uses it to strike a policeman.   According to the present decision, it would seem that he is guilty." [66]   Such
a result must be regrettable.[67]   Of course, if he knew that he had

59 *Cf*. the definition in the Public Order Act 1936, s. 4.
60 Firearms Act 1968, s. 54.
61 *R*. v. *Jura* [1954] 1 Q.B. 503, decided under the provisions of the Prevention
   of Crime Act 1953 (below, p. 262).
62 See *Evans* v. *Wright* [1964] Crim.L.R. 466.   See also *Harrison* v. *Thornton*
   [1966] Crim.L.R. 388; *Grieve* v. *Macleod* [1967] Crim.L.R. 424.   These cases
   were decided under the provisions of the Prevention of Crime Act 1953 (below,
   p. 292).
63 See *Wong Pooh Yin* v. *Public Prosecutor* [1955] A.C. 93.
64 See *Sambasivam* v. *Public Prosecutor* [1950] A.C. at p. 469 (P.C.); see also
   R. v. *Cugullere* [1961] 1 W.L.R. 858 (below, p. 294).
65 *R*. v. *Pierre* [1963] Crim.L.R. 513.
66 [1963] Crim.L.R. 514.
67 *Ante*, p. 35.

something with him which fired gas, he should be convicted even though he did not know that a gas pistol was a firearm for the purposes of the Act. This would be a mistake of law and irrelevant.[68]

Section 21[69] of the Act prohibits the possession of firearms or ammunition by certain categories of persons convicted of crime, and makes it an offence [**summary conviction:** *Imp.* 6 *months and* £400 *fine*; **indictment:** *Imp.* 3 *years and fine*]. The persons to whom this prohibition applies are:

(1) A person who has been sentenced to preventive detention, imprisonment[70] or corrective training for a term of three years or more (or sentenced in Scotland to be detained for such a period in a young offenders' institution) shall not have firearms or ammunition in his possession at any time.

(2) A person who has been sentenced to Borstal training, to corrective training of less than three years, or to imprisonment[70] for more than three months but less than three years, or who has been sentenced to a detention centre for three months or more (or a young offenders' institution in Scotland), shall not have firearms or ammunition in his possession at any time before the expiration of five years from the date of his release.

(3) A person who is the holder of a licence issued under the Children and Young Persons Act 1933, s. 53 (or the Children and Young Persons (Scotland) Act 1937)[71]; or is subject to a recognisance to keep the peace, or to be of good behaviour, a condition of which is that he shall not possess, use or carry a firearm; or is subject to a probation order containing such a requirement (or in Scotland has been ordained to find caution, a condition of which is that he shall not possess use or carry a firearm). Such a person shall not have a firearm or ammunition in his possession during the currency of such licence, order, recognisance or finding.

It is further an offence [similarly punishable] for a person to sell, or transfer a firearm or ammunition to, or to repair, test or prove a firearm or ammunition for a person whom he knows or has

---

[68] *Ante*, p. 47.
[69] As amended by the Courts Act 1971, Sched. 9.
[70] A suspended sentence is not within the section: *R.* v. *Fordham* [1970] 1 Q.B. 77.
[71] Which provides for the detention of children and young persons convicted of serious crime, but enables them to be discharged on licence by the Secretary of State.

reasonable ground for believing to be prohibited by the section from having such a firearm or ammunition in his possession, **section 21 (5).**

Possession of Arms by Minors

The Act separates minors into three distinct groups: those under 17, those under 15 and those under 14. It is an offence for a person under 17 to *purchase* or *hire* any firearms or ammunition [**summary conviction:** *Imp. 6 months and £400* [72] *fine*; **section 22 (1)**] or subject to certain exemptions [73] to have an air weapon with him in a public place, except an air gun or air rifle which is so covered with a securely fastened gun cover that it cannot be fired [**summary conviction, section 22 (5):** £50 *fine*]. It is an offence for a person under the age of 15 to have with him an assembled shot gun except (a) while under the supervision of a person of or over the age of 21 or (b) while the gun is covered as above, **section 21 (3).** A person under the age of 14 commits an offence if he has in his possession any firearm or ammunition to which section 1 of the Act applies, except where he comes within the provisions of section 11 [**summary conviction:** *Imp. 6 months and £400* [74] *fine*]; **section 22 (2)** or subject to s. 23 of the Act to have with him an air weapon or ammunition for an air weapon [**summary conviction:** £100 *fine*],[75] **section 22 (4).**

In relation to air weapons, certain exemptions arise in respect of clubs and shooting galleries **(section 23)** but abuse of those provisions is an offence [**summary conviction:** £100 [76] *fine*].

In so far as other persons are concerned, it is an offence [**summary conviction:** *Imp. 6 months and £400* [77] *fine*] for a person

(a) to sell or to let on hire any firearm or ammunition to a person under 17;

---

[72] Increased from £200 by the Criminal Justice Act 1972, s. 28 (5), not in force July 1, 1972.

[73] See s. 23.

[74] Increased from £200 by the Criminal Justice Act 1972, s. 28 (5), not in force July 1, 1972.

[75] Increased from £50 by the Criminal Justice Act 1972, s. 28 (5), not in force July 1, 1972.

[76] Increased from £50 by the Criminal Justice Act 1972, s. 28 (5), not in force July 1, 1972.

[77] Increased from £200 by the Criminal Justice Act 1972, s. 28 (5), not in force July 1, 1972.

(*b*) to give or lend any firearm or ammunition to which section 1 of the Act applies to any person under 14 or to part with the possesion of such firearm or ammunition to such a person (unless exempted under the provisions of s. 11).

Also it is an offence [**summary conviction:** £100 [78] *fine*] to give a shot gun, or ammunition for a shot gun to a person under 15; or to give an air weapon or ammunition for an air weapon to a person under the age of 14 or to part with possession of an air weapon or ammunition for an air weapon to a person under 14 (except in the circumstances envisaged by section 23 above) [**summary conviction:** £100 *fine* [79]], **section 24.**

It is a defence to prove in proceedings under section 24 (above) that the accused believed the person concerned to be over the age mentioned and to show that he had reasonable grounds for the belief, **section 24 (5).**

Enforcing the Act

Wide powers are conferred upon the police for the purpose of enforcing the Act. **Section 48** provides that a constable may demand any person whom he believes to be in possession of any firearm or ammunition to which section 1 of the Act applies, or of a shot gun the production of his firearms or shot gun certificate. If he fails to do so, or to permit the officer to read it or otherwise show that he is entitled to be in possession, the officer may seize the firearm, shot gun or ammunition and may require that person to give his name and address immediately. Failure to do so is an offence [**summary conviction:** £50 *fine* [80]].

Section 46 provides for the issue of search warrants which warrants extend to the seizure of firearms and ammunition and to the inspection of the books of registered firearms dealers.

A constable who has reasonable cause to suspect that a person has a firearm with or without ammunition with him in a public place, or is committing or about to commit elsewhere than in a public place an offence under sections 18 (1) and (2) and 20 of the Act may

---

[78] Increased from £50 by the Criminal Justice Act 1972, s. 28 (5), not in force July 1, 1972.
[79] *Ibid.*
[80] Increased from £20 by the Criminal Justice Act 1972, s. 28 (5), not in force July 1, 1972.

(a) search that person and detain him for the purpose of doing so;

(b) stop and search and detain a vehicle which he suspects to be employed for the purpose;

(c) may require such person to hand over any firearm or ammunition for examination.

It is an offence [**summary conviction:** *Imp*. 3 *months and* £200 [81] *fine*] for a person to fail to comply with (c) above, **section 47.** A constable may arrest without warrant:

(a) any person found on premises he is searching under authority of a search warrant issued under section 46 and whom he has reason to believe to be guilty of an offence under the Act (except an offence under section 22 (3) or one relating specifically to air weapons);

(b) any person whom he has reasonable cause to suspect to be committing an offence under sections 19, 20, 21 or 47 (2) of the Act, and for the purpose of exercising this power he may enter any place;

(c) any person who refuses to declare his name and address when required to do so under section 48 (2) or whom in such a case he suspects of giving a false name and address or of intending to abscond: **section 50.**

The Act provides for the forfeiture and disposal of firearms and for the cancellation of certificates by the convicting court **(section 52).**

The normal rule as to limitation of proceedings under section 104 of the Magistrates' Courts Act 1952 does not apply to offences under the Act. **Section 51** provides a period of four years (with certain exceptions) but provides that no proceedings shall be instituted after the six month period unless by or on the direction of the Director of Public Prosecutions.[82]

SECTION 2.   OTHER OFFENSIVE WEAPONS

Section 1 of the **Prevention of Crimes Act 1953** provides that any person who without lawful authority or reasonable excuse,

---

[81] Increased from £100 by the Criminal Justice Act 1972, s. 28 (5), not in force July 1, 1972.

[82] The list of offences triable is numerous and not all are specifically dealt with. For a full list see Sched. 6 of the Act as amended by the Criminal Justice Act 1972, s. 28 and Sched. 6.

the proof whereof shall be on him, has with him in any public place [83] any offensive weapon commits an offence **[summary conviction:** *Imp.* 3 *months and* £200 *fine* or **indictment:** *Imp.* 2 *years and fine]*.[84]

The expression " offensive weapon " is defined [85] as meaning any article made or adapted for use for causing injury [86] to the person, or intended by the person having it with him for such use by him. " A cosh, a knuckle-duster and a revolver are examples of articles in the first class," [87] *i.e.* made for causing injury. In the second class, *i.e.* articles adapted for causing injury, would be a razor blade inserted into a potato or a bottle broken for the purpose.[88] In the third class, *i.e.* articles with which the accused intends to cause injury, would come any other kind of articles, *e.g.* a shot gun,[89] a sandbag, a razor,[90] a studded belt [91] or a sheath knife.[92] In the case of the first and second classes, the prosecution does not have to prove that the accused had the article with him with the intention of using it to cause injury to the person [93]; once it is proved that they come within that class, the burden of proof will be upon the accused to show reasonable excuse. In the case of articles in the third class the prosecution will have to prove that the accused intended to cause injury with them before the burden of proof shifts.[94]

Where an article is not in either of the first two classes, it may be difficult to prove that the accused intended to use it for the purpose of injuring someone. In *Woodward* v. *Koessler* [95] Donovan J. said that if the accused has in fact used the article for injuring someone, then he is presumed to have had it with him for that purpose. But even if it is presumed conclusively that the accused had a shot gun (for example) with him for the purpose of injuring

[83] Defined in s. 1 (4) in the same terms as in the Firearms Act 1968 (*ante*, p. 287).
[84] As amended by the Criminal Justice Act 1967, s. 92 (1) and (8) and Sched. 3.
[85] s. 1 (4).
[86] It is not enough that its use would cause fright, unless of a degree which might produce injury through shock : *R.* v. *Edmonds* [1963] 2 Q.B. 142.
[87] *R.* v. *Petrie* [1961] 1 W.L.R. at p. 361.
[88] Smith and Hogan, p. 285.
[89] *R.* v. *Sparks* [1965] Crim.L.R. 113.
[90] *R.* v. *Petrie* [1961] 1 W.L.R. at p. 361.
[91] *McMahon* v. *Dolland* [1965] Crim.L.R. 238.
[92] *Woodward* v. *Koessler* [1958] 1 W.L.R. 1255.
[93] *Davis* v. *Alexander* (1970) 54 Cr.App.R. 398.
[94] See *R.* v. *Petrie* [1961] 1 W.L.R. 358.
[95] [1958] 1 W.L.R. 1255.

someone because he did injure someone with it, he should still be
acquitted if he is able to prove that he had lawful authority or
reasonable excuse (see above [96]) for having the gun with him. So
in *R.* v. *Jura* [97] the accused was firing a rifle at a shooting gallery
when in a moment of anger he turned round and shot a female
companion. The Court of Criminal Appeal held that he had
reasonable excuse for carrying the gun and his appeal was therefore
allowed. The court pointed out that the Offences against the Person
Act 1861 provided appropriate punishment for the accused's conduct and that the 1953 Act was meant to deal with persons who
go out with offensive weapons. With respect, this would seem to
have been the correct decision, and it is unfortunate that in *R.* v.
Powell [98] the Court of Criminal Appeal confined the decision in
Jura to its special facts. In this case the accused had hit someone
with a toy pistol. The accused alleged that he was looking after
the pistol for someone else. It was held that at the time that he
used it he had no reasonable excuse to have the pistol, although
he may have had such an excuse earlier. His appeal was accordingly dismissed. This conflicts with the *Jura* decision because,
applying the reasoning in the *Powell* case, at the time the accused
used the rifle he would have had no reasonable excuse. The
result of the *Powell* case is that anyone who intentionally injures
someone with any inanimate object commits an offence against
section 1 of the Act unless the injury was not unlawful, *e.g.* the
accused was acting in self-defence. The court in the *Powell* case,
it is submitted with respect, confused " having the pistol " with
" using the pistol." If the accused had a reasonable excuse for
having the pistol with him, that excuse was not lost when he *used*
it improperly.

Provided that a person does not have this reasonable excuse,
it does not matter if the accused's possession of the offensive
weapon was temporary. In one case a person who picked up a
stone to throw at someone unlawfully was held to have been
properly convicted of an offence against the Act.[99] This case does
not conflict with the *Jura* case, because in that case it was held
that he had a reasonable excuse when he picked up the rifle.

[96] *Ante*, p. 287.
[97] [1954] 1 Q.B. 503.
[98] [1963] Crim.L.R. 511.
[99] *Harrison* v. *Thornton* [1966] Crim.L.R. 388.

Mens rea. It was held by the Court of Criminal Appeal in *R.* v. *Cugullere* [1] that it must be proved that the accused knew that he had the offensive weapon with him. In view of the decision in *R.* v. *Pierre* [2] it is not clear whether the accused must also have known the facts that made the thing an offensive weapon.

In addition to section 1, section 4 of the Public Order Act 1936, makes it an offence to have an offensive weapon at a public meeting without lawful authority. [3]

Finally, the **Restriction of Offensive Weapons Act 1959** [4] prohibits the distribution of " flick knives." **Section 1** of the Act makes it an offence [**summary conviction:** *Imp.* 3 *months and* £50 *fine*; *second or subsequent offence, Imp.* 6 *months and* £200 *fine*] for any person to manufacture, sell or hire or offer for sale or hire, or expose for sale or have in his possession for the purposes of sale or hire, or to lend or give to any other person any " flick or gravity knife." The Act describes these weapons more fully. It is sufficient to say that the characteristic of both kinds of knives is that the blade is normally concealed in the handle or sheath and the blade either flicks out automatically or, after being otherwise released, locks into place.

[1] [1961] 1 W.L.R. 858.
[2] [1963] Crim.L.R. 513.
[3] *Ante,* p. 195.
[4] As amended by the Restriction of Offensive Weapons Act 1961.

CHAPTER 22

OFFENCES AGAINST THE ROAD TRAFFIC LAWS

SECTION 1. INTRODUCTION

THERE are those who consider that the law in relation to motorists falls entirely outside the scope of the criminal law,[1] nevertheless a work of this comprehensive nature would be incomplete without reference to some of the more important aspects of this subject, since a great deal of the time of the criminal courts is taken up with motoring offences.[2] A number of statutes deal with such offences, of which the **Road Traffic Acts, 1960, 1962** and **1972** are the principal.

In addition to the more general punishments of fine and imprisonment, the courts have power upon convicting motoring offenders to disqualify them from driving for a period, and to order that particulars of convictions be endorsed upon their driving licences.[3]

SECTION 2. DANGEROUS AND CARELESS DRIVING

By **section 35** of the **Offences against the Person Act 1861** it is an offence [*Imp.* 2 *years*] for anyone having the control of any carriage or vehicle, by wanton or furious driving or racing, or any other wilful misconduct, or by wilful neglect, to do or cause to be done any bodily harm to any person whatsoever.[4]

By **section 1** of the **Road Traffic Act 1972** it is an offence [*Imp.* 5 *years*] [5] for any person to cause the death of another person by the driving of a motor-vehicle on a road recklessly, or at a speed or in a manner which is dangerous to the public, having regard to all the circumstances of the case, including the nature, condition and use of the road, and the amount of traffic which is

---

[1] See " Should traffic offences be classed as crime? " by P. J. Morrish, 134 J.P.N. p. 787.
[2] See, generally, Wilkinson, *Road Traffic Offences.*
[3] Road Traffic Act 1972, Pt. III, ss. 93–105.
[4] *R.* v. *Swindall and Osborn* (1846) 2 Cox C.C. 141 ; *R.* v. *Phillip Cooke* [1971] Crim.L.R. 44.
[5] *Ibid.*, Sched. 4.

actually at the time, or which might reasonably be expected to be, on the road.[6]

By **section 2 of the Road Traffic Act 1972** it is an offence punishable on **indictment** [*Imp. 2 years and fine*] or on **summary conviction** [£100 *fine and Imp. 4 months (6 months on second or subsequent conviction)*] [7] for a person to drive a motor-vehicle on a road recklessly, or at a speed or in a manner which is dangerous to the public, having regard to all the circumstances, etc.[8]

By **section 3** of the **Road Traffic Act 1972** it is an offence punishable on **summary conviction** [£100 *fine; second or subsequent conviction* £100 *fine and Imp. 3 months*] [9] for a person to drive a motor-vehicle on a road without due care and attention or without reasonable consideration for other persons [10] using the road.[11]

A number of points arise in connection with these offences.

Driving. Although normally there is no difficulty in determining whether a person is driving, difficulties can arise if the vehicle is moving without the engine on. It has been held that steering a vehicle down a hill without the engine on does constitute driving.[12] Otherwise, steering a vehicle that is being towed is not driving,[13] and the same, probably, applies to a vehicle being pushed,[14] unless the same person is pushing and controlling the steering.[15] It has been held that pedalling a moped with its engine out of action is " driving." [16]

---

6 See the article " Causing death by dangerous driving: a suggestion " by Sir Brian MacKenna [1970] Crim.L.R. 67. As to manslaughter, see p. 441, *post*.
7 *Ibid.*, Sched. 4.
8 This section creates three separate offences. They may be charged conjunctively (*i.e.* with an " and ") but not disjunctively (*i.e.* with an " or "): *R.* v. *Clow* [1965] 1 Q.B. 598.   9 *Ibid.*, Sched. 4.
10 This includes passengers in the accused's vehicle: *Pawley* v. *Wharldall* [1966] 1 Q.B. 373.
11 This section creates two separate offences. See above, note 8. There is provision for an alternative finding under this section when the court is of the opinion that a charge under s. 2 has not been proved: *ibid.*, Sched. 4, Pt. IV, para. 4.
12 *Saycell* v. *Bool* [1948] W.N. 232; *R.* v. *Kitson* (1955) 39 Cr.App.R. 66 (*ante*, p. 101); *cf. R.* v. *Roberts* [1965] 1 Q.B. 85. See also *R.* v. *Wibberley* [1966] 2 Q.B. 214.   13 *Wallace* v. *Major* [1946] K.B. 473.
14 *R.* v. *Arnold* [1964] Crim.L.R. 664; *R.* v. *Roberts* [1965] 1 Q.B. 85 at p. 88; but *contra Shimmell* v. *Fisher* [1951] W.N. 484 (which was said in *R.* v. *Roberts* at p. 88 to be a special case) and *R.* v. *Spindley* [1961] Crim.L.R. 486.
15 See *Floyd* v. *Bush* [1953] 1 W.L.R. 242 (bicycle with auxiliary motor); *R.* v. *Roberts* [1965] 1 Q.B. 85 at p. 88; *R.* v. *Whitlow* [1965] Crim.L.R. 170 (motorbike); see also [1965] Crim.L.R. at pp. 59–60. But *contra R.* v. *Munning* [1961] Crim.L.R. 555 (motor-scooter).   16 *R.* v. *Tahsin* [1970] R.T.R. 88.

It is not necessary to be in the driving seat in order to be driving. In one case, for example, it was held that the accused, who was sitting in the passenger's seat, drove when he pulled the starter with the car in gear so that it jerked forward.[17]

If a vehicle requires one person to steer the vehicle and another to work the other controls, both are driving for the purposes of sections 2 and 3.[18] Even an ordinary vehicle can be " driven " by two people. It has been held that an instructor who had one hand on the steering wheel and the other hand on the hand brake was driving as well as the pupil who was in the driver's seat.[19] But it is not sufficient that the instructor was ready to assume control.[20]

Motor-vehicle. A motor-vehicle is defined in the Act as " a mechanically propelled vehicle intended or adapted for use on roads." [21] A vehicle that has been mechanically propelled ceases to be mechanically propelled when " there is no reasonable prospect of the vehicle ever being made mobile again." [22] Whereas the mere removal of the engine may not be sufficient,[23] the fact that the engine is incomplete and does not work, that the tyres are all flat and one is missing, that there is no gearbox and no battery may be sufficient to take the vehicle out of the category of motor-vehicles.[24]

Even though a vehicle is undoubtedly mechanically propelled, it may not be intended or adapted for use on roads. The mere fact that the vehicle was found on a road does not necessarily bring it within the category. On the other hand, however deficient it may be in the ordinary attributes of a motor-vehicle—brakes, silencer, mirrors, horns, lights, etc.—it will be regarded as a

---

[17] *R.* v. *Levy* [1956] Crim.L.R. 340.
[18] s. 196 (1). A hovercraft within the meaning of the Hovercraft Act 1968 (referred to in the Road Traffic Act 1972, as a hover vehicle) is a motor vehicle for the purpose of the Act, whether or not it is adapted or intended for use on roads.
[19] *Langman* v. *Valentine* [1952] W.N. 475.
[20] *Evans* v. *Walkden* [1956] 1 W.L.R. 1019.
[21] s. 190 (1).
[22] *Smart* v. *Allen* [1963] 1 Q.B. 291 at p. 298. It may be that a different test applies to pedal cycles fitted with an auxiliary motor, see *Lawrence* v. *Howlett* [1952] W.N. 308, where it is suggested that the test is " is the motor in working condition? " If so, then it is clearly a motor-vehicle even though the engine is not being used: *Floyd* v. *Bush* [1953] 1 W.L.R. 242.
[23] *Newberry* v. *Simmonds* [1961] 2 Q.B. 345.
[24] *Smart* v. *Allen* [1963] 1 Q.B. 291.

motor-vehicle if it is found being driven [25] along a road for a substantial distance or period. The problem arises with a mechanically propelled vehicle which is used primarily off roads but is found on a road not being driven along it for any substantial distance or period. The test is whether a reasonable person looking at *this* [26] vehicle would say that some general use on the roads is contemplated as one of the users,[27] the intention of the manufacturer, or the driver for the time being, probably not being relevant.[28] It has been held that a motor dumper used primarily on construction sites did not become a motor-vehicle because of an occasional use on the roads adjoining the sites.[29] On the other hand, a Euclid earth scraper, too large to be transported and capable of doing 45 m.p.h. has been held to be within the definition.[30] It has also been held that a go-kart found on an isolated occasion on a road [31] and a saloon car considerably modified for racing being towed to a racing circuit [32] were not motor-vehicles. A hovercraft is a motor-vehicle.[33] An invalid carriage complying with the prescribed requirements of the **Chronically Sick and Disabled Persons Act 1970** and used in accordance with the prescribed conditions is not a motor-vehicle for the purposes of the Road Traffic Regulation Act 1967 and the Road Traffic Act 1972, even though mechanically propelled.[34]

Road. "Road" is defined as "any highway and any other road to which the public have access, and includes bridges over which a road passes." [35] In order for a piece of land to be a road it must lead from one place to another.[36] So normally a

---

[25] See *Brown* v. *Abbott* [1965] Crim.L.R. 493, below, n. 32.
[26] In *Burns* v. *Currell* [1963] 2 Q.B. 433 at p. 441, Lord Parker C.J. seems to suggest that regard should be had to the general user of this class of vehicles. This appears to conflict with other parts of the judgment (at p. 440) and would appear to be out of line with the cases on dumpers and the case cited in the previous note.
[27] *Burns* v. *Currell* [1963] 2 Q.B. 433 at p. 440.
[28] *Daley* v. *Hargreaves* [1961] 1 W.L.R. 487 at p. 492; *Burns* v. *Currell* [1963] 2 Q.B. 433 at p. 440.
[29] *Daley* v. *Hargreaves* [1961] 1 W.L.R. 487.
[30] *Childs* v. *Coghlan* (1968) 112 S.J. 175.
[31] *Burns* v. *Currell* [1963] 2 Q.B. 433.
[32] *Brown* v. *Abbott* [1965] Crim.L.R. 493.
[33] See fn. 18.
[34] Chronically Sick and Disabled Persons Act 1970, s. 20 (1); Road Traffic Act 1972, Sched. 7.
[35] Road Traffic Act 1972, s. 196 (1) *supra.*
[36] See fn. 58 on p. 302, *post.*

car-park will not be a road.[37]   Also the public must have access
to it.   So a private road may be a "road" for the purposes of
the Act if the public are *in fact allowed on to it*.[38]   What is meant
by the word "public" is the public generally (even though a
charge may be made [39]) and not a special class of members of the
public, *e.g.* members of a club.   A vehicle was deemed to be on
a "road" when it was partly on the road and partly on private
land.[40]

Dangerous and careless driving.   The standard expected of the
driver is that of the reasonable driver, *i.e.* these offences punish
negligence or carelessness.

> "That standard is an objective standard, impersonal and
> universal, fixed in relation to the safety of other users of the
> highway.   It is in no way related to the degree of proficiency
> or degree of experience attained by the individual driver." [41]

It might be thought that dangerous driving should be grossly
careless driving that is dangerous.   However, it has been held
that a person can be convicted of dangerous driving even if his
driving was only slightly careless.[42]   The test is objective, and the
degree of negligence is thus irrelevant.   If there is actual danger
to other road users, then it matters not whether the accused driver
was deliberately reckless, careless, momentarily inattentive or even
doing his incompetent best.[43]   The prosecution do not have to
prove an *intention* to drive badly, but the offence requires an element of "fault" on the part of the driver.   It is not an absolute
offence.   The fault need not be the sole cause of the situation but
it must be a cause.   The fault involves a failure, a falling below
the care or skill of a competent or experienced driver in relation
to the manner of driving and the conditions of the case.[44]   The
effect of the decision in *R.* v. *Evans* (*supra*) is to blur the distinction

---

[37] *Griffin* v. *Squires* [1958] 1 W.L.R. 1106.
[38] *Harrison* v. *Hill*, 1932 S.C. (J.) 13 (Scotland); approved in *Griffin* v. *Squires*
[1958] 1 W.L.R. 1106.
[39] *Glynn* v. *Simmonds* [1952] W.N. 289.
[40] *Randall* v. *Motor Insurers' Bureau* [1969] 1 All E.R. 21.
[41] *McCrone* v. *Riding* (1938) 158 L.T. 253 at p. 254.
[42] As to the application of the principle *res ipsa loquitur* see *Rabjohns* v. *Bulgar*,
Butty v. *Davey*, and *Wright* v. *Wenlock* [1972] Crim.L.R. 46, 48, 49.
[43] *R.* v. *Evans* [1963] 1 Q.B. 412 and see *R.* v. *Stevens* [1970] Crim.L.R. 158.
[44] *R.* v. *Gosney* [1971] 2 Q.B. 674, disapproving *R.* v. *Ball and Loughlin* (1966)
50 Cr.App.R. 266.

between the two offences. If an accident involving someone other than the accused has actually occurred, it is likely that the accused, once shown to have been driving carelessly, will be found to have driven dangerously.[45] Furthermore, there will be, at least, an element of danger in most careless driving, since the rules of good driving, which the accused has violated, are designed to prevent danger.[46] Clearly, if the accused suddenly and unforseeably collapses at the wheel because of a heart attack, or is attacked in the classic hypothetical case by a swarm of bees, or even where the steering fails as the result of an unforeseeable defect[47] then he cannot be said to be negligent in the circumstances. The position is of course otherwise, where the driver allows himself to be overcome by sleep,[48] or knowing that he is subject to blackouts or dizzy spells still drives, or where he drives, knowing that he has a defective tyre, which bursts causing an accident.[49]

In a charge of causing death by dangerous driving, the judges have found it convenient to direct juries that the accused's dangerous driving must have been a " substantial " cause of the death.[50] On the other hand it has been recently held by the Court of Appeal, in *R*. v. *Hennigan*[51] that there is nothing in the Act itself which requires the manner of the driving to be a substantial, or major, or any other description of, the cause of the accident. So long as the driving is *a cause* and something more than *de minimis* the Act applies.

SECTION 3. UNFITNESS TO DRIVE

By **section 5 (1)** of the **Road Traffic Act 1972** it is an offence punishable on **indictment** [*Imp. 2 years and fine*] or **summary conviction** [£100 *fine and Imp. 4 months (6 on second or subsequent conviction)*][51a] for a person, when driving or attempting to drive a motor-vehicle[52] on a road[53] or other public place, to be unfit through drink or drugs.

---

[45] *Cf. R*. v. *Evans, supra* at p. 418.
[46] " As the law now stands, the question whether the defendant is brought into court on the major or the minor charge depends merely on the discretion of the prosecution, without governing rules ": Glanville Williams, p. 117.
[47] *R*. v. *Atkinson* (1971) 55 Cr.App.R. 1.
[48] *Kay* v. *Butterworth* (1946) 110 J.P. 75.
[49] *R*. v. *Robert Millar (Contractors) Ltd. and Robert Millar* [1970] 2 Q.B. 54.
[50] *R*. v. *Curphey* (1957) 41 Cr.App.R. 78; *R*. v. *Gould* (1964) 47 Cr.App.R. 241.
[51] [1971] Crim.L.R. 285.   [51a] *Ibid.*, Sched. 4.
[52] Above, p. 298.   [53] Above, p. 299.

By **section 5 (2)** it is an offence punishable on **indictment** [*Imp.* 12 *months and fine*] or on **summary conviction** [*Imp.* 4 *months and* £100 *fine*] [54] for a person, when in charge of a motor-vehicle which is on a road or other public place, to be unfit to drive through drink or drugs. [55]   A person is deemed for the purposes of this subsection not to have been in charge of a motor-vehicle if he proves that at the material time the circumstances were such that there was no likelihood of his driving the vehicle so long as he remained unfit to drive through drink or drugs.

By **section 5 (4)** a person shall be taken to be unfit to drive if his ability to drive properly is for the time being impaired. [56]

Public place.   In the same way as a private road may become a " road " for the purposes of the Road Traffic Act, [57] so a private piece of land may become a " public place."   A clear example of a public place is a car-park attached to and owned by a public-house. [58]

Drink or drugs.   " Drink " probably means alcoholic drink. [59] " Drug " means any medicine given to cure, alleviate or assist an ailing body and includes insulin. [60]

In charge.   In *Haines* v. *Roberts* [61] Lord Goddard C.J. said that a person remains in charge of his car until he has put it in charge of someone else.   So even if a person is standing next to the car with the ignition key, he may be acquitted if he was waiting for someone who had agreed to drive the car. [62]   But if no such arrangement has been made, he will continue *in charge* although he has no intention of driving [63] or his friends have no intention of allowing him to drive. [64]   The proviso that a person is deemed

---

54 *Ibid.*, Sched. 4.
55 A constable may arrest without a warrant a person whom he reasonably thinks is committing an offence under this section : s. 5 (5) as interpreted in *Wiltshire* v. *Barrett* [1966] 1 Q.B. 312.
56 *Ibid.*, s. 5 (3).
57 *Ante*, p. 299.
58 See *Elkins* v. *Cartlidge* (1947) 177 L.T. 519; *R.* v. *Waters* (1963) 47 Cr.App.R. 149. *Cf. Pugh* v. *Knipe* [1972] Crim.L.R. 247.
59 *Armstrong* v. *Clark* [1957] 2 Q.B. 391 at p. 394.
60 *Ibid.*
61 [1953] 1 W.L.R. at p. 311.
62 *Crichton* v. *Burrell*, 1951 S.L.T. 365.
63 *Jowett-Shooter* v. *Franklin* (1949) 65 T.L.R. 756.
64 *Haines* v. *Roberts* [1953] 1 W.L.R. 309.

not to have been in charge if there was no likelihood of his driving while unfit, etc.,[65] mitigates the harshness that would otherwise arise by reason of such a wide definition. This proviso may even save the person " dead drunk " and asleep in his own car[66] if he can prove (which might be difficult) that there was no likelihood of his driving until fit.

Proof. Proof of this offence has never been easy, depending as it does essentially, upon the evidence of the particular medical witnesses called to support or refute the case. Poor court personalities, medical technicalities, differing theories and personal opinions have always proved susceptible to cross-examination, and led already sympathetic juries to acquit. Since the enactment of the Road Safety Act 1967, now consolidated in the Road Traffic Act 1972, charges under this section are brought less often. By **section 7 (1)** of the **Road Traffic Act 1972** the court shall have regard to the proportion or quantity of alcohol or drugs in the accused's blood or body as ascertained by a blood[67-68] or urine test. If the accused refuses[69] to provide a specimen for the test upon being requested to do so by a constable, his refusal *may*[70] be treated as supporting Crown evidence or rebutting defence evidence with respect to his condition.

In the case of both blood and urine specimens, the accused must be supplied with a specimen himself if he requests one. Also a constable,[71] when requesting a specimen, must offer the accused one. If the accused's request is refused, the evidence is inadmissible.[72] If the constable fails to offer a specimen, the judge has a discretion to refuse to admit the evidence.[73]

The Act does not help the court in deciding whether, on the evidence of the proportion of alcohol, the accused was impaired.

---

[65] Above, p. 302.
[66] *John* v. *Bentley* [1961] Crim.L.R. 552.
[67-68] The *blood* must be taken with the accused's consent by a medical practitioner: s. 12 (2).
[69] For what constitutes a refusal, see s. 7 (2).
[70] Unless reasonable cause therefor is shown. See *R.* v. *Dick-Cleland* [1965] Crim.L.R. 440, where a conviction was quashed because of a direction that the jury " should " or " would " hold the refusal against him.
[71] The section refers only to a " constable " and does not therefore, apply if a doctor makes the request: *R.* v. *Lewis* [1965] Crim.L.R. 50.
[72] s. 10 (5) (*b*).
[73] *R.* v. *Mitten* [1966] 1 Q.B. 10.

SECTION 4. BLOOD/ALCOHOL OFFENCES

Part I of the **Road Safety Act 1967** created five new offences, all of
which are now incorporated into the Road Traffic Act 1972. Under
section 6 (1) it is an offence punishable on **summary conviction**
[*Imp. 4 months and £100 fine, or Imp. 6 months on second or
subsequent conviction*] or on **indictment** [*Imp. 2 years and fine*] [74]
for a person to drive or attempt to drive on a road [75] or other
public place, having consumed alcohol [76] in such a quantity that
the proportion in his blood, as ascertained from a laboratory test
for which he subsequently provides a specimen under section 9
of the Act, exceeds the prescribed limit at the time he provides
the specimen.   Under **section 6 (2)** it is an offence punishable
on **summary conviction** [*Imp. 4 months and £100 fine*] or on
indictment [*Imp. 12 months and fine*] [76a] to be in charge of a motor-
vehicle on a road or other public place in similar circumstances.
A person cannot, however, be convicted of being in charge of a
motor-vehicle if he proves that at the material time the circumstances were such that there was no likelihood of his driving it so
long as there was any probability of his having alcohol in his
blood in a proportion exceeding the prescribed limit: **section 6 (3)**. [77]

In determining the likelihood of a person's driving a motor-
vehicle when he is injured or the vehicle is damaged, the fact that
he has been injured or that the vehicle has been damaged may be
disregarded by a court: **section 6 (4)**.

The **prescribed limit** is 80 milligrammes of alcohol in 100
millilitres of blood: **section 12 (1)**: 107 milligrammes of alcohol in
100 millilitres of urine is equivalent to 80 milligrammes of alcohol
in 100 millilitres of blood: **section 12 (4)**.

The object of **section 6** of the Act is to avoid as far as possible
the necessity for relying on medical and scientific evidence of the
kind put before juries in cases under section 5 of the Road Traffic
Act 1972, and to make the result of a laboratory test given in

---

[74] *Ibid.*, Sched. 4.   See " The Road Safety Bill " by J. D. J. Havand in [1967]
Crim.L.R. 151; " Offences under the Road Safety Act 1967 " [1969] Crim.L.R.
292 and " Driving to drink " [1970] Crim.L.R. 683, both by P. Seago.

[75] Defined at p. 299, *ante*.

[76] At the time of driving or attempting to drive; see, *e.g. R.* v. *Hamilton* [1970]
3 All E.R. 284, affirmed in the House of Lords [1971] 1 W.L.R. 647.

[76a] *Ibid.*, Sched. 4.

[77] The defendant must prove that there was no likelihood of his driving in the
future so long as there was any probability of the alcohol in his blood exceeding
the prescribed limit: *Northfield* v. *Pinder* [1969] 2 Q.B. 7.

accordance with the provisions of the Act conclusive evidence of
the excess, if any, of alcohol in the blood over the prescribed
limit.[78] The section is directed at the person who has consumed
alcohol at the time of driving or attempting to drive. In *Rowlands*
v. *Hamilton* [79] the House of Lords held that the quantity of alcohol
consumed by a driver before he ceased driving can only be
validly ascertained from a laboratory test (within the meaning of
section 9) so as to prove an offence, if the specimen is taken at a
time when no additional alcohol has entered the driver's body
after he has ceased to drive and before he gives the specimen.[79a]
Where a person consumes alcohol after he has ceased to drive and
before the police are able to obtain a specimen, he is thus in a
position to frustrate the procedures under the Act.[79b]

Before any charge can be brought under section 6 (1) or (2),
the procedure laid down by the Act itself, from the taking of the
first breath test to the production of the analyst's certificate must
be closely observed. This procedure hedges the erring motorist
around with every possible safeguard against indiscriminate or
arbitrary treatment by the police and the appellate courts in many
decisions on the Act have declared it to be a highly formalised
procedure which must be strictly adhered to.

The starting point is **section 8 (1)** which provides that a constable in uniform [80] may require any person driving or attempting to
drive [81] a motor-vehicle on a road or other public place to provide
a specimen of breath for a breath test [82] there or nearby [83] if the
constable has reasonable cause [84]

---

[78] s. 10 (1). See the observations of Lord Parker C.J. in *R.* v. *Durrant* [1970] 1
W.L.R. 29.

[79] [1971] 1 W.L.R. 647, H.L. affirming *R.* v. *Hamilton* [1970] 3 All E.R. 284.

[79a] A different view has been taken of these provisions in Scotland, where the
tenor of the decisions of the High Court of Justiciary is that the evidence of
subsequent consumption may *modify* the evidence provided by the analyst's
certificate but does not necessarily *eliminate* it: *Wood* v. *Brown* [1970] Crim.
L.R. 162; *H.M. Advocate* v. *Laurie* 1971 S.L.T. 29; both quoted in the commentary to *Ritchie* v. *Pirie* [1972] Crim.L.R. 251.

[79b] A deliberate act of consuming alcohol to frustrate the procedure under the
Act may amount to wilful obstruction of a police constable, contrary to the
Police Act 1964, s. 51 (3) (see p. 172, *ante*): *Ingleton* v. *Dibble* [1972] 1 Q.B.
480 at p. 485 D.C.

[80] See *Wallwork* v. *Giles* [1970] R.T.R. 117; and *Cooper* v. *Rowlands* [1972]
Crim.L.R. 53.

[81] See below for what is meant by these expressions.

[82] Defined in s. 12 (1). [83] See p. 308, *post*.

[84] Whether a constable has reasonable cause to suspect is *prima facie* a question
of fact for the justices (or, it is submitted, for the jury), but if there is no
evidence on which a reasonable bench of justices could have concluded that

(a) to suspect him of having alcohol in his body; or

(b) to suspect him of having committed a traffic offence while the vehicle was in motion,[85] and provided that, in this case, the requirement is made as soon as is reasonably practicable after the commission of the traffic offence.[86]

Section 8 (2) provides that if an accident [87] occurs owing to the presence of a motor-vehicle on a road or other public place, a constable in uniform may require any person whom he has reasonable cause to believe was driving or attempting to drive the vehicle at the time of the accident to provide a specimen of breath for a breath test—(a) except while that person is at a hospital as a patient, either at or near the place where the requirement is made or, if the constable thinks fit, at a police station specified by the constable; (b) in the said excepted case, at the hospital; but a person shall not be required to provide such a specimen while at a hospital as a patient if the medical practitioner in immediate charge of his case is not first notified of the proposal to make the requirement or objects to the provision of a specimen on the ground that its provision or the requirement to provide it would be prejudicial to the proper care or treatment of the patient.[88]

A number of important questions arise on the interpretation of section 8. " **Breath test** " is defined [89] as a test for the purpose of obtaining an indication [90] of the proportion of alcohol in a person's blood carried out by means of a device of a type approved for the purpose of such test by the Secretary of State, on a specimen of breath provided by that person.

The " approved device " is that known as the Alcotest, comprising an indicator tube (marked with the name " Alcotest "), a

the constable had reasonable cause, the Divisional Court is entitled to, and will, interfere: *Williams* v. *Jones* [1972] Crim.L.R. 50. The reasonable suspicion must precede the test.

[85] " Traffic offence " means an offence under any provision of the Road Traffic Act 1972, except Part V, or under any provision of Part III of the Road Traffic Act 1960 or the Road Traffic Regulation Act 1967: Road Traffic Act 1972, s. 8 (8).

[86] See p. 308, *post.*

[87] As to whether there has been an accident or not, see *R.* v. *Pico* [1971] Crim.L.R. 599, and as to the meaning of " accident," see *R.* v. *Morris* [1972] 1 W.L.R. 228.

[88] The burden of proof is on the prosecution to establish that the proper procedure has been followed. See, *e.g. Jones* v. *Brazil* [1971] Crim.L.R. 47.

[89] s. 12 (1).

[90] It is no more than an indication.

mouthpiece and a measuring bag, and supplied to police forces in England and Wales in a container marked with the name " Alcotest (R) 80." After a number of appeals concerning the approval of the device, it was said by the Court of Appeal (Criminal Division) in *R.* v. *Jones* [91] that a court, including a jury may now take judicial notice of the fact that the " Alcotest (R) 80 " device is of an approved type, and formal proof is no longer necessary. The device must be identified as an " Alcotest (R) 80 " but it need not be produced in court.[92] It was held in *Director of Public Prosecutions* v. *Carey* [93] that there is no absolute requirement expressed or implied in the Act that a test in order to be a breath test within the Act must be conducted in perfect compliance with the manufacturer's instructions. A departure from those instructions does not vitiate the test, if it is carried out in good faith and is reasonable, it is essential that the device be properly assembled, and where the defence takes the point that the device used was not of an approved type and was not properly assembled, these issues must be left to the jury.[94]

Driving or attempting to drive. Under section 8 (1) a breath test may only be required of a person " driving or attempting to drive," and the meaning of these words has given the courts some difficulty. In *R.* v. *Price* [95] the Divisional Court sought to equate such a person with " what one might generally call the driver." Somebody who is not only at the steering wheel while the vehicle is in motion, but somebody who is in the driving seat while the vehicle is stationary and what is more somebody who has got out of the driving seat, albeit temporarily, and can still be described in general terms as " the driver." In *Pinner* v. *Everett*,[96] however, a House of Lords case, Lord Upjohn criticised the use of the word " driver " which does not appear in the section. The House of Lords decided that the question is not necessarily determined by whether the vehicle is in motion, but is a question of degree and fact in each case. A person who is going into his house, having

---

[91] [1970] 1 W.L.R. 16; and see *Cooper* v. *Rowlands* [1972] Crim.L.R. 53.
[92] *Miller* v. *Howe* [1969] 1 W.L.R. 1510. A bag with a hole in it is not the device approved: *Rayner* v. *Chief Constable of Hampshire* [1971] R.T.R. 15.
[93] [1970] A.C. 1072. See also *Gill* v. *Forster* [1972] Crim.L.R. 45.
[94] *R.* v. *Coates* [1971] Crim.L.R. 370.
[95] [1968] 1 W.L.R. 1853.
[96] [1969] 1 W.L.R. 1266.

finished driving, is not " driving or attempting to drive " [97] nor is
a defendant who has left his car to speak to the police on another
matter [98] nor where he has stopped his vehicle for the purpose of
continuing a conversation with his passengers [99] or where he
stopped voluntarily and left his car for the purpose of making a
telephone call [1] or where he was asked to take a first breath test
fifteen minutes after he had left his car [2] or where he had
abandoned his vehicle and was caught later by the police.[3]

In each of these cases the initial suspicion was not that the
motorist had alcohol in his body but that he had committed a
crime. It appears that where a motorist is stopped or approached
by the police for reasons totally unconnected with driving, as for
example where they wish to speak to him on another matter,
that motorist is not " driving or attempting to drive " within the
meaning of the section. A motorist who has been effectively prevented from driving by having his ignition keys taken from him
is not driving.[4]

At the trial, the question whether the defendant was driving or
attempting to drive, may be for the jury or for the judge to decide,
according to the circumstances. There are cases where there is a
dispute as to the primary facts, and in those cases the question
must be left to the jury like any other issue of fact.[5] On the other
hand there are those cases where there is no dispute as to the
primary facts, and where there is no question left for decision by
anyone except the question of law, namely, whether the facts
disclose that the defendant was " driving or attempting to drive "
at the time. Such a matter is one of law and the trial judge must
give a ruling.[6]

There or nearby. The requirement [7] for a breath test should
be made " there or nearby " and it must be made as soon as is

---

[97] *Campbell* v. *Tormey* [1969] 1 W.L.R. 189.
[98] *Pinner* v. *Everett* (*supra*).
[99] *Stevens* v. *Thornborrow* [1970] R.T.R. 31.
[1] *R.* v. *Kelly* [1970] 1 W.L.R. 1050.
[2] *R.* v. *Bove* [1970] 1 W.L.R. 949.
[3] *Anthony* v. *Jenkins* [1971] R.T.R. 19. See also *Erskine* v. *Hollin* [1971]
Crim.L.R. 243.
[4] *Harman* v. *Wardrop* (1971) 135 J.P. 256. See also *Wright* v. *Brobyn* [1971]
Crim.L.R. 241; *Erskine* v. *Hollin* [1971] Crim.L.R. 243.
[5] *R.* v. *Kelly* [1970] 1 W.L.R. 1050; *R.* v. *Wall* [1969] 1 W.L.R. 400.
[6] *R.* v. *Kelly* (*supra*).
[7] As to when a " request " amounts to a " requirement " see *R.* v. *Clarke* [1969]
1 W.L.R. 1109.

" reasonably practicable " after the commission of a moving traffic offence.[8] Whether or not these requirements are satisfied is a matter for the trial court, and are matters of degree and fact.[9] " Near or thereby " is used in a purely geographical sense.[10] It is not necessary for the validity of the requirement for a breath test that it should be made while the motorist is still driving, so long as the request forms part of a relevant single transaction or chain of events. In *R.* v. *Jones* [11] the Court of Appeal (Criminal Division) held that " both as a matter of reasonable approach and on well established authority " [12] a requirement under section 8 (1) may be made off the road so long as it is made " in the course of a chain of action following sufficiently closely on an observed driving on the road. . . ." This case was expressly approved by the House of Lords in *Sakhuja* v. *Allen.*[13] There is no distinction to be drawn between a driver who knows he is being pursued and one who does not.[14-15]

Failure to provide a breath test. Failure to provide a breath sample without reasonable excuse is an offence [£50 *fine*] [16] and, if the constable has reasonable cause to believe that the person has alcohol in his body and the person is not in hospital he may be arrested. If the breath test is given and proves positive he may also be arrested. **Section 8 (7)** provides that a person arrested under the provisions of section 5 (5) or 8 must be given an oppor-

---

[8] In *Director of Public Prosecutions* v. *Carey* (*supra*) Lord Diplock said that the statutory right conferred on a constable, under s. 8, to require a breath-test, carried with it by necessary implication the right to require a person to remain there or nearby until the effect of recently consumed alcohol has worn off sufficiently to enable him to provide a specimen of breath, which when used in the approved device will give a reliable reading of his true blood/alcohol level.

[9] *Arnold* v. *Chief Constable of Hull* [1969] 1 W.L.R. 1499.

[10] *Donegani* v. *Ward* [1969] 1 W.L.R. 1502.

[11] [1970] 1 W.L.R. 211, followed in *Sasson* v. *Taverner* [1970] 1 W.L.R. 338.

[12] Citing the " hot pursuit " cases on arrest, *e.g. R.* v. *Howarth* (1828) 1 Mood. C.C. 207 and *Harvey* v. *Boultbee* (1830) 4 C. & P. 350 and *Griffith* v. *Taylor* (1876) 2 C.P.D. 194.

[13] As was *Sasson* v. *Taverner* (*supra*); [1972] 2 W.L.R. 116 H.L. The House of Lords overruled the decisions in *Trigg* v. *Griffin* [1970] R.T.R. 53, *Campbell* v. *Tormey* [1969] 1 W.L.R. 189, and *R.* v. *Wall* [1969] 1 W.L.R. 400, which suggested that the requirement must be made on a road or public place.

[14-15] *R.* v. *Sakhuja* [1971] Crim.L.R. 289.

[16] s. 8 (3), " failure " means " refusal " : s. 12 (1), but inability to take the test by reason of defective equipment does not amount to failure: *Hoyle* v. *Walsh* [1969] 2 Q.B. 13. See also *R.* v. *Clarke* [1969] 1 W.L.R. 1109 and *R.* v. *Wagner* [1970] R.T.R. 422. It does not amount to duress for a constable to warn a defendant that failure is punishable with imprisonment (which it is not): *Bryant* v. *Morris* [1972] Crim.L.R. 115.

tunity to provide a specimen of breath for a breath test at the police station.[17]

Arrest. Section 9, which relates to the taking of the sample for analysis depends for its validity upon an arrest, whether under section 8 (4) or under section 5 of the Act. A person can be required to provide a specimen under section 9 only where he has been so arrested.[18] The whole question of arrest is vital, and where the fact of arrest is challenged by a defendant, the matter is for the jury to decide.[19] Two main points arise:

(1) there must be an arrest based upon the preconditions of section 8 (or in accordance with the provisions of section 5 (5)), that is, the officer must have been in uniform; the defendant must have been driving or attempting to drive, on a road or other public place etc.; and

(2) the purported arrest of the defendant must have amounted to a valid arrest in law.[20]

Laboratory tests. Section 9 (1) provides that a person who has been arrested under either section 5 (5) or section 8 may, while at a police station,[20a] be required by a constable to provide a specimen for a laboratory test [21] (which may be a specimen of blood or urine), if he has previously been given an opportunity to provide a specimen of breath for a breath test at that station, under section 8 (7) and either—

(a) it appears to a constable in consequence of the breath test [22] that the device by means of which the test is carried out

---

[17] The breath test, the requirement of and the actual giving of the specimen must all take place at the same police station: *Butler* v. *Easton* [1970] R.T.R. 109. Where the defendant has taken a breath test at the station, even if it is the first, he is not entitled to insist upon taking a second at the same station: *Rooney* v. *Houghton* [1970] 1 W.L.R. 550.

[18] For the position where the arrest is made under s. 5 (5), and the proceedings are brought under s. 6, see *Humphreys* v. *Thompson* [1970] R.T.R. 228; *Coneys* v. *Nicholson* [1970] R.T.R. 231 and *Atkinson* v. *Lumsden* [1970] R.T.R. 235.

[19] *R.* v. *Ayres* [1970] R.T.R. 398; *R.* v. *Veevers* [1971] Crim.L.R. 174.

[20] *Alderson* v. *Booth* [1969] 2 Q.B. 216; *R.* v. *Gordon* [1970] R.T.R. 125; *R.* v. *Way* [1970] R.T.R. 348 and *Wheatley* v. *Lodge* [1971] R.T.R. 22.

[20a] It was held in *Butler* v. *Easton* [1970] R.T.R. 109 that the specimen must be given at the same police station as that at which the request was made. In Scotland it has been held otherwise: *Milne* v. *McDonald* [1972] Crim. L.R. 254.

[21] " The analysis of a specimen provided for the purpose ": s. 12 (1). A specimen of blood must be taken by a doctor: s. 12 (2).

[22] See pp. 306–307, *ante.*

indicates that the proportion of alcohol in his blood exceeds the prescribed limit; or

(b) when given the opportunity to provide that specimen he fails to do so.[23]

Section 9 (2) provides that a person while at a hospital as a patient may be required by a constable to provide at the hospital [24] a specimen for a laboratory test—

(a) if it appears to the constable in consequence of a breath test carried out on that person under section 8 (2) that the device by means of which the test is carried out indicates that the proportion of alcohol in his blood exceeds the prescribed limit; or

(b) if that person has been required, whether at the hospital or elsewhere to provide a specimen of breath for a breath test, but fails to do so and a constable has reasonable cause to suspect him of having alcohol in his body.

A person cannot, however, be required to provide a specimen for a laboratory test under this subsection if the medical practitioner in immediate charge of his case is not first notified of the proposal to make the requirement, or objects to the provision of a specimen on the ground that its provision or the requirement to provide it or a warning under section 9 (7) would be prejudicial to the proper care or treatment of the patient.[25]

---

[23] A driver who refuses to wait while a constable sends for breath test equipment may be guilty of a " failure " to provide a specimen of breath: *R.* v. *Wagner* [1970] R.T.R. 422 C.A.

[24] The specimen must be provided at the hospital or the procedure under s. 9 (1) must be followed: *Bosley* v. *Long* [1970] 1 W.L.R. 1411. In Scotland it has been held that this protection extends to a person who is at the hospital as an outpatient: *MacNeil* v. *England* [1972] Crim.L.R. 255.

[25] Whether the medical practitioner objects or does not object is a matter of fact, and evidence of it is not to be treated as hearsay: *R.* v. *Chapman* [1969] 2 Q.B. 436. As to the position where the medical practitioner sanctions blood yet urine is required see *R.* v. *Green* [1970] 1 All E.R. 408; *Ward* v. *Keene* [1970] R.T.R. 127 and *Jones* v. *Brazil* [1970] R.T.R. 449. The constable must tell the doctor that the patient will be warned of the consequences of refusal, namely, imprisonment, a fine and disqualification. If he fails to tell the doctor this the doctor cannot decide whether the taking of the specimen will be prejudicial to the patient's health: accordingly, a subsequent refusal by the patient will not be an offence under s. 9 (3). A request is sufficient if made in the honest and reasonable belief that it would be, and is being, understood by the person required, even if it turns out that the words have not in fact been heard or understood because, *e.g.* the defendant was in a dazed or confused condition after the accident: *R.* v. *Nicholls* [1972] 1 W.L.R. 503.

Section 9 (3) provides that a failure, without reasonable excuse,[26] to provide a specimen is an offence and—

(a) if it is shown that at the revelant time [27] the defendant was driving or attempting to drive [28] a motor vehicle on a road or other public place he shall be liable to be proceeded against and punished as if the offence charged were an offence under section 6 (1) of the Act; and

(b) in any other case, if it is shown that at the time he was in charge of a motor vehicle on a road or other public place, he shall be liable to be proceeded against and punished as if the offence charged were an offence under section 6 (2).

However, under section 9 (5), a person shall not be treated as having refused unless—

(a) he is first requested to provide a specimen of blood but refuses to do so;

(b) he is then requested to provide two specimens of urine [29] within one hour of the request, but fails to provide them within the hour or refuses at any time within the hour to provide them; and

(c) he is again requested to provide a specimen of blood but refuses to do so.

Section 9 (7) provides that a constable shall, on requiring any person under section 9 to provide a specimen for a laboratory test, warn him that failure to provide a specimen of blood or urine may render him liable to imprisonment, fine and disqualification, and if the constable fails to do so, the court before which that person is charged with an offence under section 6 or 9 of the Act may [30] direct an acquittal or dismiss the charge as the case may require.

---

26 It is a question of law whether a matter put forward as a reasonable excuse is capable of being such. If it is capable of coming within this definition it is a matter of fact and degree whether it is a " reasonable " excuse." *Procaj* v. *Johnstone* [1970] R.T.R. 49; *R.* v. *Clarke* [1969] 1 W.L.R. 1109; *Law* v. *Stephens* [1971] Crim.L.R. 369, and, *post*, p. 313.

27 Defined in the Act.

28 p. 307, *ante*.

29 The first specimen is disregarded.

30 " May " does not mean " must ": *R.* v. *Brush* (1968) 52 Cr.App.R. 717. The court's decision whether or not to direct an acquittal would depend on whether or not in the opinion of the court the accused was prejudiced by the failure: *R.* v. *Forbes* [1971] Crim.L.R. 174.

A failure to give the warning does not render a specimen necessarily invalid, but it may show that prejudice has arisen and the judge may on that ground direct an acquittal.[31]

Section 11 provides that a person required to provide a specimen under section 9 (1) may be detained at a police station until a breath test indicates that the proportion of blood does not exceeed the prescribed limit.

Without reasonable excuse. The refusal or failure to provide a blood or urine sample must be without reasonable excuse. A similar phrase is used under section 7, but there the failure to provide such a specimen merely reinforces the prosecution's case which must rest on other evidence. In so far as the proof of reasonable excuse is concerned the burden of raising the issue is on the motorist, because that is a fact peculiarly within his own knowledge. He must show a reasonable excuse for refusing to give both blood and urine. Once such evidence is adduced the burden is upon the prosecution to rebut such a defence to the satisfaction of the Court.[32] If reasonable excuse is established there must be an acquittal. Of course, it follows, that the jury should not be directed that it is for the defendant to prove that there was reasonable excuse. Whether embarrassment, physical injuries or mental condition can provide the basis for a reasonable excuse for failure to provide a specimen is a matter of fact and degree. The Divisional Court has suggested that mental condition or physical injuries would have to be of a very extensive character before they could operate in such a way.[33] A reasonable excuse for failure to provide urine does not automatically operate as a reasonable excuse to provide blood.[34] Where a defendant consents to give a blood sample the specimen of blood must be taken by a doctor. It is for the doctor to decide from which part of the body the most satisfactory speci-

---

[31] On a trial on indictment the judge must hold a " trial within a trial " to determine the issue whether or not the warning was given and whether prejudice has arisen: *R.* v. *Brush* [1968] 1 W.L.R. 1740 and *R.* v. *Forbes* [1971] Crim.L.R. 174. *Cf.* where the question arises under s. 9 (3) *R.* v. *Dolan* [1969] 1 W.L.R. 1479.

[32] *R.* v. *Clarke* [1969] 1 W.L.R. 1109.

[33] *R.* v. *Clarke* (*supra*). See also *Rowland* v. *Thorpe* [1970] 3 All E.R. 195 D.C. and *Scible* v. *Grain* [1970] R.T.R. 358. Where there is no evidence on which a jury could find reasonable excuse, the judge should withdraw the issue from their consideration: *R.* v. *Clarke* (*supra*); *R.* v. *Wallace* [1972] Crim.L.R. 186.

[34] *Ibid.* and see *R.* v. *Harling* [1970] 3 All E.R. 902.

men can be obtained with the least danger to the defendant's health. In *Solesbury* v. *Pugh* [35] it was held that it would be reasonable to refuse to give a blood specimen from an infected arm but not reasonable to specify an unsuitable part, such as a big toe. If a consenting defendant offers blood from an unsuitable part of his body and will not agree to the doctor's suggestion of another part he should be requested under section 9 (5) by a constable to give urine samples followed by a request, if urine is refused, for blood. The physical inability to pass water could be a reasonable excuse for not providing a urine sample. [36] Once a motorist has given his final refusal under section 9 (5) (*c*) it was held in *Law* v. *Stephens* [37] that it was too late for him to change his mind even though he had refused saying he wanted legal advice from his solicitor and on the arrival of his solicitor shortly after and acting on his solicitor's advice he offered to supply a specimen.

The provisions of section 9 (5) (6) requiring the accused to be supplied with a specimen if he requests one apply to specimens required under either section 5 or section 9 [38] and a constable requiring a specimen must warn the defendant of the consequences of failure to provide one. Section 9 (7) makes this procedure mandatory, and where the evidence on this point is challenged, the issue must be left to the jury since they might regard the issue as highly relevant to the question whether the defendant had a reasonable excuse for refusal. [39]

SECTION 5. OTHER OFFENCES

Among the numerous offences concerned with road traffic should be mentioned the following:

No insurance. By **section 143 (1)** of the **Road Traffic Act 1972** [40] it is unlawful for a person to use, or to cause or permit any other

---

35 [1969] 1 W.L.R. 1114.

36 *R.* v. *Brush* [1968] 1 W.L.R. 1740.

37 (1971) 115 S.J. 369 D.C., *Projac* v. *Johnstone* (*supra*) applied; *cf. Rooney* v. *Haughton* (*supra*).

38 A number of cases establish that the specimen of blood should be capable of analysis in a reasonable time. *Earl* v. *Roy* [1969] 1 W.L.R. 1050. *Cf. Kierman* v. *Willock* [1972] Crim.L.R. 248; *Doctorine* v. *Watt* [1970] R.T.R. 305; *Braddock* v. *Whittaker* [1970] R.T.R. 288; *R.* v. *Weil* [1970] R.T.R. 284; *Smith* v. *Cole* [1970] R.T.R. 459.

39 *R.* v. *Dolan* [1969] 1 W.L.R. 1479; *cf. R.* v. *Brush* [1968] 1 W.L.R. 1740.

40 As to civil liability in relation to passengers, see The Motor Vehicles (Passenger Insurance) Act 1971.

person to use, a motor vehicle on a road unless there is in force in relation to the user of the vehicle by that person or that other person, as the case may be, such a policy of insurance or such a security in respect of third party risks as complies with the requirements of the Act.[40a] The offence is punishable on **summary conviction** [*Imp.* 3 *months and* £50 *fine*]. The section imposes an absolute prohibition on using an uninsured vehicle or causing or permitting it to be used on a road. Knowledge is immaterial. However, a person charged with using a motor vehicle in contravention of this section must not be convicted if he proves that the vehicle did not belong to him and was not in his possession under a contract of hiring or of loan, that he was using the vehicle in the course of his employment and that he neither knew nor had reason to believe that there was not in force in relation to the vehicle such a policy of insurance as security as complies with the requirements of the Act.[41]

Failure to stop after an accident. By **section 25** of the **Road Traffic Act 1972** if, owing to the presence of a motor-vehicle on a road, an accident occurs whereby personal injury is caused to a person other than the driver of that motor-vehicle or damage is caused to a vehicle other than that motor-vehicle or a trailer drawn thereby or to an animal [42] (other than one in that motor-vehicle or trailer drawn thereby), the driver of the motor-vehicle shall stop and, if required to do so by any person having reasonable grounds for so requiring, give his name and address and also the name and address of the owner and the identification marks of the vehicle. If, in the case of any such accident, he does not give his name and address, he must report the accident to a police station or police constable within twenty-four hours. Failure to do so is punishable on summary conviction [£50 *fine or Imp.* 3 *months* [43]].

It has been held that no offence is committed against this section if the driver was unaware that he had been involved in an accident.[44]

[40a] The onus of proving that a policy of insurance is in force lies upon the defendant as it is peculiarly within his own knowledge: *R.* v. *Oliver* [1944] K.B. 68; *Philcox* v. *Carberry* [1960] Crim.L.R. 563 approved in *Leathley* v. *Drummond* [1972] Crim.L.R. 227.
[41] s. 143 (2).
[42] " Animal " is defined as " any horse, cattle, ass, mule, sheep, pig, goat, or dog ": s. 25 (3).   [43] Road Traffic Act 1972, Sched. 4.
[44] *Harding* v. *Price* [1948] 1 K.B. 695; *Butler* v. *Whittaker* [1955] Crim.L.R. 317.

Taking motor-vehicles without authority.[45]   The provisions of this offence will be found elsewhere.[46]   By **section 29** it is also an offence to get onto a vehicle or tamper with its mechanism without lawful authority or reasonable cause.

Forgery, false statements.   The forgery of documents, licence plates etc., and making of false statements for the purpose of obtaining licences etc., are punishable by **sections 169** to **174.**

Section 26 of the **Vehicles (Excise) Act 1971** punishes on **summary conviction** [£200 *fine*] or on **indictment** [*Imp*. 2 *years*] any person who forges or fraudulently alters or uses, or fraudulently lends or allows to be used by any other person

(a) any mark to be fixed or sign to be exhibited on a mechanically propelled vehicle in accordance with section 19 or 21 of the Act; or

(b) any trade plates or replacements such as are mentioned in section 23 (c) of the Act; or

(c) any licence or registration document under the Act.

The same section punishes [*similar penalties*] any person who

(a) in connection with an application for a licence or for the allocation of temporary licences or registration marks makes a declaration which to his knowledge is false or in any material respect misleading; or

(b) being required by virtue of the Act to furnish particulars which to his knowledge are false or in any material respect misleading.

Mens rea.   Courts have not interpreted motor-vehicle offences in any consistent manner as regards the requirement of *mens rea*. For example, it has been held that absence of *mens rea* is a defence to a charge of failing to report an accident (above), but that the offences of failing to comply with a traffic sign [47] and using a vehicle with a defective braking system [48] impose absolute liability.   A more satisfactory conclusion has been reached as

---

[45] Theft Act 1968, s. 12.

[46] *Post*, p. 504.

[47] *Rees* v. *Taylor*, October 19, 1939, unreported; *Brooks* v. *Jefferies* [1936] 53 T.L.R. 34.

[48] *James and Son Ltd.* v. *Smee*; *Green* v. *Burnett* [1955] 1 Q.B. 78.

regards the offence of failing to accord precedence. The Divisional Court has recently held that [49]

" . . . A sudden removal of control over the vehicle occasioned by a latent defect of which the driver did not know and could not *reasonably* be expected to know would render the subsequent failure to accord precedence no offence, provided he is in no way at fault himself." [50]

Although the court does not make the point clear, it would seem that the court is imposing liability for negligence rather than interpreting the offence as one of strict liability.[51]

---

[49] *Burns* v. *Bidder* [1967] 2 Q.B. 227 at p. 241.
[50] Italics added.
[51] See also *Leicester* v. *Pearson* [1952] 2 Q.B. 668, discussed in Glanville Williams, pp. 233–234; *ante*, p. 47; Glanville Williams, " Absolute Liability in Traffic Offences " [1967] Crim.L.R. 142, 194.

CHAPTER 23

BETTING, GAMING AND LOTTERIES

SECTION 1. INTRODUCTION

THE law of gambling is to be found principally in the Betting, Gaming and Lotteries Acts 1963 to 1971, the Gaming Act 1968 and the Pool Competitions Act 1971. The following four Sections deal with the different forms of gambling: betting, gaming, lotteries and amusements with prizes.

Gambling may be defined as the hazarding of a stake upon the result of an event—the unsuccessful person losing his stake.[1] All forms of gambling may be divided into two kinds:

(1) two persons agree that the one among them who chooses the correct result will win from the other a certain sum of money (or other prize)[2]; and

(2) a number of persons agree, among themselves or with a third party, that a sum of money (or other prize), which they have contributed, will be given to the person, or persons, among them who choose or otherwise achieve the correct result.

Within the first category come, for example, betting with a bookmaker, or playing poker. Within the second category come, for example, totalisator betting, football pools, bingo and other lotteries.

SECTION 2. BETTING

Part I of the **Betting, Gaming and Lotteries Act 1963** regulates betting. Part I divides all betting into pool betting and other betting.

Pool Betting in this Act has the same meaning as in section 10 of the Betting and Gaming Duties Act 1972.[3] That section defines it as a method of betting where a number of persons make bets—

---

[1] See *Lockwood* v. *Cooper* [1903] 2 K.B. 428 at p. 431; *Tote Investors Ltd.* v. *Smoker* [1968] 1 Q.B. 509.

[2] Such an agreement is not enforceable at law: see Cheshire and Fifoot, p. 262 *et seq.* But nothing in the Gaming Acts 1710–1892 shall affect the validity of, or any remedy in respect of, any cheque which is accepted in exchange for cash or tokens to be used by a player in gaming on licensed or registered premises under Pt. II of the Gaming Act 1968: Gaming Act 1968, s. 16 (4).

[3] Betting, Gaming and Lotteries Act 1963, s. 55, as amended by Sched. 11 to the Gaming Act 1968, Sched. 5 to the Betting and Gaming Duties Act 1972; and see Pool Competitions Act 1971, s. 2 (5) (c).

(a) on terms that the winnings of such of those persons as are winners shall be, or be a share of, or be determined by reference to, the stake money paid or agreed to be paid by those persons, whether the bets are made by means of a totalisator, or by filling up and returning coupons or other printed or written forms, or otherwise howsoever, or

(b) on terms that the winnings of such persons are winners shall be, or shall include, an amount (not determined by reference to the stake money paid or agreed to be paid by those persons) which is available in any proportions among such of those persons as are winners, or

(c) on the basis that the winners or their winnings shall, to any extent, be at the discretion of the promoter or some other person.

A bet is deemed, under the section, to be made by way of pool betting unless it is at fixed odds.

Betting other than pool betting may be defined as **fixed odds betting**—a term not used in the principal Act but used in the Betting and Gaming Duties Act 1972. Under that Act a bet is at fixed odds only if each of the persons making it knows or can know, at the time he makes it, the amount he will win, except in so far as that amount is to depend on the result of the event or events betted on, or on any such event taking place or producing a result, or on the numbers taking part in any such event, or on the starting prices or totalisator odds for any such event, or on there being totalisator odds on any such event, or on the time when his bet is received by any person with or through whom it is made. So " tote odds " offered by a bookmaker are fixed odds.[4]

Part I of the Act also draws a distinction between on-track betting and off-track betting. Off-track betting is of two kinds—betting in person or by postal or telephonic means.

The Betting, Gaming and Lotteries Act 1963, s. 52, provides

---

4 However, a bookmaker can offer " tote odds " on either " recognised horse races " (*post*, p. 322) or dog races on " licensed tracks " (*post*, p. 323) only with the permission of, respectively, the Horserace Totalisator Board and the management of the totalisator, for which permission a charge may be made: ss. 14 (1), 17 (2). Only a civil remedy is available for breach of these provisions: ss. 14 (2), 17 (3).

for two main penalties, which may conveniently be referred to as the major and minor penalty.[5]

Major penalty. Punishment on **summary conviction** by £100 fine and on second or subsequent conviction for an offence under the same provision £200 fine and 3 months' imprisonment.[6] Punishment on **indictment** by £500 fine and on second or subsequent conviction for an offence under the same provision £750 fine and 1 year's imprisonment.[7]

Minor penalty. Punishment on **summary conviction** by £50 fine and on second or subsequent conviction for an offence under the same provision £100 fine and 2 months' imprisonment.[8] Punishment on **indictment** by £300 fine and on second or subsequent conviction for an offence under the same provision £500 fine and 6 months' imprisonment.[9]

The expression " same provision " includes a corresponding provision repealed by this Act.[10]

Fixed Odds Betting

By **section 1 (1) (b)** of the **Betting, Gaming and Lotteries Act 1963** it is provided that, save as provided below, no person shall either use any premises for the purposes of effecting any betting transaction [11] other than a pool betting transaction (*i.e.* a fixed odds betting transaction) with persons resorting to those premises, or cause or knowingly permit any premises to be used by any other person for that purpose [*major penalty*]. Section 1 (2) provides that any person who, for any purpose connected with the effecting of a betting transaction, resorts to any premises being used in contravention of section 1 (1) (*b*) shall be liable on **summary conviction** [£50 *fine*]. Once a person is proved to have been on such premises, it is then for him to prove that he was on the premises for bona fide purposes which were not connected with the effecting of a betting transaction.[12]

---

5 See Loewe, " The Compleat Gambler " [1964] Crim.L.R. at p. 809.
6 s. 52.   7 *Ibid.*
8 *Ibid.*
9 *Ibid.*
10 s. 52 (3).
11 Defined in s. 55 (1) to include the collection or payment of winnings on a bet and any transaction in which one or more of the parties is acting as a bookmaker.   12 s. 1 (3).

Section 1 (1) (*b*) is a difficult section and requires some explanation. The expression " premises " includes any house, office, room, etc., and is defined by the Act to include " any place " and, for the purposes of section 1, also any vessel.[13] If the place in question is outdoors, then it will be a " place " for the purposes of this section if it is sufficiently definite [14] or localised [15] so that persons wishing to make a bet will not have difficulty in finding the person who is alleged to have used the place.[16] So a stand, stool or a conspicuous umbrella at a racecourse [17] have been held to be " places." However, for example, a bookmaker at a course who has no sign to indicate where he can be found and wanders around the enclosure probably would not be said to be using a place.[18]

The expression " use " has been given a restricted meaning. In particular it has been held to involve the idea of business. A person is not said to use premises unless:

(i) there is an element of repetition,[19] and

(ii) " he has such a degree of control [albeit without the knowledge or consent of the occupier [20]] over them that it can be said that the premises are a place where he is carrying on his betting *business*," [21] and

(iii) by his user " he [is] indicating that he [is] using that place as a place where he [can] be found and [is] carrying on his *business*." [22]

So it has been held, for example, that members of a club who bet with each other do not use the premises for betting,[23] unless the club consists of bookmakers with whom other members bet.[24]

---

[13] s. 55.

[14] *Powell* v. *Kempton Park Racecourse Co.* [1899] A.C. 143 at p. 162 (Betting Act 1853).

[15] *Brown* v. *Patch* [1899] 1 Q.B. 892 at p. 900 (Betting Act 1853).

[16] *Ibid.*

[17] See *Brown* v. *Patch* [1899] 1 Q.B. 892, and the cases cited in that case.

[18] *Powell* v. *Kempton Park Racecourse Co.* [1899] A.C. 143 at p. 196, *per* Lord James of Hereford. However, the authority of this dictum is somewhat diminished in that his Lordship relied on the *ejusdem generis* rule of statutory interpretation which, although it is applied to the words of the Betting Act 1853 could not apply to the present Act.

[19] *Milne* v. *Commissioners of Police for City of London* [1940] A.C. 1 at p. 44. See also *Whitehurst* v. *Fincher* (1890) 62 L.T. 433.

[20] *R.* v. *Porter* [1949] 2 K.B. 128.

[21] *Milne* v. *Commissioners of Police for City of London* [1940] A.C. 1 at p. 28. Italics added.

[22] *Brown* v. *Patch* [1899] 1 Q.B. 892 at p. 900. Italics added.

[23] *Downes* v. *Johnson* [1895] 2 Q.B. 203.

[24] *R.* v. *Corrie* (1904) 68 J.P. 294.

The expression "resorting" has been defined as involving physical presence. A person does not resort to a place to which he sends letters or telegrams.[25]

There are a number of exceptions to section 1 (1) (*b*), one of which is to be found in the proviso to section 1 (1). This states that paragraph (*b*) shall not apply if both the persons using the premises and the persons with whom the betting transactions are effected:

(i) either reside or work on those premises or on premises of which those premises form part; or

(ii) are, or are acting on behalf of, holders of bookmakers' permits [26] which are for the time being in force.

The other exceptions to section 1 (1) (*b*) will be dealt with separately below.

Having examined section 1 (1) (*b*), it is now intended to consider fixed odds betting from the point of view of on-track betting, off-track betting in person and off-track betting by postal or telephonic means.

On-track betting. Section 1 (5) provides that section 1 (1) (*b*) does not apply to anything done on an *approved horse racecourse* on a day on which horse races but no other races take place thereon. An "approved horse racecourse" means a horse racecourse approved by the Totalisator Board,[27] the constitution and functions of which are set out in the Act.[28]

Section 1 (5) further provides that section 1 (1) (*b*) does not apply to anything [29] done on *any track*:

(i) provided that the occupier of the track consents to bookmaking being carried on there [30]; and

(ii) provided that bookmaking shall not take place—

---

[25] *R.* v. *Brown* [1895] 1 Q.B. 119.
[26] *Post*, p. 329.
[27] s. 13. One of the conditions of this appoval is that bookmakers must be allowed on the track: *ibid.*
[28] Respectively ss. 12 and 14.
[29] This does not operate so as to exempt from s. 1 (1) (*b*) bookmaking on any permanent structure other than a structure used by the bookmaker in common with members of the public, nor any bookmaking in any position specially appropriated for the use of the particular bookmaker: s. 1 (6).
[30] s. 20.

    (*a*) on more than 104 days in the same year [31]; or

    (*b*) on any Good Friday, Christmas Day or Sunday [*major penalty*] [32]

    (*c*) on more than 14 days in any one month except on an approved horse racecourse [*major penalty*] and

(iii) provided that, unless

    (*a*) the track is an approved horse racecourse which is being used on the day in question solely for the purpose of horse races, and unless

    (*b*) bookmaking has not taken place on more than seven days in the previous year [33] and notice [34] has been given to the chief officer of police for the area

    a track betting licence has been obtained by the occupier of the track from the local authority [*major penalty*].[35]

Further restrictions on betting on dog racecourses [36] are provided by section 7,[37] which prohibits betting, on such a course, on more than eight races or for more than a continuous period of four hours [*minor penalty*]. An exception is made for what are called " special betting days." [38]

Off-track betting in person. Off-track betting in person, like on-track betting is generally prohibited by section 1 (1) (*b*), to the extent to which it comes within that section. That section is, however, subject to **section 9,** which regulates the establishment of licensed betting offices. Section 9 provides that if, in the case of any premises, there is for the time being in force a licence authoris-

---

[31] Or in relation to a dog racecourse which is a licensed track, 130 days: Betting, Gaming and Lotteries (Amendment) Act 1971. Being a period beginning with July 1 in each year.

[32] s. 5, amended by the Betting, Gaming and Lotteries (Amendment) Act 1971, s. 1. An offence will also normally have been committed against s. 1 (1) (*b*).

[33] Being a period beginning with July 1 in any year.

[34] Seven clear days' notice is required.

[35] s. 6, amended by the Betting, Gaming and Lotteries (Amendment) Act 1971, ss. 1 and 2. An offence will, normally, also have been committed against s. 1 (1) (*b*).

[36] " ' Dog race ' means a race in which an object propelled by mechanical means is pursued by dogs, and ' dog racecourse ' shall be construed accordingly ": s. 55.

[37] As amended by the Betting, Gaming and Lotteries (Amendment) Act 1971, s. 1. As to the notification of betting days, see *ibid*. s. 2.

[38] s. 7 (2), as amended by the Betting, Gaming and Lotteries (Amendment) Act 1971, s. 1.

ing the holder of that licence to use those premises as a betting office, section 1 (1) shall not apply to the use of those premises for the effecting of betting transactions with or through the holder of the licence or any servant or agent of his.

Betting office licences are granted by justices of the peace upon the conditions laid down in the First Schedule. These licences can be held only [39] by a holder for the time being,[40] of a " bookmaker's permit "[41] or a " betting agency permit,"[42] both of which are granted by the justices,[43] may be forfeited [44] and must be produced to a constable on request.[45]

The Fourth Schedule lays down detailed rules for the management of licensed betting offices. Contravention of these rules by a licensee or his servant or agent is punishable on **summary conviction** [£100 *fine*].[46] The Schedule imposes, *inter alia*, the following requirements:

(i) No person under the age of 18 may be admitted to, or allowed to remain on, the premises.

(ii) The licensee must display the betting office licence on the premises.

(iii) No facilities for watching television or listening to the wireless may be provided or allowed on the premises.[47]

(iv) No other kind of entertainment may be provided or allowed on the premises nor may any refreshment be served.

Provision is made in section 10 for the expulsion from licensed betting offices of drunken, violent, quarrelsome or disorderly persons. If such persons fail to leave upon being requested to do

---

[39] They can also be held by the Horserace Totalisator Board; *post*, p. 327.

[40] If the permits are cancelled, the licence ceases to be in force: Sched. 1, para. 32.

[41] *Post*, p. 329.

[42] These are granted to accredited agents either of a holder of a bookmaker's permit or of the Horserace Totalisator Board: s. 9 (2) (c) and Sched. 1, para. 17 (a).

[43] s. 9 (2) and Sched. 1, para. 1.

[44] s. 11.

[45] *Post*, p. 329.

[46] s. 10 (1). However, where any person is charged with an offence under this subsection by reason only of his being the licensee, it shall be a defence to prove that the contravention took place without his consent or connivance and that he exercised all due diligence to prevent it; and see *Mallon* v. *Allon* [1964] 1 Q.B. 385.

[47] This does not include any broadcast made by the " blower " (a private means of telephonic communication from track to office), provided that the matter relates only to the events on which bets have been made.

so, they may be convicted on **summary conviction** [£5 *fine*].[48] Also
a constable may, upon request, help to expel such a person.[49]

A constable may enter a licensed betting office to see whether
the provisions of the Fourth Schedule are being complied with.
Obstruction of a constable in the exercise of this power is punishable
on **summary conviction** [£10 *fine*].[50]

Finally, section 10 prohibits advertising in connection with
licensed betting offices, an exception being made in favour of certain
advertisements on or near the premises [*minor penalty*].

Off-track betting by postal or telephonic means. Since the
posting or telephoning of a bet to premises does not constitute
" resorting " to those premises,[51] section 1 (1) (*b*) has no application
to this kind of betting. There are no requirements particular to this
kind of betting which need concern us.

Pool Betting

On-track pool betting. Section 1 (1) (a) provides that no person
shall use any premises, or cause or knowingly permit any premises
to be used, as a place where persons resorting thereto may effect
pool betting transactions. Section 1 (2) and (3), the terms of which
have already been noted, also apply.[52] The words " use,"
" premises " and " resorting " have already been defined [53]—in
particular, a bookmaker's stand at a race meeting can constitute
" premises." [54]

Section 1 (1) (*a*) is stated to be subject to **section 4 (1).** Section
4 (1) provides that no pool betting business shall be carried on on
any track except in accordance with paragraphs (*a*) and (*b*), which
deal, respectively, with horse races and dog races [*major penalty*].[55]
The term " pool betting business " [56] probably would not include
pool betting by friends, although it has been suggested that it would
include charitable betting pools.[57]

[48] s. 10 (2).   [49] s. 10 (3).
[50] s. 10 (4).   [51] *Ante*, p. 322.
[52] *Ante*, p. 320.
[53] *Ante*, pp. 321–322.
[54] *Ante*, p. 321.
[55] A person committing an offence against s. 4 (1) may (and usually will) also
have committed an offence against s. 1 (1) (*a*) if he has used premises to which
persons may resort in order to carry on his pool betting business.
[56] Defined in s. 55.
[57] See [1964] Crim.L.R. 76.

Section 4 (1) (*a*) allows pool betting business carried on on an *approved horse racecourse* [58] on a day on which horse races but no other races take place thereon and carried on by the Horserace Totalisator Board, or, with the authority of that Board, by the management of the racecourse.

Although section 4 (1) (*a*) makes pool betting business on approved horse racecourses the exclusive preserve of the Totalisator Board, a proviso to section 4 (1) allows persons to receive or negotiate bets with a view to those bets being made with the Totalisator Board, or with the racecourse management if it is providing pool betting facilities with the authority of the Board. This proviso protects persons who take other people's bets to the totalisator for them in return for a fee or gratuity.

Section 4 (1) (*b*) allows pool betting business on a licensed *dog racecourse* [59] by means of a totalisator operated by the occupier of the track, or by a person authorised by the occupier, in accordance with certain conditions.[60]   A licensed racecourse is a course in respect of which a track betting licence has been granted by the local authority.[61]   There is no proviso similar to the proviso to section 4 (1) (*a*).[62]

Having regard to sections 1 (1) (*a*) and 4 (1) (*a*) and (*b*) it follows that the use of premises to which persons resort for all other pool betting is unlawful. Charitable pool betting on a " donkey-derby " is, almost certainly, unlawful, unless it comes within the provisions of the Pool Competitions Act 1971.[63]

Sections 5 and 7, both of which have been considered above,[64] apply equally to pool betting.

Off-track pool betting in person. We have already seen above [65] that section 1 (1) (*a*) prohibits the use of premises for pool betting

---

[58] *Ante*, p. 322.
[59] *Ante*, p. 323, n. 36.
[60] See s. 16, as amended by the Betting, Gaming and Lotteries (Amendment) Act 1971, s. 1 (v). Bookmakers must be allowed onto the track if a totalisator is being operated (s. 16 (2)) and failure to allow bookmakers on is an offence against s. 16 (2) [major penalty] and also apparently s. 4 (1) (*b*), but a bookmaker may be excluded from a particular place on the track: *R.* v. *Greyhound Racing Association Ltd.* (1955) 119 J.P. 501.
[61] ss. 6, 55 and Sched. 3, para. 6 (2) as amended by the Betting, Gaming and Lotteries (Amendment) Act 1971, s. 1 ; and, *ante*, p. 323.
[62] Above.
[63] See, *post*, p. 348 ; and   [1964] Crim.L.R. 76.
[64] *Ante*, p. 323.
[65] *Ante*, p. 325.

transactions. Section 1 is, however, stated to be subject to **section 9 (1),** the effect of which, in conjunction with other sections, is to provide that an exception is made in favour only of the Horserace Totalisator Board, or an " accredited agent " [66] of that Board, who, if they hold betting office licences,[67] may use premises in respect of which the licence was granted for the purposes of carrying on pool betting in any form on any recognised horse race.[68] A " recognised horse race " is defined as a horse race run on an approved horse racecourse on a day when horse races and no other races take place on that racecourse.[69] All off-track pool betting in person other than that carried on by the Totalisator Board or an accredited agent is an offence against section 1 (1) (a) if the provisions of that section are otherwise satisfied.[70]

Off-track pool betting by postal or telephonic means. Section 1 (1) (a), set out above,[71] does not apply to off-track betting not done in person, because there will be no " resorting." [72] However, **section 4 (2)** provides that no person shall carry on any pool betting business otherwise than on a track unless he is a registered pool promoter [*major penalty*]. The pool betting business carried on by any registered pool promoter must take the form of the promotion of competitions for prizes for making forecasts as to sporting or other events.[73] Registration is with the local authority and the business must be carried on in accordance with the conditions set out in the Second Schedule to the Act.[74] This requirement of registration does not apply to the Totalisator Board nor, probably, to an " accredited agent " [75] of that Board.[76] The requirement of registration would, however, apply to persons authorised [77] by the Board

---

[66] That is, an agent accredited by the Board for the purposes of receiving or negotiating bets with a view to those bets being made with or through the Board: s. 9 (2) (c).

[67] *Ante*, p. 324.

[68] This is, apparently, the combined effect of ss. 9 (1), 55 and 14 (1).

[69] s. 55.

[70] An offence may also be committed against s. 47, *post*, p. 347.

[71] *Ante*, p. 325.　　　　　　　　　　　　　　　　　[72] *Ante*, p. 322.

[73] But see the Pool Competitions Act 1971, s. 7 (2) in relation to registered pool promoters licensed under that Act. Sched. 2, para. 13. See *Singette Ltd.* v. *Martin* [1971] 2 W.L.R. 13, pp. 20–22, where the general and predominant character of the competitions was that the prizes were for holding numbers which happened to be lucky in a particular week.

[74] See also the Pool Competitions Act 1971, s. 2 (5) (a).

[75] Defined in n. 66, above.

[76] Proviso to s. 4 (2) and s. 55.

[77] In accordance with s. 14 (1) (c).

to carry on pool betting business in any form on a recognised horse race.

No person may carry on off-track pool betting business in any form on any recognised horse race [78] without the authority of the Totalisator Board.[79] The only remedy for a breach of this provision is by civil suit.[80]

Finally, section 47 (set out later [81]) provides that no person, other than the Totalisator Board or an accredited agent of that Board, or any person whose only trade or business is that of a bookmaker,[82] may carry on pool betting as part of a trade or business. It also provides that no pool betting at all may be *conducted* [as opposed to advertised] through a newspaper.

Miscellaneous Provisions

Section 8 provides that any person frequenting or loitering [83] in a street or public place, on behalf either of himself or of any other person, for the purposes of bookmaking, betting, agreeing to bet, or paying, receiving or settling bets, shall be liable on **summary conviction** [£100 *fine*; 2nd conviction, £200 *fine*; 3rd or subsequent conviction,[84] £200 *fine and 3 months' Imp.*; and on any conviction, forfeiture of betting articles found in his possession]. A proviso makes an exception in favour of anything done on any ground used, or adjacent to ground used, for a racecourse for racing with horses on a day on which horse races take place on that racecourse. A constable may arrest without a warrant any person found committing an offence under this section and may seize and detain any articles liable to forfeiture.[85]

---

[78] Defined above.   [79] s. 14 (1) (*a*).
[80] s. 14 (2).
[81] *Post*, p. 347.
[82] The use of the word " only " seems unduly restrictive—it would appear to prevent a bookmaker, who, quite incidentally, has another trade or business, from conducting pool betting as part of his trade or business as bookmaker. See also the Pool Competitions Act 1971, s. 1 (6).
[83] The meaning of the expression " frequenting " is not clear (see *R*. v. *Clarke* (1884) 14 Q.B.D. 92; *Clarke* v. *Taylor* (1948) 112 J.P. 639; *Cook* v. *Fretwell* (1928) Stone's *Justices' Manual*, 1972, p. 749). It is clear that the expression " loitering " has a wider meaning and can take place on a single occasion: *Williamson* v. *Wright*, 1924 S.C.(J.) 57. See also *Bland* v. *Cowan* [1963] 2 Q.B. 735.
[84] Notwithstanding s. 52 (3) (*ante*, p. 320), a conviction under the repealed Street Betting Act 1906 shall be deemed to have been a conviction for an offence under this section only if the offence was committed after December 1, 1961: s. 8 (3).
[85] s. 8 (2).

The expression "street" is defined as including any bridge, road, lane, footway, subway, square, court, alley, or passage, whether a thoroughfare or not, which is for the time being open to the public.[86] The doorways and entrances of premises abutting upon, and any ground adjoining and open to, a street shall be treated as forming part of the street.[87]

The expression "public place" is not defined in the Act but, probably, means a place to which the public have an unrestricted right of access and would therefore, for example, exclude a public-house.[88]

Bookmakers. **Section 2** provides that no person shall act as a bookmaker [89] *on his own account* unless he holds a bookmaker's permit granted by the justices [*major penalty*].[90]

A bookmaker's permit [91] must be produced to a constable upon request and refusal or failure without reasonable cause to produce it is punishable on **summary conviction** [£10 *fine*].[92]

The expression "bookmaker" is defined in the Act [93] as any person who, whether on his own or another's account, *by way of business* receives or negotiates bets or conducts pool betting operations, other than the Totalisator Board [94] or a person employed by that Board, or a person who operates or is employed in operating a totalisator.

Bookmakers' servants or agents. **Section 3** provides that no person shall by way of business receive or negotiate bets as servant or agent to another bookmaker or to the Totalisator Board unless:

    (i) he is 21 years old; and
    (ii) he has the written authority of the bookmaker or Board; and

---

86 s. 8 (4).   87 *Ibid.*
88 *Brannan* v. *Peek* [1948] 1 K.B. 68. This case was decided on the Street Betting Act 1906 which actually defined " public place " in this way, but Lord Goddard C.J. apparently thought that a public-house would not be a public place in any event. *Cf.*, *post*, 334, nn. 19, 20.
89 Defined in s. 55 (1).
90 This does not, however, apply to registered pool promoters: *ibid.* Where there is a partnership every partner who acts as a bookmaker must have a permit: *Dungate* v. *Lee* [1969] 1 Ch. 545.
91 And also a betting agency permit (*ante*, p. 324): s. 9 (5).
92 s. 10 (3).
93 s. 55.
94 Or the management of an approved racecourse carrying on pool betting on that course with the authority of the Board.

(iii) the bookmaker has a bookmaker's permit or a betting agency permit.

If any bets are made in contravention of this section the servant or agent and the bookmaker or Board are liable on **summary conviction** [£10 *fine; 2nd or subsequent conviction, £50 fine*].

A register of all such persons must be kept and failure to do so is punishable on **summary conviction** [as above].[95] To refuse, or without reasonable cause to fail, to produce to a constable upon request either a written authority or the register is punishable on **summary conviction** [£10 *fine*].[96]

However, section 3 does not apply to the following persons:

(i) persons themselves holding a bookmaker's permit or a betting agency permit, or

(ii) persons who receive or negotiate bets on the premises of a holder of one of these permits or of the Board, or

(iii) persons who receive or negotiate bets made by way of pool betting as servants or agents to a registered pool promoter.

Young Persons. **Section 21** provides that it is an offence [*minor penalty*] for any person to—

(i) have any betting transaction with a person under the age of 18,

(ii) employ such a person in the effecting of any betting transaction or in a licensed betting office, or

(iii) receive or negotiate any bet through such a person.

However, it is further provided that a person is not guilty of this offence by reason of

(i) the employment of a person under the age of 18 in the effecting of betting transactions by post, or

(iii) the carriage by such a person of a communication relating to a betting transaction for the purposes of its conveyance by post.

It is further provided that no offence will have been committed if the accused did not know, nor ought to have known, that the

[95] s. 3 (3).
[96] s. 3 (4).

person was under the age of 18 *unless* he was " apparently " under that age.[97]

Section 22 prohibits the sending of circulars advertising anything to do with betting to persons whom the sender knows to be under 18 years of age [*minor penalty*]. It is provided that if the circular is sent to any place of education, the sender is deemed to have known that the addressee was under that age unless he proves that he had reasonable grounds for believing him to be of full age.[98]

Offences by occupiers of licensed tracks. Although the occupier of a licensed track [99] need not admit bookmakers [1] (except where the occupier of a licensed dog racecourse is operating a totalisator [2]), if he does so **section 18** provides that he will commit an offence [*minor penalty*] if:

(i) he charges a bookmaker more than five times the entrance fee to that part of the track, or

(ii) he charges the bookmaker's assistant more than the ordinary entrance fee to that part of the track, or

(iii) he charges different amounts to different bookmakers, or their assistants, who are admitted to the same part of the track, or

(iv) he receives any other payment, etc., as consideration for special facilities for a particular bookmaker.

Section 19 provides that it is an offence for occupiers of licensed tracks (or lessees or licensees having an interest or right over the track) to have any interest in bookmaking thereon [*minor penalty*].

Right of entry. **Section 23** grants constables and other persons so authorised by the licensing authority a right of entry onto tracks. Obstruction of a constable or such a person in the exercise of his powers is punishable on **summary conviction** [£10 *fine*].

Horserace Betting Levy Board. To encourage horse racing and breeding and veterinary science the Betting, Gaming and Lotteries Act 1963 provides for the establishment of a Horserace Betting

[97] s. 21 (2).
[98] s. 22 (3), as amended by the Family Law Reform Act 1969, s. 1 (3), Sched. 1, Pt. I.
[99] *Ante,* pp. 322, 323.
[1] s. 20.
[2] s. 16 (*ante,* p. 326).

Levy Board which makes a levy on bookmakers and the Horserace Totalisator Board.[3]

Betting, Gaming, Bingo and Gaming Machine Licence Duties. Provision is made in the Betting and Gaming Duties Act 1972[4] (which consolidates the law relating to excise duties for betting and gaming) for the collection of an excise duty on betting, both pool betting and fixed odds betting, on gaming, bingo, and gaming machines. Various penalties are provided in Schedule 15, para. 15, for failure to pay duty, the contravention or failure to comply with any of the provisions of any of the regulations of the Act, the obstruction of any officer in the exercise of his functions in relation to betting duties, the making of false statements or the fraudulent evasion of such duties.

SECTION 3. GAMING

Part II of the Betting, Gaming and Lotteries Act 1963 has now been superseded by the **Gaming Act 1968** which was passed in an attempt to put an end to the commercial exploitation of gaming, and the abuses which had arisen as a result of the previous relaxation of the law.[5] The broad policy of the Act was to permit gaming on premises licensed for gaming but to prohibit it elsewhere. " Gaming " is defined in the 1968 Act[6] as the " playing of a game of chance for winnings in money or money's worth, whether any person playing the game is at risk of losing any money or money's worth or not." [7] " A game of chance " includes, saving athletic games or sports, any game of chance and skill combined, and any pretended game of chance, or of chance and skill combined.[8]

In order for there to be a game, although the participators need not necessarily be on the same premises, there must be sufficient participation to constitute the playing of a game.[9] Thus, it has

---

[3] ss. 24–31.
[4] Effective from June 11, 1972.
[5] By the 1960 Act. The Gaming Act 1968 repeals ss. 32–39 inclusive and ss. 49 (4) and (5) of the 1963 Act.
[6] s. 52 (4).
[7] s. 52 (4). This change in the definition abrogates the effect of the decision in *McCollom* v. *Wrightson* [1968] A.C. 522.
[8] s. 52.
[9] *D.P.P.* v. *Armstrong* [1965] A.C. 1262; *D.P.P.* v. *Regional Pool Promotions* [1964] 2 Q.B. 244, both decisions under the previous legislation.

been held that a game of " postal bingo " did not satisfy this requirement, where there were some 100,000 " players " who were allocated, or could choose, cards by post, where the draw was made by
the promoters privately and subsequently announced on the radio
and in the newspapers, and where the winners were notified by post
so that it made no difference whether they listened to the results
or not.[10]

Under the Gaming Act 1968, gaming is divided into three
categories, namely

    (a) what may be called private gaming, that is gaming which
        may take place elsewhere than on premises licensed or
        registered under the Act;

    (b) gaming on licensed or registered premises;

    (c) gaming by means of machines.

Gaming on Private Premises

Private gaming. What may be described as private gaming, that is
gaming other than on licensed or registered premises is controlled
by Part I of the Act which makes all gaming unlawful except in
accordance with the permission and subject to the control provided
for in the Act. By **section 2** no gaming may take place except on a
domestic or private occasion in a private dwelling, or where
certain conditions are fulfilled, in a hostel or hall of residence or
similar establishment, where the game is a " bankers game " or if
by its nature it does not offer chances equally favourable to all
players. This prohibits games where (a) the game involves playing
or staking against a bank, whether the bank is held by one of the
players or not; (b) the nature of the game is such that the chances
in the game are not equally favourable to all the players [11]; (c) the
nature of the game is such that the chances in it lie between the
player and some other person, or (if there are two or more players)
lie wholly or partly between the players and some other person,
and these chances are not as favourable to the player or players
as they are to that other person.[12] **Section 3** prohibits gaming under

10 *D.P.P.* v. *Armstrong* (*supra*).
11 The numerous cases decided on this matter before the coming into force of
    the Act are to be found in a specialised work, such as Paterson's *Licensing*
    Acts (80th ed. 1972).
12 *Ibid.*

Part I where (apart from any stakes hazarded) any charge [13] in money or money's worth is made in respect of the gaming. **Section 4** prohibits gaming under Part I where any levy is charged on any of the stakes or the winnings of the players.

It is an offence punishable on **summary conviction** [£400 *fine*] or on **indictment** [*Imp. 2 years and a fine*] [14] to organise or manage any gaming in contravention of sections 2–4 (above) or knowingly to allow any premises, vessel [15] or vehicle [16] to be used for such a purpose.

Gaming in a public place: Section 5 prohibits gaming in any street,[17] or subject to an exemption in favour of licensed premises, in any other place to which, whether on payment or otherwise, the public have access. Gaming in such circumstances is an offence punishable on **summary conviction** [£50]. The prohibition under section 5 does not extend to the playing of dominoes and cribbage and other games of equal chance authorised by the appropriate liquor licensing authority in public houses and hotels licensed for the sale of liquor.[18] Such gaming must however comply with the terms of sections 2–4 of the Act. The expression " place to which the public have access " would exclude a club, because clubs are not normally places to which the public have access.[19] However it would include a place, such as a public house, the occupier of which reserves the right to refuse admission.[20]

Gaming with persons under the age of eighteen: section 7 forbids absolutely any gaming by persons under eighteen in public houses and hotels. The offence is punishable on **summary conviction** [£20 *fine*]. There is no other provision in Part I which restricts gaming by young people in the premises to which Part I applies.

Commercial Gaming

The object of Part II of the Act, is the control of gaming on a commercial scale. It deals with gaming for money by games of

---

[13] Defined in s. 52 (7).
[14] s. 8.
[15] See s. 52.   [16] *Ibid.*
[17] Defined in s. 5 (3).
[18] Apart from premises with restaurant or residential licences only.
[19] See *Panama (Piccadilly) Ltd.* v. *Newberry* [1962] 1 W.L.R. 610.
[20] *Glynn* v. *Simmonds* [1952] W.N. 289; *Capper* v. *Baldwin* [1965] 2 Q.B. 53 at p. 60; *Blytheway* v. *Oakes* [1965] Crim. L.R. 37.

chance such as roulette, baccarat, etc. To this end it provides for the licensing and registration of premises where such gaming is to take place, and the lynch pin around which the controls revolve is the Gaming Board, with its supervisory jurisdiction. The procedure for licensing, and that for the registration of clubs and miners' institutes, is set out in the Second and Third Schedules to the Act, respectively.

In relation to the licensing of premises generally, the **Second Schedule** [21] provides that the licensing authority shall be the authority responsible for the grant, renewal and revocation, etc. of bookmakers' permits and betting office licences, and it lays down in detail the procedure for application, grant, renewal and revocation of such licences. Similar provisions in the **Third Schedule** [22] relate to the registration of clubs and miners' welfare institutes.

The Gaming Board set up by the Act,[23] as its prime duty, has to " keep under review the extent and character of gaming " throughout the country and " in particular to keep under review the extent, character and location of the facilities provided." [24] In addition to its primary duty, the Board is required to:

(a) advise the Home Secretary as to the need for legislation [25];

(b) advise the licensing authorities as to the exercise of their powers [26]; and

(c) appear before licensing authorities to oppose applications for the grant or renewal of licences, or to move for the cancellation of a licensing or registration certificate.[27]

The Board has effective control of the grant of applications for licences since the **Second Schedule** provides [23] that an application to the licensing authority shall be of no effect unless the Board has issued a certificate of consent to show its approval of the application.

In addition, the Board investigates the trustworthiness of all applicants for licences, and has powers of approving gaming supervisors, gaming operatives in casinos and also selected operatives in

[21] As amended by the Finance Acts 1969 and 1970 and the Betting and Gaming Duties Act 1972, the Courts Act 1971.
[22] *Ibid.*
[23] s. 10.
[24] s. 10 (3).
[25] s. 51 (2).
[26] Sched. 2 as amended.
[27] *Ibid.* para. 31 as amended by the Courts Act 1971, Scheds. 5 and 9.
[28] Para. 3.

bingo clubs, and retailers of gaming and amusement machines.[29] Through its inspectorate it assists the police in the detection of breaches of conditions or restrictions attached to licences and in the detection of fraudulent play.[30]

Gaming, Licensed or Registered Premises. In relation to gaming upon licensed or registered premises, **section 12** of the Act prohibits a person from participating in the gaming:

(1) if he is not present on the premises at the time when the gaming takes place there, or if he is participating on behalf of another person who is not present on the premises at the time; although where the gaming consists of a game which involves playing or staking against a bank, the holder of the licence or a person acting on his behalf may hold the bank or have a share or interest in it.[31]

(2) unless he is a member of the club specified in the licence who, at the time when he begins to take part, is eligible so to do or is a bona fide guest of such a person; provided that he has complied with the requirements of eligibility.[32] The mere fact that such a guest has made a payment lawfully required under section 14 does not preclude him from being a bona fide guest.[33]

(3) if he is the holder of the licence or person acting on his behalf or employed in the premises in question.

Where the premises are registered under the Third Schedule, similar provisions are to be found in relation to members and bona fide guests. " Participation " is defined [34] for the purposes of the section as:

(a) taking part in the game as a player [35];
(b) where the game involves playing or staking against a bank, holding the bank or having a share in it.

Section 13 while preserving the general provisions of section 2 games in relation to gaming under Part II does permit the relaxation of the prohibition by means of regulations and an exemption has

---

[29] s. 19 and Sched. 5; s. 27 and Sched. 6.
[30] s. 43.
[31] s. 12 (4).
[32] s. 12 (3).
[33] s. 12 (5).
[34] s. 12 (7).
[35] Defined in s. 52 (8), incorporating s. 55 (1) of the 1963 Act. The fact that a player, by reason of his not being a member of the club, would not be allowed to receive winnings does not mean that he is not participating: *Wheeler* v. *Gibbins* [1970] 1 W.L.R. 268; *cf. Tote Investors Ltd.* v. *Smoker* [1968] 1 Q.B. 509.

already been made [36] in favour of pontoon and *chemin de fer* in registered premises. **Section 14** permits the imposition of charges, which would otherwise be unlawful by reason of section 3, in relation to premises under Part II [37]; and **section 15** permits a levy on stakes or winnings, otherwise unlawful by virtue of section 4, to be made in respect of licensed (but not registered) premises. **Section 16** prohibits the giving of credit by the holder of the licence or a person acting under his behalf either to enable a person to take part in the gaming, in respect of his losses, and imposes restrictions on the acceptance of cheques in exchange for cash or tokens. **Section 17** excludes persons under eighteen from premises except where bingo clubs or gaming for prizes is concerned. **Section 18** restricts gaming on Sundays.

Bingo club premises. Special provisions are made in respect of bingo club premises, that is, clubs specified in a licence under the Act, where restrictions have been imposed [38] limiting the gaming to the playing of bingo. It is provided by **section 20** that where a game of bingo is played simultaneously on different bingo club premises where

(*a*) all the players take part in the same game at the same time and all are present at that time on one or more of the premises, and

(*b*) the draw takes place on one or other of the premises while the game is being played, and

(*c*) any claim of one of the players to have won is indicated to all the other players before the number is called

then the restrictions on participation imposed by section 12 (1) do not apply provided that:

(*a*) the aggregate amount paid to players as winnings does not exceed the aggregate amount of the stakes hazarded by the players in playing that game, and

(*b*) the aggregate amount paid to players as winnings in respect of that game, together with the aggregate for the week in respect of those premises does not exceed £1,000.

Certain other exemptions are made in favour of such premises.[39]

---

[36] Gaming Act (Registration under Pt. II) Regulations 1969, reg. 2.
[37] As to amount see Gaming Act (Registration under Pt. II) Regulations 1969, reg. 2. In relation to licensed gaming clubs see the Gaming Clubs (Bankers Games) Regulations 1970. [38] Under para. 25 of Sched. 2.
[39] s. 20.

Gaming for prizes. Where the gaming concerned under Part II of the Act is gaming for prizes and

(*a*) the amount paid by any person for any one chance to win a prize does not exceed five new pence; and

(*b*) the aggregate amount taken by way of the sale of chances in any one determination of winners of prizes does not exceed two pounds and fifty new pence, and the sale of these chances and the declaration of the result takes place on the same day and on the premises on which and at the time when the game is played; and

(*c*) no money prize exceeding five new pence is distributed or offered; and

(*d*) the winning or the purchase of a chance to win a prize does not entitle any person to any further opportunity to win money or money's worth by taking part in any other gaming or in any lottery; and

(*e*) the aggregate amount or value of the prizes on any one determination of winners does not exceed two pounds and fifty new pence

then, in relation to premises licensed under the Second Schedule the provisions of sections 13, 17, and 20 (8) are relaxed.[40]

Where a contravention of sections 12–20, or of any regulation made under section 22 occurs on any premises, the holder of any licence,[41] or every officer of a club or institute registered under the Act shall be guilty of an offence punishable on **summary conviction** [*Fine* £400] or on **indictment** [*Imp. 2 years and fine*].[42] It shall, however, be a defence for such a person to prove both that the contravention occurred without his knowledge and that he exercised all such care as was reasonable in the circumstances to secure that the provisions in question would not be contravened.[43] There are also wide powers of disqualification.[44] If a person for the purpose of obtaining for himself or another a certificate of approval issued by the Board, or reinstatement of a certificate revoked by the Board

---

[40] s. 21. See the Decimal Currency Act 1969, s. 10 (1).
[41] And under s. 16 (3). In relation to cheques " every person concerned in the organisation or management."
[42] s. 23 (4).
[43] s. 23 (3).
[44] ss. 24 and 25.

makes a statement which he knows to be false in a material particular or recklessly makes a statement which is false in a material particular, he commits an offence punishable on **summary conviction** [*Fine* £200].[45]

Whist drives, etc. Section 41 operates to exclude "gaming [46] carried on at an entertainment promoted for raising money to be applied for purposes other than private gain" [47] from the provisions of Part I.

The gaming must be carried on at an entertainment (*e.g.* a social evening) but it has been held that bingo and whist are themselves an entertainment and that no further entertainment is needed.[48] The expression " private gain " is defined as not including payment into the general funds of the club.[49] Nor are proceeds being applied for purposes of private gain if hire or maintenance charges are being paid in respect of the machines out of the proceeds, *unless* these charges are calculated as a percentage of the stake-money.[50]

The four conditions which must be observed are as follows:

    (i) that not more than one payment (whether by way of entrance fee or stake or otherwise) is made by each player in respect of all the games played at the entertainment, and that no such payment exceeds fifty new pence;

    (ii) that not more than one distribution of prizes is made in respect of all the games played at the entertainment, and that the total value of all prizes so distributed does not exceed £50 [51];

---

[45] s. 23 (6).

[46] Is not gaming to which Pt. II of the Act applies or gaming by means of a machine to which Part III of the Act applies, and does not constitute the provision of amusements with prizes in the circumstances specified in ss. 48 (1) or 49 (1) of the Betting, Gaming and Lotteries Act 1963.

[47] The Betting, Gaming and Lotteries Act 1963, s. 54 (1) and (3) (construction of certain references to private gain) shall have effect for the purposes of this section.

[48] *Bow* v. *Heatley*, 1960 S.L.T. 311. On the other hand, *chemin-de-fer* has been held not to be an entertainment in its own right: *De Horsey* v. *Rignell* (1962) 106 S.J. 1070.

[49] s. 54 (3) of the 1963 Act preserved by s. 41 (11) of the 1968 Act.

[50] s. 54 (2).

[51] *Ibid.* s. 41 (4): exceptionally, this can be increased to £100 or more: ss. 41 (8) and (9), Gaming Act 1968.

     (iii) that all the payments mentioned in (i), after allowing for the expenses and the cost of the prizes, be applied for purposes other than private gain;

     (iv) that only a reasonable allowance be made for expenses.[52]

Gaming by means of machines

Part III of the Act seeks to control, not only the use of gaming machines,[52a] but also their sale and supply. **Section 26** defines the machines to which this part of the Act applies including slot machines for playing a game of chance in which the element of chance is provided by the machine itself.

Sale and supply of machines: section 27 imposes a general restriction on the sale or supply of such machines unless the seller or supplier holds a certificate issued by the Board, or is the servant or agent of such a person. There are exemptions in favour of the sale or supply to dealers [53]; for transactions by finance companies,[54] or for the sale of machines as scrap or as fixtures.[55] Certificates are not required where the machines are to be used exclusively at fairs, in amusement places or on pleasure piers.[56] **Section 28** confers powers on the Secretary of State to make regulations restricting the terms and conditions of sale and maintenance of machines.

Use of machines for gaming. **Section 35** absolutely prohibits the use of machines for gaming, except in licensed or registered premises;[57] at non-commercial entertainments;[58] or for amusements with prizes.[59] The provisions for registration and licensing of premises are to be found in the Seventh and Eighth Schedules to the Act. Part III sets up a registration scheme for clubs who desire to have one or two gaming machines but do not wish to have any

[52] s. 41 (7) makes detailed provisions for a series of entertainments.
[52a] For the meaning of " gaming machine " see the Betting and Gaming Duties Act 1972, s. 26.
[53] s. 27 (2) (a).
[54] s. 27 (2) (b).
[55] s. 27 (2) (c).
[56] s. 27 (3).
[57] s. 35 (a).
[58] s. 35 (b).
[59] s. 35 (c).

other form of gaming. This scheme applies to members' and proprietary clubs.[60] On such premises the following rules apply:

(a) not more than two machines may be available for gaming unless permission for more is granted by the licensing authority;

(b) only cash may be inserted and that only up to a maximum of five new pence at a time;

(c) all prizes must be in coin and no other benefit or advantage is permitted;

(d) the use of the machines when the public have access is prohibited.

Use of machines for amusements with prizes. Machines are permitted without authority or limit on prizes or numbers, where they are incidental to non-commercial entertainments such as fêtes, bazaars and the like, and at pleasure fairs or on pleasure piers.[61]

SECTION 4. LOTTERIES

Part III of the **Betting, Gaming and Lotteries Act 1963** deals with lotteries. What constitutes a lottery is not defined in the Act. It has been described as a distribution of prizes by lot or chance.[62] For a competition to be a lottery the winning of a prize must depend solely on chance and not on skill.[63] This definition would include many kinds of gaming.[64] An absolutely free and gratuitous distribution of chances is not a lottery.[65] Nor would it probably be

---

[60] *Tehrani* v. *Rostron* [1972] 1 Q.B. 182. It is otherwise under Pt. II of the Act.   [61] s. 27 (3).

[62] *Taylor* v. *Smetten* (1883) 11 Q.B.D. 207 at p. 210; *Moore* v. *Elphick* (1945) 110 J.P. 66; *D.P.P.* v. *Bradfute and Associates Ltd.* (*supra*) and the cases set out in the speech of Lord Pearson in *Singette Ltd.* v. *Martin* [1971] 2 W.L.R. 13 (H.L.) at p. 22. The problem of what constitutes " chance " has much exercised the courts: see Halsbury, Vol. 18, pp. 239–240. An essential feature of a lottery is that the receipt of a prize must depend entirely on chance: *Hall* v. *Cox* [1899] 1 Q.B. 198; and see *Atkinson* v. *Murrell* [1972] 2 Q.B. 274 at p. 279.

[63] *Singette Ltd.* v. *Martin* (*supra*) at p. 22, *per* Lord Pearson: " In deciding whether a competition is a lottery or not, a realistic view should be taken and regard should be had to the way in which the competition is actually conducted." *Ibid.* In a chain-letter scheme, any payment is dependent upon the chance that the chain will not break before any particular person's name reaches the top of the list: *Atkinson* v. *Murrell* (*supra*).

[64] *i.e.* those kinds of gaming in which no skill is involved. " There is no limit to the ingenuity of the devisers of projects such as this, and there is accordingly, no end to the variety of schemes which may constitute a lottery ": *Barnes* v. *Strathern* 1929, J.C. 41, at p. 46.

[65] *Willis* v. *Young and Stembridge* [1907] 1 K.B. 448 at p. 455.

a lottery unless a person who does not win loses his stake.[66] So Premium Bonds are not stakes in a lottery. But a person may be regarded as losing his stake even though the net result of the transaction is that he acquires something of economic value, win or lose. So a company which offers prizes to the purchasers of one of their products with the winning number on it is organising a lottery,[67] as also a company which offers money to a person having one of their products in the house when a representative of the company calls. To prevent such offers from being lotteries, in practice, some element of skill (e.g. a question) is usually introduced. However, as a result of recent decisions even the presence of a skill-testing question may not prevent a scheme from being a lottery. In one case, on the inside of the label attached to a tin of cat food was printed a " bingo " game. The game was played by matching numbers, also printed on the label, with the bingo numbers. On the successful completion of a line, a purchaser was entitled to attempt a question which required some skill in order to answer it. It was held that the scheme could be divided into two stages and that, since on completing the line, the purchaser obtained something of value, i.e. the right to attempt the question, the scheme constituted a lottery.[68] To avoid the consequences of this decision, promoters of such competitions will have to be prepared to give away the chance to play the game even though no particular item is bought.

It is not an essential feature of a lottery that there should be a prize fund or profit out of which prizes are provided,[68a] although it is essential that the participants make a payment or contribution for the purchase of their chance.[68b]

Section 41 [69] provides that subject to certain exceptions all lotteries are unlawful. Notwithstanding this, no offence will have

---

[66] If he does not lose his stake, there is no element of wagering: see *Lockwood* v. *Cooper* [1903] 2 K.B. 428 and *Waring* v. *Wildgoose* [1964] Crim.L.R. 268; also *Tote Investors Ltd.* v. *Smoker* [1968] 1 Q.B. 509. But lotteries may not require this element of wagering: see *Wallingford* v. *Mutual Society* (1880) 5 App.Cas. 685 at p. 697 and Halsbury, Vol. 18, pp. 238–239.

[67] *Hunt* v. *Williams* (1888) 52 J.P. 821; *Taylor* v. *Smetten* (1883) 11 Q.B.D. 207; *Willis* v. *Young and Stembridge* [1907] 1 K.B. 448.

[68] *D.P.P.* v. *Bradfute and Associates Ltd.* [1967] 2 Q.B. 291.

[68a] *Atkinson* v. *Murrell* [1972] 2 Q.B. 274 (a chain-letter scheme).

[68b] *Ibid.*; See also *Whitbread & Co. Ltd.* v. *Bell* [1970] 2 Q.B. 547; *Douglas* v. *Valente* 1968 S.L.T. 85; *Atkinson* v. *Murrell* [1972] 3 W.L.R. 465 at p. 470, H.L.

[69] As amended by the Gaming Act 1968, Sched. 11.

been committed unless the provisions of section 42 are contravened.[70]

Section 42 [71] provides that it is an offence [*major penalty* [72]] for any person in connection with any *unlawful* lottery, promoted in Great Britain or elsewhere,[73] to do any of the following:

(i) print any tickets for use in the lottery;

(ii) sell or distribute tickets;

(iii) offer or advertise tickets for sale or distribution;

(iv) have tickets in his possession for the purposes of sale or distribution;

(v) print, publish or distribute or have in his possession for the purpose of publication or distribution—

    (*a*) any advertisement of the lottery;

    (*b*) any list [74] of winning tickets;

    (*c*) any matter calculated to induce people to participate in that or other lotteries;

(vi) bring into Great Britain, or invite any person to send into Great Britain, for the purpose of sale or distribution any ticket in, or advertisement of, the lottery;

(vii) send or attempt to send out of Great Britain any money, ticket, etc., in connection with the lottery;

(viii) use any premises, or cause or knowingly permit any premises to be used, for purposes connected with the promotion or conduct of the lottery;

(ix) cause, procure or attempt to procure any person to commit the acts enumerated above.

It is a good defence for the accused to prove that he reasonably believed that the lottery was lawful or that it amounted to lawful gaming. Although the burden of proving this defence lies upon the accused he must establish it only upon the balance of probabilities.[75]

---

[70] *Sales-Matic Ltd.* v. *Hinchcliffe* [1959] 1 W.L.R. 1005.

[71] As amended by the Gaming Act 1968, Sched. 11.

[72] *Ante*, p. 320.

[73] Betting Duties Act 1972.

[74] Whether complete or not.

[75] *R.* v. *Carr-Briant* [1943] K.B. 607, and see p. 595.

Section 43 provides that certain " small lotteries " promoted as an incident of an entertainment [76] shall not be unlawful. But the section further provides that if the following conditions are not satisfied, every person concerned in the promotion or conduct of the lottery shall be guilty of an offence [77] [*major penalty*]. These conditions are:

(i) that the whole proceeds of the entertainment and lottery (making a deduction for, only, the expenses of the entertainment, printing costs for lottery tickets and a sum not exceeding £10 for prizes) be devoted to purposes other than private gain [78];

(ii) that none of the prizes in the lottery be money prizes;

(iii) that the tickets are sold and the results declared on the premises where the entertainment is held and during the course of the entertainment;

(iv) that the lottery, or the lottery and other gaming [79] or amusements with prizes,[80] shall not be the only, or the only substantial, inducement to persons to attend the entertainment.

Section 44 provides that " private lotteries " are not unlawful. A private lottery is a lottery in Great Britain which is promoted for, and *in which the sale of tickets* [81] *is confined to*, either:

(i) members of a society [82] established and conducted for purposes not connected with gaming, betting or lotteries; or

(ii) persons all of whom work or, alternatively, reside on the same premises,

and which is promoted only by such members [83] or persons.

---

[76] The expression " entertainment " is defined as meaning bazaars, sales of work, fêtes, dinners, dances, sporting or athletic events and other entertainments of a similar character, whether limited to one day or extended over two or more days: s. 43 (3).

[77] It is a good defence if the accused can prove that the contravention occurred without his consent or connivance and that he exercised all due diligence to prevent it.

[78] As to the meaning of private gain, see, *ante*, p. 339, but s. 54 (2) does *not* apply.

[79] Under s. 41 of the Gaming Act 1968.

[80] Under s. 48 (3) as amended by the Gaming Act 1968, Sched. 11.

[81] s. 44, especially s. 44 (2) (*d*), seems to imply that only the promoters themselves can sell the tickets.

[82] Defined to include a club, institution, etc.: *ibid.* (1) (*c*).

[83] The members must have the written authorisation of the governing body of the society: *ibid.* (1) (*c*) .

The precise meaning of the expression "established and conducted for purposes not connected with gaming," etc., is not clear. It has been held that if a club (in the particular case, a football supporters' club), the object of which is to raise money, runs a lottery, then this section does not protect it.[84] If the object of the club is not to raise money, then, at least, if the lotteries are not held often, this section will protect it for otherwise "it would make nonsense of the definition, for it would be impossible to hold a lottery and remain within it."[85] If, on the other hand, it holds lotteries regularly, it may well lose the protection of the section.[86] In any event, societies are advised to register in accordance with section 45 (discussed below) because it is not safe to rely on section 44 for these reasons.

Section 44 further provides that, if the following conditions are not satisfied, each of the promoters and any other person contravening a condition commit an offence[87] [*major penalty*]. These conditions are:

   (i) that the whole proceeds (after deducting only expenses incurred for printing and stationery) shall be devoted to providing prizes and, additionally or alternatively, in the case of a society, to the purposes of the society;

  (ii) that no written advertisements of the lottery shall be distributed or exhibited other than advertisements exhibited on the premises of the society, or, as the case may be, the premises where the participators work or reside, and other than such advertisements as are contained on the ticket;

 (iii) that the price of every ticket shall be the same and be stated on the ticket;

 (iv) that on the ticket there appears the name and address of each of the promoters and a statement to the effect that the only persons who may buy the tickets are those persons for whom the lottery is promoted (above) and that

---

[84] *Pearse* v. *Hart* [1955] 1 W.L.R. 57; *Maynard* v. *Williams, ibid.* at p. 54.

[85] *Maynard* v. *Williams* [1955] 1 W.L.R. 54 at p. 64, *per* Devlin J.; but *cf.* the judgment of Lord Goddard C.J. in the same case, particularly at p. 58.

[86] See *Maynard* v. *Williams* (*ubi supra*). See also *Payne* v. *Bradley* [1962] A.C. 343 at p. 359.

[87] It is a good defence for a person charged by reason only of being a promoter to prove that the contravention occurred without his consent or connivance and that he exercised all due diligence to prevent it.

a prize may only be given to a person who, himself, bought
a ticket;

(v) that no prize be otherwise distributed;

(vi) that tickets may only be bought, that no credit may be given
and that no stake be returned;

(vii) that no tickets be sent through the post.

Section 45 [88] provides that certain lotteries, otherwise unlawful,
which are conducted for charitable, sporting or other purposes are
lawful. This section applies to lotteries promoted in Great Britain
on behalf of a society [89] which is registered with the local
authority [90] and which is conducted wholly or mainly for one or
more of the following purposes:

(i) charitable purposes [91];

(ii) participation in or support of athletic sports or games [92]
or cultural activities [93];

(iii) or *other* purposes not being for private gain [94] or for
any commercial undertaking.

Section 45 further provides that, if the following conditions are
not satisfied, the promoter and any other person who is party to
the contravention commit an offence [95] [*major penalty*]. These
conditions are:

(i) that the promoter be a member of the society authorised
in writing by the governing body of the society;

(ii) that no remuneration in respect of the lottery be paid
to the promoter or to any person engaged in betting
business who is employed by the promoter;

---

[88] Pool Competitions Act 1971, s. 1 (2).

[89] Defined to include a club, institution, etc.: s. 45 (2).

[90] In accordance with Sched. 7. The local authority are bound to register unless
certain narrow and specified requirements are not satisfied. Promoters are
obliged to make a return to the local authority showing proceeds, etc. Failure
to do so or making a false return is punishable on summary conviction
[£20 *fine*]: *ibid*.

[91] For the meaning of charitable purpose, see Halsbury, Vol. 4, p. 213 *et seq*.

[92] This means that lotteries of the kind in *Maynard* v. *Williams* [1955] 1 W.L.R.
54 can now be carried on lawfully.

[93] Nothing in the present Act affects the operation of the Arts Union Act 1846
and any lottery promoted and conducted in accordance with that Act shall not
be unlawful: s. 46.

[94] If it is calculated to benefit the society, it does not matter that it would also
benefit an individual: s. 45 (2).

[95] There is a defence identical to that to s. 44; *ante*, p. 345, n. 87. There is also
a particular defence in connection with the conditions concerning the expenses
of, and prizes for, the lottery: s. 45 (5) (*b*).

(iii) that no prize shall exceed £100 and that no ticket be sold for more than 5p;

(iv) that the whole proceeds (after deducting sums for expenses[96] and prizes) are applied to the purposes of the society (above);

(v) that the price for every ticket shall be the same and stated on the ticket;

(vi) that the total value of tickets sold shall not exceed £750[97];

(vii) that no written advertisement shall be distributed otherwise than to members or exhibited otherwise than on the society's premises;

(viii) that every ticket and advertisement shall specify the name of the society, the name and address of the promoter and the date of the draw or other determining event;

(ix) that no ticket shall be sent through the post to a person who is not a member of the society[98];

(x) that no person shall be allowed to participate in the lottery unless the promoter has received[99] the whole price of the ticket and that the stake, once received by the promoter, shall not be returned;

(xi) that no payment on account of expenses or prizes shall be made out of the moneys of the society other than the proceeds of the lottery;

(xii) that no ticket shall be sold by or to a person under 16 years of age.

Restrictions on certain prize competitions. Section 47 provides that it shall be an offence [*major penalty*][1] to conduct in or through any newspaper,[2] or in connection with any trade or business[3] or the sale of any article to the public—

96 The maximum sum that may be spent on expenses is specified in s. 45 (3) (*e*).
97 Further provisions are made for lotteries promoted on the same day by the same society: s. 45 (3) (*g*).
98 *N.B.* The sale of tickets to non-members is not forbidden.
99 Not necessarily directly from that person.
1 The accused may also be proceeded against under s. 42, where applicable: s. 47 (2).
2 Defined in s. 55.
3 That is, trade or business *other than* sponsored pool betting or pool betting operations carried on by a person whose only trade or business is that of a bookmaker.

(i) any competition in which prizes are offered for forecasts
of the result either—
  (a) of a future event[4]; or
  (b) of a past event the result of which is not yet
  ascertained or not yet generally known;
(ii) any other competition success in which does not depend to
a substantial degree upon the exercise of skill.

The expression " competition " has been held to include pool
betting[5]—thus considerably widening what, at first sight, might
be thought to be the scope of this section, but a competition which
having no element of skill, is an unlawful lottery under Part III
cannot be lawful pool betting under Part I.[6]

In *Ladbroke's (Football) Ltd.* v. *Perrett*[7] the defendants conducted a " spot-ball " competition published in a newspaper. A
competitor had to decide, after studying a photograph of an
incident in a football match from which the ball had been
eliminated, in which eight of a grid of superimposed squares the
ball was most likely to be. After the competition had been published
a panel of experts met and decided in which eight squares the ball
was most likely to be and the prizes were awarded to competitors
who selected the same squares as the panel. The Divisional Court
held that the deliberation of the panel was a future event, and their
decision was a result. They held further that since the competitors
were exercising their skill in selecting eight squares and were
attempting to forecast the panel's decision, the competition infringed
section 47 1 (a) (i).

The **Pool Competitions Act 1971**[8] permits a registered pool
promoter, holding a certificate from the Gaming Board to be
granted a licence by the board to hold competitions for prizes
subject to certain conditions. A competition of this sort must be
one where (a) the allocation of prizes depends upon the outcome
of sporting events, and (b) each competitor has the right to forecast
the outcome of those events, and (c) prizes can be won both where
the competitor forecasts the outcome and where he does not. A

4 See *Ladbrokes (Football) Ltd. & Others* v. *Perrett* [1971] 1 W.L.R. 110.
5 *Elderton* v. *United Kingdom Totalisator Co. Ltd.* [1946] Ch. 57.
6 *Singette Ltd.* v. *Martin* [1971] A.C. 407.
7 [1971] 1 W.L.R. 110.
8 The Act permits competitions such as that declared unlawful in *Singette* v.
Martin, ante, p. 341, where they are conducted for the benefit of charitable
and other societies.

certificate will be issued by the Board only where it is shown that
during the period of twelve months ending November 24, 1970
the promoter has held at least nine competitions, each of which was
a competition for prizes depending upon the outcome of sporting
events and each was for the benefit of a society established and
conducted wholly or mainly for (i) charitable purposes, or (ii)
participation in, or support of athletic sports or games or cultural
activities, or (iii) other purposes being neither for private gain nor
commercial undertaking, provided that each of the competitions
would have constituted pool betting business on the assumption
that the entries and entry moneys were bets and stakes, that all
the competitors had made forecasts as to the outcome of sporting
events and the prizes had been for making such forecasts.

The board may attach conditions to such a licence and a person
who fails to comply with any term or condition of the licence
commits an offence punishable on **summary conviction** [£400 *fine*]
or on **indictment** [*a fine*].[9]

Part IV of the Betting, Gaming and Lotteries Act 1963 and Part III
of the Gaming Act 1968 deal with amusements with prizes. The
expression " amusement with prizes " includes a machine operated
by chance (*e.g.* a fruit machine or pin table).[10]

Amusements at non-commercial entertainments. Section 48 [11]
permits the provision at an entertainment (within the meaning of
section 43 [12]) of amusements with prizes. Such amusements are
exempt from sections 41 or 42.

Section 48,[13] however, further provides that if any of these
sections would have been contravened, then, unless the following
conditions are satisfied, an offence [*minor penalty* [14]] will be committed by any person concerned in the provision or conduct of
the amusement, unless he proves that the contravention occurred

[9] Pool Competitions Act 1971, s. 3 (8).
[10] *Capper* v. *Baldwin* [1965] 2 Q.B. 53. For the meaning of " gaming machine "
see Betting and Gaming Duties Act 1972, s. 26.
[11] As amended by the Gaming Act 1968, Sched. 11.
[12] *Ante*, p. 344.
[13] As amended by the Gaming Act 1968, Sched. 11.
[14] *Ante*, p. 320.

without his consent or connivance and that he exercised all due
diligence to prevent it. These conditions are:

(i) that the whole proceeds of the entertainment (including the
proceeds of any such amusements) after deducting—

(a) the expenses of the entertainment and of these
amusements (including prizes); and

(b) any of the expenses authorised to be deducted
under the first condition to section 43,[15]

will be devoted to purposes other than private gain;

(ii) that the opportunity to win prizes by this means or by
this means and also by lotteries or by gaming is not the
only, or the only substantial, inducement to persons to
attend the entertainment.

Amusements at commercial entertainments. Section 49 [16]
provides that sections 41 or 42 shall not apply to the provision of
amusements with prizes—

(i) on any premises in respect of which a permit granted
by the local authority [17] is in force;

(ii) on any premises in respect of which a permit granted under
section 34 of the Gaming Act 1968 is for the time being in
force used mainly for the purposes of amusements by means
of machines; or

(iii) at any pleasure fair consisting wholly or mainly of amusements provided by travelling showmen which is held on
premises not used in the preceding year on more than
twenty-seven days for the holding of such a fair.

Section 49 provides that, if either of these sections would have
applied, then, unless the following conditions are satisfied, an
offence [*minor penalty*] will be committed by any person concerned
in the provision or conduct of that amusement, unless he proves
that the contravention occurred without his consent or connivance
and that he exercised all due diligence to prevent it. These
conditions are:

(i) that the stake does not exceed 5p;

[15] *Ante*, p. 344.
[16] As amended by the Betting, Gaming and Lotteries Act 1964 and the Gaming
Act 1968, Sched. 11.
[17] See para. 1 of Sched. 6 to the 1963 Act and para. 1 of Sched. 9 of the Gaming
Act 1968.

   (ii) that the total amount of the stakes does not exceed £2·50p, that the sale of stakes and declaration of result take place on the same day and on the premises on which, and during the time when, the amusement is provided;

  (iii) that a successful player is not *entitled* [18] (whether on payment or otherwise) to any further opportunity to win prizes by taking part in any amusement with prizes or in any gaming or lottery [19];

  (iv) that, in the case of pleasure fairs, the opportunity to win prizes at these amusements is not the only, or the only substantial, inducement to persons to attend the fair;

  (v) that no money prize exceeding five new pence is distributed or offered. No permit under section 49 (as amended) shall be granted in respect of any premises where a licence under the Gaming Act 1968 is for the time being in force in respect of them or where a club or a miners' welfare institute is for the time being registered in respect of them under Part II of that Act, and, where such a licence is granted or a club or miners' welfare institute is so registered in respect of any premises and a permit under section 49 is then in force in respect of those premises, the permit thereupon ceases to have effect.

Section 6. Search Warrants

Search warrants in respect of premises may be issued by a justice under both the 1963 and 1968 Acts. Under the 1963 Act the warrant entitles any constable to enter and seize money, documents etc. which he has reasonable cause to believe may be required as evidence for an offence under this Act and to arrest and search any person found on the premises whom he has reasonable cause to believe to be committing or to have committed any such offence.[20] Under the Gaming Act 1968 gaming inspectors and constables are given rights of entry into licensed (but not registered premises); while search warrants may be executed in either registered or licensed premises. The Gaming Board and Chief Officers of police

---

[18] In contrast, presumably, to " allowed."
[19] s. 49 (3) (*b*).
[20] s. 51.

are entitled to demand information from both licensed and registered clubs.[21]

SECTION 7. CHEATING

Section 17 of the **Gaming Act 1845** [22] provides that any person who obtains any money or valuable thing by any fraud or unlawful device or ill practice in playing at or with cards, dice etc. or in betting on the event of any game, sport etc. commits an offence punishable on **summary conviction** [*Imp. 6 months and £200 fine*] or on **indictment** [*Imp. 2 years*].

SECTION 8. MARINE INSURANCE

By **section 1** of the **Marine Insurance (Gambling Policies) Act 1909** it is provided that—

(i) if any person effects a contract of marine insurance without having any bona fide interest in the safe arrival of the ship, or in the preservation of the subject-matter insured, or a bona fide expectation of acquiring such an interest, and

(ii) if any person in the employment of the owner of a ship, not being a part-owner of the ship, effects a contract of marine insurance in relation to the ship, the contract being made " interest or no interest " or subject to a similar term,

the contract is deemed to be a contract by way of gambling on loss by maritime perils and the person effecting it is punishable on **summary conviction** [*Imp. 6 months and £100 fine*].

Any broker or other person through whom such a contract is effected, and any insurer with whom it is effected, is liable to the same punishment if he knew that the contract was of the above nature.

In either case the accused may elect to be tried on indictment.

Proceedings under the Act cannot be instituted without the consent of the Attorney-General.

---

[21] s. 43.
[22] As amended by the Theft Act 1968, s. 33 (2) and Sched. 2.

CHAPTER 24

INTOXICATING LIQUOR

SECTION 1. INTRODUCTION

THE purpose of statutory regulation of the sale of intoxicating liquor is twofold:

(1) To ensure the proper conduct of the retail trade. In order to achieve this purpose nearly all retailers of intoxicating liquor are required to have a justices' licence, and there are numerous provisions regulating the conduct of the trade. The principal Act is the Licensing Act 1964.

(2) To obtain revenue from the manufacturing, wholesaling or retailing of intoxicating liquor. In order to achieve this purpose the manufacturers and wholesalers of liquor are required, subject to a few exceptions, to have excise licences, which are issued by the Commissioners of Customs and Excise. The principal Act is the Customs and Excise Act 1952.

The purpose of this chapter is to provide a general outline of the law on the topic.

SECTION 2. CUSTOMS AND EXCISE ACT 1952

Only those provisions of this Act which deal with licensing will be mentioned here. Licences are granted in respect of a named person (or persons) and named premises.

Manufacturers. An excise licence is required for:

(i) the manufacture of spirits [1];
(ii) the brewing of beer other than for the brewer's domestic use or for consumption by farm labourers employed by him in the actual course of their labour or employment; or for the brewing of beer (with the authority of the Commissioners and subject to compliance with their conditions) solely for the purposes of research or of experiments in brewing.[2]

---

[1] Angostura bitters are deemed not to be spirits: Finance Act 1970, s. 6 (2).
[2] s. 125, as amended by the Finance Act 1963, s. 6 and the Finance Act 1967, ss. 1 (5), 4 (1), (6) (*d*), Sched. 5, para. 4 (3).

353

(iii) the making of intoxicating liquor from fruit and sugar or of any wine and cider, provided that the cider has been artificially strengthened to more than 15 proof.[3]

Wholesalers.　No person may deal wholesale in spirits, beer or any wine without an excise licence.[4]　Retailers of liquor require a justices' licence but not an excise licence.[5]　A licence is either an " on-licence," authorising the holder to sell liquor for consumption on the premises, or an " off-licence," authorising the sale for consumption off the premises only.[6]

Certain sales of intoxicating liquor are exempted from the requirements of a wholesaler's excise licence.　These include sales for medicinal purposes.[7]

Clubs.　As we shall see later,[8] the supply of liquor to members in certain kinds of clubs is not regarded as a " sale," and until 1959 an excise licence was not required for them.　These clubs, however, have to be registered under the Licensing Act 1964.[9] Clubs which are not registered require a justices' licence.

Section 3.　Selling Liquor Without a Licence

By **section 160** of the **Licensing Act 1964** [10] it is an offence [*Imp. 6 months and* £200 *fine* [11]] for any person to

(a) sell or expose for sale by retail [12] any intoxicating liquor [13] without holding a justices' licence or canteen licence authorising the sale of that liquor, or

(b) holding such a licence, sells, etc. except at the place for which that licence authorises him to hold an excise licence for the sale of that liquor.[14]

---

[3] s. 139, as amended by the Finance Act 1956, s. 2 (1), and the Finance Act 1962, s. 1 (4).
[4] s. 146 as amended.
[5] Retail excise licences were abolished by the Finance Act 1967.
[6] s. 149.
[7] ss. 157, 166, 238.　S. 166 makes specific provision for Cambridge University and the Vintners' Company.
[8] *Post*, p. 356.　　　　　　　　　　　　　　　[9] *Post*, p. 356.
[10] As amended by the Finance Act 1967.
[11] Provision is also made for forfeiture of the licence and disqualification.
[12] See Licensing Act 1964, s. 201.
[13] Defined in s. 201 to include spirits, beer, wine, cider.
[14] Where intoxicating liquor is sold in contravention of the section, every occupier who was privy or consenting to the sale commits the offence: s. 160 (2).

Exceptions to section 160. There are a number of exceptions to section 160. These include places for the sale of such things as [15]:

(1) Registered clubs in respect of the *sale* of liquor to non-members for consumption on the premises.[16]

(2) The House of Commons.[17]

(3) Certain liqueur chocolates.[18]

(4) Licensed [19] theatres.[20]

(5) Passenger aircraft, passenger vessels and railway passenger vehicles.[21]

(6) Medicated or methylated spirits.[22]

(7) Spirits made by registered medical practitioners or registered pharmacists as medicine.[23]

(8) Certain naval, air force and army canteens authorised by the Secretary of State.[24]

(9) A place in respect of which an occasional licence is in force.[25]

Justices' licence. A justices' licence [26] authorises the holder to sell by retail, intoxicating liquor on the premises named in the licence. Justices' licences are either on- or off-licences.[27]

The owner of the premises does not have to hold the licence, provided that his manager or agent does.[28] Sales by the licence holder's servants or agents do not contravene section 160.[29]

Sells. The offence of " selling " under section 160 is an absolute one and it matters not that the defendant honestly thought that he was supplying to a member of a registered club.[30] Some difficulty arises when members of a club purchase drinks from the

---

[15] There are also exceptions in favour of Cambridge University and the Vintners: Licensing Act 1964, s. 199.

[16] *Ibid.* s. 49 (1), *post,* p. 357.

[17] *R.* v. *Graham-Campbell, Ex p. Herbert* [1935] 1 K.B. 594.

[18] *Ibid.* s. 167.   [19] *Ante,* p. 248.

[20] *Ibid.* s. 199; as amended by the Finance Act 1967 and Theatres Act 1968, Sched. 2.

[21] Licensing Act 1964, s. 199 as amended; Customs and Excise Act 1952, s. 155.

[22] Licensing Act 1964, s. 199 as amended.

[23] *Ibid.*   [24] *Ibid.*

[25] See the Licensing Act 1964, s. 180.

[26] Granted by the licensing justices in the particular licensing district.

[27] *Ante,* p. 354.

[28] *Mellor* v. *Lydiate* [1914] 3 K.B. 1141.

[29] *Williamson* v. *Norris* [1899] 1 Q.B. 7.

[30] *French* v. *Hoggett* [1968] 1 W.L.R. 94.

club. Clubs can be conveniently divided up into members' clubs and proprietary clubs. A members' club is a club in which the property, including the liquor, is owned by all the members of the club, trustees or a company, provided that if it is owned by trustees or a company, the property is being held on behalf of the members so that the real interest in the property, including the liquor, remains in the members of the club.[31] In this case the transaction is regarded as a release of the property and not a sale. A proprietary club, on the other hand, is a club in which the members have no proprietary interest, e.g. the ordinary night-club. In this case the purchase of drinks is undoubtedly a sale.

This distinction would not be of too much importance but for an apparent gap in the Licensing Act. As we shall see later, section 39 provides for the *registration* of clubs which satisfy certain conditions. If these conditions are satisfied, then the club would normally be a members' club. But there is no positive provision which allows the *sale* of liquor to members of registered (but not licensed) clubs (which is necessary if they are *not* members' clubs) or to their guests (which would be necessary whether they are members' clubs or not). Ironically, there is a special provision [32] for allowing the *sale* of drinks to persons who are admitted to the club as neither members nor guests of members, unless a condition restricting or prohibiting such sales has been attached to the registration certificate.

Even if this gap could be filled judicially, the distinction between sales and supply could still be important. A member who purchases liquor at an unregistered members' club can only be convicted of an offence against section 39 and not section 160.

Canteen licences. By section 148 [33] special provision is made for the sale of intoxicating liquor at seamen's canteens. The licence is granted by the licensing justices.

SECTION 4. CLUBS AND RESTAURANTS

Clubs. By **section 39** of the **Licensing Act 1964** it is an offence [*Imp.* 6 *months and* £200 *fine*] to supply intoxicating liquor on any

---

[31] *Trebanog Club* v. *Macdonald* [1940] 1 K.B. 576.
[32] s. 49.
[33] As amended by the Finance Act 1967, Sched. 7, para. 6.

club premises by or on behalf of the club to a member or guest unless the club is registered in respect of those premises or the liquor is supplied under the authority of a justices' licence held by the club for the premises. It is also an offence [£10 *fine*] for a registered club to supply liquor for consumption off the premises other than to members in person or to supply liquor off the premises in respect of which the club is registered.[34]

A registration certificate is granted by a magistrates' court and will not be granted unless, *inter alia*, there is an interval of two days between nomination or application and admission; the club is established and constructed in good faith as a club and has not less than twenty-five members; intoxicating liquor is supplied only by or on behalf of the club; the purchase and supply of intoxicating liquor is managed by the club in general meeting [35] or an elective committee; no person receives at the expense of the club any commission on purchases of liquor and no person derives any pecuniary benefit from the supply of liquor (other than the general gain to the club).[36] Objections to the issue or renewal of a certificate may be made as well as requests for cancellation on the grounds that the qualifying conditions are not satisfied.[37]

As already noted above,[38] there is a special provision allowing for the *sale* of intoxicating liquor to persons other than members or their guests. To prevent this from being abused the magistrates' court has power, in certain circumstances, to restrict this right.

Restaurants and guest houses. Provision is made in Part IV of the Licensing Act 1964 for the granting of special justices' on-licences (called Part IV licences in the Act) for restaurants and guest houses. There are three kinds of licences—restaurant, residential and residential and restaurant licences.

A restaurant licence is granted for premises structurally adapted and bona fide used for the purpose of habitually providing the customary main meal at midday or in the evening, or both, for the accommodation of persons frequenting the premises. It is

---

[34] There is an exception to this in s. 39 (3) which covers places other than its premises which the registered club is using on a special occasion.
[35] There must be an annual general meeting and, subject to exceptions, all members must be entitled to vote: Sched. 7.
[36] s. 41. See also ss. 43, 44.
[37] s. 44.
[38] *Ante*, p. 355.

granted subject to the condition that intoxicating liquor shall not be sold or supplied on the premises otherwise than to persons taking table meals there and for consumption by such a person as an ancillary to his meal.[39]

A residential licence is granted for premises bona fide used for the purpose of habitually providing for reward board and lodging, including breakfast and one other at least of the customary main meals. It is granted subject to the condition that intoxicating liquor shall not be sold or supplied on the premises otherwise than to persons residing there or their private friends bona fide entertained by them at their own expense, and for consumption by such a person or his private friend so entertained by him either on the premises or with a meal supplied at or to be consumed off the premises.[40]

A restaurant and residential licence is granted for premises which satisfy the conditions set out above for a restaurant licence *and* a residential licence. It is granted subject to the condition that intoxicating liquor shall not be sold or supplied otherwise than as permitted by the conditions of a restaurant licence or by those of a residential licence.[41]

There is provision for forfeiture of the licence, disqualification from holding a licence and refusal to grant or renew a licence unless certain conditions are satisfied.[42]

SECTION 5. PERMITTED HOURS

By **section 59** of the **Licensing Act 1964** it is an **offence** [£100 *fine*] for a person except during permitted hours—

(a) himself or by his servant or agent to sell or supply to any person in licensed premises or premises in respect of which a club is registered any intoxicating liquor, whether to be consumed on or off the premises; or

(b) consume in or take from such premises any intoxicating liquor.

---

[39] s. 94; for the offence committed if this condition is broken, see *post*, p. 361.
[40] *Ibid.*
[41] *Ibid.*
[42] s. 98; s. 100 amended by the Refreshment Houses Act 1964; the Theft Act 1968, and the Late Night Refreshment Houses Act 1969.

There are a number of exceptions to section 59.

(1) It does not apply to the sale of intoxicating liquor under an occasional licence.[43]

(2) Where any intoxicating liquor is supplied in any premises during the permitted hours, the section does not prohibit or restrict—

(a) during the first ten minutes after the end of any period forming part of those hours, the consumption of the liquor on the premises, nor, unless the liquor was supplied or is taken away in an open vessel, the taking of the liquor from the premises;

(b) during the first half-hour after the end of such a period, the consumption of the liquor on the premises by persons taking meals there, if the liquor was supplied for consumption as an ancillary to their meals.[44]

(3) The section does not prohibit or restrict—

(a) the sale or supply to, or consumption by, any person of intoxicating liquor in any premises where he is residing[45];

(b) the ordering of intoxicating liquor to be consumed off the premises, or the dispatch by the vendor of liquor so ordered;

(c) the sale of intoxicating liquor to a trader for the purposes of his trade, or to a registered club for the purposes of the club; or

(d) the sale or supply of intoxicating liquor to any canteen or mess.[46]

(4) The section does not prohibit or restrict as regards *licensed premises*—

(a) the taking of intoxicating liquor from the premises by a person residing[47] there; or

(b) the supply of intoxicating liquor for consumption on the premises to any private friends of a person residing there

[43] s. 59 (3). [44] s. 63.

[45] " Person residing " includes a person not residing but carrying on or in charge of the business on the premises: s. 63 (4).

[46] s. 63. As to canteens, see *ante*, p. 356. " Mess " means an authorised mess of H.M. naval, military or air forces.

[47] Above, note 45.

who are bona fide entertained by him at his own expense, or the consumption of intoxicating liquor by persons so supplied; or

(c) the supply of intoxicating liquor for consumption on the premises to persons employed there for the purposes of the business carried on by the holder of the licence, or the consumption of liquor so supplied, if the liquor is supplied at the expense of their employer or of the person carrying on or in charge of the business premises.[48]

(5) The section does not apply to certain international airports.[49]

(6) The section does not apply to the sale of liqueur chocolates,[50] the sale of intoxicating liquor in passenger aircraft, vessels and railway vehicles for which an excise licence has been taken out,[51] the sale of medicated or methylated spirits,[52] the sale by registered medical practitioners or registered pharmacists of spirits made up in medicine,[53] the sale of intoxicating liquor by wholesale[54] and the sale or consumption of intoxicating liquor in canteens.[55]

Licensed premises. It will be noticed that section 59 applies to licensed premises and registered clubs. "Licensed premises" means premises in respect of which a justices' licence is in force or any premises or place, other than a licensed canteen, where intoxicating liquor is sold by retail under a licence.[56] Thus theatres which hold an *excise* licence are licensed premises.

Permitted hours. The permitted hours can vary from place to place and vary according to the kind of premises. Particular provision is made for registered clubs, restaurants and places kept for dancing, music and other public entertainment.[57]

---

[48] s. 63.
[49] s. 87.
[50] s. 167.
[51] s. 199 and see *ante*, p. 355.
[52] s. 199.
[53] s. 199.
[54] *Ibid*.
[55] *Ibid*. As to "canteens," see *ante*, p. 356. For further exceptions, see *ante*, p. 355, n. 15.
[56] Licensing Act 1964, s. 200.
[57] *Ibid*. Part III.

SECTION 6. CONDUCT OF LICENSED PREMISES

There are a number of offences concerning the conduct of licensed premises, the more important of which will be mentioned here. Besides the prospect of being convicted for these offences, the licence holder faces the prospect of his licence not being renewed if the premises are not kept under control.[58]

By **section 161** of the **Licensing Act 1964** it is an offence [*Imp. 6 months and £200 fine*] for the holder of a justices' on-licence knowingly to sell or supply intoxicating liquor to persons to whom he is not permitted by the conditions of the licence to sell or supply it. By the same section it is an offence, similarly punishable, for the holder of a Part IV licence [59] knowingly to permit intoxicating liquor sold in pursuance of the licence to be consumed on the premises by persons for whose consumption there he is not permitted by the conditions of the licence to sell it.

By **section 164,** where a person, having purchased intoxicating liquor from the holder of a justices' licence which does not cover the sale of that liquor for consumption on the premises, drinks the liquor—

(a) in the licensed premises, or
(b) in premises which adjoin or are near the licensed premises and which belong to the holder of the licence or are under his control or used by his permission, or
(c) on a highway adjoining or near those premises,

then, if the drinking is with the privity or consent of the holder of the licence, the holder of the licence commits an offence [£10 *fine; second or subsequent conviction* £20]. If the holder of a justices' off-licence sells any spirit or wine in an open vessel he commits an offence [£20 *fine*].[60]

By **section 166** it is an offence [£30 *fine*] in any licensed premises,[61] licensed canteen or the premises of any registered club to sell or supply intoxicating liquor unless it is paid for at the time it is sold or supplied. There are exceptions in favour of liquor sold or supplied with meals or to persons resident in licensed premises. In these cases it is sufficient that payment for the liquor

---

58 See the Licensing Act 1964, s. 3.
59 *Ante*, p. 357.
60 s. 164 (4) added by the Finance Act 1967, Sched. 7, para. 14.
61 *Ante*, p. 360.

and the meal or the accommodation, as the case may be, is made together.

Unless otherwise stated, the following offences are punishable by £20 fine and on a second or subsequent conviction by £30 fine. In the following offences, the expression " holder of a justices' licence " includes the holder of a canteen licence and occasional licence [62] and the expression " licensed premises " has the meaning given above [63] but also includes a licensed canteen.[64]

By **section 172** the holder of a justices' licence shall not permit drunkenness or any violent, quarrelsome or riotous conduct to take place in the licensed premises nor shall he sell intoxicating liquor to a drunken person.[65] To " permit " drunkenness, etc. the licence holder must have knowledge of it.[66] But the offence of selling liquor to a drunken person is an offence of strict liability.[67]

By **section 173** it is an offence to procure intoxicating liquor in licensed premises for consumption by a drunken person or to aid a drunken person in obtaining or consuming liquor [*Imp. 1 month or £2 fine*].

By **section 175** the holder of a justices' licence shall not knowingly allow the licensed premises to be the habitual resort or place of meeting of reputed prostitutes, whether the object of their resorting or meeting is or is not prostitution; but this section does not prohibit his allowing any such person to remain in the premises for the purpose of obtaining reasonable refreshment for such time as is necessary for that purpose.

By **section 176** it is an offence for the holder of a justices' licence to permit [68] the licensed premises to be a brothel [69] [£20 fine].[70]

By **section 177** it is an offence for the holder of a justices' licence to suffer any game to be played in the premises in such circumstances that an offence under the Gaming Act 1968 [71] is

---

[62] s. 179.
[64] s. 179.
[63] *Ante*, p. 360.
[65] The holder of the licence may refuse to admit and may expel a drunken, violent or disorderly person and failure to comply with a request to go is an offence: s. 174.
[66] *Somerset* v. *Wade* [1894] 1 Q.B. 574.
[67] *Cundy* v. *Le Cocq* (1884) 13 Q.B.D. 207. *Ante*, p. 44.
[68] See the comment on s. 172 above.
[69] *Ante*, p. 244.
[70] Provision is also made for forfeiture of the licence and disqualification: ss. 176 (2), 9 (1).
[71] *Ante*, p. 334.

committed or a requirement or restriction for the time being in force under section 6 (d) [72] of that Act is contravened. The word " suffer," apparently, imports *mens rea* here.[73]

By **section 178** of the **Licensing Act 1964** it is an offence for the holder of a justices' licence—

(*a*) knowingly to suffer any constable to remain on the licensed premises during any part of the time appointed for the constable's being on duty.

(*b*) to supply any liquor or refreshment to any constable on duty except by authority of a superior officer of the constable, or

(*c*) to bribe or attempt to bribe any constable.

In spite of the absence of the word " knowingly " in (*b*), *mens rea* is required.[74]

Vicarious responsibility. The principles of vicarious responsibility as they apply to licensing offences have already been noted.[75]

SECTION 7.   OFFENCES CONCERNING YOUNG PERSONS

In the following sections the expression " holder of a justices' licence " includes the holder of a canteen licence [76] and the expression " licensed premises " or a " bar in licensed premises " includes a licensed canteen or bar in such a canteen.[77] The expression " bar " includes any place exclusively or mainly used for the sale and consumption of intoxicating liquor.[78] But in the following sections the expression " bar " does not include a bar at any time when it is usual in the premises in question for it to be, and it is—

(*a*) set apart for the service of table meals; and

(*b*) not used for the sale or supply of intoxicating liquor otherwise than to persons having table meals there and for consumption by such a person as an ancillary to his meal.[79]

---

[72] *Ante*, p. 334 (this deals with dominoes and cribbage).
[73] See *Somerset* v. *Hart* (1884) 12 Q.B.D. 360.
[74] *Sherras* v. *De Rutzen* [1895] 1 Q.B. 918. *Ante*, p. 44.
[75] *Ante*, p. 55.
[76] s. 179. However, parts of s. 169 and all of s. 171 do not apply to licensed canteens.
[77] *Ante*, p. 362; s. 179.
[78] s. 201.
[79] s. 171.

By **section 168** of the **Licensing Act 1964** it is an offence [£2 *fine; second or subsequent conviction* £5] for the holder of a justices' licence to allow a person under fourteen to be in the bar of the licensed premises during the permitted hours. It is also an offence, similarly punishable, to cause or procure, or attempt to cause or procure, any person under fourteen to be in the bar of licensed premises during the permitted hours. No offence is committed under this section if the person under fourteen—

(*a*) is the licence-holder's child; or

(*b*) resides in the premises, but is not employed there; or

(*c*) is in the bar solely for the purpose of passing to or from some part of the premises which is not a bar and to or from which there is no other convenient means of access or egress.[80]

By **section 169 (1),** it is an offence [£25 *fine; second or subsequent conviction* £50 [81]] for the holder of a licence [82] or his servant knowingly to sell intoxicating liquor on the licensed premises to a person under eighteen or knowingly to allow a person under eighteen to consume intoxicating liquor in a bar or for the holder of the licence knowingly to allow any person to sell intoxicating liquor to a person under eighteen. By **section 169 (2)** it is an offence [£20 *fine*] for a person under eighteen in licensed premises to buy or attempt to buy intoxicating liquor, or to consume intoxicating liquor in a bar. However, neither of these subsections prohibits the sale to or purchase by a person who has attained the age of sixteen of beer, porter, cider or perry for consumption at a meal in a part of the premises usually set apart for the service of meals which is not a bar.

By **section 169 (3)** it is an offence for any person [£25 *fine; second or subsequent conviction* £50 [83]] to buy or attempt to buy intoxicating liquor for consumption in a bar in licensed premises by a person under eighteen.

By **section 169 (5)** it is an offence, similarly punishable, for the holder of a licence or his servant knowingly to deliver, or for the holder of the licence knowingly to allow any person to deliver,

---

[80] There is also an exception in favour of railway refreshment-rooms and similar premises: s. 168 (5).

[81] There is also provision for forfeiture of the licence if the offence was committed by the licence-holder: s. 169 (8).

[82] *i.e.* any licence, not only a justices' licence.   [83] Above, note 81.

to a person under eighteen intoxicating liquor sold in the licensed premises for consumption off the premises, except where the delivery is made at the residence or working place of the purchaser.

By **section 169 (6)** it is an offence, similarly punishable, for a person knowingly to send a person under eighteen for the purpose of obtaining intoxicating liquor sold or to be sold in licensed premises for consumption off the premises, whether the liquor is to be obtained from the licensed premises or other premises from which it is delivered in pursuance of the sale. . Neither of these subsections applies where the person under eighteen is a member of the licence-holder's family or his servant or apprentice and is employed as a messenger to deliver intoxicating liquor.

By **section 170,** the holder of a licence commits an offence [£5 *fine; second or subsequent conviction* £20] if any person under eighteen is employed in any bar in the licensed premises at a time when the bar is open for the sale or consumption of intoxicating liquor.[84]

Section 186 (1) provides that a constable may, at any time, enter licensed premises, a licensed canteen or premises for which a special hours certificate is in force for the purpose of preventing or detecting the commission of any offence against the Act, other than an offence under section 155 or 157 thereof, which deal with the prohibition of sale, etc., of intoxicating liquor in canteens outside permitted hours, or for consumption off the premises.[85] Failure to admit a constable who demands entry under such circumstances is an offence [£5; *second or subsequent conviction* £10] under **section 186 (2).** A search warrant may be issued by a justice of the peace if he is satisfied by information on oath that there is reasonable ground for believing that any intoxicating liquor is sold by retail or exposed or kept for sale by retail at any place where that liquor may not lawfully be sold by retail.

---

[84] There is an exception for employees passing through the bar and delivering messages to the bar: s. 170 (2).

[85] A police officer cannot demand admission unless he has reasonable grounds for suspecting that an offence is being or is about to be committed. A police inspector, in the course of making a routine visit to certain licensed premises, a club, twice demanded admission to inspect the premises, and was twice refused admission by the club's doorman. Held, that since the visit was a routine visit, the inspector had no ground to demand admission under s. 186 (1). *Valentine* v. *Jackson* [1972] 1 W.L.R. 528 D.C. (*Duncan* v. *Dowding* [1897] 1 Q.B. followed; *R.* v. *Dobbins* (1883) 48 J.P. 182 not followed).

Section 8. Parties Organised for Gain

Sections 84 and 85 of the **Licensing Act 1964** prohibit the supply or consumption of intoxicating liquor outside general licensing hours at parties organised for gain taking place in premises kept or habitually used for parties so organised, other than licensed premises, a place in respect of which an occasional licence has been granted, canteens, messes and registered clubs. A party is deemed to have been organised for gain if any pecuniary advantage accrued or was intended to accrue to any person concerned in its organisation as a result of the party. In determining whether any such advantage so accrued or was intended to accrue no account shall be taken of any expenditure incurred in connection with the party.[86]

[86] However, a party shall not be deemed to be organised for gain merely because an organiser takes part in the playing of any game or the making of bets: s. 84 (4).

CHAPTER 25

OFFENCES RELATING TO MERCHANT SHIPPING

CERTAIN offences are created by the **Merchant Shipping Acts 1894-1970.** They may be divided into three categories, according to the purpose they are designed to serve—the safety of ships at sea, the rendering of assistance at sea and the protection of seamen.[1] Unless otherwise stated offences are punishable on **indictment** [*Imp. 2 years and a fine*] or on **summary conviction** [6 *months and* £100 *fine*].[2]

Safety of ships at sea. It is made an offence by **section 27** of the **Merchant Shipping Act 1970** for the master or any member of the crew[3] of a ship registered in the United Kingdom to do any act which causes or is likely to cause the loss or destruction of, or serious damage to, the ship; or the death of, or serious injury to a person on board the ship; or to omit to do anything required to preserve the ship from loss, destruction or serious injury, if the act is deliberate or amounts to a breach or neglect of duty[4] or if he is under the influence of drink or a drug[5] at the time: On **indictment** [*Imp. 2 years and a fine*]; *on* **summary conviction** [£200 *fine*]. Such acts or omissions also constitute an offence where committed in the United Kingdom or Isle of Man by a ship's pilot, whether the ship is British or foreign.[6]

---

1 The provisions of Pts. II and III of the Merchant Shipping Act 1906 are repealed by the Merchant Shipping Act 1970, and these matters will now form the subject of Regulations. See also the Merchant Shipping (Disciplinary Offences) Regulations 1972 (S.I. 1972, No. 1294) when the 1970 Act (in note 1, above) comes into force.

2 Merchant Shipping Act 1894, s. 680.

3 The section applies to a person who goes to sea in a ship without the consent of the master, or of any other person authorised, or is conveyed in a ship in pursuance of section 62 (5) (*b*) of the Act: *ibid.* s. 32. (The Act was not in force on July 1, 1972.)

4 This includes, except in relation to the master any disobedience to a lawful command: s. 27 (2).

5 In proceedings for an offence under this section it is a defence to prove that at the time the defendant was under the influence of a drug taken by him for medical purposes, and either that he took it on medical advice and complied with any directions given as part of that advice, or that he had no reason to believe that the drug might have the influence it had: s. 33.

6 Pilotage Act 1913, ss. 46 and 61.

It is an offence for a seaman employed in a ship registered in the United Kingdom, while on duty, to be under the influence of drink or a drug [5] to such an extent that his capacity to carry out his duties is impaired [**summary conviction:** £50 *fine*] [7] or for such a seaman [8] wilfully to disobey a lawful command relating to or likely to affect the operation of the ship or its equipment: [**summary conviction:** £50 *fine*].

It is an offence punishable on **summary conviction** [£50 *fine*] [9] for a seaman employed in a ship registered in the United Kingdom, persistently and wilfully to neglect his duty, or persistently and wilfully to disobey lawful commands [10] or to combine with other seamen employed in that ship to disobey lawful commands or to neglect duty, or to impede the navigation of the ship or the progress of a voyage.[11]

It is an offence punishable on **summary conviction** [£100 *fine*] [12] for a seaman employed in a ship registered in the United Kingdom to be absent without leave and thereby to delay the ship, or for it to go to sea without him, if he is absent deliberately and without reasonable cause, or recklessly.

The sending of ships to sea in an unseaworthy condition is made an offence by section 457 of the **Merchant Shipping Act 1894.** The section applies only to British ships, and the condition of the ship must be such that its being sent to sea might endanger life. It is a defence to show either that all reasonable means were taken to ensure that the ship was sent to sea in a seaworthy state, or that the sending of the ship to sea was reasonable and justifiable in the circumstances. By the same section it is an offence on the part of the master to take the ship to sea in an unseaworthy state. A master has a defence if he can prove that it was, under the circumstances, reasonable and justifiable to take the ship to sea. A prosecution under this section may be by way of indictment only and must be brought by, or with the consent of, the Ministry of Transport.[13]

It is also an offence to take or send a British ship registered in the United Kingdom to sea when overloaded [**indictment:** *a fine.*

---

[7] s. 28.   [8] See n. 3.
[9] s. 29.   [10] See n. 4.
[11] See n. 3.   [12] s. 30.
[13] The section originally stipulated for the prosecution to be brought by, or with the consent of, the Board of Trade. The function has, by delegated legislation, been transferred to the Department of the Environment.

Summary conviction: £400 *fine*].[14] A ship is overloaded for these purposes if the Plimsoll marks on both sides of the ship are submerged when the ship is floating on an even keel in salt water.[15]

Offences in connection with the discharge of oil into the sea are created by the **Prevention of Oil Pollution Act 1971.**[16]

Rendering of assistance at sea. At common law the master of a British ship was under a duty to assist anyone from his own vessel who was in danger at sea. The Merchant Shipping Act 1894 extended this duty, making it an offence for the master of a British ship to fail to assist the master, crew and passengers of a ship with which his own vessel had been in collision if he could have rendered such assistance without jeopardising his own vessel, crew and passengers.[17]

There is a general duty to assist, created by the Maritime Conventions Act 1911. As a result of this Act it is an offence for the master of a vessel to fail to assist anyone, even an alien enemy, in danger of being lost at sea.[18] Without prejudice to this general duty, it is an offence for the master of a British ship to fail to proceed to the assistance of any vessel or aircraft when he knows from distress signals or any other source of information that the vessel or aircraft is in distress.[19]

Protection of seamen. The provisions formerly contained in the Merchant Shipping Act 1906, calculated to discourage the practice of leaving seamen behind or discharging them before the voyage has ended, now form part of regulations [20] made by the Department of Trade and Industry under the Merchant Shipping Act 1970.

Fishing vessels' safety. The Fishing Vessels (Safety Provisions) Act 1970 [21] gives power for rules to be made by the Board of

---

[14] Merchant Shipping (Load Lines) Act 1967, s. 4.
[15] Merchant Shipping (Safety Convention) Act 1949, s. 44.
[16] See p. 225, *ante*. As to civil liability see the Merchant Shipping (Oil Pollution) Act 1971.
[17] s. 422.
[18] s. 6.
[19] Merchant Shipping (Safety Convention) Act 1949, s. 22. It is intended that these provisions should be repealed: Merchant Shipping Act 1970, s. 100 (3) and Sched. 5.
[20] Not published by July 1, 1972.
[21] To be brought into force by statutory instrument.

Trade relating to the safety of such vessels.[22]   By **section 1 (4)** it is
an offence punishable on **summary conviction** [£400 *fine*] for the
owner or master of such a vessel to contravene the fishing vessel
construction rules.[23]   **Section 4** makes it an offence punishable on
summary conviction [£50] for the owner or master of such a vessel
to go or attempt to go to sea without the appropriate fishing vessel
certificate.[24]   **Section 5** makes it an offence [*punishable as under
section 4 above*] for the owner of such a vessel to fail to give
written notice of alterations to his vessel in regard to its hull,
equipment, machinery or life-saving appliances.

22 Not published by July 1, 1972.
23 Not published by July 1, 1972.
24 Issued under s. 3.

CHAPTER 26

OFFENCES AGAINST THE BANKRUPTCY AND COMPANY LAWS

SECTION 1. BANKRUPTCY

THE purpose of the law of bankruptcy is twofold, namely to make what is left of the bankrupt's property available to all the creditors and to protect those persons with whom an undischarged bankrupt subsequently has dealings. The law on these matters is contained in the Bankruptcy Act 1914 as amended by the Bankruptcy (Amendment) Act 1926, and the Deeds of Arrangement Act 1914. The offences under these Acts are too numerous to be dealt with in a work of this nature but some of the more important are mentioned here.

It is an offence [1] for a person who has been adjudged bankrupt, or in respect of whose estate a receiving order has been made to fail to make full disclosure and deliverance up of all assets and all documents relating to his affairs, including previous transactions.[2] The court will then know what property is available and what previous transactions can and ought to be set aside for the benefit of the creditors. It is also an offence for such a person to dispose of any of his property with intent to defraud creditors [3] and an offence for him to leave or attempt to leave England taking with him £20 or more with intent to defraud his creditors.[4]

It is an offence for an undischarged bankrupt to get credit for £10 or upwards or to engage in trade or business under a name

---

[1] Punishable on *summary conviction* [*Imp.*: 12 *months*] and on *indictment* [*Imp.*: 2 *years*] under the Bankruptcy Act 1914, s. 164 as amended by the Bankruptcy (Amendment) Act 1926, s. 10; the Administration of Justice (Miscellaneous Provisions) Act 1933, s. 10; Sched. III; and the Criminal Law Act 1967, Sched. III, Pt. III.

[2] Bankruptcy Act 1914, s. 154 as amended by the Bankruptcy (Amendment) Act 1926, and the Criminal Law Act 1967, Sched. 2, para. 12 (2), Pt. VII.

[3] 1914 Act, s. 156 as amended by the Theft Act 1968, s. 32 (3) and Sched. III, punishable both on *summary conviction* and *indictment* [*Imp.*: 1 *year*]. By s. 6 of the Bankruptcy (Amendment) Act 1926, if a man causes his property to be taken in execution or connives at such a taking, he is deemed to have disposed of it within the meaning of s. 156.

[4] Bankruptcy Act 1914, s. 159.

other than that under which he was adjudicated bankrupt without disclosing, in the former case, that he is an undischarged bankrupt and in the latter the name under which he was adjudicated bankrupt.[5] However, the debtor may apply for a certificate of misfortune and if successful will not be subject to these disabilities. It is an offence for a bankrupt to obtain credit by deception.[6] Credit under section 155 of the Bankruptcy Act 1914, however, seems to be limited to the payment or repayment of a sum of money. The receipt of money on a promise to render services or deliver goods in the future is apparently not obtaining credit within the meaning of the Act.[7]

SECTION 2. COMPANIES

Because of the advantageous position which directors and officers of a company enjoy as against shareholders, creditors and the public at large, the opportunities for peculation and fraud are numerous. Much of this field is covered by the ordinary provisions of the criminal law, but in order to strengthen the law a number of offences with particular reference to companies and corporations have been created by statute. The principal Acts may be said to be the **Companies Acts 1948** and **1967**, the Prevention of Fraud (Investments) Act 1958 and the Protection of Depositors Act 1963. It is only possible to deal with a few of the provisions here.

(1) Offences relating to the ordinary management of the company. **Section 18 of the Theft Act 1968** [8] safeguards shareholders against dishonesty by providing that in certain circumstances directors and officers of companies and other bodies corporate are liable for offences committed under sections 15, 16 and 17 of the

---

[5] Bankruptcy Act 1914, s. 155. It seems that " credit " under this section is limited to the payment or repayment of a sum of money. The receipt of money on a promise to render services or deliver goods in the future is apparently not within the section. See " Bankrupt Obtaining Credit " by Alec Samuels at [1966] Crim.L.R. 148. Cf. s. 16 of the Theft Act 1968 at p. 514, post. See also R. v. Doubleday (1964) 49 Cr.App.R. 62. The offence is complete when credit to the amount of £10 has been obtained, even if the sum is made up of smaller amounts obtained on separate occasions: R. v. Hartley [1972] 2 W.L.R. 101.

[6] See Theft Act 1968, s. 16, obtaining pecuniary advantage by deception.

[7] See n. 5, supra.

[8] Not dealt with in this book.

Theft Act,[9] committed by the corporation. **Section 19** makes it an offence [*Imp.* 7 *years*] for an officer of a body corporate or unincorporated association, with intent to deceive members or creditors about its affairs, to publish or concur in publishing a written statement or account which to his knowledge is or may be misleading, false or deceptive in a material particular. By **section 15 of the Protection of Depositors Act 1963** [10] it is an offence punishable on **summary conviction** [*Imp.* 3 *months and* £200 *Fine*] or on **indictment** [*Imp.* 2 *years and a Fine*] for an officer of a company to cause or permit to be included in any account, notice or other document required or authorised to be delivered to the Registrar or the Board of Trade any statement which to his knowledge is false in a material particular. A *similar penalty* is incurred under **section 114 of the Companies Act 1967** in relation to certain false explanations and statements.

Further offences to protect the public from " share pushing " have been created by the **Prevention of Fraud (Investments) Act 1958** as amended.

(2) Those relating to the winding up of a company. The object of a winding up is to gather up all the assets so that distribution can be made to those entitled. The officers of the company must make a full disclosure and deliver up all the company's assets and all the documents relating to the affairs of the company. It is a defence for the accused to prove that he had no intent to defraud. The officers of the company must not conceal, destroy, mutilate or falsify, or be privy to such concealment, destruction, etc. of any book or paper, or make or be privy to the making of any false entry in any book or paper, or fraudulently part with, or alter or make an omission in, or be privy to the fraudulent parting with, alteration or making of any omission in any document, affecting or relating to the property or affairs of the company or after the commencement of the winding up or at any meetings of the creditors of the company within twelve months next before the commencement of the winding up to attempt to account for any part of the property of the company by fictitious losses or expenses, or pawn, pledge or dispose of any property of the company which has been obtained on credit and has not been paid for, unless such

---

[9] See under Offences Against Property, Chap. 35, *post.*
[10] Amended by the Companies Act 1967, s. 130 and Sched. 8, Pt. VII.

pawning, pledging or disposing is in the ordinary way of the business of the company; or be guilty of any false representation or other fraud for the purpose of obtaining the consent of the creditors of the company or any of them to an agreement with reference to the affairs of the company or to the winding up. It is a good defence for the accused to prove that he had no intent to conceal the state of affairs of the company or to defeat the law.[11] They must not dispose of or cause or connive at the levying of any execution against the property of the company with intent to defraud creditors of the company.[12] There is provision for preventing offenders from becoming directors of companies within a specified period (not to exceed five years) from conviction.[13]

Section 3. Friendly Societies

The **Friendly and Industrial and Provident Societies Act 1968,** as amended by the **Friendly Societies Act 1971,** redefines the auditing and accounting requirements of these societies and by section 18 provides that any contravention by a society of any provision of the Act and any direction given by the registrar under section 4 of the Act is an offence under the appropriate registration Act.[14]

---

[11] Companies Act 1948, s. 328, as amended by the Criminal Law Act 1967.
[12] *Ibid*. s. 330. The cancellation of a debt owed to the company by the prisoner himself is not a transfer of property " within the section," *R. v. Davies* [1955] 1 Q.B. 71.
[13] *Ibid*. s. 188.
[14] See *e.g.* Friendly Societies Acts 1896–1971, Industrial and Provident Societies Act 1965, Building Societies Acts 1874–1962 and the Industrial Relations Act 1971.

CHAPTER 27

OFFENCES RELATING TO BUSINESS, TRADE
AND PROFESSIONS

SECTION 1. OCCUPATIONS REQUIRING SOME
PARTICULAR QUALIFICATION

BY numerous statutes the exercise of various professions, trades
and occupations is prohibited except by persons possessing certain
qualifications, or in accordance with prescribed regulations. The
following are some of the principal examples:

(1) Solicitors. By **section 19** of the **Solicitors Act 1957** it is
made an offence for any unqualified person to pretend that he
is qualified to act as a solicitor [**summary conviction:** £50 *Fine*].
By **section 18** [1] of the Act, it is provided that no unqualified person
should act as a solicitor in any court of civil or criminal jurisdiction, or in any cause or matter, civil or criminal, to be heard or
determined before any justice or justices or any commissioners of
Her Majesty's revenue [*Fine and Imp.*]. This offence constitutes a
contempt of the court in which the unqualified person acted. A
further penalty of £50 may be recovered in the High Court or any
county court by the Law Society acting with the consent of the
Attorney-General. By **section 20** it is provided that, subject to
exceptions, no person who is not a qualified solicitor may draw or
prepare:

(*a*) any instrument of transfer or charge for the purposes of
the Land Registration Act 1925 or make any application [2]
or lodge any document for registration under that Act at
the registry; or

(*b*) any other instrument relating to real or personal estate,
or any legal proceeding [**summary conviction:** £50 *fine*].[3]

---

[1] Amended by the Courts Act 1971, Sched. 11.
[2] If it is for registration: *Carter* v. *Butcher* [1966] 1 Q.B. 526.
[3] The subsection does not apply to barristers, duly certificated notaries public,
public officers acting in the course of their duty, and persons employed merely
to engross any instrument, application or proceeding. The expression " instrument " in paragraph (*b*) excludes wills, agreements under hand only, or letter
or power of attorney or a transfer of stock containing no trust or limitation
thereof.

375

It is a defence to prove that the act was done without fee.   By
section 21 it is also made an offence for any person who is not
qualified as a solicitor [4] to act in the preparation of papers for
probate [**summary conviction: £10** *fine*].   Again, it is a defence
to prove that the act was done without fee.

(2) **Doctors.**   By **section 31** of the **Medical Act 1956** it is made
an offence for anyone wilfully and falsely [5] to pretend that he is a
qualified doctor, surgeon, apothecary, etc., or to take any title or
description implying that he is registered under the Act,[6] or that he
is recognised by law as a doctor, surgeon, apothecary, etc.
[**summary conviction:** £500 *fine*].

There is no prohibition on the actual practice of medicine by
unqualified persons, but the **Abortion Act 1967, section 1,** exempts
from the provisions of the criminal law, only a pregnancy terminated by a registered medical practitioner, upon the opinion of two
registered medical practitioners and by the **Venereal Disease Act
1917** it is an offence for anyone other than a duly qualified person
to treat venereal disease [**indictment:** *Imp.* 2 *years*; **summary:
conviction:** £100 *fine or Imp.* 6 *months*].

(3) **Dentists.**   By **section 35** of the **Dentists Act 1957** a person
who is not a registered dentist or a registered medical practitioner
may not use the title of dentist, dental surgeon or dental practitioner, or use any title or description implying that he is a registered
dentist [**indictment:** £500 *fine*; **summary conviction:** £100 *fine*].
By **section 34** it is an offence, similarly punishable, for anyone who
is not a registered dentist or a registered medical practitioner to
practise or to hold himself out as practising or as being prepared
to practise dentistry.   This does not apply (i) to extractions performed without anaesthetic by a registered pharmaceutical chemist
where the call is urgent and no registered medical or dental practitioner is available or (ii) to the performance in a public dental
service of minor dental work by a person under the supervision
of a registered dentist.

---

[4] There is an exception in favour of barristers and notaries public.
[5] If a man honestly thinks that he is qualified, then he commits no offence:
Wilson v. *Inyang* [1951] 2 K.B. 799; but see the observations of Lord Goddard
C.J. in *Younghusband* v. *Luftig* [1949] 2 K.B. 354. *Semble*, it would be no
defence to show that one did not know one had to be qualified: see *Arrowsmith*
v. *Jenkins* [1963] 2 Q.B. 561, *ante*, p. 218.
[6] Medical Act 1956, s. 31.

(4) Opticians. By **section 22** of the **Opticians Act 1958** any individual who uses the title of ophthalmic, dispensing, registered or enrolled optician when not registered or enrolled as such commits an offence [**indictment**: £250 *fine*; **summary conviction**: £100 *fine*]. By **section 20** anyone who is not a registered medical practitioner or registered ophthalmic optician may not test the sight of another person [*similarly punishable*]. By **section 21** no one may sell any optical appliance unless the sale is effected by or under the supervision of a registered medical practitioner or registered optician [*similarly punishable*].

(5) Chemists. **Section 19** of the **Pharmacy Act 1954** makes it an offence for anyone who is not a registered pharmaceutical chemist to use the title of pharmaceutical chemist, chemist and druggist, member of the Pharmaceutical Society, etc., or to use the title of chemist in connection with the sale of goods by retail [**summary conviction**: £100 *fine*]. This provision is to be repealed by the Medicines Act 1968 when the Sixth Schedule to that Act comes into force. Under **section 78** of that Act it is an offence for anyone who is not lawfully conducting a retail pharmacy business to take or use the title of chemist and druggist, druggist, dispensing chemist and dispensing druggist or to take or use the title of chemist in connection with the sale of any goods by retail [**summary conviction**: £100 *fine*].

The same section makes it an offence in connection with retail sales to use the description pharmacy except in respect of a registered pharmacy or in respect of the pharmaceutical department of a hospital or a health centre [**summary conviction**: £100 *fine*]. Also, under the same section it is an offence for a person who is not a pharmacist to take or use the title of pharmaceutical chemist, pharmaceutist, pharmacist, member of the Pharmaceutical Society, and Fellow of the Pharmaceutical Society and no persons shall take or use any of those titles in connection with a business consisting of the retail sale of goods unless those premises are a registered pharmacy of a hospital or health centre [**summary conviction**: £100 *fine*]. However, it is submitted that a pharmacist can use any of those titles even on unregistered premises.

The same section further makes it an offence for anyone in connection with any business to use a title, description or emblem suggesting that he or any person employed in the business possesses a qualification with respect to the sale, manufacture or assembly of medicinal products which he does not in fact possess [**summary conviction:** £100 *fine*].

(6) Nurses. By **section 27** of the **Nurses Act 1957** as amended by the **Nurses Act 1969** anyone who is not a registered nurse commits an offence by taking the title of nurse [7] or registered nurse. Also a person whose name is included in any part or parts of the nursing register but not in another part, commits an offence by taking or using any name, title, addition, description, uniform or badge, or otherwise doing any act of any kind, implying that his name is included in that other part. By **section 28** of the Act of 1957,[8] any person who is not an enrolled nurse commits an offence by taking the title of nurse or enrolled nurse [**summary conviction:** £10 *fine*].

(7) Veterinary surgeons. By **section 1** of the **Veterinary Surgeons Act 1966** no individual shall practise, or hold himself out as practising, or as being prepared to practise, veterinary surgery unless he is a registered veterinary surgeon [**indictment:** *fine*; **summary conviction:** £100 *fine*]. Veterinary surgery is defined as including veterinary surgery, medicine and diagnosis.[9] Regulations may exempt from this section the performance of minor treatments and operations.

By **section 20** it is an offence [*similarly punishable*] for an unregistered person to take or use the title of veterinary surgeon.

(8) Architects. By **section 1** of the **Architects Registration Act 1938** subject to exceptions,[10] it is an offence for any person to practise or carry on business under any name, style or title containing the word " architect " [11] unless he is registered under the Architects (Registration) Act 1931 [**summary conviction:** £50 *fine*]. By **section 12** of the **Architects Registration Acts 1931** to **1969** it is an offence to obtain registration by a false representation [**summary conviction:** £50 *fine*].

---

[7] An exception is made in favour of children's nurses. The Minister of Health may make regulations creating further exceptions: see S.I. 1961 No. 1213.
[8] As amended by Nurses (Amendment) Act 1961, Sched. 2.
[9] s. 27. See *Lawson* v. *Towse* [1967] Crim.L.R. 369.
[10] See the proviso to s. 1.
[11] A reference to " Dipl.Ing.Arch." on notepaper has been held not to come within this section: *Jacobowicz* v. *Wicks* [1956] Crim.L.R. 697.

There are further provisions in various Acts relating to qualifications which must be obtained before a person can either hold himself out as being of a particular occupation or practise such occupation. Patent agents, for example, are covered by the **Patents Act 1949**, and the **Professions Supplementary to Medicine Act 1960** covers such occupations as chiropodists, radiographers and remedial gymnasts.

Section 2.   Licences and Registration

Numerious statutes provide that licences are required, or some registration procedure must be complied with, in order to conduct certain activities and that failure to license or register is an offence. Sometimes it is the person concerned and sometimes the premises which must be licensed or registered.

Some of these provisions have already been noted or will be noted separately in the chapter or section on: Customs and Excise [12]; Animals [13]; Licensing of Places of Entertainment [14]; Betting, Gaming and Lotteries [15]; Intoxicating Liquor [16]; Occupations requiring some Particular Qualification [17]; Moneylending [18]; Scrap Metal [19]; Pedlars [20]; Pawnbrokers [21]; Road Traffic.[22]

Besides these, there are numerous licensing and registration requirements under individual Acts of Parliament covering such various topics as adoption societies, canal boats, caravan sites, charities, child minders, common lodging houses, hearing aids, homes for the mentally disabled, knackers' yards, marine store dealers, nursing homes, pleasure boats, premises connected with the sale of food and drugs, slaughterhouses, theatrical employers, and many others.[23]

Section 3.   Hearing Aid Dispensers

By **section 1** of the **Hearing Aid Council Act 1968** it is an offence on **summary conviction** [£100 *fine*] for any person other than a

[12] *Ante*, p. 153.
[14] *Ante*, p. 248.
[16] *Ante*, p. 353.
[18] *Post*, p. 381.
[20] *Post*, p. 380.
[21] *Post*, p. 383.
[22] *Ante*, p. 316.
[13] *Post*, p. 413.
[15] *Ante*, p. 318.
[17] *Ante*, p. 375.
[19] *Post*, p. 385.
[23] A comprehensive list will be found in Morrish and McLean *A Practical Guide to Appeals in Criminal Courts*, 1971.

registered dispenser of hearing aids or a person whose name has been notified to the registrar of the council and who is undergoing full time training with a view to being registered as a dispenser of hearing aids and is acting under the supervision of a registered dispenser to act as a dispenser of hearing aids or for such person to employ an unregistered person.

SECTION 4. PEDLARS

For the law concerning this occupation one must have recourse to the **Pedlars Acts 1871 and 1881.** This section will be confined to the provisions concerning certificates and licensing. The statutory provisions regarding hawkers have now been repealed.[24]

Pedlars. A pedlar is a person who goes on foot from town to town or from house to house.[25] A person who comes within this definition is required, unless he comes within the permitted exemptions,[26] to obtain a pedlar's certificate. Such a certificate authorises a pedlar to ply his trade throughout the entire United Kingdom.[27] It is obtained from the chief officer of police for the area in which the applicant has resided for at least one month prior to the application and remains in force for one year from date of issue. The officer must be satisfied that the applicant is over seventeen, is of good character and in good faith intends to carry on the trade of pedlar.[28]

An offence is committed by a pedlar if he acts as such without a certificate [**summary conviction:** 50p *fine* (£1 *for a second or subsequent conviction*)]. It is an offence to refuse to show the certifi-

---

[24] Local Government Act 1966, Sched. 6, repealing Hawkers Act 1888.

[25] One would not be a pedlar if one carried one's goods in a car. If, however, one left the car at the top of a street and went from house to house on foot (as in practice would be the case) one would become a pedlar: *Sample* v. *Hulme, Walmsley* v. *Hulme* [1956] 1 W.L.R. 1319.

[26] The Pedlars Act 1871, s. 23, exempts:
  (i) commercial travellers, other persons selling goods to dealers who buy for re-sale purposes and persons selling books being agents authorised in writing by the publishers,
  (ii) vendors of vegetables, fresh fruit or victuals,
  (iii) persons selling goods in any lawful mart, market or fair.

[27] Pedlars Act 1881, s. 2.

[28] Pedlars Act 1871, s. 5. S. 16 provides that a court of summary jurisdiction may summon a pedlar before it to show that he is in good faith carrying on the trade of pedlar. If he fails to appear or if, on appearance, he fails to satisfy the court that he is in good faith carrying on the trade of pedlar, the court must deprive him of his certificate.

cate to anyone entitled to demand production of it [**summary conviction:** 25p *fine*].[29] It is an offence for a pedlar to refuse to allow a police officer to inspect his pack [**summary conviction:** £1 *fine*].[30] If the pedlar refuses to show his certificate or has no certificate or refuses to show the contents of his pack, he may be arrested by any person entitled to demand production of the certificate.[31]

Where a pedlar is convicted of any offence the court may deprive him of his certificate; if he is convicted of begging the court must do this. If a pedlar is convicted of an offence against the Pedlars Acts, then the court must, if the certificate is not ordered to be forfeited, direct that particulars of the conviction be indorsed on it.[32]

SECTION 5.   MONEYLENDERS

The restrictions imposed on moneylenders are to be found in the **Moneylenders Acts 1900 to 1927.** The expression " moneylender " is defined in section 6 of the 1900 Act as including " every person whose business is that of moneylending." [33] By the same section certain persons and bodies are exempt from the Acts. These include pawnbrokers, any person carrying on the business of banking [34] or insurance and any person carrying on business not having

---

[29] s. 17. The following persons may demand production of the certificate:
  (i) a Justice of the Peace,
  (ii) a police officer,
  (iii) anyone to whom the pedlar offers his goods for sale,
  (iv) anyone in whose private grounds or premises he is found.

[30] s. 19.

[31] s. 18.

[32] ss. 14 and 16.

[33] Hire-purchase firms are not as a rule caught by the Act. Their transactions take one of two forms: there may be a sale of property from the dealer to the finance house, from whom the third party takes the property on hire-purchase, or the property may be sold by the dealer to the third party, payment to be made by instalments, and in return for payment of the purchase price by the finance house the dealer will assign to the finance house the debt owed by the third party. Both methods entail the payment out of a lump sum by the finance house, but such a lump sum is not a loan, it is the purchase price of the property or debt, as the case may be, and so the transactions are outside the Act: *Olds Discount Co.* v. *Playfair* (1938) 159 L.T. 332; *Olds Discount Co.* v. *Cohen* (1938) 159 L.T. 335n.

[34] As to what constitutes a bank, see *United Dominions Trust Ltd.* v. *Kirkwood* [1966] 2 Q.B. 431. The Board of Trade's Certificate that a person is a banker is conclusive evidence of that fact for the purposes of the Acts: Companies Act 1967, s. 123 (1).

for its primary object the lending of money in the course of which and for the purpose whereof he lends money.[35]

By **section 1** of the 1927 Act all moneylenders must take out in respect of every address at which they carry out business an excise licence from the appropriate county or county borough council.[36] Such licences may not be granted to anyone who has not obtained from the magistrates' court [37] having jurisdiction in the area in which business is to be carried on a certificate for each licence which is required.[38] Contravention of section 1 is an offence carrying an excise penalty of £100. For a second or subsequent conviction imprisonment for three months may be ordered.[39]

Licences and certificates must show the true name of the moneylender and also the address in respect of which the licence is to be in force. If the moneylender carries on business in some authorised name [40] other than his own name, this also must appear on the certificate and licence. Breach of these requirements incurs the penalty already described.[41]

Section 5 of the 1927 Act imposes restrictions on the power of moneylenders to advertise. No person may send to any person without his written request any circular advertising the name, address or telephone number of a moneylender or containing an invitation to borrow money from a moneylender; nor may any person disseminate such particulars or invitation by means of advertisements in newspapers or by posters or placards. This is subject to one exception, namely, that an advertisement either in a newspaper or on a poster or placard exhibited at the authorised

---

[35] If the sole purpose for lending the money is to keep a client " sweet " so that business will be benefited indirectly, this is not moneylending: *Premor Ltd.* v. *Shaw Brothers* [1964] 1 W.L.R. 978. The lending must also be " in the course of one's business " and that requires that it be done with reference to some specific transaction or transactions: *ibid*.

[36] See Finance Act 1949, s. 15, and S.I. 1950 No. 30.

[37] If the business is to be carried on in the metropolitan police district, the certificate must be obtained from a stipendiary magistrate.

[38] s. 2, as amended by the Justices of the Peace Act 1949, s. 46 (2) and Sched. 4, Pt. II.

[39] Companies are dealt with by increasing the excise penalty to £500.

[40] This may be some name under which he trades as an individual or the name of a firm in which he is a partner: for details, see s. 2 (3) (*b*) and (*c*).

[41] Failure to carry out the requirements in respect of a certificate would render the licence void. Failure to disclose one's true name on a licence makes it void (s. 1 (2)) and a licence which does not show the authorised name and address would not be a " proper moneylenders' licence " for the purpose of s. 1 (5) (*b*).

address of the moneylender will be legal provided that the requirements concerning use of names are observed [42] and provided the
advertisement confines itself to specified heads of information.[43]

The same section prohibits the employment of any person by
a moneylender for the purpose of touting for custom and also the
entry into such employment by any person. Contravention of
any of the provisions of section 5 is an offence [**indictment:** £100
fine and Imp. 3 *months*; **summary conviction:** £25 *fine and Imp.* 1
month].

By **section 4** of the 1900 Act, any moneylender who, by any
false, misleading, or deceptive statement, representation or promise,
or by any dishonest concealment of material facts, fraudulently
induces or attempts to induce any person to borrow money or to
agree to the terms on which money is or is to be borrowed, commits an offence punishable on **indictment** [*Imp.* 2 *years and* £500
fine].

Where the holder of a certificate has been convicted of any
offence against the Moneylenders Acts 1900 to 1927, or under
sections 2 or 4 of the Betting and Loans (Infants) Act 1892,[44]
the court may order suspension or forfeiture of the certificate. If
forfeiture is ordered, the court may direct further that the person
convicted be disqualified from obtaining another certificate during
such time as the court thinks fit. Where a person has been so
convicted, particulars of the conviction and any order arising
thereout must be indorsed on the certificate.[45]

SECTION 6. PAWNBROKERS

The major enactments on this topic are the **Pawnbrokers Acts 1872
and 1960.** A pawnbroker is a person whose business is that of
taking goods and chattels in pawn. To prevent evasion of the Act,
transactions which, though technically not a pawning, do amount
to a loan of money on the security of goods are also subjected to

---

[42] These requirements are dealt with in s. 4 of the Act.
[43] Any authorised address at which the moneylender carries on business,
including the telegraphic address and telephone number, any address where
he formerly carried on business, a statement that he lends money with or
without security, the highest and lowest sum of money that he is prepared
to lend and the date on which his business was first established.
[44] These sections prohibit the sending to infants of invitations to borrow money
and the soliciting of infants to make affidavits in connection with loans.
[45] s. 3.

the provisions of the Act.[46]   The Act is not applicable to transactions involving more than fifty pounds.[47] If, therefore, any such
transactions are effected, the pawnbroker will not be entitled in
respect of that business to the benefit of section 6 (a) of the Moneylenders Act 1900.   He will therefore have to comply with the
provisions concerning moneylenders.[48]

A pawnbroker as so defined is required to take out for each
shop at which he carries on his business a yearly [49] excise licence.
This is obtained from the county or county borough council for
the area in which business is carried on.[50]   A licence may not be
granted, however, unless the applicant holds a certificate authorising the grant.   If business is to be carried on in the metropolitan
police district, then a certificate is required to be obtained from a
stipendiary magistrate.   Elsewhere, if there is a stipendiary magistrate having jurisdiction in the area, the application is made to
him; if not, then the application is made to the county borough or
the county district council.[51]   If a certificate is being sought for the
first time, notice of the application must be given in accordance
with the statutory requirements.[52] A certificate may not be refused
unless the applicant fails to give evidence of good character or
unless it appears that the shop or any adjoining premises owned or
occupied by him are frequented by thieves or persons of bad
character or unless, in the case of a first application, the provisions
as to notice have not been complied with.[53]   Acting as a pawn-

---

[46] s. 5. A pawn exists where possession only of the goods or chattels is given
to the pawnbroker. A transaction whereby title passes on the understanding
that the borrower may repurchase on payment of the loan is a mortgage, and,
were it not for s. 5, would be outside the Act.

[47] Pawnbrokers Act 1960, s. 1.

[48] S. 6 (a) exempts from the Moneylenders Acts " any pawnbroker in respect of
business carried on by him in accordance with . . . the Acts for the time
being in force in relation to pawnbrokers." Hence, if the transactions are
outside the Act there will be no exemption.

[49] Pawnbrokers Act 1872, s. 37; Finance Act 1949, s. 15; S.I. 1950 No. 130.

[50] Ibid.

[51] Pawnbrokers Act 1872, ss. 39, 40; Local Government Act 1894, ss. 27, 32.

[52] Pawnbrokers Act 1872, s. 42, as amended, provides as follows:
   (i) at least 21 days before the application is made notice must be sent
       by registered post to the rating authority for the area (in London one
       applies to the rating authorities in their capacity as overseers) and also
       to the superintendent of police for the area ;
   (ii) a notice must have been affixed to the door of the church or chapel
        in the parish or place on two consecutive Sundays within the 28 days
        preceding the application.

[53] Ibid. s. 43.

broker without a licence is an offence punishable by an excise penalty of fifty pounds.[54]

Among the numerous offences that can be committed by pawnbrokers is taking an article in pawn from an intoxicated person or from a person under the age of fourteen, whether on his own or another's behalf.[55] Among the offences that can be committed by a pawner is giving false information to a pawnbroker as to the ownership of an article or giving a false name and address.[56] All these offences are punishable on summary conviction [£10 *fine*].[57] If a person pawns an article which is not his and which he does not have the authority to pawn, he also commits an offence [*forfeits £5 and any sum not exceeding the value of the pledge*].[58]

SECTION 7.   SCRAP METAL DEALERS

It is provided by **section 1** of the **Scrap Metal Dealers Act 1964** that if anyone carries on business as a scrap metal dealer, he must register certain information with the county borough or county district council where he carries on his business.   Registration is cancelled at the end of three years but may be renewed for successive periods of three years.   The carrying on of business as a scrap metal dealer without registration of such information is an offence [**summary conviction:** £100 *fine*].

To prevent dishonesty, there are stringent provisions designed to ensure none of the dealer's transactions goes unrecorded.   By **section 2**, dealers are required to keep a book and to enter into that book information concerning all scrap metal received at the store (including a description of the metal) [59] and all scrap metal processed at or dispatched from the store.   The dealer may, if he wishes, use two books, one for recording loads of metal received and one for recording dispatches, but at no time may more than one book be used for each.   Thus there will be in one or two books a complete record of the dealer's transactions.   Breach of the provisions of section 2 is an offence [**summary conviction:** £100

---

[54] *Ibid.* s. 37, as amended.
[55] *Ibid.* s. 32; Children and Young Persons Act 1933, s. 8.   The pawning of certain articles is also made illegal by statute.
[56] Pawnbrokers Act 1872, s. 34.
[57] *Ibid.* s. 45.   Provision is made for compensating an injured party.
[58] *Ibid.* s. 33.   The forfeitures are paid to the injured party.
[59] What is deemed to be a fair description of the metal depends in each case on the circumstances: *Jenkins* v. *Cohen (A.) & Co. Ltd.* [1971] 1 W.L.R. 1280.

fine].   Special provisions are made in section 3 for itinerant collectors.

Section 4 provides that a court may direct that other requirements set out in the section [60] must be satisfied by a scrap metal dealer who is convicted of an offence against section 1 or 2 or any offence involving dishonesty.

By **section 5** a scrap metal dealer who acquires scrap metal from a person under the age of sixteen (on his own or another's behalf) and any person who on selling scrap metal to a dealer gives a false name or address commits an offence [**summary conviction: £10** *fine*].

By **section 6,** if an officer of a local authority reasonably believes that a place in the area which is not registered as a scrap metal store is, in fact, being used as such, he may, if authorised thereto in writing by the authority, enter that place for the purpose of verifying his belief.   Likewise, if a place is registered as a scrap metal store any constable may enter and inspect it.   He also has a right to be shown the books (of which he may make copies) and any scrap metal in the place.   Anyone who obstructs such persons or refuses to produce the book or books when validly required to do so commits an offence [**summary conviction: £20** *fine*].   An entry may not be effected by force without the authority of a warrant granted by a Justice of the Peace.

Section 8.   Food and Drugs

The law relating to food and drugs is now contained principally in the **Food and Drugs Act 1955,** which consolidated, with amendments, the existing statutory provisions.

By section 106 of the Act of 1955, any offence under the Act, unless a special penalty is provided by the Act, is punishable on summary conviction [61] [*Imp. 3 months and £100 fine and, in the case of a continuing offence, a further fine of £5 per day*].

The Act of 1955 is divided into six parts.   **Part I** [sections 1–27] contains general provisions as to food and drugs; **Part II** [sections 28–48] deals with milk, dairies and cream substitutes;

---

[60] These are (i) no scrap metal shall be received between 6.0 p.m. and 8.0 a.m., and (ii) all scrap metal shall be kept in the condition in which it was received for 72 hours.   Penalty for non-compliance is £100 fine.

[61] s. 108 (1).   The only exception is disclosure of information under s. 5 (3).

Part III [sections 49–61] deals with the provision and regulation of markets; **Part IV** [sections 62–81] deals with slaughterhouses, knackers' yards and cold-air stores; **Part V** [sections 82–121] deals with administration; **Part VI** [sections 122–137] contains miscellaneous and general provisions.

The principal offences under the Act are:

(1) For any person to add any substance to food, to use any substance as an ingredient in the preparation of food, to abstract any constituent from food, or to subject food to any other process or treatment so as to render the food injurious to health, with intent that the food shall be sold for human consumption in that state [**section 1 (1)**].

(2) For any person to add any substance to, or abstract any constituent from, a drug so as to affect injuriously the quality, constitution or potency of the drug, with intent that the drug shall be sold in that state [**section 1 (2)**].[62]

(3) For any person to:

(a) sell for human consumption, offer, expose or advertise for sale for human consumption, or have in his possession for the purpose of any such sale, any food rendered injurious to health by means of any operation described in section 1 (1) [**section 1 (3) (a)**];

(b) sell, offer, expose or advertise for sale, or have in his possession for the purpose of sale, any drug injuriously affected in its quality, constitution or potency by means of any operation described in section 1 (2) [**section 1 (3) (b)**].[63]

In proceedings for any offence under this section consisting of the advertisement for sale of any food or drug, it is a defence for the person charged to prove that, being a person whose business it is to publish, or arrange for the publication of, advertisements, he received the advertisement for publication in the ordinary course of business [**section 1 (6)**].

(4) For any person to sell to the prejudice of the purchaser any food or drug which is not of the nature, or not of the sub-

---

[62] This subsection will be repealed by the Medicines Act 1968, s. 135 (2), Sched. 6, when it comes into force.

[63] This subsection will be repealed by the Medicines Act 1968, s. 135 (2), Sched. 6, when it comes into force.

stance, or not of the quality, of the food or drug demanded by the purchaser [**section 2 (1)**].

In proceedings for any offence under this section it is not a defence to allege that the purchaser bought for analysis or examination and therefore was not prejudiced [**section 2 (2)**].

This section creates three separate offences, and hence an indictment alleging that food " was not of the nature or not of the substance or not of the quality demanded " would be bad for uncertainty.[64] Where the alleged offence consists of a " foreign body " in food, the correct charge is that the food is " not of the substance " demanded; and there must be evidence that the foreign body is harmful in some way.[65]

By **section 3** of the Act, in proceedings under section 2 of the Act for an offence consisting of the sale of food to which any substance has been added, or in the preparation of which any substance has been used as an ingredient, or from which any constituent has been abstracted, or which has been subjected to any other process or treatment, other than food thereby rendered injurious to health, it is a defence for the person charged to prove that the operation in question was not carried out fraudulently, and that the article was sold having attached thereto a notice of adequate size, distinctly and legibly printed and conspicuously visible, stating explicitly the nature of the operation, or was sold in a wrapper or container displaying such a notice [**section 3 (1)**]. In proceedings for any offence under section 2 of the Act in respect of any food or drug containing some extraneous matter, it is a defence for the defendant to prove that the presence of that matter was an unavoidable consequence of the process of collection or preparation [**section 3 (3)**]. In proceedings for any offence under section 2 of the Act in respect of diluted whisky, brandy, rum or gin, it is a defence for the defendant to prove that the spirit in question had been diluted with water only and that its strength was still not lower than thirty-five degrees under proof [**section 3 (4)**].

(5) For any person to give with any food or drug sold by him, or to display with any food or drugs exposed by him for sale, a label, whether attached to or printed on the wrapper or container or not, which:

---

[64] *Bastin* v. *Davies* [1950] 2 K.B. 579; *Moore* v. *Ray* [1951] 1 K.B. 58.
[65] *Edwards* v. *Llaethdy Meirion* [1957] Crim.L.R. 402; *Lovell* v. *Andover Corporation* [1958] Crim.L.R. 46.

(*a*) falsely describes the food or drug, or

(*b*) is calculated to mislead as to its nature, substance or quality,

unless he proves that he did not know, and could not with reasonable diligence have ascertained, that the label was of such a character as aforesaid [**section 6 (1)**].

(6) For any person to publish, or be a party to the publication of, an advertisement (not being such a label so given or displayed by him as aforesaid) which:

(*a*) falsely describes any food or drug, or

(*b*) is calculated to mislead as to the nature, substance or quality of any food or drug,

and in proceedings against the manufacturer, producer or importer of the food or drug, it shall rest on the defendant to prove that he did not publish, and was not a party to the publication of, the advertisement [**section 6 (2)**]. But in proceedings under section 6 (3) it is a defence for the defendant to prove either:

(*a*) that he did not know, and could not with reasonable diligence have ascertained, that the advertisement was of such a character as is therein described; or

(*b*) that, being a person whose business it is to publish, or arrange for the publication of, advertisements, he received the advertisement in the ordinary course of business [**section 6 (3)**].

For the purposes of section 6 of the Act, a label or advertisement which is calculated to mislead as to the nutritional or dietary value of any food is calculated to mislead as to the quality of the food [**section 6 (4)**].

(7) For any person to:

(*a*) sell, or offer or expose for sale, or have in his possession for the purpose of sale or of preparation for sale, or

(*b*) deposit with, or consign to, any person for the purpose of sale or of preparation for sale,

any food intended for, but unfit for, human consumption [**section 8 (1)**].

Where food in respect of which an offence under paragraph

(a) has been committed was sold to the offender by some other person, that person also is guilty of an offence [**section 8 (2)**].

Where a person is charged with an offence under paragraph (b) or under section 8 (2), it is a defence for him to prove either:

(a) that he gave notice to the person with whom he deposited or to whom he consigned or sold the food in question that it was not intended for human consumption, or

(b) that, at the time when he delivered or dispatched it to that person, either it was fit for human consumption or he did not know, and could not with reasonable diligence have ascertained, that it was unfit for human consumption [**section 8 (3)**].

(8) For any person to sell, or offer or expose for sale, or have in his possession for the purpose of sale or preparation for sale, for human consumption any part of, or product derived wholly or partly from, an animal which has been slaughtered in a knacker's yard or of which the carcass has been brought into a knacker's yard [**section 12 (1)**].

Legal proceedings. The following are the principal rules with regard to legal proceedings under the Act:

(1) Where a sample has been procured under the Act in the case of milk, no prosecution in respect of the article sampled shall be commenced more than twenty-eight days after it was procured, or, if the justice before whom the information was laid is satisfied on oath that it was not practicable to lay it at an earlier date and gives a certificate to that effect, forty-two days [66] [**section 108**]. In any other case the normal period is two months. If the requisite certificate is obtained from a justice, there is no time limit.

(2) A person against whom proceedings are brought under the Act shall, upon information duly laid by him, and on giving to the prosecution not less than three clear days' notice of his intention, be entitled to have brought before the court in the proceedings any person to whose act or default he alleges that the offence was due, and, in such a case, that person may be convicted and the original defendant, if he proves that he has used due diligence to

---

[66] But where the article of food is taken by a sanitary inspector, not a sampling officer, this limitation has no application; *Leach* v. *United Dairies* [1949] W.N. 225.

secure that the provisions in question were complied with, may be acquitted [**section 113**].[67]

(3) In the case of any prosecution under Part I, II or III of the Act in respect of selling, etc., an article not of a nature, substance or quality entitling a person to sell or deal with it under the description or in the manner under or in which the defendant dealt with it, it is a defence for him to prove:

(a) that he purchased it as being an article of such a nature, substance and quality as would have so entitled him and with a written warranty to that effect,[68] and

(b) that he had no reason to believe at the time of the commission of the alleged offence that it was otherwise; and

(c) that it was then in the same state as when he purchased it.[69]

But a warranty is a defence to proceedings under the Act only:

(a) if the defendant has not later than three clear days before the hearing sent to the prosecutor a copy of the warranty with a notice stating that he intends to rely on it and specifying the name and address of the person from whom he received it and has also sent a similar notice to that person; and

(b) in the case of a warranty given by a person resident outside the United Kingdom, the defendant proves that he had taken reasonable steps to ascertain, and did in fact believe in, the accuracy of the statements contained therein; and

(c) in the case of a prosecution in respect of a sample of milk, the defendant has, within sixty hours, after the sample was procured, served a notice complying with provisions contained in the Seventh Schedule to the Act.

For the purposes of this and the next section, a name or description entered in an invoice is to be deemed a written war-

---

[67] An original defendant who gives the required notice and lays an information against the person to whose act he alleges the offence is due can take advantage of this defence even if such person absconds and is not in fact before the court: *Malcolm* v. *Cheek* [1948] 1 K.B. 400. But an original defendant must be convicted if he cannot satisfy the court that the contravention was due to the other person and that he himself used all due diligence: *Moore* v. *Ray* [1951] 1 K.B. 58; *Simmons* v. *London Central Meat Co.* [1958] Crim.L.R. 47.

[68] Including an excise certificate for the removal of duty-paid spirits under the Customs and Excise Act 1952, s. 242; *Follett* v. *Luke* [1947] K.B. 289.

[69] Any alteration whatever by the defendant, even though it be totally unconnected with the defect alleged, will deprive him of this defence: *Hall* v. *Owen-Jones* [1967] 1 W.L.R. 1362.

ranty that the food or drug to which the entry refers is of such a nature, substance and quality that a person can sell or otherwise deal with it under that name or description without contravening the Act or any regulations made thereunder [**section 115**].

A defendant who in any proceedings under the Act wilfully applies to any food or drug a warranty or certificate of analysis given in relation to any other food or drug is guilty of an offence.

A person who, in respect of any food or drug sold by him, gives to the purchaser a false warranty *in writing* is guilty of an offence, unless he proves that when he gave the warranty he had reason to believe that the statements or descriptions therein contained were accurate [**section 116**]. Proceedings in respect of the giving of a false warranty must be commenced within twelve months of the date of the offence [**section 108**].

The Food and Drugs Act 1955, and regulations made thereunder, contain numerous provisions relating to the manufacture, sale and designations of milk and cream.[70]

By **section 32** any person who

(a) adds any water or colouring matter, or any dried or condensed milk or liquid reconstituted therefrom, to milk intended for sale for human consumption; or

(b) adds any separated milk or mixture of cream and separated milk to unseparated milk intended for such sale; or

(c) sells, or offers or exposes for sale, or has in his possession for the purpose of sale for human consumption, any milk to which any addition has been made in contravention of the foregoing provisions;

(d) sells, or offers or exposes for sale, under the designation of milk any liquid in the making of which any separated milk or any dried or condensed milk has been used, is guilty of an offence.

By **section 47** any person who sells, or offers or exposes for sale, for human consumption under a description or designation including the word " cream " any substance which appears to be

---

[70] Of course, offences against the other sections may also be committed. *Cf. Hall v. Owen-Jones* (*supra*) where an offence against s. 2 was held to have been committed (excess penicillin in milk).

cream but which is not is guilty of an offence. This does not apply to artificial cream, provided that it is described as such.

The **Fertilisers and Feeding Stuffs Act 1926** [71] has elaborate provisions imposing fines on anyone who sells any article for use as a fertiliser of the soil or as food for cattle or poultry without giving to the purchaser, in the prescribed manner, particulars of the nature, substance and quality of the article, and, in some cases, of its ingredients, or who gives false particulars, or who sells or offers for sale for use as food for cattle or poultry, or has in his possession packed or prepared for sale for such use, any article containing any ingredients deleterious to cattle or poultry.

By the **Plant Varieties and Seeds Act 1964** [72] provisions are made imposing fines and/or imprisonment for various offences relating to the breeding of plant varieties or to transactions concerning seeds or seed potatoes.

SECTION 9. WEIGHTS AND MEASURES

The principal Act on this subject is the **Weights and Measures Act 1963** of which the following are the most important provisions. Unless otherwise stated, the punishment for any of the following offences under this Act is a *fine of* £100 (£250 *in the case of a second or subsequent conviction under the same provision*) *and* 3 *months' imprisonment*.[73] All offences under the Act are punishable only on **summary conviction.**

(1) Subject to two minor exceptions,[74] it is an offence to use for trade [75] any units and instruments of weight or measurement which are not specified in, respectively, Schedule 1 and Schedule 3 to the Act [**section 10**]. These are imperial [76] and metric units, and instruments measuring or weighing in such units.[77]

---

[71] This Act will be repealed by the Agriculture Act 1970, ss. 87 (1), 113 (3), Sched. 5, Pt. V, when it comes into force.

[72] As amended by the Agriculture (Misc. Provns.) Act 1968; The Trade Descriptions Act 1968.

[73] s. 52, amended by the Criminal Justice Act 1967, Sched. 3.

[74] ss. 60 and 62 (1).

[75] Defined in s. 9.

[76] *i.e.* the normal British measurements of miles, yards, gallons, pounds etc.

[77] It is provided that jewellers may use carat and troy weight measurements for trade, and that apothecaries may use " ounce apothecaries." The Board of Trade may provide that " ounce apothecaries " may not be used at all for trade after January 31, 1969: s. 10 (2) (3) (9).

(2) Equipment may not be used for weighing and measuring for trade unless it has been passed by an inspector [78] as fit for such use, and stamped to indicate that it has been so passed [**section 11**] [£20 *fine* [79]].

(3) It is an offence to forge or counterfeit such a stamp, or to alter the machine after stamping so as to make it false or unjust, or knowingly to use for trade or to sell, offer or expose for sale a machine which has been so stamped or is false or unjust as a result of such an alteration [**section 15**].

(4) It is an offence to use for trade or to have in one's possession for use for trade any weighing or measuring equipment which is false or unjust [80] or to commit any fraud in the using of any [81] weighing or measuring equipment for trade [**section 16**].[82]

(5) It is an offence for anyone to sell or purport to sell a quantity less than that asked for, but if a purchaser gets what he may reasonably be taken to have asked for, no offence is committed [83] [**section 24**].

(6) Quite apart from giving short weight, which is covered by section 24, it is set out in Schedules 4, 5, 6, 7 and 8 that certain other requirements must be satisfied in relation to the sale of goods. Food is covered by Schedule 4, which specifies, *inter alia*, the quantities in which various articles may be sold. Beer and cider, for example, may be sold by retail only in third-pints, half-pints or multiples of half a pint. Failure to observe such requirements is an offence [**section 22**].

Defences. The Act sets out a number of defences available to a person charged with offences against sections 24 and 22. Two of these defences, namely, warranty and default of another person are very similar to those in the Food and Drugs Act 1955.[84] The present Act provides a third defence, to the effect that the person charged may be acquitted if he can prove:

[78] The obstruction of an inspector is made an offence by s. 49 [£20 *fine*].
[79] s. 52 (1).
[80] This offence and the offence under s. 15 may often overlap. In such a case, a conviction will more easily be secured by alleging a contravention of this part of s. 16, which, apparently, creates an offence of strict liability.
[81] The machine need not be false or unjust.
[82] An offence may also be committed, it seems, against s. 24 (below).
[83] See *Marshall* v. *Searles* [1964] Crim.L.R. 667, where it was held that a request for a pint of Guinness may be taken to be a request for a pint consisting of 94 per cent. Guinness and 6 per cent. froth.
[84] *Ante*, pp. 391, 392.

    (i) that the commission of the offence was due to a mistake or accident or some other cause beyond his control; and

    (ii) that he did everything that could reasonably be expected in order to avoid committing the offence [**section 26**].

SECTION 10. THE TRADE DESCRIPTIONS ACT 1968

The **Trade Descriptions Act 1968,** which replaces the Merchandise Marks Acts 1887–1953, is concerned with consumer protection. It creates a number of offences of giving inaccurate or inadequate information to customers in the course of business transactions relating to the supply of goods or services. The object of the Act is to protect the public and it relates only to business or commercial transactions. It is not intended to apply to domestic bodies or households, and is not designed to protect a husband from his wife or the members of a club from the club.[85] Subject to certain provisions of the Act itself, and in particular section 24,[86] the offences created are principally of strict or absolute liability.[87] Offenders are liable on **summary conviction** [£400 *fine*] or on **indictment** [*Imp.* 2 *years and fine*].[88]

    Section 1 makes it an offence for any person in the course of trade or business [89]

    (*a*) to apply a false trade description [90] to any goods, or

    (*b*) to supply or offer to supply [91] any goods [92] to which a false trade description is applied.

---

[85] *John* v. *Matthews* [1970] 2 Q.B. 443.

[86] See *post*, p. 400.

[87] See *ante*, p. 40.

[88] s. 18.

[89] See s. 39 (2) for meaning of this phrase. Where a car hire business as part of its normal practice buys or disposes of cars, the selling of a car and the application of a trade description in the course of that sale is an integral part of the business carried on as a car hire firm: *Havering London Borough Council* v. *Stevenson* [1970] 1 W.L.R. 1375, D.C.

[90] The fact that a false trade description is a trade mark within the meaning of the Trade Marks Act 1938 does not prevent it being a false trade description when applied to any goods, except where the conditions under s. 34 are satisfied.

[91] A person offering goods for supply or having goods in his possession for supply shall be deemed to offer to supply: s. 6 and see *North West Gas Board* v. *Aspden* [1970] Crim.L.R. 301 as to the distinction between a positive offer and an invitation to treat.

[92] " Goods " includes ships and aircraft, things attached to land and growing crops: s. 39 (1). See the Customs and Excise Act 1952, s. 32, for the provisions governing goods sold for export, or for use as stores.

The expression " trade description " is defined in **section 2** as an " indication," direct or indirect, and by whatever means given, of any of the following matters with respect to any goods or parts of goods, that is to say (i) quantity,[93] size or gauge; (ii) method of production, processing or reconditioning; (iii) composition; (iv) fitness for purpose, strength, performance, behaviour or accuracy; (v) any physical characteristic not included in the preceding paragraphs; (vi) testing by any person and the results thereof; (vii) approval by any person or conformity with a type approved by any person; (viii) place or date of manufacture, production, processing or reconditioning; (ix) person by whom manufactured, produced, processed or reconditioned; (x) other history, including ownership or use.

The above matters must be taken (*a*) in relation to any animal to include sex, breed or cross, fertility or soundness; (*b*) in relation to semen, to include the identity and characteristics of the animal from which it was taken, and the measure of dilution.[94] There are certain exceptions, mainly in favour of fertilisers and animal feeding stuffs [95] and in regard to matters dealt with by the Food and Drugs Act 1955.[96] Section 1 does not apply to goods supplied or offered to be supplied in the course of certain market research experiments.[97]

In certain circumstances under **section 21** a person can, in the United Kingdom, be an accessory to offences committed abroad provided that the act if committed in the United Kingdom in respect of the goods concerned would be an offence under section 1 of the Act.

The expression " false trade description " is defined in **section 3** as a " trade description which is false to a material degree." [98] It has been held under previous legislation that a trade description may be false on account of what it omits, although it is literally true.[99] A trade description which though not false is misleading, that is to say it is likely to be taken for such an indication of any

---

[93] " Quantity " includes length, width, height, area, volume, capacity, weight and number: s. 2 (3).
[94] s. 2 (2).
[95] s. 2 (4).
[96] s. 2 (5).
[97] s. 37.
[98] This does not apply to ss. 11–15 of the Act.
[99] *R.* v. *Kylsant* (*Lord*) [1932] 1 K.B. 442; *R.* v. *Bishirgian* (1936) 154 L.T. 499; *cf. Curtis* v. *Chemical Cleaning and Dyeing Co. Ltd.* [1951] 1 K.B. 805.

of the matters specified in section 2 (16) as would be false to a material degree,[1] is deemed to be a false trade description; as is anything which, though not a trade description is likely to be taken for an indication of any of those matters, and as such an indication would be false to a material degree [2] or a false indication, or anything likely to be taken as an indication which would be false, that any goods comply with a standard specified or recognised by any person or implied by the approval of any person, if there is no such person or no standard so specified, recognised or implied.[3]

By section 4 a person is said to apply a trade description to goods if he:

(a) affixes or annexes to it, or in any manner marks it or incorporates it with—

(i) the goods themselves, or

(ii) anything in, on, or with which the goods are supplied [4]; or

(b) places the goods in, on, or with anything which the trade description has been affixed or annexed to, marked on, or incorporated with, or places any such thing with the goods; or

(c) uses the trade description in any manner likely to be taken as referring to the goods.

An oral statement may amount to the use of a trade description. Where goods are supplied in pursuance of a request in which a trade description is used, and the circumstances are such as to make it reasonable to infer that the goods are supplied as goods corresponding to that trade description, the person supplying the goods shall be deemed to have applied that trade description to the goods.

By **section 5** special provisions apply in relation to trade descriptions contained in advertisements.[5]

The Act empowers the Board of Trade to make definition orders [6] marking orders [7] and to impose requirements as to the information contained in advertisements.[8]

---

[1] s. 3 (2).   [2] s. 3 (3).

[3] s. 3 (4).

[4] e.g. in a bottle: Stone v. Burn [1911] 1 K.B. 927.

[5] " Advertisement " includes a catalogue, circular or price list: s. 39.

[6] s. 7.

[7] s. 8.   [8] ss. 9 and 10.

Section 11 (1) makes it an offence for any person offering to supply goods of any description to give, by whatever means, any false indication to the effect that the price at which the goods are offered is equal to or less than a recommended price, or the price at which the goods, or goods of the same description, were previously offered by him, or is less than such a price by a specified amount. **Section 11 (2)** makes it an offence for such a person to give, by whatever means, any indication likely to be taken as an indication that the goods are being offered at a price less than that at which they are in fact being offered.[8a] For the purposes of section 11 an indication that goods were previously offered at a higher price or at a particular price is treated, unless the contrary is expressed, as an indication that they were so offered within the preceding six months for a continuous period of not less than twenty-eight days: **section 11 (3).**[8b]

By **section 12** it is an offence to make false representations in the course of any trade or business as to royal approval or award. By **section 13** it is an offence for any person in the course of any trade or business to give, by whatever means, any false indication, direct or indirect, that any goods or services supplied by him are of a kind supplied to any person.

Section 14 is an important section. It deals with false or misleading statements as to services etc. Under the section it is an offence for any person, in the course of any trade or business [9]—

    (*a*) to make a statement which he knows to be false [10] or

    (*b*) recklessly [11] to make a statement which is false, as to any of the following matters—

[8a] The words of this subsection are very wide. *Cf. Doble* v. *David Greig Ltd.* [1972] 1 W.L.R. 703, D.C.; *N.W. Gas Board* v. *Aspden* [1970] Crim.L.R. 301.

[8b] The burden of proving the falsity of such an allegation is on the prosecution: *House of Holland* v. *Brent London Borough Council* [1971] 2 Q.B. 304.

[9] A statement after a contract has been completed and the price paid may come within the section: *Breed* v. *Cluett* [1970] 2 Q.B. 459.

[10] " False " means false to a material degree: s. 14 (4). Actual knowledge of the facts in question may be imputed in law in circumstances where a person deliberately refrains from making inquiries, the results of which he may not care to have. See *Mallon* v. *Allon* [1964] 1 Q.B. 385 at p. 394. But mere neglect to ascertain what could have been found out by reasonable inquiries is not tantamount to knowledge: *Taylors Central Garages Ltd.* v. *Roper* (1951) 115 J.P. 445; *cf. London Computator Ltd.* v. *Seymour* (1944) 109 J.P. 10.

[11] For the meaning see below n. 13 and *R.* v. *Grunwald* [1963] 1 Q.B. 935.

(i) the provision in the course of any trade or business of any services,[12] accommodation or facilities;

(ii) the nature of such services, accommodation or facilities provided in the course of any trade or business;

(iii) the time at which, the manner in which, or the persons by whom such services etc., are to be so provided;

(iv) the examination, approval or evaluation by any person of such services etc., so provided; or

(v) the location or amenities of any accommodation so provided.

For the purposes of this section anything, whether or not a statement as to any of the matters specified above, likely to be taken for such a statement as to any of those matters as would be false, shall be deemed to be a false statement as to that matter; and a statement made regardless of whether it is true or false shall be deemed to be made recklessly [13] whether or not the person making it had reasons for believing that it might be false.[14]

Statements for the purposes of section 14 are not confined to those statements inducing a person into entering into a contract. In *Breed* v. *Cluett* [15] Lord Parker C.J. said: " There may well be statements made after a contract is completed, a contract for repairs to my motor car, a contract for repair to my roof, stating the effect of what has been done by way of repair, which may constitute an offence if made recklessly, even though the contract has been completed and payment has been made." If a statement is true at the time it is made for example, that there are available at a hotel twin bedded rooms with a terrace; and the defendants have contracted with the hotel management that those rooms should be kept for their customers, then subsequent negligence in ensuring that the rooms were in fact allocated to those customers,

---

12 " Services " does not include anything done under a contract of service: s. 14 (4). In relation to any services consisting or including the application of any treatment or process, or the carrying out of any repair, the matters specified shall be taken to include the effect of the treatment process or repair.

13 Thus importing the common law definition of " recklessly " laid down in *Derry* v. *Peek* (1889) 14 App.Cas. 337: *Sunair Holidays Ltd.* v. *Dodd* [1970] 1 W.L.R. 1037.

14 s. 15 which concerns orders defining terms for the purposes of s. 14 must be read together with the section.

15 [1970] 2 Q.B. 459 at p. 462.

has no bearing on whether the statement is made falsely or recklessly.[16]

Section 20 provides that where an offence has been committed by a body corporate, and it is proved that it was committed with the consent and connivance of, or is attributable to any neglect on the part of any director, manager,[17] secretary, or other similar officer of the body corporate, or any person purporting to act in that capacity, he, as well as the body corporate shall be guilty of the offence and liable to be proceeded against and punished accordingly. By **section 23** where the commission of an offence under the Act is due to the act or default of another person that other person shall be guilty of an offence and may be charged with and convicted of the offence, whether or not proceedings are taken against the first mentioned person.

A defence to any provisions of the Act is provided by **section 24** if the person charged proves:

(*a*) that the commission of the offence was due to a mistake or to reliance on information supplied to him, or to the act or default of another person, an accident, or some other cause beyond his control; and

(*b*) that he took all reasonable precautions and exercised all due diligence to avoid the commission of such an offence by himself or by any person under his control.

Subsection 24 (1) (*a*) provides five alternative defences, namely (i) mistake; (ii) reliance on information supplied to him; (iii) the act or default of another person; (iv) an accident; and (v) some other cause beyond his control.[18] A mistake under section 24 (1) (*a*) means a mistake of the person charged, not a mistake by another person.[19]

Any person can be " another person " within section 24 (1) (*a*) provided that in a case where a defendant is an individual such a person is someone other than that individual, and in a case where the defendant is a company or other corporate body he is some

---

[16] *Sunair Holidays Ltd.* v. *Dodd* [1970] 1 W.L.R. 1037.
[17] The word " manager " in this section refers to someone in the position of managing the affairs of the company and not to the branch manager of a store: *per* Fisher J. in *Tesco Ltd.* v. *Nattrass* [1971] 1 Q.B. 133 referring to *Registrar of Restrictive Trading Agreements* v. *W. H. Smith & Sons Ltd.* [1969] 1 W.L.R. 1460.
[18] *Birkenhead and District Co-operative Society Ltd.* v. *Roberts* [1970] 1 W.L.R. 1497 and *Tesco Ltd.* v. *Nattrass* [1971] 1 Q.B. 133.
[19] *Birkenhead and District Co-operative Society Ltd.* v. *Roberts* (*supra*).

person, not being a person within section 20 [20] carrying out the functions of such person. A shop manager can be "another person" for the purposes of the section, where the act or default of his which it is sought to rely on is something actually done by him.[21]

In order to bring himself within the defence afforded by section 24 a defendant must not only prove one of the five alternatives in section 24 (1) (a) but must also show that he exercised all due diligence etc. In the case of a corporate body the taking of such precautions involves two things: first, the setting up of an efficient system for the avoidance of offences under the Act. Secondly, the proper operation of the system. In *Tesco Ltd.* v. *Nattrass*,[22] the Divisional Court said, that inevitably the second part will involve in most cases delegation by the company to employees falling outside those classed in section 20. The court was of opinion that if such a person failed to carry out that duty, then the company was unable to show that they had satisfied the requirements of section 24 (1) (b). The House of Lords, on appeal,[23] took an entirely different view, namely that in the case of a large-scale business, it would be consistent with the taking of reasonable precautions and the exercise of due diligence to institute an effective system to avoid the commission of offences under which superior servants were instructed to supervise inferior servants whose acts might lead to the commission of offences. In the case of a limited company a failure to exercise due diligence would only arise where the failure was that of a director or senior manager in actual control of the company's operations who could be identified with the controlling mind and will of the company.[24] A subordinate manager's failure to exercise supervisory functions over other servants of the company would constitute "an act or default of another person" *i.e.* a person other than the company.

Section 24 (2) provides that where it is proposed to rely on the defence or act or default of another person, or reliance on information supplied, the defendant will not be allowed, without leave of the court to rely on the defence unless he has given seven clear

---

[20] See *ante*, p. 400.
[21] *Beckett* v. *Kingston Bros. (Butchers) Ltd.* [1970] 1 Q.B. 606.
[22] [1971] 1 Q.B. 133.
[23] [1972] A.C. 153.
[24] See pp. 104–106, *ante*.

days' notice in writing to the prosecutor identifying or assisting to identify that other person.

Section 24 (3) provides a defence in proceedings under the Act for an offence of supplying or offering to supply goods to which a false trade description is applied, if the person charged proves that he did not know and could not with reasonable diligence have ascertained that the goods did not conform to the description or that the description had been applied to the goods.

Section 25 provides a defence in relation to an offence committed by the publication of an advertisement, in which case the person charged must prove that he is a person whose business it is to publish or arrange for the publication of advertisements, and that he received the advertisement for publication in the ordinary course of business and did not know and had no reason to suspect that its publication would amount to an offence under the Act.

Section 28 provides for the enforcement of the Act by means of search warrants, and wide powers of inspection, entry, seizure and detention by authorised officers of a local weights and measures authority, which is the enforcement authority under the Act, or of a government department. Obstruction of [25] the officers is an offence punishable on **summary conviction** [£50 *fine*].[26]

No prosecution shall be commenced under the Act after the expiration of three years from the commission of the offence or one year from its discovery by the prosecutor [27] whichever is the earlier.[28] A magistrates' court may try an information for an offence under the Act if it was laid within twelve months of the commission of the offence.[29] Except in certain specified cases [30] no prosecution may be instituted by a local weights and measures authority unless they have given notice of intended prosecution to the Department of Trade and Industry, and either twenty-eight days

---

[25] Before there can be obstruction under s. 29 (1) (*a*) it must be shown that the officer was validly exercising his powers. Before he can be said to be validly exercising his powers under s. 28 (1) (*a*) it must be shown that an offence under the Act could have been committed: see *e.g. John* v. *Matthews* [1970] 2 Q.B. 443.

[26] s. 29.

[27] See as to the calculation of the period *Goldsmith* v. *West Metropolitan Rail Co.* [1904] 1 K.B. 1.

[28] s. 19 (1).

[29] s. 19 (2). But see the subsection as to the circumstances when it does not apply.

[30] Disclosing manufacturing processes or trade secrets under s. 28 (5) and obstructing authorised officers under s. 29.

have elapsed from the giving of the notice or the Department of Trade and Industry has issued its certificate.[31]

By **section 59** of the **Trade Marks Act 1938** it is an offence to make or cause to be made a false entry in the register of trade marks kept under the Act, or a writing falsely purporting to be a copy of an entry in any register, or producing or tendering or causing to be produced or tendered in evidence any such writing, knowing the entry or writing to be false.

By **section 1** of the **Trade Descriptions Act 1972** [31a] it is an offence to supply or offer to supply goods which were manufactured or produced outside the United Kingdom bearing a United Kingdom name or mark or a name or mark likely to be taken as such unless either there is also a conspicuous indication of the country of origin or the name or mark was not visible in the state in which the goods were supplied nor likely to become visible. As to defences, see section 2 (1).

The **Trading Representations (Disabled Persons) Act 1958** provides that it is an offence in selling goods from house to house or by post to represent that blind or disabled persons are employed in the production of the goods or that such persons will benefit from the sale unless the seller is registered with the Department of Employment and Productivity [**summary conviction:** *Imp. 3 months and* £100 *fine*]. The Department will refuse registration unless it is satisfied that the representations are correct. A number of organisations do not have to be registered nor is it necessary for a substantially disabled person who produces and sells the goods himself to be registered.

SECTION 11. AUCTIONS

An auction is a manner of selling or letting property by bids, and usually to the highest bidder by public competition.[32]   Where, for example, agreements are made not to bid, or where the right to bid is restricted, this end is defeated and offences may be committed.

Thus, the **Auctions (Bidding Agreements) Acts 1927** and **1969** are aimed at dealers who form " rings," and by agreeing not to bid against one another ensure that any lot or lots are knocked down

---

[31] s. 30 (2).
[31a] Comes into force December 29, 1972.
[32] Halsbury's Laws, Vol. 2, p. 69. Where a reserve price is stated the property will not necessarily be sold to the highest bidder.

to one of their number at a cost much less than its true value, the profit being subsequently shared out. The Act of 1927 provides that any dealer [33] who agrees to give, or gives, or offers any gift or consideration to any other person or an inducement or reward for abstaining or for having abstained from bidding at a sale by auction, or any person who agrees to accept, or accepts, or attempts to obtain from any dealer any such gift or consideration, commits an offence [**summary conviction:** £400 [34] *fine and Imp. 6 months*; **indictment:** *Imp. 2 years and a fine*].[35] A prosecution for such an offence may not be brought without the consent of the Attorney-General or Solicitor-General.

The offences are exceptions to section 104 of the Magistrates' Courts Act 1952, which provides a limit of six months on the institution of proceedings. By section 1 (2) of the 1969 Act offences under section 1 of the 1927 Act may be tried by a magistrates' court, if information is laid within five years of the commission of the offence, and within three months after the date on which evidence, sufficient in the opinion of the Attorney-General to justify proceedings, comes to his knowledge.[36]

The **Mock Auctions Act 1961** makes it an offence to promote, to conduct, or to assist in the conduct of a mock auction [**indictment:** £1,000 *fine and Imp. 2 years*; **summary conviction:** £100 *fine and Imp. 3 months*]. An auction becomes a mock auction if any of the following happens during the course of the sale:

(*a*) any articles are given away or offered as gifts;

(*b*) certain articles specified in the Act [37] are sold at a price lower than that bid for them;

(*c*) the right to bid for certain articles specified in the Act [38] is restricted or stated to be restricted to persons who have already bought or agreed to buy one or more articles.[39]

---

[33] A " dealer " is a person who, in the normal course of his business, attends sales by auction for the purpose of purchasing goods with a view to reselling them: s. 1 (2).

[34] Increased from £100 by the Criminal Justice Act 1967, s. 92 and Sched. 3, Pt. I.

[35] Added by s. 1 (1) of the 1969 Act in relation to offences committed after October 22, 1969. As to other orders which may be made on conviction, see s. 2 of the 1969 Act.

[36] s. 1 (2) of the 1969 Act in relation to offences committed after October 22, 1969.

[37] Plate, plated articles, linen, china, glass, books, pictures, prints, furniture, jewellery, articles of household or personal use or ornament or any musical or scientific instrument or apparatus: s. 3 (2).

[38] *Ibid.*   [39] *Semble*, not necessarily those specified in the Act.

SECTION 12. CONSUMER PROTECTION ACT 1961

The **Consumer Protection Acts 1961** and **1971** provide that the Secretary of State may make regulations prescribing the design, construction, packing etc., of particular goods or classes of goods and stipulate that they must be accompanied by certain warnings and instructions where such regulations are expedient to prevent or reduce risk of death or personal injury.[40] **Sections 2** and **3** of the **1961** Act [41] make it an offence punishable on **summary conviction** [£100 *fine; second or subsequent conviction £250 fine and Imp. 3 months*] to sell or have in possession for the purposes of sale [42] any goods or the component parts of such goods which do not comply with the regulations. Section 2 provides for a number of exceptions. Section 3 provides that where the commission by any person of an offence under the section is due to the act or default of some other person, that other person shall be guilty of an offence, and may be charged with and convicted of it, whether or not proceedings are taken against the first-mentioned person.[43] Section 3 [44] states that it is a defence for a person to prove that he took all reasonable precautions and exercised all due diligence to avoid the commission of such an offence. If the particular regulations so prescribe, an officer authorised in writing by the local authority may inspect goods or component parts of goods kept in the area for the purpose of sale and the local authority may purchase such goods or components to determine whether there is compliance with the regulations.[45]

SECTION 13. UNSOLICITED GOODS

The **Unsolicited Goods Act 1971** creates a number of offences in relation to unsolicited goods, that is, goods sent to a person without any prior request made by him or on his behalf.[46] **Section 2 (1)** makes it an offence punishable on **summary conviction** [*fine: £200*]

---

[40] Regulations have been made regarding, *inter alia*, heating appliances and children's nightdresses.

[41] Amended by s. 1 of the 1971 Act.

[42] If the particular regulations so provide, the provisions of the Act apply to lettings under a hire-purchase scheme or lettings for hire: s. 2 (6).

[43] s. 3 (2) (*a*) inserted by the Consumer Protection Act 1971, s. 1.

[44] s. 3 (2) (*b*) inserted by the Consumer Protection Act 1971, s. 1.

[45] s. 1 (3).

[46] s. 6 (1). " Send " includes deliver: *ibid.*

for any person who not having reasonable cause to believe there is a right to payment yet, in the course of any trade or business, demands payment, or asserts a present or prospective right to payment for such goods sent to another with a view to his acquiring them.[47] **Section 2 (2)** makes it an offence punishable on **summary conviction** [£400 *fine*] for a person with a view to obtaining payment for such goods to threaten to bring legal proceedings or to place or cause to be placed the name of the recipient of the goods on a list of defaulters or debtors, or to threaten to do so, or to invoke or cause to be invoked any other collection procedure, or to threaten to do so.

Section 3 makes it an offence punishable on **summary conviction** [£400 *fine*] for a person to make unlawful demands, or assertions of a present or prospective right to payment of a charge or part of a charge for including or arranging the inclusion of a person's name in a business or trade directory, without any prior request by such a person.[48]

SECTION 14. HIRE-PURCHASE AND CREDIT-SALE TRANSACTIONS

Sections 21, 22 and **23** of the **Hire-Purchase Act 1965** require that a person entitled to enforce a hire-purchase agreement, credit-sale agreement or a conditional-sale agreement[49] against a hirer, buyer or guarantor shall, within four days of receiving a request and the sum of 12½p from such person, supply him with a full statement of the account, including the amount paid and payable. A guarantor is also entitled to request a copy of the agreement. Until the request is fulfilled neither the agreement nor any right to recover the goods can be enforced. If the default continues for a month, the defaulter commits an offence [**summary conviction:** £25 *fine*].

Section 24 provides that it is an offence, similarly punishable, for a hirer or buyer not to inform the owner or seller, when requested in writing to do so, where the goods are to be found.

The **Advertisements (Hire-Purchase) Act 1967** regulates the content of advertisements for goods available for disposal by way of hire-purchase or credit-sale and makes it an offence not to

---

[47] For the rights of the recipient see s. **1**.
[48] In the form required by s. 3 (1) (3).
[49] The Act does not apply to transactions where the total purchase price exceeds £2,000: s. 2.

comply with the Act. The purpose of the Act is to force the advertiser who wishes to disclose some information about the terms of the agreement to disclose other information that he might not otherwise disclose, *e.g.* the total number of instalments, the cash price and the total price under the agreement.

SECTION 15. OFFENCES IN RELATION TO INDUSTRIAL DISPUTES

At common law there were opinions to the effect that combinations in restraint of trade were punishable as conspiracies.[50] By section 2 of the Trade Union Act 1871 [51] the purposes of any trade union [52] were not, *by reason only that they are in restraint of trade,* deemed to be unlawful, so as to render any member of such trade union liable to criminal prosecution for conspiracy or otherwise. These words are now included in **section 135** of the **Industrial Relations Act 1971.**

After the Act of 1871 was passed it was made clear by the courts that a combination in restraint of trade is not *per se* a criminal conspiracy.[53] Hence the above-mentioned provisions are now regarded as simply declaratory of the common law.[54]

The effect of an opinion expressed in 1872 [54] was that workmen striking or threatening to strike could be found guilty of a criminal conspiracy to coerce their employer at common law, though no crime was committed by any individual. In response to this, section 3 of the Conspiracy and Protection of Property Act 1875 provided that an agreement or combination by two or more persons to do or procure to be done any act in contemplation or furtherance of an industrial dispute [55] is not indictable as a conspiracy if such act committed by one person would not be punishable as a crime.[56]

---

[50] See *Hilton* v. *Eckersley* (1855) 6 E. & B. 47; *Walsby* v. *Anley* (1861) 3 E. & E. 516.

[51] Repealed by the Industrial Relations Act 1971, Sched. 9.

[52] " Trade Union " is defined " as an organisation of workers which is for the time being registered as a trade union " under the Industrial Relations Act 1971; *ibid.* s. 61 (3). Note the distinction in s. 61 between Trade Unions and organisations of workers.

[53] See *Mogul Steamship Co.* v. *McGregor, Gow & Co.* [1892] A.C. 25.

[54] *R.* v. *Burn* (1872) 12 Cox C.C. 316.

[55] Within the meaning of the Industrial Relations Act 1971. See s. 167 (1) (5) of that Act.

[56] The expression " crime " as defined by the section means an offence punishable on indictment or on summary conviction and for which the offender is liable to be imprisoned either absolutely or as an alternative to some other punishment.

Nothing in this section, however, exempts from punishment any persons guilty of a conspiracy for which punishment is awarded by statute or affects the law relating to riot, unlawful assembly, breach of the peace or sedition, or any offence against the state or Sovereign.

By **section 7** of the **Conspiracy and Protection of Property Act 1875** every [57] person who, with a view to compel any other person to abstain from doing, or to do, any act [58] which such other person has a legal right to do or abstain from doing, wrongfully and without legal authority:

(a) Uses violence to, or intimidates, such other person, or his wife or children, or injures his property [59]; or

(b) Persistently follows him about from place to place; or

(c) Hides his tools, clothes, or other property, or hinders him in the use thereof; or

(d) Watches or besets his house, or other place where he resides, or works, or carries on business, or happens to be, or the approach to such house or place (usually known as picketing); or

(e) Follows him with two or more other persons in a disorderly manner through any street or road,

commits an offence punishable on **summary conviction** [*Imp.* 3 *months or* £20 *fine*].[60]

By **section 134** of the **Industrial Relations Act 1971** [61] where one or more pickets, in contemplation or furtherance of an industrial dispute,[62] attend at or near a place where a person works or carries on business, or any place where a person happens to be, not being a place where he resides, and they do so only for the purpose of *peacefully* obtaining information from him or *peacefully* communicating information to him or *peacefully* [63] persuading him to

---

[57] This word makes the law of general application and does not restrict it to industrial disputes, though in practice the offence most frequently occurs in connection therewith.

[58] The particular act must be specified in the summons and conviction, since it is the prevention of it which forms the " gist and pith " of the offence: *R.* v. *McKenzie* [1892] 2 Q.B. 519 at p. 521.

[59] The particular property injured must be specified in the summons and conviction: *Smith* v. *Moody* [1903] 1 K.B. 56.

[60] s. 9 provides that the accused may elect trial on indictment.

[61] The Trades Disputes Act 1906 is repealed.

[62] Defined in s. 167 (1) (5).

[63] Contrary to popular opinion, the violent acts of pickets during the miners' strike of January–February 1972 are in no way excused or condoned by law.

work or not to work, their attendance shall not *of itself* constitute an offence under section 7, or under any other enactment or rule of law.

By **section 5** of the Act of 1875, it is a similar offence for *any person* wilfully and maliciously to break a contract of service or hiring, knowing or having reasonable cause to believe that the probable consequences of his so doing, either alone or in combination with others, will be to endanger human life, or cause serious bodily injury, or to expose valuable property to destruction or serious injury.[64]

SECTION 16.   CONTRACTS OF EMPLOYMENT AND REDUNDANCY
PAYMENTS

By **section 4** of the **Contracts of Employment Act 1963**[65] an employer is required not later than thirteen weeks after the beginning of an employee's period of employment to give to the employee a written statement setting out the terms of the employment, including the name of the parties, the date the contract began, the scale of remuneration, the intervals at which it is paid (*e.g.* weekly, monthly, etc.), the terms and conditions relating to hours of work and terms relating to holidays, sickness and pension rights. The employer is also required to give a written statement concerning any changes. It is sufficient to inform the employee in the statement that the particulars may be discovered in a document which the employee has reasonable opportunities of reading in the course of his employment or is otherwise reasonably accessible to him. It is not necessary to give the employee the statement if he is given a copy of the contract of employment which sets out the particulars.

The section does not apply to an employee normally employed for less than twenty-one hours weekly. Also it does not apply to certain dockers and seamen and to an employee whose father, mother, husband, wife, son or daughter is the employer.[66]

Section 5 of the Act made a failure to comply with section 4 an offence. However, section 5 was repealed by section 38 of the Redundancy Payments Act 1965, except in respect of failures to

[64] As to the effect of a strike notice on this section see the Industrial Relations Act 1971, s. 147 (2) (*c*).
[65] Substituted by the Industrial Relations Act 1971, Sched. 2, Pt. II.
[66] s. 6.

comply with section 4 before an appointed day, *i.e.* December 6, 1965.[67]   Failures to comply with section 4 and disputes concerning the section are now to be referred to a tribunal.

By the **Redundancy Payments Act 1965**, which provides for employers to make redundancy payments to certain employees, it is an offence [68] when making a redundancy payment otherwise than in pursuance of the decision of a tribunal not to give the employee a written statement indicating how the amount has been calculated.

Section 17.   Factories, Etc.

By the **Factories Act 1961** and the **Offices, Shops and Railway Premises Act 1963** and numerous other Acts, Rules, and Orders, many regulations have been made as to the sanitary arrangements of such buildings, the safety of machinery etc., used therein, the periods of employment of children and women, the education of children, accidents, and innumerable other matters.   For breaches of these regulations, which are outside the scope of this book, pecuniary penalties, and in some cases imprisonment, may be imposed.

Section 18.   The Fire Precautions Act 1971

The **Fire Precautions Act 1971** provides that a fire certificate be required in respect of certain premises [69] specifying their use, the means of escape provided, the type, location and number of means for warning of fire and fighting fires.[70]   Amongst other offences created by the Act, **section 7** of the **Act** makes it an offence: **summary conviction** [*fine*: £400]: **Indictment** [*Imp. 2 years and a fine*] for the occupier of such premises not to have a certificate in force, or for any person to contravene the requirements of such

---

[67] Redundancy Payments Act (Appointed Day) Order 1965 (S.I. 1965 No. 1757).
[68] Punishable on **summary conviction** [£20 *fine*] s. 5 (2).   Also, if after failure by the employer to give an employee a written statement indicating how the amount of the redundancy payment has been calculated, the employer without reasonable excuse fails to comply with a written notice from the employee requiring the employer to give a written statement as to how the amount of the redundancy payment has been calculated, the employer commits an offence punishable on **summary conviction** [£20 *fine on first conviction and* £100 *fine in any other case*] s. 5 (3).
[69] See ss. 1–3.
[70] s. 6.

a certificate. **Section 8** makes it an offence [*similar penalty as above*] for an occupier of premises to which a certificate applies, to carry out material extensions or alterations to the premises, or to keep explosive or highly inflammable materials in the building, or more than the quantity of such materials prescribed, without giving notice to the fire authority. Certain other offences in relation to the inspection of premises, and the forging and falsification of documents and statements etc., are also dealt with under the Act. A general defence to charges brought under the Act is provided by **section 25** for a person who proves that he took all reasonable precautions and exercised all due diligence to avoid the commission of an offence.

SECTION 19.   LANDLORD AND TENANT

Only a very short summary of those provisions of the Acts dealing with rented premises which create offences can be attempted here.

By section 85 of the **Rent Act 1968,** a person commits an offence [£100 *fine*] who as a condition of the grant, renewal or continuance of a protected tenancy [71] requires or receives, in addition to the rent the payment of any premium or the making of a loan. A court before whom an offender is convicted may order the premiums to be repaid. It is also an offence [£100 *fine*] under **section 86** if anyone requires or receives a loan or premium as a condition of the assignment of such a tenancy, and a similar offence is created under **section 87** in relation to furnished lettings. By **section 89** it is an offence [£100 *fine*] for any person who, in connection with the proposed grant, renewal, continuance or assignment of a protected tenancy on terms which require the purchase of furniture, to offer or otherwise seek to obtain a price for the furniture which he knows or ought to know is unreasonably high; or to fail to furnish a written inventory of the furniture, specifying the price sought for each item.

The **Landlord and Tenant Act 1962** makes it an offence [**summary conviction:** £50 *fine; second or subsequent conviction:* £100 *fine*] for a landlord not to provide a rent book to a weekly tenant.

By **section 30** of the **Rent Act 1965,**[71a] it is an offence punishable on **summary conviction:** [*Imp.* 6 *months and* £400 *fine*] or on **indict-**

---

[71] See s. 1 of the Act.
[71a] Amended by the Criminal Justice Act 1972, s. 30.

ment [*Imp. 2 years and a fine*] for any person unlawfully to deprive a tenant who is occupying premises as a residence of his occupation of the premises unless he proves that he believes that the person had ceased to reside in the premises. It is an offence similarly punishable to harass the person or persistently withdraw services with intent to cause the person to give up the occupation.[71b] In almost all cases in which a tenant [72] is in occupation of premises as a dwelling-place it is now unlawful to evict him without a court order, whether the original lease or agreement has come to an end or not.[73] Unless such a court order has been obtained an eviction will constitute an offence against section 30.

Provisions similar to those contained in **section 30** apply in relation to the occupiers of caravan sites: **section 3, Caravan Sites Act 1968.**

[71b] See *R.* v. *Abrol* [1972] Crim.L.R. 318 where it was held that there must be deliberate continuity in withholding services coupled with the necessary intent.

[72] The Acts do not protect mere licensees.

[73] Rent Act 1965, ss. 31, 32; Rent Act 1968, s. 11.

CHAPTER 28

ANIMALS

SECTION 1. DOGS

Dogs worrying livestock. The owner or in certain circumstances the person in charge of a dog which worries livestock on any agricultural land is guilty of an offence [1] [**summary conviction: £20** *fine* [2]]. If a police officer finds a dog on what appears to him to be agricultural land and he reasonably believes the dog to have been worrying livestock there and no one present will admit to being its owner, he may seize the dog and it will then be treated as a stray.[3]

Dangerous dogs.[4] Any court of summary jurisdiction may hear a complaint [5] by any [6] person that a dog is dangerous and not kept under proper control. If the court is satisfied that the dog is dangerous, then the court may order either:

(i) that the dog be kept under proper control; or, alternatively,
(ii) that the dog be destroyed.

Failure to comply with such an order is an offence [**summary conviction: £1** *fine for every day of non-compliance* [7]].

Whether a dog is or is not dangerous is clearly a question of degree. Arising out of the same facts there may be a complaint

---

1 Dogs (Protection of Livestock) Act 1953, s. 1 (1) (6). Where a dog causes damage by killing or injuring livestock, any person who is a keeper of the dog is liable for the damage in the civil courts; subject to certain statutory exceptions: Animals Act 1971, ss. 3, 5; and the defence under s. 9 repealing the provisions of the Dogs Act 1906 ss. 1 (1)–(3) and amending the Dogs (Amendment) Act 1928.

2 The fine was increased to £20 by the Criminal Justice Act 1967, Sched. 3. Where the owner has been previously convicted on a charge arising out of depredations committed by the same dog, then the fine is £50.

3 See *post*, p. 414.

4 Dogs Act 1871, s. 2.

5 Not an information. A complaint and the making of an order is a civil proceeding: *R.* v. *Nottingham Justices, ex p. Brown* [1960] 1 W.L.R. 1315.

6 Not necessarily the person aggrieved: *Smith* v. *Baker* [1961] 1 W.L.R. 38.

7 The justices have no power to order destruction of the dog on an information laid for non-compliance with an order to keep a dog under proper control. The justices can act only in the manner required by the Act and the Act requires a complaint that the dog is dangerous and not kept under proper control: *Rhodes* v. *Heritage* [1951] W.N. 221.

brought under the 1871 Act and an information laid under the 1953 Act. Since the one is a civil proceeding and the other criminal, the information should be heard before the complaint and not vice versa lest evidence admissible in civil cases and not admissible in criminal cases continue to operate on the minds of the justices when they come to hear the criminal information.[8]

An order cannot be made in relation to a person, who although the owner of the dog at the time it was alleged to be dangerous and not kept under proper control, has bona fide transferred ownership of the dog to another person before the date of the hearing[9]: although in those circumstances an order may be made against the new owner.[10]

Ferocious dogs. It is an offence to allow to be at large[11] in the metropolis[12] or in any street in a town to which the Town Police Clauses Act 1847, s. 28, applies any unmuzzled ferocious[13] dog [**summary conviction:** £20 *fine or Imp.* 14 *days*].

Stray dogs.[14] A stray dog if found in a highway or place of public resort[15] may be seized and detained by any police officer. Such a dog is then to be kept for seven clear days following upon the seizure, after which it may be sold or destroyed, unless the owner upon or previous to the expiry of the seven days has claimed the dog and paid all expenses arising out of its detention. Where the dog's address appears on the collar, or the owner of the dog is known, a notice in writing should be sent to the address given or to the owner giving information of the seizure and of the dog's liability to be sold or destroyed. The seven clear days do not begin to run in such case until service of the notice has been effected.[16]

---

[8] *R.* v. *Dunmow Justices, ex p. Anderson* [1964] 1 W.L.R. 1039.

[9] *R.* v. *Jones, ex p. Daunton* [1963] 1 W.L.R. 270.

[10] *R.* v. *Leicester Justices, ex p. Workman* [1964] 1 W.L.R. 707.

[11] A dog is not at large when on a lead, unless the lead is so long as to preclude any control over the dog. Provided control is possible (even though not exercised) the dog is not at large: *Ross* v. *Evans* [1959] 2 Q.B. 79.

[12] Metropolitan Police Act 1839, s. 54.

[13] " Ferocious " and " Dangerous " are not synonymous. Hence dismissal of an information under s. 28 of the Town Police Clauses Act would not necessarily prevent an order being made under the 1871 Act—a dog can be dangerous without being ferocious; *Keddle* v. *Payn* [1964] 1 W.L.R. 262.

[14] See Dogs Act 1906, s. 3.

[15] This is a place to which the public in fact goes, as distinct from a place to which the public has absolute right to go.

[16] As to which, see Dogs Act 1906, s. 3 (3).

Any dog which is on the highway or in a place of public resort without a collar on which is inscribed the name and address of the owner may, without more ado, be seized and treated as a stray.[17] The same facts also constitute an offence on the part of the owner and any person in charge of it [**summary conviction:** £50 *fine*].[18]

It is also an offence to allow a dog to be on any road designated by the local authority for the area unless it is on a lead [**summary conviction:** £5 *fine*].[19]

SECTION 2.   REQUIREMENTS OF LICENSING AND REGISTRATION

Dog Licences Act 1959.   This Act makes it an offence to keep a dog [20] aged over six months without obtaining a licence for it [**summary conviction:** £10 *fine* [21]].   It is also an offence for anyone having a licence to fail to produce it to an authorised officer [22] or constable within a reasonable time after request [*similarly punishable*].   The licence may be obtained from a post office.   It is valid for twelve months dating from the first day of the month on which it was taken out.

By the **Pet Animals Act 1951,** the **Animal Boarding Establishments Act 1963,** and the **Riding Establishments Acts 1964 to 1970,** one must obtain a licence from the local authority before one may keep—

(a) a petshop;

(b) a boarding establishment for dogs and/or cats [23];

(c) a riding establishment.[24]

Failure to obtain the appropriate licence is an offence [**summary conviction:** *Imp.* 3 *months and* £25 *fine*, but under the Riding

---

[17] Control of Dogs Order, S.R. & O. 1930 No. 399.

[18] *Ibid.*

[19] Road Traffic Act 1972, s. 31 (1).

[20] There are certain exceptions in favour of guide dogs, sheep dogs and hounds aged under twelve months which have not yet hunted with the pack: ss. 2 (2), 3 and 4.   It is no longer necessary for owners of sheep dogs to obtain certificates of exemption: Local Government Act 1966, s. 36.

[21] The fine was increased by the Local Government Act 1966, s. 36 (4).

[22] An officer of the county or county borough council who is authorised to request production of dog licences: s. 13.

[23] " Animal " is defined in the Act as " any dog or cat ": Animal Boarding Establishments Act 1963, s. 5 (2).

[24] This is a place where horses are let out for hacking or where riding lessons are given for profit: Riding Establishments Act 1964, s. 6.

Establishments Acts, *Imp.* 3 *months and* £50 *fine* [25]. In making its decision whether or not to grant a licence the local authority is directed to take into account such considerations as the suitability of the accommodation and the efficiency of the precautions taken against disease.[26]

A licence may not be granted where the applicant is disqualified from keeping the type of concern in respect of which the licence is sought, *e.g.* where one is disqualified from keeping a petshop, one will be unable to get a petshop licence.[27] Upon conviction of certain offences a licence, once granted, may be cancelled, and the offender disqualified from keeping dogs,[28] keeping a petshop,[29] keeping a boarding establishment for animals,[30] keeping a riding establishment [31] or from having the custody of animals at all.

Keeping dogs, or keeping animals at all in the face of a disqualification order, amount to offences in their own right [**summary conviction:** £50 *fine and Imp.* 3 *months*]. No such separate offence is created by the Pet Animals Act 1951, the Animal Boarding Establishments Act 1963, or the Riding Establishments Acts 1964 to 1970. The offence with which a person would be charged under these Acts would merely be that of keeping the establishment without a licence [32] [**summary conviction:** £25 *fine and Imp.* 3 *months*].

25 Increased by the 1970 Act, s. 4.

26 Pet Animals Act 1951, s. 1 (5); Animal Boarding Establishments Act 1963, s. 1 (5); Riding Establishments Act 1964, s. 1 (4). In the case of an application for a riding establishment licence, the authority is not to make its decision until it has received a veterinary report on the premises: Riding Establishments Act 1964, s. 1 (3).

27 Pet Animals Act 1951, s. 1 (2). In certain cases a licence must be refused even when the disqualification to which one is subject is not a disqualification from keeping the establishment for which one is seeking the licence, *e.g.* if one is disqualified from keeping an animal boarding establishment, one cannot be granted a riding establishment licence.

28 Offences involving cruelty to dogs: Protection of Animals (Cruelty to Dogs) Act 1933, s. 1 (1).

29 Offences against the Pet Animals Act 1951; Protection of Animals Act 1911; Pet Animals Act 1951, s. 5 (3).

30 Offences against the Animals Boarding Establishments Act 1963; Pet Animals Act 1951; Protection of Animals Act 1911: Animal Boarding Establishments Act 1963, s. 3 (3).

31 Offences against the Riding Establishments Act 1964; Animal Boarding Establishments Act 1963; Pet Animals Act 1951; Protection of Animals Act 1911; Riding Establishments Act 1964, s. 4 (3).

32 This is made possible by the fact that one cannot obtain a licence if one is disqualified. There is, however, a possibility that by non-disclosure of convictions one may obtain a licence notwithstanding a disqualification order. The Riding Establishments Act 1964, s. 3 (2), caters for this by making it an offence to make a false statement for the purpose of obtaining a licence. No such provision, however, appears in the Pet Animals Act 1951, or the Animal Boarding Establishments Act 1963.

SECTION 3.   SPECIFIC OFFENCES INVOLVING CRUELTY TO ANIMALS

The main offences are contained in the **Protection of Animals Acts, 1911–1964.**[33]   The animals protected by these Acts are domestic animals and captive animals.[34]   A captive animal is an animal, not being a domestic animal, which is in captivity or confinement.[35] Whether an animal is in captivity or not has been judicially considered in two cases—*Steele* v. *Rogers*[36] and *Rowley* v. *Murphy*.[37] It appears from these that the fact that an animal is temporarily immobilised, whether by agency of man or by force of circumstances, is not sufficient.   An animal is " in captivity " only when some dominion is exercised over it, as where animals are kept in a zoo.[38]

Offences: (1) Cruelly to beat, kick, ill-treat, over-ride, over-drive, over-load, torture, infuriate or terrify any animal, or cause unnecessary suffering to any animal as a result of any wanton or unreasonable act or omission.[39]   Since cruelty is the essence of the offence it is necessary to know what the word signifies in this context.   The mere fact that pain is caused is not by itself sufficient.   What must be proved is that the pain was inflicted without good reason.[40]

(2) To convey or carry any animal in such manner or position as to cause that animal unnecessary suffering.[41]

---

[33] Protection of Animals Act 1911; Protection of Animals Act (1911) Amendment Act 1912; Performing Animals (Regulation) Act 1925; Protection of Animals Amendment Act 1927; Protection of Animals (Cruelty to Dogs) Act 1933; Protection of Animals Act 1934; Protection of Animals (Amendment) Act 1954; Protection of Animals (Anaesthetics) Act 1954; Abandonment of Animals Act 1960; Animals (Cruel Poisons) Act 1962; Protection of Animals (Anaesthetics) Act 1964.

[34] Protection of Animals Act 1911, s. 15.

[35] *Ibid.*

[36] (1912) 22 Cox C.C. 656 (whale stranded on a beach when the tide went out).

[37] [1964] 2 Q.B. 43 (stag, trapped under a van, dragged into a nearby enclosure and killed).

[38] *Ibid.* at p. 47, *per* counsel *arguendo.*

[39] Protection of Animals Act 1911, s. 1 (*a*).

[40] A sufficiently good reason for this purpose can be that the infliction of pain is necessary if the animal is to be of any use to man; the breaking-in of horses may be justified on this principle.   The fact that by the infliction of pain a slight profit will accrue to the owner has been held insufficient: *Ford* v. *Wiley* (1889) 23 Q.B.D. 203 (dishorning of cattle).

[41] Protection of Animals Act 1911, s. 1 (*b*).

(3) To cause, procure or assist at the fighting or baiting of any animal.[42]

(4) Wilfully and without reasonable cause to administer any poisonous or injurious drug or substance to any animal.[43]

(5) To subject an animal to an operation which is performed without due care and humanity.[44] By the **Protection of Animals (Anaesthetics) Act 1954**,[45] subject to certain exceptions,[46] an operation on an animal [47] which involves interference with sensitive tissues or bone structure will be deemed to be performed without due care and humanity unless an effective anaesthetic is used.[48]

(6) Being the owner, or having charge or control of any animal, without reasonable cause to abandon it, whether permanently or not, in circumstances likely to cause the animal unnecessary suffering.[49] All these offences are punishable by a £50 *fine and Imp.* 3 *months*.[50]

The Acts do not apply to: (1) The hunting of any captive animal, provided that it is first liberated in such a place that it has a reasonable chance of escape and that it is not by reason of mutilation, injury or exhaustion incapacitated from escaping. On recapture, the Act applies once more.[51]

(2) The slaughter of animals for human consumption, provided that no unnecessary suffering is inflicted.[52]

(3) Anything lawfully done under the Cruelty to Animals Act, 1876.[53] This Act regulates vivisection, *i.e.* experiments performed on living animals for the advancement of science. The main requirements of the Act are that the person performing the experiment be licensed by the Home Secretary and that the subject of the

[42] *Ibid*. s. 1 (*c*). See also Town Police Clauses Act 1847, s. 36, and Cockfighting Act 1952.
[43] Protection of Animals Act 1911, s. 1 (1) (*d*).
[44] *Ibid*. s. 1 (1) (*e*).
[45] As amended by the Protection of Animals (Anaesthetics) Act 1964.
[46] Protection of Animals (Anaesthetics) Act 1954, s. 1 (2) and Sched. I as amended.
[47] In this Act, " animal " does not include birds, reptiles or fish.
[48] But see below the provisions as to vivisection contained in the Cruelty to Animals Act 1876.
[49] Abandonment of Animals Act 1960, s. 1.
[50] Protection of Animals Act 1911, s. 1 (1), as amended by Protection of Animals (Amendment) Act 1954, s. 3.
[51] Protection of Animals Act 1911, s. 1 (3) (*b*).
[52] *Ibid*. s. 1 (3) (*a*).
[53] *Ibid*. s. 1 (3).

experiment be fully anaesthetised throughout, if the experiment is calculated to give pain. Sometimes, however, the purpose of an experiment may be frustrated if the animal is not fully conscious, and in such a case if the requisite certificate [54] be obtained, the operation may be carried out without anaesthetic being used.

[54] Cruelty to Animals Act 1876, s. 3 (proviso), s. 11.

CHAPTER 29

THE GAME LAWS AND WILD LIFE CONSERVATION

SECTION 1. POACHING

Poaching by night. By **section 1** of the **Night Poaching Act 1828,** as amended by **section 1** of the **Night Poaching Act 1844,**[1] and the **Wild Creatures and Forest Laws Act 1971,** any person who by night (*i.e.* from one hour after sunset to one hour before sunrise [2])—

   (i) unlawfully takes or destroys any game (*i.e.* hares, pheasants, partridges, grouse, heath or moor game, black game, and bustards [3]) or rabbits on any land, whether open or enclosed, or upon any road, highway, or path; or

  (ii) unlawfully enters or is on any land, whether open or enclosed, with any gun, net or other instrument for the purpose of taking game,

commits an offence punishable on **summary conviction** in the case of the first offence [*Imp.* 3 *months*] and second offence [*Imp.* 6 *months*] and on **indictment** in the case of the third offence [7 *years*].

By **section 2** of the Act, as similarly amended, it is provided that where any person is found committing any such offence it shall be lawful for the owner or occupier of the land, and, in case of the first of such offences, the owner or occupier of the land adjoining such road, etc., or the lord of the manor in which the land is situated or a gamekeeper or servant of any of such persons, or anyone assisting them, to arrest the offender, and if the latter assaults or offers violence with any gun, stick, club or other offensive weapon to anyone authorised to arrest him, he is guilty of an offence [*Imp.* 7 *years*].

By **section 9** of the Act, as similarly amended, it is an offence [*Imp.* 14 *years*] *for three or more persons* by night unlawfully to enter or be upon any land, open or enclosed, or any road, etc., for the purpose of taking or destroying game or rabbits, if *any*

---

[1] This Act extended the provisions of the Act of 1828 to unlawfully taking, etc., game on roads, highways, etc.
[2] Act of 1828, s. 12.
[3] *Ibid.* s. 13.

of such persons is *armed* with any gun, stick, club or other offensive weapon. To support a charge under this section it is not necessary that three persons, so armed, should actually enter or be upon the land; it is sufficient if some are on the land while others are giving them aid outside the land.[4] It is to be noted that all who are present may be convicted if any one is armed within the meaning of the section.[5]

A stick is not necessarily an offensive weapon, unless the jury finds that it was taken for the purpose of offence.[6] But anything —even a stone—may be an offensive weapon if it is capable of inflicting serious injury and was brought for that purpose.[7]

The prosecution for any offence punishable under the Act of 1828, as amended by the Act of 1844, must be commenced within twelve months from the offence.[8]

Poaching by day. The law relating to poaching by day is contained principally in the **Game Act 1831** as amended by the Wild Creatures and Forest Laws Act 1971. Any person who by day commits any trespass in pursuit of game, woodcock, snipe or rabbits is punishable on **summary conviction** [£20 *fine; or, if the trespass is by five or more persons, £50 fine*].[9] If the trespass is by five or more persons and any one of them is armed with a gun and uses violence or intimidation to prevent the approach of anyone entitled to require them to quit the land or give their names and addresses, a further offence is committed by all of them [£5 *fine*].[10] The expression " game " has the same meaning as in the 1828 Act, except that bustards are no longer game for the purposes of the 1831 Act.[11]

If the trespasser does not give his real name and address or wilfully continues or returns upon the land when required to quit and give his name and address by the person having the right to

---

4 R. v. *Passey* (1836) 7 C. & P. 282; R. v. *Lockett* (1836) 7 C. & P. 300; R. v. *Whittaker* (1848) 2 C. & K. 636.
5 R. v. *Goodfellow* (1845) 1 C. & K. 724. Unless, probably he was so armed without the knowledge of the rest: see R. v. *Southern* (1821) R. & R. 444.
6 R. v. *Palmer* (1831) 1 M. & Rob. 70; R. v. *Fry* (1837) 2 M. & Rob. 42; R. v. *Turner* (1849) 3 Cox 304.
7 R. v. *Grice* (1837) 7 C. & P. 803; R. v. *Sutton* (1877) 13 Cox 648.
8 Act of 1828, s. 4.
9 s. 30, as amended by the Protection of Birds Act 1954, Sched. 6; Game Laws (Amendment) Act 1960, s. 5 (1).
10 s. 31. See below for the persons entitled so to require.
11 See s. 2, as amended by the Protection of Birds Act 1954, Sched. 6.

the game, or by the occupier of the land, or by the servant of, or a person authorised by, either of them or by a police constable, he may be apprehended by the person so requiring, and he also commits an offence [£5 *fine*].[12]

By the **Poaching Prevention Act 1862** any constable or peace officer may in any highway, street or public place search any person whom he has good cause to suspect of coming from any land where he has been unlawfully in search of game, and of having in his possession any game unlawfully obtained, or any gun, part of a gun, cartridges, nets, snares, etc., used for taking game, and if any game, gun, etc., is found upon a person so searched the constable, etc., may apply for a summons, and if such person has obtained such game by unlawfully going on land in search of it, or has used such gun, etc., for unlawfully killing or taking game, or has been accessory thereto, he may be fined £50 and will also forfeit the game, gun, etc.[13]

In section 1 of the Act " game " is defined as including hares, pheasants, partridges, eggs of pheasants and partridges, woodcocks, snipes, rabbits, grouse, black or moor game, and eggs of grouse, black or moor game.

The following offences are created by **section 32** of and the **First Schedule** to the **Theft Act 1968**.

Deer and Fish. An offence of poaching is re-enacted in the **First Schedule** to the **Theft Act**,[14] which provides that a person who unlawfully takes or kills or attempts to kill (i) any deer in inclosed lands where deer are usually kept, or (ii) who unlawfully takes or destroys or attempts to take or destroy any fish in water which is private property, or in which there is any private right of fishery, commits an offence punishable on **summary conviction** in the case of a first offence with a fine of £50 and after previous conviction for the same offence with a fine of £100 and three months' imprisonment. Any person may arrest without warrant anyone who is or whom with reasonable cause he suspects to be

---

[12] s. 31, as amended by the Game Laws (Amendment) Act 1960, s. 1 (2). If the trespasser has not been asked his name and address, then the apprehension is unlawful. Nevertheless, if the trespasser uses more force than is necessary to avoid such unlawful apprehension, he may be convicted of assault: *R.* v. *Wilson* (1955) 39 Cr.App.R. 12.

[13] s. 2, as amended by the Game Laws (Amendment) Act 1960, s. 3 (2).

[14] For the reasons for its inclusion in the Theft Act 1968, see Cmnd. 2977, para. 53.

committing such offences. In the case of fish, a poacher commits the above offence only where he angles unlawfully between one hour after sunset and one hour before sunrise. During the day the offence committed is a separate one [on summary conviction: £20 *fine*].

SECTION 2. CONSERVATION OF GAME AND OTHER WILD LIFE

By **section 3** of the **Game Act 1831,** as amended by the **Game Act 1970,** it is an offence to kill or take game [15] or use any dog, gun or instrument for that purpose on a Sunday or Christmas Day [£5 *fine*] or to kill or take game during the close seasons set out in the section for the various kinds of game [16] [£5 *fine for each head of game*].[17]

By **section 24** the taking or destruction (except by a person having authority to shoot the game) of the eggs of any game bird or of any swan, wild duck, teal or widgeon or the possession of such eggs is an offence [25p *for each egg*].

By the **Hares Preservation Act 1892** it is an offence to sell or expose for sale between March and July hares and leverets unless imported from abroad. Under the **Ground Game Act 1880** the shooting of hares or rabbits between the expiration of the first hour after sunset and the commencement of the last hour before sunrise is forbidden.

The use of poison for killing game is prohibited by the **Game Act 1831, s. 3,** and for the killing of any animals or birds, other than vermin, by the **Protection of Animals Act 1911, s. 8,** and the **Protection of Animals (Amendment) Act 1927, s. 1.** If poison is used for invertebrates or vermin reasonable precautions must be taken to prevent injury to dogs, fowl, etc. However, poisonous gas may be used in rabbit holes.[18]

The use of any traps for killing or taking game birds is forbidden by the Protection of Birds Act 1954 (below). The use of any but approved traps for the killing or taking of any animals is forbidden by the **Pests Act 1954, s. 8,** and by **section 9** of that Act the use of a spring-trap for the killing or taking of hares or rabbits elsewhere than in a rabbit hole is also forbidden. It is also an

---

[15] See above, p. 420.
[16] There is no close season for hares under this Act.
[17] Penalty increased from £1 by the Game Act 1970.
[18] Prevention of Damage by Rabbits Act 1939, s. 4.

offence by **section 12** to use a rabbit infected with myxomatosis to spread the disease among uninfected rabbits.

The **Deer Act 1963** regulates the hunting of deer. The killing or taking of deer is forbidden at night or during close seasons [18a] or with traps or poisons or with certain kinds of weapons.

By **section 4** of the **Game Licences Act 1860** [19] it is an offence [£20 *fine*] to take or kill, or to assist in the taking or killing or to use any dog, gun or other instrument for the purpose of taking or killing any game (within the meaning of the 1831 Game Act), or any woodcock, snipe, rabbits or deer without a licence.[20] There are a number of exceptions. These include the hunting of hares, rabbits and deer by the owner of *enclosed* lands [21] or by someone with his permission; the coursing of hares with greyhounds or the hunting of hares with beagles or other hounds; the hunting of deer with hounds; the giving of assistance to a person who is duly licensed.[22] The **Game Act 1831,**[23] and the **Game Licences Act 1860,** also require that a person dealing wholesale or retail in game shall have a game dealer's licence and a further excise licence.

The legislation dealing with the licensing of guns is dealt with elsewhere.[24]

Turning now, briefly, to the **Protection of Birds Act 1954, section 1** of the Act prohibits the killing, injury or taking of any wild bird or the taking or destruction of the nest or eggs of any wild bird other than game birds. In respect of certain rare birds [25] the penalty is £25 fine and imprisonment for one month for the first offence, and £25 fine and imprisonment for three months for a second or subsequent offence. In respect of the other birds the penalty is a £5 fine. Certain wild birds and their eggs and nests (*e.g.* crows, magpies, sparrows, wood-pigeons) may be destroyed

---

[18a] See *e.g. Traill* v. *Buckingham* [1972] 1 W.L.R. 459, D.C. where it was held that it is no defence to a charge of shooting deer during the close season that it was damaging crops on land *adjacent* to that on which it was shot.

[19] As amended by the Birds Protection Act 1954, Sched. 6.

[20] In the case of game only, failure to have this licence may also be an offence under the 1831 Act. Licences may be obtained from most post offices.

[21] The Act distinguishes between enclosed land and moorland; farmland is enclosed land; *Jemmison* v. *Priddle* [1972] 1 Q.B. 489.

[22] See ss. 5, 6.

[23] As amended by the Game Act 1970.

[24] *Ante*, Chap. 21.

[25] Sched. 1 to the Act. S. 4 of the Protection of Birds Act 1967 makes it an offence wilfully to disturb this category of birds while they are nesting.

at any time of the year by the occupiers of land (not, therefore, everyone) or persons acting with their authority and certain other authorised persons. Certain other wild birds (*e.g.* snipe, wild duck, wild geese, woodcock) may be killed or taken outside the close seasons, unless pursuant to section 7 of the Protection of Birds Act 1967, during a period of severe weather, a special protection order has been made. The eggs of black-head gulls and common gulls may be taken for consumption by humans and poultry and lapwing eggs may be taken or destroyed before the fifteenth day of April in any year.

Section 5 [26] of the Act prohibits certain methods of killing any wild birds, including game birds. These methods include the use of traps, springs, snares, poison, gas, live or injured birds as decoys, a shot-gun of which the barrel has an internal diameter of more than one and three-quarter inches, artificial light. Again there are exceptions. In particular, cage-traps and nets may be used to take those wild birds which may be destroyed at any time of the year.

Section 6 restricts the sale of live and dead wild birds and their eggs.[27] **Section 8** prohibits the use of bird cages which are too small. Section 5 of the 1967 Act makes it an offence, subject to exceptions, to ring or mark wild birds.

Much of the Act may be varied by the Secretary of State, *e.g.* the lists of wild birds specified in the Schedules.

A brief reference should be made to the **Salmon and Freshwater Fisheries Act 1923,** as amended by subsequent legislation. This Act prohibits fishing for salmon, trout and freshwater fish other than freshwater fish which migrate to and from tidal waters and other than eel.[28] Fishing with lights, snares, spears, stones or other missiles, roe, explosives and poisons is forbidden. Fishing outside the close season is forbidden and the use of nets for fishing is closely regulated. It was held in the case of *Edwards* v. *Morgan* [29] that water bailiffs appointed under the Act when on

[26] As amended by the Protection of Birds Act 1967, s. 6.
[27] In the case of *Partridge* v. *Crittenden* [1968] 1 W.L.R. 1204 it was held by the Divisional Court that an advertisement in a " for sale " newspaper column " bramble finch cocks, bramble finch hens, 25s. each " was not an offer for sale contrary to s. 6 (1) of the Act, but an invitation to treat, although, on the facts of the case there was plainly a sale, and a possession for sale, both of which could have been charged. It is unfortunate that the courts tend to give the word " offer " its contractual meaning in interpreting statutes of this kind.
[28] For the meaning of " tidal waters," see *Ingram* v. *Percival* [1969] 1 Q.B. 548.
[29] [1967] Crim.L.R. 40.

patrol and not exercising one of the special authorities under the Act such as searching boats, examining nets, seizing fish, etc., were clearly deemed to be on duty as constables and did not have to produce their instruments of appointment before they could act by virtue of s. 67 (4), as they would have had to do if they been exercising one of those special authorities under the Act.

The Conservation of Seals Act 1970 regulates the killing of seals. **Section 1** prohibits, subject to certain exceptions,[30] the killing or taking of seals by the use of any poisonous substance, or the use for the killing, injuring or taking of seals of any firearm other than of a type prescribed by the Act. **Section 2** prescribes an annual close season for certain types of seal and makes it an offence to infringe that close season. Offences and attempts to commit offences are punishable on **summary conviction** [£50 *fine*] or in the case of a second or subsequent conviction [£100 *fine*]. Powers of search, arrest and seizure are conferred upon constables by section 4 and powers of forfeiture upon the courts by section 6.

[30] For statutory defences, see ss. 9 and 10.

PART III

OFFENCES AGAINST THE PERSON

CHAPTER 30

HOMICIDE

SECTION 1. INTRODUCTION

THREE offences fall to be considered in this chapter, all of which
are termed homicide:

  (i) murder;
  (ii) manslaughter;
  (iii) infanticide.

Causing death by dangerous driving is also homicide but this
offence will be dealt with separately.[1]

Since the Suicide Act 1961 it is no longer an offence for a person to attempt to commit suicide. It is, however, a crime to aid
or procure the suicide of another[2] and a person who kills another
in pursuance of a suicide pact is guilty of manslaughter.[3]

SECTION 2. ACTUS REUS OF HOMICIDE

The *actus reus* of all three types of homicide is traditionally described in the words of Sir Edward Coke[4] as being the unlawful
killing of any reasonable creature " in being " and under the
Queen's peace, the death following within a year and a day.

Unlawful killing. Although a person has the required *mens rea*
for either murder or manslaughter, it will not be homicide unless
the killing was unlawful. It is common to classify a killing which
is not unlawful as either justifiable homicide or excusable homicide.[5] The only important difference between the two disappeared
with the Forfeiture Act 1870, and it has therefore been felt more
satisfactory not to use the old classification here.

---

[1] *Ante*, p. 296.
[2] s. 2.
[3] *Post*, p. 439.
[4] 3 Inst. 47.
[5] Arch. para. 2550.

A killing is not unlawful in the following cases:

(1) where the lawful sentence of a competent court is being executed in a lawful manner by a person whose duty it is to carry out the sentence [6];

(2) where an officer of justice [7] is forcibly resisted in the lawful execution of a duty to arrest,[8] detain,[9] seize property [10] or make a search [11] as part of criminal or civil process, provided that he uses no more force than is reasonably necessary to protect himself and execute his duty [12];

(3) where a private person is aiding an officer of justice in the lawful execution of one of the duties enumerated in (2) above, provided he uses no more force than is reasonably necessary [13];

(4) where a private person is effecting a *lawful* arrest [14] of a person suspected of having committed a criminal act, provided he uses no more force than is reasonably necessary [15];

(5) where a person is preventing the commission of a crime provided that he uses no more force than is reasonably necessary [16];

---

[6] Arch. para. 2529.

[7] *e.g.* constable, court officer (*e.g.* a tipstaff or a county court bailiff), sheriff, J.P., or any person detailed by a court to execute a particular order.

[8] See *Southam* v. *Smout* [1964] 1 Q.B. 308, in which case it was held that where an officer of the county court enters a house by virtue of his warrant to execute civil process or a landlord enters under a legal right to levy a distress he may enter by the ordinary means of access by turning a handle, or lifting a latch, or pushing open a door which is shut but not locked and such an entry is lawful and is not a breaking in. Also, it was held that though an officer of the law enters a stranger's house to execute civil process at his peril, his entry is justified if the goods or the person sought are found in the stranger's house; *Morrish* v. *Murray* (1844) 13 M. & W. 52 applied.

[9] For powers of arrest and detention in criminal matters, see *post*, p. 552, and in civil matters, see *e.g.* Halsbury, Vol. 8, p. 20 *et seq.* (writs of attachment, orders of committal).

[10] See *Vaughan* v. *McKenzie* [1969] 1 Q.B. 557 in which case it was held that an officer executing civil process might not lawfully enter the dwelling-house of an execution debtor if the debtor physically resisted his entry, even if the door was unfastened, and that therefore, he was not acting in the execution of his duty when he was assaulted. *Broughton* v. *Wilkerson* (1880) 44 J.P. 781, D.C. and *Rossiter* v. *Conway* (1893) 58 J.P. 350, applied. *Southam* v. *Smout* (*supra*) considered.

[11] *Post*, p. 562.

[12] Arch. para. 2527, and below, n. 22.

[13] *Ibid.*

[14] For the powers of arrest, see *post*, p. 555.

[15] Arch. para. 2527, and below, n. 22. Criminal Law Act 1967, s. 3.

[16] Criminal Law Act 1967, s. 3 (1). At common law there were elaborate rules for determining whether a killing in self-defence, in defence of others and in defence of property was lawful. Since the rules depended in part on the distinction between felony and misdemeanour, they have now been abolished: *ibid*. s. 3 (2). For the defence of mistake, see *R.* v. *Rose* (1884) 15 Cox 540.

(6) where a person is preventing civil trespass to land or goods, provided that the trespasser has first refused to comply with a request to cease trespassing and has been given a reasonable time to comply with the request and provided that no more force is used than is reasonably necessary[17];

(7) where a person accidentally kills another in circumstances where some harm is foreseen, but the harm is not unlawful because:

  (i) the victim was being lawfully chastised[18]; or

  (ii) the victim was being operated on lawfully[19]; or

  (iii) the harm was inflicted during the course of a game and by voluntarily playing the game the victim consented to, and by law was able to consent to, the infliction of that kind of harm[20]; or

  (iv) the victim consented to, and by law was able to consent to, the infliction of the harm.[21]

Reasonable force.[22] To determine whether force is reasonable all the circumstances must be examined. So in the case of (5) (prevention of crime) an intentional killing might be justified in an extreme case, whereas in the case of a very minor offence it might not be reasonable to use the slightest force.

The use of force would not be regarded as reasonable if there were alternative practicable methods of preventing the wrong, e.g. asking the wrongdoer to desist.

"Any person set by his master to watch a garden or yard, is not at all justified in shooting at or injuring in any way, persons who may come into those premises, even in the night; and if he saw them going into his master's hen roost, he would still not be justified in shooting them. He ought *first* to go

---

17 Salmond, p. 71; Russell, pp. 490–491. But see Arch. para. 2512.
18 To be lawful the force must be moderate (Arch. para. 2509) and the person must be entitled to chastise, e.g. parent, teacher or other person having control over a child: Children and Young Persons Act 1933, s. 1 (7); *Cleary* v. *Booth* [1893] 1 Q.B. 465.
19 Certain operations are unlawful, *post*, p. 448. See also manslaughter by criminal negligence, *post*, p. 444.
20 See *R.* v. *Brashaw* (1878) 14 Cox 83; Arch. para. 2495, and *post*, p. 455.
21 *Post*, p. 455.
22 See p. 439, *post*, as to reasonable force in relation to self-defence. If the force is more than is reasonable in the circumstances, the justification or excuse fails and the offender is liable for the offence disclosed by the evidence.

and see if he could not take measures for their apprehension." [23]

Killing. It is essential, of course, that the accused must have killed or been a party to the killing of the deceased. The difficult problems of causation and liability for omissions have already been dealt with,[24] and it will be noted that the majority of cases are concerned with homicide.

Any reasonable creature in being. The term " reasonable creature " means any human being. An infant is " in being " only when it is both completely extruded from its mother's body and in a living state.[25] It will be homicide if an infant, who is born alive, dies from injuries inflicted before or during birth or as a result of premature birth effected by acts which cause it to be born before it is capable of maintaining an independent existence.[26] Although a person who inflicts injuries which prevent a child from being born alive is not guilty of homicide, he may be guilty of the offence of child destruction.[27]

Of a person under the Queen's peace. This requirement is commonly stated to exclude only an alien enemy killed in the actual heat and exercise of war and, possibly, also a rebel killed in the actual practice of rebellion.[28]

The death following within a year and a day. Death must occur within a year and a day of the injury; the period to include the day of the injury.[29]

The absence of a body. The prosecution must prove the fact of death, like other facts, beyond a reasonable doubt. It is not necessary that a body or any part of the body alleged to be killed

---

[23] *R. v. Scully* (1824) 1 C. & P. 319, italics added.
[24] *Ante,* respectively p. 21 and p. 17.
[25] Arch. para. 2476. There does not have to be severance of the umbilical cord: *R. v. Reeves* (1839) 9 C. & P. 25. A child is in a living state when it is " breathing and living by reason of breathing through its own lungs alone, without deriving any of its living or power of living by or through any connection with its mother ": *R. v. Handley* (1874) 13 Cox 79 at p. 81.
[26] *R. v. West* (1848) 2 C. & K. 784.
[27] *Post,* p. 451.
[28] Arch. para. 2477. For the *jurisdictional* limits on the competence of an English court to try a person accused of homicide, see *post,* p. 691.
[29] *R. v. Dyson* [1908] 2 K.B. 454.

should be discovered,[30] the fact of death may be proved by circumstantial evidence.

SECTION 3. MENS REA OF MURDER

The requisite mental element of murder, or " malice aforethought " as it used to be called, is satisfied where it is proved that the accused intended to cause the death of, or grievous bodily harm to,[31] any person, whether such person is the person actually killed or not.[32] If this mental element is present, and the *actus reus* of homicide is proved, then the offence will be murder, unless the accused was insane, suffering from diminished responsibility, acting under grave and sudden provocation, or in pursuance of a suicide pact, or unless, in the case of a mother, the offence amounts only to infanticide.

Grievous bodily harm. Although it is clear that if the accused foresaw the the death of the victim he will have satisfied the mental requirement of murder, the sufficiency of foresight of grievous bodily harm has been criticised [33] and has led to difficulties of definition. It is clear, however, on the authorities that a mere foresight of grievous bodily harm is sufficient.[34] In *Director of Public Prosecutions* v. *Smith* [35] Viscount Kilmuir defined " grievous bodily harm " [36] as " really serious harm " although it need not necessarily be likely to kill.[37]

---

30 *R.* v. *Onufrejczyk* [1955] 1 Q.B. 388.
31 *R.* v. *Vickers* [1957] 2 Q.B. 664 at p. 670; see also *R.* v. *Ward* [1956] 1 Q.B. 351 and *D.P.P.* v. *Smith* [1961] A.C. 290.
32 *R.* v. *Gross* (1913) 23 Cox 455; Arch. paras. 2516, 2517. In *D.P.P.* v. *Smith* (*supra*) the House of Lords held that the mental element of murder was present where (*a*) the accused was " unlawfully " and voluntarily doing something to someone, and (*b*) the ordinary responsible man would, in all the circumstances of the case, have contemplated grievous bodily harm as the natural and probable result; it being immaterial that the accused did not himself foresee the likelihood of death or grievous bodily harm: *ibid.* at p. 327. This case was heavily criticised, and expressly and forcibly disapproved of by the High Court of Australia in *Parker* v. *The Queen* noted in [1963] Crim.L.R. 675. Following a report entitled " Imputed Intent " by the Law Commissioners, *Smith's* case was overturned by the Criminal Justice Act 1967, s. 8, *q.v.* p. 52, *ante.*
33 Law Commission, Imputed Intent, H.M.S.O. 1967.
34 See cases cited *supra*, n. 31.
35 [1961] A.C. 290.
36 For the purposes of ss. 18 and 20 of the Offences Against the Person Act 1861.
37 Viscount Kilmuir's definition was followed in *R.* v. *Metharam* (1961) 45 Cr.App.R. 304.

The test of the accused's intention is the subjective one introduced by the Criminal Justice Act 1967, s. 8.[38]

Insanity. This topic has already been dealt with separately.[39]

Diminished responsibility. Although a person, who has killed
or was a party to the killing of another, may have the required
common law *mens rea* for murder, it will be a good defence, under
section 2 of the **Homicide Act 1957**, to a charge of murder if that
person was, at the time of the killing, suffering from diminished
responsibility, that is:

> "was suffering from such abnormality of mind (whether
> arising from a condition of arrested or retarded development
> of mind or any inherent causes or induced by disease or
> injury) as substantially impaired his mental responsibility for
> his acts and omissions in doing or being a party to the
> killing." [40]

This defence is only available to an accused person charged with
murder and has the effect, if established, of reducing the offence to
manslaughter.[41] It is for the defence to prove diminished responsibility[42] but on the balance of probability and not beyond a
reasonable doubt.[43] The court will not accept a plea of guilty of
manslaughter on the grounds of diminished responsibility, but will
require the issue, as in cases of insanity, to be left to the jury.[44]

Whether or not the accused was suffering from " such abnormality of mind . . . as substantially impaired his mental responsibility " is a question of fact for the jury[45] and " a proper
explanation of the terms of the section as interpreted in *R. v.*

---

[38] *R.* v. *Wallett* [1968] 2 Q.B. 367.
[39] *Ante*, p. 88.
[40] s. 2 (1).
[41] s. 2 (3).
[42] s. 2 (2).
[43] *R.* v. *Dunbar* [1958] 1 Q.B. 1.
[44] *R.* v. *Matheson* [1958] 1 W.L.R. 474 at pp. 479–480.
[45] *R.* v. *Byrne* [1960] 2 Q.B. 396 at pp. 403, 404; *R.* v. *Jennion* [1962] 1 W.L.R.
317 at p. 321. In *R.* v. *Byrne* it was said, at pp. 403–404, that the jury should
approach the questions " in a broad common-sense way " and should take
into account all the evidence and not only the medical evidence, which, subject
to one exception, they are not bound to accept; and see to the same effect
R. v. *Simcox* [1964] Crim.L.R. 402. The exception is expert evidence on the
cause of the abnormality. The jury's verdict may however be set aside if it
is not supported by the evidence: *R.* v. *Matheson* [1958] 1 W.L.R. 474.

Byrne [46] ought to be put before them." [47] In that case the terms were explained in the following manner. "Abnormality of mind" was said to mean "a state of mind so different from that of ordinary human beings [of the accused's racial type [48]] that the reasonable man would term it abnormal." The accused's "perception of physical acts and matters" and "ability to form a rational judgment as to whether an act is right or wrong" were in this regard material. "The expression 'mental responsibility for his acts' points to a consideration of the extent to which the accused's mind is answerable for his physical acts which must include a consideration of the extent of his ability to exercise will power to control his physical acts." [49]

The defence must prove that the abnormality of mind resulted from at least one of the causes set out in section 2 (1).[50] The Court of Criminal Appeal said in *R. v. Di Duca* [51] that it was doubtful whether the transient effect of alcohol, even if it was toxic, could amount to an injury affecting the mind.[52] In a later case the Court of Criminal Appeal also declined to come to any decision as to whether a person could successfully plead diminished responsibility if, at the time of the killing, he suffered from a combination of inherent abnormality of mind and drink.[53]

When on a trial for murder the accused contends that he was suffering from diminished responsibility, the prosecution may bring evidence to show that the accused was in fact insane.[54]

---

[46] [1960] 2 Q.B. 396.

[47] *R. v. Terry* [1961] 2 Q.B. 314 at p. 322. The explanation in *R. v. Byrne* was also accepted by the Privy Council as " authoritative and correct " in *Rose v. R.* [1961] A.C. 496 at p. 507.

[48] *R. v. King* [1965] 1 Q.B. 443; [1964] Crim.L.R. 133. The accused, a native of Uganda, was charged with the murder of four people. A doctor called on his behalf said that Africans were more likely to kill when provoked than other races. McNair J. said that if his mental condition was not peculiar to him but of a kind to be expected from his racial type, then it was not abnormality. The summing-up of the learned judge on this point was said to be entirely correct by the Court of Criminal Appeal [1965] 1 Q.B. 443 at p. 454.

[49] *R. v. Byrne* [1960] 2 Q.B. 396 at p. 403.

[50] *R. v. King* [1965] 1 Q.B. 443; [1964] Crim.L.R. 133.

[51] (1959) 43 Cr.App.R. 167 at p. 173.

[52] The summing-up to the jury by Donovan J. in *R. v. Dowdall, The Times*, January 22, 1960, and a number of Scottish authorities support this proposition; see [1962] Crim.L.R. 838.

[53] *R. v. Clarke and King* [1962] Crim.L.R. 836; see also *R. v. Dowdall, The Times*, January 22, 1960; *cf. Att.-Gen. for Northern Ireland v. Gallagher* [1963] A.C. 349, *ante*, pp. 34, 94–96.

[54] Criminal Procedure (Insanity) Act 1964, s. 6.

Provocation. The fact that the accused was acting under what amounts in law to provocation when he killed or was a party to the killing operates, like diminished responsibility, to reduce to manslaughter what would otherwise be murder.[55] " Provocation in law consists mainly of three elements—the act of provocation, the loss of self-control, both actual and reasonable, and the retaliation proportionate to the provocation." [55a] Unlike diminished responsibility the burden is on the prosecution to eliminate provocation,[56] so that if there is any doubt as to whether or not there was sufficient provocation, the jury must not convict the accused of murder.[57] Like diminished responsibility the defence of provocation applies solely to a charge of murder.[58]

Where the defence of provocation is in issue, the judge must decide whether " the case is one in which the view might fairly be taken . . . that the accused was in fact acting under the stress of . . . provocation," [59] so that he was temporarily deprived of the power of self-control, as a result of which he committed the unlawful act which caused death.[60] If the evidence can support the view that there was provocation, then the issue as to whether or not the accused was acting under provocation should be left to the jury.[61] In deciding this, account should be taken of any evidence which suggests, *inter alia*, that:

> (i) the fatal blow was not " really due to a sudden unpremeditated gust of passion " but, having regard to the type of weapon used and the nature of the blow, was the result of " preparation and malicious premeditation " [62];

---

[55] *Att.-Gen. for Ceylon* v. *Kumarasinghege Don Juan Perera* [1953] A.C. 200 at p. 206 (P.C.); *Lee Chun-Chuen* v. *R.* [1963] A.C. 220 at pp. 227–228 (P.C.); *contra* a dictum by Viscount Simon in *Holmes* v. *D.P.P.* [1946] A.C. 588 at p. 598. See also *R.* v. *Martindale* [1966] 1 W.L.R. 1564.

[55a] *Lee Chun-Chuen* v. *The Queen* [1963] A.C. 220, *per* Lord Devlin at p. 231.

[56] *R.* v. *Ives* [1970] 1 Q.B. 208. And see *ante*, p. 49.

[57] *R.* v. *McPherson* (1957) 41 Cr.App.R. 213.

[58] *R.* v. *Cunningham* [1959] 1 Q.B. 288. *Cf. R.* v. *Bruzas* [1972] Crim.L.R. 367.

[59] *Holmes* v. *D.P.P.* [1946] A.C. 588 at p. 597. This is merely an example of the judge's task to decide whether on the available evidence an issue should be left to the jury.

[60] *Mancini* v. *D.P.P.* [1942] A.C. 1 at p. 9.

[61] *Holmes* v. *D.P.P.* [1946] A.C. 588 at p. 597.

[62] *Ng Yiu-Nam* v. *R.* [1963] Crim.L.R. 850 at p. 851 (Supreme Court of Hongkong); and see also *R.* v. *Thomas* (1837) 7 C. & P. 817; but see *R.* v. *Fantle* [1959] Crim.L.R. 584, and comment thereon in Elliott, " Interpretation of the Homicide Act " [1960] Crim.L.R. at pp. 10–11.

(ii) the accused had cooled down after the alleged act of provocation and, activated possibly by a desire for revenge,[63] " had shown thought, contrivance and design . . . for the exercise of contrivance and design denoted rather the presence of judgment and reason, than of violent and ungovernable passion." [64]

It is, however, not sufficient merely to show that the accused was *himself* provoked. There is a much-criticised rule that it will be murder and not manslaughter if, in the estimation of the jury, a reasonable man would not have lost his self-control, or, if having lost it, he would have regained it by the time of the killing.[65] When provocation is relied on, the matter is governed by **section 3** of the **Homicide Act 1957**:

" Where on a charge of murder there is evidence on which the jury can find that the person charged was provoked (whether by things done or by things said or by both together) to lose his self-control, the question whether the provocation was enough to make a reasonable man do as he did shall be left to be determined by the jury; and in determining that question the jury shall take into account everything both done and said according to the effect which, in their opinion, it would have on a reasonable man." [66]

In considering what the reaction of the accused was, **section 8 of the Criminal Justice Act 1967** requires the jury to consider what the intention of the accused was when he acted as he did.[67]

In deciding whether " the provocation was enough to make a reasonable man do as he did " the jury should " consider [*inter alia*] whether a sufficient interval has elapsed since the provocation to allow a reasonable man time to cool." [68]

[63] *R.* v. *Thomas* (1837) 7 C. & P. 817 at p. 819; and see *R.* v. *Lynch* (1832) 5 C. & P. 324.

[64] *R.* v. *Hayward* (1833) 6 C. & P. 157 at p. 159.

[65] *Mancini* v. *D.P.P.* [1942] A.C. 1 at p. 9; but *cf. R.* v. *Southgate* [1963] Crim.L.R. 570.

[66] This section remedied what were thought to be defects in the common law doctrine of provocation, as to which see *Holmes* v. *D.P.P.* [1946] A.C. 588.

[67] *R.* v. *Ives* [1970] 1 Q.B. 208 at 216.

[68] *Mancini* v. *D.P.P.* [1942] A.C. 1 at p. 9. " The presence of cooling time certainly seems to be of no more than evidentiary significance after the Homicide Act, 1957 ": Cross and Jones, p. 146. Prior to that Act a judge could direct a jury that it was not open to them on the evidence to find a verdict of manslaughter on the grounds of provocation, because a reasonable

The reasonable man, to whose powers of endurance in the face of provocation the jury are referred, is not blessed with any " *peculiar* physical qualities," [69] nor is he an " unusually excitable or pugnacious individual," [70] nor is he " temporarily made excitable or pugnacious by self-induced intoxication." [71] If, because of a peculiar characteristic, the alleged provocation had caused the accused to kill but it would not have caused a reasonable man, not endowed with this characteristic, to kill, it will be murder and not manslaughter. So in *Bedder* v. *Director of Public Prosecutions* [72] the accused, who was sexually impotent and was attempting unsuccessfully to have intercourse with a prostitute, had killed her because she jeered at his incapacity and subsequently struck him. He pleaded provocation. The House of Lords upheld his conviction for murder, on the grounds that the test to be applied is that of the effect of the provocation on the reasonable man and the reasonable man is not invested with any of the peculiar physical characteristics of the accused. So in *R.* v. *McCarthy* [73] the accused, who had had a considerable amount of drink, had killed a man by beating his head on the roadway. It was alleged by the defence that the dead man had indecently assaulted him and had suggested they commit sodomy and that this had caused the accused to lose his temper and attack the deceased. The Court of Criminal Appeal dismissed his appeal against conviction for murder. Lord Goddard C.J., reading the judgment of the court, said [74] that " drunkenness which may lead a man to attack another in a manner which no reasonable sober man would do cannot be pleaded as an excuse reducing the crime to manslaughter if death results."

In *R.* v. *Brown* [75] the Court of Appeal (Criminal Division) said that " when considering whether the provocation was enough to

man would not have been so provoked: see *Holmes* v. *D.P.P.* [1946] A.C. 588. If, therefore, a judge decided that there had been time for cooling and a reasonable man would not have acted as the accused had done, he could withdraw the issue from the jury; but see *R.* v. *Fisher* (1837) 8 C. & P. 182, where the jury appear to have disregarded the judge's ruling. After the Act, the judge must leave the question as to the effect of the provocation on a reasonable man entirely to the jury.

[69] *Bedder* v. *D.P.P.* [1954] 1 W.L.R. 1119 at p. 1122, italics added.
[70] *Mancini* v. *D.P.P.* [1942] A.C. 1 at p. 9; approving *R.* v. *Lesbini* [1914] 3 K.B. 1116.
[71] *R.* v. *McCarthy* [1954] 2 Q.B. 105 at p. 112.
[72] [1954] 1 W.L.R. 1119.
[73] [1954] 2 Q.B. 105.
[74] At p. 112.
[75] [1972] 2 Q.B. 229.

make a reasonable man do as the accused did, it is relevant for a jury to compare the words or acts or both of these things which are put forward as provocation with the nature of the act committed by the accused. It may be for instance that the jury might find that the accused's act was so disproportionate to the provocation alleged that no reasonable man would have so acted."* The court said that a jury should be instructed to consider the relationship of the accused's acts to the provocation when asking themselves the question " Was it enough to make a reasonable man do as he did? " [76-78]

Self-defence. Self-defence is an answer to a charge of murder just as it is to one of assault, and basically the same principles apply.[79] No more force must be used than is reasonably necessary.[80] Where the force used in defence exceeds what is reasonably necessary in the circumstances, the justification of self-defence fails and is eliminated from the case. The jury will then have to consider whether on the facts of the case, the actions of the accused amount to murder or manslaughter. There is no general rule of law that homicide resulting from the use of excessive force in self-defence amounts to manslaughter only.[81]

Suicide pacts. Although a person has the requisite common law *mens rea* for murder, it will not be murder but manslaughter if he killed or was a party to a killing in pursuance of a suicide pact. Under the **Homicide Act 1957, s. 4,** as amended by the **Suicide Act 1961, Sched. 2**:

> " (1) It shall be manslaughter, and shall not be murder, for a person acting in pursuance of a suicide pact between him and another to kill the other or be a party to the other . . . being killed by a third person.

> " (2) Where it is shown that a person charged with the murder of another killed the other or was a party to his . . .

[76-78] The precise words of Viscount Simon L.C. in *Mancini* v. *Director of Public Prosecutions* [1942] A.C. 1 at p. 9 that " the mode of resentment must bear a reasonable relationship to the provocation " should be avoided by judges, unless it is made clear that it is not a rule of law which the jury have to follow: *Phillips* v. *The Queen* [1969] 2 A.C. 130, P.C., *per* Lord Diplock at p. 137; *R.* v. *Brown* [1972] 2 Q.B. 229 at p. 234.

[79] See p. 455, *post.*

[80] Criminal Law Act, 1967, s. 3 (1).

[81] *Palmer* v. *The Queen* [1971] A.C. 814; *R.* v. *McInnes* [1971] 1 W.L.R. 1600.

being killed, it shall be for the defence to prove that the person
charged was acting in pursuance of a suicide pact between him
and the other.

" (3) For the purposes of this section ' suicide pact ' means
a common agreement between two or more persons having for
its object the death of all of them, whether or not each is to
take his own life, but nothing done by a person who enters
into a suicide pact shall be treated as done by him in pursuance
of the pact unless it is done while he has the settled intention
of dying in pursuance of the pact."

Irresistible impulse.   In the absence of insanity or diminished
responsibility, the fact that the accused acted under an irresistible
impulse is no defence to a charge of murder.[82]   But where it is
shown that the accused is suffering from a disease of which one of
the symptoms is such an impulse, then that may be evidence that
he was insane within the M'Naghten Rules.[83]

Thabo Meli's case.   In *Thabo Meli* v. *The Queen* [84] the accused
struck the deceased over the head with intent to kill him.   Thinking
that they had succeeded in killing him they rolled over a small
cliff what they thought was his corpse in order to make the death
appear to be an accident.   Medical evidence showed that he was
alive at the moment he was rolled over the cliff and that he died
later of exposure.   The Privy Council affirmed their conviction for
murder.   Although, admittedly, the first act, which was accompanied by *mens rea*, was not the cause of death and the second
act, which caused the death, was not accompanied by *mens rea*,
the Privy Council felt it impossible to divide up " what was really
one transaction in this way " [85] so that it would not be murder.
Although it is possible to envisage difficulties arising when it is
necessary to decide whether or not the accused's acts constituted
one transaction, the decision seems right.   More difficulty arises
when the accused only foresaw grievous bodily harm and not death

[82] *R.* v. *King* [1965] 1 Q.B. 443; [1964] Crim.L.R. 133; and see further *ante,*
Chap. 2.
[83] *Att.-Gen. for South Australia* v. *Brown* [1960] A.C. 432 at pp. 449–450.
[84] [1954] 1 W.L.R. 228.
[85] *Ibid.* at p. 230.

as resulting from his acts but thought, mistakenly, that he had killed the victim. In *R.* v. *Church* [86] the Court of Criminal Appeal apparently thought that it would still be murder.

SECTION 4. PUNISHMENT FOR MURDER

Where an accused person is found guilty of murder he must be sentenced to imprisonment for life. **Section 1** of the **Murder (Abolition of Death Penalty) Act 1965** provides that on sentencing a person convicted of murder to imprisonment for life, a court may at the same time declare the period which it recommends to the Secretary of State as the minimum period which in its view should elapse before he is released on licence.[87] In addition, special provisions have been made for the release on licence of such persons.[88]

SECTION 5. MANSLAUGHTER

Manslaughter is traditionally classified as either voluntary or involuntary manslaughter. Voluntary manslaughter consists of those killings which would have been murder but are only manslaughter because the accused either:

(i) was suffering from diminished responsibility,[89] or

(ii) was acting under provocation,[90] or

(iii) killed or was a party to the killing in pursuance of a suicide pact.[91]

What constitutes involuntary manslaughter is still not entirely clear, and this topic must be approached with caution. As Widgery L.J. said in *R.* v. *Lipman* [92]:

" Manslaughter remains a most difficult offence to define because it arises in so many different ways and, as the mental

---

[86] [1966] 1 Q.B. 59; and see the note thereon in [1965] Crim.L.R. 303.
[87] No right of appeal exists against such a recommendation: *R.* v. *Aitken* [1966] 1 W.L.R. 1076.
[88] *Post*, p. 861.
[89] *Ante*, p. 434.
[90] *Ante*, pp. 437–439.
[91] *Ante*, p. 394.
[92] [1970] 1 Q.B. 152 at p. 159.

element (if any) required to establish it varies so widely, any general reference to *mens rea* is apt to mislead."

If the *actus reus* of homicide is proved, then it will apparently be manslaughter if, it not being murder:

   (i) the accused was intentionally or recklessly either threatening harm to or actually harming the deceased [93] *and* this threat of harm or harm:

      (a) caused the deceased's death,

      (b) constituted a criminal offence, and, in the case of threats,

      (c) was " such as all sober and reasonable people would inevitably recognise must subject the other person to, at least, the risk of some harm resulting therefrom, albeit not serious harm " [94] or

   (ii) the death of the deceased resulted from the accused's " criminal negligence."

The courts have traditionally drawn a distinction between these two different kinds of involuntary manslaughter that is death caused by an unlawful act and death caused by criminal negligence. In *R*. v. *Larkin* [95] Humphreys J. said:

" Perhaps it is as well once more to state the proposition of law which has been stated by judges for generations, and, so far as we are aware, never disputed or doubted. If a person is engaged in doing a lawful act, and in the course of doing that lawful act behaves so negligently as to cause the death of some other person, then . . . it will not amount to manslaughter unless the negligence is of a very high degree. . . . That is the law where the act is lawful. Where the act which a person is engaged in performing is unlawful, then if at the same time it is a dangerous act, that is, an act which is likely to injure another person, and quite inadvertently the doer of the act causes the death of that other person by that act, then he is guilty of manslaughter."

---

[93] Or another person; see *ante*, p. 48, and *R*. v. *Larkin* (1942) 29 Cr.App.R. 18 (below).

[94] *R*. v. *Church* [1966] 1 Q.B. 59 at p. 60. *Quaere* whether the objective test still applies in view of s. 8 of the Criminal Justice Act 1967, and see *R*. v. *Lipman* [1970] 1 Q.B. 152 at p. 158.

[95] (1942) 29 Cr.App.R. 18 at p. 23.

An Unlawful Act causing Death

Threats of harm. In *R.* v. *Larkin* [96] the deceased woman had died as a result of her throat having been cut by a razor held by the accused. The accused admitted that he was flourishing the razor for the purpose of threatening another person but said in evidence that the woman had drunkenly blundered against it. The trial judge directed the jury that even if they accepted the accused's evidence, it would still be manslaughter. It was held by the Court of Criminal Appeal, affirming his conviction for manslaughter, that the act of flourishing the razor in a threatening manner was unlawful [97] and was at the same time likely to injure another person, and it was therefore manslaughter. Similarly it has been held [98] to be manslaughter where the accused inadvertently killed a person while unlawfully threatening him with a gun.

Actual harm. It is still not entirely clear what kind of unlawful harm is sufficient. It is clear that the act must be " unlawful " in the criminal sense of that word [99] and not merely from the angle of civil liabilities.[1] It would seem that the harm must have been intentionally or recklessly inflicted.[2] In *R.* v. *Lamb* [3] the accused, in jest, with no intention of doing any harm, pointed a revolver at the deceased, his best friend. The revolver had two bullets in the chambers, but neither bullet was in the chamber opposite the barrel. The revolver was an old-fashioned one, and, although the accused was unaware of this, it rotated clockwise each time the trigger was pulled, thus placing the fatal bullet in the chamber opposite the barrel where it was struck by the firing pin. It was held in the Court of Appeal Criminal Division, that as regards this class of manslaughter, there was no evidence of any unlawful act, in the absence of the intent requisite for an assault. In *Andrews* v. *Director of Public Prosecutions* [4] the House of Lords held that to kill a person while driving recklessly or at a speed or in a manner which was dangerous to the public (contrary to what was then

---

[96] (1942) 29 Cr.App.R. 18.

[97] The crime of assault ; *post*, p. 453.

[98] *Kwaku-Mensah* v. *The King* [1946] A.C. 83 at p. 91 and *R.* v. *Cashmore* [1959] Crim.L.R. 850.

[99] *R.* v. *Lamb* [1967] 2 Q.B. 981 at p. 988.

[1] *Ibid.*; and see *R.* v. *Franklin* (1883) 15 Cox C.C. 163.

[2] Glanville Williams, " Constructive Manslaughter " [1957] Crim.L.R. at p. 300.

[3] [1967] 2 Q.B. 981.

[4] [1937] A.C. 576.

section 11 of the Road Traffic Act 1930 [5]) was not manslaughter in the absence of " criminal negligence ": in other words, this is not the kind of unlawful act which would *ex necessitate* lead to conviction for manslaughter if someone was killed.

Even though it may not be clear what kind of unlawful harm does *ex necessitate* lead to a conviction for manslaughter in such circumstances, it seems clear, at least, that if death results from a criminal abortion, it is manslaughter. So in *R.* v. *Buck and Buck* [6] the Court of Criminal Appeal, following *R.* v. *Lumley,* [7] held that it is manslaughter if death results from a criminal abortion, " an offence which involves a considerable risk to the person, no matter with what care it may be committed." [8]

No specific or ulterior intent is necessary to support a conviction for manslaughter based on a killing in the course of an unlawful act. [9] In this way it differs from manslaughter by neglect.

Criminal Negligence

The best-known definition of criminal negligence is probably that in *R.* v. *Bateman.* [10] In that case a doctor had been convicted of the manslaughter of a woman whose confinement he had attended. On his appeal his conviction was quashed. Lord Hewart C.J. said [11]:

> " To support an indictment for manslaughter the prosecution must prove the matters necessary to establish civil liability (except pecuniary loss), and, *in addition*, must satisfy the jury that the negligence or incompetence of the accused went beyond a mere matter of compensation and showed such disregard for the life and safety of others as to amount to a crime against the state and conduct deserving punishment."

In *Andrews* v. *D.P.P.* [12] Lord Atkin doubted [13] whether the expressions used by Lord Hewart C.J. were, or were intended to be,

---

[5] Now s. 2 of the Road Traffic Act 1972.
[6] (1960) 44 Cr.App.R. 213.
[7] (1912) 76 J.P. 208.
[8] (1960) 44 Cr.App.R. 213 at pp. 219–220.
[9] See generally *R.* v. *Lipman* [1970] 1 Q.B. 152.
[10] (1925) 19 Cr.App.R. 8.
[11] At p. 13, italics added.
[12] [1937] A.C. 576.
[13] At p. 583.

a precise definition, but he said [14] that " the substance of the judgment is most valuable, and in my opinion is correct."

To define criminal negligence the word " reckless " is sometimes used.[15] But this is only confusing because " reckless," as we have seen,[16] is used to denote the state of mind of a person who foresees the likelihood of a certain consequence resulting from his act but either is indifferent as to whether it occurs or not or does not wish it to occur. Whereas if a man's conduct does not measure up to the standard of a reasonable man and causes harm which he did not foresee, then as we have also seen,[17] he is said to have been negligent.[18]

It should be noted that " cases of manslaughter in driving motor-cars are but instances of a general rule applicable to all charges of homicide by negligence." [19] However, the reluctance of juries to convict a driver of manslaughter led to the creation in 1956 of a new offence of causing death by dangerous driving. This has been examined above.[20] The creation of this offence has not affected the power of the court to convict a driver of manslaughter, but prosecutions for manslaughter of this kind are now rare.

Accessories

A person can be convicted as an accomplice to an involuntary manslaughter caused by an unlawful and dangerous act even though not present at the time of the act.[21]

Punishment and Procedure

Upon an indictment for murder, if the jury acquit the accused, then, if the evidence so warrants, they may return a verdict of manslaughter.[22]

The maximum punishment for manslaughter is imprisonment for life.[23]

[14] *Ibid.*
[15] *e.g.* in *Andrews* v. *D.P.P.* [1937] A.C. 576 at p. 583; *R.* v. *Bonnyman* (1942) 28 Cr.App.R. 131 at p. 135; *R.* v. *Church* [1966] 1 Q.B. 59 at p. 68.
[16] *Ante*, p. 35.   [17] *Ante*, p. 46.
[18] If the courts mean reckless in its usual sense, then (likewise) the word " negligence " is completely out of place; see further Russell, p. 592 *et seq.*
[19] *Andrews* v. *D.P.P.* [1937] A.C. 576 at p. 583.
[20] *Ante*, p. 296.
[21] *R.* v. *Creamer* [1966] 1 Q.B. 72.
[22] Criminal Law Act 1967, s. 6 (1).
[23] Offences against the Person Act 1861, s. 5, as amended by the Criminal Justice Act 1948, s. 1 and Sched. 10.

Section 6.   Attempts to Commit Murder

Any attempt to commit murder is punishable with life imprisonment.[24]   In order to be convicted of attempted murder, the accused must have intended to kill.   It is not sufficient that he merely intended to cause grievous bodily harm.[25]

Section 7.   Conspiracy, Incitement and Threats to Murder

By **section 4** of the **Offences against the Person Act 1861**, it is an offence [*Imp.* 10 *years*] to conspire [26] to murder any person or to solicit, encourage, persuade or endeavour to persuade, or to propose to anyone to murder any person,[27] whether he be a British subject or not, and whether he be in the British dominions or not.   By **section 16** of the Act, it is an offence [*Imp. life*] for any person maliciously to send, deliver, utter, or directly or indirectly cause to be received, knowing the contents thereof, any letter or writing threatening to kill or murder any person.

Section 8.   Infanticide

Like diminished responsibility, the effect of the **Infanticide Act 1938** is to reduce what would otherwise be murder to a lesser offence, in this case infanticide.

By **section 1** of that Act, it has been provided (1) that where a woman by any wilful act or omission causes the death of her child, being a child under the age of twelve months, in circumstances which, but for the Act, would have amounted to murder, but, at the time of such act or omission, the balance of her mind was disturbed by reason of her not having fully recovered from the effect of giving birth to the child, or by reason of the effect of lactation consequent upon the birth of the child, she shall be guilty of the offence of infanticide and *punishable as for manslaughter*;

---

[24] Criminal Law Act 1967, s. 7 (2).   In practice attempted manslaughter is not an offence known to the law.   Cf. *R.* v. *Bruzas* [1972] Crim.L.R. 367.

[25] *R.* v. *Whybrow* (1951) 35 Cr.App.R. 141.

[26] As to conspiracy, see *ante*, p. 63.

[27] Where A solicited B, who was at the time pregnant, to murder her child at birth and subsequently the child was born alive, it was held that there was a soliciting to murder " a person " within the meaning of this section: *R.* v. *Shephard* [1918] 2 K.B. 125.

(2) that if in such circumstances she is tried for murder the jury may return a verdict of infanticide. Subsection (3) [28] provides that if a mother is charged with the murder of her child, then, notwithstanding the Act, it is still open to the jury, if the evidence so warrants, to find a verdict of manslaughter.

---

[28] As amended by the Criminal Law Act 1967, Sched. 3.

CHAPTER 31

OFFENCES CONCERNING CHILDBIRTH

SECTION 1.   INTRODUCTION

AT common law it was not murder to kill a child in the womb or while in the process of being born.   Such an act was a common law misdemeanour, but today it will amount either to the statutory offence of abortion, or where the child is capable of being born alive, to the offence of child destruction.

SECTION 2.   ABORTION

By **section 58** of the **Offences against the Person Act 1861** it is an offence [*Imp. life*]—

(i) for any pregnant woman unlawfully to administer [1] to herself any poison or other noxious thing or to use any instrument or other means whatsoever [2] with intent to procure her own miscarriage;

(ii) for any person unlawfully to administer [1] to any woman whether pregnant or not, or to cause to be taken by her, any poison or other noxious thing with intent to procure miscarriage, or to use any instrument or other means whatsoever [2] with like intent.

It must be shown that the substance is a " poison " or " noxious thing."

A number of points arise as to the meaning of this section.   If the thing administered is a recognised poison, the offence may be committed although the quantity given is so small as to be incapable of doing any harm.[3]   If a substance produces a miscarriage, it is certainly a noxious thing.[4]   Even if it cannot produce a miscarriage, it may still be a noxious thing [5]—provided that, in the quantity

---

[1] For the meaning of the word " administer," see Arch. para. 2623.
[2] See *R.* v. *Spicer* (1955) 39 Cr.App.R. 189.
[3] *R.* v. *Cramp* (1880) 5 Q.B.D. 307 at pp. 309–310.
[4] *R.* v. *Hollis* (1873) 12 Cox 463 at p. 467.
[5] *R.* v. *Marlow* (1964) 49 Cr.App.R. 49. *Contra, R.* v. *Hollis* (*ubi supra*). See also Russell, p. 603, n. 23.

administered,[6] it can have some effect on the human system.[7] If the substance administered is a poison or other noxious thing or if any instrument or other means is used to procure an abortion, then, provided that there was an intent to procure miscarriage, the fact that no miscarriage was or could be produced is immaterial.[8]

Not all abortions are unlawful. By **section 1** of the **Abortion Act 1967** [9] it is not an offence under the law relating to abortion (which by section 6 of the Act is taken to be both sections 58 and 59 of the 1861 Act and any rule of law relating to the procurement of abortion), for a registered medical practitioner to terminate a pregnancy, provided *two* registered medical practitioners are of the bona fide opinion that either:

(a) continuance of the pregnancy would involve risk to the life of the pregnant woman, or injury to her physical or mental health or any existing children of her family (taking into account the pregnant woman's actual or reasonably foreseeable environment) greater than if the pregnancy were terminated; or

(b) there is substantial risk that if the child were born it would suffer from such physical or mental abnormalities as to be seriously handicapped.

Such abortions must be carried out in a National Health Service Hospital.

Where, however, a registered medical practitioner is of the bona fide opinion that a pregnancy must be terminated immediately in order to save the life or prevent grave permanent injury to the physical or mental health of the pregnant woman, the requirement as to the opinions of two registered medical practitioners does not apply, nor is it necessary for the operation to be performed in a National Health Service Hospital.

By **section 2**, the Minister of Health may make regulations providing for—

(a) the certification in the form required by the regulations of the requisite opinion of the practitioner or practitioners concerned;

---

6 *R.* v. *Brown* (1899) 63 J.P. 790.

7 *R.* v. *Hennah* (1877) 13 Cox 547.

8 *R.* v. *Cramp* (1880) 5 Q.B.D. 307 and *R.* v. *Spicer* (1955) 39 Cr.App.R. 189.

9 The Act is intended to clarify the former common law, for which see *R.* v. *Bourne* [1939] 1 K.B. 687 (formerly the leading case) and *R.* v. *Newton and Stungo* [1958] Crim.L.R. 469.

(b) the giving of notice by any registered medical practitioner who terminates a pregnancy of such termination;

(c) the prohibition of any disclosure, except to prescribed persons or for prescribed purposes, of any information published or notice given under the regulations.

By **section 4,** persons having conscientious objections to any treatment authorised by the Act are under no duty to participate therein (the burden of proof lying on the party relying on the section) except that the duty to participate in treatment necessary to save the life or prevent grave permanent injury to the physical or mental health of a pregnant woman is not affected.

Conspiracy and aiding and abetting. It should be noted that in (i) it is essential that the woman be pregnant, whereas that is not the case in (ii). However it has been held that a woman, even though she is *not* pregnant, may be convicted of *conspiring* [10] with other persons, or of *aiding* and *abetting* [11] other persons, to administer *to her* any poison, etc., contrary to the second part of section 58. So if a woman allows others to attempt to abort her unlawfully, then she will be guilty of a criminal offence even though she may not in fact be pregnant.

Attempt. Although this topic has already been examined,[12] a brief reference needs to be made here. If a woman administers to herself any poison, etc., but is not pregnant and therefore unable to commit the main offence, it would seem that she cannot be convicted of the crime of attempt.[13] There are conflicting authorities as to whether the crime of attempt will have been committed if the substance which is taken or administered is not in fact either poisonous or noxious.[14]

Indictment for child destruction. By **section 1 (3)** of the **Infant Life (Preservation) Act 1929** a person indicted for child destruction may, if the evidence so warrants, be convicted of administering poison, etc., with intent to procure abortion.[15]

---

[10] *R.* v. *Whitchurch* (1890) 24 Q.B.D. 420. As to conspiracy, see *ante,* p. 63.
[11] *R.* v. *Sockett* (1908) 1 Cr.App.R. 101. As to aiding and abetting generally, see *ante,* p. 73.   [12] *Ante,* p. 57.
[13] See *R.* v. *Whitchurch* (1890) 24 Q.B.D. 420 at pp. 421–422.
[14] *R.* v. *Osborn* (1920) 84 J.P. 83 and *R.* v. *Brown* (1899) 63 J.P. 790; and see *ante,* p. 62.
[15] Not affected by the Abortion Act 1967: s. 5, *ibid.*

By **section 59** of the **Offences against the Person Act 1861** it is an offence [*Imp.* 5 *years*] for *any person* unlawfully to supply or procure any poison or other noxious thing, or any instrument or thing whatsoever, knowing that it is intended to be unlawfully used with intent to procure the miscarriage of any woman, whether pregnant or not.

The word "procure" has been defined to mean getting possession from another person.[16]

SECTION 3. CHILD DESTRUCTION

By **section 1** of the **Infant Life (Preservation) Act 1929** any person who, with intent to destroy the life of a child capable of being born alive, by any wilful act causes it to die *before* it has an existence independent of its mother shall be guilty of the offence of child destruction [*Imp. life*].[17] The Abortion Act 1967 [18] does not apply to the offence of child destruction.[19] But it is provided that no person is to be found guilty of an offence under section 1 of the Infant Life (Preservation) Act 1929 unless it is proved that the act which caused the death of the child was not done in good faith for the purpose *only* of preserving the life of the mother. The word "life" has been given a liberal interpretation.[20] The burden of showing bad faith is on the Crown.[21]

Evidence. For the purposes of the Act, evidence that a woman had at any material time been pregnant for a period of twenty-eight weeks or more shall be prima facie proof that she was at that time pregnant of a child capable of being born alive.[22]

Indictment for other offences. A person tried for the murder or manslaughter of a child or for infanticide or for an offence under **section 58** of the **Offences against the Person Act 1861** [23] may be convicted of child destruction.

---

16 *R.* v. *Mills* [1963] 1 Q.B. 526.
17 See note 15, *supra.*
18 See *ante*, p. 449.
19 Abortion Act 1967, s. 5.
20 See *R.* v. *Bourne* [1939] 1 K.B. 687.
21 *R.* v. *Newton and Stungo* [1958] Crim.L.R. 469, a decision on s. 58 of the Offences against the Person Act 1861.
22 s. 1 (2).
23 *Ante* p. 448.

SECTION 4.   CONCEALMENT OF BIRTH

By **section 60** of the **Offences against the Person Act 1861,** if any woman is delivered of a child, *every person* who by any secret disposition of the dead body of the child, whether it died before, at or after its birth, endeavours to conceal the birth is guilty of an offence [*Imp.* 2 *years*].

Mere denial of the birth is not sufficient without some actual and *secret* disposition of the body.[24] " What is a secret disposition must depend upon the circumstances of each particular case." [25] The test is the probability of the body being found; there may therefore be a secret disposition if the body is put in any secluded place, even though it is not concealed from view,[26] and conversely there may not be a secret disposition even though the body has been concealed from view.[27]

In order to convict a woman of endeavouring to conceal the birth of her child a dead body must, as a rule, be found and identified as that of the child of which she is alleged to have been delivered.[28]

---

[24] *R.* v. *Turner* (1839) 8 C. & P. 755.
[25] *R.* v. *Brown* (1870) L.R. 1 C.C.R. 244 at p. 246.
[26] *Ibid.*
[27] *R.* v. *George* (1868) 11 Cox 41.
[28] *R.* v. *Williams* (1871) 11 Cox 684; see also *ante,* p. 432. But in *R.* v. *Kersey* (1908) 1 Cr.App.R. 260 it was held that a confession by the accused was sufficient evidence.

CHAPTER 32

ASSAULTS AND OTHER PERSONAL INJURIES

SECTION 1. ASSAULT AND BATTERY

THE term " assault " is commonly used today in its wider sense of including an " assault " and a " battery," but it is in fact a separate offence and should be treated as such. An " assault " is any act which intentionally—or possibly recklessly—causes another person to apprehend immediate and unlawful violence.[1] The term " battery " means the actual application of unlawful force, however slight, to another, whether directly or indirectly.

It will be an assault intentionally to strike at another with a stick, or to draw a knife upon a person, or to point a gun,[2] or to throw a brick at another, even if it misses. The *mens rea* of assault is the causing of the apprehension; so if a man strikes at another, where there is no possibility of the blow connecting, then this is no assault.[3] An unlawful detention or imprisonment may amount to an assault.[4] If A unlawfully touches B in a hostile manner [5] or throws or shoots something at B, or if A digs a hole for B to fall into, and B does [6] or if A trips B this is a battery. Also, kissing a woman without her consent would be a battery. It has been held that the communication of a disease by one person to another cannot constitute a battery.[7]

A battery is not " unlawful " in the same circumstances that a killing is not unlawful.[8] It was seen in the chapter on Homicide [9] that in the following circumstances harm is lawful:

(i) Where a person is being lawfully [10] chastised;
(ii) Where a person is being operated on lawfully;

---

[1] *Per* James J. in *Fagan* v. *Commissioner for Metropolitan Police* [1969] 1 Q.B. 439.
[2] If the victim thinks it is loaded; *cf. R.* v. *Lamb* [1967] 2 Q.B. 981.
[3] See Arch. para. 2631.
[4] See Arch. para. 2632.
[5] See Hawk c. 62, s. 2.
[6] *R.* v. *Clarence* (1888) 22 Q.B.D. 23, but *cf. ibid.* at p. 50.
[7] *Ibid.*
[8] *Ante,* pp. 430–431; Arch. paras. 2641–2649.
[9] *Ante,* p. 431.
[10] *Ibid.* and n. 17 *infra.*

(iii) Where a person consents to the use of force in a game, and is by law able so to consent;

(iv) Where a person otherwise consents to, and is able to consent to, the use of force.

Apart from the obvious case of unlawful abortions,[11] it is not clear when an operation is unlawful. In one case Denning L.J., after discussing the few authorities on the matter, said that an operation done without just cause and excuse is unlawful although the person consents to it. The learned judge suggested that a sterilisation operation performed so that a man could have the pleasure of sexual intercourse without the responsibilities attached would be unlawful as injurious to the public interest.[12] However, the other two learned judges expressly dissociated themselves from this view.[13]

Discussing the law regarding games which involve the use of force, Stephen J. in *R.* v. *Coney* said [14]:

"The principle as to consent seems to me to be this: When one person is indicted for inflicting personal injury upon another, the consent of the person who sustains the injury is no defence to the person who inflicts the injury, if the injury is of such a nature, or is inflicted under such circumstances, that its infliction is injurious to the public as well as to the person injured. . . .

"In cases where life and limb are exposed to no serious danger in the common course of things, I think that consent is a defence to a charge of assault, even when considerable force is used as, for instance, in cases of wrestling, single-stick, sparring with gloves, football, and the like; but in all cases the question whether consent does or does not take from the application of force to another its illegal character is a question of degree depending upon circumstances."

In that case the court held that persons who participate in prize fighting are guilty of assault.

---

[11] *Ante*, p. 448.
[12] *Bravery* v. *Bravery* [1954] 1 W.L.R. 1169 at p. 1180.
[13] *Ibid*. at p. 1175.
[14] (1882) 8 Q.B.D. 539 at p. 539.

It has been held that a person cannot necessarily prevent the application of bodily harm from being an assault merely because he consents to that application. In *R.* v. *Donovan* [15] it was held that the accused, who for sexual gratification had given a girl a caning to which she had consented, could still be convicted of assault if " the blows struck by the prisoner were likely or intended to do bodily harm." Bodily harm was defined as " hurt or injury calculated to interfere with the health or comfort of the victim," not necessarily permanent but " more than merely transient and trifling." [16] The court held that the infliction of such harm in order not to amount to an assault had to come within one of the recognised exceptions, *e.g.* lawful chastisement, sports.

Self-defence is an answer to a charge of assault, even an aggravated assault, but the force used must be no more than is reasonably necessary for the purposes of self-defence.[17] In order to determine in a particular case what is reasonable, all the circumstances must be examined. One of the factors to be taken into consideration in determining reasonableness is whether the accused retreated, if only in mind.[18] To avail himself of the justification of self-defence an accused must have demonstrated by his actions that he is prepared to temporise and disengage, even to make a physical withdrawal.[19] This does not mean that he is obliged to keep off the streets, or refrain from going to a place to which he is lawfully entitled to go, because he has reason to believe that he will be attacked. The duty to " retreat " does not arise until the parties are within sight of each other, and the threat to the person relying on self-defence becomes so imminent that he is able to demonstrate his unwillingness to fight.[19a] The burden of eliminating self-defence lies upon the Crown.[20]

A person's right of defence is not limited to defending his person and property, but extends at least to defending his spouse, parent, child or servant; and where an arrestable offence is apprehended, even to defending a complete stranger.[21]

[15] [1934] 2 K.B. 498.
[16] *Ibid.* at 509.
[17] Criminal Law Act 1967, s. 3 (1).
[18] *R.* v. *McInnes* [1971] 1 W.L.R. 1600.
[19] *R.* v. *Julian* (1969) 53 Cr.App.R. 407.
[19a] *R.* v. *Field* [1972] Crim.L.R. 435, C.A.
[20] *R.* v. *Wheeler* (1967) 52 Cr.App.R. 28.
[21] *R.* v. *Duffy* [1967] 1 Q.B. 63.

If self-defence is eliminated, then the nature of the assault will depend upon the circumstances of the case.

Duress will vitiate consent,[22] but it is not clear how far fraud will vitiate it. In *R. v. Clarence* [23] the accused was charged with assault. He had had intercourse with his wife at a time when he knew, but his wife did not know, that he was suffering from gonorrhoea. It was held that the communication of a disease did not itself constitute an assault [24] and that concealing the disease from his wife did not vitiate her consent to the intercourse, although she would not have consented had she known the truth. Stephen J. held that: " The only cases in which fraud indisputably vitiates consent in these cases are matters of fraud as to the nature of the act done." So, the learned judge said, if the consent was obtained by wrongfully representing that the application of force was part of a surgical operation or examination it would be an assault.[25] Stephen J. went on to say that it was not clear whether fraud as to identity vitiates consent, although he thought the better view was that it did.[26]

A physical interference with a young child in circumstances of indecency which might not be an ordinary assault because of the presence of consent now constitutes the offence of indecent assault by virtue of statute.[27]

SECTION 2. COMMON AND AGGRAVATED ASSAULTS

By **section 42** of the **Offences against the Person Act 1861,**[28] where any person unlawfully assaults or beats another, two justices *upon complaint by or on behalf of the person aggrieved* may hear and determine the charge, and may inflict upon the defendant a *fine of £50 or imprisonment for 2 months* in addition to any costs which they may order him to pay.

By **section 43,**[29] where a person is charged before two justices with an assault or battery upon a child, whose age does not in their

---

[22] See, *e.g. R. v. Nichol* (1807) R. & R. 130; *R. v. Day* (1841) 9 C. & P. 722 and see generally *ante*, p. 97.
[23] (1888) 22 Q.B.D. 23.
[24] Above at p. 453.
[25] At p. 43–44.
[26] *Ibid.*
[27] *Post*, p. 471.
[28] As amended by the Criminal Justice Act 1925, s. 39; Criminal Justice Act 1967, Sched. 3.
[29] *Ibid.*

opinion exceed fourteen years, or upon any female, *either upon the complaint of the party aggrieved or otherwise,* and the justices are of opinion that such assault or battery is of so aggravated a character that it cannot be sufficiently punished under the provisions of the preceding paragraph, they may hear and determine the charge in a summary way and may punish the defendant by a *fine of* £100 *or imprisonment for* 6 *months,* in addition to any costs which they may order him to pay.

If upon the hearing of any such case of assault and battery upon the merits, where the complaint was preferred by or on behalf of the party aggrieved, under either of the two preceding sections, the justices deem the offence not to be proved, or find the assault or battery to have been justified, or so trifling as not to merit any punishment, and shall accordingly dismiss the complaint, they shall forthwith make out a certificate under their hands stating the fact of such dismissal and shall deliver it to the party against whom the complaint was made.[30]   If a person obtains such a certificate or, having been convicted, pays the fine imposed or suffers the imprisonment awarded, he is released from all further or other proceedings, civil or criminal, for the same cause.[31]

Where, however, the justices are of opinion that the assault or battery complained of is, from any circumstance, a fit subject for prosecution by indictment, they must abstain from adjudication and deal with the case in all respects as if they had no authority finally to determine it: nothing, moreover, in these sections authorises any justices to hear and determine any case of assault or battery in which any question arises as to the title to any lands, tenements or hereditaments, or any interest therein or accruing therefrom, or as to any bankruptcy or insolvency, or any execution under the process of any court of justice.[32]

By **section 47** of the **Offences against the Person Act 1861** a common assault is also an **indictable offence** [*Imp.* 1 *year*].

---

[30] s. 44.
[31] *Ibid.* s. 45. The words " for the same cause " do not mean for the same *act,* but for the same accusation. A conviction for assault is therefore no bar under this section to an indictment for manslaughter. Nor would it enable the common law plea of *autrefois convict* to be set up: *R.* v. *Morris* (1867) L.R. 1 C.C.R. 90; but see *Masper* v. *Brown* (1876) 1 C.P.D. 97. For a full discussion of ss. 44, 45, see North, " Civil and Criminal Proceedings for Assault " (1966) 26 M.L.R. 16.
[32] Offences against the Person Act 1861, s. 46, as amended by the Criminal Law Act 1967, Sched. 3.

A person who commits an assault occasioning actual bodily harm is guilty of an offence [*Imp.* 5 *years*]. The term " actual bodily harm " includes any hurt or injury calculated to interfere with the health or comfort of the prosecutor; it need not be of a permanent nature, nor amount to grievous bodily harm.[33]

A number of aggravated assaults have already been examined or will be examined later. These are: (i) indecent assaults,[34] (ii) assaults with intent to rob,[35] (iii) assaults with intent to commit buggery,[36] (iv) assaults upon police and other public officers,[37] (v) assaults with intent to resist arrest [38] and (vi) assaults by poachers.[39]

SECTION 3.   OTHER MALICIOUS INJURIES

The following are offences under the **Offences against the Person Act 1861**. A number of them require some specific or ulterior intent, *e.g.* malicious wounding *with intent* to cause grievous bodily harm. The meaning of the word " intent " has been examined earlier.[40]   Most of the offences also include the words " unlawfully " and " maliciously." We have already seen when harm is lawful,[41] and have examined the legal definition of the word " malice." [42]   The expression " maliciously " in these sections of the Offences against Person Act 1861 imports *mens rea,* although the Court of Appeal has said [43] that the definition laid down in *R.* v. *Cunningham* [44] is not appropriate, and that in relation to a charge of malicious wounding, the word " maliciously " merely imports an awareness on the part of the accused that his act may have the consequence of causing some physical harm, albeit of a minor character, to some other person.[45]

Grievous bodily harm; wounding. By **section 18** of the Act [46] it is an offence [*Imp. life*] unlawfully and maliciously by any means

---

[33] *R.* v. *Donovan* [1934] 2 K.B. 498 at p. 509; Arch. paras. 2634 and 2654.   It includes a hysterical or nervous condition: *R.* v. *Miller* [1954] 2 Q.B. 282.
[34] *Post,* p. 471.   [35] *Post,* p. 507.
[36] *Post,* p. 478.   [37] *Ante,* p. 171.
[38] *Ante,* p. 193.
[39] *Ante,* p. 420.
[40] *Ante,* p. 39.
[41] *Ante,* pp. 430, 431, 453.
[42] *Ante,* p. 42.
[43] *R.* v. *Mowatt* [1968] 1 Q.B. 421.
[44] [1957] 2 Q.B. 396; see also *Wilkins* v. *An Infant* [1965] Crim.L.R. 730.
[45] *Cf. R.* v. *Solanke* (1970) 54 Cr.App.R. 30, a case under s. 16 of the Act.
[46] As amended by the Criminal Law Act 1967, Sched. 3.

whatsoever to wound or cause any grievous bodily harm to any person with intent to do some grievous bodily harm or with intent to resist or prevent the arrest or detainer of any person.[47]

By **section 20** it is an offence [*Imp. 5 years*] [48] unlawfully and maliciously to wound or inflict any grievous bodily harm upon any person either with or without any weapon or instrument.

"Grievous bodily harm" means any really serious bodily injury.[49] It is not necessary that it should be either permanent or dangerous.[50] To constitute a "wound" the whole skin must be broken, a mere abrasion or separation of the cuticle is not sufficient.[51]

"Causing" or "inflicting" grievous bodily harm is of course much wider than the definition of assault, and grievous bodily harm may be caused or inflicted indirectly, where a charge of assault would not lie. Thus, a person who deliberately causes a panic in a theatre so that persons are severely injured may be said to "cause" grievous bodily harm.[52] The same is the case where the accused has so threatened a person that his victim tries to escape and in doing so injures himself.[53] It has been held, however, that a person who communicates to another a disease cannot be convicted of these offences.[54]

Strangling. By **section 21** it is an offence [*Imp. life*] for any person by any means whatever to attempt to choke, suffocate or strangle any person, or by means calculated to choke, etc., to attempt to render any person insensible or incapable of resistance, with intent to commit or to enable or assist any other person to commit any indictable offence.

Administration of drugs and poisons, etc. By **section 22** it is an offence [*Imp. life*] for any person unlawfully to apply or administer [55] to, or cause to be taken by, or attempt to cause to

47 See also *ante*, p. 193.
48 As amended by the Penal Servitude Act 1891, s. 1 (1), repealed by Criminal Justice Act 1948, s. 1.
49 *Director of Public Prosecutions* v. *Smith* [1961] A.C. at 290, pp. 334–335; followed in *R.* v. *Metharam* (1961) 45 Cr.App.R. 364, C.C.A.
50 *R.* v. *Ashman* (1858) 1 F. & F. 88.
51 *R.* v. *McLoughlin* (1838) 8 C. & P. 635.
52 *R.* v. *Martin* (1881) 8 Q.B.D. 54, followed in *R.* v. *Chapin* (1909) 74 J.P. 71.
53 *R.* v. *Halliday* (1890) 61 L.T. 701; *R.* v. *Lewis* [1970] Crim.L.R. 647; *R.* v. *Roberts* (1972) 56 Cr.App.R. 95.
54 *R.* v. *Clarence* (1888) 22 Q.B.D. 23.
55 As to what constitutes "administering," see Arch. para. 2623.

be administered to, etc., any other person any chloroform, lauda-num, or other stupefying or overpowering drug or matter with intent to commit or to enable or assist any other person to commit any indictable offence.

The offence of administering drugs to obtain or facilitate inter-course is dealt with later.[56]

By **section 23** it is an offence [*Imp.* 10 *years*] for any person unlawfully and maliciously to administer to, or cause to be admini-stered to or taken by, any person any poison,[57] or other destructive or noxious thing,[58] so as thereby to endanger the life of such per-son, or to inflict on him any grievous bodily harm.

By **section 24**[59] it is an offence [*Imp.* 5 *years*] for any person unlawfully, etc., to administer, etc., to any other person any poison etc., with intent to injure, aggrieve or annoy such person.[60]

Explosions. By **section 28** it is an offence [*Imp. life*] for any person unlawfully and maliciously by the explosion of gunpowder or any other explosive substance to burn, maim, disfigure, disable[61] or do grievous bodily harm to any person.

By **section 29** it is an offence [*Imp. life*] for any person unlaw-fully and maliciously to cause any gunpowder, etc., to explode, or send or deliver to, or cause to be taken or received by, any person any explosive substance or any other dangerous or noxious thing, or to put at any place, or throw at or upon or otherwise apply to any person, any corrosive fluid, or any destructive or explosive substance, with intent in any of such cases to burn, maim, disfigure, disable[61] or do grievous bodily harm to any person, whether any bodily injury be effected or not.

By **section 30** it is an offence [*Imp.* 14 *years*] for any person unlawfully and maliciously to place or throw on, upon, against or near any building, ship or vessel any gunpowder, etc., with intent to do bodily injury to any person, whether or not any explosion takes place or any bodily injury be effected.

---

[56] *Post*, p. 468.
[57] *Ante*, pp. 448, 449.
[58] *Ibid.* and see *R.* v. *Weatherall* [1968] Crim.L.R. 115.
[59] As amended by the Penal Servitude Act 1891, s. 1 (1).
[60] A person indicted under s. 23 may be convicted under s. 24: s. 25.
[61] As to the meaning of these terms, see Arch. para. 2654.

By **section 64** [62] it is an offence [*Imp.* 2 *years*] for any person knowingly to have in his possession, or make, any gunpowder, explosive substance, or any dangerous or noxious thing, or any machine or instrument with intent to commit, or enable another to commit, any offence in the Act for which a person (not previously convicted) may be tried on indictment otherwise than at his own instance.

Spring-guns, man-traps.   By **section 31** [63] it is an offence [*Imp.* 3 *years*] for any person to set or place or cause to be set, etc., any spring-gun, man-trap or other engine [64] calculated to destroy human life or inflict grievous bodily harm, with the intent that or whereby it may destroy or inflict grievous bodily harm upon a trespasser or other person coming in contact therewith.[65]

Whoever knowingly and wilfully permits any such spring-gun etc., though previously set by another person, to continue set etc. in any place subsequently coming into his possession is to be deemed to have set it with such intention.

The section provides, however, that nothing herein shall make it illegal to set such traps as are usually set for the destruction of vermin, or to set a spring-gun, etc., in a dwelling-house, between sunset and sunrise, for the protection thereof.

Offences concerning railways.   By **section 32** it is an offence [*Imp. life*] for any person unlawfully and maliciously (i) to put or throw upon any railway any wood, stone or other thing; (ii) to remove or displace any rail, sleeper, or other thing belonging to a railway; (iii) to turn, move, or divert any points or other machinery belonging to a railway; (iv) to make, show, hide, or remove any signal or light upon or near a railway; (v) to do or cause to be done any other matter or thing, with intent in any of such cases to endanger the safety of persons travelling or being upon the railway.

By **section 33** it is an offence [*Imp. life*] for any person unlawfully and maliciously to throw, or cause to strike, at, against, upon or into any railway engine, carriage, or truck, any wood, stone, etc.,

---

[62] As amended by the Criminal Law Act 1967, Sched. 2.
[63] As amended by the Penal Servitude Act 1891, s. 1 (1).
[64] An engine has been held to mean a mechanical contrivance and does not include an arrangement of electric wires: *R.* v. *Munks* [1964] 1 Q.B. 304.
[65] If death ensues it will be at least manslaughter (Arch. para. 2543) and maybe murder.

with intent to injure or endanger the safety of any person upon such engine, etc., or any other engine, etc., forming part of the same train.

By **section 34** it is an offence [*Imp.* 2 *years*] for any person by any unlawful act, or by any wilful omission or neglect, to endanger or cause to be endangered the safety of any person conveyed or being in or upon a railway.[66] A person who carelessly endangers the safety of the passengers does not commit this offence, because his conduct will not be " wilful." [67] However, if the accused is an employee of a railway company, he may commit a **summary offence** [*Imp.* 2 *months or* £10 *fine*] under **section 17** of the **Railway Regulation Act 1842,** which punishes wilful or negligent conduct liable to endanger persons.[68]

Furious driving. Section 35 of the **Offences against the Person Act 1861** punishes furious driving.[69] This offence is dealt with in Chapter 22.

SECTION 4. FALSE IMPRISONMENT

False imprisonment is a common law offence [*fine and Imp.*]; it may also be the subject of civil proceedings.

The prosecution need only to prove the imprisonment by the defendant, who must then show that it was justified.[70] The circumstances in which it is justifiable will be explained later.[71]

" Every confinement of the person is an imprisonment, whether it be in a common prison or in a private house . . . or even by forcibly detaining one in the public streets." [72] It must, however, amount to a total restraint of liberty for some time, however short; merely to prevent a person from going along a particular road or

---

[66] It is sufficient that the defendant causes a source of danger, he need not cause an accident: *R.* v. *Pearce* [1967] 1 Q.B. 150.

[67] See *R.* v. *Senior* [1899] 1 Q.B. 283, *post* p. 481. However, he may be guilty of manslaughter if his negligence causes death and is " criminal," *ante,* p. 444.

[68] An offence will also be committed against this Act if the employee is drunk while employed in the railway or if he contravenes any rule or by-law of the company.

[69] See *R.* v. *Phillip Cooke* [1971] Crim.L.R. 44.

[70] Arch. para. 2804.

[71] *Post,* pp. 555–567.

[72] Arch. para. 2803. It is not clear whether the person imprisoned needs to know that he is imprisoned, *e.g.* can a sleeping person be falsely imprisoned? See *Herring* v. *Boyle* (1834) 6 C. & P. 496; *cf. Meering* v. *Graham-White Aviation Co. Ltd.* (1919) 122 L.T. 44.

in a particular direction is not an imprisonment.[73] But there may be an imprisonment although the person is not touched, but submits to the restraint, as, *e.g.* if a person is told by a constable to go with him and obeys.

The imprisonment must be by the defendant himself or by his orders. Thus, if a police officer arrests B as a result of an order given by A, there is an imprisonment by A; but there is no imprisonment by A if he merely states the facts to the police officer who, acting on his own initiative, arrests B.[74] Nor is there an imprisonment by A if the opinion and judgment of a judicial officer are interposed between the charge and the " imprisonment," *e.g.* if A makes a charge against B to a magistrate, who issues a warrant for the arrest of B.[75]

It is usual in such cases to describe the imprisonment as " unlawful and injurious " in the indictment. In *R.* v. *Hosein and Hosein* [75a] Shaw J. directed the jury that the word " injurious " in relation to the imprisonment, meant an imprisonment which was to the victim's detriment; confinement which was not to her advantage, and was against her interest and against her will.

Section 5.   Kidnapping

In *Russell on Crime* it is stated [76]:

" The stealing and carrying away, or secreting of any person of any age or either sex against the will of such person, or if he be a minor against the will of his friends or lawful guardians,[77] sometimes called *kidnapping,* is an offence at common law, punishable by fine and imprisonment.[78] The most aggravated form of kidnapping is the forcible abduction or stealing and carrying away of any person from his own country into some other, or to parts beyond the seas, whereby he is deprived of the friendly assistance of the laws to redeem him from captivity."

---

[73] *Bird* v. *Jones* (1845) 7 Q.B. 742.
[74] *Sewell* v. *National Telephone Co.* [1907] 1 K.B. 557; see also *Grinham* v. *Willey* (1859) 4 H. & N. 296.
[75] *Austin* v. *Dowling* (1870) L.R. 5 C.P. 534.
[75a] Unreported but tried at the Central Criminal Court in the autumn of 1970.
[76] At p. 692, footnotes omitted.
[77] See also *post*, p. 481.
[78] See p. 201, *ante*, fn. 59.

In *R.* v. *Reid* [78a] a husband entered the house where his wife was staying with a relative, and holding a knife at her throat, threatened to kill her unless she packed her things and left with him. The Court of Appeal (Criminal Division) held [78b] that if a husband treated his wife with hostile force, and that force resulted in carrying her away from the place where she wished to remain, the offence of kidnapping was committed.

[78a] [1972] 3 W.L.R. 395.
[78b] In the absence of English authority the Court considered the American cases of *People* v. *Carvalho* (1952) 256 Pacific Reporter 2d, 950; and *People* v. *Ford* (1964) 388 Pacific Reporter 2d, 892.

CHAPTER 33

RAPE AND OTHER SEXUAL OFFENCES AND ABDUCTION

SECTION 1. RAPE

BY **section 1 (1)** of the **Sexual Offences Act 1956** rape is an offence [*Imp. life; attempted rape, Imp. 7 years* [1]].[2]

A person commits rape if he has sexual intercourse with a woman without her consent, either

(i) by force or fear of bodily harm [3];

(ii) by fraud, *i.e.* where an apparent consent is vitiated by fraud, *e.g.* where the woman only consented because she thought that the accused was performing a medical operation upon her [4] or where the accused impersonated the woman's husband [5];

(iii) when she is asleep or unconscious, or so mentally defective [6] or so young [7] as to be unable to understand the nature of the act and thus not be in a position to decide whether to consent or resist.

It follows from the requirement of *mens rea* that the accused must not have believed that the woman consented, although there is no English authority to this effect.[8] This may be of particular importance if the accused was drunk at the time.[9]

Evidence of penetration only, without emission, is sufficient proof of intercourse.[10] Penetration of the slightest kind is suffi-

---

1 *Ibid*. Sched. 2.
2 A person indicted for rape may be convicted of a number of other offences: *ibid*. Sched. 2, as amended by the Criminal Law Act 1967, Sched. 2. On a charge of rape the accused may be convicted of indecent assault by virtue of the Criminal Law Act 1967, s. 6 (3); *R.* v. *Mochan* (1969) 54 Cr.App.R. 5.
3 *R.* v. *Hallett* (1841) 9 C. & P. 748.
4 *R.* v. *Flattery* (1877) 2 Q.B.D. 410. See also *R.* v. *Williams* [1923] 1 K.B. 340.
5 Sexual Offences Act 1956, s. 1 (2).
6 *R.* v. *Barratt* (1873) L.R. 2 C.C.R. 81; *cf. R.* v. *Fletcher* (1866) L.R. 1 C.C.R. 39. See also *post*, p. 468.
7 *R.* v. *Harling* (1937) 26 Cr.App.R. 127; *R.* v. *Howard* [1966] 1 W.L.R. 13.
8 *Cf.* The position in Australia (*R.* v. *Burles* [1947] V.L.R. 392) and in Canada (*R.* v. *Vandervoort* [1961] O.W.N. 141).
9 *R.* v. *Boucher* [1963] 2 C.C.C. 241.
10 Sexual Offences Act 1956, s. 44.

cient, and, if no penetration is proved, the accused may be convicted of attempt.[11]

A husband cannot be convicted as a principal [12] in a rape upon his wife, unless he is separated from his wife by a separation order or separation agreement.[13]   He may, however, be convicted of assault or aggravated assault.[14]   It is, however, no defence that the woman was his mistress or that she was a prostitute, though such circumstances may be of importance in determining whether she consented.

A boy of under fourteen years cannot be convicted of rape or of unlawful sexual intercourse, whatever his actual capacity,[15] but he may be convicted of an indecent assault,[16] and (probably) of an attempt.[17]   And a boy under fourteen or even a woman may be convicted as accomplices to rape.[18]   It is essential that where two or more defendants are charged with rape on the same woman, each rape be charged in a separate count.[19]   A verdict of indecent assault still remains open to a jury on an indictment for rape.[20]

Section 2.   Unlawful Sexual Intercourse

The expression " unlawful sexual intercourse " appears in a number of offences in the Sexual Offences Act 1956.   As we shall see, the meaning of the word " unlawful " is various.   In all offences of unlawful sexual intercourse evidence of penetration only, without emission, is sufficient proof of intercourse.[21]

Consent is no defence in a case of unlawful sexual intercourse and although the girl consents or even incites the commission of the offence she is not punishable.[22]

---

11 Arch. para. 2879.
12 If a husband is present aiding and abetting another person to commit rape upon her, he may be convicted as an accomplice: Arch. para. 2880 and *Lord Audley's Case* (1631) 3 St.Tr. 401.
13 *R.* v. *Clarke* (1949) 33 Cr.App.R. 216; *R.* v. *Miller* [1954] 2 Q.B. 282.
14 *R.* v. *Miller* [1954] 2 Q.B. 282.
15 Arch. para. 2880: *R.* v. *Waite* [1892] 2 Q.B. 600.
16 *R.* v. *Williams* [1893] 1 Q.B. 320.
17 *Ibid.*
18 Arch. para. 2880.   As to aiding and abetting by means of encouragement see *R.* v. *Clarkson* (1971) 55 Cr.App.R. 445.
19 *R.* v. *Holley and Others* (1969) 53 Cr.App.R. 519.
20 By virtue of the Criminal Law Act 1967, s. 6 (3); *R.* v. *Mochan* (1969) 54 Cr.App.R. 5.   An alternative verdict of unlawful sexual intercourse with a girl under 16 years cannot now be left to the jury. *Ibid.*
21 Sexual Offences Act 1956, s. 44.
22 *R.* v. *Tyrell* [1894] 1 Q.B. 710; and see *R.* v. *Beale* (1865) L.R. 1 C.C.R. 10.

Children. By **section 5** of the **Sexual Offences Act 1956** unlawful [23] sexual intercourse with *a girl under thirteen* is an offence [*Imp. life* [24]]; and so is the attempt [*Imp. 7 years*].[25] It is clear that *mens rea* as to the age of the girl is not required.[26] It is immaterial that the girl consented. By **section 6** it is an offence to have or attempt to have unlawful [27] sexual intercourse with a girl between thirteen and sixteen.[28] Again it is immaterial that the girl consented but a man is not guilty of an offence under section 6 if he was under the age of twenty-four and had not previously been charged [29] with a like offence [30] and he proves [31] that he reasonably believed that the girl was sixteen years of age or over.[32] This defence does not apply if the accused had not directed his mind to the question of the girl's age: he must both have had reasonable cause to believe and must have actually believed that she was over sixteen.[33] Nor does it apply to the offence of indecent assault.[34] In any proceedings against a person charged with this offence it is a defence for him to prove [35] that at the time of the offence he had reasonable cause to believe that the girl in question was his wife.[36]

By **section 26** it is an offence for an owner, occupier or manager of any premises or person assisting in the management thereof to induce or knowingly suffer any girl between thirteen and sixteen to be on such premises for any unlawful [37] sexual intercourse, whether with any particular man or generally.[38] In the case of a

---

[23] The word " unlawful " would appear to add nothing.

[24] Sched. 2.

[25] Sched. 2, as amended by Indecency with Children Act 1960, s. 2 (1) (*a*), (3).

[26] See *R.* v. *Prince* (1868) L.R. 1 C.C.R. 150.

[27] See n. 23 above.

[28] It is a defence to prove (s. 47) that the accused, at the time of the offence, had reasonable cause to believe that the girl was his wife: s. 6 (2). No prosecution for this offence can be commenced more than 12 months after its commission: *ibid.* Sched. 2.

[29] The expression " charged " means appearing before a court having jurisdiction to determine the matter: *R.* v. *Rider* [1954] 1 W.L.R. 463; Arch. para. 2918.

[30] For the definition of " like offence," see s. 6 (3).

[31] s. 47.

[32] s. 6 (3).

[33] *R.* v. *Banks* [1916] 2 K.B. 621; *R.* v. *Harrison* (1938) 26 Cr.App.R. 166.

[34] *R.* v. *Forde* [1923] 2 K.B. 400. The offence is discussed *post*, p. 471.

[35] s. 47.

[36] s. 6 (2).

[37] It is difficult to see what the word " unlawful " adds to the section.

[38] It is not clear whether it would be a good defence that the accused thought the girl to be over sixteen (*i.e.* whether *mens rea* is necessary as to the ingredient of age). *Cf.* s. 27, *post*, p. 468.

girl under thirteen this offence carries a heavier sentence [*Imp. life* [39]] [**section 25**].

Use of drugs. By **section 4,** it is an offence for a person to administer to or cause to be taken by any woman any drug or other matter with intent to stupefy or overpower her so as to enable any man [40] to have unlawful [41] sexual intercourse with her [42].

Defectives. By **section 7,**[43] it is an offence for a man to have or attempt to have unlawful [44] sexual intercourse with a woman who is a defective, provided that a person is not guilty of this offence if he proves [45] that he did not know and had no reason to suspect her to be a defective.[46] This proviso has been interpreted subjectively. It means that if the accused himself " did not know and that he, himself, had no reason to suspect the woman to be a defective," [47] then he is entitled to be acquitted.

By **section 27** it is an offence for a person, being the owner or occupier of any premises or having or acting in the management thereof, to induce or knowingly suffer any female defective to resort to or be on such premises for the purpose of unlawful [48] sexual intercourse with any man; provided that he is not guilty of this offence if he proves that [49] he does not know and has no reason to suspect her to be a defective.

By **section 128** of the **Mental Health Act 1959** [50] it is also an offence [51] for a person employed in a hospital to have unlawful sexual intercourse with an in-patient being treated for mental disorder or to have unlawful sexual intercourse on the premises with

---

[39] Sched. 2.
[40] *i.e.* the accused or some other man. The essence of the offence is the *administration* of the drug. If there has been only one administration there is only one offence however many men it is intended should have unlawful sexual intercourse with her: *R.* v. *Shillingford* (1968) 52 Cr.App.R. 188 C.A.
[41] " Unlawful " presumably means either otherwise criminal (*e.g.* the girl is under sixteen years of age) or " without her consent."
[42] Corroboration is required if the evidence is that of one witness only: s. 4 (2).
[43] As substituted by the Mental Health Act 1959, s. 127 (1) (*a*).
[44] The word " unlawful " appears to add nothing other than that it would probably exclude intercourse between married persons.   [45] s. 47.
[46] Defined in s. 45, as substituted by the Mental Health Act 1959, s. 127 (1) (*b*).
[47] *R.* v. *Hudson* [1966] 1 Q.B. 448 at p. 454.
[48] It is difficult to see what the word " unlawful " adds to this section.
[49] s. 47.
[50] This replaces s. 8 of the Sexual Offences Act 1956, which is in Sched. 8 to the 1959 Act.
[51] The consent of the Director of Public Prosecutions is required before proceedings are instituted: s. 128 (4).

an out-patient being so treated; provided that it shall not be an offence if the accused proves [52] that he did not know and had no reason to suspect her to be a mentally-disordered patient. **Section 1 (4)** of the Sexual Offences Act 1967 extends section 128 to include buggery and gross indecency with such persons.

Procuration. The following offences, also to be found in the **Sexual Offences Act 1956,** prohibit the procuring of girls and women for unlawful sexual intercourse. The term " procuring " means " persuading," so if the woman needed no persuading the accused has not committed the offence.[53] If unlawful sexual intercourse does not actually take place, the accused should be charged with an attempt.[54] If the unlawful intercourse takes place and itself constitutes an offence by the man having intercourse, the " procurer " would be guilty as an accomplice to that offence whether the woman needed persuading or not.

By **section 23,** it is an offence for a person to procure or attempt to procure a girl under the age of twenty-one to have unlawful [55] sexual intercourse in any part of the world with a third person.[56]

By **sections 2 and 3** it is an offence for a person to procure, or attempt to procure by threats or intimidation or to procure by false representations, any woman or girl to have any unlawful [57] sexual intercourse (whether with himself or another [58]) in any part of the world.[59]

By **section 9** it is an offence for a person to procure, or attempt to procure, a woman who is a defective to have unlawful [60] sexual intercourse (with another or, probably, with himself [61]) in any part of the world; provided that he is not guilty of this offence if he proves [62] that he does not know and has no reason to suspect her to be a defective.[63]

---

[52] s. 128 (5).
[53] *R.* v. *Christian* (1913) 78 J.P. 112.
[54] *R.* v. *Johnson* [1964] 2 Q.B. 404.
[55] Presumably intercourse which is " extra-marital " but not " criminal " will also be unlawful: see *post*, p. 473, n. 6.
[56] Corroboration is required if the evidence is that of one witness only: s. 23 (2).
[57] It is difficult to see what the word " unlawful " adds in this section, but it might exclude marital intercourse: *post*, p. 473, n. 6.
[58] *R.* v. *Williams* (1898) 62 J.P. 310, but *cf. R.* v. *Cook* [1954] 1 W.L.R. 125.
[59] Corroboration (n. 56, above) is required: ss. 2 (2) and 3 (2).
[60] The word " unlawful " would appear to add nothing to this section.
[61] *Supra*, n. 59.
[62] s. 47.
[63] As to this proviso, see *supra* p. 468.

By **section 28** it is an offence for a person to cause or encourage [64] the commission of unlawful [65] sexual intercourse with a girl under the age of sixteen for whom he is responsible.[66]   A person shall be deemed to have so caused or encouraged if he knowingly allowed the girl to consort with or be employed by a prostitute or person of known immoral character.[67]

Incest. By **section 10,** any male person who has sexual intercourse with a female who is to his knowledge his grand-daughter, daughter, sister, or mother is guilty of an offence [*Imp. 7 years, or if the female is under thirteen, for life* [68]].[69]   It is immaterial that the sexual intercourse was with the consent of the female person.[70]

An *attempt* by a male person to commit the offence is likewise an offence [*if the girl is under thirteen, Imp. 7 years* [71]*; otherwise, Imp. 2 years* [72]].   By **section 38** of the Act, upon a conviction for either of these offences upon a female under twenty-one years of age, the court may divest the offender of all authority over such female and may appoint any person to be her guardian during minority.

By **section 11** of the Act, a female of or above the age of sixteen years who permits her grandfather, father, brother, or son (knowing him to be such) to have sexual intercourse with her commits an offence [*Imp. 7 years* [73]].   An attempt is also an offence [*Imp. 2 years* [74]].

To constitute the commission of this offence by a woman there must be permission as distinct from mere submission.[75]   By these sections it is equally an offence whether the brother or sister be the half-brother or half-sister of the offender, and whether the relationship is illegitimate or traced through lawful wedlock.

---

[64] Not to prevent sexual intercourse may, in certain conditions, be " causing " or " encouraging ": R. v. *Ralphs* (1913) 9 Cr.App.R. 86.

[65] It is difficult to see what the word " unlawful " adds to this section.

[66] The persons who are " responsible " include, *inter alia*, parents, guardians, persons having actual possession and control: s. 28 (3) (4).

[67] s. 28 (2).   [68] Sched. 2.

[69] A person indicted under this section may be convicted of a number of other offences: Sched. 2 as amended by the Criminal Justice Act 1967, Sched. 2.

[70] But in that case she may be an accomplice, whose evidence against the prisoner requires corroboration: R. v. *Draper* (1929) 21 Cr.App.R. 147.

[71] Sched. 2 as amended by Indecency with Children Act 1960, s. 2 (2), (3).

[72] Sched. 2.

[73] Sched. 2.

[74] *Ibid.*

[75] R. v. *Dimes* (1911) 7 Cr.App.R. 43.

No prosecution for incest, except when undertaken by or on behalf of the Director of Public Prosecutions, can be commenced without the sanction of the Attorney-General.[76]

SECTION 3.   INDECENT ASSAULT AND INDECENCY WITH CHILDREN

Indecent assault. By **section 14** of the **Sexual Offences Act 1956** it is an offence for any person, male or female, to make an indecent assault upon a female [*if the girl is under thirteen, Imp. 5 years,*[77] *otherwise Imp. 2 years*[78]]. By **section 15** it is an offence for any person, male or female,[79] to make an indecent assault on a male [*Imp. 10 years*[80]].

The expression " assault " is used in its wide sense to include both assault and battery.[81]   There will, of course, be no assault if the person alleged to have been assaulted consented[82] to the assault.   But this is subject to the decision in *R.* v. *Donovan*[83] (above[84]), and also to statutory exceptions which apply to these two offences only.   These exceptions[85] provide that neither a child under the age of sixteen[86] nor a person whom the accused knew or had reason to suspect[87] to be a defective[88] can give any consent which would prevent an act being an assault for the purposes of these two crimes.[89]   So if A indecently handles a child of fifteen he is guilty of an offence, even though the child may *in fact* have consented.

Because of the requirement that there must be an assault, it has been held that a mere invitation to somebody to touch the body of the person making the invitation cannot, *in the absence*

---

[76] Sched. 2.

[77] Sexual Offences Act 1956, Sched. 2, as amended by Indecency with Children Act 1960, s. 2 (1) (*b*), (3).

[78] Sched. 2.

[79] See *R.* v. *Hare* [1934] 1 K.B. 354.   [80] Sched. 2.

[81] *Ante*, p. 453; *R.* v. *Rolfe* (1952) 36 Cr.App.R. 4.

[82] An apparent consent may be vitiated by fraud, *ante*, p. 456.

[83] [1934] 2 K.B. 498.   [84] *Ante*, p. 455.

[85] Sexual Offences Act 1956, ss. 14 (2), (4); 15 (2), (3).

[86] *Mens rea* as to the age of the child is presumably not required: *R.* v. *Prince* (1875) L.R. 2 C.C.R. 154.   If a man inserts his finger into the vagina of a girl under 16, this is an indecent assault, however willing or co-operative the girl may be: *R.* v. *McCormack* [1969] 2 Q.B. 442.

[87] *Ante*, p. 468.   [88] *Ante*, p. 468, n. 46.

[89] However, in the case of a girl under 16, it is a defence for a man to prove (s. 47) that, at the time of the offence, he had reasonable cause to believe that the girl was his wife: s. 14 (3).

of any threats, amount to an assault.[90]   So if A invites a child to masturbate him and the child does so, but A does not threaten the child in any way, it is not an indecent assault.[91]   This part of the law has been thrown into some confusion recently.

In *R.* v. *Mason* [92] it was held that sexual intercourse with a person under sixteen does not *per se* constitute an indecent assault in the absence of any use of force or hostile act.   Yet this decision must surely be questioned in view of the case of *R.* v. *McCormack* [93] in which it was held that if a man inserts his finger into the vagina of a girl under sixteen this is an indecent assault, however willing the girl may be.

To discover whether an assault is indecent, all the circumstances must be examined.[94]   The same act may be decent or indecent according to the circumstances.   To pull a child towards one is obviously not necessarily indecent, but may be so if accompanied by exposure of the person.[95]

By **section 28** of the **Sexual Offences Act 1956** it is an offence for a person to cause or encourage [96] the commission of an indecent assault on a girl under the age of sixteen for whom he is responsible.[97]   A person shall be deemed to have so caused or encouraged if he knowingly allowed the girl to consort with or be employed by a prostitute or person of known immoral character.[98]

By **section 1** of the **Indecency with Children Act 1960** any person who commits an act of gross indecency with or towards a child under the age of fourteen, or incites a child under that age to do such an act with him or another, commits an offence, punishable on **indictment** [*Imp. 2 years*] or on **summary conviction** [*Imp. 6 months and £400 fine*].[99]

---

[90] *Fairclough* v. *Whipp* (1951) 35 Crim.App.R. 138; *D.P.P.* v. *Rogers* [1953] 1 W.L.R. 1017; for what is an extension of these cases, see *Williams* v. *Gibbs* [1958] Crim.L.R. 127, and the commentary thereon.
[91] *D.P.P.* v. *Rogers* [1953] 1 W.L.R. 1017.   [92] (1968) 53 Cr.App.R. 12.
[93] [1969] 2 Q.B. 442 and see Arch. para. 2985.
[94] *Beal* v. *Kelley* [1951] W.N. 505.
[95] *Ibid.* See also *R.* v. *George* [1956] Crim.L.R. 52, in which it was held that something more than just a *secret* indecent motive must be shown.
[96] *Ante,* p. 470, n. 64.
[97] *Ante,* p. 470, n. 66.   [98] s. 28 (2).
[99] The Sexual Offences Act 1967, s. 8, which provides that no proceedings be instituted except with the consent of the Director of Public Prosecutions against any man for gross indecency or certain other offences where any person is under twenty-one does not apply to proceedings under the Indecency with Children Act 1960: Criminal Justice Act 1972, s. 48 (not in force at July 1, 1972).

SECTION 4.   ABDUCTION AND DETENTION OF WOMEN, GIRLS, CHILDREN AND DEFECTIVES

Women and girls. By **section 17** of the **Sexual Offences Act 1956** any person is guilty of *an offence* [*Imp.* 14 *years* [1]] who, with the intention that she shall marry or have unlawful [2] sexual intercourse [3] with that or any other person *takes away* or *detains* a woman against her will, if she is so taken away or detained either by force or for the sake of her property or expectations of property.

For the purposes of the section the reference to " expectations of property " relates only to property of a person to whom she is next-of-kin or one of the next-of-kin, and " property " includes any interest in property. [4]

By the **Act of 1956** the following are offences [*Imp.* 2 *years* [5]].

By **section 24** it is an offence to *detain* any woman or girl against her will on any premises with intent that she may have unlawful [6] sexual intercourse with any particular man or generally or in any brothel. Where a woman or girl is in or upon premises for the purposes of having unlawful sexual intercourse or is in a brothel, the withholding of her clothes or other property with intent to compel or induce her to remain there, or the threat of legal proceedings if she takes away clothes provided for her by him or on his directions, is deemed to constitute a detention. [7]

By **sections 19 and 20** it is an offence to take out of the possession and against the will of her parent, or other person having the lawful care or charge of her:

(1) Any unmarried girl under eighteen with intent that she may have unlawful [8] sexual intercourse with any man. It is a defence for the accused to prove [9] that he had reasonable cause to believe that the girl was over eighteen.

(2) Any unmarried girl under sixteen without lawful authority or excuse.

---

[1] Sched. 2.
[2] It is difficult to see what the word " unlawful " can add to these offences.
[3] For the definition of sexual intercourse see *ante*, p. 466.
[4] s. 17 (2).   [5] Sched. 2.
[6] It is difficult to see what the word " unlawful " adds to this section, although it may exclude marital intercourse.
[7] s. 16 (2).   A woman who takes away clothes in these circumstances in order to escape is not liable civilly or criminally: s. 16 (3).
[8] The word " unlawful " has been held to mean extra-marital: *R*. v. *Chapman* [1959] 1 Q.B. 100.
[9] s. 47.

The taking need not be by force actual or constructive, and the fact that the girl consents or proposes the plan is no defence if the accused " made a bargain with her to take her away " [10] or if by preconcerted arrangement the girl leaves her home in order to meet and go away with the accused.[11]   But if without any persuasion or agreement a girl leaves her home and goes to the accused he is not guilty of " taking " merely because he does not restore her.[12] There may, however, be a taking out of possession where a girl is " taken " while absent from her home if her absence is for a mere temporary purpose which does not interrupt the possession of the person in lawful charge of her.[13]   It is not necessarily a defence that the taking was merely for a short time, and without any intent to keep her away from her home permanently.[14]

There is a taking against the will of the parent, etc., if, though he consented, his consent was induced by the fraudulent representations of the accused.[15]

It has been held that these offences are not committed if the accused honestly (and reasonably [16]) believed that the girl was not under the lawful charge of any person or that the person in lawful charge had consented.[17]   But, in the case of an offence against section 20, it is no defence that the accused honestly and upon reasonable grounds believed that the girl was over sixteen.[18]   The offence may be committed either by a male or female, and the absence of any corrupt motive is no defence.[19]

Children.   By **section 56** of the **Offences against the Person Act 1861** it is an offence [*Imp. 7 years*] for anyone unlawfully either by force or fraud to lead or take away or decoy or entice away or detain any child under the age of fourteen years, with intent to deprive any parent, guardian, or other person having the lawful care or charge of such child of its possession, or with intent to

---

10 *R.* v. *Robins* (1844) 1 C. & K. 456 at p. 460.
11 *R.* v. *Manktelow* (1853) 6 Cox C.C. 143.
12 *R.* v. *Olifier* (1866) 10 Cox C.C. 402; *R.* v. *Jarvis* (1903) 20 Cox C.C. 249.
13 *R.* v. *Mycock* (1871) 12 Cox C.C. 28.
14 *R.* v. *Timmins* (1860) 8 Cox C.C. 401; *R.* v. *Baillie* (1859) 8 Cox C.C. 238.
15 *R.* v. *Hopkins* (1842) C. & M. 254.
16 But see *ante*, p. 47.
17 *R.* v. *Hibbert* (1869) L.R. 1 C.C.R. 184; and see *R.* v. *Prince* (1875) L.R. 2 C.C.R. 154 at p. 175.
18 *R.* v. *Prince* (1875) L.R. 2 C.C.R. 154.
19 *R.* v. *Booth* (1872) 12 Cox C.C. 231.

steal any article upon or about its person, or with any such intent to receive or harbour any such child knowing it to have been so taken away, etc., or detained. This offence cannot, however, be committed by anyone who claims any right to the possession of the child or by its mother or, in the case of an illegitimate child, by one who claims to be its father.

Fraud exercised either upon the child or its parent, etc., is sufficient to constitute the offence.[20] It is not necessary to prove an intent to deprive the parent, etc., permanently of the possession of the child.[21]

If the child taken is a boy over fourteen but under eighteen or a girl over sixteen and under eighteen, and the taking is without the consent of the parents, the accused could, perhaps, be charged with kidnapping—a common law offence.[22]

Defectives. By **section 1** of the **Sexual Offences Act 1956** it is an offence for a person, with intent that any female defective shall have unlawful[23] sexual intercourse with any man, to take such defective out of the possession of her parent or any person having lawful charge of her against his will; provided that he is not guilty of this offence if he proves[24] that he does not know and has no reason to suspect her to be a defective.[25]

SECTION 5. OFFENCES CONCERNING PROSTITUTION

Those offences concerning prostitution which are more properly treated as part of the law of nuisance have already been examined and a meaning has been given to the expressions " prostitute " and " brothel." [26] The following are also offences [*Imp. 2 years*, except where the contrary is stated].[27]

By **section 22** of the **Sexual Offences Act 1956** it is an offence for a person to procure or attempt to procure any woman to become a common prostitute in any part of the world, or to leave the United Kingdom with intent that she may become an inmate

---

[20] *R.* v. *Bellis* (1893) 62 L.J.M.C. 155.
[21] *R.* v. *Powell* (1914) 24 Cox C.C. 229.
[22] Arch. para. 2801.
[23] The word " unlawful " would appear to add nothing to this section.
[24] s. 47.
[25] As to this proviso, see, *ante*, p. 468.
[26] *Ante*, p. 244.
[27] Sexual Offences Act 1956, Sched. 2.

of or frequent a brothel elsewhere, or to leave her usual place of abode in the United Kingdom with intent that she may become an inmate of or frequent a brothel in any part of the world.[28]

By **section 24** (noted above [29]) detaining a woman in a brothel is an offence.

By **section 28** it is an offence for a person to cause or encourage [30] the prostitution of a girl under the age of sixteen for whom he is responsible.[31] A person shall be deemed to have so caused or encouraged if he knowingly allowed the girl to consort with or be employed by a prostitute or person of known immoral character.[32]

By **section 29** it is an offence for a person to cause or encourage the prostitution in any part of the world of a woman who is a defective,[33] provided that he is not guilty of an offence if he proves [34] that he does not know and has no reason to suspect her to be a defective.[35]

By **section 3** of the **Children and Young Persons Act 1933** [36] any person having the custody, charge or care of a child between four and nineteen who allows it to reside in or frequent a brothel is punishable on **indictment** or **summarily** [£25 *fine and Imp. 6 months*].

By **section 30** of the **Sexual Offences Act 1956** [37] it is an offence punishable on **indictment** [*Imp. 7 years*] or **summarily** [*Imp. 6 months*] for a man knowingly to live wholly or in part on the earnings of prostitution. A man who lives with or is habitually in the company of a prostitute, or who exercises control, direction or influence over a prostitute's movements in a way which shows he is aiding, abetting or compelling her prostitution with others, is presumed to be knowingly living on the earnings of prostitution unless he proves to the contrary.[38]

The circumstances in which a man can be said to be living on the earnings of prostitution can be divided into three categories.

---

[28] Corroboration is required if the evidence is that of one witness only: s. 22 (2).
[29] *Ante*, p. 473. [30] *Ante*, p. 470, n. 64.
[31] *Ante*, n. 66 on p. 470.
[32] s. 28 (2).
[33] *Ante*, p. 468, n. 46. [34] s. 47.
[35] As to this proviso, see *ante*, p. 468.
[36] As amended by the Sexual Offences Act 1956, Sched. 4 and the Children and Young Persons Act 1963, Sched. 5.
[37] And Sched. 2, as amended by the Street Offences Act 1959, s. 4.
[38] s. 30 (1).

First, where the man is maintained by her. Secondly, "if he is paid by prostitutes for goods or services supplied by him to them for the purpose of their prostitution which he would not supply but for the fact that they were prostitutes." [39] So a person who provides premises to a prostitute to be used only at certain times of the day and only for prostitution [40] or who publishes a directory of prostitutes [41] and, in either case, receives a fee (whether reasonable or not) for so doing is guilty of the offence. Thirdly, a person who provides premises or goods, for prostitutes which are normally provided for other people will be guilty of this offence, if, and only if, he charges an exorbitant price.[42]

By **section 5** of the **Sexual Offences Act 1967** it is an offence, similarly punishable, for a man or woman knowingly to live wholly or in part on the earnings of prostitution of another man.

By **section 31** of the **Sexual Offences Act 1956** [43] it is an offence punishable on **indictment** [*Imp. 7 years*] or **summarily** [*Imp. 6 months*] for a woman for purposes of gain to exercise control, direction or influence over a prostitute's movements in a way which shows she is aiding, abetting or compelling her prostitution.

SECTION 6. UNNATURAL OFFENCES

By **section 12** of the **Sexual Offences Act 1956** it is an offence to commit buggery.[44] [*Imp. life if with a boy under the age of sixteen or with a woman or an animal. Imp. 10 years if with a man who did not consent. Imp. 5 years if he consented and was under twenty-one and the accused was, or was over, twenty-one. Otherwise Imp. 2 years.*[45]] The evidence is similar to that required to prove rape, with two exceptions: (i) subject to the Sexual Offences Act 1967 the consent of the person upon whom it was

[39] *Shaw* v. *D.P.P.* [1962] A.C. 220 at p. 264.
[40] *R.* v. *Thomas* [1957] 1 W.L.R. 747. See also *Calvert* v. *Mayes* [1954] 1 Q.B. 342.
[41] *Shaw* v. *D.P.P.* [1962] A.C. 220.
[42] *R.* v. *Thomas* [1957] 1 W.L.R. 747; *Shaw* v. *D.P.P.* [1962] A.C. 220 at pp. 265–266, 271
[43] And Sched. 2, as amended by the Street Offences Act 1959, s. 4.
[44] That is, sexual intercourse *per anum* by a man with a man or a man with a woman, or sexual intercourse *per anum* or *per vaginam* by a man or woman with an animal: Arch. para. 2968.
[45] Sched. 2, as amended by Sexual Offences Act 1967.

perpetrated is no defence; (ii) both parties, if consenting, are equally guilty; but if one of the parties is a boy under the age of fourteen years, it is an offence in the other only.[46]

Any attempt to commit this crime, or any assault with intent to commit the same [**section 16**], is also an offence. [*For attempt: Imp.* 10 *years if with a boy under the age of sixteen, or with a woman or an animal, otherwise the maximum period for the substantive offence. For assault: Imp.* 10 *years.*[47]] The offence of indecent assault has been noted above.[48]

By **section 13** it is an offence [*Imp.* 2 *years or Imp.* 5 *years if by a man of, or over, the age of twenty-one with a man under that age*[49]] for a male person, either in public or private, to commit or be a party to the commission, or to procure or attempt to procure the commission, by any male person, of an act of gross indecency[50] with another male person. Consent is no defence,[51] subject however, to the provisions of the Sexual Offences Act 1967.

Section 1 of the **Sexual Offences Act 1967** provides that a homosexual act (defined as buggery or gross indecency between men) in private shall not be an offence, provided that the parties consent and have attained the age of twenty-one.[52] An act is not done in private if more than two persons take part or are present, or if done in a lavatory to which the public have, or are permitted to have access, whether on payment or otherwise. A man suffering from severe abnormality within the meaning of the Mental Health Act 1959 cannot in law give the necessary consent, but a homosexual act with such a person is not an offence if the accused proves that he did not know and had no reason to suspect the man to be so suffering. Section 1 does not prevent an act from being an offence under any provision of the Army Act 1955, the Air Force Act 1955, or the Naval Discipline Act 1957, and, by section 2, a homosexual act on board a United Kingdom merchant ship continues to be an offence.

---

[46] Arch. para. 2970.
[47] Sched. 2, as amended by Sexual Offences Act 1967.
[48] *Ante*, p. 471.
[49] Sched. 2, as amended by Sexual Offences Act 1967.
[50] Physical contact is not necessary: *R.* v. *Hunt* (1950) 34 Cr.App.R. 135.
[51] *R.* v. *Hall* [1964] 1 Q.B. 273.
[52] The burden of proving that the act was not in private, etc., is upon the prosecutor: Sexual Offences Act 1967, s. 1 (6).

Section 4 (1) makes it an **indictable** offence [*Imp.* 2 *years*] for a man to procure another man to commit with a third man an act of buggery which, by reason of section 1, is *not* an offence (if it were an offence the punishment would be the same as for the substantive offence because the procurer would then be an accomplice). Section 4 (3) provides that it shall not be an offence under section 13 of the 1956 Act to procure another man to commit an act of gross indecency with the procurer, which act is not an offence by virtue of section 1. It, therefore, remains an offence for the procurer to procure another man to commit an act of gross indecency with a third man, albeit the act is not an offence because of section 1. Although this may seem strange, it must be remembered that the word procure in section 13 (as in other sections of the 1956 Act and in section 4 (1) of the 1967 Act) means persuading an unwilling person to commit the act. Furthermore, although it is necessary for the act to be committed, it is not necessary for the act to be a criminal offence.[53] If the act procured does constitute an offence, then the procurer will, in any case, be an *accomplice* to the offence.

Section 8 of the **Sexual Offences Act 1967** provides that no proceedings shall be instituted except by or with the consent of the Director of Public Prosecutions against any man for the offence of buggery with, or gross indecency with, another man, for attempting to commit either offence, or for aiding, abetting, counselling, procuring or commanding its commission where either of those men was at the time of its commission under the age of twenty-one.[53a] **Section 7** of the Act imposes a time limit on prosecutions.

SECTION 7. SOLICITING BY MEN

By **section 32**[54] it is an offence punishable on **indictment** [*Imp.* 2 *years*] or on **summary conviction** [*Imp.* 6 *months*] for a man persistently to solicit or importune in a public place for immoral purposes. The expressions " solicit " and " public place " have already been defined.[55] There must be an element of persis-

---

[53] *Ante*, p. 476.
[53a] This section does not apply to offences under the Indecency with Children Act 1960: Criminal Justice Act 1972, s. 48 (not in force at July 1, 1972).
[54] And Sched. 2.
[55] *Ante*, pp. 246 and 334.

tence [56] and it would not seem to matter that he is soliciting for himself, other men or women. It has recently been held that a man who solicits women to have intercourse with him does not commit this offence.[57]

CHAPTER 34

CHILDREN

THE offences found in this chapter arise mainly under the **Children and Young Persons Acts 1933 to 1969.** The classification of offences adopted by the 1933 Act—those relating to the safeguarding of children from moral and physical danger and those relating to employment—will be followed here.

By **section 1** [1] it is an offence for any person being over sixteen and having the care or custody of any child under that age wilfully to assault, neglect, abandon, etc., such person or to procure the assault, neglect, abandonment, etc., of such person in a manner likely to cause unnecessary suffering or injury to health [**indictment:** £100 *fine and Imp.* 2 *years;* **summary conviction:** £100 *fine and Imp.* 6 *months*]. The section does not create a number of separate offences of assaulting, neglecting, abandoning, etc., it creates a single offence dealing with a number of forms of cruelty.[2]

The section further provides that a parent or other person legally liable to maintain a child under sixteen shall be deemed to have neglected him in a manner likely to cause injury to his health if he has failed to provide adequate food, clothing, medical aid or lodging for him, or if, having been otherwise unable to make this provision, he has failed to take steps to procure it to be provided under the Welfare Acts. A person who has attained sixteen is also deemed to have neglected the child if it is proved that the death of a child under three was caused by suffocation (not due to disease, etc.) while the child was in bed with that person and the person was drunk.

In *R. v. Senior* [3] the accused was charged with manslaughter. He was a member of a sect, called the Peculiar People, who believed that the use of doctors and drugs to cure the sick was contrary to the Bible. The accused, in accordance with his beliefs, had failed to provide medical assistance for one of his children, who had as a result died. The accused's conviction was confirmed

---

[1] As amended by s. 31 and Sched. 5 to the 1963 Act, and the Criminal Law Act 1967.
[2] *R. v. Hayles* [1969] 1 Q.B. 364.
[3] [1899] 1 Q.B. 283.

on appeal. The court held that the accused had wilfully neglected the child contrary to the provisions of the predecessor of the present section 1. Lord Russell C.J. said [4]:

> " ' Wilfully ' means that the act is done deliberately and intentionally, not by accident or inadvertence, but so that the mind of the person who does the act goes with it. Neglect is the want of reasonable care—that is, the omission of such steps as a reasonable parent would take. . . . "

Since the accused had, in committing an offence, caused the death of the child, he was automatically guilty of manslaughter.[5] The decision has been criticised on the basis that the court did not give full scope to the doctrine of *mens rea* imported expressly by the word "wilfully," but it is still the leading case on the subject. The *actus reus* of the offence is apparently committed if the accused failed to take reasonable care or if the refusal to allow medical aid was unreasonable.[6] However, it could be argued that the accused does not have the necessary *mens rea* unless he believed that such reasonable medical assistance was necessary. In *R*. v. *Senior* there was some evidence that the accused thought, on an interpretation of a passage in the Bible, that God would cure his child better than any doctor.[7]

Section 4 [8] makes it an offence [**summary conviction:** £25 *fine and Imp.* 3 *months*] for any person to cause or procure a child under sixteen or, having the custody, charge or care of such a child, to allow him to be in any street, premises or place for the purposes of begging, whether or not there is any pretence of performing or offering anything for sale. If any person while performing or offering anything for sale in a street or public place has with him a child who has been lent or hired out to him, the child shall be deemed to be there for the purposes of begging.

Section 5 [9] makes it an offence [**summary conviction:** £10 *fine*] for any person to give or cause to be given to any child under the age of five years any intoxicating liquor, except upon the order of a duly qualified medical practitioner or in case of sickness.

---

4 At pp. 290–291.
5 *Ante*, p. 19.
6 *Oakey* v. *Jackson* [1914] 1 K.B. 216 at p. 220.
7 [1899] 1 Q.B. 283 at p. 284.
8 As amended by the Children and Young Persons Act 1963, Sched. 5.
9 As amended by the Criminal Justice Act 1967, Sched. 3.

A number of other offences concerning intoxicating liquor and
children are to be found in the Licensing Act 1964 which is
discussed elsewhere.[10]

Section 7 [11] makes it an offence for any person to sell to a
person apparently under the age of sixteen years any tobacco or
cigarette papers whether for his own use or not [**summary conviction:** *first offence, £25 fine; second offence, £50 fine; third offence,
£100 fine*]. Where the charge is brought in respect of a sale of
tobacco otherwise than in the form of cigarettes, the accused is not
guilty if he did not know and had no reason to believe that the
tobacco was for the use of the person to whom it was sold.

Section 7 also provides that if an automatic machine for the
sale of tobacco kept on any premises is being extensively used by
persons apparently under the age of sixteen, then a complaint may
be made to a court of summary jurisdiction, which may order the
owner of the machine or the person on whose premises it is kept
to remove it; alternatively, it may order that precautions be taken
to prevent the machine being so used. Failure to comply with the
order is an offence [**summary conviction:** £50 *fine and* £10 *for each
day of non-compliance*].

If a constable or park-keeper (when in uniform) finds a person
apparently under the age of sixteen smoking in any street or public
place he may seize any tobacco and cigarette papers which are in
that person's possession.[12]

Other provisions regarding children may be found in the sections dealing with pawn-brokers,[13] scrap-metal dealers,[14] betting,
and gaming.[15]

By **Part II** of the **Children and Young Persons Act 1933** numerous restrictions are imposed on the employment of children and
young persons.[16] The principal provisions with regard to employment are as follows:

---

[10] *Ante*, p. 353.
[11] As amended by the Children and Young Persons Act 1963, s. 32.
[12] s. 7 (3). The provisions of s. 7 relating to sale and seizure do not apply
where the person to whom the tobacco was sold or in whose possession it
was found had bought the tobacco or had it in his possession in his capacity
as employee of a dealer or manufacturer in tobacco or, if in uniform, as a
boy messenger employed by a messenger company: s. 7 (4).
[13] *Ante*, p. 383.   [14] *Ante*, p. 385.
[15] *Ante*, p. 318.
[16] The provisions of this Part of the Act have been substantially amended and
supplemented by the Children and Young Persons Act 1963, and the
Childrens Act 1972

By **section 18,**[17] no child may be employed until he has attained the age of thirteen. No child may be employed before the close of school hours on any day on which he is required to attend school. No child may be employed before 6 a.m. or after 8 p.m. No child may be employed for more than two hours on any day on which he is required to attend school. No child may be employed on a Sunday for more than two hours. No child may be employed to handle anything so heavy as to be likely to cause injury to him.

By the same section local education authorities[18] are empowered to make by-laws imposing additional restrictions.

The by-laws may, for example, prescribe an age-limit higher than that specified in the Act or they may impose more stringent requirements as to the hours during which children may be employed. No by-law may, however, prevent a child from taking part in an entertainment in accordance with a licence granted for that purpose.[19]

In addition to the requirements of section 18 and of any by-laws made thereunder, it is further provided by section 20 that a person must have attained the age of sixteen years before he may engage in or be employed in street trading.[20]

Contravention of any of the provisions relating to employment contained in this Part of the Act or in by-laws made by authority thereof is an offence [**summary conviction:** £20 *fine or* £50 *in the case of a second or subsequent conviction*]. No offence is committed by the person employed. As we have seen, however, it is an offence for a person to engage in street trading on his own behalf [**summary conviction:** £10 *fine or* £20 *in the case of a second or subsequent conviction*].

By **section 23,**[21] no person under the age of sixteen may take part in any public performance in which his life or limbs are endangered, and anyone who causes or procures or, being his parent or guardian, allows such a person to take part in such a

---

[17] As amended by the Education (Miscellaneous Provisions) Act 1948, s. 11 and Sched. 1.

[18] See s. 96 of the 1933 Act.

[19] See below. If one has a licence one is also exempt from the requirement that the child be not employed for more than two hours on any school day or before 6.0 a.m. and after 8.0 p.m.

[20] The local education authorities have power to make by-laws allowing persons under 16 to be so employed by their parents. By-laws may also be made raising the minimum age requirement to 18.

[21] As amended by the Criminal Justice Act 1967, Sched. 3.

performance commits an offence [**summary conviction:** £50 *fine or* £100 *in the case of a second or subsequent conviction*].   Proceedings under this section may be brought only by a chief officer of police or someone acting under his authority.

The training of persons for performances of a dangerous nature is covered by **section 24.**[22]   This imposes an absolute prohibition on the training of anyone who has not attained the age of twelve years.   One may train a person over twelve but under sixteen provided that one obtains a licence from a magistrates' court.[23] The training of a person under twelve, or the training without a licence of a person over twelve but under sixteen, amounts to an offence on the part of anyone who caused or procured it or, being parent or guardian, allowed it [**summary conviction:** £20 *fine or* £50 *in the case of a second or subsequent conviction*].

It may be added that the **Shops Act 1950** and the **Young Persons (Employment) Acts 1938 and 1964** regulate the hours of persons who, being under the age of eighteen, are employed in shops and warehouses and in certain specified occupations, and impose penalties for the breach.

[22] *Ibid.*
[23] Not a local authority as in s. 22.

PART IV

OFFENCES AGAINST PROPERTY

Chapter 35

THEFT

Section 1. Theft

BEFORE the revision and simplification of the law of theft and kindred offences by the **Theft Act 1968,** the greater part of the law relating to the dishonest appropriation of property was unnecessarily complicated. The reasons for this state of affairs may be found by tracing in detail the historical development of the criminal law in general and the concept of larceny in particular. This has been done elsewhere and cannot serve any useful purpose in a work of this nature. The difficulty which faces both author and student is to know to what extent the old law [1] should be examined. Where the law has been extensively revised by a single Act of Parliament, which is the position in relation to the law of theft, some of the older authorities may still be relevant to offences under the new Act. In this chapter, the old law and the authorities arising under it will only be discussed in so far as they serve to illustrate some point under the Theft Act. To do otherwise will only lead to confusion.

By **section 7** of the **Theft Act 1968** theft is an indictable offence punishable with imprisonment for 10 years.[2]

The Act provides that a person is guilty of theft if he dishonestly appropriates property belonging to another with the intention of permanently depriving the other of it; and " thief " and " steal " are to be construed accordingly.[3] It is immaterial whether the appropriation is made with a view to gain, or is made for the thief's own benefit.[4]

It will be seen that the offence consists of four ingredients, that is to say:

(1) dishonest;

---

[1] Before January 1, 1969, the law of larceny was contained in the common law and the extensions of the common law contained in the Larceny Acts 1861 and 1916.

[2] The numerous statutory punishments for different forms of larceny under the Acts of 1861 and 1916 are all abolished.

[3] Theft Act 1968, s. 1 (1).

[4] *Ibid.* s. 1 (2).

    (2) appropriation;

    (3) of property which is capable of being stolen, belonging to
         another;

    (4) with intent permanently to deprive.[5]

It might be convenient to examine those four ingredients in that order, yet it is probably more useful to consider first what property is capable of being stolen, and thus forming the subject-matter of a charge of theft.

What property is capable of being stolen?

The definition of " property " in the Act is very wide [6] including as it does, " money and all other property, real or personal, including things in action and other intangible property." This definition is subject to only one qualification, namely that the property must be capable of appropriation, since the appropriation of property belonging to another is the *actus reus* of the offence of theft. Perhaps the only thing that comes immediately to mind as being incapable of appropriation is electricity [7] and to put that matter beyond doubt the abstraction of electricity is made the subject of a special offence in the Act.[8] Water and gas, at least when piped, come within a slightly different category, and there would seem to be no reason why they should not be capable of appropriation.[9]

Land and things forming part of the land. The Act starts with the general principle that a person cannot steal land,[10] or things forming part of the land and severed from it by the offender or by his directions,[11] but goes on to detail three cases in which the general proposition does not apply. First, it may be theft where the offender is a trustee or personal representative, or is authorised by power of attorney, or as liquidator of a company, or otherwise, to sell or dispose of land belonging to another, and he appropriates the land or anything forming part of it by dealing with it in breach

---

[5] *R.* v. *Lawrence* (1970) 114 S.J. 864; affirmed [1972] A.C. 626 H.L.

[6] Theft Act 1968, s. 4 (1).

[7] See the doubts expressed by the Criminal Law Revision Committee on whose report (Cmnd. 2977) the Act is based, para. 85 at p. 379.

[8] s. 13.

[9] *R.* v. *White* (1853) Dears. 203; *R.* v. *Firth* (1869) L.R. 1 C.C.R. 172; *Ferens* v. *O'Brien* [1883] 11 Q.B.D. 21.

[10] Not including incorporeal hereditaments.

[11] s. 4 (2).

of the confidence reposed in him.[12] Secondly, it may be theft where the offender is not in possession of the land and appropriates anything forming part of the land by severing it or causing it to be severed, or after it has been severed. Thus where a stranger, not being in possession of land, cuts and appropriates grass growing on the land this may be theft.[13] The position will be the same if such a person removes a gate from its hinges and appropriates it.[14] Where a person encroaches on the land of his neighbour by moving the boundary fence, this is not theft; nor would it seem to be theft where a person in possession of land digs gravel from the soil and appropriates it. The third exception [15] makes it theft where a person in possession of land under a tenancy [16] appropriates the whole or part of any fixture or structure let to be used with the land.[17]

Incorporeal hereditaments such as easements, rights of way, rents and profits are expressly excluded from the definition of land [18] but since they appear to come within the definition of " property " under the Act [19] although such cases must be rare indeed, they are, in theory, capable of being stolen.

Things growing wild on land are within the general definition of " property " under the Act and may form the subject-matter of a charge of theft, provided that they are first severed from the land, and where they are appropriated by a person not in possession of the land. A special exemption, however, is provided [20] in the case of a person who picks mushrooms [21] growing wild on any land, or who picks flowers, fruit or foliage from a plant [22] growing wild on any land. Such a person does not (although he is not in

---

[12] Which amounted to fraudulent conversion under the old law.

[13] s. 4 (2) (b).

[14] Cf. R. v. Foley (1889) 17 Cox C.C. 142; cf. R. v. Skujins [1956] Crim.L.R. 266.

[15] s. 4 (2) (c).

[16] Tenancy means a term of years or any less period and includes an agreement for such a tenancy; a person " holding over " as a statutory tenant or otherwise is also treated as having possession under a tenancy.

[17] In Billings v. Pill [1954] 1 Q.B. 70 the Divisional Court held that an army hut secured by bolts to a concrete base was not a " structure " and could be removed without damaging the freehold.

[18] s. 4 (2).

[19] In s. 4 (1); although it is difficult to envisage the theft of an easement or right of way in practice.

[20] s. 4 (3).

[21] Including any fungus.

[22] Including any shrub or tree.

possession of the land) steal what he picks, unless he does so for reward or for sale or for other commercial purpose. Thus a person who picks brambles in a hedgerow or takes elderberries from a tree on the land of another does not steal them if he intends them for consumption by his family, but only where he intends, for instance, to market the former or make wine for sale from the latter. This exemption only applies to things growing wild; to take fruit from another's orchard is still theft. There is a distinction between a person who " picks " fruit, etc., growing wild, and a person who takes and uproots the whole plant. The latter is guilty of theft. Injury to growing plants, trees and the like will come within the ambit of the offence of criminal damage.[23]

Animals. Certain domestic animals which are not traditionally used for labour or food were not the subject of larceny at common law, being regarded as of no value. Among this class were included dogs, cats, monkeys, ferrets, parrots and canaries, etc.[24] It would be strange in England for dogs to be treated thus, and they together with certain other animals and birds were made larcenable by statute.[25] Under the Theft Act 1968 animals are clearly within the definition of " property "[26] and domestic animals are capable of being stolen. Wild creatures, tamed or untamed, are regarded as property,[27] but the Act provides[28] that a person cannot steal a wild creature " not tamed nor ordinarily kept in captivity " or the carcase of such a creature, unless either[29]—

(i) it has been reduced into possession by or on behalf of another person *and* possession of it has not since been lost or abandoned; or

(ii) another person is in course of reducing it into possession.

The effect of the Act is that as a general proposition *wild* creatures are an exception to the rule. Where the wild creature has been tamed, or is ordinarily kept in captivity, *e.g.* a jackdaw which has been caged or a deer in a deerpark, then if it is appropriated that is

---

[23] See below, *post*, pp. 530 *et seq.*
[24] 1 Hawk. c. 33, s. 23.
[25] Larceny Act 1861, ss. 3, 18, 21, 22.
[26] In s. 4 (1) *ante*, p. 490.
[27] s. 4 (4).
[28] *Ibid.*
[29] It is submitted that this refers to the specific animal and not to the genus or species. As to what amounts to " captivity " and a comparison with the status of the Children of Israel see *Rowley* v. *Murphy* [1964] 2 Q.B. 43.

theft. The same is the case in relation to zoo animals, that is wild animals reduced into possession and ordinarily kept in captivity. If such an animal is appropriated from the zoo this is theft. If such an animal escapes from the zoo, and while at large it is appropriated, then this will be theft if possession has not been "lost or abandoned " by the zoo. Whether this stage has been reached is one of degree in the particular circumstances of the case.

If a poacher enters upon land and takes a hare or pheasant or is in the course of doing so, when a third person, not being in possession of the land takes the game from him, this is theft. The case is the same if A drives his car upon the land of B and kills a pheasant, then if A takes the carcase this is not theft, but if C driving behind takes the carcase from A this is theft.

An offence of poaching is to be found in the **First Schedule** to the **Theft Act.**

Things in action such as trade marks, copyrights, debts, etc., though intangible, may be stolen, but few cases are likely to arise.

Value. To be the subject of theft, a thing must have some value, but it need not apparently be of the value of any coin known to the law.[30]

Property belonging to another

Since theft is concerned with the dishonest appropriation of property belonging to another, the property must not only be capable of being stolen, and therefore be in existence and be ascertainable so that it can be appropriated, but it must belong to another. It follows that to appropriate property which cannot or does not belong to another is not theft.

Certain property cannot belong to anyone. It has always been a principle of English law that a human corpse cannot be owned. There could be no theft of a corpse at common law.[31] Property does not belong to another if that other has abandoned it, but whether there has in fact been an abandonment will often be a difficult question of fact. A person who loses property does not necessarily intend to abandon it, even where he has given up the search for it.[32] Again, an owner may intend, in a manner of

---

[30] Arch. para. 1483.
[31] *R.* v. *Handyside* (undated) 2 East P.C. 652 ; *R.* v. *Sharpe* (1856) Dears. & B. 160.
[32] *Hibbert* v. *McKiernan* [1948] 2 K.B. 142.

speaking, to abandon his property and yet still intend to exclude others from it, and this would be no abandonment in law. In *Hibbert* v. *McKiernan*,[33] a golf club which intended to exclude the general public from its land was held to have a special property in golf balls lying on the course after being lost, despite the fact that their original owners had given up the search for them.[34] It was held in *Williams* v. *Phillips*[35] that refuse put into the dustbin is not abandoned, since it remains in the householder's possession until it is taken away, when it becomes the property of the local authority. A dustman who dishonestly appropriates refuse in such circumstances may be guilty of theft. The mere fact that an owner of property does not intend to make further use of some article, and it is thus of no value to him, does not mean that he has abandoned it.[36] If the accused holds an honest belief that property has been abandoned, then, of course, apart from any question of whether or not that is the case, he would not be acting dishonestly and would be entitled to be acquitted.[37]

The Theft Act regards property as belonging to any person having possession or control of it, or having in it any proprietary right or interest (not being an equitable interest arising only from an agreement to transfer or grant an interest).[38] Theft is an offence against possession or control rather than ownership. There are no grounds for qualifying the words "possession or control" in the section so as to read into them such an implied meaning as "lawful possession" or a "right of possession superior to that of the taker."[39]

In general, it may be said that possession or control requires an intention on the part of the possessor to possess or control, although he may yet at any given moment in time not have the particular article in mind or indeed know where it is. In *Hibbert* v. *McKiernan*[40] the officials of the club did not know at any given moment the exact number or position of the abandoned golf balls. The Electricity Board may not know how many coins are in a

[33] n. 32, *supra*.
[34] The position might have been different on a public course.
[35] (1957) 41 Cr.App.R. 5.
[36] *Digby* v. *Heelan* (1952) 102 L.J. 287, D.C.
[37] *Cf. R.* v. *White* (1912) 7 Cr.App.R. 266.
[38] s. 5 (1).
[39] *R.* v. *Turner* (*No.* 2) (1971) 55 Cr.App.R. 336.
[40] [1948] 2 K.B. 142.

meter, but they have possession of them.[41] So does a householder have possession of the whole contents of his house even though he may not be able to itemise them.[42]

Any proprietary rights or interest in land. The law protects all interests in property, and for the purposes of the law of theft the only interest excluded from this protection is the " equitable interest arising only from an agreement to transfer or grant an interest." A person with a greater proprietary interest may " steal " the chattel from a person with a lesser interest. A servant may steal from his master property which may be under the former's control; and a trustee may " steal " property in which a beneficiary has only an equitable interest. A person having a proprietary right or interest in a chattel may steal from a person having mere custody of it. In *R.* v. *Turner*[43] the owner of a car took it to a garage to be repaired. He said he would come back the next day and pay for the repairs and take the car away. The same day, without telling the garage proprietor, he took the car away from near the garage. The Court of Appeal agreed with the trial judge that quite apart from any questions of lien or hire purchase, the test was " Was the garage proprietor in fact in possession or control of the car? " A conviction for theft was upheld. It is theft where a person removes his own property dishonestly from a repairer who has possession[44]; or where he dishonestly removes it from the possession of an auctioneer.[45] A person who owns, possesses or has control of property has a proprietary right in that property; any power to exclude others will suffice.[46] Co-owners and joint partners each have a proprietary right or interest in the joint property, and it will be theft where one dishonestly appropriates any of the property from the other.[47]

The Act provides for certain special cases, where difficulty may arise in defining property as " belonging to another." The first of these cases refers to trust property. In general the dishonest appropriation of trust property by a trustee will fall within the

[41] *Martin* v. *Marsh* [1955] Crim.L.R. 781 but see [1956] Crim.L.R. 74.
[42] See Smith and Hogan, *op. cit.*, p. 362.
[43] (1971) 55 Cr.App.R. 336.
[44] *e.g. Rose* v. *Matt* [1951] 1 K.B. 810.
[45] *Dennant* v. *Skinner* [1948] 2 K.B. 164.
[46] For a detailed examination of this question see Smith and Hogan, *op. cit.*, pp. 363–364.
[47] *R.* v. *Bonner* (1970) 54 Cr.App.R. 257.

ambit of the general definition,[48] for the beneficiary will have a proprietary interest in the trust property. There are, however, trusts which do not fall strictly within the general definition—the obvious example being a " purpose " trust where the object of the trust is to effect some purpose [49] rather than to benefit some individual. Such property will fall within the extended definition and the Act provides [50] that the persons to whom such property " belongs " shall be regarded as including any person having a right to enforce the trust; and the Act provides that an intention to defeat the trust shall be regarded as an intention to deprive of the property any person having that right.

Property received for a particular purpose. Where a number of persons subscribe money for a particular purpose, for instance, for a holiday club or a Christmas fund, and that money is held by a treasurer, then to whom does the money belong? [51] In strict law one must concede that the money belongs to the treasurer, but this clearly gives rise to difficulties where the treasurer steals the money. The Theft Act deals with this as a special case and provides [52] that where a person receives property from or on account of another and is under an obligation to the other to retain and deal with that property or its proceeds in a particular way, the property or proceeds shall be regarded *as against him* as belonging to another. Therefore where the treasurer or stake-holder dishonestly appropriates any of the subscribed funds, the criminal law takes the view *as against him* that the property belongs to the subscribers, and he may be convicted of theft. It has been suggested [53] that this provision may cover the common case of a workman who has undertaken to do certain work, and has received an advance for the particular purpose of purchasing materials, who then dishonestly uses the money for his own purposes.[53a] It is

---

[48] In s. 5 (1).
[49] Generally charitable.
[50] s. 5 (2).
[51] *R. v. Hassal* (1861) Le. & Ca. 56 is a classic example.
[52] s. 5 (3).
[53] Smith and Hogan, *op. cit.*, p. 365.
[53a] But very clear proof of the obligation is required. In *R. v. Hall* [1972] 3 W.L.R. 381 a travel agent received payments and deposits from projected charter flights. The firm did not prosper and he was unable to arrange the flights or repay the money. It was held that the mere fact that the sums were paid into his trading account was not conclusive. It was not established that his clients expected him to retain and deal with the money in a particular way or that an obligation to do so was undertaken by him.

essential for the purposes of section 5 (3) that dishonesty is present at the time of the appropriation.[53b]

Property obtained by mistake. The old law of larceny was bedevilled by problems of the moment at which and the circumstances in which the property in some article passed. Cases arise with considerable frequency in which an offender obtains possession of property by reason of a mistake on the part of the person from whom the property is obtained. The classic textbook example is that of *R.* v. *Ashwell.*[54] In the dark Ashwell was handed by the prosecutor a sovereign in mistake for a shilling. He appropriated it. In *R.* v. *Hudson*[55] the accused received and appropriated to his own use a cheque clearly intended for someone else of the same name. In *Moynes* v. *Coopper*[56] an employee received more money in his pay packet than he was entitled to do, owing to the error of a pay clerk. He appropriated the extra amount. In this class of case there is no longer any room for argument as to whether the property passed to the thief, or what the prosecutor intended to pass. The Theft Act provides[57] that where a person gets property by another's mistake, and is under an obligation to make restoration in whole or in part, of the property or its proceeds or of the value of it, then to the extent of that obligation the property or proceeds shall be regarded *as against him* as belonging to the person entitled to its restoration, and an intention not to make restoration is regarded by the Act as an intention to deprive that person of the property or proceeds.

Property of a corporation sole. Finally, the Act regards the property of a corporation sole as belonging to the corporation, notwithstanding a vacancy in the corporation.[58]

Husband and wife. Under the Theft Act spouses are liable for offences under the Act by one spouse against the property of another, as if they were not married.[59]

[53b] *R.* v. *Hall (supra)*.
[54] (1885) 16 Q.B.D. 190.
[55] [1956] 2 Q.B. 252.
[56] [1956] 1 Q.B. 439.
[57] s. 5 (4).
[58] s. 5 (5).
[59] s. 30.

The appropriation

The *actus reus* of theft being the dishonest appropriation of property belonging to another, it is logical to consider next the meaning of appropriation. The word was intended [60] to mean the same as " conversion." [61] It envisages some act or dealing, as the Act puts it, rather than a mere mental intention to assume rights of ownership. Appropriation is defined in the Act as follows [62]:

" Any assumption by a person of the rights of an owner amounts to an appropriation, and this includes, where he has come by the property (innocently or not) without stealing it, any later assumption of a right to it by keeping it or dealing with it as owner."

This definition is very wide. The Act substitutes for the concept of " taking and carrying away " under the old law of larceny, the concept of assuming the rights of ownership. The rights of ownership can be assumed in numerous ways, so numerous that it would be idle to attempt to categorise them. Ownership clearly carries with it the right to dispose of property by sale or loan, or pledge, or even by destruction. A person who usurps the right of the owner to sell or to pledge property or to destroy that property may be convicted of theft, where the other ingredients of the offence are present.[63] The owner has the right to use property, and logically it might follow that it is an assumption of ownership to use another's property. But English law does not recognise the concept of *furtum usus*, except in relation to the theft of a conveyance.[64] In order to constitute theft the " use " would need to involve the permanent deprivation of the owner of the property.[65] A *conditional* appropriation will not suffice.[65a]

A problem arises in deciding whether an appropriation of property amounts to theft where the owner consents or apparently consents to the assumption of rights of ownership. Under the old law the words " without the consent of the owner " were part of

---

[60] By the Criminal Law Revision Committee. See Cmnd. 2977, paras. 34 and 35.
[61] In the offence of fraudulent conversion under s. 20 (1) (iv) of the Larceny Act 1916.
[62] s. 3 (1).
[63] *i.e.* the *mens rea* below, p. 499.
[64] *Post*, p. 504.
[65] See below, p. 502.
[65a] See, *e.g.* R. v. *Easom* [1971] 2 Q.B. 315 discussed at p. 503, *post*.

the definition of larceny, and where the owner consented to the taking and carrying away there was no larceny. These words are, however, no part of the definition of theft under the Act, and the Court of Appeal has taken the view [66] that they were deliberately omitted. The court drew this distinction between real and apparent consent:

> "Where there has been true consent by the owner of the property to its appropriation by another, a charge under, . . . the Theft Act would fail because the essential element of *dishonesty* would not have been established. If, however, the apparent consent was brought about by dishonesty there was nothing in the words, or by reason of any implication that could properly be read into the words, to make such apparent consent relevant as providing a defence."

Consent obtained by intimidation is clearly no true consent; nor is consent obtained by dishonesty.[67] Where the owner of property assists the thief in appropriating it in order to facilitate his apprehension [68] there seems to be no reason under the Act why the thief should not be convicted, despite the limited nature of the " apparent consent."

It seems clear that under the definition of " appropriation " in the Act, there will be theft by an innocent finder who later decides to assume rights of ownership over the property found, also by a person who obtains property through the mistake of another, and even by a parent where property is brought home by a child under the age of criminal responsibility.

There may be cases of theft by omission, as where a person lawfully borrows a motor-car from a friend on the understanding that he will return it, and after that period of time has elapsed he omits to return it, dishonestly intending to retain it. Again, where the innocent finder of property discovers the true owner and then dishonestly omits to return the property, there is theft. The Act provides a special exception [69] in favour of a person who buys

---

[66] *R.* v. *Lawrence* [1971] A.C. 373. See also *R.* v. *Greenberg* [1972] Crim.L.R. 331.

[67] See *R.* v. *Lawrence* (*supra*) as to the difficulty in distinguishing between theft and obtaining by deception under s. 15 (1) of the Theft Act, in certain cases.

[68] *Cf.* such cases as *R.* v. *Egginton* (1801) 2 Leach 913; *R.* v. *Williams* (1843) 1 C. & K. 195; *R.* v. *Turvey* (1946) 31 Cr.App.R. 154 and *R.* v. *Miller and Page* (1965) 49 Cr.App.R. 241 examined at Arch. para. 1475.

[69] s. 3 (2).

property for value in good faith and then later discovers that the seller has no title.

Dishonesty

The appropriation, in order to amount to theft, must be effected " dishonestly " and with the " intention of permanently depriving the other " of the property. These two elements constitute the *mens rea* of the offence of theft. Dishonesty is at the root of the whole concept of theft under the Act, but it is one of the most difficult elements to define. The Criminal Law Revision Committee [70] regarded dishonesty as something the layman would easily recognise,[71] and considered that the word could stand alone as a layman's concept without definition. The Act contains only a partial definition of dishonesty to deal with one or two special circumstances. It is immaterial for the purposes of the sections governing theft whether or not an appropriation is made with a view to gain, or for the thief's own benefit.[72] Thus a person who appropriates property belonging to another merely so that he can destroy it, even though he himself does not gain from this act, may commit theft.

Under the Act a person's appropriation of property belonging to another is not to be regarded as dishonest if he appropriates the property in the belief that he has in law a right to deprive the other of it, on behalf of himself or a third person.[73] This is known as a claim of right. Thus, where the offender honestly believes that he is owed £5 by another, and takes a lesser sum from that person's purse believing that he has a right to do so, then his actions, though unwise, are not to be described as dishonest under the Act.[74] And the position is the same if the offender is asserting honestly what he believes to be his right, even if that right is unfounded either in law or in fact.[75]

Again, appropriation in the belief that the offender would have the consent of the person from whom he takes it, if that other knew of the appropriation and the circumstances of it, is not

---

[70] Cmnd. 2977, para. 39.
[71] Although three judges apparently had some difficulty in doing so in *Sinclair* v. *Whybrow* [1967] 2 Q.B. 279.
[72] s. 1 (2).
[73] s. 2 (1) (*a*).
[74] See *e.g.* under the old law the cases of *R.* v. *Clayton* (1920) 15 Cr.App.R. 45 and *R.* v. *Bernhard* [1938] 2 K.B. 264.
[75] *R.* v. *Bernhard* (*supra*).

regarded as dishonest.[76] The classic and simple case of the woman going to a neighbour's and taking some article of household property comes to mind. If she takes it in the belief that the other woman would consent this is not dishonest. A more difficult case arises on the facts of *R.* v. *Flynn.*[77] The appellant was convicted of theft. He was employed as a part-time manager of a services' cinema. He had cashed a cheque which was not met and he had been ordered to repay the money without delay. He took £6 belonging to the cinema to repay the money. He maintained at his trial that he took the money in the form of an advance on his following week's salary, something he did frequently for his junior employees, and he believed that his employers would have consented had they known of the facts. The appeal was in fact decided on the unsatisfactory nature of the trial, but it is submitted that if he honestly held such a belief, then he would have had a defence under the Act. *Flynn's* case should, however, be distinguished from those cases where the defendant takes money for his own purposes, knowing that he has no immediate possibility of repayment, although in the genuine hope or expectation of being able to repay the money at some future date. Such conduct never amounted to a defence to larceny, and does not, under the Theft Act, prevent the conduct being dishonest.[78]

The last exemption dealt with in the Act, as part of the partial definition of dishonesty, deals with the appropriation of goods found. A person's appropriation of property belonging to another is not regarded as being dishonest (except where the property comes to him as trustee or personal representative) if he appropriates the property in the belief that the person to whom the property belongs cannot be discovered by taking reasonable steps. Again, as in the case of a claim of right, the subjective test operates. Did the accused believe that the owner could not be found, not whether the court believes that the owner could be found.[79] Whatever the original belief of the finder, if he subsequently discovers the whereabouts or identity of the other person, yet decides to

[76] s. 2 (1) (*b*).
[77] [1970] Crim.L.R. 118: See also the Hong Kong case of *Pang Hei Chung* v. *The Queen* [1971] Crim.L.R. 440.
[78] *R.* v. *Williams* [1953] 1 Q.B. 660; *R.* v. *Cockburn* [1968] 1 W.L.R. 281; *Halstead* v. *Patel* [1972] 1 W.L.R. 661 at p. 514, *post.*
[79] *R.* v. *Knight*, 12 Cox C.C. 102.

appropriate the property with intent to deprive the other permanently of it, this will be theft.

A person's appropriation of property belonging to another may be dishonest notwithstanding that he is willing to pay for the property.[80]

The intention to deprive

Coupled with the dishonest state of mind, there must be, to constitute theft, an intention in the mind of the offender permanently to deprive the other person of the property. If the appropriator merely has in mind to deprive the owner of such of his property as, on examination proves worth taking, and having discovered that it is valueless to him, leaves it to hand to be repossessed by the owner, this is not theft.[81] Although the Act makes new law in certain respects, it has not abandoned the basic conception both of the common law and of earlier legislation, that there can be no theft without the intention of permanently depriving another of his property.[82] There is nothing in the Act which provides that the intention must be formed at the time of the dishonest appropriation. The concept is not clarified by the Act which purports [83] to clarify the meaning of the words " intention of permanently depriving " in certain respects and giving illustrations of the dishonest intentions required in the definition of theft.

> " A person appropriating property belonging to another without meaning the other permanently to lose the thing itself, is nevertheless to be regarded as having the intention of permanently depriving the other of it, if his intention is to *treat the thing as his own to dispose of* regardless of the other's rights; and a borrowing or lending of it may amount to so treating it if, but only if, the borrowing or lending is for a period and in circumstances making it equivalent to an outright taking or disposal." [84]

[80] s. 2 (2).
[81] *R.* v. *Easom* [1971] 2 Q.B. 315.
[82] *R.* v. *Warner* (1971) 55 Cr.App.R. 93.
[83] See, *e.g.* s. 6.
[84] Theft Act 1968, s. 6 (1). This section is not intended to water down the definition of theft in s. 1 (1): *R.* v. *Warner* (1971) 55 Cr.App.R. 93.

This is in effect a conversion. Nevertheless, in *R.* v. *Easom* [85] it was held not to be theft where the appellant picked up a handbag in the cinema, and after sorting through it found nothing of value and left it in front of the seat he had vacated.

Where a person, having possession or control (lawfully or not) of property belonging to another, parts with the property under a condition as to its return which he may not be able to perform, this (if done for purposes of his own and without the other's authority) amounts to treating the property as his own to dispose of regardless of the other's rights.[86] Thus, the offence of theft extends to instances where the person appropriating the property does not literally intend to deprive the owner of it permanently. An example would be where the thief intends to abandon the property in such circumstances that the likelihood of the owner recovering it is to the thief's knowledge remote. Again it would be theft if the thief intends to return it only after his own use of the property has rendered it useless to the owner, or where he intends to sell it back to the owner under a representation that it is his, the thief's, own property.

SECTION 2. REMOVAL OF ARTICLES FROM PUBLIC GALLERIES, ETC.

There are a number of offences in the nature of theft which have received particular legislative treatment. Legislation was enacted to deal with those persons who remove works of art or articles of value from a building or its grounds open to the public, without authority. The types of building covered by this section are museums, art galleries, stately homes and those parts of royal palaces open to the public. By virtue of **section 11 (5)** of the **Theft Act 1968,** such an offence is an indictable one [*5 years*].

Section 11 (1) provides that:

" Subject to subsections (2) and (3) below, where the public have access to a building in order to view the building or part of it, or a collection or part of a collection housed in it, any person who without lawful authority removed from the building or its grounds the whole or part of any article displayed or kept for display to the public in the

---

[85] n. 81, *supra.*
[86] *Ibid.* s. 6 (2); and Arch. para. 1458.

building or that part of it or in its grounds shall be guilty
of an offence."

A collection includes one put together for a temporary purpose,
but excludes one made or exhibited for sales or other commercial
dealings [**section 11 (2)**]. In the case of an article not forming part
of a permanent exhibition, the offence is only committed if the
removal is effected on a day on which the public have access
[**section 11 (2)**]. It is a defence if the accused believed he had
lawful authority or would have it had the person entitled to give
it known of the removal and the circumstances [**section 11 (3)**].

The mischief at which the section is apparently aimed is the
abuse of the privilege of the public to view public or private
collections, and the need for punishing those who come within the
section, where it may be difficult to show " intention permanently
to deprive " or indeed " dishonesty." Thus persons who do such
acts to draw attention to themselves or to a cause would come
within this section. Where as in the *Goya* case a ransom is
demanded for the return of the article then the offence is one of
theft.

SECTION 3. TAKING A CONVEYANCE WITHOUT AUTHORITY

By **section 12** of the **Theft Act 1968** [87] a person commits an offence
[*Imp. 3 years*] if

(*a*) without the consent of the owner or other lawful authority,
    he takes any conveyance for his own or another's use, or

(*b*) he drives or allows himself to be driven in it knowing
    that it has been taken without such authority.

The offence is expressly made an arrestable offence [**section 12
(3)**] and on indictment the jury may convict of such an offence
as an alternative on a charge of theft [**section 12 (4)**]. " Conveyance " is defined in the section as meaning any conveyance
constructed or adapted for the carriage of a person or persons
whether by land, water [88] or air, excluding conveyances which are
not constructed or adapted for use only under the control of a
person not carried in or on it. The " owner " of a conveyance

---

[87] Superseding the offences under the Road Traffic Act 1960, s. 217 and the
Vessels Protection Act 1967. But see the Road Traffic Act 1972, ss. 29, 30.
[88] Vessels Protection Act 1967 (rep.).

which is subject to a hiring or a hire-purchase agreement is the person entitled to possession under the agreement [**section 12 (7)**]. A pedal cycle is excluded from the main provisions of the section, but a separate summary offence [£50] is created by **section 12 (5)** covering persons who do the same acts in relation to pedal cycles.

The *actus reus* of the offence under (*a*) above is the " taking " and not as under former legislation [89] a " taking and driving away." A servant who during the period of his employment makes unauthorised use of his master's vehicle for the purpose of some frolic of his own, does not commit this offence, since he is in lawful possession of the vehicle.[90] But the position is otherwise when he drives the vehicle after working hours, after an interval of time, and at a time when he does not intend to drive it that day to his employer's premises; and this is so even where he retains " custody " of the vehicle having left it outside his own house.[91] In every case where a person is charged with an offence of this nature, it must be shown, if he was not the actual taker, that he was acting in concert with the taker as part of a joint enterprise.[92] The fact that a person is found sitting in a car, or riding on a pillion of a motor cycle may be some evidence from which this can be inferred, but it does not of itself prove that he was a party to the original taking.[93]

Under the old legislation it was held that a person cannot be said to be the " driver " of a vehicle unless he is in the driving seat or in control of the steering wheel and also had something to do with the propulsion of the vehicle [94] although it has been held that a person who propels the vehicle by pushing it, can be said to drive it for the purposes of certain sections of the Road Traffic Acts.[95] It might be that in view of the definition of the word " drive " in **section 12** of the Act, " drive " may receive a different interpretation in regard to an offence of driving a conveyance taken without authority.

A person does not commit the offence of theft of a conveyance by anything done in the reasonable belief that he has lawful

---

[89] Road Traffic Act 1960, s. 217 (rep.).
[90] *Mowe* v. *Perraton* (1952) 35 Cr.App.R. 194 D.C.
[91] *R.* v. *Wibberley* (1965) 50 Cr.App.R. 51.
[92] *A.* v. *Bundy* (1960) 125 J.P. 89 and *R.* v. *Stally* (1960) 44 Cr.App.R. 5.
[93] *R.* v. *Stally*; and *D* (*an Infant*) v. *Parsons* [1960] 1 W.L.R. 797.
[94] *R.* v. *Roberts* [1965] 1 Q.B. 85 ; 48 Cr.App.R. 296.
[95] *e.g.* s. 28 (1) Road Traffic Act 1960 (rep.). See *Shimmell* v. *Fisher* [1951] 2 All E.R. 672.

authority to do it or that he would have the owner's consent if the owner knew of his doing it and the circumstances of it [**section 12 (6)**].[96] Where the accused fails to return a vehicle on the completion of an agreed purpose and goes on to use it for another purpose and without any such reasonable belief, he commits an offence under the section. A false representation by the accused which is not of a fundamental nature, namely that he wants the vehicle in order to go to A, when in fact he wants it to go to B, does not apparently vitiate the apparent consent of the owner.[97]

---

[96] *R.* v. *McGill* (1970) 54 Cr.App.R. 300.
[97] *R.* v. *Peart* [1970] 2 Q.B. 672. *Quaere* whether a false representation of a fundamental character would vitiate the owner's consent: *ibid.*

CHAPTER 36

AGGRAVATED FORMS OF THEFT—GOING EQUIPPED

SECTION 1. ROBBERY

BY **section 8** of the **Theft Act 1968,**[1] a person is guilty of robbery [*Imp. Life*][2] if (i) he steals and (ii) immediately before or at the time of doing so, and in order to do so, he

(*a*) uses force on any person or

(*b*) puts or seeks to put any person in fear of being then and there subjected to force.

Robbery is an aggravated form of theft; it must therefore be proved that the accused stole from the person who is alleged to have been robbed. Any defence to a charge of theft, such as a claim of right [3] will be a defence to robbery. Where an attempted theft only is disclosed, if the conduct of the accused amounted to an assault, he may be convicted of an assault with intent to rob.[4] Whether the accused may be convicted of common assault will depend on the nature of the allegations in the indictment.[5]

It was intended that the statutory definition of robbery under the Act should overcome the requirement formerly supposed to exist under the old law that the theft must be from the person or in the presence of the person on whom the force was used, or who was threatened.[6] **Section 8** requires, not that the property should be in the " immediate and personal care and protection " of the person robbed, but that the force should be used or threatened " for the purpose of the theft "; although it is restricted to that used or threatened immediately before or at the time of the theft.[7] It is not robbery to use force for the purpose of escape, once the theft has been completed. There is no requirement in the

[1] s. 32 (1) (*a*) abolishes the common law offence of robbery.
[2] s. 8 (2).
[3] See *e.g. R.* v. *Skivington* [1968] 1 Q.B. 66.
[4] Under the provisions of s. 6 (3) of the Criminal Law Act 1967.
[5] *R.* v. *Springfield* (1969) 53 Cr.App.R. 608.
[6] Cmnd. 2977, para. 65.
[7] *Ibid.*

507

section that the force or threats must be used on the person from whom the property is stolen.[8]

The mere snatching of a handbag or an ear-ring from the person will not necessarily amount to robbery, unless possibly where the victim offers resistance which has to be overcome.[9] Where the conduct of the accused amounts to putting a person in fear, the only threats which fall within the section are threats of being then and there subjected to force. Threats of a more remote nature, such as threats to expose or accuse of unnatural offences fall more naturally within the ambit of the offence of blackmail,[10] and do not constitute robbery.

SECTION 2. BURGLARY

By **section 9** of the **Theft Act 1968** [11] a person commits the offence of burglary [*Imp.* 14 *years*] [12] if:

(*a*) he enters any building (including an inhabited vehicle or vessel [13]) or part of a building as a trespasser and with intent to steal anything in the building or that part of it in question, or to inflict on any person therein any grievous bodily harm, or to rape any woman therein, or to do unlawful damage to the building or anything in it; or

(*b*) having entered any building or part of a building as a trespasser he steals or attempts to steal anything in the building or that part of it or inflicts or attempts to inflict on any person therein any grievous bodily harm.

The offence depends upon entering a building as a trespasser, and the Theft Act has abandoned the highly technical concept of breaking, which formed a part of the former offences of burglary and housebreaking, nor is there any distinction drawn under the Act between offences committed by day or at night.

Any building may be the object of burglary provided that it has some degree of permanence. The section expressly includes within the definition of building, an inhabited vehicle or vessel, and such a vehicle or vessel is included at times when the person

---

[8] See *Smith* v. *Desmond* [1965] A.C. 960.   [9] Cmnd. 2977, para. 65.
[10] *Post*, p. 524. As *e.g.* in *R.* v. *Pollock, R.* v. *Divers* [1967] 2 Q.B. 1145.
[11] The former statutory offences of burglary, housebreaking, etc., under the Larceny Act 1916, ss. 24–27 were abolished by the Theft Act, s. 32 (1) (*a*) and see " Burglary under the Theft Act " by Professor Smith [1968] Crim. L.R. 295.
[12] s. 9 (4).   [13] s. 9 (3).

having habitation in it is not there as well as at times when he is.[14] A tent is not within the section.[15] It is sufficient to constitute burglary if the trespassory entry takes place in part of a building, so that a tenant may commit burglary by entering the room of another tenant, and a guest at a hotel may commit burglary by entering another guest's room with intent to steal, inflict grievous bodily harm, rape or to unlawfully damage the room or anything in it, or indeed, the tenant or guest having entered another tenants' or guests' room, steals or attempts to steal anything in the room or inflicts or attempts to inflict on any person therein any grievous bodily harm. It should be noted that there is a distinction between section 9 (1) (*a*) of the Act under which it must be proved that the defendant entered with intent to commit one of four ulterior offences and that under subsection (*b*) where he must have entered and committed or attempted to commit one of two only of those ulterior offences, namely, stealing or inflicting grievous bodily harm.[16]

It seems likely that the old cases may usefully be referred to in assisting in determining what amounts to an entry; for the commission of the offence depends upon a trespassory entry. Under the old law, it was sufficient if there was the least degree of entry with any part of the body or with any instrument or weapon inserted *for the purpose of removing goods*, but not merely because an instrument used for the breaking penetrated into the house.[17] Thus A opens a window and introduces a crowbar to force a shutter three inches inside the window. This was no entry if no part of A's body was within the window.[18]

To enter as a trespasser means essentially to enter without right or authority. Whether the common law doctrine of trespass *ab initio* [19] has any application, is doubtful.[20] Where consent is obtained to entry, and that consent is obtained by fraud [21] then, if that apparent consent is in reality no consent at all, there is a

---

[14] s. 9 (3). [15] Cmnd. 2977.
[16] For a clear explanation of what constitutes burglary in the particular circumstances relating to the meaning of the kinds of ulterior offences which an offender intends to commit or has to commit or attempts to commit, see Smith and Hogan at pp. 416 and 417.
[17] *R.* v. *Hughes* (1785) 1 Leach 407; *R.* v. *Bailey* (1818) R. & R. 341; *R.* v. *Davis* (1823) R. & R. 499; *R.* v. *Rust* (1828) 1 Mood.C.C. 183.
[18] *R.* v. *Rust* (1828) 1 Mood.C.C. 183.
[19] See *Chic Fashions (West Wales) Ltd.* v. *Jones* [1968] 2 Q.B. 299.
[20] See Smith and Hogan, *op. cit.*, p. 410.
[21] As in *R.* v. *Boyle* [1954] 2 Q.B. 292.

trespass. On an indictment for burglary the defendant may be convicted of theft.[21a]

Section 3. Aggravated Burglary

The offence of aggravated burglary [*Imp. Life*] under **section 10** of the **Theft Act 1968** is committed where a person commits burglary under **section 9** and, at the time,[22] has with him [23] any firearm, or imitation firearm, any weapon of offence, or any explosive.

Firearm or imitation firearm is defined in the section, the former to include an air gun or air pistol and the latter as anything " which has the appearance of being a firearm whether capable of being discharged or not." [24]

Weapon of offence is much wider in its ambit than the term " offensive weapon " [25] since the section defines it as " any article made or adapted for use for causing injury to or incapacitating a person, or intended by the person having it with him for such use." An article made for incapacitating a person clearly goes far beyond what one would associate with an offensive weapon, and would clearly include ammonia, pepper, chloroform or other stupefying drugs, and also bonds, ropes, gags and other such articles.

Explosive within the section, means any article manufactured for the purpose of producing a practical effect by explosion, or intended by the person having it with him for this purpose.[26]

Section 4. Going Equipped for Theft, etc.

By **section 25** of the **Theft Act 1968** [27] a person commits an offence [*Imp. 3 years*] if, when not at his place of abode, he has with

---

[21a] *R.* v. *Lillis* [1972] 2 Q.B. 236; under the provisions of the Criminal Law Act 1967, s. 6 (3), for which see *post*, p. 751.

[22] " At the time " means that in a charge of entry with intent, at the time of entry, and where the charge is one of committing or attempting to commit the theft or inflicting grievous bodily harm, means at the time of the commission of the offence.

[23] " Has with him " imputes knowledge that, he had such a firearm or weapon with him and that it was such a firearm or weapon of aggravation.

[24] *Cf.* Firearms Act 1968, s. 7 (1).

[25] *Cf.* Prevention of Crimes Act 1953, s. 1 (4).

[26] *Cf.* Explosives Act 1875, s. 3 (1).

[27] Replacing s. 28 of the Larceny Act 1916.

him any article for use in the course of, or in connection with any burglary,[28] theft [29] or cheat.[30]   The offence is expressly made arrestable, although carrying less than 5 years imprisonment. This section is wider than the provisions which it replaces.[31]

Proof that the accused had with him an article made or adapted for use in connection with burglary or theft, may be evidence that he had it with him for use in the course of, or in connection with burglary or theft.[32] Where it is proved on a charge under this section that a person had such an article on him, then the burden of proof is in effect cast upon him [33] to give an explanation of his possession which negatives his intent to use it in the manner alleged.[34]

---

[28] Under s. 9.
[29] Under s. 7 and including s. 12 : s. 21 (5).
[30] Which means an offence of deception under s. 15 : s. 21 (5).
[31] It is submitted that it will include, *e.g.* a motor vehicle used to carry the stolen property from a burglary, or a carrier bag used for shoplifting.
[32] *R.* v. *Harrison* [1970] Crim.L.R. 415, C.A. The fact is evidence, but not conclusive evidence.
[33] Subject to the usual rules, for which see *post*, p. 592.
[34] s. 25 (3).

CHAPTER 37

OBTAINING BY DECEPTION

SECTION 1. PROPERTY

BY **section 15** of the **Theft Act 1968** a person who, by any deception, dishonestly obtains property belonging to another, with the intention of permanently depriving that other of it, commits an offence punishable on **indictment** [*Imp.* 10 *years*]. A person is to be treated as " obtaining " property if he obtains ownership, possession or control of it, and " obtaining " includes obtaining for another, or enabling another to obtain or retain.[1] The offence covers all instances which would have amounted to obtaining by false pretences under the old law, and indeed, in view of the substitution of the intent as " dishonestly " for that of " fraudulently " under the old law, may be wider in ambit than its predecessor.[2]

Property. There is a distinction between " property " under this section and property which may be the subject of theft.[3] The property which may be obtained by deception includes " money and all other property real or personal, including things in action and other intangible property "[4] belonging to another. On the other hand,[5] land or an interest in land may be obtained by deception although it may not be stolen.[6] Wild creatures although property, are not capable of ownership and are therefore excluded.[7] The owner of property may obtain possession of his own property by deception, just as he may steal it.[8]

---

[1] Theft Act 1968, s. 15 (2).
[2] See the observations of the Court of Appeal (Criminal Division) in *R.* v. *Potger* (1970) 55 Cr.App.R. 42. As to the distinction between obtaining property by deception and theft by a trick see *R.* v. *Lawrence* [1970] 3 W.L.R. 1103; approved *sub nom. Lawrence* v. *Metropolitan Police Commissioner* [1971] 2 W.L.R. 225.
[3] ss. 4 (1), 4 (3) and 5 (1) of the Act are incorporated into s. 15; s. 4 (2) and 4 (4) are not.
[4] See *ante*, p. 490.
[5] See *ante*, p. 490.
[6] See *ante*, p. 490.
[7] See *ante*, p. 492.
[8] *Cf. R.* v. *Turner* (*No.* 2) [1971] 1 W.L.R. 901.

512

The deception. "Deception" means any deception whether deliberate or reckless by words or conduct, as to fact or law, including a deception as to the present intentions of the person using the deception or of any other person.[9] It was intended[10] that subject to the overriding requirement of dishonesty the deception should cover recklessness in the sense of not caring whether the statement was true or false[11] but not mere carelessness. Whether a statement of opinion is within the definition of deception is not clear. It was not capable of amounting to a false pretence under the old law.[12] It must be shown in order to constitute an offence under the section that the accused deliberately or recklessly used the deception concerned, and that he did so dishonestly, and that the deception operated on the mind of the victim thus obtaining the property.

A simple act may carry with it implications of deception. In *R.* v. *Page*[13] the Court of Appeal held that the drawer of a cheque implied (*a*) that he had an account with the bank named; (*b*) that he had authority to draw on it for the amount shown and (*c*) that in the ordinary course of events the cheque will be honoured on presentation.

The deception need not be used towards the person from whom the property is obtained.[14] On the other hand as a general rule it must be shown that the deception operated upon the mind of the prosecutor, otherwise there will be an attempt only. This element is usually afforded by direct evidence from the mouth of the person defrauded.[15] In an exceptional case such proof may be afforded by indirect evidence, if the facts are such that the alleged deception is the only reason which could be suggested as having operated on the mind of the victim,[16] but the Court of Appeal has said that this principle should not be extended.[17] Where a loan of money is obtained by lying about the purpose for which it is required it is no defence to say that one intends to repay the money.[18]

---

[9] s. 15 (4). [10] By the Criminal Law Revision Committee.
[11] As in *Derry* v. *Peek* (1889) 14 App.Cas. 337.
[12] *R.* v. *Bryan* (1857) D. & B. 265.
[13] (1971) 55 Cr. App.R. 229; considered in *Halstead* v. *Patel* (below).
[14] *Cf. R.* v. *Robinson* [1915] 2 K.B. 347.
[15] *R.* v. *Laverty* [1970] 3 All E.R. 432.
[16] *R.* v. *Sullivan* (1945) 30 Cr.App.R. 132.
[17] *R.* v. *Laverty* (*supra*).
[18] *R.* v. *McCall* (1971) 55 Cr.App.R. 173.

Dishonesty. The deception must be deliberate or reckless and must be accompanied by dishonesty.[19] An obtaining may be by means of a deliberate or reckless deception and yet not be dishonest.[20] Dishonesty is nowhere defined for the purposes of this section, and even the partial definition applicable in cases of theft [21] is not applicable to this offence. One is left with the intention that it should be a layman's concept.[22]

In *Halstead* v. *Patel*,[22a] the defendant was a postman who opened a giro account with the Post Office, arranging for his wages to be paid directly into the account. During the postal strike of 1971, knowing that there were no wages being paid in, and that there were no facilities for overdrawing, he continued to withdraw sums in cash from the account. The Court of Appeal (Criminal Division) held that the appellant had acted dishonestly, in that he knew there were no funds to meet the withdrawals from his account, and he intended to deprive the Post Office of the actual coins and notes paid out to him.

SECTION 2. A PECUNIARY ADVANTAGE

BY **section 16** of the **Theft Act 1968** [23] a person commits an offence punishable on **indictment** [*Imp.* 5 *years*] if he, by any deception,[24] dishonestly obtains for himself a pecuniary advantage. This, in effect, punishes the obtaining of credit by deception. The meaning of " pecuniary advantage " in the section is restricted to the following cases [25]: where

(*a*) any debt or charge for which a person makes himself liable or is or may become liable (including one not legally enforceable) is reduced or in whole or in part evaded [26] or deferred; or

---

[19] It is essential that a jury should be directed on this: although there may be cases where the deception could only have been made dishonestly and failure to direct the jury will not result in an appeal being allowed: *R.* v. *Potger* (1969) 114 S.J. 906; *cf. R.* v. *McCall* (*supra*) and *R.* v. *Waterfall* [1970] 1 Q.B. 164.

[20] *R.* v. *Wright* [1960] Crim.L.R. 366; *R.* v. *Griffiths* (1965) 49 Cr.App.R. 279 at p. 286.

[21] See *ante*, p. 500.   [22] See *ante*, p. 500.

[22a] [1972] 1 W.L.R. 661, considering *R.* v. *Williams* [1953] 1 Q.B. 660 and *R.* v. *Cockburn* (1968) 52 Cr.App.R. 134. See *ante*, p. 501.

[23] *Cf.* Debtors Act 1869, s. 13, now repealed.

[24] Defined by s. 15 (4) which is applied to s. 16 by s. 16 (3).

[25] s. 16 (2).

[26] Which means evading payment of the debt: *R.* v. *Locker* [1971] 2 Q.B. 321; *R.* v. *Page* [1971] 2 Q.B. 330.

(b) he is allowed to borrow by way of overdraft, or to take out a policy of insurance or annuity contract, or obtains an improvement of the terms on which he is allowed to do so; or

(c) he is given an opportunity to earn remuneration or a greater remuneration in an office or employment or to win money by betting.[27]

Dishonesty is once again the overriding consideration, and in a trial on indictment the jury must be directed as to the need for dishonesty.[28] The test is a subjective one, and the issue is whether the defendant had an honest or dishonest mind. Where the question of dishonesty arises in regard to a debt incurred by the accused, the issue is whether the accused had an *honest* belief that the debt would be repaid; whether he had any reasonable grounds for the belief ought to be considered, but it is not a test which can be regarded as conclusive.[29]

In R. v. *Aston and Hadley*[30] the appellants entered a betting shop shortly before a race was due to start. The bet was accepted and it was understood that the stake was immediately payable in cash. The race started, and one of the appellants started to count out the stake money slowly and deliberately. Once the progress of the race had been observed on the screen and the particular animal was seen to have lost all chance of winning, the appellants gathered up the stake money and left the shop. The indictment was laid under section 16 (2) (a); the prosecution therefore undertaking to prove (i) that there was a debt for which the appellants had made themselves liable; and that the appellants had (ii) dishonestly, (iii) by a deception, (iv) obtained the evasion of that debt. The Court of Appeal held that the case was not within the framework of section 16 (2) (a) although it might have been brought under section 16 (2) (c). The deception must be such as to operate on the mind of the victim; and under the former subsection it must deceive the victim so as to influence

---

27 See R. v. *Royle* [1972] Crim.L.R. 42 and " Restatement of a Judicial Nightmare—section 16 of the Theft Act 1968 " by Professor Smith at [1972] Crim. L.R. 4. See also " The Deception of s. 16 " by Tony Waters [1972] Crim. L.R. 400.

28 R. v. *Potger* [1970] 55 Cr.App.R. 42.

29 R. v. *Waterfall* [1970] 1 Q.B. 148.

30 [1970] 1 W.L.R. 1584.

him to do or to refrain from doing something whereby the debt
is deferred or evaded. The court was of opinion that the slow
counting of the money in the circumstances did not qualify as
such an inducement.

In *R.* v. *Locker* [31] the accused owed his landlord rent, which
should have been paid in advance, although it was not. He was
given notice to quit and then gave a cheque drawn on a bank
at which he had no account. The Court of Appeal held that
although the appellant might have practised a deception with
the intention of inducing the landlord to refrain from requiring
payment on the due date, there was no evidence that the deception
caused the landlord to refrain from pressing for payment, and
therefore the offence was not made out.

SECTION 3. CHEATING AND PERSONATION

Cheating. The offence at common law of cheating, except as
regards offences relating to the public revenue, is abolished by
section 32 of the Theft Act 1968. To make a false statement
(whether written or not) relating to income tax with intent to
defraud the Revenue, or to deliver or cause to be delivered a
false document relating to income tax with similar intent amounts
to common law misdemeanour and is indictable as such. [32]

Personation. It is a common law misdemeanour to personate
a juryman, and it is not necessary to prove that the personator had
any corrupt motive or anything to gain by his conduct or any
specific intention to deceive other than that which is involved in
his going into the jury box and taking the oath in the name of
another. [33] It is no answer that he did not know he was doing
wrong.

By statute special provisions are also made with regard to the
personation of particular classes of persons, *e.g.* the personation of
police, school-teachers, etc., in order to receive any pay, pension or
gratuity due to them. [34]

---

[31] [1971] 2 Q.B. 321; see also *R.* v. *Royle* [1971] 1 W.L.R. 1764.
[32] *R.* v. *Hudson* [1956] 2 Q.B. 252; Arch. para. 3547.
[33] *R.* v. *Clark*, 82 J.P. 295 (Avory J.); Arch. para. 1602.
[34] See Arch. paras. 1603–1610.

CHAPTER 38

FALSE ACCOUNTING AND DESTRUCTION, ETC. OF DOCUMENTS

SECTION 1. FALSE ACCOUNTING

BY **section 17 of the Theft Act 1968** [1] it is an offence [*Imp. 7 years*] for a person dishonestly, with a view to gain for himself or another, or with intent to cause loss to another, (*a*) to destroy, deface, conceal or falsify any account or any record or document made or required for any accounting purpose; or (*b*) in furnishing information for any purpose, to produce or make use of any account, or any such record or document as aforesaid, which to his knowledge is or may be misleading, false or deceptive in a material particular. For the purposes of the section a person who makes or concurs in making in an account or other document, an entry which is or may be misleading, false or deceptive in a material particular, or who omits or concurs in omitting a material particular from an account or other document, is to be treated as falsifying the document. [2]

This offence is wider in scope than the former enactments which it replaces [3] and covers falsification to the prejudice of any person. [4] The section is however restricted to records and documents "required for any accounting purpose." The falsification of a mechanical means of accounting is clearly within the section. Thus in *R.* v. *Solomons,* [5] A was a driver in the service of a taxi cab company and was bound to pay over to the company a percentage of the daily receipts as indicated by his taximeter. While driving certain passengers he put his taximeter out of action so that it registered nothing, and appropriated the fares paid by them. It was held that he could be convicted of falsifying an account. [6]

---

[1] Replacing ss. 82 and 83 of the Larceny Act 1861 and the Falsification of Accounts Act 1875.

[2] s. 17 (2).

[3] The essence of the former offences was an intention to defraud an employer: see Cmnd. 2977, para. 103.

[4] Not just an employer.

[5] [1900] 2 **K.B.** 980.

[6] Within s. 1 of the Falsification of Accounts Act 1875.

False accounting may be based on an intention of temporary gain and does not involve an intention of permanent gain as in theft.[7] Because an accused is guilty of theft, it does not follow that he is guilty of false accounting.

Section 18 of the Act seeks to put the management of corporate bodies under a positive obligation to prevent irregularities by providing that senior officers of bodies corporate who are shown to have consented or connived at the commission of an offence under section 17 are liable to be similarly proceeded against and punished.

SECTION 2. DESTRUCTION, SUPPRESSION, ETC. OF DOCUMENTS

By section 20 [8] of the Theft Act 1968 it is an offence punishable on **indictment** [*Imp. 7 years*] for a person dishonestly, with a view to gain for himself or another, or with intent to cause loss to another, to destroy, deface or conceal any valuable security,[9] any will or other testamentary document, or any original document of or belonging to, or filed or deposited in, any court of justice or any government department.[10] By **section 20 (2)** [11] a person commits an offence [*similarly punishable*] who dishonestly, with a view to gain for himself or another or with intent to cause loss to another, by any deception [12] procures the execution of a valuable security.[13] The subsection applies in relation to the making, acceptance, indorsement, alteration, cancellation or destruction·in whole or in part of a valuable security, and in relation to the signing or sealing of any paper or other material [14] in order that it may be made or converted into, or used or dealt with as, a valuable security, as if that were the execution of a valuable security.

---

[7] *R.* v. *Eden* (1971) 55 Cr.App.R. 139, C.A.

[8] Replacing offences under ss. 27–30 of the Larceny Act 1861.

[9] Defined in s. 20 (3) as "any document creating, transferring, surrendering or releasing any right to, in or over property, or authorising the payment of money or delivery of any property, or evidencing the creation, transfer, surrender or release of any such right, or the payment of money or delivery of any property, or the satisfaction of any obligation."

[10] The section does not cover local government documents which the Criminal Law Revision Committee considered adequately covered by statutory provisions, Cmnd. 2977, para. 106.

[11] Replacing s. 32 (2) of the Larceny Act 1916.

[12] Which has the same meaning as in s. 15 of the Act: s. 20 (3).

[13] See n. 9.

[14] *Quaere* whether "material" would cover the hide of A. P. Herbert's *Negotiable cow.*

CHAPTER 39

HANDLING STOLEN GOODS

By **section 22 (2)** of the **Theft Act 1968** it is an offence punishable on **indictment** [*Imp.* 14 *years*] to handle stolen goods. A person handles stolen goods if (otherwise in the course of stealing) he, knowing or believing them to be stolen goods, dishonestly receives the goods, or dishonestly undertakes or assists in their retention, removal, disposal or realisation by or for the benefit of another person, or if he arranges so to do **(section 22 (1))**. Any number of receivers or handlers at different times of the stolen property may be charged in the same indictment[1] though not in the same count, and may be tried together.[2] A person cannot, on the same facts, be convicted of theft and handling.[3]

The principal offence. The *actus reus* of the offence consists in receiving or otherwise handling stolen goods. Therefore it must be proved that the property in question qualifies as stolen goods. " Goods " include money and every other description of property except land, and include things severed from the land by stealing.[4] " Stolen goods " include goods obtained in England and Wales or elsewhere, by theft, blackmail, or deception.[5] They also include goods obtained elsewhere than in England and Wales by an act which would have amounted to an offence by the law of that other country and would have been theft, blackmail or obtaining by deception under English law.[6] In addition to the goods originally stolen, the term " stolen goods " includes goods directly or indirectly representing, or having at any time represented such goods in the hands of the thief as being the proceeds of any disposal or realisation of the whole or the part of the goods stolen.[7] Whether goods amount to

---

[1] Theft Act 1968, s. 27 (1).
[2] *Ibid.*
[3] But see *R.* v. *Froggett* [1966] 1 Q.B. 152 in relation to charges of conspiracy to steal and handling stolen goods.
[4] Theft Act 1968, s. 34 (2) (*b*).
[5] *Ibid.* s. 24 (4).
[6] *Ibid.* s. 24 (1).
[7] *Ibid.* s. 24 (2).

stolen goods is a matter for the jury.[8] Although the theft must
be proved, the circumstances in which the accused received or
handled the property may of themselves be sufficient to satisfy
a jury that they were stolen, and also that at the time the accused
handled them he knew or believed them to be stolen.[9] If when the
property came to be handled by the accused it had not formed
the subject of theft as defined above, then no offence can be
committed under section 22.

The handling. Handling may be committed in one of several
ways.[9a] It is handling to receive stolen goods in the sense of
taking possession or control of them, even if it be merely as a
bailee.[10] It is not necessary that the accused should have taken
the goods into his house or shop or that he should have them
about his person. He may be in " constructive possession " of
them if they are in the hands of an associate [11] or of an employee,[12]
provided they were received by that person with the knowledge
and authority of the accused,[13] for in such a case they are in the
actual control of a person over whom the accused has control and
who would be likely to obey his orders as to their disposal.[14] If
the stolen goods are found on the accused's premises, then the
jury will probably find that they are in his possession,[15] but it
should be shown that they are there at his invitation or that he
was aware of their presence and that he exercised some control
over them.[16] Where the wife of the accused is also charged it
must be shown that she acted independently of her husband in
handling the property.[17]

---

[8] *R. v. Young* (1953) 36 Cr.App.R. 200.
[9] See the line of cases *R. v. Sbarra* (1918) 13 Cr.App.R. 118; *R. v. Fuschillo*
(1940) 27 Cr.App.R. 193; *Noon* v. *Smith* [1964] 1 W.L.R. 1450, D.C.; *cf.*
Cohen v. *March* [1951] 2 T.L.R. 402, D.C.
[9a] Where the prosecution rely on different methods of handling, these different
methods should form the subject-matter of separate counts in the indictment:
R. v. Sloggett [1972] 1 Q.B. 430; followed in *R. v. Marshall* (1972) 56
Cr.App.R. 263. *Cf. Griffiths* v. *Freeman* [1970] 1 W.L.R. 659 (a magistrates' court case). See also *R. v. Ikpong* [1972] Crim.L.R. 432.
[10] *R. v. Mills* (1853) 6 Cox 353.
[11] *R. v. Smith* (1855) Dears. 494.
[12] *Ibid.*
[13] *R. v. Pearson* (1908) 1 Cr.App.R. 79.
[14] *R. v. Smith* (*supra*).
[15] *R. v. Lewis* (1910) 4 Cr.App.R. 96.
[16] *R. v. Cavendish* [1961] 1 W.L.R. 1083.
[17] s. 30.

Mere physical handling of stolen goods does not necessarily amount to possession but of course the conduct of the accused may fall within one of the headings of the definition. It is handling to assist in the retention of stolen property, but mere failure to reveal to the police that stolen property is on the premises does not amount to assisting in its retention, although it may be strong evidence of it.[18] A person who by arrangement brings transport to remove stolen goods is assisting in their removal.[19] Under section 22 (1) of the Act in a count of handling stolen goods, where the offence is alleged to have been committed by assisting in the retention of the stolen goods, there should be included the words " by or for the benefit of another person " because that is an ingredient of the offence.[20]

Resumption of possession by owner. Goods cease to be stolen goods if the owner has resumed possession before they are handled by the accused [21] and the Theft Act [22] provides that goods shall not be regarded as having continued to be stolen goods after they have been restored to the person from whom they were stolen *or to other lawful possession or custody*,[23] or after that person and any other person claiming through him have otherwise ceased as regards those goods to have any right to restitution in respect of the theft.[24]

Knowledge and intention. It must be proved that the accused, at any time when he handled the goods, knew or believed them to be stolen, and was acting dishonestly, that is, had guilty knowledge. This may be proved directly or circumstantially by evidence of facts from which knowledge may be inferred, *e.g.* that he bought the goods at a price very much under their value. The circumstances in which the accused handled the goods may of

---

[18] *R.* v. *Brown* [1970] 1 Q.B. 105.

[19] *R.* v. *Crispin* (1971) 55 Cr.App.R. 310 and if the goods have already been removed, he is guilty of an attempt: *ibid.*

[20] *R.* v. *Sloggett* [1972] 1 Q.B. 430 and see *R.* v. *Freeman* [1970] 1 W.L.R. 659.

[21] *e.g. R.* v. *Schmidt* (1886) L.R. 1 C.C.R. 15; *cf. R.* v. *Villensky* (1892) 2 Q.B. 597.

[22] s. 27 (2).

[23] Where police seize property without the authority of the owner, this clearly comes within the section; *cf. R.* v. *King* [1938] 2 All E.R. 662.

[24] If the owner of goods obtained by criminal deception chooses, on discovering the deception, to ratify his disposal: Cmnd. 2977, para. 139.

themselves be sufficient to show guilty knowledge.[25] Besides such knowledge or belief, there must be an intention to act dishonestly. Therefore if a person receives stolen goods, believing them to be stolen, but with the intention of handing them over to the authorities, the offence is not committed.[26] Where there is an innocent receipt, a subsequent intention to appropriate the property may now in certain circumstances amount to handling.[27] It is not sufficient just to show that the goods were received in circumstances which would have aroused suspicions in a reasonable man, the question is a subjective one, and it must be shown that the accused was aware of the theft, or that he believed the goods to be stolen, or that suspecting them to be stolen he deliberately shut his eyes to the facts.[28]

Evidence. By **section 27 (3)** of the **Theft Act 1968,** where a person is being proceeded against for handling stolen goods, then at any stage of the proceedings, if evidence has been given of his having or arranging to have in his possession the goods the subject of the charge, or of his undertaking or assisting in, or arranging to undertake or assist in, their retention, removal, disposal or realisation, the following evidence shall be admissible for the purpose of proving that he knew or believed the goods to be stolen goods: (a) evidence that he has had in his possession, or has undertaken or assisted in the retention, removal, disposal or realisation of, stolen goods from any theft taking place not earlier than twelve months before the theft charged [29]; and (b) provided that seven days' notice in writing has been given to him of the intention to prove the conviction, evidence that he has within the five years preceding the date of the offence charged been convicted of theft or handling stolen goods. It is not necessary for the purposes under this section to charge the previous conviction of the defendant in the indictment. There are special

---

[25] *R.* v. *Fuschillo, etc., ante,* p. 520.

[26] *R.* v. *Matthews* (1950) 34 Cr.App.R. 55.

[27] For a dicussion of this topic, see Prof. Smith, *op. cit.,* paras. 484–485.

[28] *Atwal* v. *Massey* [1971] 3 All E.R. 881.

[29] Under the corresponding section (s. 43 (1)) of the Larceny Act 1916, evidence might be given as to the circumstances in which it was found, and any statements made at the time by the accused in explanation of its being found: *R.* v. *Smith* [1918] 2 K.B. 415 the court has a discretion to exclude the evidence; *R.* v. *List* [1966] 1 W.L.R. 9; *R.* v. *Herron* [1967] 1 Q.B. 107. See also *R.* v. *Davis* [1972] Crim.L.R. 431.

provisions in relation to the theft of anything in the course of transmission, or handling the proceeds of such a theft.[30]

If the accused is found in possession of property which it is proved has been stolen (or obtained by blackmail or by criminal deception shortly before it was found in his possession) an inference may be drawn, in the absence of any satisfactory explanation, that the accused stole the property or handled it knowing it to be stolen property, as the case may be.[31] This rule, sometimes erroneously called the " doctrine " of recent possession, is merely a common-sense rule of evidence. The burden of proving the dishonest handling remains upon the prosecution.[32]

Advertising Rewards for Return of Stolen or Lost Goods

By **section 23** of the **Theft Act 1968.** Where any public advertisement of a reward for the return of any goods which have been stolen or lost uses any words to the effect that no questions will be asked, or that the person producing the goods will be safe from apprehension or inquiry, or that any money paid for the purchase of the goods or advanced by way of loan on them will be repaid, the person advertising the reward and any person who prints or publishes the advertisement is guilty of an offence, punishable on summary conviction [£100 *fine*].

---

[30] s. 27 (4), Theft Act 1968.
[31] See generally Arch. paras. 1571–1572.
[32] See *e.g. R.* v. *Fallon* (1963) 47 Cr.App.R. 160 at p. 164; and see *D.P.P.* v. *Nieser* [1959] 1 Q.B. 254 at p. 266.

CHAPTER 40

BLACKMAIL [1]

By **section 21** of the **Theft Act 1968** [2] a person is guilty of blackmail [*Imp*. 14 *years*] if, with a view to gain for himself or another,
or with intent to cause loss to another, he makes any unwarranted
demand with menaces; and for this purpose a demand with
menaces is unwarranted unless the person making it does so in
the belief (*a*) that he has reasonable grounds for making the
demand; and (*b*) that the use of the menaces is a proper means of
reinforcing the demand. **Section 21 (2)** states that the nature of
the act or omission demanded is immaterial, and it is also
immaterial whether the menaces relate to action to be taken by
the person making the demand. It is probably irrelevant that
the victim is unmoved by the menaces. [3]

The demand. The nature of the demand is immaterial, but
it must be made with a view to gain or intent to cause loss.
Where the demand is made by letter, it is made when the letter
leaves the accused so as to be beyond recall on its way to the
intended victim. [4] The essential feature of the offence was intended
to be demanding something with menaces when the accused
knows either that he has no right to make the demand, or that
the use of the menaces is improper. The section requires that
the demand should be unwarranted. In testing whether a demand
is unwarranted or not, the test is intended to be the subjective one,
whether the person honestly believed that he had the right to
make the demand. [5] Such a test must needs lead to criticisms [6]
but it is probably the only workable test, as blackmail is an
offence in the nature of dishonesty. The size of the demand
may give some lead as to whether the accused was seeking

---

[1] This is now the technical name for the offence, not merely a colloquial name
for " demanding with menaces."
[2] Replacing ss. 29–31 of the Larceny Act 1916.
[3] *R.* v. *Clear* [1968] 1 Q.B. 670.
[4] *Treacy* v. *D.P.P.* [1971] A.C. 537, H.L.
[5] *Ibid.* See also *R.* v. *Lambert* [1972] Crim.L.R. 422.
[6] " Blackmail: A Criticism " by Sir Bernard MacKenna [1966] Crim.L.R. 467
at p. 473 ; see also Professor Hogan at [1966] Crim.L.R. 474.

genuine compensation or merely trying to make unlawful gain. In *R.* v. *Dymond* [7] a girl wrote a letter to the prosecutor threatening to summon him for indecently assaulting her, and suggesting that he either pay or be summoned, and adding that she would let the whole town know about his goings on. In *R.* v. *Bernhard* [8] a Hungarian woman threatened a married man that unless he paid her money which she claimed he owed her under an agreement in consideration of her having been his mistress, she would tell his wife and the Press of their association. She had previously consulted a Hungarian lawyer who had wrongly advised her that the agreement was binding. These cases, if the facts were established, would now both come within the subjective test. The offence is committed in England where the defendant posted a letter in England written by him and addressed to and received by one X in Germany, making an unwarranted demand with menaces. [4]

Menaces. In *Thorne* v. *Motor Trade Association* [9] Lord Wright said: "I think the word 'menace' is to be liberally construed and not as limited to threats of violence but as including threats of any action detrimental to or unpleasant to the person addressed."

This definition is the basis of an offence of blackmail [10] and in order to bring himself within the defence under section 21 (1) (*b*), the accused must show that he believed the use of the menaces was a proper means of reinforcing his demand. [11] "Proper" is intended to "direct the mind to consideration of what is morally and socially acceptable." [12] Once again, the test is whether the accused believes in the propriety of doing so.

---

[7] [1920] 2 K.B. 260.
[8] [1938] 2 K.B. 264.
[9] [1937] A.C. 797 at p. 817.
[10] Cmnd. 2977, para. 123.
[11] *Ibid.*
[12] *Ibid.*

CHAPTER 41

OFFENCES IN RELATION TO THE POST OFFICE

OFFENCES of stealing and handling mailbags were formerly the subject of legislation both under the Larceny Act 1916 and the Post Office Act 1953. The Theft Act 1968 repealed such provisions and a number of other minor offences outside the scope of the Larceny Act. Stealing and handling mail is now punishable under the general provisions of the Theft Act, leaving only a number of offences dealing particularly with mail and post office services to be prosecuted under the **Post Office Acts 1953** and **1969.**[1] Offences under the Post Office Acts 1953 and 1969 may be conveniently divided into two categories; namely, those which can be committed only by persons engaged in the business of the Post Office authority, and those which can be committed by any person.

Offences by persons engaged in the business of the Post Office authority

(1) It is an offence [*Imp. 7 years*] for any person engaged in the business of the Post Office authority to secrete a postal packet in course of transmission by post [**Post Office Act 1953, s. 57**[2]].

(2) It is an offence [*Imp. 2 years and fine*] for such a person, contrary to his duty, to open, or procure or suffer to be opened, any postal packet in course of transmission by post, or wilfully to detain or delay, or procure or suffer to be detained or delayed, any such postal packet. The provision does not extend, of course, to the opening, detaining or delaying of such a packet returned for want of a true direction, or because the addressee has refused it, or has refused or neglected to pay the postage, or where the packet cannot for any other reason be delivered [*ibid.* **s. 58**].[3]

(3) It is an offence for any such person to grant or issue a money order with a fraudulent intent [*Imp. 7 years*]. If any such

---

[1] But see the Theft Act 1968, s. 14 and the Post Office Act 1953, s. 70 as substituted by the Theft Act 1968, s. 33 (1), (2) and Sched. 3.

[2] As amended by the Theft Act 1968, Scheds. 2 and 3; the Post Office Act 1969, Sched. 4; and the Schedule to the Criminal Damage Act 1971.

[3] As amended by the Theft Act 1968, Sched. 2 and the Post Office Act 1969, Sched. 4.

officer reissues a money order previously paid he is deemed to have issued it with fraudulent intent [*ibid*. **s. 22**].[4]

(4) It is an offence [*Imp*. 12 *months*] for any person having official duties connected with the Post Office, or acting on its behalf, contrary to his duty, to disclose or make known or intercept the contents of any telegraph message or any message entrusted to the Post Office for the purpose of transmission [**Telegraph Act 1868, s. 20** [5]].

(5) It is an offence punishable **summarily** [£400 *fine*] or on **indictment** [*Imp*. 2 *years and fine*] for any person to disclose information obtained in the course of the provision of data processing services in accordance with the Post Office Act 1969, without the consent of the person for whom those services are provided, except for the purpose of providing those services or as required by law [**Post Office Act 1969, s. 65**].

(6) Carelessness, negligence or misconduct by persons employed in carrying or delivering mail bags or postal packets is an offence punishable on **summary conviction** [£20 *fine* [6]].

Offences which may be committed by any person

(1) It is an offence [*Imp*. 5 *years*] for any person unlawfully to take away or open a mail bag sent by any ship, vehicle or aircraft employed by or under the Post Office authority for the transmission of postal packets under contract, or unlawfully to take a postal packet in the course of transmission out of a mail bag so sent [**Post Office Act 1953, s. 53** [7]].

(2) It is an offence [*Imp*. 2 *years and fine*] for any person fraudulently to retain, or wilfully to secrete, or keep or detain, or when required by a person engaged in the business of the Post Office authority, to neglect or refuse to deliver up any postal packet which is in the course of transmission by post and which ought to have been delivered to any other person, or any such postal packet or mail bag which has been found by him or any other person [*ibid*. **s. 55** [8]].

---

[4] As amended by the Theft Act 1968, Sched. 2 and the Post Office Act 1969, Sched. 4.

[5] As amended by the Post Office Act 1969. As to persons in the employ of a telegraph company, see Post Office (Protection) Act 1884, s. 11 as amended by the Criminal Justice Act 1967, Sched. 3.   [6] Post Office Act 1953, s. 59.

[7] As amended by the Theft Act 1968, Sched. 2.

[8] As amended by the Criminal Law Act 1967, s. 7 (1) and the Theft Act 1968, Sched. 2 and the Post Office Act 1969, Sched. 4.

(3) It is an offence [*Imp.* 6 *months or* £50 *fine*] for any person not engaged in the business of the Post Office authority, wilfully and maliciously, with intent to injure any other person, to open or cause to be opened any postal packet which ought to have been delivered to that other person, or to do anything whereby the due delivery of the postal packet is impeded. This provision does not apply where the person opening etc. the packet is a parent or in the position of a parent or guardian of the person to whom the packet is addressed [*ibid*. **s. 56** 9].

(4) It is an offence punishable **summarily** [£100 *fine*] or on **indictment** [*Imp.* 12 *months*] for any person to send or attempt to send a postal packet, save as the Post Office authority may either generally or in any particular case allow, which encloses any explosive, dangerous, noxious or deleterious substance, any filth, any sharp instrument not properly protected, or any living creature or other thing whatever which is noxious or likely to injure other postal packets or a person engaged in the business of the authority [*ibid*. **s. 11** 10]. The same section makes it an offence to send indecent or obscene matter through the post. This part of the section is dealt with elsewhere.11

(5) It is an offence for any person to place or attempt to place in or against any post office letter box or telephone kiosk or cabinet, any fire, match, light, explosive, dangerous, noxious or deleterious substance, or any fluid, or to commit any nuisance in or against such letter box, kiosk or cabinet, or to do anything or attempt to do anything likely to injure it, its appurtenances or contents punishable on **indictment** [*Imp.* 12 *months*] or on **summary conviction** [£100 *fine*] [*ibid*. **s. 60** 12].

(6) It is a **summary offence** [£10 *fine*] for any person to affix notices on, or paint, or disfigure any Post Office letter box or other property belonging or used on behalf of the authority [*ibid*. **s. 61** 13].

(7) It is a **summary offence** [£10 *fine*] for any person without due authority to imitate any British or foreign stamp or mark [*ibid*. **s. 62** 14] and an offence [£20 *fine*] for any person to make,

---

9   Subject to the Mental Health Act 1959, s. 36 (6).
10 As amended by the Schedule to the Post Office Act 1961; the Criminal Justice Act 1967, Sched. 3; and the Post Office Act 1969, Scheds. 4 and 11.
11 *Ante*, pp. 236–237.
12 As amended by the Criminal Justice Act 1967, Sched. 3.
13 *Ibid*.   14 *Ibid*.

alter, use, deal in or be in possession without lawful excuse of any fictitious stamp which purports to be a representation of a British or foreign stamp unless made etc. in conformity with regulations [*ibid.* **s. 63** [15]].

(8) It is an offence [*Imp.* 1 *month and* £10 *fine*] for any person wilfully to obstruct or molest a person engaged in the business of the Post Office authority in the execution of his business or, whilst in Post Office premises to obstruct the course of business of the Post Office [*ibid.* **s. 65** [16]]. A person who commits such an offence may be removed from such premises by a person engaged in the business of the Post Office authority or by a constable.

(9) It is an offence punishable on **indictment** [*Imp.* 2 *years*] or on **summary conviction** [*Imp.* 3 *months and* £100 *fine*] for any person dishonestly to use a public telephone or telex system (including a system provided under licence, otherwise than by the Post Office authority) with intent to avoid payment [*ibid.* **s. 65A** [17]].

---

[15] As amended by the Schedule to the Post Office Act 1961, and the Post Office Act 1969, Sched. 8.
[16] As explained in the Post Office Act 1969, Sched. 4.
[17] As substituted by the Theft Act 1968, Sched. 2 and amended by the Post Office Act 1969, Sched. 4.

CHAPTER 42

CRIMINAL DAMAGE TO PROPERTY

SECTION 1. INTRODUCTION

THE **Criminal Damage Act 1971** marks a further step in codifying the criminal law. The Act creates[1]:

(1) a simple offence of destroying or damaging the property of another;

(2) an aggravated offence of destroying or damaging property whether belonging to another or not, with the intention of endangering life, or being reckless in that regard;

(3) two subsidiary offences: (*a*) making threats to destroy or damage property; and (*b*) possessing anything with intent that it should be used for destroying or damaging property.

SECTION 2. CRIMINAL DAMAGE

Thus, by **section 1 (1)** of the Act it is an offence [*Imp.* 10 *years*[2] *but Imp. life if committed by destroying or damaging property by fire*][3] for any person, without lawful excuse, to destroy or damage any property belonging to another, intending to destroy or damage such property or being reckless as to whether such property would be destroyed or damaged.

By **section 1 (2)** it is an offence [*Imp. Life*][4] for any person, without lawful excuse, to destroy or damage any property, whether belonging to himself or another—

(*a*) intending to destroy or damage any property, or being reckless as to whether any property would be destroyed or damaged; and

(*b*) intending by the destruction or damage to endanger the life of another, or being reckless as to whether the life of another would be endangered.

---

[1] Repealing the Malicious Damage Act 1861 (with the exception of four sections) and see the Schedule to the Act, and the passage at paras. 91–98 of the Law Commission Report (Law Com. No. 29) upon which the Criminal Damage Act 1971 is based.

[2] s. 4 (2).   [3] s. 4 (1). The offence is still charged as " arson."

[4] s. 4 (1). Offences under s. 1 (1) or s. 1 (1) and (3) or under s. 2 or s. 3 are triable summarily with the consent of the accused: Criminal Justice Act 1972, s. 47, nullifying the decision in *R. v. Aylesbury C.C., ex p. Simons* [1972] Crim.L.R. 555.

By **section 2** it is an offence [*Imp*. 10 *years*] [5] for a person without lawful excuse to make to another a threat, intending that that other should fear that it would be carried out—

(*a*) to destroy or damage any property belonging to that other or a third person; or

(*b*) to destroy or damage his own property in a way which he knows is likely to endanger the life of that other or a third person.

By **section 3** it is an offence [*Imp*. 10 *years*] [6] for a person, without lawful excuse, to have anything in his custody or under his control intending to use it or permit another to use it—

(*a*) to destroy or damage any property belonging to some other person; or

(*b*) to destroy or damage the user's property in a way which he knows is likely to endanger the life of some other person.

The simple offence under section 1 (1) is intended [7] to be a comprehensive one covering the destruction of or damage to any type of tangible property by any means. Damage to intangible property, *e.g.* patents, copyright, goodwill, trade secrets is excluded from the Act.[8] The mental element of the simple offence under section 1 (1) is an intention to destroy or damage the property of another, or recklessness as to whether another person's property would be destroyed or damaged. The same mental element forms part of that required to constitute the aggravated offence under section 1 (2) coupled with an intention by the destruction or damage to the property to endanger the life of another, or recklessness in that regard. In place of the old concept of " unlawfully and maliciously," the Act substitutes the condition that the damage or destruction to property must be without lawful excuse, a concept to be found frequently in modern statutes.

Without lawful excuse. The absence of lawful excuse is made an element of each of the offences under the Act, and the burden of proving such absence lies upon the prosecution.[9] The phrase

[5] s. 4 (2).
[6] *Ibid.*
[7] See Report of the Law Commission (Law Com. No. 29) App. A, Clause I. Explanatory notes.
[8] *Ibid.*
[9] *Cf.* s. 19, Firearms Act 1968 and s. 2 (2), Homicide Act 1957.

" without lawful excuse " is deliberately used in the Act in place
of the words " unlawfully and maliciously " frequently found in
the legislation which it replaces.[10] There is in general a clear
distinction between the mental element constituting the offence,
the ulterior or specific intention, and the element of unlawful-
ness. Under the Act, despite the fact that damage may have
been done to property, there will be no offence if one or other of
these elements is absent. In certain circumstances a person is
entitled to damage or destroy property belonging to another. A
person is entitled to kill a dog attacking him[11]; a person may
dismantle and remove a building unlawfully put up on his
property[12]; a person effecting a lawful arrest or executing a
search warrant may break down doors after admittance has been
demanded and refused[13]; and in the execution of non-criminal
court orders, damage may be lawfully caused to property in
certain circumstances, although outer doors and windows may
not be broken open.[14] In order to abate a nuisance a person may
damage property. In *Webb* v. *Stansfield*[15] it was held that a
person was entitled to force the quarter light of a car which blocked
the entrance to his garage in order to move the car.

Claim of right. Although the claim of right in the law of
theft has long been recognised, its application to the law of
malicious damage to property was uncertain.[16] **Section 5** of the
Act is intended to put this matter beyond doubt for the purposes
of the simple offence under section 1 (1) and offences under
sections 2 (*a*), 3 (*a*).[17]

Section 5 (2) provides that a person charged with an offence
to which this section applies shall, whether or not he would be

---

[10] Law Com. No. 29, para. 48 *et seq.*
[11] *Hanway* v. *Boultbee* (1830) 4 C. & P. 350.
[12] *R.* v. *Dyer* (1952) 36 Cr.App.R. 155.
[13] Halsbury, Vol. 10, pp. 354, 356, 357, and see Criminal Law Act 1967, s.
   2 (6).
[14] Halsbury, Vol. 16, pp. 42–43, and see also *Southam* v. *Smout* [1964] 1
   Q.B. 308.
[15] [1966] Crim.L.R. 449.
[16] Law Com. No. 29, paras. 51–53. See *e.g. R.* v. *Twose* (1879) 14 Cox 327;
   R. v. *Day* (1844) 8 J.P. 186; *R.* v. *Clemens* (1898) 1 Q.B. 556. *Cf. R.* v.
   James (1837) 8 C. & P. 131; *R.* v. *Langford* (1842) C. & M. 602. See also
   Gott v. *Measures* [1948] 1 K.B. 234 and *Workman* v. *Cowper* [1961] 2
   Q.B. 143.
[17] s. 5 (1).

treated for the purposes of this Act as having a lawful excuse apart from this subsection, be treated for those purposes as having a lawful excuse—

(a) if at the time of the act or acts alleged to constitute the offence he believed that the person or persons whom he believed to be entitled to consent to the destruction of or damage to the property in question had so consented, or would have so consented to it if he or they had known of the destruction or damage and its circumstances,[18] or

(b) if he destroyed or damaged or threatened to destroy or damage the property in question or, in the case of a charge of an offence under section 3 of the Act, intended to use or cause or permit the use of something to destroy or damage it, in order to protect property belonging to himself or another, or a right or interest in property [19] which was or which he believed to be vested in himself or another, and at the time of the act or acts alleged to constitute the offence he believed—

   (i) that the property right or interest was in immediate need of protection; and

   (ii) that the means of protection adopted or proposed to be adopted were or would be reasonable having regard to all the circumstances.[20]

By **section 5 (3)** it is immaterial for the purposes of the section whether a belief is justified or not if it is honestly held.[21] The excuse thus provided will cover cases where the defendant mistakenly believes that he or some other person has a right which requires protection, subject of course to the conditions that (1) he had an honest belief in the immediate necessity of its protection and (2) that he had an honest belief in the reasonableness of the means used or proposed to be used.

---

[18] This subsection reinforced by subsection (3) makes it clear that honest though unjustified belief in the consent of the owner will constitute such a lawful excuse (Law Com. No. 29), App. A, Clause 5.

[19] For the purposes of this subsection a right or interest in property includes any right or privilege in or over land, whether created by grant, licence or otherwise: s. 5 (4).

[20] Cf. *Goodway* v. *Becher* [1951] 115 J.P. 435; applied in *Workman* v. *Cowper* [1961] 2 Q.B. 143.

[21] Nullifying *Gott* v. *Measures* [1948] 1 K.B. 234.

Property. For the purposes of the Act, under section 10 (1) " property "[22] means property of a tangible nature,[23] whether real or personal, including money and (a) including wild creatures which have been tamed or are ordinarily kept in captivity, and any other wild creatures or their carcases if, but only if, they have been reduced into possession which has not been lost or abandoned or are in the course of being reduced into possession; but (b) not including mushrooms[24] growing wild on any land or flowers, fruit or foliage of a plant[25] growing wild on any land. Under **section 10 (2)** property is treated for the purposes of the Act as belonging to any person—(a) having the custody or control of it; (b) having in it any proprietary right or interest (not being an equitable interest arising only from an agreement to transfer or grant an interest); or (c) having a charge on it. By **section 10 (3)** where property is subject to a trust, the persons to whom it belongs shall be so treated as including any person having a right to enforce the trust. By **section 10 (4)** the property of a corporation sole is to be treated as belonging to the corporation notwithstanding a vacancy in the corporation.

Damage. The expression " damage " means perceptible damage.[26] Walking across a lawn will not normally cause any perceptible damage and thus not be an offence, although it might constitute a civil trespass. Trampling down long grass on the other hand, has been held to be sufficient.[27]

Powers of search by section 6 of the Act.[28] If it is made to appear by information on oath before a justice of the peace that

---

[22] The definition of property in the Criminal Damage Act 1971 follows closely that contained in the Theft Act 1968, the main differences being that (i) both real and personal property are included in the term and (ii) no intangible property is included.

[23] See *ante*, p. 493.

[24] Includes any fungus: s. 10 (1).

[25] Includes any shrub or tree: *ibid.*

[26] *Eley* v. *Lytle* (1885) 50 J.P. 308.

[27] *Gayford* v. *Chouler* [1898] 1 Q.B. 316 a case under the Malicious Damage Act 1861.

[28] This section is parallel to s. 26 of the Theft Act 1968. Its purpose is to authorise the issue of a warrant to search for and seize anything used or intended to be used for committing the offence of criminal damage, and to regulate the search and seizure, and the disposal of such property. It is wider than the corresponding powers under s. 55 of the Malicious Damage Act 1861.

there is reasonable cause to believe that any person has in his custody or under his control or on his premises anything which there is reasonable cause to believe has been used or is intended for use without lawful excuse—

(a) to destroy or damage property belonging to another; or

(b) to destroy or damage any property in a way likely to endanger the life of another,

the justice may grant a warrant authorising any constable to search for and seize that thing.

A constable who is authorised under this section to search premises for anything, may enter (if need be by force) and search the premises accordingly and may seize anything which he believes to have been used or to be intended to be used as aforesaid.[29]

Evidence. By **section 9** [30] a person shall not be excused, by reason that to do so may incriminate that person or the wife or husband of that person of an offence under this Act—

(a) from answering any question put to that person in proceedings for the recovery or administration of any property, for the execution of any trust or for an account of any property or dealings with property; or

(b) from complying with any order made in any such proceedings;

but no statement or admission made by a person in answering a question put or complying with an order made as aforesaid shall, in proceedings for an offence under this Act, be admissible in evidence against that person or (unless they married after the making of the statement or admission) against the wife or husband of that person.

Compensation. The courts have wide powers of ordering the payment of compensation under the **Criminal Justice Act 1972.**[31]

[29] The Police (Property) Act 1897 (disposal of property in the possession of the police) shall apply to property which has come into the possession of the police under this section as it applies to property which has come into the possession of the police in the circumstances mentioned in that Act.

[30] The counterpart of s. 31 (1) of the Theft Act 1968.

[31] *Post*, p. 820.

Ouster of jurisdiction. It will be seen later [32] that where there is a dispute as to title to real property, the jurisdiction of a magistrates' court is ousted, on the basis that magistrates are not normally qualified to adjudicate in such disputes. In relation to offences under the Criminal Damage Act 1971, however, it is expressly provided by **section 7 (2)** that no rule of law ousting the jurisdiction of a magistrates' court to try offences where a dispute of title to property is involved, shall preclude such a court from trying offences under the Act or any other offences of destroying or damaging property.

SECTION 3. ENDANGERING PROPERTY BY EXPLOSIVES

By **section 2** of the **Explosive Substances Act 1883** it is an offence [*Imp. life*] for any person *unlawfully and maliciously* to cause by any explosive substance an explosion of a nature likely to *endanger life or cause serious injury to property*, whether any injury to person or property has been actually caused or not.

By **section 3** of the same Act it is an offence [*Imp*. 20 *years*] for any person *unlawfully and maliciously*—

(1) To do any act with intent to cause by an explosive substance, or to conspire to cause by an explosive substance, an explosion in the United Kingdom of a nature likely to endanger life or cause serious injury to property.

(2) To make, or knowingly have in his possession or under his control, any explosive substance, with intent by means thereof to endanger life, or cause serious injury to property in the United Kingdom, or to enable any other person by means thereof to do so, whether any explosion does or does not take place and whether any injury to person or property has been actually caused or not.

By **section 4** of the same Act it is an offence [*Imp*. 14 *years*] for any person to make or knowingly have in his possession, etc., any explosive substance under such circumstances as to give rise to a reasonable suspicion that he is not making it or does not have it in his possession, etc., for a lawful object,[33] unless he can show that he made it or has it in his possession for a lawful object. Other

---

[32] *Post*, p. 645.
[33] *Cf*. Firearms Act 1968, at p. 237, *ante*.

provisions dealing with explosives have been noted elsewhere in the book.[34]

SECTION 4. OTHER INJURIES TO PROPERTY

Railways, etc. By **section 35 of the Malicious Damage Act 1861** [35] it is an offence [*Imp. life*] unlawfully or maliciously (i) to place or throw upon any railway any wood, stone or other matter, or (ii) to take up, remove or displace any rail, sleeper or other matter belonging to any railway; or (iii) to turn or divert any points or other machinery belonging to any railway; or (iv) to make, show, hide or remove any signal or light upon or near to any railway; or (v) to do or cause to be done any other thing, with intent in any of such cases to obstruct, overthrow, injure or destroy any engine, carriage or truck using such railway.

By **section 36** [36] it is an offence [*Imp. 2 years*] by any unlawful act, or by any wilful omission or neglect, to obstruct or cause to be obstructed any engine or carriage using any railway, or to aid and assist therein.

Electric lines. By **section 22** of the **Electric Lighting Act 1882,** it is an **offence** [*Imp. 5 years*] for any person unlawfully and maliciously to cut or injure any electric line or work with intent to cut off any supply of electricity.

Navigation Marks, etc. By **section 47** of the **Malicious Damage Act 1861** it is an offence [*Imp. life*] [37] unlawfully to mask, alter or remove any light or signal, or to exhibit any false light or signal, with intent to bring any vessel into danger, or unlawfully and maliciously to do any act tending to the immediate loss or destruction of any vessel, and for which no punishment is provided by any preceding section.

And by **section 48** of the same Act it is an offence [*Imp. 7 years*] [38] unlawfully and maliciously to cut away, remove, alter, destroy, etc., or to do any act with intent to cut away, etc., or in any other manner to injure or conceal any boat, buoy, etc., used for the guidance of seamen for the purpose of navigation.

---

[34] *Ante,* p. 221 and p. 460.
[35] This section was not repealed by the Criminal Damage Act 1971.
[36] *Ibid.*
[37] This section was not repealed by the Criminal Damage Act 1971.
[38] *Ibid.*

CHAPTER 43

FORGERY [1]

SECTION 1. INTRODUCTION

THE forging or uttering of forged documents, which at common law was a misdemeanour, is now governed by statute. The Forgery Act 1913 deals specifically with a large number of documents. Other classes of documents are dealt with by the Forgery Act 1861 and numerous other statutes. Section 4 of the Forgery Act 1913 (below), operates as a " catch-all " provision in that it makes it an offence to forge *any* document.

SECTION 2. THE FORGERY ACT 1913

Forgery

By **section 1 (1)** of this Act it is provided that " for the purposes of this Act, forgery is the making of a false document in order that it may be used as genuine, and in the case of the seals and dies mentioned in this Act the counterfeiting of a seal or die."

By **section 1 (2),** " A document is false within the meaning of this Act if the whole or any material part thereof purports [2] to be made by or on behalf of or on account of a person who did not make it nor authorise its making; or if, though made by . . . [etc.] the person by whom or by whose authority it purports to have been made, the time or place of making, where either is material, or, in the case of a document identified by number or mark, the number or any distinguishing mark identifying the document, is falsely stated therein; and in particular a document is false—

    (*a*) If any material alteration, whether by addition, insertion, obliteration, erasure, removal, or otherwise, has been made therein;

---

[1] The Law of Forgery is being reviewed by the Law Commission (Working Paper No. 26). See " The Law Commission's Working Paper on Forgery " [1970] Crim.L.R. 548.

[2] It is the purport of the document which must be false, that is, the document must tell a lie about itself : see *R.* v. *Dodge and Harris* [1972] Q.B. 416.

(b) If the whole or some material part of it purports to be made by or on behalf of a fictitious [3] or deceased person;

(c) If, though made in the name of an existing person, it is made by him or by his authority with the intent that it should pass as having been made by some person, real or fictitious, other than the person who made or authorised it." [3a]

By **section 1 (3)** of the Act the crossing on any cheque, draft on a banker, post office money order, postal order, coupon, or other document the crossing of which is authorised or recognised by law is a material part thereof. The same subsection also provides (i) that it is immaterial in what language a document is expressed or in what place within or without the Queen's dominions it is expressed to take effect; (ii) that forgery of a document may be complete even if the document when forged is incomplete, or is not or does not purport to be such a document as would be binding or sufficient in law.

Section 1 (2) specifically refers to a number of different kinds of forgeries. However, the list is not exhaustive. By **section 35 (1)** of the **Criminal Justice Act 1925** it is declared that a document may be a false document for the purposes of the Forgery Act 1913 notwithstanding that it is not false in such a manner as is described in section 1 of that Act.

By **section 2** of the **Forgery Act 1913** the forgery of the following documents, if committed *with intent to defraud*, is made an offence—

(1) Any will, codicil, or other testamentary document, or any probate or letters of administration;
Any deed or bond, or any assignment of any deed or bond, or any attestation of the execution of any deed or bond;
Any bank note,[4] or any indorsement on or assignment of any bank note [*Imp. life*].

---

[3] See, *e.g. R.* v. *Hassard and Devereux* (1970) 54 Cr.App.R. 295 where the accused had assumed a fictitious name " for the purposes of fraud."

[3a] Subsection 1 (2) (c) does not extend to the case of a document which is signed with authority, bears on its face no falsity, yet has been brought into being for an ulterior dishonest purpose: *R.* v. *Vincent* (1972) 56 Cr.App.R. 281.

[4] This expression is defined by s. 18 (1) as amended by the Post Office Act 1969, Sched. 11, it includes (*inter alia*) any note or bill of exchange of the

(2) Any valuable security [5] or assignment thereof, or indorsement thereon, or in the case of a bill of exchange, any acceptance thereof; and

Any document of title to land or goods [6] or assignment thereof or indorsement thereon;

Any power of attorney or authority to transfer any share or interest in any stock, annuity or public fund, or in the debt of any public body, company, or society or in the capital stock of any such company or society, or to receive any dividend or money in respect of such share or interest, or any attestation of any such power of attorney or authority;

Any entry in any book or register which is evidence of any person's title to any such share, dividend, etc.;

Any policy of insurance or assignment thereof or indorsement thereon;

Any charterparty or assignment thereof;

Any certificate of the Commissioners of Inland Revenue or any other Commissioners acting under the Income Tax Acts [*Imp*. 14 *years*].

By **section 3** the forgery of a large number of public documents, if committed *with intent to defraud or deceive*, is made an offence. These include—

(1) Any register or record of births, baptisms, marriages, deaths, and burials, and any certified copy of any such register, and any copy of any such register, etc., directed or required by law to be transmitted to any Registrar or other officer;

Bank of England or Bank of Ireland, or of any other person, body corporate, or company carrying on the business of banking in any part of the world. By s. 1 of the Counterfeit Currency (Convention) Act 1935, it also includes currency notes issued by or on behalf of the government of any country outside the United Kingdom, *i.e.* any notes which, by whatever name called, are legal tender in the country of issue.

[5] Defined by s. 18 (1) of the Act, as amended by s. 35 of the Criminal Justice Act 1925 and the Post Office Act 1969, Sched. 11. By s. 23 of the Post Office Act 1953, a post office money order is a " valuable security " within the Forgery Act 1913. A national insurance stamp issued under the National Insurance Act 1965 was held to be a " valuable security " in *Att.-Gen. of Hong Kong* v. *Pat Chiuk Wak* (1971) 55 Cr.App.R. 342, P.C.

[6] The terms " document of title to land " and " document of title to goods " are defined by s. 18 (1) of the Act as amended by the Post Office Act 1969, Sched. 11.

Any certified copy of a record purporting to be signed
by an assistant keeper of the Public Records in England;
Any wrapper or label provided by or under the authority
of the Commissioners of Inland Revenue or of Customs
and Excise [*Imp*. 14 *years*].[7]

(2) Any official document of a court of justice or issued by
the judge, magistrate, or any officer of such a court;
Any register or book kept under the provisions of any
law in or by the authority of any court of justice, and any
certificate, office copy or certified copy thereof or of any
part thereof;
Any document which a magistrate or the authority having
jurisdiction under Part VIII of the Mental Health Act
1959[8] is authorised or required by law to make or issue;
Any document which any person authorised to administer
an oath under the Commissioners for Oaths Act 1889 is
authorised or required by law to make or issue;
Any document made by a law officer of the Crown or
officer of state upon which any court of justice or any officer
might act;
Any document or copy thereof intended to be used in
evidence in any court of record, or any document made
evidence by law;
Any certificate required by any Act for the celebration of
marriage;
Any licence for the celebration of marriage;
Any certificate, declaration, or order under any enactment
relating to the registration of births or deaths;
Certain certificates, declarations, bills of sale, etc., under
the Merchant Shipping Acts 1894 to 1970;
Any permit, certificate, or similar document granted by
the Commissioners of Customs and Excise [*Imp*. 7 *years*].

By **section 4** of the Act[9] the forgery of any **document,** if
committed *with intent to defraud*, or, in the case of a **public
document,** *with intent to defraud or deceive*, is an offence [*Imp*. 2
years].

---

[7] As to counterfeiting documents, seals, etc., in Customs and Excise matters, see
also Customs and Excise Act 1952, s. 302, *ante*, p. 153.
[8] Mental Health Act 1959, Sched. 7.
[9] As amended by the Criminal Law Act 1967, Sched. 3.

By **section 5** of the Act the forgery of certain seals and dies, if committed *with intent to defraud or deceive*, is an offence. These include—

(1) The seals of the Public Record Office in England, or any court of record, and of the office of the Registrar-General of Births, Deaths and Marriages [*Imp. life*].

(2) The seal of any register office relating to birth, baptisms, marriages, or deaths, or of any burial board, or any office for the registry of deeds or titles to lands [*Imp.* 14 *years*].

(3) The seal of any court of justice other than a court of record, or of the Court of Protection [10] [*Imp.* 7 *years*].

(4) Any die provided, made or used by the Commissioners of Inland Revenue or of Customs and Excise or required or authorised by law to be used for marking or stamping gold and silver [*Imp.* 14 *years*].[11]

(5) Any stamp or die provided, made or used in pursuance of the Local Stamp Act 1869 [*Imp.* 7 *years*].

What can be forged. Section 1 (1) makes it clear that only documents and, to a limited extent, seals and dies can be forged. As far as the kind of documents specifically mentioned in sections 2 and 3, there is no difficulty. A difficulty does, however, arise with section 4, which prohibits the forgery of *any* document.[12] It has been suggested that for something to be a document there must be some writing on it, " so that a painting, photograph, plan, map or drawing is not a document, unless, of course, it contains sufficient writing to make it a document " or unless it is " attached to and referred to in what is otherwise a document." [13] Furthermore, " if a thing is not otherwise a document, the addition of a name cannot make it one." [14] Thus a faked painting in the style of a particular artist with a copy of the artist's signature added to it is not a " document," [15] although a certificate of a painting's authenticity would be.[16]

---

[10] Mental Health Act 1959, Sched. 7.
[11] As to counterfeiting documents, seals, etc., in Customs and Excise matters, see also Customs and Excise Act 1952, s. 302, *ante*, p. 153.
[12] See Glanville Williams, " What is a document?" (1948) 11 M.L.R. 150.
[13] *Ibid.* p. 157; but *cf.* Russell, p. 1218 *et seq.*
[14] Glanville Williams, *op. cit.*, p. 157.
[15] *R. v. Closs* (1858) D. & B. 460 and see *R. v. Douce* [1972] Crim.L.R. 105 and the commentary thereon.
[16] *R. v. Pryse-Hughes* (1958) *The Times*, May 14.

Even though something has writing on it (and thus satisfies the test above) it may still not be a document. It was said in *R*. v. *Smith*[17] that a label or wrapper on goods for sale was not a document. But ballot papers, licences,[18] registers[19] and football pool coupons[20] are documents.[21]

The falsity. Section 1 (1) states that forgery is the making of a false document in order that it may be used as genuine, and section 1 (2) lists some (but not all[22]) of the different ways in which a document can be rendered false. In *R*. v. *Hopkins and Collins*[23] the Court of Appeal held that:

> " If a man has a cash book and proceeds to make false entries in it so that it does not represent the truth and does not represent what he received and what he paid out, that book is a false document, and it is made false by the person who keeps it."

In the particular case the accused, who were officials of a supporters' club, had falsely entered into the club's books lesser amounts than they had in fact received, greater amounts than they had actually paid out and made further alterations to other entries and with the result that the documents gave " a wholly false impression of the amount that ought to have been in the hands of the appellants."[24] In the circumstances they had, therefore, made a false document in order that it could be used as genuine.

Hopkins and Collins has been strongly criticised[25] on the grounds that what the appellants had done would certainly not have been a forgery at common law.[26] However, the court said[27]:

---

[17] (1858) D. & B. at p. 574.

[18] Arch. para. 2172.

[19] *R*. v. *Potter* [1958] 1 W.L.R. 638.

[20] *R*. v. *Butler* (1954) 38 Cr.App.R. 57.

[21] See further Glanville Williams, *op. cit.*, pp. 159–160, where it is suggested that to be a document the thing ought to be an " instrument," as to which see *post*, p. 546, n. 38.

[22] *Ante*, p. 538.

[23] (1957) 41 Cr.App.R. 231 at p. 234.

[24] *Ibid.* at p. 235.

[25] See, *e.g.* Kenny, p. 388 *et seq.*; Smith and Hogan, p. 440 *et seq.*

[26] See *Re Windsor* (1865) 10 Cox 118 and the authorities cited in n. 25, above. At common law the document had " to tell a lie about itself," *e.g.* purport to be made by someone who did not make it or, in the case of a cheque, for an amount of money greater than the amount for which it had originally been made. " Forgery is the false making of an instrument purporting to be that which it is not; it is not the making of an instrument which purports to be what it really is, but which contains false statements. Telling a lie does not become a forgery because it is reduced into writing ": *Re Windsor, ibid.* at p. 123.

[27] (1957) 41 Cr.App.R. 231 at p. 235 (footnote added).

"Forgery no longer depends on the common law. . . . It depends simply on the statute of 1913 [28] and, in the opinion of the court, this case clearly falls within it."

The intent. The accused must have committed the forgery with intent to defraud or, in the case of public documents, with intent to defraud or deceive. The distinction between these two intents has been explained as follows:

"To deceive is, I apprehend, to induce a man to believe that a thing is true which is false, and which the person practising the deceit knows or believes to be false. To defraud is to deprive by deceit: it is by deceit to induce a man to act to his injury. More tersely it may be put, that to deceive is by falsehood to induce a state of mind; to defraud is by deceit to induce a course of action." [29]

The point was more fully discussed by Lord Denning in *Welham* v. *Director of Public Prosecutions* [30]:

"'To deceive' here conveys the element of deceit which induces a state of mind, without the element of fraud, which induces a course of action or inaction. Take the case of a private document. For instance, where a man fabricates a letter so as to puff himself up in the opinion of others. Bramwell B. put the instance: 'If I were to produce a letter purporting to be from the Duke of Wellington inviting me to dine, and say, "See what a respectable person I am"': *R.* v. *Moah.*[31] There would then be an intent to deceive but it would not be punishable at common law or under the statute, because then it would not be done with intent to defraud. Take next the case of a public document. For instance, a parish register. If a man should falsify it so as to make himself appear to be descended of noble family, for the sake of his own glorification, he would not be guilty of an intent to defraud and would therefore not be punishable at common

---

28 See also *Welham* v. *D.P.P.* [1961] A.C. 103 at pp. 123, 130.
29 *Re London, etc., Finance Corporation Ltd.* [1903] 1 Ch. 728 at p. 732. This passage was described by Goddard L.C.J. as the " locus classicus, which has been cited with approval over and over again " (*R.* v. *Wines* (1954) 37 Cr.App.R. 197 at p. 199).
30 [1961] A.C. 103 at p. 133.
31 (1858) 7 Cox 503 at p. 504.

law (see *R*. v. *Hodgson* [32]), but he would have an intent to deceive and he would be punishable under the present statute, as indeed he was under its predecessors, such as the Forgery Act, 1861, s. 36."

In *Welham's* case the House of Lords decided that the expression "intent to defraud" was not to be confined in its meaning to intend to cause economic loss. In the words of Lord Denning [33]:

"If a drug addict forges a doctor's prescription so as to enable him to get drugs from a chemist, he has, I should have thought, an intent to defraud, even though he intends to pay the chemist the full price and no one is a penny the worse off."

By **section 17 (2)** of the Act it is provided that where an intent to defraud or an intent to deceive is one of the constituent elements of an offence punishable under the Act or under any other Act relating to forgery or any kindred offence for the time being in force, it shall not be necessary to allege in the indictment or to prove an intent to defraud or deceive any particular person.

Uttering

By **section 6** [34] of the Act every person who utters any forged document, seal or die is guilty of an offence and liable to the same punishment as if he himself had forged the document, etc. By this section a person "utters a forged document, seal, or die, who knowing the same to be forged, and with either of the intents necessary to constitute the offence of forging the said document, seal, or die, uses, [35] offers, publishes, delivers, disposes of, tenders in payment or in exchange, exposes for sale or exchange, exchanges, tenders in evidence, or puts off the said forged document, seal, or die." The section is in sufficiently wide terms to include the posting of a letter enclosing a forged document. [36]

---

[32] (1856) D. & B. 3 at p. 8.
[33] [1961] A.C. 103 at p. 131.
[34] As amended by the Criminal Law Act 1967, Sched. 3.
[35] A forged document is "used" when a copy is made of it (*e.g.* a photostatic copy) and the copy is sent away with a view to deceiving or defrauding the recipient: *R*. v. *Harris* [1966] 1 Q.B. 184 at p. 196. It is not clear whether the forgery would be "used" if the copy was not sent on but merely put in a drawer (for example): *ibid.*
[36] *R*. v. *Owen and Others* [1957] 1 Q.B. 174.

Demanding money on forged instruments

By **section 7** every person is guilty of an offence [*Imp.* 14 *years*] who, with intent to defraud, demands, receives or obtains, or causes or procures to be delivered or transferred to any person, or endeavours to receive, obtain, or cause, etc., to be delivered, etc., to any person, any money or security for money or other property—

(a) Under, upon or by virtue of [37] any forged instrument [38] whatsoever, knowing the same to be forged; or

(b) Under, etc., any probate or letters of administration, knowing the will or other testamentary writing on which such probate, etc., was granted to have been forged, or knowing such probate, etc., to have been obtained by any false oath, affirmation or affidavit.

Possession of forged documents and implements for forgery

By **sections 8** [39] and **9** of the Act any person is guilty of an offence who, without lawful authority or excuse,[40] *the proof of which lies on the accused*—

(1) Purchases or receives from any person, or has in his custody or possession, a forged bank note, knowing the same to be forged; or

(2) Has in his custody or possession, knowing the same to be forged, any forged die required or authorised by law to be used for marking gold or silver plate or wares, or any such wares bearing the impression of such forged die; or any forged stamp or die as defined by the Stamp

---

[37] A person satisfies this (wide) requirement if he forges a hire-purchase proposal form for a vehicle in the office of a finance company and later takes receipt of the vehicle from a garage: *R.* v. *Hurford* [1963] 2 Q.B. 398.

[38] The word "instrument" is not confined to documents of a formal character; it bears the same meaning as in s. 38 of the Forgery Act 1861 (where it was held to apply to a telegram, see *R.* v. *Riley* [1896] 1 Q.B. 309), and includes any business document, or "writing which, if accepted and acted upon, would establish a business relation and lead directly to business dealings with another person" (*R.* v. *Cade* [1914] 2 K.B. 209).

[39] As amended by the Justices of the Peace Act 1949, Sched. VII.

[40] In *R.* v. *Wuyts* [1969] 2 Q.B. 474, C.A. It was said that it is a defence to such a charge if the defendant proves on the balance of probabilities that he retained the note, etc., solely in order to hand it over to the police. The fact that he did not do so at the first available opportunity is not necessarily fatal to that defence.

Duties Management Act 1891; or any forged wrapper or label provided by or under the authority of the Commissioners of Inland Revenue or of Customs and Excise [*Imp.* 14 *years*].

(3) Makes, uses, or knowingly has in his custody or possession any paper intended to resemble the paper used for making bank notes, Treasury bills, etc., or any instrument for making the same; or engraves or otherwise makes on any plate, stone, etc., any words, device, etc., used on any bank note or any document of title to any share or interest in any public stock, fund or debt, or in any stock, etc., of any corporation, company or society; or uses or knowingly has in his custody or possession any plate upon which such words, devices, etc., have been engraved or made, or any paper upon which they have been printed or made [*Imp.* 7 *years*].

By **section 10** of the Act any person who, without lawful authority or excuse, *the proof of which lies on the accused*, purchases, or receives, or knowingly has in his custody or possession any special paper used for making Treasury bills, etc., before such paper has been duly stamped, signed and issued for public use, or any die peculiarly used in the manufacture of such paper, is guilty of an offence [*Imp.* 2 *years*].

By **section 15** a person is deemed to have a document, etc., in his custody or possession (i) if he has it in his personal custody or possession; (ii) if he knowingly and wilfully has it in the actual custody or possession of any other person, or in any building, field or other place, whether occupied by himself or not.

SECTION 3. FORGERY AND SIMILAR OFFENCES UNDER OTHER STATUTES

Some offences under statutes other than the Forgery Act 1913 have been mentioned elsewhere.[41] Others include:

Registers of births, etc. To insert or cause to be inserted in any register of births, baptisms, marriages, deaths and burials deposited or kept under various statutes a false entry of any birth, etc., or to give any false certificate, or to certify any writing to be a copy of

---

41 *Ante*, pp. 153, 316.

or extract of any such register, knowing the same to be false [*Imp. life*].[42]

Court records. For the clerk or the appropriate officer of any court, or other officer having the custody of the records of any court, to utter any false copy or certificate of any record, knowing the same to be false, or to deliver to any person any paper falsely purporting to be the process of any court or a copy thereof, or to be any judgment, decree or order of any court or a copy thereof, or acting or professing to act under any such false process, knowing the same to be false [*Imp. 7 years*].[43]

Passports. By **section 36** of the **Criminal Justice Act 1925**,[44] it is an offence [*Imp. 2 years* and *fine*] for any person to forge any passport or to make a statement which is to his knowledge untrue for the purpose of procuring a passport, whether for himself or for any other person.

Stamps. The forgery of stamps is dealt with in the Stamp Duties Management Act 1891.

Road Fund Licences, etc. The forgery of road fund licences, trade plates, etc., is dealt with in the Vehicles (Excise) Act 1971, and the forgery of licences, test certificates etc., by the Road Traffic Act 1972.

---

[42] Non-Parochial Registers Act 1840, s. 8, as amended by the Criminal Damage Act 1971, Schedule; Burials Act 1857, s. 15, as amended by the Schedule to the Forgery Act 1913; Forgery Act 1861, ss. 36 and 37, as also so amended.
[43] Forgery Act 1861, s. 28, as amended by the Schedule to the Forgery Act 1913. See also County Courts Act 1959, ss. 186, 188.
[44] As amended by s. 92 (8) of the Criminal Justice Act 1967.

PART V

PROCEDURE UPON PROSECUTION OF INDICTABLE AND SUMMARY OFFENCES

CHAPTER 44

THE PROSECUTION AND INVESTIGATION OF CRIME

SECTION 1. INTRODUCTION

THE prosecution of offences is not in the hands of any central body, nor indeed in the hands of any one official. Most local authorities of any size have a prosecuting authority, responsible for giving legal advice to the local authority and to the police force, but there is no official in England and Wales comparable with the continental Public Prosecutor or even the American District Attorney. Even the Director of Public Prosecutions (created by the Prosecution of Offences Act 1879) is concerned essentially with giving advice to the police and other bodies on the conduct of prosecutions, although he is able to exercise control over prosecutions in two ways: First, an Act of Parliament may require his consent or that of the Attorney-General before a particular prosecution may be brought. Secondly, in certain classes of cases he generally undertakes the conduct of the prosecution. He does so where (i) the offence is punishable with death or is one of a class formerly undertaken by the Treasury Solicitor; (ii) where an order is given so to do by the Home Secretary or the Attorney-General; and (iii) where it appears to the Director that the offence is of such a character that a prosecution is required in the public interest and that owing to the importance or difficulty of the case or other circumstances, his action is necessary to ensure the due prosecution of the offender.

In cases other than those undertaken by the Director, the prosecution may be in the hands of a local authority, a government department, a police officer, or even in many cases in the hands of a private individual.

In the absence of any central body, it will be seen at once that much of the burden of prosecution falls upon the police, yet as a general rule, it will be seen that they have few powers greater than an ordinary citizen to enable them to carry out their duties. It is the citizen who has all the rights and privileges. Although the task of preserving law and order, protecting life and property, detecting and apprehending offenders is imposed upon the police, the citizen has no more than a moral or social duty to assist them in this task. The common law required a citizen to disclose to the authorities all material facts relevant to certain grave crimes such as treason or felony, of which he had definite knowledge. He was required to disclose the name of the offender if he knew it, the place of the offence and other similar facts. If he failed to do so he might be prosecuted for misprision of treason or felony as the case may be. The former crime is still on the Statute Book,[1] the latter was abolished by the Criminal Law Act 1967. The common law also required a citizen to assist a police constable in the execution of his duty to preserve the peace. Failure so to do is still an indictable offence.[2]

Apart from these duties there is little legal liability imposed by the law. A member of the public whom the police wish to interview may go of his own free will to a police station to " assist the police in their inquiries." He is under no obligation to do so, unless he is arrested. He may refuse to answer questions, he may refuse to co-operate in any way. He has the right to do so.[3] There is of course a difference between preserving silence or failing to co-operate with the police in their investigation and deliberately putting them on a false scent or giving false or misleading information.[4] The common law never dealt adequately with this matter, although the offence of effecting a public mischief was sometimes used to punish such behaviour.[5] The Criminal Law Act 1967 makes it a summary offence to cause wasteful employment of the police, and this includes giving false reports tending to show that an offence has been committed, or that a person has information material to a police inquiry.[6]

SECTION 2. THE POWERS OF A POLICE OFFICER

There is no exhaustive definition of the powers and obligations of the police but it has been said that they include a duty to take all necessary steps to achieve their task of preserving law and order, protecting life and property, and detecting and apprehending

[1] See *ante*, p. 128.   [2] See *ante*, p. 173.
[3] See the Judges' Rules 1964; Arch. para. 1119.
[4] See the observations of Lord Parker C.J. in *Rice* v. *Connolly* [1966] 2 Q.B. 414.
[5] See *ante*, p. 175.
[6] s. 5 (2), *ante*, p. 175.

offenders. The cardinal principle in England is that "what is officially done must be done in accordance with the law." [7] There exist no police powers under which the government may act in a general way for the preservation of public peace and safety. The police must in general point to some specific provision of the law to justify any executive act which may be called in question. English law looks upon police constables as citizens in uniform, and as such they have no greater powers in carrying out their duties than the ordinary citizen unless some power is expressly conferred upon them. This principle imports an element of risk into the duties of a police officer. In a recent case,[8] Lord Denning said this:

" . . . the police have got to get the consent of the householder to enter, if they can; or, if not, to do it by stealth or force. Somehow they seem to manage. No decent person refuses them admission. If he does, he is probably implicated in some way or other. So the police risk an action for trespass. It is not much of a risk."

This element of risk runs through much of the work of the police, particularly at the investigatory stage. The police officer who seeks to enter premises takes a risk of being sued in trespass. The officer who seeks to search premises must act with the authority of the householder or with that of a search warrant. Where he has neither he takes a risk. The officer who wishes to question a suspect and that suspect refuses to go with him, takes a risk. He must make up his mind whether to let him be or run the risk of an action for wrongful arrest if he oversteps his powers.

Where an officer acts properly and reasonably according to the powers conferred upon him, or according to his powers as an ordinary citizen, he is acting in the execution of his duty. Once he oversteps these powers he runs the risk of having his efforts nullified in the courts, by having the evidence which he has obtained excluded from the proceedings, and of being sued or even prosecuted for his conduct.

At first sight it may seem that the whole subject of police powers is fraught with lack of power, and that such a lack of

[7] *Per* Sir John Latham C.J. in the Australian case of *Arthur Yates & Co. (Property) Ltd.* v. *The Vegetable Seeds Committee* (1945) 72 C.L.R. at p. 66.
[8] *Ghani* v. *Jones* [1970] 1 Q.B. 693.

power must stultify their operations, but in practice it is not so. The liberty of the private citizen is paramount in England. Every interference with individual liberty is unlawful unless it can be justified at common law or by statute, but not every trivial interference with a citizen's liberty amounts to conduct sufficient to take an officer outside the scope of his duties. As has been said quite recently,[9] in relation to the police officer's duty of preventing and detecting crime:

> " The common law has always recognised that the discharge of this duty may justify some interference with the rights of innocent citizens which would in other circumstances be entitled to protection. . . . The balance of the inviolability of personal liberty and the pursuit of the public weal came down upon the side of him who acted reasonably in the intended performance of what right-minded men may deem a duty to their fellow men—the prevention and detection of crime."

It is this element of reasonableness which alleviates the dangers of the risks run by individual police officers. It is worth examining some of the special powers possessed by the police, and the extent to which they are subject to control by the courts.

SECTION 3. THE POWER TO QUESTION

A police officer has the right to question any person, whether suspected or not, from whom he thinks useful information may be obtained. The suspect may refuse to answer, and he cannot be prosecuted for that refusal in the absence of statutory authority. In relation to interrogation, however, the courts keep a wary eye open for evidence that questioning has been oppressive or unfair. The whole of this topic is so bound up with the admissibility of evidence, that it is better to deal with it under that heading. The police have no power to detain for questioning unless an arrest has been made. As Devlin J. has said[10]:

> " You may sometimes read in novels and detective stories, perhaps written by people not familiar with police procedure, that persons are sometimes taken into custody for questioning.

---

[9] Per Diplock L.J. in *Chic Fashions (West Wales) Ltd.* v. *Jones* [1968] 2 Q.B. 299.

[10] *R.* v. *Roberts* (1953) quoted in *Street on Torts*, 5th ed., p. 93. See also *Rice* v. *Connolly* [1966] 2 Q.B. 414; *Ludlow and others* v. *Burgess* [1971] Crim.L.R. 238.

There is no such power in this country. A man cannot be detained unless he is arrested."

Nor can a person be arrested unless the person making the arrest thinks that the person arrested is guilty of the offence. In the words of Lord Porter [11]:

"Those who arrest must be persuaded of the guilt of the accused; they cannot bolster up their assurance or the strength of the case by seeking further evidence and detaining the man arrested meanwhile or taking him to some spot where they can or may find further evidence."

To overcome the difficulties of the law in this respect, the police may, of course, invite a person to come to the police station to help inquiries. However, if the person concerned wishes to leave, he must be allowed to do so unless it is decided then and there to arrest him, and it must be remembered that no one is under an obligation to answer any question put by a policeman unless there is some statutory authority to the contrary in a particular case.[12] Another legitimate way of overcoming the difficulty is to arrest the suspect on a minor charge with a view to further investigation of a graver charge.[13] However, the arrest for the minor charge must be a lawful arrest and will not be made lawful merely because the person arrested was in fact guilty of the graver charge.[14]

Section 4. Arrest Without Warrant

Subject to a few exceptions, at common law only a felon or suspected felon could be arrested without a warrant. **Section 2** of the **Criminal Law Act 1967** created a new category of offences: "arrestable offences." An arrestable offence is defined as an offence for which the sentence is fixed by law or for which a person (not previously convicted) may under or by virtue of any enactment be sentenced to imprisonment for a term of five years and to attempts to commit any such offence.[15]

---

[11] *John Lewis & Co. Ltd.* v. *Tims* [1952] A.C. 676 at p. 691.
[12] *Ante*, p. 137.
[13] *Christie* v. *Leachinsky* [1947] A.C. 573 at p. 593.
[14] *Ibid.* at p. 604.
[15] Extended by the Theft Act 1968, s. 12 (3) to include offences under that section of taking or attempting to take a conveyance. As to the arrest of children and young persons, see *post*, p. 680.

Section 2 (2) provides that any person [16] may arrest without warrant anyone who is, or whom he, with reasonable cause, suspects to be, in the act of committing an arrestable offence. **Section 2 (3)** provides that where an arrestable offence has been committed, any person may arrest without warrant anyone who is, or whom he, with reasonable cause, suspects to be, guilty of the offence.

Section 2 (4) provides that where a constable, with reasonable cause, suspects that an arrestable offence has been committed, he may arrest without warrant anyone whom he, with reasonable cause, suspects to be guilty of the offence. **Section 2 (5)** provides that a constable may arrest without warrant any person who is, or whom he, with reasonable cause, suspects to be, about to commit an arrestable offence.

A constable, then, has the additional power over other persons of being able to arrest a person whom he suspects with reasonable cause of having committed an arrestable offence, even though no such offence has been committed by that person. In the case of a private person, the arrest will not be lawful unless the offence has actually been committed.[17] A constable also has the additional power of being able to arrest a person about to commit an arrestable offence.

Unfortunately, the section does not specifically deal with the criminal liability of a person who makes an arrest which is unlawful by virtue of section 2. For example, where a private person honestly, even though unreasonably, thinks that an arrestable offence is being or has been committed by X, that person should be protected from criminal liability for false imprisonment.[18] It may be concluded from the wording of the subsections that, in this kind of case, the person making the arrest would not be protected from criminal liability.

Section 2 (7) provides that the section does not prejudice any power of arrest conferred by law apart from this section. At common law, any person has the right to arrest a person in order to stay a breach of the peace which is being committed in his presence or which he has reasonable grounds to believe will be

16 " A person " will include under, *e.g.* the Criminal Damage Act 1971, the owner of the property or his servants.
17 This is in line with the position at common law: *Walters* v. *W. H. Smith and Son* [1914] 1 K.B. 595.
18 *Ante*, p. 462.

renewed.[19] Also a judge of a court of record may order a person to be arrested for contempt committed in the face of the court.[20] A constable also has certain rights to arrest persons granted bail. This will be discussed later.

Statutory powers of arrest without warrant exist in many cases, of which the following are the most important [21]—

(i) Offenders against the **Night Poaching Act 1828** may be arrested by the owner of the land and his servants.[22]

(ii) Most of the offences under the **Theft Act 1968,** the **Offences Against the Person Act 1861,** and the **Criminal Damage Act 1971** are arrestable. However, the offences of taking motor-vehicles, etc., without authority [23] and of going equipped for theft [24] although punishable only with three years' imprisonment, are expressly made arrestable by the Act.

(iii) Any person may arrest without warrant a person found committing any offence against the **Coinage Offences Act 1936,**[25] or any offence against the **Vagrancy Act 1824,**[26] or the **Official Secrets Acts.**[27]

(iv) Any person may arrest without warrant a person found committing an indictable offence by night.[28]

(v) Anyone may arrest without a warrant a person found committing an offence under **section 32** of the **Sexual Offences Act 1956** (which relates to soliciting by men).[29]

(vi) Any person may arrest without warrant a person who, in a public place and while drunk, is guilty of disorderly behaviour.[30]

(vii) A constable may arrest without warrant any person whom he reasonably suspects of having committed an offence under **section 22** or **23** of the **Sexual Offences Act 1956,** or **section 5** of the **Sexual Offences Act 1967.**[31]

---

[19] Arch. para. 2810. As to the meaning of the expression "breach of the peace," see *ante,* p. 194.

[20] Arch. para. 2813, *ante,* p. 176.

[21] See further Arch. paras. 2811, 2812. [22] s. 2.

[23] Theft Act 1968, s. 12. [24] s. 25.

[25] s. 11.

[26] s. 6. See *ante,* p. 240.

[27] See s. 6 of the Act of 1911.

[28] Prevention of Offences Act 1851, s. 11.

[29] Sexual Offences Act 1956, s. 41, as amended by the Criminal Law Act 1967, Sched. 3.

[30] *Ante,* p. 247. [31] See s. 40 of the 1956 Act and s. 5 (3) of the 1967 Act.

(viii) A constable may arrest without warrant any person whom he reasonably suspects is committing an offence against **section 1, 4** or **5** of the **Public Order Act 1936**,[32] or **section 1** of the **Prevention of Crime Act 1953**.[33]

(ix) The more serious offences under the **Firearms Act 1968** are arrestable offences, but certain extra powers of arrest without warrant are also given to constables.[34]

(x) A constable may arrest without warrant any person who within his view commits the offences of either dangerous driving or careless driving unless that person gives his name or address or produces his licence,[35] or any person who is committing the offence of driving while under the influence of drink or drugs [36] and blood/alcohol over the prescribed limit.[37]

(xi) A constable may arrest a common prostitute who loiters or solicits in a street or public place for the purpose of prostitution.[38]

(xii) A constable has also, under the **Children and Young Persons Act 1933,** certain powers of arrest without warrant for offences mentioned in the First Schedule to that Act.[39]

(xiii) A constable may arrest without a warrant anyone whom he finds in a street or in any other place to which, whether on payment or otherwise, the public have access and whom he suspects with reasonable cause to be taking part in gaming.[40]

(xiv) A constable and an immigration officer have wide powers of arrest under the **Immigration Act 1971**.[41]

---

[32] Public Order Act 1936, s. 7 (3).

[33] Prevention of Crime Act 1953, s. 1 (3). However there are certain limitations on the power to arrest in these circumstances: *ibid.*

[34] *Ante*, p. 292.

[35] Road Traffic Act 1972, s. 164.

[36] *Ibid.* s. 5 (5). This subsection has been interpreted as giving a constable the power to arrest if he reasonably believes the driver to be committing an offence: *Wiltshire* v. *Barrett* [1966] 1 Q.B. 312.

[37] Road Traffic Act 1972, s. 8 (4). For powers of arrest under that Act, see *ante*, p. 310.

[38] Street Offences Act 1959, s. 1 (3).

[39] See s. 13 and see Children and Young Persons Act 1969, s. 29, regarding the release or further detention of children or young persons arrested with or without warrant.

[40] Gaming Act 1968, s. 5 (1) (2).

[41] Immigration Act 1971, Part III (in force from January 1, 1972).

(xv) Under the **Misuse of Drugs Act 1971** [42] a constable may arrest without warrant [43] a person who has committed, or whom the constable, with reasonable cause, suspects to have committed, an offence under the Act, if—

> (a) he, with reasonable cause, believes that that person will abscond unless arrested; or
>
> (b) the name and address of that person are unknown to, and cannot be ascertained by, him; or
>
> (c) he is not satisfied that a name and address furnished by that person as his name and address are true.

(xvi) Persons absent from institutions, within the jurisdiction of a local authority, community homes, etc., may be arrested without warrant under the provisions of **section 32** of the **Children and Young Persons Act 1969.**

Where a statute gives power to arrest an " offender " the question whether this term includes a person reasonably suspected of being an offender depends upon the language of the statute. [44]

SECTION 5. THE USE OF FORCE IN MAKING AN ARREST

Section 3 of the **Criminal Law Act 1967** provides that a person may use such force as is reasonable in the circumstances in effecting or assisting in the lawful arrest of offenders or suspected offenders or of persons unlawfully at large. **Section 2 (6)** provides that for the purpose of arresting a person under any power conferred by section 2 a constable may enter, if need be by force, and search any place where that person is or where the constable, with reasonable cause, suspects him to be. This right is not conferred upon a private citizen. At common law a constable has a similar power to enter a place, by force if necessary, to effect an arrest with a warrant. [45] An arrest need not be effected by actual touching or seizing; it may be effected by a mere form of words, provided that they are calculated to bring to the arrested person's

---

[42] s. 24.

[43] Without prejudice to his other powers of arrest: s. 24 (2).

[44] *Barnard* v. *Gorman* [1941] A.C. 378. See also *Wiltshire* v. *Barrett* [1966] 1 Q.B. 312.

[45] *Burdett* v. *Abbot* (1811) 14 East 1, at pp. 158, 162.

attention, and do so, the fact that he is under compulsion, and thereafter he submitted to that compulsion.[46]

Where a person is arrested with a warrant, he should be shown the warrant if the arresting officer has it in his possession or, if not, he should be told the reason for his arrest and should be shown the warrant as soon after the arrest as is practicable, if he requests to see it.[47] Where a person arrests another without a warrant, " he must in ordinary circumstances inform the person arrested of the true ground of arrest." " He is not entitled to keep the reason to himself or to give a reason which is not the true reason." " If the citizen is not so informed but is nevertheless seized, the policeman [or private person], apart for certain exceptions, is liable for false imprisonment." " The requirement that the person arrested should be informed of the reason why he is seized naturally does not exist if the circumstances are such that he must know the general nature of the alleged offence for which he is detained." " The requirement that he should be informed does not mean that technical or precise language need be used." [48] A deaf person can be lawfully arrested, although he does not realise that he has been arrested.[49]

Where a private person makes an arrest, his duty is to take the arrested person before a justice or to a police station as soon as he reasonably can but not necessarily forthwith.[50] Thus it is permissible for a store detective who has arrested a person to take him before a senior officer of the company to consider the case before deciding to send for the police.[51]

However, a constable has greater power in this respect. In the words of Lord Denning M.R.[52]:

" When a constable has taken into custody a person reasonably suspected of felony [or, presumably, made any lawful arrest], he can do what is reasonable to investigate the matter, and to see whether the suspicions are supported or not by further evidence. He can, for instance, take the person sus-

---

[46] *Alderson* v. *Booth* [1969] 2 Q.B. 216.
[47] *Magistrates' Courts Act* 1952, s. 102 (4).
[48] *Christie* v. *Leachinsky* [1947] A.C. 573 at p. 587.
[49] *Wheatley* v. *Lodge* [1971] 1 W.L.R. 29, D.C. Where an original arrest does not comply with these requirements, subsequent compliance may validate the arrest: *R.* v. *Kulynycz* [1971] 1 Q.B. 367.
[50] *John Lewis & Co. Ltd.* v. *Tims* [1952] A.C. 676.
[51] *Ibid.*
[52] *Dallison* v. *Caffery* [1965] 1 Q.B. 348 at p. 367.

pected to his own house to see whether any of the stolen property is there, else it may be removed and valuable evidence lost. He can take the person suspected to the place where he was working, for there he may find persons to confirm or refute his alibi. The constable can put him up on an identification parade to see if he is picked out by the witnesses. So long as such measures are taken reasonably, they are an important adjunct to the administration of justice."

Where a constable has arrested a person with a warrant, the warrant will state that the arrested person should be brought before a justice forthwith or at a certain time,[53] or that the arrested person should be released on bail.[54] Where a constable has arrested a person without a warrant or has taken into custody a person lawfully arrested by a private citizen, he should take the arrested person to a police station as soon as is reasonable.[55]

After a person has been brought to a police station he should be charged as soon as there is sufficient evidence against him and a copy of the charge given to him. Where the arrested person is interrogated, police officers should conform with the Judges' Rules, otherwise any confession may be inadmissible.

If it is not practicable to take a person who has been arrested for an offence without a warrant before a magistrates' court within twenty-four hours [56] of his being taken into custody, then he must be released on bail conditioned for his appearance at a magistrates' court if the offence is not a serious one.[57] Alternatively, if inquiries into the case cannot be completed forthwith, he may be released on bail [58] conditioned for his appearance at a police station at a future date. In such a case where that person is apparently under seventeen the recognisance may be taken from his parent or guardian.[59] Where a person is taken into custody for an offence without a warrant [60] and is retained in custody, he shall be brought before

---

[53] *Post*, p. 575.
[54] *Post*, p. 569.
[55] *Dallison* v. *Caffery* [1965] 1 Q.B. 348.
[56] This includes a Sunday or public holiday.
[57] Magistrates' Courts Act 1952, s. 38 (1), as amended by the Children and Young Persons Act 1969, Sched. 6 and *post*, p. 568.
[58] *Ibid.* s. 38 (2) and *post*, p. 569.
[59] Magistrates' Courts Act 1952, s. 38 (3), as amended by the Children and Young Persons Act 1969, s. 72 (4), Sched. 6.
[60] This does not cover the case of an arrest without warrant under s. 8 of the Road Traffic Act 1972 after a positive breath test: *R.* v. *McKenzie* [1971] 1 All E.R. 729.

a magistrates' court as soon as is practicable.[61] Separate provisions apply to the detention and bail of young persons under the age of seventeen.[62]

Where a person has been arrested without a warrant for an offence and it becomes clear that no charges are to be preferred against him, he should be released at once.[63]

Where a child or young person is arrested such steps must be taken by the person who arrested him as may be practicable to inform at least one person whose attendance may be required under section 34 (2) of the Children and Young Persons Act 1933.[64]

As we have seen,[65] a person may be arrested by a private citizen to prevent the renewal of a breach of the peace and may be arrested by a constable if he is about to commit an arrestable offence. Where such an arrest has been made, the arrested person should be liberated when a reasonable time has elapsed.[66] This period may, however, be utilised in an appropriate case to obtain an order under section 91 of the Magistrates' Courts Act 1952,[67] binding the person over to keep the peace, or an order authorising his detention in a mental hospital under the Mental Health Act 1959.

SECTION 6. POWER TO SEARCH

(A) The power to enter premises. In the course of an investigation, police officers may wish to enter upon private property for the purposes of obtaining evidence, or questioning the persons thereon, or for the purposes of searching the premises and seizing incriminating evidence. Every invasion of private property, however slight, is technically a trespass.[68] Nobody has the right to enter private property except strictly in accordance with authority,[69] nor is a police officer in any better position in this regard than an ordinary member of the public, unless he is backed by the authority of the law. An officer is not entitled to enter premises merely because he

---

[61] s. 38 (4).
[62] *Post*, p. 680.
[63] *Wiltshire* v. *Barrett* [1966] 1 Q.B. 312.
[64] As amended by the Children and Young Persons Act 1969, s. 72 (3) (4); Sched. 5, para. 3; Sched. 6. See as to the special provisions for juveniles, *post* p. 680.
[65] *Ante*, p. 556.
[66] See *Williams* v. *Glenister* (1824) 2 B. & C. 699.
[67] *Post*, p. 792.
[68] See *Semayne's Case* (1605) 5 Co.Rep. 919.
[69] *Per* Lord Camden C.J. in *Entick* v. *Carrington* (1765) 19 St.Tr. 1030.

suspects that something is amiss, although probably no reasonable householder would object to him doing so, if the entry were bona fide and no damage was caused.[70]

The following general rules may be formulated:

(1) It is a defence to an action for trespass, open to a police officer as much as to any other citizen, to show that he was upon property with the leave and licence of the owner.[71] An officer, like any other member of the public, has an implied licence and leave from the householder to enter a garden gate and walk up to the front door, and to knock on that door for the purpose of making inquiries.[72] If he exceeds his licence, or remains on land after that licence is revoked, he becomes a trespasser, and an officer who acts thus is no longer acting in the execution of his duty[73]; although he is entitled to a reasonable opportunity to leave.[74]

(2) A police officer may enter premises to prevent a breach of the peace[75] and, probably, to prevent the commission of any offence which he believes to be imminent or likely to be committed,[76] and in such circumstances he may be said to enter by virtue of a licence given by law, that is, with the authority of the law.[77]

The old cases seem to support the proposition that an officer may enter premises where he hears an affray in progress, and may even break in to suppress it or arrest an offender[78]; and may break in to prevent an affray which he believes, on reasonable grounds, may take place on private premises[79]; and he may break open doors to gain entry (a) to prevent the commission of an arrestable offence, or where an arrestable offence has been committed in order to make an arrest; and he may do the same where an affray occurs in the presence of the officer, and an

[70] *Per* Atkin L.J. in *Great Central Ry. Co.* v. *Bates* [1921] 3 K.B. 578 at p. 582.
[71] Clerk and Lindsell, 11th ed., Chap. 16.
[72] *Robson* v. *Hallett* [1967] 2 Q.B. 939.
[73] *Davies* v. *Lisle* [1936] 2 K.B. 434 and see *McArdle* v. *Wallace* [1964] Crim. L.R. 467.
[74] *Robson* v. *Hallett* (*supra*).
[75] *Thomas* v. *Sawkins* [1935] 2 K.B. 249.
[76] *Ibid. per* Lord Hewart C.J.
[77] Clerk and Lindsell, 11th ed., Chap. 16.
[78] Clerk and Lindsell, 11th ed., Chap. 16.
[79] *Handcock* v. *Baker* (1800) 2 Bos. & P. 260.

offender runs away and hides in a house; or (*b*) where any person in lawful custody escapes and takes refuge in a house.[80]

(3) An officer enters premises with the authority of the law where he has authority under a warrant to search the premises.

(B) The power to search premises, persons and vehicles. As we have already seen, where the police have no warrant, they have got to obtain the consent of the householder to enter his premises, or if not, to do it by stealth or force. The cardinal principle in entering premises for the purpose of search is that where the householder refuses his consent, a search warrant must be obtained. At common law that was the only authority, and in no other case was an officer permitted to enter a house and seize goods.[81] On the principle that " Every man's house is his castle "[82] the law was always strictly construed in favour of the householder, but on the other hand, it was equally recognised that a man's house was not to be used " as a hiding place for thieves or a receptacle for stolen goods." At common law, the search for stolen goods was the classic case but the issue of search warrants is now covered by statute.

The present position is as follows : (i) in certain limited circumstances a constable has a power of search without a warrant, *e.g.* under section 47 of the Firearms Act 1968, section 23 of the Misuse of Drugs Act 1971 and other statutes; (ii) also, in certain localities,[83] where a constable has reason to suspect that anything stolen or unlawfully obtained may be found in or upon any vessel, boat, cart or carriage, he may stop, search and detain such vessel, etc., and also any person whom he may reasonably suspect of having or conveying in any manner anything stolen or unlawfully obtained.[84]

---

[80] *R.* v. *Marsden* (1868) L.R. 1 C.C.R. 131 and see generally Stone, 104th ed., p. 397.

[81] See Denning M.R. in *Ghani* v. *Jones* [1970] 1 Q.B. 693.

[82] *Per* Lord Coke in *Semayne's Case* (1605) 5 Co.Rep. 919.

[83] *e.g.* London under s. 66 of the Metropolitan Police Act 1839; Birmingham under the Birmingham Corporation (Consolidation) Act 1883; the City of London under the City of London Act 1839. Newcastle under the Newcastle upon Tyne Improvement Act 1841, s. 39.

[84] Following the substance of the Metropolitan Police Act 1839, s. 66; which words are used in similar or identical terms in many local Acts.

Under the Theft Act 1968 [85] an officer of police not below the rank of superintendent may authorise in writing a constable to search premises for stolen goods where the person in occupation of the premises has been convicted within the preceding five years of certain offences of dishonesty, and the statute authorises any such officer to enter and search the premises accordingly and to seize any goods he believes to be stolen goods.

(C) Magistrate's power to issue a search warrant. A magistrate may issue his warrant to search premises where such warrant can be founded on some provision of the common law or some statute. At common law a justice of the peace may issue a search warrant upon sworn information by a complainant that he has reason to suspect that property of his, which need not be specified, has been stolen and is in the possession of another.[86] Apart from this, there is at common law no power in any magistrate to grant a warrant for the general search of premises.[87] By statute, search warrants may be granted in many other cases, *e.g.* for explosive substances,[88] for anything which there is reasonable cause to believe is intended for use, without lawful excuse, to destroy or damage the property of another,[89] for forged documents and implements of forgery,[90] for counterfeit coin and coinage tools,[91] for children believed to be ill-treated or neglected,[92] for obscene books and pictures,[93] for sketches, plans and documents which are evidence of an offence under the Official Secrets Acts,[94] for blasphemous and seditious libels,[95] for dangerous drugs,[96] for a woman detained for an immoral purpose,[97] for firearms,[98] for evidence of the commission

---

[85] s. 26 (2).
[86] *Jones* v. *German* [1897] 1 Q.B. 374.
[87] *Leach* v. *Money* (1765) 19 St.Tr. 1001 at p. 1027 and *Entick* v. *Carrington* (1765) 19 St.Tr. 1029.
[88] Offences against the Person Act 1861, s. 65, amended by the Criminal Law Act 1967, Sched. 2; Explosives Act 1875, ss. 73–75, 86.
[89] Criminal Damage Act 1971, s. 6 (1).
[90] Forgery Act 1913, s. 16.
[91] Coinage Offences Act 1936, s. 11 (3).
[92] Children and Young Persons Act 1933, s. 40, amended by the Children and Young Persons Act 1963, s. 64 and Sched. III.
[93] Obscene Publications Act 1959, s. 3, but only on an information laid by the Director of Public Prosecutions: Criminal Justice Act 1967, s. 25.
[94] Official Secrets Act 1911, s. 9.
[95] Criminal Libel Act 1819, s. 1.
[96] Misuse of Drugs Act 1971, s. 23.
[97] Sexual Offences Act 1956, s. 43.
[98] Firearms Act 1968, s. 46.

of an offence under the Incitement to Disaffection Act 1934,[99] for evidence of an offence under the Public Order Act 1936,[1] where trading in prostitution is alleged,[2] under the Licensing Act 1964,[3] the Customs and Excise Act 1952,[4] the Children Act 1958,[5] the Mental Health Act 1959,[6] and the Protection of Birds Act, 1954.[7]

Again, by **section 43** of the **Sexual Offences Act 1956** a justice of the peace may, on the oath of a parent, relative, or guardian of any woman or girl, or other person who, in the opinion of such justice, is bona fide acting in her interest, that there is a reasonable cause to suspect that such a woman or girl is unlawfully detained for immoral purposes in any place within his jurisdiction, issue a warrant to search such place for, and when found to detain, such woman or girl until she be brought before him, and then may order her to be delivered up to her parents or guardians. And he may also cause any person accused of unlawfully detaining such woman or girl to be apprehended and brought before him. A woman or girl is deemed to be unlawfully detained for immoral purposes if she is so detained for the purpose of being unlawfully and carnally known by any man, and either (i) is under the age of sixteen years; or (ii) if of or over that age, and under the age of eighteen years, is detained against her will, or that of her father, mother, or other person having the lawful charge of her, or (iii) if of or above the latter age, is detained against her will.

The above examples are not meant to be exhaustive, but they offer an indication of the cases in which a magistrates' court is authorised to grant a search warrant. It is interesting to note that—

> " No magistrate, no judge even, has any power to issue a search warrant for murder. He can issue a search warrant for stolen goods, and for some statutory offences such as coinage, but not for murder, not to dig for the body nor to look for the axe, the gun or the poison dregs." [8]

The circumstances must fall within the provisions of a particular statute, or the power to issue a warrant does not exist. The common law does not permit officers to ransack a person's house or to

---

[99] s. 2.
[1] s. 2 (5).
[2] Sexual Offences Act 1956, s. 43.
[3] s. 145.
[4] ss. 296–298.
[5] s. 135.   [6] s. 136.
[7] s. 6.   [8] *Per* Lord Denning in *Ghani* v. *Jones* (*supra*).

search for papers or articles therein or to search his person merely to see if he has committed some offence.

(D) The power to search persons after arrest. On arrest there is a right to search the person arrested for articles material to a criminal charge.[9]   There are clearly good reasons for this, including: (a) the safe custody of the prisoner's property; (b) the necessity of taking from him anything with which he might cause injury to himself or others or to assist him in escaping; and (c) obtaining evidence which might reasonably be considered as evidence connecting him with either the offence charged or some other offence.[10] The test to be applied both in (a) and (c) is " reasonableness." If a constable has reasonable grounds for believing that the person arrested has evidence, or potentially dangerous articles about his person, the search would be justified.   If the search is justified, the removal of the articles is justified.

A person in custody may be searched where, by reason of his violence, language or conduct, a search is prudent both for his own protection and for the protection of others.   There is no authority for the customary search of a prisoner's premises after his arrest, but no doubt a warrant could be readily obtained.[11]   If a police officer who has lawfully entered premises makes a general search of the premises without having a search warrant, and takes away documents, he is protected against the consequences of what would otherwise be a trespass if the documents subsequently prove to be relevant on a charge of a criminal nature against anyone.   The police are also entitled to retain any property properly taken from any person or premises until the conclusion of any charge on which such property is material.[12]

SECTION 7. THE POWER TO SEIZE AND DETAIN PROPERTY

Where police officers enter a house by virtue of a warrant or arrest a man lawfully, with or without a warrant for a serious offence they are entitled to take possession of any goods which they find in his house or in his possession, which they reasonably believe to be

[9] *Bessell* v. *Wilson*, 17 J.P. 567; *Elias* v. *Pasmore* [1934] 2 K.B. 164.
[10] Articles which are evidence of an offence by a third person may be removed but damages may be recovered for wrongful removal.
[11] See *R.* v. *Lushington, ex p. Otto* [1894] 1 Q.B. 420 for the observations of Wright J. at p. 423.
[12] *Elias* v. *Pasmore* [1934] 2 K.B. 164.

material evidence of the crime for which he is arrested or for which they enter. If in the course of their search they come upon other goods which show him to be implicated in some other crime they may take those also; provided they act *reasonably* and detain them no longer than is necessary.[13] To justify the police in taking possession of an article where no one has been arrested or charged, the following requisites must be satisfied: First, the police must have reasonable grounds for believing that (i) a serious offence has been committed and that (ii) the article in question is either the fruit of the crime or the instrument by which the crime was committed, or is material evidence to prove the commission of the crime. Secondly they must believe that the person in possession of the article committed the crime or is implicated in it or is an accessory to it, or at any rate that his refusal to allow the police to have the article is quite unreasonable. Thirdly, the police must not keep the article or prevent its removal for any longer than is reasonably necessary to complete their investigations or preserve it for evidence. The lawfulness of their actions is to be judged by the position at the time of their acts and not by what happens afterwards. The police are entitled to retain articles for production in court [14] provided they are relevant [15] but not for longer than the time necessary for the trial and subsequent appeal.[16]

SECTION 8. BAIL BY THE POLICE

Here it is intended to deal with that part of the law of bail applicable to the period of time after a person's arrest and before he has either been tried by a magistrates' court or committed by a magistrates' court for trial by jury.

By **section 38** [17] of the **Magistrates' Courts Act 1952**, on a person's being taken into custody for an offence without a warrant, a police officer not below the rank of inspector, or the police officer in charge of the police station to which the person is brought, may, and, if it will not be practicable to bring him before a magistrates' court within twenty-four hours after his being taken into custody,

---

[13] *Ghani* v. *Jones* (*supra*); *Garfinkel* v. *Metropolitan Police Commissioner* [1972] Crim.L.R. 44 and see *R.* v. *Waterfield* [1964] 1 Q.B. 164.
[14] *R.* v. *Lushington, ex p. Otto*, 58 J.P. 282.
[15] *R.* v. *Barnett* (1829) 3 C. & P. 600; *R.* v. *Frost* (1839) 9 C. & P. 129.
[16] *Gordon* v. *Metropolitan Police Commissioner* [1910] 2 K.B. 1080.
[17] As amended by the Children and Young Persons Act 1969, Sched. 6.

must inquire into the case and, unless the offence appears to the officer to be a serious one, release him on his entering into a recognisance, with or without sureties for a reasonable amount, conditioned for his appearance before a magistrates' court at the time and place named in the recognisance. Where, on a person's being taken into custody for an offence without a warrant, it appears to any such officer as aforesaid that the inquiry into the case cannot be completed forthwith, he may release that person on his entering into a recognisance, with or without sureties, for a reasonable amount, conditioned for his appearance at such police station and at such time as is named in the recognisance unless he previously receives a notice in writing from the officer in charge of that police station that his attendance is not required; and any such recognisance may be enforced as if it were conditioned for the appearance of that person before a magistrates' court for the petty sessions area in which the police station named in the recognisance is situated. Where a person is taken into custody for an offence without a warrant and is retained in custody, he must be brought before a magistrates' court as soon as practicable.

The purpose of granting bail to a person at this time is to prevent him from having to wait in custody at a time when it is not known whether he is guilty of the offence or not. In order to be granted bail, *i.e.* be released from custody, the accused and, if so ordered, other persons will be required to enter into a recognisance for his appearance. A recognisance is an acknowledgment that on the non-appearance of the accused, the persons entering into the recognisance will pay certain stipulated sums of money to the Queen. Persons other than the accused who enter into recognisances for his appearance are called sureties.

By **section 93** of the **Magistrates' Courts Act 1952** it is provided that the justice on issuing a warrant may indorse it with a direction that the person arrested shall on arrest be released on his entering into such a recognisance, with or without sureties, conditioned for his appearance before a magistrates' court, as may be specified in the indorsement; and the indorsement must fix the amounts in which the principal and the sureties, if any, are to be bound. A warrant thus indorsed is commonly said to be " backed for bail." Where such an indorsement has been made, then, on that person's being taken to the police station on arrest under the warrant, the officer in charge of the police station shall release him on his entering into a recognisance, with or without sureties approved by the officer, in accordance with the indorsement, conditioned for his appearance before a magistrates' court at the time and place named in the recognisance.

The granting of bail to young persons under the age of seventeen will be dealt with later.[18]

SECTION 9. MISCELLANEOUS POWERS

The police have a number of miscellaneous powers under various statutes. Examples of these are the power to enter and inspect premises under the Theatres Act 1968; [19] and a power under the same Act for an officer of or above the rank of superintendent to examine and copy scripts of plays.[20]

---

18 *Post*, p. 680.
19 *Ibid*. s. 15.
20 *Ibid*. s. 10.

CHAPTER 45

PROCESS TO COMPEL APPEARANCE— BAIL BY JUSTICES

THE first step in the prosecution of any offence is to secure the appearance of the alleged offender. This may be effected—by summons or by arrest with or without a warrant.

SECTION 1. SUMMONS AND ARREST BY WARRANT

By **section 1** of the **Magistrates' Courts Act 1952,** it is provided that upon an information [1] being laid before a justice of the peace [2] for any county or borough that any person has, or is suspected of having, committed an offence, the justice may take one of two courses—

(a) he may issue a summons directed to that person requiring him to appear before the court to answer to the information; or

(b) he may issue a warrant to arrest that person and bring him before the court.

Section 24 (1) of the **Criminal Justice Act 1967,** provides that a warrant for the arrest of any person who has attained the age of seventeen shall not be issued under section 1 of the Magistrates' Courts Act 1952, unless—

(a) the offence to which the warrant relates is an indictable offence or is punishable with imprisonment; or

(b) the address of the defendant is not sufficiently established for a summons to be served on him.

The decision to issue a summons or a warrant is one for the justice and is discretionary. If he refuses to issue either, the High

---

[1] An information is simply the statement by which the magistrates are informed of the offence. As to the form and contents, see the Magistrates' Courts Rules 1968, rr. 1 (2), 1 (3) and 83 and Magistrates' Courts (Forms) Rules 1968, Form 1. Where the informant has reason to believe that the alleged offender is a juvenile, there is a duty to inform the appropriate local authority: Children and Young Persons Act 1969, s. 5 (8) and see *ibid.* s. 9, for the corresponding duty upon the local authority.

[2] Informations other than those to be substantiated on oath may be laid before the clerk to the justices who may issue a summons: Justices' Clerks Rules 1970.

Court will not compel him to review his decision unless his discretion was exercised on improper or extraneous grounds.[3]   It is no exercise of discretion to make a practice of always refusing applications of a certain type.[4]   But to enable a justice to issue a warrant in the first instance, it is necessary that an information in writing, and substantiated on oath or affirmation, should be laid before him. If a summons only is to be issued in the first instance, the information need not be in writing or on oath.

By **section 1 (2) (a)** of **the Act,** a justice of the peace may issue a summons or warrant in any case where an offence has been committed, or is suspected to have been committed, within the county or borough.   Where the offence has been committed on the boundary between two or more local jurisdictions, or within five hundred yards of such a boundary, or in any harbour, river, arm of the sea or other water lying between two or more local jurisdictions, the offence may be treated as having been committed in any of those jurisdictions (section 3 (1)).   An offence begun in one local jurisdiction and completed in another may be treated as having been wholly committed in either (section 3 (2)), and an offence which has been committed on any person or on or in respect of any property, in or on a vehicle or vessel engaged on any journey or voyage through two or more local jurisdictions, may be treated as having been committed in any of those jurisdictions (section 3 (3)).

By **section 1 (2) (b)** of **the Act,** a justice of the peace may also issue a summons or warrant where it appears to him necessary or expedient, with a view to the better administration of justice, that the person charged should be tried jointly with, or in the same place as, some other person who is charged with an offence, and who is in custody, or is being or is to be proceeded against, within the county or borough.   But there must be a sufficient nexus between the cases, and the justices should bear in mind the interests of the prosecution and the defence.[5]

By **section 1 (2) (c)** of **the Act,** a justice may issue a summons or warrant in respect of an *indictable offence* [6] if the person charged

---

[3] *R.* v. *Kennedy* (1902) 86 L.T. 753 ; 20 Cox 230.

[4] *R.* v. *Beacontree Justices, ex p. Mercer* [1970] Crim.L.R. 103.

[5] *R.* v. *Blandford and Freestone* (1955) 39 Cr.App.R. 51, in which the Court of Criminal Appeal held that the justices' discretion under this paragraph had been properly exercised.

[6] See p. 646.

resides or is, or is believed to reside or be, within the county or borough, even though the offence was not committed within the county or borough. Where the offence charged is *not an indictable offence*, a summons may not be issued by virtue only of that paragraph, and any warrant issued must require the person charged to be brought before a magistrates' court having jurisdiction to try the offence.

By **section 1 (2) (e)** a justice may issue a summons or warrant if the offence was committed outside England and Wales and, where it is an offence exclusively punishable on summary conviction, if a magistrates' court for the county or borough would have jurisdiction to try the offence if the offender was before them.[7]

By **section 1 (5)** of **the Act,** one justice of the peace has, in every case, jurisdiction to issue a summons or warrant under section 1 upon an information being laid before him, notwithstanding any enactment requiring the information to be laid before two or more justices.

By **Rule 83** of the **Magistrates' Courts Rules 1968** every information, summons, warrant or other document laid, issued or made for the purposes of, or in connection with, any proceedings before a magistrates' court for an offence shall be sufficient if it describes the specific offence with which the accused is charged, or of which he is convicted, in ordinary language avoiding as far as possible the use of technical terms and without necessarily stating all the elements of the offence, and gives such particulars as may be necessary for giving reasonable information of the nature of the charge.[8] If the offence charged is one created by or under any Act, the description of the offence shall contain a reference to the section of the Act, or, as the case may be, the rule, order, regulation, by-law or other instrument creating the offence.

However, by **section 100** of **the Act,** no objection is to be allowed to any information, or to any summons or warrant to procure the presence of the defendant, for any defect in it in substance or form, or for any variance between it and the evidence adduced on behalf of the prosecutor or complainant at the hearing of the information or complaint. But if the variance between the

---

[7] Added by the Courts Act 1971, Sched. 8.
[8] If insufficient particulars are given, application for sufficient particulars may be made at any time after the charge is preferred: *R.* v. *Aylesbury Justices, ex p. Wisbey* [1965] 1 W.L.R. 339.

summons or warrant and the evidence adduced is such that, in the opinion of the court, the defendant has been misled, the court must adjourn the hearing.[9]

Section 72 of the **Criminal Justice Act 1967** grants a justice of the peace power to issue warrants for the arrest of escaped prisoners and mental patients.

The summons.[10] By **Rule 81,** the summons must be signed by the justice issuing it, or state his name and be authenticated by the signature of the clerk to the justices. A summons may now be issued by the clerk himself.[11] It must state shortly the matter of the information or complaint and the time and place at which the defendant is required by the summons to appear. A single summons may be issued against a person in respect of several informations or complaints; but the summons must state the matter of each information or complaint separately, and it has effect as several summonses, each issued in respect of one information or complaint. A summons to a juvenile may include the parent or guardian.[12]

Rule 82 provides for the service of the summons in one of three ways. It may be effected—

(a) by delivering it to the person to whom it is directed; or

(b) by leaving it for him with some person at his last known or usual place of abode; or

(c) by sending it by post in a registered letter or in a recorded delivery letter addressed to him at his last known or usual place of abode.

In the case of an offence, other than one which is a summary offence and not also an indictable offence, if the person summoned fails to appear in answer to a summons served by methods (b) or (c), the service will not be treated as proved unless it is proved that the summons came to his knowledge; and for that purpose any

---

[9] Notwithstanding the words of s. 100, where such a variance is apparent, the court may, instead of adjourning the case, either continue to hear it after the information has been amended if the accused does not object, or dismiss the information, leaving it to the prosecution to charge the accused under a new information: *Meek* v. *Powell* [1952] 1 K.B. 164; *Hunter* v. *Coombs* [1962] 1 All E.R. 904. See also *Wright* v. *Nicholson* [1970] 1 W.L.R. 142; *Hutchinson (Cinemas) Ltd. and Others* v. *Tyson* (1969) 134 J.P. 202.

[10] Magistrates' Courts (Forms) Rules, 1968, Form 2.

[11] *i.e.* under the Justices Clerks' Rules 1970.

[12] Magistrates' Courts (Children and Young Persons) Rules 1970, r. 26.

letter or other communication purporting to be written by him or on his behalf in such terms as reasonably to justify the inference that the summons came to his knowledge is admissible as evidence of that fact.[13]

A summons requiring the attendance at court of any person to give evidence or produce a document or thing cannot be served by registered post, nor can any summons be served by this method outside England and Wales.[14]

Service of a summons on a corporation is effected by delivering it at, or sending it by post to, the registered office of the corporation, or, if the corporation has no registered office in England and Wales, to any place in England and Wales where the corporation trades or conducts its business.[15]

In practice, a summons is usually served by recorded delivery or by a constable on the accused personally, or delivered to some person for him at his last or most usual place of abode.

The warrant of arrest.[16] By **Rule 78,** every warrant under the Act must be signed by the justice issuing it unless signature by the clerk to the justices is permitted.[17] By **Rule 79,** a warrant of arrest must require the persons to whom it is directed, that is to say, the constables of the police area in which the warrant is issued, or any persons named in that behalf in the warrant, to arrest the person against whom the warrant is issued. The warrant must name or otherwise describe the person for whose arrest it is issued, and must contain a statement of the offence charged in the information, or, as the case may be, the ground on which the warrant is issued.

By **section 102** of **the Act,** it is provided that a warrant of arrest remains in force until it is executed (*i.e.* the accused person is duly apprehended) or withdrawn. The issue or execution of any warrant of arrest is as effectual on Sunday as on any other day. The warrant may be executed anywhere in England and Wales by any person to whom it is directed or by any constable acting within his police area.

By **section 102 (4)** of the **Magistrates' Courts Act 1952** a warrant to arrest a person charged with an offence may be executed

---

[13] Magistrates' Courts Rules 1968, r. 82 (2). [14] *Ibid.* r. 82 (5).
[15] *Ibid.* r. 82 (3).
[16] Magistrates' Courts (Forms) Rules 1968, Form 3.
[17] *i.e.* under the Magistrates' Courts Rules 1968, r. 93, the Magistrates' Courts (Forms) Rules 1968 or the Justices' Clerks Rules 1970.

by a constable notwithstanding that it is not in his possession at the time; but the warrant shall, on the demand of the person arrested, be shown to him as soon as practicable.

By **section 6** of the **Constables Protection Act 1750** a constable who makes an arrest under the authority of a justice's warrant and does not exceed the authority of the warrant is protected against any action brought in consequence of any want of jurisdiction in the justice who signed the warrant.

A *general* warrant is as a rule void, *e.g.* a warrant to apprehend the authors, printers and publishers of a libel, without naming them.[18] But in certain cases a warrant may be issued to arrest all persons found on particular premises, *e.g.* any house or place suspected of being used as a common gaming house.[19]

Warrants of arrest issued elsewhere in Great Britain. In order to enable a warrant issued in England to be executed in Scotland, Northern Ireland or the Channel Islands and vice versa it must be backed, *i.e.* a justice of the county or place where it is to be executed must make an indorsement upon it, signed with his own name, authorising its execution within the area of *his* jurisdiction. The warrant may then be executed by the persons who have brought the warrant or the local police.[20] However, in the case of warrants issued in Scotland for the apprehension of a person charged with an offence, they may also be executed in England without backing by any constable acting within his police area.[21]

It appears that warrants issued in Northern Ireland or the Channel Islands cannot be executed in England on Sundays [22] and that the person making the arrest must have the warrant in his possession.[23] The Scottish warrants may be executed in England on Sundays and without possession of the warrant only by a constable acting within his area.[24]

---

[18] *Money* v. *Leach* (1765) 1 W.Bl. 555.
[19] Betting, Gaming and Lotteries Act 1963, s. 51 (1) (*b*).
[20] Indictable Offences Act 1848, ss. 12–15, amended by the Courts Act 1971, Sched. 8.
[21] Criminal Justice (Scotland) Act 1963, s. 39. Special provisions have also been made for the border counties: Police (Scotland) Act 1967, s. 18.
[22] As they do not come within the provisions of the Magistrates' Courts Act 1952, s. 102 (3).
[23] *Sed quaere* whether s. 102 (4) of the Magistrates' Courts Act 1952 (above), applies to these warrants.
[24] Criminal Justice (Scotland) Act 1963, s. 39.

Warrants of arrest issued elsewhere in the Commonwealth. The **Fugitive Offenders Act 1967** provides for the issue in England of warrants of arrest for persons found in England, who are accused of a relevant offence in a Commonwealth country, or a Dependency of the United Kingdom, or for a person who is unlawfully at large after conviction in such a country.

Warrants of arrest issued in the Republic of Ireland. Warrants of arrest for indictable offences and summary offences punishable with more than six months' imprisonment issued in Ireland may be backed by a justice in accordance with the provisions of the **Backing of Warrants (Republic of Ireland) Act 1965.** They may then be executed in that part of England which comprises the area under the jurisdiction of the justice who has backed the warrant in the same manner as if the warrant had been originally issued in England.[25] A justice may also issue a " provisional warrant " at the request of a constable who has received an urgent request to detain a person for whose arrest a warrant has been issued in Ireland, but who has not yet come into the possession of the warrant.

SECTION 2. BAIL BY JUSTICES

At any time before beginning to inquire into an offence as examining magistrates or at any time during the inquiry, or at any time before or during a summary trial, a magistrates' court may adjourn the inquiry or trial and remand the accused in custody or remand him on bail.[26] **Section 105** of the **Magistrates' Courts Act 1952** states that the court, when granting bail, must take from him a recognisance, with or without sureties,[27] conditioned for his appearance before the court either at the end of the period of remand, or at every time and place to which the hearing may from time to

25 Backing of Warrants (Republic of Ireland) Act 1965, s. 1 (4). For a detailed consideration of the procedure applicable in such a case see *R.* v. *Governor of Brixton Prison, ex p. Keane* [1972] A.C. 204.

26 Magistrates' Courts Act 1952, ss. 6 (1), 14 (1) (4), 105, as amended. See also ss. 16 (1), 26 (2), as amended.

27 The recognisances of the sureties may be taken before, after or at the same time as the recognisance of the principal: Criminal Justice Administration Act 1914, s. 24. The power of the Crown Court under the Courts Act 1971, s. 13 (5) to permit " other security " to be given does not apparently apply to magistrates' courts unless they are taking sureties on behalf of the Crown Court, under s. 13 (5) (6).

time be adjourned (called continuous bail). The section also provides that instead of the court taking the recognisances, the court may fix the amount of the recognisances with a view to their being taken subsequently in accordance with section 95 and meanwhile remand the accused in custody. **Section 95** states that where the court has fixed the amount in which the principal (*i.e.* the accused) and his sureties, if any, are to be bound, the recognisances may be taken by any of a list of prescribed persons.[28]

Section 105 (4) provides that a person shall not be remanded on bail for a period exceeding eight clear days unless he and the prosecution consent.[29]

Section 106 provides for further remands and enlargement of the recognisances on the failure of the accused to appear for reasons of illness, accident or other reasons.[30]

Section 21 of the **Criminal Justice Act 1967** provides that the court, before granting bail, may impose conditions which are likely to result in the accused's appearance or which are necessary in the interests of justice or for the prevention of crime. These conditions might include daily reporting to the police station, observing a stipulated curfew, delivering up a passport or staying at a stipulated address.[31] However, the section states that the court may not require the accused to find sureties in respect of the conditions.

Section 19 of the **Criminal Justice Act 1967** provides that a justice of the peace shall not take part in trying the issue of a defendant's guilt on the summary trial of an information if in the course of the same proceedings the justice has been informed, for the purpose of determining the question of the defendant's admission to bail, that he has one or more previous convictions.

SECTION 3. PRINCIPLES OF BAIL

Categories of offence. We have already seen that the police may only grant bail on the arrest of a person without warrant if the

---

[28] This list includes any justice of the peace, the clerk of any magistrates' court, any police officer not below the rank of inspector, the officer in charge of any police station, the governor or keeper of a prison: Magistrates' Courts Rules 1968, r. 72.

[29] There are exceptions to this, see s. 105 (4) (c) and s. 26 (1), as amended by the Criminal Justice Act 1967, Sched. 6.

[30] As to the powers of the clerks to the justices to remand further on bail, see the Justices' Clerks Rules 1970.

[31] *Cf.* the power of the Crown Court to take " other security " under the Courts Act 1971, s. 13 (5).

offence is not a serious one.[32] A magistrates' court has a wide discretion to grant bail, but there are some statutory limitations on their powers to grant or refuse bail for certain kinds of offences, and certain general principles must be borne in mind.[33]

Section 8 of the **Magistrates' Courts Act 1952** provides that a person charged with treason must not be admitted to bail except by order of a judge of the High Court or the Secretary of State.

Section 18 of the **Criminal Justice Act 1967** provides that, subject to certain provisions, a magistrates' court *must* remand a person who has attained the age of seventeen [34] on bail if:

(*a*) he is charged with a summary offence which is not also an indictable offence and is punishable with not more than six months' imprisonment; or

(*b*) the court has started to try him summarily for an offence that is either both summary or indictable and is punishable on summary conviction with not more than six months' imprisonment or an indictable offence which is triable summarily and, after he has pleaded to the charge, the trial is adjourned; or

(*c*) he is charged with a summary offence for which it is intended that he will be tried by a jury and the preliminary inquiry is adjourned or he is committed for trial.

Section 18 (4) provides that the section does not require the granting of bail where a proper recognisance or satisfactory sureties are not forthcoming.

Section 18 (5) provides that the section does not require that a person should be granted bail:

" (*a*) where he is charged with an offence punishable by that court with imprisonment for a term of not less than six months and it appears to the court that he has been previously sentenced to imprisonment or borstal training;

(*b*) where it appears to the court that, having been released on bail on any occasion, he has failed to comply with the conditions of any recognisance entered into by him on that occasion;

---

[32] *Ante*, p. 568.
[33] See *post*, p. 580.
[34] Special provisions apply to juveniles, see *post*, p. 680 and the Children and Young Persons Act 1969, ss. 23, 24 and 29.

(c) where he is charged with an offence alleged to have been committed while he was released on bail;

(d) where it appears to the court that it is necessary to detain him to establish his identity or address;

(e) where it appears to the court that he has no fixed abode or that he is ordinarily resident outside the United Kingdom;

(f) where the act or any of the acts constituting the offence with which he is charged consisted of an assault on or threat of violence to another person, or of having or possessing a firearm, an imitation firearm, an explosive or an offensive weapon, or of indecent conduct with or towards a person under the age of sixteen years;

(g) where it appears to the court that unless he is remanded or committed in custody he is likely to commit an offence; or

(h) where it appears to the court necessary for his own protection to refuse to remand or commit him on bail."

Section 18 (6) provides that the section does not apply where a trial is adjourned for the purpose of enabling a medical examination and report to be made on the defendant if it appears impracticable to obtain such a report without remanding him in custody.

Section 18 (7) [34a] provides that where a court refuses to grant bail to any person who has attained the age of seventeen, the court shall, if he is not represented by counsel or a solicitor, (a) in a case of committal, inform him that he may apply to a judge of the High Court, or to the Crown Court, to be admitted to bail, and (b) in any other case, inform him that he may apply to a judge of the High Court for that purpose.

Section 18 (8) provides that where a magistrates' court refuses bail to a person coming within section 18 (1), (2) or (3), written reasons for the refusal shall be given to a person who is unrepresented or to a person who is represented if counsel or solicitor so requests.

Other factors. The object of requiring bail is to secure the presence of the prisoner, and it should not be withheld merely as a punishment. The question for the consideration of the justices is

[34a] Amended by the Criminal Justice Act 1972, Sched. 5. (Not in force on July 1, 1972.)

whether it is probable that if bail is granted the accused will appear to stand his trial. In applying this test they must consider (i) the nature of the charge, (ii) the evidence in support of it, (iii) the severity of the punishment for the offence, (iv) whether the sureties are independent or indemnified by the accused.[35] After justices have decided to commit a prisoner for trial, it is proper that, on their asking whether the police object to bail, they should be told of the prisoner's previous convictions[36]; and they should not ordinarily grant bail to persons with bad criminal records.[37] Where a person is charged with the more serious crimes, bail will not normally be granted.

The amount of the bail is a matter for the discretion of the justice, but by the Bill of Rights 1688 excessive bail must not be required.[38] If any sureties are required, they must be able to answer for the sum in which they are bound and may be examined on oath as to their means.

If a justice denies or delays bail where it ought to be granted he is guilty, at common law and by statute, of an offence.[39]

SECTION 4. REVIEW OF BAIL

By **section 94** of the **Magistrates' Courts Act 1952** where a magistrates' court has committed a person to custody in default of finding sureties, the court may, on application by the person committed, and after hearing fresh evidence, reduce the amount in which it is proposed that any surety should be bound or dispense with any of the sureties or otherwise deal with the case as it thinks just.

Section 22 of the **Criminal Justice Act 1967** provides that where a person has been refused bail or has been given or offered bail on terms unacceptable to him by a magistrates' court, he may apply for bail to a High Court judge in chambers.[40] If he is

---

[35] Arch. para. 203 and the authorities there cited.

[36] *R.* v. *Fletcher* (1949) 113 J.P. 365.

[37] *R.* v. *Wharton* [1955] Crim.L.R. 565.

[38] See *Ex p. Thomas* [1956] Crim.L.R. 119.

[39] *R.* v. *Badger* (1843) 4 Q.B. 468; Statute of Westminster I (1275), Habeas Corpus Act (1679), and Bill of Rights (1688–89). But as his duty in respect of admitting to bail is judicial and not ministerial he is not liable to an action for refusing bail without proof of malice or improper motive: *Linford* v. *Fitzroy* (1849) 13 Q.B. 240.

[40] For the procedure, see Rules of the Supreme Court 1973, Ord. 79, r. 9.

refused bail by that judge, he may make no fresh application to any other judge, or to the Divisional Court or the Court of Appeal.[41]

The High Court may admit the applicant to bail or direct his admission to bail [42] or, where he has been admitted to bail, may vary any conditions on which he was so admitted or reduce the amount in which he or any surety is bound or discharge any of the sureties.[43] Where a person is committed to the Crown Court in custody, that court may admit or direct his admission to trial, under section 13 (4) (a) of the Courts Act 1971. This power is additional to the powers of the High Court to grant bail. The two systems are complementary and a person committed by magistrates in custody may apply either to the Crown Court or to the High Court.[44] If the amount fixed by the justices be so excessive that the defendant cannot avail himself of it, application may also be made *ex parte* to the Divisional Court for a writ of habeas corpus on the ground that the imposition of such excessive bail amounts to a grant of no bail and contravenes the Bill of Rights 1688, and thus makes the applicant's imprisonment unlawful.[45]

Section 5. Position of the Sureties

A person who is released on bail upon the recognisances of sureties is treated as being in their custody. If they fear that he is about to break the recognisance, they may arrest him and bring him before a justice, who will then remand him in custody in discharge of the bail unless other sureties can be found.[46] **Section 23 (1)** of the **Criminal Justice Act 1967** gives a surety the power to have the accused arrested by a constable.

An agreement by an accused person to indemnify his sureties if the recognisances are forfeited for non-appearance, constitutes a common law conspiracy.[47]

---

[41] *Ibid.*

[42] See the Criminal Justice Act 1948, s. 37 (3) and the Criminal Justice Act 1967, s. 22 (3), as amended by the Courts Act 1971, Sched. 8.

[43] Criminal Justice Act 1967, s. 22, as amended.

[44] Procedure is governed by Rules 17 and 22 of the Crown Court Rules 1971. Application may be heard by a Crown Court judge in chambers: s. 22.

[45] *Ex p. Thomas* [1956] Crim.L.R. 119.

[46] Arch. para. 201.

[47] *R.* v. *Porter* [1910] 1 K.B. 369.

Section 6. Termination and Forfeiture

In the previous Section, it was seen that the sureties may terminate the bail by bringing the accused, or having him brought, before a justice. Bail is also terminated, of course, if the accused appears at the time, or times, and place specified.

Section 23 (1) of the **Criminal Justice Act 1967** provides that a constable may arrest without warrant any person who has been admitted to bail—

(*a*) if the constable has reasonable grounds for believing that that person is likely to break the condition that he will appear at the time and place required or any other condition on which he was admitted to bail, or has reasonable cause to suspect that the person is breaking or has broken any such other condition; or

(*b*) on being notified in writing by any surety for that person that the surety believes that that person is likely to break the first-mentioned condition and for that reason the surety wishes to be relieved of his obligations as surety.

Section 23 (2) provides that a person arrested under subsection (1)—

(*a*) shall, except where he was so arrested within the period of twenty-four hours immediately preceding an occasion on which he is required by virtue of a condition of his bail to appear before any court, be brought as soon as practicable and in any event within twenty-four hours after his arrest before a justice acting for the petty sessions area in which he was arrested; and

(*b*) in the excepted case shall be brought before the court before which he is required to appear.

Section 23 (3) provides that a justice before whom such a person is brought may, if of the opinion that the accused has broken or is likely to break any condition of his bail, remand him in custody or release him on his original recognisance or a new recognisance, and, if not of the opinion, shall release him on his original recognisance.

Section 96 of the **Magistrates' Courts Act 1952** [48] provides that where any recognisance is conditioned for the appearance of a

---

[48] As amended by the Criminal Justice Act 1967, Sched. 6 and the Courts Act 1971, Sched. 8.

person before a magistrates' court or for his doing any other thing connected with a proceeding before a magistrates' court, and the recognisance appears to be forfeited, the court may adjudge the persons who gave the recognisance to pay the sum in which they are bound, or a lesser sum, or the court may remit the sum.[49] Payment of any sum adjudged shall be enforced as a fine.[50]

Section 97 provides that where any person on bail fails to appear in accordance with his recognisance, the court may issue a warrant for his arrest.

[49] There is no right of appeal: *R.* v. *Durham JJ., ex p. Laurent* [1945] K.B. 33.
[50] Magistrates' Courts Act 1952, s. 96 (4), as amended by the Criminal Justice Act 1967, Sched. 6.

CHAPTER 46

LEGAL AID

THE statutory provisions relating to legal aid in criminal cases are to be found in Part IV of the Criminal Justice Act 1967.[1] Appeals by way of case stated and proceedings by way of the prerogative orders to the Divisional Court, and appeals from that court to the House of Lords are treated for the purposes of legal aid as civil proceedings and governed by Part I of the Legal Aid and Advice Act 1949.

By **section 73** of the **Criminal Justice Act 1967** legal aid is available in the following circumstances:

> . . . Where a person is charged with an offence before a magistrates' court or appears or is brought before a magistrates' court to be dealt with, the court may order that he shall be given legal aid for the purpose of the proceedings before the court [2] and any other magistrates' court to which the case is remitted in pursuance of section 56 (1) of the Children and Young Persons Act 1933.

> Where a person convicted by a magistrates' court desires to appeal to the Crown Court, either of those courts may order that he shall be given legal aid for the purpose of the appeal and where any such person gives notice of appeal, either of those courts may order that the other party to the appeal shall be given legal aid for the purpose of resisting the appeal.[3]

> Where a person—

>> (*a*) is or is to be brought before a juvenile court under section 1 of the Children and Young Persons Act 1969; or

---

[1] Amended by the Children and Young Persons Act 1969, Sched. 1, the Courts Act 1971, Sched. 8 and the Criminal Justice Act 1972, Sched. 5. See in relation to magistrates' courts the Legal Aid in Criminal Proceedings (General) Regulations 1968 (S.I. 1968 No. 1231), as amended by the Legal Aid General Proceedings (General Amendment) Regulations 1970, and the Legal Aid in Criminal Proceedings (Assessment of Resources) Regulations 1968 (S.I. 1968 No. 1265), as amended by the Legal Aid in Criminal Proceedings (Assessment of Resources) (Amendment) Regulations 1970.

[2] Criminal Justice Act 1967, s. 73 (2), as amended by Sched. 1 to the Children and Young Persons Act 1969, and the Courts Act 1971, Sched. 8.

[3] *Ibid.* s. 73 (3).

(b) is the subject of an application to a magistrates' court under section 15 or section 21 of that Act; or

(c) is or is to be brought before a juvenile court under section 31 of that Act,

the court may order that he shall be given legal aid for the purpose of proceedings before the court and, in a case falling within paragraph (a) of this subsection, before any juvenile court to which the case is remitted.[4]

Where a person desires to appeal to the Crown Court in pursuance of section 2 (12), 3 (8), 16 (8), 21 (4) or 31 (6) of the said Act of 1969, that court or the court from whose decision the appeal lies may order that he be given legal aid for the purpose of the appeal.[5]

Where a person is committed to or appears before the Crown Court for trial or sentence, or appears or is brought before the Crown Court to be dealt with, the court which commits him or to which he is committed, or before which he appears or is brought, may order that he shall be given legal aid for the purpose of the trial or other proceedings before the Crown Court.[6]

Where a person desires to appeal to the Court of Appeal under Part I of the Criminal Appeal Act 1968, the criminal division of the Court of Appeal may order that he shall be given legal aid for the purpose of the appeal and any proceedings preliminary or incidental thereto.[7]

Where either party to an appeal to the criminal division of the Court of Appeal . . . desires to appeal to the House of Lords from a decision of . . . [that court], the court which gave the decision may order that the person to whose conviction or sentence the appeal relates shall be given legal aid for the purpose of the appeal and any proceedings preliminary or incidental thereto.[8]

Where the criminal division of the Court of Appeal or the House of Lords orders a person to be retried by the

---

4 Ibid. s. 73 (3A) inserted by the Children and Young Persons Act 1969, Sched. 1.
5 Ibid. s. 73 (3B) inserted by the Children and Young Persons Act 1969, Sched. 1, later amended by the Courts Act 1971, Sched. 8.
6 Ibid. s. 73 (4).
7 Ibid. s. 73 (5), amended by the Courts Act 1971, Sched. 8, and the Criminal Justice Act 1972, s. 38. (The latter was not in force on July 1, 1972.)
8 Ibid. s. 73 (7), further amended by the Courts Act 1971, Sched. 8.

Crown Court under section 7 of the Criminal Appeal Act 1968 (new trials in cases of fresh evidence), the former court or the House of Lords, as the case may be, or the latter court may order that he shall be given legal aid for the purposes of the retrial.[9]

Where a person makes an application to a magistrates' court for a review of a compensation order under section 3 of the Criminal Justice Act 1972, the court may order that legal aid be given for the purpose of the proceedings before the court.[9a]

Section 74 [10] defines legal aid as meaning representation by a solicitor and counsel assigned by the court, including advice on the preparation of that person's case for the proceedings. However, for the purpose of any proceedings before a magistrates' court, representation by only a solicitor should normally be ordered and for the purpose of section 73 (5) (appeal to the Court of Appeal) representation by only counsel may be ordered.[11]

Section 74 also provides that a legal aid order for a trial or appeal therefrom shall be authority to the solicitor or counsel, as the case may be, to advise whether there are reasonable grounds of appeal from that trial or appeal and to assist in the making of notices of appeal, etc.

Section 74 further provides that a person summoned or arrested for an offence and either appearing before the court *or due to appear before the court* may apply for legal aid.

Section 75 [12] provides that the power to make a legal aid order shall be exercisable by a court having power under section 73 of this Act to do so where it appears to the court desirable to do so in the interests of justice. It has been said [13] that legal aid is desirable in the interests of justice:

(*a*) where the charge is a grave one in the sense that the accused is in real jeopardy of losing his liberty or livelihood or suffering serious damage to his reputation;

---

[9] *Ibid.* s. 73 (8).

[9a] *Ibid.* s. 73 (8A) inserted by the Criminal Justice Act 1972, Sched. 5.

[10] As amended by the Children and Young Persons Act 1969, Sched. 1, and the Courts Act 1971, Sched. 8, and the Criminal Justice Act 1972, Sched. 2.

[11] s. 74 (2) and (4).

[12] As amended by the Children and Young Persons Act 1969, Sched. 1.

[13] The Departmental Committee on Legal Aid in Criminal Proceedings quoted in Brian Harris's *Criminal Jurisdiction of Magistrates*, 2nd ed. at p. 267.

(b) where the charge raises a substantial question of law;

(c) where the accused is unable to follow the proceedings and state his own case because of his inadequate knowledge of English, mental illness or other mental or physical disability;

(d) where the nature of the defence includes tracing and interviewing witnesses or the expert cross-examination of a witness for the prosecution;

(e) where legal representation is desirable in the interest of someone other than the accused as, *e.g.* in the case of several offences against young children when it is undesirable that the accused should cross-examine the witnesses in person.

A court having power to do so must make such an order—

(a) where a person is committed for trial on a charge of murder; or

(b) where the prosecutor appeals or applies for leave to appeal from the criminal division of the Court of Appeal to the House of Lords.

However, a court must not make a legal aid order for the giving of aid to any person for the purpose of any criminal proceedings or any other purpose unless it appears to the court that his means are such that he requires assistance in meeting the costs which he may incur for that purpose.[14] Where a doubt arises whether a legal aid order should be made, the doubt shall be resolved in the applicant's favour.[15]

Section 76[16] empowers the courts to order a person to whom legal aid has been granted to pay contributions in respect of the relevant costs, either in one sum or by instalments; the collecting authority is the clerk to the magistrates' court named in the order by the court making the order of contribution.[17] By **section 77**[18] the court may refer the matter to the Supplementary Benefits Committee for an inquiry into that person's means.

---

[14] s. 75 (2).
[15] s. 75 (5).
[16] Amended by the Children and Young Persons Act 1969, Sched. 1 and the Courts Act 1971, Sched. 8.
[17] *Ibid.*
[18] Amended by the Children and Young Persons Act 1969, Sched. 6, and the Administration of Justice Act 1970, s. 43, and Sched. 10.

Section 80 gives power in certain circumstances to the court to amend or revoke any order made.

Part IV of the Act departs from the former law in requiring a person granted legal aid to make a contribution towards, or repay, the costs incurred if so ordered. The court is empowered, after disposing of a case, to make such order as appears reasonable having regard to the person's resources and commitments, the computation of which is governed by regulations. The court granting legal aid must require the applicant or an "appropriate contributor" to furnish a written statement of his means [19] and may refuse to make a legal aid order until a payment, on account of any contribution or repayment to which he may be liable, is made.[20]

The **Children and Young Persons Act 1969** [21] gives to the courts the power, in respect of legally assisted persons who have not attained the age of sixteen, to order a contribution, if any, to be paid by an appropriate contributor, that is, "his father or any person who has been adjudged to be his putative father, and, whether or not he is legitimate, his mother." [22]

Any practising barrister or solicitor may be assigned by the court to act for a legally assisted person unless, after a complaint made to, and proved against him by, a special tribunal, he is excluded from giving such assistance.[23]

Section 81 (2) of the Criminal Justice Act 1967 provides that, subject to regulations under section 83 of this Act, the costs of legal aid ordered to be given to a legally assisted person for the purpose of any proceedings shall include sums on account of the fees payable to any counsel or solicitor assigned to him and disbursements reasonably incurred by any such solicitor for or in connection with those proceedings.

Transcripts. Where it has been necessary in order to prepare an appeal to pay for a copy of the transcript or short transcript [24] of the trial, the costs of that transcript would seem to be a proper

[19] It is an offence under s. 89 of the Act to make a false statement.
[20] s. 75 (3) and (4).
[21] Sched. 1.
[22] *Ibid.*
[23] s. 82.
[24] *Post*, p. 846.

disbursement for the purposes of section 65 (2). Alternatively, application may be made to the Court of Appeal for a free transcript.[25]

Procedure for recovery. The procedure for the recovery of legal aid contributions in criminal cases is governed by the **Administration of Justice Act 1970, s. 43** and **Sched. 10.** The collecting court is the magistrates' court from which the accused was committed in respect of proceedings on indictment or that magistrates' court which is specified by the court of trial.

[25] *Post,* p. 846.

CHAPTER 47

EVIDENCE[1]

SECTION 1. INTRODUCTION

A COURT of law has to conduct its proceedings, and make its determinations, in the light of the admissible evidence which is laid before it; and nothing ought to be taken into account in reaching a verdict or finding which is not supported by admissible evidence. This " admissibility " is determined by the Law of Evidence, which seeks to lay down (1) what facts may be properly led in order to determine in a criminal case the guilt or innocence of an accused person; and (2) how, and by whom, and in what circumstances, such facts may be presented to the court. Evidence is described as direct when it immediately establishes the fact sought to be proved; it is described as circumstantial where it establishes other facts, so relevant to, or connected with, the fact to be proved that they support an inference or presumption as to its existence. Thus, for example: if A is charged with the murder of B, the evidence of a witness who actually saw A murder B would be direct proof; but, in the absence of any such direct evidence, circumstantial proof would be afforded by evidence (i) that A was in B's company shortly before the murder and was heard quarrelling with B; (ii) that B was stabbed by a knife belonging to A; (iii) that bloodstains were found on A's clothes.

Both direct and circumstantial evidence are equally *admissible,* but it is impossible to make any absolute comparison of their *cogency* (*i.e.* persuasiveness). If proof is direct, the only uncertainties are as to the truth and accuracy of the witnesses, who may be deliberately lying or honestly mistaken; if it is circumstantial there is also an uncertainty as to what is the correct inference. The weight of circumstantial evidence, therefore, depends largely upon the number of independent facts which support the same inference,

---

[1] This chapter is based upon that prepared for the 21st ed. by J. Mickleburgh, LL.M., Lecturer in Law at the University of Newcastle-upon-Tyne, but has been considerably amended.

and where there are many such facts it will be as cogent as the testimony of one or two witnesses giving direct evidence.[2]

Proof

Proof of a fact may be said to be the satisfaction of the court as to its existence by means of admissible evidence.

Burden of proof. Where a party to proceedings seeks to establish some issue of fact as part of his case, it is said that the burden of proving that issue lies upon him. It is a general rule of principle that he who affirms must prove. A person who asserts the existence or non-existence of any fact or circumstance must prove what he alleges; the burden of proof is upon him. In a criminal case, it is a fundamental principle of English law that a person accused of an offence is presumed to be innocent until he is proved guilty. Thus, where an accused pleads " not guilty " to a charge or to the count of an indictment; the prosecution is obliged to prove at the trial every fact or circumstance stated in the charge or counts, which is material and necessary to establish the offence alleged. This means, that as a general rule (apart from any special provision to the contrary [3]) the burden of proving guilt lies upon the prosecution, and it is not for the defence to establish innocence. The court must be sure of the guilt of the accused.[4]

If at the end of the proceedings there is a reasonable doubt in the mind of the court [5] or on indictment in the minds of the jury,[6] caused by evidence given by the prosecution or by the defence, the prosecution have not discharged the burden upon them; and the defendant is entitled to be acquitted.[7] This general rule, however, is subject to a number of exceptions:

(1) The burden of establishing unfitness to plead,[8] and the

---

[2] " [C]ircumstantial evidence is very often the best. It is evidence of surrounding circumstances which, by undesigned coincidence, is capable of proving a proposition with the accuracy of mathematics. It is no derogation of evidence to say that it is circumstantial ": *R.* v. *Taylor* (1928) 21 Cr.App.R. 20 at p. 21.

[3] Below.

[4] *R.* v. *Bradbury* (1969) 113 S.J. 70, C.A.

[5] *e.g.* the magistrates in a summary proceeding.

[6] At the Crown Court all matters of fact are for the jury.

[7] *Woolmington* v. *D.P.P.* [1935] A.C. 462.

[8] *R.* v. *Podola* [1960] 1 Q.B. 325.

defences of insanity [9] and diminished responsibility [10] lie upon the defence, if these issues are raised.

(2) The burden of proving some particular issue may be laid by statute upon the defence, *i.e.* lawful authority or reasonable excuse.[11]

(3) The proof of some matter may be presumed by statute unless the contrary is proved by the accused.[12]

(4) Where in summary proceedings a defendant to an information or complaint relies for his defence on any exemption, exception, proviso, excuse or qualification, the burden of proving it rests on him.[13]

The older common law principle is " that what comes by way of proviso in a statute must be insisted on by way of defence by the party accused; but where exceptions are in the enacting part of a law, it must appear in the charge that the defendant does not fall within any of them," [14] and it applies to any statutory offence. However, there is no authority which establishes that where an accused raises a defence contained in a proviso to an enacting section establishing the offence, he bears the legal burden of proving he is within the proviso, although clearly he is under an evidential burden of adducing some evidence in support.[15]

(5) Where a statute makes it an offence to do something without a licence, authorisation or specified excuse. The principle in *R.* v. *Turner* [16] seems to lay down that in such cases the prosecution is obliged only to give evidence of the forbidden act; but not that the accused does not come within one of the permitted exceptions. Thus where the accused was charged with driving a motor-vehicle without a licence, it was held that the prosecution need not show that he had no licence.[17] It is for the accused to show that he had the necessary licence, authorisation or excuse because " if a nega-

---

[9] *McNaghten's Case* (1843) 10 Cl. & Fin. 200.
[10] Homicide Act 1957, s. 2 (2).
[11] *e.g.* s. 4 of the Explosive Substances Act 1883; and ss. 8, 9 and 10 of the Forgery Act 1913. See also the Prevention of Crimes Act 1953 and the Misuse of Drugs Act 1971.
[12] Prevention of Corruption Act 1916, s. 2.
[13] Magistrates' Courts Act 1952, s. 81.
[14] *R.* v. *Jarvis* (1756) 1 East 643n.; *R.* v. *James* [1902] 1 K.B. 540.
[15] See the cases on the effect of the proviso to s. 57 of the Offences against the Person Act 1861; *R.* v. *Curgerwen* (1865) L.R. 1 C.C.R. 1; *R.* v. *Jones* (1883) 11 Q.B.D. 118; *R.* v. *Audley* [1907] 1 K.B. 383.
[16] (1816) 5 M. & S. 206.
[17] *John* v. *Humphreys* [1955] 1 W.L.R. 325. See also *R.* v. *Scott* (1921) 86 J.P. 69; *R.* v. *Oliver* [1944] K.B. 68; *R.* v. *Cohen* [1951] 1 K.B. 505.

tive averment be made by one party, which is peculiarly within the knowledge of the other, the party within whose knowledge it lies, and who asserts the affirmative, is to prove it, and not he who avers the negative." [18]

This principle has been applied in a number of cases, but in none of them was it made quite clear whether the accused was under a legal burden of proving he came within a permitted exception or was simply obliged to adduce evidence to that effect. It may be that the principle in *R.* v. *Turner* merely casts an evidential burden on the accused,[19] namely if the accused does adduce some evidence of having, for example, the necessary licence, he must be acquitted unless the jury are convinced he had no licence.[20]

It should be noted that a burden of proof is cast upon the accused of proving the common law defences of consent, accident, duress,[21] self defence,[22] non-insane automatism,[23] provocation [22] or justification generally.[24] In such cases, while it is for the defence to raise the issue, once raised the burden lies upon the prosecution of eliminating it.[25] The same principle applies where the accused puts forward an alibi.[26]

Standard of proof. Whosoever bears the legal burden of proof in respect of a given issue must adduce evidence which attains a certain degree of cogency in order to succeed on that issue. The degree of cogency required is higher in a criminal than a civil case.[27]

In a civil action the party who bears the legal burden of proof (usually the plaintiff) must satisfy the jury that his version of the

---

[18] *R.* v. *Turner, supra,* at p. 211. Note that the rule does *not* apply to *positive* facts " peculiarly within the knowledge of [the accused] "; see *R.* v. *Spurge* [1961] 2 Q.B. at p. 212.

[19] *R.* v. *Cohen* [1951] 1 K.B. 505; but see *R.* v. *Oliver* [1944] K.B. 68 which was expressly followed in *R.* v. *Ewens* [1967] 1 Q.B. 322.

[20] *i.e.* the legal burden of proving the accused did not have a licence ultimately rests on the prosecution. *Cf.* the situation where the accused must first raise the defences of provocation, accident, self-defence and non-insane automatism ; only then does the prosecution bear the legal burden of disproving them: see *Bratty* v. *Att.-Gen. for Northern Ireland* [1963] A.C. 386.

[21] *R.* v. *Bone* [1968] 1 W.L.R. 1885.

[22] *R.* v. *Wheeler* [1967] 1 W.L.R. 1531.

[23] *R.* v. *Dervish* [1968] Crim.L.R. 37; *Cook* v. *Aitchison* [1968] Crim.L.R. 266.

[24] *R.* v. *Cascoe* (1970) 50 Cr.App.R. 401.

[25] *Bratty* v. *Att.-Gen. for Northern Ireland* [1963] A.C. 386.

[26] *R.* v. *Woods* [1968] Crim.L.R. 104.

[27] *R.* v. *Carr-Briant* [1943] K.B. 607; *Miller* v. *Minister of Pensions* [1947] 2 All E.R. 372.

facts is more probable than the other party's. "That degree [of proof] is well settled. It must carry a reasonable degree of probability. . . . If the evidence is such that [the jury] can say: 'We think it more probable than not' the burden is discharged, but if the probabilities are equal, it is not." [28]

As regards a criminal case the prosecution, who, except in certain instances,[29] bear the legal burden of proof, must establish the guilt of the accused beyond reasonable doubt so that the magistrates or jury feel sure of the guilt of the accused [30]; and "if, at the end of and on the whole of the case, there is a reasonable doubt created by the evidence given by either the prosecution or the prisoner . . . the prosecution has not made out the case and the prisoner is entitled to an acquittal." [31]

However, where the legal burden of proof on any issue is on the accused he is not obliged to convince the jury beyond reasonable doubt but simply on the balance of probabilities, *i.e.* to the degree of cogency normally required in a civil action.[32]

What Must be Proved

In a criminal case, the general rule is that where the accused pleads not guilty, every essential matter bearing upon his guilt must be proved, in order for the prosecution to succeed. Once more, however, the rule is subject to exceptions:

1. There is no need for a fact to be proved, where it is formally admitted under **section 10** of the **Criminal Justice Act 1967.**[33]

2. A court will take judicial notice (*i.e.* accept as established without the giving of evidence) of (i) all branches of English law,[34] including all public statutes and all statutes passed since 1850 unless the contrary is provided,[35] and the procedure and jurisdiction of the Divisions of the High

---

[28] *Miller* v. *Minister of Pensions, supra,* n. 27.
[29] *Supra,* at p. 592.
[30] *R.* v. *Bradbury* (1969) 113 S.J. 70, C.A.
[31] *Woolmington* v. *Director of Public Prosecutions* [1935] A.C. 462 at p. 481.
[32] *R.* v. *Carr-Briant* [1943] K.B. 607; *R.* v. *Dunbar* [1958] 1 Q.B. 1; *R.* v. *Patterson* [1962] 2 Q.B. 429.
[33] See p. 743, *post.*
[34] But not of Scots, colonial or foreign law, which must be proved by expert witnesses: *Mostyn* v. *Fabrigas* (1774) 1 Cowp. at p. 174. The House of Lords takes judicial notice of Scottish law, and the Privy Council of colonial law.
[35] Interpretation Act 1889, s. 9.

Court; (ii) matters of common knowledge [36] and general custom judicially ascertained and established [37]; (iii) the relations of Great Britain with foreign states [38]; (iv) the territorial and administrative divisions of the country; (v) various official seals and signatures; (vi) weights and measures and the currency.

3. The standard of proof may be lightened, although not eliminated by means of presumptions. A presumption is a conclusion which the law says may be drawn from a certain basic set of facts. Sometimes one speaks of presumptions of fact, and of conclusive or irrebuttable presumptions of law. Neither of these is a true presumption, for the first is merely an inference which may or may not be drawn by a court, whereas the second is really a principle of law. The only true presumption is the rebuttable presumption of law, that is a presumption which must be drawn in the absence of rebutting evidence.

Examples are:

(1) The presumption of the death of a person who has not been heard of for seven years by those who, if he were alive, would have been likely to hear of him.[39]

(2) The presumption *omnia rite esse acta, i.e.* " that everything is to be presumed rightly done unless the contrary appear," [40] *e.g.* the presumptions (i) that a person who has acted in a public capacity was duly appointed,[41] (ii) that a document was made on the day whose date it bears.[42]

(3) The presumption that a child born during the subsisting marriage of its mother is legitimate.[43]

---

[36] *R.* v. *Luffe* (1807) 8 East 193. In *R.* v. *Jones* (1969) 54 Cr.App.R. 63, the Court of Appeal held that a court (including a jury) is entitled to take judicial notice of the fact that the Alcotest R. 80 device is of an approved type.

[37] *Brandao* v. *Barnett* (1846) 12 Cl. & F. 787.

[38] *Taylor* v. *Barclay* (1828) 2 Sim. 213; *Duff Development Co.* v. *Kelantan* [1924] A.C. 797; where there is any doubt the court will inquire of a Secretary of State, whose reply is conclusive.

[39] *Prudential Co.* v. *Edwards* (1877) 2 App.Cas. 509; *Re Rhodes* (1887) 36 Ch.D. 586; *Chipchase* v. *Chipchase* [1939] P. 391; *Chard* v. *Chard* [1956] P. 259 at p. 272; *Bullock* v. *Bullock* [1960] 1 W.L.R. 975.

[40] *R.* v. *Catesby* (1824) 2 B. & C. at p. 820.

[41] *Berryman* v. *Wise* (1791) 4 T.R. 366.

[42] *Anderson* v. *Weston* (1840) 6 Bing.N.C. 296.

[43] *Morris* v. *Davies* (1837) 5 Cl. & Fin. 163; *Preston-Jones* v. *Preston-Jones* [1951] A.C. 391: *F.* v. *F.* (*No.* 2) [1968] P. 506.

The weight of evidence required to rebut a presumption varies according to the presumption involved. Thus to rebut the presumption of legitimacy, the evidence must establish beyond reasonable doubt that the child is illegitimate,[44] *i.e.* the effect of the presumption is to cast a legal burden on the party against whom it operates to disprove the presumed fact. But the presumption of death merely casts an evidential burden on the party who seeks to rebut it and this he satisfies by adducing some evidence for the jury.[45] The legal burden of proving the death is therefore still borne by the party in whose favour the presumption operates.

Where a presumption operates against an accused in a criminal trial its effect is only to cast an evidential burden on him, *i.e.* to put some evidence before the jury which raises a reasonable doubt in their mind as to the presumed fact.[46]

SECTION 2. RESTRICTIONS ON THE ADMISSION OF EVIDENCE

Relevancy

It is a general rule that nothing may be given in evidence during the trial of a criminal charge which does not tend directly to the proof or disproof of the facts in issue between the prosecution and the defence. The facts in issue are (1) the facts relating to the constituents of the offence charged and denied by virtue of the plea of not guilty (and not admitted by him under the provisions of section 10 of the Criminal Justice Act 1967)[47]; and (2) the facts alleged by the defence and denied by the prosecution, such as an alibi, or matters of justification or excuse. All such facts in issue are relevant and evidence of them may be admitted. Also admissible under this general heading is evidence of facts relevant to the issue. These are facts which support or rebut any inference or presumption as to the existence or non-existence of a fact in issue, or which explain any fact in issue. So where, for example, the issue is whether an act was committed by A, the following facts, *inter alia*, are relevant: (i) facts showing motive or opportunity;

---

[44] *Morris* v. *Davies, supra.*

[45] *Prudential Assurance Co.* v. *Edmonds* (1877) 2 App.Cas. 487.

[46] *Woolmington* v. *D.P.P.* [1935] A.C. 462, where it was said that the legal burden of proof is only on the accused when he raises the defence of insanity (to which must be added those instances noted *ante,* p. 592).

[47] See p. 743.

(ii) his previous conduct, such as threats or acts of preparation; (iii) his subsequent conduct, if apparently influenced by the doing of the act, *e.g.* attempts to destroy evidence against him or to procure false evidence.[48]

A fact which is not directly relevant may become indirectly relevant, as *e.g.* by affecting the credibility of a witness, or the admissibility of evidence, as, for example, facts on which the admissibility of a confession depends.

In *Kuruma* v. *The Queen* [49] Lord Goddard C.J. said: " The test to be applied in considering whether evidence is admissible is whether it is relevant to the matters in issue. If it is, it is admissible and the court is not concerned with how the evidence was obtained." There are however two notable qualifications to this general rule. First, when one comes to consider the admissibility of statements made in answer to the police and alleged extra-judicial confessions a much stricter rule applies.[50] Secondly, the judge in every criminal case has a discretion to disallow evidence, even if, in law, it is relevant and therefore admissible, if its admission would operate unfairly against the accused. In considering whether admission of the evidence would operate unfairly against an accused the judge may consider whether the evidence has been obtained in an oppressive manner, by force, or against the wishes of the accused.[51] In *R.* v. *Murphy*,[52] the Lord Chief Justice of Northern Ireland, Lord MacDermott, said that " Unfairness to the accused is not susceptible of close definition. It must be judged in the light of all the material facts and findings and all the surrounding circumstances. The position of the accused, the nature of the investigation and the gravity or otherwise of the suspected offence may all be relevant."

---

[48] *R.* v. *Palmer* (1856); *Moriarty* v. *L.C. & D. Ry.* (1870) L.R. 5 Q.B. 314.
[49] [1955] A.C. 197.
[50] See p. 610, *post.*
[51] *Callis* v. *Gunn* [1964] 1 Q.B. 495 (a case on fingerprints). See also *R.* v. *Payne* [1963] 1 All E.R. 848 (doctor's examination); *King* v. *The Queen* [1969] 1 A.C. 304 (drugs found as the result of an illegal search); *R.* v. *Senat and Sin* (1968) 52 Cr.App.R. 282; *R.* v. *Stewart* [1970] 1 W.L.R. 1112; *R.* v. *Keeton* (1970) 54 Cr.App.R. 267.
[52] [1965] N.I. 138 (C.-M.A.C.); and see also *R.* v. *Harz* [1967] 1 A.C. 760 and *Sneddon* v. *Stevenson* [1967] 2 All E.R. 1277. The Scots cases of *Lawrie* v. *Muir*, 1950 S.C.(J.) 19; *Fairley* v. *Fishmongers of London*, 1951 S.C.(J.) 14 (an unfair trick); *H.M. Advocate* v. *Turnbull*, 1951 S.C.(J.) 96 (unfairness to the accused) are also of interest.

Evidence of Similar Facts

" When a prisoner is charged with an offence . . . the facts laid before the jury should consist exclusively of the transaction which forms the subject of the indictment." [53] This remains the general rule, and the fact that the accused has committed similar acts on other occasions may not be proved in evidence " for the purpose of leading to the conclusion that the accused is a person likely, from his criminal conduct or character, to have committed the offence for which he is being tried." [54]

Nevertheless, there are obviously circumstances in which evidence of similar facts becomes relevant to an issue before the court, and in those circumstances, becomes admissible. The commission of similar acts done by the accused on other occasions may be proved for the following purposes, and subject to the following conditions:

(1) Where such acts are so connected with the act which is the subject of the charge as to form part of one and the same transaction, they may be proved in order to explain and show the nature of the act which is impeached.[55] Where the prisoners were charged with breaking into a booking-office at a railway station, evidence was given that they had broken into three other railway booking-offices on the same night, each of the cases being mixed up with the other.[56]

(2) Where the fact of the prisoner having done the thing charged is proved, evidence that he has on other occasions done similar acts is admissible to prove intent, guilty knowledge or any other condition of mind. Thus, on a charge of uttering counterfeit coin knowing it to be such, evidence that the prisoner has previously and subsequently uttered other counterfeit coin is admissible to prove his knowledge that it was counterfeit.[57] In *R.* v. *Sporle and*

---

[53] *R.* v. *Bond* [1906] 2 K.B. 389 at p. 397.

[54] *Makin* v. *Att.-Gen. for N.S.W.* [1894] A.C. 57 at p. 65.

[55] This was the rule at common law. The enactment of the Indictments Act 1915, s. 4, Sched. 1, results in less reliance having to be put upon this principle.

[56] *R.* v. *Cobden* (1862) 3 F. & F. 833.

[57] *R.* v. *Bond* [1906] 2 K.B. 389; *R.* v. *Mortimer* (1936) 25 Cr.App.R. 150. Note that *subsequent* similar facts *may* not be admissible to prove guilty intent with respect to an earlier occurrence, since the necessary intent may not have been formed until after the acts on which the charge was founded: *R.* v. *Boothby* (1933) 24 Cr.App.R. 112. But evidence of subsequent similar acts has been admitted on occasions (*e.g. R.* v. *Geering* (1849) 18 L.J.M.C. 215) and will usually be relevant to establishing intent.

Others,[58] where S and D were convicted of corruption, contrary to section 1 of the Public Bodies Corrupt Practices Act 1889, and unlike S, D faced only one count and the allegation was that after S, a local authority councillor, had improperly furthered the interests of D's employers in relation to council contracts he received a corrupt payment from D. Similar allegations were made against S in respect of other defendants. The Court of Appeal held that evidence of S's conduct in relation to other defendants was admissible in the case against D, since the state of S's mind in supporting the cause of D's employers was relevant, and evidence of system was admissible for this purpose. The fact that the conduct was that of S and not of D did not detract from the relevance of the evidence.

(3) Where the act which is the subject of the charge is one of a series of similar acts committed by the prisoner, *or* where the charge relates to one of a series of similar occurrences with which he was connected, evidence of such acts or occurrences is admissible in order to rebut a defence of accident, mistake, or the existence of honest motive, or the suggestion that an innocent inference may be drawn from the facts.[59] The particular defence must be really in issue, that is, raised by the accused.[60]

Where the defence is raised, that the act complained of was accidental, then evidence of similar acts is admissible to show the contrary. Thus, in the leading case of *Makin* v. *Att.-Gen. for N.S.W.*,[61] A was charged with the murder of a child whose body was found buried in the garden of A's house. The child had been received from its mother on payment of a sum insufficient for its maintenance and on a representation that A wished to adopt it. Evidence that other children had been received on similar representations, and that other bodies had been found in gardens of houses occupied by A, was admissible to rebut the defence that the death was accidental. It is admissible *not* because it tends to show that

---

[58] (1972) 56 Cr.App.R. 31 at p. 45 approving *R.* v. *Bond* [1906] 2 K.B. 389.
[59] *Makin* v. *Att.-Gen. for New South Wales* (*supra*). *Harris* v. *D.P.P.* [1952] A.C. 707. But not apparently where the defence is that the act was involuntary: *R.* v. *Harrison-Owen* 35 Cr.App.R. 108.
[60] *R.* v. *Rodley* [1913] 3 K.B. 468; *Perkins* v. *Jeffrey* [1915] 2 K.B. 702. " It must have been raised in substance if not in so many words. . . . The prosecution cannot credit the accused with fancy defences in order to rebut them at the outset with some damning piece of prejudice ": *Thompson* v. *R.* [1918] A.C. 221 at p. 232; but see *R.* v. *G. and U.* [1965] Crim.L.R. 37.
[61] [1894] A.C. 57.

A has a propensity for murdering children, but since it is relevant to A's defence.[62]

Likewise, similar fact evidence may be adduced to rebut the defence of mistake or honest motive. So where A was charged with attempting to obtain an advance from a pawnbroker upon a ring by the false pretence that it was a diamond ring, the fact that A had obtained and attempted to obtain other loans from other pawnbrokers upon similar false pretences was relevant, as tending to show that he was pursuing a course of similar acts and was not acting under a mistake.[63] But if the other false pretences had been *different*, evidence of them would not have been admissible, as it would merely tend to show that the prisoner was of dishonest character.[64]

The accused may allege that, although he committed the act complained of, he had no guilty intent. Thus in *R. v. Hall*[65] A was charged in separate counts with acts of gross indecency on different occasions with B, C and D: part of his defence was that the acts with B and C were done in the course of medical treatment. It was held that the evidence of B and C as to what took place was admissible on every count to show criminal intent.[66] But had the defence been that the meeting with C had never taken place, then B's evidence would have been inadmissible. In *R. v. Chandor*,[67] where A was charged with indecent assaults on B in the Lake District and on C and D at Croydon, A alleged the meeting with B never took place. Held, that the evidence of C and D was not admissible as regards the alleged meeting with B; " Evidence that an offence was committed by the accused against [C] at Croydon could not be any evidence that the accused met [B] in the Lake District and committed an offence there." If the *identity* of the accused had been in issue, then evidence of B and C would have been admissible; see below. In many cases, of course, whether such evidence is admissible or not, will depend upon the

---

[62] See also *R. v. Geering* (1849) 18 L.J.M.C. 215; *R. v. Armstrong* [1922] 2 K.B. 555.
[63] *R. v. Francis* (1874) L.R. 2 C.C.R. 128.
[64] *R. v. Fisher* [1910] 1 K.B. 149.
[65] [1952] 1 K.B. 302. See also *R. v. Sims* [1946] K.B. 531.
[66] Since it was highly unlikely that both would be mistaken as to the nature of the alleged medical treatment. But the evidence must be of *similar* indecent acts and even then must not be of a " tenuous " nature: *R. v. Doughty* [1965] 1 W.L.R. 331. *Cf. Att.-Gen., Jersey* v. *Norton* [1967] 1 A.C. 464.
[67] [1959] 1 Q.B. 545.

nature of the defence raised. Evidence may not be admissible where the accused merely denies the commission of the offence, which would be admissible if he alleged accident, innocent association or sought to set up an alibi.[68]

(4) Where the evidence of similar acts goes to identify the accused as the doer of the act in issue, it is admissible. So in *R.* v. *Hall* [69] A also alleged that he had never seen D. It was held that the evidence of B and C was admissible as tending to show by the similarity of their accounts that A had been involved with D. Normally such evidence will be relevant to identifying the accused as perpetrator of the crime charged, because it shows a *highly peculiar propensity* which the accused possessed.[70] Hence where the accused was charged with the murder of a young girl by manual strangulation, evidence of two other murders committed by the accused was admitted to show that the accused was the murderer in the present case. The similarities between all three deaths were: (i) the victim was a young girl; (ii) death was caused by manual strangulation; (iii) there was no attempt at sexual interference, or sign of a struggle; (iv) no attempt had been made to hide the bodies.[71]

(5) Similar fact evidence may also be adduced where it corroborates the evidence of a prosecution witness, since it renders the evidence of the witness more credible.[72] So where A was charged with unlawful carnal knowledge of B, and B gave evidence that A had told her of similar conduct with another girl, evidence was admitted of that conduct as it " tended to shew that [A] was guilty of the offence with which he was charged, for if he had made that statement to [B] at the time alleged by her, that fact would strongly corroborate her evidence that [A] was the person who had had connection with her." [73]

---

[68] *R.* v. *Horwood* [1970] 1 Q.B. 133; *R.* v. *King* [1967] 2 Q.B. 338; *R.* v. *Dean* [1967] Crim.L.R. 633.

[69] [1952] 1 K.B. 302, *supra*.

[70] *Thompson* v. *R.* [1918] A.C. 221; *R.* v. *Ball* [1911] A.C. 47. But see *R.* v. *Robinson* (1953) 37 Cr.App.R. 95.

[71] *R.* v. *Straffen* [1952] 2 Q.B. 911. The accused's plea of " not guilty " was said to put the defence of identity in issue. See *R.* v. *Morris* [1970] Crim. L.R. 97 but *cf. R.* v. *Ferrier* [1968] Crim.L.R. 501. See also *R.* v. *Sims* [1946] K.B. 531.

[72] *R.* v. *Chitson* [1909] 2 K.B. 945; *R.* v. *Kennaway* [1917] 1 K.B. 25; *R.* v. *Lovegrove* [1920] 3 K.B. 643.

[73] *R.* v. *Chitson, supra*, at p. 947.

Evidence of similar facts, before it is admissible must be probative in some real degree that the accused committed the offence,[74] and even if such evidence is properly admissible under one of the above heads, the judge is under a duty to set the essentials of justice above the technical rule if the strict application of the latter would operate unfairly against the accused.[74] " In all such cases the judge ought to consider whether the evidence which it is proposed to adduce is sufficiently substantial, having regard to the purpose to which it is professedly directed, to make it desirable in the interest of justice that it should be admitted. If, so far as that purpose is concerned, it can in the circumstances of the case have only trifling weight, the judge will be right to exclude it." [75] The matter is one for the discretion of the trial judge, and the Court of Appeal will not lightly intervene.[76]

Evidence of Character

The fact that the **accused** is of good character, *i.e.* good *general reputation*, may be relevant in order to suggest that he is not likely to have committed the offence with which he is charged.[77] As has just been stated in the preceding paragraph, the fact that he is of bad character may not be proved merely to suggest that he is likely to have committed the offence charged, though the commission of similar acts may in certain cases be proved to explain the nature of an act by the accused person or to show his state of mind in doing an act or to establish a systematic course of conduct. The fact that the accused person is of bad character or has committed or been convicted of other offences may become relevant in the following circumstances:

(1) Where he gives evidence of his good character, or has put questions to witnesses for the Crown and has obtained or attempted to obtain from them any admission that he is a man of good

---

[74] *Harris* v. *D.P.P.* [1952] A.C. 694 at p. 707; *R.* v. *Fitzpatrick* [1963] 1 W.L.R. 7.

[75] *Noor Mahomed* v. *R.* [1949] A.C. 182 at p. 192.

[76] *R.* v. *Morris* (1969) 54 Cr.App.R. 69.

[77] It is now more usual to describe character as going to credibility: *e.g. R.* v. *Bellis* (1965) 50 Cr.App.R. 88; *R.* v. *Islam* [1969] Crim.L.R. 263. There is no duty imposed upon the judge to refer to good character in his summing-up: *R.* v. *Smith* [1971] Crim.L.R. 531, C.A. The evidence should be relevant to the offence, so, *e.g.* if he is charged with obtaining by deception, such evidence should be directed towards his honesty.

character, and has thus put his character in issue, the prosecution may, in rebuttal, give evidence of his bad character.[78]

(2) Where the fact that he has been previously convicted is an essential element of the charge against him.[79]

(3) Where he gives evidence on his own behalf he may in certain cases be cross-examined, not only as to similar acts which are relevant under the rules stated in the preceding paragraph, but also as to his commission of, or conviction for, previous offences and as to his character generally.[80]

(4) After conviction, evidence of his good or bad character or of his commission of, or conviction for, other offences is admissible in order to determine the punishment.[81]

The character of a **witness,** including a prosecutor who gives evidence, is relevant as affecting his credibility, and evidence-in-chief may be given of his general reputation [82]; he may also be cross-examined as to specific acts of misconduct, but if he denies them he cannot as a rule be contradicted.[83]   But, save as affecting his credibility as a witness, the character of the **prosecutor** is irrelevant except in cases of rape and similar offences.[84]   Medical evidence is admissible to show that a witness suffers from a disease or defect of mind which affects the reliability of his evidence.[85]

Opinion Evidence

A witness must, as a general rule, give evidence only of facts within his knowledge and recollection, and not of his opinions: it is for the court and jury to draw opinions from his testimony.[86]   In so far as criminal proceedings are concerned [86a]:

(1) The opinion of experts is admissible upon all subjects for which special study or experience is necessary to the formation of

---

[78] *R.* v. *Rowton* (1865) 10 Cox 25 ; *R.* v. *Butterwasser* [1948] 1 K.B. 4. Again the evidence should be directed towards the accused's general reputation.
[79] *e.g.* on a charge under the Coinage Offences Act 1936, s. 5 (5). See further *ante*, p. 133.
[80] Criminal Evidence Act 1898, s. 1 (*f*); *post*, p. 629.
[81] *Post*, p. 753.
[82] *R.* v. *Brown* (1867) L.R. 1 C.C.R. 70.
[83] See further, *post*, p. 627.   [84] *Post*, p. 628.
[85] *Toohey* v. *Metropolitan Police Commissioner* [1965] A.C. 595, overruling *R.* v. *Gunewardene* [1951] 2 K.B. 600 on this point. Such evidence may contain details of the diagnosis and of the extent to which the witness's credibility is affected. And see *R.* v. *Dunning and Others* [1965] Crim.L.R. 372 ; *R.* v. *Eades* [1972] Crim.L.R. 99.
[86] *Carter* v. *Boehm* (1776) 3 Burr. at p. 1918.
[86a] See the Civil Evidence Acts 1968 and 1972 in relation to civil proceedings.

an opinion, *e.g.* matters of science, art, medicine or foreign law.[87] Whether the witness is competent to give expert evidence is for the judge to decide.[88]

The duty of experts " is to furnish the judge or jury with the necessary scientific criteria for testing the accuracy of other evidence, so as to enable the judge or jury to form their own independent judgment by the application of these criteria to the facts proved in evidence." [89] An expert may refer to textbooks or other treatises to explain or confirm his opinion.[90]

(2) In matters with respect to which a witness cannot give positive testimony, he may speak as to his opinion or belief, *e.g.* for the identification of persons, things or handwriting, or in questions of physical or mental conditions.[91]

Evidence excluded by Public Policy

No evidence is admissible of any facts the disclosure of which would prejudice the public interest, *e.g.* state secrets and communications between Government offices on public matters.[92] So, also, in *public* prosecutions no evidence is admissible of the means by which information is obtained leading to the detection of offences,[93] except, perhaps, where the strict enforcement of the rule would lead to a miscarriage of justice.[94]

Hearsay Evidence

If a witness says that A told him something, or produces a writing signed by A, this may or may not be hearsay; if it is hearsay it is, in general, inadmissible. The mere fact that the evidence of a witness includes evidence as to words spoken by another person who is not called is no objection to its admissibility. Words spoken are facts just as much as any other action by a human being: If the speaking of the words is a relevant fact, a witness may give evidence that

---

[87] *Folkes* v. *Chadd* (1782) 3 Doug.K.B. 157.
[88] *Bristow* v. *Sequeville* (1850) 5 Exch. 275.
[89] *Per* Lord President Cooper in *Davie* v. *Edinburgh Magistrates*, 1953 S.C. 34 at p. 46. As to the classification of dogs, bloodhounds, etc., as experts, see the article by A. H. Hudson in [1967] Crim.L.R. 110. As to experts in handwriting cases, see p. 637, *post.*
[90] *R.* v. *Somers* [1963] 1 W.L.R. 1306.
[91] *Fryer* v. *Gathercole* (1849) 4 Exch. 262.
[92] *Duncan* v. *Cammell, Laird & Co. Ltd.* [1942] A.C. 624; see *Conway* v. *Rimmer* [1967] 1 W.L.R. 1031 where the conflicting authorities are reviewed.
[93] *Marks* v. *Beyfus* (1890) 25 Q.B.D. 494.
[94] *Ibid.*

they were spoken.[95] Whether it is hearsay or not depends, as a rule, upon whether the *making* of the statement or its *truth* is in issue.[96]

The mere making of a statement is a *fact*, which, like any other fact, may be proved if it is (i) in issue, as a libel; or (ii) relevant to the issue, as statements accompanying and explaining the nature of a transaction (*e.g.* seditious speeches or inscriptions on banners carried by a crowd)[97]; or (iii) indirectly relevant, as affecting the credibility of a witness (*e.g.* contradictory statements made by him on other occasions).[98]

But a statement, whether oral or written,[99] made by a person who is not called as a witness is not admissible to prove the *truth* of any matter contained in that statement: "The rule against the admission of hearsay evidence is fundamental. It is not the best evidence and it is not [except rarely] delivered on oath. The truthfulness and accuracy of the person whose words are spoken to by another witness cannot be tested by cross-examination, and the light which his demeanour would throw on his testimony is lost."[1] Thus evidence by A that he *heard* B say "The accused shot X" is inadmissible as proof of that fact. Likewise where the issue is as to the authenticity of a deed, a statement by a deceased witness to the deed that he forged it is inadmissible.[2]

However, to this basic rule many exceptions have been created both at common law[3] and by statute, and for our present purposes the following are the most important cases in which hearsay evidence is admissible: (i) where the statement or fact is part of the *res gestae*; (ii) where the statement relates to the existence of any bodily or mental condition of the maker; (iii) complaints;

---

[95] *Ratten* v. *The Queen* [1972] A.C. 378, P.C.
[96] *Subramaniam* v. *Public Prosecutor* [1956] 1 W.L.R. 965 at p. 969. See also *R.* v. *McLean* (1968) 52 Cr.App.R. 8: *Mawji Khan* v. *R.* [1967] 1 All E.R. 80; *R.* v. *Chapman* [1969] 2 Q.B. 436.
[97] *R.* v. *Hunt* (1820) 3 B. & Ald. 566.
[98] Arch. para. 1352.
[99] The rule applies equally to documents. Where it is sought to prove the truth of facts contained in them, the maker must be called: *R.* v. *Gillespie* 51 Cr.App.R. 172; *Hill* v. *Baylis* [1958] 1 Q.B. 271; *Myers* v. *D.P.P.* [1965] A.C. 1001 but see Criminal Evidence Act 1965, *post*, p. 615. *Cf. T. H. Brown Ltd.* v. *Baggott (No. 2)* [1970] R.T.R. 323 D.C.
[1] *Teper* v. *R.* [1952] A.C. 480 at p. 486.
[2] *Stobart* v. *Dryden* (1836) 1 M. & W. 615.
[3] It seems that the courts will not now create any further exceptions: *Myers* v. *D.P.P.* [1965] A.C. 1001. The particular decision has now been reversed by statute: Criminal Evidence Act 1965, *post*, p. 615.

(iv) declarations made by deceased persons; (v) confessions; (vi) statements contained in public documents; (vii) trade or business records; (viii) certain depositions.

Where the Statement or Fact is Part of the Res Gestae

All statements and conduct which are contemporaneous with, or part of,[4] a fact in issue or relevant to the issue can be proved in order to explain that fact.[5] So where A, the victim of a running-down accident, explained immediately afterwards to B how he had been run over, evidence given by B of A's statement was admitted as proof of the cause of the accident.[6]

In *Ratten* v. *The Queen*[7] the Privy Council said that the test is whether the making of the statement was in some sense part of the transaction or event. The evidence may be admitted if the statement producing it is made in such conditions (always being those of approximate but not exact contemporaneity) of involvement or pressure as to exclude the possibility of concoction or distortion to the maker, or the disadvantage of the accused.

Statement as to the Bodily or Mental Condition of the Maker

Where the statement relates to the existence of any bodily or mental condition, and is made by a person whose condition at the time of making the statement is in issue,[8] it is admissible only so far as it relates to the nature and effects of the condition. Nothing is admissible which is in the nature of a narrative as to how, or by whom, the condition was caused.[9]

Complaints

On charges of sexual offences against females, and of gross indecency with and indecent assaults on young males,[10] a complaint of the victim is admissible in certain circumstances and for certain purposes.

---

[4] See Phipson, pp. 88–91.
[5] *Teper* v. *R.* [1952] A.C. 480.
[6] *R.* v. *Foster* (1834) 6 C. & P. 325.
[7] [1972] A.C. 378, P.C. See also *Teper* v. *The Queen* [1952] A.C. 480, P.C. *Cf. R.* v. *Parker* (1960) 45 Cr.App.R. 1.
[8] *R.* v. *Johnson* (1847) 2 C. & K. 354; *Aveson* v. *Kinnaird* (1805) 6 East 188.
[9] *R.* v. *Nicholas* (1846) 2 C. & K. 1246 at p. 248; *R.* v. *Gloster* (1888) 16 Cox 471.
[10] *R.* v. *Camelleri* [1922] 2 K.B. 122.

The complaint must have been voluntary; but the mere fact that it was made in answer to questions will not render it inadmissible unless it was induced by questions of a *suggestive or leading* nature.[11] So a complaint will *not* be inadmissible because it was made in answer to a natural question put by a mother or person in charge, such as " What is the matter?" or " Why are you crying?"[12] However, the complaint must be made " at the first opportunity after the offence which reasonably offers itself."[13]

If these conditions are satisfied the complaint is then admissible as evidence " of the consistency of the conduct of the prosecutrix with the story told by her in the witness-box, and as being inconsistent with her consent to that of which she complains."[14] The judge must warn the jury that it is only relevant for these purposes.[15]

Declarations made by Deceased Persons

Declarations made by deceased persons are admissible in certain cases, of which the following are the most important:

(1) Declarations **against the pecuniary or proprietary interest** of the deceased.[16] Such a declaration need not be made contemporaneously with the fact recorded,[17] and is evidence not only of such facts as were against interest but of all connected facts to which it refers.[18] Thus a statement by a deceased person that he was illegitimate is admissible as being against both his pecuniary and his proprietary interest[19]; an entry by a deceased surgeon of payment of his fees for attending a confinement on a certain date is evidence, not only of the receipt of the money, which is a declaration against his pecuniary interest, but also of the date of

[11] *R.* v. *Osborne* [1905] 1 K.B. 551.
[12] *Ibid.* at p. 556.
[13] *Ibid.* at p. 561.
[14] *R.* v. *Lillyman* [1896] 2 Q.B. 167 at p. 170. Strictly speaking it is only when the complaint is admitted to negative the fact of consent that an exception to the hearsay rule is created. Thus if the victim gives no evidence, the complaint is inadmissible: *R.* v. *Wallworth* (1958) 42 Cr.App.R. 153; *Sparks* v. *R.* [1964] A.C. 964.
[15] *R.* v. *Osborne* [1905] 1 K.B. 551 at p. 561.
[16] No interest other than " pecuniary or proprietary " will suffice. Thus it is not sufficient that the declaration is of an act done by the declarant which would expose him to prosecution and as to which it is in his interest to keep silent: *Sussex Peerage Case* (1844) 11 Cl. & F. 85.
[17] *Doe* v. *Turford* (1832) 3 B. & Ad. 890 at p. 898.
[18] *Taylor* v. *Witham* (1876) 3 Ch.D. 605.
[19] *Re Perton* (1885) 53 L.T. 707.

the child's birth and the names of its parents [20]; and an entry in the books of A (deceased) that he has paid a quarter's rent for the premises he occupies is evidence, not only that he was a tenant and not owner (this being the declaration against his proprietary interest), but also of the amount and payment of the rent,[21] and that the person to whom it was paid was the owner.[22]

(2) Declarations made **in the discharge of a duty** and contemporaneously with the facts recorded *and* without any motive to misrepresent *and* relating only to acts by the declarant.[23] Such declarations are admissible only to prove acts which it was the declarant's *duty* both to do and to record, and not of any other facts contained in the declaration. So an entry of delivery of beer made in A's books on the evening of the delivery, and signed by a deceased drayman, whose duty it was to deliver the beer and sign the entry, is admissible to prove the delivery of the beer.[24] But a certificate of arrest annexed to the writ by a deceased sheriff's officer is only relevant to prove the fact and time of the arrest, but not the place, it being no part of the officer's duty to record the place of arrest.[25]

(3) **Dying declarations,** which are admissible only if (i) the charge is one of the murder or manslaughter of the declarant [26]; (ii) the declaration relates to the circumstances of the death [27] and (iii) at the time when the declaration was made the declarant was in " settled, hopeless expectation of death." [28] Any hope of recovery in the mind of the declarant, however slight, renders the declaration inadmissible.[29] But it is not inadmissible because a hope of recovery arose subsequently in the mind of the declarant,[30] or because the doctor thought that recovery was possible.[31]

---

[20] *Higham* v. *Ridgway* (1808) 10 East 109.
[21] *R.* v. *Exeter Guardians* (1869) L.R. 4 Q.B. 341.
[22] *Peaceable* v. *Watson* (1811) 4 Taunt. 16.
[23] *The Henry Coxon* (1878) 3 P.D. 156.
[24] *Price* v. *Torrington* (1703) 1 Salk. 285.
[25] *Chambers* v. *Bernasconi* (1834) 1 C.M. & R. 347.
[26] *R.* v. *Mead* (1824) 2 B. & C. 605. A dying declaration is inadmissible if on its face it is incomplete: *Waugh* v. *R.* [1950] A.C. 203. There seems no reason why a dying declaration should not be admissible in a case of death by dangerous driving.
[27] *R.* v. *Mead, supra.*
[28] See *R.* v. *Perry* [1909] 2 K.B. 697.
[29] *R.* v. *Jenkins* (1869) L.R. 1 C.C.R. 187.
[30] *R.* v. *Austin* (1912) 8 Cr.App.R. 27.
[31] *R.* v. *Mosley* (1825) 1 Mood. 97 ; *R.* v. *Peel* (1860) 2 F. & F. 21.

Whether or not the declarant had such an expectation of death is a question for the judge.[32]

The declaration, if it satisfies these requirements, is only admissible to prove the cause and circumstances of the death.[33] If, on the face of the declaration, it is incomplete, it is inadmissible.[34]

(4) Declarations as to a **public or general right or custom,** or a matter of **public or general interest,**[35] if made by a person of the class who would know it, and made before the commencement of any controversy as to its existence.[36]

Extra-Judicial Confessions

A confession of a crime is only admissible in evidence against the accused where *it is shown by the prosecution* that it was voluntary, *i.e.* that " it has not been obtained from him either by fear of prejudice or hope of advantage exercised or held out by a person in authority." [37] It is for the judge to decide by holding a " trial within a trial " in the absence of the jury whether the confession is admissible, and the accused is entitled to give evidence and call witnesses to show it was not voluntary.[38]

A confession will therefore be inadmissible where an inducement to confess has been held out by a person in authority, *i.e.* by someone engaged in the prosecution, arrest, detention or examination of the prisoner by the person wronged by the offence,[39] or by someone else in the presence and without the dissent of a person in

---

[32] *R.* v. *Whitmarsh* (1898) 62 J.P. 711.

[33] *R.* v. *Mead, supra.*

[34] *Waugh* v. *The King* [1950] A.C. 203.

[35] *Lord Dunraven* v. *Llewellyn* (1850) 15 Q.B. 791.

[36] *Sturla* v. *Freccia* (1880) 5 App.Cas. 623 at p. 641.

[37] *Ibrahim* v. *R.* [1914] A.C. 599 at p. 609. The prosecution must establish *beyond reasonable doubt* that the confession was voluntary: *R.* v. *Thompson* [1893] 2 Q.B. 12; *R.* v. *Sartori, Gavin and Phillips* [1961] Crim.L.R. 397. The admissibility of an alleged confession does not depend on whether or not there has been compliance with the Judges' Rules (see *post,* p. 612), but on whether it has been shown that the confession has been made voluntarily: *R.* v. *Prager* [1972] 1 W.L.R. 260, C.A. Once the issue has been raised the judge *must* give a ruling on it, he cannot do so properly without hearing the evidence the defence wish to adduce: *R.* v. *Moore* [1972] Crim.L.R. 372.

[38] *R.* v. *Cowell* [1940] 2 K.B. 49. If the judge rules the confession inadmissible, the accused is entitled, during the trial before the jury, to cross-examine the witnesses again as to the circumstances in which the confession was made: *R.* v. *Murray* [1951] 1 K.B. 391.

[39] *R.* v. *Wilson* [1967] 2 Q.B. 406, *Deokinanan* v. *The Queen* [1969] 1 A.C. 20 (P.C.).

authority.[40] The prisoner's employer is not a person in authority unless the offence was committed against him.[41]

The inducement itself must be of some worldly advantage held out or threat made which is calculated to make the confession untrue. It need not necessarily relate to the charge or contemplated charge.[42] Persuasion on moral or religious grounds will not make the confession inadmissible,[43] but it now seems that, a promise to let the prisoner see his wife [40] may render his subsequent confession inadmissible,[44] or to allow time to have other matters taken into consideration,[45] or to let him have bail.[46]

A threat of violence, or the use of violence, will clearly render a confession inadmissible.[47]

The inducement must be the actual cause of the accused making the confession. A confession made *after* the inducement has ceased to influence the accused is admissible.[48]

A confession is not inadmissible because it was obtained under a promise of secrecy [49] or merely as the result of questions put by a person in authority [50] or by the police [51]; but the court may refuse to allow evidence of a confession obtained by questions by the police after the prisoner was in custody if the method of questioning was improper or unfair.[52] The test of admissibility is voluntariness. Admissibility is a matter of law and is for the judge to decide without the assistance, and in the absence, of the jury. If the judge allows a confession to be admitted in evidence, its value and evidence is a matter for the jury, and " voluntariness " is only one of the factors for them to take into account in assessing the weight

---

40 *R.* v. *Taylor* (1839) 8 C. & P. 733 ; *R.* v. *Laugher* (1846) 2 C. & K. 225 ; *R.* v. *Cleary* (1963) 48 Cr.App.R. 116.

41 *R.* v. *Moore* (1852) 2 Den. 522.

42 *Commissioners of Customs and Excise* v. *Harz* [1967] A.C. 760.

43 *R.* v. *Baldry* (1852) 2 Den. 430. " The words ' You had better tell the truth ' seem to have acquired a sort of technical meaning, importing either a threat or a benefit ": *R.* v. *Jarvis* (1867) L.R. 1 C.C.R. 96 at p. 99.

44 *Harz's Case, supra,* disapproving *R.* v *Lloyd* (1834) 6 C. & P. 393.

45 *R.* v. *Northam* (1967) 52 Cr.App.R. 97.

46 *R.* v. *Zaveckas* [1970] 1 All E.R. 413. And see generally the observations of Winn L.J. in *R.* v. *Richards* [1967] 1 W.L.R. 653.

47 *Cf. R.* v. *Parratt* (1831) 4 C. & P. 570 ; *R.* v. *Smith* [1959] 2 Q.B. 35.

48 *R.* v. *Smith, supra.* Much will depend on the circumstances of each case, and in particular on the lapse of time between the inducement and the confession.

49 *R.* v. *Thomas* (1836) 7 C. & P. 345.

50 *Ibrahim* v. *R.* [1914] A.C. 599.

51 *R.* v. *Best* [1909] 1 K.B. 692.

52 *R.* v. *Smith* [1961] 3 All E.R. 972, and the cases cited therein.

to attach to it.[53] The judge ought, in directing the jury, to tell them that the weight they attach to the confession must depend on all the circumstances in which they find it was taken, and it is their right to give it such weight as they think fit.[54]

A confession by one accused is not evidence against another.[55] Where, however, two prisoners are jointly tried, a confession by one which implicates the other may be given in evidence against the maker; but the judge should warn the jury that it is not evidence against the co-accused.[56]

General rules for the guidance of the police[57] in questioning suspects and obtaining statements have been approved by the judges.[58] A police officer has a right to question any person, whether suspected or not, from whom he thinks useful information as to the commission or perpetrator of an offence may be obtained.[59] As soon as an officer has evidence which would afford reasonable grounds for suspecting that a person has committed an offence he must caution that person before putting to him any further questions relating to that offence.[60] Similarly, where a person is charged with or informed that he may be prosecuted for an offence he must be cautioned.[61] Thereafter, only in exceptional circumstances should a person be questioned further, after the appropriate caution.[62] But the fact that a person is questioned without any caution, even after his arrest, does not render his statements inadmissible,[63] though it is a fact to be taken into account by the judge, who may in his discretion refuse to allow the statement

[53] *Chan Wei Kung* v. *The Queen* [1967] 2 A.C. 160.
[54] *R.* v. *Burgess* [1968] 2 Q.B. 112. Approving *Chan Wei Kung* (*supra*).
[55] *Surujpaul* v. *R.* [1958] 1 W.L.R. 1050 at p. 1056.
[56] *R.* v. *Gunewardene* [1951] 2 K.B. 600.
[57] Professional investigators of any description ought to comply with the rules. In *R.* v. *Nichols* [1967] Crim.L.R. 296 it was held they did not apply to a store manager. *Quaere* whether the rule should not have applied in that case, since the questioning was in the presence of a store detective.
[58] See Arch. paras. 1119–1124 which contain Home Office Circular No. 31/1964 which relates to the Rules; notes thereon; administrative directions or instructions and the taking of statements. The rules, known as the "Judges' Rules," are rules of practice only and do not have the force of law, but they are there to be obeyed: *R.* v. *Roberts* [1970] Crim.L.R. 464.
[59] R. 1.
[60] R. 2: the caution shall be in the following terms: "You are not obliged to say anything unless you wish to do so but what you say may be put into writing and given in evidence." The phrase "and given in evidence *against you*" must *not* be used.
[61] R. 3 (*a*).
[62] R. 3 (*b*).
[63] *R.* v. *Prager* [1972] 1 W.L.R. 260, C.A.

to be given in evidence [64]: but if the judge allows proof of the statement, a conviction need not be quashed unless there has been a miscarriage of justice.[65]

Any statement made should, if possible, be taken down in writing and signed by the person making it, who should be asked to make any corrections he wishes.[66]

Where a statement by one of two persons charged with the same offence, or informed that they may be so prosecuted, is handed to the other by a police officer, nothing should be said or done to invite any reply or comment.[67]

Although a confession of the accused is inadmissible because it is involuntary, nonetheless any relevant facts discovered in consequence of that confession may be proved, and the same is presumably the case where the statement is in breach of the judges' rules. So if A in the course of an improperly induced confession states that stolen property is hidden in her house, and that property is subsequently found there, the fact of the finding is admissible.[68] It may well be that *at least* so much of the involuntary confession that relates to the subsequent discovery may also be adduced against the accused.[69] But where documents are produced by the accused as a direct result of the improper inducement, they are not admissible, since they " stand on precisely the same footing as an oral or written confession which is brought into existence as the result of such promise, inducement or threat." [70]

A confession may be made by acceptance of another's statement. Accordingly, statements made in the presence or hearing of a person are admissible against him (i) if made upon an occasion on which he might reasonably be expected to make some observation, explanation or denial, and (ii) if and in so far as he has accepted the statement so as to make it in effect his own. He may accept by words, conduct or demeanour, whether he has done so being a question for the jury; if the circumstances demanded an answer, silence may amount to an acceptance, and even a denial may be

---

[64] *R. v. Voisin* [1918] 1 K.B. 531.
[65] See *Ibrahim* v. *R.* [1914] A.C. 599, where the authorities are reviewed.
[66] R. 4.
[67] R. 5.
[68] *R. v. Warickshall* (1783) 1 Leach 263. See *R. v. Griffin* (1809) Russ. & Ry. 151; *R. v. Gould* (1840) 9 C. & P. 364; *Kuruma* v. *R.* [1955] A.C. 197.
[69] The authorities conflict on this point: see cases cited *supra* and *R. v. Berriman* (1854) 6 Cox C.C. 388.
[70] *R. v. Barker* [1941] 2 K.B. 381 at p. 385.

made in such a manner as to cause the jury to disbelieve him and to constitute evidence from which acceptance may be inferred.[71] The mere fact that a person, having been charged with an offence and given a formal caution, declines or refuses to say anything is not a consideration for the jury tending to prove his guilt.[72] Whether an accused person has been cautioned or not, his silence when told by a police officer of an allegation by a third party, cannot by itself amount to an acknowledgment of the truth of the allegation.[73]

An admission made by the prisoner on oath in any previous proceedings is admissible against him unless (i) he is specially protected by statute,[74] or (ii) he was in such proceedings improperly compelled to answer incriminating questions.[75]

Statements Contained in Public Documents

Statements contained in such documents are admissible in proof of the facts recorded. These documents, of which there are many, include: (i) the *Gazette*, which at common law is " an authoritative means of proving " all matters of state and public acts of the Government [76]; (ii) judicial and quasi-judicial inquisitions, records and reports (English or foreign) if made under public legal authority and for a public purpose [77]; (iii) official registers (English or foreign), provided that they are kept under the sanction of public authority and are recognised by the tribunals of the country where they are kept as public records [78]; and, generally, (iv) any document made under public authority " for the purpose of the public making use of it and being able to refer to it." [79] Many registers and

[71] *R.* v. *Christie* [1914] A.C. 545 at pp. 554, 565.

[72] *R.* v. *Leckey* [1947] 1 K.B. 80. See also *R.* v. *Naylor* [1933] 1 K.B. 685.

[73] *R.* v. *Hall* (1970) 55 Cr.App.R. 108.

[74] See *e.g.* Bankruptcy Act 1914, s. 166, as amended by the Theft Act 1968, *cf. R.* v. *Harris and anor.* [1970] 1 W.L.R. 1252. See also Arch. para. 1101.

[75] *R.* v. *Garbett* (1847) 2 C. & K. 474; *R.* v. *Coote* (1873) L.R. 4 P.C. 599; and see Arch. para. 1102.

[76] *R.* v. *Holt* (1793) 5 T.R. 436 at p. 444. By statute also the *Gazette* is evidence of various matters, as, *e.g.* under s. 137 of the Bankruptcy Act 1914, by which a copy of the *London Gazette* containing notice of a receiving order or an order adjudging a debtor bankrupt is conclusive evidence of the order having been made and of its date.

[77] *Sturla* v. *Freccia* (1880) 5 App.Cas. 623. See also *Att.-Gen.* v. *Antrobus* [1905] 2 Ch. 188.

[78] *Lyell* v. *Kennedy* (1889) 14 App.Cas 437.

[79] *Sturla* v. *Freccia* (1880) 5 App.Cas. 623 at p. 643.

certificates are by different statutes made evidence of the facts authorised to be registered and certified.[80]

Trade or Business Records

The **Criminal Evidence Act 1965**[81] creates a further exception to the hearsay rule by enacting that in any criminal proceedings where direct oral evidence of a fact would be admissible, any statement contained in a document and tending to establish that fact shall on production of the document be admissible as evidence of that fact,[82] provided (i) the document[83] is a record relating to any trade or business[84] and was compiled for that purpose by persons with personal knowledge of the information supplied,[85] and (ii) the person who supplied the information is dead, or abroad, or unfit to attend as a witness, or cannot be identified or found, or cannot reasonably be expected to recollect the matters dealt with in the information he supplied.[86]

Depositions

(1) Depositions in preliminary proceedings. By **section 13** of the **Criminal Justice Act 1925**[87] the deposition before examining justices of a witness in respect of whom a conditional witness order was made, or who is proved at the trial to be dead or insane, or so ill as not to be able to travel, or to be kept out of the way by or on behalf of the accused, may without further proof be read at the trial, provided that the conditions of the section have been complied with.[88] This section also applies to written statements tendered in evidence in committal proceedings pursuant to section 2 of the Criminal Justice Act 1967.[89]

---

[80] See, *e.g.* the Bankers' Books Evidence Act 1879.
[81] Amended by the Post Office Act 1969, Sched. 4.
[82] s. 1.
[83] Which includes any device by means of which information is recorded or stored: s. 1 (4). So, *e.g.* microfilm and computer cards are within the Act.
[84] Which includes any public transport, public utility or similar undertakings carried on by a local authority and the activities of the Post Office: s. 1 (4).
[85] s. 1 (1) (*a*).
[86] s. 1 (1) (*b*).
[87] Amended by the Criminal Procedure (Attendance of Witnesses) Act 1965, Sched. 2.
[88] See *post*, p. 739.
[89] Criminal Justice Act 1967, s. 2 (7).

By **section 12 (4)** of the Act (as substituted by the **Magistrates' Courts Act 1952, s. 131** and **Sched. 5),** any statement made by the accused before examining justices may also be given in evidence if the provisions of the rules made under section 15 of the Justices of the Peace Act 1949 have been complied with.[90] If he gives evidence on his own behalf it is admissible at the trial although he then declines to give evidence.[91]

Depositions taken before coroners are admissible on the death of the witness, if they are signed by the coroner and the witness and the prisoner had full opportunity for cross-examination.[92] A deposition before the coroner made by the prisoner is also admissible.[93]

(2) *Depositions for the perpetuation of testimony.* By **section 41** of the **Magistrates' Courts Act 1952** where a person appears to a justice of the peace to be able and willing to give material information relating to an indictable offence or to any person accused of an indictable offence, and the justice is satisfied, on a representation made by a duly qualified medical practitioner, that the person is dangerously ill and unlikely to recover, then, if it is not practicable to take the evidence of the sick person in accordance with the Act and rules, the justice may take in writing the deposition of the sick person on oath. The deposition so taken may be given in evidence before examining justices or at the trial only if (i) the declarant is dead or it is proved that there is no reasonable probability that he will ever be able to travel or give evidence, and (ii) the declaration purports to be signed by the justice by or before whom it was taken, and (iii) the person against whom it is to be used had reasonable notice of the intention to take the statement, and full opportunity of being present and cross-examining the person making it.[94]

(3) *Depositions of children and young persons.* By **section 42** of the **Children and Young Persons Act 1933** where, in respect of an offence against a child or young person set out in the First Schedule,[95] a justice of the peace is satisfied by the evidence of a

---

[90] See *post,* pp. 671–672.
[91] *R.* v. *Bird* (1898) 15 T.L.R. 26.
[92] *R.* v. *Cowle* (1907) 71 J.P. 152 ; *R.* v. *Black* (1910) 74 J.P. 71.
[93] Arch. para. 1097.
[94] Criminal Law Amendment Act 1867, s. 6, as amended by the Magistrates' Courts Act 1952, s. 131 and Sched. 5 and the Courts Act 1971, Sched. 11. For rules governing the taking of the deposition of a person dangerously ill, see Magistrates' Courts Rules 1968, r. 29.
[95] For these offences, see Arch. para. 2755.

qualified medical practitioner that the attendance before the court of that child or young person would seriously endanger his life or health, he may take the deposition out of court; and by **section 43** depositions taken in accordance with the previous section are admissible in evidence provided reasonable notice of the intention to take the deposition was served upon the accused, and that he or his counsel or solicitor had an opportunity of cross-examination. The written statement of a child is also admissible in a preliminary inquiry into a sexual offence under **section 27** of the **Children and Young Persons Act 1963.**[96]

SECTION 3. PROOF BY ORAL EVIDENCE

Proof of a fact by means of oral evidence, *i.e.* the testimony of witnesses, necessitates the consideration of (i) how the *attendance* of witnesses in court may be secured, (ii) how their evidence is to be given, (iii) whether a particular witness is *competent* to give evidence, and, if so, whether he can be *compelled* to do so, (iv) how the examination of a witness is conducted, (v) in what circumstances a witness may refuse to answer a question or produce a document on the grounds of *privilege,* and (vi) where *corroboration* of his evidence is required.

Attendance of Witnesses

By **section 1** of the **Criminal Procedure (Attendance of Witnesses) Act 1965,** examining justices at preliminary proceedings must make a *witness order* in respect of all witnesses examined by them (except the accused and his character witnesses, if any), requiring them to attend and give evidence at the trial of the accused.[97] Where the evidence of such a witness is unlikely to be required or disputed at the trial the justices may make a conditional witness order, requiring the witness to attend if notice to that effect is given to him.[98] **Section 2 (10)** of the **Criminal Justice Act 1967** extends

---

[96] See *post,* p. 671.

[97] ss. 1 (4) and 7 (2) abolish the binding over of witnesses by examining justices and coroners to secure their attendance at the trial. By s. 7 (1) the provisions of the Act relating to witness orders may be applied by rules under s. 25 (2) of the Coroners (Amendment) Act 1926, to proceedings in case of persons charged by a coroner's inquisition.

[98] s. 1 (2) (*a*) (*b*).

this provision to persons whose written statements are tendered in evidence in committal proceedings under the Act.

As regards criminal proceedings at the Crown Court any other witness may be served with a *witness summons* requiring him to attend and give evidence or produce a document or thing,[99] but the witness may apply to the Crown Court or to the High Court, and if he satisfies the court that he cannot give or produce any material evidence, the court may direct that the summons shall be of no effect.[1]

Disobedience without just excuse to either a witness order or summons requiring attendance before a court is a contempt of that court.[2]

Where a witness is unlikely to obey a witness order or summons and evidence *on oath* is given which satisfies a High Court judge to that effect, the judge may issue a warrant to arrest the witness and bring him before the court he is required to attend.[3]

If a witness fails to comply with a witness order or summons and attend before the Crown Court, that court may either (i) cause him to be served with a notice requiring his attendance; or (ii) issue a warrant for his arrest bringing him before the court if it is satisfied that there are reasonable grounds for believing he has failed to attend without just excuse, or if he has failed to comply with a notice under (i) above.[4]

A witness brought before a court by means of a warrant issued under the Act may be remanded in custody or on bail until the court receives his evidence or punishes him for contempt.[5]

---

[99] s. 2 (1). The witness summons may be issued out of the Crown Court or the High Court. No *subpoena ad testificandum* or *subpoena duces tecum* may be issued where a witness summons is issuable: s. 8.

[1] s. 2 (2), as amended by the Courts Act 1971, Sched. 8.

[2] s. 3 (1). No term of imprisonment exceeding three months may be imposed for such contempt: s. 3 (2).

[3] s. 4 (1). No warrant shall be issued in respect of a witness subject to a conditional witness order unless notice has been given to him requiring his attendance; nor in respect of a witness summons unless the judge is satisfied by evidence on oath that the witness is likely to be able to give or produce material evidence at the trial: *ibid.*

[4] s. 4 (2). For the purposes of s. 13 of the Act, such a warrant is treated as a warrant issued in the Crown Court: Courts Act 1971, Sched. 8, but in the case of a warrant of arrest for a witness, only a High Court judge may issue such a warrant out of the Crown Court.

[5] s. 4 (3).

Giving of Oral Evidence

All oral evidence is given either:

(1) On *oath* upon the New Testament or, in the case of Jews, upon the Old Testament [6] or in the Scottish form [7] or in any form which, according to his religion or nationality, binds the conscience of the witness.[8] In all cases in which an oath may lawfully be administered the party is bound by the oath administered, provided it has been administered in such form and with such ceremonies as he may declare to be binding.[9] And, if an oath has been duly administered and taken, the fact that the witness has no religious belief does not affect the validity of the oath.[10]

(2) On *affirmation,* which is permissible where the witness objects to take an oath, either (i) because he has no religious belief, or (ii) because the taking of oaths is contrary to his religious belief. An affirmation so made has the same force and effect as if the witness had taken an oath.[11] A person may also be permitted, or required, to affirm where it is not reasonably practicable without inconvenience or delay to administer an oath in the manner appropriate to his religious belief.[12]

(3) By **section 38** of the **Children and Young Persons Act 1933** where, in any proceeding against any person for an offence, any child of tender years [13] who is tendered as a witness does not, in the opinion of the court, understand the nature of an oath, the evidence of that child may be received, though not given upon oath, if, in the opinion of the court, the child is possessed of sufficient intelli-

---

[6] The form of and manner of taking the oath is now prescribed by s. 2 of the Oaths Act 1909. The person taking the oath must hold the New Testament, or, in the case of a Jew, the Old Testament, in his uplifted hand and must repeat after the officer administering the oath the words " I swear by Almighty God that . . . ," followed by the words of the oath prescribed by law. The words to be used by children and young persons are: " I promise before Almighty God . . .": Children and Young Persons Act 1963, s. 28 (1). The officer shall (unless the person about to take the oath *voluntarily objects* thereto or is physically incapable of so taking the oath) administer the oath in this form and manner without question.

[7] Oaths Act 1888, s. 5.

[8] Arch. para. 1354; and see *Omichund* v. *Barker* (1744) 1 Atk. 25.

[9] Oaths Act 1838, s. 1. See also s. 15 (1) of the Perjury Act 1911.

[10] Oaths Act 1888, s. 3.

[11] Oaths Act 1888, s. 1; see *R.* v. *Clark* [1962] 1 W.L.R. 180.

[12] Oaths Act 1961, s. 1 (1) (2), reversing the decision in *R.* v. *Pritam Singh* [1958] 1 W.L.R. 143.

[13] Which is a matter for the good sense of the court: *R.* v. *Campbell* [1956] 2 All E.R. 272 at p. 274. It is undesirable in any case to call a child of five: *R.* v. *Wallwork* (1958) 122 J.P. 299.

gence to justify the reception of the evidence and understands the duty of speaking the truth.[14] Such unsworn evidence is to be deemed a deposition though not taken on oath, but no person can be convicted upon such testimony unless it is corroborated by some other material evidence in support thereof implicating him.[15] The mere refusal by the accused to make a statement or to disclose his defence before the committing justices does not as a general rule amount to a corroboration.[16]

By section 42 of the Children and Young Persons Act 1933 provisions are also made for taking out of court the depositions of a child or young person against whom any offence in the First Schedule to the Act [17] has been committed, if attendance in court would involve serious danger to its life or health, and by section 43 such depositions are admissible in evidence where the conditions of the section are satisfied.[18]

(4) The accused may make an *unsworn statement* from the dock, usually before counsel for the prosecution addresses the jury at the close of the trial.[19]

Competence and Compellability of Witnesses

A witness is said to be competent if he can lawfully be called to give evidence. Formerly a person who had any interest in the result of the trial or had been convicted of certain crimes was incompetent to give evidence. But by **section 1** of the **Evidence Act 1843** it was provided that no person offered as a witness should thereafter be excluded by reason of incapacity from crime or interest from giving evidence. But the fact that a witness has been so convicted or is of bad character is relevant to his credibility.

At the present day, therefore, subject to special rules affecting the prisoner and his or her wife or husband, all persons are compe-

---

[14] It is the duty of the presiding judge to satisfy himself whether the witness should be sworn or not: *R.* v. *Surgenor* (1940) 27 Cr.App.R. 175.

[15] If the only evidence implicating the prisoner is that of unsworn children, the judge should stop the case; for corroboration cannot be provided by other unsworn evidence: *R.* v. *Campbell* (1956) 40 Cr.App.R. 95. The unsworn evidence of a child is not, in law, capable of corroborating the evidence of the complainant in the trial of a sexual offence: *R.* v. *Hester, The Times,* April 22, 1972, C.A. (*R.* v. *Campbell* (*supra*) not followed). As to corroboration generally, see *post,* p. 634.

[16] *R.* v. *Keeling* (1942) 28 Cr.App.R. 121.

[17] As amended by the Sexual Offences Act 1956, Scheds. 3, 4; the Suicide Act 1961. See also the Indecency with Children Act 1960, s. 1 (3).

[18] *Ante,* p. 617.   [19] Arch. para. 557.

tent to give evidence unless, in the opinion of the judge, they are, through infancy, drunkenness or insanity, unable to understand the nature of an oath or the duty of speaking the truth or to give rational evidence.[20] A person who suffers from partial delusions is not incompetent to give evidence upon matters not connected with his delusions, but if his evidence appears tainted with insanity the jury may disregard it.[21] Children are competent witnesses provided they understand the nature and consequences of the oath, but by virtue of section 38 of the Children and Young Persons Act 1933 a child of tender years may give unsworn evidence in criminal trials in certain circumstances.[22]

A person who is a competent witness is also a compellable witness, *i.e.* can be required to give his evidence, although he may refuse to answer certain questions on the grounds of privilege.[23] There are, however, several important exceptions to the general rules of competence and compellability.

The common law rule is that the *accused* is not a competent witness for the prosecution. One effect of this rule is that one co-prisoner is not competent to give evidence on behalf of the prosecution against another.[24]

The accused is a competent witness for the defence [25] whether charged solely or jointly with any other person,[26] but he cannot be called as a witness *except on his own application.*[27] In *Redfern* v. *Redfern* [28] Bowen L.J. said: " It is one of the inveterate principles

---

[20] Any examination by the judge of a witness in order to ascertain his competence must be in open court, otherwise it will invalidate a conviction: *R.* v. *Dunne* (1929) 21 Cr.App.R. 176.

[21] *R.* v. *Hill* (1851) 2 Den. 254.

[22] See *ante*, p. 619.

[23] See *post*, p. 628.

[24] *R.* v. *Grant* [1944] 2 All E.R. 311; *R.* v. *Sharrock* [1948] 1 All E.R. 145. A co-prisoner becomes competent for the prosecution when (i) a *nolle prosequi* is filed with reference to his case, (ii) an order for separate trials is obtained, (iii) no evidence is offered against him and he is acquitted, or (iv) he pleads guilty. See *R.* v. *Boal* [1965] 1 Q.B. 402 at p. 411. In the last instance he should normally be sentenced before he is called.

[25] *i.e.* he can give evidence on his own behalf or on behalf of a co-accused.

[26] Criminal Evidence Act 1898, s. 1.

[27] *Ibid.* s. 1 (*a*); *Comet Products U.K. Ltd.* v. *Hawkex Plastics Ltd.* [1971] 2 Q.B. 67, in which case it was decided that, since an application to commit for contempt in a civil action on the alleged breach of an interim injunction had a quasi-criminal aspect and the proposed cross-examination of the defendant would be likely to cover broad issues in the action, as a matter of discretion the cross-examination ought not to be allowed.

[28] [1891] P. 139, quoted with approval by Lord Denning M.R. in *Comet Products U.K. Ltd.* v. *Hawkex Plastics Ltd. and Another* (*supra*).

of English law that a party cannot be compelled to discover that which, if answered, would tend to subject him to any punishment, penalty, forfeiture, . . . ' no one is bound to criminate himself.' " Moreover, the prosecution may *not* comment upon his failure to give evidence.[29] In only one case is the accused a competent and compellable witness for the prosecution—by **section 1** of the **Evidence Act 1877,**[30] on the trial of any indictment or other proceeding for a nuisance to any public highway, river or bridge, and other indictment or proceeding instituted for the purpose of trying or enforcing a civil right only.

Again the *accused's spouse* is generally not a competent witness for the prosecution,[31] except that he or she is competent and compellable (i) in proceedings under the Evidence Act 1877, and (ii) in criminal proceedings involving a charge of personal violence by the accused against his or her spouse.[32]

The Theft Act 1968 empowers a husband and wife to prosecute each other for any offence (whether under that Act or not) as if they were not married.

Where proceedings are brought by one spouse against another, then the one bringing the proceedings is a competent witness for the prosecution at every stage of the proceedings. Where one spouse is charged in proceedings not brought by the other with having committed any offence against the other or the other's property, the other shall be competent to give evidence at every stage of the proceedings whether for the defence or for the prosecution and whether the accused is charged solely or jointly with any other person. There are however two provisos to this general rule [33] : (a) the wife or husband [34] shall not be compellable either

---

[29] *Ibid*. s. 1 (*b*); but the trial judge may comment: *R.* v. *Rhodes* [1899] 1 Q.B. at pp. 83–84; and so may a co-accused: *R.* v. *Ferrara* (1971) 55 Cr.App.R. 199; *R.* v. *Pratt* [1971] Crim.L.R. 234; *R.* v. *Bathurst* (1968) 52 Cr.App.R. 251.

[30] As amended by the Highways Act 1959, Sched. 25; and as far as London is concerned by the London Government Act 1963, Sched. 6.

[31] A divorced husband or wife of the accused remains an incompetent witness for the prosecution in respect of any matters relating to the period of marriage. The same rule applies where there has been a decree of nullity on the the ground of impotence, as the marriage is valid until decree: *R.* v. *Algar* [1954] 1 Q.B. 279.

[32] *R.* v. *Lapworth* [1931] 1 K.B. 117. For the meaning of a charge of personal violence, see Arch. para. 1332 and the cases cited therein.

[33] Theft Act 1968, s. 30 (2), subject of course to the consent of the Director of Public Prosecutions where appropriate under s. 30 (4) of the Act.

[34] Unless compellable at common law.

to give evidence or, in giving evidence, to disclose any communication made to the other during the marriage; (b) failure to give evidence shall not be commented upon by the prosecution.[35]

The spouse is also rendered competent but not compellable [36] for the prosecution in the case of certain offences specified in the Schedule to the Criminal Evidence Act 1898 [37] and subsequent statutes.[38] The consent of the accused is *not* required.[39]

The accused's spouse is a competent witness for the defence [40] *upon the application of the accused,*[41] but again is not compellable,[42] except in the case of proceedings under the Evidence Act 1877, and in criminal charges of personal violence by the accused against his or her spouse.[43]

The Examination of Witnesses

The witnesses may be (i) examined in chief; (ii) cross-examined; (iii) re-examined.

When the case is called on, or at any time during the trial, the court at the request of either party may order the witnesses, or such as have not been examined, to leave the court until called for, in order that each may be examined out of the hearing of the others. If the order be disobeyed the witness may be punished for his contempt, but his evidence cannot be rejected, though it may be made the subject of comment to the jury by the judge.[44]

Examination-in-chief must be confined to matters in issue or directly relevant to the issue.

In examination-in-chief and re-examination **leading questions** are not as a rule permitted, *i.e.* questions so framed as to suggest

---

[35] Theft Act 1968, s. 30 (3). [36] *Leach* v. *R.* [1912] A.C. 305.
[37] Amended by the Theft Act 1968, Sched. 3.
[38] These arise under the following enactments: (i) the Sexual Offences Act 1956, s. 39; (ii) the Infant Life (Preservation) Act 1929, s. 2 (5); (iii) the Children and Young Persons Act 1933, s. 15; (iv) the National Assistance Act 1948, s. 51, amended by the Ministry of Social Security Act 1966, Sched. 8 (persistent refusal to maintain self or any person whom he is liable to maintain); (v) the Mental Health (Scotland) Act 1960, s. 96; the foregoing have been added by those Acts to the Schedule to the Act of 1898; (vi) the Criminal Justice Administration Act 1914, s. 28 (3) (bigamy), the foregoing Acts containing provisions exactly similar to those of the Act of 1898.
[39] Criminal Evidence Act 1898, s. 4 (1), as amended.
[40] *Ibid.* s. 1. The defence includes both the accused and co-accused.
[41] *Ibid.* s. 1 (*c*). As regards offences mentioned in footnote 38, *supra*, the consent of the accused is *not* required: *ibid.* s. 4 (1).
[42] *Leach* v. *R., supra.*
[43] *Supra.*
[44] Arch. para. 1372.

to the witness what answer is required. A witness must give his own account of what he saw or heard or of any transaction as to which he speaks. If, therefore, the question is what a witness saw or heard, he should be asked: " What did you see? " or " What did you hear? " If he is asked: " Did you see such-and-such? " or " Did you hear such-and-such? " the question is a leading one and objection may be taken to it.

Leading questions are, however, permitted (i) in matters which are undisputed or merely introductory; (ii) to identify persons or things; (iii) in order to obtain a direct contradiction of a fact sworn to by another witness.[45] An improper leading question should always be objected to by counsel on the other side before the witness has time to answer it.

A witness must speak only of matters within his own knowledge and recollection; he cannot therefore read his evidence but he may refresh his memory by reference to any memorandum if (i) made at or about the time of the fact to which it refers, and (ii) either made by himself or seen by him when the facts were fresh in his mind and then recognised to be correct.[46] A tape recording used by a police officer to record conversations may be used by the officer to refresh his memory.[47] Records of conversations obtained by telephone tapping may be admissible in the same way.[48] The opposite party may see any such memorandum and cross-examine upon such parts as are referred to without making them evidence against him, but if he examines on any other parts they become evidence against him.[49]

A party may not discredit his own witness by giving general evidence of his bad character, but he may contradict him by other

---

[45] *Ibid.* para. 1378.

[46] *Lau Pak Ngam* v. *The Queen* [1966] Crim.L.R. 443. Nor is there any objection to a witness refreshing his memory from a previous statement made near to the date of the offence before giving evidence: *R.* v. *Richardson* [1971] 2 Q.B. 484. An *expert* witness may refer to works published by others in order to refresh his memory or correct his opinion. See the *Sussex Peerage Case* (1844) 11 Cl. & Fin. 185 at p. 117.

[47] *R.* v. *Mills and Rose* [1962] 1 W.L.R. 1152. Great caution must be exercised in the admission of such recordings: *R.* v. *Ali and Hussain* [1966] 1 Q.B. 688; particularly where it is contended that the recording is not the original, or has been fabricated: *R.* v. *Stevenson & Others* [1971] 1 W.L.R. 1. See *R.* v. *Robson, R.* v. *Harris* [1972] 1 W.L.R. 651, *post* p. 638.

[48] *R.* v. *Senat, R.* v. *Sin* (1968) 52 Cr.App.R. 282.

[49] *Gregory* v. *Tavernor* (1833) 6 C. & P. 280.

relevant evidence,[50] and if the witness is, in the opinion of the judge, hostile, he may, by leave of the judge, prove that he has made at other times a statement inconsistent with his present testimony, but before such last-mentioned proof can be given, the circumstances of the statement must be mentioned to the witness and he must be asked whether or not he made it.[51] If the previous inconsistent statement is proved, then the judge must warn the jury not only that the witness is unreliable, but that the previous statement does not constitute evidence on which they can act,[52] *unless* it amounts to an admission.

The object of **cross-examination** is (i) to obtain from the witness admissions as to any part of the case of the cross-examining party, (ii) to diminish the weight of the evidence given by the witness by showing that it is inaccurate, improbable or contradictory, or that he himself is not worthy of belief.

An accused person is at liberty to cross-examine a co-accused or any witness (not called by him) whether or not the evidence given by the witness is adverse to his case.[52a]

As a general rule a witness should be cross-examined upon any part of his evidence which is intended to be disputed, the failure to cross-examine being usually considered as an acceptance of the evidence.[53] Thus, if a witness has given an account of a conversation or transaction, and the cross-examining counsel intends to challenge its accuracy by calling evidence to the contrary, he should put to the witness his own client's version of the conversation or transaction in order to give him the opportunity of admitting or denying it. Any fact which an accused person intends to prove as part of his case should also be put to those witnesses for the prosecution whom it affects, in order to give them an opportunity of denying it. Incautious cross-examination may, however, let in evidence of matters not admissible in the first instance, as, *e.g.* of parts of a memorandum which have *not* been referred to by a

---

[50] *Ewer* v. *Ambrose* (1825) 4 B. & C. 25. That is to say, if one witness gives evidence contrary to what is expected, the party calling him is not precluded from improving his case by other witnesses.

[51] Criminal Procedure Act 1865, s. 3. The word " adverse " means that the witness is hostile, not merely that he gives unfavourable evidence: *Greenough* v. *Eccles* (1859) 5 C.B.(N.S.) 786.

[52] *R.* v. *Golder* [1960] 1 W.L.R. 1169; approved in *R.* v. *Oliva* [1965] 1 W.L.R. 1028. This applies whether the previous statement is sworn or unsworn.

[52a] See *R.* v. *Hilton* [1972] 1 Q.B. 421 where the authorities are considered.

[53] *R.* v. *Hart* (1932) 23 Cr.App.R. 202. This obviously does not apply in cases where a party is representing himself.

witness, or of a conversation which would otherwise have been excluded. Leading questions are permissible in cross-examination.[54]

The weight of the evidence given by a witness depends upon his knowledge of the facts and his truthfulness; accordingly cross-examination is not limited to matters in issue or directly relevant to the issue, but may extend to any matters which affects the credibility of the witness, who may accordingly be asked any question which:

(1) Tests his sources of knowledge in relation to the facts of which he has spoken, his reasons for believing the facts to be as he has stated, the circumstances attending their occurrence, as, *e.g.* whether it was light or dark, whether he was near or distant when it occurred, and what opportunities he had for observation; his powers of memory and judgment; or

(2) Impeaches his credit by showing: (i) his interest, bias or partiality [55]; (ii) that he has on other occasions made statements inconsistent with his present testimony [56]; (iii) that he is of bad general reputation or that he has at any time been convicted of any indictable offence.[57]

In cross-examination which goes to the matter in issue, it is not improper for counsel to put questions suggesting fraud, misconduct or the commission of any criminal offence (even though he is not able or does not intend to exercise the right of calling affirmative evidence to support or justify the imputation they convey) if he is satisfied that *the matters suggested are part of his client's case* and has no reason to believe that they are only put forward for the purpose of impugning the witness's character. Questions which affect the credibility of a witness by attacking his character, but are not otherwise relevant to the actual inquiry, ought not to be

---

[54] *Parkin* v. *Moon* (1836) 7 C. & P. 408 at p 409.

[55] *Thomas* v. *David* (1836) 7 C. & P. 350; *Att.-Gen.* v. *Hitchcock* (1847) 1 Ex. 91.

[56] Criminal Procedure Act 1865, ss. 4 and 5. In *R.* v. *Oyesiku* (1972) 56 Cr.App. R. 240 it was held by the Court of Appeal (Criminal Division) that if the credit of a witness is impugned on a material fact on the ground that his account is a late invention or reconstructed, an earlier statement by the witness to the same effect, if made contemporaneously at a time sufficiently early to be inconsistent with the allegation, is admissible.

[57] *Ibid.* s. 6. When an accused person gives evidence such questions may be asked him only in the special circumstances provided for by the Criminal Evidence Act 1898; *post*, pp. 629–632.

asked unless the cross-examiner has reasonable grounds for thinking that the imputation conveyed by the question is well founded
or true.[58]

An opposing witness may be contradicted by independent evidence on all matters which are directly relevant.[59] But on matters
which are relevant only as affecting his credit a witness's answers
in cross-examination cannot be contradicted by independent
evidence,[60] except:

   (i) Where he denies having previously made a statement
      inconsistent with his present evidence. Before proof of
      such a statement can be given the circumstances under
      which it was made must be mentioned to the witness,
      and he must be asked whether he did make it.[61] If the
      previous statement was in writing, and it is intended to
      contradict him by the writing, his attention must, before
      such contradictory proof is given, be called to the parts
      of the writing which are to be used for the purpose of
      contradicting him; the judge may, however, at any time
      during the trial require the production of the writing
      for his inspection and make such use of it as he may
      think fit,[62] e.g. he may call attention to other parts of
      it to which no reference has been made.[63]
  (ii) Where he denies interest, bias or partiality.[64]
 (iii) Where he denies a previous conviction for an indictable
      offence.[65]
 (iv) Where he denies a reputation for untruthfulness.[66]

---

[58] Rules approved by the Bar Council on November 6, 1950; see Arch. para.
1390.   [59] R. v. Phillips (1936) 26 Cr.App.R. 17.
[60] Harris v. Tippett (1811) 2 Camp. 637.
[61] Criminal Procedure Act 1865, s. 4.
[62] Criminal Procedure Act 1865, s. 5. Therefore, although a witness may be
cross-examined as to what he said before examining justices and for that
purpose the deposition may be put into his hands without reading it as part
of the evidence of the cross-examining party, the latter is bound by the answer
of the witness unless the deposition is put in to contradict him, and it is not
permissible to say that the deposition does contradict him unless it is so put
in: Arch. para. 1391. Even when put in, it is only evidence that the witness
is a liar. " Such use " in s. 5 means such proper use as he may think fit. It
does not entitle the judge to rule that the deposition is evidence against the
person on trial: R. v. Birch (1924) 18 Cr.App.R. 26. And see R. v. Golder
[1960] 1 W.L.R. 1169.
[63] R. v. Birch (1924) 18 Cr.App.R. 26.
[64] Thomas v. David (1836) 7 C. & P. 350.
[65] Criminal Procedure Act 1865, s. 6.
[66] R. v. Brown (1867) L.R. 1 C.C.R. 70; R. v. Gunewardene [1951] 2 K.B. 600.

In the case of rape, attempt to rape and indecent assault, the prosecutrix may be cross-examined: (i) as to her general immoral character; (ii) as to previous connections with the prisoner; (iii) as to previous connections with other men. The defence may contradict her by independent evidence of her general immoral character,[67] and of previous connections with the prisoner (which are directly relevant upon the issue of consent); but not of previous connections with other men.[68]

After a witness has been cross-examined he may be **re-examined** in order to explain any answers given by him in cross-examination. But re-examination should be strictly limited to this purpose; the re-examiner may not without the leave of the judge ask questions which he might have put and ought to have put in examination-in-chief. " I think the counsel has a right, upon re-examination, to ask all questions which may be proper to draw forth an explanation of the sense and meaning of the expressions used by the witness on cross-examination, if they be in themselves doubtful, and, also, of the motive by which the witness was induced to use those expressions; but, I think, he has no right to go further, and to introduce matter new in itself, and not suited to the purpose of explaining either the expressions or the motives of the witness." [69] Thus, a witness who has been cross-examined as to some part of a conversation may be re-examined as to all connected parts of such conversation, but not as to unconnected statements made at the same time.[70] Leading questions are not permitted in re-examination.

Privilege

Privilege from self-incrimination. A witness *other than an accused person* cannot in general be compelled to answer any question or produce any document which he swears will tend to expose him to any criminal charge, penalty or forfeiture,[71] whether

---

[67] *R.* v. *Clarke* (1817) 2 Stark. 241.
[68] *R.* v. *Riley* (1887) 18 Q.B.D. 481.
[69] *The Queen's Case* (1820) 2 B. & B. 284 at p. 297.
[70] *Prince* v. *Samo* (1838) 7 Ad. & El. 630.
[71] *R.* v. *Boyes* (1861) 1 B. & S. 311 ; *Pye* v. *Butterfield* (1864) 5 B. & S. 829. See also the Evidence Act 1851, s. 3. By the Witnesses Act 1806, it is expressly provided that a witness cannot refuse to answer merely on the ground that his answer would show that he owed a debt or would expose him to a civil action.

by virtue of English or foreign law.[72] To entitle a witness to this
" privilege of silence, the court must see from the circumstances of
the case and the nature of the evidence which the witness is called
to give that there is reasonable ground to apprehend danger to the
witness from his being compelled to answer "; if, however, " the fact
of the witness being in danger be once made to appear, great lati-
tude should be allowed to him in judging for himself of the effect of
any particular question "; but " the danger to be apprehended must
be real and appreciable." [73] If a witness, after claiming privilege, is
improperly compelled to answer, his answer cannot, on a subsequent trial for such criminal charge, be given in evidence against
him.[74] The fact that a witness answered an incriminating question
in ignorance of his privilege will not prevent his answer from being
used in evidence, either in the case in which it was given, or in
subsequent criminal proceedings against him.[75] By some statutes,
however, it is provided that a witness cannot refuse to answer
questions as to certain matters on the ground that they would
incriminate him, but that his answers shall not be admissible against
him in criminal proceedings arising out of the same.[76]

As regards an *accused person* who gives evidence it is provided,
by **section 1 (e)** of the **Criminal Evidence Act 1898,** that he may be
asked any question in cross-examination notwithstanding that it
would tend to criminate him as to the offence charged.[77] But one
of two persons jointly charged is entitled to give evidence not
merely on his own behalf, but for the defence generally. If, however, he gives evidence on behalf of his co-accused, he may be
cross-examined to show his own guilt [78]; if he gives evidence on his
own behalf only, he may be cross-examined to incriminate his co-
accused [79]; if he gives evidence incriminating his co-accused, he
may be cross-examined as to his own guilt.[80]

---

[72] Provided the existence of the foreign law is established or admitted: *U.S.A.*
v. *M'Rae* (1867) L.R. 3 Ch. 79. But see *Re Atherton* [1912] 2 K.B. 251 at
pp. 255–256.
[73] *R.* v. *Boyes* (1861) 1 B. & S. 311 at p. 330; approved in *Ex p. Reynolds*
(1882) 20 Ch.D. 294.
[74] *R.* v. *Garbett* (1847) 2 C. & K. 474.
[75] *R.* v. *Coote* (1873) L.R. 4 P.C. 599.
[76] See, *e.g.* the Bankruptcy Act 1914, s. 166 amended by the Theft Act 1968,
Sched. 2.
[77] *i.e.* tend to connect him with the commission of the offence charged: *Jones*
v. *Director of Public Prosecutions* [1962] A.C. 635 at p. 663.
[78] *R.* v. *Rowland* [1910] 1 K.B. 458.
[79] *R.* v. *McFarlane* [1920] 2 K.B. 183.
[80] *R.* v. *Hadwen* [1902] 1 K.B. 882.

By **section 1 (f)** of the Act, however, the accused may not be asked, and, if asked, may not be required to answer,[81] any question tending to show that he has committed or been convicted of or been charged with [82] any offence other than that wherewith he is then charged, or is of bad character,[83] *except in the following specified circumstances* [84]:

(1) Where the proof that he has committed or been convicted [85] of another offence is admissible evidence to show that he is guilty of the offence wherewith he is charged.[86] This permits the accused to be cross-examined as to the other offence where it is relevant to the offence charged as evidence of similar facts.[87]

(2) Where he has personally or by his advocate asked questions of the witnesses for the prosecution with a view to establishing his own good character, or has given evidence of his good character.[88]

The accused, however, does not put his good character in evidence by mere assertions of innocence or repudiation of guilt, nor by giving reasons for such assertion or repudiation.[89] So it was held that this exception did not operate where prosecution witnesses were asked questions with a view to negative fraudulent intent on the part of the accused.[90] But *any* direct reference by the accused to his good character is usually sufficient to permit cross-examina-

---

[81] The judge should stop such questions himself without waiting for counsel for the accused to object; and, if the question has been put, tell the jury to disregard it: *R.* v. *Ellis* [1910] 2 K.B. 746 at p. 764.

[82] *i.e.* charged before a criminal court and not merely suspected or accused without prosecution: *Stirland* v. *Director of Public Prosecutions* [1944] A.C. 315 at pp. 323–324.

[83] The expression "tending to show" means "to reveal to the jury for the first time"; so if, for example, the accused has already made known in his examination-in-chief that he has committed or been convicted of or charged with another offence, or is of bad character, then cross-examination on the same matter will not be prohibited by s. 1 (*f*): *Jones* v. *Director of Public Prosecutions* [1962] A.C. 635 at pp. 659, 663, 689.

[84] A question prohibited by s. 1 (*f*) is *not* permissible under s. 1 (*e*) on the ground that it is relevant to the offence charged, as tending to incriminate the accused: *Jones* v. *Director of Public Prosecutions* at pp. 658, 662, 682; but see at pp. 668, 701. Even if the question be permissible it must be relevant to an issue before the jury or to the accused's credibility as a witness: *Maxwell* v. *Director of Public Prosecutions* [1935] A.C. 309 at p. 321. Note that the whole of s. 1 (*f*) is subject to s. 16 (2) of the Children and Young Persons Act 1963 which enacts that an accused person of or over the age of 21 cannot be asked about offences of which he was found guilty while under the age of 14.

[85] *Not* charged and acquitted: *R.* v. *Cokar* [1960] 2 Q.B. 207.

[86] s. 1 (*f*) (i).

[87] As to similar fact evidence generally, see *ante*, p. 599.

[88] s. 1 (*f*) (ii).   [89] *R.* v. *Ellis* [1910] 2 K.B. 746.

[90] *Ibid.* but see *R.* v. *Samuel* (1956) 40 Cr.App.R. 8.

tion. Thus statements that the accused attended Mass regularly,[91] or had been earning an honest living for a long time,[92] have been sufficient to put his character in issue; but where a defence witness volunteers a statement as to the accused's character the prosecution are not entitled to cross-examine the witness as to the accused's true character.[93]

Once the accused has put his character in issue he is to be regarded as putting the *whole* of it in issue. " He cannot assert his good conduct in certain respects without exposing himself to inquiry about the rest of his record, so far as this tends to disprove a claim for good character." [94]

(3) Where the nature or conduct of the defence is such as to involve imputations on the character of the prosecutor or the witnesses for the prosecution.[95]

There is no general rule [96] that where the nature of the defence necessarily involves the imputation the judge's discretion should be exercised in favour of the defendant.[97]

Whenever counsel for the prosecution proposes to cross-examine the accused as to his character he should make an express application for leave to the judge before so proceeding.[98] The judge may feel in his discretion that the questions relating to the character of the accused " immeasurably outweigh " the result of questions by the defence and make a fair trial impossible. On the other hand in the ordinary and normal case he may feel that if the character of the prosecutor and his witnesses has been attacked the jury should have the material before them on which they can form a judgment whether the accused is more worthy of belief.[99] Nor should questions be put in such a way as may involve the accused inadvertently attacking the character of a prosecution witness [1]; or admitting that he has been in prison or committed perjury.[2]

[91] *R.* v. *Ferguson* (1909) 2 Cr.App.R. 250.
[92] *R.* v. *Baker* (1912) 7 Cr.App.R. 252.
[93] *R.* v. *Redd* [1923] 1 K.B. 104.
[94] *Stirland* v. *Director of Public Prosecutions* [1944] A.C. 315 at p. 327 but see *R.* v. *Thompson* [1966] 1 W.L.R. 405.
[95] s. 1 (*f*) (ii). The object of cross-examination under this subsection is really to affect the credit of the accused. See, *e.g. R.* v. *Vickers* [1972] Crim.L.R. 101.
[96] As was suggested in *R.* v. *Flynn* [1963] 1 Q.B. 729 at p. 737.
[97] *Selvey* v. *Director of Public Prosecutions* [1970] A.C. 304.
[98] *R.* v. *McLean* (1926) 19 Cr.App.R. 104.
[99] See *R.* v. *Jenkins*, 31 Cr.App.R. 1 at p. 15; approved in *Selvey* v. *D.P.P.* (*supra*).   [1] *R.* v. *Eidinow* (1932) 23 Cr.App.R. 145.
[2] *R.* v. *Haslam* (1916) 12 Cr.App.R. 10.

(4) Where he has given evidence against any other person charged with the same offence.[3]

Before an accused can be cross-examined under this exception by a co-accused [4] or the prosecution, the co-accused must be charged *with the same offence*.[5]

Since one accused is not a competent witness for the prosecution against a co-accused,[6] the evidence against a co-accused can only arise during the examination-in-chief or cross-examination of the accused when giving evidence on his own behalf. He cannot be said to have given such evidence simply because his version of the facts disagrees with that of his co-prisoner [7]; evidence against a co-accused means evidence which supports the prosecution's case against a co-accused in a material respect or which undermines the defence of the co-accused.[8] The test is an objective one, *i.e.* what is the effect of the evidence on the jury, and in this respect it is irrelevant that the evidence against the co-accused was not given with any hostile intent, or that it was given reluctantly.[9]

Once it is established that the accused has given evidence against a co-accused, the trial judge has no discretion, but is bound to allow cross-examination by the co-accused.[10] However, where it is the prosecution who wish to question the accused, the judge does have a discretion to refuse such cross-examination.[11]

Marital communications. All communications between a husband and wife made during the marriage are privileged from disclosure.[12] The privilege can only be claimed by the spouse to whom the communication was made; and there is no rule of law

---

[3] s. 1 (*f*) (iii).

[4] *R.* v. *Hadwen* [1902] 1 K.B. 882.

[5] See *R.* v. *Roberts* [1936] 1 All E.R. 23 ; *R.* v. *Meek* [1967] Crim.L.R. 44 and *R.* v. *Russell* [1971] 1 Q.B. 151.

[6] *Ante*, p. 621.

[7] *R.* v. *Stannard* [1965] 2 Q.B. 1.

[8] *Murdoch* v. *Taylor* [1965] A.C. 574 at p. 592 but see *R.* v. *Hoggins* (1967) 51 Cr.App.R. 444.

[9] *Murdoch* v. *Taylor* (*supra*) at p. 590.

[10] *Murdoch* v. *Taylor, supra* ; *R.* v. *Stannard, supra* ; *R.* v. *Ellis* [1961] 1 W.L.R. 1064.

[11] *Murdoch* v. *Taylor* [1965] A.C. 574 at p. 593.

[12] Criminal Evidence Act 1898, s. 1 (*d*) ; Evidence Amendment Act 1853, s. 3 and see Theft Act 1968, s. 30: By virtue of s. 16 (3) of the Civil Evidence Act 1968 this provision applies now only in relation to criminal proceedings.

which prevents the communication being disclosed in evidence by someone other than the spouse witness.[13]

The privilege only subsists *during the marriage,* so a communication made during the marriage is not privileged from disclosure where the marriage has been determined by death or dissolution.[14]

Professional privilege. Professional privilege protects from disclosure in evidence documents and communications of two kinds:

(1) *Confidential communications between a client and his legal adviser, whether made directly or through an agent.* It is the client's privilege and it is the duty of his legal adviser to claim it; but the client may waive the privilege by authorising disclosure, in which case the communication is admissible in evidence. The privilege in this case exists whether or not any litigation is pending, and applies to communications between client and solicitor, whether the relationship is existing or in contemplation, in respect of all matters within the ordinary scope of the latter's professional employment, *e.g.* the sale or purchase of property.[15] But it does not extend to everything learnt by a legal adviser in the course of his dealing with his client, but only to confidential communications made for the purpose of obtaining his advice.[16] Thus a solicitor may be compelled to disclose collateral matters which have incidentally come to his knowledge, such as his client's address,[17] or name,[18] or matters which occurred at the execution of a deed which he attested.[19]

(2) Confidential communications made or documents called into existence for the purpose of providing or obtaining information, advice or legal assistance *with reference to existing or contemplated litigation.*[20] In this case the privilege is not limited to communications between a person and his legal adviser, but extends to communications between either of them and a third party[21] or to

---

[13] *Rumping* v. *Director of Public Prosecutions* [1964] A.C. 814. As to disclosure *otherwise than in evidence before a court,* see *Argyll* v. *Argyll* [1967] Ch. 302.
[14] *Shenton* v. *Tyler* [1939] Ch. 620.
[15] *Minter* v. *Priest* [1930] A.C. 558.
[16] *Wheeler* v. *Le Marchant* (1881) 17 Ch.D. 675.
[17] *Ex p. Campbell* (1870) L.R. 5 Ch. 703.
[18] *Bursill* v. *Tanner* (1885) 16 Q.B.D. 1 at p. 5.
[19] *Crawcour* v. *Salter* (1881) 18 Ch.D. 30 at p. 36.
[20] *Wheeler* v. *Le Marchant, supra,* at pp. 681, 685.
[21] *M'Corquodale* v. *Bell* (1876) 1 C.P.D. 471.

documents made by a third party; provided that, in each case, they were made for the purposes of the litigation.[22]

The privilege does not, however, in either case, extend to communications made *in furtherance of* any criminal or fraudulent purposes.[23] And it extends only to legal advisers, including their clerks; it does not apply to communications to or from medical advisers or clergymen.[24]

There is no privilege entitling a journalist to refuse to disclose the name of an informant.[25]

Corroboration

As a general rule a jury is entitled to act upon the evidence of a single witness as to a particular fact, and there is no requirement that such evidence must be corroborated, *i.e.* confirmed or supported by further independent evidence. However, in certain circumstances corroborative evidence is required.

When corroboration is required. Corroborative evidence may be required either by statute or the common law.

Certain statutes require corroboration by providing that:

(1) the evidence of two or more witnesses is necessary before the accused can be convicted of a particular offence[26];

(2) no person shall be convicted of an offence under the Act *solely* upon the evidence of one witness as to a particular fact[27];

(3) no person shall be convicted of an offence under the Act upon the evidence of one witness unless the witness is corroborated in some material particular by evidence implicating the accused: **Sexual Offences Act 1956, ss. 2–4, 22** and **23,** relating to the procuration of women and girls for prostitution;

(4) no person shall be convicted of an offence where unsworn evidence of a child is given[28] on behalf of the prosecution unless

---

[22] *Anderson* v. *Bank of British Columbia* (1876) 2 Ch.D. 644.

[23] *R.* v. *Cox and Railton* (1884) 14 Q.B.D. 153 and as to the interest and duty of a Crown Department to prosecute offenders see *Butler* v. *Board of Trade* [1971] Ch. 680.

[24] *Wheeler* v. *Le Marchant, supra.*

[25] *Mulholland and Foster* v. *Att.-Gen.* [1963] 2 Q.B. 477.

[26] See, *e.g.* the Places of Religious Worship Act 1812; the Representation of the People Act 1949, s. 146 (5), which deals with impersonation at elections.

[27] The Perjury Act 1911, s. 13; Road Traffic Regulation Act 1967, s. 78A inserted by the Road Traffic Act 1972, s. 203 (2), and see *Nicholas* v. *Penny* [1950] 2 K.B. 466.

[28] In accordance with the provisions of the Children and Young Persons Act 1933, s. 38; *ante,* p. 619.

that evidence is corroborated by some other material evidence implicating the accused: **Children and Young Persons Act 1933, s. 38 (1).**

Even where corroboration is not required by statute a judge may in his discretion warn the jury in certain circumstances that it would be dangerous to rely upon the uncorroborated evidence of a witness, but that nonetheless they are perfectly entitled to do so. It is now established that in the following circumstances the judge *must* so warn the jury [29]:

(1) Where there is evidence given on behalf of the prosecution against the accused by an *accomplice*.[30] Accomplices are witnesses who are (i) *participes criminis* in respect of the crime charged, *i.e.* persons actually committing, procuring or aiding and abetting an offence and persons committing, procuring or aiding and abetting a misdemeanour; (ii) handlers giving evidence at the trial for theft of those from whom they received the goods; and (iii) parties to any other crime of the accused which may be proved as similar fact evidence.[31] It has been held that the following are *not* accomplices: an agent provocateur [32]; a child victim of a sexual offence [33]; a woman upon whose immoral earnings the accused is charged with having lived [34]; and a co-accused who gives evidence which implicates the accused.[35]

It is for the judge in doubtful cases to decide whether there is any evidence tending to show that a particular witness is an accomplice, but for the jury to decide whether in fact that person is an accomplice within the above definition.[36]

---

[29] Failure to give the warning will normally mean that the conviction will be quashed on appeal, unless the Court of Appeal applies the proviso to s. 2 (1) of the Criminal Appeal Act 1968 which allows them to dismiss any appeal if no miscarriage of justice has occurred: but the proviso will not normally be invoked where there has been a failure to give the warning: *R.* v. *Trigg* [1963] 1 W.L.R. 305 at pp. 309–310; but see *R.* v. *Todd* [1964] C.L.Y. 745.

[30] *Davies* v. *Director of Public Prosecutions* [1954] A.C. 378.

[31] *Ibid.* at p. 400. As to similar fact evidence, see *ante*, p. 599.

[32] *R.* v. *Mullins* (1848) 3 Cox C.C. 526; *R.* v. *Bickley* (1909) 2 Cr.App.R. 53. See further *Brannan* v. *Peek* [1948] 1 K.B. 68 considered in *R.* v. *Murphy* [1965] N.I. 138 and in *Sneddon* v. *Stevenson* [1967] 1 W.L.R. 1051; *R.* v. *Birtles* [1969] 1 W.L.R. 1047.

[33] *R* v. *Pitts* (1912) 8 Cr.App.R. 126.

[34] *R.* v. *King* (1914) 10 Cr.App.R. 117.

[35] Since he is not a witness for the prosecution: *Davies* v. *Director of Public Prosecutions* [1954] A.C. 378 at p. 399. See *R.* v. *Stoneley* [1965] Crim.L.R. 491.

[36] *Davies* v. *Director of Public Prosecutions* [1954] A.C. 378 at p. 402; *R.* v. *Vernon* [1962] Crim.L.R. 35.

(2) Where the evidence is given by a witness who is the victim of a sexual offence.[37]

(3) Where *sworn* evidence is given by a child.[38]

What amounts to corroboration. Corroboration is independent evidence which confirms the evidence in need of corroboration in some material particular, and which implicates the accused as to the crime with which he is charged.[39] It is the duty of the judge to explain to the jury what is meant in law by corroboration,[40] and it is for the jury to decide whether or not the evidence before them does amount to corroboration.[41]

Before evidence can amount to corroboration it must be *independent* of the witness to be corroborated. Accordingly on a charge of unlawful sexual intercourse with a girl, a statement made by her to a third person after the offence, even if admissible as a complaint,[42] does not amount to corroboration of her evidence.[43] But any independent evidence will suffice, whether it be testimony of another witness; or the evidence of the accused himself[44]; or statements made by him[45]; or his similar conduct on other occasions.[46]

However, the unsworn evidence of one child cannot corroborate the sworn[47] or unsworn[48] evidence of another; but the sworn

---

[37] *R. v. Jones* (1925) 19 Cr.App.R. 40; *R. v. Freebody* (1935) 25 Cr.App.R. 69; *R. v. Burgess* (1956) 40 Cr.App.R. 144.

[38] *R. v. Campbell* [1956] 2 Q.B. 432. Unsworn evidence of a child must also be corroborated: Children and Young Persons Act 1933, s. 38 (1).

[39] *R. v. Baskerville* [1916] 2 K.B. 658 at p. 667.

[40] Unless there is no evidence capable of amounting to corroboration, because to explain the meaning in such circumstances might confuse the jury: *R. v. Fisher* [1965] 1 W.L.R. 464.

[41] Where there is evidence capable of amounting to corroboration, if believed by the jury, the judge should refer to it in general terms in his summing-up: *R. v. Goddard* [1962] 1 W.L.R. 1282 at p. 1286; doubting *R. v. Zielinski* [1950] 2 All E.R. 1114.

[42] *Ante*, p. 607.

[43] *R. v. Whitehead* [1929] 1 K.B. 99; see also *R. v. Christie* [1914] A.C. 545. Nor is silence in the face of an accusation a sufficient inference that the accused accepts the truth of a statement (except in special circumstances) *R. v. Whitehead* (*supra*); *R. v. Keeling* [1942] 1 All E.R. 507. *Hall* v. *The Queen* [1972] Crim.L.R. 34, disapproving *R. v. Feigenbaum* [1919] 1 K.B. 431. Failure to give evidence does not amount to corroboration: *R. v. Jackson* (1953) 37 Cr.App.R. 43; *R. v. Blank* [1972] Crim.L.R. 176.

[44] *R. v. Dossi* (1918) 13 Cr.App.R. 158.

[45] *R. v. Hook* (1858) Dears. & B. 606. But the fact that the accused, when charged and cautioned, did not deny the charge is not corroboration: *R. v. Whitehead, supra.*

[46] *R. v. Chitson* [1909] 2 K.B. 945; *R. v. Kennaway* [1917] 1 K.B. 25; *R. v. Lovegrove* [1920] 3 K.B. 643; see *ante*, p. 602.

[47] *R. v. E.* [1964] 1 W.L.R. 671.

[48] *R. v. Manser* (1934) 25 Cr.App.R. 18.

evidence of a child can corroborate the sworn or unsworn evidence of another child.[49]

The evidence of one accomplice cannot be corroborated by the evidence of another accomplice [50]; but the evidence of an accomplice's wife can be corroboration of her husband's testimony.[51]

SECTION 4. PROOF BY DOCUMENTARY EVIDENCE

Proof of the Execution of Documents

Public documents as a rule require no authentication.[52] The execution of a private document may be proved by calling the attesting witness, if any, or by proof of the handwriting or signatures.[53]

Handwriting may be proved (i) by the writer; (ii) by anyone who saw the document written; (iii) by anyone who has seen the party write on any other occasion [54]; (iv) by anyone who has had any opportunity of becoming acquainted with the handwriting of the party through correspondence with him or through seeing documents written by him [55]; (v) by comparison with genuine documents.[56] Where a jury is asked to make a comparison between the handwriting on two documents an expert should in general be available to help them. The Court of Appeal has expressed the view that to invite a jury to compare specimens of handwriting without expert assistance is irregular.[57] In *R.* v. *O'Sullivan* [58] however the Court realised that such a situation might be unavoidable, and contented itself with saying that a jury should never be deliberately invited or exhorted to make comparisons, and should be warned of the dangers of doing so.

---

[49] *R.* v. *Campbell* [1956] 2 Q.B. 432.
[50] *R.* v. *Noakes* (1832) 5 C. & P. 326.
[51] *R.* v. *Allen and Evans* [1965] 2 Q.B. 295.
[52] See *ante,* p. 614.
[53] Evidence Act 1938, s. 3. Where, although not required by law, a document has been attested, it is not necessary to call the attesting witnesses; and the document may be proved as if there had been no attesting witnesses: Criminal Procedure Act 1865, s. 7.
[54] *Doe* v. *Suckermore* (1837) 5 Ad. & El. 703.
[55] *Ibid.*; *R.* v. *Slaney* (1832) 5 C. & P. 213.
[56] Criminal Procedure Act 1865, s. 8.
[57] *R.* v. *Smith* (1968) 52 Cr.App.R. 648; *R.* v. *Tilley* [1961] 1 W.L.R. 1309; *R.* v. *Harden* [1963] 1 Q.B. 8. But the evidence need not be that of a *professional* expert: *R.* v. *Silverlock* [1894] 2 Q.B. 766.
[58] [1969] 2 All E.R. 237.

The following presumptions operate with regard to the execution of documents:

(1) A document purporting to be a deed, if signed and attested, is presumed to have been duly sealed and delivered.[59]

(2) Documents are presumed to have been executed on the date they bear, and (if more than one) in the proper order for effecting their purpose.[60]

(3) A document twenty years old which is produced from proper custody is presumed to be valid.[61]

(4) Alterations in a will are presumed to have been made after execution; alterations in a deed before execution.[62]

Proof of the Contents of a Document

The contents of documents must, as a rule, be proved by *primary* evidence, that is, by the production of the document itself; all evidence in substitution for the document, whether a copy or verbal evidence of its contents, is *secondary*, and, except when made admissible by statute, may not be given until the absence of the document has been accounted for; the law does not permit a man to give evidence which from its very nature shows that there is better evidence in existence.[63] The same principle appears to apply to tape recordings, where it is sought to introduce them in evidence. In *R.* v. *Robson, R.* v. *Harris*,[63a] Shaw J. held that the judge was required to do no more than satisfy himself that a prima facie for originality had been made out. He was of opinion in that case that, on the balance of probabilities, the recordings were originals and authentic and that their quality was adequate to enable a jury to form a fair assessment of the conversations recorded in them. There are no degrees of secondary evidence, and hence if any secondary evidence is admissible, all kinds are equally admissible though they may differ in weight.[64]

---

[59] *Re Sandilands* (1871) L.R. 6 C.P. 411.
[60] *Anderson* v. *Weston* (1840) 6 Bing.N.C. 296.
[61] Evidence Act 1938, s. 4. As to the meaning of proper custody, see *Meath* v. *Winchester* (1836) 3 Bing.N.C. 183.
[62] *Doe* v. *Catomore* (1851) 16 Q.B. 745.
[63] *Macdonnell* v. *Evans* (1852) 11 C.B. 930.
[63a] [1972] 1 W.L.R. 651.
[64] *Doe* v. *Ross* (1840) 7 M. & W. 102. This does not apply to any public documents with regard to which some particular kind of secondary evidence is by statute admissible in order to avoid the necessity of producing the original.

Secondary evidence is admissible in the following cases:

(1) Where the original is destroyed, or cannot be found after reasonable search,[65] or cannot conveniently be produced in court, as in the case of inscriptions on walls or tombstones.[66]

(2) Where the original is in the hands of the opposite party, who does not produce it, provided that he has been given proper notice to produce it or that notice to produce it is unnecessary.[67]

Notice to produce is unnecessary (i) where the opponent or his solicitor has the document in court [68]; (ii) where the document is a notice, as, *e.g.* a notice to the accused of an intent to charge him with being an habitual criminal [69]; (iii) where from the nature of the case the opposite party must know that he is called upon to produce the document.[70]

(3) Where the original is in the possession of a third person who is out of the jurisdiction and refuses to produce it, or being within the jurisdiction has been served with a witness summons and justifiably refuses to produce it on the ground of privilege.[71]

(4) Where the original is a *public or official document* of which some particular kind of secondary evidence is permitted by statute or rule of court.

(5) **Section 14** of the **Evidence Act 1851** provides that wherever any book or document is of such a public character as to be admissible in evidence upon its mere production from the proper custody, and no statute exists which renders its contents provable by means of a copy, its contents may be proved by an *examined copy, i.e.* a copy produced by a witness who swears that he has examined it with the original, or by a *certified copy, i.e.* a copy signed and certified by an officer who has charge of the original.

---

[65] *Brewster* v. *Sewell* (1820) 3 B. & Ald. 296.
[66] *Mortimer* v. *M'Callan* (1840) 6 M. & W. 58.
[67] *Dwyer* v. *Collins* (1852) 7 Ex. 639.
[68] *Dwyer* v. *Collins, supra.*
[69] *R.* v. *Turner* [1910] 1 K.B. 346.
[70] *R.* v. *Aickles* (1784) 1 Leach 294; *R.* v. *Elworthy* (1867) L.R. 1 C.C.R. 103 at p. 105.
[71] If the refusal is wrongful, secondary evidence is not admissible: *R.* v. *Llanfaethly* (1853) 23 L.J.M.C. 33.

CHAPTER 48

PROCEEDINGS IN THE MAGISTRATES' COURT

SECTION 1. CONSTITUTION

THE expression " magistrates' court " is defined as " any justice or justices of the peace acting under any enactment or by virtue of his or their commission or under the common law." [1]

The vast majority of criminal cases are tried in a magistrates' court. A magistrates' court must not try an information summarily except when composed of at least two justices unless the trial or hearing is one that by virtue of any enactment may take place before a single justice.[2]

The Magistrates' Courts Act 1952 makes a distinction between a petty sessional court-house and an occasional court-house.

A petty sessional court-house is a court-house or other place at which justices are accustomed to assemble for holding special or petty sessions, or which is for the time being appointed as a substitute for such court-house or place, and also any court-house or place at which any metropolitan police magistrate, or other stipendiary magistrate, is authorised by law to do any act authorised to be done by more than one justice.[3]

The justices acting for a petty sessions area not a borough may appoint as an occasional court-house any place that is not a petty sessional court-house.[4] Public notice of the appointment must be given and there may be more than one for each petty sessions area. The occasional court-house may be outside the petty sessions area for which it is appointed.[5]

---

[1] Magistrates' Courts Act 1952, s. 124 (1).

[2] s. 98 (1) of the Magistrates' Courts Act 1952. Very few Acts confer this power: see, e.g. Vagrancy Act 1824, ss. 3, 4 and the Licensing Act 1872, s. 12. See also s. 121 (1) below. A single justice may issue a summons or warrant (s. 1 (5), *ante*, p. 571) and may discharge the functions of examining justices (s. 4 (1), *post*, p. 665).

[3] Interpretation Act 1889, s. 13 (3) as amended by the Justices of the Peace Act 1968, Sched. 5.

[4] Magistrates' Courts Act 1952, s. 123 (1). In boroughs every sitting and acting of the justices at any place appointed is deemed a petty sessions; Petty Sessions Act 1849, s. 1.

[5] Magistrates' Courts Act 1952, s. 123 (2) (3).

A magistrates' court must sit in a *petty sessional court-house* for the purpose of trying summarily an information for an indictable offence, but it may try an information for an offence that is not indictable or hold an inquiry into the means of an offender,[6] or impose imprisonment when sitting in either a petty sessional court-house or an *occasional court-house.*[7] Unless there is any specific enactment to the contrary, a magistrates' court must sit in open court,[8] that is in the presence of the public, whether they are sitting as examining justices [9] or otherwise.

A magistrates' court composed of a single justice, or sitting in an occasional court-house, must not impose imprisonment for a period exceeding fourteen days or order a person to pay more than £1.[10] The justices composing the court before which any proceedings take place must be present during the whole of the proceedings, but this does not preclude a justice from absenting himself during the course of the proceedings provided that he takes no further part therein.[11] It is expressly provided that the court which sentences the accused or otherwise deals with him need not be composed of the same justices as the court which convicted him.[12]

These provisions do not apply [13] to a stipendiary magistrate sitting in a place appointed for the purpose; he is deemed to be a court of summary jurisdiction consisting of two or more justices.[14]

SECTION 2. JURISDICTION

The jurisdiction of a magistrates' court is limited territorially, by the age of the defendant, and by the category of the offence charged. A magistrates' court for a country or borough has jurisdiction to try all summary offences committed within the county or borough.[15] A magistrates' court also has jurisdiction where a person appears or is brought before the court in answer to a summons or a warrant

---

[6] For the purposes of section 44 of the Criminal Justice Act 1967.
[7] s. 98 (3), as amended by the Criminal Justice Act 1967, Sched. 6.
[8] s. 98 (4).
[9] Criminal Justice Act 1967, s. 6 (1).
[10] *Ibid.* s. 98 (5).
[11] *Ibid.* s. 98 (6).
[12] *Ibid.* s. 98 (7).
[13] Magistrates' Courts Act 1952, s. 121 (1). As amended by Administration of Justice Act 1964, Sched. 5 and the Justices of the Peace Act 1968, Sched. 5.
[14] Interpretation Act 1889, s. 13 (12) as amended by the Justices of the Peace Act 1968, Sched. 5.
[15] Magistrates' Courts Act 1952, s. 2 (1).

issued under section 1 (2) (b) of the Act [16] (which relates to the trial of a person jointly with another person who is in custody, or is being or is to be proceeded against, within the county or borough).

Where a magistrates' court is trying a person for an offence, the court also has jurisdiction to try him for any *summary* offence which could be tried by a magistrates' court for any other area.[17]

Where an offence has been committed on the boundary between two or more local jurisdictions, or within 500 yards of such boundary, or in any harbour, river, arm of the sea or other water lying between two or more local jurisdictions, the offence may be treated as having been committed in any of those jurisdictions [18]; and an offence begun in one local jurisdiction and completed in another may be treated as having been wholly committed in either.[19] Where an offence has been committed on any person, or on or in respect of any property, in or on a vehicle [20] or vessel engaged on any journey or voyage through two or more local jurisdictions, the offence may be treated as having been committed in any of those jurisdictions; and where the side or any part of a road or any water along which the vehicle or vessel passed in the course of the journey or voyage forms the boundary between two or more jurisdictions, the offence may be treated as having been committed in any of those local jurisdictions.[21]

Where any district within which any court has jurisdiction is situate on the coast of any sea, or abuts on any bay, river, etc., such court has jurisdiction over any vessel on, or lying or passing off that coast, or in such bay, etc., and over all persons thereon as if the vessel or persons were within the limits of the original jurisdiction of the court.[22]

A person who aids, abets, counsels or procures the commission by another person of a summary offence may be tried (whether or not he is charged as a principal) either by a court having jurisdiction to try that other person or by a court having, by virtue of his own offence, jurisdiction to try him.[23]

---

[16] *Ante*, p. 572.
[17] Criminal Justice Act 1967, s. 28.
[18] s. 3 (1) of the Magistrates' Courts Act 1952.
[19] *Ibid*. s. 3 (2).
[20] Not merely the unlawful use of the vehicle: *Wardhaugh (A. F.) Ltd.* v. *Mace* [1952] W.N. 305.
[21] *Ibid*. s. 3 (3).
[22] Merchant Shipping Act 1894, s. 685.
[23] Magistrates' Courts Act 1952, s. 35. Amended by the Tokyo Convention Act 1967, s. 1 (3).

"When a crime is committed in England a secondary party (accessory or abettor) can be punished even though he was not within British territorial jurisdiction at the time when the crime was committed or when he gave his assistance, at least if he is a citizen of the United Kingdom." [24]

A statute may also specifically provide that a summary offence created by that statute can be dealt with in some other jurisdiction than that in which it was committed, *e.g.* Poaching Prevention Act 1862.

Conduct which would constitute a summary offence if committed in England is not an offence if committed below the high-water mark in the absence of statutory provision. Section 3 of the Continental Shelf Act 1964,[25] section 7 of the Oil in Navigable Waters Act 1971, sections 8 and 10 of the Mineral Working (Offshore Installations) Act 1971, make exceptions, respectively, for conduct on installations over the continental shelf.[26-27] Whereas section 685 of the Merchant Shipping Act 1894 is merely concerned with venue and does not extend the ambit of the criminal law, section 686, which is dealt with later [28] in relation to trials on indictment, provides that when a British subject commits an offence abroad, and then in due course comes within the jurisdiction of a court sitting within the United Kingdom, then that court has jurisdiction to try him provided that the necessary preconditions laid down in the section are fulfilled.

There are a number of statutes creating summary conviction offences for conduct in territorial waters, on the high seas and even in other countries.[29] If the statute does not specifically deal with venue (*i.e.* which magistrates' court has jurisdiction to try the offence), the courts will find that it has impliedly created a jurisdiction for any magistrates' court to try it.[30]

---

[24] Prof. Glanville Williams, quoted with approval in *R.* v. *Robert Millar (Contractors) Ltd.* [1970] 2 Q.B. 54.

[25] *Post*, p. 694.

[26-27] *Ibid.*

[28] *Post*, p. 693; see *e.g. R.* v. *Liverpool Justices, ex p. Molyneux* [1972] 2 W.L.R. 1033.

[29] See *e.g.* Merchant Shipping Act 1894; Salmon and Freshwater Fisheries Act 1923; Representation of the People Act 1949; Wireless Telegraphy Act 1949; Protection of Birds Act 1954; Marine, etc., Broadcasting (Offences) Act 1967.

[30] *R.* v. *Kent Justices, ex p. Lye* [1967] 2 Q.B. 153. As a matter of convenience the justices of the area " opposite " the commission of any offence committed off the coast should take jurisdiction: *ibid.*

By **section 46 (1)** of the **Children and Young Persons Act 1933** [31] charges against a child or young person may not be heard by a court of summary jurisdiction which is not a juvenile court except in certain specified cases. [32]

In the case of indictable offences triable summarily and offences triable either on indictment or summarily, a magistrates' court has jurisdiction over any such offence committed by a person who appears or is brought before the court, whether or not the offence was committed within the county or borough. [33]

The provisions of section 3 of the Continental Shelf Act 1964, section 7 of the Oil in Navigable Waters Act 1971, sections 8 and 10 of the Mineral Working (Offshore Installations) Act 1971, and section 686 of the Merchant Shipping Act 1894, [34] apply to this category of offences. The indictable offence of making a false statutory declaration contrary to section 5 of the Perjury Act 1911, which is triable summarily, may be committed by making such a declaration in any place outside England. [35]

Limitations on the right to prosecute. As in the case of indictable offences, the consent of the Attorney-General or the Director of Public Prosecutions may be required before the proceedings are instituted. For example, the consent of the Attorney-General is required to institute proceedings under section 3 of the Criminal Justice Act 1967, which makes it an offence to report committal proceedings. [36]

Whereas in the case of most indictable offences there is no limitation of time preventing the institution of proceedings, there is such a limitation for most summary conviction offences. Except as otherwise expressly provided, a magistrates' court shall not try an information unless the information was laid within six months from the time when the offence was committed. [37] Although this applies to offences which are both indictable and summary when tried summarily, it does not apply to indictable offences which are tried summarily.

[31] Amended by the Education Act 1944, Sched. 9, Justices of the Peace Act 1949, Sched. 7, Children and Young Persons Act 1969, Sched. 5. See also the Children and Young Persons Act 1963, s. 18.
[32] See *post*, pp. 683, 684.
[33] Magistrates' Courts Act 1952, s. 2 (3).
[34] At p. 693.   [35] Perjury Act 1911, s. 8.
[36] *Post*, p. 665.
[37] Magistrates' Courts Act 1952, s. 104.

Ouster of jurisdiction. Where a dispute as to title over real property or interests in real property arises in a magistrates' court, the court has no jurisdiction to determine the dispute as a general rule, but this rule does not preclude the court from trying offences under the Criminal Damage Act 1971 or any other offences of destroying or damaging property.[38] If the offence is only a summary offence, no further criminal proceedings may be taken until the dispute is settled.[39] If the offence is triable on indictment, *e.g.* an assault, then the justices should proceed as examining justices.[40]

The following statement of the rule is taken from *Russell on Crime* [41] :

" (i) It is a presumption of the common law. . . .

 (ii) It is sometimes confirmed in statutes; for example in section 46 of the Offences against the Person Act 1861.

(iii) The purpose or language of a statutory provision may be such as necessarily to exclude the rule. . . .

(iv) The scope of the rule is restricted to disputes as to rights in real property. . . .

 (v) The justices may not adjudicate upon title to land, but it is for them, in the first instance, to decide whether, in the case before them, there is in fact a dispute as to title to land. . . .

(vi) . . . The defendant must do more than make a mere assertion that such a dispute is before them . . . There must be some show of reason in the claim. . . .

(vii) The application of the principle of ouster is not affected by the absence or existence of an honest belief by the defendant that he was justified in acting as he did, nor is the question of *mens rea* relevant . . . The use of such phrases as a ' bona fide claim of right ' is misleading and has caused much confusion in some cases. . . .[42]

(viii) . . . Where a defendant's case is seen to rest upon a contention that he has some right to land which the law does

---

[38] Criminal Damage Act 1971, s. 7 (2).

[39] See *Burton* v. *Hudson* [1909] 2 K.B. 564.

[40] See *R.* v. *Holsworthy Justices, ex p. Edwards* [1952] 1 All E.R. 411.

[41] Appendix 2. Footnotes omitted and footnote below added.

[42] See for example *White* v. *Feast* (1872) L.R. 7 Q.B. 353, where it was held, on an interpretation of s. 14 (1) of Criminal Justice Administration Act 1914 (repealed by the Criminal Damage Act 1971) that the jurisdiction of the court was ousted when a fair and reasonable claim was made out.

not recognise, it is plain that there is no dispute as to title upon which the court is called to adjudicate. . . ."

An example of (viii) might be a claim by a defendant, charged with unlawful fishing,[43] that, as a member of the public, he had a right to fish in a non-navigable river from the bank. Although members of the public may be allowed to fish in such a river with the consent of the owner, in the absence of such consent (which may be removed at any time), the law of real property does not recognise that they have any right of fishery. So the claim by a defendant to such a right would be so without merit that jurisdiction would not be ousted.[44] If, on the other hand, the defendant claimed that the owner of the fishery had executed a deed granting him the right to fish and, for example, the effect of the deed were disputed, the jurisdiction of the court would be ousted.

SECTION 3. CATEGORIES OF OFFENCES

Subject to one exception,[45] all offences are either tried summarily by a magistrates' court or tried on indictment, that is at the Crown Court with a jury. Before a person can be tried on indictment, he must, as a general rule,[46] be committed for trial by a magistrates' court. The process of deciding whether a person should be committed for trial is a "preliminary inquiry," sometimes called "committal proceedings."

Offences may be classified as follows:

1. Those more serious matters, triable on indictment only;
2. Indictable offences triable summarily in certain circumstances—"the schedule offences";
3. Those triable either summarily or on indictment—"hybrid offences";
4. Those summary offences triable in certain circumstances on indictment;
5. Summary offences.

Until recently, legislation, setting out the definition of, or the punishment for, any serious offences used the expressions "felony"

---

[43] Contrary to Theft Act 1968.

[44] See *Hudson* v. *Macrae* (1863) 4 B. & S. 585.

[45] Contempt of court may be tried summarily in any court having jurisdiction over the contempt (see further *ante*, p. 177). For another exception, see *post*, p. 703.

[46] There are exceptions, see *post*, p. 703.

or " misdemeanour " to describe them. Since the Criminal Law
Act 1967 these expressions have become obsolete. Modern legislation, *e.g.* Misuse of Drugs Act 1971, Firearms Act 1968, refers only
to offences as being punishable (i) on indictment, or (ii) summarily
or (iii) either on indictment or summarily. All offences which were,
before the passing of the 1967 Act, either felonies or misdemeanours
may now be described as " indictable offences."

Of the five categories listed above, there is no difficulty with
indictable offences or summary offences. The other categories must,
however, be examined further.

Indictable offences which may be tried summarily. Indictable
offences are serious offences and the superior courts often urge
that such offences must be dealt with on indictment.[47] Obviously,
however, there are many cases which are properly tried summarily
in a magistrates' court. In the case of those indictable offences
set out in the **First Schedule** to the **Magistrates' Courts Act 1952,**[48]
an accused person who has attained the age of seventeen may *give
his consent to summary trial*. By **section 19** [49] of the Act, if at any
time during the inquiry into the offence it appears to the court,
having regard to any representations made in the presence of the
accused by the prosecutor or made by the accused, and to the
nature of the case that the punishment that the court has power to
inflict under the section would be adequate and that the circumstances do not make the offence one of serious character and do not
for other reasons require trial on indictment, the court may proceed
with a view to summary trial.[50] For the purpose of proceeding in
this way, the court must cause the charge to be written down, if this
has not already been done, and read to the accused and must tell
him that he may, if he consents, be tried summarily instead of
being tried by a jury and, if the court thinks it desirable for his
information, may tell him before what court he would be tried if
tried by a jury and explain what is meant by being tried summarily.[51] The court must warn the accused that if he is tried

---

[47] See for recent examples, *R.* v. *Coe* [1969] 1 All E.R. 65 and *R.* v. *Everest*
(1968) 118 S.J. 820.

[48] As amended by the Obscene Publications Act 1959, s. 2 (2); the Suicide Act
1961, s. 3 (2), the Theft Act 1968, s. 29 and Sched. 3 and the Schedule to
the Criminal Damage Act 1971.

[49] Amended by the Criminal Justice Act 1967, s. 43, the Criminal Law Act 1967,
Sched. 3 and the Courts Act 1971, Scheds. 8, 11.

[50] s. 19 (2). The expedience of summary trial must be decided judicially:
R. v. *Bodmin Justices* [1947] K.B. 321.   [51] *Ibid.*, s. 19 (3).

summarily and convicted, and that if the court, on obtaining information of his character and antecedents is then of opinion that a greater punishment should be inflicted than the court has power to inflict, he may be committed to the Crown Court for sentence under **section 29** of the Act [52] in accordance with the provisions of **section 29** of the **Criminal Justice Act 1948.**[53] The accused must then be asked whether he wishes to be tried by a jury or tried summarily.

If the accused gives his consent, the court may then proceed to summary trial.[54]   Consent ought to be given by the accused himself, although where it is given in his presence and hearing by his legal representative and not contradicted, this will suffice.[55] The consent must be entered in the court register.[56]   The accused may withdraw his consent at any time before the evidence is given but not afterwards.[57]   The consent of the prosecution is not necessary except in a case affecting the property or affairs of Her Majesty or of a public body (as defined by the Public Bodies Corrupt Practices Act 1889 [58]) or in a case in which the prosecution is being carried on by the Director of Public Prosecutions.[59]

A person summarily convicted of an indictable offence is liable to imprisonment for a term not exceeding six months or a fine not exceeding £400 or both,[60] but by **section 108** of the **Magistrates' Courts Act 1952,** where two or more terms of imprisonment are

[52] As substituted by the Courts Act 1971, Sched. 8, para. 27.
[53] *Ibid.,* s. 19 (4), as amended by the Criminal Law Act 1967, Sched. 3. If this warning is not given and the accused is convicted by the magistrates' court, the conviction will be quashed: *R.* v. *Kent Justices* [1952] 2 K.B. 355.
[54] At any time before the conclusion of the prosecution's evidence, the court may resume the inquiry as examining justices but not thereafter: Criminal Justice Act 1925, s. 13 ; Magistrates' Courts Act 1952, s. 24.
[55] *R.* v. *Latham, ex p. Roberts* (1943) 41 L.G.R. 99 ; a representative may consent on behalf of a corporation but if no representative appears, consent to summary trial is not required. Magistrates' Courts Act 1952, Sched. 2, paras. 3 and 5.
[56] Magistrates' Courts Rules 1968, r. 19.
[57] *R.* v. *Craske etc.* [1957] 2 Q.B. 591 ; *R.* v. *Ibrahim* (1957) 42 Cr.App.R. 38 ; *R.* v. *Bennett* [1960] 1 W.L.R. 102 ; *R.* v. *Southampton City Justices, ex p. Briggs* [1972] 1 W.L.R. 277.
[58] The expression " public body " includes a county or borough council and local and public authorities of all descriptions: Public Bodies Corrupt Practices Act 1889, s. 7 ; Prevention of Corruption Act 1916, s. 4 (2).
[59] Magistrates' Courts Act 1952, s. 19 (7).
[60] *Ibid.,* s. 19 (6) as amended by the Criminal Justice Act 1967, s. 43 (1). But where a person is convicted of an offence of inciting to commit a summary offence, he is not liable to a greater penalty than he would have been liable to on being summarily convicted of the last-mentioned offence: *ibid.,* s. 19 (8). So also where a person is convicted of an attempt, he is not liable to a greater penalty than he would have been on conviction for the completed offence: *ibid.,* s. 19 (9).

imposed to run consecutively, the aggregate of the terms may, in certain circumstances, exceed six months but may not exceed twelve months.

By **Rule 19** of the **Magistrates' Courts Rules 1968,** where a magistrates' court, having begun to inquire into an information as examining justices, decides to proceed summarily, then unless the accused pleads guilty, the court must recall for cross-examination any witnesses who have already given evidence, except any not required by the accused or the prosecutor to be recalled for that purpose. By **section 23** of the **Magistrates' Courts Act 1952,** in such a case any evidence already given before the court shall be deemed to have been given in and for the purposes of the summary trial.[61]

The following are among the more important offences listed in the **First Schedule** to the **Magistrates' Court Act 1952** [62]:

(*a*) Offences under section 1 (1) or section 1 (1) and (3) of the Criminal Damage Act 1971 or section 2 or section 3 of that Act, except offences of arson.

(*b*) Offences under sections 20, 27, 47 and 60 of the Offences against the Person Act 1861.

(*c*) Offences under section 5 of the Perjury Act 1911, in relation to statements in statutory declarations.

(*d*) Offences under section 2 (2) (*a*) of the Forgery Act 1913, in relation to any document being an authority or request for the payment of money or for the delivery or transfer of goods and chattels, where the amount of the money or the value of the goods or chattels does not exceed one hundred pounds; or under paragraph (*a*) of section 7 of that Act, where the amount of the money or the value of the property in respect of which the offence is committed does not exceed one hundred pounds;

(*e*) Any indictable offence under the Theft Act 1968, except:
　　(i) robbery, aggravated burglary, blackmail and assault with intent to rob; and

---

[61] This does not apply to the written evidence of children admitted under Children and Young Persons Act 1963, s. 27 (see s. 27 (3) of that Act) or to the written evidence of any person admitted in evidence under the Criminal Justice Act 1967, s. 2 (see s. 2 (9) of that Act).

[62] As amended by the Criminal Justice Administration Act 1962, Sched. 3, Criminal Law Act 1967, Sched. 3; Criminal Justice Act 1967, s. 27 and Sched. 7; Criminal Law Act 1967, s. 4 (5); Obscene Publications Act 1959, s. 2 (2); the Suicide Act 1961, s. 3 (2); the Theft Act 1968, s. 29, Sched. 3; the Schedule to the Criminal Damage Act 1971 and the Criminal Justice Act 1972, s. 47.

(ii) burglary in a dwelling if entry to the dwelling or the part of it in which the burglary was committed, or to any building or part of the building containing the dwelling, was obtained by force or deception or the use of any tool, key or appliance, or if any person in the dwelling was subjected to violence or the threat of violence; and

(iii) burglary comprising the commission of, or an intention to commit an offence which is not included in the schedule; and

(iv) handling stolen goods from an offence not committed in the United Kingdom.

(*f*) Committing an indecent assault upon a person, whether male or female.

(*g*) Offences under section 4 (1) of the Sexual Offences Act 1967 (procuring others to commit homosexual acts) and section 13 of the Sexual Offences Act 1956 (gross indecency between men).

(*h*) Concealing offences contrary to section 5 (1) of the Criminal Law Act 1967.

(*i*) Assisting offenders contrary to section 4 (1) of the Criminal Law Act 1967.

(*j*) Aiding, abetting, counselling or procuring the commission of any offences listed in the Schedule, attempting to commit any such offence and attempting to commit any offence that is both an indictable offence and a summary offence.

(*k*) Any offence consisting in the incitement to commit a summary offence or to commit any offences listed in the above paragraphs.

Offences triable either on indictment or summarily. Some offences are, *by virtue of the statute creating them,* triable either on indictment or summarily, *e.g.* a number of offences under the Road Traffic Act 1972 and the Firearms Act 1968. **Section 18 (1) of the Magistrates' Courts Act 1952** [63] provides that a magistrates' court dealing with an information charging such an offence must, where the accused has attained the age of seventeen, proceed as examining justices unless the prosecutor applies to the court

[63] Amended by the Children and Young Persons Act 1969, s. 6 (2).

for the information to be tried summarily.[64] The application must be made before any evidence is called and if the accused fails to appear, may be made in his absence.[65] If the court, on the application of the prosecutor,[66] decides to proceed summarily, it may, at any time before the close of the evidence for the prosecution, discontinue the summary trial and proceed as examining justices.[67] However, even if the court does not decide to proceed summarily at this time, the court may subsequently proceed to try the case summarily if, at any time during the inquiry it appears to the court, having regard to any representations made by the prosecutor or the accused and to the nature of the case, that it is proper to do so.[68] If the court decides to proceed summarily, the court must, before asking the accused whether he pleads guilty, cause the charge to be written down, if this has not already been done, and read to him.[69] By **section 23** in such a case any evidence already given before the court shall be deemed to have been given in and for the purposes of summary trial.[70] The power under section 29 of the Act to commit to the Crown Court for sentence arises only where the accused is tried summarily under subsection (3) and not under subsection (1). Where a person is wrongly committed under subsection (1) after summary trial, the proceedings are null and void.[71]

---

[64] It is recommended that the clerk of the court should ask the prosecutor whether he is proceeding summarily: *James* v. *Bowkett* [1952] W.N. 341. If the court proceeds summarily the accused may still elect trial by jury under s. 25. But if he does elect trial by jury he may be given the sentence that he would have been given had the prosecution proceeded by indictment (*R.* v. *Gibbs* [1965] 2 Q.B. 281) and further counts may be added (*R.* v. *Roe* [1967] 1 W.L.R. 634).

[65] *Ibid.*, s. 18 (2).

[66] Normally the prosecutor is asked whether he is electing summary trial: see also *James* v. *Bowkett* [1952] W.N. 341.

[67] *Ibid.*, s. 18 (5). In all other cases, once the magistrates' court has decided to try an indictable offence summarily, it cannot thereafter proceed as examining justices: *ibid.*, s. 24.

[68] *Ibid.*, s. 18 (3). But if the prosecution is being carried on by the Director of Public Prosecutions, the court may not act under that subsection without his consent. Only if the court proceeds to try the case summarily under s. 18 (3) may the accused be committed to the Crown Court for sentence. There is no such power if the court proceeds to summary trial under s. 18 (1) (see *ibid.*, s. 29, and *R.* v. *South Greenhoe JJ.* [1950] 2 K.B. 558).

[69] *Ibid.*, s. 18 (4).

[70] See above, note 61.

[71] *R.* v. *South Greenhoe Justices, ex p. D.P.P.* [1950] 2 K.B. 558; *R.* v. *Jones (Gwyn)* [1969] 2 Q.B. 33.

Summary offences which may be tried on indictment. By **section 25 (1)** of the **Magistrates' Courts Act 1952,**[72] where a person who has attained the age of seventeen is charged before a magistrates' court with a summary offence for which he is liable, or would if he were adult be liable, to be sentenced by the court to imprisonment for a term exceeding three months, he may claim to be tried by a jury, unless the offence is an assault [73] or an offence under sections 30, 31 or 32 [74] of the Sexual Offences Act 1956, or an offence under section 5 of the Sexual Offences Act 1967. The claim can be made only by a defendant who appears in person [75] and it must be made before he pleads to the charge.[76] In any summary case where the accused has a right to claim trial by jury, the court must inform him of his right before asking him whether he pleads guilty and, if the court thinks it desirable for the information of the accused, may tell him before what court he would be tried if tried by a jury and explain what is meant by being tried summarily. The court must then ask him whether he wishes, instead of being tried summarily, to be tried by a jury.[77] The vital point is that the accused should be told that he may be tried before a jury. It is not enough to ask if he wishes to be tried summarily.[78] The caution must be put to the accused himself [79] although his answer may be given by his legal representative in his hearing [80] and this answer will be sufficient if not contradicted.[81] If the caution is not explained to the accused personally a subsequent committal for sentence will be invalid.

---

[72] As amended by the Sexual Offences Act 1956, Sched. 3, and Sexual Offences Act 1967, s. 5 (2), the Criminal Law Act 1967, Sched. 3; the Children and Young Persons Act 1969, s. 6 (2) and the Courts Act 1971, Scheds. 8 and 11.

[73] This includes an aggravated assault, such as an assault upon a police officer while in the execution of his duty: *Toohey* v. *Woolwich Justices* [1967] 2 A.C. 1.

[74] Where, however, the immoral act solicited is a homosexual act, the defendant may claim trial by jury: Sexual Offences Act 1967, s. 9.

[75] It is sufficient, however, where the defendant's legal representative elects in the presence and hearing of the defendant who does not object: *R.* v. *Salisbury and Amesbury JJ., ex p. Greatbatch* [1954] 2 Q.B. 142 but the election must be put to the accused himself.

[76] Magistrates' Courts Act 1952, s. 25 (2) and entered in the register.

[77] *Ibid.,* s. 25 (3).

[78] *R.* v. *Salisbury and Amesbury Justices, ex p. Greatbatch* [1954] 2 Q.B. 142.

[79] *R.* v. *Kettering JJ., ex p. Patmore* [1968] 1 W.L.R. 436. A caution has no application to a written plea of guilty under the Magistrates' Courts Act 1957, s. 1: *R.* v. *Bishop's Stortford Justices, ex p. Shields* [1969] Crim.L.R. 201, D.C.

[80] *Ex p. Greatbatch (supra).*

[81] *Ibid.* and see *R.* v. *Latham, ex p. Roberts* (1943) 41 L.G.R. 99.

A corporation may consent or object to summary trial by its representative, but the court may deal with the case summarily where the representative does not appear. Where a corporation is charged jointly with an individual, then, if the offence is one for which an accused has the right to claim trial by a jury, the court shall not try either of the accused summarily if the other exercises that right.[82]

A right to claim trial by jury also arises under a number of other enactments, *e.g.* the Explosives Act 1875, s. 92; the Conspiracy and Protection of Property Act 1875, s. 9; the Cruelty to Animals Act 1876, s. 15; and the Witnesses (Public Inquiries) Protection Act 1892, s. 3.[83] The procedure to be followed in these cases appears to be the same as that under section 25 of the Act of 1952.

If, under **section 25** of the Magistrates' Courts Act 1952 or any other enactment, an accused person exercises his right to be tried by a jury for a summary offence, the court must deal with the information in all respects as if it were for an indictable offence and the offence is deemed to be an indictable offence.[84]

Section 25 of the Act applies only where more than three months' imprisonment can be imposed in the first instance, not where it can be imposed in default of payment of a fine.[85] Where the offence charged is one which is punishable by more than three months' imprisonment only upon proof of previous convictions for the same offence (*e.g.* under section 33 of the Sexual Offences Act 1956), the court must explain to the accused that he may have a right to claim trial by jury and, after giving him the same information as is given in the ordinary case, must ask him whether, if he has that right, he wishes, instead of being tried summarily, to be tried by jury.[86]

Where the accused is charged with an offence that is both a summary offence for which he may claim trial by jury and an indictable offence, then, if the court, having begun under section 18 (1) to proceed as if the offence were not a summary one,

---

[82] Magistrates' Courts Act 1952, s. 36 and Sched. 2.
[83] As amended by the Courts Act 1971, Sched. 8. In the case of this offence, the prosecution may also demand trial by jury, but the demand must be made before the accused pleads (Magistrates' Courts Act 1952, s. 25 (2) (6)).
[84] *Ibid.*, s. 25 (6).
[85] *Carle* v. *Elkington* (1892) 67 L.T. 374.
[86] Magistrates' Courts Act 1952, s. 25 (4).

proceeds under section 18 (3) with a view to summary trial, it shall, before asking the accused whether he wishes to be tried by a jury, explain to him that if he is tried summarily he may be committed to the Crown Court for sentence under section 29.[87]

Where the Crown Court obtains jurisdiction by reason only of the fact that the accused has elected trial by jury under section 25, the prosecution may not in the indictment substitute another count for the original count or add other counts [88] nor may a greater sentence be imposed upon him than could have been imposed by the justices had they dealt with the case summarily.[89] Such counts can only be added if they are founded on evidence before the justices and the court of trial has an inherent jurisdiction to ensure that the defendant is not prejudiced by varying or adding counts.[90]

SECTION 4. PROCEDURE ON SUMMARY TRIAL

Where a charge or information is tried summarily in a magistrates' court, the procedure is governed partly by practice and partly by the **Magistrates' Courts Acts 1952** and **1957** and the **Magistrates' Courts Rules 1968.** The practice of magistrates' courts, in so far as the matters which are not covered by statute are concerned, is based essentially upon the practice of trials upon indictment, shorn however of those technicalities required on indictment to provide for the presence of a jury.[91]

Open court. " It is one of the essential qualities of a court of justice that its proceedings should be open to the public, and that all persons who may be desirous of hearing what is going on, if there be room in the place for that purpose—provided they do not interrupt the proceedings and provided there is no specific reason why they should be removed—have a right to be present for the purpose of hearing what is going on." [92] This requirement is made statutory by **section 98** of the **Magistrates' Courts Act 1952**

---

[87] s. 25 (5).
[88] *R.* v. *Phillips* [1953] 2 Q.B. 14, *cf.* the authorities cited in note 64 above.
[89] *R.* v. *Furlong* [1962] 2 Q.B. 161, *cf.* the authorities cited in note 64, above.
[90] *R.* v. *Nisbet* [1972] 2 Q.B. 37 in which case *R.* v. *Phillips* was not followed.
[91] Lord Parker C.J. said in *Simms* v. *Moore* [1970] 2 Q.B. 327 " Magistrates have always had an inherent power to regulate the procedure in their courts in the interests of justice and a fair and expeditious trial."
[92] *Daubney* v. *Cooper* (1829) 10 B. & C. 237.

and **section 6** of the **Criminal Justice Act 1967** which provide that a magistrates' court shall sit in open court, subject to the provisions of any enactment to the contrary.[93] No magistrates' court is however obliged to allow its proceedings to be interrupted by organised and noisy protests or disturbance. Although the court is not a court of record, and the magistrates have no power to commit for contempt, nevertheless they have power to eject such persons as conduct themselves in this manner, or even to issue a summons returnable instanter before another bench, calling upon the offenders to show cause why they should not be bound over.[94] Refusal to be bound over can be punished by imprisonment for up to six months.[95]

Appearance of parties. A party to any proceedings before a magistrate's court may be represented by counsel or solicitor.[95a] Also, it would seem that, even in a criminal case, any person, whether he be a professional man or not, may attend as a friend of either party, may take notes, may quietly make suggestions, and give advice, provided that he does not seek to take part in the proceedings as an advocate.[95b] As a general rule no trial should take place in the absence of one of the parties, and this applies particularly in a magistrates' court where there is no power to proceed in the absence of the accused unless there is express statutory authority.[95c] By **section 15** of the **Magistrates' Courts Act 1952**, where at the time and place appointed for the trial or adjourned trial of an information the prosecutor appears but the accused does not, the court may proceed in his absence or, if the information has been substantiated on oath issue a warrant for his arrest. Where the court adjourns the trial after having received any evidence, however, whether on that occasion or on a previous occasion, or after having convicted the accused under **section 13** of the **Magistrates' Courts Act 1952** or **section 1 (2)** of the **Magistrates' Courts Act 1957**,[96] the court must not issue a warrant

---

[93] See *e.g.* Official Secrets Act 1920, s. 8 (4); Criminal Justice Act 1967, s. 6; Children and Young Persons Act 1933, ss. 37 and 47 (2).
[94] See p. 177, *ante.*
[95] Magistrates' Courts Act 1952, s. 91.
[95a] Magistrates' Courts Act 1952, s. 94.
[95b] *Collier* v. *Hicks* (1831) 2 B. & Ad. 663. A dictum of Lord Tenterden C.J. approved in *McKenzie* v. *McKenzie* [1971] P. 33. (Such a person being sometimes referred to as a " McKenzie man.")
[95c] *Cf.* the position in committal proceedings. See *post*, p. 666.
[96] See p. 658, below.

unless it thinks it undesirable by reason of the gravity of the offence, to continue the trial in the absence of the accused. Nor must a warrant be issued unless the offence is punishable with imprisonment, or the court having convicted the defendant proposes to impose a disqualification from driving upon him. Of course, where a summons has been issued, the court must not begin to try the information in the absence of the accused or issue a warrant unless either it is proved to the satisfaction of the court on oath or in such other manner as may be prescribed, that the summons was served on the accused within what appears to the court to be a reasonable time before the trial or adjourned trial or the accused has appeared on a previous occasion to answer to the information.

Where a summons has been issued and the court has begun to try the information to which the summons relates, then if the defendant at any time during or after the trial, makes a statutory declaration that he did not know of the summons or the proceedings until a date specified in the declaration, being a date after the court has begun to try the information; and also within fourteen days of that date the declaration is served on the clerk to the magistrates' court, then without prejudice to the validity of the information, the summons and all subsequent proceedings are treated as void. The information is then tried again before a different bench.

Where at the time and place appointed for the trial or adjourned trial the accused appears or is brought before the court, and the prosecutor does not appear, by **section 16** of the **Magistrates' Courts Act 1952** the court may either dismiss the information or, if evidence has been received on a previous occasion, proceed in the absence of the prosecutor. If the court adjourns the trial at this stage, the accused should not be remanded in custody unless he has been brought from custody or cannot be remanded on bail by reason of his failure to enter into a recognisance or find sureties.

By **section 17** of the Act where neither the prosecutor nor the accused appears, the court may dismiss the information or, if evidence has been received on a previous occasion, proceed in their absence.

Where the defendant appears and answers the charge, a conviction will not be set aside on the ground of some defect or irregularity in the process by which he is brought before the court, provided that the magistrates had jurisdiction in respect of time and place over the offence.[97] Thus, a conviction has been held good although the accused was arrested upon a warrant which was illegal because it had not been substantiated on oath.[98] On the other hand, where the defect is one which goes to jurisdiction, such as a summons which is served after the time prescribed by statute for its service, the position is otherwise.

Information. A magistrates' court must not proceed to the trial of an information that charges more than one offence.[99] Where one accused person appears charged with two informations, they can only be heard together with his consent,[99a] otherwise they must be heard separately,[1] the court adjudicating upon the first before hearing the second.[2]

Where two accused persons are charged jointly they may apply to be tried separately,[3] but if they are tried together they can each be convicted of having committed the offence independently.[4]

Plea of guilty. If the accused appears the court must state to him the substance of the information and ask him whether he pleads guilty or not guilty.[5] If the accused pleads guilty, the court may convict him without hearing evidence.[6]

It is of the utmost importance that before a conviction is recorded on a plea of guilty, the court is satisfied that the accused intends to admit his guilt of the offence charged. A plea of guilty accompanied by words denying an essential element of the offence is really a plea of not guilty.[7] The accused may sometimes plead guilty to theft on the basis that he took the property, only to say

---

[97] *R.* v. *Hughes* (1879) 4 Q.B.D. 614.
[98] *Ibid.*
[99] Magistrates' Courts Rules 1968, r. 12.
[99a] *R.* v. *Ashbourne Justices, ex p. Maden* [1950] W.N. 51; and see *R.* v. *Dunmow Justices, ex p. Anderson* [1964] 1 W.L.R. 1039.
[1] *Brangwynne* v. *Evans* [1962] 1 W.L.R. 267.
[2] *R.* v. *Fry* (1898) 62 J.P. 457.
[3] *R.* v. *Hoggins and others* [1967] 1 W.L.R. 1223.
[4] *Director of Public Prosecutions* v. *Merriman* [1972] 3 W.L.R. 547 H.L.
[5] Magistrates' Courts Act 1952, s. 13 (1).
[6] *Ibid.*, s. 13 (3).
[7] See *R.* v. *Golathan* (1955) 79 J.P. 270; *R.* v. *Durham Quarter Sessions, ex p. Virgo* [1952] 2 Q.B. 1.

in mitigation that he thought it was his own propery, or that he was only borrowing it, or some such phrase which will indicate an intention to deny dishonesty. It is good practice, adopted in many courts, not to record a conviction until all the information is before the court.

Where the accused pleads guilty [8] there is in general no need for evidence to be given. The prosecutor outlines the facts of the case and gives an account of the antecedents of the accused person. It is usual to ask the accused whether he agrees with the facts as outlined, and whether he admits any previous convictions which have been cited. The court is also provided with copies of probation or medical reports which may be relevant to the case. The accused or his legal representative will then address the court in mitigation, and the court will then proceed to sentence.

At any time before sentence, the accused is entitled to apply to the court to change his plea from guilty to not guilty, and the court must then decide whether the interests of justice require that this is permitted.[9]

Section 1 of the **Magistrates' Courts Act 1957** provides a special procedure for a defendant to plead guilty in writing without attending the court. It is most frequently used in the case of traffic summonses but is not confined to such matters. The section provides that where a summons has been issued requiring a person to appear before a magistrates' court (other than a juvenile court) to answer an information for a summary offence, not being either (a) an offence which is also triable on indictment; or (b) an offence for which the accused is liable to be sentenced to be imprisoned for a term exceeding three months, then if

(i) the clerk of the court is notified by the prosecutor that the accused has been served with the summons accompanied by the prescribed notice containing a statement as to the effect of the

---

[8] The plea must be entered in the register: Magistrates' Courts Rules 1968, r. 54 (3).

[9] *S (an infant)* v. *Manchester City Recorder* [1971] A.C. 481. In allowing a plea of guilty to be withdrawn, a court decides that the defendant should not be bound by his confession of fact, which would otherwise have resulted in immediate conviction. The question whether the confession made by his plea of guilty has any *probative* value remains open for consideration: *R.* v. *Rimmer* [1972] 1 W.L.R. 268. Whether, in any particular case, the evidence as to the previous plea and its withdrawal should be admitted in the subsequent proceedings is a matter for the discretion of the court, considering whether it has any probative value and whether, if it has, it would exceed the prejudice to the accused: *ibid.*

section and a concise statement in the prescribed form of such facts relating to the charge as will be placed before the court by or on behalf of the prosecutor, if the accused pleads guilty without appearing before the court; and

(ii) the accused [10] has notified the clerk of the court in writing signed by him or his solicitor that he desires to plead guilty without appearing before the court,

the court may hear and dispose of the case in the absence of the accused. Any submissions made by the accused with a view to mitigation of penalty must be read to the court.[11]

The court may decide that procedure under this section is not appropriate. In these circumstances the court must adjourn for the purpose of dealing with the case as if the notification had been given.[12] If the court does so, or if, after convicting the accused under section 1, the court desires his presence in order to sentence him, the court may not issue a warrant for his arrest under **section 15** of the **Magistrates' Courts Act 1952**, nor may the trial be resumed unless the court is satisfied that the defendant has received notice of the date and place of resumption and the reasons for adjournment. If the court is so satisfied and the defendant does not appear, then a warrant under **section 15** may be issued if the provisions of that section are satisfied.[13]

Plea of not guilty. The following is a short account of the procedure laid down in the case of a plea of not guilty.

The prosecutor calls the evidence for the prosecution and before doing so may address the court.[14]

[The provisions of sections 9 and 10 of the Criminal Justice Act 1967 in relation to proof by written statements and formal admissions apply to summary trials as to trials on indictment.[15]

The provisions of section 77 of the Magistrates' Courts Act give a justice the power to secure the attendance of witnesses.[16]]

---

[10] In the case of a corporation the plea may be notified by a director or the secretary: Criminal Justice Act 1967, s. 29 (3).

[11] As to the effect of failure to observe this provision see *R.* v. *Oldham Justices, ex p. Morrissey* [1959] 1 W.L.R. 58 and *R.* v. *Davis* (1959) 43 Cr. App.R. 215.

[12] s. 1 (2) (*b*).

[13] s. 1 (3).

[14] Magistrates' Courts Rules 1968, r. 13 (1).

[15] See p. 740.

[16] See p. 743.

Evidence given before a magistrates' court must be on oath,[17] or affirmation.[18] Children of tender years may give unsworn evidence where this is permitted.[19] Undisputed plans and drawings may be proved by certificate.[20] Each witness is examined by the person calling him, or by the clerk of the court,[21] cross-examined by the other party, and if necessary re-examined.

At the conclusion of the case for the prosecution, the accused may address the court, whether or not he afterwards makes an unsworn statement or calls evidence.[22] This is for the purpose of submitting that he has no case to answer.[23]

Before the defendant gives evidence the court should advise him of his right to remain silent, or to make an unsworn statement from the dock, or to give evidence on oath or affirmation and call witnesses. Where the defendant calls evidence, he himself must be heard before his witnesses.[24]

At the conclusion of the evidence, if any, for the defence the prosecution may call evidence to rebut that evidence.[25]

In the absence of special circumstances, it is wrong for justices to allow evidence to be adduced after they have retired, and indeed probably after the defence have closed their case.[25a]

At the conclusion of the evidence for the defence and any unsworn statement which the accused may make and the evidence if any in rebuttal, the accused may address the court if he has not already done so.[26]

Either party may, with the leave of the court, address the court a second time, but where the court grants leave to one party it shall not refuse the other.[27]

Where both parties address the court twice the prosecutor shall address the court a second time before the accused does so.[28]

[17] Magistrates' Courts Act 1952, s. 78.
[18] Interpretation Act 1889, s. 3.
[19] Children and Young Persons Act 1933, s. 38.
[20] Criminal Justice Act 1948, s. 41.
[21] See *Simms* v. *Moore* [1970] 2 Q.B. 327.
[22] Magistrates' Courts Rules 1968, r. 13 (2).
[23] As to the meaning of submitting no case see *Practice Note* [1962] 1 All E.R. 448.
[24] *R.* v. *Morrison* (1911) 75 J.P. 272; *R.* v. *Smith* [1968] 1 W.L.R. 636.
[25] Magistrates' Courts Rules 1968, r. 13.
[25a] *Webb* v. *Leadbetter* [1966] 1 W.L.R. 245.
[26] Magistrates' Courts Rules 1968, r. 13.
[27] *Ibid.*
[28] *Ibid.*

Adjournment of trial. By **section 14** of the **Magistrates' Courts Act,** the court may at any time, whether before or after beginning to try an information, adjourn the trial, and may do so, notwithstanding anything in the Act, when composed of a single justice.[29] The court may when adjourning either fix the time and place at which the trial is to be resumed, or, unless it remands the accused, leave the time and place to be determined later by the court; but the trial must not be resumed at that time and place unless the court is satisfied that the parties have had adequate notice thereof. The court may, for the purpose of enabling inquiries to be made or of determining the most suitable method of dealing with the case, exercise its power to adjourn after convicting the accused and before sentencing him or otherwise dealing with him; but, if it does so, the adjournment must not be for more than four [30] weeks at a time. On adjourning the trial of an information the court may remand the accused in custody or on bail and, where the accused has attained the age of seventeen, must do so if (i) the offence is not a summary one; or (ii) the court has proceeded to summary trial under section 18 (3) of the Act [31] after having begun to inquire into the information as examining justices; and, where the court remands the accused, the time fixed for the resumption of the trial must be that at which he is required to appear or be brought before the court in pursuance of the remand.[32] The provisions of section 105 dealing with remand and the principles regarding bail (including the important provisions of section 18 of the Criminal Justice Act 1967) have already been noted.[33]

Decision of the court. The court may only convict the accused on the information or dismiss the information. There is no power to convict of a lesser offence not charged.[34] Where more than one justice is present the decision is that of the majority present and adjudicating, and the chairman has no casting vote; if the court is

---

[29] Nowadays it will be rare that a reasonable request for an adjournment will be refused: see *e.g. M (J)* v. *M (K)* [1968] 1 W.L.R. 1897.
[30] The period was increased by the Criminal Justice Act 1967, s. 30.
[31] *Ante,* pp. 650, 651.
[32] Justices may not use remand in custody as an excuse for a real, though unavowed, purpose of detaining an offender in prison: *R.* v. *Brentford Justices* (1941) 166 L.T. 57.
[33] *Ante,* p. 577 *et seq.*
[34] *Lawrence* v. *Same* [1968] 2 Q.B. 93.

equally divided, the case may be heard on a fresh information or complaint or adjourned to the next sitting, when it may be reheard before another bench. If the court declines to adjourn it must dismiss an information.

Section 14 of the **Magistrates' Courts Act 1952** gives the court power to adjourn after conviction and before sentence in order to enable inquiries to be made about the defendant.

By **section 26** of the Act,[35] if on the trial by a magistrates' court of an offence punishable on summary conviction with imprisonment, the court is satisfied that the offence has been committed by the accused, but is of opinion that an inquiry ought to be made into his physical or mental condition before the method of dealing with him is determined, the court must adjourn the case to enable a medical examination and report to be made and must remand him; but the adjournment must not be for more than for three weeks where the court remands him in custody or four weeks where he is remanded on bail. If the accused is remanded on bail, it must be a condition of the recognisance that he must undergo medical examination in such place and in such manner as may be specified in the recognisance.[36]

On the resumed hearing, the court need not be composed of the same justices who convicted the defendant.[37]

A magistrates' court may, under **section 22** of the **Criminal Justice Act 1972**,[38] with the consent of the offender, defer passing sentence on him for a specified period, not exceeding six months, for the purpose of having regard, in determining his sentence, to his conduct after conviction (including where appropriate the making by him of reparation for his offence) or to any change in his circumstances. Once deferred, sentence may not be deferred a second time. If the offender commits a further offence, then he may be brought back for sentence before the date of deferment has expired, a summons or warrant being issued to bring him before the court. A magistrates' court is not obliged to remand an offender

---

[35] Amended by the Mental Health Act 1959, Scheds. 7 and 8, the Criminal Justice Act 1967, Sched. 6 and the Children and Young Persons Act 1969, Sched. 6.

[36] 1952 Act, s. 26 (1) (3). The provisions of s. 18 (1) and (2) of Criminal Justice Act 1967 (*ante*, p. 579), do not apply to remand under this section: Criminal Justice Act 1967, s. 18 (6).

[37] Magistrates' Courts Act 1952, s. 98 (7).

[38] Not in force as at July 1, 1972.

under s. 14 (4) of the Magistrates' Courts Act 1952, when sentence is deferred.[39]

Section 26 of the **Criminal Justice Act 1967** provides that a magistrates' court shall not, in a person's absence, sentence him to imprisonment or make an order that a suspended sentence passed on him shall take effect. Nor shall any disqualification be imposed upon a person in his absence unless, pursuant to section 14,[40] the court has adjourned the trial after conviction and the defendant has been notified of the time and place for the resumption of the trial and the reasons for the adjournment.[41]

By **section 41** of the **Criminal Justice Act 1972,** a magistrates' court may vary or rescind a sentence or other order imposed or made by it when dealing with an offender,[42] provided that this power is only exercisable on the day when the sentence or order was imposed or made, or where the court comprised three or more Justices, by a court which consists of or comprises a majority of those Justices; and only by a court constituted in the same manner as the court by which the sentence or order was imposed or made.[43] Where a person has pleaded not guilty before a magistrates' court, or the court has proceeded in his absence and he is found guilty, and it subsequently appears to the court that it would be in the interests of justice that the case should be heard again by different justices, then the court may so direct,[44] subject to the same restrictions as in the case of sentence, above. Where the court gives such a direction, the finding of guilty and any sentence or other order imposed or made in consequence is of no effect, and the general powers of remand under the Magistrates' Courts Act 1952, apply.[45-46]

SECTION 5. THE PRELIMINARY INQUIRY

Where, in view of the category of the offence, or the election of the accused person, the case before the court is not to be heard summarily, an inquiry is held by the magistrates, sitting as examining justices, in order to decide whether to commit the accused for trial on indictment at the Crown Court. This inquiry is known as a

[39] s. 22 (6).
[40] *Ante*, p. 662.
[41] s. 20 (2) and (3). See also *R.* v. *Mason* [1965] 2 All E.R. 308.
[42] s. 32 (1).
[43] *Ibid.*, s. 32 (4).
[44] *Ibid.*, s. 32 (2).
[45-46] *Ibid.*, s. 32 (3).

"preliminary inquiry," and the proceedings are sometimes described as "committal proceedings."[47] Every indictable offence must be investigated in this way unless:

    (i) it is one of those offences which may be and is dealt with summarily,[48] or

    (ii) the bill of indictment is preferred by the direction of the Court of Appeal or by the direction or with the consent of a judge of the High Court[49]; or

    (iii) the bill of indictment is preferred pursuant to an order made under section 9 of the Perjury Act 1911[50] or

    (iv) the offender is committed for trial on a coroner's inquisition.[51]

It is not the duty of the examining justices to decide the guilt or innocence of the accused. "The duty of the magistrates is simply, upon hearing the evidence for the prosecution, and evidence, if it is to be adduced, on the part of the defence, to consider and decide whether there is a presumption of guilt,"[52] or whether there is "such evidence, that, uncontradicted at the trial, a reasonably minded jury would convict upon it."[53] Where the accused gives evidence for his defence at the committal proceedings, it is open to the magistrates to refuse to commit for trial, if on the whole of the evidence, they are satisfied that no reasonable jury would convict.[54]

The rules governing the procedure at the preliminary inquiry are to be found in the **Magistrates' Courts Act 1952**, the **Criminal Justice Act 1967** and the **Magistrates' Courts Rules 1968**.

---

[47] A magistrates' court before which a person is charged with an indictable offence begins to act as examining justices as soon as he appears or is brought before the court, unless the court has already determined under s. 18 of the Magistrates' Courts Act 1952, to proceed summarily: Criminal Justice Act 1967, s. 35.

[48] *Ante*, p. 646.

[49] *Post*, p. 703.

[50] *Ante*, p. 186.

[51] This procedure is only very rarely used. For the procedure see Coroners Act 1887; Coroners (Amendment) Act 1926; Coroners Rules 1953, S.I. 1953, No. 205; Coroners (Indictable Offences) Rules 1956, S.I. 1956, No. 1692, and Coroners (Indictable Offences) Rules 1965, S.I. 1965, No. 1668. See generally "Committal on Inquisition," J. D. J. Havard [1960] Crim. L.R. 44.

[52] *R.* v. *Carden* (1879) 44 J.P. 122 at p. 137 *per* Cockburn C.J.

[53] *R.* v. *Brixton Prison Governor, ex p. Bidwell* [1937] 1 Q.B. 305 *per* Swift J. approved in *Kwesi Armah* v. *Government of Ghana* [1968] A.C. 192, H.L.

[54] *Re Roberts* [1967] 1 W.L.R. 474.

By **section 2 (3)** of the **Magistrates' Courts Act 1952,** a magistrates' court for a county or borough has jurisdiction as examining justices over any offence committed by a person who appears or is brought before the court, whether or not the offence was committed within the county or borough.

By **section 6** of the Act, the court may, before beginning to inquire into an offence as examining justices, or at any time during the inquiry, adjourn the hearing, and if it does so must remand the accused in custody or on bail.[55] The court must, when adjourning fix the time and place at which the hearing is to be resumed; and the time fixed shall be that at which the accused is required to appear or be brought before the court in pursuance of the remand.

The functions of examining justices may be discharged by a single justice.[56] **Section 6** of the **Criminal Justice Act 1967,** provides that examining justices shall sit in open court except where any enactment contains an express provision to the contrary and except where it appears to them as respects the whole or any part of committal proceedings that the ends of justice would not be served by their sitting in open court.

Restrictions on reporting. Section 3 of the **Criminal Justice Act 1967,**[57] provides that it is an offence punishable on **summary conviction** [£500 *fine*][58] to publish[59] in Great Britain a written report, or to broadcast in Great Britain a report, of any committal proceedings in England and Wales containing any matter other than that permitted by subsection (4). However, a magistrates' court must order that a report may be published or broadcast if the defendant or one of the defendants so requests.[60] Where one of several defendants applies for reporting restrictions to be lifted, the magistrates must make the order and have no power to limit the reporting of the proceedings to that part of the case affecting the applicant.[61] The application may be made as soon

---

[55] *Ante*, p. 577.
[56] Magistrates' Courts Act 1952, s. 4 (1).
[57] Amended by the Children and Young Persons Act 1969, Sched. 5.
[58] Criminal Justice Act 1967, s. 3 (5). Proceedings may only be instituted with the consent of the Attorney-General: *ibid.*, s. 3 (6).
[59] The offence is only committed by the proprietors, editors or publishers of the newspaper or, where the report is broadcast, the broadcasting corporation and any person having functions relating to the programme corresponding to the editor of a newspaper: see *ibid.*, s. 3 (5).
[60] *Ibid.*, s. 3 (2).
[61] *R.* v. *Russell, ex p. Beaverbrook Newspapers Ltd.* [1969] 1 Q.B. 342.

as the defendants are before the court and does not apply to the proceeding of taking depositions only.[62] Once an order is made it cannot be subsequently revoked.[63] **Section 3 (3)** provides that it shall not be unlawful to publish or broadcast a report of committal proceedings after the court has decided not to commit for trial, or after the conclusion of the trial of the defendant, or, where there is more than one defendant, after the conclusion of the trial of the last defendant to be tried. The subsection also provides that where during the inquiry the court proceeds to try the case of one or more of the defendants summarily,[64] it shall not be unlawful to publish or broadcast as part of the report of the summary trial a report of so much of the committal proceedings containing any such matter as takes place before the determination.[65]

Committal proceedings. By **section 4 (3)** of the **Magistrates' Courts Act 1952,** evidence given before examining justices must be given in the presence of the accused, and the defence is at liberty to put questions to any witness at the inquiry but notwithstanding these provisions, by **section 45** of the **Criminal Justice Act 1972** [65a] examining justices may allow evidence to be given before them in the absence of the accused if—

    (a) they consider that by reason of his disorderly conduct before them it is not practicable for the evidence to be given in his presence; or

    (b) he cannot be present for reasons of health but is represented by counsel or a solicitor and has consented to evidence being given in his absence.

By **Rule 4 (2)** of the **Magistrates' Courts Rules 1968,** a magistrates' court inquiring into an offence as examining justices must

---

[62] R. v. *Bow Street Magistrate, ex p. Kray* [1968] 2 Q.B. 473. See also R. v. *Vincent* [1968] Crim.L.R. 405, D.C.

[63] R. v. *Blackpool Justices, ex p. Beaverbrook Newspapers Ltd.* [1972] 1 W.L.R. 95.

[64] Under Magistrates' Courts Act 1952, ss. 10, 18, 19 and Children and Young Persons Act 1969, s. 6.

[65] Any report in a newspaper, and any broadcast report, of committal proceedings in a case where publication is permitted by virtue only of s. 3 (3) of this Act, published as soon as practicable after it is so permitted is treated for the purpose of s. 3 of the Law of Libel Amendment Act 1888 (privilege of contemporaneous newspaper reports of court proceedings), and s. 9 (2) of Defamation Act 1952 (extension of the said s. 3 to broadcasting), as having been published or broadcast contemporaneously with the committal proceedings: Criminal Justice Act 1967, s. 5.

[65a] Not in force on July 1, 1972.

cause the evidence of each witness, including the evidence of the accused, but not including any witness of his merely as to character, to be put into writing; and as soon as may be after the examination of such a witness must cause his deposition to be read to him in the presence and hearing of the accused, and must cause the witness to sign the deposition. By **Rule 4 (3),** the deposition must be authenticated by a certificate signed by one of the examining justices.[66]

These provisions must be strictly complied with. Accordingly, where nothing was taken down in writing at the hearing but the witnesses were examined from statements previously made by them, copies of which were handed to the justices, it was held by the Court of Criminal Appeal that the committal of the accused for trial was unlawful, that a document purporting to be an indictment, upon which they were tried and convicted, was not an indictment at all, that their trial was therefore a nullity and that the court could either order a proper trial or quash the conviction.[67] In a later case Q was brought before examining justices on various charges of obtaining goods by false pretences and fraud. After numerous witnesses had been examined in a regular manner P was brought before the justices as a co-defendant, and it became necessary to repeat the evidence of those witnesses as it incriminated P with regard to seven charges which were subsequently contained in seven counts of an indictment against P and Q. To save time the deposition of each of those witnesses was read to him and he was asked whether it was correct. P and Q were committed for trial and P was convicted upon sixteen counts of the indictment. It was held by the Court of Criminal Appeal that so far as concerned the seven counts his conviction must be quashed.[68]

The attendance of witnesses may be enforced by summons and, in default of obedience thereto, by warrant, or if the justices are satisfied by evidence on oath that the witness will not otherwise

---

[66] Where there has been a failure by the examining magistrate to sign the depositions, the trial cannot proceed. But where some of the depositions are unsigned the trial may proceed if the evidence contained in the signed depositions justifies the committal: *R. v. Edgar and Others* (1958) 42 Cr. App.R. 192.

[67] *R. v. Gee, Bibby & Dunscombe* [1936] 2 K.B. 442.

[68] *R. v. Phillips & Quayle* [1939] 1 K.B 63. These cases, although decided on the wording of s. 17 of the Indictable Offences Act 1848 (now repealed), must still be taken to apply to the similar wording of s. 4 (3) of the 1952 Act and r. 4 (2) of the 1968 Rules.

attend, by warrant in the first instance. The justices may also summon a witness to produce any document or articles.[69] If any person refuses without just excuse to give evidence or to produce any document or articles, the justices may commit him to custody for a period not exceeding seven days.[70] These powers may be exercised in respect of any person who is in England or Wales.

By **section 1** of the **Criminal Procedure (Attendance of Witnesses) Act 1965,**[71] a magistrates' court acting as examining justices shall in respect of each witness examined by the court, other than the accused and any witness of his merely to his character, make an order,[72] called a witness order, requiring him to give evidence before the Crown Court at which the accused is to be tried. Where it appears to the court, after taking into account any representation made by the accused or prosecutor, that the attendance at the trial of any witness is unnecessary on the ground that his evidence is unlikely to be required or is unlikely to be disputed, then the court may make a conditional witness order in respect of that witness.[73]

If a conditional witness order is made the court must inform the person committed for trial of his right to require the attendance of such witness at the trial, and the steps he must take for the purpose of enforcing the witness's attendance.

Where a person without just excuse disobeys a witness order requiring him to attend before a court, he shall be guilty of contempt and may be punished summarily by *that* court as if his contempt had been committed in the face of the court. However, the maximum period of imprisonment is 3 months.[74] Further available processes to secure the attendance of witnesses will be examined later.[75]

Rule 5 of the **Magistrates' Courts Rules 1968** provides that a witness order shall be served on the witness as soon as practicable after the accused has been committed for trial; except in the case of a conditional order which shall be served on the witness imme-

---

[69] Application for process may be made by the applicant in person or by his counsel or solicitor: Magistrates' Courts Rules 1968, r. 88 (1). The Justices' Clerk may himself issue summonses: Justices' Clerks Rules 1970.
[70] Magistrates' Courts Act 1952, s. 77.
[71] As substituted by the Courts Act 1971, Sched. 8, para. 45 (1).
[72] See generally Rules 5 and 6 of the Magistrates' Courts Rules 1968.
[73] *Ibid*. s. 1 (2).
[74] *Ibid*. s. 3 (2).
[75] *Post*, p. 742.

diately after the deposition has been signed. If a witness order has been made and the court then determines not to commit the accused for trial, it shall give notice to the witness that he is no longer required to attend.[76] **Rule 6** provides for the procedure to be observed by either the prosecution or the accused to procure the attendance at trial of a witness subject to a conditional order.[77]

Section 2 of the **Criminal Justice Act 1967** provides that in committal proceedings a written statement,[78] by any person [79] shall be admissible as evidence to the extent as oral evidence to the like effect by that person,[80] if the following conditions are satisfied:

(a) the statement purports to be signed by the person who made it;

(b) the statement contains a declaration by that person to the effect that it is true to the best of his knowledge and belief and if over the age of fourteen years that he made the statement knowing that, if it were tendered in evidence, he would be liable to prosecution if he wilfully stated in it anything which he knew to be false or did not believe to be true, or if he has not attained the age of 14 years that he understands the importance of telling the truth in it [81];

(c) before the statement is tendered in evidence, a copy of the statement is given,[82] by or on behalf of the party proposing to tender it, to each of the other parties [83] to the proceedings; and

---

[76] Rule 5 (4).

[77] s. 1 (3) of the Criminal Procedure (Attendance of Witnesses) Act 1965, provides that, where a conditional witness order has been made, the court must explain to the accused how he can procure the presence at his trial of that witness if he wishes him to be present.

[78] Such a statement may be one prepared for the purpose of the proceedings from one or more original statements made by the witness: *Practice Note* [1969] 3 All E.R. 1033.

[79] The Criminal Justice Act 1972, s. 46 (1) extends this procedure to written statements made in Scotland or Northern Ireland. Section 46 (2) extends it to written statements made outside the United Kingdom but with the omission of ss. 2 (2) (b), 2 (3A) and 2 (7).

[80] Any document or object referred to as an exhibit and identified in a written statement tendered in evidence under this section shall be treated as if it had been produced as an exhibit and identified in court by the maker of the statement: *ibid*. s. 2 (6).

[81] The Children and Young Persons Act 1969, Sched. 5.

[82] Not served on him, *cf*. s. 9: A copy must also be given to the clerk of the court: Magistrates' Courts Rules 1968, r. 58 (2).

[83] It is sufficient if given to the party's solicitor: *R*. v. *Bott* [1968] 1 W.L.R. 583.

(*d*) none of the other parties, before the statement is tendered in evidence at the committal proceedings, objects to the statement being so tendered under this section.[84]

If such a statement is admitted, the provisions of the Criminal Procedure (Attendance of Witnesses Act) 1965 apply.[85]

The following requirements must also be satisfied:

(*a*) if the statement is made by a person under the age of twenty-one, it shall give his age;

(*b*) if it is made by a person who cannot read it, it shall be read to him before he signs it and shall be accompanied by a declaration by the person who so read the statement to the effect that it was so read; and

(*c*) if it refers to any other document as an exhibit, the copy given to any other party to the proceedings under paragraph (*c*) of the last foregoing subsection shall be accompanied by a copy of that document or by such information as may be necessary in order to enable the party to whom it is given to inspect that document or a copy thereof.[86]

Even though a person's written statement may be admissible, the court on its own motion or at the application of a party to the proceedings may require that person to attend and give evidence.[87]

Unless the court commits the defendant for trial by virtue of section 1 of the Criminal Justice Act 1967,[88] or the court otherwise directs, any written statement admitted into evidence shall be read aloud and where the court does so direct, an oral account of the statement shall be given.[89]

Section 89 of the **Criminal Justice Act 1967** provides that if any person in a written statement tendered in evidence by virtue of this section wilfully makes a statement material in those proceedings which he knows to be false or does not believe to be true, he commits an offence punishable on **indictment** [*Imp. 2 years and fine*]. The section also provides that the Perjury Act 1911 shall have effect as if the section were contained in that Act.

---

[84] *Ibid.* s. 2 (2).
[85] *Ibid.* s. 2 (10).
[86] *Ibid.* s. 2 (3).
[87] *Ibid.* s. 2 (4).
[88] *Post*, pp. 677–679.
[89] *Ibid.* s. 2 (5).

Section 27 (1) of the **Children and Young Persons Act 1963** provides that in any preliminary investigation inquiring into a sexual offence [90] a child shall not be called as witness for the prosecution, but any statement made in writing by or taken in writing from the child shall be admissible in evidence of any matters of which his oral testimony would be admissible. However this subsection does not apply—

(*a*) where at or before the time where such a statement is tendered in evidence the defence objects to the application of that subsection; or

(*b*) where the prosecution requires the attendance of the child for the purpose of establishing the identity of any person; or

(*c*) where the court is satisfied that it has not been possible to obtain from the child a statement that may be given in evidence under this section; or

(*d*) where the inquiry into the offence takes place after the court has discontinued to try it summarily and the child has given evidence in the summary trial.[91]

Any such statement received in evidence must be made an exhibit.[92]

Rule 4 (4) of the **Magistrates' Courts Rules 1968** provides that before a written statement is received in evidence under section 27 (1), the court must explain the effect of that subsection to the accused in ordinary language and, if the defence does not object to the application of that subsection, must inform him that he may ask questions about the circumstances in which the statement was made or taken.

By **Rule 4 (6),** after the evidence for the prosecution has been given and after hearing any submission, if any is made, the court must, unless it then decides not to commit for trial, cause the charge to be written down, if this has not already been done, and read to the accused and must explain to him its nature in ordinary language.

The court must then say to the accused [93]: " You will have an opportunity to give evidence on oath before us and to call wit-

---

[90] " Sexual offence " means any offence under the Sexual Offences Act 1956, or the Indecency with Children Act 1960, or any attempt to commit any such offence : 1963 Act, s. 27 (4).

[91] *Ibid.* s. 27 (2).

[92] Magistrates' Courts Rules 1968, r. 4 (5).

[93] *Ibid.* r. 4 (7).

nesses. But first I am going to ask you whether you wish to say anything in answer to the charge. You need not say anything unless you wish to do so. Anything you say will be taken down and may be given in evidence at your trial. You should take no notice of any promise or threat which any person may have made to persuade you to say anything. Do you wish to say anything in answer to the charge? " or words to that effect.

Whatever the accused says in answer to the charge must be put into writing, read over to him and signed by one of the examining justices and also, if the accused wishes, by him.[94] Whether or not the accused has made any statement in answer to the charge, the court must then give him an opportunity to give evidence himself and to call witnesses.[95]

Where the accused is represented by counsel or a solicitor, his counsel or solicitor must be heard on his behalf, either before or after the evidence for the defence is taken, at his discretion, and may, if the accused gives evidence himself and calls witnesses, be heard on his behalf with the leave of the court both before and after the evidence is taken.[96] Where two defence speeches are made, the prosecution is entitled to be heard immediately before counsel or the solicitor for the accused is heard the second time.[97]

Before the accused is committed, **Rule 4 (9)** requires that the court say to the accused:

> "I must warn you that if this court should commit you for trial you may not be permitted at that trial to give evidence of an alibi or to call witnesses in respect of an alibi unless you have earlier given particulars of the alibi and the witnesses. You may give these particulars now to this court or to the solicitor for the prosecution not later than seven days from the end of these committal proceedings "

or words to that effect.[98]

---

[94] The statement of the accused thus made may be given in evidence at the trial without further proof thereof; Criminal Justice Act 1925, s. 12 (4) as substituted by the Magistrates' Courts Act 1952, s. 131 and Sched. V. Such a statement forms part of the evidence for the prosecution: *R. v. Bird* (1898) 62 J.P. 760. Normally the accused will reserve his defence.

[95] *Ibid.* r. 4 (10).

[96] *Ibid.* r. 4 (11).

[97] *Ibid.*

[98] And rule 4 (13) requires the Clerk of the Court to give written notice of the relevant provision.

The court is not required to give this warning in a case where it appears that having regard to the nature of the offence with which the accused is charged it is unnecessary to do so.

By **section 7 (1)** of the **Magistrates' Courts Act 1952,** if a magistrates' court inquiring into an offence as examining justices is of opinion, on consideration of the evidence and of any statement of the accused, that there is sufficient evidence to put the accused upon trial by jury for any indictable offence, the court must commit him for trial [99]; and, if it is not of that opinion, it must, if he is in custody for no other cause than the offence under inquiry, discharge him. By **section 7 (2)** the court may commit a person for trial either (i) in custody, that is to say, by committing him to custody there to be safely kept until delivered in due course of law, or (ii) on bail, that is to say, by taking from him a recognisance, with or without sureties, conditioned for his appearance at the time and place of trial. The same principles of bail which were discussed earlier [1] apply here.

By **Rule 7** of **the Rules,** the court must, on committing any person for trial, cause to be entered in the register and must specify in the warrant of commitment or, as the case may be, in the conditions of the recognisance, the location of the Crown Court at which that person is to be tried. By **section 18 (7)** of the **Criminal Justice Act 1967,** where the court refuses to commit a person who has attained the age of seventeen on bail, it must, if he is not represented by counsel or solicitor, inform him that he may apply to a Judge of the High Court to be admitted to bail.[2]

When committing a person for trial, a magistrates' court must, by virtue of **section 7** of the **Courts Act 1971,** specify the place at which he is to be tried, and in selecting the place must have regard to:

(*a*) the convenience of the defence, the prosecution and the witnesses,

(*b*) the expediting of the trial, and

---

[99] Where the justices are equally divided in opinion they have power to adjourn the hearing for rehearing before themselves or a differently constituted tribunal: *R.* v. *Hertfordshire JJ.* [1926] 1 K.B. 191.

[1] *Ante,* p. 578. Note that the Criminal Justice Act 1967, s. 18 (*ante,* p. 579), requires the magistrate to release a person committed for trial on a summary offence, unless one of the exceptions applies.

[2] As to the powers of the Crown Court in regard to bail see *post,* p. 713, the Courts Act 1971, s. 13 (4).

(*c*) any directions given by or on behalf of the Lord Chief Justice with the concurrence of the Lord Chancellor.

For the purposes of the business of the Crown Court, the centres at which it sits are classified as:

   (i) first-tier centres, which deal with both civil and criminal cases and are served by both High Court and Circuit judges;

  (ii) second-tier centres which deal with criminal cases only but are served by both High Court and Circuit judges;

 (iii) third-tier centres which deal with criminal cases only and are served by Circuit judges only.

Directions given by the Lord Chief Justice under section 4 (5) of the Courts Act 1971,[3] and dated October 14, 1971, classify all offences, for the purpose of trial in the Crown Court as follows:

Class 1 offences, including murder, treason and offences under section 1 of the Official Secrets Act 1911, which must be tried by a High Court judge;

Class 2 offences, such as manslaughter, abortion, rape, incest, which must be tried by a High Court judge unless a particular case is released for trial by a Circuit judge or Recorder, by or on the authority of a presiding judge of a circuit;

Class 3 offences which may be listed for trial before a High Court judge, Circuit judge or Recorder and which are offences which do not fall within classes 1, 2 and 4; and

Class 4 offences, such as wounding, burglary, robbery and and a host of others, which may be tried by a High Court judge but will normally be listed for trial before a Circuit judge or Recorder.

In committing a person for trial, the directions of the Lord Chief Justice state that the magistrates' court must, if the offence or any of the offences is included in classes 1 to 3, specify the most convenient location of the Crown Court where a High Court judge regularly sits, and if the offence is in class 4, then in general, the court must specify the most convenient location of the Crown Court. However, if in the view of the justices, committing a person for trial for an offence in class 4, the case should be tried by a High

---

[3] Set out in full at p. 708, *post*.

Court judge, they must indicate their view, giving reasons, in a notice to be included with the papers sent to the Crown Court, and must then commit him to the most convenient location of the Crown Court where a High Court judge regularly sits. The following considerations should influence the justices in favour of trial by a High Court judge, namely, where:

    (i) the case involves death or serious risk to life (excluding cases of dangerous driving, or causing death by dangerous driving, having no aggravating features);

    (ii) widespread public concern is involved;

    (iii) the case involves violence of a serious nature;

    (iv) the offence involves dishonesty in respect of a substantial amount of money;

    (v) the accused holds a public position or is a professional or other person owing a duty to the public;

    (vi) the circumstances are of unusual gravity in some other respect;

    (vii) a novel or difficult point of law is likely to be involved, or a prosecution for the offence is rare or novel.

In selecting the most convenient location of the Crown Court a magistrates' court must have regard to the considerations referred to in section 7 (1) of the Courts Act 1971, and to the location or locations of the Crown Court designated by a presiding judge as the location or locations to which cases should normally be committed from their petty sessions area. If a person is committed on one occasion in respect of a number of offences, all the committals must be to the same location of the Crown Court and that location must be the one where a High Court judge regularly sits if such a location is appropriate for any of the offences.

By **section 7 (2)** of the **Courts Act 1971,** the Crown Court may still give directions, or further directions, altering the place of any trial on indictment, varying the decision of a magistrates' court or the previous decision of the Crown Court, and the defendant or the prosecutor, if dissatisfied with the place of trial as fixed by the magistrates' court, or by the Crown Court, may apply to the Crown Court for a direction, or further direction, varying the place of trial; and the Crown Court must take the matter into consideration and, as it thinks fit, comply with or refuse the application, or give a direction not in compliance with the application. An application of this nature is heard in open court.

Section 4 of the **Criminal Justice Act 1967** provides that where a person has been committed for trial or the court has decided not to commit him, the clerk of the court shall, on the day on which the committal proceedings are concluded or the next day, display in a part of the court house to which the public have access a notice—

(a) giving that person's name, address and age (if known);

(b) in a case where the court so commits him, stating the charge or charges on which he is committed and the court to which he is committed;

(c) in a case where the court dismisses the charge, describing the offence charged and stating that it has dismissed the charge.

By **section 10 (3)** of the **Children and Young Persons Act 1969,** however, such a notice must not contain the name or address of any child or young person unless the justices in question have stated that he should be mentioned in it for the purposes of avoiding injustice to him.

By **Rule 10 (2)** of the **Magistrates' Courts Rules 1968,** as soon as practicable after the committal of any person for trial, and in any case before the first day of sitting of the court to which he is committed, the clerk of the magistrates' court that committed him must send to the appropriate officer of the Crown Court [4]:

(a) the information, if it is in writing;

(b) the depositions and written statements tendered in evidence, together with a certificate authenticating the depositions and statements, and any admission of facts made for the purposes of the committal proceedings under section 10 of the Criminal Justice Act 1967 and not withdrawn;

(c) all statements made by the accused before the magistrates' court;

(d) a list of the names, addresses and occupations of the witnesses in respect of whom witness orders have been made;

(e) if the accused is committed for trial on bail, the recognisance of the accused;

---

[4] This provision is subject to s. 5 of the Prosecution of Offences Act 1879, which relates to the sending of recognisances, informations, depositions and other documents and things to the Director of Public Prosecutions.

(*f*) any recognisance entered into by any person as surety for the accused;

(*g*) a list of the documents and articles produced in evidence before the justice or treated as so produced;

(*h*) such of the documents and articles referred to in the last preceding sub-paragraph as have been retained by the justices [5];

(*i*) a certificate showing whether the accused was informed at the committal proceedings of the requirements of section 11 of the Criminal Justice Act 1967 (notice of alibi) and a record of any particulars given by him to the magistrates' court under that section;

(*j*) if the committal was under section 1 of the Criminal Justice Act 1967 (committal for trial without consideration of the evidence), a statement to that effect;

(*k*) if the magistrates' court has made an order under section 3 (2) of the Criminal Justice Act 1967 (removal of restrictions on reports of committal proceedings), a statement to that effect;

(*l*) the certificate of the examining justices as to costs of prosecution;

(*m*) if any person under seventeen is concerned in the committal proceedings, a statement whether the magistrates' court has given a direction under section 39 of the Children and Young Persons Act 1933 (prohibition of publication of certain matter in newspapers).

By **Rule 11,** the person having custody of the depositions on which any person has been committed for trial must, as soon as is practicable after application is made to him by or on behalf of the accused, supply to the accused copies of the depositions, the list of witnesses and, if the information is in writing, of the information.[6]

Section 1 committal proceedings. Section 1 of the **Criminal Justice Act 1967** provides that a magistrates' court inquiring into an offence as examining justices may, if satisfied that all the

---

[5] R. 10 (1) provides that a magistrates' court that commits a person for trial shall, unless there are reasons for not doing so, retain any documents and articles produced by a witness who is subject to a conditional witness order. As a matter of convenience all documents and articles produced by a witness who is subject to a witness order will be retained by the court.

[6] The accused is entitled, at the time of the trial, to inspect all the depositions or copies thereof without fee or reward: 6 & 7 Will. 4, c. 114, s. 4.

evidence before the court (whether for the prosecution or for the defence) consists of written statements tendered to the court under section 2 of the Act with or without exhibits, commit the defendant for trial for the offence without consideration of the contents of those statements, unless:

    (*a*) the defendant or one of the defendants is not represented by counsel or a solicitor;

    (*b*) counsel or a solicitor for the defendant or one of the defendants, as the case may be, has requested the court to consider a submission that the statements disclose insufficient evidence to put that defendant on trial by jury for the offence.[7]

The procedure for this type of committal proceedings is laid down in **Rule 3** of the **Magistrates' Courts Rules 1968.** The court must cause the charge to be written down, if this has not already been done, and read to the accused and must then ascertain whether he wishes to:

    (*a*) object to any of the prosecution statements being tendered in evidence;

    (*b*) give evidence himself or call witnesses, or

    (*c*) submit that the prosecution statements disclose insufficient evidence to put him on trial by jury for the offence with which he is charged.

If the court is satisfied that the accused, or each of them if there are more than one, do not wish to take any of those steps, and determines after receiving any written statements tendered by the prosecution and the defence, under section 2 of the Criminal Justice Act 1967, to commit the accused for trial without consideration of the evidence, then the court may say to the accused:

    " You will be committed for trial by jury, but I must warn you that at that trial you may not be permitted to give evidence of an alibi or to call witnesses in support of an alibi unless you have earlier given particulars of the alibi and of the witnesses. You may give those particulars now to this court or at any time within the next seven days to the solicitor for the prosecution "

or words to that effect.

---

[7] s. 7 (1) of the Magistrates' Courts Act 1952 (above p. 673) does not apply to such a committal: Criminal Justice Act 1967, s. 1 (2).

The court is not required to give this warning where it appears, having regard to the nature of the offence with which the accused is charged, that it is unnecessary to do so.

If the accused or any of them is not represented, or if any one of them wishes to take any of the steps open to them as above, then the proceedings revert to the conventional committal proceedings under rule 4.

Section 44 of the **Criminal Justice Act 1972** [7a] enables a person under the age of seventeen to be committed in accordance with this procedure in like manner as a person of or over that age. [8]

[7a] Not in force on July 1, 1972.
[8] Thus nullifying the decision in *R.* v. *Coleshill Justices, ex p. Whitehouse* [1971] 1 W.L.R. 1684.

CHAPTER 49

SPECIAL PROVISIONS RELATING TO JUVENILES

SPECIAL provisions apply to the trial of children and young persons. The Children and Young Persons Act 1969 takes a further step in the direction of removing children and young persons from the ambit of the Criminal Law and the criminal courts. The care proceedings introduced under that Act can hardly be dealt with in a work of this general nature, but some of the important provisions relating to the prosecution of such persons for criminal offences are dealt with in this chapter. The expression " child " means for most purposes a person under fourteen [1] and the expression " young person " means a person who has attained the age of fourteen but is under the age of seventeen.[2]

SECTION 1. ARREST AND BAIL

By **section 28 (4)** of the **Children and Young Persons Act 1969** a constable who arrests a child without warrant otherwise than for homicide, shall as soon as practicable after doing so, secure that the case is inquired into by a police officer not below the rank of inspector or by the officer in charge of a police station, and that officer, on completing the inquiry shall either release the person in question or, if he thinks that he ought to be detained further in his own interests or because of the nature of the alleged offence, shall make arrangements for his detention in a place of safety and inform him, and take such steps as are practicable to inform his parent or guardian, of his right to apply to a justice of the peace for his release. It is lawful to detain the person in question in accordance with any such arrangements, but it is not lawful for a child so arrested, unless for homicide, to be detained after the expiration of eight days beginning with the day on which he was arrested; and if during that period he applies for his release, the justice of the

---

[1] Children and Young Persons Act 1933, s. 107 (1). Children and Young Persons Act 1969, s. 70.
[2] Under Part II, Sched. 3 and ss. 27, 63, 64 and 65 of the Children and Young Persons Act 1969 it means a person under eighteen and a person who has attained eighteen and is under a care order: Children and Young Persons Act 1969, s. 70 (1).

peace shall direct that he be released forthwith unless he considers that he ought to be detained further in his own interests or because of the nature of the alleged offence.

By **section 29** of **the Act,** where a person is arrested with or without a warrant and cannot be brought immediately before a magistrates' court, then if he appears to be a child and his arrest is for homicide, or he appears to be a young person and his arrest is for any offence, the officer in charge of the police station to which he is brought, or another officer not below the rank of inspector shall forthwith inquire into the case and shall release him unless he considers that in his own interests he ought to be detained; or the officer has reason to believe that he has committed homicide or another grave crime or that his release would defeat the ends of justice, or that if he were released (where he was arrested without a warrant) he would fail to appear in answer to any charge which might be made. A person arrested in pursuance of a warrant must not be released unless he or his parent or guardian, with or without sureties, enters into a recognisance for his attendance at the hearing of the charge; and such a recognisance may be conditioned for the appearance of the guardian or parent at the hearing in addition to the person arrested. This last provision applies also to a person arrested without a warrant if the officer concerned has decided that an information should be laid in respect of an offence alleged to have been committed by him.[2a]

If the officer decides not to release the person to whom the inquiry relates he must, unless he certifies that it is impracticable to do so or that he is of so unruly a character as to make it inappropriate to do so, make arrangements for that person to be taken into the care of the local authority and detained by the authority. This legalises his detention, and the certificate must be produced at court. Such a person must be brought before a magistrates' court within seventy-two hours of the time of his arrest unless an officer not below the rank of inspector certifies to a magistrates' court that by reason of illness or accident he cannot be brought before a court within that period. Where that person is brought before a magistrates' court or a certificate is produced to the court, and the court does not proceed to inquire into the case forthwith then the court shall order that person's release, or where he was arrested in pursuance of a warrant, or the court considers that he ought in his own

[2a] Criminal Justice Act 1972, s. 43. (Not in force on July 1, 1972.)

interest to be detained, the court shall remand him. Where he is remanded otherwise than on bail, and he is not represented by solicitor or counsel, he must be informed of his right to apply to a judge in chambers, and he must be given a written notice of the reasons for remanding him.

By **section 34 (2)** of the **Children and Young Persons Act 1933**,[3] the person who arrests a child or young person must take such steps as are reasonably practicable to inform at least one of his parents or guardians.

SECTION 2. CONSTITUTION OF JUVENILE COURTS

No justice is qualified to sit as a member of a juvenile court unless he is a member of the juvenile court panel of justices for that petty sessional area.[4] The panel is chosen from justices who are specially qualified in dealing with juvenile cases.[5] With the exception of stipendiary magistrates, who are *ex officio* members of the panel, no justice may be a member of the panel after he has attained the age of sixty-five unless a special exception is made by the Lord Chancellor.[6] Each juvenile court shall consist of not more than three justices and shall include a man and a woman.[7] Special provisions have been made for London.[8]

By **section 47**[9] of the **Children and Young Persons Act 1933** a juvenile court shall not sit in a room in which sittings of a court other than a juvenile court are held if a sitting of that other court has been or will be held there within an hour before or after the sitting of the juvenile court. No person may be present at any sitting of a juvenile court except (*a*) members and officers of the court; (*b*) parties to the case, their solicitors and counsel, and witnesses and other persons directly interested in the case; (*c*) bona fide representatives of the Press; (*d*) such other persons as the court may specially authorise to be present.

By **section 49**[10] no newspaper report of any proceedings in a juvenile court[11] may reveal the name, address or school, or include

---

[3] As amended by the 1969 Act, Sched. 5.
[4] Children and Young Persons Act 1933, s. 45 and Sched. 2 (as substituted by the Children and Young Persons Act 1963).
[5] *Ibid.* and see Juvenile Courts (Constitution) Rules, S.I. 1954 No. 1711.
[6] *Ibid.* rr. 2 and 5.   [7] *Ibid.* r. 12.
[8] Children and Young Persons Act 1933, Sched. 2, as substituted.
[9] As amended by Children and Young Persons Act 1963, s. 17 (2).
[10] As amended by Children and Young Persons Act 1969, s. 10.
[11] Including any other magistrates' court or the court in which an appeal is brought: *ibid.*

any particular calculated to lead to the identification, of any child
or young person concerned in those proceedings, either as being the
person against or in respect of whom the proceedings are taken or
as being a witness, nor may any picture be published in any newspaper as being or including a picture of any such child or young
person. Any person who publishes any matter in contravention of
this section is liable on summary conviction to a fine of £50 for each
offence. The court or the Secretary of State may, however, if it is
appropriate to do so for the purpose of avoiding injustice to a child
or young person, by order dispense with the requirements of this
section in relation to him to such extent as may be specified in the
order; and thus permit names, etc., to be published.

On an appeal from a juvenile court to the Crown Court or on
the commitment by a juvenile court of a person for sentence by
such a court, the judge is assisted by two members of a juvenile
court panel, sitting as judges and not only as assessors.

Section 3. Trial of Offences

By **section 46** [12] of the **Children and Young Persons Act 1933** no
charge against a child or young person and no application whereof
the hearing is by rules made under the section assigned to juvenile
courts, is to be heard by a court of summary jurisdiction which is
not a juvenile court. But a charge made jointly against a child or
young person and a person who has attained the age of seventeen
must be heard by a court other than a juvenile court. And, where
a child or young person is charged with an offence, the charge *may*
be heard by a court other than a juvenile court if a person who has
attained the age of seventeen is charged at the same time with
aiding, abetting, causing, permitting, etc., that offence. There is
special provision [13] for the case where, in the course of proceedings
in a magistrates' court, it appears that an accused is a child or
young person. In such circumstances the court is entitled to
proceed with the hearing and determination of those proceedings.

Where the special procedure in relation to pleading guilty in
writing under section 1 of the Magistrates' Courts Act 1957 is

---

[12] As amended by the Education Act 1944, Sched. 9 and the Children and
Young Persons Act 1969, Sched. 5.
[13] s. 46 (1), proviso (c).

involved if such a notification is received and the magistrates' court has no reason to believe that the accused is a child or young person, then if he is, he shall be deemed to have attained the age of seventeen for the purpose of this section.

Section 18 of the **Children and Young Persons Act 1963,** also provides that, notwithstanding section 46, a magistrates' court which is not a juvenile court may hear an information against a child or young person if he is charged—

(a) with aiding, abetting, causing, procuring, allowing or permitting an offence with which a person who has attained the age of seventeen is charged at the same time; or

(b) with an offence arising out of circumstances which are the same as or connected with those giving rise to an offence with which a person who has attained the age of seventeen is charged at the same time.

By **section 6** of the **Children and Young Persons Act 1969,**[14] where a person under the age of seventeen appears or is brought before a magistrates' court on an information charging him with an offence, other than homicide, which is an indictable offence within the meaning of the Magistrates' Courts Act 1952, he shall be tried summarily unless either he is a young person and the offence is such as is mentioned in section 53 (2) of the Children and Young Persons Act 1933 (under which young persons convicted on indictment of certain grave crimes may be sentenced to be detained for long periods) and the court considers that if he is found guilty of the offence it ought to be possible to sentence him in pursuance of that section, or unless he is charged jointly with a person who has attained the age of seventeen and the court considers it necessary in the interests of justice to commit them both for trial. In that case, the court, if it is of opinion that there is sufficient evidence to put him on his trial, or it has power under section 1 of the Criminal Justice Act 1967 to commit him without consideration of the evidence,[15] commits him for trial on indictment in the usual way.

---

[14] Replacing the Magistrates' Courts Act 1952, ss. 20 and 21.

[15] Inserted by the Criminal Justice Act 1972, Sched. 5, which by s. 44 permits a person under the age of seventeen falling within paras. (a) or (b) of s. 6 (1) of the 1969 Act to be committed for trial under s. 1 in like manner as a person of or over the age of seventeen. (Not in force on July 1, 1972.)

The right to claim trial by jury under **section 25** of the **Magistrates' Courts Act 1952** [16] is confined to a person who has attained the age of seventeen.

Section 27 of the **Criminal Justice Act 1967** provides that where a court remands a person charged with or convicted of an offence, or commits him for trial or sentence, and he is not less than seventeen but under twenty-one, and is not released on bail, then if the court is informed by the Home Secretary that a remand centre is available for the reception of persons of his class or description, it shall commit him to the remand centre. If the court is not notified, it must commit him to prison.

By **section 23** of the **Children and Young Persons Act 1969,** where a court remands or commits for trial a child charged with homicide or remands a child convicted of homicide, or remands a young person charged with or convicted of one or more offences, or commits him for trial or sentence, and he is not released on bail, then the court must commit him to the care of a local authority in whose area it appears that he resides or in which one of the offences was committed. If, however, the court certifies that a young person is of so unruly a character that he cannot safely be committed to the care of the local authority, then if it is notified that a remand centre is available it shall commit him there, and if it is not available it must commit him to prison.

Procedure in juvenile courts. The procedure in relation to offenders tried in juvenile courts is governed by the **Magistrates' Courts (Children and Young Persons) Rules 1970.**[17-18]

Except where a child or young person is legally represented the court must allow his parent or guardian to assist him in conducting his defence and cross-examining the witnesses for the prosecution. If the parent or guardian cannot be found or cannot reasonably be required to attend, the court may for the purposes of these Rules allow any relative or other responsible person to take his place [**Rule 5**].

The court must explain to the child or young person the substance of the charge in simple language suitable to his age and

---

[16] As amended by the Children and Young Persons Act 1969, s. 6 (2).

[17-18] Part II reproduced here (Rules 5–12) is concerned with " offence " cases. Part III of the Rules relates to care proceedings and proceedings in respect of care, supervision or fit person orders ; Part IV relates to proceedings under s. 3 of the 1963 Act.

understanding [**Rule 6**] and must ask him whether he admits it [**Rule 7**].

If the child or young person does not admit the charge the court then hears the evidence of the witnesses in support of the charge who may be cross-examined by or on behalf of the child, etc. If the child or young person is not legally represented or assisted in his defence under the provisions of **Rule 5** and, instead of asking questions by way of cross-examination, makes assertions, the court must put to the witness such questions as it thinks necessary, and for this purpose may question the child in order to bring out or clear up any point arising out of such assertions [**Rule 8 (2)**].

If a prima facie case is made out, the child or young person must be told that he may give evidence or make a statement, and the evidence of any witnesses for the defence is heard [**Rule 9**].

Where the child or young person is found guilty of an offence whether after a plea of guilty or otherwise, he and his parent or guardian, if present, must be given an opportunity of making a statement. The court must also, take into consideration such information as to his general conduct, home surroundings, school record and medical history as may enable it to deal with the case in his best interests, and in particular any information furnished under section 9 of the Act, and if such information is not fully available may remand him in order to allow inquiries to be made [**Rule 10**].

The court may consider any report without it being read aloud, but if it does so the substance of it must be communicated to the child etc. [**Rule 10**].

Before finally disposing of the case or remitting it to another court the court must inform the child and his parent or guardian etc., of the manner in which it proposes to deal with the matter and allow representations to be made [**Rule 11 (1)**].

On making an order the court must explain its effect to the child etc. [**Rule 11 (2)**].

Sentencing. Provisions regarding sentencing will be dealt with later.[19]

Section 56 of the **Children and Young Persons Act 1933** [20] provides that a court before which a child or young person is found guilty of an offence other than homicide, must unless satisfied that

---

[19] *Post*, p. 799.
[20] As amended by the Children and Young Persons Act 1963, Sched. 3 and the Children and Young Persons Act 1969, Sched. 5.

it would be undesirable to do so, remit the case to a juvenile court, which may deal with him in any way in which it might have dealt with him if he had been tried and convicted there.   In the case of a magistrates' court, **section 7 (8)** of the **Children and Young Persons Act 1969** requires the court to remit a child or young person to the juvenile court unless the court decides to deal with the case, merely by an order of absolute or conditional discharge, a fine, damages or costs, an order requiring a parent or guardian to enter into recognisances, or an order of disqualification or endorsement under the Road Traffic Act 1972.

Chapter 50

TRIAL AT THE CROWN COURT—PART I

Section 1. The Indictment

A BILL of indictment is a written or printed accusation of crime made at the suit of the Queen against one or more persons.[1] It is preferred before the Crown Court by delivering the bill to the appropriate officer of the Crown Court,[2] and when signed by him becomes an indictment.

Form and contents of an Indictment. The common law rules as to the form of indictments were greatly simplified by the **Indictments Act 1915,** which also conferred upon courts wide powers of amending defects.

By **Rule 4 (1)** of the **Indictment Rules 1971,** an indictment must be in the form set out in Schedule 1 to the Rules, or in a form substantially the same. Thus:

Court of Trial ....

The Queen v. ....

Statement of Offence

Robbery, contrary to section 8 of the Theft Act 1968.

Particulars of Offence

A B on the —— day of —— robbed C D of £200.

....
Appropriate officer of the court

Where more than one offence is charged in an indictment, the statement and particulars of each offence must be set out in a separate paragraph called a count; and the counts must be numbered consecutively.

---

[1] Arch. para. 1.

[2] Indictments (Procedure) Rules 1971, r. 4 (S.I. 1971 No. 2084 (L.51)). The " appropriate officer " is any such officer as may be designated for the purpose in question by arrangements made by or on behalf of the Lord Chancellor: *ibid.* r. 2. Precedents of indictments are to be found in the Appendix, *post,* p. 865.

Thus:

First Count

Statement of Offence

Blackmail contrary to section 21 (1) of the Theft Act 1968.

Particulars of Offence

A B on the —— day of —— with a view to gain for himself or with intent to cause loss to another made an unwarranted demand upon C D for £100 with menaces.

Second Count

Statement of Offence

Theft contrary to section 1 of the Theft Act 1968.

Particulars of Offence

A B on the —— day of —— stole £100 the property of C D.

The prosecution, or the appropriate officer of the Crown Court, are entitled to require that the terms of the indictment should be settled by counsel if they think fit. Both the prosecution and the accused should be informed when an indictment contains counts which differ materially from, or are additional to, the charges upon which the accused was committed for trial. Where additional charges are preferred, based on fresh facts, which were not the subject of committal, the Court of Appeal has said that the police should see the accused as soon as it is decided to formulate the charges and caution him.[3]

A person charged on indictment must, if he so requests, be supplied by the proper officer of the court of trial with a copy of the indictment free of charge,[4] and those engaged in the defence of such a person should obtain a copy of it at the earliest possible moment.[5]

Every indictment consists of three parts: (A) the **commencement** (including the statement of the court of trial and the presentment), (B) the **statement of offence** (or statements of offences), and (C) the **particulars of offence** (or offences).

---

[3] *R.* v. *Dickson* (1969) 53 Cr.App.R. 263.
[4] Indictment Rules 1971, r. 10 (1). The cost of supplying such a copy is treated as part of the costs of the prosecution: *ibid.* r. 10 (2).
[5] *R.* v. *Dickson* (*supra*).

A. The commencement. At common law it was an important feature of the commencement that it stated the venue, that is the area or neighbourhood for which the court sat, and from which the jurors were drawn, and in which, as a rule, the offence was committed. By **section 6** of the **Courts Act 1971** all proceedings on indictment must be brought before the Crown Court, which is a single court though sitting in a number of locations. The Crown Court has thus exclusive jurisdiction in proceedings on indictment for offences wherever committed, including proceedings on indictment for offences within the jurisdiction of the Admiralty of England.[6] The common law rule that jurisdiction was local, that is that the accused had to be tried before a court having jurisdiction over the place where the offence was committed, is no longer of importance, since the Crown Court has jurisdiction throughout England and Wales. We have already examined the considerations governing the committal by examining justices to one location or another.[7]

The position when it comes to offences committed abroad is another matter. The criminal jurisdiction of the common law courts was territorial; they could not, unless by statutory authority, try a person for a crime committed abroad, even if the offence was committed by a British subject. The general rule is still, that in the absence of statutory authority, no British subject can be tried under English law for an offence committed on land abroad.[8] Of course if a person in a foreign country initiates acts which take effect in England and are criminal by English law, then such a person may be tried in England and Wales for that offence.[9] Where the appellant in Northern Ireland sent letters to firms in England containing fraudulent football pool claims, the Court of Appeal held that the English courts had jurisdiction to try him for attempting to obtain property by deception.[10] Much will depend upon the technical elements of the offence charged. It has been held that the offence of blackmail is complete when a letter sending an unwarranted demand is posted beyond recall,

---

[6] Courts Act 1971, s. 6 (2).
[7] *Ante*, p. 673.
[8] See Arch. para. 67.
[9] *R.* v. *Oliphant* [1905] 2 K.B. 67; *R.* v. *De Marny* [1907] 1 K.B. 388.
[10] *R.* v. *Baxter* (1971) 55 Cr.App.R. 214, following *R.* v. *Oliphant* (*supra*) and *R.* v. *Rogers* (1877) 3 Q.B.D. 28.

therefore if a letter is posted from England or Wales to a person abroad, the offender can be tried in England.[11]

A foreigner is not liable under English law for an offence committed on land abroad,[12] except where there is statutory authority therefor,[13] or in the case of treason, where the foreigner has previously resided within the Queen's dominions, and at the time of the treasonable act still owes allegiance to the Crown.[14] The chief offences [15] which can now be tried in England when committed abroad are piracy, whether committed by a British subject or not [16]; hijacking, whether committed by a British subject or not [17]; murder and manslaughter committed on land out of the United Kingdom by a British subject (and whether of a British subject or not) [18]; bigamy [19]; offences against the Foreign Enlistment Act 1870 [20]; the Official Secrets Acts 1911 and 1920 [21] and the Perjury Act 1911 [22]; offences by colonial governors [23] or persons employed in any public service [24]; offences committed in a foreign country by any British subject employed with Her Majesty's Government in the service of the Crown and purporting to act in the course of his employment,[25] and offences against the Unlawful Oaths Acts.[26]

---

[11] *Treacey* v. *Director of Public Prosecutions* (1971) 55 Cr.App.R. 113, H.L.

[12] Arch. para. 67. See *e.g.,* R. v. *Doot* [1972] 3 W.L.R. 33.

[13] See *e.g.* R. v. *Oliphant (supra).*

[14] *Joyce* v. *Director of Public Prosecutions* [1946] A.C. 347. As to the position where a person abroad aids and abets the commission of an offence in England, see R. v. *Millar and Another* [1970] 2 Q.B. 54.

[15] For complete list and details, see Arch. paras. 68–88.

[16] See Arch. para. 82 and *ante*, p. 158.

[17] Hijacking Act 1971, ss. 1, 2.

[18] Offences against the Person Act 1861, ss. 9, 10, as amended by the Criminal Law Act 1967, Sched. 3. Triable in any county or place in which the offender is apprehended or is in custody. For an example of the exercise of this jurisdiction in a case of murder, see R. v. *Page* [1954] 1 Q.B. 170.

[19] *Ibid.* s. 57, as amended by the Criminal Law Act 1967, Sched. 3.

[20] See ss. 16, 17. Triable where the offence was committed or where the accused is.

[21] See s. 10 of the Act of 1911.

[22] See s. 8.

[23] Governors of Plantations Act 1698, as amended by the Criminal Justice Act 1948, Sched. X, and by the Criminal Law Act 1967, Sched. 2 ; see R. v. *Eyre* (1868) L.R. 3 Q.B. 487.

[24] Criminal Jurisdiction Act 1802, s. 1, as amended by the Criminal Law Act 1967, Scheds. 2 and 3.

[25] Criminal Justice Act 1948, s. 31 (1). Triable in any place in England in which the offender is apprehended or is in custody: s. 31 (2).

[26] Act of 1797, s. 6, Act of 1812, s. 7, both as amended by the Criminal Law Act 1967, Sched. 3.

Admiralty jurisdiction.[27] The Admiralty jurisdiction referred to in section 6 (2) of the Courts Act 1971 extends over **British ships** on the high seas and in foreign rivers " within the flux and reflux of the tides and where great ships go," [28] but not over ships in English rivers, or creeks, or arms of the sea within the body of a county, except in cases of piracy [29] in respect of which the Admiralty had exclusive jurisdiction, and in cases of murder or maiming committed on ships in great rivers below the bridges, in respect of which the Admiralty jurisdiction is concurrent with that of the common law courts.[30] The jurisdiction extends to all persons on the ship, whether British subjects or foreigners.[31] For the purposes of jurisdiction over offences the area of territory may be extended by use of the royal prerogative [32] or by Parliament.[33]

Offences, other than piracy, if committed on a **foreign** ship were not at common law within the Admiralty jurisdiction,[34] but by **section 2** of the **Territorial Waters Jurisdiction Act 1878** an offence committed by any person, whether or not a British subject, on the open sea within the territorial waters [35] of Her Majesty's dominions is an offence within the Admiralty jurisdiction although committed on board or by means of a foreign ship.

---

[27] The common law courts had no jurisdiction to try offences committed at sea, because the commissions of the judges applied only to counties and the jurors were summoned only to try cases within counties. Such crimes were, however, within the jurisdiction of the Admiralty, and were originally tried in the court of the Lord High Admiral, and, from the reign of Henry VIII, by commissioners of oyer and terminer, of whom one was the judge of the Admiralty Court.

[28] *R.* v. *Anderson* (1868) L.R. 1 C.C.R. 161. " The expression ' high seas ' when used with reference to the jurisdiction of the Court of Admiralty, included all oceans, seas, bays, channels, rivers, creeks, and waters below low-water mark, and where great ships could go, with the exception only of such parts of such oceans, etc., as were within the body of some county ": *per* Lindley L.J. in *The Mecca* [1895] P. 95, quoted with approval in *R.* v. *Liverpool Justices, ex p. Molyneux* [1972] 2 W.L.R. 1033 at p. 1036. See also *R.* v. *Carr and Wilson* (1882) 10 Q.B.D. 76 and *The Tolten* [1946] P. 135.

[29] Piracy may be piracy *jure gentium*, *i.e.* robbery within the Admiralty jurisdiction, or piracy by statute, *e.g.* under the Piracy Acts. For details, see p. 157, *ante*, and Arch. paras. 3051, 3059–3066.

[30] Arch. para. 83 ; and see *R.* v. *Keyn* (1876) 2 Ex.D. 63.

[31] *R.* v. *Anderson, ubi supra* ; *R.* v. *Carr* (1882) 10 Q.B.D. 76.

[32] *R.* v. *Kent Justices, ex p. Lye* [1967] 2 Q.B. 153 ; *Post Office* v. *Estuary Radio* [1967] 1 W.L.R. 1396.

[33] Sea Fisheries Act 1883 ; Fishery Limits Act 1964 ; Wireless Telegraphy Act 1949, s. 6, as amended by the Wireless Telegraphy Act 1967, s. 9 ; Antarctic Treaty Act 1967.

[34] *R.* v. *Keyn* (1876) 2 Ex.D. 63.

[35] *i.e.* within one marine league from low-water mark (3 nautical miles): s. 7. See *R.* v. *Kent Justices, ex p. Lye* [1967] 2 Q.B. 153 for an analysis of ss. 2 and 7; and see the Mineral Workings (Offshore Installations) Act 1971.

And by **section 687** of the **Merchant Shipping Act 1894**[36] the Admiralty jurisdiction extends over all offences against property or person committed either ashore or afloat by any person, British subject *or foreigner,* who at the time of the offence is employed in any British ship, or was so employed within three months before the offence.

By **section 686** of the **Merchant Shipping Act 1894** it is further provided that any British subject who commits an offence on board any British ship on the high seas,[37] or in any foreign port, or on board any foreign ship to which he does not belong, or any person *not being a British subject* who commits an offence on a British ship, may be tried by any court of justice within the jurisdiction of which he is found (*i.e.* found to be at the time of trial), provided that he could have been tried by that court if the offence had been committed on board a British ship within the limits of its ordinary jurisdiction.

All offences within the jurisdiction of the Admiralty may now be tried at the Crown Court.[38]

By **section 1 (1)** of the **Tokyo Convention Act 1967**[39] any act or omission taking place on a *British controlled aircraft* while in flight elsewhere than in or over the United Kingdom which, if taking place in, or in a part of, the United Kingdom, would constitute an offence under the law in force in, or in that part of the United Kingdom shall constitute that offence, and by *subsection* 1 (3) for the purpose of conferring jurisdiction, any offence under the law in force in, or in a part of, the United Kingdom committed on board an aircraft in flight shall be deemed to have been committed in any place in the United Kingdom, or as the case may be, in that part, where the offender may for the time being be.

Section 2 of the **Hijacking Act 1971** goes further, in providing that where a person of *whatever nationality* does on board *any aircraft, wherever registered,* and while outside the United Kingdom, any act which, if done in the United Kingdom (or as the case may be, in England, Wales, Northern Ireland or in Scotland)

---

[36] As amended by the Criminal Law Act 1967, Sched. 3.
[37] *H.M. Advocate* v. *Cameron and Others,* 1971 S.L.T. 202, in which case Lord Cameron held that " Jurisdiction is specifically extended by s. 686 of the Merchant Shipping Act 1894 to cover persons, being British subjects, who are charged with having committed any offence on board any British ship on the high seas or in any foreign port or harbour or . . .''
[38] Courts Act 1971, s. 6 (2).
[39] Repealing s. 62 of the Civil Aviation Act 1949.

would constitute the offence of murder, attempted murder, manslaughter,[40] or assault or an offence under certain sections [41] of the Offences against the Person Act 1861, or section 2 of the Explosive Substances Act 1883, his act, if it is done in connection with the offence of hijacking committed by him or attempted by him on board that aircraft, will constitute such an offence.

By **section 3** of the **Continental Shelf Act 1964** any act or omission which (*a*) takes place on, under or above an installation in a designated area or any waters within 500 metres of such an installation; and (*b*) would if taking place in any part of the United Kingdom, constitute an offence under the law in that part, shall be treated for the purposes of that law as taking place in that part.[42]

B. The Statement of Offence. By **section 3** of the **Indictments Act 1915** " every indictment shall contain, and shall be sufficient if it contains, a statement of the specific offence or offences with which the accused person is charged, together with such particulars as may be necessary for giving reasonable information as to the nature of the charge." The section also provides that " notwithstanding any rule of law or practice, an indictment shall, subject to the provisions of this Act, not be open to objection in respect of its form or contents if it is framed in accordance with the Rules under this Act."

By **Rule 5** of the **Indictment Rules 1971,** subject only to the provisions of Rule 6 (below), every indictment must contain, and will be sufficient if it contains, a statement of the specific offence with which the accused person is charged describing the offence shortly, together with such particulars as may be necessary for giving reasonable information as to the nature of the charge. An indictment for a specific offence will not be open to objection in respect of its form if it is framed in accordance with a form of indictment for that offence for the time being approved by the Lord Chief Justice.[42a]

---

[40] Or culpable homicide in Scotland.

[41] ss. 18, 20, 21, 22, 23, 28 or 29.

[42] See also the Oil in Navigable Waters Act 1971, and the Mineral Workings (Offshore Installations) Act 1971.

[42a] None published by July 1, 1971. See Appendix.

C. Particulars of the Offence. By **Rule 6** where the specific offence with which an accused person is charged in an indictment is one created by or under an enactment, then (without prejudice to the generality of rule 5 above) the statement of offence must contain a reference to the section of, or the paragraph of the Schedule to, the Act creating the offence in the case of an offence created by a provision of an Act; the provision creating the offence in the case of an offence created by a provision of a subordinate instrument and the particulars must disclose the essential elements of the offence. Provided that an essential element need not be disclosed if the accused person is not prejudiced or embarrassed in his defence by the failure to disclose it. It is not necessary to specify or negative an exception, exemption, proviso, excuse or qualification.

By **Rule 7** where an offence created by or under an enactment states the offence to be the doing or the omission to do any one of any different acts in the alternative, or the doing of or the omission to do any act in any one of any different capacities, or with any one of any different intentions, or states any part of the offence in the alternative, the acts, omissions, capacities or intentions, or other matters stated in the alternative in the enactment or subordinate instrument may be stated in the alternative in an indictment charging the offence.

By **Rule 8** it is sufficient to describe a person whose name is not known as a person unknown.

By **Rule 9** charges for any offences may be joined in the same indictment if those charges are founded on the same facts, or form or are a part of a series of offences of the same or a similar character.

Amendment of indictments. By **section 5** of the **Indictments Act** it is provided that " where, before trial, or at any stage of a trial, it appears to the court that the indictment is defective, the court shall make such order for the amendment of the indictment as the court thinks necessary to meet the circumstances of the case, unless, having regard to the merits of the case, the required amendments cannot be made without injustice." [43]

---

[43] s. 5 (1). The order for amendment is indorsed on the indictment, which is then treated as if it had been signed by the proper officer in the amended form : s. 5 (2).

This section merely enables the court to remedy a *defect* in an indictment, as *e.g.* where a section in an Act has been repealed and re-enacted, by substituting the earlier section for the later section in a case in which the later section was not in force at the time of the offence,[44] or where an indictment charges an offence not disclosed in the depositions and fails to charge an offence which is disclosed,[45] or where the indictment charges burglary, alleging that the defendant entered a building as a trespasser and stole six keys, is amended by substituting the allegation that he entered the building as a trespasser with intent to steal, on the ground that this amendment merely corrected a misdescription of the original offence.[46] It does not enable the court to alter the substance of the charge at the end of the case for the Crown by amending a count which discloses no offence; nor does it enable the court to strike out of the indictment the name of a prisoner who has been arraigned and given into the charge of the jury.[47] But an amendment may be made even if the indictment is not bad in law on its face.[48] The section is very wide, and expressly provides for amendment at any stage of the trial. There is nothing to preclude amendment after arraignment, either by the addition of a new count or otherwise.[49] On the other hand the amendment of the indictment during the course of the trial is likely to prejudice the accused, and the longer the interval between arraignment and amendment the more likely it is that injustice will be caused. In every case it is essential to consider with great care whether the accused will be prejudiced thereby.[50] It is submitted that where a further count is added, the defendant must be called upon to plead to it, and must be put in charge of the jury on it, even if this is part way through the trial. The proper time to apply for an amendment is before the accused is arraigned.

---

[44] *R.* v. *Tuttle* (1929) 21 Cr.App.R. 85. But if there had been a *conviction* under a wrong section, the C.C.A. will quash it; see *Meek* v. *Powell* [1952] 1 K.B. 164, *per* Goddard L.C.J.

[45] *R.* v. *Martin* [1962] 1 Q.B. 221 at p. 227.

[46] *R.* v. *Norton* [1970] Crim.L.R. 282.

[47] *R.* v. *Michalski* (1955) 39 Cr.App.R. 22.

[48] *R.* v. *Pople* [1950] W.N. 420; [1950] 2 All E.R. 679.

[49] *R.* v. *Johal, R.* v. *Ram* [1972] 3 W.L.R. 210 considering *R.* v. *Martin* [1962] 1 Q.B. 221 and *R.* v. *Harden* [1963] 1 Q.B. 22. See also *R.* v. *Smith* [1950] 1 K.B. 53.   [50] *R.* v. *Johal, R.* v. *Ram* [1972] 3 W.L.R. 210.

If as a result of any amendment the court is of opinion that the postponement of the trial is expedient the court shall make such order as to its postponement as appears necessary and may in the meantime release the accused on bail.[51]

Joinder of defendants in one indictment. It is not possible to try more than one person at the same time on separate indictments.[52] However, it is possible to try more than one person at the same time on a single indictment which charges the defendants in the same count or separate defendants in separate counts. For example, A and B may be tried on a single indictment which charges in one count that A and B did assault X, or they may be tried on a single indictment which charges in one count that A assaulted X and in another count that B assaulted X.

Where two persons are jointly charged in one count of an indictment with one offence, the count, in effect, alleges against each defendant a separate offence committed on the same occasion and as part of the same transaction, the connection between the separate offences being no more than that as against each defendant not only his own physical acts but also the physical acts of the other defendant may be relied upon by the prosecution as an *actus reus* of the offence with which he is charged.[53] It is not necessary, as was suggested by the Court of Appeal in *R.* v. *Scaramanga*,[54] for the Crown, in order to secure the conviction of each defendant to prove that each was acting in concert with the other. It is sufficient to show against any and each of the defendants that either he himself did a physical act which is an essential ingredient of the offence charged, or that he helped another defendant to do such an act, and that in doing that act or in helping the other defendant to do it, he himself had the required criminal intent.[55-61]

---

[51] s. 5 (4) (5) (*post*, p. 713).
[52] *Crane* v. *Director of Public Prosecutions* [1921] 2 A.C. 299. The trial is in such a case a nullity, and a *venire de novo* must be awarded, *i.e.* a fresh jury must be summoned to re-try the case.
[53] *Director of Public Prosecutions* v. *Merriman* [1972] 3 All E.R. 42, H.L.
[54] [1963] 2 Q.B. 807 followed in *R.* v. *Parker* (1969) 53 Cr.App.R. 289 and *R.* v. *Holley* (1969) 53 Cr.App.R. 519. All these cases were overruled by the House of Lords in *Director of Public Prosecutions* v. *Merriman* where the authorities are reviewed.
[55-61] *Director of Public Prosecutions* v. *Merriman* (*supra*) approving the Australian case of *R.* v. *Fenwick* (1953) 54 S.R.N.S.W. 147.

In **R. v. Assim** [62] the Court of Criminal Appeal laid down the general rules applicable to the joinder on one indictment of several defendants for separate offences. The court said [63]:

" As a general rule it is, of course, no more proper to have tried by the same jury several offenders on charges of committing individual offences that have nothing to do with each other than it is to try before the same jury offences committed by the same person that have nothing to do with each other. Where, however, the matters which constitute the individual offences of the several offenders are upon the available evidence so related, whether in time or by other factors, that the interests of justice are best served by their being tried together, then they can properly be the subject of counts in one indictment and can, subject always to the discretion of the court, be tried together. Such a rule, of course, includes cases where there is evidence that several offenders acted in concert but is not limited to such cases.

Again, while the court has in mind the classes of case that have been particularly the subject of discussion before it, such as incidents which, irrespective of there appearing a joint charge in the indictment, are contemporaneous (as where there has been something in the nature of an affray) or successive (as in protection racket cases), or linked in a similar manner, as where two persons individually in the course of the same trial commit perjury [64] as regards the same or a closely connected fact, the court does not intend the operation of the rule to be restricted so as to apply only to such cases as have been discussed before it.

If examples are needed it is sufficient to say . . . it would be obviously irregular to charge two men in separate counts of the same indictment with burglary simply and solely

---

[62] [1966] 2 Q.B. 249.

[63] *Ibid.* at p. 261.

[64] The court purported to overrule *R.* v. *Leigh and Harrison* [1966] 1 All E.R. 687, in which Megaw J., following earlier settled authority, quashed a joint indictment for perjury. See further M. Buckley, " Joinder of Defendants in Indictments for Perjury " [1967] Crim.L.R. 162.

because they had purely by coincidence separately broken [65] into the same house at different times on the same night. . . ."

All accomplices and persons who have given assistance to offenders, contrary to section 4 of the Criminal Law Act 1967, should be tried on the same indictment as the principal.

In one case, statute has specifically authorised the joinder of defendants in one indictment. **Section 27 (1)** of the **Theft Act 1968** provides that in an indictment for handling stolen goods, any number of persons who have at different times thus handled the property or any part of it, may be charged and tried together.

Where persons jointly indicted plead not guilty, the court may order them to be tried separately if the interests of justice so require. A judge is under no duty to direct separate trials, however, unless he is of opinion that " there is some special feature of the case which would make a joint trial of the several counts embarrassing to the defendants and separate trials are required in the interests of justice." [66] Where an essential part of one accused's defence is an attack upon another the judge should take this into account in considering whether to order separate trials.[67]

This joinder of defendants may be made the subject of appeal, or the court may quash the indictment.[68] However, if objection is not taken before plea, the Court of Appeal is reluctant to quash the conviction.[69]

Joinder of offences in one count of an indictment. As a general rule, an indictment must not be double, that is to say, no *one count* should charge the prisoner with having committed more than one offence [70] unless the offences charged are part of " one act and one entire transaction," [71] as *e.g.* an assault on two persons at the same

[65] Or entered as trespassers under the Theft Act 1968.
[66] *Ludlow* v. *Metropolitan Police Commissioner* (1970) 54 Cr.App.R. 233, H.L.
[67] *R.* v. *Grondkowsky and Another* [1964] K.B. 369. See further A. Samuels, " Separate Trials " [1966] Crim.L.R. 303.
[68] Arch. para. 127.
[69] See *R.* v. *Assim* [1966] 2 Q.B. 249 at p. 259.
[70] Arch. para. 122. See *R.* v. *Johnson* [1945] 1 K.B. 419; *R.* v. *Ballysingh* (1953) 37 Cr.App.R. 28.
[71] *R.* v. *Giddings* (1842) 1 C. & M. 634, and see *R.* v. *Wilmot* (1933) 24 Cr. App.R. 63, and cases there mentioned.

time.[72] So, for example, section 1 of the Dangerous Drugs Act 1965,[73] makes it an offence for an occupier of premises to permit those premises to be used for the purpose of smoking cannabis or dealing in cannabis. It has been held that this section created two separate offences and that, therefore, they must not be charged in the same count.[74]

Duplicity may be objected to and the court may quash the indictment or it may be a ground of appeal, but it cannot be made the subject of a motion in arrest of judgment.

Joinder of several offences in different counts. A person cannot be put in charge on more than one indictment at the same time, and any trial on more than one indictment at the same time is a nullity.[75] But, by **section 4** of the **Indictments Act 1915,**[76] and **Rule 9** of the **Indictment Rules 1971,** charges for more than one offence may be joined in the same indictment in different counts if the charges are founded on the same facts or are part of a series of offences of the same or a similar character. Offences of attempted theft and robbery are offences of " similar character " within the meaning of rule 9 and may be properly joined in one indictment. Rule 9 does not imply that joinder of offences cannot be sanctioned unless the offences arise out of the same facts or are part of a system of conduct. A sufficient nexus must however be shown to exist between the offences and this is clearly established if evidence of one offence would be admissible on the trial of the other, but the rule is that the offences should exhibit such similar features as to establish a prima facie case that they can properly and conveniently be tried together in the general interests of justice. These interests include the interests of the defendants, the Crown, witnesses and the public, also the prejudice likely to arise in the second trial from the extensive press reports of the first trial, if the offences are tried separately.[77] Thus a person may be charged

---

[72] *R.* v. *Giddings* (1842) 1 C. & M. 634.
[73] To be repealed and replaced by the Misuse of Drugs Act 1971, s. 8.
[74] *Ware* v. *Fox* [1967] 1 W.L.R. 579. See further Glanville Williams, " The Count System and the Duplicity Rule " [1966] Crim.L.R. at p. 257 *et seq.*
[75] *R.* v. *McDonnel* (1928) 20 Cr.App.R. 163.
[76] As amended by Criminal Law Act 1967, Sched. 3.
[77] *R.* v. *Kray and Others* [1969] 1 Q.B. 125 approved in *Ludlow* v. *Metropolitan Police Commissioner* (*supra*), where it was held that the required

in one count of an indictment with forging a cheque, in a second count with uttering a forged cheque, and in a third count with obtaining or attempting to obtain money by the false pretence that the cheque was genuine.[78]

By **section 5 (3)** it is further provided that where, before trial, or at any stage of a trial, the court is of opinion that the accused may be prejudiced or embarrassed in his defence by reason of being charged with more than one offence in the same indictment, or that for any other reason it is desirable to direct that he should be tried separately for any one or more offences charged in an indictment, the court may order a separate trial of any count or counts in such indictment.[79]

The object of adding separate counts may be either to charge distinct offences committed by different acts (*e.g.* a series of false representations) or to charge the same act as constituting two offences, either in the alternative (*e.g.* theft and handling) or where the same act may constitute either a more serious or a less serious offence (*e.g.* an assault with a particular intent and assault occasioning actual bodily harm). Each count is, for the purpose of evidence, verdict and judgment, equivalent to a separate indictment,[80] and charges which can be made in separate counts of one indictment ought not to be preferred in several indictments.[81] Where a prisoner is indicted for an offence, it is not necessary to add a count for an attempt to commit it, or for an included offence, because, by **section 6** of the **Criminal Law Act 1967,** he may be convicted of the attempt or included offence.

At the trial the Crown may elect to proceed only with some of the counts and, if this is done, the court may order that the other counts should not be proceeded upon without leave of the court.[82]

---

nexus was a feature of similarity which in all the circumstances of the case enables the offences to be described as a series.

[78] Arch. para. 130. See also *R.* v. *Clayton-Wright* [1948] 2 All E.R. 763.

[79] See *R.* v. *Hall* [1952] 1 K.B. 302 ; *R.* v. *Fitzpatrick* [1963] 1 W.L.R. 7.

[80] Arch. para. 131 ; see *R.* v. *Phillips and Quayle* [1939] 1 K.B. 63.

[81] *R.* v. *Carver* (1927) 20 Cr.App.R. 3. Counts charging other offences may be included in an indictment, including a count for murder or manslaughter : *Practice Direction* [1964] 1 W.L.R. 1244. More than one murder may be charged in the same indictment : Homicide Act 1957, s. 6 (2).

[82] See *R.* v. *Riebold* [1967] 1 W.L.R. 674 and *post,* p. 726.

Limitations on the right to prosecute. As a general rule, there is no restriction on the right to take criminal proceedings. There are, however, some exceptional cases in which a prosecution may not be instituted without the order of a judge or the direction or consent of the Attorney-General or Solicitor-General or the Director of Public Prosecutions or some other authority.[83]

In the absence of any statutory limitation for a particular prosecution, a prosecution may be commenced at any length of time after the offence (*nullum tempus occurrit regi*).[84]

The exceptions [85] include:

(1) *Treason* committed in Great Britain, except by endeavouring to assassinate the sovereign, for which the *indictment* must be signed within *three years* of the offences [86];

(2) Unlawful sexual intercourse with or an attempt to have unlawful sexual intercourse with a girl between the ages of thirteen and sixteen years, for which the *prosecution* must be *commenced* not more than *twelve months* after the offence.[87]

Previous convictions. Section 5 (4) of the Coinage Offences Act 1936 provides for an increased penalty for persons, who, having been previously convicted of certain offences, utter counterfeit coin. Similar provisions for increased penalties on subsequent convictions may be found in section 1 of the Night Poaching Act 1828. There are also a number of summary offences which carry an increased penalty for second or subsequent convictions, and for which the accused may be able to elect trial by jury, *e.g.* sections 33–36 of the Sexual Offences Act 1956.

Miscellaneous provisions of the Act. By **section 6** of the **Indictments Act 1915,** if an indictment is of unnecessary length or is materially defective, the court may make such order as it thinks fit as to the payment of any part of the costs of the prosecution which have been incurred thereby.

---

[83] Arch. para. 291.

[84] This does not apply to offences punishable only on summary conviction, with regard to which, proceedings must, as a rule, be commenced within six months from the offence: Magistrates' Courts Act 1952, s. 104 (*ante*, p. 644).   [85] For a full list, see Arch. paras. 152–160.

[86] Treason Act 1695, ss. 5, 6.

[87] Sexual Offences 1956, s. 37 and Sched. 2.

By **section 7** (as amended by the *Third Schedule* to the *Administration of Justice Act* 1933), "Nothing in this Act shall prevent an indictment being open to objection if it contravenes or fails to comply with any other enactment."

By **section 8,** nothing in the Act or Rules is to affect the law or practice relating to the jurisdiction of a court or the place where an accused person can be tried, or prejudice or diminish the obligation to establish by evidence according to law any acts, omissions, or intentions which are legally necessary to constitute the offence with which the person accused is charged, or otherwise affect the law of evidence in criminal matters.

SECTION 2. PREFERRING AND SIGNING THE BILL OF INDICTMENT

Preferment of a Bill of Indictment. The preferment of a bill of indictment is governed by the **Administration of Justice (Miscellaneous Provisions) Act 1933** and the **Indictments (Procedure) Rules 1971** made thereunder.

Section 2 [88] of the Act provides as follows:

(1) A bill of indictment charging any person with an indictable offence may be preferred by any person before a court in which the person charged may lawfully be indicted for that offence, and where a bill of indictment has been so preferred the proper officer of the Crown Court must, if he is satisfied that the requirements of the next subsection have been complied with, sign the bill, and it shall thereupon become an indictment and be proceeded with accordingly :

Provided that if the judge is satisfied that the said requirements have been complied with, he may, on the application of the prosecutor or of his own motion, direct the proper officer to sign the bill and the bill shall be signed accordingly.

(2) Subject as hereinafter provided no bill of indictment charging any person with an indictable offence shall be preferred unless either—

(*a*) the person charged has been committed for trial for the offence; or

(*b*) the bill is preferred by the direction of the Court of Appeal or by the direction or with the consent of a

[88] As amended by the Criminal Appeal Act 1964, s. 5, Sched. 2; the Criminal Justice Act 1967, s. 2 (8); and the Courts Act 1971, Sched. 11.

judge of the High Court or pursuant to an order made under section 9 of the Perjury Act 1911:

Provided that—

(i) where the person charged has been committed for trial, the bill of indictment against him may include, either *in substitution for or in addition* to counts charging the offence for which he was committed, any counts founded on facts or evidence disclosed in any examination or deposition taken before a justice in his presence or in any written statement admitted in evidence under section 2 of the Criminal Justice Act 1967, being counts which may lawfully be joined in the same indictment [89];

(ii) a charge of a previous conviction of an offence or of being an habitual drunkard may, notwithstanding that it was not included in the committal or in any such direction or consent as aforesaid, be included in any bill of indictment.

(3) If a bill of indictment preferred otherwise than in accordance with the provisions of the last foregoing subsection has been signed by the proper officer of the court, the indictment shall be liable to be quashed:

Provided that—

(*a*) if the bill contains several counts, and the said provisions have been complied with as respects one or more of them, those counts only that were wrongly included shall be quashed under this subsection; and

(*b*) where a person who has been committed for trial is convicted on any indictment or any count of an indictment, that indictment or count shall not be quashed under this subsection in any proceedings on appeal, unless application was made at the trial that it should be so quashed.

[89] The charges that may be added are not confined to charges similar to the committal charge: *R.* v. *Roe* [1967] 1 W.L.R. 634 at pp. 640–641. A charge upon which the justices refused to commit may be added: *R.* v. *Morry* [1946] K.B. 153. Where additional charges are preferred on fresh facts, which were not the subject of committal, it has been said that the police ought to see the defendant as soon as it is decided to formulate those charges and caution him: *R.* v. *Dickson* [1969] 1 W.L.R. 405. Where there has been a committal for a non-existent offence no charge can be validly added, since such a committal is a nullity: *R.* v. *Lamb* (*Thomas*) [1968] 1 W.L.R. 1946. See also *R.* v. *William* [1972] Crim.L.R. 436.

By the same section it is provided that, save as aforesaid, nothing in the section shall affect any enactment restricting the right to prosecute in particular classes of cases.

The procedure is further governed by the **Indictments (Procedure) Rules 1971. Rule 4** provides that a bill of indictment is preferred before the Crown Court by delivering it to the appropriate officer [90] of the court. Where, with the assent of the prosecutor, the bill is prepared by, or under the supervision of, the appropriate officer, then it is not necessary for the bill to be delivered to him, but as soon as it has been settled to his satisfaction, it is deemed to have been duly preferred.

By **Rule 5,** where a defendant has been committed for trial, the bill of indictment must be preferred within twenty-eight days of the committal, or within such longer period as a judge of the Crown Court may allow.

Application for a Voluntary Bill of Indictment. Where an application is made to the court for a voluntary bill of indictment under section 2 (2) (*b*) of the Administration of Justice (Miscellaneous Provisions) Act 1933, such an application may be made, by virtue of **Rule 6,** to a judge of the High Court. By **Rule 7** such application must be in writing, signed by the applicant or his solicitor. The application must, by **Rule 8,** be accompanied by the bill of indictment which it is proposed to prefer, and unless the application is made by or on behalf of the Director of Public Prosecutions, must be accompanied by an affidavit of the applicant, or if the applicant is a corporation, by an affidavit by some director or officer of the corporation, that the statements contained in the application are, to the best of the deponent's knowledge, information and belief, true; and the application must state whether or not any application has previously been made under the Rules,[91] and whether there have been any committal proceedings, and the result of any such application or proceedings.

Where there have been no committal proceedings, by **Rule 9** an application for a voluntary bill must state the reason why it is desired to prefer a bill without such proceedings and the application must be accompanied by proofs of the evidence of the

---

[90] Such officer as may be designated for the purpose in question by arrangements made by or on behalf of the Lord Chancellor.

[91] Or any rules revoked by the 1971 Rules, *ibid.*

witnesses whom it is proposed to call in support of the charge, and the application must embody a statement that the evidence shown by the proofs will be available at the trial and that the case disclosed by the proofs is, to the best of the knowledge, information and belief of the applicant, substantially a true case.

Where there have been committal proceedings,[92] and the justice or justices have refused to commit the accused for trial, **Rule 9 (2)** requires that the application be accompanied by a copy of the depositions[93] and proofs of any evidence which it is proposed to call in support of the charges so far as that evidence is not contained in the depositions. The application must also embody a statement regarding the evidence and depositions such as has to be included under **Rule 9 (1).** Where the accused has been committed for trial, the application must state why it is made and must be accompanied by proofs of any evidence which it is proposed to call in support of the charges, in so far as it is not contained in the depositions, and, unless the depositions have already been transmitted to the judge to whom the application is made, must be accompanied by a copy of them, and a statement as to knowledge, information etc., as is required by Rules 9 (1) and 9 (2) **(Rule 9 (3)).** Any person in charge of the depositions is under a duty to give to any person desiring to make an application as above a reasonable opportunity to inspect the depositions taken and, if required to do so by him, supply him with a copy of the depositions or any part of them **(Rule 11).**

By **Rule 10,** unless the judge otherwise directs in any particular case, his decision on the application must be signified in writing on the application without requiring the attendance before him of any applicant or of any of the witnesses. If the judge thinks fit, however, to require the attendance of the applicant or any of the witnesses,[94] their attendance *must not* be in *open court*. If an applicant is required to attend, he may attend by solicitor or counsel.

SECTION 3. PROCESS TO COMPEL APPEARANCE

If a person against whom a bill of indictment has been preferred is present or in the custody of the Crown Court he may be arraigned

---

[92] Defined in Rule 2.
[93] Defined in Rule 2.
[94] As to process, see below.

at once. If he has been bound over by recognisances to appear, he is called upon to surrender and may also be arraigned at once. Where any person charged with or convicted of an offence has entered into a recognisance conditioned for his appearance at the Crown Court and in breach of the recognisance fails to appear, the Crown Court may, without prejudice to the enforcement of the recognisance, issue a warrant for his arrest.[95] On issuing a warrant the Crown Court may indorse it for bail and in any such case the person arrested must, unless the Crown Court otherwise directs, be taken to a police station and the officer in charge of that station must release him from custody if he, and any sureties required by the indorsement and approved by the officer, enter into recognisances of such amount as may be fixed by the indorsement.[96]

A person in custody in pursuance of a warrant issued by the Crown Court with a view to his appearance before the Crown Court shall be brought forthwith before either the Crown Court or a magistrates' court and if he is brought up before a magistrates' court:

(a) that court must commit him in custody, or release him on bail until he can be brought or appear before the Crown Court at the time and place appointed by the latter court;

(b) if the warrant is indorsed for bail, but the person in custody is unable to satisfy the conditions indorsed, the magistrates' court may vary the conditions if satisfied that it is proper so to do.[97]

Such a warrant can be executed in Scotland [98] and a magistrates' court has jurisdiction and a justice of the peace may act in such a matter whether or not the offence was committed or the arrest was made within the court's area, or the area for which he was appointed.[99]

Where an indictment has been signed although the person charged has not been committed for trial, the Crown Court may

---

[95] Courts Act 1971, s. 13 (3).
[96] *Ibid.* s. 13 (6).
[97] Courts Act 1971, s. 13 (7).
[98] *Ibid.* s. 13 (8) and the Summary Jurisdiction (Process) Act 1881, s. 4.
[99] Courts Act 1971, s. 13 (9).

issue a summons requiring him to appear before the Court, or issue a warrant for his arrest.[1]

If he is in the custody of another court, he may be removed by *habeas corpus ad respondendum* and brought up to plead. If recognisances have been entered into for him to appear to take his trial for any offence at any court of criminal jurisdiction, and an indictment has been signed against him and he is then in the prison belonging to the jurisdiction of such court, under warrant of commitment, or under sentence for some other offence, the court may, by order in writing, direct the governor of the prison to bring him up for trial without a writ of habeas corpus.[2] Alternatively, if he is lawfully confined anywhere under any sentence or under commitment for trial or otherwise, he may be brought up for trial under an order in writing of a Secretary of State.[3]

There is no statutory procedure for ensuring the attendance of a defendant against whom an indictment has been preferred under section 2 (2) (*b*) of the Administration of Justice (Miscellaneous Provisions) Act 1933 (where the bill of indictment is preferred by the direction of a judge of the High Court). The only method seems to be by way of a bench warrant.[4]

SECTION 4. DISTRIBUTION OF CROWN COURT BUSINESS

Directions have been given by the Lord Chief Justice, dated October 14, 1971,[5] classifying offences for the purposes of trial in the Crown Court, and allocating proceedings to the various locations of the Crown Court.

Classification of Offences. The directions classify all offences under four heads, thus:

Class 1. The following offences, which are to be tried by a High Court judge:

(1) Any offences for which a person may be sentenced to death.

(2) Misprision of treason and treason felony.

(3) Murder.

---

[1] *Ibid.* s. 13 (2).
[2] Criminal Law Amendment Act 1867, s. 10.
[3] Criminal Justice Act 1961, s. 28.
[4] *R.* v. *Harrison* [1954] Crim.L.R. 39; *R.* v. *Clark and Richardson* [1957] Crim.L.R. 80.
[5] *Practice Direction* [1971] 3 All E.R. 829.

(4) Genocide.

(5) An offence under the Official Secrets Act, 1911, s. 1.

(6) Incitement, attempt or conspiracy to commit any of the above offences.

Class 2. The following offences, which are to be tried by a High Court judge unless a particular case is released by or on the authority of a presiding judge, that is to say, a High Court judge assigned to have special responsibility for a particular circuit: manslaughter; infanticide; child destruction; abortion (Offences against the Person Act 1861, s. 58); rape; sexual intercourse with girl under thirteen; incest with girl under thirteen; sedition; an offence under the Geneva Conventions Act 1957, s. 1; mutiny; piracy; incitement, attempt or conspiracy to commit any of the above offences.

Class 3. All indictable offences other than those in classes 1, 2 and 4. They may be listed for trial by a High Court judge [6] or by a circuit judge or recorder.[7]

Class 4. (1) All offences which may, in appropriate circumstances, be tried either on indictment or summarily. They include—

  (*a*) indictable offences which may be tried summarily (Magistrates' Courts Act 1952, s. 19, Sched. 1);

  (*b*) offences which are both indictable and summary (Magistrates' Courts Act 1952, s. 18);

  (*c*) offences punishable on summary conviction with more than three months' imprisonment where the accused may claim to be tried on indictment (Magistrates' Courts Act 1952, s. 25).

(2) Conspiracy to commit any of the above offences.

(3) The following offences:

  (*a*) Causing death by reckless or dangerous driving (Road Traffic Act 1972, s. 1).

  (*b*) Wounding or causing grievous bodily harm with intent (Offences against the Person Act 1861, s. 18).

---

[6] High Court judge includes a Deputy High Court judge.

[7] A presiding judge may vary the allocation of cases to a particular Crown Court centre, *e.g.* in Greater London some class 4 offences, namely, robbery, causing grievous bodily harm and causing death by dangerous driving have been cited as Class 3 cases and are committed for trial at a 2nd tier court centre.

(c) Burglary (Theft Act 1968, s. 9) in a dwelling in circumstances set out in Schedule 1, paragraph 11 (c) of the Magistrates' Courts Act 1952.

(d) Robbery, or assault with intent to rob (Theft Act 1968, s. 8).

(e) Offences under Forgery Act 1913 (being offences under that Act which are not triable summarily, i.e. other than offences under section 2 (2) (a) or section 7 where the value of the property does not exceed £100).

(f) Incitement, attempt or conspiracy to commit any of the above offences.

(g) Conspiracy to commit an offence which is in no circumstances triable on indictment or an act which is not an offence.

(4) Any offence in class 3, if included in class 4 in accordance with directions (which may be either general or particular) given by a presiding judge or on his authority.

When tried on indictment offences in class 4 may be tried by a High Court judge, circuit judge or recorder but will normally be listed for trial by a circuit judge or recorder.

Allocation. The Directions given by the Lord Chief Justice allocate the business of the Crown Court as follows:

(i) Class 1 and 2 offences must be tried by a High Court judge, unless, in the case of a class 2 offence, the case is released by or under the authority of a presiding judge having regard to all the circumstances. Where the prosecution of such an offence has been undertaken by the Director of Public Prosecutions, the Director's views must, where practicable, be obtained before the case is considered for release.

(ii) Class 3 offences will be listed for trial by a High Court judge unless, after having regard to the considerations set out in paragraph 2 of the directions,[8] the officer responsible for listing decides that the case should be listed for trial by a circuit judge or recorder. This decision may only be taken after consultation with a presiding judge (or a judge

---

[8] See *ante*, p. 675.

acting for him) or in accordance with directions given, whether general or particular, by a presiding judge.

(iii) Class 4 offences will be listed for trial by a circuit judge or recorder unless, bearing in mind the considerations set out in paragraph 2 of the directions [9] and the views if any put forward by the justices,[10] the officer responsible for listing decides that the case should be tried by a High Court judge. Again, such a decision may only be taken after consultation with a presiding judge, or in accordance with directions given by him.

These three items in paragraph 12 deal with the business of the Crown Court in proceedings on indictment. In so far as the other business of the court is concerned, the Directions provide as follows:

(iv) Where a probation order, care order or order for conditional discharge has been made, or a suspended sentence passed, by a High Court judge, and the offender is committed to or brought before the Crown Court, his case will be listed for hearing by a High Court judge unless, in accordance with the decision of the officer responsible for listing, his case is listed for hearing by a circuit judge or recorder. Such a decision can only be taken after consultation with a presiding judge, or in accordance with directions, general or particular, given by him.

(v) All other proceedings before the Crown Court (excluding an application for a direction or further direction varying the place of trial) including appeals, committals for sentence or to be dealt with, and proceedings under the original civil jurisdiction of the Crown Court will normally be listed for hearing by a court presided over by a circuit judge or recorder.

The Directions of October 14, 1971 [11] lay down that the hearing of an appeal or of proceedings under the civil jurisdiction of the Crown Court will take place at the location of the Crown Court designated by a presiding judge as the appropriate location for such proceedings originating in the areas concerned.

[9] See *ante*, p. 675.
[10] See *ante*, pp. 674–675.
[11] *Practice Direction* [1971] 3 All E.R. 829, para. 10.

SECTION 5. TIME AND PLACE OF TRIAL—BAIL

In addition to the selection of the location for trial by the committing magistrates [12] and the power of the Crown Court to vary that location, under **sections 7 (1)** and **7 (2)** of the **Courts Act 1971,** [13-14] the Directions given by the Lord Chief Justice, dated October 14, 1971 also provide that the Crown Court may give directions for the transfer from one location to another of (i) appeals; (ii) proceedings on committal for sentence, or to be dealt with; and (iii) proceedings under the original jurisdiction of the Crown Court where this appears desirable for the expediting of the hearing or the convenience of the parties. These directions may be given in a particular case by an officer of the Crown Court, or generally, in relation to a class or classes of case, by a presiding judge or a judge acting on his behalf. If dissatisfied with the directions given by an officer of the court, any party to the proceedings may apply to a judge of the Crown Court who may hear the application in chambers.

The trial of a person committed by a magistrates' court must not, by virtue of **section 7 (4)** of the **Courts Act 1971** and **Rule 19** of the **Crown Court Rules 1971,** begin until the expiration of 14 days beginning with the date of his committal, except with his consent and the consent of the prosecutor, and unless the Crown Court has otherwise ordered, must begin not later than the expiration of eight weeks beginning with the date of his committal. The trial is deemed to begin when the accused is arraigned. The trial may still be postponed on the application of either the prosecution or the defence.[15] They must, however, satisfy the court that there is sufficient cause for the postponement, such as the illness of the defendant, or the unavoidable absence or illness of a necessary and material witness, or the existence of prejudice in the jury.

By **section 5 (4) (5)** of the **Indictments Act 1915** it is provided that where, before trial, or at any stage of a trial, the court is of opinion that the postponement of the trial is expedient as a consequence of the exercise of any power of the court under the Act to amend an indictment or order a new trial, the court shall make such order as to the postponement as appears necessary.

[12] See *ante*, pp. 674–675.
[13-14] This power is exercisable only by a judge of the Crown Court: s. 7 (5).
[15] *Practice Direction* [1971] 3 All E.R. 829, para. 14.

Where under this section an order is made for a separate trial or for the postponement of a trial:

> (i) if such an order is made during a trial the court may order the jury to be discharged from giving a verdict on the count, or counts the trial of which is postponed or on the indictment, as the case may be; and

> (ii) the procedure on the separate trial of a count shall be the same as if the count had been in a separate indictment and the procedure on the postponed trial shall be the same (if the jury has been discharged) as if the trial had not commenced; and

> (iii) the court may make such order as to costs and as to admitting the accused person to bail, and otherwise as it thinks fit.

Bail by the court of trial. In relation to trials upon indictment,[16] the Crown Court, by virtue of **section 13 (4)** of the **Courts Act 1971,** may admit to bail or direct the admission to bail of any person who has been committed in custody for appearance before the court or who is in the custody of the Crown Court pending the disposal of his case by the court. The time during which such a person is on bail does not count as part of any term of imprisonment or detention under his sentence.

There is nothing to prevent an application for bail being made to the Court during the hearing of proceedings. Where the application is not made at that stage, however, the procedure is governed by **rule 17** of the **Crown Court Rules 1971,** and by the Directions given by the Lord Chief Justice, dated October 14, 1971.[17]

A notice in writing of intention to apply for bail must be given to the Crown Court. Where a person who desires to apply for bail has not been able to instruct a solicitor to apply on his behalf for bail, he may give notice in writing to the Crown Court of his desire to apply, requesting that the Official Solicitor should act for him in the application, and the Court may if it thinks fit assign the Official Solicitor to act for the applicant accordingly.[18] If the applicant requests the Official Solicitor to act for him in his

---

[16] Bail may also be granted in other cases: Courts Act 1971, s. 13 (4) (b) (d) (e).
[17] *Practice Direction* [1971] 3 All E.R. 829, para. 15.
[18] r. 17 (6).

application, it will be heard by a Crown Court judge in London. In any other case the application will be heard at the location of the Crown Court where the proceedings in respect of which the application arises took place or are due to take place.[19] Notice in writing, in the prescribed form,[20] of the intention to apply to the Crown Court for bail must be given to the prosecutor, and to the Director of Public Prosecutions if the prosecution is being carried on by him, at least twenty-four hours before the application is made.[21] The prosecutor or the Director must then notify the appropriate officer of the Crown Court and the applicant of whether he opposes the application and whether he wishes to be represented at the hearing. If he does oppose it he must give to the appropriate officer, for the consideration of the Court, a written statement of his reasons for so doing, at the same time sending a copy of the statement to the applicant.[22]

The applicant is not entitled to be present on the hearing of the application unless the Crown Court gives him leave.[23] **Rule 18 (2)** provides that on hearing an application for bail the Crown Court may order that the applicant be released from custody on entering into a recognisance, with or without sureties, or giving other security before an officer of the Crown Court, a justice of the peace or any other person authorised by virtue of section 95 (1) of the Magistrates' Courts Act 1952.[24] A person who proposes to enter into a recognisance or give other security in pursuance of an order of the Crown Court, before a justice of the peace or other person, must give twenty-four hours' notice before he does so.[25] The justice or other person must transmit the recognisances to the Crown Court.[26]

---

[19] *Practice Direction (supra)*, para. 15.
[20] r. 17 (2). The prescribed form is to be found in Sched. 2 to the Rules. The applicant must inform the Crown Court on the form of any previous applications to the High Court or the Crown Court in relation to the same proceedings: r. 18 (1).
[21] This procedure may be dispensed with if the Official Solicitor is assigned: r. 17 (7).
[22] r. 17 (3).
[23] r. 17 (5).
[24] Crown Court Rules 1971, r. 18 (2).
[25] *Ibid.* r. 18 (3).
[26] *Ibid.* r. 18 (4).

Chapter 51

TRIAL AT THE CROWN COURT—PART II

Section 1. Public Trial

It may here be observed that at common law a trial on indictment must be held in a public court with open doors, but it sometimes happens that the judge may in certain cases request women and young children to leave the court, and he has power to exclude or eject persons who disturb the proceedings.[1] By **section 37** of the **Children and Young Persons Act 1933,** where a person who, in the opinion of the court, is a child or young person is called as a witness in any proceedings in relation to an offence against, or any conduct contrary to, decency or morality, the court may direct that all persons (other than bona fide representatives of a newspaper or news agency) not being members or officers of the court, or parties to the case, or their solicitors or counsel, or persons otherwise directly concerned in the case, shall be excluded from the court during the taking of the evidence of such child or young persons. By **section 36** of the Act it is also provided that no child (other than an infant in arms or a messenger, clerk, etc., who is required to attend at any court for purposes connected with his employment) shall be permitted to be present in court during the trial of any person charged with an offence, or during any proceedings preliminary thereto, unless he is the person charged with the offence or his presence is required as a witness or otherwise for the purposes of justice.

Section 2. Recording the Proceedings

By **section 32 (1)** of the **Criminal Appeal Act 1968** Rules of Court may provide for the making of a record (whether by means of shorthand notes by mechanical means, or otherwise) of any proceedings in respect of which an appeal lies (with or without leave) to the Court of Appeal. **Rule 18** of the **Criminal Appeal Rules 1968** provide that the whole of any proceedings in respect of which

---

[1] Arch. para. **541.**

an appeal lies (with or without leave) to the court must be recorded by means of shorthand notes, or with the permission of the Lord Chancellor, by mechanical means. Where such proceedings are recorded by means of shorthand notes it is not necessary to record the opening or closing addresses to the jury on behalf of the prosecution or an accused person unless the judge of the court of trial otherwise directs, or any other part of such proceedings which the judge of the court of trial directs need not be recorded. Where it is not practicable for such proceedings to be recorded by means of shorthand notes or by mechanical means, the judge of the court of trial must direct how and to what extent the proceedings must be recorded.

It is the duty of the judge, counsel and court officials to see that the evidence and summing up in a criminal trial is properly recorded. Where it is known that no shorthand writer or no fully competent shorthand writer is present, the greatest care should be taken to ensure that an unchallengeable note is made. It is the judge's duty to do all that is practicable to see that an adequate record is made. He can make a note of his summing up either before or after delivering it when it is fresh in his mind. Counsel should make their own notes and should be entirely free to raise any query with the judge.[2]

SECTION 3. RIGHTS OF AUDIENCE

The traditional position by which counsel only had the right of audience in the superior courts has been, to some extent, modified by the **Courts Act 1971. Section 12** empowers the Lord Chancellor to direct that solicitors be able to appear in, conduct, defend and address the court in any, or any specified category of, proceedings in the Crown Court. By directions which came into force on January 1, 1972,[3] solicitors are permitted to appear for specified purposes at the sittings of the Crown Court at certain locations (Caernarvon, Barnstaple, Bodmin, Doncaster and Lincoln) where

---

[2] R. v. *Payne and Spillane* [1971] 1 W.L.R. 1779. The mere fact that there is no shorthand note will not, of itself, be a ground for saying that the trial was unsafe or unsatisfactory within section 2 (1) (a) of the Criminal Appeal Act 1968. In order to show such a state of affairs it must be established that there was an actual irregularity in the course of the trial or an error in the summing-up: R. v. *Le Caer* [1972] Crim.L.R. 546. See also R. v. *Elliott* (1909) 2 Cr.App.R. 172.

[3] [1972] 1 All E.R. 144.

they had rights of audience before the coming into force of the Act. In addition, by directions which came into force on March 1, 1972,[4] a solicitor is empowered to appear in, conduct, defend and address the court in

(a) criminal proceedings in the Crown Court on appeal from a magistrates' court or on committal of a person for sentence or to be dealt with, *if he, or any partner of his, or any solicitor in his employment or by whom he is employed, appeared on behalf of the defendant in the magistrates' court,* or

(b) in certain civil proceedings in the Crown Court. There seems to be no reason why, a defendant at the Crown Court should not have the right to have a friend with him to advise, take notes and generally assist, on the principle enunciated by Lord Tenterden in *Collier* v. *Hicks* and considered in *McKenzie* v. *McKenzie*,[4a] provided that such person does not seek to take part in the proceedings as an advocate.

SECTION 4. ARRAIGNMENT

The first step in a trial on indictment is the arraignment of the accused person. This consists of three parts, namely:

(i) Calling the defendant to the bar by name;
(ii) Reading to him the substance of the indictment;
(iii) Asking him whether he is guilty or not.

The defendant must be brought to the bar without any shackles or other restraint unless there is any reason to believe that he will attempt to escape or be guilty of violence, in which case the judge may order him to be brought up in irons and kept in irons during the trial.[5] Once he has been arraigned, and the jury has been sworn, it is not necessary for the defendant to remain in court. He has, of course, a right to be present at his trial, provided that he does not abuse that right. If he does so, for the purpose of obstructing the proceedings, by unseemly, indecent or outrageous behaviour, the judge may have him removed and the trial may proceed in his absence, or the jury may be discharged and the

---

[4] [1972] 1 All E.R. 608.
[4a] See p. 655, *ante*, in relation to the position in a Magistrates' court.
[5] 2 Hawk. c. 28, s. 1.

trial commenced again at a later stage. The accused may also, by his conduct, waive his right to be present, as by absconding during the trial. In such a case the judge has a discretion to proceed with the trial in his absence.[6]

Where an indictment contains several counts, each count should be put to the defendant separately, and he should be asked to plead to each count as it is read to him.[7]

If, on being called upon to plead, the defendant stands mute of malice, or will not answer directly, the court may order a plea of not guilty to be entered for him.[8] If, however, there is any doubt whether he is standing mute of malice or by the visitation of God,[9] a jury, which may consist of any twelve persons present, must be empanelled and sworn to try this issue. If the jury find him mute of malice a plea of not guilty will be entered for him; if they find him mute by the visitation of God they may then be sworn again to try whether he is unfit to plead.[10] If he is found fit to plead, a plea of not guilty will be entered. The same jury may be used for these preliminary issues but a different jury must be used for the trial, unless the court directs otherwise under **section 4 (4) (b)** of the **Criminal Procedure (Insanity) Act 1964.**[11]

Each of the courses which may be taken by the accused will now be considered.

1. Plea of " Guilty." If the accused pleads that he is guilty and that plea is accepted by the court,[12] no further proof or trial is necessary, and the court proceeds to judgment on his " own confession." Before doing so, however, it hears the main facts of the case from the prosecuting counsel and also any statements which the prisoner or his counsel may desire to make. Also, with a view to fixing the punishment, the court obtains such information as to the character of the accused as may be relevant and available.[13]

---

[6] *R.* v. *Jones (R.E.W.) (No. 2)* [1972] 2 All E.R. 731 approving the Australian case of *R.* v. *Abrahams* (1895) 21 V.L.R. 343.

[7] *R.* v. *Boyle* [1954] 2 Q.B. 292.

[8] Criminal Law Act 1967, s. 6 (1) (*c*).

[9] As, *e.g.* where he is deaf and dumb, or so deaf that he cannot hear the indictment when read; see Arch. para. 428.

[10] *Ante,* p. 88.

[11] Courts Act 1971, s. 35 (5) (*b*).

[12] The trial judge may refuse to accept the plea of guilty where he is of the opinion that the plea proceeds from fear, duress, weakness or ignorance: *R.* v. *Cole* [1965] 2 Q.B. 388 at p. 394.　　　　[13] See *post,* p. 753.

Where, on arraignment on a single count, the prosecution allege that the offence is part of a series, while the defendant alleges that it is an isolated act, it is wrong for the judge to hold a trial within a trial for the purpose of deciding the matter. If the judge feels that justice cannot be done by accepting the defendant's version he should allow a voluntary bill charging the other acts to be preferred or permit the indictment to be amended.[13a]

When a person is arraigned on indictment he may plead not guilty to the offence specifically charged in a count, but guilty to another offence of which he might be found guilty on that count.[14] But the accused must himself plead guilty.[15] If there is nothing in the depositions which can be said to reduce the charge, counsel for the Crown should refuse to accept the plea of guilty.[16] Even if counsel agrees to accept it in these circumstances, the trial judge has a discretion not to accept it.[17] If the plea of guilty is not accepted, the plea is deemed to be withdrawn so that he cannot be sentenced on it if he is then acquitted by the jury.[18] However, it is open to the prosecution during the trial to lead evidence that the accused pleaded guilty on the lesser included charge and, if the accused raises a defence inconsistent with his plea, he may be cross-examined on the point.[19] If the plea of guilty is accepted, his conviction for that offence shall constitute an acquittal of the other.[20]

Where a person is charged on two (or more) counts and he pleads guilty to one count and not guilty to another, then, if he is tried and acquitted on the latter charge, he may still be sentenced on the former.[21]

A plea of not guilty may by leave of the judge be withdrawn and a plea of guilty substituted, but where this is done after the

---

[13a] *R.* v. *Huchison* [1972] 1 W.L.R. 398.
[14] Criminal Law Act 1967, s. 6 (1) (*b*).
[15] It is not sufficient for the accused's counsel to say that he wishes to plead guilty: *R.* v. *Heyes* [1951] 1 K.B. 29.
[16] *R.* v. *Soanes* (1948) 32 Cr.App.R. 136.
[17] *Ibid.*
[18] *R.* v. *Hazeltine* [1967] 2 Q.B. 857.
[19] *Ibid.*
[20] Criminal Law Act 1967, s. 6 (5), and this is also so when the two offences are charged in separate counts: *ibid.*
[21] If the counts are alternative, *e.g.* robbery and receiving (now handling stolen goods), a plea of guilty to the receiving does not prevent a trial for robbery and if he is convicted on the more serious count, the plea of guilty on the lesser alternative count should remain on the file and sentence not be proceeded with: *R.* v. *Cole* [1965] 2 Q.B. 388.

prisoner has been put in charge of the jury the verdict of the jury must be taken.[22] A plea of guilty may by the leave of the judge be withdrawn before, but not after, sentence.[23]

A plea of guilty by one accused is in no sense to be regarded as evidence against a co-accused.[24]

Plea bargaining. The situation arose in recent years whereby some defendants appealed to the Criminal Division of the Court of Appeal on the ground that they had not had a free choice of plea when appearing for trial on indictment. As a result in the case of *R.* v. *Turner* [25] the Court of Appeal gave the following directions:

1. Counsel must be completely free to do what is his duty—to give the accused the best advice he can and, if need be, in strong terms. It will often include advice that a guilty plea, showing an element of remorse, is a mitigating factor which might enable the court to give a lesser sentence.

2. The accused, having considered counsel's advice, must have a complete freedom of choice whether to plead guilty or not guilty.

3. There must be freedom of access between counsel and judge. Any discussion, however, must be between the judge and both counsel. If a solicitor representing the accused is in court he should be allowed to attend the discussion if he so desires.

Such freedom of access is important because there might be matters calling for communication or discussion of such a nature that counsel cannot in his client's interests mention them in open court. For example, counsel may by way of mitigation wish to tell the judge that the accused has not long to live, is suffering, maybe from cancer, of which he should remain ignorant. Again, counsel on both sides may wish to discuss with the judge whether it would be proper, in a particular case, for the prosecution to accept a plea to a lesser offence.

It is, of course, imperative that so far as possible justice must be administered in open court. Counsel should, therefore, ask to see the judge only when it is felt to be really necessary.

---

[22] If this is not done the trial is a nullity: *R.* v. *Heyes* [1951] 1 K.B. 29. See Arch. para. 525.

[23] *R.* v. *Plummer* [1902] 2 K.B. 339; *R.* v. *Campbell, ex p. Hoy* [1953] 1 Q.B. 585; *R.* v. *McNally* (1954) 38 Cr.App.R. 90. As to the effect of a plea of guilty withdrawn see *R.* v. *Rimmer* [1972] 1 W.L.R. 268, *ante*, p. 658.

[24] *R.* v. *Moore* (1956) 40 Cr.App.R. 50.

[25] [1970] 2 Q.B. 321; 54 Cr.App.R. 352, C.A.

4. The judge should, subject to one exception, never indicate the sentence which he is minded to impose. A statement that on a plea of guilty he would impose one sentence but that on a conviction following a plea of not guilty he would impose a more severe sentence, should never be made. That could be taken to be undue pressure on the accused, thus depriving him of that complete freedom of choice which is essential. Such cases, however, are, in the experience of the court, happily rare. What on occasions does appear to happen, however, is that a judge will tell counsel that, having read the depositions and the antecedents, he can safely say that on a plea of guilty he will, for instance, make a probation order, something which might be helpful to counsel in advising the accused. The judge in such a case is no doubt careful not to mention what he would do if the accused were convicted following a plea of not guilty. Even so, the accused may well get the impression that the judge was intimating that in that event a severer sentence, maybe a custodial sentence, would result, so that again he may feel under pressure. That must also not be done. The only exception is that it should be permissible for a judge to say, if it be the case, that whatever happens, whether the accused pleads guilty or not guilty, the sentence will or will not take a particular form. Finally, where any such discussion on sentence has taken place between judge and counsel, counsel for the defence should disclose it to the accused and inform him of what took place.

Therefore, it can be seen that it is essential that a defendant has freedom of choice as regards his plea and that he or his counsel must not be pressurised during the trial to plead guilty. In *R*. v. *Barnes* [26] the Court of Appeal described the trial judge's conduct as " wholly improper " where he had, half-way through the prosecution case and in the absence of the jury, stated in effect that the accused was plainly guilty and that the time of the court was being wasted because, amongst other things, it was putting extreme pressure on the accused to plead guilty, whereas after advice from his counsel, the choice of plea was his.[27]

2. Motion to quash indictment. A motion to quash the indictment may be made on the ground of some invalidity on the

[26] (1970) 55 Cr.App.R. 100, C.A.
[27] See also *R*. v. *Brook* [1970] Crim.L.R. 600, C.A.

face of it or some irregularity which would make erroneous any judgment given upon it.

If the defect is merely formal the motion to quash should be made before plea pleaded and the defect may then be amended by the court.[28] If the defect is substantial, as, *e.g.* where the court has no jurisdiction, the motion to quash may be made after plea pleaded.[29] If the indictment is clearly bad the court will quash it, but if there is any doubt, especially in serious cases, the court will refuse to quash it, and will leave the defendant to his remedy by demurrer or motion in arrest of judgment.[30]

3. Demurrer. A demurrer is an objection by which the defendant admits the facts alleged against him in the indictment to be true, but denies that they amount in law to the offence with which he is charged.[31] In the recent case of *R.* v. *Deputy Chairman of Inner London Sessions, ex p. Metropolitan Police Commissioner* [32] Lord Parker C.J. said " I hope that now demurrer in criminal cases will be allowed to die naturally."

4. Other pleas. The prisoner, if he does not plead " guilty," may (A) Plead to the jurisdiction; (B) Plead specially in bar; (C) Plead that he is unfit to stand trial; (D) Plead the general issue, *i.e.* " not guilty." A plea of not guilty may be entered with these special pleas.[33]

A. Plea to the jurisdiction. Where an indictment is for an offence over which the court has no jurisdiction the accused may plead to the jurisdiction without answering to the charge. A plea to the jurisdiction is rare, for any objection on the ground of want of jurisdiction is better taken by motion to quash or motion in arrest of judgment or under the general issue,[34] or the defendant, if convicted, may appeal.[35]

---

[28] See s. 5 (1) of the Indictments Act 1915, *ante*, p. 695.
[29] Arch. para. 235; *R.* v. *Heane* (1864) 4 B. & S. 946; *R.* v. *Thompson* [1914] 2 K.B. 99.
[30] *R.* v. *Lynch* [1903] 1 K.B. 444.
[31] Arch. para. 430. Owing to the wide powers of amendment given by the Indictments Act 1915, demurrers are practically obsolete: *ibid.*
[32] [1970] 2 Q.B. 80 D.C.
[33] *Ibid.*
[34] See *R.* v. *Jameson* [1896] 2 Q.B. 425.
[35] See, generally, Arch. para. 429.

A plea to the jurisdiction must be in writing, in the following form:

The Queen v. A B

(*Court of Trial*)

A says that the court ought not to take cognisance of the indictment against him because, etc.

The form of the replication to this plea is:

The Queen v. A B

(*Court of Trial*)

H A (the appropriate officer of the Crown Court) joins issue on behalf of the Queen.

B. Special pleas are also rare, since all matters of justification and excuse may as a general rule be given in evidence under the general issue. Only the following need be mentioned here [36]:

(i) **Autrefois acquit** and **autrefois convict.** These pleas are grounded on the common law maxim that " a man shall not be brought into danger . . . for one and the same offence more than once." [37] " Where a criminal charge has been adjudicated upon by a court having jurisdiction to hear and determine it, that adjudication, whether it takes the form of an acquittal or conviction, is final as to the matter so adjudicated upon, and may be pleaded in bar to any subsequent prosecution for the same offence." [38] It is immaterial whether the first conviction or acquittal was on indictment or on summary proceedings, provided that it was before a court of competent jurisdiction after a hearing on the merits.[39] And, if a person has been convicted, it is immaterial that he has not been sentenced.

Thus, in *R.* v. *Sheridan*,[40] the accused was charged at petty sessions with an indictable offence and consented to be dealt with summarily. Evidence was given against him and by him and the

---

[36] For the special plea of *justification* on a charge of libel, see Libel Act 1843, s. 6. Arch. paras. 3622, 3645.

[37] 2 Hawk. c. 35, s. 1.

[38] *R.* v. *Miles* (1890) 24 Q.B.D. at p. 431. S. 33 of the Interpretation Act 1889 extended the rule laid down in *R.* v. *Miles* to statutory offences: see *R.* v. *Thomas* [1950] 1 K.B. 26.

[39] *Wemyss* v. *Hopkins* (1875) L.R. 10 Q.B. 378.

[40] (1936) 26 Cr.App.R. 1.

justices announced that they found him guilty, but instead of sentencing him committed him to quarter sessions (now the Crown Court) for trial upon the same charge. At quarter sessions he raised the plea of *autrefois convict*, but it was overruled and he was convicted. *Held*, by the Court of Criminal Appeal that his conviction must be quashed. So also if a person has pleaded guilty it is immaterial that he has not been sentenced.[41]

These pleas can, however, succeed only where the accused was actually in danger on the first proceedings; if by reason of any defect in the indictment or process, he was not on the first proceedings lawfully liable to suffer judgment for the offence then charged, he cannot set up such proceedings as a bar to a subsequent indictment [42]; a judgment on demurrer is therefore no bar to a subsequent indictment.[43]

Nor can either plea be set up unless either (i) the subsequent indictment is based on the same acts or omissions in respect of which the previous acquittal or conviction was made and some statute directs that a defendant shall not be tried or punished twice in respect of the same acts or omissions,[44] or (ii) the acquittal or conviction was for the same offence or substantially the same offence as that charged on the subsequent indictment. With respect to the latter class of cases, Lord Morris in *Connelly* v. *Director of Public Prosecutions* [45] said that both principle and authority establish:

> " (1) That a man cannot be tried for a crime in respect of which he has previously been acquitted or convicted; (2) that a man cannot be tried for a crime in respect of which he could on some previous indictment have been convicted; (3) that the same rule applies if the crime in respect of which he is being charged is in effect the same, or is substantially the same, as either the principal or a different crime in respect of which he has been acquitted or could have been convicted or has been convicted; (4) that one test as to whether the rule applies is whether the evidence which is necessary to support the second indictment, or whether the facts which constitute

---

41 *R.* v. *Grant* (1936) 26 Cr.App.R. 8.
42 *R.* v. *Drury* (1849) 3 C. & K. 193; *R.* v. *Marsham* [1912] 2 K.B. 362; see also *Halstead* v. *Clark* [1944] K.B. 250.
43 *R.* v. *Richmond* (1843) 1 C. & K. 240.
44 See Arch. para. 437.
45 [1964] A.C. 1254 at pp. 1305–1306.

the second offence, would have been sufficient to procure a legal conviction upon the first indictment either as to the offence charged or as to an offence of which, on the indictment, the accused could have been found guilty [46]; (5) that this test must be subject to the proviso that the offence charged in the second indictment had in fact been committed at the time of the first charge; thus if there is an assault and a prosecution and conviction in respect of it there is no bar to a charge of murder if the assaulted person later dies [47]; (6) that on a plea of autrefois acquit or autrefois convict a man is not restricted to a comparison between the later indictment and some previous indictment or to the records of the court, but that he may prove by evidence all such questions as to the identity of persons, dates and facts as are necessary to enable him to show that he is being charged with an offence which is either the same, or is substantially the same, as one in respect of which he could have been convicted; (7) that what has to be considered is whether the crime or offence charged in the later indictment is the same or is in effect or is substantially the same as the crime charged (or in respect of which there could have been a conviction) in a former indictment and that it is immaterial that the facts under examination or the witnesses being called in the later proceedings are the same as those in some earlier proceedings; . . . (9) that, apart from cases where indictments are preferred and where pleas in bar may therefore be entered, the fundamental principle applies that a man is not to be prosecuted twice for the same crime."

In that case the appellant was alleged to have taken part in an armed robbery, in the course of which one of the robbers shot and killed a man. On these facts he could have been charged with both murder and robbery. He was tried and convicted of murder, but by reason of a misdirection his conviction was quashed by the Court of Criminal Appeal. The House of Lords held that he could be tried afresh on the robbery charge. Lord Morris said [48]:

---

[46] Applying this proposition, it follows that an acquittal on an indictment for murder is a bar to a subsequent indictment for manslaughter, because on the first indictment the defendant could have been convicted of manslaughter: see *R.* v. *Barron* [1914] 2 K.B. 570 at p. 574.

[47] See *R.* v. *Thomas* [1950] 1 K.B. 26.

[48] [1964] A.C. 1254 at pp. 1309–1310.

" The test is, therefore, whether such proof as is necessary to convict of the second offence, would establish guilt of the first offence or of an offence for which on the first charge there could be a conviction. Applying to the present case the law as laid down, the question is whether proof that there was robbery with aggravation would support a charge of murder or manslaughter. It seems to me quite clear that it would not. The crimes are distinct. There can be robbery without killing. There can be killing without robbery. Evidence of robbery does not prove murder or manslaughter. Conviction of robbery cannot involve conviction of murder or manslaughter. Nor does an acquittal of murder or manslaughter necessarily involve an acquittal of robbery. Nor on a charge of murder could a man be convicted of robbery."

However, Lord Devlin said [49] that:

" As a general rule a judge should stay an indictment (that is, order it remain on the file not to be proceeded with) when he is satisfied that the charges therein are founded on the same facts as the charges in a previous indictment on which the accused has been tried, or form or are a part of a series of offences of the same or a similar character as the offences charged in the previous indictment."

Lord Devlin said [50] that this rule would not, of course, apply where a trial judge has, or would have, ordered separate trials for charges in the same indictment. Nor did it apply in this case because, at that time,[51] there was a rule of practice that prevented the joinder of other charges with a charge of murder.

Both pleas should be in writing and signed by counsel, but, if pleaded orally, the court will assign counsel to prepare the plea in proper form for the defendant.[52]

The form of the plea is as follows:

The Queen v. A B

(Court of Trial)

A B says that the Queen ought not further to prosecute the

---

[49] At pp. 1359–1360. In *R.* v. *Riebold* [1967] 1 W.L.R. 674, Barry J. held that Lord Devlin's view was that of the majority of the court and applied it to the facts of that case.   [50] *Ibid.*

[51] The rule was changed in 1964 (*ante*, p. 701, note 81).

[52] Arch. para. 446.

indictment against him because he has been lawfully acquitted (or convicted) of the offence charged therein.

Where a defendant pleads *autrefois acquit* or *convict*, issue is then joined by the Crown and a jury is sworn to try the issue. The Courts Act 1971 [53] expressly permits the jury who have tried the special plea to try the accused on the general issue.

(ii) **Issue estoppel.** There is some authority to the effect that where it can be shown that a verdict of not guilty involves a particular determination of fact, the Crown may not thereafter make an allegation contrary to that finding.[54] This rule (if it exists) might either operate to prevent a contrary allegation being made during a trial or could, in the appropriate circumstances, justify a special plea of issue estoppel. For example, a plea of issue estoppel would seem to be justified in the following circumstances. A is acquitted on a charge of theft of a book. At his trial he admitted (as he is entitled to do under section 10 of the Criminal Justice Act 1967) all the elements of theft as proved other than the issue of claim of right. Later he is charged with criminal damage to the book. Since claim of right is also a defence to a charge of criminal damage, the Crown would be estopped from denying that he had that claim. Thus an essential element of the crime would be missing.

(iii) **Pardon.** The Queen's pardon may be pleaded in bar to the indictment or after verdict in arrest of judgment, or after judgment in bar of execution. But it must be pleaded at the first opportunity, otherwise the defendant is deemed to have waived the benefit of it.[55]

C. Unfit to stand trial. The question of what constitutes unfitness to stand trial has already been discussed.[56] In this Chapter we are concerned only with the procedure. **Section 4** of the **Criminal Procedure (Insanity) Act 1964** provides that the

---

[53] s. 35 (5) (c).
[54] See *Connelly* v. *Director of Public Prosecutions* [1964] A.C. 1254; *Mills* v. *Cooper* [1967] 2 Q.B. 459 and the authorities cited in those cases but see also *R.* v. *Maskell* (1970) 54 Cr.App.R. 429 in which it was held on appeal that there was no authority for the proposition that relevant evidence must be excluded on an elastic principle of unfairness or that issue estoppel applied where the parties in the proceedings were not the same.
[55] Arch. para. 459.
[56] *Ante*, p. 88.

following provisions shall have effect where on the trial of a person the question arises (at the instance of the defence or otherwise) whether the accused is fit to be tried. These provisions are—

(1) The court may postpone consideration of the question of fitness to plead until any time up to the opening of the case for the defence if the court, having regard to the nature of the supposed disability,[57] is of the opinion that it is expedient and in the interests of the accused so to do. If the jury then acquit the accused, the question of fitness to plead shall not be determined.[58] The issue of fitness to plead should not be decided before arraignment, but should be postponed until some time before the defence is opened, if there are reasonable chances of the evidence for the prosecution being successfully challenged so that the defence will not be called on.[59] The decision in *R*. v. *Burles*[60] laid down that the judge should first consider the strength or weakness of the prosecution's case as disclosed on the depositions. If the prosecution properly propose to offer no evidence or if their case is so weak that, whatever the degree of disability, it appears to the judge to be expedient to postpone the trial of the issue of fitness to plead, he should do so and afford the defendant the opportunity of acquittal, but if the case for the prosecution is not to that extent weak, the judge should consider the nature and degree of the suggested disability and then decide whether it would be expedient and in the interests of the defendant to postpone the trial of the issue.

(2) Subject to (1), the question of fitness to plead shall be determined as soon as it arises.[61]

(3) The question of fitness to plead shall be determined by a jury: and—

(a) where it falls to be determined on the arraignment of the accused, then if the trial proceeds the accused shall be tried by another jury;

(b) where it falls to be determined at any later time it shall be determined by a separate jury or by the jury by whom the accused is being tried, as the court may direct.[62]

[57] The subsection applies to any disability, such that, apart from the Act, it would constitute a bar to the defendant being tried: *R*. v. *Burles* [1970] 2 Q.B. 191.
[58] *Ibid*. s. 4 (2).
[59] *R*. v. *Webb* [1969] 2 Q.B. 278.
[60] *Supra*.
[61] *Ibid*. s. 4 (3).
[62] *Ibid*. s. 4 (4).

(4) Where a person is found unfit to plead, the trial shall not proceed.[63]

Where a person is found unfit to plead, the court must make an order that the accused be admitted to such hospital as may be specified by the Secretary of State.[64] A person so admitted is treated for the purposes of the Mental Health Act 1959, as if he had been admitted pursuant to a hospital order made under section 60 of that Act, together with an order restricting discharge made under section 65 of that Act without limitation of time.[65] These sections are dealt with later.[66] The effect of section 65 is that the accused cannot be released without the authority of the Secretary of State.

Where a person is detained after being found unfit to plead, the Secretary of State, after consultation with the responsible medical officer, may remit the person to custody for trial if he is satisfied that the person can properly be tried.[67] However, he may subsequently still be found to be unfit for trial by a jury.

Special provisions have been made for an appeal against a finding that a person is unfit to stand trial. These will be noted later.[68]

D. The **general issue** is pleaded by the defendant orally at the bar in the words " not guilty," by which he is deemed to have put himself upon the country (*super patriam*) for trial. This plea throws on the prosecutor the burden of proving every essential ingredient of the offence as stated in the indictment. The defendant in answer may prove not only everything which rebuts the allegations in the indictment, but all matters of justification and excuse, and, in case of a statutory offence, all matters which bring him within any proviso contained in the statute creating the offence.

Where a person pleads not guilty and the prosecutor proposes to offer no evidence against him, the court may, if it thinks fit, order that a verdict of not guilty shall be recorded without the defendant being given in charge to the jury, and the verdict shall have the same effect as if the defendant had been tried and acquitted on the verdict of a jury.[69]

---

[63] *Ibid.* s. 4 (5).
[64] *Ibid.* s. 5 (1).
[65] *Ibid.* Sched. 1, para. 2 (1).
[66] *Post*, p. 796.
[67] *Ibid.* s. 5 (4). This cannot be done, however, if, pursuant to s. 66 of the Mental Health Act 1959, the Secretary of State has ordered that the person shall cease to be subject to the special restrictions set out in s. 65 of that Act: Criminal Procedure (Insanity) Act 1964, Sched. 1, para. 2 (2).
[68] *Post*, p. 840.
[69] Criminal Justice Act 1967, s. 17.

CHAPTER 52

TRIAL AT THE CROWN COURT—PART III
PROCEDURE AFTER A PLEA OF NOT GUILTY [1]

SECTION 1. SELECTION OF JURORS

THE **Courts Act 1971** [2] makes the Lord Chancellor responsible for summoning jurors for service. He has designated the chief clerk at each location of the Crown Court as the appropriate officer for summoning jurors for all courts at that location except coroners' courts. In theory jurors may be required to serve at any place in England or Wales, but the requirement of **section 31 (2)** of the Act that regard must be had to their convenience and to their places of residence, and the desirability of selecting jurors within reasonable travelling distance of the place they are to attend [3] means that in practice they will be summoned to the petty sessional area from which persons are normally committed to that location of the Crown Court. They will be summoned by notice in writing sent by post or delivered by hand.

A panel of jurors is prepared by the appropriate officer of the Crown Court from those persons summoned to attend for a specified period. A party to the proceedings in which the jurors are or may be called upon, to try an issue, and any person acting on his behalf, is entitled without payment, to reasonable facilities for inspecting the panel. [4]

If it appears that a jury to try an issue before the court is incomplete, or may be, the court may, at its discretion, require any persons who are in, or in the vicinity of, the court and who are qualified to serve as jurors, [5] or any other persons who although not qualified, and even though their names do not appear in the register of electors, appear to the court to be responsible or suitable persons, to be summoned without written notice, up to such number as is needed, allowing for refusals and challenges, to make

---

[1] For procedure on a plea of guilty, see *ante*, p. 718.
[2] s. 31 (1).
[3] s. 31 (2).
[4] s. 32 (2) (3) (4).
[5] The qualification of jurors is outside the scope of a work of this nature but a proportion of the panel must be composed of women.

up a full jury.[6] The names of these persons are added to the panel and challenges may be made in the usual manner, the court proceeding as if those so summoned had been included in the panel in the first instance. This was formerly known as " praying a tales."

The jury are selected by the clerk of the court calling their names as he selects them from a ballot box. As their names are balloted they are asked to answer to them and take their place in the jury box. When twelve persons are seated in the jury box the clerk of the court addresses the accused as follows " Prisoner at the Bar, the names of the persons I am about to call are the persons who will form a jury to try you. If you have any objection to them, or to any of them, you must make your objection as they severally come to the Book to be sworn and before they are sworn, and your objection shall be heard." This gives the accused the right of challenge. Each juror is called by name, and called upon to take the oath. Each juror must be sworn separately, and they need no longer be sworn in the presence of each other.

Challenges are effected by the accused or his counsel calling out " challenge " or by the prosecuting counsel calling out " stand by for the Crown " as the juror's name is called and before he actually takes the oath.

By the **Juries Act 1949**,[7] and regulations made thereunder, provisions have been made for the grant of travelling and subsistence allowances and compensation for loss of earnings to persons attending a summons to serve on a jury.

Challenges may be (1) **peremptory,** *i.e.* without assigning any cause, or (2) **for cause,** *i.e.* for some specific reason which must be alleged and proved.

Seven **peremptory** challenges may be made by the defence.[8] There is, however, no right in addition to the peremptory challenges for a defendant to stand by prospective jurors and not challenge for cause until the panel is exhausted. Such right is confined to the Crown. In an exceptional case the judge himself may stand by a juror or allow the defendant to do so.[9] Where the defendant is denied his right of peremptory challenge and is con-

---

[6] s. 33.

[7] As amended by the Juries Act 1954, and the Courts Act 1971, Sched. 11.

[8] Criminal Justice Act 1948, s. 35, as amended by Criminal Law Act 1967, Sched. 3 and the Courts Act 1971, Sched. 11.

[9] *R.* v. *Chandler* [1964] 2 Q.B. 322.

victed the trial is a nullity and a retrial may be ordered.[10]   The prosecution has no right of peremptory challenge, but may ask that a juror or jurors should "stand by," and, unless a sufficient jury cannot be made up without them, is not required to show any cause.[11]

Any juror or jurors may be challenged **for cause,** either by the prosecution or the defence.[12] The challenge may be either to the array or to the polls.

(i) **Challenge to the Array. Paragraph 3 (1)** of **Schedule 4** to the **Courts Act 1971** preserves the right of challenge to the array. This is a right of challenging the entire jury on the grounds that the summoning officer has been biased or has acted improperly when summoning the jury. A challenge to the array should be in writing and made before any juror is sworn, and should state specifically the grounds of the objection. If both parties agree to the challenge the jury panel must be quashed. If one party challenges and the other party counter pleads the judge should appoint two triers from the jury panel to decide the facts of the matter on oath, in the presence of the judge.

(ii) **A challenge to the polls** is a challenge to individual jurors on the ground of some disqualification, and may be made after an unsuccessful challenge to the array. It may be made orally and must be made when the juror comes to be sworn and before the officer begins to administer the oath to him.[13]

A challenge to the polls is also *either principal or for favour.*

Principal challenges are either:

Propter honoris respectum—where a peer or lord of parliament is sworn on a jury for the trial of a commoner, or

Propter defectum, i.e. on account of some personal objection, such as infancy or want of the requisite qualification, or

Propter affectum, i.e. on the ground of some partiality or

Propter delictum, i.e. on account of conviction for some infamous crime.

Challenges *for favour* may be made where there is ground for suspecting partiality though not sufficient for a principal challenge *propter affectum.*

---

[10] *R.* v. *Williams* (1927) 19 Cr.App.R. 67. But see *R.* v. *Berkley* [1969] 2 Q.B. 446.

[11] See Arch. para. 508.

[12] See note 8 above.   [13] For fuller details see Arch. para. 515 *et seq.*

Any question as to the validity of a challenge for cause must be determined by the judge or other person before whom the proceedings are to be heard.[14]

The mere fact that there has been a previous trial resulting in a verdict adverse to the defendant and that this has been widely reported in the press with comments on the evidence does not ordinarily provide a case of probable bias or prejudice in jurors empanelled on a later trial of the defendant. It may be otherwise where newspapers knowing that there is to be a subsequent trial have widely publicised discreditable allegations whether of fact or fiction. In *R. v. Kray and Ors.*,[15] the trial judge ruled that those facts led to a prima facie presumption that persons who had read that information would find it difficult to reach a verdict in a fair minded way. In the exceptional circumstances he permitted defending counsel to examine the jurors as they came into the box to be sworn.

A sufficient number of jurors having been obtained, they are then **sworn.** The judges have expressed the opinion that the following form of oath should be used in all cases: " *I swear by Almighty God [or I do solemnly, sincerely and truly declare and affirm] that I will faithfully try the several issues joined between our Sovereign Lady the Queen and the prisoner(s) at the bar and give a true verdict according to the evidence.*" Each juror should be separately sworn and should read the oath from a printed card held in his hand.[16]

The prisoner is then put in charge of the jury by the clerk of the court of trial as follows: " Members of the jury the prisoner at the bar A. B. stands indicted in that he . . . (stating the substance of the offences charged). To this indictment he has pleaded not guilty, and it is your charge to say, having heard the evidence, whether he be guilty or not."

The court may permit the jury to separate at any time before they retire to consider their verdict,[17] but once they have retired they may not separate even with the leave of the court, except that the court may allow a separation in cases of evident necessity.[18]

---

[14] Criminal Justice Act 1948, s. 35 (2).
[15] (1969) 53 Cr.App.R. 412.
[16] (1957) 41 Cr.App.R. 4; statement of Lord Goddard C.J.
[17] s. 35 (4).
[18] *R. v. Neal* [1949] 2 K.B. 500.

By **section 1 (1)** of the **Criminal Justice Act 1965** it is provided that when in the course of a criminal trial any juror dies, or is discharged by the court for illness or any other reason, but the number of its members is not reduced below nine, the jury shall nevertheless be considered as remaining properly constituted for the purposes of that trial and a verdict may be given accordingly. However, the provisions of subsection (1) do not apply on the trial of a person for murder or for an offence punishable with death unless the prosecution and the defendant give written assent thereto.[19]   Also, on the death or discharge of a juror, the court may order, in any case where it sees fit to do so, the discharge of the jury notwithstanding the provisions of subsection (1).[20]

The jury selected by any one ballot must try only one issue, but any juror is liable to be selected on more than one ballot.[21]   Except however, that this provision does not prevent the trial of two or more issues by the same jury if the trial of the second or last issue begins within twenty-four hours from the time when the jury is constituted, or the trial of fitness to plead by the same jury as that by whom the accused is being tried, if that is so directed by the court under section 4 (4) (*b*) of the Criminal Procedure (Insanity) Act 1964, or in a case beginning with a special plea, the trial of the accused on the general issue by the jury trying the special plea.[22]   The court may, on the trial of the second or any subsequent issue, instead of proceeding with the same entire jury, order any juror to withdraw, if the court considers he could be justly challenged or excused, or if the parties to the proceedings consent, and the juror to replace him is selected by ballot in open court, except that if he is summoned after balloting has begun he need not be balloted in open court.[23]

Section 2. Order of Proceedings at the Trial

It is only intended at this stage to give a rough outline of the procedure.   Various matters will be discussed more fully below.

---

[19] Criminal Justice Act 1965, s. 1 (2).
[20] *Ibid.* s. 1 (3). By regulations made under the Juries Act 1949 as amended by the Juries Act 1954, and the Courts Act 1971, section 36, provision has been made for the grant of travelling and subsistence allowances, and compensation for loss of earnings to persons attending a criminal trial: Juror's Allowances Regulations 1971 (S.I. No. 136 of 1971].
[21] Courts Act 1971, s. 35 (4).
[22] *Ibid.* s. 35 (5) (*a*) (*b*) (*c*).
[23] *Ibid.* s. 35 (6).

In the first place counsel for the prosecution opens the case to the jury, stating the principal matters on which he intends to rely. He then calls his witnesses, who, having been sworn, are examined by him, cross-examined by the defence, and then re-examined by him upon any matters referred to in cross-examination.

At the conclusion of the case for the prosecution, the defence may submit to the judge that there is *no evidence* to prove an essential element of the offence or offences charged in the indictment or that the evidence of the prosecution on any count or counts is such that no reasonable tribunal could safely convict upon it.[24] If the judge upholds a submission in respect of the whole indictment, he will then direct the jury to return a verdict of not guilty. If he upholds the submission in respect of one or more of the counts only, he will direct them to return a verdict of not guilty in respect of such count or counts. Once a decision to direct a verdict of not guilty has been made by the judge, he cannot thereafter change his mind upon hearing the evidence for the defence.[25]

If no such submission is made or if, being made, it fails, the subsequent steps depend upon whether any evidence, oral or documentary, other than the evidence of the defendant himself and witnesses only as to character, is adduced for the defence and whether the defendant is or is not represented by counsel. All witnesses, including the defendant if he gives evidence, may be cross-examined and re-examined.

1. *If any evidence is to be adduced other than the evidence of the defendant himself and witnesses only as to character, then*:

    (i) The defendant, or if he is represented by counsel, his counsel, may, if he so desires, open his defence.[26]

    (ii) The witnesses for the defence, including the defendant, if he desires to give evidence, are then examined.

[24] *R.* v. *Young* (1964) 48 Cr.App.R. 292.

[25] See *Practice Direction* [1962] Crim.L.R. 160 and *R.* v. *Plain* [1967] 1 W.L.R. 565.

[26] Criminal Procedure Act 1865, s. 2. An accused prisoner may, if he so wishes, conduct his own defence, and if he is refused the right to do so and is convicted, the conviction will be quashed: *R.* v. *Woodward* [1944] K.B. 118. An unrepresented defendant must be told by the judge that he may either go into the witness-box and give evidence on oath and be cross-examined like any other witness, or may make a statement to the jury from the dock and he must also be informed of his right to call witnesses. If he is not so informed his conviction may be quashed: *R.* v. *Andrews* (1938) 27 Cr.App.R. 12; *R.* v. *Carter* (1960) 44 Cr.App.R. 225.

  (iii) If the defendant does not desire to give evidence he may make an unsworn statement.[27]

  (iv) Counsel for the prosecution sums up the evidence on behalf of the prosecution.[28]

  (v) The defendant, or if he is represented, his counsel, sums up the evidence for the defence.[29]

2. *If no evidence is adduced other than that of the defendant himself and witnesses as to character, then*:

  A. *if the defendant is represented by counsel—*

    (i) The defendant, if he so desires, gives his evidence or makes an unsworn statement [30] and witnesses as to character give their evidence.

    (ii) Counsel for the prosecution *may* sum up his case.[31]

    (iii) Counsel for the defence sums up his case.[32]

  B. *if the defendant is not represented by counsel—*

    (i) The defendant, if he so desires, gives his evidence and witnesses as to character give their evidence.

    (ii) The defendant addresses the jury in his own defence.[33]

If two or more persons are jointly indicted and represented by different counsel, then, in the absence of agreement between counsel, the court will call on them to cross-examine and address the jury in the order in which the names of the persons whom they represent stand on the indictment.[34]

At the conclusion of the evidence, if any, for the defence, the Crown may in certain circumstances introduce rebutting evidence.[35] Such evidence may even be introduced after the conclusion of defence counsel's final address to the jury, but not after the conclu-

---

[27] The Criminal Evidence Act 1898 which allows a prisoner to give evidence on his own behalf (see *ante*, p. 621) did not take away his right to make an unsworn statement upon which he cannot be cross-examined. For the duty of the trial judge with respect to such a statement when he is summing up to the jury, see *R.* v. *Frost and Hale* (1964) 48 Cr.App.R. 284.

[28] Criminal Procedure Act 1865, s. 2; Criminal Procedure (Right of Reply) Act 1964, s. 1.

[29] *Ibid.*

[30] Above, note 27.

[31] Criminal Procedure Act 1865, s. 2.

[32] Criminal Procedure Act 1865, s. 2.

[33] The prosecutor has no right of reply.

[34] Arch. para. 553.

[35] See Arch. paras. 554, 555.

sion of the summing up to the jury by the judge.[36] If introduced after the defence counsel's final address the defence counsel would be entitled to comment on the evidence.[37]

After the conclusion of the defence counsel's final address to the jury, and before the jury consider their verdict, the judge sums up the evidence and directs them on the applicable law.

Duties of counsel for the prosecution. Prosecuting counsel should regard himself as a " minister of justice " assisting in the administration of justice rather than as an advocate. Thus he should not press for a conviction or make unfair observations likely to prejudice the jury against the accused.[38] Other obligations of a similar kind are noted below.

Among the other duties of counsel for the prosecution are—

(1) the duty to make available to the defence a witness from whom the prosecution have taken a statement and whom they know can give material evidence, although there is no duty to supply the defence with a copy of the statement [39];

(2) the duty to inform the defence of the known bad character of the victim of the crime [40] (*e.g.* the complainant or the owner of the property), although there is no duty to search every kind of record, *e.g.* bankruptcy proceedings, to see whether anything exists against him [41];

(3) the duty to inform the defence if a witness who has been called by the prosecution and given evidence on a material issue has earlier made a conflicting statement which is in the possession of the prosecution and, although there is no duty to hand over any such statement, the judge may order that it should be handed over.[42]

Counsel's address to the jury. When counsel either for the prosecution or defence is summarising his case to the jury before calling his witnesses, he should be careful not to refer to any evidence the admissibility of which is in doubt. Counsel for the

[36] See *R.* v. *Flynn* (1957) 42 Cr.App.R. 15.
[37] Arch. para. 554.
[38] *R.* v. *Puddick* (1865) 4 F. & F. 497 at p. 499; *R.* v. *Banks* [1916] 2 K.B. 621.
[39] *R.* v. *Bryant and Dickson* (1946) 31 Cr.App.R. 146.
[40] This person is sometimes referred to as the prosecutor or prosecutrix.
[41] *R.* v. *Collister and Warhurst* (1955) 39 Cr.App.R. 100.
[42] Arch. para. 1374.

prosecution must not comment on the failure of the accused, or of his spouse, to give evidence.[43] Nor should counsel for the accused state to the jury as existing facts any matters about which the defendant has told him but which he does not propose to prove in evidence.

Witnesses. At the request of either party, the court will order witnesses who have not yet given their evidence to leave the court until they are called.

All the witnesses whose names are on the back of the indictment (*i.e.* all the witnesses who gave evidence for the Crown at the preliminary inquiry) ought to attend,[44] except witnesses in respect of whom only a conditional witness order [45] is in force or whose testimony will not be given orally. This rule obliges the Crown to take all reasonable steps to secure their attendance. If, despite all such steps, it proves impossible to secure the presence of a witness, for instance because he has gone abroad, the judge may in his discretion permit the trial to proceed provided that no injustice is done thereby.[45a] The prosecutor has a wide discretion as to whether he should call every witness whose name appears on the back of the indictment. Where such a witness's evidence is capable of belief, it is the prosecutor's duty to call him either for examination by himself in the normal way or only for cross-examination by the defence, even though the evidence that he is going to give is inconsistent with the case sought to be proved. But where the evidence of such a witness is manifestly unreliable, the prosecutor is not obliged to call him.[46]

The discretion whether or not to call a witness whose name appears on the back of the indictment must be exercised in a manner which is calculated to further the interest of justice and at the same time be fair to the defence. If the prosecution appears to be exercising the discretion improperly, the trial judge may invite the prosecutor to call a particular witness and on his refusal to do so, the judge may call the witness himself.[47]

---

[43] Criminal Evidence Act 1898, s. 1 (*b*).
[44] *R.* v. *Oliva* [1965] 1 W.L.R. 1028 at p. 1035. See also *Adel Muhammed El Dabbah* v. *Att.-Gen. for Palestine* [1949] A.C. 156.
[45] *Ante*, p. 668.
[45a] *R.* v. *Cavanagh and Shaw* [1972] 1 W.L.R. 676, where the considerations affecting the exercise of this discretion are considered.
[46] *R.* v. *Oliva* [1965] 1 W.L.R. 1028 at pp. 1035–1036.
[47] *Ibid.* This is particularly the case where the evidence has been opened to the jury: *R.* v. *Sterk* [1972] Crim.L.R. 391.

Additional witnesses may also be called by the prosecution provided that notice of the intention to do so, with a copy of their proposed evidence, is sent to the defendant and to the court.[48]

Although the evidence of witnesses is usually given orally, section 13 (3) of the Criminal Justice Act 1925, and section 9 of the Criminal Justice Act 1967, provide that, in certain circumstances, a written statement of the evidence of a witness is admissible.

Section 13 (3) of the **Criminal Justice Act 1925** [49] provides that where any person has been committed for trial for any offence, the deposition of any person taken before the examining justices may without further proof be read as evidence on the trial of that person, whether for that offence or for any other offence arising out of the same transaction, or set of circumstances, as that offence, provided that the following conditions are satisfied:

(*a*) The deposition must be the deposition either of a witness in respect of whom a conditional witness order has been made, or of a witness who is proved at the trial by the oath of a credible witness to be dead or insane, or so ill as not to be able to travel, or to be kept out of the way by means of the procurement of the accused or on his behalf;

(*b*) It must be proved at the trial, either by a certificate purporting to be signed by the justice before whom the deposition purports to have been taken, or by the clerk to the examining justices, or by oath of a credible witness, that the deposition was taken in the presence of the accused and that the accused or his counsel or solicitor had full opportunity of cross-examining the witness;

(*c*) The deposition must purport to be signed by the justice before whom it purports to have been taken:

Provided that these provisions shall not have effect in any case in which it is proved:

(i) That the deposition or certificate was not in fact signed by the justice by whom it purports to have been signed; or

---

[48] Arch. para. 1375.

[49] As amended by the Magistrates' Courts Act 1952, Sched. 6 and the Criminal Procedure (Attendance of Witnesses) Act 1965.

(ii) Where the deposition is the deposition of a witness in respect of whom a conditional witness order has been made, that the witness has been duly notified that he is required to attend the trial.[50]

Section 2 (7) of the **Criminal Justice Act 1967** provides that section 13 (3) (other than subsection (b)) of the Criminal Justice Act 1925 shall apply to any written statement tendered in evidence in committal proceedings pursuant to section 2, as it applies to a deposition taken in such proceedings. However, the signature of the examining justice, which is required on a deposition pursuant to section 13 (3) (c), is not required on a written statement if he signs a certificate authenticating one or more such statements.

Section 9 (1) of the **Criminal Justice Act 1967** provides that in any criminal proceedings, other than committal proceedings, a written statement by any person [51] shall be admissible as evidence to the like extent as oral evidence to the like effect [52] by that person if such of the following conditions as are applicable are satisfied. These conditions, which are set out in **subsection (2),** are:

(a) the statement purports to be signed by the person who made it;

(b) the statement contains a declaration by that person to the effect that it is true to the best of his knowledge and belief and that he made the statement knowing that, if it were tendered in evidence, he would be liable to prosecution if he wilfully stated in it anything which he knew to be false or did not believe to be true [53] or in the case of

---

[50] In *R.* v. *Collins* (1938) 26 Cr.App.R. 177, the accused pleaded guilty before the examining justices and the witnesses were bound over conditionally to attend the trial. At the trial he pleaded not guilty and applied for an adjournment to prove an alibi. His application was refused and, since no witnesses were present, their depositions were read to the jury, who convicted him. *Held,* by the Court of Criminal Appeal, that such a course was not desirable and should not be adopted again. The provisions of s. 13 (3) were not intended to apply to cases where the accused changes his plea.

[51] By the Criminal Justice Act 1972, s. 46 (1), s. 9 is extended to written statements made in Scotland or Northern Ireland.

[52] Any document or object referred to as an exhibit and identified in a written statement tendered in evidence under this section shall be treated as if it had been produced as an exhibit and identified in court by the maker of the statement: s. 8 (7).

[53] If any person in a written statement tendered in evidence by virtue of s. 8 wilfully makes a statement material in those proceedings which he knows to be false or does not believe to be true, he commits an offence: Criminal Justice Act 1967, s. 89 (1). The Perjury Act 1911 shall have effect as if s. 89 were contained in that Act: s. 89 (2).

a statement, which indicates that the person making it has not attained the age of fourteen, that he understands the importance of telling the truth in it [54];

(*c*) before the hearing at which the statement is tendered in evidence, a copy of the statement is served, by or on behalf of the party proposing to tender it, on each of the other parties to the proceedings [55]; and

(*d*) none of the other parties or their solicitors, within seven days from the service of the copy of the statement, serves a notice on the party so proposing objecting to the statement being tendered in evidence under this section:

Provided that the conditions mentioned in paragraphs (*c*) and (*d*) shall not apply if the parties agree before or during the hearing that the statement shall be so tendered.

Section 9 (3) provides that the following provisions shall also have effect in relation to any written statement tendered in evidence under this section, that is to say—

(*a*) if the statement is made by a person under the age of twenty-one, it shall give his age;

(*b*) if it is made by a person who cannot read it, it shall be read to him before he signs it and shall be accompanied by a declaration by the person who so read the statement to the effect that it was so read; and

(*c*) if it refers to any other document as an exhibit, the copy served on any other party to the proceedings under paragraph (*c*) of subsection (2) shall be accompanied by a copy of that document or by such information as may be necessary in order to enable the party on whom it is served to inspect that document or a copy thereof.

Section 9 (4) provides that notwithstanding that a written statement made by any person may be admissible as evidence by virtue of this section—

(*a*) the party by whom or on whose behalf a copy of the statement was served may call that person to give evidence; and

(*b*) the court may, of its own motion or on the application of

[54] Inserted by the Children and Young Persons Act 1969, Sched. 5.
[55] For the requirements of valid service, see s. 9 (8).

any party to the proceedings,[56] require that person to attend before the court and give evidence.

Turning now to the methods of securing the presence of witnesses at the trial we have already seen that failure to comply with a witness order made by a magistrates' court acting as examining justices is an offence.[57] **Section 2** of the **Criminal Procedure (Attendance of Witnesses) Act 1965** [58] provides that for the purpose of any criminal proceedings before the Crown Court a *witness summons* may be issued out of that court or out of the High Court. A witness summons is a summons requiring the person to whom it is directed to attend before the court and give evidence or produce any document or thing specified in the summons.[59] Failure to comply with a witness summons is punishable by the court issuing the summons in the same way as failure to comply with a witness order.[60]

Section 4 (1) of the Act provides that if a judge of the High Court is satisfied by evidence on oath that a witness in respect of whom a witness order or witness summons is in force is unlikely to comply with the order or summons, the judge may issue a warrant to arrest [61] the witness and bring him before the court before which he is required to attend:

Provided that a warrant shall not be issued under this subsection in the case of a witness subject to a conditional witness order unless notice has been given requiring him to attend the trial, nor in the case of a witness subject to a witness summons unless the judge is satisfied by such evidence as aforesaid that the witness is likely to be able to give material evidence or produce any document or thing likely to be material evidence in the proceedings.

Section 4 (2) provides that where a witness who is required to attend before the Crown Court by virtue of a witness order or a witness summons fails to attend in compliance with the order or summons, that court may:

---

[56] In the case of a court other than a magistrates' court, this application may be made to the court before the hearing: s. 9 (5).

[57] *Ante*, p. 668.

[58] Amended by the Courts Act 1971, Sched. 8.

[59] Application may be made to the Crown Court or to the High Court to direct that the summons shall be of no effect where no material evidence can be given or produced: s. 2 (2).

[60] s. 3, *ante*, p. 668.

[61] Such a warrant is treated as if issued out of the Crown Court: Courts Act 1971, Sched. 8.

(a) in any case, cause to be served on him a notice requiring him to attend the court forthwith or at such time as may be specified in the notice;

(b) if the court is satisfied that there are reasonable grounds for believing that he has failed to attend without just excuse, or if he has failed to comply with a notice under paragraph (a) above, issue a warrant to arrest him and bring him before the court.

A witness brought before the court in pursuance of a warrant under section 4 may be remanded in custody or on bail (with or without sureties).[62]

Right of the judge to call a witness. A judge at a criminal trial has the right to call a witness not called by either the prosecution or the defence, without the consent of either the prosecution or the defence, if in his opinion that course is necessary in the interests of justice. However, in order that injustice should not be done to the defendant, a judge should not as a general rule call a witness after the case for the defence is closed except in a case where a matter arises *ex improviso*, which could not be foreseen.[63]

Proof by formal admission. Section 10 of the **Criminal Justice Act 1967** provides that, subject to the following provisions, any fact of which oral evidence may be given in any criminal proceedings may be admitted for the purpose of those proceedings by or on behalf of the prosecutor or defendant, and the admission by any party of any such fact under this section shall as against that party be conclusive evidence in those proceedings of the fact admitted. An admission under this section:

(a) may be made before or at the proceedings;

(b) if made otherwise than in court, shall be in writing;

(c) if made in writing by an individual, shall purport to be signed by the person making it and, if so made by a body corporate, shall purport to be signed by a director or

---

[62] s. 4 (3).

[63] See *R. v. Cleghorn* [1967] 2 Q.B. 584. For an example of an exception to the rule, see *R. v. Tregear* [1967] 2 Q.B. 574. The power of the judge to call a witness seems to stand on much the same footing as the power of allowing rebutting evidence to be called (see p. 745, *post*): *R. v. Sullivan* (1922) 16 Cr.App.R. 121; *R. v. Joseph* (1972) 56 Cr.App.R. 60.

manager, or the secretary or clerk, or some other similar
officer of the body corporate;

(d) if made on behalf of a defendant who is an individual, shall
be made by his counsel or solicitor;

(e) if made at any stage before the trial by a defendant who is
an individual, must be approved by his counsel or solicitor
(whether at the time it was made or subsequently) before
or at the proceedings in question.

An admission under this section for the purpose of proceedings
relating to any matter shall be treated as an admission for the
purpose of any subsequent criminal proceedings relating to that
matter (including any appeal or retrial).[64]   However, with the leave
of the court, an admission may be withdrawn in the proceedings
for the purpose of which it is made or any subsequent criminal
proceedings relating to the same matter.[65]

Notice of alibi. Section 11 (1) of the **Criminal Justice Act 1967**
provides that on a trial on indictment the defendant shall not,
without the leave of the court,[66] adduce evidence in support of
an alibi [67] unless, before the end of the prescribed period, he gives
notice of particulars of the alibi.[68]   **Section 11 (2)** provides that
the defendant shall not, without the leave of the court,[69] call any
other person to give such evidence unless:

(a) the notice includes the name and address of the witness
or, if the name or address is not known to the defendant
at the time he gives the notice, any information in his
possession which might be of material assistance in
finding the witness;

(b) if the name or the address is not included in that notice,
the court is satisfied that the defendant, before giving

---

[64] s. 10 (3).   [65] s. 10 (4).

[66] Leave of the court shall not be refused if it appears that the defendant was
not informed at the preliminary inquiry of the requirements of the section:
s. 11 (3). The discretion of the court with regard to allowing or refusing
the evidence to be given must be exercised judicially: *R.* v. *Sullivan* [1971]
1 Q.B. 253.

[67] The expression " evidence in support of an alibi " is defined in s. 11 (8).

[68] The section envisages the commission of an offence at a particular time and
place. The statutory requirements only apply if the alibi relates to the time
when the offence is alleged to have been committed: *R.* v. *Lewis* [1969] 2
Q.B. 1; similarly where the offence charged is a continuing one, such as
living on immoral earnings, difficulties may arise as to what amounts to
" evidence in support of an alibi ": *R.* v. *Hassan* [1970] 1 Q.B. 423.

[69] See note 66 above.

the notice, took and thereafter continued to take all reasonable steps to secure that the name or address would be ascertained;

(c) if the name or the address is not included in that notice, but the defendant subsequently discovers the name or address or receives other information which might be of material assistance in finding the witness, he forthwith gives notice of the name, address or other information, as the case may be; and

(d) if the defendant is notified by or on behalf of the prosecutor that the witness has not been traced by the name or at the address given, he forthwith gives notice of any such information which is then in his possession or, on subsequently receiving any such information, forthwith gives notice of it.

The notice must be given in court during, or at the end of, the proceedings before the examining justices or be given in writing to the solicitor for the prosecutor *within seven days of the end of those proceedings.*[70]

Rebutting evidence. As a general principle evidence which is clearly relevant to the issue, and within the possession of the Crown should be advanced by the Crown as part of its case, and such evidence cannot properly be admitted after evidence for the defence, by way of rebuttal.[71] But where the evidence is in no sense probative of the guilt of the defendant, but is directed towards disproving the truth of the defence the position is otherwise and the judge has a discretion to admit the evidence.[72] In *R. v. Frost* [73]:

" There can be no doubt about the general rule, that where the Crown begins a case (as it is with an ordinary plaintiff), they bring forward their evidence, and cannot afterwards

---

[70] s. 11 (6) (8). In the case of a notice under s. 11 (2) (c) or (d) it must be in writing: s. 11 (6). The requirements for a valid notice are set out in s. 11 (7). The period of seven days excludes Sundays and other specified holidays: s. 11 (9).

[71] *R. v. Rice* [1963] 1 Q.B. 857; *R. v. Levy and Tait* (1966) 50 Cr.App.R. 198.

[72] *R. v. Milliken*, 53 Cr.App.R. 389. No evidence may be received after the completion of the summing-up: *R. v. Corless* (1972) 56 Cr.App.R. 341 where the authorities are reviewed. See also *R. v. Doran* [1972] Crim.L.R. 392.

[73] (1839) 9 C. & P. 129 at p. 159; *R. v. Day* (1940) 27 Cr.App.R. 168; *R. v. Levy and Tait* (1966) 50 Cr.App.R. 198; *R. v. Joseph* (1972) 56 Cr.App.R. 60.

support their case by calling fresh witnesses, because there may be evidence in the defence to contradict it. But if any matter arises *ex improviso,* which the Crown could not foresee, supposing it to be entirely new matter, which they may be able to answer only by contradictory evidence, they may give evidence in reply."

The question whether the prosecution will be allowed to call rebutting evidence or not is in the discretion of the trial judge.[74]

Until 1967, rebuttal evidence was often used to meet an alibi raised for the first time by the accused at the trial. The Criminal Justice Act 1967 provides that any evidence tendered to disprove an alibi may, subject to any directions by the court as to the time it is to be given, be given before or after evidence is given in support of the alibi.[75] However, in practice rebuttal evidence will not normally be admissible where notice has been given under that Act.[76]

Argument in the absence of the jury. Where any legal arguments arise during the course of the trial, *e.g.* regarding the admissibility of evidence, the jury should retire if their presence in court would unfairly prejudice the defendant's case.

Evidence in absence of the jury. In regard to evidence, however, apart from evidence on the question of the admissibility of a confession, it is most exceptional for evidence to be permitted in the absence of the jury.[77]

View. The judge may, even without the consent of the prosecutor, allow the jury to view the *locus in quo* at any time during the trial, even after the summing-up, if it is within the jurisdiction, but precautions ought to be taken to secure that the jury shall not improperly receive evidence out of court, in the

---

[74] *R.* v. *McKenna* (1956) 40 Cr.App.R. 65; *cf. Phelan* v. *Back* [1972] 1 W.L.R. in which case it was decided that a recorder or chairman of quarter sessions (now the Crown Court), when sitting alone or with justices, when hearing an appeal and not sitting with a jury, had a discretion to allow evidence to be called after the normal point at which such evidence would be excluded, if the interests of justice required it.

[75] s. 11 (4).

[76] See *R.* v. *Flynn* (1958) 42 Cr.App.R. 15 at pp. 18–19.

[77] See *R.* v. *Reynolds* [1950] 1 K.B. 606; *R.* v. *Sutton* (1969) 53 Cr.App.R. 504.

absence of the judge and the prisoner.[78] There is a dearth of English authority on this matter, although the Privy Council has dealt with the principles on at least two occasions. It would seem that the jury is entitled to go to a simple view without witnesses or judge being present. Where, however, witnesses are to be present, then the accused and the judge ought to be present also. After the view the witnesses should be recalled in order to give evidence in respect of the place viewed.[79]

Summing up. Before the jury consider their verdict the judge sums up the evidence, directing them as to the law applicable and particularly on whom the burden of proof lies,[80] and calling their attention to the salient points of the evidence. He may also, in his discretion, comment on the absence of evidence which might have been expected, including the failure of the prisoner to give evidence.[81] The trial judge may tell the jury that in giving weight to the accused's explanation, they may take into account his failure to say anything to the police earlier. However, they must be told that he has no duty to say anything and the trial judge cannot say such things as: " Can you imagine an innocent man behaving like that? "[82] He must leave to the jury everything in the indictment about which sufficient evidence has been given and direct the jury upon the law relating to every count in the indictment.[83] He must put the defence to the jury.[84] There is no obligation to direct the jury where the defendant relies on an alibi that it is for the prosecution to negative it, unless the jury seem in danger of supposing that the burden is on the defence.[85] He

[78] R. v. Martin (1867) L.R. 1 C.C.R. 387. The Crown Court Rules 1971 may make provisions as respects views by jurors. The places to which a juror may go to view are not restricted to any particular county or area: Courts Act 1971, Sched. 4.

[79] Karamat v. The Queen [1956] A.C. 256; Tameshawar v. The Queen [1957] A.C. 476.

[80] R. v. Rees (1928) 21 Cr.App.R. 35; R. v. Hepworth and Fearnley [1955] 2 Q.B. 600.

[81] R. v. Rhodes [1899] 1 Q.B. 77.

[82] See R. v. Ryan (1966) 50 Cr.App.R. 144; R. v. Hoare [1966] 1 W.L.R. 762; R. v. Sullivan (1967) 51 Cr.App.R. 102.

[83] R. v. Lincoln (1944) 29 Cr.App.R. 191; see also R. v. Lester (1938) 27 Cr.App.R. 8.

[84] R. v. Mills (1935) 25 Cr.App.R. 138; R. v. Tillman [1962] Crim.L.R. 261, and this applies whether or not the accused gives evidence: R. v. Jarman (1962) 106 S.J. 838. See also R. v. Porritt (1961) 45 Cr.App.R. 348; R. v. Kachikwu (1968) 52 Cr.App.R. 538.

[85] R. v. Wood (1968) 52 Cr.App.R. 74.

must explain the rules regarding a majority verdict and he must not use expressions which may convey that the minority should try to agree with the majority.[86] Misdirection or failure to direct the jury on questions of law or fact may be a ground of appeal.

SECTION 3. VERDICT AND JUDGMENT

After the summing-up the jury consider their verdict. For this purpose they may, if they desire, retire from the court under the charge of an officer of the court. From the time they begin to consider their verdict they may not separate or leave the place in which they are deliberating until they have returned their verdict or have been discharged, and any breach of this rule renders the whole trial void.[87] Nor, after they have retired, may they obtain any further assistance or information except in open court from the judge in the presence of the defendant.[88] The judge may, in answer to a question by the jury, give a further direction on the material points, and if the form of the jury's question indicates that they are proceeding on a wrong premise, such further direction must be given.[89]

The verdict of the jury, whether guilty or not guilty, must be:

(a) unanimous[90]; or
(b) in a case where there are not less than eleven jurors, the verdict of at least ten jurors; or
(c) in a case where there are ten jurors, the verdict of nine jurors.[91]

However, the court must not accept a majority verdict on a verdict of guilty unless the foreman of the jury has stated in open court the number of jurors who respectively agreed to and dissented from

[86] R. v. Mills [1939] 2 K.B. 90.
[87] R. v. Neal [1949] 2 K.B. 500.
[88] R. v. Green (1949) 34 Cr.App.R. 33. But see R. v. Furlong (1950) 34 Cr.App.R. 79. This does not include further evidence being given. The jury is bound to try the case and return their verdict on the evidence already before them.
[89] R. v. Adair (1958) 42 Cr.App.R. 227.
[90] Where it appears that the jury cannot agree, the judge should direct them in the light of R. v. Walheim (1925) 36 Cr.App.R. 167, but see R. v. Davey [1960] 1 W.L.R. 1287 as to the need for emphasising unanimity. See also R. v. Kalinsky [1967] 1 W.L.R. 699.
[91] Criminal Justice Act 1967, s. 13 (1). And then only after a direction given by the judge dealing with the circumstances in which the court is prepared to receive a majority verdict.

the verdict.[92] He must not state in open court the number of jurors who respectively agreed to and dissented from the verdict where the verdict is one of not guilty. Nor must a court accept such a verdict unless it appears to the court that the jury have had not less than two hours and ten minutes [between the time when the last member of the jury has left the jury box to go to the jury room and the time when there is put to the jury the question as to whether at least ten (nine as the case may be) have agreed upon their verdict?] for deliberation or such longer period as the court thinks reasonable having regard to the nature and complexity of the case.[93]

The verdict must be delivered in open court, in the presence of all the jurors, whose assent to it is then conclusively presumed.[94]

If the jurors cannot after a reasonable time come to a unanimous or lawful majority verdict they are discharged and the prisoner may be tried again.

Once the defendant is in charge of the jury the trial cannot end until the jury return a verdict or express their disagreement,[95] unless there are alternative counts (e.g. for stealing and handling stolen goods). Since a defendant cannot be guilty of both stealing and handling the same property, if the jury convict on one count, they should be discharged from giving a verdict on the other.[96] It may, however, here be noted that a nolle prosequi to stay proceedings upon an indictment or information pending in any court may be entered, by leave of the Attorney-General, at the instance of either the prosecutor or the defendant, at any time after the indictment has been signed, and before judgment.[97] A nolle prosequi puts an end to the prosecution, but the prisoner remains liable to be reindicted.[98]

A verdict may be either:

(i) General, i.e. guilty or not guilty on the whole charge;

[92] Ibid. s. 13 (2).
[93] Ibid. s. 13 (3) and see Practice Direction (1970) 54 Cr.App.R. 373.
[94] R. v. Roads [1967] 2 Q.B. 108 and the procedure to be followed is laid down in the Practice Direction (supra) set out in Arch. para. 574. As to the propriety of following that direction see R. v. Georgiou (1969) 53 Cr.App.R. 428. See also R. v. Bateson (1969) 54 Cr.App.R. 11.
[95] R. v. Heyes [1951] 1 K.B. 29.
[96] R. v. Seymour (1954) 38 Cr.App.R. 68.
[97] A nolle prosequi may be granted, e.g. where in cases of misdemeanour a civil action is pending for the same cause.
[98] Arch. paras. 293, 294.

(ii) *Partial,* *e.g.* a conviction on one or more counts of the indictment, or of an offence other than the offence charged;

(iii) *Special,* where the jury find the facts alone and leave to the court the question of their legal effect.[99]

A verdict is not complete until it is accepted by the judge and recorded, and the judge is not bound to receive the first verdict of the jury but may request them to reconsider it, and the verdict which they ultimately return will then be their verdict.[1] If the verdict is so defective or ambiguous or inconsistent that a judgment cannot be founded thereon the judge may discharge the jury,[2] and if in such cases a verdict of guilty is recorded the conviction will be quashed. So also a conviction was quashed where, on a charge of obtaining food and money by false pretences,[3] the jury found the verdict of "guilty of obtaining food and money under false pretences, but whether or not there was any intent to defraud the jury consider there is not sufficient evidence," this finding negativing a material allegation in the indictment, namely, the intent to defraud.[4] But the jury have a right to return a general verdict of guilty or not guilty, and if they insist on so doing the judge is bound to accept it.[5] Where the verdict of a jury is plain and unequivocal and unambiguous the judge should not put any questions to them in order to ascertain the grounds of their verdict.[6]

When several persons are joined in one indictment the jury may convict some and acquit others. In some cases, however, the acquittal of one may render the conviction of the other or others impossible; in conspiracy, for example, at least two of the prisoners must be convicted, and in riot at least three, unless those convicted

---

[99] As, *e.g.* in *R.* v. *Dudley* (1884) 14 Q.B.D. 273, where the jury found the facts and left it to the court to say whether the prisoners were guilty of murder.

[1] *R.* v. *Yeadon* (1861) L. & C. 81; *R.* v. *Meany* (1862) L. & C. 213; *R.* v. *Harris* [1964] Crim.L.R. 54.

[2] *R.* v. *Murphy* (1869) L.R. 2 P.C. 535 at p. 548.

[3] Under the old Larceny Act 1916, now obtaining property by deception under the Theft Act 1968.

[4] *R.* v. *Gray* (1891) 17 Cox 299.

[5] *R.* v. *Allday* (1837) 8 C. & P. 136; and see *R.* v. *Meany* (1862) L. & C. 213; *R.* v. *Farnborough* [1895] 2 Q.B. 484.

[6] *R.* v. *Larkin* [1943] K.B. 174.

are charged with having been engaged in the conspiracy or riot with some other person or persons not tried upon that indictment.[7]

Alternative verdicts. In this section we are dealing with the power of the jury to convict a person charged with an offence of a lesser included offence or another offence or an attempt to commit the offence. This alternative offence does not have to be put into a separate count. Where the prosecution believe that a person may be guilty of a lesser or other offence but, in accordance with the rules set out below, a verdict for that offence is not possible on a charge of the greater offence, then the lesser or other offence should be included in a separate count.

Section 6 (3) of the **Criminal Law Act 1967** provides that where on a person's trial on indictment for any offence except treason or murder, the jury find him not guilty of the offence specifically charged in the indictment, but the allegations in the indictment amount to or include (expressly or by implication) an allegation of another offence falling within the jurisdiction of the court of trial, the jury may find him guilty of that other offence or of an offence of which he could be found guilty on an indictment specifically charging that other offence. Where the indictment does not set out particulars of the matters relied on to prove the offence charged, the correct test for ascertaining whether it contains allegations which expressly or impliedly include an allegation of a lesser offence is whether it is a necessary step towards proving the offence charged to prove the commission of the lesser offence; that is to say whether the lesser offence is an essential ingredient of the offence charged.[8] Thus a charge of unlawful sexual intercourse with a girl under 16 necessarily involves an allegation of indecent assault.[9]

Attempts. For purposes of subsection (3) any allegation of an offence shall be taken as including an allegation of attempting to commit that offence; and where a person is charged on indictment with attempting to commit an offence or with any assault or other act preliminary to an offence, but not with the completed offence,

---

[7] Arch. para. 572.

[8] *R.* v. *Springfield* (1969) 53 Cr.App.R. 608. This can be shown by striking out of the indictment all the averments which have not been proved, and seeing what is left: *R.* v. *Lillis* [1972] 2 Q.B. 236, C.A. See also *R.* v. *Snewing* [1972] Crim.L.R. 267.

[9] *R.* v. *McCormack* [1969] 2 Q.B. 442.

then (subject to the discretion of the court to discharge the jury with a view to the preferment of an indictment for the completed offence) he may be convicted of the offence charged notwithstanding that he is shown to be guilty of the completed offence.

Assisting offenders.   Section 4 (2) provides that if on the trial of an indictment for an arrestable offence the jury are satisfied that the offence charged (or some other offence of which the accused might on that charge be found guilty) was committed, but find the accused not guilty of it, they may find him guilty of any offence under subsection (1) of that section (assisting offenders) of which they are satisfied that he is guilty in relation to the offence charged (or that other offence).

In addition to these general sections, there are a number of provisions dealing with particular offences. The following are the more important:

(i) On an indictment for murder a person found not guilty of murder may be found guilty:

(*a*) of manslaughter, or of causing bodily harm with intent to do so; or

(*b*) of an offence of which he may be found guilty under an enactment specifically so providing (see below (ii)), or under section 4 (2) of this Act (above); or

(*c*) of an attempt to commit murder, or of an attempt to commit any other offence of which he might be found guilty;

but may not be found guilty of any offence not included above.[10]

(ii) Upon the trial of a woman for the murder of her child under the age of twelve months the jury may, in certain special circumstances, return a verdict of infanticide instead of one of murder.[11]

(iii) On an indictment for child destruction the jury may convict of an offence under section 58 of the Offences against the Person Act 1861.[12]

---

[10] Criminal Law Act 1967, s. 6 (2).

[11] Infanticide Act 1938, s. 1 (2).

[12] Infant Life (Preservation) Act 1929, s. 2 (3). Offences under s. 58 of the Offences against the Person Act 1861 relate to administering drugs or using instruments to procure abortion.

(iv) On an indictment for rape, the jury may convict of any of the offences under sections 2 to 4, 8 or 14 of the Sexual Offences Act 1956,[13] and of indecent assault but not of unlawful sexual intercourse with a girl under sixteen.[14]

(v) On an indictment for incest by a man the jury may convict of any of the offences under section 5 or 6 of the Sexual Offences Act 1956.[15]

Special verdict of insanity. If it appears to the jury that a defendant is insane, they must return a special verdict that he is not guilty by reason of insanity, and the court must then order him to be detained in a hospital until ordered by the Home Secretary to be discharged.[16]

Motion in arrest of judgment. After conviction and before judgment the defendant may move the court in arrest of judgment. Such a motion can be grounded only on some objection arising on the face of the record, as, for example, some want of sufficient certainty in the indictment in the statement of the facts and circumstances constituting the offence, which has not been amended during the trial, or cured by verdict.[17] A verdict may cure an imperfect allegation, which might have been held bad on demurrer. So, where a defendant was charged with " corrupt practices " without specifying what corrupt practices he had committed, the imperfect allegation was cured by a verdict that he was guilty of bribery, *i.e.* one species of corrupt practices.[18]

If the motion is successful the defendant is discharged, but may be indicted again on the same facts.

Judgment. Before sentence the court should be informed by a police officer of the defendant's character, circumstances and

---

[13] Sexual Offences Act 1956, Sched. II, 1, col. 4, as amended by Criminal Law Act 1967, Sched. 2.
[14] *R.* v. *Mochan* [1969] 1 W.L.R. 1331.
[15] Sexual Offences Act 1956, Sched. II, 14, col. 4, as amended by Criminal Law Act 1967, Sched. 2.
[16] Trial of Lunatics Act 1883, s. 2 (as amended by the Criminal Procedure (Insanity) Act 1964, s. 1); Criminal Procedure (Insanity) Act 1964, s. 5. The defence of insanity is dealt with *ante* at p. 90.
[17] See Arch. para. 611.
[18] *R.* v. *Stroulger* (1886) 17 Q.B.D. 327. See also *R.* v. *Goldsmith* (1873) L.R. 2 C.C.R. 74 at p. 79. " If the issue joined be such as necessarily required on the trial proof of the facts so defectively or imperfectly stated or omitted and without which it is not to be presumed that either the judge

history, in order that a proper punishment may be awarded.[19] In a Practice Direction the judges of the Queen's Bench Division have laid down the procedure which should be followed with regard to the previous convictions and antecedents of the defendant[20]:

> "(1) Details of previous convictions must always be supplied by the police to the defending solicitor, or if no solicitor is instructed to defending counsel, on request. The judges are of opinion that there is no obligation on a police officer to satisfy himself that the prisoner has authorised a statement of previous convictions to be given as it is clearly within the ordinary authority of solicitor and counsel to obtain this information. In order that the defence may be properly conducted, the prisoner's advisers must know whether they can safely put the prisoner's character in issue.

> "(2) There is no need for police officers to supply a list of previous convictions to the court before conviction because the prisoner's previous convictions are always set out in the confidential calendar with which the judge is supplied by the governor of the gaol whose duty it is to supply it.[21] The police will, of course, give any information to the governor that he may require to enable him to perform his duty.

> "(3) A proof of evidence should be prepared by a police officer containing particulars of the prisoner's age, education and employment, the date of arrest, whether the prisoner has been on bail, and a statement summarising any previous convictions and any previous findings of guilt (including findings of guilt excluded from the details of previous convictions by reason of the Children and Young Persons Act

would direct the jury to give or the jury would have given the verdict, such defect, imperfection, or omission is cured by the verdict by the common law."

[19] For this purpose hearsay evidence is, in the first instance, admissible, but if it is challenged or contradicted by or on behalf of the defendant the judge should either direct proper proof to be given or should disregard the information (R. v. Campbell (1911) 6 Cr.App.R. 131; R. v. Marquis (1951) 35 Cr. App.R. 33). The court should be informed of everything known to the police which is in favour of the defendant: R. v. Van Pelz [1943] K.B. 157. See also R. v. Crabtree (1952) 36 Cr.App.R. 161.

[20] [1966] 1 W.L.R. 1184.

[21] Since this statement was made, the practice of providing such a confidential calendar has fallen into abeyance. The court is now provided with the antecedents of the defendant by the police.

1963, s. 16 (2)). It should also set out the date (if known) of the last discharge from prison or other place of custody. It may also contain a short and concise statement as to the prisoner's domestic and family circumstances, his general reputation and associates.

"Attached to the proof of evidence should be a factual statement of any convictions and of any previous findings of guilt which should be supplied in accordance with paragraph (1) above (except those excluded by operation of the Children and Young Persons Act 1963, s. 16 (2)).

"This proof, other than the attachment, should be given either with his brief or at the outset of the case to counsel for the prosecution. Subject in any particular case to a direction by the presiding judge to the contrary, counsel for the prisoner (or the prisoner if not legally represented) should be entitled to be supplied with a copy of such proof of evidence as relates to his client (or himself if not represented):

    (a) in the case of a plea of not guilty as soon as the jury retire to consider their verdict,

    (b) in the case of a plea of guilty as soon as the plea is entered.

"A copy of the proof of evidence shall be given to the shorthand writer when the officer is called to prove the contents. He may use it to check his note but must only transcribe so much as is given in evidence."

Where the defendant *admits* [21a] that he has committed other offences which are still untried and desires that they should be taken into account in determining his sentence, it is desirable that the court should do so if the other offences are of the same character as that of which he has been convicted and are offences which it has jurisdiction to try.[22] If the defendant has been committed for

---

[21a] Charges other than those contained in the indictment can never be taken into consideration by a court in sentencing a prisoner unless, on being asked, he *admits the truth* of those charges: *R.* v. *Berkofsky* (1935) 25 Cr.App.R. 66. No pressure should be put on the defendant to admit outstanding offences, though there should be an explicit inquiry by the judge whether the defendant admits his guilt: *R.* v. *Nelson* [1967] 1 W.L.R. 449.

[22] *R.* v. *Warn* (1937) 26 Cr.App.R. 115; *R.* v. *Batchelor* [1952] W.N. 244. Offences against the Road Traffic Acts involving disqualification for driving or indorsement of licence ought not to be taken into consideration when sentencing a prisoner for another class of offence: *R.* v. *Collins* (1947) 32 Cr.App.R. 27, although where a defendant is convicted of an offence for

such other offences, the court, before dealing with them, should ascertain whether the prosecution agrees, and should not as a matter of course deal with them if the prosecution for sufficient reason desires that they should be separately tried. If there has been a committal in another jurisdiction for another class of offence the judge ought not to take it into consideration unless the prosecution consents, and even then he should consider whether the public interest requires a separate investigation.[23]

It is not strictly necessary for the defendant to be present when judgment is given, although in practice he always is.

Punishments and orders upon conviction are dealt with later.[24]

Deferment of sentence. The Crown Court, without prejudice to its powers to bind an offender over to come up for judgment when called upon,[25] also has the power under **section 21** of the **Criminal Justice Act 1972**[26] to defer passing sentence on an offender, for the purpose of enabling the court to have regard, in determining his sentence, to his conduct after conviction, including where appropriate, the making by him of reparation for his offence, and to any change of circumstances.[27] Such deferment may be to any date specified by the court, but not more than six months after the date of conviction, and once deferred, sentence may not be deferred again.[28] The power to defer sentence is only exercisable if the offender consents, and the court is satisfied, having regard to the nature of the offence and the character and circumstances of the offender, that to exercise such power would be in the interests of justice.[29] If, during the period of deferment, the offender is again convicted, in Great Britain the court is empowered to pass sentence before the period of deferment expires,[30] in which case process, either by summons or warrant, must be issued to bring him before the court.[31]

---

which he is liable to be disqualified, another offence of the same class may be taken into consideration: *R.* v. *Jones* [1970] 1 W.L.R. 1494. Nor should the court take into consideration the breach of a probation order or of a condition of discharge: *R.* v. *Webb* [1953] 2 Q.B. 390. *The Crown Court—An Index of Common Penalties and Formalities*, 4th ed. 1972 by Peter Morrish and Ian McLean.

[23] *R.* v. *Maclean* [1911] 1 K.B. 332.
[24] *Post*, p. 759 *et seq.*
[25] For which see p. 792.
[26] Not in force as at July 1, 1972.
[27] s. 22 (1).
[28] s. 22 (2).   [29] s. 22 (3).
[30] s. 22 (4).   [31] s. 22 (5).

CHAPTER 53

PROCEDURE ON TRIAL OF CORPORATIONS

THE criminal responsibility of corporations has been discussed earlier.[1] In this chapter we are concerned with the procedure applicable on the trial of corporations.

Magistrates' courts. Proceedings against a corporation in a magistrates' court are governed by the provisions of **Schedule 2** to the **Magistrates' Court Act 1952** and **section 29** of the **Criminal Justice Act 1967.** In general, the procedure is the same as in the case of an individual accused, but some special provisions apply, thus:

A representative [2] may on behalf of the corporation enter a plea of guilty or not guilty.[3]

Where a corporation is charged jointly with an individual with an offence before a magistrates' court, then:

(a) if the offence is not a summary offence, but one that may be tried summarily with the consent of the accused, the court shall not try either of the accused summarily unless each of them consents to be so tried.

(b) if the offence is a summary offence, but one for which an accused has the right to claim trial by a jury, the court shall not try either of the accused summarily if the other exercises that right.[4]

A magistrates' court may commit a corporation for trial by an

---

[1] *Ante,* p. 104.

[2] The expression "representative" means any person duly appointed by the corporation to represent it for the purposes of this section, and the appointment need not be under seal, but may be by a statement in writing purporting to be signed by a managing director of the corporation, or any person having the management of the affairs of the corporation, and such a statement shall be prima facie evidence of the appointment: Criminal Justice Act 1925, s. 33 (6).

[3] Criminal Justice Act 1967, s. 29. Notification for the purposes of s. 1 (2) of the Magistrates' Courts Act 1957 (trial in the absence of an accused who pleads guilty: *ante,* p. 658) may be given by a director or secretary: *ibid.* s. 29 (3).

[4] Magistrates' Courts Act 1952, Sched. 2.

order in writing empowering the prosecutor to prefer a bill of indictment in respect of the offence named in the order.[5]

A representative may, on behalf of the corporation, make a statement before examining justices in answer to the charge. Where a representative appears, any requirement of the Act that anything is to be done in the presence of the accused, or is to be read or said to the accused, must be construed as a requirement that that thing shall be done in the presence of the representative or read or said to the representative. Where a representative does not appear, any such requirement, and any requirement that the consent of the accused shall be obtained for summary trial, does not apply.[6]

The provisions of the Magistrates' Courts Act 1952, relating to committal to the Crown Court for sentence [7] do not apply on the trial of a corporation.[8] Apart from this provision and the provisions set out above the provisions of the Magistrates' Court Act relating to the inquiry into and trial of indictable offences and the trial by jury of certain summary offences shall apply to a corporation as they apply to an adult.[9]

Trial on indictment. On arraignment of a corporation the corporation may enter in writing by its representative a plea of guilty or not guilty, and if either the corporation does not appear by a representative or, though it does not appear, fails to enter any plea, the Crown Court must order a plea of not guilty to be entered, and the trial will proceed as though the corporation had duly entered a plea of not guilty.[10]

---

[5] Magistrates' Courts Act 1952, Sched. 2.
[6] *Ibid.*
[7] *Post*, p. 761.
[8] Magistrates' Courts Act 1952, Sched. 2.
[9] *Ibid.*
[10] Criminal Justice Act 1925, s. 33 (3) as amended by the Courts Act 1971, Sched. 8.

CHAPTER 54

PUNISHMENTS AND ORDERS

IN this chapter the chief punishments and orders which may be imposed or made are dealt with. The next chapter will deal with punishments and orders in special cases (*e.g.* hospital orders, provisions regarding juveniles) and the chapter following that will deal with a number of miscellaneous orders.

SECTION 1. DEATH

Sentence of death may be pronounced (in the case of persons not being subject to military, naval or air force law) only on conviction for treason, and offences against section 2 of the Piracy Act 1837.[1] Sentence of death cannot be pronounced on a person convicted of such offences if it appears to the court that at the time when the offence was committed he was under the age of eighteen years,[2] nor upon a woman found to be pregnant.[3]

SECTION 2. IMPRISONMENT UPON SUMMARY CONVICTION

The powers of a magistrates' court to impose sentences of imprisonment are limited by statute. The minimum sentence of imprisonment [4] which may be passed by a magistrates' court is one of five days.[5] The maximum sentence depends upon the

[1] Sentence of death for murder was abolished by the Murder (Abolition of Death Penalty) Act 1965. Sentence of death under the Dockyards Protection Act 1772 was abolished by the Criminal Damage Act 1971.

[2] Children and Young Persons Act 1933, s. 53 (1), as substituted by the Murder (Abolition of Death Penalty) Act 1965; such a person is sentenced to be detained during H.M. pleasure and may be kept in such place as the Secretary of State directs.

[3] Sentence of Death (Expectant Mothers) Act 1931.

[4] Other than for default in payment of a fine, Magistrates' Courts Rules, r. 45 (1).

[5] Magistrates' Courts Act 1952, s. 107. A person may, however, be detained on the order of a court, in a police cell or other place of detention certified by the Home Secretary, for a period of not more than four days: Magistrates' Courts Act 1952, s. 107; and instead of passing a sentence of imprisonment, a magistrates' court may order that the offender be detained within the precincts of the court, or at any police station until such hour, not later than 8 p.m. on the day of the conviction, as the court may direct: *ibid.* s. 110; but the court must not make an order under this section if it will deprive the offender of a reasonable opportunity of returning to his abode on the day of the order: *ibid.*

class of offence. The question of whether a defendant can be imprisoned at all depends upon his age, and upon his previous character.

A magistrates' court may not impose a sentence of imprisonment on any person under seventeen years of age.[6] By **section 17 (2)** of the **Criminal Justice Act 1948,** the court may not impose a sentence of imprisonment on a person under twenty-one years of age unless there is no other appropriate method of dealing with him, and the court must state its reason for that opinion and cause it to be specified in the warrant and entered in the register. **Section 14** of the **Criminal Justice Act 1972** extends that principle to persons over twenty-one, not previously sentenced to imprisonment, and requires the court, for the purpose of determining whether any other method of dealing with him is appropriate, to obtain and consider information about the circumstances and take it into account together with any relevant information about his character and mental and physical condition.[7]

The maximum period of imprisonment depends upon the statute creating the offence, but the court may reduce the period prescribed unless the statute, being one passed after 1879, expressly provides to the contrary.[8] A magistrates' court trying a person summarily for an indictable offence (under section 19 of the Magistrates' Courts Act 1952) may, on conviction, sentence him to a maximum term of six months' imprisonment [9]; or in the case of a person tried summarily (under sections 18 or 19 of the Act) commit him to the Crown Court for sentence.[10]

By section 108 of the Act, a magistrates' court may pass consecutive sentences of imprisonment upon a person, but the aggregate term must not exceed six months, unless the sentences include at least two sentences for indictable offences dealt with summarily by consent, in which case the term must not exceed twelve months. These restrictions do not operate where a person has been sentenced to imprisonment and a fine for the same offence and a

---

[6] Magistrates' Courts Act 1952, s. 107.
[7] The First Offenders Act 1958 is repealed by this Act. The section does not affect the powers of the Crown Court to pass a sentence fixed by law: *ibid.* s. 13 (4). The Criminal Justice Act 1972 was not in force on July 1, 1972.
[8] Magistrates' Courts Act 1952, s. 27 (1).
[9] *Ibid.* s. 19 (6). There are, however, exceptions to this rule, the most important of which is under the Misuse of Drugs Act 1971, where under Sched. 4 a magistrates' court may impose a sentence of 12 months' imprisonment for a single offence.
[10] See below.

period of imprisonment is imposed for non-payment of the fine or for want of sufficient distress to satisfy the fine.

It must always be made clear to a convicted person whether sentences are to run concurrently or consecutively, and as a general rule two consecutive sentences should not be passed for two offences arising from one and the same act.

SECTION 3. COMMITTAL TO THE CROWN COURT FOR SENTENCE OR TO BE DEALT WITH

Where a magistrates' court exercises its powers under section 18 [11] or 19 [12] of the Magistrates' Courts Act 1952 to try summarily a person accused of an indictable offence, and that person is convicted, then if that person is not less than seventeen years of age, and the court, on obtaining information about his character and antecedents,[13] is of opinion that they are such that greater punishment should be inflicted for the offence than a magistrates' court has power to inflict, the court may, by virtue of **section 29** of the **Magistrates' Courts Act 1952,**[14] and, in accordance with section 56 of the Criminal Justic Act 1967, commit him in custody or on bail [15] to the Crown Court for sentence in accordance with the provisions of section 29 of the Criminal Justice Act 1948.

The foundation of the jurisdiction to deal summarily with an indictable offence is that it should have appeared to the magistrates *inter alia* that the circumstances of the offence were not so serious as to require trial on indictment. Only, therefore, if aggravating features emerge upon conviction may this procedure be adopted.[16]

By **section 62** of the **Criminal Justice Act 1967,** if a prisoner released on licence under section 60 or 61 of that Act [17] is

---

[11] See p. 650, *ante.*

[12] See p. 647, *ante.*

[13] As to what constitutes " antecedents " see the Practice Direction [1966] 1 W.L.R. 1184. See also *R.* v. *Vallett* [1951] W.N. 4 and *R.* v. *King's Lynn Justices, ex p. Carter* [1969] 1 Q.B. 488.

[14] Amended by the Criminal Law Act 1967, Sched. 3, the Criminal Justice Act 1967, s. 56 (4) and Sched. 3 and the Courts Act 1971, Sched. 8.

[15] The circumstances must be rare in which magistrates can properly commit on bail under this section, since its purpose is to enable a longer prison term to be imposed than the justices have power to impose: *R.* v. *Coe* [1968] 1 W.L.R. 1950. The Crown Court may grant bail: Courts Act 1971, s. 13 (4) (*a*). For procedure see p. 713, *ante.*

[16] *R.* v. *Tower Bridge Magistrates, ex p. Osman* [1971] 1 W.L.R. 1109.

[17] See pp. 861, 862, *post.*

convicted by a magistrates' court of an offence punishable on indictment with imprisonment, the court may, instead of dealing with him in any other way, commit him in custody to the Crown Court for sentence in accordance with section 29 of the Criminal Justice Act 1948.

Where a person is committed for sentence under section 29 of the Magistrates' Courts Act 1952, or under section 62 of the Criminal Justice Act 1967, he is committed by the magistrates to the most convenient location of the Crown Court, having regard to the location or locations designated by a presiding judge as that or those to which cases should normally be committed from the particular petty sessions area.[18] Such cases will normally be listed for hearing before a court presided over by a circuit judge or recorder.[19]

Section 29 of the **Criminal Justice Act 1948**[20] provides that where an offender is committed for sentence under the above provisions, the Crown Court must inquire into the circumstances of the case, and it has power to deal with the offender in any manner in which it could deal with him as if he has been convicted on indictment before it. In relation to a prisoner on licence committed under the provisions of section 62, the Crown Court, whether or not it passes any other sentence upon him, may revoke his licence.[21]

The committal for sentence by the magistrates is not an order made on conviction,[22] and there is therefore no right of appeal to the Crown Court against the committal,[23] the only remedy being by means of one of the prerogative orders.[24] This does not mean that there is no appeal against the summary conviction upon which the committal is based. Where the accused has pleaded guilty in the magistrates' court, and has been committed to the Crown Court for sentence, the Crown Court has power to entertain an application for change of plea, subject to the

---

[18] Directions given by the Lord Chief Justice, dated October 14, 1971, paras. 8 and 9.
[19] *Ibid.* para. 12 (5).
[20] As substituted by the Courts Act 1971, Sched. 8.
[21] Criminal Justice Act 1967, s. 62 (10) as amended by the Courts Act 1971, Sched. 8. He cannot thereafter be released for at least one year from the revocation of the licence.
[22] See p. 828, *post.*
[23] *R.* v. *London Sessions Appeal Committee, ex p. Rogers* [1951] 2 K.B. 74.
[24] *R.* v. *Warren* [1954] 1 W.L.R. 531; *R.* v. *Jones (Gwyn)* [1969] 2 Q.B. 33.

usual rules.[25] If the application is refused that is an end of the matter; if the application is granted, the case will be remitted to the magistrates' court for trial.[26]

Committals to the Crown Court to be dealt with arise in a number of other ways, thus:

(1) A person convicted by a magistrates' court under **section 5** of the **Vagrancy Act 1824** may be committed to the Crown Court to be dealt with as an incorrigible rogue[27];

(2) A person between the ages of seventeen and twenty-one who is convicted by a magistrates' court of an offence punishable on summary conviction with imprisonment may be committed to the Crown Court with a view to a sentence of borstal training being imposed, under **section 28** of the **Magistrates' Courts Act 1952**[28];

(3) A person in whose case a probation order or an order for conditional discharge has been made by the Crown Court, and who is convicted by a court of summary jurisdiction of an offence committed during the probation period or the period of conditional discharge may be committed to custody or released on bail until he can be brought or appear before the Crown Court: **section 8 (4)** of the **Criminal Justice Act 1948**[29];

(4) A person convicted by a magistrates' court of an offence punishable with imprisonment, during the operational period of a suspended sentence imposed by the Crown Court may commit such a person by virtue of **section 42 (1) (a)** of the **Criminal Justice Act 1967**[30] to the Crown Court to be dealt with in respect of the suspended sentence;

(5) A person convicted by a magistrates' court of an offence punishable on summary conviction with imprisonment may be committed to the Crown Court with a view to a hospital order coupled with a restriction order being made: **section 67 (1)** of the **Mental Health Act 1959**.[31]

[25] See p. 719, *ante.*
[26] *R.* v. *Mutford and Lothingland Justices, ex p. Harber* [1971] 2 Q.B. 291.
[27] Vagrancy Act 1824, as amended, s. 10.
[28] As amended by the Courts Act 1971, s. 53 and Sched. 8. And see *post,* pp. 808–810.
[29] Amended by the Courts Act 1971, Sched. 8. See *post,* p. 787.
[30] Amended by the Courts Act 1971, Sched. 8. See *post,* p. 770.
[31] Amended by the Courts Act 1971, Sched. 8. See *post,* p. 798.

(6) A person in whose case a probation order was made by the Crown Court, and who has failed to comply with the requirements of the order (otherwise than by the commission of a further offence) may, in an appropriate case, be committed to custody or released on bail until he can be brought before the Crown Court to be dealt with: **section 6** of the **Criminal Justice Act 1948.**

(7) A person proved before a magistrates' court to have been in breach of a community service order made by the Crown Court, may be committed in custody or on bail to the Crown Court to be dealt with under **section 17 (3) (b)** of the **Criminal Justice Act 1972.**

(8) Where it appears to a magistrates' court that it would be in the interests of justice, having regard to the circumstances which have arisen since the making of a community service order by the Crown Court, that the order should be revoked or that the offender should be dealt with in some other manner for the offence in respect of which the order was made, that person may be committed, in custody or on bail, until he can be brought before the Crown Court, under **section 18 (2)** of the **Criminal Justice Act 1972.**

(9) A prisoner on licence who is convicted by a magistrates' court of an offence punishable on indictment with imprisonment may be committed in custody or on bail to the Crown Court, with a view to the revocation of his licence, under **section 62 (6)** of the **Criminal Justice Act 1967.**

By virtue of **section 56 (1)** of the **Criminal Justice Act 1967** a person may be committed for sentence in respect of an offence that is only triable summarily. That section provides that where a magistrates' court—

(a) has convicted a person of an offence punishable with imprisonment, or of an offence for which he may be disqualified from driving under the Road Traffic Act 1972, or has power to deal with a person who has committed an offence while under a suspended sentence; and

(b) commits that person to the Crown Court as an incorrigible rogue or for sentencing under section 29, or commits him to the Crown Court after convicting him of an

offence committed while under a probation or conditional
discharge order, or while under a suspended sentence or
committed after being released from prison on licence [32];

the magistrates' court may commit him to the Crown Court to
be dealt with in respect of the offence.[33]

The location of the Crown Court to which such persons should
be committed will depend upon the circumstances of the case.
Where a probation order or order for conditional discharge has
been made, or a suspended sentence passed, and the offender is
committed to the Crown Court to be dealt with for the original
offence or in respect of the suspended sentence:

(a) If the order was made or the suspended sentence was
passed by the Crown Court, he should be committed to
the location of the Crown Court where the order was
made or the suspended sentence was passed, unless it is
inconvenient or impracticable to do so;

(b) If he is not so committed and the order was made by a
High Court judge or, before the Crown Court came into
existence, by a court of assize, he should be committed
to the most convenient location of the Crown Court where
a High Court judge regularly sits;

(c) In all other cases, he should be committed to the most
convenient location of the Crown Court, having regard
to the location or locations of the Crown Court designated
by a presiding judge as that or those to which cases
should normally be committed from the particular petty
sessions area.[34]

Where a probation order, care order, or order for conditional
discharge has been made, or a suspended sentence passed, by a
High Court judge, and the offender is committed to or brought
before the Crown Court, his case will be listed for hearing by

[32] *Post*, pp. 861, 862.
[33] Having committed the defendant for sentencing, the magistrates court must
make no further orders regarding the punishment of the defendant but must
leave the making of such orders to the Crown Court: s. 56 (5). However,
this does not apply to the power to order disqualification from driving, which
may still be exercised pending sentencing: s. 56 (8). See also the Road
Traffic Act 1972, s. 103.
[34] Directions given by the Lord Chief Justice, dated October 14, 1971, paras.
5–9.

a High Court judge unless, in accordance with the decision of the officer responsible for listing, his case is listed for hearing before a circuit judge or recorder, but only then after consultation with, or on the directions of a presiding judge. All other proceedings of this nature before the Crown Court will normally be listed for hearing before a circuit judge or recorder.[35]

SECTION 4. IMPRISONMENT [36] AFTER CONVICTION ON INDICTMENT [37]

The Crown Court may not sentence a person to more than the maximum term provided by the statute creating the offence, unless that person is a persistent offender who may, in certain circumstances be liable to an extended sentence.[38] Where a person is convicted on indictment of an offence against any **enactment** and is for that offence liable to be sentenced to imprisonment, but the sentence is not by any enactment either limited to a specified term or expressed to extend to imprisonment for life, the person so convicted shall be liable to imprisonment for not more than two years: **Criminal Justice Act 1967, s. 7 (1).** A person convicted on indictment of an **attempt** to commit an offence for which a maximum term of imprisonment or a maximum fine is provided by any enactment shall not be sentenced to imprisonment for a term longer, nor to a fine larger, than that to which he could be sentenced for the complete offence: *ibid.* **section 7 (2).** Where an offence is a **common law** offence and no penalty is provided by statute, there is no maximum term of imprisonment, but the sentence must not be inordinate.[39] In the case of conspiracy to commit an offence, it is only in very exceptional circumstances that the sentence should be greater than that which could have been imposed for the substantive offence.[40]

No court may pass a sentence of imprisonment on a person who has attained the age of twenty-one and has not previously been sentenced to imprisonment unless the court is of opinion that no

---

[35] *Ibid.* para. 12 (iv), (v).

[36] Penal servitude was abolished by the Criminal Justice Act 1948. Any enactment empowering a court to impose penal servitude is to be read as conferring the power to impose a sentence of imprisonment for a term not exceeding the maximum term for which a sentence of penal servitude could have been passed before the Act: *ibid.* s. 1 (1).

[37] See generally *The Crown Court: An Index of Common Penalties and Formalities* by Peter Morrish and Ian McLean.

[38] See below p. 772.

[39] *R.* v. *Morris* [1951] 1 K.B. 394.

[40] *Verrier* v. *Director of Public Prosecutions* [1967] 2 A.C. 195.

other method of dealing with him is appropriate, and for the purpose of dealing with that question, the court must obtain and consider information about the circumstances, and must take into account such information and any other information before the court which is relevant to his character and his physical and mental condition.[41]

By **section 11** of the **Courts Act 1971,** a sentence imposed, or order made, by the Crown Court when dealing with an offender shall take effect from the beginning of the day on which it is imposed, unless the court otherwise directs. Such a sentence or order may be varied or rescinded by the court within twenty-eight days, beginning on the day when the sentence or order was imposed or made.[42] But where two or more persons are jointly tried on an indictment, a sentence or order imposed or made on any of those persons on the indictment may be varied or rescinded by the court not later than the expiration of which ever is the shorter of the following periods—(a) twenty-eight days beginning with the date of the conclusion of the joint trial, (b) fifty-six days beginning with the day on which the sentence or other order was imposed or made.[43] The joint trial for this purpose is concluded on the latest of the following dates, that is, any date on which any of the persons jointly tried is sentenced, or is acquitted, or on which a special verdict is brought in.[44]

Where a sentence or other order is varied or rescinded in this way, it may only be so varied or rescinded by the court constituted as it was when the order or sentence was made or imposed, or where that court comprised one or more justices a court so constituted except for the omission of any one or more of those justices.[45] A sentence or order so varied or rescinded shall take effect from the beginning of the day on which it was originally imposed or made unless the court otherwise directs.[46] In relation to section 18 (2) of the Criminal Appeal Act 1968, however,

---

[41] Criminal Justice Act 1972, s. 14 (1).

[42] s. 11 (1); The Crown Court Rules may, where two or more persons are tried separately on the same or related facts alleged in one or more indictments, provide for extending the period: s. 11 (6).

[43] s. 11 (2).

[44] s. 11 (3).

[45] Courts Act 1971, s. 11 (4); this means in effect that where a court consisted of a presiding judge and two justices or more, the judge who presided can vary or rescind the sentence or order.

[46] *Ibid.* s. 11 (5).

which provides for the time limit for notice of appeal or application for leave to appeal, the sentence or order is regarded as being imposed or made on the day on which it was varied.[47]

The length of any sentence of imprisonment is treated as reduced by any period during which the offender was in custody by reason only of having been committed to custody by an order of a court made in any proceedings relating to that sentence or the offence for which it was passed or any proceedings from which those proceedings arose. But where the offender was previously subject to a probation order,[48] an order for conditional discharge[49] or a suspended sentence[50] in respect of that offence, any such period falling before the order was made or suspended sentence passed shall be disregarded for the purposes of this section.[51] So, for example, if a person is committed in custody to the Crown Court for sentencing under section 29 of the Magistrates' Courts Act 1952,[52] any sentence of imprisonment which he may be given is treated as reduced by the term spent in custody after committal and before sentencing.

Where a convicted person is already serving a sentence of imprisonment, a further sentence should be expressed to run consecutively to the total period of imprisonment to which he is already subject,[53] unless it is intended that it should run concurrently.[54] Where a person is convicted and is to be sentenced to imprisonment on different counts on the same indictment, it must be made clear to him by the judge whether the sentences are to run consecutively or concurrently.[55] Ordinarily, two consecutive sentences should not be passed for two offences which arise from one and the same act.[56] It is wrong to pass a sentence partly concurrent with and partly consecutive to another sentence passed on a different indictment.[57]

Provisions regarding the computation of a sentence imposed by the Court of Appeal and by a court on a retrial will be noted later.[58]

---

[47] Courts Act 1971, s. 11 (5).
[48] Post, p. 782.
[49] Post, p. 786.
[50] Post, p. 769.
[51] Criminal Justice Act 1967, s. 67 (1).
[52] As substituted by the Courts Act 1971, Sched. 8.
[53] See Practice Direction [1959] 1 W.L.R. 491.
[54] i.e. that it should date from the day it is imposed.
[55] Arch. para. 637.
[56] R. v. Torr [1966] 1 W.L.R. 52 ; Arch. para. 637.
[57] R. v. Mills [1969] 1 W.L.R. 455.
[58] Post, p. 854.

SECTION 5. SUSPENDED SENTENCES [59]

The **Criminal Justice Act 1967,** gave courts the power to suspend a sentence of imprisonment. By **section 39** of that Act, a court which passes a sentence of imprisonment [60] for a term of not more than two years may [61] order that the sentence shall not take effect unless, during a period specified in the order (called the " operational period ") being not less than one year and not more than two years [62] from the date of the order, the offender commits in Great Britain another offence punishable with imprisonment, and thereafter a court having power to do so orders that the original sentence shall take effect. [63]

By **section 40** where such a person is convicted of an offence punishable with imprisonment while under that suspended sentence, any court having jurisdiction for the purpose, must consider his case and must deal with him either :

(*a*) by ordering that the suspended sentence take effect with the original term unaltered;

(*b*) by ordering that the sentence take effect with the substitution of a lesser for the original term;

(*c*) by varying the original order and substituting for the period specified therein a period expiring not later than two years from the date of the variation; or

(*d*) by making no order with respect to the suspended sentence.

The court ought to make an order under paragraph (*a*) unless it is of opinion that it would be unjust to do so in view of all the circumstances which have arisen since the suspended sentence was imposed, including the facts of the subsequent offence, and

---

[59] See generally on the subject *The Crown Court: An Index of Common Penalties and Formalities* by the same authors.

[60] Where two or more sentences are imposed at the same time the court imposing them may order them to be concurrent or consecutive, Magistrates' Courts Act 1952, s. 108.

[61] The mandatory suspension of sentences of six months or less imposed by the Criminal Justice Act 1967, s. 39 (3) was abolished by the Criminal Justice Act 1972, s. 11 (1). (This Act was not in force on July 1, 1972.)

[62] Substituted for 3 years by the Criminal Justice Act 1972, s. 11 (2).

[63] A fine may be imposed on the same occasion as a suspended sentence : *R.* v. *Leigh* (1970) 53 Cr.App.R. 169; a suspended sentence should not be made consecutive to an immediate sentence passed on the same occasion : *R.* v. *Sapiano* (1968) 51 Cr.App.R. 674; *R.* v. *Morris* [1970] Crim.L.R. 172; A suspended sentence should not be imposed where probation is appropriate : *R.* v. *O'Keefe* [1969] 1 All E.R. 426, but see now p. 771, *post*, as to suspended sentence supervision orders.

where it does not put it into effect the court must state its reasons.[64] The proper approach is to pass sentence on the offender for the subsequent offence, and then to decide whether or not the suspended sentence shall take effect consecutively or concurrently.[65] The comparative triviality of the subsequent offence may be a ground for not ordering the suspended sentence to take effect, particularly where it is of a different category from the original offence, but the mere fact that the offences are of a different nature is not of itself a ground for not making an order.[66]

Conveniently, it is provided that the court to deal with a person convicted of an offence while under a suspended sentence is, with an exception, the court that convicts him of this subsequent offence. An offender may be dealt with in respect of a suspended sentence by the Crown Court, or where the sentence was passed by a magistrates' court by any magistrates' court before which he appears or is brought.[67] If the sentence was imposed by a superior court, the magistrates' court should commit him to the Crown Court [67a] to be dealt with there and, if it does not do so, shall give written notice to the clerk of the court which passed the suspended sentence.[68]

Section 56 (1) of the Criminal Justice Act 1967 [68a] which gives a magistrates' court the power, in certain circumstances to commit a person for sentence in respect of a summary offence, also enables the court in those circumstances to commit to the Crown Court a person whom the court has the power to deal with in respect of a suspended sentence.[69]

---

[64] s. 40 (1).

[65] R. v. Ithell [1969] 1 W.L.R. 272: Normally it should be consecutive: R. v. Brown (1970) 54 Cr.App.R. 176; and Harris, The Times, November 9, 1968.

[66] R. v. Moylan [1970] 1 Q.B. 143; R. v. Saunders (1970) 53 Cr.App.R. 247. A subsequent conviction which results in a probation order or a conditional discharge does not qualify as a conviction for this purpose: R. v. Tarry [1970] 2 Q.B. 561. It is not part of the court's function, when considering whether or not to activate a suspended sentence, to review the propriety of the original sentence, but there are cases where justice cannot be done without fitting into the pattern of events leading to the subsequent conviction the facts which gave rise to the passing of the suspended sentence. To that extent it may be necessary to inquire into them in order that a proper assessment may be made of the overall position: R. v. Munday (1972) 56 Cr.App.R. 220.

[67] Ibid. s. 41 (1) as amended by the Courts Act 1971, Sched. 11.

[67a] See p. 761.

[68] Ibid. s. 41 (1), (2).

[68a] Ante, p. 764.

[69] See generally, p. 761, ante.

Where the court that convicts a person of an offence committed during the operational period does not deal with him in respect of the suspended sentence, the court which passed the suspended sentence may deal with him. **Section 42** [69a] sets out the procedure for obtaining the presence before that court of such a person. The procedure is similar to that under section 8 of the Criminal Justice Act 1948 [70] for obtaining the presence before a court of a person convicted of an offence while under a probation or conditional discharge order.

Suspended sentence supervision order. A difficulty in the administration of the law as to suspended sentences was that a probation order could not be made, if at the same time the court imposed on a defendant a suspended sentence. This has now been rectified. By **section 12** of the **Criminal Justice Act 1972,** where a court imposes a suspended sentence of *more than six months*, it may make a suspended sentence supervision order, placing the offender under the supervision of a supervising officer for a period not exceeding the period which is the operational period in relation to the suspended sentence. The supervising officer is a probation officer, and much in the same way as in the case of an ordinary probation order, an offender must keep in touch with his supervising officer in accordance with such instructions as he may be given by him, and must notify him of any change of address. The order may be discharged on the application of the offender or the supervising officer, by the appropriate magistrates' court, or in proper cases by the Crown Court, and in any event it ceases to have effect if, before the end of the period, a court orders that the suspended sentence take effect, or if the order is discharged or replaced by a further order. Where a court varies a suspended sentence, by extending the operational period, it may make a new supervision order.

In the same way as an ordinary probation order, an offender may be dealt with for breach of the new provisions of a supervision order. If at any time while a supervision order is in force it appears on information to a justice of the peace for the appropriate petty sessional division, that the offender has failed to comply with any of the requirements of the order, he may issue a summons requiring

[69a] As amended by the Courts Act 1971, Scheds. 8 and 11.
[70] At pp. 788, 789.

him to attend, or a warrant for his arrest. If it is proved to the satisfaction of the court that the offender has failed to comply, without reasonable excuse, with any of the requirements of the order, he may be fined up to £50.

Supplementary provisions. A suspended sentence which has not taken effect is treated as a sentence of imprisonment for the purposes of all enactments and instruments made under enactments except any enactment or instrument which provides for disqualification for or loss of office, or forfeiture of pensions, of persons sentenced to imprisonment.[70a] A person may therefore appeal against the imposition of a suspended sentence by any court and may also appeal against any order made after being convicted of any subsequent offence.[71]

SECTION 6. EXTENDED SENTENCES FOR PERSISTENT OFFENDERS

Section 37 of the **Criminal Justice Act 1967** abolished preventive detention and corrective training. Instead, a person who has committed an offence and who has shown that he is a persistent offender may, in certain circumstances, be sentenced to a term extended beyond the term which the judge would have imposed if the section had not been enacted.[71a] **Section 37 (2)** provides that where an offender is convicted *on indictment* of an offence punishable with imprisonment for a term of two years or more and the conditions set out below are satisfied, then, if the court is satisfied, by reason of his previous conduct and of the likelihood of his committing further offences, that it is expedient to protect the public from him for a substantial time, the court may impose an extended term of imprisonment. It has been said[72] that the whole object of an extended sentence and the protection of the public is to be found not merely in the length of the sentence imposed, but also in the licensing provisions contained in the Act.[72a]

The conditions referred to in section 37 (4) are:

> (*a*) the offence was committed before the expiration of three years from a previous conviction of an offence

[70a] Criminal Justice Act 1967, s. 39 (9) (*a*).
[71] Criminal Justice Act 1967, s. 40 (9), and see the Criminal Appeal Act 1968, s. 11 (4).
[71a] *D.P.P.* v. *Ottewell* [1970] A.C. 642.
[72] *R.* v. *Goody* (1970) 54 Cr.App.R. 328.　　　　　　[72a] *i.e.* in s. 59.

punishable on indictment with imprisonment for a term of two years or more or from his final release [73] from prison after serving a sentence of imprisonment, corrective training or preventive detention passed on such a conviction; and

(b) the offender has been convicted on indictment [73a] on at least three previous occasions [74] since he attained the age of twenty-one of offences punishable on indictment with imprisonment for a term of two years or more; and

(c) the total length of the sentences of imprisonment, corrective training or preventive detention to which he was sentenced on those occasions [75] was not less than five years and—

(i) on at least one of those occasions a sentence of preventive detention was passed on him; or

(ii) on at least two of those occasions a sentence of imprisonment (other than a suspended sentence which has not taken effect) or of corrective training was so passed and of those sentences one was a sentence of imprisonment for a term of three years or more in respect of one offence or two were sentences of imprisonment each for a term of two years or more in respect of one offence.[76]

For the purpose of determining whether the conditions specified in subsection (4) are satisfied in relation to an offender, no account shall be taken of any previous conviction or sentence unless notice has been given to the offender at least three days before the later sentence is passed on him that it is intended to prove

---

[73] The expression "final release" includes a release on licence under s. 60 or 61 of the Criminal Justice Act 1967 (*post*, p. 861) but does not include a temporary discharge: s. 38 (5).

[73a] This includes a person sentenced at the Crown Court after being summarily convicted by a magistrates' court: s. 38 (2).

[74] A conviction in N. Ireland does not qualify for inclusion in the notice, by reason of s. 104 (3) of the Act: *R.* v. *Wynne* (1971) 55 Cr.App.R. 384. This applies equally to convictions in the Channel Islands and the Isle of Man.

[75] A period by which a sentence is reduced under s. 67 (1) of the Criminal Justice Act 1967 (above, p. 768), should not be taken into account: s. 67 (4).

[76] s. 37 (4). Where an extended term is imposed, the court shall issue a certificate to that effect: s. 37 (5). Three days' notice of an intention to prove a previous sentence or conviction must be given to the defendant: s. 38 (3).

the previous conviction or sentence to the court.[76a] Before passing
sentence the court should ask the prisoner whether he has been
served with such a notice with a view to the possibility of an
extended sentence and whether he admits the offences set out
in the notice.[77] The period of a suspended sentence cannot be made
part of a term of extended imprisonment.[77a]

A persistent offender may be sentenced up to a *total* of ten
years' imprisonment where the ordinary maximum for the offence
is five years or more and not more than ten years; *e.g.* if the
maximum for an offence is five years a person convicted of that
offence who is a persistent offender may be sentenced up to ten
years' imprisonment. A persistent offender may be sentenced up
to a *total* of five years' imprisonment where the ordinary maximum
is less than five years. Where the ordinary maximum exceeds ten
years, there is no greater maximum for the persistent offender.[78]
An extended term should be passed in the form of a single
term of imprisonment and not in the form of an ordinary term
followed by an extended term.[79]

SECTION 7. FINES AFTER CONVICTION ON INDICTMENT

Section 7 (3) of the **Criminal Law Act 1967** provides that where
a person is convicted on indictment of any offence other than an
offence for which the sentence is fixed by law, the court, if not
precluded from sentencing the offender by its exercise of some
other power (such as the power to make a probation order),[80] may
impose a fine in lieu of or in addition to dealing with him in any
other way in which the court has power to deal with him, subject
however to any enactment limiting the amount of the fine that may
be imposed or requiring the offender to be dealt with in a particular
way. There is no statutory limit to a common law fine, except the
provisions of **Magna Carta** and the **Bill of Rights** against excessive
fines.[81]

76a Criminal Justice Act 1967, s. 38 (3).
77 *R.* v. *Concannon* [1970] 1 W.L.R. 1159.
77a *R.* v. *Barrett* [1969] 1 W.L.R. 1336.   78 See s. 37 (3).
79 *R.* v. *Pearson* (1970) 55 Cr.App.R. 157. For the correct approach where it is
   intended to impose an extended sentence and also to bring into operation a
   suspended sentence see *R.* v. *Roberts* [1971] 1 W.L.R. 894.
80 The court has no power to impose a fine in addition to imposing a probation
   order (*R.* v. *Parry* [1951] 1 K.B. 590) or a conditional discharge order (*R.* v.
   McClelland (1951) 35 Cr.App.R. 22).
81 See also *R.* v. *Morris* [1951] 1 K.B. 394.

Section 14 of the **Criminal Justice Act 1948** [82] provides that where a fine is imposed, or any amount is due under a recognisance, the court may allow time for payment or may direct payment by instalments. **Section 47 (1)** of the **Criminal Justice Act 1967** provides that the court shall fix a term of imprisonment which the defendant is to undergo if the sum which he is liable to pay is not duly paid, but the term must not exceed twelve months' imprisonment.[83] Where the offender is committed to the Crown Court for sentence,[84] the term fixed in default is not limited to that laid down in the First Schedule to the Magistrates' Courts Act 1952, or in section 258 of the Customs and Excise Act 1952, unless the offence was committed under section 56 of the Criminal Justice Act 1967.[85] However, because of **section 47 (2)** a time for payment must normally be allowed. That section provides that no person shall *on the occasion when a fine is imposed on him by the* court be committed to prison in pursuance of such an order unless:

(*a*) in the case of an offence punishable with imprisonment, he appears to the court to have sufficient means to pay the sum forthwith;

(*b*) it appears to the court that he is unlikely to remain long enough at a place of abode in the United Kingdom to enable payment of the sum to be enforced by other methods; or

(*c*) on the occasion when the order is made the court sentences him to immediate imprisonment for that or another offence, or he is already serving a term of imprisonment.[86]

For the purposes of collecting, enforcing and remitting [87] a fine imposed by the Crown Court, the fine shall be treated as having

---

[82] As amended by the Criminal Justice Act 1961, s. 5 (5); and the Courts Act 1971, Sched. 8.

[83] Criminal Justice Act 1948, s. 14; *i.e.* on any one count.

[84] See p. 761.

[85] As to the provisions for default in the case of juveniles see pp. 805 and 806.

[86] Where (*c*) applies, the court may order that the period of imprisonment ordered in default of paying the fine should run consecutively to any period that he is serving or is then ordered to serve: Criminal Justice Act 1948, s. 14 (3). See also *H.M. Treasury* v. *Harris* [1957] 2 Q.B. 516.

[87] However, a magistrates' court may not remit the whole or any part of a fine imposed by a High Court judge without the consent of a judge of the High Court; or, where the fine was imposed before the Crown Court, without the consent of that court: s. 47 (8).

been imposed on conviction by the magistrates' court specified
by the court or, if no such order is made, by the magistrates' court
which committed him for trial.[88]

The term of imprisonment specified in any warrant of commitment issued by a magistrates' court in default of payment
shall be the term fixed by the Crown Court subject to any reduction
to which the defendant is entitled by reason of part payment[89]
or by reason of remission of the fine.[90]

Section 8. Fines after Summary Conviction and Enforcement of all Fines

A magistrates' court, trying a person summarily for an indictable
offence under section 19 of the Magistrates' Courts Act 1952, may
sentence him to a maximum fine of £400.[91] In the case of a
young person the limit is £50,[92] in the case of a child £10.[93]

The *maximum* fine depends upon the statute creating the
offence, but the court may reduce any fine prescribed by statute
unless the statute expressly provides to the contrary and was
passed after 1879.[94] Moreover, whenever a court has power under
any Act passed after 1879 to sentence an offender to imprisonment for an offence punishable on summary conviction, it may,
though not given authority under the particular Act, impose,
instead of imprisonment, a fine not exceeding £100.[95]

In fixing the amount of any fine the court must take into consideration, among other things, the means of the offender so far
as they appear or are known to the court, but the amount of the
police fees payable in the case must not be taken into considera-

---

[88] s. 47 (3) as amended by the Courts Act 1971, Sched. 8 and see further below
in Section 7.
[89] Below, p. 779.
[90] s. 47 (6) as amended by the Courts Act 1971, Sched. 8 and below, p. 778. See
also note 87 above.
[91] *Ante*, p. 648.
[92] Children and Young Persons Act 1969, s. 6 (3), see also p. 805.
[93] Magistrates' Courts Act 1952, s. 32 and Children and Young Persons Act
1969, s. 34 (5). See also p. 805.
[94] Magistrates' Courts Act 1952, s. 27 (1).
[95] *Ibid.* s. 27 (3) as amended by the Magistrates' Courts Act 1957, s. 5 and
the Criminal Justice Act 1967, s. 43. But the amount of the fine must not
be such as to subject the offender, in case of non-payment, to a longer term
of imprisonment than he would be liable to in the first instance under the
Act authorising the imprisonment: *ibid.*

tion; and payment of those fees must not be required in addition to the fine.[96]

A magistrates' court may allow time for payment or may order payment by instalments.[97] Where time for payment has been allowed, the court may, if so requested, allow further time or order payment by instalments.[98]

Enforcement. Where a person is in default in paying a fine, a magistrates' court may issue a warrant committing him to prison for a certain period or may issue a warrant of distress.[99] Where a warrant of distress has been issued and, after its enforcement, it appears that his goods are insufficient to satisfy the sum, the court may issue a warrant of commitment.[1] The term of imprisonment for which an offender may be committed may not exceed the period applicable to the case under the Third Schedule to the Magistrates' Courts Act 1952.[2]

Normally, because of **section 44 (2)** of the **Criminal Justice Act 1967,** the offender must be allowed time for payment. This section provides that a magistrates' court shall not *on the occasion of convicting an offender* issue a warrant of commitment for a default in paying the fine unless at least one of three conditions is satisfied.[3] These are the same conditions that apply to the Crown Court under section 47 (2) of the Act.[4]

If the court does not issue a warrant of commitment in any of the circumstances mentioned in section 44 (2) it *may* at that time fix the term of imprisonment to be served in the event of default and postpone the issue of the warrant.[5] Thereafter the warrant may be issued at any time without a further hearing.

---

[96] Magistrates' Courts Act 1952, s. 31 (1) (2). In this section the expression "police fees" means all fees payable to a constable: *ibid*. s. 31 (3).

[97] *Ibid*. s. 63 (1). Where payment by instalments has been ordered and default is made in the payment of one instalment, proceedings may be taken as if default had been made on all unpaid instalments: s. 63 (3). The power to refuse time to pay is restricted: Criminal Justice Act 1967, s. 44 (2).

[98] *Ibid*. s. 63 (2). The clerk may allow further time for payment of such a sum: Justices' Clerks Rules 1970.

[99] *i.e.* seizure of the defendants' goods for sale. See further Magistrates' Courts Rules 1968, rr. 44 and 78.

[1] Magistrates' Courts Act 1952, s. 64 but see the Criminal Justice Act 1967, s. 44.

[2] As amended by Criminal Justice Act 1967, s. 93.

[3] Where a warrant is issued on the grounds that one of these conditions is satisfied, that fact and the ground shall be specified in the warrant: Criminal Justice Act 1967, s. 44 (7).   [4] See p. 775, *ante*.

[5] Magistrates' Courts Act 1952, s. 65.

If the court does not at the time of the conviction, issue a warrant or fix a term and postpone the issue of the warrant, then no warrant of commitment may subsequently be issued unless the offender is already in prison or the court has, *since the conviction*, inquired into his means in his presence.[6] Furthermore, when the court does inquire into his means in his presence, the court may still not issue a warrant of commitment at that time or thereafter unless:

(*a*) in the case of an offence punishable with imprisonment, the offender appears to the court to have sufficient means to pay the sum forthwith; or

(*b*) the court has considered or tried all other methods of enforcing payment of the sum and it appears to the court that they are inappropriate or unsuccessful.[7]

If the court does not issue a warrant of commitment at the time of the means inquiry, it may at that time fix the term of imprisonment to be served in default and postpone the issue of the warrant of commitment.[8] If the court follows this procedure, the warrant of commitment may be issued by it thereafter without a further hearing.

If, at the time of inquiring into the offender's means, the court does not either issue a warrant of commitment or fix the term of imprisonment to be served in default while postponing the issue of the warrant of commitment, then, if it wishes, on a later occasion, either to issue a warrant or fix a term, this may only be done at a hearing at which the offender is present unless the offender is already in prison.[9] If on this later occasion a term of imprisonment is fixed and the issue of the warrant postponed, then the warrant may be issued thereafter without a further hearing.

The magistrates' court may, on inquiring into the offender's means, remit the whole or any part of the fine imposed upon him

---

[6] Criminal Justice Act 1967, s. 44 (4). By at least two justices in open court: Magistrates' Courts Act 1952, s. 98 (2) and (3). Particulars of the inquiry must be recorded: Magistrates' Courts Rules 1968, r. 53.

[7] *Ibid.* s. 44 (5). s. 44 (7) also applies here.

[8] See Magistrates' Courts Act 1952, s. 65.

[9] Criminal Justice Act 1967, s. 44 (6). For provisions regarding the process for securing the attendance of the offender, see *ibid.* and Magistrates' Courts Act 1952, s. 70 (2)–(5).

if the court thinks it just to do so having regard to any change in the circumstances since his conviction.[10]

If imprisonment is imposed for non-payment of a fine, the term must be reduced proportionately if part of the sum is paid after committal and the offender must be released if the whole sum in default is paid.[11]

Community Service Order. In any case in which a magistrates' court has power to issue a warrant of commitment for default in paying a sum adjudged to be paid by a conviction of a magistrates' court, the court may make a community service order in respect of that person in default in lieu of issuing a warrant of commitment.[12] The provisions of the Criminal Justice Act 1972,[13] in relation to such orders then have effect so that the power under section 17 (3) to impose a fine of up to £50 for failure to comply with any requirement of the order does not apply,[14] but the power under section 17 (3) (a) and section 18 (1) (b) of the Act to deal with an offender for the offence in respect of which the order was made[15] is construed as a power to deal with the person in respect of whom the order was made for his default in paying the sum in question. Where a community service order is made in such circumstances, the order ceases to have effect on payment of the whole sum to any person authorised to receive it, or on payment of part of the sum, the total number of hours for which the person in question was required to work under the order is reduced proportionally.[16] A fine imposed by the Crown Court is not treated, under this section, as having been imposed on conviction by a magistrates' court.[17]

---

[10] Criminal Justice Act 1967, s. 44 (10). Where the court does this after a term of imprisonment has been fixed, it shall proportionately reduce the term: *ibid.* Note that where a magistrates' court wishes to remit a fine imposed before the Crown Court, this remission can be granted only if the required consent is obtained. This is subject to the exceptions in s. 44 (11). Substituted by the Courts Act 1971, Sched 8, " Fine " for this purpose does not include " any other sum adjudged to be paid on conviction, whether as a pecuniary penalty, forfeiture, compensation or otherwise."

[11] Magistrates' Courts Act 1952, s. 67.

[12] Criminal Justice Act 1972, s. 49 (1) (not in force on July 1, 1972).

[13] ss. 15–19 (not in force on July 1, 1972).

[14] See p. 786, *post.*

[15] See p. 786, *post.*

[16] Criminal Justice Act 1972, s. 49 (3) (not in force on July 1, 1972).

[17] As would normally be the case under the Criminal Justice Act 1967, s. 47 (3): Criminal Justice Act 1972, s. 49 (4) (not in force on July 1, 1972).

Because the provisions set out in section 44 may be unnecessarily elaborate where the offence charged is minor, two alternative procedures are available upon a person's failure to pay a fine. Notwithstanding section 44, a magistrates' court may order a person in default to be detained in accordance with **section 110** of the **Magistrates' Courts Act 1952,** until 8 p.m. on the day of conviction or be detained in accordance with **section 111** of that Act. Section 111 provides that a magistrates' court may issue a warrant for the detention of the defaulter. Unless the sum adjudged is paid, this warrant authorises any police constable to arrest the defaulter and take him to a police station and shall require the officer in charge of the station to detain him there until eight o'clock in the morning of the day following that on which he is arrested, or, if he is arrested between midnight and eight o'clock in the morning, until eight o'clock in the morning of the day on which he is arrested. However, the officer may release him at any time within four hours before eight o'clock in the morning if the officer thinks it expedient to do so in order to enable him to go to his work or for any other reason appearing to the officer to be sufficient.[18]

Supervision order. Where any person is adjudged to pay a sum by a summary conviction and the convicting court does not commit him to prison forthwith in default of payment, the court may, either on the occasion of the conviction or on a subsequent occasion, order him to be placed under the supervision of such person [19] as the court may from time to time appoint.[20] A person so placed under supervision cannot subsequently be imprisoned for default unless the court has considered a report supplied by the supervisor on the offender's conduct and means.[21]

Enforcement by other means. Section 45 of the **Criminal Justice Act 1967,**[22] enables fines to be enforced by civil proceedings in the High Court and county court against income, assets, etc.

---

[18] If the alternative procedures are used, the power to commit to prison cannot be exercised: ss. 110 (1) and 111 (1) as amended.

[19] This is usually a probation officer.

[20] Magistrates' Courts Act 1952, s. 71 (1).

[21] *Ibid.* s. 71 (6). However, this does not apply if, after taking all reasonable steps, the report cannot be obtained: *ibid.* Nor does it apply to detention under s. 111.

[22] As amended by the Administration of Justice Act 1970, s. 42.

By **section 1 (3)** of the **Attachment of Earnings Act 1971** [23] a magistrates' court may make an attachment of earnings order to secure the payment of any sum adjudged to be paid by a conviction or treated by any enactment relating to the collection and enforcement of fines, costs, compensation or forfeited recognisances, as so adjudged or paid, or the payment of any sum required to be paid by a legal aid contribution order. An application for such an order may be made by the person to whom payment is required to be made, or by the debtor. Such an order is directed to the person who appears to have the debtor in his employment and instructs him to make periodical deductions from the debtor's earnings and pay the amounts deducted to the court collecting officer. The order must specify the normal deduction rate, that is the amount of money per week, month, etc., as the court thinks reasonable, and the protected earnings rate, below which the court considers that the debtor's earnings should not be reduced. The employer is bound to comply with the order, provided that if the debtor leaves his employment or is no longer employed by him, he must notify the court within ten days. There is power under **section 9** to vary and discharge the order. Where an employer ceases to have the debtor in his employment, the order lapses, but the debtor is required to inform the court in writing of any change of employment together with details of the new employment. Failure by the debtor or by the employer to comply with the provisions of the Act are punishable on summary conviction.

Searching of defendants. Where a person has been adjudged to pay a sum by a conviction, the court may order him to be searched and any money found on him, either on his apprehension or when so searched, or which may be found on him when taken to prison or a detention centre in default of payment of that sum, may, unless the court otherwise directs, be applied towards the payment of the sum so adjudged to be paid, and the surplus, if any, shall be returned to him. But the money must not be so applied if the court is satisfied that it does not belong to the person on whom it was found, or that the loss of the money will be more injurious to his family than his detention.[24]

---

[23] Replacing in so far as criminal proceedings are concerned the provisions of ss. 46, 79 and Sched. 1 to the Criminal Justice Act 1967, and repealing similar provisions in the Administration of Justice Act 1970. And see the Attachment of Earnings Rules 1971.   [24] Magistrates' Courts Act 1952, s. 68.

Transfer of fine order. A "transfer of fine order" may be made under which all the functions of a court of summary jurisdiction in relation to any sum adjudged to be paid may, if the defendant appears to be residing in some division or place other than that for which the convicting court acted, be exercised by the court of summary jurisdiction in such other division or place.[25]

SECTION 9. PROBATION ORDERS AND COMMUNITY SERVICE ORDERS

Probation Orders. A court before which a person who has attained the age of seventeen [26] is convicted of an offence for which the sentence is not fixed by law can make a probation order, instead of sentencing such offender, if it is of opinion that, having regard to the nature of the offence and the character of the offender, it is expedient so to do.[27] Such an order requires the offender to be under the supervision of a probation officer for not less than one nor more than three years.[27] The order must name the petty sessional division in which the offender resides and a probation officer of that division must, unless the offender changes his residence, be appointed to supervise him.[28] The order may impose such requirements as the court considers necessary, having regard to the circumstances of the case, for securing the offender's good conduct or for preventing the repetition of the offence or the committing of further offences by him.[29] Common requirements are: to be of good behaviour and keep the peace; to notify the probation officer of any change of address; to keep in touch with the probation officer in accordance with such instructions as he may from time to time give; and, in particular, if the probation

[25] *Ibid.* s. 72; Criminal Justice Act 1972, s. 50.
[26] Amended by the Children and Young Persons Act 1969, s. 7 (2). Probation is no longer available in the case of juvenile offenders. As to supervision orders in relation to children and young persons, see p. 803, *post.*
[27] Criminal Justice Act 1948, s. 3 (1). A court may not make a probation order on one count and impose a suspended sentence on another. Criminal Justice Act 1967, s. 39 (2); or commit to a detention centre on the other: *R.* v. *Evans* [1959] 1 W.L.R. 26; or impose a fine in addition to an order for the same offence: *R.* v. *Parry* [1951] 1 K.B. 590. *R.* v. *McClelland* [1951] 1 All E.R. 557 (although a fine may be imposed on a separate offence: *R.* v. *Jones* [1968] Crim.L.R. 120. A probation order may not be imposed currently with an immediate custodial sentence: *R.* v. *Emmett* (1968) 53 Cr.App.R. 203. The power to award damages as compensation under the Criminal Justice Act 1948, s. 11 (2) was repealed by the Criminal Justice Act 1972, Sched. 6 but see now *post*, p. 820. The court may order the offender to pay costs: Courts Act 1971, s. 48 (1)). [28] 1948 Act, s. 3 (2).
[29] Criminal Justice Act 1948, s. 3 (3). And see statement by Lord Goddard C.J. reported in (1952) 35 Cr.App.R. 207.

officer so requires, to receive visits from the probation officer at the offender's home.[30] The order may contain conditions as to residence in an approved probation home or hostel or other specified institution, but such an order is not to be made unless the court considers the home surroundings of the offender.[31] Before making a probation order the court is required to explain in ordinary language its terms and effect to the offender and to warn him that if he fails to comply with its terms or commits another offence he will be liable to be sentenced for the original offence.[32]

The Departmental Committee on the Probation Service [33] concluded that there was an *a priori* case for the use of probation where four conditions exist—

(a) The circumstances of the offence and the offender's record must not be such as to demand, in the interests of society, that some more severe method be adopted in dealing with him.

(b) The risk, if any, to society through setting the offender at liberty must be outweighed by the moral, social and economic arguments for not depriving him of it.

(c) The offender must need continuing attention, since otherwise, if condition (b) is satisfied, a fine or discharge will suffice.

(d) The offender must be capable of responding to this attention while at liberty.

Where the court is satisfied on the evidence of a duly qualified practitioner,[34] that the mental condition of the offender is such as requires and may be susceptible to mental treatment, but is not such as to warrant his detention in pursuance of a hospital order,[35] the probation order may require the offender to receive such treatment for not more than twelve months, as a resident or non-resident patient at an institution or as a patient of a specified medical practitioner.[36]

[30] See " The Sentence of the Court," H.M.S.O., 1969, para. 27.
[31] s. 3 (4) (a). Where an order requires a person to reside in an institution other than a mental hospital, a copy of it must be sent to the Secretary of State: s. 3 (7). Every order must name the institution and state length of residence: s. 3 (4) (b).
[32] s. 3 (5).
[33] 1962, Cmnd. 1650, para. 15.
[34] He must also be approved for the purposes of the Mental Health Act 1959, s. 28.   [35] *Post*, p. 796.
[36] s. 4, amended by Mental Health Act 1959, Scheds. 7, 8.

The Criminal Justice Act 1972 envisages the setting up of day training centres, at which probationers may be required to attend. **Section 20** [37] of the Act provides that where a court makes a probation order in the case of an offender, it may include in the order a requirement that the probationer attend, during the probation period, at a centre specified in the order, provided that he consents to such a requirement.[38] It is not possible to include such a requirement in an order, however, unless the court has been notified by the Secretary of State that a suitable centre exists in the appropriate petty sessions area, and that arrangements can be made for his attendance at that centre.[39] Such a requirement cannot be included in an order which is to include a requirement for mental treatment under section 4 of the Criminal Justice Act 1948.[40] Such a probationer is required in accordance with the instructions of the probation officer supervising him to attend on not more than sixty days at the centre specified in the order, and while attending, to comply with the instructions given by, or under the authority of the person in charge of the centre.[41] The hours of attendance, the records, and the appointment of persons to run such centres are the subject of rules made under the Act.[42]

Probation orders may be amended or discharged on application to the magistrates' court of the petty sessional division named in the order. However, in the case of a probation order made by the Crown Court, the power to discharge shall, if the court so directs when the order is made, be exercised only by that court.[43] Where a court has the power to discharge, it may instead substitute for the probation order a conditional discharge order.[44]

Probation officers are appointed in each probation area to undertake the supervision of persons in respect of whom probation orders are made by any court. The duties of a probation officer are to visit and receive reports from the person under supervision, to see that he observes the conditions of his recognisance, to report to the court on his behaviour, to assist him

---

[37] Not in force as at July 1, 1972.
[38] s. 20 (1).
[39] s. 20 (2).
[40] *Ibid.*
[41] s. 20 (4).
[42] s. 20 (6).
[43] Criminal Justice Act 1948, Sched. I, and Criminal Justice Act 1967, s. 54 (1) amended by the Courts Act 1971, Sched. 8.
[44] Criminal Justice Act 1967, s. 53.

generally and to help him to find employment.[45] As to breach of a probation order, see below under conditional discharge.

Community Service Orders. By the **Criminal Justice Act 1972,** a court, before whom a person of seventeen or over is convicted of an offence punishable with imprisonment, may, instead of dealing with him in any other way, make a community service order, requiring him to perform unpaid work in accordance with the provisions of the Act, for such number of hours, not being in the aggregate less than forty or more than two hundred and forty, as specified in the order of the court.[46] A court will only be able to make such an order if the offender consents to it, if the court is notified by the Secretary of State that arrangements exist for such a person to do such work, and if it is satisfied after considering any report about the offender by a probation officer, that the offender is a suitable person to do such work, and that arrangements can be made for him to do so.[47] A court, when making such an order is not prevented from also making an order for costs, or an order for compensation or restitution, or of disqualification from driving.[48]

An offender in respect of whom a community service order is made, will have to report to the relevant officer, and notify him from time to time of any change of address, and perform for the number of hours specified in the order such work at such times as he may be instructed by that officer.[49] The instructions given must, so far as practicable, be such as to avoid any conflict with the offender's religious beliefs and any interference with the times, if any, at which he normally works or attends a school or other educational establishment. In general, the work will have to be performed within twelve months, beginning with the date of the order.[50] The performance of such work will be regulated by Community Service Rules, made under the Act.[51] Wide powers are given to the courts to extend the period beyond twelve months, and to amend or revoke the order.[52]

---

[45] For administrative provisions relating to the appointment, payment and expenses of probation officers and as to probation areas and committees, see Criminal Justice Act 1948, Sched. I.

[46] s. 15 (1), not in force July 1, 1972.   [47] s. 15 (2), not in force July 1, 1972.

[48] s. 15 (8), not in force July 1, 1972.   [49] s. 16 (1), not in force July 1, 1972.

[50] s. 16 (2), not in force July 1, 1972.

[51] Made under s. 19, not in force July 1, 1972.

[52] s. 18, not in force July 1, 1972.

If at any time while such an order is in force, it appears on information to a justice of the peace acting for the area specified in the order that the offender has failed to comply with any of the requirements of the Act,[53] including failing satisfactorily to perform the work which he has been instructed to do, then that justice may issue a summons, or where appropriate a warrant, to bring him before a magistrates' court for the area specified in the order.[54] That court, if satisfied that the offender has failed, without reasonable excuse to comply with any of the requirements of the Act, will be able, without prejudice to the continuance of the order, to impose on him a fine of up to £50, or if the order was made by a magistrates' court, revoke the order and deal with the offender in any manner in which he could have been dealt with if the order had not been made, or if the order was made by the Crown Court, commit the offender in custody or on bail to that court.[55]

Section 10. Order for Absolute or Conditional Discharge

Absolute and conditional discharge. The **Criminal Justice Act 1948, s. 7,**[56] provides that where a court by which a person is convicted of an offence, other than one for which the sentence is fixed by law, is of opinion, having regard to the circumstances, the nature of the offence and the character of the offender, that it is inexpedient to inflict punishment and that a probation order is not appropriate, it may make an order discharging him absolutely or conditionally. Where an order for absolute discharge is made, the offender is free to go and the matter is at an end.[56a] Where an order for conditional discharge is made, however, there is a condition attached to it that the offender shall commit no further offence for a period of not more than three years from the date of the order.[57] The effect of such order is to be explained to the offender in ordinary language; if he does commit an offence within

---

[53] *i.e.* those in s. 16.
[54] s. 17 (1), (2).
[55] s. 17 (3) (*b*).
[56] As amended by Criminal Justice Act 1967, s. 52.
[56a] s. 7 (3) and (4). On absolute discharge of an offender by a magistrates' court the words " discharged absolutely C. J. Act 1948, s. 7 " must be entered in the register.
[57] Criminal Justice Act 1948, s. 7 (1) as amended by the Criminal Justice Act 1967, s. 52. This is the only condition.

the period specified in the order, he may be sentenced for the original offence.[58]

Breach of a probation or conditional discharge order. A breach of a probation order may arise either by virtue of a failure to comply with one of the administrative conditions of the order, such as reporting or working or living in a prescribed place, or by the commission of a further offence. The two forms of breach are distinct, and are provided for by **sections 6 and 8** of the **Criminal Justice Act 1948** respectively. **Section 6**[59] provides that if at any time during the probation period it appears on information to a justice with jurisdiction for this purpose[60] that the probationer has failed to comply with any of the requirements of the order, the justice may issue a summons requiring the probationer to appear at the court of the petty sessional division for which the justice acts at the time specified therein, or may, if the information is in writing and on oath, issue a warrant for his arrest and appearance before that court.

If it is proved to the satisfaction of the court before which a probationer appears or is brought under this section that the probationer has failed to comply with any of the requirements of the probation order, that court may without prejudice to the continuance of the probation order, impose on him a fine not exceeding £50,[61] or make in respect of him a community service order,[62] or may:

(a) if the probation order was made by a court of summary jurisdiction, deal with the probationer, for the offence in respect of which the probation order was made in any manner in which the court could deal with him if it had just convicted him of that offence;

---

[58] A breach of the condition should not be merely taken into consideration when sentence is passed for another offence, but should be separately dealt with: *R.* v. *Webb* (1953) 37 Cr.App.R. 82.

[59] Amended by the Criminal Justice Act 1967, s. 54 (5) and the Courts Act 1971, Sched. 8.

[60] If the probation order was made by a court of summary jurisdiction, any justice acting for a petty sessional division or place for which that court or the supervising court acts. In any other case, any justice acting for the petty sessional division or place for which the supervising court acts: Criminal Justice Act 1948, s. 6 (2) amended by the Criminal Justice Act 1967, s. 54 (5).

[61] Increased from £20 by the Criminal Justice Act 1972, s. 21 (1) (not in force on July 1, 1972).

[62] *Ibid.*, s. 21 (2).

(b) if the probation order was made by the Crown Court, commit him in custody [63] or release him on bail (with or without sureties) until he can be brought or appear before the Crown Court.[64]

Where the probationer is brought or appears before the Crown Court, and it is proved to the satisfaction of that court that he has failed to comply with any of the requirements of the probation order, that court may deal with him, for the offence in respect of which the probation order was made, in any manner in which the court could deal with him if he had just been convicted before that court of that offence.[65] Alternatively, the court may impose upon the probationer a fine of £50,[66] or make in respect of him a community service order.[67]

The procedure under section 6 does not apply to a probationer who is convicted of a further offence.[68] Where a probationer or a person under a conditional discharge order commits a further offence, the procedure under **section 8** [69] of the Act applies. That section provides that if it appears to a judge or justice of the peace having jurisdiction for this purpose [70] that a person in whose case a probation order or an order for conditional discharge has been

---

[63] If he is committed in custody, he may later be released on bail: Criminal Justice Act 1967, s. 54 (4).

[64] Criminal Justice Act 1948, s. 6 (3), as amended by Criminal Justice Act 1967, s. 54 (5) and the Courts Act 1971, Sched. 8. As to committals for sentence, see p. 761, *ante*. In *R.* v. *Devine (Practice Note)* (1956) 40 Cr.App.R. 45 the procedure to be followed on a breach of a probation order was laid down. When the prisoner is brought before the court, the breach alleged should be put to him in the clearest possible terms and he should be asked to say whether he admits it or not. If the prisoner admits the breach, then the court can deal with him; if he does not, then a trial takes place, albeit without a jury, and the prisoner may give evidence and call witnesses. The court then decides whether the breach has been proved.

[65] Criminal Justice Act 1948, s. 6 (4) (b) as amended by the Courts Act 1971, Sched. 8.

[66] Criminal Justice Act 1967, s. 54 (5) as amended by the Courts Act 1971, Sched. 8 and the Criminal Justice Act 1972, s. 21 (1).

[67] Criminal Justice Act 1972, s. 21 (2) (not in force on July 1, 1972).

[68] Criminal Justice Act 1948, s. 6 (6).

[69] As extended by the Courts Act 1971, Sched. 8.

[70] Where the probation order or order for conditional discharge was made by the Crown Court/a judge of the Crown Court. At the Crown Court this fact is determined without a jury: Criminal Justice Act 1948, s. 11 (1). If the order was made by a court of summary jurisdiction, a justice acting for the petty sessional division or place for which that court acts. In the case of a probation order, a justice acting for the petty sessional division or place for which the supervising court acts: Criminal Justice Act 1948, s. 8 (2) amended by the Criminal Justice Act 1967, s. 56 (3) and the Courts Act 1971, Scheds. 8 and 11.

made has been convicted by a court in any part of Great Britain of an offence committed during the probation period or during the period of conditional discharge, and has been dealt with in respect of that offence, the judge or justice may issue a summons requiring that person to appear at the place and time specified therein, or may issue a warrant for his arrest.[71]

A summons or warrant issued under this section shall direct the person so convicted to appear or to be brought before the court by which the probation order or the order for conditional discharge was made, or, where the summons or warrant was issued by a justice acting for the petty sessional division for which the supervising court acts, before the supervising court.[72]

A magistrates' court that convicts a person who is under a probation or conditional discharge order made by the Crown Court, may commit him in custody or release him on bail, with or without sureties, to be brought or appear before that court.[73] The Crown Court before which a person under a probation or conditional discharge order made by a magistrates' court is convicted or committed for sentence, also has the power to deal with him for the offence for which the order was made.[74] A magistrates' court before which a person under a probation or conditional order made by another magistrates' court is convicted also has the power to deal with him for the offence for which the order was made, if the consent of that court is obtained or if, in the case of a probation order the consent of that court or of the supervising court is obtained.[75]

Where, under any of the above provisions, a court has the power to deal with a person under a probation or conditional discharge order who has been convicted of another offence, that court may deal with him in any manner in which it could deal with

[71] A justice may issue a summons only on an information and may issue a warrant only on an information in writing and on oath: proviso to s. 8.

[72] Ibid. s. 8 (3) as amended by the Criminal Justice Act 1967, s. 56 (3) and the Courts Act 1971, Sched. 11.

[73] Ibid. s. 8 (4) as amended by Criminal Justice Act 1967, s. 55 (3) and the Courts Act 1971, Scheds. 8 and 11. If under this subsection the offender would be committed to the Crown Court and, by virtue of another enactment, a magistrates' court commits him to the Crown Court to be dealt with in respect of another offence, he shall be committed to the Crown Court in respect of both offences: Criminal Justice Act 1967, s. 56 (7).

[74] Criminal Justice Act 1948, s. 8 (6) as amended by the Courts Act 1971, Sched. 8.

[75] Ibid. s. 8 (7) amended by the Criminal Justice Act 1967, s. 56 (3).

him if it had just convicted him of the offence in respect of which the order was made.[76] However, the Crown Court when dealing with a person under a probation or conditional discharge order made by a magistrates' court has only the same powers as a magistrates' court would have.[77]

Supplementary provisions. The court on making a probation or conditional discharge order may, if it thinks it expedient for the purpose of the reformation of the offender, allow any person who consents to do so to enter into recognisance for the good behaviour of the offender.[78]

Probation orders and orders for absolute and conditional discharge are not deemed to be a conviction for any purpose other than the purpose of the proceedings in which the order is made and any subsequent proceedings in respect of the order.[79] Such an order is to be disregarded for the purposes of any enactment that confers or authorises any disqualification or disability on convicted persons.[80] However, there is an exception in the case of motoring offences.[81] Though the making of such an order is not a " conviction " in the full sense, it does not prejudice the right of the offender to appeal against the conviction or to rely on the order in bar of subsequent proceedings for the same offence.[82]

---

[76] *Ibid.* s. 8 (5) (7). As to the approach to sentence in such a case see *R.* v. *Stuart* (1964) 129 J.P. 125; *R.* v. *Evans* (1961) 125 J.P. 134. Where a probationer is sentenced for the offence for which he was placed on probation, the probation order ceases to have effect: s. 5 (4).

[77] *Ibid.* s. 8 (6) as amended by the Courts Act 1971, Sched. 8.

[78] *Ibid.* s. 11 (1).

[79] Criminal Justice Act 1948, s. 12 (1).

[80] *Ibid.* s. 12 (2). But the fact that the offender committed the offence is admissible as evidence of bad character for the purpose of proving that he is a " suspected person " within the meaning of s. 4 of the Vagrancy Act 1824: *R.* v. *Harris* (1950) 34 Cr.App.R. 184. Breaches of such an order should not be taken into consideration but should be dealt with separately so that the sentence passed on the breach may rank as a conviction: *R.* v. *Webb* [1953] 2 Q.B. 390.

[81] s. 12 (2) does not apply to those motoring offences, listed in Sched. 4 to the Road Traffic Act 1972, which carry obligatory or discretionary disqualification from driving or obligatory endorsement. Orders of disqualification and endorsement are to be made notwithstanding the fact that a probation or discharge order is made. Furthermore, where a person has committed an offence for which he has been disqualified from driving or for which his licence was endorsed and a probation or discharge order was made, that offence shall be taken into account in determining liability to punishment or disqualification for any offence listed in Sched. 1 committed subsequently, notwithstanding s. 12 (1): Criminal Justice Act 1967, s. 51.

[82] *Ibid.* s. 12 (3) (*a*). This provision is necessary because an accused person has no right of appeal unless he has been convicted. See further, *post,*

For the purposes of revesting or the restoration of any property in consequence of the conviction of any person a probation order or order for absolute or conditional release is, however, treated as a conviction.[83]

Right of appeal. A person convicted by a magistrates' court has no right of appeal against the imposition of a probation or conditional discharge order; but when sentenced for an offence in respect of which such an order was made after breaching a requirement of the probation order or committing another offence, then he may appeal against the sentence.[84] A person convicted at the Crown Court may appeal against the imposition of a probation or conditional discharge order and may appeal against a sentence imposed after breaking a requirement of the probation order or committing another offence whether convicted by that court or committed to that court for sentence.[85-94]

SECTION 11. RECOGNISANCES (BINDING OVER)

A recognisance is an obligation of record [95] entered into before a court or official authorised to take it by a person who is thereby bound to the performance of some condition. In form a recognisance is an acknowledgment of a debt to the Queen, with a provision that if the person entering into the recognisance performs the condition thereby imposed, the recognisance shall be void. If, on the other hand, the condition is not fulfilled, the recognisance may be forfeited and estreated, upon which the person bound and his sureties will become absolute debtors to the Crown for the sum named.

Recognisances are used in many circumstances and for many different purposes.

At common law a person convicted of any misdemeanour whether summarily [96] or on indictment may, in addition to or in substitution for any other punishment, be required to enter

---

pp. 828, 841. Note that under s. 83 of the Magistrates' Courts Act 1952, these orders do not rank as " sentences " for the purpose of appealing to the Crown Court, see p. 829.

[83] *Ibid.* s. 12 (3) (*b*).

[84] Magistrates' Courts Act 1952, s. 83 and see generally p. 829, *post*.

[85-94] Criminal Appeal Act 1968, ss. 9, 10 as amended by the Courts Act 1971, Sched. 8.

[95] See Magistrates' Courts (Forms) Rules 1968, Form 119.

[96] *R.* v. *Sandbach* [1935] 2 K.B. 192.

into a recognisance with or without sureties, to keep the peace and be of good behaviour.[97] By virtue of the Criminal Law Act 1967, which assimilates the law and practice relating to felonies to that of misdemeanours, this rule now applies to all indictable offences. Imprisonment may be ordered until the recognisances are entered into.

By **section 1 (7)** of the **Justices of the Peace Act 1968** it is provided that any court of record having a criminal jurisdiction has, as auxiliary to that jurisdiction, the power to bind over to be of good behaviour a person who or whose case is before the court, by requiring him to enter into his own recognisances or to find sureties or both and committing him to prison if he does not comply.

Recognisances may also be employed by way of " preventive justice," even though no offence has actually been committed. By **section 91** of the **Magistrates' Courts Act 1952,** a magistrates' court may, by order on complaint,[98] adjudge any person to enter into a recognisance, with or without sureties, to keep the peace or to be of good behaviour towards the complainant, and if that person fails to comply with the order the court may commit him to custody for a period not exceeding six months or until he sooner complies with the order.

The Crown Court instead of imposing any other punishment has power, except in the case of murder, to require a convicted person to enter into recognisances with or without sureties to come up for judgment when called upon.[99] This power used to be exercised by Assizes and Quarter Sessions after conviction and before sentence, because they could not in those circumstances grant bail. Now, however, **section 13 (4) (c)** of the **Courts Act 1971**

---

[97] *R.* v. *Dunn* (1847) 12 Q.B. 1026; Arch. para. 669. Notwithstanding anything in any enactment whereby power is conferred on a court, on a person's conviction of an offence, to bind him over to keep the peace or be of good behaviour, that power may be exercised without sentencing the person convicted to a fine or to imprisonment: Criminal Law Act 1967, s. 7 (4). This is not to be confused with binding over to come up for judgment if called upon to do so. See below.

[98] Under s. 45 of the Act. But Lord Goddard C.J. suggested in *Wilson* v. *Skeock* (1949) 113 J.P. 294 at p. 296 that justices can exercise their power and bind over to keep the peace any person brought before them for any offence. As to procedure see *Sheldon* v. *Bromfield Justices* [1964] 2 Q.B. 573 and *R.* v. *Aubrey-Fletcher, ex p. Thompson* [1969] 1 W.L.R. 872.

[99] Arch. para. 721. Preserved by the Courts Act 1971, s. 6. Nor is this power affected by the Criminal Justice Act 1972 which gives to the Crown Court the power to defer sentence for up to six months. See p. 756 *ante.*

gives express power to grant bail to a person who is in the custody of the Crown Court pending the disposal of his case by that court.

Security for the peace can be demanded by any person who swears that another has threatened to do him or his wife or child any bodily harm, and that in consequence he has reasonable ground for fear.[1] Security for good behaviour is more comprehensive than and includes security for the peace. It can be required from any person whose acts or language are shown to be likely to endanger the public peace, even though no one is put to any bodily fear,[2] as, for example, from any person who uses or threatens to use in public places language the natural consequence of which is to cause others to commit a breach of the peace, *e.g.* a Protestant lecturer who uses language offensive and insulting to Roman Catholics.[3] The order of a magistrates' court is not a conviction, but a person directed to enter into recognisances has an appeal to the Crown Court under the Magistrates' Courts (Appeals from Binding Over Orders) Act 1956.

It is not open to the judge or magistrate to insert any kind of condition in a recognisance to keep the peace or be of good behaviour. Thus the court cannot impose a condition that the offender shall return to his own country and not return to England for a specified period.[4] However, a convicted person may be bound over in the Crown Court to come up for judgment [5] when called upon and in such a case a condition that the offender should leave the country and not return could be imposed.[6]

By **section 95** of the **Magistrates' Courts Act 1952** a magistrates' court has power, in any case where it may take a recognisance, to fix the amount in which the principal and his sureties, if any, are to be bound with a view to the recognisances being taken later; and where this is done, the recognisance need not be entered into before that court, but may be entered into before any other court of summary jurisdiction, or before a clerk of such a court, or before a superintendent or inspector of police or police officer in charge of any police station, or if any of the parties is

[1] Hawk. c. 60, s. 6; *R.* v. *Dunn* (1840) 12 Ad. & E. 599.
[2] *Lansbury* v. *Riley* [1914] 3 K.B. 229; *R.* v. *Sandbach* [1935] 2 K.B. 192.
[3] *Wise* v. *Dunning* [1902] 1 K.B. 167.
[4] *R.* v. *McCartan* [1958] 1 W.L.R. 933; *R.* v. *Flaherty* [1958] Crim.L.R. 556; as explained in *R.* v. *Ayu* [1958] 1 W.L.R. 1264.
[5] Courts Act 1971, s. 6 (4) (*b*).
[6] *R.* v. *Ayu* [1958] 1 W.L.R. 1264.

in prison, before the governor or keeper of such prison.[7] The recognisances of sureties may be taken separately and either before or after the recognisances of the principal.

Where in the case either of an imprisonment or a fine there is prescribed a requirement for the offender to enter into recognisances and to find sureties for keeping the peace and observing some other condition, or to do any such things, the court may dispense with any such requirement or any part thereof.[8]

Where a person has been committed to prison by a magistrates' court for default in finding sureties, the court may, on application made to them by him or someone on his behalf, inquire into his case, and if, on new evidence, or proof of a change of circumstances, the court think it is just to do so, they may reduce the amount for which it is proposed the surety or sureties, should be bound, or dispense with the surety or sureties, or otherwise deal with the case as they think just.[9]

Forfeiture of recognisances. Breach of recognisances can only be punished by forfeiture. Where a recognisance is forfeited before the Crown Court, the provisions of section 14 of the Criminal Justice Act 1948 [10] and section 47 of the Criminal Justice Act 1967 [11] apply. The provisions of these sections have already been noted when dealing with fines after conviction on indictment.[12] They apply equally to forfeited recognisances.

Where a recognisance to keep the peace or to be of good behaviour has been entered into before a magistrates' court or any recognisance is conditioned for the appearance of a person before a magistrates' court or for his doing any other thing connected with a proceeding before a magistrates' court, and the recognisance appears to the court to be forfeited, the court may declare the recognisance to be forfeited and adjudge the persons bound thereby, whether as principal or sureties, or any of them, to pay the sum in which they are respectively bound. But the court has no power to declare a recognisance to keep the peace or to be of good behaviour forfeited except by order on complaint. The court which declares the recognisance to be forfeited may,

---

[7] Magistrates' Courts Rules 1968, rr. 72–74.
[8] Magistrates' Courts Act 1952, s. 27 (2).
[9] Magistrates' Courts Act 1952, s. 94.
[10] As amended by the Criminal Justice Act 1967, and the Courts Act 1971, Sched. 8.
[11] As amended by the Courts Act 1971, Sched. 11.   [12] *Ante*, p. 775.

instead of adjudging any person to pay the whole sum in which he is bound, adjudge him to pay part only of the sum or remit the sum. Payment of such a sum including any costs awarded against the defendant may be enforced in the same way as a fine imposed after a summary trial of an offence not punishable with imprisonment, provided that at any time before the issue of the warrant of commitment or before the sale of goods under a warrant of distress, the court may remit the whole or any part of the sum either absolutely or as the court thinks just.[13]

Position of surety.   Where a surety to a recognisance to keep the peace or to be of good behaviour entered into before a magistrates' court [14] has reason to suspect that the person bound as principal has been or is about to be guilty of conduct which was or would be a breach of the condition of the recognisance, he may make complaint to any justice of the peace having jurisdiction either in the place in which the said person is or is believed by the informant to be or in the place where the magistrates' court by which the recognisance was ordered to be entered into was held, and that justice may thereupon, if in his discretion he thinks fit, issue a warrant or summons against the said person.[15]

The magistrates' court before which the said person is brought under any such warrant or before which he appears in answer to any such summons may, unless it adjudges the recognisance to be forfeited, order the recognisance to be discharged and order the principal to enter into a new recognisance, with or without sureties, to keep the peace or to be of good behaviour.[16]

Appeals.   The **Magistrates' Courts (Appeals from Binding Over Orders) Act 1956** [17] provides for a right of appeal to the Crown Court where a person is ordered by a magistrates' court to enter into a recognisance to keep the peace or be of good behaviour.

---

[13] Magistrates' Courts Act 1952, s. 96, as amended by Criminal Justice Act 1967, Sched. 6 and the Courts Act 1971, Sched. 8. However, so much of s. 44 (10) of the Criminal Justice Act 1967 (*ante*, p. 778) as empowers a court to remit sums shall not apply to the sum but so much thereof as relates to remission after a term of imprisonment has been imposed shall so apply: *ibid.* para. 17.

[14] There is no equivalent provision for recognisances entered into before the Crown Court.

[15] Magistrates' Courts Act 1952, s. 92 (1); by the proviso to that subsection, a warrant may not be issued unless the complaint is in writing and substantiated on oath.   [16] Magistrates' Courts Act 1952, s. 92 (2).

[17] Amended by the Criminal Justice Act 1967, Sched. 7, and the Courts Act 1971, s. 53 and Sched. 9.

CHAPTER 55

PUNISHMENTS AND ORDERS IN SPECIAL CASES

SECTION 1. HOSPITAL ORDERS

Section 60 of the **Mental Health Act 1959**[1] provides that where a person is convicted before the Crown Court of an offence other than an offence the sentence for which is fixed by law, or is convicted by a magistrates' court of an offence punishable on summary conviction with imprisonment, and the following conditions are satisfied:

   (*a*) the court is satisfied, on the written or oral evidence of two medical practitioners—

      (i) that the offender is suffering from mental illness, psychopathic disorder,[2] subnormality[3] or severe subnormality[4]; and

      (ii) that the mental disorder[5] is of a nature or degree which warrants the detention of the patient in a hospital for medical treatment, or the reception of the patient into guardianship under this Act; and

   (*b*) the court is of opinion, having regard to all the circumstances including the nature of the offence and the character and antecedents of the offender, and to the other

---

[1] Amended by the Children and Young Persons Act 1969, Scheds. 5 and 6 and by the Courts Act 1971, Sched. 8.

[2] " Psychopathic disorder " means a persistent disorder or disability of mind (whether or not including subnormality of intelligence) which results in abnormally aggressive or seriously irresponsible conduct on the part of the patient, and requires or is susceptible to medical treatment: Mental Health Act 1959, s. 4 (4).

[3] " Subnormality " means a state of arrested or incomplete development of mind (not amounting to severe subnormality) which includes subnormality of intelligence and is of a nature or degree which requires or is susceptible to medical treatment or other special care or training of the patient: *ibid.* s. 4 (3).

[4] " Severe subnormality " means a state of arrested or incomplete development of mind which includes subnormality of intelligence and is of such a nature or degree that the patient is incapable of living an independent life or of guarding himself against serious exploitation, or will be so incapable when of an age to do so: *ibid.* s. 4 (2).

[5] " Mental disorder " means mental illness, arrested or incomplete development of mind, psychopathic disorder, and any other disorder or disability of mind; and " mentally disordered " shall be construed accordingly: *ibid.* s. 4 (1).

796

available methods of dealing with him, that the most suitable method of disposing of the case is by means of an order under this section,

the court may by order authorise his admission to and detention in such hospital as may be specified in the order or, as the case may be, place him under the guardianship [6] of a local health authority or of such other person approved by a local health authority as may be so specified.

Such an order is authority for the patient's detention for one year in the first instance. This authority can be renewed if the medical officer responsible for the defendant's treatment recommends that further detention is necessary in the interests of the patient's health or the protection or safety of others. The hospital managers are not bound to agree. In the case of a patient over sixteen, he or his nearest relatives may apply at certain intervals to a mental health review tribunal who may direct his discharge. Under a section 60 order the patient may be discharged at any time by the hospital managers, or by the responsible medical officer, or by the review tribunal. Their powers appear to be unlimited. Once discharged the patient is no longer liable to recall and a patient absent without leave cannot be retaken into custody and ceases to be liable to be detained if he is over twenty-one, and of certain classification, either six months, and in certain cases after twenty-eight days' absence.[7]

Where a person is charged before a magistrates' court with any act or omission as an offence and the court would have power, on convicting him of that offence, to make an order under subsection (1) of this section in his case as being a person suffering from mental illness or severe subnormality, then, if the court is satisfied that the accused did the act or made the omission charged, the court may, if it thinks fit, make such an order without convicting him.[8]

A hospital or guardianship order shall not be made unless arrangements have been made for the offender.[9] Where an order is made under this section, the court shall not pass a

---

[6] The effect of a guardianship order is to confer on the authority or person named as guardian, to the exclusion of any other person, all such powers as would be exercisable by them or him if they or he were the father of the patient and the patient were under the age of 14 years: *ibid.* s. 34 (1).

[7] *R.* v. *Gardiner* [1967] 1 W.L.R. 464 at p. 468.

[8] Mental Health Act 1959, s. 60 (2).   [9] *Ibid.* s. 60 (3) (4).

sentence of imprisonment [10] or impose a fine or make a probation order in respect of the offence or make any such order as is mentioned in paragraphs (b) or (c) of section 7 (7) of the Children and Young Persons Act 1969 in respect of the offender, but may make any other order which the court has power to make apart from this section.[11]

An application may be made to a mental health review tribunal for discharge of a person in respect of whom a hospital or guardianship order has been made either by the patient within six months, or by the nearest relative within twelve months, of the making of the order.[12]

By **section 65** [13] the Crown Court, when making a hospital order, may further order that the offender should not be released without the consent of the Secretary of State either during an unlimited period or during a specified period. An order restricting discharge may be made when it appears to the court, having regard to the nature of the offence, the antecedents of the offender and the risk of his committing further offences if set at large, that it is necessary for the protection of the public to do so.

The effect of making a restriction order under section 65 is that (i) there is authority to detain the patient for the duration of the order though the Secretary of State may terminate it, at any time, if satisfied that it is no longer required for the protection of the public; (ii) the patient can only be discharged by, or with the consent of the Secretary of State; and (iii) the discharge may be conditional, in which case the patient remains liable to recall during the period of the restriction order.[14]

Where a magistrates' court convicts a person over the age of fourteen of an offence punishable with imprisonment and the court think that an order restricting discharge should be made, he may be committed to the Crown Court to be dealt with by that court.[15]

[10] Including a sentence or order for detention: s. 60 (6).
[11] *Ibid.* s. 60 (6) amended by the Children and Young Persons Act 1969, Sched. 5.　　　　　　　　　　　　　　[12] *Ibid.* s. 63 (4).
[13] Amended by the Courts Act 1971, Sched. 8.
[14] *R.* v. *Gardiner* [1967] 1 W.L.R. 464. The Secretary of State may direct that a person should cease to be subject to the provisions of s. 65: *ibid.* s. 66.
[15] *Ibid.* s. 67, as amended by the Criminal Justice Act 1967 and the Courts Act 1971, Sched. 8. S. 29 of the Criminal Justice Act 1948, as substituted by the Courts Act 1971, Sched. 8, and s. 15 of the Criminal Justice Administration Act 1962 (*ante*, p. 762) apply to a committal under this section: Mental Health Act 1959, s. 67 (2).

An appeal lies against any hospital order (with or without an order restricting discharge) or a guardianship order made under section 60 or 65.[16]

SECTION 2. JUVENILES

Imprisonment. No court may impose imprisonment on a person under seventeen years of age.[17] No court may impose a sentence of imprisonment on any person under the age of twenty-one, unless it is of opinion that no other method of dealing with the offender is appropriate after considering the circumstances and the offender's character and mental and physical condition.[18] Where a person under twenty-one years of age is sentenced to imprisonment by the Crown Court or a magistrates' court, the court must give its reasons for its opinion that no other method of punishment is appropriate.[19]

No court may pass a sentence of imprisonment on a person within the limits of age which qualify for borstal training [20] except:

(a) for a term not exceeding six months; or
(b) (where the court has power to pass such a sentence) for a term not less than three years.[21]

However, this does not apply to a person already serving a sentence of imprisonment [22] and in relation to a person who has served a previous term of imprisonment of not less than six months, or a previous sentence of borstal training, a reference to eighteen months shall be substituted for three years.[23]

Section 63 of the **Criminal Justice Act 1967** makes provision for the supervision of young short-term offenders after release.

---

[16] Mental Health Act 1959, s. 70, as amended by the Children and Young Persons Act 1969, Sched. 6.

[17] Magistrates' Courts Act 1952, s. 107 (2).

[18] Criminal Justice Act 1948, s. 17 (2). Young prisoners are segregated from other prisoners and, where given long sentences, are removed to selected prisons or parts of prisons, known as Young Prisoners' Centres.

[19] Magistrates' Courts Act 1952, s. 107 (3).

[20] That is between 15 and 21: see p. 808 but see n. 17 *infra*.

[21] Criminal Justice Act 1961, s. 3 (1). If a person is sentenced to imprisonment on more than one count, then it is the aggregate total of consecutive terms that must not exceed six months or must not be less than three years: *R.* v. *Scully* [1966] 1 W.L.R. 1294.

[22] Criminal Justice Act 1961, s. 3 (2).

[23] *Ibid.* s. 3 (3). See *e.g. R.* v. *Hughes* [1968] 1 W.L.R. 560; *R.* v. *Leonard* (1964) 108 S.J. 425.

They are made subject to the same supervisory procedures applicable to persons released from detention centres.[24]

If on trying a young person summarily under section 6 (1) of the Children and Young Persons Act 1969, the court finds him guilty it may impose a fine not exceeding £50 or may exercise the same powers as it *could* have exercised if he had been found guilty of an offence punishable with three months' imprisonment.[25]

A person convicted of an offence who appears to the court to have been under the age of eighteen years at the time the offence was committed must not, if he is convicted of homicide, be sentenced to imprisonment for life, nor may sentence of death be pronounced on any such person; but in lieu thereof the court must sentence him to be detained during Her Majesty's pleasure, and if so sentenced he is liable to be detained in such place and under such conditions as the Secretary of State may direct.[26] The court may also direct detention by a local authority in a community home [27] provided that the offender is not detained in that manner after he attains the age of nineteen.

Where a child or young person is convicted on indictment of any offence punishable in the case of an adult with imprisonment for fourteen years or more, not being an offence the sentence for which is fixed by law, and the court is of opinion that none of the other methods in which the case may legally be dealt with is suitable, the court may sentence the offender to be detained for such period not exceeding the maximum term of imprisonment with which the offence is punishable in the case of an adult as may be specified in the sentence; and where such a sentence has been passed the child or young person is, during that period, liable to be detained in such place and on such conditions as the Secretary of State may direct.[28]

The **Children and Young Persons Act 1969** takes a further step in curtailing the powers of the courts to punish juvenile offenders.

---

[24] *Post*, p. 808.

[25] Children and Young Persons Act 1969, s. 6 (3). A sentence of imprisonment is not possible because of s. 107 (2) (above). See further the Criminal Justice Act 1961, s. 4, as amended by the Courts Act 1971, Sched. 8.

[26] Children and Young Persons Act 1933, s. 53 (1), as substituted by the Murder (Abolition of Death Penalty) Act 1965, s. 1 (5).

[27] Children and Young Persons Act 1969, s. 30 (1). For the provisions in relation to " community homes," see *ibid.* s. 35 *et seq.*

[28] Children and Young Persons Act 1933, s. 53 (2), as amended by the Criminal Justice Act 1961, s. 2 and Sched. 4.

Section 7 abolishes the powers in criminal proceedings against persons under seventeen years of age, to make probation orders, approved school orders, fit person orders and orders committing to a remand home. In addition it repeals section 5 of the Criminal Justice Act 1961, which provides for the detention of juveniles for default in the payment of fines, etc.

In place of these orders (subject to section 53 (1) of the Children and Young Persons Act 1933, which provides for the detention of young persons for certain grave crimes), where a child is found guilty of homicide or a young person is found guilty of any offence before any court, that court, or the court to which he is remitted, shall have power:

(a) if the offence is punishable in the case of an adult with imprisonment, to make a care order in respect of him; or

(b) to make a supervision order in respect of him; or

(c) with the consent of his parent or guardian, to order the parent or guardian to enter into a recognisance to take proper care of him and exercise proper control over him.

Care order. A care order commits the child to the care of the local authority in whose area he appears to the court to habitually reside. If he does not appear to reside habitually in the area of any local authority, the court may commit him to the care of the local authority in whose area it appears that the offence was committed.[29] Unless the order is discharged [30] or extended [31] it ceases to have effect when the child reaches the age of eighteen, or if he was already sixteen when the order was made, when he attains the age of nineteen.

The powers and duties of the local authority are to be found in sections 11 [32]–13 [33] of the Children Act 1948, and in section 27 of the Children and Young Persons Act 1969. In general it may be said that there is a general duty to use their powers so as to further the best interests of the child, and afford him opportunity for the proper development of his character and abilities, although they are now bound to take any necessary step for the

29 Children and Young Persons Act 1969, s. 20.
30 *Ibid.* s. 21 (1).
31 *Ibid.* s. 20 (3).
32 Substituted by s. 27 (1) of the 1969 Act.
33 Substituted by s. 49 of the 1969 Act.

protection of the public even if that step may not further the best interests of the child.

Section 13 of the Children Act 1948, empowers a local authority to accommodate a child or young person by boarding him out with foster parents, by maintaining him in a community home or to allow him to be under the charge and control of a parent, guardian, relative or friend.

The local authority has a duty to review the case of every child every six months. If the child has been committed to their care by a care order, they are required to consider whether to make an application for discharge.[34]

If it appears to a juvenile court, on the application of the local authority in respect of a care order, which would cease to have effect because the subject of it has attained the age of eighteen, that such a person is accommodated in a community home, or a home provided by the Secretary of State, and that by reason of his mental condition or behaviour it is in his interest, or the public interest, for him to continue to be so accommodated after he attains the age of eighteen; then if the person in question is before the court, the court may order that the care order continue in force until he is nineteen.[35]

If it appears to the juvenile court, on the application of the local authority or on the application of a person committed to their care, that it is appropriate to discharge the order, the court may either discharge the order, and where the person concerned has not attained the age of eighteen make a supervision order in respect of him or dismiss the application, in which case no further application may be made, except with the consent of the juvenile court, within the next three months.[36] An appeal lies to the Crown Court in respect of the extension of an order to the age of nineteen, the dismissal of an application to discharge, or imposition of the supervision order.[37]

Where a person who has attained the age of fifteen, is committed to the care of a local authority by a care order and is accommodated in a community home, and the local authority consider he ought to be removed to a borstal institution, they may

[34] Children and Young Persons Act 1969, s. 27 (4).
[35] Ibid. s. 21 (1).
[36] Ibid. s. 21 (2) and (3).
[37] Ibid. s. 21 (4).

bring him with the consent of the Secretary of State before a juvenile court.[38] If that court is satisfied that his behaviour is such that it will be detrimental to the persons accommodated in the community home, for him to be accommodated there, the court may order his removal to a borstal institution.[39] The care order will then cease to have effect [40] and for most purposes [41] he will be treated as a person sentenced to borstal training. Where the court is not in a position to decide whether to make such an order, it has power to remand him to a remand centre for a period not exceeding twenty-eight days,[42] although in certain circumstances that period may be varied or extended by that court or by any other magistrates' court acting for the same area.[43]

Supervision order. This order replaces the probation order in respect of persons under seventeen years of age. The supervisor must be either a local authority designated by the order or a probation officer.[44] Where a local authority is designated it will normally be the authority in whose area it appears to the court that the supervised person resides or will reside. The court has power to designate another authority but only if that authority agrees. The court may only designate a probation officer as supervisor in the case of a child, where the local authority so request and a probation officer has already been exercising his statutory duties or has done so, in relation to another member of the household to which the child belongs.[45]

By **section 17** of the **Children and Young Persons Act 1969** an order lasts for three years or shorter period if specified by the court. During that period it is the duty of the supervisor to advise, assist and befriend the supervised person. In addition to this general duty, the court has power to insert into a supervision order a number of different requirements. Apart from the general provision that the order may contain such prescribed provisions as the court considers appropriate for facilitating the performance by the supervisor of his duties, the following should be noted:

---

[38] *Ibid.* s. 31 (1).
[39] *Ibid.* s. 31 (2).
[40] *Ibid.* s. 31 (3).
[41] Subject to paras. (*a*) and (*b*) of s. 31 (3).
[42] *Ibid.* s. 31 (4).
[43] *Ibid.* s. 31 (5).
[44] Children and Young Persons Act 1969, s. 11.
[45] *Ibid.* s. 13.

(1) An order that he comply with the directions of his supervisor to reside with a named individual **(section 12 (1))**; (2) to reside for a single specified period at a specified place: **(section 12 (2) (a))**; (3) to live in a specified place or places for a period or periods specified; to present himself to a specified person or persons at a specified place or places on a specified day or days; to participate in specified activities on specified days **(section 12 (2) (b))**.

By **section 12 (4)** of the **Act,** where a court is satisfied on the evidence of an approved [46] medical practitioner that the mental condition of the supervised person is such as requires, or may be susceptible to, treatment; but is not such as to warrant the making of a hospital order, the court may include in a supervision order a requirement that the supervised person shall for a period specified in the order submit to:

  (i) treatment by or under the direction of a fully registered medical practitioner specified in the order;

 (ii) treatment as a non resident patient at a place specified in the order;

(iii) treatment as a resident patient in a hospital or mental nursing home (but not a specified hospital).

Although the treatment is not limited to a period of twelve months, it may not extend beyond his eighteenth birthday, and if the supervised person is over fourteen it can only be made with his consent.

By **section 15** of the **Act** a juvenile court may, while a supervision order is in force in respect of a person who has not reached the age of eighteen, either on the application of that person or of the supervisor, make an order discharging the order or varying it by cancelling any requirement inserted or adding or substituting a further requirement which might have been inserted at the time when the order was made. If the order is discharged a care order may be made.

Where the supervised person has attained the age of eighteen, an adult magistrates' court has power to vary or cancel any requirement inserted in the original order by virtue of section 12 (1) or 12 (2), but not to add to such requirements or make a care order. In effect **section 15 (3)** and **section 15 (4)** of the **Act** give the adult

---

[46] Under the Mental Health Act 1959, s. 28.

court the powers it would have in relation to a person over eighteen on a probation order.

Fine or recognisances, etc. Where a person under the age of seventeen is tried summarily in a magistrates' court under section 6 of the Children and Young Persons Act 1969, the court may on finding him guilty impose a fine not exceeding £50, or in the case of a child not exceeding £10.[47]

Where a child or young person is found guilty of any offence for the commission of which a fine or costs or a compensation order under section 1 of the Criminal Justice Act 1972 may be imposed, if the court is of opinion that the case would best be met by the imposition of a fine, costs, or the making of such an order the court may, and must if the offender is a child, order such fine, etc., to be paid by the parent or guardian, unless it is satisfied that he cannot be found or has not conduced to the commission of the offence by neglecting to exercise due care or control over the child or young person.[48] No order under this section may be made against a parent or guardian without giving him an opportunity of being heard except where, having been required to attend, he has failed to do so.[49]

The parent or guardian may appeal against an order made under this section (a) if made by a court of summary jurisdiction, to the Crown Court, (b) if made by the Crown Court to the Court of Appeal.[50]

Fines imposed on juveniles, as opposed to fines imposed on their parents or guardians can now be enforced only by attachment of earnings or by an attendance centre order.

A person who has reached seventeen but not reached twenty-one may not be committed to prison in respect of the non-payment of a sum which he has been adjudged to pay by a conviction of a court of summary jurisdiction *and for the payment of which he has been allowed time* unless he has been placed under supervision in respect of that sum. Where, however, the court is satisfied that it is undesirable or impracticable to place him under supervision, a warrant (which must state the grounds on which the court or a justice is so satisfied) may be issued.[51]

[47] Children and Young Persons Act 1969, s. 6 (3) and s. 34 (5).
[48] Children and Young Persons Act 1933, s. 55 (1) as amended.
[49] Children and Young Persons Act 1933, s. 55 (3), as amended.
[50] *Ibid.* s. 55 (5) as amended.　[51] Magistrates' Courts Act 1952, s. 71 (4) (5).

Where a court has power to commit a person to prison for any term for a default and that person has reached the age of seventeen and is detained in a detention centre under a previous sentence or warrant, the court may commit him to a detention centre for a term not exceeding the term aforesaid or six months whichever is the shorter.[52]

Attendance centres. Section 19 (1) [53] of the **Criminal Justice Act 1948** provides that where a court of summary jurisdiction has power, or would, but for the statutory restrictions upon the imprisonment of young offenders, have power to impose imprisonment on a person who is under twenty-one years of age, or to deal with any such person under section 6 of this Act for failure to comply with any of the requirements of a probation order, the court may, if it has been notified by the Secretary of State that an attendance centre is available for the reception from that court of persons of his class or description, order him to attend at such a centre, to be specified in the order, for such number of hours as may be so specified; provided that no such order shall be made in the case of a person who has been previously sentenced to imprisonment, borstal training or detention in a detention centre, or has been ordered to be sent to an approved school.

The aggregate number of hours specified is usually twelve but must not be more than twenty-four.[54] The times which he is required to attend should be such as to avoid interference with his school or working hours.[55] Provision is made for varying or discharging the order and for dealing with a person who fails to attend at the centre or commits a breach of the rules of the centre.[56]

Attendance centres are available only in populated areas. They are usually run by police officers in their free time and most are in schools, police premises or youth clubs. It is hoped that the staff will be able to teach the offender a respect for the law and to use his leisure time constructively.[57]

Detention centres. Section 4 of the **Criminal Justice Act 1961** [58] provides that in any case where a court has power, or would have

---

[52] Criminal Justice Act 1961, s. 5 (1) substituted by the Children and Young Persons Act 1969, Sched. 5.   [53] As amended.
[54] See Criminal Justice Act 1961, s. 10 (2).
[55] Criminal Justice Act 1948, s. 19 (2).   [56] *Ibid.* s. 19 (3) (7) (8).
[57] See " The Sentence of the Court," H.M.S.O. 1969, para. 44.
[58] Amended by the Courts Act 1971, Sched. 8.

power but for the statutory restrictions upon the imprisonment of young offenders, to pass sentence of imprisonment on an offender under twenty-one but not less than fourteen years of age, the court may, subject to the provisions of this section, order him to be detained in a detention centre.

An order for the detention of an offender may be made for the following term—

(a) where the offender has attained the age of seventeen or is convicted before the Crown Court, and the maximum term of imprisonment for which the court could (or could but for any such restriction) pass sentence in his case exceeds three months, any term of not less than three or more than six months;

(b) in any other case, a term of three months.[59]

An order under this section shall not be made in respect of a person who is serving or has served a sentence of imprisonment for a term of not less than six months or a sentence of borstal training unless it appears to the court that there are special circumstances (whether relating to the offence or to the offender) which warrant the making of such an order in his case.[60]

Section 5 of the **Criminal Justice Act 1961** [61] provides that where a court has power to commit a person to prison for any term for a default and that person has attained the age of seventeen and is detained in a detention centre under a previous sentence or warrant, the court may commit him to a detention centre for a term not exceeding the aforesaid, or six months whichever is the shorter.

The court may, in the case of a person who has reached the age of seventeen, direct that the term of detention ordered should commence on the expiration of any other term for which that person is liable to be detained in a detention centre and which was imposed by that or another court.[62] If the court does this, a term of less than that which must ordinarily be given by virtue of section 4 or 5 may be ordered.[63] The aggregate of the terms for

[59] Criminal Justice Act 1961, s. 4 (2) as amended by the Children and Young Persons Act 1969, Sched. 6.
[60] *Ibid.* s. 4 (4) as amended. The court shall consider any report made in respect of him by the Secretary of State and, in the case of a magistrates' court where there is no such report, shall adjourn until the report is made: *ibid.*
[61] As substituted by the Children and Young Persons Act 1969, Sched. 6.
[62] *Ibid.* s. 7 (1) (2) as amended by the Children and Young Person's Act 1969, Sched. 6.
[63] *Ibid.* s. 7 (3). Amended by the Children and Young Persons Act 1969, Sched. 6.

which a person may be ordered to be detained in a detention centre by virtue of any two or more orders made by the same court on the same occasion shall not in any case exceed six months.[64] Furthermore, the total term for which a person may be detained in a detention centre shall not exceed nine months at a time; and accordingly so much of any term for which a person is ordered to be so detained as, together with any other term on which it is wholly or partly consecutive, exceeds nine months shall be treated as remitted.[65]

The First Schedule to the Act provides for the supervision of persons released from detention centres.[66] A person detained in a detention centre in pursuance of an order under section four shall, after his release and until the expiration of the period of twelve months from the date of his release, be under the supervision of such society or person as may be specified in a notice to be given to him by the Secretary of State on his release, and shall, while under that supervision, comply with such requirements as may be so specified.[67] On failure to comply with a requirement he may be recalled to the detention centre to complete the unexpired portion of his term of detention (if any) or for a period of fourteen days.[68]

Borstal. Section 20 (1) [69] of the **Criminal Justice Act 1948** provides that where a person is convicted on indictment of an offence punishable with imprisonment, then if on the day of his conviction [70] he is not less than fifteen but under twenty-one years of age and a sentence of borstal training is available in his case under section 1 (2) of the Criminal Justice Act 1961, the court may, in lieu of any other sentence, pass a sentence of borstal training. **Section 28** [71] of the **Magistrates' Courts Act 1952** provides that where a person is convicted by a magistrates' court of an offence punishable on summary conviction with imprisonment, then, if on the day of the conviction he is not less than fifteen but under twenty-one years old and is a person who, under section 1 (2) of the Criminal Justice Act 1961 may be committed for a sentence of

[64] *Ibid.* s. 7 (4).
[65] *Ibid.* s. 7 (5).
[66] Remission may be obtained for good conduct.
[67] Criminal Justice Act 1961, Sched. 1, para. 1. Provision is made for varying the requirements: *ibid.*
[68] *Ibid.* para. 2. A person may not be recalled more than once: *ibid.*
[69] As substituted by Criminal Justice Act 1961, Sched. 6.
[70] *R.* v. *Baxter* [1970] 1 W.L.R. 13.
[71] *Ibid.* as amended by the Criminal Justice Act 1967, Sched. 6, and the Courts Act 1971, Sched. 8.

borstal training, the court may commit him in custody or on bail to the Crown Court[72] for sentence in accordance with the provisions of section 20 of the Criminal Justice Act 1948.[73]

Section 1 (2) of the **Criminal Justice Act 1961**[74] provides that the power of a court to pass a sentence of borstal training is exercisable in any case where the court is of opinion, having regard to the circumstances of the offence and after taking into account the offender's character and previous conduct, that it is expedient that he should be detained for training for not less than six months; but such a sentence shall not be passed on a person who is under seventeen on the day of his conviction unless the court is of opinion that no other method of dealing with him is appropriate.

Before passing a sentence of borstal training in the case of an offender of any age, the court must consider any report made in respect of him by or on behalf of the Secretary of State. The same provisions apply in relation to an unrepresented offender being sent to borstal for the first time as apply in the case of imprisonment.[75]

A person sentenced to borstal training is detained in a borstal institution for such period, not extending beyond two years after the date of sentence and not being less than six months from that date, as the Secretary of State may determine, and must then be released. However, the Secretary of State may direct that any such person shall be released before the expiration of six months.[76]

Borstal training is designed for persons who are not suitable or who are too old for the alternative sanctions discussed above, but who are not eligible for imprisonment.

A person, after his release from a borstal institution and until the expiration of two years from the date of his release, is under the supervision of such society or person as may be specified in a notice to be given to him by the Secretary of State on his release, and must, while under that supervision, comply with such requirements as may be so specified.[77]

---

[72] As to the proper location see *ante*, p. 711.

[73] Where the court decides not to sentence him to borstal, the court may deal with him in any manner in which the court of summary jurisdiction might have dealt with him: Criminal Justice Act 1948, s. 20 (5), as substituted by Criminal Justice Act 1961, Sched. 6.

[74] Amended by the Children and Young Persons Act 1969, Sched. 6.

[75] Criminal Justice Act 1972, s. 37. See p. 760, *ante*.

[76] Prison Act 1952, s. 45 (2) as substituted by S.I. 1963 No. 597.

[77] Prison Act 1952, s. 45 (3) as amended by Criminal Justice Act 1961, Sched. 4. The requirements may be modified: *ibid.*

If before the expiration of two years from the date of his release the Secretary of State is satisfied that a person who is under supervision after his release from a borstal institution has failed to comply with any requirement for the time being specified in the notice given to him, he may by order recall him to a borstal institution and he is liable to be detained until the expiration of two years from his sentence or the expiration of six months from his being taken into custody under the order, whichever is the later.[78]

Section 12 of the **Criminal Justice Act 1961** provides that where a person sentenced to borstal training:

(a) being under supervision after his release from a borstal institution; or

(b) having escaped from a borstal institution

is convicted whether on indictment or summarily of an offence for which the court has power, or would have power but for the statutory restrictions upon the imprisonment of young offenders, to pass sentence of imprisonment, the court may, instead of dealing with him, order that he be returned to a borstal institution.[79]

Before making such an order the court must consider argument made by or on behalf of the Secretary of State on the offender's response to the training already undergone [80] unless the court proposes to deal with him otherwise than by making an order under that section.[81] Any adjournment for the purposes of obtaining a report may be on bail or in custody.[82]

Where such an order is made by the Crown Court on committal by a magistrates' court, that person has a right of appeal to the Court of Appeal (Criminal Division).[83]

SECTION 3. DEPORTATION ORDER

In certain circumstances, a court has the power to recommend the deportation of aliens and Commonwealth immigrants.

---

[78] Prison Act 1952, s. 45 (4), as amended by Criminal Justice Act 1961, Sched. 4.

[79] A person ordered to be returned under this section is treated as if he had been recalled under Prison Act 1952, s. 45 (above): s. 12 (2). A youth undergoing borstal training should not be given a suspended sentence of imprisonment if he is convicted of a further offence: *R.* v. *Baker* (1971) 55 Cr.App.R. 182 (not in force on July 1, 1972).

[80] s. 12 (3).

[81] Criminal Justice Act 1972, s. 42 (2).

[82] *Ibid.* s. 42 (2).

[83] Criminal Justice Act 1972, s. 42 (1).

By the **Immigration Act 1971** a person who is not patrial [84] is liable to deportation from the United Kingdom if, after he has attained the age of seventeen, he is convicted of an offence for which he is punishable with imprisonment and on his conviction is recommended for deportation by a court. Any court may recommend his deportation, which has power to sentence him for the offence, unless he is committed to be sentenced or otherwise dealt with by another court. [85] Where it is intended to recommend deportation, the court must give the offender no less than seven days' notice in writing. [86] The order will not be put into effect until the time for appealing has elapsed. [87]

The Court of Appeal has said that a court considering a recommendation of deportation is concerned simply with the crime committed, the offender's past record and the potential detriment to this country if he remains here. [88]

SECTION 4. DRUNKENNESS

Habitual drunkenness. The expression "habitual drunkard" means a person who, not being a mentally disordered person within the meaning of the Mental Health Act 1959, is notwithstanding, by reason of habitual intemperate drinking of intoxicating liquor, at times dangerous to himself or herself or others, or incapable of managing himself or herself, and his or her affairs. [89] The **Inebriates Act 1898** provides that where a person is convicted on indictment of an offence punishable with imprisonment, if the court is satisfied that the offence was committed under the influence of drink, or that drunkenness was a contributory cause of the offence, and the offender admits that he is, or is found by the jury to be, an habitual drunkard, the court may, in addition to or substitution for any other sentence, order him to be detained for a term not exceeding three years in any State inebriate reformatory,

---

[84] As defined in s. 2 (5) of the Act. There is a special exemption in s. 7 for persons in this country at the end of July 1971, who have been ordinarily resident for five years, unless at the end of July or during five years he was undergoing imprisonment of six months or more. (This Act was still not in force on July 1, 1972).

[85] s. 6 (1). [86] s. 6 (2).

[87] s. 6 (6).

[88] *R. v. Caird and Others* (1970) 54 Cr.App.R. 499.

[89] Habitual Drunkards Act 1879, s. 3. A person may be an habitual drunkard, although in the intervals between bouts of drinking he is a sober man: *Eaton v. Best* [1909] 1 K.B. 632.

or in any certified inebriate reformatory the managers of which are willing to receive him.[90]

In the proceedings on the indictment the offender is in the first instance arraigned on so much only of the indictment as charges such offence, and if he pleads guilty or is found guilty, the jury shall, unless he admits that he is an habitual drunkard, be charged to inquire whether he is an habitual drunkard, and in that case it is not necessary to swear the jury again. Unless evidence that the offender is an habitual drunkard has been given before he is committed for trial, not less than seven days' notice must be given to the proper officer of the court by which the offender is to be tried, and to the offender, that it is intended to charge habitual drunkenness in the indictment.[91]

Any person who commits any of the offences mentioned in the First Schedule to the Act,[92] and who within the twelve months preceding the date of the commission of the offence has been convicted summarily at least three times of any such offence, and who is an habitual drunkard, is liable on conviction on indictment, or if he consents to be dealt with summarily, on summary conviction, to be detained for a term not exceeding three years in any certified inebriate reformatory the managers of which are willing to receive him.[93]

By the Habitual Drunkards Act 1879 (as continued and amended by the Inebriates Acts 1888 and 1898), provision was made for the licensing by local authorities of retreats for the control, care and curative treatment of habitual drunkards, who, subject to certain conditions prescribed by the Act, may be admitted on their own application, and when admitted may not, unless discharged by the order of a justice under the Act, leave the retreat until the expiration of the time specified in the application, not exceeding, however,

---

[90] Inebriates Act 1898, s. 1.

[91] Inebriates Act 1898, s. 1.

[92] These consist of offences against (i) s. 12 of the Licensing Act 1872; (ii) s. 58 of the Metropolitan Police Act 1839; (iii) ss. 29 and 61 of the Town Police Clauses Act 1847; (iv) s. 28 of the London Hackney Carriages Act 1843; (v) s. 287 of the Merchant Shipping Act 1894; (vi) s. 2 (3) of the Licensing Act 1902; and (vii) certain Scottish and Irish Acts. A number of these offences will be replaced by Criminal Justice Act 1967, s. 91, when that section comes into force.

[93] 1898 Act, s. 2. The offence for which a person may be detained under this section is a compound offence consisting of (i) commission of one of the offences specified in the First Schedule to the Act; (ii) a conviction for at least three times of one of these offences; and (iii) being an habitual drunkard: *R.* v. *Briggs* [1909] 1 K.B. at pp. 386, 387.

a period of two years. All such retreats are governed by Rules made by the Secretary of State and are inspected twice a year by inspectors appointed by the Secretary of State.

The **Criminal Justice Act 1972** envisages the setting up of treatment centres for alcoholics to which a police officer may take persons whom he is empowered to arrest for certain offences involving drunkenness.[94]

---

[94] See *ante*, p. 247.

CHAPTER 56

MISCELLANEOUS ORDERS AND CONSEQUENCES

SECTION 1. COSTS

THE subject of costs is now principally governed by the **Costs in Criminal Cases Act 1952.** A consolidation measure, the Costs in Criminal Cases Bill 1972, has been introduced in Parliament and as it will, on enactment, form the basis of the law in this field, the first part of this chapter has been written with reference to its provisions.

By **clause 3** of that Bill it is provided that the Crown Court before which any person is prosecuted or tried on indictment [1] may order (i) the payment out of central funds [2] of the costs of the prosecution; (ii) if the accused is acquitted, the payment out of central funds of the costs of the defence.

Where an appeal is brought to the Crown Court against a conviction by a magistrates' court of an indictable offence, or against the sentence imposed on such a conviction, the Crown Court may order (i) the payment out of central funds of the costs of the prosecution; (ii) if the appeal is against conviction, and the conviction is set aside in consequence of the decision on the appeal, the payment out of central funds of the costs of the defence. The costs payable under this clause are such sums as appear to the court reasonably sufficient to compensate the prosecutor, or as the case may be, the accused, for the expenses properly incurred by him in carrying on the proceedings, and to compensate any witness for the prosecution, or as the case may be for the defence, for the expense, trouble or loss of time properly incurred in or incidental to his attendance.

Each case must be considered on its own facts.[3] A defendant is not entitled to costs merely by reason of the fact that he is

---

[1] The Crown Courts' powers to award costs are the same in a trial on indictment as in a committal for sentence under ss. 28 and 29 of the Magistrates' Courts Act 1952; a committal under the Mental Health Act 1959, Pt. V, and a committal as an incorrigible rogue under the Vagrancy Act 1824, or of an appeal under that Act; Costs in Criminal Cases Bill 1972, cl. 17.

[2] Central funds means money provided by Parliament: Costs in Criminal Cases Bill 1972, cl. 12.

[3] *R.* v. *Sansbury* (1959) 44 Cr.App.R. 14.

acquitted; the power to award him costs should be exercised only in cases where it is right to do so. To be taken into consideration are such matters as whether the prosecution acted unreasonably in starting or continuing proceedings and whether the accused by his conduct has, in effect, brought the proceedings, or their continuation, upon himself.[4] But even where no order is made as to payment of the defendant's costs, such sums may be awarded to defence witnesses as are reasonably sufficient to compensate them for the expense, trouble or loss of time incurred by them in attending the hearing,[5] and a witness as to character only, may be compensated under this clause where the court certifies that the interests of justice required his attendance, but no sum shall be paid to such a witness in respect of whom no such certificate is given.[6] " Witness " in this connection means a person properly attending to give evidence whether or not he gives evidence and includes a person called to give evidence at the instance of the court, whether or not he is a witness for the defence. The amount of the costs so ordered to be paid under clause 3 of the Bill must be ascertained as soon as practicable by the appropriate officer of the court. The costs of carrying on the defence that may be awarded to any person under this clause may include the costs of carrying on the defence before the examining justices who committed him for trial, or as the case may be before the magistrates' court who convicted him. By section 32 (2) of the Criminal Justice Act 1967,[7] sections 1, 3 and 7 of the Act apply in relation to a medical practitioner making a written report to a court in pursuance of a request, to which section 32 (3) of the Criminal Justice Act 1967 applies as it applies to a person called to give evidence at the instance of the court.

Clause 4 of the Bill provides that where a person is prosecuted or tried on indictment [8] the Crown Court may order (i) the accused if he is convicted to pay the whole or any part of the costs, incurred in or about the prosecution and conviction, including any proceedings before the examining magistrates, (ii) the prosecutor to pay the whole or any part of the costs incurred in or about the

---

[4] See [1959] 1 W.L.R. 1090.
[5] The amounts to be allowed are prescribed in the Witnesses' Allowances Regulations 1971.
[6] s. 3 (5).
[7] Costs in Criminal Cases Bill 1972, Sched. 1.
[8] The Crown Court has the same powers in those circumstances to award costs as between parties.

defence including any proceedings before the examining magistrates, if the accused is acquitted. Once the discretion of the court has been exercised in awarding costs, there is no further discretion to limit the amount awarded.[9] The amount of such costs except where a specific amount has been ordered to be paid must be ascertained as soon as practicable by the appropriate officer. It has been said that it is not appropriate to make an order for costs when giving a convicted person a considerable sentence, unless he has private capital.[10] It is unsatisfactory to order payment of " one quarter " of the prosecution's costs by a defendant. It is better for an estimate to be made of the costs and a predetermined figure laid down.[11]

Where an offender is dealt with under section 6, 8 or 9 of the Criminal Justice Act 1948 (breach of requirement of a probation order or conviction of a further offence during the currency of a probation order or an order for conditional discharge) or under section 40 (1) of the Criminal Justice Act 1967, in respect of a suspended sentence, the Crown Court has the same powers to award costs out of central funds or to award costs between the parties as if the offender had been tried in those proceedings for the offence for which the order was made or sentence was passed.[12]

Where a person is brought before the Crown Court for failure to comply with a condition of a recognisance to keep the peace or be of good behaviour, which he entered into on conviction of an indictable offence, the court's powers to order the payment of costs out of central funds are the same, with modifications, as if the failure was an indictable offence.[13-14]

By **clause 1** of the **Costs in Criminal Cases Bill 1972** a magistrates' court, (i) dealing summarily with an indictable offence, or inquiring into any offence as examining justices, may order the payment out of central funds of the costs of the prosecution; (ii) dealing summarily with an indictable offence and dismissing the information, or inquiring into any offence as examining justices and determining not to commit the accused for trial, may order the payment out of central funds of the costs of the defence. The amount of costs to be awarded under this clause is the same as that to be awarded by the Crown Court under clause 3. Also,

[9] *Practice Direction* [1968] 1 W.L.R. 389 (Crime: Costs); *R.* v. *Bow Street Magistrates, ex p. Palmer* [1969] Crim.L.R. 658 (*Preliminary Inquiry*).
[10] *R.* v. *Gaston* [1971] 1 W.L.R. 85.   [11] *R.* v. *Judd* [1971] 1 W.L.R. 89.
[12] s. 17.   [13-14] *Ibid.* s. 17 (5).

as in clause 3, defence witnesses may be compensated even if no order is made as to the payment of the defendant's costs.

By **clause 2** of the Bill,[15] on the summary trial of an information a magistrates' court has power to make such order as to costs (i) on conviction, to be paid by the accused to the prosecutor; (ii) on dismissal of the information, to be paid by the prosecutor to the accused, as it thinks just and reasonable. But where the court orders payment upon conviction of any sum as a fine, penalty, forfeiture or compensation and such sum does not exceed 25p, no costs are to be ordered unless in any particular case the court thinks fit.[16] Where examining justices determine not to commit the accused for trial and are of the opinion that the charge was not made in good faith, they may order the prosecutor to pay the whole or any part of the costs incurred in or about the defence.[17-19]

Clause 5 provides for costs to be awarded by a divisional court of the Queen's Bench Division or by the House of Lords on appeal therefrom out of central funds.

Clause 6 provides for costs to be awarded by the Court of Appeal (Criminal Division) at their discretion when they allow an appeal against conviction, or against a verdict of not guilty by reason of insanity or against a finding of disability in favour of the appellant. Such costs are payable out of central funds and include costs incurred in or about his defence in the Crown Court. By **clause 7** the Court of Appeal are also empowered to order the payment out of central funds of such sums as appear reasonably sufficient to compensate a person properly attending to give evidence on an appeal, or any proceedings preliminary or incidental thereto, whether or not he gives evidence, for the expense, trouble or loss of time properly incurred in or incidental to his attendance; also the court may direct that the expenses of an appellant not in custody in appearing before the court on the hearing of his appeal etc., be paid to him out of central funds. **Clause 8** provides that when the Court of Appeal dismiss an appeal or an application for leave, they may order the appellant to pay

---

[15] cl. 2 (2) (*a*).

[16] cl. 2 (2) (*a*). Where the accused is under 17 years old, the amount of the costs, ordered to be paid by the accused himself is not to exceed the amount of any fine ordered to be paid: cl. 2 (2) (*b*).

[17-19] cl. 2 (4). An appeal lies to the Crown Court against such an order if the amount ordered to be paid exceeds £25: cl. 2 (5).

any person named in their order, the whole or any part of the costs of the appeal or application, including the cost of the transcript.

On an application for leave to appeal from the Court of Appeal to the House of Lords, if an application is made by the prosecutor and is dismissed by the Court of Appeal or the House of Lords, or an appeal is determined by the House of Lords in favour of the accused, whether the appeal is by him or by the prosecutor, then the Court of Appeal (if the application for leave is dismissed by them) or the House of Lords in any other case may, by virtue of **clause 9** order the payment to the accused out of central funds of such sums as appear reasonably sufficient to compensate him for his expenses. When the Court of Appeal or the House of Lords dismiss an application by the accused for leave to appeal to the House, then either court may, if they think fit, order him to pay such person as is named in their order, the whole or any part of the costs of the application: **clause 10.**

Where a court orders the payment of costs by the accused or the prosecutor and also orders the payment of costs out of central funds, the costs, so far as they are payable under both orders, are primarily payable out of central funds; and the court must give notice to the Secretary of State of the order for the payment of costs by the accused or the prosecutor to the extent that any costs are primarily payable out of central funds by an order (under this or any other Act) and have been paid out of those funds. The Secretary of State is entitled to be reimbursed out of any money due under any other court order for the payment of those costs, and to take any proceedings for the enforcement of any such other order providing for payment of costs by the prosecutor.[20]

Section 41 of the **Administration of Justice Act 1970** [21] provides for the recovery of costs awarded by a magistrates' court and the superior courts and allows the imposition of terms of imprisonment to be specified in default of payment. Collection and enforcement is undertaken where the order is made by a magistrates' court by that court and in any other case, such magistrates' court as may be specified in the order.

---

[20] Costs in Criminal Cases Bill 1972, cl. 10 and see the Crown Court Rules 1971 (S.I. 1971 No. 1292) rr. 12, 13, 14, 15, 16 as regards the taxation of costs.
[21] As amended by the Courts Act 1971, Sched. 6.

SECTION 2. FORFEITURE AND DEPRIVATION OF PROPERTY

Forfeiture of property to the Crown and the punishment of being placed outside the protection of Her Majesty have been abolished.[22] **Section 23** of the **Criminal Justice Act 1972,** however, gives to the courts the power to deprive a person of property used or intended for use for the purposes of crime.[23]   Where a person is convicted of an offence punishable on indictment with not less than two years' imprisonment and the court by or before which he is convicted is satisfied that any property which was in his possession or under his control at the time of his apprehension has been used for the purpose of committing, or facilitating the commission of any offence, or was intended by that person to be used for that purpose, the court may make an order under **section 23** of the Act, depriving the offender of his rights, if any, in the property, and the property, if not already in their possession, will be taken into the possession of the police.[24]   In such a case the Police (Property) Act 1897 will apply, but any application must be made under that Act by any claimant within six months of the date on which the deprivation order was made, and the claimant's application will not succeed unless he satisfies the court either that he had not consented to the offender having possession of the property, or that he did not know, and had no reason to suspect that the property was likely to be used for the purpose of committing or facilitating the commission of any offence.[25]   " Facilitating the commission of an offence," includes, for the purposes of the Act, the taking of any steps after it has been committed for the purpose of disposing of any property to which it relates or of avoiding apprehension or detection.[26]

The Crown Court, but only that court, has power under the **Criminal Justice Act 1972, s. 24,**[27] where a person is convicted before it of an offence punishable on indictment with not less than two years' imprisonment, or, having been convicted of such an offence, is committed for sentence under section 29 of the Magistrates' Courts Act 1952, if satisfied that a motor vehicle was used

---

[22] Forfeiture Act 1870, s. 1 ; Criminal Law Act 1967, s. 7 (5) although forfeiture of specific articles identified in an indictment is available under a number of Acts *e.g.* Immigration, Firearms, Drugs, Coinage etc.

[23] Not in force as at July 1, 1972.

[24] Criminal Justice Act 1972, s. 23 (1), (2).

[25] *Ibid.* s. 23 (3).

[26] *Ibid.* s. 23 (6).

[27] Not in force as at July 1, 1972.

by that person or by anyone else for the purpose of committing, or facilitating the commission of, the offence, may order such person to be disqualified for holding or obtaining a driving licence, for such period as the court thinks fit. Facilitating the commission of an offence includes taking any steps after it has been committed for the purpose of disposing of any property to which it relates or of avoiding apprehension or detection.[28]

Section 3. Disqualification from Public Office

Disqualification from holding public office follows a conviction for treason.[29]   A person is disqualified from being elected or being a member of a local authority if he has within five years before the day of his election or since his election, been convicted in the United Kingdom, the Channel Islands or the Isle of Man, of any offence and ordered to be sentenced to imprisonment for a period of not less than three months without the option of a fine.[30]

Section 4. Compensation

Under the provisions of the **Forfeiture Act 1870,**[31] and the **Magistrates' Courts Act 1952,**[32] any court convicting a person of an indictable offence might order him to pay compensation for any loss or damage to property (other than loss or damage due to an accident arising out of the presence of a motor vehicle on a road) suffered by the applicant through or by means of the offence, but not exceeding £400. Under the **Criminal Justice Act 1948**[33] compensation might be ordered when a probation order or an absolute or conditional discharge is made. There were also provisions for ordering compensation under the **Protection of Animals Act 1911,**[34] and the **Criminal Damage Act 1971.**[35]   All these provisions had disadvantages, the chief of them being that, under the provisions of the Forfeiture Act 1870, damages might not be awarded for injury to the person, and also under that Act, the

[28] s. 23 (6) of the Criminal Justice Act 1972.
[29] Forfeiture Act 1870, s. 2 as amended by the Criminal Law Act 1967, Sched. 3.
[30] Local Government Act 1933, s. 59 (1) (e).
[31] s. 4 as amended by the Criminal Law Act 1967, Sched. 2.
[32] s. 34 as amended by the Criminal Law Act 1967, Sched. 2.
[33] s. 11 (2).
[34] s. 4
[35] s. 8.

person aggrieved had to make an application for compensation,[36] giving evidence of such loss,[37] immediately after conviction. This meant that if the applicant was for any reason not available, through illness or incapacity or mere ignorance of his rights, the order could not be made. A further disadvantage was that under all the enactments mentioned above, compensation could only be awarded in respect of the offence for which the offender was convicted, and no compensation could be ordered in respect of offences taken into consideration on sentence, whatever the amount of loss or damage suffered by the victims of such offences.

The **Criminal Justice Act 1972**[38] repeals all the above provisions[39] and substitutes for them a single order of compensation in far wider terms. Under **section 1** of the Act, a court by or before whom a person is convicted of an offence may, in addition to dealing with him in any other way, make an order requiring him to pay compensation (a) in respect of any personal injury caused by that offence or by any other offence which is taken into consideration by the court in determining his sentence; (b) in respect of any loss of or damage to property, caused as aforesaid; and (c) where such offence of which he was convicted or which was taken into consideration is one under the Theft Act 1968,[40] and the property is recovered, but has been damaged, in respect of that damage, however caused.[41] No compensation may be ordered under these provisions in respect of loss suffered by dependants of any such person in consequence of his death,[42] and the restrictions as to motor accidents is maintained in relation to (a) and (b) above, but not in relation to (c).[43]

In determining whether to make such an order, and in determining the amount of the order, the court is obliged to have regard to the means of the offender as they appear to the court.[44] A magistrates' court continues to be restricted to a limit of £400

---

[36] R. v. Melksham (1971) 115 S.J. 548, C.A.

[37] R. v. Bowman (1928) 20 Cr.App.R. 90.

[38] Not in force as at July 1, 1972.

[39] s. 1 (6).

[40] s. 1 (1).

[41] A compensation order is in addition to and not in substitution for punishment for the offence: R. v. Lovett (1870) 11 Cox C.C. 602.

[42] But see Criminal Law Act 1826, s. 30 amended by the Criminal Law Act 1967, Sched. 2.

[43] Criminal Justice Act 1972, s. 1 (2).

[44] s. 1 (3).

in respect of any offence of which they have convicted an offender [45] but the Crown Court is not restricted in this regard. A compensation order under the Criminal Justice Act 1972 is treated, when made on conviction on indictment, as an order for the restitution of property, and is so treated for the purpose of an appeal to the Court of Appeal.[46] There are provisions in the Act, relating to the suspension of such orders pending, and on appeal.[47] The Crown Court, in making an order may allow time for payment or direct payment by instalments.[48]

There are provisions in the Act, whereby a compensation order may become the subject of review. At any time before the order has been complied with, or fully complied with, the magistrates' court for the time being having functions in relation to the enforcement of the order, on the application of the person against whom the order was made, will be able to discharge the order, or reduce the amount which remains to be paid, if it appears that the injury, loss or damage in respect of which the order was made, has been held in civil proceedings to be less than it was taken to be for the purposes of the order; or in the case of an order made in respect of the loss of any property, that the property has been recovered by the person in whose favour the order was made.[49] Where a compensation order has been made in favour of a person in respect of any loss, damage or injury, then any damages in civil proceedings will be assessed without regard to the order, but where the whole or part of the order has been paid, the damages awarded in the civil proceedings shall not exceed the amount by which they exceed the amount paid under the order.[50]

SECTION 5. RESTITUTION

Section 28 of the **Theft Act 1968** [51] provides that where any goods [52] have been stolen, and either a person is convicted of any offence with reference to the theft (whether or not the stealing is the gist of

---

[45] s. 1 (5) and see this subs. for the position in respect of the aggregate amounts of several orders.
[46] s. 2 (1).
[47] s. 2 (1)–(3).
[48] Criminal Justice Act 1972, s. 40.
[49] s. 3 (1).
[50] s. 4.
[51] *e.g.* s. 28 (1), (2), (3) substituted by the Criminal Justice Act 1972, Sched. 3.
[52] " Goods " includes all kinds of property except land.

his offence, *e.g.* obtaining property by deception, or blackmail, or handling goods which are stolen, or obtained by deception or blackmail [53]) or a person is convicted of any other offence but such offence as aforesaid is taken into consideration in determining his sentence, the convicting court may (*a*) order any person having possession or control of the goods to restore them to any person entitled to recover them from him; or (*b*) on the application of a person entitled to recover from the person convicted any other goods directly or indirectly representing the first mentioned goods (as being the proceeds of any disposal or realisation of those goods, the whole or part of them, or all goods so representing them) order those other goods to be delivered or transferred to the applicant; or (*c*) order that a sum not exceeding the value of the first mentioned goods be paid out of any money of the person convicted which was taken out of his possession at the time of his apprehension to any person who would be entitled to recover the goods from him if they were still in his possession.[54] In general, complicated questions of restitution are not suitable for summary disposal by a criminal court.[55]

Section 6 (3) of the **Criminal Justice Act 1972** [56] extends the power of the court to make restitution orders to cases not only where a person is convicted of an offence, but also to cases where, on the conviction of a person of any other offence, the court takes an offence such as is specified in section 28 of the Theft Act 1968 into consideration.

Under **section 30 (4)** of the **Criminal Appeal Act 1968** there is a right of appeal against the making of a restitution order in the Crown Court,[57] and this is extended by **section 6 (4)** of the **Criminal Justice Act 1972** [58] to cases where an order has been made in respect of offences taken into consideration. Such an order ceases to have effect if the person convicted successfully appeals against his conviction for the offence, or all the offences for which he was

---

[53] And possibly, conspiracy to steal, attempted stealing, and assisting offenders after such offences have been committed.

[54] s. 28 (1). As substituted by the Criminal Justice Act 1972, Sched. 3, not in force as at July 1, 1972.

[55] *Stamp* v. *United Dominions Trust (Commercial) Ltd.* [1967] 1 Q.B. 418; *R.* v. *Church* (1970) 55 Cr.App.R. 65 (C.A.).

[56] Not in force as at July 1, 1972.

[57] Theft Act 1968, s. 28 (5); *R.* v. *Parker* (1970) 54 Cr.App.R. 339, C.A.

[58] Not in force as at July 1, 1972.

convicted in the proceedings in which the order was made.[59]   A restitution order made in the magistrates' court is an order made on conviction for the purposes of section 83 of the Magistrates' Courts Act 1952, and appeal therefore lies from the making of it to the Crown Court.   The order must be suspended until the expiration of the time prescribed for the giving of notice of appeal, or where notice is given within the period, until the determination of the appeal.[60]

A restitution order may be made in respect of money found on the prisoner or in the hands of his agent which is the subject of the charge or the proceeds of the sale of stolen property.[61]   Where any person has been summarily convicted of an offence that is not a summary offence, the magistrates' court may make the like order for the restitution of property as might have been made by the court before which the offender would have been tried had he been tried on indictment [62]; where property is in the possession of the police by virtue of an order made under section 23 of the Criminal Justice Act 1972, special restrictions apply.[63]   Where stolen property has been pledged to a pawnbroker for less than £50 the restitution order may be made either with or without payment to the pawnbroker of all or any part of the loan according to the circumstances of the case.[64]

By the **Police (Property) Act 1897,** a court of summary jurisdiction may make orders as to property coming into the possession of the police in connection with any criminal charge or under a search warrant, or in proceedings under section 1 of the Children and Young Persons Act 1969,[65] or section 34 of the Pawnbrokers Act 1872.[66]   The Theft Act 1968 does not affect the right of the

---

[59] Criminal Justice Act 1972, s. 6 (4) not in force as at July 1, 1972. The operation of a restitution order must be suspended pending an appeal to the Court of Appeal: Criminal Appeal Act 1968, s. 30 (1); and pending an appeal to the House of Lords: *ibid.* s. 42 (1).

[60] Criminal Justice Act 1972, s. 6 (5) not in force as at July 1, 1972.

[61] *R.* v. *Justices of Central Criminal Court* (1886) 18 Q.B.D. 314. This is still the case, although this decision was based on the old law.

[62] Magistrates' Courts Act 1952, s. 33 (1).

[63] See p. 819, *ante.*

[64] Pawnbrokers Act 1872, ss. 10 and 30, as amended by Pawnbrokers Act 1960, s. 1.

[65] Children and Young Persons Act 1969, s. 72 (3), Sched. 5, para. 1, and see S.I. 1970 No. 1498, Sched. 1 App.A.

[66] Where a pawnbroker detains a person under s. 34 of the Pawnbrokers Act 1872 the property the subject of the offence must be taken before a justice of the peace, if at all possible

police or any person claiming the property to apply to a magistrates' court under the Police (Property) Act 1897, for an order for the delivery of the property to the person appearing to the court to be the owner.

When property is taken from a person charged before a magistrates' court with any offence punishable on indictment or summary conviction and the court is of opinion that the property or any part thereof can be returned consistently with the interests of justice and the safe custody of the person charged, it may direct such property or part thereof to be returned to the person charged or such other person as he may require.[67]

Section 6. Criminal Bankruptcy Orders

The **Criminal Justice Act 1972** envisages the setting up of a procedure for depriving offenders of any gain accruing to them from the proceeds of crime. When the system comes into operation, a person convicted of an offence before the Crown Court may have a criminal bankruptcy order made against him in respect of that offence, or any other offence or offences of which he is convicted in the same proceedings, or has taken into consideration for the purpose of sentence, if it appears to the court that those offences have caused any person or persons whose identity is known to the court, to suffer loss of or damage to property of an amount of £15,000 or more.[68] It will be possible for an order to be made against two or more offenders in respect of the same loss or damage.[69] The order will have to specify the amount of loss or damage appearing to the court to have been caused by the offence, or each of the offences, the person or persons appearing to the court to have suffered that loss or damage, and the amount of that loss or damage which it appears to the court each of those persons has suffered and the operative date.[70]

Where a criminal bankruptcy order is made against any person, that person will be treated as a debtor who has committed an act of bankruptcy on the date on which the order is made,[71] and any person specified in the order as having suffered loss or damage of

---

[67] Magistrates' Courts Act 1952, s. 39.
[68] ss. 7 (1), (2).
[69] *Ibid.* s. 7 (4).
[70] *Ibid.* s. 7 (3).
[71] *Ibid.* Sched. 1, para. 2.

any amount will be treated as a creditor for a debt of that amount provable in the bankruptcy of the person against whom the order is made.[72] For the purpose of proving such a debt in the proceedings, a copy of the order of the court will be treated as sufficient evidence of the debt, unless it is shown by any party to the proceedings that the amount of the relevant loss or damage is greater or less than the amount specified in the order, or that the offence or offences specified in the order did not in fact cause it.[73] No one may contend, however, in such proceedings that the offence or offences specified in the order were not committed by the person against whom the order is made.[74] If it is shown that the amount of relevant loss or damage is greater than that specified in the order, then the debt will be deemed to be the greater amount.[75]

In general, subject to the provisions of the Criminal Justice Act 1972, the ordinary procedures of the Bankruptcy Act 1914 will apply. A criminal bankruptcy petition will be presented to the High Court, subject to the court's power to transfer the proceedings to any other court.[76] A petition may not be presented by the debtor himself.[77] Where a criminal bankruptcy order has been made by the Crown Court, and a bankruptcy petition is presented in respect of the offender, otherwise than under the Criminal Justice Act 1972, before or after the bankruptcy order is made, the court having jurisdiction in relation to the bankruptcy may be able, on the application of the official petitioner, to dismiss the petition, rescind any receiving order made in pursuance thereof, or if that person has been adjudicated bankrupt, annul the adjudication on such terms, if any, as the court thinks fit.[78] The official receiver will be the trustee in bankruptcy of the estate of a person adjudged bankrupt in criminal bankruptcy proceedings.[79]

The **Criminal Justice Act 1972, section 9,** sets up the office of official petitioner, the Director of Public Prosecutions occupying that post *ex officio*.[80] His functions will be to consider whether in any particular case, it is in the public interest that he himself should

---

[72] *Ibid*. Sched. 1, para. 3 (1).
[73] *Ibid*. Sched. 1, para. 3 (2).
[74] *Ibid*. Sched. 1, para. 3 (4).
[75] *Ibid*. Sched. 1, para. 3 (2).
[76] *Ibid*. Sched. 1, para. 4 (1).
[77] *Ibid*. Sched. 1, para. 4 (2).
[78] *Ibid*. Sched. 1, para. 5.
[79] *Ibid*. Sched. 1, para. 8.
[80] *Ibid*. s. 9 (1).

present the bankruptcy petition, and if he considers it in the public interest, to do so; to make payments, in such cases as he may determine, towards those expenses incurred by other persons in connection with criminal bankruptcy proceedings, and generally to exercise, in the public interest, such powers as are conferred upon him by the **Schedule** to the Act.[81]

No appeal will lie against the making of a criminal bankruptcy order [82] but where a person successfully appeals to the Court of Appeal against his conviction of an offence by virtue of which such an order was made, the Court of Appeal will be able, in certain circumstances, to rescind the order, or amend it.[83]

SECTION 7. FINGERPRINTS

By **section 40** [84] of the **Magistrates' Courts Act 1952,** a magistrates' court before which a person not less than **fourteen** years of age is charged may, if the accused has been taken into custody or appears in answer to a summons for an offence punishable with imprisonment, order that his fingerprints and palmprints be taken by a constable and the constable may use such reasonable force as is necessary. The application must be made by an officer of police not below the rank of inspector. If the accused is acquitted or discharged, or the information is dismissed, the fingerprints and all copies and records thereof must be destroyed.

[81] *Ibid.* s. 9 (2), and see Sched. 1, paras. 13–15.
[82] *Ibid.* s. 8 (1).
[83] *Ibid.* s. 8 (2)–(5).
[84] As amended by Criminal Justice Act 1967, s. 33.

CHAPTER 57

APPEALS FROM MAGISTRATES' COURTS—
CROWN PRACTICE

Section 1. Appeals

AN appeal from the decision of a magistrates' court in a criminal case lies either to the Crown Court, whence there is, in some circumstances, a further appeal by way of case stated to the Queen's Bench Division, or, in a suitable case, by way of case stated direct to the Queen's Bench Division, and from there in certain circumstances to the House of Lords.

Appeal to the Crown Court. In the case of a conviction by a magistrates' court there is a general right of appeal[1] to the Crown Court,[2] if the convicted person:

(a) pleaded guilty, against his sentence;

(b) pleaded not guilty, against both conviction and sentence.

A person who deliberately and unequivocally pleads guilty to a charge or information in a magistrates' court has no right of appeal against his consequent conviction. His right of appeal is restricted to an appeal against sentence. This principle applies only to a valid plea of guilty. In order to be effective such a plea must be unambiguous. It must amount to an admission of the offence charged. It not infrequently happens that an apparent plea of guilty, when considered together with the explanation given by the accused, or the statement which he has made to the police, or even something said by him in mitigation of sentence, is clearly no plea of guilty at all. Where it appears to the Crown Court that a person is seeking to appeal upon an apparent plea of guilty, the court is bound to determine the validity of that plea as a preliminary issue, and where it is raised, the court is bound to determine it.[3] The

---

[1] Under the Magistrates' Courts Act 1952, s. 83 (1) as amended by the Courts Act 1971, Sched. 8.

[2] By the Courts Act 1971, s. 8 and Sched. 1, the appellate and other jurisdiction conferred on the courts of quarter sessions before their abolition is vested in the Crown Court.

[3] *R.* v. *Marylebone Justices, ex p. Westminster City Council* [1971] 1 W.L.R. 567.

court may look only at what happened before the magistrates' court. Once it is shown that nothing occurred there which can cast any doubt upon the validity of the plea of guilty, it is too late to permit a change of plea or to remit the case to the court below on the basis that the appellant did not intend to plead guilty.[4] If the Crown Court is satisfied that the plea entered below was effective and binding then it will not entertain an appeal against conviction.[5] On the other hand, if after inquiring into the matter the court is satisfied from what was said or done in the magistrates' court that the plea entered was ambiguous or equivocal, then the matter will be remitted to the lower court for a plea of not guilty to be entered and the matter tried.[6]

In relation to an appeal against sentence, the expression " sentence " includes [7] any order made on conviction by a magistrates' court, not being (i) a probation order [8] or an order for conditional discharge; (ii) an order for the payment of costs; (iii) an order for the destruction of an animal under the Protection of Animals Act 1911, s. 2; or (iv) an order made in pursuance of any enactment under which the court has no discretion as to the making of it, or of its terms.[9] Although no appeal lies against the imposition of a probation order or order of conditional discharge, appeal does lie in respect of any sentence imposed upon the breach of such an order.[10] It has been held that an order of examining justices committing an accused for trial on indictment is not an " order made on conviction " [11]; nor is a committal to the Crown Court for sentence under the provisions of sections 28 and 29 of the Magistrates' Courts Act 1952 [12] although appeal will lie against the conviction on which such a committal is based.[13] An " order made on conviction " will include such orders as those for the restitution of stolen goods, forfeiture of firearms or offensive weapons, orders for the endorsement of licences or the disqualification from holding

[4] Ibid.
[5] R. v. Durham Quarter Sessions, ex p. Virgo [1952] 2 Q.B. 1.
[6] R. v. Tottenham Justices, ex p. Rubens [1970] 1 W.L.R. 800.
[7] Magistrates' Courts Act 1952, s. 83 (3).
[8] A supervision order under the Children and Young Persons Act 1969 is within the meaning of " sentence."
[9] e.g. on obligatory disqualification under the Road Traffic Act 1972.
[10] Magistrates' Courts Act 1952, s. 83 (2).
[11] For a full discussion of this question see A Practical Guide to Appeals in Criminal Courts, Morrish and McLean.
[12] R. v. London Sessions Appeal Committee, ex p. Rogers [1951] 2 K.B. 74.
[13] See, e.g. R. v. Tottenham Justices, ex p. Rubens [1970] 1 W.L.R. 800.

or obtaining a driving licence in certain circumstances.[14] An order for deportation under the Commonwealth Immigrants Act 1962 is such an order.[15]

A person sentenced to pay a fine for the breach of a community service order has a right of appeal to the Crown Court.[15a]

The prosecutor has no right of appeal to the Crown Court against the dismissal of an information unless such a power is expressly given by statute.[16]

Other rights of appeal. A list of enactments conferring rights of appeal to the Crown Court is to be found in the **Ninth Schedule** to the **Courts Act 1971.** A detailed account of appeal rights and procedure under the various enactments can hardly be dealt with in a work of this size.[17]

The procedure for initiating an appeal in a criminal case is governed by the **Magistrates' Courts Act 1952** and the Rules made under **section 15** of the **Courts Act 1971.**

Initiating an appeal. The **Crown Court Rules 1971**[18] regulate and prescribe the procedure to be followed in the Crown Court, both on appeal[19] and generally. They make provision for the time within which notice of appeal[20] must be given and the circumstances in which further time may be allowed; they provide for the particulars to be included in the notice, the persons on whom the notice must be served and the particulars if any to accompany the notice. The Rules provide for the abandonment of the appeal; for the circumstances in which a person concerned with the decision appealed against is disqualified from hearing the appeal, and a host of other administrative matters.

By **section 89** of the **Magistrates' Courts Act 1952** if the appellant is in custody he may be released on giving notice of appeal and on entering into a recognisance, with or without

---

[14] See generally for the principles governing orders made on conviction *R.* v. *London Sessions Appeal Committee, ex p. Beaumont* [1951] 1 K.B. 557.

[15] *R.* v. *Edgehill* [1963] 1 Q.B. 593.

[15a] Criminal Justice Act 1972, s. 17 (5) (not in force on July 1, 1972).

[16] *e.g.* under the Customs and Excise Act 1952, s. 283 (4) and the Diseases of Animals Act 1950, s. 81.

[17] See n. 11, *supra*.

[18] ss. 83 *et seq.*

[19] Crown Court Rules 1971, rr. 7–9.

[20] *Ibid*. r. 7 (21 days).

sureties, conditioned to appear at the hearing of the appeal.[21]   If bail is refused, or the conditions of bail are unacceptable, the defendant may apply to the High Court to grant bail or vary those conditions.[22]

Constitution of the appeal court. The Crown Court in its appellate jurisdiction consists of a judge of the High Court, or a Circuit judge or a Recorder sitting with not less than two and not more than four justices of the peace.[23]   The judge or Recorder presides over the hearing, and if the members of the court are equally divided he has a second or casting vote, the decision on an appeal being by a majority.[24] The Crown Court Rules authorise or require the judge in specified circumstances, to enter on, or continue with proceedings with less than the required number, or where one or more of the justices comprising the original court has withdrawn or is absent.[25] It is expressly provided that a judge or justice of the peace is not disqualified from acting as a judge of the Crown Court for the reason that the proceedings are not at a place within the area for which he was appointed, or because the proceedings are not related to that area in any other way.[26] There is no right to take any objection to a decision of the Crown Court on the basis that it was not constituted as required, unless objection was taken on that ground by or on behalf of a party to the proceedings, not later than the time when the proceedings were entered on, or the alleged irregularity began.[27]

The appeal hearing. If neither party appears at the hearing either personally or by advocate, the appeal will be dismissed. If the respondent alone appears the conviction or order will generally be affirmed. If the appellant alone appears, the appeal may be allowed on proof that all the requirements as to notice, recognisances etc. have been complied with.

---

[21] s. 89 (2) states that this provision does not apply where the accused has been committed to the Crown Court for sentence under section 28 or 29. However, the failure to repeal this provision appears to be an oversight because, by s. 20 of the Criminal Justice Act 1967 persons committed for sentence may now be released on bail.

[22] Criminal Justice Act 1967, s. 22.

[23] Courts Act 1971, s. 5 (1). The number and qualifications of justices is prescribed by the Crown Court Rules, r. 3.

[24] s. 5 (8). As to juvenile appeals see *ante*, p. 683.

[25] s. 5 (6) and r. 4.

[26] s. 5 (8).

[27] s. 5 (7).

The proceedings on appeal before the Crown Court are in the nature of a rehearing of the whole case, and the evidence is led afresh. This was the procedure at quarter sessions, and **section 9 (5)** of the **Courts Act 1971** provides expressly that the transfer to the Crown Court of the previous appellate jurisdiction of quarter sessions shall not affect the customary practice or procedure of such an appeal or the extent to which such an appeal was by way of rehearing.[28] Where the appeal is against sentence only, it is usual for the facts of the case to be outlined and the evidence led as to character and antecedents, before the court hears argument as to sentence. Where the appeal is against conviction, the prosecutor begins again and is bound to prove his case afresh, Neither side is limited to the witnesses called below, and fresh evidence may be tendered.[29] All the attributes of a rehearing apply. The court is not limited to reviewing the decision of the court below, it must form its own opinion on the subject matter of the appeal and may substitute that opinion for the opinion of the lower court.[30]

Powers of the court. By **section 9** of the **Courts Act 1971** the Crown Court may, in the course of hearing any appeal, correct any error or mistake in the order or judgment incorporating the decision which is the subject of the appeal. On determination of the hearing of the appeal the Crown Court:

(a) may confirm, reverse or vary the decision appealed against, or

(b) may remit the matter with their opinion thereon to the authority whose decision is appealed against,[31] or

---

[28] A great part of the appellate proceedings before quarter sessions was customary, although the jurisdiction and powers of the court were statutory, being founded upon the Quarter Sessions Act 1849, and the Summary Jurisdiction Acts 1879 and 1933, all of which are repealed by the Courts Act 1971.

[29] It is undesirable that the Crown Court should have before it the notes of evidence taken in the magistrates' court. Nevertheless, such notes of evidence should be sent to the appropriate officer of the Crown Court so that they can be shown to the Judge or Recorder if necessary, *e.g.* in order to decide an application for legal aid or to judge the length of the appeal for listing purposes. *Practice Note* [1956] 1 Q.B. 451; *R.* v. *Grimsby Borough Q.S., ex p. Fuller* [1956] 1 Q.B. 36.

[30] See *Sagnata Investments Ltd.* v. *Norwich Corporation* [1971] 2 Q.B. 614, approving the observations of Lord Goddard C.J. in *Stepney Borough Council* v. *Joffe* [1949] 1 K.B. 499, and of Lord Parker C.J. in *R.* v. *Essex Quarter Sessions, ex p. Thomas* [1966] 1 W.L.R. 359 at p. 362; but disapproving of *Godfrey* v. *Bournemouth Corporation* [1969] 1 W.L.R. 47.

[31] The lower court is bound to give effect to that opinion: *R.* v. *Tottenham Justices, ex p. Rubens, supra* [1970] 1 W.L.R. 800.

(c) make such other order in the matter as the court thinks just, and by any such order exercise any power *which the said authority might have exercised.*

If the appeal is against conviction *or* sentence, their powers include the power to award any punishment, whether more or less severe than that awarded by the magistrates' court provided that it is a punishment which the lower court had power to award.[32]

Further appeal from the Crown Court by way of case stated. Any order, judgment or other decision of the Crown Court, other than one given in relation to a trial on indictment, or given under the Betting, Gaming and Lotteries Act 1963, the Licensing Act 1964 or the Gaming Act 1968, may be questioned on the ground that it is wrong in law or in excess of the jurisdiction of the court by applying to the Court to state a case for the opinion of the Queen's Bench Division.[33] The procedure is governed by the rules under the Judicature Act 1925 which apply as if the case stated was an appeal to the High Court.[34]

By **section 13 (4)** of the **Courts Act 1971** the Crown Court may admit to bail, or direct the admission to bail, of any person who has applied to state a case. Where bail is refused by the Crown Court or the conditions of bail are unsatisfactory, application may be made to the High Court [35] which has power to grant bail.[36]

Appeal from justices by way of case stated. Any person who was a party to any proceeding before a magistrates' court or is aggrieved by the conviction, order, determination or other proceeding of the court may question the proceeding on the ground that it is *wrong in law* or is in *excess of jurisdiction,* by applying to the justices composing the court to state a case for the opinion of the High Court on the question of law or jurisdiction involved.[37]

---

[32] *Cf.* the powers of the Court of Appeal under the Criminal Appeal Act 1968, s. 11, and on a retrial under the Criminal Appeal Act 1968, Sched. 2.

[33] Courts Act 1971, s. 10.

[34] Since the jurisdiction of the Crown Court is wholly statutory, the common law powers of quarter sessions to state a case (see, *e.g. R.* v. *Northumberland Justices* [1965] 1 W.L.R. 700) is probably abolished by the repeal of s. 20 of the Criminal Justice Act 1925, unless it can be said that power is preserved by the Courts Act 1971, Sched. 1.

[35] Criminal Justice Act 1967, s. 22.

[36] Criminal Justice Act 1948, s. 37 (1) (*b*), substituted by the Courts Act 1971, Sched. 8.

[37] Magistrates' Courts Act 1952, s. 87 (1).

Application for a case stated operates as an abandonment of the right to appeal to the Crown Court.[38] An application must be made in writing within fourteen days after the day on which the decision was given, and must be delivered to the clerk of the magistrates' court whose decision is questioned, or sent to him by post.[39] If the applicant for the case to be stated is in custody, the court may release him on bail on his entering into a recognisance, with or without sureties, conditioned for his appearance before the magistrates' court within ten days after the judgment of the High Court has been given, unless the determination in respect of which the case is stated is reversed by that judgment.[40] The case must be stated within three calendar months after the date of the application.[41] It must set out the findings of fact made by the justices, which are conclusive, but not the evidence on which they were based (unless one of the questions on which the opinion of the High Court is sought is whether there was evidence on which the magistrates' court could come to its decision).[42] It may be stated on behalf of the justices whose decision is questioned by any two or more of them.[43]

If the justices are of opinion that the application is frivolous, but not otherwise, they may refuse to state a case unless the application is made by or under the direction of the Attorney-General. If they refuse, they must, on request by the applicant, give him a signed certificate of refusal; the applicant can then apply to the High Court for an order of mandamus requiring them to do so, and if the court makes the order, the justices must state the case upon the appellant entering into the prescribed recognisance.[44]

When the case has been stated by the justices the appellant must within ten days lodge it in the High Court and must within four days of lodging it give to the respondent written notice of the appeal and a copy of the case, and there must be at least eight clear days between the service of the notice and the day named therein for the hearing.[45]

---

[38] *Ibid.* s. 87 (4).
[39] Magistrates' Courts Rules 1968, r. 65. The court may require the applicant to enter into recognisances for costs: Magistrates' Courts Act 1952, s. 90.
[40] Magistrates' Courts Act 1952, s. 89. S. 22 of the Criminal Justice Act 1967 applies here also.
[41] Magistrates' Courts Rules 1968, r. 67.
[42] *Ibid.* r. 68. See *Practice Direction* [1972] 1 W.L.R. 3.
[43] *Ibid.* r. 66.   [44] Magistrates' Courts Act 1952, s. 87 (5) (6).
[45] Rules of Supreme Court, Ord. 56, r. 6.

Hearings of an appeal by way of case stated. The appeal is heard by a Divisional Court of the Queen's Bench Division.[46] On an appeal from a magistrates' court, the Divisional Court must hear and determine the questions of law arising upon the case, and (i) reverse, affirm, or amend the determination in respect of which the case was stated; or (ii) remit the matter to the justice or justices with the opinion of the court thereon; or (iii) make such other order as may seem just.[47] On an appeal from the Crown Court, the Divisional Court may give any judgment, or make any order which ought to have been given or made by that court, or may remit the order and the conviction with the order and the case stated on it, with the opinion or direction of the court, for rehearing and determination by the Crown Court, or may remit the case for restatement.

The High Court no longer has an original jurisdiction to grant bail on appeal. Application must first be made to the court from which the appeal is being taken.[48]

Section 2. Crown Proceedings

The High Court possesses an inherent power at common law to supervise inferior courts and tribunals. This power is limited and extends essentially to matters of jurisdiction. The means by which the court exercises its power is by the issue of the writ of habeas corpus, and the orders of mandamus, certiorari and prohibition. The particular order which is appropriate will depend upon the matter to be challenged, or the stage at which the proceedings which are to be questioned have reached. The writ of habeas corpus lies to test the validity or want of jurisdiction of an order depriving a person of his liberty. The order of mandamus lies to compel an inferior court to exercise its jurisdiction; certiorari lies to quash the decision of an inferior court which has exercised jurisdiction which it does not have; and prohibition lies to restrain an inferior court from assuming jurisdiction which it does not possess. The writ of habeas corpus is issued to the person responsible for the detention, and in criminal matters generally to the

[46] *Ibid.* rr. 1 and 5.
[47] Summary Jurisdiction Act 1857, s. 6, as amended by the Magistrates' Courts Act 1952, Sched. 5, and Administration of Justice Act 1960, s. 19 (1).
[48] Criminal Justice Act 1967, s. 22, repealing the Criminal Justice Act 1948, s. 37 (1) (2) and (3), in this respect.

governor of the prison in which the detained person is to be found. The prerogative orders lie against a magistrates' court and against the Crown Court in its appellate jurisdiction but not in relation to its jurisdiction relating to trials on indictment. Where an order of certiorari is sought against the Crown Court, bail may be granted, either by the Crown Court or by the High Court.

Habeas corpus. The writ of habeas corpus is available in respect of imprisonment by the civil or military courts. Its most important aspect today in criminal matters is to test the validity of committals, by a metropolitan magistrate, of persons detained for extradition under the provisions of the Extradition Act 1870 and the Fugitive Offenders Act 1967. In hearing an application for the issue of the writ, the High Court does not sit as a court of appeal. It does not rehear the matters which were decided below but merely considers whether the court or other tribunal had authority to issue the warrant of commitment.

Mandamus. A mandamus is a remedy granted to compel the performance of an imperative public duty where a party with a legal right to its performance has made a demand for its performance and has been refused and has no other remedy. Thus, as has been already stated, where a court of summary jurisdiction or the Crown Court refuses to state a case the applicant may apply for a mandamus to compel it to do so.

The remedy of mandamus is available only to compel the performance by justices of ministerial acts as to which they have no discretion, or to compel them to exercise their judicial functions where they have failed to exercise a proper judicial discretion, or have declined jurisdiction. Thus, it is obligatory upon justices to hear and consider an application for the issue of a summons, and if they refuse to do so, they may be compelled by mandamus. But if, having considered the application, they bona fide exercise their discretion and bring their minds to bear upon the question whether they ought to grant it or not, the Queen's Bench Division will not interfere by mandamus,[49] unless they have taken into consideration something " extraneous and extra-judicial " which ought not to have affected their decision.[50] So

[49] *Ex p. Lewis* (1888) 21 Q.B.D. 191.
[50] *R.* v. *Adamson* (1875) 1 Q.B.D. 201.

also if justices, upon a mistaken view of the law, refuse to adjudicate on the merits of the case, a mandamus may issue.[51] But if, however, erroneously, they have adjudicated upon the merits of the case, a mandamus will not lie unless they have taken into consideration matters which are absolutely outside the ambit of their jurisdiction.[52]

Certiorari. By certiorari the proceedings of a court of summary jurisdiction or of the Crown Court other than its jurisdiction in matters relating to trial on indictment [53] may be removed to the Queen's Bench Division for the purpose of being examined and, if necessary, quashed. The right to this remedy exists in every case as a matter of common law, unless expressly taken away by statute.[54] It exists, as a general rule, for (i) a defect or informality on the face of the proceedings, or (ii) where the justices have had no jurisdiction or have exceeded their jurisdiction, or (iii) where a conviction has been obtained fraudulently.

Prohibition. In a proper case an order of prohibition may be obtained in the Queen's Bench Division to restrain justices or the Crown Court, other than in its jurisdiction in matters relating to trial on indictment,[55] from proceeding without jurisdiction or in excess of their jurisdiction.

Procedure. The procedure for an application for an order of mandamus, certiorari or prohibition is to be found in Order 56 of the Rules of the Supreme Court. Application is made to the Divisional Court of the Queen's Bench Division.

SECTION 3. APPEALS TO THE HOUSE OF LORDS

Section 1 of the **Administration of Justice Act 1960,** as amended by the Criminal Appeal Act 1968, Sched. 7, provides for a right of appeal to the House of Lords from a decision of the Divisional Court in a criminal cause or matter with the leave of that court or the House of Lords. The provisions of those Acts will be dealt with later in their application to appeals from the Criminal

---

[51] See *R.* v. *Kennedy* (1902) 86 L.T. 753.
[52] *R.* v. *Cotham* [1898] 1 Q.B. 802.
[53] Courts Act 1971, s. 10 (5).
[54] The right has been taken away by many statutes.
[55] Courts Act 1971, s. 10 (5).

Division of the Court of Appeal.[56] They apply equally to appeals from the Divisional Court.

SECTION 4. APPEALS AGAINST SENTENCE IMPOSED AFTER COMMITTAL TO THE CROWN COURT

The power of a magistrates' court under section 29 of the Criminal Justice Act 1948 [57] to commit a person convicted summarily before that court for sentencing by the Crown Court has been dealt with.[58]

Section 10 of the **Criminal Appeal Act 1968** [59] provides for rights of appeal against sentence when a person is dealt with by the Crown Court (otherwise than on appeal from a magistrates' court) for an offence of which he was not convicted on indictment.

Thus, the proceedings from which an appeal against sentence lies under the section are those where an offender convicted of an offence by a magistrates' court is committed by that court to be dealt with for his offences before the Crown Court and therefore includes a committal under section 29 (above) or where an offender having been made the subject of a probation order or an order for conditional discharge or given a suspended sentence, appears or is brought before the Crown Court to be further dealt with for his offence.

Appeal lies to the criminal division of the Court of Appeal in the following cases only:

(a) where, either for that offence alone or for that offence and other offences for which sentence is passed in the same proceeding,[60] he is sentenced to six months' imprisonment or more; or

(b) where the sentence is one which the court convicting him had not power to pass; or

(c) where the court in dealing with him for the offence makes in respect of him—

(i) a recommendation for deportation; or

(ii) an order disqualifying him from holding or obtaining a licence to drive a motor-vehicle under Part II of the Road Traffic Act 1960,[60a]

---

[56] *Post*, p. 859.
[57] As substituted by the Courts Act 1971, Sched. 8, para. 27.   [58] *Ante*, p. 761.
[59] As substituted by the Courts Act 1971, Sched. 8, para. 57.
[60] The expression "same proceeding" is defined in s. 10 (4).
[60a] Now Road Traffic Act 1972, Pt. III.

(iii) an order under section 40 of the Criminal Justice Act 1967 [61] (suspended sentences);

(iv) an order under section 12 of the Criminal Justice Act 1961, returning an offender to borstal on reconviction.[62]

The provisions of section 11 of the Criminal Appeal Act 1968 which deal with the powers of the court on an appeal against a sentence imposed after a trial or indictment and which will be noted later, apply to an appeal against sentence imposed after committal.[63]

---

[61] p. 769.

[62] s. 10 (3) added by the Criminal Justice Act 1972, s. 42 (1) (not in force on July 1, 1972).

[63] *Post*, p. 854 and see *post*, pp. 843 *et seq.*

CHAPTER 58

APPEALS FROM TRIALS ON INDICTMENT

SECTION 1. APPEALS FROM THE CROWN COURT TO
THE COURT OF APPEAL

FROM an early period it was a general practice for a judge of assize to reserve any difficult question of law in order to consult thereon with the other judges of the common law courts. By the Crown Cases Act 1848, the Court for Crown Cases Reserved was created, and it was provided that whenever a person was convicted of any treason, felony or misdemeanour before a court of assize or quarter sessions the court before whom he was tried might reserve any question of *law* arising on the trial for the consideration of the justices of either Bench and Barons of the Exchequer, who might thereupon finally determine such question and reverse, affirm or amend any judgment, or " make such other order as justice may require. " By the Judicature Act 1873, all jurisdiction under this Act in relation to questions of law arising in criminal trials was transferred to the judges of the High Court.

But, unless a question of law was thus reserved or the case was one of a very limited class in which relief could be obtained by writ of error or, in misdemeanours,[1] by a new trial there was nothing in the nature of an appeal even on a question of law, and there was in no case an appeal from the verdict of the jury.

The Criminal Appeal Act 1907 provided for the establishment of the Court of Criminal Appeal and gave certain rights of appeal to that court to persons convicted on indictment against their conviction and sentence. The Court of Criminal Appeal was abolished in 1966, but by **section 1** of the **Criminal Appeal Act 1966** [2] a new Criminal Division was created in the Court of Appeal. The jurisdiction of that court is wholly statutory and is regulated by the Criminal Appeal Acts 1964, 1966 and 1968, and the rules of court made under the Acts of 1966 [3] and 1968 [4] and the Supreme Court

---

[1] See *R.* v. *Bertrand* (1867) L.R. 1 P.C. 520.
[2] As amended by the Criminal Appeal Act 1968, Sched. 5.
[3] s. 2 (5).
[4] s. 46.

of Judicature (Consolidation) Act 1925.[5] The Criminal Appeal Act 1907 is expressly repealed by the **Criminal Appeal Act 1968** which consolidates the law and practice relating to appeals to the new Criminal Division. In relation to jurisdiction, the effect is that the Criminal Division now exercises all the jurisdiction of the Court of Appeal under Parts I and II of the 1968 Act, and all other jurisdiction exercised immediately before the commencement of the Act by the former Court of Criminal Appeal.[6]

The Criminal Division sits throughout much of the year in several courts. In general, one court is presided over by the Lord Chief Justice of England, while the other court or courts are presided over either by a Lord Justice of Appeal or one of the judges of the High Court. A court of this division is duly constituted if it consists of an uneven number of judges, not being less than three [7] and indeed usually the number is three. A court of the division is duly constituted, but not for the purpose of (*a*) determining an appeal; or (*b*) determining an application for leave to appeal to the House of Lords; or (*c*) of refusing an application for leave to appeal to the Criminal Division in certain circumstances— where the court consists of two judges only.[8] Again, where one judge of the court maintains that an appeal should be allowed, but the other two consider that it should be dismissed, there is power for the dissenting judge to ask for the appeal to be re-argued before a larger court.[9]

The court is not bound by its own decisions and because of the need for certainty in the criminal law only one judgment is given unless the presiding judge otherwise authorises.[10] This power is seldom exercised.[11]

Right of appeal. By virtue of **sections 1, 9, 10, 12 and 15** of the **Criminal Appeal Act 1968,** a person convicted on indictment may appeal to the Criminal Division of the Court of Appeal:

(*a*) against his conviction, whether he pleaded guilty or not;

---

[5] s. 99.
[6] Criminal Appeal Act 1966, s. 1 as amended by the 1968 Act, Sched. 5.
[7] Administration of Justice Act 1970, s. 9 (1).
[8] *Ibid.* s. 9 (2).
[9] See, *e.g. R.* v. *Norman* [1924] 2 K.B. 315.
[10] Criminal Appeal Act 1966, s. 2 (4).
[11] For examples of separate judgments under the equivalent provision of the 1907 Act, see *R.* v. *Norman* [1924] 2 K.B. 315; *R.* v. *Head* [1958] 1 Q.B. 132.

(b) against any sentence (not fixed by law) passed on him for an offence, whether passed on his conviction or in a subsequent proceeding;

(c) against a verdict of not guilty by reason of insanity; or

(d) against a finding that he was under a disability, where a jury has so determined.[12]

There is no appeal by the Crown against the acquittal of an accused person on indictment or against any order adverse to the Crown made in such proceedings, but in certain circumstances such a case may be referred to the court by the Attorney-General.[13] The court has no power to hear an appeal in relation to an interlocutory matter, however, such as the refusal of the trial judge to order particulars of a count in an indictment.[14] An appeal under (a) (c) or (d) lies as of right on any ground of appeal involving a question of law alone, or with leave of the Court of Appeal or upon the certificate of the trial judge that it is a fit case for appeal, on any ground which involves a question of fact alone, or a question of mixed law and fact, or upon any other ground which appears to the court to be sufficient.[15] An appeal against sentence, lies only with leave of the Court of Appeal.[16]

There is no jurisdiction to hear an appeal after the death of the appellant, although it has been suggested [17] that in such a case it is open, in certain circumstances, to the personal representatives of the deceased to petition the Secretary of State for relief. The Secretary of State has powers to refer a case to the Court of Appeal.

" Conviction " includes conviction on a plea of guilty, or upon the verdict of a jury, but if a plea of guilty has been recorded on indictment, the court will only entertain an appeal against the conviction :

(i) if it appears that the appellant did not appreciate the nature of the charge; or

---

[12] *i.e.* under the Criminal Procedure (Insanity) Act 1964, s. 4. The court also has the power to entertain an appeal against conviction on the ground that the hearing of a preliminary issue with regard to fitness to plead was open to objection or error in law so that the prisoner should not have been tried on the substantive charge : *R.* v. *Podola* (1959) 43 Cr.App.R. 220.

[13] Under the Criminal Justice Act 1972, s. 36. See *post*, p. 859. (This provision was not in force on July 1, 1972.)

[14] *R.* v. *Collins* [1970] 1 Q.B. 710.

[15] ss. 1, 12, 15.

[16] s. 11.

[17] *R.* v. *Jefferies* [1969] 1 Q.B. 120; see also *R.* v. *Rowe* [1955] 1 Q.B. 573.

(ii) if the appellant did not intend to admit that he was guilty of it; or

(iii) if, upon the admitted facts, the appellant could not have been convicted in law of the offence charged.[18]

No appeal lies against the conviction of an incorrigible rogue committed to the Crown Court for sentence, since the conviction is by the committing magistrates. An appeal lies, however, against any sentence imposed by the Crown Court.[19]

" Sentence " includes " any order made by a court in dealing with an offender." [20] A recommendation for deportation under the Immigration Act 1971 is expressly included,[21] as is a hospital order under the Mental Health Act 1959.[22] An order for the payment of costs is part of the sentence,[23] and so is an order for the payment of compensation made under the Criminal Justice Act 1972.[24] A restitution order, made under the provisions of the Theft Act 1968,[25] may be the subject of an appeal to the court [26]; but no appeal lies against the making of a criminal bankruptcy order.[27]

A person disqualified from holding or obtaining a driving licence may appeal to the court.[28] An order estreating bail for non-appearance, is not part of the sentence,[29] nor is a term of imprisonment passed in default of the payment of estreated bail.[30]

A person who is dealt with at the Crown Court [31] (otherwise than on appeal from a magistrates' court) for an offence of which he was not convicted on indictment has a right of appeal [32] against any sentence imposed at the Crown Court:

---

[18] See, e.g. R. v. Forde [1923] 2 K.B. 400 at p. 403.

[19] R. v. Johnson [1909] 1 K.B. 438.

[20] Criminal Appeal Act 1968, s. 50 and Courts Act 1971, s. 57 (1).

[21] Courts Act 1971, s. 57 (1) (b).

[22] Criminal Appeal Act 1968, s. 50. See ante, p. 796.

[23] Courts Act 1971, s. 57 (1).

[24] Criminal Justice Act 1972, s. 2 (not in force on July 1, 1972); Criminal Appeal Act 1968, ss. 30 and 42 (1).

[25] s. 28, substituted by the Criminal Justice Act 1972, s. 64 (1) and Sched. 5. See post, p. 822.

[26] Criminal Appeal Act 1968, ss. 9, 50; Criminal Justice Act 1972, s. 6 (4) (b) (not in force on July 1, 1972).

[27] Criminal Justice Act 1972, s. 8 (1) (not in force on July 1, 1972).

[28] Road Traffic Act 1972, s. 94 (1); R. v. Surrey Quarter Sessions [1963] 1 Q.B. 990.

[29] R. v. Thayne [1970] 1 Q.B. 441.

[30] R. v. Harman [1959] 2 Q.B. 134.

[31] See ante, p. 838.

[32] Criminal Appeal Act 1968, s. 10 as amended.

(a) where, after summary conviction, he was committed by the magistrates' court to be dealt with; or

(b) where, having been made the subject of a probation order or conditional discharge, or given a suspended sentence, he appears or is brought before the Crown Court to be further dealt with for his offence.

In such circumstances, however, the right of appeal is restricted by section 10 of the Criminal Appeal Act 1968 to cases where:

(i) either for that offence alone or for that offence and others, for which sentence is passed at the same proceeding, he was sentenced to six months imprisonment or more; or

(ii) the sentence is one which the convicting court had no power to impose; or

(iii) the court in dealing with the offender for the offence (a) made a recommendation for his deportation, (b) made an order of disqualification under Part II of the Road Traffic Act 1960 [32a] (c) made an order as to an existing suspended sentence under section 40 of the Criminal Justice Act 1967,[33] or (d) where the court made in respect of him an order, under section 12 of the Criminal Justice Act 1961, returning him to borstal on reconviction.[34]

Grounds of appeal. Instances of grounds of appeal involving a question of law might be that the indictment was defective, that evidence was wrongly admitted or rejected, that the judge of the court of trial misdirected the jury, that required corroboration was not forthcoming, that at the close of the case for the prosecution there was no case to go to the jury, or that a material irregularity occurred in the conduct of the trial.

Where it is alleged that the indictment was defective, the court will take into consideration the gravity of the defect before deciding whether or not to quash the conviction. Where the defect is of a less serious nature the court will be reluctant to interfere [35] and may apply the proviso,[36] or resort to its power to substitute a con-

---

[32a] Now Road Traffic Act 1972, Pt. III.

[33] See *ante*, p. 769.

[34] Inserted by the Criminal Justice Act 1972, s. 64 (1) and Sched. 5 nullifying the effect of *R.* v. *Bebbington* [1969] 1 W.L.R. 1348.

[35] See, *e.g. R.* v. *Disney* [1933] 2 K.B. 138; *R.* v. *McVitie* [1960] 2 Q.B. 483; *R.* v. *Miller and Hannoman* [1959] Crim.L.R. 50.

[36] To ss. 2 (1), 13 (2), 16 (1) of the Criminal Appeal Act 1968. See *post*, p. 849.

viction for some other offence.[37]   Where, however, the defect is a
serious one such as where the count was bad for duplicity,[38] then
the court will quash the conviction, even though no objection was
taken to the defect at the trial.[39]   Where an objection was raised
and wrongly overruled by the judge of the court of trial the court
will quash the conviction,[40] and it will also do so where the defect
may have caused real embarrassment to the accused.[41]

Where evidence has been wrongly admitted at the trial the court
will generally quash the conviction unless, upon a consideration of
the nature of the evidence admitted, and the directions of the trial
judge in regard to it, it can be said that that evidence cannot
reasonably be said to have affected the minds of the jury in arriving
at their verdict, and that they would or must have arrived at the
same verdict if the evidence had not been admitted.   The test is
" Whether on a fair consideration of the whole proceedings . . .
[the court] . . . must hold that there is a probability that the
improper admission of evidence turned the scale against the appellant." [42]   Similar principles apply in relation to the wrongful
exclusion of evidence.

Initiating the appeal.   Where a person convicted desires to
appeal under the Criminal Appeal Act 1968 or to obtain the leave
of the court to appeal, he must give notice to the registrar on the
appropriate form within twenty-eight days from the date of the
conviction, verdict or finding appealed against, or in the case of
appeal against sentence, from the date on which sentence was
passed, or in the case of an order made or treated as made on
conviction, from the date of the making of the order.[43]   He must
state his grounds for appealing which will be presented to the court
together with any other matters which he desires to be brought to
the notice of the court.   Except in the case of a conviction involving

---

[37] *Ibid.* s. 3.
[38] See *ante,* pp. 699, 700.
[39] *R.* v. *Molloy* [1921] 2 K.B. 364; *R.* v. *Wilmot* (1933) 24 Cr.App.R. 63.
[40] *e.g. R.* v. *Stoddart* (1909) 2 Cr.App.R. 217; *R.* v. *Miller and Hannoman*
(*supra*).
[41] *R.* v. *Edwards and Gilbert* [1913] 1 K.B. 287; *R.* v. *Thompson* [1914] 2
K.B. 99.
[42] A test propounded by Lord Normand in *Teper* v. *The Queen* [1952] A.C.
480 and adopted in *R.* v. *Parker* (1960) 45 Cr.App.R. 1. See *R.* v. *Lewis*
[1969] 2 Q.B. 1; *R.* v. *Hassan* [1970] 1 Q.B. 423.
[43] Criminal Appeal Act 1968, s. 18. The appropriate form is set out in the
Schedule to the Criminal Appeal Rules 1968. It must be signed by the
appellant himself or on his behalf. See also r. 2 set out in Arch. para. 871.

sentence of death, the time within which notice of appeal or of an application for leave to appeal may be given may be extended at any time by the court.[44]

Preparation of appeal. The registrar is responsible for preparing the appeal for hearing by the court, and it is from his office that the appellant obtains any documents or things, copies or reproductions of documents required for the purposes of the appeal.[45] The registrar may make arrangements for the inspection of documents or exhibits by an interested party [46] and a transcript of the record of any proceedings or any part of the proceedings may be obtained from him, if in his possession or from the official shorthand writer of the trial court. The registrar gives notice of the date on which the appeal, or the application, is to be heard, both to the appellant or any person having him in custody and to any other interested party whom the court requires to be represented at the hearing.

Record of proceedings. The present practice is for the registrar of the Criminal Division to require a " short transcript " to be prepared for the use of the court or any judge thereof when application is made for leave to appeal against sentence or conviction. A short transcript includes the plea, the summing-up of the trial judge, the verdict, evidence as to character, any speech in mitigation of sentence and any observations of the judge upon passing sentence. It will also include any rulings made during the trial on the admissibility of evidence. On the request of the court or the registrar, the full transcript may be supplied.[47]

The appellant, any " party interested " in the appeal and any other person who is granted leave of the court may obtain a copy of the transcript on payment of the charges laid down by the Treasury. The appellant may also receive a copy of so much of the transcript as is supplied to the court at a reduced rate, or a free copy if the court so directs.[48]

---

[44] Criminal Appeal Act 1968, s. 18. And see r. 2 of the Criminal Appeal Rules 1968.
[45] Criminal Appeal Act 1968, s. 21.
[46] Criminal Appeal Rules 1968, rr. 7 (4) and 8.
[47] Criminal Appeal Act 1968, s. 32 and Criminal Appeal Rules 1968, r. 19.
[48] Provided that in the case of an interested party who has been given legal aid under s. 73 (5) of the Criminal Justice Act 1967, for the purpose of the appeal or any proceedings preliminary or incidental thereto such a transcript must be supplied free. Criminal Appeal Rules 1968, r. 19 (2) ; Arch. para. 887.

Representation by counsel. The appellant may be represented upon the hearing of the appeal or upon the hearing of any application preliminary or incidental thereto.[49]   In practice appellants are not normally represented at applications for appeal, etc.

The Crown is not normally represented at a hearing of an application for leave to appeal or a hearing of an appeal against sentence.   For appeals against conviction counsel are instructed by local prosecuting authorities.   The Director of Public Prosecutions appears on appeal when he prosecuted at the trial, or when he considers it desirable to assume responsibility for the defence of the appeal, or when he is instructed to do so by the court.

Legal Aid. By **section 47** of the **Criminal Appeal Act 1968,** the court may at any time assign to an appellant, a solicitor and counsel, or counsel only, in his appeal or in proceedings preliminary or incidental thereto, where it appears desirable in the interests of justice that he should have legal aid and that he has not sufficient means to enable him to obtain it.   Where it appears to the registrar of the court that a solicitor and counsel or counsel only ought to be assigned to an appellant under Part I of the Act, although no application for legal aid has been made, he must report the fact to the court, or a judge of the Court of Appeal or of the Queen's Bench Division so that the judge may consider whether legal aid should be granted.   Where an appellant's application for legal aid is refused by the judge, the appellant can have his application decided by the court.[50]

Bail. The court has power to admit an appellant to bail if it thinks fit, pending the hearing of an appeal [51] but the court has expressed the view [52] that this should be rarely done and then only in special circumstances.[53]   Where an application for bail is refused by the single judge, the application may be determined by the full court.   There are provisions governing the revocation and forfeiture of bail where granted.[54]

---

[49] Where the appellant is represented upon an application for leave to appeal, the full court would normally hear it.

[50] See *ante*, p. 585 for the provisions as to legal aid generally.

[51] Criminal Appeal Act 1968, s. 19.

[52] *R.* v. *Rowe* (1968) 118 New L.J. 1149.

[53] *Ibid.* and see cases cited at Arch. para. 882.

[54] Criminal Appeal Rules 1968, rr. 5 and 6.

Right of appellant to be present. An appellant, notwithstanding that he is in custody, is entitled to be present, if he desires it, on the hearing of his appeal, except where the appeal is on some ground involving a question of law alone, but in that case and on an application for leave to appeal and on any proceedings preliminary or incidental to an appeal, he is not entitled to be present except when the court gives him leave.[55] The power of the court to pass any sentence under the Act may be exercised notwithstanding that the appellant is for any reason not present.[56]

Single judge procedure. Section 31 of the **Criminal Appeal Act 1968** provides that the powers of the court to give leave to appeal and to decide other preliminary and incidental applications in relation to an appeal, *e.g.* extensions of time in which to appeal, bail, may be exercised by any judge of the court.[57] These powers may be exercised by any judge of the High Court, whether or not he is entitled by virtue of a request from the Lord Chief Justice to be a member of the criminal division at that time.[58]

Abandonment of Appeals. An appellant may at any time abandon his appeal by giving notice of abandonment to the registrar in the prescribed form.[59] The effect of such a notice is that the appeal is deemed to have been dismissed by the court.[60]

However, if any application is refused by a single judge, the appellant is entitled to have the application determined by a court of the criminal division, *i.e.* before not less than three judges.[61] But his application must be returned within fourteen days of the receipt by him of the refusal, or such longer period as the judge of the court may fix.[62]

---

[55] Criminal Appeal Act 1968, s. 22 (1).

[56] *Ibid.* s. 22 (3).

[57] A judge sitting alone considers the case in his private room.

[58] s. 45 (2) of the Criminal Appeal Act 1968, amended by the Administration of Justice Act 1970, s. 9 (3).

[59] Criminal Appeal Rules 1968, r. 10.

[60] The court will not allow a notice of abandonment to be withdrawn unless the appellant shows that there was some fraud or mistake or misapprehension as to what had happened with regard to the appeal or the notice of appeal: *R.* v. *Healey* (1956) 40 Cr.App.R. 40; *R.* v. *Moore* (1957) 41 Cr.App.R. 179. Quite unusual circumstances must be shown to exist: *R.* v. *Sutton (Philip)* [1969] 1 W.L.R. 375 and see *R.* v. *Noble* [1971] 1 W.L.R. 1772.

[61] Criminal Appeal Act 1968, s. 31 (3).

[62] Criminal Appeal Rules 1968, r. 12. See *R.* v. *Gaston* (1970) 55 Cr.App.R. 88; the power to extend the time under r. 12 (1) may be exercised by any

It is more usual for applications for leave to appeal against conviction to go to the full court sitting in public. Applications for leave to appeal against sentence are usually considered by a single judge.[63]

Determination of appeal. Section 2 of the **1968 Act** provides that the Court of Appeal, on any appeal against conviction shall allow the appeal and quash the conviction, if they think that the verdict of the jury should be set aside on the ground

    (a) that under all the circumstances of the case the verdict of the jury is unsafe or unsatisfactory;

    (b) that the judgment of the trial court before whom the appellant was convicted should be set aside on the ground of a wrong decision of any question of law; or

    (c) that there was a material irregularity in the course of the trial

and in any other case the court shall dismiss the appeal.

In deciding whether the verdict is unsafe or unsatisfactory, the court asks itself the subjective question, " whether it is content to let the matter stand as it is, or whether there is not some lurking doubt in their minds which makes them wonder whether an injustice has been done." This is a reaction which need not be based strictly on evidence as such; it is a reaction which can be produced by a general feel of the case: [64]

Provided that the court may, notwithstanding that they are of opinion that the point raised in the appeal might be decided in favour of the appellant, dismiss the appeal if they consider that no miscarriage of justice has actually occurred.

It is not every irregularity that is a ground for quashing the conviction. It happens from time to time that something is done in the course of a trial which is not strictly in accordance with recognised procedure. If that is so, the court has to consider whether or not " it is an irregularity which goes to the root of the

    judge of the court, not necessarily the judge who refused the application: *R.* v. *Ward* (1971) 55 Cr.App.R. 509. See also *R.* v. *Doherty* [1971] 1 W.L.R. 1454.

[63] For a definition of " single judge " see s. 45 (2) of the 1968 Act, amended by the Administration of Justice Act 1970, Sched. 11. For powers of single judge see the Criminal Appeal Act 1968, s. 31.

[64] *Per* Widgery L.J. in *R.* v. *Cooper* [1969] 1 Q.B. 267; see also *R.* v. *Smith* (1967) 51 Cr.App.R. 22 and *R.* v. *Husein* (1968) 52 Cr.App.R. 291.

case." [65] Such an irregularity may arise in a number of cases, such as where the trial is said to have been unfairly conducted; or where the jury may have been tampered with; or where the trial judge has failed to inform an unrepresented defendant of his rights.

There have been many decisions on the question when the court should make use of the proviso, but for general principles reference may be made to *Maxwell* v. *Director of Public Prosecutions* [66] and *Stirland* v. *Director of Public Prosecutions*,[67] both decisions of the House of Lords. However, when examining these decisions it should be borne in mind that the 1966 and 1968 Acts deleted the word "substantial" which appeared before "miscarriage."

Sentence when appeal allowed on part of an indictment. Section 4 of the Act provides that where a person appeals against conviction on an indictment containing two or more counts, and the Criminal Division of the Court of Appeal allow the appeal in respect of part of the indictment, they may in respect of any count on which he remains convicted pass such sentence, in substitution for any sentence passed thereon at the trial, as they think proper and as authorised by law for the offence of which he remains convicted on that count.

However, the court shall not under this section pass any sentence such that the appellant's sentence on the indictment as a whole will, in consequence of the appeal, be of greater severity than the sentence, taken as a whole, which was passed at the trial for all offences of which he was convicted on the indictment.

Power to substitute conviction of alternative offence. Section 3 of the Act provides that where an appellant has been convicted of an offence and the jury could on the indictment have found him guilty of some other offence, and on the finding of the jury it appears to the Court of Appeal that the jury must have been

---

[65] *Per* Lord Goddard C.J. in *R.* v. *Furlong* (1950) 34 Cr.App.R. 79.

[66] [1935] A.C. 309. "The rule which has been established is that if the conviction is to be quashed on the ground of misreception of evidence, the proviso cannot operate unless the evidence objected to is of such a nature and the circumstances of the case are such that the court must be satisfied that the jury must have returned the same verdict even if the evidence had not been given ": *ibid.* at p. 322.

[67] [1944] A.C. 315. See also Arch. paras. 925, 926.

satisfied of facts which proved him guilty of that other offence, the court may, instead of allowing or dismissing the appeal, substitute for the verdict found by the jury a verdict of guilty of that other offence, and pass such sentence in substitution for the sentence passed at the trial as may be authorised by law for that other offence, not being a sentence of greater severity.[68]

Disposal of appeal against conviction on special verdict. Section 5 of the Act provides that where on the conviction of an appellant the jury have found a special verdict (*i.e.* a finding on the facts alone [69]) and the court consider that a wrong conclusion has been arrived at by the court of trial on the effect of that verdict, the court may, instead of allowing the appeal, order such conclusion to be recorded as appears to the court to be in law required by the verdict and pass such sentence in substitution for the sentence passed at the trial as may be authorised by law.

Substitution of finding of insanity or unfitness to plead. Section 6 (1) of the Act provides that where on an appeal against conviction the Court of Appeal are of opinion that the proper verdict would have been not guilty by reason of insanity; or that the case is not one where there should have been a verdict of acquittal, but that there should have been a finding that the accused was under disability the court shall make an order that the accused be admitted to such hospital as may be specified by the Secretary of State.

Examination of witnesses. Under section 23 of the **1968 Act** the court has power, if it thinks it necessary or expedient in the interests of justice, to order any witnesses who would have been compellable witnesses in the proceedings from which the appeal lies to attend for examination and be examined before the court, whether they were or were not called in those proceedings, or to order the examination of any such witnesses to be conducted before any judge or officer of the court or other person appointed by the court for the purpose, and allow the admission of any

---

[68] So, where there was a charge of murder and the defence of provocation was raised but the judge in his summing-up did not refer to that defence, the court substituted for a verdict of murder a verdict of manslaughter: *R.* v. *Cobbett* (1940) 28 Cr.App.R. 11; see also *R.* v. *Davenport* (1954) 38 Cr.App.R. 37.

[69] *Ante,* p. 750.

depositions so taken as evidence before the court. The court likewise has power, to receive the evidence, if tendered, of any such witness, including the appellant, who is a competent but not compellable witness, and, if the appellant makes an application for the purpose, of the husband or wife of the appellant in cases where the evidence of the husband or wife could not have been given at the proceedings except on such an application.

Section 23 also provides that, unless the court is satisfied that the evidence if received would not afford a ground for appeal, the court shall receive evidence tendered if:

(a) it appears to them that the evidence is likely to be credible and would have been admissible in the proceedings from which the appeal lies on an issue which is the subject of the appeal; and

(b) they are satisfied that it was not adduced in those proceedings, but that there is a reasonable explanation for the failure so to adduce it.

It is only in the most exceptional cases that the court is prepared to admit further evidence [70] and the principles upon which the court may be said to act are these:

(a) The evidence must be such as was not available at the trial [70a] (although the court has on occasion departed from this principle).

(b) The evidence must be relevant to the issues, although it is not necessarily limited to evidence of witnesses who speak to the offence or the offender [71]

(c) It must be evidence that is credible, that is well capable of belief. [72]

---

[70] See *R.* v. *Stafford* [1968] 3 All E.R. 752. As to medical and scientific opinion as fresh evidence, see *R.* v. *Lomas* (1969) 53 Cr.App.R. 256 and *R.* v. *Merry* (1970) 54 Cr.App.R. 274.

[70a] The Court of Appeal must in general be satisfied that the evidence could not with reasonable diligence have been obtained for use at the trial: *R.* v. *Beresford* (1972) 56 Cr.App.R. 143 at p. 149.

[71] *e.g.* the conduct of the presiding judge: *R.* v. *Hircock* [1970] 1 Q.B. 67 but hearsay evidence is not admissible, see *R.* v. *Dallos* [1971] Crim.L.R. 90, C.A.

[72] *R.* v. *Parks* (1962) 46 Cr.App.R. 29; *R.* v. *Jordan* (1956) 40 Cr.App.R. 152; *R.* v. *Flower and Others* (1966) 50 Cr.App.R. 22. See also *R.* v. *Ditch* (1969) 53 Cr.App.R. 256; *R.* v. *James* [1971] Crim.L.R. 476. This means well capable of belief in the context of the circumstances as a whole, including the other evidence in the case directed to the issue under consideration: *R.* v. *Beresford* (1972) 56 Cr.App.R. 143 at pp. 149, 150.

Where the evidence is in fact admitted, then the court will go on to consider whether there might have been a reasonable doubt in the minds of the jury as to the guilt of the appellant, if that evidence had been given, together with the other evidence at the trial.[73] If the court considers that there might have been that reasonable doubt it will quash the conviction.[74] Where fresh evidence is heard the court will adopt the same principle as is followed on the application of the proviso to section 2 of the Act and will dismiss the appeal if satisfied after considering the fresh evidence " that no reasonable jury, properly directed would or could have come to any other conclusion than that to which they did come, and that no miscarriage of justice has actually occurred." [75]

Power to order a new trial. Section 7 of the Act provides that where an appeal against conviction is allowed by reason only of evidence received or available to be received by that court under section 23 of the Act and it appears to the court that the interests of justice so require, the court may order the appellant to be retried.

An appellant shall not be retried by virtue of this section for any offence other than:

(a) the offence of which he was convicted at the original trial and in respect of which his appeal is allowed;

(b) an offence of which he could have been convicted at the original trial on an indictment for the first-mentioned offence; or

(c) an offence charged in an alternative count of the indictment in respect of which the jury were discharged from giving a verdict in consequence of convicting him of the first-mentioned offence.

The appellant is retried on a fresh indictment preferred by the Court of Appeal.[76] The Court of Appeal may make such orders as appear to be necessary regarding the custody or admission to bail of the appellant.[77]

---

[73] R. v. Parks (supra).
[74] R. v. Harding (1936) 25 Cr.App.R. 190.
[75] R. v. Collins (1950) 34 Cr.App.R. 146.
[76] Criminal Appeal Act 1968, s. 8 (1) as amended by the Courts Act 1971, Sched. 11.
[77] Ibid. s. 8 (2).

On a retrial neither the depositions taken at the preliminary inquiry nor any written statement made pursuant to section 2 of the Criminal Justice Act 1967 (both of which are, in certain circumstances, admissible in a trial on indictment [78]) are admissible if the person who made the deposition or statement gave evidence at the first trial. However, a transcript of the record of the evidence given by any witness at the original trial may, with the leave of the judge, be read as evidence—

(*a*) by agreement between the prosecution and the defence; or

(*b*) if the judge is satisfied that the witness is dead or unfit to give evidence or to attend for that purpose, or that all reasonable efforts to find him or to secure his attendance have been made without success:

and in either case may be so read without further proof if verified in accordance with rules of court.[79]

Where a person ordered to be retried is again convicted on the retrial, the court before whom he is convicted may pass in respect of the offence any sentence authorised by law, not being a sentence of greater severity than that passed on the original conviction.[80]

Determination of an appeal against sentence. Section 11 (3) of the **Criminal Appeal Act 1968** provides that, on an appeal against sentence, the court, if it considers that the appellant should be sentenced differently for an offence for which he was dealt with by the court below may:

(*a*) quash any sentence or order which is the subject of the appeal; and

(*b*) in place of it pass such sentence or make such order as it thinks appropriate for the case and as the court below had power to pass or make when dealing with him for the offence;

but the court shall so exercise its powers under this subsection that, taking the case as a whole, the appellant is not more severely dealt with on appeal than he was dealt with by the court below.[81]

[78] *Ante*, pp. 739, 740.   [79] Criminal Appeal Act 1968, Sched. 2.
[80] *Ibid*. But see *R.* v. *Turner* (*No.* 2) [1971] 1 W.L.R. 901.
[81] The Court of Appeal also has power to deal with an appellant in respect of a suspended sentence: *ibid*. s. 11 (4).

Under this section the court will not alter a sentence merely on the ground that they might, if they had been trying the appellant, have passed a different sentence: the sentence must be manifestly excessive or wrong in principle before the court will interfere.[82] Appeal against sentence of death is regulated by section 48 of the Act, and the Fourth Schedule.

Computation of sentence. Where an appellant is admitted to bail under section 19 of the Act pending the hearing of his appeal or application to appeal, the time during which he is at large after being so admitted shall be disregarded in computing the term of any sentence to which he is for the time being subject.[83] However, the time during which an appellant is in custody shall, subject to any direction which the Court of Appeal may give to the contrary, be reckoned as part of the term of any sentence to which he is for the time being subject. No such direction may be given when leave to appeal has been granted or a certificate has been given under section 1 of the Act[84] and when giving such a direction the court must state their reasons.[85] It will be made only when the appeal is totally without merit.[86]

The term of any sentence passed by the Court of Appeal under sections 3, 4, 5, 11 or 13 (4) of the Act shall, unless the court otherwise directs, begin to run from the time when it would have begun to run if passed in the proceedings from which the appeal lies.[87]

Appeal against verdict of not guilty by reason of insanity. Section 12 of the Act provides that a person in whose case a verdict of not guilty by reason of insanity is returned may appeal against the verdict to the Court of Appeal:

(a) on any ground of appeal which involves a question of law alone, and

(b) with the leave of the Court of Appeal or upon the certificate of the judge of the court of trial[88] that it is a fit case for

---

[82] See the cases cited in Arch. paras. 939–940B.

[83] s. 29 (3).

[84] *Ante*, p. 842.

[85] s. 29 (2).

[86] *Practice Direction* [1970] 1 W.L.R. 663, C.A.

[87] s. 29 (4).

[88] " The judge of the court of trial " means, where the Crown Court comprises justices of the peace, the judge presiding. s. 51 (1) as substituted by the Courts Act 1971, Sched. 8, para. 57 (3).

appeal, on any ground of appeal which involves a question of fact alone or a question of mixed law and fact or any other ground which appears to the court to be a sufficient ground of appeal;

and the Court of Appeal under **section 13** of the Act on any such appeal shall allow the appeal if they think that the verdict should be set aside on the ground that there was a material irregularity in the course of the trial, or that the order of the court giving effect to the verdict should be set aside on the ground of a wrong decision of any question of law or on the ground that under all the circumstances of the case the verdict was unsafe or unsatisfactory, and shall in any other case dismiss the appeal.

The Court of Appeal may dismiss such an appeal under section 12 of the Act, if of opinion that, notwithstanding that the point raised in the appeal might be decided in favour of the appellant, no miscarriage of justice has actually occurred.

Where:

(a) an appeal under section 12 of the Act would fall to be allowed, and

(b) none of the grounds for allowing it relates to the question of the insanity of the accused,

the Court of Appeal may dismiss the appeal if of opinion that but for the insanity of the accused, the proper verdict would have been that he was guilty of an offence other than the offence charged.

Where an appeal under section 12 of the Act is allowed:

(a) if the ground, or one of the grounds, for allowing the appeal is that the finding of the jury as to the insanity of the accused ought not to stand and the Court of Appeal are of opinion that the proper verdict would have been that he was guilty of an offence (whether the offence charged or any other offence of which the jury could have found him guilty), the court shall substitute for the verdict of not guilty by reason of insanity a verdict of guilty of that offence, and shall have the like powers of punishing or otherwise dealing with the appellant, and other powers, as the court of trial would have had if the jury had come to the substituted verdict [89];

(b) in any other case, the Court of Appeal shall substitute for the verdict of the jury a verdict of acquittal.

Hospital order on disposal of appeal. Section 14 of the Act provides: where on an appeal under section 12, the court is of opinion that there should not have been an acquittal but that there should have been a finding that the accused was under disability, the court shall make an order that the appellant be admitted to a hospital specified by the Secretary of State. Similarly,[90] where the court substitutes a verdict of acquittal [91] and they are of opinion that the appellant is suffering from mental disorder of a nature or degree which warrants his detention in a hospital under observation for at least a limited period and that he ought to be detained in the interests of his own health or safety or with a view to the protection of other persons, the court shall make an order that he be admitted for observation to a hospital specified by the Secretary of State.

Appeal against finding of disability. By section 15 of the Act where there has been a determination [92] of the question of a person's fitness to be tried and the jury has returned a finding that he is under a disability, that person may appeal to the court against that finding, on any ground of appeal which involves a question of law alone, and with the leave of the court of appeal, on any ground which involves a question of fact alone or a question of mixed law and fact or any other ground which appears to the court to be sufficient. If the judge of the court of trial grants a certificate that the case is fit for appeal on a ground involving a question of fact or mixed law and fact, then the leave of the court of appeal is not required. By **section 16** the court must allow such an appeal if they are of opinion:

---

[89] The court has no power under subs. (a) to sentence any person to death, but where under that para. they substitute a verdict of guilty of an offence for which apart from the subsection they would be required to sentence the appellant to death, their sentence shall (whatever the circumstances) be one of life imprisonment, s. 15 (5).

[90] s. 14 (2).

[91] In accordance with s. 13 (4) (b) of the Act.

[92] Under s. 4 of the Criminal Procedure (Insanity) Act 1964.

(a) that the finding of the jury should be set aside on the
     ground that under all the circumstances of the case it is
     unsafe or unsatisfactory; or
(b) that the order of the court giving effect to the finding should
     be set aside on the ground of a wrong decision of any
     question of law; or
(c) that there was a material irregularity in the course of the
     determination of the question of fitness to be tried.[93]

Subject to the proviso as to no miscarriage of justice, the court
must dismiss the appeal in any other case, subject to one exception.[94] Where the question of fitness to be tried was determined
later than on arraignment, then notwithstanding that the finding
was properly come to, the court must allow the appeal if it is of
opinion that the case is one in which the accused should have been
acquitted before the question of fitness to be tried was considered.
In such a case the court may, in addition to quashing the finding,
direct a verdict of acquittal (but not a verdict of not guilty by
reason of insanity) to be recorded.

Reference by Home Secretary. Section 17 of the Act empowers
the Home Secretary,[95] if he thinks fit, where a person has been
convicted on indictment, found not guilty on indictment by
reason of insanity, or found by a jury to be under a disability,
either to:

(a) refer the whole case to the court, the case then being
     treated as an appeal by that person[96]; or
(b) if he desires the assistance of the court on any point arising
     in the case, refer that point to the court for an opinion
     thereon. In such a case the court will consider the point[97]
     and furnish the Home Secretary with their opinion.

Disposal of groundless appeal. Section 20 of the Act provides
that where a notice of appeal purporting to be on a ground of

---

[93] The appellant may then be tried for the offence with which he was charged:
     s. 16 (3).
[94] Under s. 16 (2).
[95] Either on an application of the person referred to, or without any such
     application: s. 17 (2).
[96] For examples of the exercise of this power under the 1907 Act see Arch. para.
     896.
[97] The Court may consider the point in private: Criminal Appeal Rules 1968,
     r. 16.

appeal which involves a question of law alone, appears to the registrar not to show any substantial ground of appeal, such an appeal may be referred by him to the court for summary determination; and where the case is so referred the court may, if they consider that the appeal is frivolous and vexatious, and can be determined without adjourning it for a full hearing, summarily dismiss the appeal, without calling on anyone to attend the hearing or to appear for the Crown thereon.

Reference to the court following an acquittal on indictment. Where a person tried on indictment has been acquitted (whether in respect of the whole or part of the indictment) the Attorney-General may, under **section 36** of the **Criminal Justice Act 1972,** if he desires the opinion of the court on a point of law which has arisen in the case, refer that point to the Court of Appeal, and that court will have to consider the point and give their opinion upon it.[98] They will be able to hear argument by, or by counsel on behalf of, the Attorney-General and by counsel on behalf of the acquitted person, or with leave, from that person himself.[99] Where the court have given their opinion, they may of their own motion, or in pursuance of an application, refer the point to the House of Lords for their opinion upon the point.[1] A reference of this nature will not, however, affect the trial in relation to which the reference is made or any acquittal in that trial.[2]

SECTION 2. APPEALS FROM THE COURT OF APPEAL TO THE HOUSE OF LORDS

Section 33 of the **Criminal Appeal Act 1968** provides that an appeal shall lie to the House of Lords, *at the instance of the defendant or the prosecutor,* from any decision of the Criminal Division of the Court of Appeal on an appeal to that court with the leave of that court or of the House of Lords. Leave shall not be granted unless it is certified by the Court of Appeal that a point of law of general public importance is involved in the decision and it appears to that court or to the House of Lords,

---

[98] s. 36 (1). (The Act was not in force on July 1, 1972.)
[99] s. 36 (2). Special provisions are laid down as to the costs of the acquitted person both in the Court of Appeal and in the House of Lords: see *ibid.* s. 36 (5) (6) (7) (8).
[1] s. 36 (3) (4).
[2] s. 36 (9).

as the case may be, that the point is one which ought to be considered by that House.[3] For the purpose of disposing of an appeal, the House of Lords may exercise any powers of the Court of Appeal or may remit the case to that court.[4]

Application for leave to appeal must be made to the Court of Appeal within fourteen days of the decision and to the House of Lords within fourteen days of the refusal of the Court of Appeal.[5]

The Court of Appeal has power to grant bail pending an appeal or application for leave to appeal.[6] Where the prosecutor appeals in a case in which, but for the decision of the Court of Appeal, the defendant would be liable to be detained, the Court of Appeal may make an order providing for the detention of the defendant or his release on bail.[7]

A defendant who is detained pending an appeal to the House of Lords shall not be entitled to be present on the hearing of the appeal or of any proceedings preliminary or incidental thereto, except where an order of the House of Lords authorises him to be present; or where the House or the Court of Appeal, as the case may be, give him leave to be present.[8]

The Court of Appeal and the House of Lords have power in certain circumstances to award costs to a defendant, whether an appellant or a respondent,[9] and also to order costs against a defendant.[10]

Reference to the House by the Court of Appeal (Criminal Division). Under the **Criminal Justice Act 1972,** where the Court

---

[3] The House of Lords is not confined to the question certified and matters relating to it: *Att.-Gen. for N. Ireland* v. *Gallagher* [1963] A.C. 349. But it would appear that where a certificate on conviction has been given the House will not hear argument in relation to sentence: *Jones* v. *D.P.P.* [1962] A.C. 635.

[4] Criminal Appeal Act 1968, s. 35 (3).

[5] *Ibid.* s. 34 (1). Except in capital cases, extension of time may be given: s. 34 (2) and see Sched. 4 of the Act.

[6] *Ibid.* s. 36.

[7] *Ibid.* s. 37. The time which a person subject to sentence, is at large after being admitted to bail under ss. 36 and 37 is to be disregarded in computing the term of his sentence. Subject to this, any sentence passed on appeal to the House of Lords in substitution for another sentence, shall, unless that House or the Court of Appeal otherwise direct, begin to run from the time when the other sentence would have begun to run: s. 43.

[8] *Ibid.* s. 38.

[9] *Ibid.* s. 39, as substituted by the Courts Act 1971, Sched. 8, para. 57 (1) (*b*), and amended by the Courts Act 1971, Sched. 11.

[10] *Ibid.* s. 40.

of Appeal (Criminal Division) have given their opinion on a point referred to them by the Attorney-General under **section 36,**[11] they may of their own motion or in pursuance of an application refer the point to the House of Lords for their opinion.[12]

[11] See p. 859, *ante.*
[12] s. 36 (3) (4).

CHAPTER 59

REMISSION, PARDON AND LICENCE

Reprieve. A reprieve is the withdrawal of a sentence for an interval of time whereby its execution is suspended. It may be granted at the discretion of either the Crown or the court of trial. A reprieve must be granted by the court when a person becomes insane after judgment.[1]

Pardon. The right to pardon is a prerogative of the Crown alone, and is exercised on the recommendation of the Home Secretary. It can be granted either before or after trial and conviction. It may be granted conditionally on the offender submitting to some lesser punishment. The grant of a free pardon or the performance of the condition in case of a conditional pardon absolves the offender from all punishment or disqualification.[2]

By the Act of Settlement 1700 it was provided that no pardon shall be pleadable in bar of an impeachment, and under the Habeas Corpus Act 1679, the Crown cannot pardon the offence of imprisoning a person out of the realm so as to evade service of a writ of habeas corpus; at common law also the Crown cannot pardon a common nuisance while it remains unredressed, nor can it pardon an offence against a penal statute after information has been brought; in the latter case, however, there is in some instances power to remit penalties.[3]

Remission for good conduct. Under rules [4] made pursuant to **section 25** of the **Prison Act 1952** prisoners may be granted remission of part of their sentence on the ground of industry and good conduct. However, the Secretary of State may direct that a " persistent offender " [5] or a person serving a sentence of eighteen months or more who was under twenty-one when the sentence was passed shall, instead of being granted remission, be released on licence at any time on or after the day on which he could have been discharged from prison if the remission had been granted.[6]

---

[1] Arch. para. 620.
[2] See Criminal Law Act 1827, s. 13 (now repealed by the Criminal Law Act 1967, Sched. 3); *Hay* v. *Tower Division Justices* (1890) 24 Q.B.D. 561.
[3] See Halsbury's *Laws of England*, Vol. 7, para. 525 *et seq.*
[4] The Prison Rules 1964, S.I. 1964 No. 388, r. 5.
[5] *Ante*, p. 772.   [6] Criminal Justice Act 1967, s. 60 (2).

Release of prisoners on licence. Part III of the Criminal Justice Act 1967 provides for the release of prisoners on licence.

Section 59 provides for the constitution of the Parole Board to advise the Secretary of State on the exercise of his powers to release prisoners on licence under sections 60 and 61 and to revoke such licences under section 62.

Section 60 empowers the Secretary of State, on the recommendation of the Board,[7] to release on licence, subject to conditions, a fixed sentence prisoner who has served one-third of his sentence or one year, whichever is the longer. The licence will remain in force until the expiration of the sentence in the cases of young prisoners and of extended sentence prisoners, and until the normal date of release on remission in the case of other prisoners.

Section 61 empowers the Secretary of State, on the recommendation of the Board, to release on licence persons sentenced to life imprisonment or to detention under section 53 of the Children and Young Persons Act 1933 (young offenders convicted of grave crimes). The Secretary of State is required to consult the Lord Chief Justice and the trial judge before releasing on licence a person sentenced to imprisonment or detention for life. The provisions of this clause replace existing enactments providing for the release on licence of such persons.

Section 62 empowers the Secretary of State and, in the event of reconviction, the Crown Court to revoke a licence.[8] In the case of a prisoner (other than a life prisoner) whose licence has been revoked by a court, the Secretary of State may not release the prisoner on licence again within a specified period. The Secretary of State may not revoke a licence unless either he has been recommended to do so by the Board or there is no time to consult the Board. A recalled prisoner may make representations about his recall and if he does so, or if his licence was revoked under the emergency procedure, the Secretary of State is to refer the case to the Board. If they recommend immediate release the Secretary of State is to give effect to the recommendation.

---

[7] In certain cases, the Secretary of State may release such person on the recommendation of a local review committee while referring the case to the Board: Criminal Justice Act 1972, s. 35 (1) (not in force on July 1, 1972).

[8] If a person subject to a licence under s. 60 or 61 of this Act is convicted by a magistrates' court of an offence punishable on indictment with imprisonment, the court may, instead of dealing with him in any other way, commit him in custody to the Crown Court for sentence in accordance with s. 29 of the Criminal Justice Act 1948. See *ante*, p. 761.

PRECEDENTS OF INDICTMENTS

(The Indictments Rules 1916, as amended, which contained an Appendix showing forms of indictment, have been repealed. The precedents which are to be framed by the Lord Chief Justice in accordance with the Indictments Rules 1971, have not yet been published. The following examples, some taken, if modified, from Archbold, 37th edition are intended to fill the gap until the new precedents are available.)

1

Statement of Offence

Murder

Particulars of Offence

A B, on the —— day of —— murdered C D.

2

Statement of Offence

Manslaughter

Particulars of Offence

A B, on the —— day of —— unlawfully killed C D.

3

Statement of Offence

Causing death by dangerous driving, contrary to section 1 of the Road Traffic Act 1972

Particulars of Offence

A B, by driving a motor vehicle on the —— day of ——, on a road, namely Station Road ——, in a manner which was dangerous to the public, caused the death of C D on the —— day of ——.

4

STATEMENT OF OFFENCE

Rape, contrary to section 1 (1) of the Sexual Offences Act 1956

PARTICULARS OF OFFENCE

A B, on the —— day of ——, had sexual intercourse with C D without her consent.

5

STATEMENT OF OFFENCE

Sexual intercourse with a girl contrary to section 6 (1) of the Sexual Offences Act 1956

PARTICULARS OF OFFENCE

A B, on the —— day of —— had unlawful sexual intercourse with C D, a girl of the age of fourteen years.

6

STATEMENT OF OFFENCE

Buggery

PARTICULARS OF OFFENCE

A B on the —— day of —— [in —— to which the public had access] committed buggery with C D.

7

STATEMENT OF OFFENCE

Incest contrary to section 10 (1) of the Sexual Offences Act 1956

PARTICULARS OF OFFENCE

A B being a male person on the —— day of —— had sexual intercourse with C D who was to his knowledge his ——.

8

STATEMENT OF OFFENCE

Gross indecency contrary to section 13 of the Sexual Offences Act 1956

PARTICULARS OF OFFENCE

A B on the —— day of —— committed an act of gross indecency with C D a male person.

9

STATEMENT OF OFFENCE

Gross indecency with child contrary to section 1 (1) of the Indecency with Children Act 1960

PARTICULARS OF OFFENCE

A B on the —— day of —— committed an act of gross indecency with C D a child of the age of —— years.

10

STATEMENT OF OFFENCE

Wounding with intent, contrary to section 18 of the Offences against the Person Act 1861

PARTICULARS OF OFFENCE

A B, on the —— day of —— wounded C D, with intent to do him grievous bodily harm.

11

STATEMENT OF OFFENCE

Unlawful wounding, contrary to section 20 of the Offences against the Person Act 1861

PARTICULARS OF OFFENCE

A B, on the —— day of —— maliciously wounded C D.

12

STATEMENT OF OFFENCE

Assault with intent contrary to section 38 of the Offences against the Person Act 1861

PARTICULARS OF OFFENCE

A B on the —— day of —— assaulted C D with intent to resist or prevent the lawful apprehension or detainer of himself the said A B.

13

STATEMENT OF OFFENCE

Assault occasioning actual bodily harm

PARTICULARS OF OFFENCE

A B on the —— day of —— assaulted C D thereby occasioning him actual bodily harm.

14

STATEMENT OF OFFENCE
Common assault

PARTICULARS OF OFFENCE
A B on the —— day of —— assaulted C D.

15

STATEMENT OF OFFENCE
Assault with intent to rob contrary to section 8 (2) of the Theft Act 1968

PARTICULARS OF OFFENCE
A B on the —— day of —— assaulted C D with intent to rob him.

16

STATEMENT OF OFFENCE
Theft, contrary to section 1 of the Theft Act 1968

PARTICULARS OF OFFENCE
A B, on the —— day of —— stole a bicycle, the property of C D.

17

STATEMENT OF OFFENCE
Robbery, contrary to section 8 of the Theft Act 1968

PARTICULARS OF OFFENCE
A B, on the —— day of —— robbed C D of a wallet and £20 cash.

18

STATEMENT OF OFFENCE
Burglary, contrary to section 9 (1) (*a*) of the Theft Act 1968

PARTICULARS OF OFFENCE
A B, on the —— day of ——, entered 9 Station Road, —— as a trespasser, with intent to steal therein.

19

STATEMENT OF OFFENCE

Aggravated burglary contrary to section 10 (1) of the Theft Act 1968

PARTICULARS OF OFFENCE

A B on the —— day of —— having entered a building at —— as a trespasser stole therein —— the property of C D and at the time of committing the said burglary had with him a weapon of offence to wit ——.

20

STATEMENT OF OFFENCE

Handling stolen goods,[1] contrary to section 22 (1) of the Theft Act 1968

PARTICULARS OF OFFENCE

A B, on the —— day of —— dishonestly received a bag, the property of C D, knowing or believing the same to have been stolen.

21

STATEMENT OF OFFENCE

Taking conveyance without authority contrary to section 12 (1) of the Theft Act 1968

PARTICULARS OF OFFENCE

A B on the —— day of —— without the consent of the owner or other lawful authority took a conveyance to wit —— for his own use.

22

STATEMENT OF OFFENCE

Being carried in motor vehicle taken without authority contrary to section 12 (1) of the Theft Act 1968

PARTICULARS OF OFFENCE

A B on the —— day of —— knowing that a motor vehicle belonging to C D had been taken without the consent of the owner or other

[1] See *ante*, p. 521 as to the modes of charging different types of handling stolen goods.

lawful authority allowed himself to be carried in the said motor vehicle without such consent or authority.

23

STATEMENT OF OFFENCE

Driving motor vehicle taken without authority contrary to section 12 (1) of the Theft Act 1968

PARTICULARS OF OFFENCE

A B on the —— day of —— knowing that a motor vehicle the property of C D had been taken without the consent of the owner or other lawful authority drove the said motor vehicle without such consent or authority.

24

STATEMENT OF OFFENCE

Having articles for theft contrary to section 25 (1) of the Theft Act 1968

PARTICULARS OF OFFENCE

A B on the —— day of —— when not at his place of abode had with him —— for use in the course of or in connection with theft.

25

STATEMENT OF OFFENCE

Blackmail, contrary to section 21 (1) of the Theft Act 1968

PARTICULARS OF OFFENCE

A B, on the —— day of ——, with a view to gain for himself or with intent to cause loss to another, in a letter dated the —— and addressed to C D at ——, made an unwarranted demand of £100 from C D with menaces.

26

STATEMENT OF OFFENCE

Arson, contrary to section 1 (1) and (3) of the Criminal Damage Act 1971

PARTICULARS OF OFFENCE

A B, on the —— day of ——, without lawful excuse, destroyed by fire a dwelling house belonging to C D, intending to destroy such property or being reckless as to whether such property would be destroyed.

27

STATEMENT OF OFFENCE

Arson contrary to section 1 (2) of the Criminal Damage Act 1971

PARTICULARS OF OFFENCE

A B on the —— day of —— without lawful excuse damaged by fire —— belonging to C D intending to damage or destroy the said —— or being reckless as to whether the said —— would be damaged or destroyed and intending by the destruction or damage to endanger the life of another or being reckless as to whether the life of another would be thereby endangered.

28

STATEMENT OF OFFENCE

Damaging property contrary to section 1 (1) of the Criminal Damage Act 1971

PARTICULARS OF OFFENCE

A B, on the —— day of —— without lawful excuse, damaged a shop belonging to C D, intending to damage such property or being reckless as to whether such property would be damaged or not.

29

STATEMENT OF OFFENCE

Obtaining property by deception, contrary to section 15 (1) of the Theft Act 1968

PARTICULARS OF OFFENCE

A B, on the —— day of ——, dishonestly obtained from C D the sum of £200 by deception, namely by falsely pretending that he intended to use the said sum for the purchase of materials for certain work, namely —— which he had undertaken to carry out at the premises of C D at ——, with the intention of permanently depriving C D of the said sum.

30

STATEMENT OF OFFENCE

First Count

Offence under section 35 of the Malicious Damage Act 1861

Particulars of Offence

A B, on the —— day of ——, maliciously displaced a sleeper belonging to British Rail with intent to obstruct upset overthrow injure or destroy an engine tender carriage or truck using the said railway.

Statement of Offence

Second Count

Obstructing railway, contrary to section 36 of the Malicious Damage Act 1861

Particulars of Offence

A B, on the —— day of ——, by unlawfully displacing a sleeper belonging to British Rail did obstruct or cause to be obstructed an engine or carriage using the said railway.

31

Statement of Offence

First Count

Forgery, contrary to section 2 (1) (*a*) of the Forgery Act 1913

Particulars of Offence

A B, on the —— day of ——, with intent to defraud, forged a certain will purporting to be the will of C D.

Statement of Offence

Second Count

Uttering forged document, contrary to section 6 (1), (2) of the Forgery Act 1913

Particulars of Offence

A B, on the —— day of —— uttered a certain forged will purporting to be the will of C D, knowing the same to be forged and with intent to defraud.

32

Statement of Offence

Endeavouring to obtain money on forged instruments contrary to section 7 (*a*) of the Forgery Act 1913

PARTICULARS OF OFFENCE

A B on the —— day of —— with intent to defraud endeavoured to obtain from C D the sum of £—— under upon or by virtue of forged —— knowing the same to be forged.

33

STATEMENT OF OFFENCE

Uttering counterfeit coin, contrary to section 5 (1) of the Coinage Offences Act 1936

PARTICULARS OF OFFENCE

A B, on the —— day of —— at the public-house called " The Red Lion " uttered a counterfeit fifty pence piece knowing the same to be counterfeit.

34

STATEMENT OF OFFENCE

Uttering counterfeit coin after a previous conviction for uttering, contrary to section 5 (5) of the Coinage Offences Act 1936

PARTICULARS OF OFFENCE

A B, having previously been convicted of an offence under section 5 (1) of the Coinage Offences Act 1936, on the —— day of ——at a public-house called " The Red Lion " uttered a counterfeit fifty pence piece knowing the same to be counterfeit.

35

STATEMENT OF OFFENCE

Perjury, contrary to section 1 (1) of the Perjury Act 1911

PARTICULARS OF OFFENCE

A B, on the —— day of —— being a witness upon the trial of an action in the Chancery Division of the High Court of Justice in England, in which one, ——, was plaintiff, and one, ——, was defendant, knowingly falsely swore that he saw one, M N, in the street called the Strand, London, on the —— day of ——.

36

STATEMENT OF OFFENCE

False accounting, contrary to section 17 (1) (*a*) of the Theft Act 1968

PARTICULARS OF OFFENCE

A B, on the —— day of ——, dishonestly and with a view to

gain for himself, falsified a record required for the accounts of his employers C D & Co. Ltd., namely a cash book kept by him, by making an entry therein purporting to show that £100 had been paid to E F.

37

STATEMENT OF OFFENCE

Assault on a constable contrary to section 51 (1) of the Police Act 1964

PARTICULARS OF OFFENCE

A B, on the —— day of —— assaulted C D a constable of the —— Police Force, while in the execution of his duty.

38

STATEMENT OF OFFENCE

Driving a motor vehicle when unfit to drive through drink contrary to section 5 (1) of the Road Traffic Act 1972

PARTICULARS OF OFFENCE

A B, on the —— day of —— when driving a motor vehicle on —— Road —— was unfit to drive through drink.

39

STATEMENT OF OFFENCE

Driving a motor vehicle with blood alcohol concentration above the prescribed limit, contrary to section 6 (1) of the Road Traffic Act 1972

PARTICULARS OF OFFENCE

A B, on the —— day of —— drove a motor vehicle on —— road ——, having consumed alcohol in such a quantity that the proportion thereof in his blood exceeded the prescribed limit at the time when he provided a specimen under section 9 of the Road Traffic Act 1972.

40

STATEMENT OF OFFENCE

Driving whilst disqualified contrary to section 99 (*b*) of the Road Traffic Act 1972

PARTICULARS OF OFFENCE

A B on the —— day of —— drove a motor vehicle on a road whilst disqualified for holding or obtaining a driving licence.

41

STATEMENT OF OFFENCE

Affray

PARTICULARS OF OFFENCE

A B, C D and E F, on the —— day of —— at —— unlawfully fought and made an affray.

42

STATEMENT OF OFFENCE

Conspiracy to defraud

PARTICULARS OF OFFENCE

A B, and C D, on divers days between the —— day of —— and the —— day of —— conspired together and with other persons unknown, to defraud such persons as should thereafter be induced to part with money to the said A B and C D by false representations that A B and C D were then carrying on a genuine business as jewellers at —— and that they were then willing and prepared and in a position to supply articles of jewellery to such persons.

43

STATEMENT OF OFFENCE

Assisting an offender contrary to section 4 (1) of the Criminal Law Act 1967

PARTICULARS OF OFFENCE

A B, on the —— day of —— C D having committed an arrestable offence, namely the theft of an overcoat, the property of E F and bearing the manufacturer's name, knowing or believing that C D had committed that offence, without lawful authority or excuse removed the name of the manufacturer with intent to impede the apprehension or prosecution of the said C D.

44

STATEMENT OF OFFENCE

Using firearm with intent contrary to section 17 (1) of the Firearms Act 1968

PARTICULARS OF OFFENCE

A B on the —— day of —— made use of a firearm with intent to resist or prevent the lawful arrest or detention of himself.

45

STATEMENT OF OFFENCE

Possessing firearm at time of committing offence contrary to
section 17 (2) of the Firearms Act 1968

PARTICULARS OF OFFENCE

A B on the —— day of —— at the time of committing an offence
to wit —— had in his possession a firearm namely ——.

46

STATEMENT OF OFFENCE

Having firearm with intent contrary to section 18 (1) of the
Firearms Act 1968

PARTICULARS OF OFFENCE

A B on the —— day of —— had with him a firearm with intent
to commit an indictable offence while he had the said firearm with
him.

47

STATEMENT OF OFFENCE

Possessing firearm with intent to endanger life contrary to section 16
of the Firearms Act 1968

PARTICULARS OF OFFENCE

A B on the —— day of —— had in his possession a firearm to wit
—— with intent by means thereof to endanger life.

48

STATEMENT OF OFFENCE

Having loaded shot gun in public place contrary to section 19 of the
Firearms Act 1968

PARTICULARS OF OFFENCE

A B on the —— day of —— without lawful authority or reasonable excuse had with him in a public place a loaded shot gun.

49

STATEMENT OF OFFENCE

Possessing firearm without certificate contrary to section 1 (1) (*a*) of
the Firearms Act 1968

PARTICULARS OF OFFENCE

A B on the —— day of —— unlawfully had in his possession a firearm to wit —— without holding a firearm certificate in force at the time.

50

STATEMENT OF OFFENCE

Possessing firearm without certificate contrary to sections 1 and 4 (4) of the Firearms Act 1968

PARTICULARS OF OFFENCE

A B on the —— day of —— unlawfully had in his possession a shot gun the barrels of which had been shortened to a length less than 24 inches without holding a firearm certificate in force at the time authorising him to have the said firearm in his possession.

51

STATEMENT OF OFFENCE

Having offensive weapon contrary to section 1 (1) of the Prevention of Crime Act 1953

PARTICULARS OF OFFENCE

A B on the —— day of —— without lawful authority or reasonable excuse had with him in a public place an offensive weapon to wit ——.

INDEX